Communications
in Computer and Information Science 754

Commenced Publication in 2007
Founding and Former Series Editors:
Alfredo Cuzzocrea, Orhun Kara, Dominik Ślęzak, and Xiaokang Yang

More information about this series at http://www.springer.com/series/7899

Alla Kravets · Maxim Shcherbakov
Marina Kultsova · Peter Groumpos (Eds.)

Creativity in Intelligent Technologies and Data Science

Second Conference, CIT&DS 2017
Volgograd, Russia, September 12–14, 2017
Proceedings

 Springer

Editors
Alla Kravets (iD)
Volgograd State Technical University
Volgograd
Russia

Marina Kultsova (iD)
Volgograd State Technical University
Volgograd
Russia

Maxim Shcherbakov (iD)
Volgograd State Technical University
Volgograd
Russia

Peter Groumpos (iD)
University of Patras
Patras
Greece

ISSN 1865-0929   ISSN 1865-0937 (electronic)
Communications in Computer and Information Science
ISBN 978-3-319-65550-5   ISBN 978-3-319-65551-2 (eBook)
DOI 10.1007/978-3-319-65551-2

Library of Congress Control Number: 2017949174

Printed on acid-free paper

This Springer imprint is published by Springer Nature
The registered company is Springer International Publishing AG
The registered company address is: Gewerbestrasse 11, 6330 Cham, Switzerland

Preface

Creativity is the process of breaking out of established patterns; it is the reorganization, recombination, or reinterpretation, of concepts and, ideas for getting something unique and previously unknown. Creating software is one of the most creative activities that humans undertake. It is developed for people and by people and people's creativity can be a good source to improvise solutions to problems for dominating complex systems such as software design and development.

This book includes the proceedings of the Second Conference on Creativity in Intelligent Technologies and Data Science 2017, which continues the previous one, CIT&DS 2015. The new conference has three main groups of topics. The first one is called "Artificial intelligence and Deep Learning Technologies for Creative Tasks." This chapter includes papers related to the following topics: (a) Knowledge Discovery in Patent and Open Sources; (b) Open Science Semantic Technologies; and (c) Computer Vision and Knowledge-Based Control. The second chapter unites articles in the framework of "Cyber-Physical Systems and Big Data-Driven World." In particular, findings related to the following are highlighted: (a) Pro-Active Modeling in Intelligent Decision-Making Support, (b) Design Creativity in CASE/CAI/CAD/PDM, (c) Intelligent Internet of Services and Internet of Things. The last chapter is titled "Intelligent Technologies in Social Engineering" and contains contributions on the topics: (a) Data Science in Social Networks Analysis; (b) Creativity and Game-Based Learning; and (c) Intelligent Assistive Technologies: Software Design and Application.

The main objective of the CIT&DS 2017 was to bring together researchers and practitioners to share ideas in using creativity to theory and practice in software engineering.

The conference on Creativity in Intelligent Technologies & Data Science 2017 was supported by the Russian Foundation for Basic Research, grant No. 17-07-20520.

July 2017

Alla Kravets
Peter Groumpos
Maxim Shcherbakov
Marina Kultsova

Organization

General Co-chairs

Vladimir Lysak   Volgograd State Technical University, Russia
Igor Kalyaev   Scientific-Research Institute Multiprocessing Computing
                      Systems of South Federal University, Russia
Dmitriy Novikov   Institute of Control Sciences of Russian Academy
                      of Sciences, Russia

Program Committee Co-chairs

Alla Kravets   Volgograd State Technical University, Russia
Peter Groumpos   University of Patras, Greece
Maxim Shcherbakov   Volgograd State Technical University, Russia
Marina Kultsova   Volgograd State Technical University, Russia

Program Committee

Peter Karsmakers   KU Leuven, Belgium
Alena Zakharova   Tomsk Polytechnic University, Russia
Ann Matokhina   Volgograd State Technical University, Russia
Dmitriy Korobkin   Volgograd State Technical University, Russia
Yasemin Allsop   University College London, UK
Sergiy Shevchenko   NTU Kharkiv Polytechnic Institute, Ukraine
Natalia Sadovnikova   Volgograd State Technical University, Russia
Olga Shabalina   Volgograd State Technical University, Russia
Nuno Escudeiro   P.Porto, Portugal
Uranchimeg   TU Chemnitz, Germany
  Tudevdagva
Takako Nakatani   The Open University of Japan, Japan
Timur Janovsky   Volgograd State Technical University, Russia
Satyadhyan Chickerur KLE Technological University, India
Andrius Zhilenas   INVENTSHIP, Lithuania
Alexey Kizim   Volgograd State Technical University, Russia
Fernando Paulo Belfo Polytechnic Institute of Coimbra, Portugal
Miltiadis Chalikias   Technological Educational Institute of Piraeus, Greece
Sergey Serebryakov   Hewlett Packard Enterprise, USA
Vladimir Gorodetsky   St. Petersburg Institute for Informatics and Automation
                      of the RAS, Russia
Vladimir Rozaliev   Volgograd State Technical University, Russia
Andrew Olyanitch   Volgograd State Agrarian University, Russia
Joao Varajao   University of Minho, Portugal

Rihito Yaegashi	Kagawa University, Japan
Adriaan Brebels	KU Leuven, Belgium
Anton Ivaschenko	Samara National Research University, Russia
Ivars Linde	ISMA, Latvia
Eduardo Sarmento	Lusofona University, Portugal
Victor Toporkov	National Research University "MPEI", Russia
Michalis Skordoulis	T.E.I. of Piraeus, Greece
Anton Anikin	Volgograd State Technical University, Russia
Alexey Finogeev	Penza State University, Russia
Andrey Andreev	Volgograd State Technical University, Russia
George Tsihrintzis	University of Piraeus, Greece
Georgiy Gerkushenko	Volgograd State Technical University, Russia
Mehran Misaghi	UNISOCIESC, Brazil
Julio Abascal	University of the Basque Country/Euskal Herriko Unibertsitatea, Spain
Bal Krishna Bal	Kathmandu University, Nepal
Leonid Chechurin	LUT, Finland
Edwin Gray	Glasgow Caledonian University, UK
Pavel Vorobkalov	Volgograd State Technical University, Russia
Anton Tyukov	Volgograd State Technical University, Russia
Jan Dekelver	Thomas More University, Belgium
Boris Lempert	Volgograd State Medical University, Russia
Maria-Iuliana Dascalu	Politehnica University of Bucharest, Romania
Igor Bessmertny	ITMO University, Russia
Vibhash Yadav	Krishna Institute of Technology, India
Kvyatkovskaya Irina	Astrakhan State Technical University, Russia
Danish Ather	College of Computing Sciences and IT, India
Irina Petrova	Astrakkhan Civil Engineering Institute, Russia
Irina Zhukova	Volgograd State Technical University, Russia
Vladimir Pavlovsky	Keldysh Institute of Applied Mathematics of RAS, Russia
Dang Phuong	University of Science and Technology - The University of Danang (UST-UD), Vietnam
Rui Rijo	Polytechnic Institute of Leiria, Portugal
Alin Moldoveanu	University Politehnica of Bucharest, Romania
Vadim Stefanuk	Institute for Information Transmission Problems, Laboratory C4, Russia
Yulia Orlova	Volgograd State Technical University, Russia
Alexander Bozhday	Penza State University, Russia
Mohammed Al-Gunaid	Volgograd State Technical University, Russia
Ionel-Bujorel Pavaloiu	University Politehnica of Bucharest, Romania
Carla Oliveira	Faculdade de Letras de Lisboa, Portugal
Olga Berestneva	Tomsk Polytechnic University, Russia
Roman Meshcheryakov	Tomsk State University of Control Systems and Radioelectronics, Russia
Anatoly Karpenko	Bauman Moscow State Technical University, Russia
Pham The Bao	University of Science, Vietnam

Nataliya Salnikova   Volgograd Institute of Management, Branch of the Russian
                            Presidential Academy of National Economy and Public
                            Administration, Russia
Christos Malliarakis   University of Macedonia, Greece
Alexander Priven   Corning, South Korea
David Moffat   Glasgow Caledonian University, UK
Fumihiro Kumeno   Nippon Institute of Technology, Japan
Hien T. Nguyen   Ton Duc Thang University, Vietnam
Germanas Budnikas   Kaunas University of Technology, Lithuania
Tadashi Iijima   Keio University, Japan
George Dragoi   University Politehnica of Bucharest, Romania
Danila Parygin   Volgograd State Technical University, Russia
Marian Hostovecky   University of SS. Cyril and Methodius, Slovakia
Nadezhda Yarushkina   Ulyanovsk State Technical University, Russia

Contents

Keynote Papers

Knowledge Discovery in Patent and Open Sources for Creative Tasks

Open Science Semantic Technologies

Computer Vision and Knowledge-Based Control

Pro-active Modeling in Intelligent Decision Making Support

Data Science in Energy Management and Urban Computing

Design Creativity in CASE/CAI/CAD/PDM

Intelligent Internet of Services and Internet of Things

Data Science in Social Networks Analysis

Creativity and Game-Based Learning

Intelligent Assistive Technologies: Software Design and Application

Keynote Papers

Creativity, Innovation and Entrepreneurship: A Critical Overview of Issues and Challenges

Peter P. Groumpos[✉]

Laboratory for Automation and Robotics,
Department of Electrical and Computer Engineering,
University of Patras, 26500 Patras, Greece
Groumpos@ece.upatras.gr

Abstract. Creativity in intelligent technologies & data science is recognized as a growing and challenging scientific field. Additional concepts of Innovation and Entrepreneurship are examined and their important role in developing theories and technologies for intelligent systems and data science is shown. The Triangle of Knowledge that contains all these concepts is presented and analyzed. The role of human intelligence in developing Intelligent Control and Cognitive Control is analyzed. The need for developing an Intelligent Cognitive Control Theory as a new unified theory is emphasized.

Keywords: Creativity · Innovation · Entrepreneurship · Deep Learning · Intelligent Control · Cognitive Control

1 Introduction

The name and main theme of this conference is Creativity in Intelligent Technologies and Data Science. Very challenging in the very interesting times we live. However all these cannot stand by themselves without taking into considerations many other scientific concepts and especially innovation and entrepreneurship [1]. Intelligent Technologies and Data Science, which are by them broad technological challenges, cover many and various scientific areas. What is more, Intelligent Technologies cannot be studied without considering the Innovation concept and Data Science without Artificial Intelligent, Big Data driven systems and data mining.

Creativity, Innovation and Entrepreneurship (CIE) have been increasingly recognized as engines to foster a new "globalized world culture", driving forward new socio-economic developments. However, their relationships from the competence-based approach aren't yet sufficiently understood [1–4]. An ongoing debate takes place at the heart of Europe 2020. In this Plenary paper an effort is made to define these important concepts, realize their interdependence and connect them with the Triangle of Knowledge (ToK) [5]. We are living in an era when the speed of innovation and inventions in the fields of science, culture, technology and industrialization is more accelerated than any other time in the history of humankind. Entrepreneurship has been identified as an engine of economic and social development which can lead to growth, can increase productivity and therefore create jobs. However, the concept of entrepreneurship is merged largely with concepts such as creativity and innovation.

© Springer International Publishing AG 2017
A. Kravets et al. (Eds.): CIT&DS 2017, CCIS 754, pp. 3–20, 2017.
DOI: 10.1007/978-3-319-65551-2_1

In this Plenary Paper an effort is also made to see how these key factors as developments can be of help for sustainable growth of communities. Definitions, of the three concepts, Creativity, Innovation and Entrepreneurship (CIE) are provided in Sect. 2. In Sect. 3 how these three concepts are creating new knowledge is analyzed and the reasons for the generation of the Cyber-Physical System (CPS), Internet of Things (IoT) and the Big Data Driven World (BDDW) are provided. The important relation of creativity to Intelligent Technologies and Data Systems is highlighted in Sect. 4, in which the definition of Intelligent Control is also provided. Section 5 relates Deep Learning (DL) to Big data systems. The challenging question of which type of control to be used, between Intelligent Control and Cognitive Control is addressed in Sect. 6. Finally Sect. 7 provides a summary of the paper and a number of future directions.

2 Creativity, Innovation and Entrepreneurship: Definitions and Aspects

Creativity: A short definition of creativity: the ability to produce original and unusual ideas, or to make something new or imaginative. Another definition: Creativity is the process of breaking out of established patterns; it is the reorganization, recombination or reinterpretation of concepts and ideas for getting something unique and previously unknown. It is the ability to transcend traditional ideas, rules, patterns, relationships, or the like, and to create meaningful new ideas, forms, methods, and interpretations.

The year 1950 has been viewed as a landmark in creativity research, when Guilford [7], first presented his Creativity address to the American Psychological Association. Until then, very few articles on creativity had been published, but after the address output grew considerably. Since the 1960s research has focused on areas such as creativity as an intellectual ability, the training of creativity thinking; the creative individual, the relationship with intelligence, creative people as divergent problem solvers and scientific understanding of creativity.

From Wikipedia we have: **Creativity** is a phenomenon whereby something new and somehow valuable is formed. The created item may be intangible (such as a concept, a scientific theory, or a musical composition) or a physical object (such as an invention, a new space machine or a nanocontrol device). Scholarly interest in creativity involves many definitions and concepts pertaining to a number of disciplines: engineering, physics, technology, manufacturing, space, economics and business, philosophy (particularly philosophy of science), education, computer science, cognitive science, psychology, theology, sociology and linguistics, covering the relations between creativity and general intelligence, mental and neurological processes, personality type and creative ability, creativity and mental health; the potential for fostering creativity through education and training, especially as augmented by technology; the maximization of creativity for national economic benefit, and the application of creative resources to improve the effectiveness of teaching and learning. The concept of creativity is extensively discussed in Wikipedia (the interested researcher should study this).

Theories of creativity have focused on a variety of factors. The dominant factors are identified as the "four Ps" 4Ps—Person, Process, Product and Place, [8]. Let us look briefly into each one of these four factors in relation to creativity.

PERSON: The person is at the center of any creative endeavor. They use their skills, the environment (or press), their creative abilities and their motivation, to create a product, from a robot arm to a clay pot. Creative abilities of an individual are not easy to measure. But they are measurable with various different indicators.

PROCESS: A focus on process is shown in cognitive approaches that try to describe thought mechanisms and techniques for creative thinking. The Process refers to the procedure used by the Person to develop the Product. Note that, the Process refers to the thought process rather than the methodology. It is the way the person thinks when he/she is attempting to solve a problem or create a new solution.

PRODUCT: Product is built by the Person and is the result of the creative Process. It is the new innovation. Product is probably the least studied factor in the field of creativity. They are generally looked at as the outcome of the Process and the Person. There is also a debate on the exact definition of the creative product. Current consensus dictates that the Product has to be both novel and useful.

PLACE (also named environmental Press): A focus on Place (or environmental Press) considers the circumstances in which creativity flourishes, such as degrees of autonomy, and access to resources. It represents the environment and the climate in which the Person operates and functions in, to create the Product. It refers to conditions conducive/prohibitive for creativity. The Place includes (but not limited to): organizational culture, resources and best practices.

In order to be creative you must also have the ability to imagine new things.

Innovation: Discussions about innovation are often made difficult because people are unclear about the exact meanings of some key terms. In particular there is confusion about the difference between creativity, innovation and invention. Let us start with some definitions: Creativity was defined above as the capability or act of conceiving something original or unusual. Innovation is the implementation of something new and Invention is the creation of something that has never been made before and is recognized as the product of some unique insight.

Innovation is the process of translating an idea or invention into a good or service that creates value or for which customers will pay. To be called an innovation, an idea must be replicable at an economical cost and must satisfy a specific need. Innovation involves deliberate application of information, imagination and initiative in deriving greater or different values from resources, and includes all processes by which new ideas are generated and converted into useful products. In business, innovation often results when ideas are applied by the company in order to further satisfy the needs and expectations of the customers. Originally Innovation was part of Technology Transfer, Fig. 1.

In a social context, innovation helps create new methods for alliance creation, joint venturing, flexible work hours, and creation of buyers' purchasing power. Innovations are divided into two broad categories: (a) Evolutionary innovations (continuous or dynamic evolutionary innovation) that are brought about by many incremental

Fig. 1. Original model of three phases of the process of Technology Transfer

advances in technology or processes (b) revolutionary innovations (also called discontinuous innovations) which are often disruptive and new.

Innovation is synonymous with risk-taking and organizations that create revolutionary products or technologies take on the greatest risk because they create new markets.

Entrepreneurship: The capacity and willingness to develop organize and manage a business venture along with any of its risks in order to make a profit. The most obvious example of entrepreneurship is the starting of new businesses. In economics, entrepreneurship combined with land, labor, natural resources and capital can produce profit. Entrepreneurial spirit is characterized by innovation and risk-taking, and is an essential part of a nation's ability to succeed in an ever changing and increasingly competitive global marketplace.

Entrepreneurship has traditionally been defined as the process of designing, launching and running a new business, which typically begins as a startup company, offering a product, process or service for sale or hire. The people who create these businesses are called entrepreneurs. It has been defined as the "capacity and willingness to develop, organize and manage a business venture along with any of its risks in order to make a profit". While definitions of entrepreneurship typically focus on the launching and running of businesses, due to the high risks involved in launching a start-up, a significant proportion of businesses have to close, due to "lack of funding, bad business decisions, an economic crisis – or a combination of all of these" [or due to lack of market demand].

Recent advances stress the fundamentally uncertain nature of the entrepreneurial attempt by anyone or a group of people. Although opportunities may exist their existence cannot be discovered or identified prior to their actualization into profits. What appears as a real opportunity ex ante might actually be a non-opportunity at all. Because the entrepreneurs lacking the necessary knowledge, business skills, experience or necessary funds. Statistics show that only four (4) out of ten (10) entrepreneurs will succeed on their first effort to start a new business.

Traditionally, an entrepreneur has been defined as "a person who starts, organizes and manages any enterprise, especially a business, usually with considerable initiative and risk. The entrepreneur is commonly seen as a business leader and innovator of new ideas and business processes.

3   How Creativity, Innovation and Entrepreneurship Are Related to Creating New Knowledge

Creating new Knowledge? YES this is the main question: how new knowledge is created!? The ability to store, aggregate, and combine data and then use the results to perform deep analyses has become ever more accessible as trends such as Moore's Law in computing, its equivalent in digital storage, and cloud computing continue to lower costs and other technology barriers. Further, the ability to generate, communicate, share, and access data has been revolutionized by the increasing number of people, devices, and sensors that are now connected by digital networks. All these have been possible thanks to the Creativity, innovation and Entrepreneurship of people and have created among many other things, the interesting Cyber-Physical Systems (CPS), Internet of Things (IoT) and Big Data Driven World (BDDW). One is for sure: all three contain Knowledge.

It is very interesting to connect all of these to the concept of the Triangle of Knowledge (ToK) Fig. 2, [5]. In Ref [5] is shown how the Triangle of Knowledge as a Driving Force for Sustainable Growth in Developing Nations.

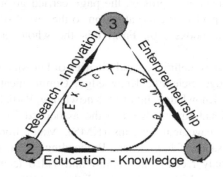

Fig. 2. The Triangle of Knowledge (ToK) based on excellence

It is very interesting to see all these, from a universal point of view. In the Triangle of Knowledge two of the three concepts been analyzed in this paper, innovation and Entrepreneurship, are the two sides of the ToK. In addition the base of the ToK, Education-Knowledge is directly related to creating new knowledge, or in other words creativity. From another point of view the circle of excellence could be consider as the creative force (creativity) to all three sides of the ToK creating new knowledge in the whole spectrum of the sides of the ToK.

But what is knowledge? The definition of knowledge is a matter of ongoing debate among philosophers and scientists for many years even from the ancient world and especially in the field of epistemology. Plato in his dialogue Theaetetus discusses the nature of knowledge, the Greek word for which is "episteme". In the dialogue, Socrates and Theaetetus provide three definitions, starting with the least satisfactory: "knowledge is nothing but perception", then "knowledge is true judgment", and, finally, "knowledge is true judgment with an account" in the original Greek text: "Ἔστιν οὖν επιστήμη δόξα". It is believed more discussion should be held over the matter. Some claim that these conditions are not sufficient, Gettier case, who gives examples allegedly demonstrate [6]. There are a number of alternatives proposed, including Robert Nozick's arguments for a requirement that knowledge 'tracks the truth' and Simon Blackburn's additional requirement that we do not want to say that those who meet any of these conditions 'through a defect, flaw, or failure' have knowledge. Richard Kirkham suggests that our definition of knowledge requires that the evidence for the belief necessitates its truth [6].

While many would agree that one of the most universal and significant tools for the transfer of knowledge is writing and reading (of many kinds), argument over the usefulness of the written word exists nonetheless, with some scholars skeptical of its impact on societies. Further discussion is needed on this issue but cannot be covered on this paper. Classical early modern theories of knowledge, especially those advancing the influential empiricism of the philosopher John Locke, were based implicitly or explicitly on a model of the mind which likened ideas to words [9]. This analogy between language and thought laid the foundation for a graphic conception of knowledge in which the mind was treated as a table, a container of content that had to be stocked with facts reduced to letters, numbers or symbols. This created a situation in which the spatial alignment of words on the page carried great cognitive weight, so much so that educators paid very close attention to the visual structure of information on the page and in notebooks [10]. From this the whole graph theory has been developed [11].

There are several, types, definitions and theories of knowledge. So for example we have: Explicit Knowledge, Scientific Knowledge, Communicated Knowledge, Tacit Knowledge, Embedded Knowledge, Intuitive Knowledge, Partial Knowledge, Situated Knowledge, Organizational Knowledge, and the associated Knowledge Management and the Knowledge Management Systems (KMS). Major libraries today can have millions of books, thousands of Journals and Proceedings of International Conferences on Knowledge. It is only recently that audio and video technology for recording knowledge has become available and the use of these still requires replay equipment and electricity. Verbal teaching and handing down of knowledge is limited to those who would have contact with the transmitter or someone who could interpret written work. Writing is still the most available and most universal of all forms of recording and transmitting knowledge. It stands unchallenged as mankind's primary technology of knowledge transfer down through the ages and to all cultures and languages of the world.

Everybody accepts that knowledge is power. Knowledge acquisition involves complex cognitive processes: perception, communication, and reasoning, while the three concepts of Creativity, Innovation and Entrepreneurship along with the ToK are the driving forces for every society to seek sustainable development, viable economic and social growth.

Two points must be made here. (1) One is the term scientific Knowledge which is related to many science and engineering problems. The development of the scientific method has made a significant contribution to how knowledge of the physical world and its phenomena is acquired. To be termed scientific, a method of inquiry must be based on gathering observable and measurable evidence subject to specific principles or laws of reasoning and experimentation. A scientific way of thinking is something that anyone can use, at any time, whether or not they are in the process of creating new knowledge. Thinking scientifically involves asking questions that can be answered analytically by performing experiments and collecting data or creating a mathematical model and then testing one's ideas or by observing physical or human made systems and record measurable data based on the observation. A scientific way of thinking inherently includes creativity in approaching explanations while staying within the confines of the data. Thinking scientifically does not mean rejecting your culture and background, but recognizing the role that they play in your way of thinking and (2) The term scientific is generic and is used for other concepts been used in this paper such for example as: scientific creativity, scientific innovation and scientific entrepreneurship.

Important remark: Scientific knowledge may not involve a claim to certainty, maintaining skepticism means that a scientist will never be absolutely certain when they are correct and when they are not. It is thus an irony of proper scientific method that one must doubt even when correct, in the hopes that this practice will lead to greater convergence on the absolute truth in general.

Until recent times, at least in the Western tradition, it was always taken for granted that knowledge was something possessed only by humans. Sometimes the notion might stretch to Society-as-such, as in (e.g.) "the knowledge possessed by the East or Arab culture" (as opposed to its individual members), but that was not assured either. Today however many scientists believes that knowledge is also part of biological domains where "knowledge" might be said to reside, include: the immune system, and in the DNA of the genetic code. In addition many also believe that knowledge is part of big machines that have tremendous amount of data that have been stored either by humans and/or automatically by permanent devices that are observing and recording data of physical and human made systems. These big data system world which are associated with the Cyber Physical Systems (CPS) and the Internet of Things (IoT) have created a new challenge as how new knowledge is created. Today a number of methods have been developed to extract the knowledge been hidden in these systems. One such method that recently is the most known is Deep Learning (DL) [12, 13].

Such considerations seem to call for a separate definition of "knowledge" to cover: (1) the biological systems and (2) the new "Big Data Driven World" (BDDW).

For biologists, "knowledge" must be usefully available to the system, though that system need not be conscious. There some criteria so we can define Knowledge of biological systems and two of them are:

(a) The system should apparently be dynamic and self-organizing and
(b) The knowledge must constitute some sort of representation of "the outside world" or ways of dealing with it, directly or indirectly.

However trying to define new truth knowledge from the second category that of "Big Data Driven World" (BDDW) is not an easy task. For one thing it is very knew and extremely complicated. For example who will guarantee that the available data on the BDDW can be trusted have been reliable and have come from the real source? There many other critical issues before we accept methods of "Data mining" and value their findings or results as new real knowledge; Knowledge that must be valid, reliable and useful.

THUS the real question is if some way exists for the system to access this "information" quickly enough and then create "knowledge" been reliable and useful. However Knowledge alone will not provide solutions to today's world problems. Knowledge (existing and new generated) must be dynamically blended and synergistically interconnected with many other components and parameters of continuous growth and sustainable development of a region. The strategy for a knowledge-based society (KBS) calls for new kinds of knowledge partnerships among disciplines as well as among the major sectors of society. These partnerships must be sought through the concepts of Creativity, Innovation, Entrepreneurship, Intelligence and the Triangle of Knowledge, Fig. 2 and references [3–5, 14]. So how intelligence gets into the discussion of Creativity, the ToK and the Big Data Driven World (BDDW)?

4 Why Creativity in Intelligent Technologies and Data Science?

Now after presenting and analyzing all the above, we would like to rise a very interesting and challenging question as to how important is to hold International conferences with these concepts as this conference on the historic city of Russia (Volgograd)? The answer is YES and we do not have enough Forums to discuss and debate these important and challenging concepts. Because they are related to the structure of our brains and understanding our minds. If one were to rank a list of civilization's greatest and most elusive intellectual challenges, the problem of "decoding" ourselves, understanding the inner workings of our minds and our brains, and how the architecture of these elements is encoded in our genome, would surely be at the top. Yet the diverse fields that took on this challenge, from philosophy and psychology to computer science, engineering, health and neuroscience, have been full of disagreement and loaded with endless discussions about the right approach. There are many reasons for this disagreement. Among them is the concept of Intelligence and Intelligent Systems. What is Intelligence? How is it related to creativity and innovation? How human intelligence is related to the brain? In addition how human intelligence is related to cognition and proactive control? All these important and challenging questions cannot be answered in a plenary paper. Therefore an attempt will be made to briefly analyze these concepts and arrive to a possible research area, which could be: **Intelligent Cognitive Control theory**. The concepts of creativity and innovation have defined and explained briefly above. It remains to define and discuss the concepts of Intelligence, Human Intelligence, Cognition, and Cognitive Control.

Intelligence can be defined as a general mental ability for reasoning, problem solving, and learning. From Wikipedia "**Intelligence** has been defined in many different ways including as one's capacity for logic, understanding, self-awareness, learning, emotional knowledge, planning, creativity, and problem solving. It can be more generally described as the ability to perceive information and to retain it as knowledge to be applied towards adaptive behaviors within an environment or context". Because of its general nature, intelligence integrates cognitive functions such as conception, apprehension, attention, learning, language, or planning. On the basis of this definition, intelligence can be reliably measured by standardized tests with obtained scores predicting several broad social outcomes such as educational achievement, job performance, health, and longevity. Intelligence is most widely studied in humans, but has also been observed in non-human animals and in plants. Another term is Artificial Intelligence (AI). It is commonly implemented in computer systems using program software.

Again from Wikipedia "Human intelligence is the intellectual power of humans, which is marked by high level cognition, motivation, and self-awareness. Intelligence enables humans to remember descriptions of things and use those descriptions in future behaviors. It is a cognitive process". It gives humans the cognitive abilities been named above. Human Intelligence enables them to experience, think and act.

Cognition is the human mental action or process of acquiring knowledge and understanding through thought, experience, reasoning, imagination, judging, remembering, comprehension, conscious thinking insight and the senses. Traditionally, the various branches of cognitive science have viewed the mind as an abstract information processor, whose connections to the outside world were of little theoretical importance. Perceptual and motor systems, though reasonable objects of inquiry in their own right, were not considered relevant to understanding "central" cognitive processes.

Proactive Control is a very recent term. There is not a well formulated definition or is there any one? More often the term cognitive control appears and is confused with proactive control. It will be shown that Proactive Control is a subset of the more generic term Cognitive Control. Furthermore attention must also be devoted and to reactive Control which is also is directly related to Cognitive Control. To understand these concepts we need to consider some other related one such proactivity. Traditionally proactivity was about being self-starting and change oriented in order to enhance personal or organizational effectiveness, such as by making improvements to work procedures or using one's initiative to solve a problem. Today on all areas (scientific and not) a shift away from the traditional work structure toward a modern one is taking place the last two decades. This shift heavily rely more on team- based and clustering work rather than individuals although the traditional proactivity characteristics for each individual remain to be the same. For example in manufacturing an employee needed to be self-reliant, have imagination and use initiatives to effectively perform his job. Today he must be able to work on a team-based environment and possess the quality of proactivity [15, 16]. Thus Proactivity is a set of self-starting, action-oriented behaviors aimed at modifying the situation or oneself to achieve greater personal or organizational effectiveness.

Until recently Cognitive Control was considered mainly only as a human process. Cognitive control examines the psychological and neural mechanisms by which people actively maintain information such as goals, instructions, plans, or specific prior events for short periods of time, and use this information to appropriately guide and control their behavior. Thus Cognitive Control is central to our notions of consciousness, feelings, agency, and will. Higher-level cognitive functions such as attention and working memory are thought to rely critically on control processes. Thus as a human process, it was believed determining the mechanisms of Cognitive Control was one of the fundamental questions for psychology, neuroscience, and philosophy.

However the last few decades Machine learning, along with many other disciplines within the field of artificial intelligence, active systems and intelligence systems, is gaining popularity, and it may in the not so distant future have a colossal impact on all the scientific fields. In simple terms, machine learning is a branch of the larger discipline of Artificial Intelligence, which involves the design and construction of computer applications or systems that are able to learn based on their data inputs and/or outputs. Basically, a machine learning system learns by experience; that is, based on specific training, the system will be able to make generalizations based on its exposition to a number of cases and then be able to perform actions after new or unforeseen events. Machine learning incorporates other data analysis disciplines, ranging from predictive analytics and data mining to pattern recognition. A variety of specific algorithms are used for this purpose. Deep Learning (DL) is a new fast growing methodology for Data mining. DL has been related to the concepts of this paper is addressed in Sect. 5.

We defined above intelligence but we did not mention Intelligent Control which has been an active research field for the last 30–40 years and is heavily related to creativity and Innovation. IEEE Control Systems Society's Technical Committee on Intelligent Control defines: "The area of intelligent control is a fusion of a number of research areas in systems and control, Computer science and operation research among others, coming together, merging and expanding in new directions …" [17]. A key sentence here is fusion of research areas which are more than the ones been included on the IEEE definition, such as neural networks, neuroscience, active systems, Robotics, Psychology and structural system theory. Today more than ever before we need to control Complex Dynamic Systems (CDS). All systems around us are complex, dynamic and nonlinear. In addition fuzziness, ambiguity and uncertainty are present on all these systems.

I am afraid that only if we wisely analyze and study the scientific and technological power of CONTROL, we can have a hope for solving all our complex problems so that the world will live in peace and realize sustainable development and steady economic growth. By wisely I mean that all related concepts-forces will act harmoniously and in perfect symmetry. Figure 2 shows that the triangle of knows must be an equilateral triangle in order to obtain the maximum area. In the same way all concepts-forces must be connected on a triangular way but again obey the rule of the triangular to be equilateral. For example in Fig. 3 the base of the triple concepts: Control-Information-Communication is control. You could generate huge amount of information and also have fantastic communication capacities. However if you do not have the

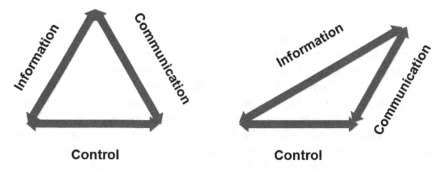

Fig. 3. The important role of control in information and communication systems

proper and reliable control your system will not operate efficiently, effectively and with the minimal cost. No one denies that over the whole scientific and technical history a number of methods of control have been growing. So we have simple open control, linear control, automatic control, continuous vs discrete control, feedback control, PID control, adaptive control, robust control, intelligent control, supervisory control, hybrid control, distributed control, fuzzy control, decentralized control, Model-Follower control, non-linear control, stochastic control and some other of special type depending the application. Now that we have clarified all related concepts that are deeply inter-connected the question arises: are all today's control concepts and methods sufficient and capable in solving the everyday world's problems and challenges that possess complexity, fuzziness, ambiguity and uncertainty? **Unfortunately** NOT. Despite the so many models and methods of CONTROL, we are not happy and satisfied. We are still looking for a unified theory of CONTROL.

Today most goal-oriented "intelligent systems" perform only those or similar tasks and "controls" they were programmed for. What is needed is an alternative approach for behavior learning, for reconfigurable "controls" and task execution. Specifically, we see cognitive flexibility and adaptability in the human brain as desirable design goals and tools for the next generation of "intelligent systems". Several cognitive architec-tures have been implemented for the purpose of testing human psychological models, but such models have not been fully adopted by the academic and scientific commu-nities. Anderson et al. presents an interesting integrated theory of the mind [18]. The human brain is known to process a variety of stimuli in parallel, ignore non-critical stimuli to execute the task in hand, and learn new tasks with minimum outside assistance. For example, humans have the capacity to receive and process enormous amount of sensory information from the environment, exhibiting integrated sensori-motor intelligence as early as two years old. Creativity and innovation are part of this dynamic process. Thus it is a challenge for "control engineers" and all scientists to find ways to realize human's robust sensorimotor mechanisms within machine learning. This process is called "**Cognitive Control**", which is unique to humans and a handful of animals. We will address the interesting scientific fields of Intelligent Control and Cognitive Control in Sect. 6.

But why Creativity in Intelligent Technologies and Data Science? Both, creativity and intelligence are mental processes or abilities. It is a long process and endless debates to get detailed knowledge about these terms. However, the basic difference between the two is: Creativity is the ability to transcend traditional ideas, rules, pat-terns, relationships, or the like, and to create meaningful new ideas, forms, methods, and interpretations. It is a subjective value while intelligence is a general ability or capacity of being very smart, knowledgeable, educated, and well informed. Intelligence is influenced by our own understanding of the concept. Intelligence is what one can improve by studies, reasoning, understanding and learning. It is most widely studied in humans, but it is also used for animals and plants.

On the other hand, creativity is a phenomenon where one tries to create something new or valuable. It is the ability to cause, to exist, or to create something of subjective value. In creativity, intelligence plays a very important role. One cannot create anything if he is not perceived to associate with intelligence. It is the process of producing something original and worthwhile. However creativity also plays an important role when intelligence is acquired either by an individual or o group of people. According to Guilford, a renowned psychologist, "creativity involves divergent thinking with respect to the traits of fluency, flexibility and originality of thought process. It means that creativity involves the thinking process in various forms with the originality and flexibility in the thought process" [7]. Thus creativity and Intelligence are strongly interconnected. Creativity is a daily thought which a person one day explores or produces. Intelligence certainly plays a part in creative thinking. So intelligence matters, it demonstrates your ability to gather knowledge and effectively use it. Creativity is the ability to go beyond the intelligence frame and capitalize on seemingly random connections of concepts.

Intelligence is also related to Big Data science and Deep Learning (DL), a topic been addressed in the next section.

5 Deep Learning and Big Data Systems

The general focus of machine learning is the representation of the input data and generalization of the learnt patterns for use on future unseen data. The goodness of the data representation has a large impact on the performance of machine learners on the data: a poor data representation is likely to reduce the performance of even an advanced, complex machine learner, while a good data representation can lead to high performance for a relatively simpler machine learner. Thus, feature engineering, which focuses on constructing features and data representations from raw data, is an important element of machine learning. Feature engineering consumes a large portion of the effort in a machine learning task, and is typically quite domain specific and involves considerable human input. Big Data represents the general realm of problems and techniques used for application domains that collect and maintain massive volumes of raw data for domain-specific data analysis e.g. speech processing, geological phenomena, computer vision, space exploration and other. Modern data-intensive technologies as well as increased computational and data storage resources have contributed heavily to the development of Big Data Driven World (BDDW) or as Big Data science has been referred by some scientists.

Deep Learning (DL) is the new big trend in machine learning. [21–23]. It had many recent successes in computer vision, automatic speech recognition and natural language processing. DL is a branch of machine learning based on a set of algorithms that attempt to model high-level abstractions in data by using multiple processing layers, with complex structures or otherwise, composed of multiple non-linear transformations. Deep learning algorithms use a huge amount of unsupervised data to automatically extract complex representation. These algorithms are largely motivated by the field of artificial intelligence, which has the general goal of emulating the human brain's ability to observe, analyze, learn, and make decisions, especially for extremely complex problems. Research in this area attempts to make better representations and create models to and particularly software tools that learn these representations from large-scale unlabeled data. DL software attempts to mimic the activity in layers of neurons in the neocortex, the wrinkly 80% of the brain where thinking occurs. The software learns, in a very real sense, to recognize patterns in digital representations of sounds, images, and other data. This basic idea is decades old, and it has led to as many disappointments as breakthroughs. But because of improvements in mathematical formulas and increasingly powerful computers, computer scientists can now model many more layers of virtual neurons than ever before. Thus DL is visiting again Artificial Intelligence (AI) and Artificial Neural Networks (ANN) with the objective to reformulate them given all recent scientific developments.

Some of the representations are inspired by advances in neuroscience and are loosely based on interpretation of information processing and communication patterns in a nervous system, such as neural coding which attempts to define a relationship between various stimuli and associated neuronal responses in the brain. There are various DL architectures such as deep neural networks, convolutional deep neural networks, deep belief networks, recurrent neural networks among other ones which are actually the same ones as those was developed in AI and ANN. A number of reviews of DL and for certain branches of AI has been reported recently. A recent one, "Deep Learning in neural networks: An overview", by Schmidhuber in 2015 [21], provides a thorough and extensive overview. This historical survey compactly summarizes relevant work, much of it from the previous millennium. Shallow and Deep Learners are distinguished by the depth of their credit assignment paths, which are chains of possibly learnable, causal links between actions and effects. The review covers deep supervised learning (also recapitulating the history of backpropagation), unsupervised learning, reinforcement learning and evolutionary computation, and indirect search for short programs encoding deep and large networks. The two key aspects of DL are: (1) models consisting of multiple layers or stages of nonlinear information processing; and (2) methods for supervised or unsupervised learning of feature representation at successively higher, more abstract layers. An extensive overview of DL algorithms is provided in Ref. [25].

6   Intelligent and Cognitive Control

We have arrived at a very critical and challenging point. We are faced with a dilemma. We need to decide between two important control scientific concepts. Which is better: Intelligent Control or Cognitive Control? And with which criteria one will make a decision, especially when a critical situation is under consideration. (a medical problem, an energy or environment urgent situation). Although the concept of Intelligent Control was analyzed above in this paper the concept of Cognitive Control has been superficially covered but is still not scientifically analyzed. Unfortunately there are quite a few terms such as: proactive, reactive, pre-active and inactive controls which are all associated with Cognitive Control. Botvinick et al. [20] presents an interesting point of conflict monitoring and Cognitive Control, which demonstrates why Cognitive Control is a difficult research area [20]. However, for the needs of this paper (and due to page limitations) only the terms proactive control, reactive control and Cognitive Control will be considered and briefly analyzed.

Cognitive Control is essential to flexible, goal-directed behavior under uncertainty, yet its underlying mechanisms are not clearly understood. Because attentional functions are known to allocate mental resources and prioritize the information to be processed by the brain. These executive functions of alerting, orienting, executive control and the interactions among them contribute to perform Cognitive Control in the presence of uncertainty and fuzzy environments. Executive functions (referred to as executive control and cognitive control) are a set of cognitive processes that are necessary for the Cognitive Control: selecting and successfully monitoring behaviors that facilitate meet the chosen goals and objectives. There is an Attentional Function Index (AFI), designed to measure perceived effectiveness in common activities requiring attention and working memory, particularly the ability to formulate plans, carry out tasks, and function effectively in daily life. According to many scientists, Cognitive Control examines the psychological and neural mechanisms by which people actively maintain information such as goals, instructions, plans, or specific prior events for short periods of time, and use this information to appropriately guide and control their behavior. Thus, Cognitive Control is central to our notions of consciousness, feelings and will.

Recent work, Braver et al. in 2007 [24], highlights a distinction between proactive and reactive modes of cognitive control, which Braver and colleagues have termed the dual mechanisms of control (DMC). Proactive Control is conceptualized as maintenance of goal-relevant information to optimally bias attention, perception and response preparation ahead of a cognitively demanding event. In contrast, reactive control reflects transient, 'on the fly' engagement of control processes at the onset of challenging tasks demands.

Both forms of cognitive control have their benefits, says Braver. Proactive control is generally more effective, but also demands more energy and is more vulnerable to interruptions. Reactive control, though, is more susceptible to interference effects, but is also less demanding than proactive control.

Today determining the mechanisms of Cognitive Control is one of the fundamental questions for all scientists in the fields of psychology, engineering, cybernetics, biology, neuroscience, and even philosophy. Currently this is one of the hottest research topics on the above scientific fields.

While these data provide evidence for the dissociation between proactive and reactive control, examining these processes within the same task has some limitations. First, reactive control is necessarily linked to contextual processes engaged during the cue, thus the reactive control measure is inherently confounded by the degree to which proactive processes are engaged. This might attenuate reactive activity in controls due to their intact proactive processes. While this may be unavoidable for any task, as individuals often engage context maintenance to guide responding, this limitation may be partially mitigated by choosing tasks specifically biased towards one type of control process.

Humans can reason about virtually any issue, and many problems may be solved. Simple and highly complex behavioral repertoires can be learned throughout the lifespan. Importantly, there are widespread individual differences in the ability to reason, solve problems, and learn which lead to human differences in the general ability to cope with challenging situations. And this is very healthy. Reasoning, problem solving, and learning are crucial facets of human intelligence.

Creativity, innovation, entrepreneurship and intelligence play an important and crucial role in solving today's difficult and challenging problems.

Engineers have long used control systems utilizing all kind of "Controls" to model and control all physical and human made systems. A recent paper by Kawamura and Gordon [19] has proposed to go from Intelligent Control to Cognitive Control. However exploring the relationships between human intelligence (intelligent control) and the brain (Cognitive Control) requires a careful analysis and consideration of the structure of human behavior and his/her careful and wise approach to solve the everyday problems that our world is facing. Thus we need both types of Control in an integrated structure such as Intelligent Cognitive Control (ICC). A unified theory is needed taking into consideration of: creativity, innovation, knowledge, intelligence, cognition and entrepreneurship. Thus we will be searching for an **Intelligent Cognitive Control theory**.

It is believed that in this effort, theories of Fuzzy Control and Fuzzy Cognitive Maps (FCM) will be useful and constructive [26, 27].

7 Summary and Future Research Directions

In this Plenary Paper a number of scientific concepts that are vital to the advancement of Science and Technology have been considered. These are: creativity, intelligence, innovation, knowledge, "kind of Controls", cognition, entrepreneurship, deep learning, machine learning, intelligent control and cognitive control. All these scientific concepts have been analyzed in details. Humans must accept that they are the only ones that must take the future of the earth on their own hands. They have the ability and ingenuity to examine and analyze all physical and human made system and make decisions and controls that will guarantee the survival of our planet earth. The ability to control our thoughts and behavior is a fundamental human characteristic. The concepts creativity, innovation, knowledge and entrepreneurship are needed to meet the above objective. The relation of the above mentioned concepts are fundamental in creating new knowledge. As a result of these new scientific challenging areas have emerged among them the Cyber-Physical Systems (CPS), Internet of Things (IoT), Deep Learning (DL) and Big Data Driven World (BDDW). The triangle of Knowledge (ToK) is also very important not only in creating new knowledge but how the process can be optimized. Deep Learning (DL) is one of the most common approach for data mining from the BDDW. The question if we should move from Intelligent Control to Cognitive Control was seriously considered and analyzed. The conclusion is that we need both and a new unified theory must be sought which is proposed to be: **Intelligent Cognitive Control.**

Future research directions according to the scientific presentation of this paper are numerous and very challenging. Intelligent control should involve both intelligence and control theory. It should be based on a serious attempt to understand and replicate the phenomena that we have always called "intelligence" e.g. the generalized, flexible, and adaptive kind of capability that we see in the human brain. Furthermore, it should be firmly rooted in control theory to the fullest extent possible; new mathematical models are needed which take into consideration the fuzzy and uncertain environments. For these new models classical methods at least in principle can be used such as: feedback control, controllability, observability, stability, reachability, autonomous systems, intelligent agents, supervisory control and other classical techniques. These developments of new designs must often be highly intuitive in the early stages, but, once these designs are specified, we should at least do our best to understand them and evaluate them in terms of the deepest possible mathematical theory. Another research topic is that of adaptive critics. They learn slowly on large problems but have generated many real-world success stories on difficult small problems. Complex adaptive critics are the only design approach that shows serious promise of duplicating critical aspects of human intelligence: the ability to cope with large numbers of variables in parallel, in real-time, in a noisy nonlinear environment. In the case of nonlinear systems and in the presence of fuzziness new models and methods are needed based on Fuzzy cognition, Fuzzy Cognitive Maps (FCM), new learning methods and algorithms. New appropriate software tools for all these new approaches must be developed and used on as many as possible real problems development In addition, there are problems in intelligent autonomous control systems that are novel and so they have not studied before at any depth.

Such is the case of hybrid systems for example that combine systems of continuous and discrete state. The marriage of all these fields can only be beneficial to all. Computer science and operation research methods are increasingly used in control problems, while control system concepts such as feedback, and methods that are based on rigorous mathematical framework ca provide the base for new theories and methods in those areas. Many more research challenges can be planned and conducted in the area of Intelligent Control.

In Cognitive Control the task of defining well future research direction is by itself a difficult task.

First of all Cognitive Control is very new scientific area having a lot of theories coming from total different fields; fuzzy theory, neuroscience, neural networks, probability theory, computer science, cybernetics, intelligent systems, experts systems, psychology, information theory, mechatronics, robotic surgery and some other ones. Thus any research challenge in each one of these fields is contributing to understand and comprehend better Cognitive Control.

A first research topic would be to define scientifically Cognitive Control and a number of potential architectures for cognitive control systems. During the past two decades, we have seen major advances in the integration of sensor technologies, artificial intelligence, machine learning and nanocontrolers into a variety of system design and operation. However there still many unsolved research problems within this integration. A next challenge for engineers will be the integration of human-like cognitive control into system design and operation as for example for the next human-kind machines. This would be the development of robots with robust sensorimotor intelligence using a Multiagent based robot control architecture and a biologically inspired intelligent control.

Human behavioral processes range from proactive to reactive and to full deliberation, cognitive control must also be able to switch between these levels to cope with the demand of task and performance, in any situation. According to a number of cognitive psychologists, cognitive control in human is performed through the working memory in the pre-frontal cortex and this switch is still a mystery to them. For example how computational modeling and convergent neuroscience methods, including functional neuroimaging, are used to investigate the neural basis of Cognitive Control. It will take many research efforts and many years to solve this research problem. Again research topics in Cognitive Control can be many, difficult and very challenging.

From all the above perhaps the most challenging research topic is how Intelligent Control and Cognitive Control can be integrated to the new proposed **Intelligent Cognitive Control theory**. If this is ever happen then a new generation of control systems would be available in which the incorporation of properties we usually associate with cognition, such as reasoning, planning, and learning would substantially increase the performance of any system for all criteria (flexibility, reliability, efficiency, adaptability, respect the environment and optimal cost).

However No One Can Predict if and When This Would be Realized
Closing this plenary paper an important question can be raised: what is our vision for the world of 2050? We certainly expect to have a population of 9–10 billion people and for whom we need; to feed them with safe food, to preserve the earth climate, and to secure energy supply to all. The world should be: healthier, better educated, more creative and innovative, have more opportunities for entrepreneurship, richer, more secure with international peace, with less inequality between rich and poor and between man and women.

For any development to be human, sustainable and global it must be centered on the human beings and must at least integrate:

- Economic development
- Social development
- Environmental stewardship
- Political stability (democracy, human rights, eliminate racism, rule of law, people and gender equality)
- Intelligent Cognitive Control theories

The Greek philosopher, Plato had said: "no man is wise enough by himself" and Confucius: "By three methods we may learn wisdom: First, by reflection, which is noblest; second, by imitation, which is easiest; and third by experience, which is the bitterest".

Thus Plato and Confucius show us the way: we must collaborate and cooperate with each other and with the spirit of creativity, innovation, intelligence, wisdom, and entrepreneurship. We must make wise decisions. Together we can do it. Each one alone cannot.

Acknowledgment. I wish to express my sincere gratitude to Mrs. Alexandra Lotsari-Groumpos for her encouragement and assisting in developing this paper as well as many thanks for editing the final version of the paper.

References

1. Edwards-Schachter, M., García-Granero, A., Sánchez-Barrioluengo, M., Quesada-Pineda, H., Amara, N.: Disentangling competences: Interrelationships on creativity, innovation and entrepreneurship. Think. Skills Creat. **16**, 27–39 (2015)
2. Amabile, T.M.: A model of creativity and innovation in organizations. Res. Organ. Behav. **10**, 123–167 (1988). JAI Press Inc.
3. Yusuf, S.: From creativity to innovation. Technol. Soc. **31**(1), 1–8 (2007)

4. Okpara, F.O.: The value of creativity and innovation in entrepreneurship. J. Asia Entrep. Sustain. **3**(2), 1–14 (2007)
5. Groumpos, P.P.: An overview of the triangle of knowledge as a driving force for sustainable growth in developing nations. IFAC Proc. **46**(8), 106–115 (2013)
6. Kirkham, R.L.: Does the Gettier problem rest on a mistake? Mind **93**(372), 501–513 (1984)
7. Guilford, J.P.: Creativity. Am. Psychol. **5**(9), 444–454 (1950)
8. Rhodes, M.: An analysis of creativity. Phi Delta Kappan **42**(7), 306–307N (1961)
9. Hacking, I.: Why Does Language Matter to Philosophy?. Cambridge University Press, Cambridge (1975)
10. Eddy, M.D.: The shape of knowledge: children and the visual culture of literacy and numeracy. Sci. Context **26**(2), 215–245 (2013)
11. Bondy, J.A., Murty, U.S.R.: Graph Theory. Graduate texts in Mathematics, vol. 244. Springer, New York (2008)
12. Goodfellow, I., Bengio, Y., Aaron-Courville, A.: Deep Learning. MIT Press, Cambridge (2016)
13. Gareth, J., Witten, D., Hastie, T., Tibshirani, R.: An Introduction to Statistical Learning: With Applications in R, 1st edn. Springer, New York (2016). Corr. 6th printing 2016 Edition
14. Groumpos, P.P.: Conceptual modeling and decision making support systems for complex dynamical systems: a critical overview. In: ELEKTRO, pp. 52–56. IEEE (2016)
15. Grant, A.M., Ashford, S.J.: The dynamics of proactivity at work. Res. Organ. Behav. **28**, 3–34 (2008)
16. Ilgen, D.R., Pulakos, E.D.: Introduction: employee performance in today's organizations. In: Ilgen, D.R., Pulakos, E.D. (eds.) The changing nature of performance, pp. 1–18. Consulting Psychologists Press, San Francisco (1999)
17. Technical Committee on Intelligent Control. IEEE Control Systems Society. http://robotics.ee.nus.edu.sg/tcic/
18. Anderson, J.R., Bothell, D., Byrne, M.D., Douglass, S., Lebiere, C., Qin, Y.: An integrated theory of the mind. Psychol. Rev. **111**(4), 1036–1060 (2004)
19. Kawamura, K., Gordon, S.: From intelligent control to cognitive control. In: 11th International Symposium on Robotics and Applications (ISORA), Budapest, Hungary, 24–27 July 2006, pp. 1–8 (2006)
20. Botvinick, M.M., Braver, T.S., Barch, D.M., Carter, C.S., Cohen, J.D.: Conflict monitoring and cognitive control. Psychol. Rev. **108**(3), 624–652 (2001)
21. Schmidhuber, J.: Deep learning in neural networks: an overview. Neural Netw. **61**, 85–117 (2015)
22. Domingos, P.: A few useful things to know about machine learning. Commun. ACM **55**(10), 78–87 (2012)
23. Arel, I., Rose, D.C., Karnowski, T.P.: Deep machine learning-a new frontier in artificial intelligence research [research frontier]. IEEE Comput. Intell. Mag. **5**(4), 13–18 (2010)
24. Braver, T.S., Gray, J.R., Burgess, G.: Explaining the many varieties of working memory variation: dual mechanisms of cognitive control. In: Conway, A.R.A., Jarrold, C., Kane, M.J., Miyake, A., Towse, J.N. (eds.) Variation in Working Memory, pp. 76–106. Oxford University Press, Oxford (2007)
25. Groumpos, P.P.: Deep learning vs. Wise learning: a critical and challenging overview. IFAC-PapersOnLine **49**(29), 180–189 (2016)
26. Kosko, B.: Fuzzy cognitive maps. Int. J. Man Mach. Stud. **24**(1), 65–75 (1986)
27. Groumpos, P.P.: Fuzzy cognitive maps basic theories and their application to complex systems. In: Glykas, M. (ed.) Fuzzy Cognitive Maps, pp. 1–22. Springer, Heidelberg (2010). doi:10.1007/978-3-642-03220-2_1

A Method and IR4I Index Indicating
the Readiness of Business Processes
for Data Science Solutions

Maxim Shcherbakov[1](✉), Peter P. Groumpos[2], and Alla Kravets[1]

[1] Volgograd State Technical University, Lenin Avenue 28, 400005 Volgograd, Russia
maxim.shcherbakov@vstu.ru
[2] University of Patras, Greece University Campus, 26504 Rio Achaia, Greece
groumpos@ece.upatras.gr
http://www.vstu.ru, https://www.upatras.gr/

Abstract. The study shows our findings regarding the initialization and implementation of data science projects in existed business processes. The index readiness for intelligence or IR4I is proposed as an indicator of understanding about the readiness of your business processes for data science solutions. The index is based on the min-min convolution of various indicators: (i) business processes maturity indicators, (ii) indicators of the level of automatization and digitalisation of business processes, (iii) extract - transform - load (ETL) processes maturity indicators, (iv) data science infrastructure and technological stacks maturity. A new method of the IR4I index calculation is provided and its contains of six steps. Use case is based on real world task related to daily electric energy consumption forecasting for daily demand ordering. This example shows the application of proposed method and possibilities for improvement of business processes towards its intelligence and efficiency.

Keywords: Data science projects · Business process analysis · Energy management

1 Introduction

Nowadays, the design of systems based on artificial intelligence, machine learning and a large amount of data processing is the hot topic for academic and practical society. The new class of system based on data-driven approaches is widely discussed [2, 15, 19]. This tendency is connected with the law of technical systems development, in particular, with the shift of human intervention to a higher or superior level. It is also known as a supervisory control [21]. At the same time, the areas of implementation of technologies based on intelligent data processing are primarily focused on well-described business processes. Nevertheless, these well-studied processes involve a human as an executor or as a decision

---

M. Shcherbakov — The reported study was partially supported by RFBR research projects 16-37-60066 mol_a_dk, and project MD-6964.2016.9.

A. Kravets et al. (Eds.): CIT&DS 2017, CCIS 754, pp. 21–34, 2017.
DOI: 10.1007/978-3-319-65551-2_2

maker. The accumulation of data regarding various situations or creating training sets in terms of machine learning allows us to talk about the possibility of replacing a human with a machine not only for routine operations implementation but for making decisions as well. In a case of large amount of information machines to work more precisely and without experts biases [11]. In addition, data mining allows detecting hidden insights in data that are useful for business or to implement predictive analytics for making preventive or proactive decisions. The second option is based on the pattern 'detect-forecast-decide-act' of proactive computing approach [5]. In this case, it is assumed that some adequate probabilistic model of the processes exists. The deployment of components for predictive analytics into existing business intelligent solutions is associated with high expectations of significant performance increasing. It may be a trap for decision makers on the high level as they expect the increasing quality of the functioning of enterprise business systems and get more profit.

There is a research question: how to evaluate the readiness of current business processes or enterprise business system for its improvement from point of view of data science? Hence, it is reasonable to define a certain indicator that allows evaluating the degree of readiness of current business processes for development of data science solutions. Also, the indicator should help to estimate the current state of readiness and find the ways for processes improving.

The paper has a deal with new findings of an index of readiness of business processes for data science solutions. The index is named IR4I which is stands for Index of Readiness for intelligence. This IR4I is calculated based on four groups indicators: (i) business processes maturity indicators, (ii) indicators of the level of automatization and digitalisation of business processes, (iii) extract - transform - load (ETL) processes maturity indicators, (iv) data science infrastructure and technological stacks maturity.

2   An Index and a Method

2.1   General Idea

The method for evaluation the readiness of business processes for the implementation of data science solutions consists of six steps. As a result of methodology, the value of index IR4I is calculated. Based on the index value, conclusions are drawn regarding possible scenarios for business process improvement for successful data science solution implementation. The index of readiness to intelligent system deployment is calculated based on four groups indicators.

1. The first group includes indicators which assess the degree of business processes formalisation. In other words, these indicators estimate the maturity of business processes from the management point of view.
2. The second group contains on indicators for detecting the maturity level of automatization and digitalisation of business processes. They show the current state of enterprise business systems.

3. Indicators in the third group estimate the maturity of extract - transform - load (ETL) processes for certain enterprise business systems.
4. The last list of indicators evaluates the quality of existed data science infrastructure and technological stacks maturity.

As a result, the IR4I is calculated based on indicators and min-min convolution operation. Figure 1 shows the scheme of proposed method.

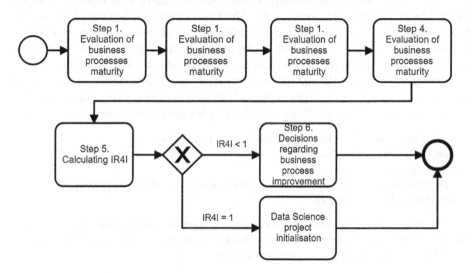

Fig. 1. A scheme for proposed method in BPMN notation. DS stands for data science, and TS is technology stack

Note, each indicator for a group has one out of three values: −1 means current state does not meet the requirements for data science solution development and implementation, 0 means current state satisfy requirements partially and 1 says about full satisfaction of requirements. This simplify way of calculation is considered as initial and can be improved using advanced techniques such as fuzzy cognitive maps [8,13].

2.2   Step 1. Evaluation of Business Processes Maturity

Before calculating of indicators, the business processes formalisation must be done. This is a standard step and is likely to be implemented in companies with an advanced level of maturity (not initial one where processes are unpredictable and poor defined). Business Process Model and Notation (BPMN) is reasonable to use for business processes formalisation and representation for further analysis. In the study, we focus on operations in business processes which are considered as checkpoint operations. It means there is a set of key performance indicators (KPI) defined and used for performance evaluation of the processes.

Checkpoint operations are subjects of evaluation of KPI's values. For such operations, KPIs are defined and formulas for KPI calculating are provided. Also, data sources containing necessary data for KPI calculating are specified. In this case, we can identify two benchmark values for business processes operations performance: (1) the desired KPI set by the manager at a higher level or driven by business requirements and (2) the mean or median KPI based on historical observations.

When the model of business processes was designed, this model is supplemented by two additional components. The first component is a structure of data flows indicating the input and output information for operations in a process's sequence. The second component is definition of data storages or data warehouses. For each data flow, a complete list of attributes for data obtained during the implementation of the operation is created. Each attribute is characterised by a name, a data type (numeric, categorical, text, images) and a range of values (optional). Data access attributes are defined for each data source:

- the type of access (manual, automatic, using API),
- the data access protocol,
- the request-response format,
- the implementation of data access mechanism e.g. data collectors, and
- access to data collectors.

The first group includes two indicators[1]. The first indicator $\alpha_1^{(1)}$ estimates the completeness of the description of business processes. The indicator has the following values according to the conditions

- $\alpha_1^{(1)} = -1$ if a business process is not described (using BMPN or another well-structured notation) or it is described partially, e.g. some operations are missed or key performance indicators are not specified,
- $\alpha_1^{(1)} = 0$ if data flows or data storages are not defined, e.g. there is no additional information about where data come from,
- $\alpha_1^{(1)} = 1$ in case of complete description of a business process.

The second indicator $\alpha_2^{(1)}$ shows the completeness of description of quality metrics or KPI for business process performance evaluation. It has the following values:

- $\alpha_2^{(1)} = -1$ if KPI is not defined or it is not assigned to a certain operation,
- $\alpha_2^{(1)} = 0$ if KPI does not have a formula for calculating or measurement tools are absent[2],
- $\alpha_2^{(1)} = 1$ if KPIs are defined completely.

Note, for $\alpha_2^{(1)}$ the typical KPI might be runtime or execution time. In this case it is reasonable to link execution time and business KPI related to the goals of companies.

---

[1] The superscripts shows the number of a group and subscripts is a number of an indicator in the group, e.g. $\alpha_j^{(i)}$ is j-th indicator in the i-th group.

[2] Also, there is no specific protocol for KPI evaluation.

2.3   Step 2. Evaluation of Automatisation Maturity

To determine maturity of business processes automatisation, it is necessary to classify the operations obtained model in the previous step. Classification can be performed based on types of operations in BPMN notation:

- tasks (actions) are operations having data as input and data as output in terms of data flow; input/output data might be represented as data frames;
- gateways (or decisions) are operations where choices made out a set of alternatives; the choice is made according to criteria;
- events (events) is an external influence on the internal process.

So the one feature inherent in all three types of activities can be single out. This feature is the existence of input and output data recorded and stored in a database. In terms of machine learning these records are considered as data sets for models training. Basically, the dataset contains on pairs of input and output vectors. From the standpoint of the readiness to implement data science solution, the existence of data sets is a crucial issue.

Consider the following indicators that are part of this group of indicators. The first indicator $\alpha_1^{(2)}$ estimates the degree of automation of business processes. The parameter takes the following values:

- $\alpha_1^{(2)} = -1$ if all actions related to information processing are performed manually;
- $\alpha_1^{(2)} = 0$ if at least one operation including information processing actions is performed manually;
- $\alpha_1^{(2)} = 1$ if all data processing operations in a business process is fully automated.

Note, in this research we consider the only activities having a deal with data or information processing.

The second indicator $\alpha_2^{(2)}$ evaluates the level of maturity for the activities related to quality evaluating procedures. The indicator might have one out three values:

- $\alpha_2^{(2)} = -1$ if values of more than one KPI are calculated or specified manually, or a manager participates in the data collecting process,
- $\alpha_2^{(2)} = 0$ if at least one KPI is calculated or set manually, or a human takes part in the collecting process and,
- $\alpha_2^{(2)} = 1$ if the quality indicators are determined automatically without a human intervention.

Finally, the third indicator $\alpha_3^{(2)}$ shows the availability of data in the format of datasets for further processing:

- $\alpha_3^{(2)} = -1$ if data does not represented as datasets (or dataframes),
- $\alpha_3^{(2)} = 0$ if data is partially represents as datasets (or dataframes) or some values are missed,
- $\alpha_3^{(2)} = 1$ if datasets (or dataframes) exist.

2.4 Step 3. Evaluation of ETL Process Maturity

ETL stands for a sequence of three types of operations over data: E – extract data from different data sources, T – transform data according to the storage structure requirements and L – load data to data storage or data warehouse. In this study, the aim is to evaluate readiness of all these operation for data science solution development and deployment. There are three indicators are considered here.

The first parameter $\alpha_1^{(3)}$ in a group characterises the maturity of the processes of data gathering from data sources. Note, the data source might be internal such as OLTP databases or external (e.g. weather forecast services). The indicator have the value

- $\alpha_1^{(3)} = -1$ if data collectors which collect data from various data sources are not exist,
- $\alpha_1^{(3)} = 0$ if data extracted manually,
- $\alpha_1^{(3)} = 1$ if data extraction is fully automated. Note, in the latter case, the schedule can be set for execution of load procedure [18].

The next indicator $\alpha_2^{(3)}$ is about the maturity of data transform process. The flowing values might be set

- $\alpha_2^{(3)} = -1$ if there are no any tools for data transform or data quality estimation,
- $\alpha_2^{(3)} = 0$ human intervention is required for data transform and quality estimation,
- $\alpha_2^{(3)} = 1$ the transform process is fully automated.

The third indicator $\alpha_3^{(3)}$ evaluates the maturity of data loading process into internal data storage for further analytics. Note, the data storage should keep raw data extracted from original data sources and transformed data according to the predefined scheme. The scheme is designed according to the requirements for further efficient data analysis. As an example, the solution can be built based on OLAP structure or HDFS with metadata storage. The indicator has one out of the three values:

- $\alpha_3^{(3)} = -1$ load tools are not available or not applicable,
- $\alpha_3^{(3)} = 0$ load requires intervention of a human,
- $\alpha_3^{(3)} = 1$ load is fully automated.

The main idea behind the indicator evaluation is a level of ETL process automation.

2.5 Step 4. Data Science Infrastructure and Technological Stacks Maturity Evaluation

Data science infrastructure is a complex of hardware and software available for generating statistical models or solutions based on machine learning approach. Note, this study uses CRISP-DM as a basic approach for data mining solution creating [3].

Consider the following indicators in this group. The indicator $\alpha_1^{(4)}$ assess the possibilities of reduction the performed in business processes task to commonly used statistical or machine learning problem. The interpretation of values for this indicator is following

- $\alpha_1^{(4)} = -1$ in case of untypical problem when it is difficult or unobvious to define a task statement,
- $\alpha_1^{(4)} = 0$ when task statement is possible to do, but it is unobvious how to reduce the task to a typical one. The term 'unobvious' means that data scientists should be involved in the processes,
- $\alpha_1^{(4)} = 1$ if the problem to solve reduce to the well-known task.

Note, the literature review shows various types of task classification [15]. The common thing of all different classifications is well-defined task statement.

One of the cost-intensive steps in the modelling process is the stage of data preprocessing or in other words preparation of data for modelling. The indicator $\alpha_2^{(4)}$ was introduced to estimate the preprocessing phase. The indicator takes the value

- $\alpha_2^{(4)} = -1$ if the preprocessing is not formalised and it is necessary to decide to make data preprocessing task statement and find methods to solve the task. Usually, $\alpha_2^{(4)} = -1$ if $\alpha_1^{(4)} = -1$,
- $\alpha_2^{(4)} = 0$ if human intervention in data preprocessing is required,
- $\alpha_2^{(4)} = 1$ if there is no need for preprocessing or preprocessing is performed automatically.

The next step is according to CRISP-DM is modelling stage [3]. It is necessary to define an indicator $\alpha_3^{(4)}$ characterising the degree of modelling automation. The indicator can be equal to one of the following values

- $\alpha_3^{(4)} = -1$ if the task is not defined, the model is not typical or modelling technologies are not defined,
- $\alpha_3^{(4)} = 0$ if an adaptation of new models (structural-parametric optimisation) is required,
- $\alpha_3^{(4)} = 1$ if the repeatable technology for modelling is developed.

The model performance evaluation is a mandatory stage of data science project. The indicator takes the value

- $\alpha_4^{(4)} = -1$ if there are no performance evaluation criteria,
- $\alpha_4^{(4)} = 0$ if it is required to adapt or test the quality criteria for applying,
- $\alpha_4^{(4)} = 1$ if the criteria are developed and experience is available.

2.6   Step 5. Calculating IR4I

The index is calculated according to the formula

$$IR4I = min_{i=1}^{n} \left(min_{j=1}^{k} \left(\alpha_j^{(i)} \right) \right),$$

(1)

where n is a number of operations in a business process, $\alpha_j^{(i)}$ – indicators mentioned in previous sections, k – a number of indicators for every operations. Assume, $\alpha_j^{(i)} \in \{-1, 0, 1\}, \forall i = \overline{1, n}, \forall j = \overline{1, k}$. The values of indicators can be interpreted as following:

- $IR4I = -1$ is a red zone does not meet requirements;
- $IR4I = 0$ is a yellow zone partially meet requirements;
- $IR4I = 1$ is a green zone, meet all requirements.

2.7   Step 6. Making Decision

The decision regarding the development and deploying data science solution for explored process is made. Also the choice of strategy for modification existed business processes is made in this step. Alternative strategies of actions are developed based on value of IR4I index and based on analyzing of included indications. So actions should increase the value of IR4I for certain business processes.

Analysis starts from the general overview of the IR4I calculated value

- $IR4I = -1$ indicates the low success rate for data science solutions implementation, so it is not reasonable to enrich existed automated system with data science components;
- $IR4I = 0$ tends to make additional analysis of the possibility (see horizontal and vertical strategies);
- $IR4I = 1$ is a green line, it is advisable to implement data science solutions.

3   Use Case

This section contains the results of application of proposed method based on new IR4I index. The use case describes the real-world problem of electricity consumption daily costs planning in an middle-size enterprise [12]. As a result of planning, the specific document is created which called *daily order* or *hourly bid*. The *daily order* containing a-day-ahead electric energy consumption demand in format of a set of raws (datetime, comsumption). Further, document sent to energy supply companies for further planning [12]. Based on the deviation of planned and actual electric energy consumption, the enterprise can be subject to a penalty in the amount according to the energy supply contract. The proposed in a paper method is applied for the certain process of daily electric energy consumption planning and daily order creating.

The middle-size manufacturing enterprise is considered as a object of energy consumption. Consequently, all indicators for IR4I are calculated for this specific case. Complementary to all calculated indicators values, the explanation is provided how calculating was made.

Figure 2 represents the business process of electric energy consumption planning in BMPN notation for middle-size manufacturing enterprise. For many countries, the special energy market exists. Specifically the marker deals with the trade and supply of energy. If an enterprise is a participant of the energy market, the special everyday process of demand request generation is needed. The process starts according to the daily schedule.

The process starts with the Step 1 called 'Collecting of energy consumption data'. All information about electric energy consumption in previous time period is stored in plain table documents. The storage *sd1* is a folder with plain table documents. The output of the first step is a set of files containing data about energy consumption in previous time periods. If the folder *sd4* contains files already, these files can be updated by new one. In the second Step 'Analysis of planned production plan', the information about planned production plan is gathered. The output of the step is files which represent union of planned production plan data with data about energy consumption in previous time periods. Finally, these files are stores on the folder *sd4*.

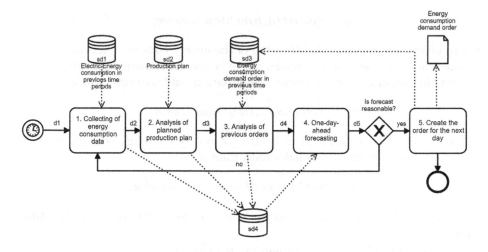

Fig. 2. A scheme for proposed method in BPMN notation

The third step titled as 'Analysis of previous orders' includes a procedure to collect data for further evaluation how data in orders varies from actual data, e.g. forecasting error evaluation. Based on data obtained in the previous steps, the forecasting of electric energy consumption is made in the step 'On-day-ahead forecasting'. The one-day-ahead forecast (KWh) is an output of the fourth step. As enterprise is a subject of fines in case of wrong demand ordering, the KPI for the processes following: mean absolute percentage error must not be exceed 15% and time for creating daily order must not exceed 2 h. The predicted values are estimated according to the manual verification procedure, and a manager who responsible for daily orders makes the decision about the finalisation of the process. The final step is creating the daily order document, signing and sending to the energy market broker.

Let consider the evaluation of described business process using declared method and IR4I index. The formalisation of the business process is high as all necessary data is provided, so $\alpha_1^{(1)} = 1$. The completeness quality metrics or KPI description is high as well, as all necessary KPI was defined precisely (time and errors). The degree of automatisation of business processes $\alpha_1^{(2)} = 0$ as all procedures for data collecting are performed manually. The level of maturity for processes of data collecting and quality metrics evaluation is middle as well $\alpha_2^{(2)} = 0$; KPI related to forecasting performance is calculated manually. The indicator $\alpha_3^{(2)} = 0$ as data stored as plain tables with different format and it is necessary to make datasets for further processing.

Let analyse indicators of the second groups $\alpha_j^{(2)}$ and the actions for improvement of operations. Consider case when all data sources are defined and all data flows are represented in a formal way. In the domain we study it might be: *sd1* – is a data source of data about electric energy consumption. Formally, the data frames stored in *sd1* has the following structure

$$df_1 = \langle objectId, timeStamp, value \rangle ,$$

where *objectId* is a unique identification of the energy consumer, a *timeStamp* is a time where the measure was made, *value* is energy consumption value at the certain time stamp. Using the same formalisation, *sd2* contains data frames

$$df_2 = \langle resourceId, timeStamp, value \rangle ,$$

where *resourceId* – a unique identification of resource (energy consumer) using during the production. *sd3* includes data frames

$$df_3 = \langle objectId, timeStamp, orderedValue \rangle ,$$

where *orderedValue* is predicted energy consumption value for the future time stamps.

Data flows in Fig. 2 can be formalized as following

- *d1* – is an event of initializations of the process;
- *d2* – dataframe with the same attributes for df_1;
- *d3* – contains two dataframes d1 and d2, where d2 has the same set of attributes as for df_2;
- *d4* – contains three data frames, two from *d3* and a dataframe with the same set as for df_3;
- *d5* – dataframe containing predicted values df_3 and a formal description of forecasting model *md*:

$$md = \langle objectId, modelId, description \rangle ,$$

where *modelId* is a unique id of a model and *description* is a high level description of the model, e.g. in *JSON* format.

In spite of data stored in electronic plain table format, $\alpha_1^{(2)} = 0$, as a manager intervention is needed for data collecting or extracting. A manager has to find a necessary file in a folder *ds1* and open the file in appropriate software for further analysis. If there is no electronic storage or some information is stored physically on the paper (book of energy consumption), then $\alpha_1^{(2)} = -1$ (the worst case). If SCADA or an energy management automation system provide the automated formatted data downloading procedure, then $\alpha_1^{(2)} = 1$. In the use case, KPI's are not calculated automatically. Moreover, the operation numbered 3 is applied for this purpose. Based on the definition in previous section, the indicator $\alpha_2^{(2)} = 0$. Forecasting model performance should evaluate according to appropriate error measurements [1,17]. Note, if time measurement is performed manually it is not efficient due to the issues of human factor. Formally, data sets exist if all data is collected in the third steps in one place (data storage). We assume, that $\alpha_3^{(2)} = 1$ in this case. Basically, the data set should not be adapted for further processing. Also, the inner data is not enough for adequate modelling and an access to external data sets need to be configured. This is might be indicated by adding a new operation in data process.

Next, we evaluate indicators in the third group. For extract data indicator evaluation we set $\alpha_1^{(3)} = 0$ as all data source are defined, but data collected manually. In practice, these data are stored in copies of original data files gathered from data storaged *ds1*, *ds2* and *ds3*. Formats of initial data files obtaining from different data sources may varying. It is evident that, the specific format of data files is an additional limitation of the extract process. Next, we estimate $\alpha_2^{(3)} = 0$ because data transformation operation is required. The main reason for this is that gathered data is stored in files with a different format. A manager makes forecast using, for instance, electronic sheets but initial files stored in CSV format. Analogously, we set $\alpha_3^{(3)} = 0$ because of human intervention is needed in the data loading process. At least a manager should point the folder there the uploading data files are located. In fact, the manual operation required due to poor data quality, e.g. missing data or abnormal values. The data quality issues are crucial for loading processes as errors may occur. Finding the wrong data is the time-consuming operation.

Continuing, the estimation of existed infrastructure for data science solution implementation is made (indicators of the fourth group). As one-day-ahead electric energy consumption forecasting is the well-known problem, the problem is reduced to the time series forecasting task. Particular, this is a problem of n-ahead forecasting of univariate time series [10]. For our case study, the indicator $\alpha_1^{(4)} = 1$. The benchmark model for the task can be auto-regression model (AR, ARMA, ARIMA). Note, that time energy series forecasting can be done based on different approaches, e.g. probabilistic approach, symbol-based approach [6]. Data preprocessing is needed due to assumptions made in previous step. The typical preprocessing is sliding window approach. It means we set $\alpha_2^{(4)} = 0$. In the literature, we can find a lot of approaches for time series forecasting [7,12,14,20]. Special attention is given to existed automated forecasting approached and packages [9]. So, the indicator $\alpha_3^{(4)} = 1$. Forecasting performance evaluation can be made using various error measurements [17]. Traditionally, the following error measurements are used for electric energy consumption forecasting: MAE, RMSE, MAPE [12, 20]. However, due to error measurement drawbacks, the choice of appropriate criteria is subject to research [4]. Anyway, we estimate $\alpha_4^{(4)} = 1$.

As the result of estimating, the current use case has the following indicators represented in the Table 1.

Table 1. Indicators for use case

level	$i = 1$	$i = 2$	$i = 3$	$i = 4$
$\alpha_{(i)}^{(1)}$	0	1	-	-
$\alpha_{(i)}^{(2)}$	0	0	1	-
$\alpha_{(i)}^{(3)}$	0	0	0	-
$\alpha_{(i)}^{(4)}$	1	0	1	1

Based on the formula 1, the final value of IR4I is equal to zero. It means, we need to explore the process in detail and define a rational strategy for improvement (see Sect. 4). As the main conclusion, the development and deployment of data science solution for the defined business process is premature.

4   Discussion

So, if IR4I is equal to one, we conclude, that data science solution can be applied over existed automated systems. In this case the standard CRISP-DM process can be applyed for design this kind of solution. On contrast, if $IR4I < 1$ re-engendering of the business process need to be done.

Modification of the process can be performed according two strategies. Conditionally, the strategies are called "*horizontal*" and "*vertical*". The *horizontal* strategy is about the consistent improvement of operations at each level, from level 1 (formalisation of business processes) and ending the last level. Each modification is aimed at increasing the values of indicators. Until the indicator gets maximal value 1. The *vertical* strategy of changing involves the study of several processes in the business process.

Note that automation is a logical step in the development of data science solution. The components of data science solutions are considered as extensions to the existed automation system. Often (as in the example above), it does not make sense to create an additional analytic software architecture, but it is reasonable to use as extensions of existing one.

If a decision is made on the appropriateness of implementing data science solutions or components based on data analysis, the following indicators should be considered. Indicator of the model interpretability $\alpha_1^{(5)}$. The indicator takes the value -1 if the model is a black box and there are no whitening approaches for the model. The parameter is set to 0 if the model is considered as a grey box or a black box with appropriate whitening methods. The proactivity of the processes $\alpha_2^{(5)}$, is characterised by the property of moving human functions to the supervisory level [16,21]. In this case, the indicator is equal to -1 if the model does not satisfy any of the properties and the human need to be involved in the implementation of the process. The indicator is set to 0 if at least one operation can be fully automated. Also, an indicator is equal to 1 if a human performs only supervision without permanent involving. The next indicator $\alpha_3^{(5)}$ - estimate the time performance for presentation of the result. Also, the indicator takes values -1 if the delivery time exceeds the time taken to perform the operation, 0 if the implementation of data science algorithms does not reduce the time of the person to perform the operation, and 1 if the time for performing is less before solution implementation.

5   Conclusion

The readiness of the current business processes for the implementation of data science solution can be formalised and evaluated. We propose the IR4I which is stands for Index of Readiness for intelligence is an index using the min-min convolution of various indicators including: (i) business processes maturity indicators, (ii) indicators of the level of automatization and digitalisation of business processes, (iii) extract - transform - load (ETL) processes maturity indicators, (iv) data science infrastructure and technological stacks maturity.

The method of evaluation is considered which is consist of six steps. The method and IR4I index can be used for the initial stage of data science solution design. However, the proposed IR4I is not sensitive for evolution of improvement. The future works should include the problem of interpretation of changes in business improvement process.

Acknowledgments. The reported study was partially supported by RFBR research projects 16-37-60066 mol a dk, and project MD-6964.2016.9. Also authors would like to thank Pavel Vorobkalov for fruitful discussion and anonymous reviewers for fruitful remarks.

References

1. Armstrong, J.S.: Evaluating forecasting methods. In: International Journal of Forecasting, vol. 30, pp. 443–472. Kluwer Academic Publishers, Norwell (2001)
2. Arnott, D., Pervan, G.: Eight key issues for the decision support systems discipline. Decis. Support Syst. **44**(3), 657–672 (2008)
3. CRISP-DM: Still the top methodology for analytics, data mining, or data science projects. http://www.kdnuggets.com/2014/10/crisp-dm-top-methodology-analytics-data-mining-data-science-projects.html. Accessed 01 Apr 2017
4. Davydenko, A., Fildes, R.: Forecast error measures: critical review and practical recommendations. In: Business Forecasting: Practical Problems and Solutions. Wiley (2016)

5. Engel, Y., Etzion, O.: Towards proactive event-driven computing. In: Proceedings of the 5th ACM International Conference on Distributed Event-Based System, pp. 125–136 (2011)
6. Golubev, A., Shcherbakov, M., Shcherbakova, N.L., Kamaev, V.: Automatic multi-steps forecasting method for multi seasonal time series based on symbolic aggregate approximation and grid search approaches. J. Fundam. Appl. Sci. **8**(3S), 2529–2541 (2016)
7. De Gooijer, J.G., Hyndman, R.J.: 25 years of time series forecasting. Int. J. Forecast. **22**(3), 443–473 (2006)
8. Groumpos, P.P.: Fuzzy cognitive maps: basic theories and their application to complex systems. Fuzzy Cogn. Maps **247**, 1–22 (2010)
9. Hyndman, R.J., Khandakar, Y.: Automatic time series forecasting: the forecast package for R. J. Stat. Softw. **27**(3), 1–22 (2008). doi:10.18637/jss.v027.i03. ISSN 1548-7660
10. Hyndman, R.J., Athanasopoulos, G.: Principles and Practice. OTexts, Melbourne (2013). http://otexts.org/fpp/
11. Kahneman, D.: Thinking, Fast and Slow. Farrar, Straus and Giroux, New York (2011)
12. Kamaev, V.A., Shcherbakov, M.V., Panchenko, D.P., Shcherbakova, N.L., Brebels, A.: Using connectionist systems for electric energy consumption forecasting in shopping centers. Autom. Remote Control **73**(6), 1075–1084 (2012)
13. Mamlook, R., Badran, O., Abdulhadi, E.: A fuzzy inference model for short-term load forecasting. Energ. Policy **37**(4), 1239–1248 (2009)
14. MIRACLE Consortium: Micro-Request-Based Aggregation. Forecasting and Scheduling of Energy Demand, Supply and Distribution (2010)
15. Nisbet, R., Elder, J., Miner, G. (eds.): Handbook of Statistical Analysis and Data Mining Applications. Academic Press, Cambridge (2009). ISBN 0123747651, 9780123747655
16. Salovaara, A., Oulasvirta, A.: A user-centric typology for proactive behaviors. In: Proceedings of the 3rd Nordic Conference on Human Computer Interaction Nordi-HCI, pp. 57–60. https://doi.org/10.1145/1028014.1028022
17. Shcherbakov, M.V., Brebels, A., Shcherbakova, N.L., Tyukov, A.P., Janovsky, T.A., Kamaev, V.A.: A survey of forecast error measures. World Appl. Sci. J. **24**(24), 171–176 (2013)
18. Sokolov, A., Tyukov, A., Sadovnikova, N., Zhuk, S., Khrzhanovskaya, O., Brebels, A.: Automatic information retrieval and preprocessing for energy management. In: Kravets, A., Shcherbakov, M., Kultsova, M., Shabalina, O. (eds.) Creativity in Intelligent, Technologies and Data Science: First Conference, CIT&DS 2015, Volgograd, Russia, September 15–17, 2015, Proceedings, pp. 462–473. Springer International Publishing, Cham (2015)
19. Stluka, P., Ma, K.: Data-driven decision support and its applications in the process industries. Comput. Aided Chem. Eng. **24**, 273–278 (2007)
20. Taylor, J.W., Espasa, A.: Energy forecasting. Int. J. Forecast. **24**(4), 561–565 (2008)
21. Tennenhouse, D.: Proactive computing. Commun. ACM **43**(5), 43–50 (2000)

Knowledge Discovery in Patent and Open Sources for Creative Tasks

"Smart Queue" Approach for New Technical Solutions Discovery in Patent Applications

Alla Kravets[1][(✉)] [iD], Nikita Shumeiko[1], Boris Lempert[2],
Natalia Salnikova[3], and Natalia Shcherbakova[1]

[1] Volgograd State Technical University,
28 Lenin av., Volgograd 400005, Russia
agk@gde.ru, nikitashumeyko92@gmail.com
[2] Volgograd State Medical University,
1 Pavshikh Bortsov Sq., Volgograd 400131, Russia
bal4224@mail.ru
[3] Volgograd Institute of Management - Branch of the Russian Presidential
Academy of National Economy and Public Administration, 8 Gagarin St.,
Volgograd 400131, Russia
ns3112@mail.ru

Abstract. This article presents an approach to the implementation of the Web-based intelligent platform of new technical solutions search and automation of the procedure of patent application examination. The main functions of this platform are submitting the patent applications and viewing information on their novelty. Patent applications are processed in the background mode through the asynchronous queue by third-party software. The architecture of the algorithms for parallel multiserver processing of uploaded applications was developed, and "Smart Queue" Approach -based multilingual intelligent platform for patent's data analysis was implemented. The patent's similarity definition algorithm is out of the scope of this article.

Keywords: Patent search · "Smart Queue" approach · Web-based intelligent platform · State of art search · Examination of patent applications · Technical solutions discovery

1 Background

Processing and verification of patents is a very time-consuming task in terms of the required volume of the analyzed information - about 10 millions of patents even since 1997 (last 20 years). To ensure the relevance of the invention, it is necessary to analyze the vast amount of information on existing patents in this and related fields to obtain an own patent. This analysis sometimes takes a lot of time and human effort at the Patent Office employees. Sometimes examiner has to make hundreds of search queries and to process thousands of existing patents manually during the examination procedure to make a decision: to approve the application or to reject it. The new patent applicants also have to ensure that the application does not duplicate existing patents, before the submission [1, 2]. The system of new technical solutions discovery and patent

© Springer International Publishing AG 2017
A. Kravets et al. (Eds.): CIT&DS 2017, CCIS 754, pp. 37–47, 2017.
DOI: 10.1007/978-3-319-65551-2_3

applications examination was designed to automate this task partially. The main components of this system are the semantic text analyzer [3, 4] carrying out an algorithm of patents comparing and patents' similarity definition within the already existing database, and a Web-based interface for users interacting with the main core of the system. The "Smart Queue" approach - based intelligent platform through which the user can request a relevance of his patent application is created and presented in this article.

Among the most common commercial products in this area we can highlight services such as Thomson Reuters (Thomson Innovation), Questel (Orbit), GridLogics (PatSeer), VantagePoint, STN Analyze Plus, STN Analyst, Invention Machine (Knowlegist, Goldfire), etc. as well as many additional toolkits: Method Patent, TEMIS, TotalPatent, Wisdomain, PatBase, ArchPatent, PatentLens, PatentBuddy, PatentTools, FreePatentsOnline, Intellogist, PriorSmart, MaxVal, BizInt SmartCharts, Espacenet, AmberScope, Acclaim IP, Innography, IFI Claims, Patent Inspiration.

However, all the above-mentioned products are conducting a search of the documents relevant to the application according to the request made by experts. So they are not the direct counterparts of the developed system. Many scientists tried to solve patent prior-art search task. The main research in patent retrieval started after the third NTCIR Workshop [5]. There is an annual track CLEF-IP, which was created to compare different approaches in different tasks related to the patent applications examination process, including prior-art search task. Xue proposed a method based on machine learning [6], D'hondt tried to use syntactic relations [7], Verma approach is based on citations and patent classes [8], Robertson created search query from patent's text and tried to extract granted patents using this query and to rank them using BM25 [9], Mahdabi used patent's summary as a query to search for relevant patents [10], Magdy used an approach based on unigrams and bigrams [11], Graf tried to use external knowledge bases [12]. The analysis of existing systems used as a Web-interface for patent searching was conducted (Table 1) [13–17].

Table 1. Compare system counterparts

Name of the system	Google patent search	US patent and trademark office	IBM's patent server
Support for asynchronous task queue	No	No	Yes
View a list of previously processed user's applications	No	No	Yes
The ability to integrate an own patent searching module	No	No	No
The ability to search the full text of the application	No	Yes	Yes
The ability to highlight matches found	Yes	Yes	Yes

2 Analysis of the Existing Patents' Search Algorithms

Nowadays, Patent Offices of different countries, European Patent Office (EPO) and The World Intellectual Property Organization (WIPO) have standard procedures of the patents' applications examination. According to results of the analysis, we defined 5 common steps of these procedures (Fig. 1) [18].

Step 1: Definition of the subject and the object of the search.
The object of the search is a specific attribute, indicating on the aim of search. Examples of search objects are a novelty, patent purity, state of the art, patentability. Mostly objects of the search are technical solutions, which are characterized by the structure, properties, and application. Factors influencing the rules of the search:

1. the functional destination of the object;
2. branch-wise application of the object;
3. the nature of the distinctive features of the object (verbal, quantitative, specific);
4. addition to the state of the art;
5. the existence of functionally independent features.

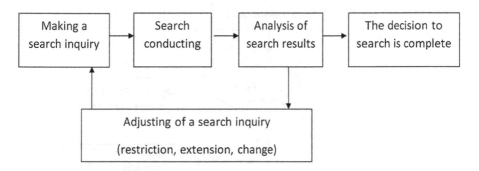

Fig. 1. General scheme of patent search

Step 2: Definition of search rules.
Patent search rules include:

1. geographical coverage of existing documents;
2. the depth of retrospections;
3. types of documents to be searched (patents, patent applications, utility models);
4. the area of search;
5. the type of information to be searched (technical features, names, dates, numbers of documents, and the legal status of documents).

Step 3: Selection a database for search (or sequence of multiple databases).
Database coverage and its search capabilities must comply with the rules of the search. Properties of search databases:

1. data coverage;
2. opportunities for the compilation of search queries;

3. presentation of search results;
4. additional tools.

Step 4: Preparation of the search strategy.
The strategy of computer searching should be drawn up by taking into account the selected database options. Search strategy includes:

1. selection of the databases' access priority;
2. preparation of search queries;
3. searches adjustment depending on the results;
4. a decision on the search ends.

Step 5: Analysis of the results.
Figure 2 contains the scheme of an application on the invention patent claim analysis algorithm.

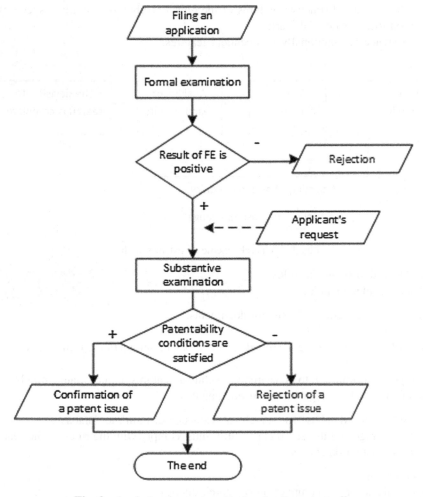

Fig. 2. Analysis of patent application by the patent office

3   The Concept of "Smart Queue" Approach -Based Intelligent Methodology

To define the requirements for the platform implemented, we have developed the algorithm of the "Smart Queue" Approach -based (SQA) intelligent methodology concept (Fig. 3).

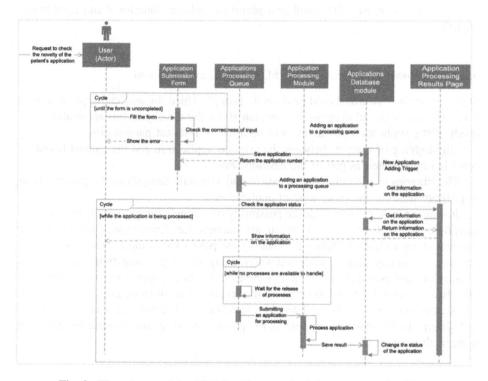

Fig. 3. The scheme of the SQA intelligent methodology concept algorithm

To find similar patents amid 10 million documents, a resource-demanding semantic analysis of these documents is necessary to compare them with the original application. It may take a long time, considering that hundreds of applications may be queued simultaneously for processing.

Therefore, SQA intelligent platform, with which the user interacts, must allow background processing of applications, while the user is viewing the report or submitting new bids.

In addition, the search for similar patents in any way should not block the process of Web-servers, keeping a TCP-user connection open. Blocking Web-server processes will lead to an excessive number of open TCP-connections, as well as significantly reduce the flexibility and scalability of the system.

In order to solve this problem, it was decided that all applications must be processed independently of the intelligent platform through which the user will upload them. Applications will be queued to be included consequently into developing processes will take data for the processing of applications, and the result will be saved at the end of the operation.

This new "Smart Queue" approach allows to provide to queue for processing applications would be a routine thread and to communicate with the network interface (getting tasks, saving the operation result), to process the queue by multiple instances (workers) located at physically distributed servers.

The concept of the SQA intelligent platform includes functional and operational requirements.

3.1   Functional Requirements for SQA Intelligent Platform

SQA intelligent platform should be created, through which the user can apply to search for patents-analogs and to obtain information about the novelty of this application. The result of the application processing will be a list of relevant patents [19].

Highlighting of matches between the original application and the patents found by color is implemented as part of the development.

The libraries of algorithms of statistical and semantic analysis of the patents listed in [20] are used for the processing of applications.

It is also necessary to provide the possibility of a simple integration of syntactic and morphological analyzer to search for patents-analogs. Key features available to the user for interacting with the system are uploading the patent application, view a brief and a complete list of applications processed with the page-by-page navigation within the list. In addition, the user should be able to see the status of his applications ("in process"/ "finished"), and detailed information on the results of its processing.

Access to the service is available by authorization. The user must be registered in the system. In the case of user forgets his password, he should be able to recover it using authorization data.

3.2   Operational Requirements for SQA Intelligent Platform

According to current trends, the SQA intelligent platform should be adopted for users of mobile devices and tablet PCs. Loading service pages must not exceed 0.5–0.8 s, including static files, resources, and images. The platform should operate correctly through Internet Explorer 9+, Mozilla Firefox 4 or higher, Google Chrome 34+ and Opera 16+ [13] browsers.

Layout and scripts must comply with W3C standards. Modern standards such as CSS 3, HTML 5 and ECMA Script 6 may be used while maintaining the performance of basic functions in the browsers listed above, which don't support these standards.

The convenient interface localization for different languages must be provided by the system because the application can be uploaded, for example, for either Russian patent or for the English one.

The platform database contains more than ten million Russian and English patents [21, 22]. When a user will send an application to the system, it will be queued for processing. Other users can handle a plurality of applications in parallel mode.

4 Implementation and Results

For the realization of the backend part, the Django Web framework written in Python has been selected. This framework was chosen due to the following criteria:

1. Django allows creating quickly flexible Web-based platforms, without wasting time on routine operations.
2. Working with the database and models is continued through ORM layer of abstraction. Support for automatic migration of the database structure can significantly reduce the time to make changes in the project design and development of new solutions.
3. Django integrates easily with Celery task queue server, which is also written in Python.
4. Django framework is free and is actively supported by a large community of developers. Security updates and fixes for vulnerabilities are available regularly.
5. There is a built-in support of users and access rights [23].

About 5–6 different services (Django, Redis, RabbitMQ, Postgresql, Postfix (for mail sent) and Nginx as a frontend for the combat environment, and Memcached for caching data and templates at Django level are required for the whole system work [23]. It makes some difficulties in deployment and configuration of these services on the developer machine, as well as in the combat environment. In order to simplify the environment deployment, container architecture was used. Each service runs in its own Docker-container, containing an isolated Unix-like environment. Containers are combined with each other to the internal network and can communicate with each other.

Automated environment assembly script is described in the configuration file docker-compose.yml. Through this, the environment for development or production can be configured and raised up by just a couple of commands.

The PostgreSQL was chosen as the database server for applications storage. It is a free high-performance and scalable database management server. According to the stability and the ability to handle large amounts of data, it can make a good competition to such commercial solutions like Oracle DB or MSSQL.

Three sets of experiments were fulfilled on the cluster (Table 2) with different tokenization methods of patents' texts: stop-words removal, synonyms replacement, N-grams (Table 3). These methods were applied both for 1 million patents' array and for patent applications processing.

All experiments' sets included two data systems:

- HDFS, where each patent as thematic vectors set processed with Latent Dirichlet Allocation (LDA) algorithm was stored in the file and all files are structured in directories according to with rules of file system;

Table 2. Cluster description

Processing 4 nodes	Data node
Processor Intel Xeon E5-2650V3 (2.3 GHz, 10- core) x2	Processor Intel Xeon E5-2660 (2.2 GHz, 8- core) x2
RAM 64 Gb DDR4	RAM 128 Gb DDR3
HDD SSD Intel 240 Gb	HDD SATA 1 Tb
Intel Xeon Phi Coprocessor 31s1p x2	Intel Xeon Phi Coprocessor 31s1p x2

Table 3. Results of experiments (fragment)

Exp. no.	Data system	Similarity definition method (on LDA vectors)	Search time, s		Precision	Recall
			Local interface	Web-interface		
Tokenization method: stop-words removal						
1.	HDFS	Cosine method	17	2	1	0.6
2.	HDFS	Element-wise vectors comparison	12	1	1	0.65
3.	PostgreSQL	Cosine method	18	2	1	0.6
4.	PostgreSQL	Element-wise vectors comparison	8	1	1	0.65
Tokenization method: synonyms replacement						
5.	HDFS	Cosine method	82	7	0.94	0.75
6.	HDFS	Element-wise vectors comparison	42	4	0.43	0.9
7.	PostgreSQL	Cosine method	90	7	0.94	0.75
8.	PostgreSQL	Element-wise vectors comparison	48	5	0.43	0.9
Tokenization method: N-grams						
9.	HDFS	Cosine method	35	3	1	0.4
10.	HDFS	Element-wise vectors comparison	26	3	1	0.4
11.	PostgreSQL	Cosine method	37	4	1	0.4
12.	PostgreSQL	Element-wise vectors comparison	22	3	1	0.4

- PostgreSQL, where all patents were stored in the database as thematic vectors set processed with LDA algorithm.

Patents and applications (Fig. 4) were processed in the SQA platform with background mode through the asynchronous queue, which includes LDA and Similarity definition methods. "Local interface" describes the software with the automatic queue, various modes of launching and operation, for example, console mode of tokenization method module.

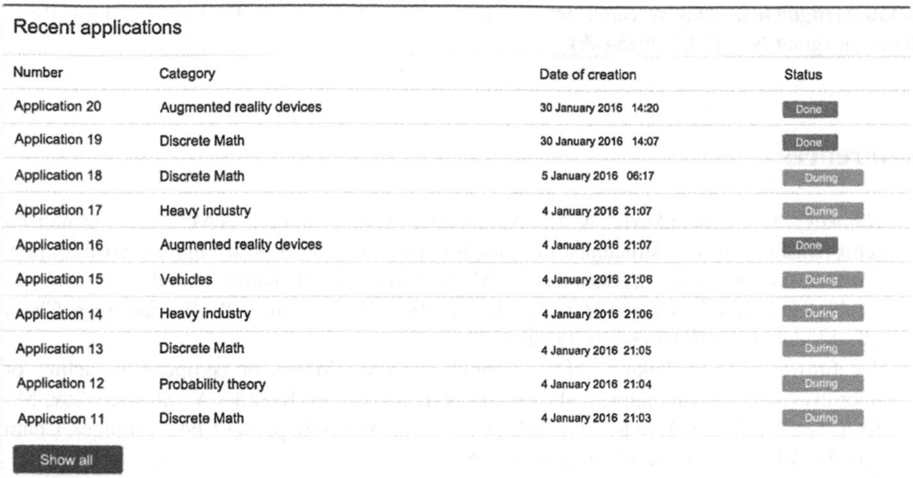

Recent applications

Number	Category	Date of creation	Status
Application 20	Augmented reality devices	30 January 2016 14:20	Done
Application 19	Discrete Math	30 January 2016 14:07	Done
Application 18	Discrete Math	5 January 2016 06:17	During
Application 17	Heavy industry	4 January 2016 21:07	During
Application 16	Augmented reality devices	4 January 2016 21:07	Done
Application 15	Vehicles	4 January 2016 21:06	During
Application 14	Heavy industry	4 January 2016 21:06	During
Application 13	Discrete Math	4 January 2016 21:05	During
Application 12	Probability theory	4 January 2016 21:04	During
Application 11	Discrete Math	4 January 2016 21:03	During

Show all

Fig. 4. A brief list of the applications' queue

Thus, proposed "Smart Queue" approach with background mode through the asynchronous queue allows decreasing the processing time on average 90% without losses in precision and recall parameters.

5 Conclusion

The main scientific contribution of this paper is the SQA intelligent methodology concept, which is implemented in the platform for new technical solutions discovery and patent applications examination. We developed the original mechanism of background mode processing through the asynchronous queue for patents' array and applications. In addition, the new approach allows integrating third-party software for processing of patents' array as well as submitted applications.

The following results were obtained:

1. The analysis of the modern mechanisms of patenting and patent analogs searching was fulfilled.
2. The existing algorithm of the patent search was studied, and a comparative analysis of the existing systems of patent search in terms of the implementation of their interfaces was done.
3. The concept and requirements of the parallel multiserver information processing algorithms implementation were developed.
4. The SQA intelligent platform was implemented on the base of Django Web framework.
5. Results of the experiments showed the decreasing of the processing time on average 90% in comparison with existing interface solutions.

Acknowledgments. This research was partially supported by the Russian Fund of Basic Research (grant No. 15-07-06254 A).

References

1. Kamaev, V.A., Salnikova, N.A., Akhmedov, S.A., Likhter, A.M.: The formalized representation of the structures of complex technical devices using context-free plex grammars. In: Kravets, A., Shcherbakov, M., Kultsova, M., Shabalina, O. (eds.) Creativity in Intelligent Technologies and Data Science. CCIS, vol. 535, pp. 268–277. Springer, Cham (2015). doi:10.1007/978-3-319-23766-4_22
2. Astafurova, O.A., Salnikova, N.A., Lopukhov, N.V.: Means of computer modeling of microwave devices and numerical methods as their base. In: Kravets, A., Shcherbakov, M., Kultsova, M., Iijima, T. (eds.) JCKBSE 2014. CCIS, vol. 466, pp. 630–642. Springer, Cham (2014). doi:10.1007/978-3-319-11854-3_55
3. Korobkin, D., Fomenkov, S., Kravets, A., Kolesnikov, S., Dykov, M.: Three-steps methodology for patents prior-art retrieval and structured physical knowledge extracting. In: Kravets, A., Shcherbakov, M., Kultsova, M., Shabalina, O. (eds.) Creativity in Intelligent Technologies and Data Science. CCIS, vol. 535, pp. 124–136. Springer, Cham (2015). doi:10.1007/978-3-319-23766-4_10
4. Kravets, A.G., Kravets, A.D., Rogachev, V.A., Medintseva, I.P.: Cross-thematic modeling of the world prior-art state. Rejected patent applications analysis. J. Fundam. Appl. Sci. 8(3S), 2542–2552 (2016)
5. Iwayama, M., Fujii, A., Kando, N., Takano, A.: Overview of patent retrieval task at NTCIR-3. In: Proceedings of NTCIR Workshop, Tokyo, 8–10 October 2002
6. Xue, X., Croft, W.B.: Automatic query generation for patent search. In: Cheung, D.W.L., Song, I.L., Chu, W., et al. (eds.) Proceedings of the 18th ACM Conference on Information and Knowledge Management. Association of Computing Machinery, New York (2009)
7. D'hondt, E., Verberne, S., Alink, W., Cornacchia, R.: Combining document representations for prior-art retrieval. In: CLEF 2011 Labs and Workshop, Notebook Papers, Amsterdam, 19–22 September 2011
8. Verma, M., Varma, V.: Exploring keyphrase extraction and IPC classification vectors for prior art search. In: CLEF 2011 Labs and Workshop, Notebook Papers, Amsterdam, 19–22 September 2011
9. Robertson, S.E., Walker, S., Beaulieu, M.M., Gatford, M., Payne, A.: Okapi at TREC-4. In: Harman, D., (ed.) Proceedings of the 4th Text Retrieval Conference (TREC-4), Gaithersburg, MD (1996)
10. Mahdabi, P., Andersson, L., Hanbury, A., Crestani, F.: Experiments: exploring patent summarization. In: CLEF 2011 Labs and Workshop, Notebook Papers, Amsterdam, 19–22 September 2011
11. Magdy, W., Jones, G.J.F.: Applying the KISS principle for the CLEF-IP 2010 prior art candidate patent search task. In: CLEF 2010 Labs and Workshop, Notebook Papers, Vienna, 31 May 2010
12. Graf, E., Frommholz, I., Lalmas, M., van Rijsbergen, K.: Knowledge modeling in prior art search. In: Cunningham, H., Hanbury, A., Rüger, S. (eds.) IRFC 2010. LNCS, vol. 6107, pp. 31–46. Springer, Heidelberg (2010). doi:10.1007/978-3-642-13084-7_4
13. Google – Search Patents. https://google.com/patents. Accessed 15 Dec 2016
14. Intellectual Property Licensing. IBM. http://www.ibm.com/patents. Accessed 15 Dec 2016
15. PostfixDocumenation. http://www.postfix.org/documentation.html. Accessed 15 Dec 2016

16. Methods of patent search. http://it4b.icsti.su/itb/ps/ps_all.html. Accessed 15 Dec 2016
17. The patent Wikipedia - the free encyclopedia. https://ru.wikipedia.org/wiki/Patent. Accessed 15 Dec 2016
18. Kravets, A.G., Korobkin, D.M., Dykov, M.A.: E-patent examiner: two-steps approach for patents prior-art retrieval. In: IISA 2015 - 6th International Conference on Information, Intelligence, Systems and Applications. Article no. 7388074 (2016)
19. Zaripova, V.M., Petrova, I.Y., Kravets, A., Evdoshenko, O.: Knowledge bases of physical effects and phenomena for method of energy-informational models by means of ontologies. In: Kravets, A., Shcherbakov, M., Kultsova, M., Shabalina, O. (eds.) Creativity in Intelligent Technologies and Data Science. CCIS, vol. 535, pp. 224–237. Springer, Cham (2015). doi:10.1007/978-3-319-23766-4_19
20. Mironenko, A.G., Kravets, A.G.: Automated methods of patent array analysis. In: IISA 2016 - 7th International Conference on Information, Intelligence, Systems and Applications. Article no. 7785341 (2016)
21. Saltykov, S., Rusyaeva, E., Kravets, A.G.: Typology of scientific constructions as an instrument of conceptual creativity. In: Kravets, A., Shcherbakov, M., Kultsova, M., Shabalina, O. (eds.) Creativity in Intelligent Technologies and Data Science. CCIS, vol. 535, pp. 41–57. Springer, Cham (2015). doi:10.1007/978-3-319-23766-4_4
22. Kravets, A.G., Mironenko, A.G., Nazarov, S.S., Kravets, A.D.: Patent application text pre-processing for patent examination procedure. In: Kravets, A., Shcherbakov, M., Kultsova, M., Shabalina, O. (eds.) Creativity in Intelligent Technologies and Data Science. CCIS, vol. 535, pp. 105–114. Springer, Cham (2015). doi:10.1007/978-3-319-23766-4_8
23. Django documentation. https://docs.djangoproject.com/en/1.9/. Accessed 10 Dec 2016

Methods of Statistical and Semantic Patent Analysis

Dmitriy Korobkin[✉], Sergey Fomenkov, Alla Kravets,
and Sergey Kolesnikov

Volgograd State Technical University, Volgograd, Russia
dkorobkin80@mail.ru

Abstract. In the paper, authors proposed a methodology to solve the problem of prior art patent search, consists of a statistical and semantic analysis of patent documents, machine translation of patent application and calculation of semantic similarity between application and patents. The paper considers different variants of statistical analysis based on LDA method. On the step of the semantic analysis, authors applied a new method for building a semantic network on the base of Meaning-Text Theory. Prior art search also needs pre-translation of the patent application using machine translation tools. On the step of semantic similarity calculation, we compare the semantic trees for application and patent claims. We developed an automated system for the patent examination task, which is designed to reduce the time that an expert spends for the prior-art search and is adopted to deal with a large amount of patent information.

Keywords: Prior-art patent search · Patent examination · LDA · Semantic analysis · Natural language processing · Big data

1 Introduction

From year to year, the number of patent applications is increasing. Around 2.9 million patent applications were filed worldwide in 2015, up 7.8% from 2014. The escalating applications flow and more than 20 million World set of granted patents (from 1980 to 2015) increase the time that patent examiners have to spend to examine all incoming applications. Sometimes examiner has to make hundreds of search queries and to process thousands of existing patents manually during the examination procedure to make a decision: to approve the application or to reject it. The increasing workload of patent offices led to need for developing new approaches for patents prior-art retrieval on the base of statistical and semantic methods of natural language processing.

Among the most common commercial products in this area we can highlight services such as Thomson Reuters (Thomson Innovation), Questel (Orbit), GridLogics (PatSeer), VantagePoint, STN Analyze Plus, STN Anavist, Invention Machine (Knowlegist, Goldfire), etc. as well as many additional toolkits: Metheo Patent, TEMIS, TotalPatent, Wisdomain, PatBase, ArchPatent, PatentLens, PatentBuddy, PatentTools, FreePatentsOnline, Intellogist, PriorSmart, MaxVal, BizInt SmartCharts, Espacenet, AmberScope, Acclaim IP, Innography, IFI Claims, PatentInspiration. However, all the

© Springer International Publishing AG 2017
A. Kravets et al. (Eds.): CIT&DS 2017, CCIS 754, pp. 48–61, 2017.
DOI: 10.1007/978-3-319-65551-2_4

above-mentioned products are conducting a search of the documents relevant to the application according to the request made by experts. So, they are not the direct counterparts of the developed system.

Many scientists tried to solve patent prior-art search task. The main research in patent retrieval started with annual tracks CLEF-IP 2009-2011, which were created to compare different approaches in different tasks related to the patent applications examination process, including prior-art search task. Magdy used an approach based on unigrams and bigrams [1], Verma's approach is based on keyphrase and citations extraction [2], Mahdabi used method based on a time-aware random walk on a weighted network of patent citations [3], Xue's approach considers an actual query as the basic unit and thus captures important query-level dependencies between words and phrases [4], D'hondt tried to compare flat classification with a two-step hierarchical system which models the IPC hierarchy [5], Bouadjenek used query with a full patent description in conjunction with generic query reduction methods [6], Kim proposed the method to suggest diverse queries that can cover multiple aspects of the query (patent) [7], Ferraro's approach consist in segmenting the patent claim, using a rule-based approach, and a conditional random field is trained to segment the components into clauses [8], Andersson used the techniques by addressing three different relation extraction applications: acronym extraction, hyponymy extraction and factoid entity relation extraction [9].

In this paper, we propose a novel approach, in which we tried to combine both statistical and semantic features to increase the accuracy of the prior-art search.

2   Methods of Statistical and Semantic Patent Analysis

2.1   Statistical Analysis

The patent statistical analysis can be performed by various methods (methods of terms extraction, storing patent databases, patents comparison). It is necessary to evaluate the effectiveness of methods of patent database statistical analysis through implementation of the following stages:

- patent document tokenization by three different methods (tokenization with removing stop-words, tokenization with replacing synonyms and tokenization based on N-grams);
- building a term-document matrix;
- clustering based on Latent Dirichlet Allocation (LDA) [10] model and using the constructed model to obtain the distribution of vectors by the clusters (unnamed topics);
- storing the obtained vectors by two different methods (storage in distributed file system HDFS, storing in PostgreSQL database);
- the comparison of the obtained vectors by four different methods (based on the standard deviation of the vectors, element-by-element comparison of the vectors, Cosine similarity, and comparison of the vector's lengths).

The basic idea of LDA is that documents are represented as random mixtures of latent topics, where each topic is characterized by a distribution according to the words from documents array. Based on the LDA model can be used a patent database statistical analysis and distribution of patents by the unnamed topics.

The first stage of the statistical analysis is the tokenization of the patent text. In this case, the tokens will be individual words or N-grams from the patent text. After tokenization is necessary to make the lemmatization, i.e. converting the extracted words to their base form for the most accurate building of term-document matrix. Tokenization must implement three different techniques: tokenization with removing stop-words, tokenization with replacing synonyms, tokenization based on n-grams.

Tokenization with removing stop words (TokenRem) involves the removal stop-words from the text that do not carry meaning in this document: prepositions, interjections, etc. The text tokenization with removing stop words takes place via Apache Lucene library.

Tokenization with replacing synonyms (TokenSyn) also involves the removal of stop-words, but beyond that, all words-synonyms are present to one word (base alias). This approach allows us to build the most accurate term-document matrix and the LDA model but slow down compared to the usual tokenization.

Tokenization based on N-grams (TokenN) divides the text into phrases of any given length. This kind of tokenization allows you to build the LDA model based on keyphrases of a document that in theory should increase the effectiveness of the patent search. For the text tokenization based on N-grams, you need to clear the text from stop-words and extracted N-gram from the text by use of Apache Lucene library.

There are various methods of constructing a term-document matrix. To build the LDA model is sufficient to make a modified version of term-document matrix based on the TF [11]. TF (term frequency) indicates the importance of specific words within the document. First you need to get a dictionary of all the words a patent database $s = \{w_1, w_2, w_3, ..., w_n\}$, where w_i is a unique word in the patent database. Then each i-th row of the term-document matrix represents the resulting dictionary, and each column - the number of occurrences of the word in i-th document.

The Big data processing framework Apache Spark and MLlib library for machine learning allow getting a dictionary of all words from the documents set and build a term-document matrix.

On the basis of the distribution vectors of patents by clusters on the base of LDA model is possible to make the selection of documents that match the query. The selection of relevant patents is made by comparing the distribution vectors. Since the comparison of multidimensional vectors can be produced based on different metrics of these vectors, and beforehand the most effective method are unknown, it is necessary to assess the effectiveness of the selected methods: element-by-element comparison (EE), calculate standard deviation (SD), compare vector size (VS), Cosine similarity (Cos).

After building the LDA model and obtain the vectors of topics per document distributions from the patent database these vectors must be stored in a data store for later retrieval and processing. In this case as a data repository for vectors can be either HDFS or PostgreSQL.

PostgreSQL allows you to store vectors of topics per document distributions in one table with two fields: ID and Vector (array of real values). Distributed file system

HDFS allows to effectively work with the patent database consisting of tens millions of documents. Framework Apache Spark allows you will store ID of the document and its vector in HDFS.

2.2 Machine Translation for Patent Examination

Patent examination on the base of prior-art retrieval from patent databases in other languages than application language needs pre-translation using machine translation tools. After analyzing was chosen statistical machine translation system Moses [12] (open-source project, licensed under the LGPL). Moses is a statistical machine translation system that allows you to automatically train translation models for any language pair. All you need is a collection of translated texts (parallel corpus). Once you have a trained model, an efficient search algorithm quickly finds the highest probability translation among the exponential number of choices. The Moses system can be integrated into any other system through XML-RPC protocol. For training Moses with GIZA ++ library used a set of several Russian-English corpora:

- training corpora based on patent families analysis (a set of patents registered in various countries (i.e. patent offices, including USPTO and Rospatent) to protect the same invention);
- fully parallel public-domain corpus consisting of 2100 United Nations General Assembly Resolutions with translations in the 6 official UN languages of the, including Russian and English;
- a collection of multilingual corpora (UMC) compiled at the Institute of Formal and Applied Linguistics (ÚFAL);
- fully parallel Russian and English corpuses from the website of Russian National Corpus;
- training corpora on the base of English and Russian version "The Art of Computer Programming" by Donald E. Knuth.

The total corpora volume was approximately 180,000 sentences (5,854,095 lexical units) in English and Russian.

The training process in Moses takes in the parallel data and uses occurrences of words and segments (known as phrases) to infer translation correspondences between the two languages of interest. Parallel Russian-English corpus was made on the basis of Patent families with using this algorithm:

- search an information about Patent Family in espacenet.com using the patent database in Russian;
- retrieval an English version of the patent in espacenet.com for this patent family;
- extract structured information such as claims from patents in English and Russian;
- proposals segmentation to obtain sentence-aligned data (parallel sentences) for the training process.

The data typically needs to be prepared before it is used in training, tokenizing the text and converting tokens to a standard case. Heuristics are used to remove sentence pairs which look to be misaligned, and long sentences are removed.

We used IRSTLM language model toolkit system to build a statistical language model. Experience with Moses revealed the difficulties with the usage of large paragraphs (more than 255 symbols) which must be segmented.

2.3 Semantic Analysis

On this step, we perform a semantic trees construction for application and patent claims. Building semantic trees and searching their intersections requires much more resources than statistical methods, which is a problem for the corpus of millions of patents. We build semantic trees using only patents claims because this part of the patent describes the invention and recites its limitations.

The text of patent claims has one feature that makes the effective use of existing solutions for building dependency trees is difficult. This feature is that the patent claims are written in one sentence, which sometimes includes hundreds of words. To solve this problem has been developed an algorithm of complex sentences segmentation [13]. Sentences are segmented on the base of transitional phrases of claims and special "marker" words such as "wherein", "such that", etc.

Then, we perform a morphological analysis of the patent text. For morphological analysis was chosen TreeTagger [14] for Russian and English language. The TreeTagger is a tool for annotating text with part-of-speech and lemma information. The TreeTagger has been successfully used to tag texts from basic world languages and is adaptable to other languages if a lexicon and a manually tagged training corpus are available.

After that, we used MaltParser [15] to perform semantic parsing (built dependency tree). Its main advantages are: it is open a source software, it allows to rich a moderate accuracy and it has pre-trained models for many languages, including Russian and English (Table 1).

Part-of-speech (POS) tags [16] are assigned to a single word according to its role in the sentence. Traditional grammar classifies words based on eight parts of speech: the verb (VB (base form), VBN (past participle), VBZ (3rd person singular present)), the noun (NN - single, NNS - plural), the Wh-determiner (WDT), the adjective (JJ), the preposition (IN), the determiner (DT), modal (MD), etc.

The Stanford typed dependencies [17] representation was designed to provide a simple description of the grammatical relationships in a sentence. It represents all sentence relationships uniformly as typed dependency relations. The current representation supports approximately 50 grammatical relations (in this example of patent dependence tree contains 11 grammatical relations: "amod" - adjectival modifier, "det" - determiner, "pobj" - object of a preposition, "nsubj" - nominal subject, "nsubjpass" - passive nominal subject, "aux" - auxiliary, "auxpass" - passive auxiliary, "nn" - noun compound modifier, "rcmod" - relative clause modifier, "prep" - prepositional modifier, "punct" - punctuation).

In the collapsed representation, dependencies involving prepositions, conjuncts, as well as information about the referent of relative clauses are collapsed to get direct dependencies between content words. We removed from dependence trees the grammatical relations such as "punct", "det", "prep", etc. The parent of removed node is transferred to the child node. So, we got dependency tree with Collapsed Stanford Dependencies (Table 2).

Table 1. Example of dependence tree in Conll'09

Index word in a sentence	Word form itself	Word's lemma or stem	POS	Index of syntactic parent	Stanford typed dependencies
1	the	the	DT	3	det
2	sandwiched	sandwiched	VBN	3	amod
3	layers	layer	NNS	6	nsubjpass
4	can	can	MD	6	aux
5	be	be	VB	6	auxpass
6	rolled	roll	VBN	0	root
7	with	with	IN	6	prep
8	dielectric	dielectric	NN	7	pobj
9	into	into	IN	6	prep
10	a	a	DT	12	det
11	compact	compact	JJ	12	amod
12	form	form	NN	9	pobj
13	that	that	WDT	14	nsubj
14	looks	look	VBZ	12	rcmod
15	like	like	IN	14	det
16	rod	rod	NN	15	pobj
17	of	of	IN	16	prep
18	metal	metal	NN	17	nn
19	.	.	SENT	6	punct

Then we use an approach based on the MTT (Meaning-Text Theory) [18]. Syntactic representations in MTT are implemented using dependency trees. According to MMT we merge collapsed Stanford Dependencies (SD) into the set of Deep syntactic relations. For sentence "The sandwiched layers can be rolled with dielectric into a compact form that looks like a rod of metal", the Stanford Dependencies, Collapsed Stanford Dependencies and Deep Syntactic Structure is representation in Table 2.

Actantial relations (I, II, III) are just numbered by increasing obliquity I for the most salient actant, II for the next, etc. We merge the following SD into actantial relation: "nsubj", "nsubjpass", "pobj", etc. The attributives relations (ATTR) cover all types of modifiers (circumstantials and attributes). We merge the following SD into relation ATTR: "amod", "rcmod", "nn", etc.

2.4   Semantic Similarity Calculation Between Application and Patents

On this step, we compare the semantic trees for application claims with trees from selected subset received on the step of the statistical analysis. We re-rank relevant patents from selected subset according to similarities between semantic trees.

In accordance with MTT trees at Deep syntactic representation level show dependency relations between terms (words) and look as networks with arrows running

Table 2. Transformation from dependence tree to semantic tree

Stanford Dependencies	Collapsed Stanford Dependencies	Deep Syntactic Structure
det(layers-3, the-1)	amod(layers-3, sandwiched-2)	ATTR(layers-3, sandwiched-2
amod(layers-3, sandwiched-2)	nsubjpass(rolled-6, layers-3)	I(rolled-6, layers-3)
nsubjpass(rolled-6, layers-3)	root(ROOT-0, rolled-6)	OPER$_2$(ROOT-0, rolled-6)
aux(rolled-6, can-4)	pobj(rolled-6, dielectric-8)	II(rolled-6, dielectric-8)
auxpass(rolled-6, be-5)	amod(form-12, compact-11)	ATTR(form-12, compact-11)
root(ROOT-0, rolled-6)	pobj(rolled-6, form-12)	III(rolled-6, form-12)
prep(rolled-6, with-7)	nsubj(looks-14, that-13)	I(looks-14, that-13)
pobj(with-7, dielectric-8)	rcmod(form-12, looks-14)	ATTR(form-12, looks-14)
prep(rolled-6, into-9)	pobj(looks-14, rod-16)	II(looks-14, rod-16)
det(form-12, a-10)	nn(rod-16, metal-18)	ATTR(rod-16, metal-18)
amod(form-12, compact-11)		
pobj(into-9, form-12)		
nsubj(looks-14, that-13)		
rcmod(form-12, looks-14)		
det(looks-14, like-15)		
pobj(like-15, rod-16)		
prep(rod-16, of-17)		
nn(of-17, metal-18)		

from predicate nodes to argument nodes. The semantic tree is built on a base of sentence "The sandwiched layers can be rolled with insulating layer into a compact form that looks like parallel sheets of metal" has 4-level view presented in Fig. 1. At the null level of a semantic trees representation are the ROOTs, at the first level are the actant relations I, II, III, etc. according to the MTT, at the second level are the attributive relations, at the last fourth level are the expanded descriptions.

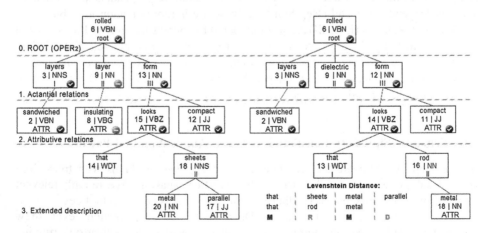

Fig. 1. Semantic trees of application (left view) and of the patent (right view).

After the stage of constructing semantic trees, the patent application is compared with each patent in the database. A comparison of the application with the i-th patent occurs by comparing each of the j-th semantic tree of the application with each k-th tree of the i-th patent.

The First Stage of Semantic Trees Comparison

According to the structure of the semantic tree, the tree's root (ROOT) is the verb (predicate). If the ROOTs of the application and the patent do not match further comparison of the trees is not performed and the comparison is made for the next semantic tree of the patent. We introduce the coefficient of two semantic trees similarity on the first 3 stages:

$$K^j_{similarity}(St_k, St_l) = \frac{\sum_{i=1}^{N_i} F_{common}(T_1, T_2)}{N_i}, \tag{1}$$

where St_k, St_l are the semantic trees of k-sentence and l-sentence of an application claim and patent claim accordingly;

j – number of semantic tree level;

$F_{common}(T_1, T_2)$ – MATCH function determines T1 и T2 terms of the compared semantic trees matches for the same parent terms;

N_i – number of terms for semantic tree St_k of application claim.

The Second Stage of Semantic Trees Comparison

If ROOTs (predicates) of trees are the same then the actant relations are compared. At this stage, each word (term) of the application is compared with each word of the corresponding patent. The tree similarity coefficient is calculated from the ratio of the number of matched words at the first level to the total number of words at the first level of the application. If the similarity coefficient (1) is less than 1/2 then a further comparison is not made.

If any term (word) is not matched on the first-third level, then the term is checked for significance. Testing the significance is based on a predetermined table that contains IDF [11] - inverse document frequency of terms in documents of patent databases. If the term's IDF is above a limit value then the term is not significant and is not taken into account of the similarity coefficient calculation.

In our example, the application semantic tree has three terms on the first level (Fig. 1). We produce a comparison: looking for matching terms with the identical actantial relations. The terms "layers" and "form" match in the application and the patent: +2/3. The term "layer" from the application did not match, check it for significance: the IDF coefficient is low than the limit value. So, the term "layer" must be taken into account in the calculation of the similarity coefficient that equal to 2/3 at the first level.

The Third Stage of Semantic Trees Comparison

At the third stage, semantic trees are compared at the 2nd level - the level of attributive relations. It is necessary that not only the application's term matches with the patent's term but also the parent terms are matched.

In the example (Fig. 1) the application has 4 attributes, at this level 3 application's terms match with the patent terms for identical parental terms. We check the non-matched term for significance, the IDF coefficient of the term "insulating" is less than the limit value, the word has a high significance, it must be taken into account when determining the similarity coefficient. Thus, the similarity coefficient for the 2nd level is 3/4.

The Fourth Stage of Semantic Trees Comparison

On the last stage compares the additional (extended) information of the third level of semantic trees.

The comparison is based on the Levenshtein distance [19]. This coefficient determines the minimum sequence of actions that need to be done to obtain another sequence of objects from the same. Actions are: insert (I), delete (D), replace (R), match (M). If the same terms from the level of attributive relations have child branches, these branches are decomposed into a linear sequence and the Levenshtein distance is determined (Fig. 1).

We introduce the coefficient of two semantic trees similarity on the 4 stage:

$$K^4_{\text{similarity}}(St_k, St_l) = \frac{LevLen}{N_i}, \qquad (2)$$

where *LevLen* – the Levenshtein distance to compare trees.

At this level of the application's semantic tree, there are 3 terms, in the case of words similarity the coefficient increases by 1/4. In the case of any similarity coefficient at the 3rd level, the patent will participate in the ranking, the value of this coefficient affects only the position in the final relevant list. In the example the Levenshtein distance is 2 (MRMD), the similarity coefficient is 2/4.

The coefficient of similarity of semantic trees is summarized for each level and the total coefficient of the application and patent similarity is the sum of trees similarity coefficients.

The coefficient of application' and patent' semantic trees similarity:

$$K_{\text{similarity}} = \sum_{z=1}^{4} (K^z_{\text{similarity}} \times 10^{4-z}), \qquad (3)$$

The coefficient of application and patent similarity:

$$K_S = \frac{\sum_{i=1}^{N_{st}} (\max_{j}(K_{\text{similarity}}(St_i, St_j)))}{\max_{i}(K_S)_i}, \qquad (4)$$

where St_i, St_j are the semantic trees of i-sentence and k-sentence of an application claim and patent claim accordingly;

N_{st} – number of semantic trees of application claim.

3 Experiments and Results

The experiments are performed using a multiprocessor computer system with distributed memory (cluster) of the Volgograd State Technical University. The cluster uses the operating systems Linux Cent'OS 6.5, 6.7. The cluster entered the 22nd edition of the Top-50 rating of the Russian supercomputers (Table 3).

Table 3. Characteristics of cluster nodes

Nodes	HDD	RAM	Cores
node21.cluster	1 TiB/2.3 TiB	7 GiB/15.6 GiB	8
node22.cluster	439 GiB/2.3 TiB	2 GiB/15.6 GiB	8
node47.cluster	355.5 GiB/708.7 GiB	2.4 GiB/62.8 GiB	20
node48.cluster	355.5 GiB/708.7 GiB	2.5 GiB/62.8 GiB	(40 with hyper-threading)

The software was installed on the nodes of the cluster:

- Apache Spark - open-source cluster-computing framework, engine for large-scale data processing;
- Library for software implementation of the LDA method – Apache Spark MLlib;
- PostgreSQL.

Statistical and semantic portraits were formed for 990,000 Russian- and English-language patents and stored in the Document Storage on the basis of the HDFS file system.

The statistic analysis software [20] produces a patent search by different methods and evaluates the efficiency of patent search. The precision and recall basic measures used in evaluating search strategies. The recall is the ratio of the number of relevant patents retrieved to the total number of relevant patents in the database. Precision is the ratio of the number of relevant patents retrieved to the total number of irrelevant and relevant patents retrieved.

$$\text{Recall} = \frac{a}{a+b} \times 100\%, \tag{5}$$

$$\text{Precision} = \frac{a}{a+c} \times 100\%, \tag{6}$$

where a – number of relevant patents retrieved in the patent database; b – number of relevant patents not retrieved; a – number of irrelevant patents retrieved (Table 4).

Table 4. Statistic analysis software testing

No	Tokenization	Vectors storage	Vectors comparison	Precision %	Recall %	Time search, c
1	TokenRem	HDFS	Cos	89	65	1.4
2	TokenRem	HDFS	VS	87	63	1.5
3	TokenRem	HDFS	SD	85	61	1.3
4	TokenRem	HDFS	EE	86	63	1.3
5	TokenRem	PostgreSQL	Cos	89	65	2.8
6	TokenRem	PostgreSQL	VS	87	63	2.9
7	TokenRem	PostgreSQL	SD	85	61	3.0
8	TokenRem	PostgreSQL	EE	86	63	2.8
9	TokenSyn	HDFS	Cos	99	81	2.3
10	TokenSyn	HDFS	VS	92	78	2.4
11	TokenSyn	HDFS	SD	94	77	2.5
12	TokenSyn	HDFS	EE	95	74	2.5
13	TokenSyn	PostgreSQL	Cos	99	81	3.2
14	TokenSyn	PostgreSQL	VS	92	78	3.4
15	TokenSyn	PostgreSQL	SD	94	77	3.5
16	TokenSyn	PostgreSQL	EE	95	74	3.5
17	TokenN	HDFS	Cos	92	77	3.7
18	TokenN	HDFS	VS	88	75	3.8
19	TokenN	HDFS	SD	87	74	4.0
20	TokenN	HDFS	EE	87	73	3.9
21	TokenN	PostgreSQL	Cos	92	77	4.1
22	TokenN	PostgreSQL	VS	88	75	4.4
23	TokenN	PostgreSQL	SD	87	74	4.7
24	TokenN	PostgreSQL	EE	87	73	4.5

On the base of statistical analysis, testing results can be concluded: the most effective method for vectors storage is storing in HDFS, comparing vectors on base Cosine similarity, patent tokenization with replacing synonyms.

We chose the coefficient "Recall" for sets of the top 50, 100, 150, 200, 250, 500 most relevant patents retrieved as a criterion of the semantic analysis effectiveness. In the tests, the Recall will be 100% when the required patent is included in the set and 0% - not included in the set. The tables indicate the average Recall value for 20 tests.

To determine the maximum software effectiveness it is necessary to perform tests with various variations of semantic analysis methods (Table 5).

Verification the term significance increases the Recall. This is due to a more accurate ranking of the trees similarity, since insignificant, commonly used words do not affect the patents ranking.

To test multilingual versions was selected a method with verification of the term's significance (Table 6).

Table 5. Semantic analysis w/ & w/o verification of term's significance

Feature	Recall@500	Recall@250	Recall@200	Recall@150	Recall@100	Recall@50
With verification of term's significance	96	95	93	92	88	81
Without verification of term's significance	89	85	84	80	76	72

Table 6. Semantic analysis for English and Russian patents

Feature	Recall@500	Recall@250	Recall@200	Recall@150	Recall@100	Recall@50
Patents on English	96	95	93	92	88	81
Patents on Russian	89	87	81	77	72	64

The results of checking the Russian- and English-language version of the semantic analyzer showed a lower Recall value for Russian patents - this is due to the complexity of Russian grammar.

4 Conclusion

For experiments with system prototype in the knowledge base were loaded the 990,000 patents from a different domain such as "Electricity", "Physics", "Mechanics" of the Russian Federation and United States patent databases.

On the first step, we compared the different variants of statistical analysis based on LDA method. Patent examination on the base of prior-art retrieval from patent databases in other languages than application language needs pre-translation using machine translation tools. On the step of the semantic analysis, we applied a new method for building a semantic network on the base of Stanford Dependencies and Meaning-Text Theory. On the step of semantic similarity calculation, we compare the semantic trees for application and patent claims.

Developed automated system prototype for the patent examination task, which is designed to help examiners in the examination process, significantly reduced search time and increased such criteria of search effectiveness as "Precision" and "Recall".

Acknowledgement. This research was partially supported by the Russian Foundation of Basic Research (grants No. 15-07-09142 A, No. 15-07-06254 A, No. 16-07-00534 A).

References

1. Magdy, W., Jones, G.J.F.: Applying the KISS principle for the CLEF-IP 2010 prior art candidate patent search task. In: Workshop of the Cross-Language Evaluation Forum, LABs and Workshops, Notebook Papers (2010)
2. Verma, M., Varma, V.: Exploring keyphrase extraction and IPC classification vectors for prior art search. In: CLEF Notebook Papers/Labs/Workshop (2011)
3. Mahdabi, P., Crestani, F.: Query-driven mining of citation networks for patent citation retrieval and recommendation. In: ACM International Conference on Information and Knowledge Management (CIKM) (2014)
4. Xue, X., Croft, W.B.: Modeling reformulation using query distributions. J. ACM Trans. Inf. Syst. **31**(2) (2013). ACM, New York
5. D'hondt, E., Verberne, S., Oostdijk, N., Boves, L.: Patent classification on subgroup level using balanced winnow. In: Lupu, M., Mayer, K., Kando, N., Trippe, A. (eds.) Current Challenges in Patent Information Retrieval. TIRS, vol. 37, pp. 299–324. Springer, Heidelberg (2017). doi:10.1007/978-3-662-53817-3_11
6. Bouadjenek, M., Sanner, S., Ferraro, G.: A study of query reformulation of patent prior art search with partial patent applications. In: 15th International Conference on Artificial Intelligence and Law (ICAIL 2015), pp. 1–11. Association for Computing Machinery (ACM), USA (2015)
7. Kim, Y., Croft, W.B.: Diversifying query suggestions based on query documents. In: Proceedings of the SIGIR 2014 (2014)
8. Ferraro, G., Suominen, H., Nualart, J.: Segmentation of patent claims for improving their readability. In: 3rd Workshop on Predicting and Improving Text Readability for Target Reader Populations (PITR). Stroudsburg, PA 18360, USA, pp. 66–73 (2014)
9. Andersson, L., Hanbury, A., Rauber, A.: The portability of three types of text mining techniques into the patent text genre. In: Lupu, M., Mayer, K., Kando, N., Trippe, A. (eds.) Current Challenges in Patent Information Retrieval. TIRS, vol. 37, pp. 241–280. Springer, Heidelberg (2017). doi:10.1007/978-3-662-53817-3_9
10. Blei, D.M.: Latent Dirichlet allocation. J. Mach. Learn. Res. **3**(4–5), 993–1022 (2003)
11. Salton, G., Buckley, C.: Term-weighting approaches in automatic text retrieval. Inf. Process. Manag. **24**(5), 513–523 (1988)
12. Durrani, N., Sajjad, H., Hoang, H., Koehn, P.: Integrating an unsupervised transliteration model into statistical machine translation. In: Proceedings of the 14th Conference of the European Chapter of the Association for Computational Linguistics (EACL), Gothenburg, Sweden (2014)
13. Korobkin, D., Fomenkov, S., Kravets, A., Kolesnikov, S., Dykov, M.: Three-steps methodology for patents prior-art retrieval and structured physical knowledge extracting. In: Kravets, A., Shcherbakov, M., Kultsova, M., Shabalina, O. (eds.) Creativity in Intelligent Technologies and Data Science. CCIS, vol. 535, pp. 124–136. Springer, Cham (2015). doi:10.1007/978-3-319-23766-4_10
14. Toutanova, K., Manning, C.D.: Enriching the knowledge sources used in a maximum entropy part-of-speech tagger. In: Proceeding EMNLP 2000, vol. 13, Hong Kong, pp. 63–70 (2000)
15. Hall, J.: MaltParser – An Architecture for Inductive Labeled Dependency Parsing, p. 92. University of Colorado, Boulder (2006)
16. Haverinen, K., Viljanen, T., Laippala, V., Kohonen, S., Ginter, F., Salakoski, T.: Treebanking finnish. In: Proceedings of the Ninth International Workshop on Treebanks and Linguistic Theories (TLT) (2010)

17. de Marneffe, M.-C., Manning, C.D.: Stanford typed dependencies manual (2016)
18. Mel'čuk, I.A.: Dependency Syntax Theory and Practice. SUNY Publ, Albany (1988)
19. Levenshtein, V.I.: Binary codes capable of correcting deletions, insertions, and reversals. Sov. Phys. Dokl. **10**(8), 707–710 (1966)
20. Korobkin, D.M., Fomenkov, S.A., Kravets, A.G., Golovanchikov, A.B.: Patent data analysis system for information extraction tasks. In: 13th International Conference on Applied Computing (AC) 2016, pp. 215–219 (2016)

Development of the Unified Technological Platform for Constructing the Domain Knowledge Base Through the Context Analysis

Nadezhda Yarushkina, Aleksey Filippov$^{(\boxtimes)}$, and Vadim Moshkin

Ulyanovsk State Technical University, Ulyanovsk, Russia
{jng, al.filippov, v.moshkin}@ulstu.ru

Abstract. The article considers the architecture of the technological platform designated for construction of the knowledge base (KB) by integrating a set of logical rules with fuzzy ontologies. Development of integration methods for a set of logical rules and fuzzy ontologies are necessary for decision support process. The KB represents the storage of knowledge and contexts of different problem areas (PrA). The PrA ontology context is a specific state of the KB content than can be chosen from a set of the ontology states. The state was obtained as a result of either versioning or constructing the KB content from different points of views.

Keywords: Knowledge base · Ontology · Context · Problem area · Fuzzy ontology

1 Introduction

In the process of any large modern organization activity, it is necessary to make urgent management decisions timely that require specialists to have deep knowledge of the problem area. Also, specialists should be able to use different decision support systems and tools for work with knowledge.

For the solution of this problem methods, knowledge discovery (KD) are used [1–4]. KD process consists of several steps:

1. preparation of the initial data set.
2. preprocessing of data.
3. transformation, normalization of data.
4. data mining.
5. postprocessing of data.

Development of a unified toolkit for KD is necessary for automation of the process of obtaining necessary knowledge about PrO. The unified toolkit should not require the users to have additional skills in knowledge engineering and ontological analysis. The unified toolkit should provide the decision support functions.

The ontology of the KB includes contexts. Contexts of the KB represent the ontology content in space and time.

© Springer International Publishing AG 2017
A. Kravets et al. (Eds.): CIT&DS 2017, CCIS 754, pp. 62–72, 2017.
DOI: 10.1007/978-3-319-65551-2_5

For example, using space contexts in the process of constructing the domain ontology allows to solve the problem of the expert level of competence in the certain subfield of the PrA. Each context is associated with a value from 0 to 1 defining the expert level of competence in the subfield of the PrA.

Time contexts allow to use versioning of the PrA ontology. Time contexts give an opportunity to monitor the dynamics of the ontology development and to return to the defined state of the ontology.

The problem of development the model of fuzzy domain KB is coming up. The ontology of KB should allow constructing the description of the PrA with contexts support. Development of integration methods for a set of logical rules and fuzzy ontologies are necessary for decision support process. The KB interface should not require a user to have additional skills in knowledge engineering and ontological analysis.

2   The Model of the Fuzzy Domain KB with Contexts Support

At the moment, the ontological approach is most often used for organization of knowledge bases of expert systems. A lot of researchers such as Bobillo and Straccia [5], Gao and Liu [6], Bianchini et al. [7], Guarino and Musen [8], Guizzardi et al. [9], Falbo et al. [10], Hotho et al. [11], Gruber [12], Medche [13], Gavrilova [14], and others are engaged in problem of integration and search of information in decision support process on the basis of an ontology.

Ontology is of a model representing knowledge of the PrA in the form of a semantic web. Ontology can be the common semantic basis in the processes of decision-making and data mining. The ontology also can unify the combination of different information systems [15, 16].

One of the KB main objectives is providing the mechanism for adapting the unified technological platform [17] to the concrete PrA with the use of methods of ontological analysis and data engineering.

The KB also support ontology context. Ontology context is a specific state of the KB content. The state was obtained as a result of versioning or constructing the KB content from different points of views.

Formally, the ontology can be represented by the following equation:

$$O = \langle T, C^{T_i}, I^{T_i}, P^{T_i}, S^{T_i}, F^{T_i}, R^{T_i} \rangle, \ i = \overline{1, t},$$

where t is a number of the ontology contexts, $T = \{T_1, T_2, \ldots, T_n\}$ is a set of ontology contexts, C^{T_i} is a set of ontology classes within the i-th context, I^{T_i} is a set of ontology objects within the i-th context, P^{T_i} is a set of ontology classes properties within the i-th context, S^{T_i} is a set of ontology objects states within the i-th context, F^{T_i} is a set of the PrA logical rules fixed in the ontology within the i-th context, R^{T_i} is a set of ontology relations within the i-th context defined as:

$$R^{T_i} = \{ R_C^{T_i}, R_I^{T_i}, R_P^{T_i}, R_S^{T_i}, R_{F_{IN}}^{T_i}, R_{F_{OUT}}^{T_i} \},$$

where $R_C^{T_i}$ is a set of relations defining hierarchy of ontology classes within the i-th context, $R_I^{T_i}$ is a set of 'class-object' ontology relations within the i-th context, $R_P^{T_i}$ is a set of 'class-class property' ontology relations within the i-th context, $R_S^{T_i}$ is a set of 'object-object state' ontology relations within the i-th context, $R_{F_{IN}}^{T_i}$ is a set of relations between $F_j^{T_i}$ logical rule entry and other instances of the ontology within the i-th context, $R_{F_{OUT}}^{T_i}$ is a set of relations between $F_j^{T_i}$ logical rule exit and other instances of the ontology within the i-th context.

The ontology presented in Fig. 1 includes 'Object' and 'Subject' classes with specific properties. These classes are the parent ones for all other ontology classes. Parent properties are inherited by children. The ontology also includes objects 'Machine', 'Component', 'Turner' and 'Smith'. Each object has own set of statements. The object 'Smith' has the statement 'hasAProfession' with a value 'Turner'.

'Working with' is the SWRL-rule [18] 'hasAProfession (Smith, Turner) → workingWith (Smith, Machine)'. This rule describes the implicit relation between 'workingWith' and objects 'Smith' and 'Machine' (Fig. 1).

The fuzzy nature of the KB appears in the process of integration of contexts of the domain ontology. The contexts are represented from different points of view Depending on a level of competence of the expert, the weight of relation of ontology can take on a value from 0 to 1. This allows defining the minimum weight of relations that can be used in the process of work with the KB content.

Formalization of the fuzzy KB can be realized with the use of the Fuzzy OWL standard [19].

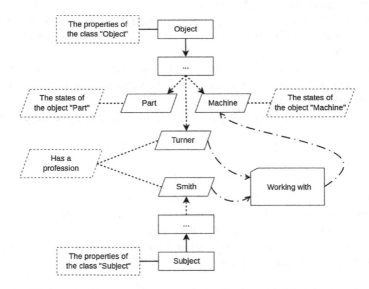

Fig. 1. The SWRL-rule represented in the form of the logical rule of the domain ontology

3 The Architecture of the Knowledge Base of the Unified Technological Platform

Figure 2 shows the architecture of the developed KB that consists of some modules:

- the module for managing the KB content;
- the module for import/export of the KB content from/to FuzzyOWL;
- the module for organizing mechanisms for obtaining and editing data with the use of dynamically generated screen forms on the basis of the KB content. This feature allows users to work with the system and not require them to have additional skills in knowledge engineering and ontological analysis;
- the module for organizing the inference according to the KB content.

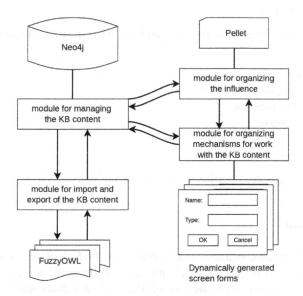

Fig. 2. The knowledge base architecture

For the development of the unified technological platform, the Java programming language and Spring Boot framework [20] were used. Such development tools have the following advantages:

1. high development rate;
2. the existence of documentation and active community of developers;
3. platform independence;
4. advanced infrastructure.

Neo4j [21] graph database is used as storage of ontologies of the KB. It has the following advantages:

1. native format for graph storages;
2. one database instance can serve graphs with billions of nodes and relations;
3. it can process graphs that do not have enough space in RAM.

Jetty servlets container with the modular architecture that allows to use only needed functions is used. Also Jetty is highly scalable for performing a lot of connections with significant downtime between the queries. It also allows serving a lot of users [22].

For modules interaction, the REST (Representational State Transfer) mechanism was used [23]. It this case, the remote procedure call represents a simple HTTP request (GET, POST, PUT, etc.), and necessary data are transmitted as parameters of the request. The main benefits of REST are the following ones:

- high performance due to the use of cash;
- scalability;
- integration system transparency;
- the simplicity of interfaces;
- portability of components;
- modification simplicity.

For inference, the Pellet reasoner was used [24]. It has the following advantages [25]:

- soundness;
- completeness;
- SROIQ(D) expressivity support;
- incremental classification;
- SWRL rules support;
- justifications;
- ABox reasoning.

All the above resources, applications, and technologies are free.

4 Experiments

A set of experiments on constructing the ontology of the PrA of the local area network (LAN) state estimation in the process of simulated traffic increase was carried out. The ontology was constructed with the use of the unified technological platform. The unified technological platform also gives the ability of the inference of expert recommendations on solving the problem situations occurred in the process of LAN functioning.

The following actions were taken:

1. The group of experts developed FuzzyOWL-ontology and the set of logical rules. Ontology and the set of logical rules were developed with the use of tools of the unified technological platform. Each expert worked with his ontology context. Weight was appropriated to each context. The weights correspond the expert level of competence in the specific field of the PrA. Figure 3 shows the fragment of the fuzzy ontology of the PrA built by a group of experts.

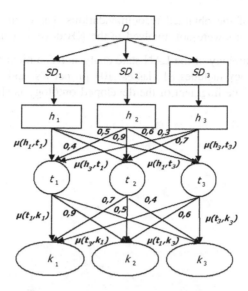

Fig. 3. The fuzzy ontology fragment

The complex problem area D can be seen on the upper level. Area D includes the merge of all the contexts of the PrA. The PrA can be divided into the corresponding subareas SD (the 2-nd level). Each subarea is characterized by its contexts (the 3-rd level). The contexts reflect the ideas of experts about categories and concepts of subareas in the context of the unified PrA D.

Experts construct the hierarchy of the PrA concepts where the 4-th level includes the basic concepts or categories of the ontology t_i, where $i = [1 \ldots n]$, the 5-th level (the lower one) includes linguistic variables related to the names of categories k_j, where $j = [1 \ldots m]$. The fuzziness of relations between the ontology categories and the concrete linguistic variable is represented in defining this relation as the value of the membership function $0 \leq \mu(t_i, k_j) \leq 1$.

In the process of developing the KB, experts match the names of categories with the keywords. Each expert is a specialist in the concrete subarea of the PrA. The weight of the expert is defined in the subareas of the PrA. The weight of the expert expressed in a value from [0, 1]. The experts should define the degree of connection between a category t_i and a keyword k_j that is also expressed in a value from [0, 1].

1. 30 problem situations of decrease of the LAN performance were simulated on the tested LAN. Technical characteristics of the tested LAN outlined in the table of the experiments' results. The reasons for the problem situation occurred should be detected.
2. The equipment performances in each simulated situation and the characteristics of the network were put into the KB. The LAN architecture also was put into the KB. The platform inference subsystem performed the output of one or several recommendations for the LAN state correction.

3. The correctness of the obtained recommendations was estimated by a group of expert. These experts were not involved in the KB development process.

The developed ontology of the LAN state analysis has a hierarchical organization. The developed ontology includes 81 classes, 104 properties, and about 200 ontology instances of classes. The fragment of the developed ontology is shown in Fig. 4.

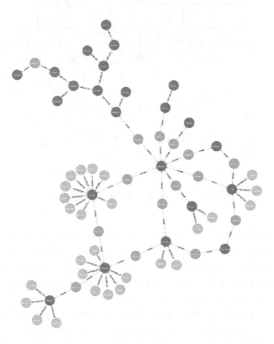

Fig. 4. The fragment of the LAN state analysis ontology

The ability to check the KB logical integrity and consistency with the use of a reasoner is the main feature of the developed technological platform. One of the main reasoner tools is testing the hierarchy of classes and their descriptions. The Pellet reasoner is used in the developed technological platform. The reasoner allows to avoid the following errors in the ontology data structure:

1. The error of consistency of classes. This error can occur if the class is inconsistent and it couldn't include instances.
2. The error of objects properties consistency. This error can occur if the object properties are contradictory.

The developed KB also includes the set of SWRL-rules represented in the ontology rules. The ontology rules are a driver in the inference process. The ontology rules are part of the domain described in the ontology.

Table 1 contains the LAN architecture. Also, that table contains some modeled problems in the process of artificial traffic increase in a network. Recommendations on solving the problems generated by the platform tools in the process of inference are presented in Table 1.

Table 1. The modeled processes of artificial traffic increase in a network

LAN architecture	Modeled problems	The recommendations of the platform inference subsystem
Star network, the number of workstations is 14, the server OS is Windows Server 2008 R2, the network switch is D-Link DGS-3420-28SC, 20 ports, the switch RAM is 2 Mb, the operating mode – 100 Mb/s Full Duplex, the media access control method is CSMA/CD, QoS is on, patch cable type is UTP, the category is 5E, port RJ-45	The fast increase of the background load, increase of the user software reaction time	The reason is an overload of the communication channel. It requires the network architecture changes. The number of stations in the overloaded domains should be reduced. The stations that create the greatest load should be connected to the switch ports
	Half Duplex mode is enabled, background load increase	The reason is the mismatch between the characteristics of a network switch and the traffic volume. It requires replacement of a switch or change of its settings
	Damage of one network patch cable; increase of collision number	The reason is the problem with connection patch cables. The reason is the wrong organization of ground of the computers connected to the local network
	Defects of switch ports, increase of CRC errors number, the background load increase	The reason is the problem of the network switch ports or the patch cable damage leading to a problem host
	Defects of an Ethernet adapter, rapid increase in a number of local and remote collisions	The reason is the problem in the domain server Ethernet adapter settings. The user should check the Ethernet adapter and the correctness of its settings

5 Comparison of the Inference on the Basis of Fuzzy and Crisp Ontologies

A set of experiments was carried in the developed unified technological platform to compare the interaction of ontological analysis and inference mechanisms on the basis of fuzzy and crisp ontologies. The possible problem situations occurred in LAN functioning in the process of traffic increase were simulated.

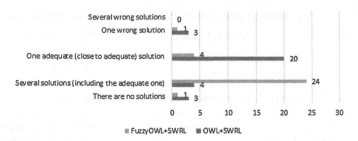

Fig. 5. The results of 30 experiments to comparison of the inference on the basis of fuzzy and crisp ontologies

The LAN of IT-department of Ulyanovsk State Technical University was chosen as an object for the experiments. The comparative analysis of the inference methodologies in the process of modeling problem situations in the LAN functioning is shown in Fig. 5.

As can be seen from the results of experiments fuzzy ontology-based on FuzzyOWL format showed a more wide range of variants. The variants are sorted by the degree of relevance of recommendations. The risks of loss of possible variants of the logical inference block are significantly reduced.

6 Conclusion

The integration of the inference mechanism and the fuzzy ontology in the context of the unified KB provide a unified toolkit of expert decision support for specialists of different organizations.

Contexts of the KB represent the ontology content in space and time. Space contexts allow solving the problem of the expert level of competence in the certain subfield of the PrA. Each context is associated with a value from 0 to 1 defining the expert level of competence in the subfield of the PrA.

Time contexts allow using versioning of the PrA ontology. Time contexts give an opportunity to monitor the dynamics of the ontology development and to return to the defined state of the ontology.

Acknowledgments. This work was financially supported by the Russian Foundation for Basic Research (Grants No. 16-47-732054 and 16-47-732120).

References

1. Rubiolo, M., Caliusco, M.L., Stegmayer, G., Coronel, M., Fabrizi, M.G.: Knowledge discovery through ontology matching: an approach based on an artificial neural network model. Inf. Sci. **194**, 107–119 (2012)
2. Renu, R.S., Mocko, G., Koneru, A.: Use of big data and knowledge discovery to create data backbones for decision support systems. Proc. Comput. Sci. **20**, 446–453 (2013)

3. Ltifi, H., Kolski, C., Ayed, M.B., Alimi, A.M.: A human-centred design approach for developing dynamic decision support system based on knowledge discovery in databases. J. Decis. Syst. **22**, 69–96 (2013)
4. Rajpathak, D., Chougule, R., Bandyopadhyay, P.: A domain-specific decision support system for knowledge discovery using association and text mining. Knowl. Inf. Syst. **31**, 405–432 (2012)
5. Bobillo, F., Straccia, U.: FuzzyDL: an expressive fuzzy description logic reasoner. In: Proceedings of the 17th IEEE International Conference on Fuzzy Systems (FUZZ-IEEE 2008), pp. 923–930. IEEE Computer Society (2008)
6. Gao, M., Liu, C.: Extending OWL by fuzzy description logic. In: Proceedings of the 17th IEEE International Conference on Tools with Artificial Intelligence (ICTAI 2005), pp. 562–567. IEEE Computer Society (2005)
7. Bianchini, D., De Antonellis, V., Pernici, B., Plebani, P.: Ontology-based methodology for e-service discovery. Inf. Syst. **31**(4), 361–380 (2006)
8. Guarino, N., Musen, M.A.: Ten years of applied ontology. Appl. Ontol. **10**(3–4), 169–170 (2015)
9. Guizzardi, G., Guarino, N., Almeida, J.P.A.: Ontological considerations about the representation of events and endurants in business models. In: La Rosa, M., Loos, P., Pastor, O. (eds.) BPM 2016. LNCS, vol. 9850, pp. 20–36. Springer, Cham (2016). doi:10.1007/978-3-319-45348-4_2
10. Falbo, R.A., Quirino, G.K., Nardi, J.C., Barcellos, M.P., Guizzardi, G., Guarino, N.: An ontology pattern language for service modeling. In: Proceedings of the 31st Annual ACM Symposium on Applied Computing, pp. 321–326 (2016)
11. Hotho, A., Staab, S., Stumme, G.: Ontologies improve text document clustering. In: Third IEEE International Conference on Data Mining, ICDM 2003, pp. 541–544 (2003)
12. Gruber, T.: Ontology. In: Liu, L., Tamer Özsu, M. (eds.) Entry in the Encyclopedia of Database Systems. Springer, New York (2008). doi:10.1007/978-0-387-39940-9_1318
13. Medche, A.: Ontology Learning for the Semantic Web. Engineering and Computer Science, vol. 665. Kluwer International, Dordrecht (2002). doi:10.1007/978-1-4615-0925-7
14. Gavrilova, T.A.: Ontologicheskii podkhod k upravleniiu znaniiami pri razrabotke korporativnykh informatsionnykh sistem (The ontological approach to knowledge management in the development of corporate information systems). Novosti iskusstvennogo intellekta (News Artif. Intell.) **2**(56), 24–29 (2003)
15. Namestnikov, A.M, Filippov, A.A., Avvakumova, V.S.: An ontology based model of technical documentation fuzzy structuring. In: CEUR Workshop Proceedings, SCAKD 2016, Moscow, Russian Federation. vol. 1687, pp. 63–74 (2016)
16. Yarushkina, N., Moshkin, V., Andreev, I., Klein, V., Beksaeva, E.: Hybridization of fuzzy inference and self-learning fuzzy ontology-based semantic data analysis. In: Abraham, A., Kovalev, S., Tarassov, V., Snášel, V. (eds.) Proceedings of the First International Scientific Conference "Intelligent Information Technologies for Industry" (IITI'16). AISC, vol. 450, pp. 277–285. Springer, Cham (2016). doi:10.1007/978-3-319-33609-1_25
17. Filippov, A.A., Moshkin, V.S., Shalaev, D.O., Yarushkina, N.G.: Uniform ontological data mining platform. In: Golenkov, V., et al. (eds) Open Semantic Technologies of Intelligent Systems (OSTIS-2016): Proceedings of VI International Science Technological Conference (Minsk, 18–20 February 2016), pp. 77-82. BSUIR, Minsk (2016)
18. SWRL: A semantic web rule language combining OWL and RuleML. https://www.w3.org/Submission/SWRL. Accessed 20 Jan 2017
19. Bobillo, F., Straccia, U.: Representing fuzzy ontologies in OWL 2. In: Proceedings of the 19th IEEE International Conference on Fuzzy Systems (FUZZ-IEEE 2010), pp. 2695–2700. IEEE Press (2010)

20. Spring Boot framework. https://projects.spring.io/spring-boot. Accessed 9 Jan 2017
21. Neo4j. https://neo4j.com/product. Accessed 10 Jan 2017
22. Greg Wilkins Jetty vs Tomcat: a comparative analysis (2008). http://www.webtide.com/choose/jetty.jsp. Accessed 9 Jan 2017
23. Representational state transfer. https://en.wikipedia.org/wiki/Representational_state_transfer. Accessed 9 Jan 2017
24. Pellet framework. https://github.com/stardog-union/pellet. Accessed 10 Jan 2017
25. Dentler, K., Cornet, R., ten Teije, A., de Keizer, N.: Comparison of reasoners for large ontologies in the OWL 2 EL profile. Semantic Web 2, April 2011, pp. 71–87 (2011)

Extraction of Physical Effects Based on the Semantic Analysis of the Patent Texts

Marina Fomenkova$^{(\boxtimes)}$, Dmitriy Korobkin ,
and Sergey Fomenkov

Volgograd State Technical University, Volgograd, Russia
mfa92@yandex.ru

Abstract. The paper represents new methodology of semantic analysis for physical effects extracting. This methodology is based on the Tuzov ontology that formally describes the Russian language. In this paper, semantic patterns were described to extract structural physical information in the form of physical effects. A new algorithm of text analysis was described. The approach is applied to the database of physical effects and to the patent texts. The results of the proposed method compared with the results of the IOFEE system that is used for the same tasks. The method described in this article allowed increasing efficiency of the physical effect elements extracting. The semantic analyzer based on the Tuzov ontology was created to increase the accuracy and completeness of the method.

Keywords: Semantic analysis · Physical effect · Fact extraction · Tuzov ontology

1 Introduction

Currently, the semantic analysis of the text is one of the most important areas in computer science. This direction is widely used in various spheres, such as trade (analysis of consumer preferences), political science and sociology (forecasting of the election results, analysis of sociological data, etc.), psychiatry (patients diagnosing), etc. However, despite its wide application, semantic text analysis is one of the most complicated mathematical problems, which consists of several stages of text processing.

In this paper, text analysis is considered as a tool for extracting structured physical knowledge in the form of physical effects (PE) [1]. Currently, the task of identifying the descriptions of PE from the texts of scientific documents for replenishing the PE base as an information basis for the development of new technical solutions is very important.

Today, there is the problem of the effectiveness of the descriptions of physical effects identifying in the texts of physical documents. Identification of descriptions of physical effects, for example, from the text of a patent is necessary to check the new incoming physical effect on the coincidence with patents existing in the database. If the descriptions of physical effects coincide in the claimed patent with descriptions in the patents from the database, the refusal in the patent application is formed.

© Springer International Publishing AG 2017
A. Kravets et al. (Eds.): CIT&DS 2017, CCIS 754, pp. 73–87, 2017.
DOI: 10.1007/978-3-319-65551-2_6

At the moment, the system for detecting descriptions of physical effects from texts based on "Semantix" semantic analyzer has been implemented [2, 3]. The disadvantage of this system is often the incorrect construction of the semantic network, due to which individual elements of physical effects can be extracted erroneously.

It is necessary to increase the effectiveness of the descriptions of physical effects identifying. In this paper, we propose a technique for identifying descriptions of physical effects from texts of documents based on the semantic templates built on the basis of the Tuzov's ontology.

2 Analysis of Software Systems and Tools for the Semantic Analysis of Text

An analysis of the effectiveness of software systems for extracting facts is presented in [3]. As shown in the paper, most existing systems do not have sufficient flexibility to customize on the subject area. Therefore, there is a need for a new approach to solving the problem of extracting elements of the PE description from the texts of scientific documents.

Analysis of the effectiveness of software systems for semantic analysis is shown in Tables 1 and 2. In these tables different program systems and tools for semantic analyses are presented. The effectiveness and semantic abilities are presented.

There are the efficiency criteria and the main points for analyzing and evaluating the systems for extracting knowledge and facts from the text sources. The following points were identified in the analysis of the subject area:

- Algorithm for identifying target entities (can be search by patterns or search based on neural network technologies).
- System flexibility - the ability to configure system parameters, the ability to add new entities to the system, etc. (These parameters can be set rigidly in the system, and can be set by the user of the system).
- License (closed or open).
- The accuracy of the retrieval of the facts sought - the percentage of correctly identified semantic units (1 - from 85%, 2 - 75–85%, 3 - below 75%).
- Completeness of extraction - the percentage of correctly extracted semantic units extracted from the total number of facts in the text (1- from 50%, 2 - to 50%).

As it can be seen from the Table 1 existing systems (except IOFFE) do not fit in the field of "Physics"; in the latter, the accuracy and completeness of the extraction of the elements of the PE structure are not high enough.

From the can be seen that these systems are oriented to the analysis of the any subject texts, they do not have the possibility of an advanced tuning to extract certain semantic structures, which significantly reduces the possibility of using them for solving the task. The most promising systems are the systems with the ability to configure flexibly templates for the subject area to improve the accuracy and completeness of retrieving the necessary information.

Table 1. Analysis of systems for extracting facts from text

Program system	An algorithm for target entities identifying	The system's flexibility (the ability to customize settings, adding new entities)	License	Accuracy extracting (1- more than 75%, 2 - 65%, 3 - 65% less)	Completeness (1 - more than 60%, 2 - less than 60%)
Extractring facts from the text files, RCO [2]	Patterns search	The parameters are hard-coded	Close	1	2
Attensity text analytics [3]	Neural network technology	The parameters are hard-coded	Close	2	1
NetOwl extractor [4]	Neural network technology	The parameters are hard-coded	Close	1	1
IOFFE [1]	Patterns search	The ability to add new patterns	Open	3	2

Table 2. Semantic analyses systems

Software	Russian support	License	Base technology	Flexibility (focus on the subject area, the ability to customize, code availability)
Stanford nlp [5]	No	Open	Machine learning technologies	No
Malt parser [6]	Yes	Open	Machine learning technologies	No
Link grammar parser [7]	No	Open	Relations grammar	No
AGFL [8]	Yes	Open	AGFL-grammar	No
Tomita parser [9]	Yes	Open	CF-grammar and key words	No

3 Semantic Text Analysis to Identify Descriptions of Physical Effect

3.1 The General Approach for PE Extracting

The general approach for PE extracting is following:

- Tokenization. At this stage, sentences are broken up into words, extra characters are deleted from the sentence.
- Morphological analysis. At this stage, all the lexemes allocated during the tokenization stage are subjected to morphological analysis. Morphological analysis is performed using a TreeTagger library. This tool is a language-independent tool for morphological markup of texts. Helmut Schmitt at the Institute of Computer Linguistics at the University of Stuttgart developed it. TreeTagger has successfully proved itself in various tasks of text processing in various languages (Russian, English, German, French, Italian, etc.).

The result is the structure that consists of three columns. The first column of the TreeTagger result is the original word received at the stage of tokenization. The second column presents the morphological characteristics of the word in the sentence (gender, number, case). In the third column, the word is presented in its initial form. If TreeTagger could not find the initial form of the word, the word <unknown> is written in the third column.

- Lemmatization. At this stage, words that were not recognized at the morphological analysis stage (the initial form of the word was not recognized) enter the input to the CstLemma application.
- Extraction of structured physical information in the form of physical effects based on semantic templates, developed based on the Tuzov's ontology.

Ontology of the Russian language [2] - a formal description of the Russian language, proposed by V.A. Tuzov (semantic roles are determined on the basis of semantic classes and morphological information). The basis of the approach is a semantic dictionary that describes more than one hundred thousand lexical units (words and phrases), and each word is described as a semantic formula consisting of basic functions.

- The language is the algebraic system $\{f_1, f_2, ... f_n, M\}$, where f_i are the basic functions in the language, and M is the language structure that represents the set of basic concepts $m_1, ... m_r$, and their hierarchy.
- Any sentence of a language can be represented as a superposition of basis functions f_i, through which the words of the language are also expressed, excluding the basic concepts m_j that enter in M. Thus, sentences represent single superposition of functions, in the mathematical sense are treated as functions.
- The grammar is related to the semantics of the language, which is based on a semantic dictionary that describes more than one hundred thousand words and phrases. They are divided into 3 levels: fundamental (consists of 1500 hierarchical classes, as well as a set of basic functions); Variable (consists of 23000 classes, connected with the fundamental, because they are described on the basis of this level and are its variations); Descriptive (words are described based on words and concepts of the first two levels). Each word is described as a semantic formula, which consists of basic functions.

The dictionary of basic concepts of the Russian language contains words that can not be expressed through other simpler concepts. It contains about 18,000 nouns that call physical and abstract objects, more than a thousand basic adjectives and about a thousand basic verbs, which, ultimately, have been replaced by verbal nouns. The remaining words - more than 90,000 words - are derived, that is, their meaning is expressed in the form of a superposition constructed from basic functions and basic concepts. The whole set of concepts is divided into a hierarchical class system.

EXPOSURE \$15142 (Caus_o (AGENT: SOMETHING \$ 1 ~ Gen, Lab (OBJECT:! Acc, LOCATION: Prep)))

In [9, 10] a formal description of the physical effect is presented. The physical effect is an objective, naturally conditioned connection between two or more physical phenomena, each of which is characterized by a corresponding physical quantity. From the content side, the PE is represented as a functional connection (arising from physical laws, their consequences) between two or more physical quantities.

To extract descriptions of physical effects, a model for representing structured physical information in a natural language text has been developed.

$$M_{PE} = <C, D, B, R_C, R_B> ,\tag{1}$$

where, C is the set of predicates (relations) that are characteristic for describing the PE in the text, $c_i \in C$; D - semantic roles and cases of arguments with predicates. $d_i \subset D$ - list of roles/ cases of arguments, consistent with the predicate c_i; $d_j \in D_i$; B - the set of elements of the description of the PE (A, B, C), $B_k \in B$.

$$\forall c_i \in C \exists d_j \in D_i d_j \longrightarrow def B_k,$$

where, $B_k \in \{input (A), output (C), object (B)\}$; def is the operator associating the role/case of the argument d_j with the predicate c_i, the set of the elements of the PE.

R_C is the relation on $C \times D$, the pair $(c_i, d_j) \in R_C$ uniquely identifies the element (s) of the PE description, consistent with the predicate role/case d_j.

R_B is the relation on $R_C \times B$, the pair $((c_i, d_j), B_k) \in R_B$ defines the set of software concepts corresponding to the element of the PE description B_k.

Let us consider an example of the application of the model.

The text containing the description of the PE: "The effect of a magnetic field on amperage in a conducting layer".

Where $C_1 = IMPACT$

$D = \{AGENT/Generic, OBJECT/VIN, LOCATION/Prev\}$

$B = \{InputPE, OutputPE, ObjectPE\}$

For the role "Agent" of the conceptual relationship c_1, which is performed by the member of the relation m_1: $z_1 = \{input of the PE\}$.

For the role of "Object", which is performed by the relation member m_2: $z_2 = \{output of the PE, object PE\}$.

For the role of "Place", which is performed by the relation member m_3: $z_3 = \{input PE, object PE\}$. $B_1 = InputPE = Magnetic field$ (Exposure (of what ?, gen), AGENT),

$B_2 = OutputPE = Amperage$ (Impact (what ?, acc), OBJECT),

$B_3 = ObjectPE = conductive layer$ (Impact (in what ?, prep), LOCATION)

The dictionary of templates contains a set of key words (predicates), which correspond to individual sets of links "Element of the description of the PE" – "Semantic role of the argument in the Tuzov ontology".

Predicates are the basic verbs or verbal nouns that characterize the descriptions of physical effects in the text, such as interaction, interaction, influence, impact, highlight, act, dependence, etc.

Let us consider an example of the application of the model.

The text containing the description of the PE: "The influence of the magnetic field on the Amperage in the conductive layer", where the predicate "EFFECT", the "Input of the PE" according to the template dictionary corresponds to the semantic role of the "Agent", the "Output of the PE" is the Object, the "Object of the PE" is the Place. We obtain the extracted elements of the PE description:

PE Input = Magnetic field (Exposure (AGENT)), PE Output = Amperage (Impact (OBJECT)),

PE object = conductive layer (Impact (LOCATION))

Based on the semantic roles in Tuzov's ontology, the structure of the semantic template was defined:

<Predicate> <input of the PE in the required case> <preposition of the output of the PE> <output of the PE in the required case> <preposition of the PE object> <PE object in the desired case>, where predicate is the keyword, selected according to the subject domain, is a verb or verbal noun (interaction, interaction, influence, allocation, isolate, action, act, depend, dependency, etc.).

In the event that there is no preposition or semantic role for the keyword in the ontology, the word null is written in the template. In the event that several prepositions and/or cases corresponded to a single semantic role, prepositions and/or cases were recorded through separators.

On the basis of the analysis of the subject area "Physics", the keywords (predicates) most frequently encountered in conjunction with unstructured descriptions of physical effects were identified. Such keywords are either verbs or other verbal parts of speech (noun, participle).

As a result, more than 100 keywords were chosen for the subject area.

Based on the semantic roles in Tuzov's ontology, the structure of the semantic template was defined:

<Predicate> <input of the PE in the required case> <preposition of the output of the PE> <output of the PE in the required case> <preposition of the PE object> <PE object in the desired case>, where predicate - the keyword, selected according to the subject domain, is a verb or verbal noun (interaction, interaction, influence, influence, influence, influence, allocation, isolate, action, act, depend, dependency, etc.);

In the event that there is no preposition or semantic role for the keyword in the ontology, the word null is written in the template. In the event that several prepositions and/or cases corresponded to a single semantic role, prepositions and/or cases were recorded through separators.

As a result, more than 100 semantic templates for the subject area were developed.

Algorithm of semantic analysis for extracting arguments Agent, Object, Place is represented in Fig. 1.

Thus, the algorithm consists of the following basic steps:

- Tokenization;
- Morphological analysis;
- Lemmatization;
- Extract the arguments of the semantic roles of the Agent, Object and Place - nouns and adjectives related to the given nouns. In addition, connections were extracted from cases - a connection was made in the genitive case, consistent with the noun corresponding to the semantic role.

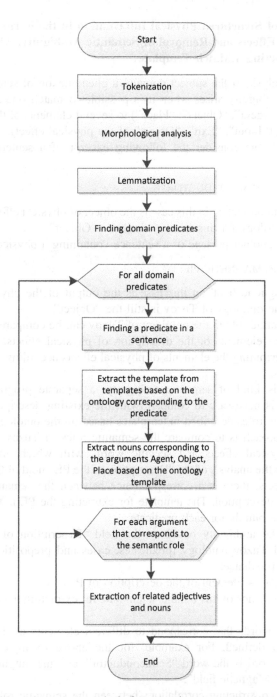

Fig. 1. Algorithm of semantic analysis for extracting arguments Agent, Object, Place

3.2   Extraction of Structured Physical Information in the Form of Physical Effects and Removal of Semantic Ambiguity. Algorithm for Constructing a Match Template

Because of the analysis of the subject domain, a phenomenon of semantic ambiguity arises. Semantic ambiguity arises when it is possible to match one semantic role in ontology. Tuzov ("Agent", "Object", "Place") to several elements of the description of the physical effect ("Input", "Exit", "Object" of the physical effect).

For example, if we consider the following excerpt of a sentence containing a physical effect:

"IMPACT ON THE SEMICONDUCTOR"

The word "semiconductor" in this case is the object of physical effect. The semantic role in Tuzov's ontology for this word is similar – "Object".

If we consider another passage of a sentence containing a physical effect:

"IMPACT ON THE MAGNETIC FIELD"

The word "magnetic field" in this case is the output of the physical effect. The semantic role in the ontology of Tuzov is still the "Object".

Thus, one semantic role in the ontology of Tuzov can be compared, depending on the context, several elements of the description of physical effects. This affects the correctness of determining the elements of physical effects according to the developed semantic templates.

To remove this kind of semantic ambiguity, a separate program module was developed, which is necessary to compare with the existing descriptions of physical effects and semantic roles described in templates based on the ontology of Tuzov. The essence of the approach is to compare the semantic roles of Tuzov, elements of the description of physical effects and specific words with which ambiguity can be revealed. Based on the analysis of the "Description of the PE" field of the description of 1200 physical effects, there is a correspondence between the semantic role and the element of the PE description. The template for extracting the PE is formed based on the statistics of this bundle for each predicate.

To eliminate the ambiguity based on the field "Description of the PE" of the database table and Tuzov ontology (predicates, cases and prepositions for semantic roles) is the correspondence:

<Semantic role> - <Element of the description of PE>.

Based on the statistics of this bundle, a template for extracting the PE is formed for each predicate.

Thus, a set of words that correspond to different elements of the description of physical effects is defined. For example, for the above example with the word "Impact", this keyword is the word "Semiconductor", and the output of the physical effect is the word "Magnetic field".

Algorithm for constructing correlations between the semantic roles of the Tuzov ontology and elements of the description of the physical effect for predicates of the domain are shown in Fig. 2.

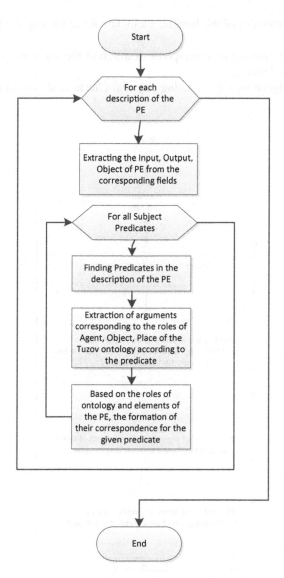

Fig. 2. The algorithm of construction of correspondences to semantic roles of Tuzov ontology to elements of the description of physical effect for predicates of the subject domain

So the essence of the approach is to compare the semantic roles of Tuzov, the elements of describing physical effects and specific words with which ambiguity can appear. To eliminate the ambiguity based on the field "Description of the PE" of the database table and Tuzov ontology (predicates, cases and prepositions for semantic roles) is the correspondence:

<Semantic role> - <Element of the description of PE>.

Based on the statistics of this bundle, a template for extracting the PE is formed for each predicate.

Thus, a set of words that correspond to different elements of the description of physical effects is defined.

The general algorithm for extracting physical effects is shown in Fig. 3.

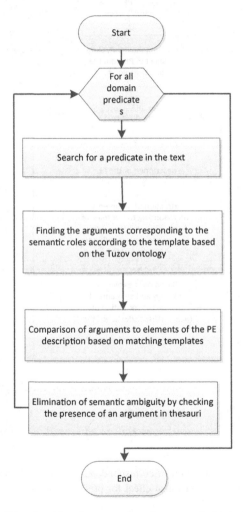

Fig. 3. The algorithm for extracting elements of physical effects

Thus, the algorithm for extracting elements of physical effects reduces to finding all the predicates of the domain and performing the following steps for them:

- Search for a predicate in the text;
- Finding the arguments corresponding to the semantic roles according to the template based on Tuzov's ontology;

- Comparison of arguments to elements of the description of the physical effect on the basis of match patterns;
- Elimination of semantic ambiguity by checking the presence of an argument in thesauri.

4 Results

The following performance criteria were developed:

- Accuracy of extraction of elements of PE description;
- Completeness of extraction of elements of PE description;
- F-measure.

The accuracy is characterized by the number of correctly extracted elements to the total number of elements of the PE description

$$P = N_r / N_f, \tag{2}$$

where, P is the accuracy of the PE extraction, Nr is the number of correctly extracted elements of the PE description, Nf is the number of elements of the FE description found in the text.

The completeness of the PE description elements extraction is a value expressed in percent, which characterizes the number of elements found in the PE description to the total number of elements of the PE description in the text.

$$R = N_f / N, \tag{3}$$

where, R is the completeness of the extraction of elements of the PE description, N_f is the number of elements of the PE found in the text, N is the total number of elements of the PE description in the text.

The F-measure is calculated by formulas 4 and 5.

$$F = \frac{(\beta^2 + 1)PR}{\beta^2 P + R}, \tag{4}$$

$$\beta^2 = \frac{1 - a}{a}, \tag{5}$$

The data was tested based on physical effects data, developed at the CAD department of Volgograd State Technical University. 100 physical effects were selected. The tests were carried out on the descriptions of physical effects in the DB of the PE and the results of the extraction were compared with the fields "Input", "Output", "Object" of the physical effect.

Also, the tests were conducted on 31 patent documents for which physical effects contained in the patent description are known in advance.

The results were compared with the results of the IOFFE program [11] based on "Semantix" semantic analyzer.

The efficiency analysis showed that the developed system increases the efficiency of extracting elements of the description of physical effects by 4% for accuracy and by 7% for completeness (Tables 3 and 4).

Table 3. Analysis of efficiency using the PE database

	Accuracy (%)	Completeness (%)	F-measure
Our system	68	59	61.5
IOFFE	57	53	54.14

Table 4. Analysis of the effectiveness using the patent array

	Accuracy (%)	Completeness (%)	F-measure
Our system	53	46	47.9
IOFFE	46	41	42.38

Sample 1. Patent description: "The photoelectric conversion element may be a photodiode having a p-n junction or a pin junction, a phototransistor, or the like. When the incident light hits the semiconductor junction of the cell, this light leads to the appearance of the photoelectric effect, in which electric charges arise." [14].

- PE Input: "Light, any other electromagnetic radiation (energy - eV)". PE Output: "The electric charge (electron emission), (J)".
- PE Object: "Photoconductive material (photoconductor)".

The results of the program show the results of the physical effect elements extraction:

- PE Input: "Light".
- PE Output: "electric charge". PE Object: "phototransistor".

Sample 2. Patent description: "In electrical circuits, any electric current produces a magnetic field and hence generates a total magnetic flux acting on the circuit".

- PE Input: "Electric current".
- PE Object: "Electrical circuit".
- PE Output: "Magnetic field".

The results of the program show the results of the physical effect elements extraction:

- PE Input: "Electric current".
- PE Object: "Electrical circuit".
- PE Output: "Magnetic field".

5 Conclusion

The method described in this article allowed increasing efficiency of the PE elements extracting. The semantic analyzer based on the Tuzov ontology was created to increase the accuracy and completeness of the method. The approach was tested on the PE database and the patent array.

Key words - predicates - (verbs, verbal nouns, participles) that can be found in sentences containing elements for describing physical effects have been identified. The corresponding descriptions are selected in the ontology.

On the basis of the ontology of Tuzov, semantic templates have been developed that consist of a keyword (predicate) - a characteristic verb or verbal form for a given field, cases of the semantic roles "Agent", "Object", "Place", and related prepositions. Then the templates of the correspondence of the semantic roles of the ontology of Tuzov and the elements of the description of physical effects are constructed. Based on the thesauri of the subject area, this allows you to extract elements of the description of physical effects from text documents.

The efficiency analysis technique included finding the accuracy and completeness of extracting elements of descriptions of physical effects from the field of describing physical effects in the database, as well as in the texts of the patent documents. Then the results were compared with the results of the IOFFE system, which was implemented based on Semantix semantic analyzer. Thus, the efficiency of the developed software was evaluated.

The results of the efficiency analysis showed that the accuracy of extraction of elements of the description of physical effects was increased by 11% for physical effects from the database and 5% for physical effects from the texts of patent documents. Completeness of extraction of elements of the description of physical effects was increased by 6% for physical effects from the database and by 7% for physical effects from the texts of patent documents.

Acknowledgement. This research was partially supported by the Russian Fund of Basic Research (grants No. 15-07-09142 A, No.15-07-06254 A, No. 16-07-00534 A).

References

1. Korobkin, D.M., Fomenkov, S.A., Kamaev, V.A., Fomenkova, M.A.: Multi-agent model of ontology- based extraction of physical effects descriptions from natural language text. In: Information Technologies in Science, Management, Social Sphere and Medicine (ITSMSSM), pp. 498–501. Atlantis Press (2016). doi:10.2991/itsmssm-16.2016.13
2. Pleshko, V.V., Ermakov, A.V.: Semantic interpretation in text analysis computer systems. J. Inf. Technol. (2009)
3. Taylor, J.: First Look – Attensity 5.5 decision, management, solutions. In: 5 International Conference on Information Technologies in Business and Industry (2017)
4. Krupka, G.R., Hausman, K.I.: Description of the NetOwl TM Extractor system as used for MUC-7. In: MUC-7 (1998)

5. Manning, C.D., Raghavan, P., Schütze, H.: Introduction to Information Retrieval. Cambridge University Press, Cambridge (2008)
6. Nivre, J., Hall, J., Nilsson, J.: MaltParser: a data-driven parser-generator for dependency parsing. In: Proceedings of the Fifth International Conference on Language Resources and Evaluation (LREC), Genoa, Italy, pp. 2216–2219 (2006)
7. Tukeyev, U.A., Melby, A.K., Zhumanov, Z.M.: Models and algorithms of translation of the Kazakh language sentences into English language with use of link grammar and the statistical approach. In: IV Congress of the Turkic World Math. Society, Baku (2014)
8. Azarova, I.: The matching of AGFL subcategories to Russian lexical and grammatical groupings. In: Proceedings of the Second AGFL Workshop on Syntactic Description and Processing of Natural Language (2002)
9. Ogogrodnik, P.B., Serebryannaya, L.V.: Text analysis with Tomita parser. In: International Conference (BSUIR), Minsk, pp. 230–231 (2014)
10. Tuzo, V.A.: Computer Linguistics. St. Petersburg State University Press, St. Petersburg (1998)
11. Korobkin, D., Fomenkov, S., Kolesnikov, S., Lobeyko, V., Golovanchikov, A.: Modification of physical effect model for the synthesis of the physical operation principles of technical system. In: Kravets, A., Shcherbakov, M., Kultsova, M., Shabalina, O. (eds.) CIT&DS 2015. CCIS, vol. 535, pp. 368–378. Springer, Cham (2015). doi:10.1007/978-3-319-23766-4_29
12. Fomenkov, S., Korobkin, D., Kolesnikov, S.: Method of ontology-based extraction of physical effect description from Russian text. In: Kravets, A., Shcherbakov, M., Kultsova, M., Iijima, T. (eds.) JCKBSE 2014. CCIS, vol. 466, pp. 321–330. Springer, Cham (2014). doi:10.1007/978-3-319-11854-3_27
13. Fomenkov, S.A., Kolesnikov, S.G., Korobkin, D.M., Kamaev, V.A., Orlova, Y.A.: The information filling of the database by physical effects. J. Eng. Appl. Sci. 9, 422–426 (2014)
14. Patent US 20100051095 A1 "Hybrid Photovoltaic Cell Using Amorphous Silicon Germanium Absorbers With Wide Bandgap Dopant Layers and an Up-Converter"
15. Salton, G., Buckley, C.: Term-weighting approaches in automatic text retrieval. J. Inf. Process. Manag. 24(5), 513–523 (1988)
16. U.S. Patent Grant Data/XML v4.3. http://www.uspto.gov/sites/default/files/products/Patent_Grant_XML_v4.3.pdf
17. Zlotin, B., Zusman, A.: Directed Evolution: Philosophy Theory and Practice. Ideation International, Southfield (2001)
18. Fey, V., Rivin, E.: Innovation on Demand: New Product Development Using TRIZ. Cambridge University Press, Cambridge (2005)
19. Blei, D.M.: Latent Dirichlet allocation. J. Mach. Learn. Res. 3(4–5), 993–1022 (2003)
20. Korobkin, D.M., Fomenkov, S.A., Kravets, A.G., Golovanchikov, A.B.: Patent data analysis system for information extraction tasks. In: 13th International Conference on Applied Computing (AC), pp. 215–219. IADIS (2016)
21. Toutanova, K., Manning, C.D.: Enriching the knowledge sources used in a maximum entropy part-of-speech tagger. In: EMNLP 2000, Hong Kong, pp. 63–70 (2000)
22. Hall, J.: MaltParser – An Architecture for Inductive Labeled Dependency Parsing. University of Colorado (2006)
23. Mel'čuk, I.A.: Dependency Syntax: Theory and Practice. SUNY Publication, New York (1988)
24. Stanford typed dependencies manual. https://nlp.stanford.edu/software/dependencies_manual.pdf

25. Korobkin, D.M., Fomenkov, S.A., Kolesnikov, S.G., Voronin, Y.F.: System of physical effects extraction from natural language text in the internet. J. World Appl. Sci. J. **24**, 55–61 (2013)
26. Dvoryankin, A.M., Polovinkin, A.I., Sobolev, A.N.: Automating the search for operation principles of technical systems on the basis of a bank of physical phenomena. J. Cybern. **14**, 79–86 (1978)
27. Arel, E.: Goldfire Innovator. Volume II: Patents and Innovation Trend Analysis User Guide. Invention Machine Corporation, Boston (2004)

Open Science Semantic Technologies

Using Weight Constraints and Masking to Improve Fuzzy Cognitive Map Models

Michal Gregor[1]([✉]), Peter P. Groumpos[2], and Milan Gregor[3]

[1] Department of Control and Information Systems,
Faculty of Electrical Engineering, University of Žilina, Žilina, Slovakia
michal.gregor@fel.uniza.sk
[2] Laboratory for Automation and Robotics,
Department of Electrical and Computer Engineering,
University of Patras, Patras, Greece
groumpos@ece.upatras.gr
[3] Department of Industrial Engineering, Faculty of Mechanical Engineering,
University of Žilina, Žilina, Slovakia
milan.gregor@fstroj.uniza.sk

Abstract. The paper presents a novel supervised learning method for fuzzy cognitive maps adapted from the theory of artificial neural networks. The main objective in designing the method was to pay closer attention to the distinctions that exist between fuzzy cognitive maps, and the original model for which the method was intended – whether it was a feedforward neural network, a recurrent network, or an energy-based model. The augmented version strives to properly build upon the various strengths of fuzzy cognitive maps – particularly on their interpretability, which arises from the close coupling that exists between their nodes and particular concepts. It is shown that the augmented method is able to outperform existing approaches. Notably, the ability of the learned model to generalize correctly, and to faithfully reconstruct the original system is studied.

Keywords: Fuzzy cognitive maps · Learning · Backpropagation · Supervised learning · Hebbian learning

1 Introduction

The complexity of tasks faced by modern industrial, medical, transport and other systems has been growing rapidly in the recent past. As a result of this growth, increasingly strong demands are being made on the performance and properties of machine learning methods designed to handle them. Typical real-world tasks that we face in practice are many-faceted, and involve various kinds of imprecision and uncertainty.

A number of approaches have been proposed in order to meet these demands and requirements. Among these are fuzzy cognitive maps, which have proved

© Springer International Publishing AG 2017
A. Kravets et al. (Eds.): CIT&DS 2017, CCIS 754, pp. 91–106, 2017.
DOI: 10.1007/978-3-319-65551-2_7

themselves very useful in modelling complex systems in the past. We may mention many challenging medical and technical applications – including applications such as advanced processing of RFID (radiofrequency identification technology) data, aiming to extract cause-effect knowledge [1,2], or vehicle navigation in intelligent RFID and sonar-based spaces [3]. The present work intends to enhance the learning potential of fuzzy cognitive maps, thereby benefiting all such existing or future applications.

We note that the distinct advantage of fuzzy cognitive maps in comparison with many other approaches, is their innate ability to make use of existing knowledge, and particularly the explicit and easily interpretable way, in which they express it.

Initially, most FCMs presented in literature were constructed by experts – making use of the very natural ways of formalizing certain kinds of knowledge that the FCM framework provides. Soon, however, the first automatic and semiautomatic methods of constructing FCMs have started to emerge. These either provide for tuning of an initial weight matrix created by a group of experts, or else for learning a weight matrix from scratch. Furthermore, by augmenting any available data with prior expert knowledge in the form of a predefined weight matrix, FCMs can be applied even when there is very little data, although many other supervised methods would struggle with overfitting under such scenarios.

A sizeable portion of FCM learning approaches arose by adapting learning methods originally developed for artificial neural networks (ANNs). Such approaches utilize the close relationship that exists between FCMs and certain types of neural networks. Many of these methods have met with a considerable amount of success, bringing FCMs forward as a viable alternative to other supervised learning methods, while keeping the advantage of their excellent interpretability.

However, a non-negligible portion of these approaches, rather than build upon the strengths of FCMs, have suffered from the fact that they were originally designed with a different kind model in mind (usually some kind of a recurrent neural network). The present paper intends to fill some of these gaps by proposing a novel learning method, adapted from the theory of artificial neural networks in such way as not to disregard the distinctions between the FCMs and the original ANN model.

Our approach is based upon backpropagation and backpropagation through time. We have already shown in previous papers that variants of the approach can be used to successfully encode attractors into the FCM and to train the FCM as a regression model for a given dataset. In such applications, the method is able to easily outperform methods such as nonlinear Hebbian learning in terms of mean square error.

The present paper is to: (a) Set forth the FCM-specific aspects of the approach. (b) To study how well the method generalizes and how closely the learned model reconstructs the original in terms of weight matrix similarity. (c) To propose augmentations, which would utilize the very distinctions between the FCM and the ANN in such way as to improve both: the learning rate, and generalization.

The paper is organised as follows. Section 2 presents a brief overview of the fundamentals concerning fuzzy cognitive maps. Section 3 presents an overview of several existing approaches to FCM learning, focusing especially on those based on Hebbian learning. Section 4 presents the baseline method used in the paper and Sects. 5 and 6 deal with the proposed augmentations. Finally, Sects. 7 and 8 presents empirical results, which verify the approach and Sect. 9 suggests lines of future inquiry.

2 Fuzzy Cognitive Maps

Fuzzy cognitive maps (FCMs) are a symbolic representation intended for the description and causal modelling of complex systems [4]. They can be expressed and visualized using a weighted directed graph such as that shown in Fig. 1.

Nodes of the graph represent concepts associated with the modelled system. The number of concepts that form any particular FCM is typically determined by experts from the corresponding field of knowledge [4]. Every concept C_i is associated with its activation value A_i. The activation values are most often from interval $[0, 1]$, or $[-1, 1]$ (this depends on the particular squashing function used – see Eq. (1) for the context).

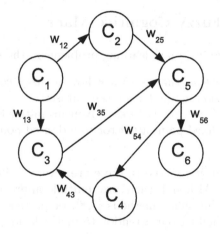

Fig. 1. Fuzzy cognitive map – an example.

Edges in the graph are directed and weighted. They express causal relationships between the concepts. An edge directed from concept C_i to concept C_j represents knowledge that a causal link exists between C_i and C_j.

Weight of an edge going from C_i to C_j is denoted $w_{ij} \in [-1, 1]$, and it specifies the meaning and the strength of the causal link. If $w_{ij} > 0$, we can say that concept C_i causes C_j to some extent – it contributes positively to its activation value. If $w_{ij} < 0$, concept C_i has negative influence on the activation value of C_j. If $w_{ij} = 0$, there is no causal link at all (such edges are not drawn).

2.1   Running the FCM

When the FCM is run, concept activation values are synchronously updated at every time step. The update rule has several distinct forms. We will include its most general form, which is as follows [5]:

$$A_i^{(k+1)} = f\left(\sum_{j=1}^{N} A_j^{(k)} w_{ji}\right), \tag{1}$$

where N is the number of concepts, $A_i^{(k)}$ is the activation value of concept C_i at time step k. f is the squashing function, which squashes the dot product into some convenient interval: most often either the sigmoid function or the hyperbolic tangent are used.

2.2   The Weight Matrix

The weight matrix of the FCM is usually constructed by experts. There are several approaches which make the task easier and more reliable – for discussion of these, the reader may refer to [4,6].

3   Learning in Fuzzy Cognitive Maps

We note that there are two main learning problems in the theory of FCMs:

- *The regression problem*, that is to say how a fuzzy cognitive map can be trained as a regression model for a given dataset;
- *The attractor problem*, that is to say given an initial fuzzy cognitive map, how can we shift a fixed-point attractor to a desired point, to encode a given limit-cycle, etc.

Of the existing learning methods, there are several, which are of interest to the problem at hand. Although there are multiple approaches based on meta-heuristics such as evolutionary methods [7,8], or particle swarm optimization [9], at this point we shall fix our attention to methods adapted from the theory of ANNs.

The reasons for focusing on this particular class of methods are two-fold: *(a)* We want to provide the essential background for discussing the approach proposed in this paper. *(b)* The meta-heuristics tend to be much more computationally expensive (often due to the fact that they operate on a population of potential solutions) and their convergence properties are typically much weaker.

3.1   Hebbian Learning

A sizeable portion of the best-known FCM learning approaches is based on Hebbian learning. The approach comes in several flavours.

There is firstly the so-called *differential Hebbian learning* (DHL) of Dickerson and Kosko [5], with a follow-up by Huerga [10], which shows that the original rule has a considerable weakness in that it cannot encode some types of sequences. The problem is partially fixed by Huerga's *balanced DHL* [10].

Then there is the *active Hebbian learning* (AHL) of Papageorgiou et al., which introduces the idea of a sequence of activation [11]. It also suggests normalizing the weight matrix to size 1 after every learning step, so as to prevent weights from growing indefinitely.

Finally, a number of papers discuss *nonlinear Hebbian learning* (NHL) – we may mention [12] as an instance. NHL is based on the Oja rule. In [13] the rule is further extended with a weight decay parameter and an additional term, which is supposed to maintain the sign of the corresponding weight (thus keeping the physical meaning of the relationship between the concepts).

In NHL learning, an initial FCM is still constructed by the experts. This is afterwards run in the standard way. However, in addition to this at every time step, the NHL learning rule is applied to the FCM.

3.2 Data-Driven Nonlinear Hebbian Learning

The work of Stach et al. [12] extends nonlinear Hebbian learning to learning an FCM from data. In this case, NHL is used to make an FCM with randomly initialized weights learn the cause-effect relationships from historical data. The authors use another randomly generated FCM to produce the historical data sequence, but the data could, naturally, come from any real system. The authors call this approach *data-driven nonlinear Hebbian learning* (DD-NHL).

4   The Baseline Method Used in the Paper

When we consider the fact that both of the learning problems outlined above (the regression problem and the attractor problem) are essentially supervised problems, it is surprising that FCM learning has so far focused almost exclusively on unsupervised approaches such as various Hebbian learning rules.

Our approach goes in a different direction altogether – the baseline is to train the FCM using backpropagation through time (BPTT) instead, which is arguably the best-known and most frequently used supervised learning method for recurrent neural networks. Since the FCM can be considered as a specific kind of a single-layer recurrent network, BPTT with gradient descent applies very well as we have already shown in [14] (concerning the attractor problem) and in [15] (concerning the regression problem). We have also shown that the approach can outperform approaches such as DD-NHL by several orders of magnitude.

We will use the approach from [14, 15] as a baseline in the present paper. For the details we refer the reader to any of those two papers.

5   The Proposed Approach

As we have already mentioned, our baseline is to use BPTT to train the FCM. This baseline is able to outperform approaches such as DD-NHL by several orders

of magnitude. However, like DD-NHL, it still does not in any way take account
of the FMC-specific aspects of the problem. This and the other objectives stated
in the introduction should be achieved in the present paper.

To meet this purpose, the current work will focus on a single variant of
the baseline approach proposed in [14,15] (the so-called One-step Delta Rule
approach). It is our belief though that the augmentations will apply equally well
to other variants, and quite possibly to other learning approaches in which the
concept of learning rate makes sense. However, this certainly remains open for
further investigation.

5.1   The Model Identification Problem

Perhaps the most important property specific to FCMs (as opposed to ANNs)
is the immediate link between a concept and a unit in the FCM. In ANNs a
single concept is usually modelled by several weights and neurons – its representation is distributed. FCMs, on the other hand, work with centralized concept
representations.

One of the consequences of this representation is that unlike ANNs, FCMs
lend themselves to be easily interpreted. We can thus see not only whether the
FCM gives correct outputs, but also whether it gives these for the right reasons.
Thus enters the *model identification problem*.

When we set-up an FCM and learn its weight matrix from data, what it
in fact does is construct a hypothesis concerning the inner workings of the real
system. The model identification problem then deals with the question whether
the hypothesis is the correct one or not (regardless of whether the FCM seems
to give the right answers).

We can also say that the question is whether the FCM *generalizes* correctly.
A further question, of course, is how to measure this (how to verify model identification). The standard approach in ANNs is to test the network on samples that
were not part of the training dataset, thus measuring the so-called *out-sample
error* (as opposed to in-sample error, which is the error on the training dataset).

However, the out-sample error too only pertains to the output of the model
and not to its internal structure. The FCM, being more interpretable, allows
us to go one step further – in addition to computing the out-sample error, we
can actually inspect the weight matrix to see whether it conforms to the way in
which the real system works.

Even for an FCM it is, in general, not easy to acquire any *quantitative* measure of how well the weight matrix matches the correct weight matrix (in terms
of mean square error or some such criterion), since in order to evaluate this, we
must already be in possession of that correct matrix. Fortunately, several of the
benchmark tasks commonly used to verify FCM learning approaches are already
laid out in such way that the correct matrix is available (the details are given in
Sect. 7).

That being said, we will also still report the out-sample error, which can be
measured regardless of whether we know what the correct weight matrix should
be beforehand, or not.

5.2   The Augmentations

Having a way to verify model identification, we may now present the augmentations to the aforementioned baseline approach. These are basically three-fold:

- The constraints augmentation;
- The presetting augmentation;
- The weight masking augmentation.

The following subsections will treat of each of these types in turn. There are, however, several common points to be laid out first.

FCMs, as we have mentioned before, are often constructed by hand – using expert knowledge. While experts may not be able to specify the precise value of every weight in the matrix, they will generally have at least some fuzzy notion of it. They are typically at least able to state whether there should be a connection between any two concepts or not. They are also usually able to tell how the connection should be oriented, and whether it should be positive or negative.

Naturally, the experts may not be equally certain of every connection. Several approaches to handling such uncertainties have in fact been proposed in the past. These include uses of fuzzy logic, or averaging knowledge gathered from multiple experts. In some of these schemes, experts themselves are awarded scores for agreeing/disagreeing with other experts, and the final weight matrix is computed as an average weighted by those scores [4]. A similar method exists for assigning a degree of confidence to every individual connection in the FCM. For more information concerning such methods, one may consult [4,6].

The purpose of our augmentations is to make the baseline learning method aware of this kind of information and to build upon it when learning the weight matrix. We also want to emphasize that this kind of information is already being collected when any of the aforementioned expert-based methods is applied – thus the information-related demands made by our approach are fairly standard for the FCM domain.

The Constraints Augmentation. Perhaps the simplest augmentation we can make is to use expert knowledge to determine polarity of each weight, and then use this information to set up constraints for the weight matrix. To this end, we may form two matrices $W^{\min}$, and $W^{\max}$, in addition to the weight matrix W, such that for every $w_{ij} \in W$, $w_{ij}^{\min} \in W^{\min}$, and $w_{ij}^{\max} \in W^{\max}$, the following constraint is to hold:

$$w_{ij}^{\min} \leq w_{ij} \leq w_{ij}^{\max} \quad \forall\, i,j. \tag{2}$$

In order to enforce the constraint, in every step, after the learning method updates the weight matrix W, the following transformation is applied:

$$W \leftarrow \max\left(\min\left(W, W^{\max}\right), W^{\min}\right). \tag{3}$$

In this work we experiment with two variants of the augmentation. In both of these the weight is constrained to $[0,1]$ if its value in the original matrix is positive, and to $[-1,0]$ if its value in the original matrix is negative.

The difference between the two variants regards the treatment of zero weights. In the first variant – *the fixed-zero variant* – zero weights remain fixed at zero. In the second variant – *the any-sign variant* – zero weights are constrained to $[-1, 1]$.

The Presetting Augmentation. The second proposal concerns the fact that the values of some weights may be known beforehand. In such case we can use the values to set up the initial weight matrix. Values of unknown weights can still be generated randomly. Learning itself may also proceed as usual.

The Weight Masking Augmentation. Finally, as stated hereinbefore, some of the existing methods for constructing weight matrices using expert knowledge are able to provide us not only with weight values, but also with their corresponding degrees of certainty. In such cases, we propose to introduce weight-specific learning rates, and set these up in such manner that the greater the degree of certainty, the lower the learning rate. Thus, weights of which we are uncertain will change their values more readily than those which are presumed to already be more or less correct.

In order to implement such behaviour, we propose multiplying the weight update matrix ΔW as computed by the learning method in every step of learning by masking matrix M, so that:

$$\Delta W \leftarrow \Delta W \circ M, \tag{4}$$

where $\Delta W \circ M$ is an element-wise product of matrices ΔW and M.

M is a matrix with elements $m_{ij} \in [0, 1]$, where 0 means that the weight is entirely fixed (all updates to the weight get multiplied by 0), and 1 means that just the original learning rate applies (updates to the weight remain unmodified by masking).

5.3   The Use of Gradient Descent

It may be noted that in the present paper we are using gradient descent to effect learning. This may seem a non-obvious choice, because there is a lot of more advanced methods with stronger performance. However, stochastic gradient descent – usually in its mini-batch form and with a rather small learning rate – is still commonly used in transfer learning, where we do not want to make very large steps in order not to disrupt the weight matrix pre-trained on the original task. Since some of the augmentations (especially presetting, of course) bring us to a very similar position, we have opted for gradient descent as well.

It may be that some of the augmentations (possibly even presetting) would work well with other, faster learning methods. In the present paper, however, we will leave this question open for future investigation.

6   Justifying the Augmentations

As far as the constraints augmentation is concerned, there should be little need for justification, since this is a fairly standard approach in other areas such as regression analysis. In such models parameters are often constrained to reasonable values. Even in the context of FCM learning, certain forms of constraining have been applied in the past, such as normalizing the size of the weight matrix. There is also the augmented version of the NHL rule, which is supposed to be able to maintain the sign of the weight [13].

It seems clear therefore that to constrain some of the parameters where possible is – in general – a reasonable idea. The utility of the particular form of constraining proposed in this paper is verified experimentally. It is true that we do take away some degrees of freedom from the learning method. It seems that this may go either way – it may result in finding a better or a worse local minimum since it does change the way in which the weight matrix slides along the error surface. Clearly, however, the effect on the model identification problem should be a positive one.

While adding constraints is clearly a sensible thing to do, adding per-weight learning rates may be seen as more controversial at first – especially with respect to its effects on convergence properties of the baseline method. It should, however, be noted that in the theory of ANNs several methods based on backpropagation and gradient descent already make use of (adaptive) per-weight learning rates. The Rprop method and its variants [16,17], which all use such per-weight learning rates, have met with excellent results and show properties that are much more robust than those of vanilla gradient descent.

Naturally, such methods are substantially different from what we propose, in that, being designed for ANNs, the learning rates arise from various heuristics – they are not (and cannot be) provided by experts as a way of incorporating prior knowledge. Their success does, however, nevertheless furnish some grounds for expecting per-weight learning rates not to have a negative impact on convergence properties – an expectation which is in fact corroborated by empirical evidence presented in the following section.

It should also be noted that the kind of information the augmentations rely upon is in most cases already available and being used in the context of manually constructed FCMs (we have already mentioned [4,6]). It is thus, in our opinion, high time to come up with methods that can effectively make use of it in the learning context.

7   Simulation Experiments

We have conducted simulation experiments to verify the proposed approach. These will be described in their turn once we have discussed the features common to all of them.

In every case, we have repeated the experiment 50 times. The results were averaged across all these runs. There is a separate section, which evaluates statistical significance of the findings in terms of p-values.

The data used for the experiment arises from the methodology of Stach et al. as given in [12]. We start with a randomly-generated weight matrix. An FCM with the matrix is then run for the period of 20 steps so as to provide historical data. The data is used to generate *(input, desired output)* pairs for learning. Finally, another randomly-initialized FCM is created, which learns its weight matrix from the data. Learning went on for the maximum of 100 epochs, and would also stop if the error went below 1.10^{-15}. The learning rate was fixed at $\gamma = 0.2$.

The training dataset consists of 10 other runs obtained from the original FCM, each time starting from a different initial state.

Verification was first done on the training dataset – this yielded the *in-sample* results; and afterwards on the testing dataset – this yielded the *out-sample* results. In all cases we report the mean square error (MSE) calculated using the following definition:

$$\frac{1}{2P} \sum_{p=1}^{P} \sum_{j} (D_j^p - O_j^p)^2, \tag{5}$$

where D_j^p and O_j^p are the j-the component of the desired and the real output vector respectively, for item p from the dataset. P is the total number of items in the dataset.

Where possible, in addition to the MSE we also verify model identification by comparing the weight matrix of the original FCM with its reconstruction as produced by the learning method. This is again given in terms of MSE – the measure is denoted as W_{MSE} in the following text.

7.1   Form of the Results

The above-mentioned indicators were computed for a number of distinct configurations of FCM size and connection density. The results will be presented in several charts. The comparison is among the following:

1. DD-NHL.
2. The baseline learning method (Baseline).
3. The baseline with anysign constraints (Constraints Anysign).
4. The baseline with fixed-zero constraints (Constraints Fixed).
5. The baseline with fixed-zero constraints and presetting (Constraints Presetting). We are presetting $1/3$ of non-zero weights – we are also adding $\mathcal{U}(-0.08, 0.08)$ noise to every preset weight.
6. The baseline with fixed-zero constraints, presetting and masking (Masking). We are lowering the learning rate for preset weights to 0.1 of its original value.

Configurations are denoted as $N; C\%$, where N is the number of concepts (size of the FCM) and C is the connection rate given as a percentage.

Note also that in the charts the in-sample and out-sample MSEs are scaled – divided by the number of concepts N – so that we have an unbiased comparison for FCMs of different sizes. The W_{MSE} is also scaled – divided by the number of non-zero weights ($N^2 C$).

7.2   In-Sample MSE

For in-sample MSE we only show the baseline, the constraints presetting and the masking variant in the chart (see Fig. 2). This is because they are all largely the same and the chart becomes rather unreadable when they are all presented.

The results are rather mixed – there is a slight improvement for smaller FMCs and a slight deterioration of performance for larger ones. In any case, the results are such that they do not bar us from applying the method, which is all that we intended to establish as far as in-sample MSE is concerned. The results concerning out-sample MSE and especially W_{MSE} will be more informative.

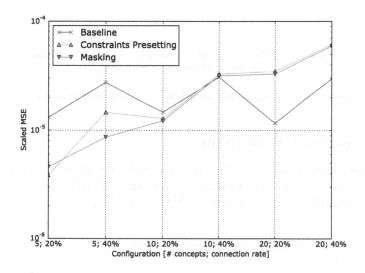

Fig. 2. In-sample MSE scaled by the number concepts.

7.3   Out-Sample MSE

As we can see in Fig. 3, there is a marked improvement in terms of out-sample MSE. This is true of all variants of our approach except the any-sign version of constraints, which is very similar to the baseline.

As we can see by comparing the any-sign version to the fixed-zero version, a very large portion of the performance gain can be ascribed to the fact that we have fixed mutual weights of non-interacting concepts to zeros.

As far as out-sample MSE is concerned, presetting should probably ideally only be used in conjunction with masking – otherwise the performance gain may not be worth the effort – there seems to be very little difference between fixed-zero constraints and presetting. When presetting is used with masking, though, the out-sample MSE is reduced notably.

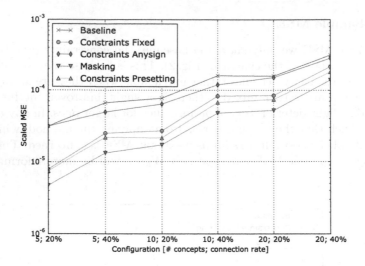

Fig. 3. Out-sample MSE scaled by the number of concepts.

7.4   Comparison with DD-NHL

Now for comparison with the DD-NHL approach. We include separate charts comparing the baseline, the masking version and DD-NHL in terms of both in-sample MSE (Fig. 4) and out-sample MSE (Fig. 5).

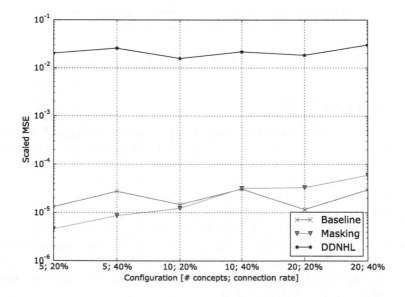

Fig. 4. In-sample MSE scaled by the number concepts; comparison with DD-NHL.

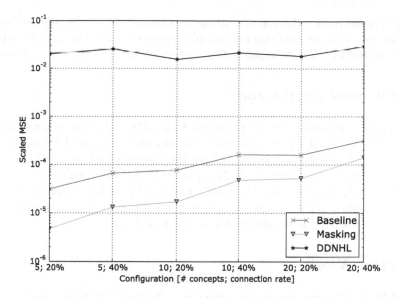

Fig. 5. Out-sample MSE scaled by the number of concepts; comparison with DD-NHL.

As we can see, there is a very significant difference – our approach outperforms DD-NHL by several orders of magnitude in both measures.

7.5   Model Identification and the W_{MSE}

Finally and most importantly there is the W_{MSE} indicator and the model identification problem. Here the results (shown in Fig. 6) are very similar to those of out-sample MSE except that they are a little more pronounced.

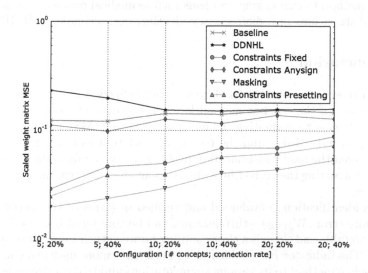

Fig. 6. Weight matrix MSE scaled by the number of connections.

This is good news – the augmentations are not only able to help generalization in the weaker sense by lowering out-sample errors; they are also able to actually improve model identification properties – generalization in the strong sense.

8   Statistical Significance

Due to space constraints, we will not present all of the data concerning statistical significance. Suffice it to say that while the any-sign version of constraints, for example, is not significantly different from the baseline for the $5; 20\%$ configuration, the difference increases for $5; 40\%$ and $10; 20\%$ and becomes very clear for the other configurations. The other approaches all perform significantly better than the baseline and the situation is very similar for other combinations of methods – with p-value ranging as far as 1e-50 or 1e-70.

9   Future Work

Several lines of future investigation are open. It should be noted that our approach could in principle be applied even in scenarios, where activation values of some of the concepts are unknown. In such cases, the backpropagation principle could be used to infer the errors. What remains unclear is to what extent this would influence generalization – this calls for further investigation.

Furthermore, it is our belief that some of the augmentations presented in this paper, may apply well to other existing FCM learning approaches – this should be verified. It also seems probable that methods now routinely used for unsupervised pre-training in ANNs would further improve model identification properties of the FCM. This approach should therefore not remain untried.

Among the lines of our possible future research is also the application of the proposed method to challenging problems such as medical problems, or advanced processing algorithms in radiofrequency identification technology (RFID).

10   Conclusion

The paper presents a novel approach to learning in fuzzy cognitive maps. Several augmentations of the baseline method have been proposed, described and evaluated. In addition to evaluating the mean square error (MSE) over the training dataset (in-sample MSE), and the testing dataset (out-sample MSE), we have also considered the model identification problem and generalization in the strong sense of constructing the correct hypothesis about the inner workings of the modelled system.

Model identification is evaluated and verified in terms of the weight matrix mean square error (W_{MSE}) – this indicator can be computed because FCMs are well interpretable and there is a close coupling between their nodes and particular concepts. The indicator has enabled us to perform a more in-depth comparison of the baseline method to its various augmentations and to data-driven nonlinear Hebbian learning (DD-NHL).

We have shown that the proposed augmentations are able to significantly improve generalization – both in the weaker (out-sample MSE) and in the stronger (W_{MSE}) sense. We have also shown that as far as in-sample and out-sample MSE is concerned there is a vast improvement in comparison to DD-NHL. The W_{MSE} is also improved. In addition, several promising lines of future research have been suggested.

Acknowledgements. This work has been supported by the Cultural and Educational Grant Agency of the Slovak Republic (KEGA) No. 038ŽU-4/2017: "Laboratory education methods of automatic identification and localization using radiofrequency identification technology".

References

1. Kim, M.C., Kim, C.O., Hong, S.R., Kwon, I.H.: Forward-backward analysis of RFID-enabled supply chain using fuzzy cognitive map and genetic algorithm. Expert Syst. Appl. **35**(3), 1166–1176 (2008)
2. Trappey, A.J., Trappey, C.V., Wu, C.R.: Genetic algorithm dynamic performance evaluation for RFID reverse logistic management. Expert Syst. Appl. **37**(11), 7329–7335 (2010)
3. Vaščák, J., Hvizdoš, J.: Vehicle navigation by fuzzy cognitive maps using sonar and RFID technologies. In: 2016 IEEE 14th International Symposium on Applied Machine Intelligence and Informatics (SAMI), pp. 75–80. IEEE (2016)
4. Groumpos, P.P.: Fuzzy cognitive maps: basic theories and their application to complex systems. In: Glykas, M. (ed.) Fuzzy Cognitive Maps, pp. 1–22. Springer, Berlin (2010)
5. Dickerson, J.A., Kosko, B.: Virtual worlds as fuzzy cognitive maps. In: Virtual Reality Annual International Symposium, pp. 471–477. IEEE (1993)
6. Stach, W., Kurgan, L., Pedrycz, W.: A survey of fuzzy cognitive map learning methods. Issues Soft Comput. Theory Appl. 71–84 (2005)
7. Stach, W., Kurgan, L., Pedrycz, W., Reformat, M.: Genetic learning of fuzzy cognitive maps. Fuzzy Sets Syst. **153**(3), 371–401 (2005)
8. Mls, K., Cimler, R., Vaščák, J., Puheim, M.: Interactive evolutionary optimization of fuzzy cognitive maps. Neurocomputing **232**, 58–68 (2017)
9. Papageorgiou, E.I., Parsopoulos, K.E., Stylios, C.S., Groumpos, P.P., Vrahatis, M.N.: Fuzzy cognitive maps learning using particle swarm optimization. J. Intell. Inf. Syst. **25**(1), 95–121 (2005)
10. Huerga, A.V.: A balanced differential learning algorithm in fuzzy cognitive maps. In: Proceedings of the 16th International Workshop on Qualitative Reasoning, vol. 2002 (2002)
11. Papageorgiou, E., Stylios, C.D., Groumpos, P.P.: Active hebbian learning algorithm to train fuzzy cognitive maps. Int. J. Approximate Reasoning **37**(3), 219–249 (2004)
12. Stach, W., Kurgan, L., Pedrycz, W.: Data-driven nonlinear hebbian learning method for fuzzy cognitive maps. In: IEEE International Conference on Fuzzy Systems. FUZZ-IEEE 2008 (IEEE World Congress on Computational Intelligence), pp. 1975–1981. IEEE (2008)
13. Papageorgiou, E.I., Groumpos, P.P.: A weight adaptation method for fuzzy cognitive map learning. Soft. Comput. **9**(11), 846–857 (2005)

14. Gregor, M., Groumpos, P.P.: Tuning the position of a fuzzy cognitive map attractor using backpropagation through time. In: Proceedings of The 7th International Conference on Integrated Modeling and Analysis in Applied Control and Automation (IMAACA 2013), Athens (2013)
15. Gregor, M., Groumpos, P.P.: Training fuzzy cognitive maps using gradient-based supervised learning. In: Papadopoulos, H., Andreou, A.S., Iliadis, L., Maglogiannis, I. (eds.) AIAI 2013. IAICT, vol. 412, pp. 547–556. Springer, Heidelberg (2013). doi:10.1007/978-3-642-41142-7_55
16. Riedmiller, M., Braun, H.: A direct adaptive method for faster backpropagation learning: The rprop algorithm. In: 1993 IEEE International Conference on Neural Networks, IEEE. pp. 586–591 (1993)
17. Igel, C., Hüsken, M.: Improving the RPROP learning algorithm. In: Proceedings of the Second International ICSC Symposium on Neural Computation (NC 2000), Citeseer pp. 115–121 (2000)

Intelligent Technologies for Large-Scale Social System Sustainable Development

Vladimir V. Tsyganov[(✉)]

V.A. Trapeznikov Institute of Control Sciences of Russian Academy Sciences,
65, Profsoyuznaya Street, Moscow 117997, Russia
vl88958@akado.ru

Abstract. Intelligent technologies based on concepts of self-organization, adaptation, and learning are proposed for control and sustainable development of the social system. Model of self-organizing evolve social system consists of several groups located in different regions is derived. Sufficient conditions about the definite direction of human capital migration between these social groups are obtained. That provides the possibility of formal definitions of concepts of human capital regional attractor and migration attractiveness, sectoral and general migration climate. A vector indicator of the attractiveness of a social group for human capital, as well as a matrix characterizing the migration climate for the entire community, is obtained. Also, adaptive technologies for straight control of the social system sustainable development are described. To avoid undesirable distortion of information it is proposed to use progressive adaptive mechanisms. Learning, self-organizing and expert control mechanisms for the sustainable development of the social system are characterized.

Keywords: Intelligent · Technology · Social · Engineering · Organization · Control · Regulation · Adaptation

1 Introduction

Problems and options for supporting social stability in large-scale systems in the context of the global crisis were examined by Kile and Dimirovsky [1]. The corresponding problems of management in social systems security were analyzed by Freeman and Stapleton [2]. To develop the ways for improving such stability, they proposed to use the methods of system engineering in the social sphere including cultural meanings and empirical data on conflicts of values (i.e. social engineering). Important for social engineering are also knowledge, communication, and creativity. In [3] considered the influence of these factors (especially creativity) on the social stability of large-scale systems in the conditions of limits of global growth, and stagnation.

Creativity is closely related to technology development. Crises and new technologies change the condition of the social groups functioning. They produce both positive and negative effects for the social system. Adaptive mechanisms for social engineering at the technology development were considered by Bagamaev with co-authors [4]. They show as a result of technology development potential of high-tech may be accumulated in some leading ("rich") social groups. To provide new high-tech

A. Kravets et al. (Eds.): CIT&DS 2017, CCIS 754, pp. 107–118, 2017.
DOI: 10.1007/978-3-319-65551-2_8

it is necessary to realize R&D, know-how etc. That needs appropriate human resources. But they drain from outsiders ("poor" social groups) to leading groups of evolving social system. The result of this is the lack of human resources in «poor» social groups. It becomes more and more difficult to adapt to changes. Therefore economical rupture between leading and lagging behind social groups is arising. That provides the likelihood of crisis of the social system, and as a consequence tensions between different social groups, human capital drain, large-scale migration etc. It gives obstacles to the realization of a more stable set of the human relations in the social system.

So crises and technological changes produce a gap between the most effective ("rich") and other ("poor") social groups of evolving social system. Some of the "poor" social groups have no possibility for adaptation to these changes and need the support. One of the important ways to diminish of the above gap is a special organizing principle for meeting human development goals is known as "sustainable development" [5]. Welfonder and Frederking consider the community of control engineers responsible for the sustainable development of a society [6]. Theoretical problems of constructing mechanisms for the sustainable development of large-scale organizations with the help of system engineering were considered by Borodin and co-authors [7].

Below we shall consider the problem of sustainable development of social system consists of social groups. For example, society is consisting of several social strata. Its sustainable development will be realized on the background of the concept of regulation and control mechanisms. Such mechanisms used intelligent technologies based on procedures of self-organization, adaptation, and learning.

In principal, the control centre of a social system can use two type intelligent technologies of sustainable development to diminish the gap between «rich» and «poor» groups. One type of them is based on regulation of self-organization of community includes social groups. Such technologies regulate the parameters of the environment to sustain the development of social groups, by managing human capital flows between «rich» and «poor» groups, large-scale migration etc.

The other type of intelligent technologies of sustainable development is based on straight control systems. To reduce their risks and likelihood of social systems instability it is possible to apply adaptive and intelligent control principles. Adequate adaptive and intelligent procedures provide identification of parameters of social groups and their environment. Finally, the centre of the social system generates the controlling actions making use of current information, obtained from the social groups, in order to achieve the optimal state of the social system as a whole. In this way, «poor» social groups obtain support corresponding to the level of the above gap in a way used in adaptive and intelligent control systems [8–10].

2 Regulation of Social Self-Organization and Migration

In this chapter, we consider technologies for social system sustainable development on the example of regulation of human capital migration. Suppose that a social group has a value system associated with an increase in its own size ("human capital"). So this social group may be considered as a self-organizing element [9]. In other words, social group is far-sighted and is capable of self-organization, by directing human resources (human investments) for development. In this model, human capital is characterized by the number of social group members. Consider the dynamic model of the social group:

$$q_{t+1} = Cq_t + Bu_t, \ q_0 = q^0, \ z_t = Aq_t, \ t = 0, 1, \ldots, \ A \geq 0, \ B \geq 0, \ C \geq 0, \ q^0 \geq 0, \tag{1}$$

where q_t is the number of members of the social group, u_t is the input human resource, z_t is the output of the social group, t is the period number. For example, z_t can be the number of new potential members of the social group (children born by social group members, members of other communities who marry members of the social group, etc.). The coefficient A associates z_t with the current number of members of the social group q_t. The term Bu_t is the actual increase in the number of the given social group, for example, at the account of the children remaining in the social group, and legal immigrants. C is the coefficient of natural loss of social group size, for example, due to mortality. B is the correction coefficient, for example, an increase in the number of legal immigrants due to family members of legal emigrants, as well as illegal immigrants.

Suppose that the social group control centre (elite) is responsible for its development. Then it is possible to consider the problem of increasing the size (human capital) of the social group. Further, it is possible to set the task of regulating of the human capital of the social group, in which elite maximizes a criterion of social group development. Based on the dynamic model of the social group (1), it is possible to consider the technology of regulation of human capital migration.

Let us believe that a community (evolve social system) consists of N social groups of the type (1) that are located in different regions. This community is headed by an elite which is capable for self-organization, by directing human resources (human investments) for the development of social groups in some regions. In this model, human capital is characterized by the number of social group members who can migrate in other regions.

Formally we shall give the notation in (1) for the evolving social group from the i-th region by the index í, $í = \overline{1, N}$. So under consideration is community includes N social groups which are increased by new neophyte members (for example, individuals who have reached a certain age). Potential (the number of members) of each group changes in accordance with the equation:

$$q_{it+1} = C_i q_{it} + B_i u_{it}, q_{i0} = q_i^0, B_i \geq 0, C_i \geq 0, q_i^0 \geq 0, í = \overline{1, N}, \ t = 0, 1, \ldots, \tag{2}$$

where q_{it} is the number of members of i-th social group, u_{it} – number of new members (neophytes) in i-th group in period t. Output (number of new potential members) of the i-th social group in period t:

$$z_{it} = A_i q_{it}, A_i \geq 0, í = \overline{1, N}, t = 0, 1, \ldots \tag{3}$$

The total increase in the number of the social group (the number of neophytes) is equal to the sum of the number of social group neophytes in both regions:

$$Z_t = \sum_{i=1}^{N} z_{it} = \sum_{i=1}^{N} A_i q_{it}, t = 0, 1, \ldots \tag{4}$$

The development of a community through self-organization suggests that elite choose regulation $u_t = (u_{1t}, \ldots u_{Nt})$ to distribute all neophytes in the period t for N social groups:

$$z_t = \sum_{i=1}^{N} u_{it}, t = 0, 1, \ldots \tag{5}$$

where u_{it} is the number of neophytes directed by the elite to i-th social group ("regional investment of human capital"). The purpose of allocation of human resources determined by (4) is to maximize goal function of the farseeing elite. So the regulation $u_t = (u_{1t}, \ldots u_{Nt})$ is aimed at maximizing the discounted current and future amount of neophytes:

$$V = \sum_{i=1}^{N} \sum_{t=0}^{T-1} \rho^t z_{it} \xrightarrow[u_{it}, i=\overline{1,N}, t=\overline{0,T-1}]{} \max, \tag{6}$$

where ρ is a discount rate, $\rho \leq 1$, T- the horizon for the elite planning (farseeing).

Let us denote optimal solution of task (2)–(6) as $u_t^* = \left(u_{1t}^*, \ldots u_{Nt}^*\right), t = \overline{0, T-1}$. We will say that social group placed in region 1 is most attractive in the community, if there are no neophytes ("investments of human capital") in other social groups:

$$u_{jt}^* = 0, j = \overline{2, N}, t = \overline{0, T-1}. \tag{7}$$

Theorem. Social group placed in region 1 is most attractive in community if

$$M_{1t} > M_{jt}, M_{it} = A_i B_i \left[1 - (\rho C_i)^t\right] / (1 - \rho C_i), i = \overline{1, N}, j = \overline{2, N}, t = \overline{0, T-1}. \tag{8}$$

Proof. Substituting (2) into (3) t + 1 times, after formal transformations we obtain:

$$z_{it+1} = A_i^t C_i [q_i^0 + B_i \sum_{k=0}^{t} A_i^{-k} u_{ik}], i = \overline{1, N}, t = \overline{0, T-1}. \tag{9}$$

Further, substituting (9) in (6), after some transformations we have that:

$$V = \sum_{i=1}^{N} C_i \left\{ \sum_{t=0}^{T-1} \left[(\rho A_i)^t q_i^0 + B_i \rho^{t+1} u_{it} (1 - (\rho A_i)^{T-t}) / (1 - \rho A_i) + (\rho A_i)^t q_i^0 \right] \right\}. \tag{10}$$

Using (8) and (10), we obtain, up to terms not contains u_{iT-1}, that
$V = \rho^T \sum_{i=1}^{N} M_{i1} u_{iT-1}$. By the statement of the theorem (8), $M_{11} > M_{j1}$, $j = \overline{2,N}$, so that
$u_{jT-1}^* = 0$. Similarly from (10), up to terms not containing u_{iT-2},
$V = \rho^{T-1} \sum_{i=1}^{N} M_{i2} u_{iT-2}$. From (8) we have $M_{12} > M_{j2}$, so that $u_{jT-2}^* = 0$, $j = \overline{2,N}$.
Repeating similar reasoning (T−2) times, we obtain (7), which was to be proved.

Substantially theorem gives sufficient conditions about the definite direction of the human capital flow between N social groups placed in different regions. Also, theorem provides the possibility of formal definitions of concepts such as community human capital regional attractor, migration attractiveness and climate, and general, specific, sectoral migration climate etc.

Community Capital Regional Attractor. According to the theorem, a social group in region 1 may be considered as the human capital attractor because of all community resources are allocated in this group: $u_{jt}^* = 0$, $j = \overline{2,N}$, $t = \overline{0, T-1}$. Thus social group in region 1 is the human regional capital attractor if condition (8) takes place. So theorem provides the background of the sustainable development of this group.

Migration Attractiveness of Group of Community. With the aid of theorem measurement means and criteria for human capital, flow monitoring can be found. In this approach vector

$$M_i = (M_{i0}, M_{i1}, \ldots, M_{iT-1}), \tag{11}$$

is the indicator of the human capital attractiveness of group of community placed in i-th region, $i = \overline{1,N}$, in periods $t = \overline{0, T-1}$. If $M_1 > M_j$, $j = \overline{2,N}$, then it should be stable income of the human capital in the group in region 1 from the community in all periods: $t = \overline{0, T-1}$. Thus vector (11) will be called the vector of migration attractiveness of the i-th region for the community. So i-th component with the index t (M_{i1}) is the migration attractiveness of i-th region in period t. Generally, members of the community will move towards a region with greater migration appeal by the vector (11).

The purpose of constructing models of migration attractiveness of the region is to study and create conditions that stimulate the influx of people into regions, branches of the economy, and even countries. This goal is achieved by modeling a regional, sectoral and state mechanism for regulating migration in a community that is a set of self-organized, far-sighted social groups. For this, a model of a self-organizing social group and a theorem on the migration attractiveness of the region are used.

Mechanisms for regulating the development of human capital in the region ensure the migration attractiveness and development of the region. For the analysis and design of mechanisms to sustain the development of a particular social group, the vector of migration attractiveness of i-th region (11) is used as a criterion. The migration attractiveness determined in this way depends on the specifics and parameters of the given social group.

Migration Climate for the Community. Consider matrix M formed on the basis of the set of vectors of migration attractiveness (11) relating to all regions:

$$M^c = (M_1, M_2, \ldots, M_N)^*, \tag{12}$$

were symbol * means transposition. Then matrix M^C characterizes migration climate for the whole community in all regions, for example, in the whole country. Adjustment of components of matrix M^C - vectors M_i and their parameters A_i, B_i, C_i, $i = \overline{1, N}$, gives the possibility to change community human capital flow in this country, i.e. to regulate migration climate. So mechanism of regulation of community sustainable development in this country may be characterized by the set of these parameters A_i, B_i, C_i, $i = \overline{1, N}$.

General Migration Climate is a generalized characteristic of the potential of human capital migration for all communities living in all regions, for example, in the whole country. For example, general migration climate characterizes the migration attractiveness of the country for members of all communities. To obtain characteristics of general migration climate, it is possible to aggregate data on migration climate for all communities living there. Denote q the number of community, $q = \overline{1, Q}$, where Q is a quantity of communities living there in all regions (for example, in the whole country). Then the above aggregation may be done by appropriate averaging over all of the vectors (11) of migration attractiveness of i-th region for all Q communities. Let denote those components obtained after averaging vectors (11) as G_1, G_2, ..., G_N. In this approach vector G_i indicates attractiveness of all Q communities placed in i-th region. Therefore G_i will be called as a vector of the human capital attractiveness of i-th region. Then matrix

$$G = (G_1, G_2, \ldots, G_N)^* \tag{13}$$

can be called the matrix of general migration climate. For example, the matrix (13) comprehensively characterizes the migration climate in all regions of the country, regardless of the communities that inhabit this country. Such approach to defining the general migration climate in the country is useful, for example, if all its regions have specific features inherent in this country (for example, specific climatic or geographic characteristics). Let there are F countries, and general migration climate in country s is G_s, $s = \overline{1, F}$. Then if $G_1 < G_j$, $j = \overline{2, F}$, it is said that the migration climate in country 1 is unfavorable than in other countries.

Sectoral Migration Climate. If there are no general (climatic, geographic, or other) features of the living environment of the communities in all its regions, it is not easy to make the above aggregation. Then it is possible to form general characteristics of the migration attractiveness of the regions for certain type (sector) of communities whose activities have a priority for all regions. The aggregated characteristic of the migration attractiveness of the regions for such communities may be determined by appropriate averaging the components of the migration attractiveness vector (11) over the set of communities belongs to this sector.

Denote p the number of community, $p = \overline{1,P}$, where P is the quantity of communities belongs to this sector. Then the above aggregation may be done by appropriate averaging over all of the vectors (11) of migration attractiveness of i-th region for all P communities. Let denote those components obtained after averaging vectors (11) as $S_1, S_2, \ldots, S_N$. In this approach vector S_i indicates attractiveness of sector including P communities placed in i-th region. Therefore S_i may be called as a vector of the sectoral human capital attractiveness of i-th region. Respectively if $S_1 > S_j$, $j = \overline{2,P}$, then sectoral migration climate in region 1 for the corresponding type of communities is more favorable than in other regions. Then matrix

$$S = (S_1, S_2, \ldots S_N)^* \tag{14}$$

can be called the matrix of sectoral migration climate. For example, the matrix (14) comprehensively characterizes the migration climate in the country for certain type of communities whose economic activities in certain branches is crucially important for all regions.

The above definitions of general and sectoral migration climate create prerequisites for the sustainable development of communities and the adoption by the authorities of the regions of decisions to improve the migration climate.

Migration Climate and Progressive Restructuring of Society. The above model allows us to describe two-stage schemes for the restructuring of society, in the form of its disaggregation, division into separate communities etc. Each of newly created communities is considered as self-organizing and is described similarly to (2)–(6). To ensure its migration attractiveness, the authorities choose the parameters of the migration climate that ensure the expanded reproduction and development of this community. In this case, we can talk about the progressiveness of the restructuring mechanism. Otherwise, restructuring leads to the emergence of artificially supported non-viable communities. The absence of a progressive restructuring mechanism leads to the drain of human capital.

Thus, a hierarchy of problems of constructing migration mechanisms arises. This hierarchy is isomorphic to the structure of society. At the lower level, there are regional migration mechanisms that determine the migration climate for particular communities. At the average level, there are specific migration mechanisms that determine the general parameters of sustainable development mechanism of a particular type of community. Finally, at the state level, the progressiveness of the migration mechanism determines legislation, participation in international organizations, etc.

Society Development Through Communities. Society as a whole can be seen as an association of communities. Implementation of the theorem on migration attractiveness for a particular community is not sufficient for the development of society at the expense of this community. After all, it is necessary to have many more potential communities that would ensure not only survival (i.e., the reproduction of society at a minimum level) but also development. The consequence of combining this assertion with the theorem on migration attractiveness is that for the development of society, many communities are needed, as well as the implementation of the conditions of migration attractiveness.

Centre of Human Capital. Let's consider some possible interpretations of the parameters of the above model. For example, q_i is the number of the i-th social group. Then C_i is the coefficient of its natural decrease in i-th region, depending on the lifespan, as well as on natural loss, mortality. Parameter B_i characterizes the effectiveness of neophytes from the point of view of their influence on the number of i-th social group, and depends on the support of neophytes in i-th region by the local population, regional and state authorities, etc.

The parameter A_i characterizes the ratio of z_i (number of new potential members of i-th social group in period t) to q_{it} - the number of members of i-th social group in period t. The parameter A_i depends on social, economic, climatic, geographic, cultural, confessional and other factors. In particular, A_i grows with such micro parameters as the birth rate g_i, and decreases with the growth of the costs H_i of the formation of the neophyte in the i-th region.

The above theorem gives the possibility to make analysis and synthesis of the migration attractiveness and climate. Suppose for example that community is placed in two regions of a single social space, in which barriers to the free movement of migrants are eliminated. The specifics of the region depend on the birth rate g_i and the costs of the formation of the neophyte H_i, $i = \overline{1,2}$. Let investigate the influence of these parameters of the regions on migration attractiveness.

Consider the situation where the only difference between the regions is that the birth rate in the region 1 is smaller than in the region 2: $g_1 < g_2$. As indicated above the parameter A_i grows with the birth rate g_i, so $A_1 < A_2$. Then according to the definition of M_i, $i = \overline{1,2}$, given in (8), $M_1 < M_2$. Therefore, according to the statement of the theorem, the social group placed in region 2 is most attractive in the community. Then the Centre of human capital in a single social space will be a region with an increased birth rate.

Consider now the situation where the only difference between the regions is that the cost of forming a neophyte in one of the regions is higher than in the other. For example, this may be due to increased pay due to harsh conditions (in particular hard climate, increased transport costs due to large territory) or other factors that determine the extreme costs of neophyte formation.

Suppose that in region 2 costs for the formation of a neophyte are increased: $H_2 > H_1$. As indicated above, the parameter A_i decreases with the growth of H_i, so $A_1 > A_2$. Then according to the definition of M_i, $i = \overline{1,2}$, given in (8), $M_1 > M_2$. Therefore, according to the statement of the theorem, the social group placed in region 1 is most attractive in the community. Thus Centre of human capital in a single social space will be a region with reduced costs for the formation of a neophyte.

On practice, globalization involves the interdependence of countries, the creation of a single social space. The specific nature of the country is determined by the costs of the formation of a neophyte, the birth rate, and other parameters of the above model. In the conditions of global liberalization, a country with increased costs for the formation of a neophyte and a low birth rate is migratory unattractive.

Example: A Country with a Harsh Climate. As region 1, we will look at a small country with warm climates like Taiwan or Singapore. The region 2 is Russia – northern country with the giant territory. Due to the coldest climate in the world,

Russian children need to buy warm clothes and eat more densely. And naturally, in the wages of parents, it is necessary to take into account the level of consumption of children, clothing, etc. We come to the conclusion that Russian parents need to pay much more than parents in Taiwan or Singapore and so on. Therefore region 1 is a region with reduced costs for the formation of a neophyte: $H_1 < H_2$. Then according to the above $A_1 < A_2$, and $M_1 < M_2$. Thus in a situation where the only difference between these regions is the costs of forming a neophyte, a country with increased costs for the formation of a neophyte (Russia) is migratory unattractive.

To avoid this, in accordance with the theorem, it is necessary to correct coefficients of the above model A_2, B_2, C_2 in order to increase the migration attractiveness and climate of region 2 (i.e. Russia). For example, it is possible to increase the coefficient C_2, increasing active life and work time of people, and reducing natural losses of the population. It is possible to increase the parameters of A_2 and B_2 by increasing the support of births by local, regional and state authorities. It can also increase the parameter A_2, reducing the cost H_2 for the maintenance and education of children, as well as improving other micro parameters - social, economic, cultural. Therefore theoretically it is possible to create a Center of human capital of Russian community at home.

Summing up, we get that the derived model and the proved theorem make it possible to analyze and synthesize the migration attractiveness and climate to regulate the sustainable development of large-scale social systems.

3   Adaptive Mechanisms for Sustainable Social Development

Evolve social system regulation to provide desirable human capital drain discussed in the previous item may be considered as an indirect way of decentralization support of the «poor» social groups. The other way is straight support of such social group from the special control centre.

The concept for designing of the optimal adaptive control mechanisms for social stability at the technology development had been derived by Bagamaev with co-authors [4]. This approach is based on the model of the adaptive mechanism of active system functioning (AMF) of the two-level organization included the Centre on the upper level and the Agent as the farseeing social group on the lower level. The role of Centre is played by the centre of evolving social system, and the role of Agent is played by the social group. AMF Σ includes both adaptive forecasting procedure F, and procedures of decision-making: planning P, resource allocation R and stimulation S: $\Sigma = \{F, P, R, S\}$. This model was developed on designing of adaptive mechanisms for sustainable development by Borodin with co-authors [7].

In fact, investigation of the problems dealing with the design of the adaptive control of the social system should include as the main component analysis and the account of the human factor effect. It may be considered as an activity manifestation of individuals or collectives (elements of the social system) is caused by the availability of their own aims, not necessary coinciding with the goal of the social system. Such elements may utilize available information channels connected with the social system control centre in order to improve the current or future state. From the other side, "active" staff deals with the process of this support may predict the results of the adaptive control procedures and to use that knowledge to reach their own aims. In fact, in many cases support given from the control centre of evolving social system to «poor» social groups had no effect because of the failure of the mechanism used (corruption, distortion of information etc.). For example, one of the important features of such failure is the activity of social system bureaucracy used their possibilities to manipulate supporting resources.

Methodology for creating such technologies to avoid undesirable distortion of information consists of designing the so-called progressive AMF. In such AMF the present value of the Agent long-term goal function corresponding to the solution of the game with the Centre increase with the growth of the efficiency of the Agent functioning [8]. Progressive AMF for social system functioning regimes are intended for eliminating undesirable Agent activity. The designing of AMF caused the sustainable development of the approach based on the obtained problem solutions of progressive AMF synthesis. Detail consideration of two main types of AMF made in [8]. The first type of AMF is intended for maintaining the processes of the state forecasting, planning, and control of the Agent. Under consideration are the adaptive procedures of time series forecasting and designing of the regressive model. The second type i.e. rank AMF is designed to provide information for learning of decision making (classification and pattern recognition). They are used mainly for adaptive estimation of the parameters of the decision-making procedure, control, and stimulation of the Agent. In some cases, both expert adaptive mechanisms and intelligent functioning mechanisms can be used.

4 Intelligent Mechanisms for Sustainable Social Development

In previous items models of indirect and direct technologies for sustainable development and diminishing rupture between groups in evolve social system had been discussed. Real social system regimes are much more comprehensive and need intelligent control systems. Drawing on experience gained in implementing intelligent control to a varied range of systems, article [9] shows the need for a multilevel self-learning and self-organized social systems.

Particular attention is directed toward adaptations of the widely used self-learning algorithms in an attempt to increase the effective applicability, the range of self-organizing control with the aid of artificial intelligence methodology. On the other hand, the possibility to control evolve the social system in dynamics with no complete information is based on intelligent information systems [9]. They realize model, identification of control objects structure and outside parameters, predictions, and forms the background of control actions on the basis of current information, received from the elements, to attain the systems aim at the whole. To avoid information distortion, passed by the elements to the centre of the social system, it is necessary to consider the problem of information system designing in a total problem of synthesis procedures such as planning, control, and stimulation accepted in the control mechanism.

The other direction in the theory develops as well as the practice control for hierarchic organizations with a stochastic structure. It has been connected with the designing of the so-called intelligent functioning mechanisms (IFM) [9, 10]. The IFM includes intelligent information systems, and procedures of planning, regulating and stimulating. In the IFM information received in the process of the social group functioning is used by the centre for decision-making and achievement of the systems aim. These IFM ensure the possibility to identify the internal structure of elements and their parameters as well as the utilization of internal elements resources in accordance with the centre goal. The important types of IFM are: Learning functioning mechanisms, Self-organizing mechanisms, Expert intelligent mechanisms.

Learning functioning mechanisms (LFM) provide the possibility of estimating the parameters of the control object potential in its dynamics, supplying more information to plan its output indices at the account of learning processes. Self-organizing mechanisms should combine learning and planning for output indices (the way it is done in LFM) with the control of its inputs, i.e. direct influence on the potential of an evolving social system. In Expert intelligent mechanisms (EIM) the expert knowledge base is the part of intelligent information systems. EIM combines learning with indistinct and qualitative commands from the centre and control on these commands basis. To design such mechanisms it is necessary to create hierarchic computerized systems with such intelligent possibility as multi-level learning. The knowledge base includes well-known dependencies, any accurate data and the results of individual and collective expertise, the social system of knowledge acquisition in an interactive mode with the decision makers who are responsible for a problem solution and answering the question: "what may actually happen, if…?".

With respect to EIM synthesis the idea of theoretical results consists in the fact that with the sufficiently flexible information usage to solve problems of planning, control and incentives the optimum will be reached. As a result – there appears the possibility of potential identifying on the extra basis of received information and gradual slow output to the required level of sustainable development. The developed approach is directed to the creation of EIM, including procedures of analysis and forecasting of objects potential with a high degree of approximation and procedure of decision-making. The approach suggested to IFM synthesis implemented to the designing of the international regimes of non-proliferation of weapons of mass destruction and technologies for its manufacture, particular intangible nuclear, chemical, biological and rocket technologies [10].

5 Conclusions

Crisis and technological changes produce a rupture between elements of evolving large-scale social system. Many social groups have no possibility for adaptation and need the support. The concept of sustainable development assumes such support. For this purpose, the regulation and control mechanisms used procedures of self-organization, adaptation, learning, and other intelligent technologies.

To provide mechanisms of regulation of self-organization migration, theorem gives the principle for comparative analysis of the human capital attractiveness of social groups of community placed in different regions. It provides the possibility of formal definitions of concepts of community human capital regional attractor, migration attractiveness and climate, and general, specific, sectoral migration climate. The above theorem also gives the possibility to make synthesis the migration climate to regulate large-scale social system sustainable development.

In control mechanisms, provision of the ability of sustainable development of evolving social system in its dynamics with incomplete information is based on the application of adaptation. It implies the consideration of a special type of human factor - activity connected with the availability of people's own goals. The centre obtains information from the social groups in the course of their functioning and uses it for estimating their states to reach the aim of the control. But the farseeing social group may predict the centre controlling action and chooses its states in such a way that its effects on the results of state estimation and adaptive control to maximize its own goal function. For this reason, the problem of the designing of progressive adaptive and intelligent mechanism (including estimation, planning, resources allocation and stimulating procedures) for the hierarchical evolve social system should be taken into account.

References

1. Kile, F., Dimirovski, G.: Choices for global social stability. In: Reports of the 17th IFAC World Congress, Seoul, pp. 6669–6674 (2008)
2. Freeman, A., Stapleton, L.: Systems security problems and cultural meanings in control and automation systems: empirical evidence for value conflicts in systems engineering. In: Reports of the 17th IFAC World Congress, Seoul, pp. 6691–6696 (2008)
3. Tsyganov, V.: Limits of global growth, stagnation, creativity and international stability. Artif. Intell. Soc. J. Knowl. Culture Commun. **29**, 259–266 (2013). Springer-Verlag, London
4. Bagamaev, R., Scherbyna, N., Tsyganov, V.: Adaptive Mechanisms for Social Stability at the Technology Development. In: Reports of the 11th IFAC Conference on Technology and International Stability, Vienna, pp. 81–86 (2004)
5. Transforming our world: the 2030 Agenda for Sustainable Development. Resolution adopted by the General Assembly of United Nation on 25 September 2015
6. Welfonder, E., Frederking, T.: Sustainable Social Economic Evolution of the Globalized Society ⇒ Joint Responsibility of Control Engineers. In: Reports of the 15th IFAC World Congress, Plenary papers, Barselona, pp. 167–178 (2002)
7. Borodin, D., Gurlev, I., Tsyganov, V.: Adaptive mechanisms for sustainable development. Syst. Sci. **1**, 280–285 (2005)
8. Tsyganov, V.: Progressive adaptive mechanisms for the international cooperation. In: Reports of the 17th IFAC World Congress, Seoul, pp. 6697–6702 (2008)
9. Tsyganov, V.: Regulation of decentralized active system development and intelligent control mechanisms. In: Reports of the 12th IFAC Symposium "Large Scale Systems. Theory and Applications", Lille, pp. 1397–1402 (2010)
10. Tsyganov, V.: Intelligent mechanisms for global evolution regulation. In: Reports of the 18th IFAC World Congress, Milan, pp. 3130–3135 (2011)

Mentally Structured Educational Technology and Engineers Preparation Quality Management

Elena V. Smirnova[✉], Anatoly A. Dobrjkov,
Anatoly P. Karpenko, and Vladimir V. Syuzev

Bauman Moscow State Technical University, Moscow, Russia
{evsmirnova, k_iu6}@bmstu.ru,
{dobrjkov, apkarpenko}@mail.ru

Abstract. The paper describes the mentally structured educational technology as a further development of "Russian method of engineers' training" which was famous in the last century ("to know how"). The modern market of intellectual work is under consideration as well, as circumstances and requirements needed for the development of educational programs and resources. Two fundamental methodological principles were applied in new educational methodology's creation.

The first principle declares, that the ultimate goal of teaching is to develop the content of subject area (acquisition of appropriate knowledge) for the student.

The second principle declares that an ultimate goal of learning and the means of its achieving change their places. The ultimate goal of learning in new technology is the formation of student's personality, which means the development of the acquisition of the mentally thinking and the accumulation of the necessary qualities.

The main idea of new mentally structured educational technology is the following. Not only the students (subjects of the educational process) need to be "adjusted" to the characteristics of the studied subject, but also the content of the subject must be adapted to the functional abilities of students in accordance with the objectively existing rules of the functional systems of the human brain. Because of these, the novel education technology was named also as subject-object technology.

The Intelligent Educational System developed by this paper's authors is the implementation of the knowledge processing paradigm. They use Knowledge Base in terms of the ontological domain model, represented as a semantic network.

Keywords: Engineer preparation · Education technology · Knowledge assessment · Software development tool

1 The Needs of Educational Technologies' Modification

Nowadays the science and technical has a feature to change technologies and new models of technical speedily. The technologies, as well as the technical devices, change their design several times during one people's generation. As a result of such a quick

© Springer International Publishing AG 2017
A. Kravets et al. (Eds.): CIT&DS 2017, CCIS 754, pp. 119–132, 2017.
DOI: 10.1007/978-3-319-65551-2_9

technical and cultural development, the student starts to study in one circumstance but when he or she graduates the university he or she came to another world and need to restudy again. From the other side, the speed of the scientific and technical progress is being dependent on the specialists' intellectual skills, first of all – of technical ones.

In accordance with the above-mentioned circumstances, the modern educational concept is being under considerable changes. It is not enough today to have good or even excellent knowledge preparation of the specialists. The modern high-quality specialist should be prepared in three directions. First, he has to have fundamental and special subject's knowledge (knowledge part), second, he should have a systematic style of thinking (mental ability should be structured) and third, he should have professionally oriented personal skills (social skills, business communication, team working and so on). The change in the educational concept requires the development of adequate educational technologies and the corresponding educational and training facilities because the quality of training of specialists' increase is impossible through organizational and structural transformations only.

Thus, the cognitive concept (the acquisition of knowledge and skills) is transformed into psychological and pedagogical concepts, oriented to the development of student's structured thinking and his personal development. Therefore, the basic paradigm of the higher education is being changed as well: from Teaching with an emphasis on instructor-led to Learning format with an emphasis on independent learning is carried out. Within this paradigm, a person learns all his life. Therefore, during the period of study at the university, the student must be "armed" with mental skills, that is, with useful "thought tool" both for knowledge acquisition and their application. An example of Learning format which is oriented to the student independent study during his engineering education in the field of digital signal processing is given in this paper also.

This paper describes the details of the Mentally Structured Educational Technology (MSET) early described in the paper [1] as a development of "Russian method of engineers' training" which was famous in the last century ("to know how"). The Bauman Moscow State Technical University is an ideological successor of such a Russian method currently.

2   Trends of the Modern Market of Intellectual Labour

The modern market of intellectual work is characterized by a high rate of change, instability, uncertainty, and vagueness of the requirements to the universities' graduates. These circumstances require the development of special education programs and of the associated educational resources. These means it should be aimed to create following features of the student added to a high level of fundamental knowledge:

- intellectual capacity, by which we consider the graduates' ability to think competently (being aware of the memory's and thinking's rules), i.e. to have a strong mental literacy (MG) and to have a strong knowledge of his relevant thinking tools;
- these tools should allow to purposefully create a student's matching set of his professionally significant personal qualities (PSPQ), such as social skills, business communication, team working and so on.

The most of the currently existing educational programs are burdened now by old methods of learning. These methods are not compatible with the new educational objectives and therefore cannot be considered as future-oriented effective tools. We need careful selection of good old and "soft" inclusion in teaching technologies of the new innovative elements.

At the market of educational services and intellectual labour, there are more and more highly-regarded harmonious developed synthetic professionals who are able to get the knowledge they need and to create new knowledge on their basis.

The quality of education is a subject to work on in recent years. In Europe, there was developed a large number of different strategies and approaches to the quality improvement, quality management, etc., which bring the highest profit and are responsible for career growth of young professionals. The problem of higher education quality is the core of the Bologna process and is seen as a goal of paramount importance for designing educational space in Europe. Russia has a Scientific Center at the Russian Academy of Science concerned with the quality of specialists' preparation [11].

The building of the mentally structured educational technology, which is competence-oriented engineers' preparation, is not an easy task. The solution consists of the educational program's structuring using two fundamentally different method-ological principles.

The first principle declares that the ultimate goal of teaching is to develop students of the content of any subject area (acquisition of appropriate knowledge). The means of achieving that aim are his psycho-physiological abilities of students.

In accordance with the second principle, the ultimate goal of learning and the means of its achieving change their places. The ultimate goal of learning in new technology is the formation of student's personality, which means the development of the acquisition of the mentally thinking and the accumulation of the necessary qualities.

3 The Concept of Mentally Structured Educational Technology (MSET)

The understanding of the functional relationship of the three pillars of professional competence: knowledge-ability (KA), mental-literacy (ML) and the necessary profes-sional personal qualities (NPPQ) can be conveniently represented in the form of "House of quality" (see Fig. 1).

The foundation of the "House of Quality" is traditional Knowledge Abilities (KA), the leading universities of Russia create a high-level KA for students. The compe-tencies which are necessary for modern professionals additionally to traditional ones are Mental Literacy (ML) and the necessary professionally significant personal quali-ties (PSPQ). In common the last two competencies could be considered as optional products of the educational process, it is shown in Fig. 1 as OIAI (Optional Intellectual Action Index). Three components KA, ML and PSPQ combine the character named as Integral Specialist's Quality Index (ISQI).

The main idea of new mentally structured educational technology (MSET) is the following. The students (subjects of the educational process) need to be "adjusted" to the characteristics of the studied subject, as well as the content of the subject must be

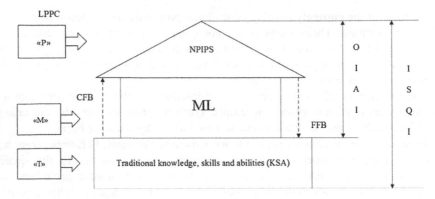

Fig. 1. Education technology "House of Quality"

adapted to the functional abilities of students too in accordance with the objectively existing rules of the functional systems of the human brain. Because of these, the novel education technology was named also as *subject-object* technology [1].

In the mentally structured educational technology (MSET) the training material needs to be humanised according to the rules that reflect the functional structure of human memory and style of thinking. This allows generating a set of subject-independent "tool of thinking" during the process of teaching through the study of mentally structured training materials.

The concept of mental literacy includes the following five parts (key competencies):

- Knowledge (cognitive) literacy (KL) means a culture of learning: the ability to perceive, understand, and independently acquire knowledge;
- Functional literacy (FL) means a culture of professional activities: the ability to apply the knowledge in a proper way;
- Creative literacy (CrL) means a culture of creativity: technological skills to generate something new, the ability to productive thinking and to innovations;
- Corporate literacy (CoL) means a culture of corporate interaction: self-development, non-confrontational group communication, the ability to make organizational and managerial decisions, the ability to bring the case to the end;
- Social literacy (SL) means a culture of situational behaviour: level of moral inter-personal communication, the ability to make socially, economically and environmentally reasonable solutions.

During the process of studying various subjects, students should have the chance to earn extra-logical knowledge that means the necessary professionally important personal skills (NIPS). In general case the structural composition of NIPS consists of the following five integrated components:

- Working ability, trainability and commitment;
- Willingness, autonomy and activity;
- Heuristic, curiosity, uninhibited;
- Self-discipline, tolerance and social responsibility;
- Communication skills and emotional stability.

The professionally significant personal qualities (PSPQ or NIPS at Fig. 1) play the role of "amps" (catalysts) which are associated functionally with key competencies. For example, the key competence which was mentioned above as knowledge of literacy is basically the first of NIPS, and it is identified as the ability to work, learning and dedication. The other paired mates of key competencies and their corresponding components are similar to PSPQ.

This five-components structure of the concept "Mental Literacy" relies on science-based, pentad structure of the brain functional systems and its higher mental functions. This structure allows building the MSET-model (competency model) of professional activities on the basis of unified methodological position.

4   Expert-Analytical Mental Literacy (ML) and Necessary Professionally Important Skills (NIPS)

Personal Skills (NIPS) Assessment

The functional relationship of the key competencies, that is, Mental Literacy (ML) and Necessary Professionally Important Personal Skills (PIPS), can be expressed in the form of Integral Specialist's Quality Index (ISQI) or generalized mental literacy (GML). Thus, it is fair the ratio:

$$GML = ISQI = ML \cup PIPS$$

The value of GML can be computed using empirical relationships:

$$GML = ISQI = [ML](FL + CrL + CoL + SL),$$

where the overline symbol means the corresponding value:

$$(ML] = 0 \_if\_ML = 0 \_and\_ [ML] = 1\_if\_ML > 0 \tag{1}$$

The multiplier [ML] in Eq. (1) reflects not only the prevailing value of the generalized. The multiplier [ML] in Eq. (1) reflects not only the prevailing value of the generalized Knowledge of Literacy and it is most important.

The multiplier [ML] is a factor, which underscores the fact that without the Knowledge Ability (KA) there is no any Mental Literacy Fundamentally as it could be seen from the formula (1), with value [ML] = 0 also [GML] = 0.

5   Mathematical and Information Support of the MSET

5.1   The Model of the Subject Ontology

Traditional training systems implement a method for creating educational materials based on "build" them from pre-developed modules (module) or shared pieces of content (SCO – Shareable Content Object). This method supports the widely known standard is SCORM [7], as well as original Russian technology, called TRACK [3].

Unlike technology SCORM, the TRACK provides interconnection between the modules by specifying relations between the concepts defined in those modules.

The current trend in the intellectual systems' development including the Intelligent Educational System (IES-MSET) developed by the authors is the implementation of the knowledge processing paradigm. In the above-mentioned intelligent educational system, IES-MSET the information component of the knowledge represents as a Knowledge Base. The last one uses the ontological domain model, represented as a semantic network [8].

The training module model in the system IES-MSET has the following description. Main terms, training modules and their principal designations are shown in Table 1.

Table 1. Terms and training modules: principal designations

Designation	Definition
mi, i = 1, 2, ...	Modules of the knowledge library
Ci, j	Input concept of the module mi
Ci = {ci, j, j ∈ [1, ni]} = CIi CEi	Set of input concept of the module mi
CIi	Input concepts, the definition of which are in theKnowledge Library
CE_i	Input concepts, the definition of which are in other Knowledge Libraries
$C_{i,j}$	Output concept of the module m_i
$C_i = \{C_{i,j}, j \in [1, n_i]\}$	Set of output concepts of the module m_i
$C_{i,j} = \{C_{i,j,k}, k \in [1: n_{i,j}]\}$	Set of concepts C_i, which is used to define the concept $c_{i,j}$
$C_{i,j} = \{C_{i,j,k}, k \in [1: n_{i,j}], k \neq j\}$	Set of concepts C_i, which is used to define the concept $C_{i,j}$.
$S(m_i)$	Semantic network of the module mi
$G(m_i)$	A directed graph without contours describes the corresponding semantic network $S(m_i)$
$K_{i,j}$	Multiplicity concepts $c_{i,j}$
l_i	The number of internal reference of the concepts used in the module m_i
$\overline{l_i}$	Number of external reference of the concepts of the module m_i

Concepts from the sets $C_{i,j}$, $C_{i,j}$ are connected (in the narrow information sense) with the Concept $C_{i,j}$. If the concept $C_{i,j}$ is connected to the concept $C_{i,k}$ and this concept $c_{i,k}$ is connected with the concept $C_{i,l}$, then we say that concepts $C_{i,j}$, $C_{i,l}$ are connected in a broad information sense.

The semantic network $S(m_i)$ of the module m_i is described as a direct graph without contours $G(m_i)$, whose vertices correspond to the concepts of sets C_i, and arcs correspond to the relations "defined concept - defining the concept" between the concepts. In other words, the arcs in the graph $G(m_i)$ correspond to the concept's communication links of the sets between each other.

Similarly, the concept's communication links are identified as an information communication links of modules. We call the modules mi and m j as information-related modules in case if one output concept of a module mi at least is the input concept for the module m j or if one output concept of a module m j at least is the input concept for the module mi.

In accordance with the idea of the TRACK, one concept can be defined in different modules of the Knowledge Library L but none of the concepts can be defined in different modules of the learning course. We call such concepts as multiple concepts.

The system IES-MSET provides the following rules for the arrangement of the concept's descriptions in the module:

- First rule - none of the concepts of the k-th level of the multilevel parallel form (MPF) of the module cannot be defined until all the concepts all located below the level of MPF are defined;
- Second rule – when performing the first rule, describe concepts of the k-th level of MPF can be entered into the module in any order [8].

Along with this, the system IES-MSET allows the use of module concepts that are not defined yet in this module but will be defined in this module later. Such concepts are referred to as internal reference concepts. In terms of MPF the link to the concept is that in the text of the module there is a concept of the above levels which is been used in the definition of the k-th level's concepts.

The reference concept may also be an external reference concept. If some module $m_{i,j}$ of the training course T used the concept, which is defined in the module $m_{i,k}$, $k > j$, then for the module $m_{i,k}$ this concept is an external reference concept. It is assumed here that if $k > j$, then the module mik in the course T is been placed textually later than module $m_{i,j}$.

Similarly, the model could be defined of the training modules' library L of training course T.

5.2   Complexity Metrics of Concepts, Modules, Libraries, and of Training Course

Let's introduce the following definitions:$\mu(c_{i,j})$ - a complexity metric of concept $c_{i,j}$; (m_i) - complexity metric of the module m_i; $\mu(L)$ - a complexity metric of the modules from library L; $\mu(T)$ - a complexity metric of the course T. The value of a complexity metric of the concept may be depended on the context under the evaluation. In the definitions of the complexity metrics, the corresponding context is indicated by the lower index. So the complexity metric ($c_{i,j}$) indicates the complexity of the concept $c_{i,j}$ within the module m_i, the complexity metric L($c_{i,j}$) - within the library L, the metric μT ($c_{i,j}$) within the course T.

Allocate two classes of the complexity metrics of concepts and modules. The complexity metric of the concept $\mu(c_{i,j})$ called context-independent metric, if $\mu(c_{i,j}) = \mu L (c_{i,j}) = \mu T (c_{i,j})$, and context-dependent metric otherwise. Similarly, a metric of the complexity of a module called context-free if, and context-sensitive – different. It is obvious that, ceteris paribus, determining the values of context-independent metrics requires less computational costs. Note that large values of all the considered metrics correspond to higher values of the complexity of the objects.

Authors have developed a significant number of the complexity metrics of concepts, modules, libraries and courses. An example of a complexity metric of the concepts (see Table 2).

Table 2. Complexity metrics of concepts: context-dependent metric, context-independent metric

Designation	Definition
$\mu 1(Ci, j) = \mu 1(\lambda, Ci, j) = \lambda$ ni, j + ni, j	Context-independent metric: the weighted number of concepts in the sets Ci, j, Ci, j; $\lambda \in [0,1]$
$\mu 2\ (c_{i,j}) = h(c_{i,j})$	Context-dependent metric: the altitude of the concepts
$\mu 3\ (c_{i,j})$	Context-dependent metric: the number of concepts, related in a broad sense with this concept Ci, j
$\mu(c) = \prod \rho\ k\ \mu\ k\ (C\ i,j),$ $k \in [1:3]$	Context-dependent metric: multimetric $\rho_k \in [0, 1]$

From the standpoint of the interpretation easiness and low computational complexity, there are following complexity metrics applied: $\mu 1(\lambda, c_{i,j})$ - weighted number of concepts through which this concept was defined, $\mu 3\ (c_{i,j})$ - the number of concepts, related to this concept in abroad sense. In other words, it is possible to recommend to use multi-metric $\mu(c_{i,j})$ for $\lambda = 0$.

5.3   The Connectedness Metrics of Academic Disciplines

In the system IES-MSET the method of determining the concepts' connectedness was applied, which is based on the fact that the search server (e.g., Yandex or Google Server) indexes a large number of training materials. Thus, to determine the proximity of concepts c1, c2 it is sufficient to determine the frequency of their occurrence in the compared documents using the Normalized Google Distance (NGD) [4]:

NGD(c1, c2) = max(logf(c1), logf(c2)) − logf(c1, c2)), logM-min(logf(c1), logf (c2)),

where M − the total number of indexed pages of documents; f (c1), f (c2) - the numbers of pages with concepts c1, c2 accordingly; f (c1, c2) − the number of pages with both c1 and c2. The value NGD = 0, if the concepts c1, c2 are together at all of the pages; NGD = ∞, if these concepts are found separately only.

6   The Software of the Mentally Structured Education Technology

6.1   The Algorithm for Constructing a Graph of Concepts' Connectedness

For a more successful students' assimilation of the knowledge, the time intervals between the studies of information-related disciplines should be minimized. Therefore the criterion of the total value minimizing of the total sum of time lags between information-related disciplines of the curriculum is been used as a decision rule in curricula's constructing taking into account the degree of their connectedness. To select the disciplines to be included in the curriculum, the above-mentioned criterion is used [1].

To create the curriculum the system ISE-MSET uses Minimum Spanning Tree method (MST), according to the table of disciplines' connectedness realised by Prima algorithm [6]. After a minimum spanning tree of the given set of disciplines is constructed, the optimal sequence of these disciplines' study by determining by traversing the skeleton of the tree.

To visualise the concepts' connectedness graph the spring algorithm Kamada-Kawai has been used with help of Graphviz Neato program [2].

The Kamada-Kawai algorithm requires the recompilation of the visualised graph's description in a special format specifying the parameters of the vertices and the connecting edges (color, line type, length and so on). The vertex's (concept) colour depends on the degree of this concept's connectedness. The length of the edge represents the Normalized Google Distance (NGD) between the relevant concepts.

6.2   Visualisation of the Training Material's Evaluation Results

The results of the discipline's evaluation are been visualised using the three following characteristics:

- Normalized Google Distance $NG\ D \in [0;\ 1]$ between two concepts calculated through Kolmogorov complexity and characterised the coherence of the discipline;
- The number Inf of indexed pages, as a result of the query string to a search engine (it consists of two concepts) $Google$, that is, the number of pages on which a given combination of concepts which characterise the information content of the discipline;
- The length $Len \in (0;\ 180]$ of the query string to a search engine $Google$, measured in a number of characters of the total length of the string (two concepts), which shows the complexity of the discipline.

Concerning to scaling, the value Inf could change in very wide range (in our experiments from 1 to 9×10^9), so let use a decimal logarithm of this quantity, that is a value log(Inf). The value 180 is an upper limit of the Len represents the maximum allowed length of the request to Google.

A set of points in the coordinate system NGD, log(Inf), Len represents the landscape of the discipline approximated by the continuous surface. The last method of the disciplines visualisation could be used to evaluate the connectedness of two disciplines' curricula.

The latter method is the discipline visualisation may be used to estimate two disciplines curricula proximity, such as the programs of the discipline of the Computer Systems and Networks Department at BMSTU and the standard program given by Ministry of Education and Science of Russian Federation. The idea is to compare topographic maps of these programs and to measure the intersecting spheres of the same colour on the maps which reflects the degree of intersection of the concepts included in the software for comparison.

6.3   The Structure of the System IES-MSET

The core modules of the system IES-MSET meet the international standards of quality assurance, in particular, the standard IEEE P. 1484.1. At the same time, while recognising the merits of the structural organisation of the IEEE P. 1484.1, corresponding to the principle of student's mental education, these paper authors consider it necessary to put the student in the centre of the subject of education as the main functional load in the system. It is also important that the interaction between the student and the learning materials is active since the student decides in what format (text, image, video or audio content) he prefers to learn the material.

According to the above mentioned, the structure of the system IES-MSET has a view at Fig. 2.

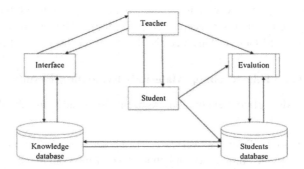

Fig. 2. The structure of the system IES-MSET

6.4   Software Development Tools

There are five subsystems at the system IES-MSET:

- United storage for databases, ontology, Knowledge databases, placed at IBM Student's physiological parameters' estimation subsystem;
- Learning materials, technology and outcomes estimation subsystem;
- Student's preparation quality subsystem;
- Interfaces for the student, teacher and expert.

The student's physiological parameters' estimation subsystem consists of a software component that calculates the speed of student's information perception. The subsystem can present information to the student in different formats: text, image or audio fragment. This subsystem stores the results of the measurements at the biometric database, so the physiological characteristics of each student in dynamics may be a subject to research. The subsystem of the training material's evaluation uses a specially designed ontology of subject knowledge, which is based on Russian educational standards.

The software development tools include an environment for object-oriented programming (Delphi, Eclipse, Dreamweaver), Java programming language, the database management system DB2, web-based interfaces, and system of user's authentication.

Authors took into account the following requirements when choosing software development tools and software design architecture:

- Open source;
- Cross-platform software (working on different platforms: Linux, Windows, etc.);
- The ability to use previous experience and to integrate different sub-tasks.

The well-established software libraries, designed to solve the problems of natural language texts, images, audio and video fragments analysis as well as to present the analysis results in text and graphic formats. These requirements led to use Java as a development language.

The process of automatic ontology creation on the basis of learning materials like textbooks, tutorials etc. include the following stages:

1. An electronic version of the textbook is downloaded to the processing computer;
2. Expert is viewing the tutorial defines the allocation of the terms in the text, for example, a glossary existence at the end of the tutorial, a list of terms at the end of each chapter, bold or italic fonts, etc. and transfer it to the computer;
3. The computer finds all the terms;
4. The computer performs a statistical analysis of terms (see details below in Sect. 7);
5. The computer creates an object of the ontology for every term;
6. For each found term there are first few references offered to the expert for the formation of the ontology object's properties;
7. for each pair of terms in processed sentences of the text of the tutorial offered by the expert for the formation of the ontology object's relationships for both terms. Such pair of terms found is a proof of the hypothesis of the connection exists between the terms;
8. Expert confirms or refuses a hypothesis about the relationship between the terms;
9. Computer establishes the relationship between the ontologies' objects;
10. If the expert confirmed the existence of a connection, the computer finds all such proposals, which refers to both terms;
11. The computer performs a statistical analysis of the relationships between the terms;
12. On the basis of these proposals, expert formulates the qualitative characteristics of the relationship.

The statistical analysis at the stages 4 and 11 includes the computation of power spectral density (PSD) [5, 9] for the terms and relationships of the terms. Authors propose to consider the term's first appearing in the current chapter, and ones introduced in the previous chapters as new and old terms accordingly. These two densities functions (PSD) have a feature of stationary random processes.

6.5 User and Expert Interfaces

An example of the interface's subsystem is shown in Fig. 3. The characteristic features of mental-structured user's and expert's interfaces as a man's faces as a result of the student competencies' evaluation and self-evaluation.

The screen form is divided into two parts "The opinion of a student" and "The opinion of the student's teacher". The figure presents the two extreme outcomes of the assessment: excellent student (as the student sees himself) and bad student (as the teacher sees his student). Certain facial features on Fig. 3 visualize the different components of the student's competence, for example, the presence of forehead wrinkles characterises his ability to work, the size of the eyes – his intelligence, etc.

The visualisation of the knowledge evaluation results and of the student's qualities is carried out in dialogue mode (Fig. 4). Screen form provides the user with the reference's access, that is an application in a separate window, which is a transcript of student's characteristic.

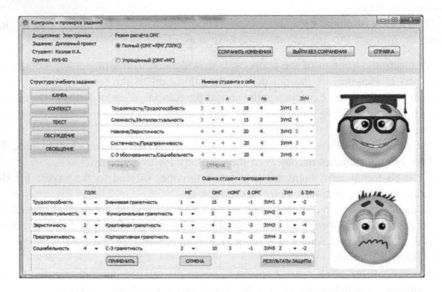

Fig. 3. Main window of the subsystem interface control and verification of student knowledge.

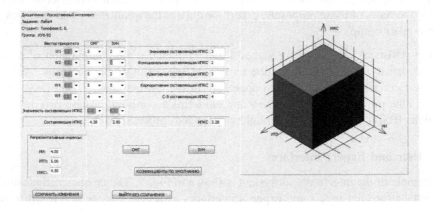

Fig. 4. Visualisation of the student competencies evaluation results in the system IES-MSET

7   Learning Form Example of the Independent Study in Engineer's Preparation

An independent study of the subject in engineering training is a critical component of the Learning format. Such independent studies are course design, homework and research work. Thus, the efficiency of a studied materials' understanding depends largely on individual tasks, received by students for independent work. These tasks should be focused on a large group of students, that is, must be a flexible and informative, allowing teachers to raise the above-described competencies.

The educational-methodical toolkit for the independent work depends on the study subjects. So the key terms in the text educational material can be successfully used for studying by students of spectral algorithms for simulation of signals in different orthogonal bases [9].

Spectral algorithms for simulation due to the choice of specific systems of basic functions are multiple and vary in accuracy and computational complexity. Independent research of various spectral views will allow the student to expand the scope of their knowledge and skills in the theory and practice of spectral processing of various objects, including semantic information.

In the article [9] there are examples which use deterministic and random signals in the framework of the correlation theory under consideration as a useful and noise components of the input signals for different management and control systems. As the initial representation of the signal in the framework of the correlation theory, there are considered their representation in the spectral domain trigonometric basis functions at a given power spectral density (PSD) [5].

Algorithms for simulation of signals in a harmonic Fourier basis can be used as a base for synthesising algorithms in arbitrary orthogonal bases. It is necessary to find the spectra of the same signal in another orthogonal basis using the Fourier spectrum and the mathematical apparatus of generalised spectrum analysis [10]. After that, the signal itself can be reconstructed through the inverse transform in this basis.

For independent work, the teacher gives to the student the PSD function and its characteristics, as well as the system of basic functions, which is the algorithm simulation. Changing the interval of definition and the number of members of the spectral series in algorithms of the simulation, students calculate a variety of amounts of realisation of the random process, building the autocorrelation function with different precision.

Thus, the task of simulation of deterministic signals in the framework of correlation theory, and spectral algorithms of its solution with respect to frequency characteristics of terms in the learning material are an effective methodological tool for the formation of a wide variety of individual tasks for all types of independent work of students - from homework, coursework and projects in scientific research work in the subject area related to the study of systems of management and control, including systems of quality management of education.

Variable parameters providing a multiplicity are the form and features of the PSD function, the intervals for determining the quantities of signals, sampling time, accuracy requirements and the complexity of the simulation and, most importantly, the system of basic functions.

8   Conclusion

The contemporary approach to the competency-based training of highly qualified specialists (technical elites) considers the changes of the mental procedures' character. The paper was about the need of new mind-software using which it would be possible to solve problems previously considered as unsolvable. It is a purpose of the IES-MSET system for automated quality control over the student's educational activities.

Acknowledgement. The work is being supported by the Russian Ministry of Education and Science (Project #2014-14-579-0144 dated 24/11/2014, ID RFMEF157714X0135).

References

1. Belous, V.V., Bobrovsky, A.V., Dobrjkov, A.A., Karpenko, A.P., Smirnova, E.V.: Multicriterion integral alternatives' estimation: mentally-structured approach to education. In: 2nd International Conference on Education and Education Management (EEM 2012), Hong Kong, China, 4–5 September 2012, vol. 3, pp. 215–224 (2012)
2. Kamada, T., Kawai, S.: An algorithm for drawing general undirected graphs. Inform. Process. Lett. **31**, 7–15 (1989)
3. Norenkov, I.P., Sokolov, N.K.: Synthesis of individual learning routes in ontology learning systems. Inf. Technol. **3**, 74–77 (2009). (in Russian)
4. Normalized Google Distance [Electronic resource]. – Access mode: https://en.wikipedia.org/wiki/Normalized_Google_distance
5. Oppenhein, A., Schafer, R.: Digital Signal Processing. Prentice-Hall, Englewood Cliffs (2012)
6. Prim's algorithm [Electronic resource]. – Access mode: https://en.wikipedia.org/wiki/Prim%27s_algorithm
7. SCORM – Project TinCan: Phase3–Capabilities. Rustici Software. [Electronic resource]. – Access mode: https://scorm.com/tincan
8. Shpak, M.A., Smirnova, E.V., Karpenko, A.P., Proletarsky, A.V.: Mathematical models of learning materials estimation based on subject ontology. In: Abraham, A., Kovalev, S., Tarassov, V., Snášel, V. (eds.) Proceedings of the First International Scientific Conference "Intelligent Information Technologies for Industry" (IITI 2016). AISC, vol. 450, pp. 271–276. Springer, Cham (2016). doi:10.1007/978-3-319-33609-1_24
9. Smirnova, E.V., Syuzev, V.V., Proletarsky, A.V., Gurenko, V.V.: Signal's simulation methodologies used in scientific and educational tasks of real-time information system's modelling. In: IATED Academy INTED2017 Proceedings, 11th International Technology, Education and Development Conference, Valencia, Spain, pp. 9140–9143 (2017)
10. Syuzev, V.V.: Introduction to digital signal processing. M.: RTSoft. (2014) (in Russian)
11. Quality of High Education site [Electronic resource]. – Access mode: http://misis.ru/spglnk/44129f80

Ontology Visualization: Approaches and Software Tools for Visual Representation of Large Ontologies in Learning

Anton Anikin[1], Dmitry Litovkin[1], Marina Kultsova[1(✉)], Elena Sarkisova[1], and Tatyana Petrova[2]

[1] Volgograd State Technical University, Volgograd, Russia
Anton@Anikin.name, marina.kultsova@mail.ru
[2] Volgograd State Socio-Pedagogical University, Volgograd, Russia
poas@vstu.ru

Abstract. In this paper, we address the issue of large ontologies visualization for learning. The ontologies can be used to improve the efficiency of the learning when the learner explores a new subject domain and needs its conceptual model. The ontologies can help to overview this new subject domain, to better understand current knowledge, the knowledge that should be got, the subject domain structure, main concepts, relationships between them and relevant information resources. However with increasing the complexity of domain structure, the number of concepts and relationships, it becomes more difficult to overview and understand conceptual model represented with the ontology. We review the approaches to ontology visualization and their implementation in the software tools that can help to resolve this issue.

Keywords: Semantic web · Ontology · Ontology visualization

1 Introduction

An ontology is a convenient tool of domain modelling for wide range of tasks, such as [2,3,18,19]:

- Exploring a new subject domain by studying its ontology-based model.
- Studying a new subject domain via ontology-based domain modeling.
- Linking the ontology concepts with relevant information resources to provide automated information retrieval during the studying a new subject domain.
- Support of inference rules allows using ontologies not only for automated information retrieval but also for learning management.

Thus, the use of ontologies in learning is well grounded and reasonable, both for studying a new subject domain by individual users, as well as within the educational process in universities to manage single courses and learning process as a whole.

© Springer International Publishing AG 2017
A. Kravets et al. (Eds.): CIT&DS 2017, CCIS 754, pp. 133–149, 2017.
DOI: 10.1007/978-3-319-65551-2_10

Within ontological modeling, the developer faces a number of problems concerning the creation, edit, distribution and sharing ontologies, and their adaptive visual representation (visualization).

The last task is topical and widely applicable due to the large scale and complexity of the domain ontologies structure. Ontologies can contain hundreds and thousands of concepts associated with different types of relationships, as well as links to the ontologies of the related domains. These makes it difficult for the user to perceive information, and so the domain ontology visualization becomes the very important task that includes adaptive visual representation of ontologies in learning, ontology navigation and search of elements within the ontology.

2   Background and Related Work

An information support plays a key role in the learning process and determines its quality and efficiency. Competency-based learning is directed to the acquirement of appropriate competencies, knowledge, and skills. Achievement of this goal is impossible without an appropriate information support of learning that implies using the relevant information and educational resources.

Information support of learning processes involves thematic information retrieval and creation of personal learning collections of information resources for some topic as a result of their retrieval and integration. The creation of such collections can be performed on the basis of user cognitive space and information space of subject domain.

A cognitive space is the set of concepts and relations among them held by a human. The cognitive space can be individual as well as shared by a group of people. Using the modern software tools the cognitive space can be mapped into conceptual model represented as a mind map, topic map, concept map (conceptual diagram) or ontology. An information space is the set of objects and relations among them held by an information system. The components of the information space for the information retrieval task include concepts, documents, words, relations among words and documents. So the information space should be consistent with the cognitive space of particular humans or groups.

An essential and actual problem is creation of the domain information space which is relevant to the personal cognitive space of subject of information process [3]. The use of ontologies for the cognitive and information spaces representation is an appropriate and promising approach to solve this problem.

Within ongoing research project, the authors proposed an ontology-based approach to the collaborative construction of the domain information space on the basis of the cognitive spaces of individuals or groups and the existing information spaces [2, 3, 18, 19]. It allows to decrease the time and increase the efficiency of retrieval and reuse of the information resources which are relevant to the subject domain and the user cognitive space. One of the important issues in the framework of this approach is representation and visualization of the domain ontology for the user.

The ontology visualization affects the efficiency of perception of domain knowledge by the learner that includes the concepts and concept hierarchy, different types of relations between the concepts, concepts properties (in the case of the domain information space - the list of information resources, corresponding to the concepts). The requirements to ontology visualization depend on tasks defined in the ontology and user competence in the subject domain. E.g., the subject domain can be totally new for the learner, the learner can know some of the concepts (and need to find it and discover the related concepts step-by-step), or he can know most of the concepts and need to find and fill the knowledge gaps in this domain.

Generally, the requirements which the visualization method and tool should be met are formulated as follows:

- One should be able to visualize all the components of the ontology, such as classes, instances, and relations.
- The tool should allow visualizing the ontology stored independently of the visualizer as well as sharing and collaborative editing the ontology by the group of users at the same time. SPARQL-endpoint can be considered as a data source to meet this requirement.
- A simple and obvious model should be used for visualization, like a graph for example.
- Some special techniques should be used for visualization of a subset of ontology elements (fragments of ontology) for navigation during the ontology studying and transformation of these fragments within the full ontology.
- The search of ontology elements (classes, individuals, relations) and visualization of search results in the full ontology and ontology fragment should be provided by the visualizer.
- As the ontology supports reasoning, the results of the reasoning should be visualized as well.

3   Approaches and Software Tools for Visual Representation of Large Ontologies

The subject domain might have a rather complex structure and cover a huge set of concepts and relations between them, that complicates extremely the study of appropriate information resources by the person who is not familiar with the domain. In this case, it is advisable to create the own domain model or use and extend the domain models created by other persons. But due to the complexity, it is difficult to overview and understand conceptual model represented with the ontology.

The usage of various approaches and tools for ontology visualization and navigation depends on the user category who work with the ontology and the use cases. The user categories considering below can be defined depending on their relation to the subject domain and role within ontology engineering process:

- Ontology Engineer: a specialist in Ontology Engineering - a research area which studies the methods and methodologies for building ontologies: formal representations of a set of domain concepts and the relationships between them. So, this type of user has high competence in the ontology engineering but does not always have enough competence in the applied subject domain.

- Domain expert: a specialist in applied subject domain who does not always have enough competence in the ontology engineering.
- Learner: ontology user that is not a specialist in the applied subject domain and needs to learn it, and who also has not enough competence in the ontology engineering.

For the task of domain information space studying the user category usually can vary from learner to an expert in this classification, but stays closer to the first one.

The following use cases are distinguished when working with ontologies [7]:

- Editing: ranges from developing a new ontology to changing a value of some property. Usually, the purpose of visualization, in that case, is to find the entity to be changed or to become linked with a new entity.
- Inspection: needs a detailed view of the ontology to see errors or deficiencies. It often implies Editing, as the user needs to see the state of the ontology before and after editing.
- Learning: means gaining knowledge about the domain the ontology covers, or learning about the ontology itself so as to use it. The view should not be so detailed as for errors discovering (for Inspection). The user often only needs to see the available classes and properties, their hierarchy and their domain/range relationships; it is actually especially for non-technical users who only want to learn the subject domain and unlikely to understand complex axioms anyway.
- Sharing: is similar to Learning, except one more actor for whom the ontology should be explained and shared with. The visualization should support displaying a part of the ontology; e.g., a picture of it can be made for an article describing the ontology.

In the case of using ontologies in the learning process by the learner, it usually implies learning and sharing use case (where the user is the second actor).

The following approaches to the ontology visualization can be distinguished [7]:

1. Zoom-Out Overview: zooming out to get a summary view of the ontology.
2. Radar View: displaying a small "minimap" of the displayed ontology.
3. Graphical Zoom: enlarging the displayed graphical elements.
4. Focus on Selected Entity: centering the view on a selected entity and its surroundings and hiding other parts of the ontology.
5. History: keeping the history of navigation steps performed by the user, thus allowing for undo/redo actions.
6. Pop-Up Window: displaying details on a chosen entity in a separate window.
7. Incremental Exploration: starting by a small part of the ontology and gradually expanding the nodes selected by the user (as detailed in [11]).
8. Search: text-based search leading to highlighting the matched entities.

9. Hide Selected Entity: hiding parts of the ontology the user is currently not interested in, thus avoiding a cluttered view.
10. Filter Specific Entity Type: e.g., hiding all object properties at once.
11. Fisheye Distortion: zooming in for a part of the graph and zooming out for the rest; focuses on a detail but keeps the context, see, e.g., [32].
12. Edge Bundles: grouping edges with similar paths, thus alleviating the clutter; implemented, e.g., in GLOW [12].
13. Drag&Drop Navigation: moving a graph that is bigger than the screen around by dragging it with the mouse.
14. Drag&Drop User Layout: allowing to move the individual nodes around.
15. Clustering: intelligent grouping of nodes or displaying a subset of important nodes, as in KC-Viz [23].
16. Integration with Editing: the user can select a visualized node or edge and edit its properties in, e.g., a pop-up window.
17. Graphical Editing: the tool supports creating new entities by, e.g., drawing edges between the displayed nodes.

Referring to [10], approaches 1–5 are associated with a criteria class called "Help and User Orientation", 6–8 with "Navigation and Browsing", 9–10 with "Dataset Reduction", 11–14 with "Spatial Organization", and 15 with "Information Coding". 16–17 have no corresponding class in [10]. In each use case category most of the 17 features should ideally be supported. However, their importance can vary.

Evidently, more low-level issues and approaches can be distinguished within each of the items above. Also, some approaches can extend the set of criteria classes.

Most of the visualization approaches and software tools are oriented to the specialists in ontological modeling and are used to solve the problem of understanding ontology ("ontology sensemaking") [23]. In this case, the relevant tasks are a search of existing ontology for reuse, optimization of large ontologies structure, when the specialist should understand the ontology structure. For this task, the tools for the high-level overviews creation can be used (1–2 in the list above), zooming (3) and element filtering (10) [23,30,33,39].

Within the tasks of learning and sharing the ontology, for efficiency knowledge sharing included into the ontology, the cognitive properties of the ontology are important that allows to user easy understanding and interpreting them. In that case the visualization of the ontology implies the visualization of some fragment of this ontology including some concepts with the context (so called "viewpoint") [1]. In [22] this problem resolved e.g., with the cognitive frame based representation of the ontology and patterns.

Also the ways of visualization below can be distinguished [21]:

1. Graph Visualizations of Ontologies [23,25,28,29,38] - a simple, understandable and convenient way for ontology presentation that almost does not require any special user knowledge and can be extended to represent special ontology properties.
2. Specific Diagram Types [15,16].

3. UML-based Ontology Visualizations [4,20,35,37] - requires special user knowledge in UML.
4. Other Diagrammatic Ontology Visualizations [5,27,36].
5. RDF Visualizations of Ontologies [14,31] - represents the ontology as RDF graph with all concepts and relations that are not useful with the large ontologies.

Also, the software tool should support the ability to extend its functionality (with plugins or source code modification) and should be open source in the last case.

So, browsing ontologies to understand their structure and content is an important activity in ontology engineering [3,22,34]. Moreover, ontologies nowadays are developed and used not only by experts but also by a wide range of non-expert users in a lot of fields, from research, health-care to daily business. The question about how to support ontology visualization and navigation in a better way has attracted a lot of attentions from researchers. A good ontology visualization system by convention [16] should support some functionalities like a high-level overview of ontology, effective scalability by concrete part of ontology, filtering options and so on.

Usually, in the early stage of the process of making sense of ontology, what user tries to do is to understand the general organization of the ontology rather than paying attention to its specific representation details. Ontology visualizer with high overview level should support user to quickly understand what main areas the current ontology is about, how it is structured. As can be seen, the issue of ontology high-level overview has never been easy, because once ontology is large enough, it is impossible to visualize the whole ontology structure on limited screen of a computer. Different approaches have been proposed to solve this issue, including:

1. Treemaps [16], which focuses to maximizing the visualized information, using space-fill solutions.
2. OwlViz visualizer [28] - a Protege plugin, which allows user to navigate through ontology by selecting, expanding, hiding nodes.
3. Ontology Navigator [23] in Neon Toolkit [8,9,25], which uses file system navigation approach to show class hierarchy of ontology.
4. KC-Viz [23,29] in Neon Toolkit [25], proposes the approach using key concepts extraction to extract most common concepts from ontology for visualization
5. Ontology Exploration Tool [17], a tool from Hozo Ontology Viewer [13], which allows user to view ontologys structure from different viewpoints in a user-friendly visualization form called Conceptual Map.
6. Ontodia [26] - online OWL and RDF diagramming tool.

3.1   Treemaps

Treemaps are solution intended for visualization of ontology with complex tree hierarchies, where tree structures are visualized as 2-D space-filling representation and 100% of visualization space is used. This effective usage of visualization space allows displaying completely large hierarchies and facilitates representation of semantic information. In treemaps, visualization space is split into bounding rectangles that representing a tree structure. The distribution of nodes into their bounding rectangles depends on the content of the nodes and can be interactively controlled. Interactive control allows user to configure the representation method in structural level (depth, boundary, etc.) as well as in information level (display of properties such as color mapping, etc.). This is in contrasts to traditional static methods of visualizing hierarchically structured information, where there are usually low effective usages of visualization space or hiding a large amount of information from users. With Treemaps, parts of hierarchy, which contain more important information can be allocated more space than parts, which contain less important information. A sample of ontology visualization by treemaps is shown in Fig. 1.

3.2   Ontology Navigator (in Neon Toolkit)

Ontology Navigator in Neon Toolkit [8,9,25] follows the classic navigation metaphor of file system, where clicking into a directory will open up its sub-directories. It allows user to navigate through hierarchy of ontology by simple clicks into classes to view subclasses. Although at first look, it is a pretty basic solution, compare to other complex visualization metaphors, this approach can be surprisingly effective thanks to two reason: (1) the navigation method is very familiar to users; (2) it allows to displaying a lot of information in a small space, in contrast to node-link approach, which can take up a lot of space. One of problems in Ontology Navigator is when clicking into a class, all of its subclasses are always shown up. It is impossible to control the number of subclasses that will be displayed or open more than one level with a single click. Also, it not allows to visualize the individuals. As can be seen, the visualization approach used in Ontology Navigator is still not enough to support making sense of the general mental model of ontology. The latest version of NeOn Toolkit is dated 2011 year. A sample of ontology visualization by Ontology Navigator is shown in Fig. 2.

3.3   KC-Viz

KC-Viz uses an innovative method based on idea of key concepts extraction to support the task of high level overview and understanding large ontologies. It provides possibility of navigation through ontology, beginning from most information-rich nodes. These nodes are extracted from ontology using algorithm of Key Concepts Extraction, which allows to create a summary of ontology. The visualization and navigation approach used in KC-Viz is analogous to visualization and navigation in maps from Geographical Information System, where large cities are displayed more noticeably than others, depending on the current level of detail. Visualization and navigation of ontology with KC-Viz begin with generation of initial summary of ontology, so that user can have general overview about ontology. A summary of ontology CodeOntology [6] (contains 65 classes, 17 individuals, 94 object properties and 13 data properties) is shown

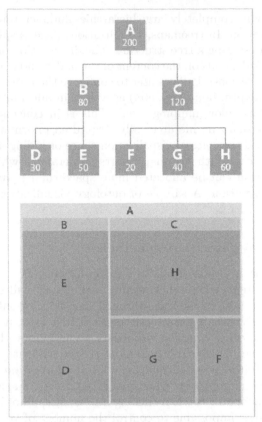

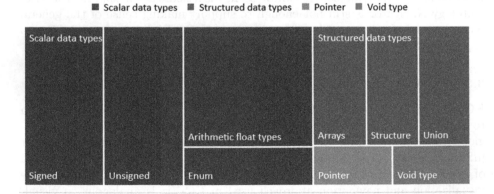

Fig. 1. Visualization of a simple tree structure with treemaps approach

Fig. 2. Visualization of the CodeOntology [6] with Ontology Navigator in NeOn Toolkit

in Fig. 3. This summary includes 16 most common classes (or may be a different amount, depending on the configuration of user) from different level, 15 of which are extracted by Key Concepts Extraction algorithm and the last concept is owl:Thing in order to create a connected graph. Grey arrows in the picture denote the direct rdfs:subClassOf relationships, and the dash green arrows denote the indirect rdfs:subClassOf relations. By hovering mouse to the indirect links, user can see the chain of direct rdfs:subClassOf relations, which summarized by indirect links. For user to capture an image of how large the current ontology is, KC-Viz displays two number inside each visualized node, indicates the number of direct and indirect subclasses of current class. Detail information about each class can be seen by hovering mouse to selected node.

So this approach is efficiency enough to visualize large ontologies regardless of the number of concepts included. It does not allow to display the instances, but the algorithm can be extended to do this.

The last version of NeOn Toolkit with KC-Viz algorithm integrated is dated 2011 year.

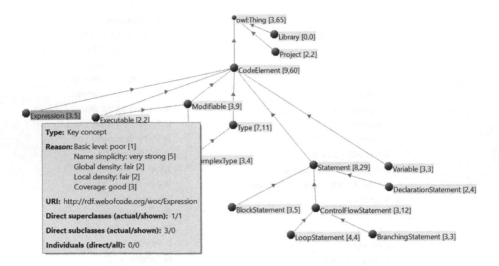

Fig. 3. Summary of CodeOntology [6] with KC-Viz

3.4   Ontology Exploration Tool (in Hozo Ontology Viewer)

Ontology Exploration Tool allows to visualize the conceptual structure of ontology as generally as possible and allows on-the-fly reorganizing some conceptual structures according to users perspective. It provides a possibility of exploring the ontology from several viewpoints to obtains an understanding of the ontology from multi-perspectives. The viewpoint is defined as a combination of a focal point and an aspect. The focal point indicates a concept to which the user pays attention as a starting point for exploration. The aspect is the manner in which the user explores the ontology. It can be the represented by a set of methods for extracting concepts according to its relations because an ontology consists of concepts and relations among them [17]. An example of ontology exploration with Ontology Exploration Tool is shown in (Fig. 4). A user sets Any (the root of ontology) as a focal point and sets Sub concepts to be the aspect of exploration. The result is that nine concepts: representation, substance, measure, Entity, attribute, location, Proposition, time, representation form are extracted, following is-a relations (rdfs:subClassOf in OWL). Next, the user focuses on concept location and selects Concepts to be referred by some relationship as an aspect, the following concepts: animal, action, basic judgment, pass, make fly, ... are extracted, following attribute-of relations (rdfs:properties in owl). As a result of this concept extraction, conceptual chains that match users interest are generated and visualized as a conceptual map. In the conceptual map, extracted concepts and followed relationships are represented as nodes and links respectively, and the nodes are located on concentric circles in which the focal point is located at the center [17].

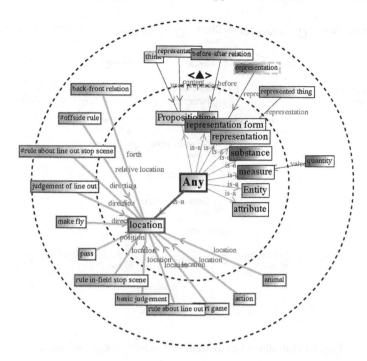

Fig. 4. Visualization of conceptual chains as a conceptual map

Even though the main purpose of Ontology Exploration Tool is about the exploration of an ontology, not the visualization itself, the way which Conceptual Map of this tool uses for visualization of the ontology structure is an effective solution for the issue of the high-level overview of ontology.

The tool allows to work effectively with large ontologies, but requires more competencies from the user in ontology engineering as well as tool interface and its options.

3.5 Ontodia - Online OWL and RDF Diagramming Tool

Ontodia [24,26] is a JavaScript-based open source solution for the ontologies visualization. It supports visualization of all types of ontology elements, including classes, individuals, all types of relations defined (Fig. 5); automatic graphs layout, export as an image, graphical zoom.

On the other hand, when the ontology is large enough, it is impossible to overview the full ontology structure when all concepts are displayed. A user can start with the blank space and drag the concepts from the panel (where they are organized as a taxonomy), sequentially disclosing the ontology elements through the selection of interested classes, individuals, and relationships (Fig. 6). But it is also can be not easy when the user does not know what concepts are main and how they are organized and linked.

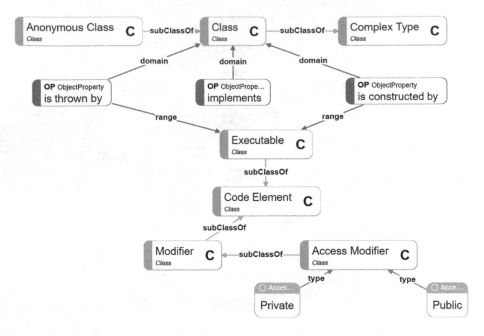

Fig. 5. Ontodia: visualization of CodeOntology fragment

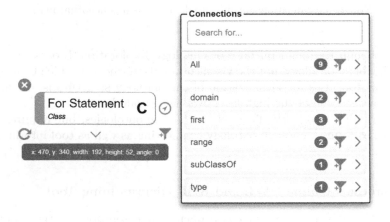

Fig. 6. Ontodia: sequential disclosure of ontology elements through the selection of interested classes, individuals and relationships

Also, this tool can work with RDF files or any SPARQL endpoint as a data source but does not work as a standalone application and requires to include the data source in the javascript code.

As it is an open source project, the functionality can be extended using different approaches including mentioned above.

4 Comparative Analysis of Software Tools for Graph-Based Ontology Visualization

We tried to compare the features of software tools mentioned above in the context of the task of graph-based visualization of large ontology. We defined the criteria for comparing that seem to us most important and informative for the considered problem. The results of the comparative analysis are presented in the Table 1.

Table 1. Comparison of software tools for graph-based ontology visualization

Software tool	Protege with OntoGraf plugin	WebVOWL	Ontology Exploration Tool (in Hozo)	KC-Viz in Neon Toolkit	Ontodia
SPARQL-endpoint as a data source	Not available	Not available	Not available	Not available	Available (endpoint is hardcoded)
Visualization of classes and instances	Yes (OntoGraf)	Classes only	Yes	Classes only	Yes
Visualization of the ontology after transformation (using visualization patterns)	No	No	No	No	No
Creation of ontology by specifying graph	No (only manual graph creation using ontology concepts)	No	No	No (only manual graph creation using ontology concepts)	No (only manual graph creation using ontology concepts)
Visualization of subset of elements/ fragment of ontology	Manual adding the ontology elements to the workspace with graph and nodes expansion (OntoGraf)	Only graph scaling and scrolling	No (only full ontology visualization)	Yes (visualization of key concepts and manual expansion of these concepts)	Manual adding the ontology elements to the workspace with graph

(continued)

Table 1. (*continued*)

Software tool	Protege with OntoGraf plugin	WebVOWL	Ontology Exploration Tool (in Hozo)	KC-Viz in Neon Toolkit	Ontodia
Search of ontology elements	Search of classes and individuals, graph visualization with graph rebuilding	Search of classes and relations with search string autocomplete, results highlighting on the graph	Search of classes	No	Sequential search of classes, individuals and relations
Visualization of the ontology with reasoning results	No	No	No	No	Yes (if supported by backend connected with SPARQL-endpoint)

5   Conclusion and Future Work

In this paper, we have compared some visualization approaches as well as software tools for the purpose of their application for visualization of large ontologies in learning. We faced this problem during our work on the project devoted to the collaborative construction of the domain information space based on the cognitive spaces of individuals or groups in learning and scientific research. The considered task defines a number of specific requirements for visual representation of the ontology, and none of the existing software tools provide the possibilities to satisfy these requirements. We chose the open-source javascript tool Ontodia as a promising visualization environment due to the following advantages. It allows connecting to the SPARQL-endpoint as a data source to separate the ontology storage and viewing/editing functions and provides collaborative developing, sharing and exploring the ontology. Also, this tool allows visualizing the ontology derived knowledge, as well as originally defined knowledge because the reasoning engine works separately from the ontology storage. Ontodia provides the possibilities for visualization of all the types of ontology elements, search and visualization of the search results, for the creation of ontology graph by different ways.

As Ontodia is open source project, it can be improved and extended with additional approaches, algorithms, and functions. The integration the KC-Viz algorithm into the Ontodia library seems to be a promising way to fix the main shortcomings and improve the usability of this tool and allows the user to start the domain ontology studying from the most important concepts.

Further evolution of the project implies extending the Ontodia diagramming tool with the functionality based on the approaches reviewed above (particularly, KC-Viz approach) that allows improving an efficiency of ontological modeling.

Acknowledgement. This paper presents the results of research carried out under the RFBR grant 15-07-03541 Intelligent support of decision making in management of large scale systems on the base of integration of different types of reasoning on ontological knowledge.

References

1. Acker, L., Porter, B.: Extracting viewpoints from knowledge bases. In: Proceedings of the Twelfth National Conference on Artificial Intelligence, AAAI 1994, vol. 1, pp. 547–552. American Association for Artificial Intelligence, Menlo Park (1994). http://dl.acm.org/citation.cfm?id=199288.199322
2. Anikin, A., Kultsova, M., Zhukova, I., Sadovnikova, N., Litovkin, D.: Knowledge based models and software tools for learning management in open learning network. In: Kravets, A., Shcherbakov, M., Kultsova, M., Iijima, T. (eds.) JCKBSE 2014. CCIS, vol. 466, pp. 156–171. Springer, Cham (2014). doi:10.1007/978-3-319-11854-3_15
3. Anikin, A., Litovkin, D., Kultsova, M., Sarkisova, E.: Ontology-based collaborative development of domain information space for learning and scientific research. In: Ngonga Ngomo, A.-C., Křemen, P. (eds.) KESW 2016. CCIS, vol. 649, pp. 301–315. Springer, Cham (2016). doi:10.1007/978-3-319-45880-9_23
4. Barzdins, J., Barzdins, G., Cerans, K., Liepins, R., Sprogis, A.: OWLGrED: a UML style graphical notation and editor for OWL 2. In: Sirin, E., Clark, K. (eds.) Proceedings of the 7th International Workshop on OWL: Experiences and Directions (OWLED 2010), San Francisco, California, USA, 21–22 June 2010. CEUR Workshop Proceedings, vol. 614. CEUR-WS.org (2010). http://ceur-ws.org/Vol-614/owled2010_submission_5.pdf
5. Catenazzi, N., Sommaruga, L., Mazza, R.: User-friendly ontology editing and visualization tools: the OWLeasyVIZ approach. In: 2009 13th International Conference Information Visualisation. pp. 283–288, July 2009
6. CodeOntology. https://doi.org/10.5281/zenodo.577939
7. Dudáš, M., Zamazal, O., Svátek, V.: Roadmapping and navigating in the ontology visualization landscape. In: Janowicz, K., Schlobach, S., Lambrix, P., Hyvönen, E. (eds.) EKAW 2014. LNCS (LNAI), vol. 8876, pp. 137–152. Springer, Cham (2014). doi:10.1007/978-3-319-13704-9_11
8. Erdmann, M., Waterfeld, W.: Overview of the NeOn toolkit. In: Suárez-Figueroa, M.C., Gómez-Pérez, A., Motta, E., Gangemi, A. (eds.) Ontology Engineering in a Networked World, pp. 281–301. Springer, Heidelberg (2012). doi:10.1007/978-3-642-24794-1_13
9. Espinoza, M., Gómez-Pérez, A., Mena, E.: Enriching an ontology with multilingual information. In: Bechhofer, S., Hauswirth, M., Hoffmann, J., Koubarakis, M. (eds.) ESWC 2008. LNCS, vol. 5021, pp. 333–347. Springer, Heidelberg (2008). doi:10.1007/978-3-540-68234-9_26

10. Freitas, C., Luzzardi, P.R.G., Cava, R.A., Winckler, M., Pimenta, M.S., Nedel, L.P.: On evaluating information visualization techniques. In: Proceedings of the Working Conference on Advanced Visual Interfaces, AVI 2002, pp. 373–374. ACM, New York (2002). http://doi.acm.org/10.1145/1556262.1556326
11. Herman, I., Melancon, G., Marshall, M.S.: Graph visualization and navigation in information visualization: a survey. IEEE Trans. Vis. Comput. Graph. **6**(1), 24–43 (2000)
12. Hop, W., de Ridder, S., Frasincar, F., Hogenboom, F.: Using hierarchical edge bundles to visualize complex ontologies in glow. In: Proceedings of the 27th Annual ACM Symposium on Applied Computing. SAC 2012, pp. 304–311. ACM, New York (2012). http://doi.acm.org/10.1145/2245276.2245338
13. Hozo: Ontology editor. http://www.hozo.jp
14. IsaViz: A Visual Authoring Tool for RDF. https://www.w3.org/2001/11/IsaViz/
15. Jambalaya - Protege plug-in. https://protegewiki.stanford.edu/wiki/Jambalaya
16. Johnson, B., Shneiderman, B.: Tree-maps: a space-filling approach to the visualization of hierarchical information structures. In: Proceedings of the IEEE Conference on Visualization, Visualization 1991, pp. 284–291, October 1991
17. Kozaki, K., Hirota, T., Mizoguchi, R.: Understanding an ontology through divergent exploration. In: Antoniou, G., Grobelnik, M., Simperl, E., Parsia, B., Plexousakis, D., Leenheer, P., Pan, J. (eds.) ESWC 2011. LNCS, vol. 6643, pp. 305–320. Springer, Heidelberg (2011). doi:10.1007/978-3-642-21034-1_21
18. Kultsova, M., Anikin, A., Litovkin, D.: An ontology-based approach to collaborative development of domain information space. In: Proceedings of the 12th International Conference on Educational Technologies (EDUTE 2016), Proceedings of the 10th International Conference on Business Administration (ICBA 2016), Barcelona, Spain, 13–15 February 2016, pp. 13–19 (2016). http://www.wseas.us/e-library/conferences/2016/barcelona/EDBA/EDBA-01.pdf
19. Kultsova, M., Anikin, A., Zhukova, I., Dvoryankin, A.: Ontology-based learning content management system in programming languages domain. In: Kravets, A., Shcherbakov, M., Kultsova, M., Shabalina, O. (eds.) CIT&DS 2015. CCIS, pp. 767–777. Springer, Cham (2015). doi:10.1007/978-3-319-23766-4_61
20. Liepins, R., Grasmanis, M., Bojars, U.: OWLGrED ontology visualizer. In: Verborgh, R., Mannens, E. (eds.) Proceedings of the ISWC Developers Workshop, Co-located with the 13th International Semantic Web Conference (ISWC 2014), Riva del Garda, Italy, 19 October 2014, CEUR Workshop Proceedings, vol. 1268, pp. 37–42. CEUR-WS.org (2014). http://ceur-ws.org/Vol-1268/paper7.pdf
21. Lohmann, S., Negru, S., Haag, F., Ertl, T.: Visualizing ontologies with VOWL. Semant. Web **7**(4), 399–419 (2016). http://dx.doi.org/10.3233/SW-150200
22. Lomov, P.: Primenenie patternov ontologicheckogo prroektirovaniya dlya sozdaniya i ispolzovaniya ontologiy v ramkah integrirovannogo prostranstva znaniy. Ontologya proektirovaniya **5**, 233–245 (2015)
23. Motta, E., Mulholland, P., Peroni, S., d'Aquin, M., Gomez-Perez, J.M., Mendez, V., Zablith, F.: A novel approach to visualizing and navigating ontologies. In: Aroyo, L., Welty, C., Alani, H., Taylor, J., Bernstein, A., Kagal, L., Noy, N., Blomqvist, E. (eds.) ISWC 2011. LNCS, vol. 7031, pp. 470–486. Springer, Heidelberg (2011). doi:10.1007/978-3-642-25073-6_30
24. Mouromtsev, D., Pavlov, D., Emelyanov, Y., Morozov, A., Razdyakonov, D., Galkin, M.: The simple, web-based tool for visualization and sharing of semantic data and ontologies. In: CEUR Workshop Proceedings, p. 77 (2015)
25. NeOn toolkit. http://neon-toolkit.org

26. OntoDia. http://www.ontodia.org
27. OntoViz. http://protegewiki.stanford.edu/wiki/OntoViz
28. OWLViz. https://protegewiki.stanford.edu/wiki/OWLViz
29. Peroni, S., Motta, E., d'Aquin, M.: Identifying key concepts in an ontology, through the integration of cognitive principles with statistical and topological measures. In: Domingue, J., Anutariya, C. (eds.) ASWC 2008. LNCS, vol. 5367, pp. 242–256. Springer, Heidelberg (2008). doi:10.1007/978-3-540-89704-0_17
30. Plaisant, C., Grosjean, J., Bederson, B.B.: Spacetree: supporting exploration in large node link tree, design evolution and empirical evaluation. In: IEEE Symposium on Information Visualization, INFOVIS 2002, pp. 57–64 (2002)
31. RDF Gravity. https://www.w3.org/2001/sw/wiki/RDFGravity
32. Sarkar, M., Brown, M.H.: Graphical fisheye views of graphs. In: Proceedings of the SIGCHI Conference on Human Factors in Computing Systems, CHI 1992, pp. 83–91. ACM, New York (1992). http://doi.acm.org/10.1145/142750.142763
33. Shneiderman, B.: Tree visualization with tree-maps: 2-D space-filling approach. ACM Trans. Graph. **11**(1), 92–99 (1992). http://doi.acm.org/10.1145/102377.115768
34. Shneiderman, B.: The eyes have it: a task by data type taxonomy for information visualizations. In: Proceedings of the 1996 IEEE Symposium on Visual Languages, VL 1996, pp. 336–343 (1996). http://dl.acm.org/citation.cfm?id=832277.834354
35. TopBraid Composer. http://www.topquadrant.com/tools/modeling-topbraid-composer-standard-edition/
36. VisioOWL. https://sites.google.com/site/semanticsimulations2/visioowl
37. Visual Ontology Modeler. http://thematix.com/tools/vom/
38. VOWL: Visual Notation for OWL Ontologies. http://vowl.visualdataweb.org/v2/
39. Wang, T.D., Parsia, B.: CropCircles: topology sensitive visualization of OWL class hierarchies. In: Cruz, I., Decker, S., Allemang, D., Preist, C., Schwabe, D., Mika, P., Uschold, M., Aroyo, L.M. (eds.) ISWC 2006. LNCS, vol. 4273, pp. 695–708. Springer, Heidelberg (2006). doi:10.1007/11926078_50

Application of Syntagmatic Patterns
to Evaluate Answers to Open-Ended Questions

Anton Zarubin[1(✉)], Albina Koval[1], Aleksey Filippov[2],
and Vadim Moshkin[2]

[1] The Bonch-Bruevich Saint-Petersburg State University
of Telecommunication, Saint-Petersburg, Russia
{azarubin, akoval}@sut.ru
[2] Ulyanovsk State Technical University, Ulyanovsk, Russia
{al.filippov, v.moshkin}@ulstu.ru

Abstract. Open-ended questions are questions that allow someone to give a free-form answer. Analysis and evaluation of answers to open-ended questions require automation. Experts who develop standards of free-form answers use uncertain information. Uncertainty may appear in cases of synonymy, polysemy, insufficiency or redundancy of the object description. Therefore, fuzziness is the most common type of uncertainty in activities related to the evaluation of answers to open-ended questions. This paper describes the methodology for evaluation free-form answers using knowledge discovery methods. Methods of knowledge discovery consider the uncertainty and fuzziness in the answers to open-ended questions. This article also describes the architecture of the expert system of electronic testing that implements the developed methodology.

Keywords: Fuzzy ontology · Open-end questions · Syntagmatic patterns · Free-form answers · Semantics · Knowledge discovery

1 Introduction

The application of distance education methods using modern pedagogical, information and telecommunication technologies is an important and promising direction of the development of the education system.

Traditional testing technologies (closed-ended questions) do not allow to evaluate the level of knowledge of distance-education students. Modification of classical models and testing techniques implies the development of tools for analyzing the free-form answers of the tested.

Fuzzy description of the state of objects in the domain does not allow us to use classical measures of distance estimation to find solutions in the space of fuzzy values. A different approach is needed, other methods and means for solving the tasks of a taxonomy of such knowledge.

Knowledge Discovery methods allow solving metric definition problems in the knowledge space described both by crisp and fuzzy data.

Hybridization of Different forms of knowledge representation allows fully describing the state of objects.

© Springer International Publishing AG 2017
A. Kravets et al. (Eds.): CIT&DS 2017, CCIS 754, pp. 150–162, 2017.
DOI: 10.1007/978-3-319-65551-2_11

Using a fuzzy representation of domain knowledge in fuzzy ontology form (FuzzyOWL) allows the effective aggregation of large arrays of knowledge with fuzzy characteristics.

Many researchers currently work in the areas of using the ontological form of knowledge representation for solving applied problems, including for extracting semantics from free-form information resources: Bobillo and Straccia [2], Gao and Liu [4], Bianchini et al. [1], Guarino and Musen [8], Guizzardi et al. [9], Falbo et al. [3], Hotho et al. [10], Gruber [7], Medche [12], Gavrilova [5], Vagin and Mikhailov [14], Gribova and Kleshev [6], Zagorulko [15], Kleschev [11], Smirnov [13].

Utilities of linguistic analysis of the text (morphology, syntax) (Russian Morphological Dictionary, StarLing, Cibola/Oleada, Mystem, Link Grammar Parser for Russian, etc.) and programs for semantic text analysis (AskNet, RussianContextOptimizer, Ontos, Google Desktop, Yandex.Server etc.) embedded in electronic testing systems to evaluate answers to open-ended questions.

These programs search for common words, calculate their density in the text, look for matches for these words in semantic tables, build tokens in accordance with the context. These programs can be a tool for search engines (Yandex, Google, etc.) and also for SEO-optimization of sites and portals. However, they cannot solve the problems of complex processing, analysis, classification, and evaluation of free-form answers without the participation of the teacher at the verification stage.

Thus, the development of fuzzy models of knowledge representation in the process of evaluating the correctness of the answer to open-ended questions and their implementation will allow us to solve the problem of automating the analysis and evaluation of the results of electronic testing.

2 Methodology for Evaluation Answers to Open-Ended Questions

2.1 Formal Knowledge Base Model

The application of mathematical and statistical approaches for evaluating of the answer to an open-ended question does not allow taking into account the morphological, semantic and syntagmatic features of natural language. It is necessary to extract concepts of the subject area in the form of syntagmatic units from the answer to evaluate answers to open-ended questions. A syntagmatic unit is a collection of several words united by the principle of semantic-grammatical-phonetic compatibility.

Features of this approach are:

- all synonyms are reduced to the same concept;
- multivalued words are assigned to different concepts;
- the links between concepts and corresponding words (terms) are described and can be used to generate a new standard of the answer;
- a standard of the answer in the expert system is presented by syntagmatic units.

It is necessary to develop fuzzy domain ontology for successful extraction of concepts from the answer and formation of its syntagmatic pattern.

Ontology is developed by an expert and contains:

- set of concepts of a subject domain,
- set of open-ended question,
- set of standards of answers to open-ended questions,
- set of terms used to form syntagmatic patterns (Fig. 1).

Formally:

$$O = \langle O^{Pr}, O^{QA}, O^L, R, SP \rangle,$$

where

O – ontology of the expert system;

O^{Pr} – the representation of the subject area in the form of a hierarchy of concepts;

O^{QA} – QA (*questions-answers*) – is the basis of the expert system, containing set of open-ended questions and standards of answers to open-ended questions;

O^L – linguistic basis of the expert system. It contains terms that describe the concepts of the domain. Also terms are used in the formation of syntagmatic patterns;

R – set of inclusion relations, synonyms and "question-object". They are used to create links between objects of the domain ontology;

SP – set of syntagmatic patterns of the domain ontology.

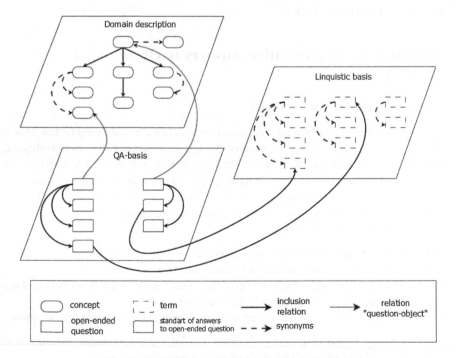

Fig. 1. The structure of the fuzzy domain ontology

Figure 2 shows a fragment of fuzzy ontology that describes the "Administration of LAN". The expert included in the ontology concept "OSI model". The concept "OSI model" includes the following concepts: "Physical layer", "Data Link layer", "Network layer", etc. In this example, we will only consider the fragment of the "LAN administration" ontology that describes the physical layer of the OSI model.

The concept of "Physical layer" is related to the relation of synonymy with the concept "Level 1 of the OSI model" and the inclusion relation with the concept "Physical layer devices". The following concepts of the domain ontology are related to devices of the physical level:

- «Network hub» is related to the relation of synonymy with the concepts «Multiport repeater» and «Hub»;
- «Repeater» is related to the relation of synonymy with the concepts «Receiver» and «Transmitter».

In addition, the expert related the open-ended question "List the devices of the 1st level of the OSI model" with the concept "Device of the physical level".

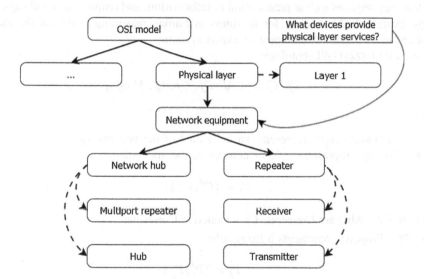

Fig. 2. Fragment of fuzzy domain ontology "Administration of LAN"

For the open-ended question "What devices provide physical layer services?" we have the syntagmatic pattern in the SWRL-rule form:

$$V^{High}(\text{network hub} \vee \text{multiport repeater} \vee \text{hub}) \wedge V^{High}(\text{repeater} \vee \text{receiver}$$
$$\vee \text{ transmitter}) \wedge W^{High} \rightarrow \text{ correct},$$

where $V = \{zero,\ low,\ below\ average,\ average,\ above\ average,\ high\}$ – probability of appearance of a syntagmatic unit of concepts of fuzzy domain ontology in answer to an open-ended question;

$W = \{low,\ below\ average,\ average,\ above\ average,\ high\}$ – the minimal weight of correct syntagmatic units of concepts of fuzzy domain ontology in the answer with which the answer to an open-ended question is considered correct.

The problem of hybridization of various approaches of representation of knowledge about the subject area in expert systems is currently relevant. The most popular models of knowledge representation in expert systems are:

- production rule system;
- frames;
- semantic networks;
- predicate logic;
- ontologies.

Hybridization of different formats of knowledge representation on an ontological basis is convenient for automated processing in expert systems and human perception.

Ontology requires a clear presentation of information, and reality can not always be clearly expressed. Accounting for fuzziness in human reasoning is one of the most important tasks in the development of expert systems

Formally FuzzyOWL-ontology:

$$I = (If,\ Cf,\ Pf,\ Af,\ Df,\ Qf,\ Lf,\ Modf),$$

where

- If – Individual simply represents an individual of the vocabulary;
- Cf – Concept, represents a fuzzy concept of the vocabulary:

$$C_f = \{C_f^A, C_f^C\},$$

where C_f^A - Abstract Concepts, C_f^C - Concrete Concepts;
- Pf – Property, represents a fuzzy role:

$$P_f = \{P_f^A, P_f^C\},$$

where P_f^A - Object Properties, P_f^C - Datatype Properties;
- Df – Axiom represents the axioms:

$$D_f = \{A_f^{ABox}, A_f^{TBox}, A_f^{RBox}\},$$

where A_f^{ABox} – The Abox contains role assertions between individuals and membership assertions, A_f^{TBox} – the Tbox contains assertions about concepts such as subsumption and equivalence, A_f^{RBox}- the RBox contains assertions about roles and role hierarchies. Some of the axioms are subclasses of FuzzyAxiom, which indicates that the axiom is not either true or false, but that it is true to some extent.

- *Of* – Degree represents a degree which can be added to an instance of FuzzyAxiom:

$$Of = \{LD_f,\, MD_f,\, ND_f,\, Var_f\},$$

LD_f – Linguistic Degrees, MD_f – Modifier Degrees, ND_f – Numeric Degrees, Var_f – Variables.

- *Lf* – Fuzzy Logic represents different families of fuzzy operators that can be used to give different semantics to the logic.

$$L_f = \{L_f^{Luk},\, L_f^{Zad},\, L_f^{Goed},\, L_f^{\mathrm{Pr}\,od}\},$$

where L_f^{Luk} - fuzzy operators logic of Lukasiewicz, L_f^{Zad} - fuzzy operators logic of Zadeh, L_f^{Goed} - fuzzy operators logic of Goedel, $L_f^{\mathrm{Pr}\,od}$ – fuzzy operators of produc logic;

- *Modf* – Fuzzy Modifier represents a fuzzy modifier which can be used to modify the membership function of a fuzzy concept or a fuzzy role. Current subclasses are Linear Fuzzy Modifier and Triangular Fuzzy Modifier.

Table 1 shows the elements of fuzzy axioms FuzzyOWL, as well as their possible representation.

Concepts and relations in natural language are the raw material for constructing the ontology. Concepts and relationships are fuzzy, inaccurate and do not have hard boundaries. Therefore, models using linguistic variables, fuzzy sets, fuzzy relationships, fuzzy graphs and fuzzy trees, fuzzy constraints, fuzzy relational and algebraic systems are an adequate means of formalizing the description of the subject area.

2.2 The Method to Evaluate Answers to Open-Ended Questions Using Syntagmatic Patterns

Formally the method to evaluate answers to open-ended questions using syntagmatic patterns:

$$F(Q,A) = \min_{k=1}^{S}\left(\hat{F}(Q_k,A)\right),\ F(Q,A) \in [0,\,1]\,, \tag{1}$$

where S – number of standard syntagmatic patterns for a particular open-ended question;

$\hat{F}(Q_k,A)$ – the value of an assessment of a correctness of the response to an open-ended question with a syntagmatic pattern of k-th standard of the answer. This value is calculated by the equation:

Table 1. Elements of fuzzy axioms in FuzzyOWL

№	Element	Possible values	Representation in FuzzyOWL

1	LD_f— Linguistic Degrees	«high», «above average», «low»	`<AnnotationAssertion>`
			
			 `<AnnotationProperty IRI="#fuzzyLabel"/>`
			
			 `<IRI>#HighLoad</IRI>`
			
			 `<Literal datatypeIRI="&rdf;PlainLiteral">fuzzyOwl2 fuzzyType="datatype";`
			
			 `Datatype type="rightshoulder"; a="15.0"; b="30.0";/fuzzyOwl2</Literal>`
			
			 `</AnnotationAssertion>`

2	MD_f— Modifier Degrees	«very», «not very»	`type="modified"`
			`modifier="very"`
3	ND_f— Numeric Degrees	$0 \leq ND \leq 1$	`Degree Value=0,6`
4	Var_f— Variables	a, b,c, k1, k2	`b="30.0";`
5	L_f— Fuzzy Logic	Zadeh, Lukasiewicz Goedel and Product	`hasSemantics="Zadeh"`
6	$Modf$— Fuzzy Modifier	Linear, Triangular	`<Datatype type="triangular" a="32.0" b="41.0" c="50.0" />`

$$\hat{F}(Q_k, A) = \max\left(1 - \frac{\text{count}(Q_k, A)}{\text{count}(A)}, \frac{\sum_{i=1}^{t}\left(V_i^{Q_K} - V_i^{A}\right)}{\sum_{i=1}^{t} V_i^{Q_K}}\right),$$

where Q_k – syntagmatic pattern of k-th standard of the answer to an open-ended question;

A – syntagmatic pattern of the answer to an open-ended question;

count(Q_k, A) – count of equal syntagmatic units in k-th standard of the answer and in answer to the open-ended question;

count(A) – count of syntagmatic units in answer to an open-ended question;

V_i^Q, V_i^A – the probability of appearance of i-th syntagmatic unit in a standard of the answer to an open-ended question and in answer to an open-ended question. If i-th syntagmatic unit is missing in answer to an open-ended question, then probability of appearance of this syntagmatic unit is zero;

t – count of syntagmatic units in the standard of the answer to an open-ended question, where the probability of appearance of this syntagmatic unit is more or equal the value of the minimal weight of correct syntagmatic unit in the answer.

Expression 1 defines the minimal distance between a syntagmatic pattern of the answer to an open question and the set of syntagmatic patterns of the standard of the answer to an open-ended question in an interval from 0 to 1. The greater this distance, the less level of correctness of answer to an open-ended question.

3   Evaluation of Answers to Open-Ended Questions Based on Syntagmatic Patterns

To evaluate the effectiveness of the algorithms developed, a series of experiments were carried out.

First Experiment. For an open-ended question: "What devices provide physical layer services?" the standard of the answer is:

network hub, repeater, Ethernet adapter, patch cable, mau, port.

In process of evaluation of answer to an open-ended question, the relation of synonymy of fuzzy domain ontology is considered. For example, instead of a syntagma *network hub* use of a syntagma *hub* is admissible.

The syntagmatic pattern of the standard of an open-ended question "What devices provide physical layer services?" is:

$$V^{High}\&\text{network hub} \wedge V^{High}\&\text{repeater}$$

$$\wedge V^{AboveAverage}\&\text{Ethernet adapter} \wedge V^{Average}\&\text{patch cable}$$

$$\wedge V^{Low}\&\text{mau} \wedge V^{Low}\&\text{port} \wedge W^{AboveAverage} \rightarrow \text{correct,}$$

where & - the set of terms that are related to the relation of synonymy of fuzzy domain ontology with the current syntagmatic unit.

On this open-ended question the following answers were given:

1. Hub, Ethernet adapter, router, a personal computer.
2. Hub, repeater.

3. Network hub, Ethernet adapter, patch cable.
4. Computer, display, first level, osi, model, repeater, Ethernet adapter.

For transform the answer to an open-ended question to a syntagmatic pattern it is necessary to extract the syntagmatic units from the text of the answer. To each syntagmatic unit, the probability of appearance of this syntagmatic unit in the answer to an open-ended question is set with taking into account the relation of synonymy of the fuzzy domain ontology. If the standard of the answer to an open-ended question is contains the syntagmatic unit of the answer to a question, then the probability of appearance of this syntagmatic unit is set as the probability of appearance of a syntagmatic unit of the standard of the answer. Otherwise, the probability of appearance of the syntagmatic unit of the answer to a question is V^{Zero}. Syntagmatic patterns for each of answers are:

$$A_1 = V^{High} \text{hub} \wedge V^{AboveAverage} \text{ethernet adapter}$$
$$\wedge V^{Zero} \text{router} \wedge V^{Zero} \text{personal computer.}$$

$$A_2 = V^{High} \text{hub} \wedge V^{High} \text{repeater.}$$

$$A_3 = V^{High} \text{network hub} \wedge V^{AboveAverage} \text{ethernet adapter} \wedge V^{Average} \text{patch cable.}$$

$$A_4 = V^{Zero} \text{computer} \wedge V^{Zero} \text{display} \wedge V^{Zero} \text{first level}$$
$$\wedge V^{Zero} \text{osi} \wedge V^{Zero} \text{model} \wedge V^{High} \text{repeater}$$
$$\wedge V^{AboveAverage} \text{ethernet adapter.}$$

After the process of defuzzification of syntagmatic patterns of the standard of answer and answer to an open-ended question "What devices provide physical layer services?" with a value of minimal weight 0.8 the values of the probability of appearance are:

- V^{High} is 1;
- $V^{AboveAverage}$ is 0.8;
- $V^{Average}$ and V^{Low} is 0 because their values of the probability of appearance 0.6 and 0.2 are less than the value of minimal weight of correct syntagmatic unit in the answer (0.8);
- V^{Zero} is 0.

After process of defuzzification the syntagmatic patterns looks like:

$$Q = \& \text{network hub } (1) \wedge \& \text{repeater } (1) \wedge \& \text{ethernet adapter}(0.8) \wedge \& \text{patch}$$
$$\text{cable } (0) \wedge \& \text{mau } (0) \wedge \& \text{port}(0).$$

$$A_1 = \text{hub } (1) \wedge \text{ethernet adapter } (0.8) \wedge \text{router}(0)$$
$$\wedge \text{personal computer } (0).$$

$$A_2 = \text{hub } (1) \wedge \text{repeater } (1).$$

$$A_3 = \text{network hub } (1) \wedge \text{ethernet adapter } (0.8) \wedge \text{patch cable } (0).$$

$$A_4 = \text{computer } (0) \wedge \text{display } (0) \wedge \text{first level } (0) \wedge \text{osi } (0)$$
$$\wedge \text{model } (0) \wedge \text{repeater } (1) \wedge \text{ethernet adapter } (0.8).$$

Calculate the values of an evaluation of a correctness of the answers to an open-ended question:

$$\hat{F}(Q, A_1) = \max\left(1 - \frac{2}{4}, \frac{(1-1) + (1-0) + (0,8-0,8)}{2.8}\right) = \max(0.5, \ 0.36) = 0.5$$

$F(Q, A_1) = 0.5.$

$$\hat{F}(Q, A_2) = \max\left(1 - \frac{2}{2}, \frac{(1-1) + (1-1) + (0,8-0)}{2.8}\right) = \max(0, \ 0.28) = 0.28$$

$F(Q, A_2) = 0.28.$

$$\hat{F}(Q, A_3) = \max\left(1 - \frac{2}{3}, \frac{(1-1) + (1-0) + (0,8-0,8)}{2.8}\right) = \max(0.34, \ 0.36) = 0.36$$

$F(Q, A_3) = 0.36.$

$$\hat{F}(Q, A_4) = \max\left(1 - \frac{1}{6}, \frac{(1-0) + (1-1) + (0,8-0,8)}{2.8}\right) = \max(0.84, \ 0.36) = 0.84$$

$F(Q, A_4) = 0.84.$

In the case of the value of a threshold of a level of a correctness of the answer to an open-ended question "What devices provide physical layer services?" equal 0.4 the correct answers are A_2 and A_3.

Second Experiment. For an open-ended question: "How does the network hub work?" the standard of the answer is:

The hub receives data from one port and forwards it to other ports.
The hub retransmits the incoming signal from one of the ports to the signal to all other (connected) ports.

The syntagmatic pattern of the standard of an open-ended question "How does the network hub works?" is:

$$V^{Low} \ \&\text{network hub} \wedge V^{High}(\&\text{recieve})$$
$$\wedge V^{High}(\&\text{incoming signal}) \wedge V^{High} \&(\text{from one} * \text{port} *)$$
$$\wedge V^{High}(\&\text{to} * \text{other}) \wedge V^{High}(\&\text{port}) \wedge W^{High} \rightarrow \text{correct},$$

where * - some number of words or symbols;
& - the set of terms that are related to the relation of synonymy of fuzzy domain ontology with the current syntagmatic unit.

On this open-ended question the following answers were given:

5. The hub retransmits data to all ports.
6. The hub concentrates the data.
7. Routes the packages.
8. The hub forwards the input data to other ports.

Calculate the values of an evaluation of a correctness of the answers to an open-ended question:

$$F(Q, A_1) = \max \left(1 - \frac{3}{5}, \frac{(1-1)+(1-1)+(1-0)+(1-0)+(1-1)}{5} \right) = \max(0.4,\ 0.4) = 0.4$$

$$F(Q, A_1) = 0.4.$$

$$F(Q, A_2) = \max \left(1 - \frac{1}{3}, \frac{(1-1)+(1-0)+(1-0)+(1-0)+(1-0)}{5} \right) = \max(0.67,\ 0.8) = 0.8$$

$$F(Q, A_2) = 0.8.$$

$$F(Q, A_3) = \max \left(1 - \frac{0}{2}, \frac{(1-0)+(1-0)+(1-0)+(1-0)+(1-0)}{5} \right) = \max(1,\ 1) = 1$$

$$F(Q, A_3) = 1.$$

$$F(Q, A_4) = \max \left(1 - \frac{4}{5}, \frac{(1-1)+(1-1)+(1-0)+(1-1)+(1-1)}{5} \right) = \max(0.2,\ 0.2) = 0.2$$

$$F(Q, A_4) = 0.2.$$

In the case of the value of a threshold of a level of a correctness of the answer to an open-ended question "How does the network hub work?" equal 0.4 the correct answers are A_1 and A_4.

4   Architecture of the Expert System

The expert system of electronic testing was developed to confirm the effectiveness of our proposed algorithms for evaluation answers to open-ended questions.

The system is aimed at automating the processes of compiling a knowledge validation package for a specific subject area and evaluating the results of testing, in which the user answers the test questions in a free-form (open-ended questions).

Features of this system are:

1. The expert system includes mechanisms for automating the process of compiling a knowledge validation package for a particular subject area in a free form (open-ended questions).
2. The expert system contains a knowledge base and tools for its extension.
3. The expert system has built-in tools for automating the process of evaluating answers to open-ended questions.
4. The system has tools to provide integration with other test systems.

The architecture of the expert system is shown in the Fig. 3.

The expert system is implemented as a web service that has API for access to all the basic functions.

The development of an expert system in the form of a web service makes it possible to apply it as a cloud solution (SaaS) and provides the process of integration with other testing systems.

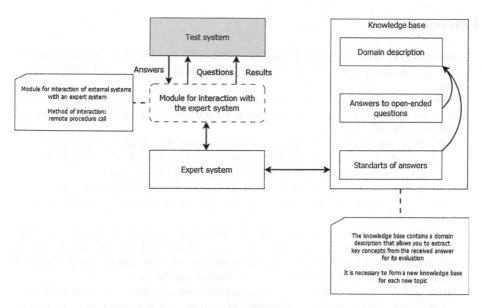

Fig. 3. Architecture of the expert system

The back-end of the expert system is implemented in the Java language using the Spring framework that facilitates the development of enterprise applications. All libraries, applications, and technologies used are free.

5   Conclusions

Thus, the mechanism of syntagmatic patterns proposed in this paper in combination with a fuzzy ontology makes it possible to effectively evaluate the answers to open-ended questions.

The developed expert system is an automated system for conducting electronic testing. The software complex is universal and can be applied in various fields of activity.

The developed software system conducts a complex analysis of the entire text:

- a certain scale is used to evaluate the answer to an open-ended question for the corresponding constructions of natural language. This scale allows for a more objective assessment.
- the system is self-learning that allows expanding the knowledge base, in the case when the mechanism of logical inference has not revealed correspondences with semantic matrices (in this case an expert is required).

Acknowledgements. This paper has been approved within the framework of the federal target project "R&D for Priority Areas of the Russian Science-and-Technology Complex Development for 2014-2020", government contract No 14.607.21.0164 on the subject "The development of architecture, methods and models to build software and hardware complex semantic analysis of semi-structured information resources on the Russian element base" (Application Code «2016-14-579-0009-0687»).

References

1. Bianchini, D., Antonellis, V.D., Pernici, B., Plebani, P.: Ontology-based methodology for e-service discovery. Inf. Syst. **31**, 361–380 (2006). doi:10.1016/j.is.2005.02.010. Elsevier Ltd.
2. Bobillo, F., Straccia, U.: FuzzyDL: an expressive fuzzy description logic reasoner. In: 17th IEEE International Conference on Fuzzy Systems, pp. 923–930. IEEE Press (2008). doi:10. 1109/FUZZY.2008.4630480
3. Falbo, R.A., Quirino, G.K., Nardi, J.C., Barcellos, M.P., Guizzardi, G., Guarino, N.: An ontology pattern language for service modeling. In: 31st Annual ACM Symposium on Applied Computing, pp. 321–326 (2016). doi:10.1145/2851613.2851840
4. Gao, M., Liu, C.: Extending OWL by fuzzy description logic. In: 17th IEEE International Conference on Tools with Artificial Intelligence, pp. 562–567. IEEE Press (2005). doi:10. 1109/ICTAI.2005.65
5. Gavrilova, T.A.: Ontologicheskii podkhod k upravleniiu znaniiami pri razrabotke korporativnykh informatsionnykh sistem (The ontological approach to knowledge management in the development of corporate information systems). Novosti iskusstvennogo intellekta (News Artif. Intell.) **2**(56), 24–29 (2003). Anakharsis. (in Russian)
6. Gribova, V.V., Kleshev, A.S.: Upravlenie proektirovaniem I realizatsiei polzovatelskogo interfeisa na osnove ontologiy (Managing the design and implementation of the user interface based on ontologies). Problemy Upravleniia (Manag. Issues) **2**, 58–62 (2006). Sensydat-Plus. (in Russian)
7. Gruber, T.: Ontology. In: Liu, L., Tamer Özsu, M. (eds.) Entry in the Encyclopedia of Database Systems, p. 1959. Springer US, New York (2009)
8. Guarino, N., Musen, M.A.: Ten years of applied ontology. Appl. Ontol. **10**(3–4), 169–170 (2015). doi:10.3233/AO-150160. IOS Press
9. Guizzardi, G., Guarino, N., Almeida, J.P.A.: Ontological considerations about the representation of events and endurants in business models. In: La Rosa, M., Loos, P., Pastor, O. (eds.) BPM 2016. LNCS, vol. 9850, pp. 20–36. Springer, Cham (2016). doi:10.1007/978-3-319-45348-4_2
10. Hotho, A., Staab, S., Stumme, G.: Ontologies improve text document clustering. In: Third IEEE Conference on Data Mining, pp. 541–544. IEEE Press (2003). doi:10.1109/ ICDM.2003.1250972
11. Kleschev, A.S.: Rol ontologii v programmirovanii. Chast 1. Analitika (The role of ontology in programming. Part 1. Analytics). Informatsionnye tekhnologii (Inf. Technol.) **10**, 42–46 (2008). New Technologies. (in Russian)
12. Medche, A.: Ontology learning for the semantic web. IEEE Intell. Syst. **16**, 72–79 (2002). doi:10.1109/5254.920602. IEEE Press
13. Smirnov, S.V.: Ontologicheskoe modelirovanie v situatsionnom upravlenii (Ontological modeling in situational management). Ontologiia proektirovaniia (Ontol. Des.) **2**(4), 16–24 (2012). New Engineering. (in Russian)
14. Vagin, V.N., Mikhailov, I.S.: Razrabotka metoda integratsii informatsionnykh system na osnove metamodelirovaniia i ontologii predmetnoi oblasti (Development of the method of integration of information systems based on metamodelling and ontology of the subject domain). Programmnye produkty I sistemy (Softw. Prod. Syst.) **1**, 22–26 (2008). CPS. (in Russian)
15. Zagorulko, Y.A.: Postroenie portalov nauchnykh znanii na osnove ontologii (Building scientific knowledge portals based on ontologies). Vychislitelnye tekhnologii (Comput. Technol.) **12**, 169–177 (2007). ICT SB RAS. (in Russian)

A Creative Model of Modern Company Management on the Basis of Semantic Technologies

Viktor Kuznetsov[1](✉), Dmitry Kornilov[2], Tatiana Kolmykova[3],
Ekaterina Garina[1], and Alexandr Garin[1]

[1] K. Minin Nizhny Novgorod State Pedagogical University,
1 Ulianova St., Nizhny Novgorod 603002, Russia
{kuzneczov-vp,e.p.garina,rp_nn}@mail.ru
[2] Nizhny Novgorod State Technical University,
41 Bolshaya Sankt-Peterburgskaya St., Nizhny Novgorod 173003, Russia
kornilov-d@yandex.ru
[3] Southwest State University, 94 50 let Oktabrya St., Kursk 305040, Russia
t_kolmykova@mail.ru

Abstract. This article is devoted to the search for a solution to a scientific and practical problem of the search for a replacement of the traditional model of company management of the form "human-human", related to high managerial expenses and the strong influence of "human factor". The purpose of the work is to develop a creative model of modern company management on the basis semantic technologies. The core of the methodology of this research is the systemic approach, which allows for the presentation of company management as a system of interconnected elements, and the "black box" approach which allows for the study of the system's reaction to the changes that take place in managerial processes. The authors offer a creative model that allows managing a modern company in the form "computer-human" with a perspective of its transformation into the form "computer-computer" with the distribution of semantic technologies. As a result of the research, the authors come to the conclusion that under the conditions of formation of the information society there appears a possibility of reducing the role of a human in the process of company management by means of automation of managerial processes. A perspective tool of the provision of such automation is semantic technologies, which allow bringing down the human's participation in the process of a modern company management to a minimum and replacing a lot of managers by one computer, as well as rationalization of managerial processes.

Keywords: Modern company management · Information society · Semantic technologies

1 Introduction

The global economic recession at the beginning of the 21st century showed the ineffectiveness of the traditional model of the modern company management, within which the managerial process has a form of "human-human", i.e., direct participation of a

© Springer International Publishing AG 2017
A. Kravets et al. (Eds.): CIT&DS 2017, CCIS 754, pp. 163–176, 2017.
DOI: 10.1007/978-3-319-65551-2_12

human as a manager and a managed subject. Firstly, this model predetermines high managerial expenses that emerge due to high expenditures for payment of managers' services and the necessity for the presence of several managers, each of which specializes only on one managerial process (e.g., financial manager, HR manager, etc.).

Most markets are peculiar for high power of consumers, which predetermines high dependence of success of business from its flexibility and the capability to offer innovational products and keep low prices. This is caused by changeability of consumer preferences and development of public needs in geometric progression, as well as the risk of reduction of payment capacity due to the reduction of the level of the population's income under the conditions of the crises that emerge within the cyclic fluctuations of the economy.

Secondly, this model is related to a high risk of incorrect (irrational) managerial decisions. A "human factor" is a reason for the non-optimal behavior of market agents, which leads to violation of the market balance and emergence of economic systems' crises. The consequences of its negative influence the company, leading to lost profit, and the society, on the whole, leading to ineffective satisfaction of public needs and non-optimal use of the existing resources.

This leads to a scientific and practical problem, related to the necessity for the development of a new model that allows eliminating these drawbacks. This research offers a hypothesis that under the conditions of formation of an information society, there appears a possibility of reducing the role of a human in the process of company management by means of automation of the managerial processes. A perspective tool of the provision of such automation is semantic technologies. The authors seek the goal of developing a creative model of the modern company management on the basis of semantic technologies.

2   Methodological Background

The sense and peculiarities of application of the existing (traditional) model of company management in various socio-economic conditions are described in the publications by [1–6, 11–13, 15, 16].

The semantic technologies were studied in a lot of works by modern authors, including [7–10, 14] etc.

The performed literature overview showed that the modern scholars agree on the necessity for improving the model of company management, but they offer no specific directions of its conduct. The works of modern authors emphasize a large potential of semantic technologies but do not describe the direct possibilities of application of these technologies in practice. This reflects the necessity for further elaboration of applied aspects of these spheres of scientific knowledge, as well as their complex study.

The core of the methodology of this research is the systemic approach, which allows presenting company management as a system of interconnected elements, and the "black box" approach, which provides the possibility for studying the reaction of the system to the changes that take place in managerial processes.

3 Perspectives of Implementing Semantic Technologies into the Managerial Processes of a Modern Company

We offer to implement semantic technologies into all managerial processes of a modern company. In the context of internal managerial processes, semantic technologies allow for the creation of a highly effective system of motivation and stimulation of personnel on the basis of personal characteristics of employees and their relations. Here we speak of automation of the processes of company's personnel management.

They also could be used for formation of highly effective teams among a company's employees on the basis of using the set inter-personal relations, this stimulating the increase of efficiency and innovational activity of personnel. This allows for automation of the process of managing the innovational activity of a company.

Semantic technologies allow for the improvement of the production process by eliminating insignificant components on the basis of existing incoming (resource capacity) and outgoing (efficiency) parameters and the priorities set by the manager. These technologies allow determining the optimal volume of production depending on the formalized results of marketing studies.

In the context of external managerial processes, semantic technologies could also be used for selecting the necessary infrastructural provision (e.g., the country of company's location, depending on the business climate, the creation of a network business all over the world depending on the set parameters of accessibility and resources' cost, etc.).

Semantic technologies have large perspectives in the aspect of managing the relations with the interested parties in a company's activity. Firstly, they allow for optimization of relations with suppliers of resources, as well as intermediaries and business partners, including decisions on participation in the market vertical and horizontal integration processes depending on the set strategic goals of business development, planned profits and risks.

These technologies allow for automation of such managerial processes and personnel hire – on the basis of the existing needs of the company in human resources and characteristics (competences) of candidates set in the digital form, attraction and usage of financial resources – on the basis of decisions on attraction of investments and taking credits from one of the potential lenders with various terms of the credit agreement, as well as attraction and usage of material resources on the basis of determination of their optimal quality and volume, on the basis of a company's capabilities in storage and sales.

Secondly, they allow for optimization of relations with consumers – directly in the B2C markets and through intermediaries in the B2B markets. Semantic technologies possess a large potential in managing the logistics and supply chains, optimization of means and directions of products sales, and marketing (consumers' loyalty management) on the basis of optimization of the marketing mix (product, price, promotion, and distribution).

Even in the relations with the state, semantic technologies are characterized by a large managerial potential. They allow for the automation of the company's accounting and its timely provision to the corresponding regulating state establishments on the basis of the set time parameters. They could also be used for optimization of taxation in case of successful formalization of qualitative parameters of the existing tax laws and peculiarities of business.

4   A Conceptual Model of Modern Company Management on the Basis of Semantic Technologies

The offered conceptual model of the modern company management on the basis of semantic technologies is shown in Fig. 1. This scheme is of a generalized character, so the system of company management is shown as a "black box".

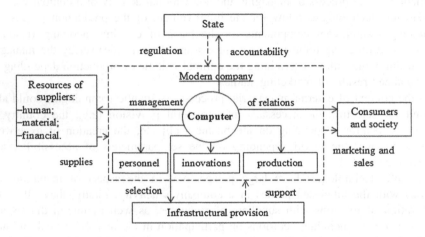

Fig. 1. Conceptual model of modern company management on the basis of semantic technologies

As is seen from Fig. 1, according to the offered model, the core of the system of modern company management is the computer, which performs all managerial functions. At that, the role of a human (manager) is brought down to the following:

- formalization of qualitative parameters of the managed objects and subjects: their qualities, connections, and relations;
- assigning weight coefficients (prioritization) to goals and tasks of the company's functioning and development.

Here we speak of simple mechanical work, though of large volume. However, it contains the elements of creativity – creative approach is necessary for the search for transferring the qualitative indicators into quantitative ones. As compared to the traditional model of company management, in the offered creative model a human (manager) performs a service function, providing the computer with the necessary information for the direct managerial decisions.

The most complicated stage of implementation of semantic technologies into the process of modern company management is the initial start of the system of automation of managerial processes, as it is a stage of the input of the main volume of parameters and of debugging of the system of computerized decision making. Of course, it is a long process, which should be done gradually, to avoid a crisis at the enterprise.

5 Modeling of Semantic Technologies Implementation into the Managerial Processes of a Modern Company

Based on the created theoretical platform, we develop the detailed models of implementation of semantic technologies into the managerial processes of a modern company.

5.1 Modeling of Implementation of Semantic Technologies into the Process of Management of Relations Between a Modern Company and the State

Application of semantic technologies in the process of management of a company's relations with the state supposes starting the system of electronic document turnover. This system includes the following four main components.

The first component: automation of the process of preparation of corporate financial and tax accounting. The system of electronic document turnover allows a user to introduce the minimum set of values of the main indicators, on the basis of which it calculated other indicators necessary for preparing the corporate financial and tax accounting. At that, the indicators that are mandatory for reflection and the indicators for internal usage, which are interesting for a company's management and accountability for higher management (business owners) are calculated.

The second component: automation of documenting a company's operation. Here we speak of delivery notes, sales slips, contracts, etc. It should be noted that most medium and large companies register all business operations in a print form. However, the electronic form does not make a document semantic.

Semantic technologies allow forming "clever documents", which are not a set of text but information accessible for computer processing. That's why completion of documents that accompany business operations of a modern company with the help of special semantic programs is a completely new form of document turnover. This allows evaluating the profitability of deals and taking them into consideration in corporate accounting before their completion, as well as performing further automatized logical processing of data depending on the emerging needs with the company's management.

The third component: tax optimization. With the presence of set parameter of the tax system, which − in case of mass distribution of semantic technologies − can be provided by tax bodies, such technologies allow evaluating the optimal characteristics of business (organizational and legal form, volume of sales, number of hired workers, region of location, use of the proper tax privileges, etc.) both at the stage of its creation and during decision making on the company's development.

The fourth component: automatized accounting for tax bodies. In certain countries − e.g., modern Russia, special requirements are set to financial and tax accounting. Moreover, the constant changes in the law lead to a change of the forms according to which corporate accounting should be completed.

In practice, this leads to the necessity for keeping a large staff who conduct the accounting of business's economic operations and to the incompatibility of the data from various years, presented in different forms. Implementation of semantic technologies due to the electronic data allows forming accounting in any form, and their automatized formula calculation allows transferring the data from one form into another, ensuring their absolute compatibility.

It is also possible to create conditions for automatic informing of tax bodies on certain or all business processes of a company. It is convenient in case of the corresponding requirements from the law. The offered model of the system of electronic document turnover of a modern company, created on the basis of semantic technologies, is presented in Fig. 2.

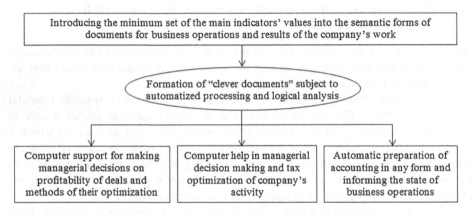

Fig. 2. The model of the system of electronic document turnover of a modern company, created on the basis of semantic technologies

5.2   Modeling of Implementation of Semantic Technologies into the Process of Managing the Infrastructural Provision of a Modern Company

Implementation of semantic technologies into the process of managing the infrastructural provision is seen in the context of automation of logistics. For that, the optimization task of the following form is prepared:

$$
\begin{cases}
\text{Profit} = \dfrac{\text{Accessibility of resources} * \text{Sales' volume}}{\text{Resources' cost} * \text{Transportation and sales' cost}} \rightarrow \max \\
\text{Accessibility of resources} \rightarrow \max \\
\text{Sales' volume} \rightarrow \max \\
\text{Resources' cost} \rightarrow \min \\
\text{Transportation's cost} \rightarrow \min
\end{cases}
\tag{1}
$$

Formula (1) sets the targeted function of a company's profit. It is given in a generalized form; in practice, it may mean revenue or pre-tax/post-tax profit, profitability, etc. Obviously, a company's profit should strive to the maximum. For that, four limitations are introduced.

First limitation: accessibility of resources should strive to the maximum. For consideration of this limitation, the parameters of resource availability are introduced (presence of resources, their volume, the complexity of obtaining the permit for their use, the level of competition for resources, etc.) for each potential territory on which the company or its structural departments could be located.

Second limitation: volume of sales should strive to the maximum. For that, the user enters the information on parameters of demand for the company's products on all potential sales territories (consumer preferences, purchasing power, market volume, etc.).

Third limitation: the cost of resources should strive to a minimum. The price of resources' usage, including official expenditures for obtaining a permit and extraction of resources, as well as unofficial expenditures (e.g., for a conspiracy with rivals, suppliers, or controlling bodies) for a company, should be minimal.

Fourth limitation: the cost of transportation of intermediary and final products should strive to a minimum. Such transportation includes transporting resources, details, and components within the production process between the structural departments of a company and shipment of the final products for all consumers.

If there are several solutions to the formulated optimization task, the user may introduce the weight coefficients, determining the priorities for limitations. In this case, the program will provide the only optimal solution for this company. The user is provided with the following information:

- the optimal number of a company's structural departments;
- territories on which they should be located;
- the preferential method of organizing such business processes as management, various intermediary productions, and final assembly of the final products (their concentration on the same territory or division between several territories);
- the optimal macro-organizational structure of company (not each separate structural department but business on the whole);
- the most profitable channels (geographical directions) of company's products' sales;
- top-priority methods (combination of methods) or transporting the company's products.

The described model of logistics automation of a modern company on the basis of semantic technologies is given in Fig. 3.

5.3 Modeling of Implementation of Semantic Technologies into the Process of Managing the Relations Between a Modern Company and Resources Suppliers

Usage of semantic technologies in the process of managing the relations between a company and resources suppliers is ensured by automation of the scenario analysis and risk management with the help of the tools of the Theory of games. Four stages of this automation are distinguished. The first type: the introduction of variables.

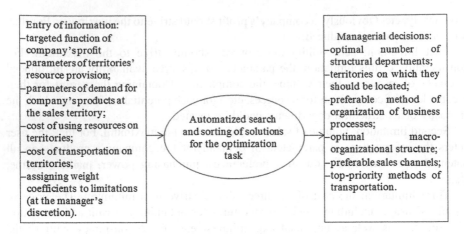

Fig. 3. Model of the system for logistics automation of a modern company on the basis of semantic technologies

Here the user has to set the company's needs for all types of resources. This admits the possibility of the versatile accounting of the resource capacity depending on the used technologies accessible for the company. At that, it is necessary to specify the cost of the technologies, if the company does not have a right for using them.

Second stage: entering the indicators of profitability. Within this approach, the user sets the existing methods of receiving the resources, necessary for the company, and their parameters. Such methods include the following:

- the conclusion of different contact for each separate type of resources with various suppliers. Here we speak of the general (human, material, financial) and detailed categories of resources (specific types of raw materials, resources, etc.);
- the conclusion of various contracts on resources with various suppliers within one type of resources;
- joining an integration association for obtaining access to all types of resources on good terms, etc.

Third stage: the introduction of risks. The information on all potential risks, probabilities of risks, and consequences of risks for the company should be provided. These might include the risks of non-shipment of resources (non-execution of concluded contracts), risks of supply of resources of improper quality, etc. Here the generalized formulations are used, though we speak of human and financial risks, apart from the material. For example, there's a risk of unfavorable change of the terms of credit agreement or non-conformity of the announced competences in the document on education to the factual competences of an employee, etc.

Fourth stage: maximization of the function "risk-profitability". Thus the stage is resulting – on the basis of all information entered by the user, the computer program provides a totality of optimal combinations of risk (which should strive to a minimum) and profitability (which should strive to maximum).

If the user specifies the detailed limitations of the risk, which the company is ready to accept, and the targeted level of expected profitability, the program can provide the only correct solution of this optimization task. In the opposite case, the manager can choose the right solution from the list provided by the program.

The solutions could be complex. For example, if one supplier of this type of resources is reliable and another offers the resource for a lower price, it is expedient to purchase this resource for maximization of the function "risk-profitability". In practice, optimal logistical schemes are very complex, especially in the sphere of large and transnational entrepreneurship – so the automatized selection of such solutions, which brings the user's decision making down to the minimum, is most preferable.

Based on the above, the model of automation of the scenario analysis and risk management of a modern company on the basis of semantic technologies is presented in Fig. 4.

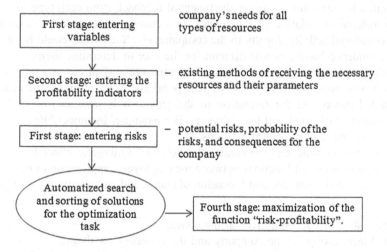

Fig. 4. Model of automation of scenario analysis and risk management of a modern company on the basis of semantic technologies

5.4 Modeling of Implementation of Semantic Technologies into the Process of Intracorporate Management of a Modern Company

Application of semantic technologies in the process of intra-corporate management of a company supposes formation of electronic databases of employees. These databases should include the following components. The first component: existing functions that should be performed by employees at the company (tasks to be realized).

It includes the detailed description of all types of works conducted by the company for the activity's spheres: management, marketing, production with a possibility of distinguishing the innovative activity and non-production activity (making order, the conduct of corporate accounting, etc.).

It is expedient to specify the labor capacity and responsibility of each type of activity in conventional (introduced by the user) items so that the program can evaluate the potential complexity of each employee's work. It is also necessary to specify knowledge, skills, and capabilities for all types of work that the employee must possess.

Second component: capabilities of each employee. It supposes specifying the set and level of knowledge, skills, and capabilities of each employee of the company. Information on such capabilities is obtained from the documents on education and additional training, as well as work experience and personal observations of the manager.

Third component: individual motives and stimuli of each employee. Detailed information on types and level of non-material and material wishes of an employee. This allows evaluating the possibilities of motivation and stimulation of the company's personnel and its preferential forms.

At that, it is important to specify the potential feedback from each type of material and non-material stimulation of employees, i.e., change of its efficiency, quality of work, innovational activity, loyalty to the company, etc. Such value could be set in the form of confidence bands, as it is difficult for the user to determine them.

Fourth component: relations between each employee and all representatives of the company's personnel (other employees). This is necessary for automatized making of managerial decisions on the formation of the teams. It is necessary to distinguish several categories of good and bad relations. For example, incompatibility, moderate enmity, strong friendship, neutral relations, etc.

The program automatically evaluates the potential synergetic effect from various methods of distribution of functions between the employees, application of the methods of motivation and stimulation, and formation of teams, and, as a result, the user gets the following information:

- optimal office of each employee at the company;
- optimal team groups at the company and the necessity for them;
- optimal structure and the scale of the system of motivation and stimulation at the company on the whole and individually for each employee, etc.

According to this, the model of the electronic database on a modern company's employees, created on the basis of semantic technologies, is shown in Fig. 5.

5.5   Modeling of Implementation of Semantic Technologies into the Process of Managing the Relationship Between a Modern Company and Consumers

Implementation of semantic technologies into the process of managing the relations between a company and consumers supposes creation of electronic databases on the customers. Such database should include the following blocks of information. The first block: individual preferences of each consumer. These are preferences and the details of his needs, i.e., the targeted qualities or technical characteristics of the company's products (color, size, taste, etc.). At that, it is necessary to specify the company's capabilities in giving its products these qualities.

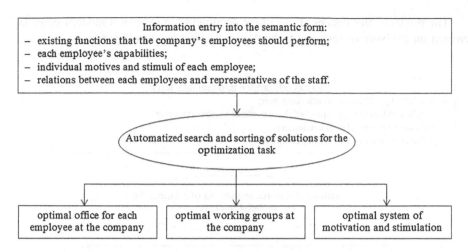

Fig. 5. Model of the system of electronic database on a modern company's employees, created on the basis of semantic technologies

The second block: weight coefficients (priorities) of these preferences for a consumer – i.e., how important these preferences are and the readiness to refuse from them. Here it is necessary to specify the probability of a consumer's refusal from purchasing the company's products in case of its lacking certain characteristics, as well as the opposite side – the probability of preferring the company's products to all other products presented in the market in case of its possessing the set characteristics.

The third block: the purchasing power of each consumer. Information on potential income of consumers and its regularity. It is necessary to specify the potential volume of purchases of the consumer and their expected total cost in the form of confidence bands.

The information on consumers' readiness to use borrowed resources is introduced – e.g., provided by the company or its partners on various terms. It is also possible to specify the preferences as to forms, volumes, and suppliers of borrowed assets, terms of credit redemption, and other terms of a credit agreement, as well as the credit history – if such information is available for the company's manager.

Fourth block: the value of each consumer for the company (frequency of purchases and their shared and total cost, the effect of prestige, etc.). Here the marketing characteristics of consumers are reflected, the most important of which is their loyalty to the company and its potential and existing business partners – if such information is available for the company's manager.

The user received the following information:

- an optimal variant of the market segmentation;
- a preferable targeted segment of the market for the company;
- optimal price for the company's products;
- the expedience of establishing the partnership relations with financial organizations for enabling the consumers to receive a credit on good terms, etc.

The model of the system of electronic document turnover of a modern company, created on the basis of semantic technologies, is visualized in Fig. 6.

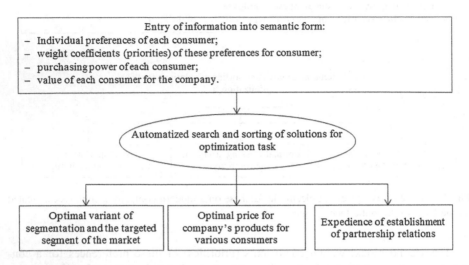

Fig. 6. Model of the system of electronic database on a modern company's consumers, created on the basis of semantic technologies

6 Conclusion

Thus, the offered hypothesis is proved, and it is shown that semantic technologies allow bringing human's participation in the process of modern company management down to the minimum and replacing a lot of managers with one computer. This ensures rationalization of managerial processes by means of elimination of the influence subject to emotions and tiredness of the "human factor", as a source of errors and risks, as well as reduction of managerial expenses, as the initial investments into adaptation and implementation of semantic technologies into the process of company management are to be returned in the mid-term.

Theoretical significance of the results of the research consists in the conceptual substantiation of the existence of perspectives for using semantic technologies for optimization of the system of modern company management. The developed creative model of modern company management on the basis of semantic technologies possesses practical value, for it can be implemented into activities of economic subjects.

In conclusion, it should be noted that semantic technologies are currently at the initial stage of their establishment. Despite the scholars' efforts for their application in the economic activity, they are still treated as technical novelties with a certain mistrust. Apart from socio-psychological factors, the mass distribution and implementation of semantic technologies into the managerial processes of a modern company are hindered by technical and organizational barriers.

One of such barriers is a very large volume of information that should be entered by a user. The announced advantage of managerial decision making on the basis of semantic technologies, which consists in the full elimination of a human from this process, cannot be achieved as of now.

Moreover, the entered information is not always mathematical and has a logical character, which allows for and even requires the usage of manager's own judgments, which, like all aspects related to a human, have a certain degree of subjectivity, reducing the precision of the initial information and distorting the final results.

It also should be noted that entering such large volume of information even with a full master of the applied software and hardware requires a lot of time. Due to this, in many cases, it is more profitable (cheaper and quicker) for a manager to make a managerial decision, instead of losing time and waiting for the program to make it.

Another barrier is caused by the fact that there's a necessity for detailed and full information on the objects of managerial decisions for automatizing this process with the help of semantic technologies. A collection of such information requires additional time and finances, extending the process of managerial decision making.

At the same time, under the condition of incomplete information, application of semantic technologies for managerial decision making is senseless, as it does not allow finding the optimal solution for the set task. As it is impossible to be sure that the company possesses full and authentic information at each moment of time, this discredits the very possibility of implementing the semantic technologies into the process of managing a modern company.

Another barrier is the necessity for timely correction of information with its update. Thus, the information entered by the manager should be constantly updated, as even the slightest changes can lead to non-optimality of the automatized decisions made on the basis of incomplete, inaccurate, or incorrect information.

That is, there's a necessity for constant monitoring of the internal and external situation, in which the company finds itself, and entering new data into semantic forms. This requires a large staff of specially trained people, which limits the circle of companies with access to the implementation of semantic technologies into managerial processes to a small number of the largest business structures.

That's why we deem it expedient to gradually enter semantic technologies into the process of a modern company management. The logical start is their partial implementation into separate managerial processes. This study distinguished five such processes: management of relations with the state, resources' suppliers, employees, consumers, and management of infrastructural provision.

This requires testing the semantic technologies at one of the managerial processes, selection of which should be predetermined by the possibilities of purchasing the necessary software and hardware and training the specialists, as well as by accessibility of information in this sphere of the company's activity.

It should be noted that the offered creative model for optimization of the system of modern company management on the basis of semantic technologies should have further conceptual and methodological development before the practical application. The most important problem on the path of its implementation is an insufficient elaboration of the means of presentation of qualitative data (qualities and ratios) in the numerical form. That's why it is necessary to pay more attention to this issue during further research devoted to studying the perspectives of practical application of semantic technologies in company management.

References

1. Agarwal, R., Ansell, J.: Strategic change in enterprise risk management. Strateg. Change **25** (4), 427–439 (2016)
2. Ahmed, I., Manab, N.A.: Influence of enterprise risk management success factors on firm financial and non-financial performance: a proposed model. Int. J. Econ. Financ. Issues **6**(3), 830–836 (2016)
3. Androsova, I., Simonenko, E.: Innovative approach to strategic management of machine-building enterprises. Econ. Ann.-XXI **157**(3–4), 94–96 (2016)
4. Belov, A.G., Kravets, A.G.: Business performance management in small and medium businesses and functional automation. World Appl. Sci. J. **24**(24), 7–11 (2013)
5. Chakravarty, D., Hsieh, Y.-Y., Schotter, A.P.J., Beamish, P.W.: Multinational enterprise regional management centres: characteristics and performance. J. World Bus. **52**(2), 296–311 (2017)
6. Chansarn, S., Chansarn, T.: Earnings management and dividend policy of small and medium enterprises in Thailand. Int. J. Bus. Soc. **17**(2), 307–328 (2016)
7. Dascalu, M.-I., Bodea, C.-N., Tesila, B., Moldoveanu, A., Ordóñez de Pablos, P.: How social and semantic technologies can sustain employability through knowledge development and positive behavioral changes. Comput. Hum. Behav. **70**, 507–517 (2017)
8. Ena, O., Mikova, N., Saritas, O., Sokolova, A.: A methodology for technology trend monitoring: the case of semantic technologies. Scientometrics **108**(3), 1013–1041 (2016)
9. Hallo, M., Luján-Mora, S., Maté, A.: Evaluating open access journals using Semantic Web technologies and scorecards. J. Inf. Sci. **43**(1), 3–16 (2017)
10. Horrocks, I., Giese, M., Kharlamov, E., Waaler, A.: Using semantic technology to tame the data variety challenge. IEEE Internet Comput. **20**(6), 62–66 (2016). 7781544
11. Popkova, E.G., Abramov, S.A., Ermolina, L.V., Gandin, E.V.: Strategic effectiveness evaluation as integral part of the modern enterprise management. Asian Soc. Sci. **11**(20), 16–21 (2015)
12. Radosavljevic, M., Barac, N., Jankovic-Milic, V., Andjelkovic, A.: Supply chain management maturity assessment: challenges of the enterprises in Serbia. J. Bus. Econ. Manag. **17** (6), 848–864 (2016)
13. Smith, A.M.J., McColl, J.: Contextual influences on social enterprise management in rural and urban communities. Local Econ. **31**(5), 572–588 (2016)
14. Sumba, X., Sumba, F., Tello, A., Baculima, F., Espinoza, M., Saquicela, V.: Detecting similar areas of knowledge using semantic and data mining technologies. Electron. Notes Theor. Comput. Sci. **329**, 149–167 (2016)
15. Tambovtseva, T.: Classification of factors influencing environmental management of enterprise. Technol. Econ. Dev. Econ. **22**(6), 867–884 (2016)
16. Wynn, M., Turner, P., Banik, A., Duckworth, G.: The impact of customer relationship management systems in small business enterprises. Strateg. Change **25**(6), 659–674 (2016)

Mechanisms for the Construction of the Service-Oriented Information System of Educational Institution Based on Technologies of Data Integration and Virtualization

Aleksandr Koskin[1(✉)], Anton Uzharinskiy[1], Andrey Averchenkov[2], Nataliya Ivkina[2], and Mihail Rytov[2]

[1] Orel State University named after I.S. Turgenev, Oryol, Russia
kts@tu-bryansk.ru
[2] Bryansk State Technical University, Bryansk, Russia

Abstract. The article contains approaches for solving the problem of building the management system of an educational institution on the basis of information resources. A model for building the IT infrastructure of an educational institution as a set of independent specialized services is proposed. A model of service interaction based on integration technology and a single data scheme is presented. The mechanism of interaction of various consumers of information resources in a single integrated environment with the use of modern technologies for accessing data and resources on the basis of standard protocols of interaction is considered. Technical aspects of implementing the integrated information system of an educational institution and the construction of a single integrating data scheme are described. The obtained results can be used to solve the problems of integration of diverse information resources within a single information space.

Keywords: Integration · Data · Data schema · Inquire model · Web-services

1 Introduction

Operating of the modern educational institution (EI) requires using and processing of large volumes of information resources of different nature of origin and structure. To date, there are no single standards describing information and management flows in the EI. Furthermore, each EI is forced to use its own solutions in the sphere of automation, oriented to internal processes and considering its specifics. Besides, the process of automation does not proceed simultaneously and consistently. As a result different independent systems are often implemented [1, 2].

Thereof following problems occur:

- the complexity of information exchange between different structural units due to the use of different data formats;

© Springer International Publishing AG 2017
A. Kravets et al. (Eds.): CIT&DS 2017, CCIS 754, pp. 177–186, 2017.
DOI: 10.1007/978-3-319-65551-2_13

- the impossibility of operative information obtaining that is necessary for acceptance of administrative decisions in real time;
- the complexity of collecting information for carrying out the analytical operation.

One of the main reasons for current problems in the sphere of information support for EI is the autonomy of information systems and the lack of a single mechanism for storing and presenting data [3]. Thereby, the task of developing mechanisms for constructing an integrated EI information system that provides common standard interfaces for data access and processing is of current interest.

2   The Role of the Integrated Information System in Management of Educational Institution

Authors consider the control system model to identify the role of the information system in the management process of the EI.

The staff involved in various fields of activity is the control object in the educational institutions. The complexity of control object is in its heterogeneity. Each employee is responsible for performing individual tasks in a separate activity field, which requires the generation of various management solutions for different groups of employees in various activity fields aimed at achieving a common management goal. The control object is characterized by some state Y(t), which is determined by the values of the internal characteristics of the object. In the field of education, such characteristics are indicators of the evaluation of the activity of the university, mainly formed by the Ministry of Education and Science.

The purpose of the control is to achieve the desired state of the control object $Y'(t)$ and define the set of actions U*(t), which allows to lead this state. In the case of the EI, the management goal will be the formation of control actions directed to the achievement of certain values of the target indicators of the university.

The influence of U(t) in education is various acts and orders directed to change certain indicators in order to achieve their expected values. The complexity of forming such an impact is provided by the fact that the control object is described by a large number of interrelated indicators; the impact on one indicator can lead to an influence on other indicators. It is also necessary to consider external influences V(t) that affect the control object. In this regard, mechanisms to evaluate the accepted control action Ym(t) and to select the optimal control in dependence of the chosen control objective are required. The application of control actions to the real object of control in search and research purposes in our case is impossible. Therefore, in order to solve the problem of searching for the optimal control action, it is necessary to create a model of a controlled system and describe the algorithm for control actions' searching.

A control system model is understood as a set of rules by which it is possible to estimate the change in the state of a managed system when applying some control. Thus, the control system model is based on a certain control law. Use of classical mathematics for the formulation of the control law is difficult to implement to the EI as a management object. The complexity of the control object is too high. Besides, the control object model must be flexible and adaptable to the altering characteristics of the real control object. It is possible to use the hierarchy analysis method and cognitive modeling as mathematical tools for constructing an EI model and generating alternative control options.

The main aim of the EI management system is the implementation of the accepted administrative influences on the management object. It was proposed to use an integrated system of web-services as a control system applied to the problem [5]. This will allow, on the one hand, to collect and aggregate diverse information about the educational institution, describing its current state with the help of a certain set of parameters. On the other hand, taking into consideration single centralized mechanism, the use of such system will allow formulating and communicating the accepted managerial influences to the personnel responsible for their implementation in the relevant field of activity [6].

The EI control circuits with the proposed integrated information system are shown in Fig. 1.

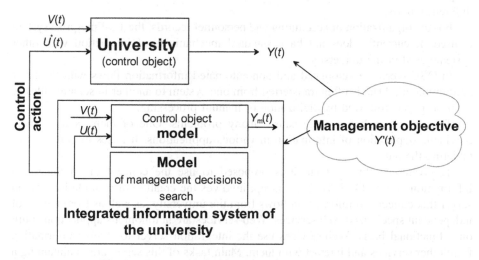

Fig. 1. The control circuit of the educational institution.

3 The Concept of Building an Integrated Information System of an Educational Institution

Let's consider the typical scheme of EI's informatization on the example of Orel State University named after I.S. Turgenev (OSU). At the OSU there is currently no centralized automated control system. A number of specialized systems are used to solve independent problems.

For the automation of learning activities, the information management system of the educational process (IMSEP) is used. The main tasks of the IMSEP are the formation of curricula and schedules, timetables, work programs of disciplines, the organization of control over the progress of students and other tasks related to educational activities. The IMSEP is an internal project of the OSU and it uses its own internal storage and data exchange formats that are incompatible with other systems. The system is built on a modular basis. Modules are designed for different groups of users: dean's office, teachers, department heads, dispatching and other services. Individual modules are combined into a single system by using a common database located on the internal server.

The OSU site is an independent module, a kind of global external interface. By operation of the website and its separate services own database is used, while some data is taken from IMSEP.

To automate the work of the library, the OSU uses its own library system with standard functionality: browsing the literature available in the library, searching for sources, viewing electronic materials, generating reports on available literature.

The information system for monitoring activities is designed to collect information on various performance indicators of structural units and staff of the OSU. At the same time, information input into this system is currently carried out manually. The process is quite laborious and often involves the input of values of the same indicators in different reports.

For the organization of accounting and personnel records, the 1C-Enterprise system is used. It currently does not have standard mechanisms of interaction with other systems used in the university.

In OSU there are automated and non-automated information flows with the latter predominating. Data is often transferred from one system to another in separate files or even on paper, followed by digitization or manual processing.

The use of such a scheme causes many problems. One of them is the almost inevitable duplication of information in various applications. It raises the problem of updating the data.

To overcome this problem it is proposed to use the concept of an integrated information system [4, 7–9]. The concept involves the creation of a single integration server that collects all information flows from the university, as well as from the set of independent specialized web services. Web-services are autonomous applications built on a functional basis. Web-services use the integration server to receive information from other services and interact with them. Main tasks of this server are: maintaining a single data model for all systems operating in the EI, maintaining data integrity in databases, organizing information exchange between applications, providing interfaces for connecting new programs and services. The use of integration technology will preserve the available information resources accumulated during the work of the organization. At the same time, they become arranged, automatic detection and correction of errors in the primary data are provided, an abstracted mechanism for access to them using a standardized interface is created. The application of integration technology for building the information system of the university has the following obvious advantages [7–10]:

- Transparency of information flows and information structure;
- Reduction of development and maintenance costs;
- Improvement in data processing performance;
- Improvement in controllability of the system.

4 Technical Aspects of Building an Integrated Information System of an Educational Institution

In the case of the resolving of tasks of combining heterogeneous applications into a single system developer often need to integrate disparate data sources into a single data representation. This integrated information is consumed by traditional applications that interact directly with databases and need access to an extended set of data sources. Method to create this single data representation is often chosen to take into account the availability of the toolkit, experience, qualifications, and level of the information culture of the organization.

The most appropriate mechanism for implementing an integrated system is the use of service-oriented technologies (SOA), based on the use of the standard SOAP protocol for data exchange between independent services, as well as methods for detecting and identifying various services [11, 12]. The architectural option of the integrated system is provided in Fig. 2.

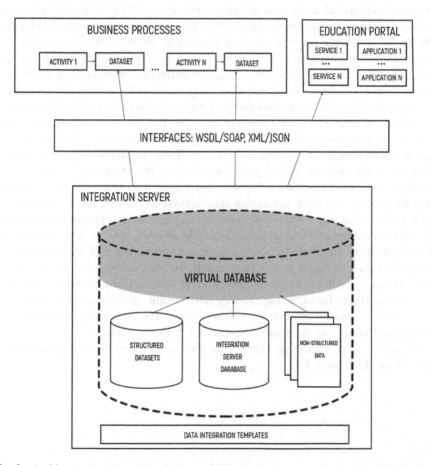

Fig. 2. Architectural option of the integrated information system of educational institution

An information service is an information system component that provides access to information from a certain domain with the rights to create, read, update and delete (CRUD). Services provide some additional processing capabilities - analytical and evaluation algorithms, data deletion rules, etc. Information services, being a basic element of the considered architecture, can appear as independent applications with their own data stores and communicate with existing integrable systems. Services often provide the additional functionality to existing applications associated with the ability to provide their data over the network and receive information from the integration server [10].

The integration server can operate as a provider as well as a service consumer using interfaces conforming to the requirements of the SOA architecture. The service consumer can access the integrated information through the integration service interface, for example, WSDL and HTTP/SOAP or another interface selected for the binding. The integration server can use the services provided by several sources of information for the purpose of integration [13].

The key mechanism implemented on the integration server is the virtualization of data through the use of an integrated data scheme (ISD). ISD is an abstract data model that describes the information resources of all the combined applications and a set of methods for extracting information from distributed information services. The main tasks of the integration server are: obtaining a request from the information service; translation and analysis of the received request; extracting information from disparate sources related to the received request; integrating and transforming information received from different sources into a single format; sending the result to the consumer.

In the context of SOA, the consumer transmits the request in a predefined query format to the integration server. The data integration server receives a request to the integrated data model. In accordance with the query translation algorithm and the description of data sources, the integration server splits the integrated query into several sub-operations and determines where the data required to respond to the integrated query are located and what operations are required to convert the various types of source views into a single integrated view. In this case, the integration server uses the ISD, which includes information on all available sources, how to interact with them, and contains query templates for sources to extract various types of information related to integrated objects. Based on this information, the integration server builds a plan to execute the query. After that, the connection to all sources is established in accordance with their interfaces for obtaining primary information, queries are performed in the databases of information sources, the results obtained are aggregated into the results of the integrated view, and the results are returned to the consumer.

The algorithm of interaction between the web service and the integration server is shown in the diagram in Fig. 3.

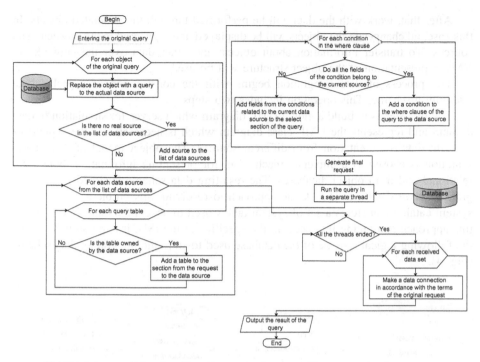

Fig. 3. Schema of the algorithm for processing a service request for data access

5   Mechanisms for Building a Virtual Database of the Server of Integration

A key element of the integration server is the virtual database. This database provides services a mechanism for accessing distributed EI resources. The task of the virtual database is to combine distributed structured and unstructured data sources and provide a universal mechanism for accessing them for different groups of services. Data sources can be relational databases, file storages, Internet resources, etc.

The basic element underlying the virtual database is the ISD. This scheme is necessary to support a single presentation of data from various sources. As a data model for constructing an integrating data scheme, it is offered to use an object model that will allow taking all advantages of object-oriented technology without binding to a specific database structure. Using the described data model, it is necessary to implement methods for mapping different types of data into a single object model. For structured relational databases, it is necessary to implement the mapping of the relationship attributes to the corresponding object fields. For unstructured sources, it is necessary to create object classes that describe the properties of these sources and allow them to detect and retrieve information. To solve this problem, it is necessary to implement mechanisms for extracting metadata from unstructured sources with their further classification and mapping to the object structure.

After that, work with the data will be performed through the generated objects. In this case, all changes in the objects will be displayed and registered in the physical data sources. To transfer information about objects and other data over the network, an XML representation of the object structure will be used.

The process of data integration begins with the construction of a global data integration scheme. This operation includes two steps.

The first step is to build a global UML diagram which serves for simulation of data domain and represents the UML class diagram which is necessary for the support of uniform data representation from different sources. The object model of data representation is chosen as a universal mechanism for presenting information, both from relational and from object databases. The resulting data schema is stored in the integration server database. The classic approach to resolving this problem is to create a system catalog that stores a set of system tables used to access the data. According to this approach and taking into account the specifics of the ISD, it is possible to define the following logical scheme of the database used to store the integrating data scheme (Fig. 4).

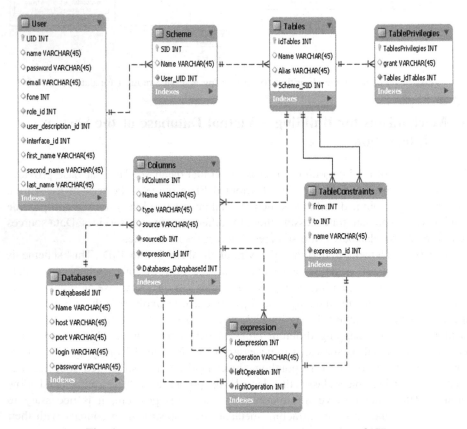

Fig. 4. The Logic diagram of the database for storage of ISD

The table «Scheme» contains the name and identifier of the integrating data scheme. Several integrated data schemes can be created in the system, however, only one scheme remains active at each time. Only one user can be the owner of the scheme. In this case, other users can access the elements of the schema in accordance with the specified access rights. Each schema contains a set of object classes stored in the table «Tables». The fields of each object class are contained in the table «Columns». In addition to standard attributes, this table has an attribute «value» that determines the condition by which the value of this field is formed based on data from real sources. As a condition, there can be both a separate field of a real source and some expression that is a composition of several fields of different sources. In this case, all the fields of real sources used to form the value of the field of the integrating data schema are written in the format: <Database name>. <Table name>. <Field name>. The table «TableConstrains» contains a description of the relationships between the elements of the integrating data schema. It contains references to connectable «from» and «to» objects and a condition for connecting tuples of these classes. The «Databases» table contains information about the integrable databases needed to access their data.

The second step involves the formulation of rules for mapping elements of existing data sources to the developed object structure. For this, it is necessary to create a specialized mathematical model. As the basis of such model, it is possible to use the apparatus of relational algebra, which must be supplemented by specialized operations on data of different structures. As a result of this process, a data model is obtained that is independent of the physical ways of representing and storing them. This model is used by services for interaction and information exchange within the framework of the integrated EI information system.

6   Conclusion

The article discusses the issues of data integration, in particular, the use of templates as the principle of working with data in relation to the integrated and temporary (virtual) representation, the data of which are actually stored in several different sources. The application of this concept allows solving the problem of creating a single information infrastructure for EI in the conditions of heterogeneity of the tasks to be solved and the means used for their solution. The application of the described system increases the controllability and control over information resources, which allows improving the quality of information services.

References

1. Eliseeva, E., Shcherba, I., Morozova, S., Shadoba, E., Petukhova, L.: Technological and methodological approaches to the design of information and educational space of modern high school. Int. Rev. Manag. Mark. 6(S1), 135–141 (2016)

2. Frolov, A.: Challenges and prospects of using information technologies in higher education. In: 2016 International Conference Education Environment for the Information Age (EEIA-2016), vol. 29 (2016). doi:10.1051/shsconf/20162902015
3. Abel, R., Brown, M., Suess, J.: A new architecture for learning. EDUCAUSE Rev., **48**(5) (2013)
4. Morris, M., Chong, F., Clark, J., Welsh, J.: Architectural Issues in Managing Web Services in Connected Systems. https://msdn.microsoft.com/en-us/library/ms954616.aspx
5. Yu, Q., Liu, X., Bouguettaya, A., Medjahed, B.: Deploying and managing web services issues solutions and directions. VLDB J. **17**(3), 537–572 (2008). doi:10.1007/s00778-006-0020-3
6. Katalin, M., Radu, L.: A system architecture based on open source enterprise content management systems for supporting educational institutions. Int. J. Inf. Manag. **36**(2), 207–214 (2016). doi:10.1016/j.ijinfomgt.2015.11.003
7. Vikhrev, V.V., Christochevskaya, A.S., Christochevsky, S.A.: To a new concept of informatization of education. Syst. Means Inf. **24**(4), 157–167 (2014)
8. Zhukova, I., Kultsova, M., Litovkin, D., Kozlov, D.: Generation of OWL ontologies from confinement models. In: Kravets, A., Shcherbakov, M., Kultsova, M., Shabalina, O. (eds.) CIT&DS 2015. CCIS, vol. 535, pp. 191–203. Springer, Cham (2015). doi:10.1007/978-3-319-23766-4_16
9. Fionova, L., Finogeev, A., Finogeev, A., Vinh, T.: Learning management system for the development of professional competencies. In: Kravets, A., Shcherbakov, M., Kultsova, M., Shabalina, O. (eds.) CIT&DS 2015. CCIS, vol. 535, pp. 793–803. Springer, Cham (2015). doi:10.1007/978-3-319-23766-4_63
10. Koskin, A.V., Uzharinsky, A.Y. Mechanisms of access to data based on a single integrated data scheme. Inf. Syst. Technol. (1), 21–30 (2015). (in Russian)
11. Hafiddi, H., Baidouri, H., Nassar, M., Kriouile, A.: Context-Awareness for Service Oriented Systems (2012). https://arxiv.org/ftp/arxiv/papers/1211/1211.3229.pdf
12. Nosenko, Y., Shyshkina, M., Oleksiuk, V.: Collaboration between research institutions and university sector using cloud-based environment. In: 12th International Conference on ICT in Education, Research and Industrial Applications, ICTERI 2016, vol. 1614, pp. 656–671 (2016)
13. Bassiliades, N., Anagnostopoulos, D., Vlahavas, I.: Web service composition using a deductive XML rule language. Distrib. Parallel Databases **17**(2), 135–178 (2005). doi:10.1007/s10619-004-0087-z

Enhancing the Quality of Nepali Text-to-Speech Systems

Rupak Raj Ghimire and Bal Krishna Bal$^{(\boxtimes)}$

Information and Language Processing Research Lab,
Department of Computer Science and Engineering,
Kathmandu University, Dhulikhel, Kavre, Nepal
rughimire@gmail.com, bal@ku.edu.np

Abstract. Text-to-speech (TTS) systems are widely studied applications in Computer Science. It is more popular among the languages which has rich set of resources such as English and not as rigorously taken up in under resourced languages such as Nepali. Nevertheless, it has wider scope of application in different areas including telephony, e-learning and telecommunication.

The underresourced languages have trouble in developing the natural sounding TTS system. This is primarily because of the linguistic resources involved in the system. The preparation of such linguistic resources is costly, time consuming and requires the involvement of linguists/experts. The general trend in this research domain is to develop natural sounding TTS out of limited resources available. Nepali, being an underresourced language has very few linguistic resources available for developing TTS system.

In this work, we modified the existing TTS system [9] by adding computational units to process the input and output, we call them post and pre processing modules. We also made the system available to the public through the desktop application and plugin for the Firefox by pruning and adding phonetic rules and normalization rules.

We evaluated the existing and modified TTS systems via the qualitative evaluation techniques where 30 users were asked to provide their evaluation of the systems being based on the parameters- intelligibility and naturalness. Our results have shown that there has been an overall improvement of 6% in terms of naturalness and intelligibility, whereas the result of comprehension and diagnostic rhyme test is increased by 12% and 10% respectively.

Keywords: Speech technology · Text-to-Speech · Natural language processing · Digital signal processing · Speech synthesis · Nepali-TTS · Unit selection · Synthesized voice

1 Introduction

Human computer interaction has always been a big issue ever since the early stages of the computing era. Making computers talk and recognize speech was the

© Springer International Publishing AG 2017
A. Kravets et al. (Eds.): CIT&DS 2017, CCIS 754, pp. 187–197, 2017.
DOI: 10.1007/978-3-319-65551-2_14

favorite tendencies of the science fiction films. Most of the computer system today uses the text input, which is sometimes very difficult across different end-users, particularly those who are visually impaired. From this perspective, text input is not the universal input and output method. To make human and computer interaction easier in every aspect, speech can be used as an alternative for such users. Most operating systems including mobile and desktop operating systems also include speech technology for the input/output. For example, voice based navigation for visually impaired peoples [1].

A lot of research on speech synthesis have been done in order to make efficient TTS and Speech recognition systems. A TTS system is a software system that can convert a given text into speech signals. The input text can be different, sometimes the text can be inputted from users through the keyboards, sometimes through the digital documents, or in the form of output of the optical character recognition (OCR) system. Whatever the input to the system, the ultimate goal of the TTS synthesis system is to create naturally sounding speech from arbitrary text. Moreover, the current trend in TTS research calls for systems that produce speech in different speaking styles with different speaker characteristics and even emotions. In order to fulfill these stringent requirements, the commonly used speech synthesis methods are formant synthesis, concatenation synthesis and articulatory synthesis. The concept of high quality TTS synthesis appeared in the mid eighties [3], as a result of important developments in speech synthesis and natural language processing techniques, mostly due to the emergence of new technologies (Digital Signal and Logical Inference Processors) [3].

1.1 Concatenative Synthesis

Concatenative synthesis is based on the concatenation (or stringing together) of segments of recorded human speech database. Generally, concatenative synthesis produces the most natural-sounding synthesized speech. However, differences between natural variations in speech and the nature of the automated techniques for segmenting the waveforms sometimes result in audible glitches in the output. The size of the database is big but the naturalness is the main advantage of this approach [6]. In this method, the computer stores multiple versions of each of the basic units of speech (phones, half-phones, syllables, etc.), and then decides which sequence of speech units sounds best for the particular text message that is being produced. There are three main sub-types of concatenative synthesis – Unit selection synthesis, Diphone synthesis and Formant Synthesis.

Unit selection synthesis uses large databases of recorded speech. During database creation, each recorded utterance is segmented into some or all of the following: individual phones, diphones, half-phones, syllables, morphemes, words, phrases, and sentences.

Unit selection provides the degree of greatest naturalness, because it applies only a small amount of digital signal processing (DSP) to the recorded speech. DSP often makes recorded speech sound less natural, although some systems use a small amount of signal processing at the point of concatenation to smoothen the waveform. The output from the best unit-selection systems is often indistinguishable from real human voices, especially in contexts for which the TTS system has been tuned. However, maximum naturalness typically requires unit-selection speech databases to be very large, in some systems ranging into the gigabytes of recorded data, representing dozens of hours of speech. Also, unit selection algorithms have been known to select segments from a place that results in less than ideal synthesis (e.g. minor words become unclear) even when a better choice exists in the database. Recently, researchers have proposed various automated methods to detect unnatural segments in unit-selection speech synthesis systems [13].

1.2 Festival

Festival [4, 11] offers a general framework for building speech synthesis systems as well as including examples of various modules. As a whole, it offers full text to speech through a number APIs: from shell level, though a Scheme command interpreter, as a C++ library, from Java, and an Emacs interface. Generally Festival uses voice built from Festvox [5], it contains tools to make new voice.

1.3 General TTS Architecture

The TTS synthesis system consists of higher and lower level of synthesis components. The higher level components of the TTS Systems is Natural Language Processing (NLP), and lower level is Digital Signal Processing (DSP), as shown in Fig. 1, [2].

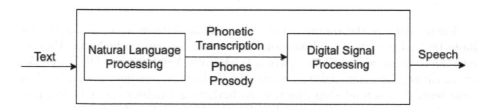

Fig. 1. General functional diagram of Text-to-Speech system [2]

The NLP module is responsible for conversion of text input into phonetic transcription and prosody information. Prosody information, which includes melody, intonation, rhythm, are necessary to make the resulting speech sounds natural. The DSP module then transforms the resulting phonetic transcription and prosody information into corresponding speech.

The state-of-the-art shows that TTS and Speech Recognition are good for the languages that are resourceful. However, good quality TTS is still not available for most of the languages. The case of Nepali language is also no different. Although, a basic prototype of TTS has been developed [9, 10], it needs to be further refined in order to get a good quality of synthesized voice. In this work, we attempt to answer the following research question – How can we make the natural sounding TTS system for Nepali out of limited resources? And we set the hypothesis as - The changes in the general architecture and addition of tokenizer and post processing module improves the naturalness and usability of the Nepali Text-to-Speech engine.

2 Related Work

TTS engine basically comprises of three parts, text normalization [12], text-phoneme generation and finally synthesis. The syntesizer produces the speech as output. There are different methods of synthesis, namely - Concatenative, Formant and Articulatory. Among these methods, Concatenative is widely used [6] for producing natural sounding TTS systems. However, diphone based or unit selection based method also can be used for the same. We took the Nepali TTS engine already developed by Language Technology Kendra [10] which is based on the unit selection method.

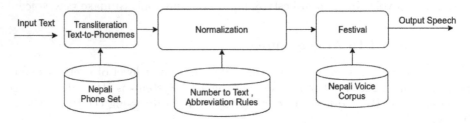

Fig. 2. Current Nepali TTS engine

Figure 2 shows the overall architecture of the current system. Firstly, the input text is fed to the Transliteration Engine, which converts the Nepali Unicode into the Romanized Nepali form, which is basically ASCII-based. The conversion or transliteration is mandatory because the Festival system does not accept Unicode text. As a second step, the text normalizer normalizes the abbreviations, numeric data based on the rules. Finally, the Festival based synthesizer [11] is used for synthesizing the text into the speech. The text pre-processing includes Natural Language Processing steps on the input text [8], if this step is not properly handled, the result would be improper normalization and transliteration. Improper normalization is mostly caused because of the non-dictionary words, numbers, email, url etc. [13]. This leads to the generation of inappropriate and unnatural speech.

3 System Architecture

After testing the current TTS engine, we identified that the output of the Nepali-TTS is highly dependent on the quality of the input text. We observed that long input to the engine causes unusual output which is messy, lacking proper intonation (too fast or too slow reading), and thus sounding unnatural. Hence, we made two major changes (addition of the tokenizer and post processing modules) in the architecture of existing Nepali-TTS Engine. The input text is sent to the tokenizer which generates a series of the tokens of standard and non-standard words. These tokens are stored in the temporary file and will be used by the post processor later in the final stage of the system. The post processor concatenates the series of the output by the Festival system by applying the prosodic rules. The major difference with the modified system is that the text will not be sent directly to the Nepali-TTS engine as in the existing system. Instead, the input text is processed and the content tokens are sent to the engine. Additionally, prosodic rules are added to the tokens which will be utilized by the system to generate the speech.

3.1 Input

The input can be fed from any client application, currently the modified system can accept input from REST API[1] and TCP consumer applications. The modified system can even accept long paragraph texts which was not the case with the existing system - it used to break down as soon the length of the input text became more than a sentence.

3.2 Pre-processing Module (Tokenizer)

This is the newly added module to the existing TTS system which splits the long input text into the manageable small tokens. The token includes both standard and non standard words (SW, NSW). The tokens are then saved into the file and will be used later by post processor. Token identifiers are the paired tags (<identifier> </identifier>). Table 1 shows the list of the tokens currently being used. The typical format of the token is as follows <identifier> TOKEN </identifier>.

Rules for Tokenization
Following are the general rules used for the tokenizer:

- the space, comma, full stop, exclamation are treated as the separator
- maximum of two words would be taken as a single token starting from the very first
- every token seg, nsw, num will be uniquely numbered starting from 1
- if we find comma (,), full stop (.) it is considered as a single token
- every words ending with dot (.) are considered as the abbreviation and are given a single token.

For example, if the input unicode text (Fig. 4) is passed to the tokenizer, then the tokenizer outputs the sequence of tokens as in Fig. 5.

---

[1] REST stands for Representational State Transfer. (It is sometimes spelled "ReST".) It relies on a stateless, client-server, cacheable communications protocol – and in virtually all cases, the HTTP protocol is used. REST is an architecture style for designing networked applications.

Table 1. Token identifiers

Identifier	Purpose
seg	Phrase segment
num	Numbers
nsw	Non standard words
abbr	NSW abbreviation
pause	Pause
pause full	Full Stop
pause small	Semi full stop for comma

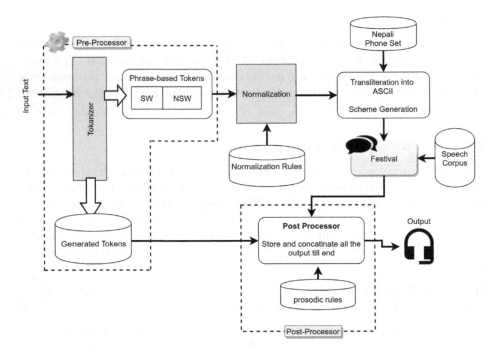

Fig. 3. Proposed Nepali TTS engine

सेकुवा पारखीमाझ डा .   दीनानाथ भण्डारीले १० बर्ष अगाडी काठमाडौँमा सुरु गरेको बाजेको सेकुवा बारे थप चर्चा गरिरहनुपर्दैन । बाजेको सेकुवा कर्नर अहिले राजधानीमा १० र राजधानीबाहिर चितवन र पोखरमा दुई गरी १२ वटा आउटलेटमा विस्तार भइसकेका छन् ।

Fig. 4. Nepali unicode text input

<seg 1>सेकुवा पारखीमाझ</seg> <nsw 2 abbr>डा</nsw> <seg 3>दीनानाथ भण्डारीले</seg> <nsw 4 num>१०</nsw> <seg 5>बर्ष अगाडी</seg> ...<seg 8>गरिरहनुपर्दैन</seg> <pause full>।</pause> <seg 9>बाजेको सेकुवा</seg> ।...

Fig. 5. Output of tokenization

3.3   Normalization

The fully normalized segment of text will be the input to this module. It converts the text in utf-8 to the text in ASCII as well as implements the linguistic features such as text-to-phoneme rules based on the Nepali phone-set. Text Normalization is the transformation of text to the pronounceable form. It includes-

- Number Converter
  The conversion depends upon the context. 1772 can have different pronunciation depending upon the context of date, phone or quantifiers. Example:
  1772 (Date): Seventeen seventy two
  1772 (Phone number): One Seven Seven Two
  1772 (Quantifier): One thousand seven hundred and seventy two
- Abbreviation Converter
  Abbreviations are expanded to full textual format. Example:
  Mrs: Misses
  St. Joseph St. - Saint Joseph Street. etc.
- Acronym Converter
  Acronims are replaced by single level components
  I.S.O: ISO.

  The output of this module is the *.scm file which is the input to the Festival engine.

3.4   Synthesis

The scm file is fed into the festival engine [4]. The engine is based on the already developed language model by the Bhasasanchar project from 2005 [9, 10]. The engine synthesizes the text based on the concatenative and unit selection methods. So it requires the speech corpus. The Nepali speech corpus was developed by Bhasasanchar Project.

3.5   Speech Corpus

Table 2 shows the details of the speech corpus used which was already developed by Bhasasanchar Project [9].

Table 2. Metadata of speech corpus used

Particular	Value
Size	170 MB
No of units	1247 Nos
Format of unit	Wav file
Average size of unit	133 KB

3.6   Post-processor

This is the another important module we added to the existing TTS engine. It collects the sequence of the output wav file from the Festival engine and concatenates them according to the sequence it is sent to the Festival. The important steps for producing natural sounding TTS systems are mostly handled here. The processor itself is based on the rules which are customizable.

Rules. Currently the prosodic rules includes the adjustable parameters as shown in Table 3.

Table 3. Adjustable parameters of prosodic rules

Parameter	Value
Pause small (for comma, exclamation, semicolon etc.)	Adjustable
Pause full (full stop)	Adjustable

4   Evaluation

4.1   Evaluation Techniques

Evaluation of TTS is essentially subjective. The main contributing factors that affects the overall quality of a TTS system are Intelligibility and Naturalness. Intelligibility answers the questions such as, how much of the spoken output can a user understand? How quickly does the user become fatigued as a listener, etc?. Whereas, Naturalness means how close to human speech does the output of the TTS synthesizer sound?

Intelligibility tests are concerned with the ability to identify what was spoken or synthesized. They are less concerned with the natural sounding signal, although naturalness is indirectly related to, and influences, intelligibility. The Comprehension Task (CT) and Diagnostic Rhyme Test (DRT) have been preformed to check the intelligibility of the TTS System.

Methodology of CT: A paragraph text of TTS output was played to the subjects and they were asked five questions out of the generated text. Based on how many questions the subjects could answer correctly, we calculated the score of the intelligibility of the system.

Methodology of DRT: Listeners were played monosyllabic words which differ only in the first consonant, and were asked to choose the word they heard from the given pairs (for example, pin/fin, hit/bit). The subjects were asked to identify five pairs of words read by the system, which gives the score for DRT.

For Naturalness test, we used Mean Opinion Score (MOS). In voice and video communication, the quality of the generated speech usually dictates whether the hearing experience was a good or a bad one. MOS gives a numerical indication of the perceived quality of the media received after being generated from the particular TTS-System. MOS is expressed in number, from 1 to 5 where 1 denotes the worst and 5 the best. It is calculated as the arithmetic mean (Eq. 1) over single ratings performed by human subjects for a given stimulus in a subjective quality evaluation test. Thus:

$$\bar{x} = \frac{1}{N} \sum_{i=1}^{N} x_i \tag{1}$$

where x_i are the individual ratings for a given stimulus by N subjects.

The Mean Opinion Score Values: Taken in whole numbers, the numbers are quite easy to grade. Following is the recommendation by ITU Telecommunication Standardization Sector (ITU-T) [7].

5. Excellent: Like face-to-face conversation or radio reception,
4. Good: Imperfections can be perceived, but sound still clear. This is (supposedly) the range for cell phones,
3. Fair,
2. Poor: Nearly impossible to communicate,
1. Bad: Impossible to communicate.

4.2 Dataset

We gathered the datasets from regular sources of the text that are used for the purpose of speech synthesis such as e-books, portable document format (PDF), websites. For each test, we took 100 sample data per subjects. For Comprehension Task, the data set is prepared in such as way that the whole text prepresents the particular theme. Diagnostic Rhyme Test (DRT) is also tested with 100 sample per subjects. In the case of MOS we selected smaller and single sentenses.

5   Results

Different tests were carried out on the old and the new Nepali-TTS system under the same experimental setup. 30 independent subjects participated in the testing process. The score given by subjects were recorded and average was calculated. Results are summarized in Table 4.

The results (Table 4) show that the comprehension of the system increased by 12% where as Diagnostic Rhyme Test is increased by 10%.

MOS mostly relies on the subject's understandability and it measures the quality of the overall system. The output of the existing system was 66% whereas the new TTS system's output is 72%, which is an improvement by 6%.

Table 4. Result of experiments

Test name	Existing Nepali-TTS	New Nepali-TTS
Comprehension task	3.2	3.9
Diagnostic rhyme test	3.4	3.9
Mean opinion score	3.3	3.6

6 Conclusion

The current work was aimed at enhancing the existing Nepali-TTS system. As a first step towards this endeavor, study of the different architectures for different TTS synthesizers for Nepali languages was done. In this work, we investigated the existing Nepali-TTS engine and added the pre- and post-processing modules in order to enhance the system. The pre-processing module acts as a language processing unit. It tokenizes the input and passes the resultant tokens to the existing TTS system. The post-processor module then merges the output of TTS system based on the prosodic rules. The merging of the output is done in the order of tokenization.

We used different testing techniques to test the enhanced and existing version of the Nepali-TTS system using various testing techniques including MOS. The output of the modified system in terms of intelligibility and naturalness is 72%, which is an improvement by 6%, whereas the result of comprehension and diagnostic rhyme test got increased by 12 % and 10% respectively.

References

1. Cha, J.S., Lim, D.K., Shin, Y.N.: Design and implementation of a voice based navigation for visually impaired persons. Int. J. Bio-Sci. Bio-Technol. **5**(3) (2013)
2. Dutoit, T.: An Introduction to Text-to-Speech Synthesis. Kluwer Academic Publishers, Dordrecht (1997). pp. 13, 14, 63, 72, 179, 196
3. Dutoit, T.: A Short Introduction to Text-to-Speech Synthesis. TTS Research Team, TCTS Lab (1999)
4. FestivalEngine (2014). http://www.cstr.ed.ac.uk/projects/festival/. Accessed 18 May 2014
5. Festvox (2014). http://festvox.org/. Accessed 10 June 2014
6. Hunt, A.J., Black, A.W.: Unit selection in a concatenative speech synthesis system using a large speech database. In: IEEE International Conference on Acoustics, Speech, and Signal Processing (ICASSP-1996) (1996)
7. ITU-T: Series P: telephone transmission quality - methods for objective and subjective assessment of quality (1996)
8. Jurafsky, D., Martin, J.H.: Speech and Language Processing, 2nd edn. Pearson Education, London (2009)
9. Nepali-TTS: Full manual of Nepali TTS (2008)
10. Nepali-TTS: http://bhashasanchar.org/textspeech_intro.php (2008). Accessed 18 Feb 2014

11. Taylor, P., Black, A.W., Caley, R.: The architecture of the festival speech synthesis system. Centre for Speech Technology Research (1998)
12. Sproat, R., Black, A.W., Chen, S., Kumar, S., Ostendorf, M., Richards, C.: Normalization of non-standard words. Comput. Speech Lang. **15**(3), 287–333 (2001). http://dx.doi.org/10.1006/csla.2001.0169
13. Wang, W.Y., Georgila, K.: Automatic detection of unnatural word-level segments in unit-selection speech synthesis. In: IEEE ASRU (2011)

Computer Vision and Knowledge-Based Control

General Approach to the Synthesis of Emotional Semantic Information from the Video

Vladimir L. Rozaliev[⊠], Yulia A. Orlova, Roman I. Guschin, and Vadim V. Verichev

Volgograd State Technical University, 28 Lenin Ave., Volgograd
Russian Federation
vladimir.rozaliev@gmail.com, yulia.orlova@gmail.com,
romanshadow3@gmail.com, vadimvv01@gmail.com

Abstract. Human emotions play an important role in the interpersonal relations. Emotions are reflected by means of a facial expression. Research and understanding of emotions are very important for human-machine interaction. This article is describing the system for automatic recognition of emotions in a video stream. The main purpose of the work is to develop a method that increases the accuracy of recognizing emotions in the video stream. The separate paragraph describes methods for recognition of the eyes and lips. The article provided the results of comparing the data obtained from the training selection. The recognition accuracy of the developed method is compared with the Artificial Neural Network algorithm. The article considers the main algorithm for obtaining key parameters from a video. The analysis of various methods used in this algorithm is made. To the end of the article annotation and classification of video recordings are described.

Keywords: Human emotions · Image identification · Facial recognition · Computer vision · Information system

1 Introduction

Nowadays videos have become a means of information transfer in such areas as education, communication, entertainment and many others. Each video and also its individual parts carry a semantic message that can be very flexible. And exactly because of this message modern movies became currently popular. Semantic of the message become known immediately for people. However, computers cannot simply understand it. For this action requires a much more complex description. The phenomenon of the gap between the understanding of human meaning and machine is usually called the semantic gap. [1] The problem becomes even more complicated when it becomes clear the extent of the video content turnover now. Obviously, to develop a special detector for each possible meaning of the message in the video is impossible, since the quantity of the concepts is incredibly powerful. Then the best way is to use common methods that are taught based on many examples. [2] Each example should represent a dependence of the "semantic information" from the "preset video".

© Springer International Publishing AG 2017
A. Kravets et al. (Eds.): CIT&DS 2017, CCIS 754, pp. 201–214, 2017.
DOI: 10.1007/978-3-319-65551-2_15

Accordingly, there are two specific objectives for learning on examples task: retrieve the key information from the video or its segment and clustering of on the videos semantic information. To solve the first objectives can be used a different kind of information in the video: metadata (author, title, and description), audio track, textual information on a specific frame, the visual information. In this paper, the concept of "Semantic information" concretize "Emotive semantics". [3] Emotional semantics is a description of human psychological feelings such as joy, anger, fear, sadness and so on. A concrete example of the use of semantic information is a system for searching video recordings at the user's request. The main feature of this request should be that the user enters text with a description of the emotion that the founded video should trigger.

The second objective is clustering video. The task of clustering is to create a system that allows to evaluate the obtained parameters of the video and create the annotation. Be aware that the video may take a few different angles for clustering. In addition, it is worth emphasizing, as noted above, you must have a feedback for results ranking and getting the best search performance.

In this paper considers the task of obtaining key information from a video. Specifically, the algorithm for face recognizing and determining their emotional component is described.

2 Obtain of the Video Recording Parameters

The obtain parameters of video recording is an algorithm with several stages:

- The division of video;
- Feature extraction;
- Presentation of video;
- Analysis of video.

The division of video is the separation of one whole video into its structural parts. Accordingly, there are different ways of defining the boundaries of these units. Also in this phase includes the tasks of identifying key personnel in a selected area and segmentation of the audio.

For further description, it is necessary to introduce the concept of structural parts of a video. The smallest semantic part is the frame. It contains information about the background color and the foreground video. Then the larger part is the installation plan is an action item in the foreground. This structural element is obtained information about movements and changes. Last, the biggest part of the video is scene. This is likely to be the sequence of actions within a single location or background.

The structural part of the video - that represent the time intervals within a single video. The most convenient method of separation is the separation of one Assembly plan. The installation plan is the time of continuous shooting from the start the camera until it stops. Or the time between one cut to another. To determine the boundaries of the scene using the graphics characteristics of each frame. Then the estimated differences between pairs of consecutive frames. If everyone is mixed, that is, have differences in several graphic options. In work [4] there are described settings that appear when you change installation, and what errors occur when the wrong choice of shifts. In accordance with the work, there are two types of ways to get the border:

- Threshold methods;
- Statistics.

Threshold methods require the installation of a certain value, which shows what is needed to increment the value to be regarded as the boundary. These methods are simple but have some inaccuracy, since the threshold value is a fixed value. As a result, to avoid problems of this type will be based on the methods of another type. Statistical methods are more advanced methods for obtaining the boundaries, as they are not just pairwise compare the footage and form a complete picture around the installation plan. And as soon as the change is rejected much of the mathematical expectation of the image parameters, this transition will be considered as the boundary of the installation plan.

The next stage is the stage of obtaining the key frames. It is obvious that to assess the video to all frames is not necessary but can worsen the performance of the system. Therefore, to avoid redundancy, it is necessary to identify the key video footage that fully reflects the contents of the installation plan. There are many methods, divided into categories:

- Sequential comparison;
- Global comparison;
- Based on the cluster;
- Based on the simplification of curves;
- Based on objects and events [5].

The first method is a consistent comparison, the same threshold method in defining the limits of the mounting frame. Selects the threshold above which a frame is considered the key and is stored for further comparison. Frames are compared sequentially, usually, the main parameter for comparison is the color histogram [6].

Most suitable for use by the method is a method of global comparison. This algorithm sets a certain target function, where the arguments are time and value of the difference between the color histograms of consecutive frames. Accordingly, the function defined on the region of the mounting frame, and after receiving all arguments is minimized, discarding unnecessary arguments.

At this stage, we have a set of key frames, and the array of intervals, dividing the video recording editing plans. Now you need to go to the bigger semantic unit scene. Typically, the data elements associated with either a specific theme or subject. It should say that the methods applied to key frames in earlier stages not applicable. This follows from the fact that the key frames do not carry sufficient information about the dynamic change. Mounting frames in one scene are linked rather meaningful story, rather than key frames.

Often applicable method is based on the assumption that all frames of the same scene have the same background. In simple cases, it is justified but not always. This method uses methods combining of similar color pixels in a rectangular region. And according to the obtained distribution the conclusion about the similarity of the images in the frame.

The most applicable assumption is that the scene change is where at the same time dramatically changes the content of both channels. For this, you can use the nearest-neighbor algorithm with a time limit. [7] However, using this approach, you need to be ready for the more tedious calculations.

Based on the information received from the video, it is now necessary to make a numerical characterization that can be used for further clustering. Was offered to the following groups of characteristics:

- The statistical characteristics of the frame;
- Object characteristics;
- Dynamic characteristics;
- Sound characteristics.

Static characteristics include characteristics selected key frames: color, texture, contours. Color in a particular frame is characterized by color histograms, color moments, color correlogram.

Texture or textural characteristics are called features, which do not depend on tone, color, and saturation of the object, and describe exactly the homogeneous/inhomogeneous effects in the images. To highlight this information from frames typically use Gabor filters [8].

Dynamic characteristics describe more semantic concepts as describe the video in for some time. You must separate two types of motion: camera motion and object motion within the frame. The movement of objects is more important from the point of view of meaning. For this, we introduce the concept of the event. An event is a change in the content of key frames. Accordingly, for the selected key frames, you must calculate the length between the current frame and the previous one. The resulting length is written to a single shared sequence. This sequence will be the signature video. The task of finding similar videos is reduced to the search of substrings in the sequence. Disadvantages of this approach are the impossibility to use the real-time.

The objects characteristics include such parameters as color, size, texture. It is one of the main tasks when working with objects is the process of defining and selecting an individual object on the image. In the considered area of the definition of emotional semantics, the objects of the human face play a special role. These objects carry a lot of information about the emotional coloration of a given keyframe. The following paragraphs describe the proposed method for face recognition.

3 Face Recognition on the Image

For this task, the Viola-Jones method is used. The basic principles on which the method based are as follows:

- Images in integral representation are used that allows calculating quickly necessary objects.
- Haar signs are used for searching the necessary object.

- The busting for a choice of the most suitable signs for a required object on this part of the image is used.
- All signs arrive on an input of the qualifier which yields the result "truly" or "lie".

Viola-Jones is one of the best methods, based on the ratio of the recognition/speed performance indicators. Also, this detector has an extremely low probability of false detection of the person. The algorithm even well works and recognizes features at a small angle, approximately to 30°. In the case of slope angle, more than 30° the percent of detection sharply falls. And it does not allow in the standard implementation to detect a person's rotated face at an arbitrary angle, which makes it difficult or makes it impossible to use the algorithm in modern production systems, taking into account their growing needs for quickly discarding windows where a person is not found.

Also, the alignment of image histograms is used to improve the recognition of "parameters" on the face.

For detection of the person on the image, we convert RGB the image into binary. For conversion of the bitmap, mean value of RGB for each pixel is calculated and if mean value less, than 110, we replace it with a black pixel, otherwise, we will replace it with a white pixel. By means of this method, we receive the bitmap from RGB (Fig. 1).

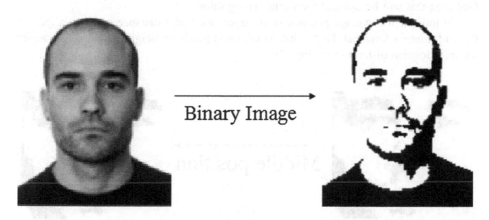

Binary Image

Fig. 1. The translation of the image in the binary mode

Then, for detection of eyes and user's lips, we try to find a forehead from the bitmap. By means of the scanning window, we find the middle of the image to find the continuous white pixels after the continuous black pixel. Then we find the maximum width of the white pixel by means of search in a vertical, with left on right the side. If the new width is less than a half of the previous maximum width, then we interrupt scanning because we reached an eyebrow. Further, we begin to cut the image of the person from home position of a forehead, and its height will make 1, 5 to increase by image width (Fig. 2).

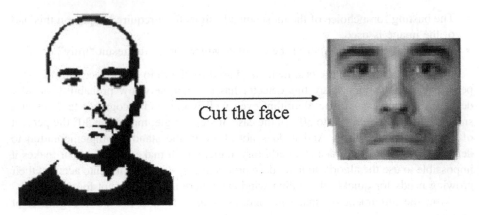

Fig. 2. Cutting optimum area for recognition of eyes and lips

4   Recognition of Eyes

Next, we are searching for the eyes on the user's face. At this stage, we use a binary cut face area that will be optimal for further recognition.

To indicate the average position of the eyes, we find a distance equal to a quarter the width user's forehead. High white continuous pixels on height between the ranges are mid position of both eyes (Fig. 3).

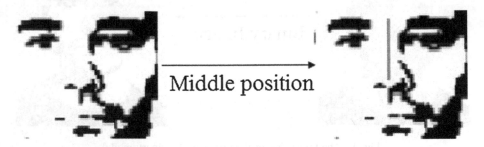

Fig. 3.   Search of average position of two eyes

Next, we search one-eighth of the width the forehead user, for the left eye and its negative value for the right eye, respectively. Between the eyebrow and the eye, there may be white dots. Then we find the right side of the left eye by looking for the black pixel in the horizontal direction from the middle position to the original position of the black pixels between the upper position and the bottom position of the left eye. And the left side for the right eye we are looking for the middle to the starting position of the black pixels between the top position and the bottom position of the right eye. The left side of the left eye is the original width of the image and the right part of the right eye ends the width of the image. Then cut the top position, the bottom position, the left side and the right side of both eyes from the RGB image. To make the eyebrow and eye joint, we place some continuous black pixels vertically from the eyebrow to the eye. The highest white continuous pixel in height between the specified ranges is the middle position of the two eyes (Figure 4).

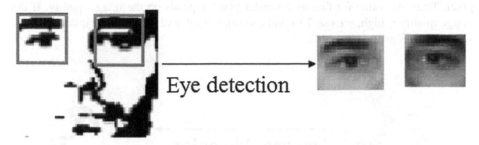

Fig. 4. Search of area of eyes on the image

5   Recognition of Lips

To detect the user's lips, we define the field in which the lips are located. Determine the area on the face in which the lips are. Then we add the distance from the smaller height of the eye to determine the upper height of the area that will contain the lips. The area will be located at the bottom of the face image. Thus, this field will contain only the lips and can some part of the nose. Cut out the RGB image according to the specified area. Then we add a distance from the lower eye height to determine the upper height of the area in which the lips are located (Fig. 5).

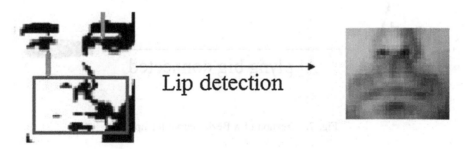

Fig. 5. Search of area of lips on the image

Thus, to detect eyes and lips, we only need to convert the RGB image to binary image and perform some search on the binary image.

6   Creation of a Bezier Curve of Lips

In the area of the lips, in addition to the lips, there may be some part of the nose. Consequently, around the area of the lips is a different skin color. Next, we transform the skin pixel into a white pixel, and the pixel of the lips, as black. Also, find those pixels that look like skin pixels and convert them to a white pixel. Here we use histograms to find the distance between the lower and middle RGB values, and above the average RGB value. If the distance is less than 70, then we use 7 to find a similar pixel, and if the distance is greater than or equal to 70, then we use 10 to find such a pixel. Thus, the value for finding a similar pixel depends on the image quality. If the image quality is high, we use 7 to find a similar pixel, and if the image quality is low, we use 10 (Fig. 6).

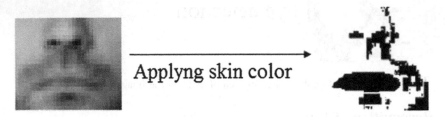

Fig. 6. Separation of lips

In a binary image, there are black areas on the lips, nose and can some other small pieces that may be slightly different from the skin color. Then we apply a large connected area to find the black area that contains the lips in the binary image. And we are sure that a large connected area is lips because, in the lip field, the lips are the largest part that differs color from the skin (Fig. 7).

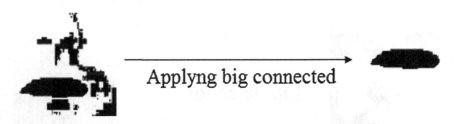

Fig. 7. Creation of a Bezier curve for lips

Then we apply the Bezier curve for the lips on a binary image. In order to apply the Bezier curve, we find the initial and final pixel of the lip in a horizontal position. Then we draw two tangent lines on the upper lip from the initial to the final pixel, and also find two points on the tangent that is not part of the lip. For the lower lip, we find two points similar to the upper lip. We use cubic curves to construct the Bezier curve on the lips. Draw two Bezier curves for the lips, one for the upper lip and one for the lower lip. The construction is applied to the binary image (Fig. 8).

Applying Bezier Curve

Fig. 8. Creation of a Bezier curve for lips

7 Creation of a Bezier Curve of Eyes

To apply the Bezier curve to the eyes, we must first remove the eyebrows from the eyes. To remove the eyebrow, we are looking for the first continuous black pixel, then a continuous white pixel, and then a continuous black pixel from the binary image of the eye area. Then remove the first solid black pixel from the area between the eyebrow and the eye, then we get the area that contains only the eye.

Now the upper area of the face that contains only the eyes. Thus, we apply a similar skin color, like the lips to find the eye area. Then we apply a large connection to find the largest connected area, and this is the eye because, in the eye box, the eyes are the biggest thing that is not like the skin color (Fig. 9).

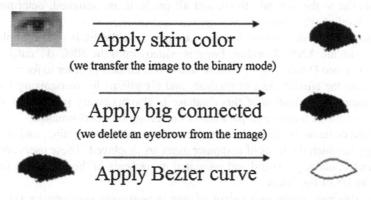

Apply skin color
(we transfer the image to the binary mode)

Apply big connected
(we delete an eyebrow from the image)

Apply Bezier curve

Fig. 9. An algorithm of creation of a Bezier curve for eyes

8 Comparison of the Obtained Data and Data from the Training Selection, Emotion Definition

Further, the Bezier curves obtained are compared with the data from the training sample. The reference points extracted with the help of Bezier curves are processed to obtain inputs for the neural network. The neural network learns to distinguish between the following emotions: neutral, happiness, sadness, anger, disgust, surprise and fear.

The training of a neural network is as follows:

- A database of images of people's faces is prepared for each of the emotions
- For training, manually marked nodal points were obtained for each of the images in the database.

- The obtained reference points were then processed to calculate the inputs mentioned earlier.
- Finally, the inputs and emotions are transmitted to the controlled neural network.

The neural network contains a hidden layer with 30 neurons.

In this approach, each neural network contains a hidden layer with 10 nodes. Each neural network is trained independently using feedback. A hidden layer with a non-linear activation function is trained to map between input-output. The outputs of each network are combined to obtain a percentage value for each emotion.

9 Computational Experiment

Artificial Neural Network (ANN) is a mathematical model, as well as its software or hardware implementation, built on the principle of the organization and functioning of biological neural networks - nerve cell networks of a living organism.

The artificial neuron imitates, in the first approximation, the properties of a biological neuron. At the input of the artificial neuron comes a set of signals, each of which is the output of another neuron. Each input is multiplied by the corresponding weight, similar to the synaptic force, and all products are summed, determining the activation level of the neuron.

The accuracy of the recognition was compared on the basis of the implemented algorithm with the ANN algorithm. For this, videos from the NRC-IIT database were used: Facial Video Database [16]. This database was created in order to form a criterion for evaluating the effectiveness of methods and algorithms for recognizing faces on a video sequence. The creation of this database is also necessary in order to study the influence of various factors and parameters on recognition performance.

The base contains 10 pairs of short videos (one video for training, and the second for testing), in which the faces of computer users are displayed. These users are in front of the monitor, making forward and rotational movements of the head. The face takes from 1/4 to 1/8 of the image.

In this database, every two videos of one person were shot one by one and the shooting conditions were the same. This database is suitable for testing the performance of the face recognition algorithm on video clips.

Comparison of the results of face recognition on video sequences between the proposed algorithm and the algorithm "Associative neural networks" (ANN) is shown in Fig. 10.

The average accuracy of face recognition on the video sequence by the proposed algorithm is 85%, and the ANN algorithm −83%.

The results of face recognition on video sequences by the proposed algorithm showed on the average a higher accuracy in comparison with the ANN algorithm.

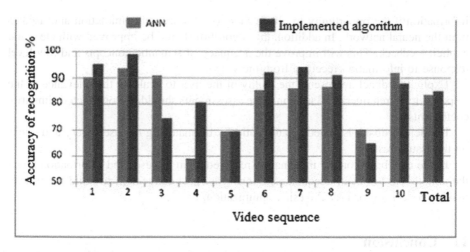

Fig. 10. Compare face recognition results to video sequences with the proposed algorithm with the ANN algorithm

10   Annotation and Classification of Video Recordings

On work [9], there was formulated the problem of video machine description. Based on the data of a graphic annotation in the form of multimedia streams. The problem is that the indexing of the video occurs using prior knowledge of the subject area. If nothing is known about the subject area, indexing will not be correct. From this, it follows that it is necessary to use an abstract method, independent of any domain.

There was proposed to use a representation based on two classes:

- Signs with the characteristics of visual contents. They include color information — histograms, textures, shapes, objects.
- Descriptive representation in the form of text and keywords. For the compilation of this description, it is possible to use a method of the layered graph of clicks of key frames.

After receiving a particular video, you need to assign certain semantic concepts of fragments (mounting frame) and classify the full video for one of the categories.

The process of assigning semantic concepts, we call the word - assigning annotations. Examples of semantic concepts - "Man walks", "car ride", "heaven". As noted above, the annotation is difficult to do based on a particular choice of concepts. Therefore, this stage needs to implement the algorithm based on training analysis and understanding video. In work [10] there was presented an FGSSMIL algorithm or "quick graph half controlled training in multiple instances". The algorithm is trained on a small number of views of videos that were also manually annotated and the annotated material. For this algorithm, possible improvements in automation of receiving the annotated video based on user comments. For example, for system YouTube, it is possible to obtain comments with the time in the video to which this review. This becomes even more true in the case of emotional search. When a sufficient amount of information if the opportunity to obtain more or less accurate annotation and used to train the neural network. In addition, this algorithm should be improved with clear and explicit feedback. This will improve the adequacy of semantic concepts and low-level response to information received from the video.

Explicit feedback represents the ability of the user to evaluate the relevance of the response to search queries. Based on these assessments should be constructed similarity coefficients.

Implicit feedback is collected automatically by matching the user query and clicks on the issued results.

In the end, based on the information received from the user and information about the annotation, to obtain adequate solutions it is most convenient to build the task of making a decision or task Bayesian optimization.

11 Conclusion

The algorithm allowing recognizing a basic set of emotions in a video stream became the result of the done operation. An algorithm it is based on Viola-Jones method, Bezier curves, and the developed neural network together with the qualifier. The system is rather steady, against lighting and additional noises on a face (points, a beard or whiskers). However, the process of detection of the person in case of bad lighting can take bigger time, than in the case of normal, daylight. The speed of operation of an algorithm allows processing a video stream in real time. From the camera, the video stream with permission of 320×240 pixels and with a frequency of 30 frames per second turns out. At the same time, during a method operating time, interruption of a flow is not watched. On the basis of the developed algorithm, it is created the auto-mated system capable to determine emotional responses of the person in real time by a video stream. Recognition accuracy very strongly depends on two criteria: accuracy of detection of "parameters" on a face and determination of the change of provision of these "parameters" in space. The accuracy of detection of breakpoints rather good. However, the main lack of a method is that determination only of a basic set of emotions, namely, neutral, happiness, grief, anger, disgust, surprise, and fear is made. For determination of more difficult emotions, for example – the alarm, shame, con-tempt, is required the analysis of the bigger quantity of frames with the use of more difficult analysis algorithms.

This work was partially supported by RFBR (grants №. 15-47-02149, 15-07-06322, 15-37-70014, 16-07-00453).

References

1. Zhao, R., William, G.: Narrowing the semantic gap-improved text-based web document retrieval using visual features. IEEE Trans. Multimedia **4**(2), 189–200 (2002)
2. Tamizharasan, C., Chandrakala, S.: A survey on multimodal content based video retrieval. Int. J. Emerg. Technol. Adv. Eng. Chennai, **3** (2013)

3. Abhishek, G., Arnab, B.: Emotion recognition from audio and visual data using f-score based fusion. In: Proceedings of the 1st IKDD Conference on Data Sciences, pp. 1–10 (2014)
4. Nigay, L., Coutaz, J.: A design space for multimodal systems: concurrent processing and data fusion. In: Proceedings of the INTERACT 1993 and CHI 1993 Conference on Human Factors in Computing Systems. New York, pp. 172–178 (1993)
5. Truong, B.T., Venkatesh, S.: Video abstraction, a systematic review and classification. ACM Trans. Multimedia Comput. Commun. **3** (2007)
6. Zhang, X.-D., Liu, T.-Y., Lo, K.-T., Feng, J.: Dynamic selection and effective compression of key frames for video abstraction. Pattern Recogn. Lett. **24**, 1523–1532 (2003)
7. Sundaram, H., Chang, S.-F.: Video Scene segmentation using video and audio features. In: 2000 IEEE International Conference on Multimedia Expo, vol. 2, pp. 1145–1148 (2000)
8. Adcock, J., Girgensohn, A., Cooper, M., Liu, T., Wilcox, L., Rieffel, E.: Fxpal experiments for trecvid 2004. In: Proceedings of the TREC Video Retrieval Evaluation (TRECVID), pp. 70–81 (2004)
9. Haase, B., Davis, M.E.: Media streams: representing video for retrieval and repurposing. Technical report (1995)
10. Zhang, T., Xu, C., Zhu, G., Liu, S., Lu, H.: A generic framework for video annotation via semi-supervised learning. IEEE Trans. Multimedia. 1206–1219 (2012)
11. Alekseev, A.V.: Automatic coloring of grayscale images based on intelligent scene analysis. In: Alekseev, A.V., Rozaliev, V.L., Orlova, Y.A. (eds.) Pattern Recognition and Image Analysis (Advances in Mathematical Theory and Applications). 25(1), pp. 10–21. Pleiades Publishing, Moscow (2015)
12. Cootes, T., Taylor, C., Cooper, D.: Active shape models-their training and application. Comput. Vis. Image Underst. **61**, 38–59 (1995)
13. Cuiping, Z., Guangda, S.: Human face recognition: a survey. J. Image Graph. **11**, 103–111 (2000)
14. Rozaliev, V.L., Bobkov, A.S., Orlova, Y.A., Zaboleeva-Zotova, A.V., Dmitriev, A.S.: Detailed analysis of postures and gestures for the identification of human emotional reactions. World Appl. Sci. J. (WASJ) **24**(24), 151–158 (2013)
15. Zaboleeva-Zotova, A.V., Orlova, Y.A., Rozaliev, V.L., Bobkov, A.S.: Emotional state recognition based on the motion and posture. In: Operations Research and Data Mining, ORADM 2012: the Workshop, 12–14 March 2012, Cancun Center for Continuous Education of the National Politechnic Institute (IPN). – Cancun, Cancun, Mexico, pp. 161–169 (2012) Eng
16. Gorodnichy, D.O.: Video-based framework for face recognition in video/D.O. Gorodnichy. In: Second Workshop on Face Processing in Video (FPiV 2005). In: Proceedings of Second Canadian Conference on Computer and Robot Vision CRV 2005, Victoria, BC, Canada, 9–11 May 2005, pp. 330–338
17. Guo, G.D., Dyer, C.R.: Learning from examples in the small sample case-face expression recognition. IEEE Trans. Syst. **35**, 477–488 (2005)
18. Havran, C., et al.: Independent Component Analysis for face authentication. In: KES 2002 Proceedings - Knowledge-Based Intelligent Information and Engineering Systems, Crema, Italy, pp. 1207–1211 (2002)
19. Rozaliev, V.L., Orlova, Y.A.: Recognizing and analyzing emotional expressions in movements. In: Isaías, P., Spector, J.M., Ifenthaler, D., Sampson, D.G. (eds.) E-Learning Systems, Environments and Approaches, pp. 117–131. Springer, Cham (2015). doi:10.1007/978-3-319-05825-2_9

20. Alekseev, A.V., Orlova, Y.A., Rozaliev, V.L., Zaboleeva-Zotova, A.V.: Two-stage segmentation method for context-sensitive image analysis. In: Kravets, A., Shcherbakov, M., Kultsova, M., Iijima, T. (eds.) JCKBSE 2014. CCIS, vol. 466, pp. 331–340. Springer, Cham (2014). doi:10.1007/978-3-319-11854-3_28

21. Shinohara, Y., Otsu, N.: Facial expression recognition using fisher weight maps. In: Proeeedings of IEEE Conference on Automatic Face and Gesture Recognition, Korea-Seoul, pp. 499–504 (2004)

22. Sujun, Z.: Facial expression recognition algorithm based on active shape model and gabor wavelet. J. Henan Univ. (Nat. Sci.) **9**, 40–45 (2010)

23. Viola, P., Jones, M.: Robust real time object detection. In: 8th IEEE International Conference on Computer Vision. Vancouver, pp. 151–155 (2001)

24. Xiaofeng, F.: Facial expression recognition based on multi-scale centralized binary pattern. Control Theory Appl. **6**, 26–32 (2009)

Visual Detection of Internal Patterns in the Empirical Data

Alena Zakharova, Evgeniya Vekhter$^{(\boxtimes)}$, Aleksey Shklyar,
and Dmitry Zavyalov

Tomsk Polytechnic University, Avenue of Lenin 30, 634050 Tomsk, Russia
{zaa,vehter,shklyarav,zda}@tpu.ru

Abstract. The article proposes the solution of the problem of the multidimensional data research. The purpose of such research is detection of internal regularities in initial data, what increases the level of knowledge and understanding the essence by the researcher.

The possibilities of using visual data models to achieve this goals are shown. Results of practical use of visual analysis of multidimensional data for justification of the choice of not determined parameters for modeling and designing oil and gas fields using given analogies. High productivity of the developed approach for solving problems of the multidimensional data analysis was confirmed.

Keywords: Cognitive graphics · Computer visualization · Decision supporting systems · Dynamic visualization · Interpretation · Visual interpretation · Visual model · Visual perception

1 Tasks of Data Analysis

In a case when the user has an experience in using visual models, actual grounds appear for explanation their effectiveness and a choice of the most effective tool [1]. Due to this, there might be an additional advantage of visual analysis, related to the reduction of time. First of all, to select the type of visual model it is necessary for the researcher to understand accurately the goal for using visual analysis tools.

The purpose of data analyses, including visual data, is to obtain an answer to the main research question [2]. While constructing a general analysis methodology, two additional circumstances should be considered. Firstly, before the completion of the analysis process, new data appears which may affect on the formulation of the main question. Secondly, the answer to the question should be considered not as the state of the visual model, but the achievement of the researcher of the necessary degree of understanding of this state.

Therefore, the meaning of the research issue, the validity of the formulation, the degree of its complexity, the correspondence between the form of the response obtained as a result of interaction with the model and the researcher's understanding of its significance become important [3]. Since getting the right idea about the result of the analysis is a priority task of the visual model, the development of expressive tools

© Springer International Publishing AG 2017
A. Kravets et al. (Eds.): CIT&DS 2017, CCIS 754, pp. 215–230, 2017.
DOI: 10.1007/978-3-319-65551-2_16

(which are a part of the visual model) need to focus on this circumstance, and not, for example, on the correspondence to the initial data.

In addition to understanding the goal, there are numbers of additional circumstances which increase the effectiveness of the process of visual analysis. There is the factor of emotional persuasiveness that allows the user to make a decision without the need for excessive verification of its reliability, as well as the ability to overcome the negative impact of such factors as a lack of concentration, fatigue or subjective rejection.

Differences in purposes of analysis form several types of models.

- **Analytical models.** Designed to find unknown patterns in the data, internal dependencies, correlation of changes in parameters, etc.
- **Controlling models.** They are used to detect inconsistencies in the visualized information to the existing understanding, inaccuracy or insufficiency of data that could not be seen or estimated by other tools.
- **Models of choice.** Are focused on granting methods of a comparison of possible variants of decisions to the researcher in those problems when the necessary choice is made by expert opinion using internal knowledge of the user or other criteria chosen by him.

2   Requirements for the Visual Solution

Solving the problem of visual analysis of data leads to obtaining new information that can have a reverse effect on the user's opinion, and therefore there are a number of requirements for the procedure for obtaining an answer to the research question. For example, the features of using visual models are associated with the concentration of attention on the object of studies [4]. This leads to the need for simultaneous visualization of both the background information and the intermediate information needed to answer the research question.

Changing the visual model during the analysis of the data creates the need to verify the correspondence of the new shape to the conditions of the initial analysis task. The phase of such assay also becomes a part of the visual image and changes its perception [5]. The output from an infinite cycle of verification of the received solutions is achieved by means of the visual model itself. For this purpose, the following characteristics have been distinguished:

- Predictability of the consequences of decision making.
- Compliance with additional criteria.
- The uniqueness or originality of the solution [6].
- Dimensionless of the representation.

3   Complex Approach to Visual Analysis

Visualization is one of the ways of modeling and it fulfills functions of the cognitive tool. While creating a visual image of the studied data, the original object S is associated with the model Z, which can have a completely different ontological affiliation.

As an object of study, S can be a real object or a complex of them, data of any kind and origin, events, as well as individual properties of P_i objects. Thus, the object of the research $S = \left\{ P_i^{(S)} \right\}$ is considered to be a set of elements localized in time (t) and space (r). The visual model Z is also an object, which consists of properties of $P_k^{(Z)}$, which are matched to the original [4].

$$S(t, r) = \{P_n^{(s)}(t, r)\} \rightarrow Z(t, r) = \{P_k^{(z)}(t, r)\}, n = 1..N(s), k = 1..K(Z),$$

where $N(S)$ is the space dimensionality of features of the original object S; $K(Z)$ is the number of perceived characteristics of the visual model associated with the original object.

In general, the dimensions of spaces of features $N(S)$ and $K(Z)$ may not coincide. In addition, some properties of the object $N^*(S)$ are not correlated to properties of the model Z. Such models - Z_A are abstract because the choice of displayed properties is arbitrary and is determined by the author of the visual model. Any visual model is abstract:

$$Z_A = \{P_k^{(Z)}(t, r)\} | F_{map} : P_{N(S)}^{(S)} \rightarrow P_{K(Z)}^{(S)}, P_{N*(S)}^{(S)} \rightarrow |P^{(Z)}\}$$

The visual image received by the observer is an artificial form, located between sensual perception and thinking. This allows to combine the visual processing of information and mental analysis of data stored in the memory of the researcher. The rationale for choosing the matching method (modeling function) F_{map} is necessary to create the most successful simulation analogy, ensuring the success of visual analysis. The purpose of the visual analysis is to obtain an answer to a question with a visual model, within the constraints.

The Statement. The effectiveness of visual analysis increases in the case of implementation of a complex approach in the function of visual modeling.

The decision to choose a matching method is taken by the author of the model. The subjectivity of the model and its interpretation determines the existence of objective $R_{map}(S)$ and conventional $C_{map}(S)$ components in the modeling function F_{map}. For abstract models Z_A, the conventional matching function of $C_{map}(S)$ becomes the main function.

$$F_{map} = \{R_{map}(S), C_{map}(S)\};$$
$$Z_A = \{P_k^{(A)}(t, r)\} | F_{map}^{(A)} : C_{map}(S) = max, R_{map}(S) = min\}$$

Thus, the choice of the mapping function (visual modeling) depends on properties of the original object S, the goal of modeling E_v and the subjective decision of the researcher H. Each of the arguments of the visual modeling function can vary in space and time.

$$C_{map} = C_{map}(S, r, t, E_v, H)$$

Subjectivity influences on the solution of the task of visual analysis twice: from the side of the author of the model and from the side of the researcher. Therefore, the control of the effectiveness of visual analysis should include management of the visual presentation of the data and management of its reading. This creates two additional components in the simulation function: the direct function E_{pr} (control of the presentation form, representation) and the inverse one E_{it} (control of the results of perception, interpretation).

$$C_{map} = <C_{map}(E_v), C_{map}(E_{pr}), C_{map}(E_{it}) >$$

Corollary A. Each component of the modeling function can be controlled and changed in time.

Corollary B. Regulation of the degree of participation of each component leads to the creation of visual models for various purposes and allows to solve problems of visual analysis of different types.

Corollary C. The effectiveness of visual analysis is determined by the time taken to obtain a solution.

Based on the proposed idea of the participation of various factors in solving problems of visual analysis, there are several definitions:

An integrated approach (to visual data analysis) is a balanced directional use of all components significant for achieving the purpose of analysis in the function of visual modeling C_{map}.

Functional approach C_{map} (E_v). The visual modeling function is responsible for matching visual data to objects based on the purpose of the analysis - E_v. Tasks of the functional approach are decomposition of the main question of analysis into research stages which have controlled effectiveness. Examples of such steps are answers for basic questions, the formulation of intermediate tasks, preservation of the research data or connection to the analysis of additional data sources.

Semiotic approach C_{map} (E_{pr}) is a function of a representation of the data, aimed at choosing the form of presentation, depending on the type and amount of data, available modeling resources, observer's awareness. The task of the presentation function C_{map} (E_{pr}) is the transfer of data to the stage of thinking in a form that ensures the achievement of the goal or corresponding to the formulated requirements. The generalization of modeling tools, which is necessary for the presentation of various data, is the basis for the transition to the concept of visual language [7].

The psychoemotional approach C_{map} (E_{it}) is a modeling function which regulates the interpretation of the visual shape [8]. It is necessary to overcome or exploit the subjective nature of visual perception. The main tasks of the interpretation function $C_{map}(E_{it})$ are the use of the cognitive potential of the researcher, managing his motivation and attitude to the analysis, reducing the time spent on making a decision.

4   The Structure of the Visual Model of Data

Data analysis is a process directed by an action which can be a sequence started with the formulation of the question and continued with the search for hypotheses contained the answer to this question. In this case, the correctness of the result of the analysis depends on two factors: the nature of the issue, which is determined by the degree of preliminary understanding of the analyzed information, and also the form of the question (see Fig. 1). The form is determined by the language of the question, by the internal structure, by logic and need for interaction with additional sources of information [9].

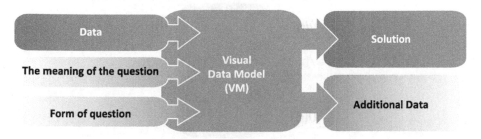

Fig. 1. Analysis of the visual shape.

The scheme of the visual analysis process demonstrated a consistent approach to the answer to the general research question (see Fig. 2), confirms the reasonableness of the integrated approach to the visual analysis. The modeling functions, combined in an integrated approach, are parallel information flows that regulate the process of analysis.

Statement. Visual data analysis is a controlled process of constructing the pattern of regularities discovered by the user in the data.

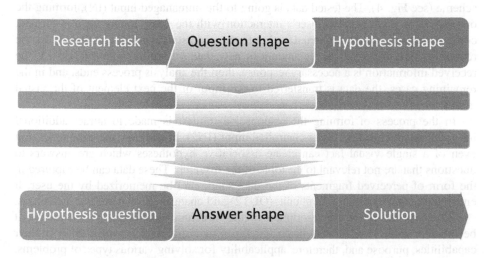

Fig. 2. The scheme of the functioning of the visual model.

Corollary A. The visual model should allow verification of regularities which are the result of the analysis.

Corollary B. The consistent nature of the analysis process allows dividing the whole process into stages which have the same properties and purpose.

The structural unit of visual analysis is an element of the visual model (see Fig. 3). The visual element is the state of the visual model, interpreted as a response to an elementary question, previously deliberated by the user. The complexity of such question is determined by the limited time of the analysis.

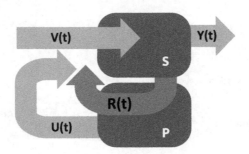

Fig. 3. The structural unit of visual analysis.

The structural unit of the visual analysis is a controlled system S with feedback R(t). The volume of the studied data comes into the uncontrolled input V(t) of the structural unit. A feature of such system is the possibility of changing the state of the controlled input of the system U(t) as a function of the obtained results Y(t). User P is a mandatory participant in the structural unit, from the point of view of an integrated approach to the visual analysis.

In general, the element of the visual model can be represented by a simple logic scheme (see Fig. 4). The tested data is going to the unmanaged input (IN), forming the original form. As a result of user's interaction with the form, a new form is formed, corresponding not to the original data, but to the understanding of their meaning by the researcher. It corresponds to the amount of new data sent to the output (OUT). If the received information is a necessary response, then the analysis process ends, and in the remaining cases, the data is transferred to the input of the next element of the visual model.

In the process of forming the response, a request is made to attract additional information which is sent to the controlled input (IN2). In addition, the comprehension even of a single visual fact can create associative hypotheses which are answers to questions that are not relevant to the topic of the research. These data can be captured in the form of perceived fragments of the data shape and be memorized by the user. It enters the output of the structural unit, (OUT2) and changes its own internal awareness.

Based on the proposed description of the structural unit of the visual model, it becomes possible to accurately determine types of visual models which differ in their capabilities, purpose and, therefore, applicability for solving various types of problems.

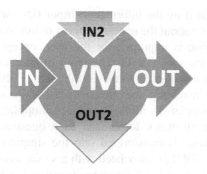

Fig. 4. Logical diagram of the structural unit.

The logical schema of the element allows declaring differences between them based on the activity of using existing links. In addition, the combination of structural units, including various types, allows analyzing and predicting the effectiveness of using visual analysis tools.

5 Selection of the Type of the Visual Model

The attraction of visual research methods is aimed at reducing the time spent on data analysis. A preliminary study of possibilities of the visual model makes it possible to determine its correspondence to conditions of analysis and, possibly, to eliminate elements that require unreasonably long time expenditure. In addition, from the point of view of an integrated approach, the basis for choosing a visual model is, not only the features of the problem being solved but also the characteristics of the researcher [5].

Based on the proposed description of the structural unit of visual analysis, the visual model can be determined by the characteristics of the activity of using information's inputs and outputs. In one of the simplest cases, the visual image is used as an indicator of the state of the observed system. The purpose of the data model is to notify the observer about a change in state or, more correctly, about the occurrence of an expected event (see Fig. 5).

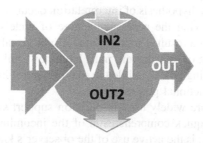

Fig. 5. Model of visual information.

The main load is tested by the information input (IN), which provides modeling functions with information about the necessary form of informing of the observer. This means that no information is important for the user, except the message about the occurrence of the expected state (OUT). The input of additional information (IN2) is not activated because the expected shape is the part of the conventional notation system. Consequently, increasing the effectiveness while solving the problem of analysis of this type is associated with the maximum simplification of the visual shape.

In addition, the control effect, formalized as a question to the stage of visual analysis (IN2), in this case, is transformed into the simplest logical switching "yes/no?". The control action (OUT2), associated with a visual assessment of the shape and the appeared emotional response, can also be reduced as much as possible, because of the use of unambiguously interpreted shapes. Thus, the transition to the next stage of visual analysis, if it exists, occurs together with a change in the state of the user's internal awareness. It arises as a realized expectation, which does not use external sources of information and does not change the amount of accumulated knowledge.

In the following case, the use of external connections of the structural element of the visual model takes the more complex character. A new visual model is designed for user's training, i.e. for information, accompanied by the verification of a new solution due to the previously generated internal awareness of the user. In a simplified form, the task of the training visual model is to transmit to the observer the necessary amount of information, which reliability is not questioned (see Fig. 6).

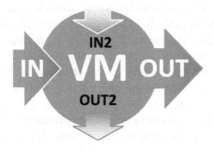

Fig. 6. A visual model of training type.

The verification of the hypothesis of interpretation occurs on the basis of previously defined criteria for achieving the necessary degree of understanding and becomes a formalized procedure. As a result, a training model or a visual model, intended for the most correct transmission of information, must have powerful information links - both incoming (IN) and outgoing (OUT), while the role of control links (IN2, OUT2) can be reduced to Minimum functional purpose.

Visual data models are widely used in decision support systems. In this case, the analysis task requires a quick comprehension of the incoming data. The determining condition for data models is the active use of the observer's knowledge and experience to obtain conclusions that influence on the further existence of the system [10]. This type of visual analysis is characterized by the active use of additional information, user's knowledge and the formulation of interim questions (see Fig. 7).

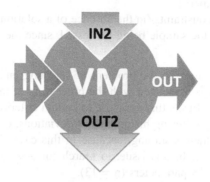

Fig. 7. Visual model for decision-making tasks.

The model's information input (IN) is used to provide the information which is necessary to construct a visual image in a form consistent with the form of the control question, which enters the input (IN2). This means that the perceived components of the model become objects that initiate the construction of response hypotheses, and therefore the choice of the type of visual representation has fundamental importance [11].

6   The Task of Data Recovery

Due to the high speed of data analysis with the help of visual models, their application in the study of empirical data, which require a large amount of computation or mental efforts, is in demand. Evaluation of the effectiveness of the use of visual methods of data analysis was held for reconstruction the missing data in the description of oil production facilities. Objects of analysis are parameters (geological, technological and other) of the oil and gas field, which are necessary for designing, modeling forecasting solutions, estimating reserves, etc. In this case, all parameters are characterized by a high cost of obtaining and not all of them are measured or identified. The hypothesis of solving this problem is the assumption of the possibility of borrowing missing data from deposits characterized by similar geological conditions, similar values of key parameters. Thus, the purpose of the visual analysis is to quickly find objects that have similar properties. The proximity criterion is determined by the user subjectively (based on the expert's judgment).

While designing the development of deposits, the search procedure for analogies is poorly formalized and in many ways is subjective - the decision always remains for the designer or expert and is often based on personal experience and is not supported by the factual material. Thus, the peculiarities of the considered problem are analogies:

- Diversity of data;
- Lack of strict formalization and methods of solution;
- Subjectivity of the received solution (Weighting factors of the parameters are determined by the expert);
- Flexible restrictions constraints (in the absence of a solution, the framework can be extended to increase the sample being processed, since the solution must be found in any case).

Traditionally, the solution to the problem of selecting analogies can be obtained statistically, this method is associated with the processing of tabular data on available deposits and identifying objects that are close to certain criteria. The visual solution of the problem can be obtained using histograms of deviations, correlation diagrams, etc. (see Fig. 8), which is time-consuming, because In this case, the expert must analyze graphs for each parameter. In this issue, to search for a solution, there is a need to construct diagrams with 13 parameters (n = 13).

Indicated solutions are associated with the processing of large amounts of data, are time-consuming and do not allow a comprehensive assessment of all available data in one model, which would make shorter the decision time. The main reason for this is that in modern conditions of growth of information volumes, traditional methods of visual data analysis based on flat two-dimensional models can not provide sufficient information to the user. It is necessary to use multidimensional data models [12].

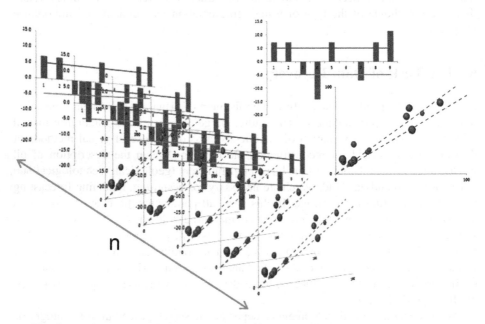

Fig. 8. A visual solution of the problem of choosing analogies in the traditional way.

To solve any problem, a model, corresponded to the type of visual decision making, is required. This indicates the need to actively engage the user's capabilities in obtaining an answer to the research question. In addition, one of the prerequisites is to reduce the analysis time. The fulfillment of this requirement can be achieved by simplifying the model to the type corresponded to the usual information, as well as by using expressive visual means that do not require long acquaintance and reflection (Table 1).

The function C_{map} (E_{pr}) is to reduce the time required for the user to get acquainted with the original data. In the situation of visualizing a significant number of parameters, C_{map} (E_{pr}) is selected to remove components that require familiarization from the shape being created. For this reason, in the model being created, the shape of an individual element, combined a given number of parameters, is represented as a three-dimensional graph.

Table 1. An example of a data structure that is examined according to the principle of analogies.

Name		Weight (1–5)	Tolerance, %	Unit of measurement	Conditions
Poro	Porosity	5	10	Unit fraction	0, 1 < Poro < 0, 25
So	Oil saturation	5	10	Unit fraction	0, 4 < So < 0, 7
Perm	Permeability	5	10	mkm^2	0, 1 < Perm < 30
m_o	Oil viscosity in reservoir conditions	4	15	мPa*s	m_o < 1, 2
ρ_o	Oil density in surface conditions	4	8	g/cm^3	0, 8 < ρ_o < 0,95
b_o	Oil-formation volume factor	4	5	Unit fraction	1, 1 < b_o < 1, 3
G	Gas content of in-place oil	4	10	$м^3/t$	30 < G < 150
h	Average net productive formation thickness	3	20	м	2 < h < 47
h_{net}	Average net oil thickness	3	15	м	0, 5 < h_{net} < 31
H	Average depth of bedding	2	5	м	2350 << 2590
NTG	Net-to gross	2	15	Unit fraction	0,42 << 0,76
p	Initial formation pressure	2	15	MPa	19 < p < 27
ρ_w	Water density in surface conditions	1	5	g/cm^3	1,005 < ρ_w < 1, 150

One of the ways to solve the problem of effective time use is to reduce the amount of excessive information for an observer. On the one hand, this is achieved by analyzing the informativeness of the obtained images and eliminating elements whose meaning is not related to the formulation of the study. But, in addition, it is possible to involve the ability of a person to mental interpolation and extrapolation of data, which makes it reasonable to reproduce in the data model only a part of them [13].

The organization of the verification procedure, performed by the interpretation function C_{map} (E_{it}), for models with the need for deep decomposition of the original question, is a complex problem. Therefore, in the studied issue, the visual model is accompanied by the maximum possible degree of interactivity of the control system (see Fig. 9), which allows to formulate a mental question at each step of the analysis in such a way that it corresponds to the speed and features of the researcher's thinking.

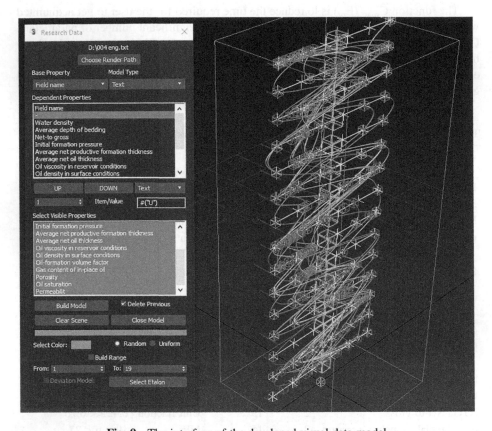

Fig. 9. The interface of the developed visual data model.

In addition to evaluating an array of heterogeneous data in one visual model, the complexity is also in the ability to perform a visual analysis of data simultaneously in several directions: absolute values, absolute and relative deviations from the standard, and data dynamics.

Within the framework of this search for analogies, the closest analogue field is selected from the sample of candidates, taking into account the weight coefficients of parameters and permissible deviations of parameters of candidates from the standard.

A conceptual diagram of the obtained visual data model for solving the problem of searching for analogies in the design of field development is presented in Fig. 10.

In 2D mode, the model allows to analyze the array of data taking into account the weight coefficients, while for a better visual perception, parameters are scaled. To solve the problem of finding analogies in the model, the comparison mode with the standard is implemented, for which a third dimension is added, which displays the deviation of

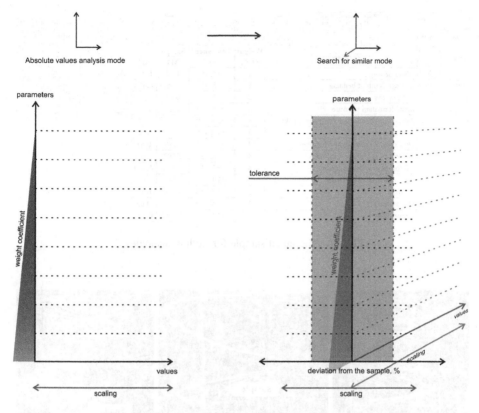

Fig. 10. Conceptual diagram of the visual data model.

parameters of each candidate from the standard. The solution of the problem is reduced to a visual assessment by the expert of deviations of parameters and the choice of the most suitable candidate.

To test the presented approach on real data, one of the Tomsk Oblast deposits was selected, where there are no own core studies which are necessary for designing the development forecast. Such studies can be taken on a similar deposit, it is necessary to find in the initial sample of candidates an analog field that is closest to the benchmark by key parameters. The initial sample includes 18 candidates (see Fig. 11). Of the total data set for each of the deposits, 13 (n = 13) key geological and physical characteristics were assigned. Weight coefficients and allowable deviations from the standard were appointed to them. The resulting visual model is shown in Fig. 12.

The created tool for visual analysis and obtaining new information is an example of visual data interpolation due to the realization in the model of the functional principle of visual analogies. Using the developed visual model allows identifying quickly in the studied empirical data objects, which are close to each other, in terms of the observer and the principles recognized by him. This approach allows you to quickly and efficiently evaluate, analyze and compare large amounts of data, which is time-consuming when using traditional methods of analysis [14].

Parameters	Weight (1-5)	Tolerance, %	Sample M1	M2
Water density	1	+5, -5	1,02	1,027
Average depth of bedding	2	+5, -5	-2406,5	-2478
Net-to gross	2	+15, -15	0,66	0,52
Initial formation pressure	2	+15, -15	25,5	25,3
Average net productive formation thickness	3	+20, -20	13,8	12,6
Average net oil thickness	3	+15, -15	6	4,8
Oil viscosity in reservoir conditions	4	+15, -15	0,56	0,61
Oil density in surface conditions	4	+8, -8	0,799	0,808
Oil-formation volume factor	4	+5, -5	1,178	1,229
Gas content of in-place oil	4	+10, -10	54	71,4
Porosity	5	+10, -10	0,14	0,15
Oil saturation	5	+10, -10	0,58	0,65
Permeability	5	+10, -10	0,0051	0,005

Fig. 11. The initial sample for finding analogies.

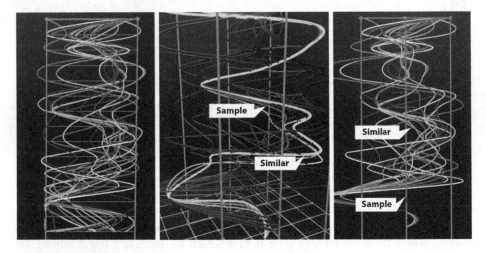

Fig. 12. The visual data model for the task of finding analogies among deposits.

In addition, such model allows to verify the data, as well as assessing the obtained forecast solution for field development, taking into account the experience of developing similar facilities (see Fig. 13).

The use of visual models adapted to rapid transformation, controlled and justified from the point of view of the impact on the observer, develops the definition of the process of visual analysis. In this case, visual analysis becomes a consistent process of investigating some information and consists in a meaningful manipulation of the visual model. The goal of such controlled transformation is a step-by-step transition to a visual model, which interpretation is analogous to the formulated answer to the general question of analysis.

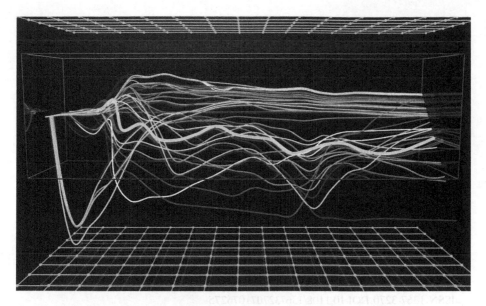

Fig. 13. An example of an estimate of the forecast solution taking into account the development experience.

7 Conclusion

Application of visual methods of the data research allows using the researcher's knowledge in creating a solution hypothesis. The creation and description of the visual, based on the proposed integrated approach, made it possible to identify main ways to increase the effectiveness of the multi-scale analysis of multidimensional data. Recusing the time of the analysis of such data is reached using interactive management of a visual shape. The offered approach of the data analysis is used to solve a problem about justifying the choice of not determined parameters for modeling and designing oil and gas fields using given analogies. This is the first time when in one visual model multidimensional and multiscale data have been comprehensively evaluated. Therefore optimum parameters of modeling a field have been selected.

This work was supported by grant 2.1642.2017/ПЧ from the Ministry of Education and Science of the Russian Federation.

References

1. Chen, C.: Mapping Scientific Frontiers: The Quest for Knowledge Visualization, 2nd edn. Springer, London (2013)
2. Korobkin, D., Fomenkov, S., Kravets, A., Kolesnikov, S., Dykov, M.: Three-steps methodology for patents prior-art retrieval and structured physical knowledge extracting. In: Creativity in Intelligent Technologies and Data Science First Conference, CIT&DS 2015, pp. 124–138. Volgograd, Russia (2015)

3. Bondarev, A.E., Galaktionov, V.A.: Multidimensional data analysis and visualization for time-dependent CFD problems. Prog. Comput. Softw. **41**(5), 247–252 (2015). doi:10.1134/S0361768815050023
4. Solovyev, R., Seryakov, V.A.: Advertisements and information objects positioning technologies based on the territorial zoning of the city of Tomsk. In: 20th International Conference for Students and Young Scientists: Modern Techniques and Technologies IOP Conference Series: Materials Science and Engineering 2014, vol. 66, Tomsk, Russia (2014)
5. Zakharova, A.A., Shklyar, A.V.: Visual presentation of different types of data by dynamic sign structures. Sci. Vis. **8**(4), 28–37 (2016)
6. Chen, C.: Top 10 unsolved information visualization problems. IEEE Comput. Graph. Appl. **25**(4), 12–16 (2005)
7. Averbukh, V.: Semiotic approach to forming the theory of computer visualization [Semioticheskij podhod k formirovaniju teorii komp'juternoj vizualizacii]. Sci. Vis. **5**(1), 1–25 (2013)
8. Kamran, S., Paul, P., Liang, H.-N., Morey, J.: Supporting sensemaking of complex objects with visualizations. Visibility Complement. Interact. Inform. **3**(4), 20 (2016). doi:10.3390/informatics3040020
9. Eppler, M., Burkhard, R.A.: Visual representations in knowledge management: framework and cases. J. Knowl. Manage. **11**(4), 112–122. QEmerald Group Publishing Limited (2007). ISSN 1367-3270 DOI:10.1108/1367327071076275
10. Shneiderman, B., Plaisant, C., Cohen, M.S., Jacobs, S.M., Elmqvist, N., Diakopoulos, N.: Designing the User Interface: Strategies for Effective Human-Computer Interaction, 6th edn. Pearson, Upper Saddle River (2016)
11. Personal visualization and personal visual analytics: Huang, D., Tory, M., Adriel Aseniero, B., Bartram, L., Bateman, S., Carpendale, S., Tang, A., Woodbury, R. IEEE Trans. Vis. Comput. Graph. **21**, 420–433 (2015)
12. Ozpeynirci, O., Ozpeynirci, S., Kaya, A.: An interactive approach for multiple criteria selection problem. Comput. Oper. Res. **78**, 154–162 (2016)
13. Zavyalov, D.A., Zakharova, A.A., Shklyar, A.V., Bagutdinov, R.A.: An integrated approach to modeling by an example of a landfill of disposal of liquid oil waste. Softw. Syst. Comput. Methods [Programmnye sistemy i vychislitel'nye metody] **1**, 22–30 (2017)
14. Zaripova, V.M., Petrova, I.Y., Kravets, A., Evdoshenko, O.: Knowledge bases of physical effects and phenomena for method of energy-informational models by means of ontologies. In: Creativity in Intelligent Technologies and Data Science First Conference, CIT&DS 2015, pp. 224–237. Volgograd, Russia (2015)

The Control System Structure for the Stable Biped Robot Motion

Alexander S. Gorobtsov[1], E.N. Ryzhov[1], A.S. Polyanina[2],
Andrey E. Andreev[1(✉)], and N.I. Kohtashvili[1]

[1] Volgograd State Technical University, Volgograd, Russia
vm@vstu.ru, A.S.Churzina@mail.ru, andan2005@yandex.ru
[2] Kamyshin Technological Institute,
Branch of the Volgograd State Technical University, Kamyshin, Russia

Abstract. The paper considers the synthesis of the controlled motion of anthropomorphic robots along given trajectories. The structure of a motion control system for walking robots is presented, including the gait generator. The gait generation unit consists of the trajectory generator of the foot points, the center of mass trajectory generator and the additional links generator. Oscillators described by nonlinear differential equations with stable limit cycles, having sections of near-rectilinear motion, are proposed to be used as a generator of trajectories of feet points. In opposite, known approaches use some analytical piecewise continuous functions. The proposed method is based on the theory of an asymptotic stability of invariant sets. Also, the stability conditions of the robot body points control under the action of the generator of additional links are analyzed. The obtained method of synthesis of the stable movement modes with the given cycles limit has been used for generation of trajectories of points feet motion of android AR-600E.

Keywords: Biped robot motion control · Stability conditions · Gait generator · Kinematics · Android AR-600

1 Introduction

The biped walking robots (further - androids) fall into an intensively developing class of robots. The development of control methods for such robots could solve various important technical problems. To date, there are several exemplars of androids in which some modes of biped walking are implemented (Fig. 1). For multidimensional spatial robotic systems, two main directions of solving the problems of motion synthesis can be distinguished. There are theoretical methods and methods based on the use of man as the operating link. The second direction has intensively been developing, for example, in medicine [1], or in the domain of walking robots, in exoskeletons. The main theoretical method of multilink mechanical systems motion synthesis is the inverse dynamics method [2]. Such method helps to define the program motions of the robot and all its drives (or actuators), implementing the given general law of motion.

    The main element of androids control systems is the gait generator, which calculates the interrelated coordinates of the motion of all robot's links. The gait generation

A. Kravets et al. (Eds.): CIT&DS 2017, CCIS 754, pp. 231–241, 2017.
DOI: 10.1007/978-3-319-65551-2_17

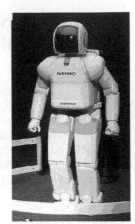

Fig. 1. Some known androids with implemented modes of biped walking (a) Boston dynamics' Atlas (b) Hubo (c) Asimo by Honda

unit consists of the trajectory generator of the foot points, the center of mass trajectory generator and the additional link generator. The trajectory generator of the foot points builds three-dimensional trajectories in a fixed coordinate system for one point on each foot. The foot trajectory on one step consists of rising, moving, lowering and a support. The shape of the trajectory is rectangular, at each section, the kinematic parameters are interpolated by trigonometric functions, which leads to the discontinuity of velocities and the acceleration jumps. In the papers [3–5] the possibility of use of other interpolation methods by means of non-linear self-oscillatory cycles and differential equations with fractional derivatives, etc. is considered.

This paper summarizes the principles behind systems that control the motion of androids along near-rectilinear trajectories [6]. In this regard, the space of admissible controls towards the introduction of nonlinearities of odd degrees of the higher order was expanded [7]. The method is based on the theory of an asymptotic stability of invariant sets.

2   The Control of Biped Robot Motion

In the present work, the problem of dynamics of kinematic chains is solved as it allows to enter a large cluster of similar structures. The synthesis of the controlled motion of the android using the inverse dynamics method is considered. The solution of the inverse dynamics method is a fairly complex mathematical and computational problem, thus obtained a solution is not always correct. To solve it, specialized software is used often, for example, SL [8], or universal software packages for modeling the dynamics of multi-bodies systems (so-called MBS packages). In this connection, there are classes of walking machines in which the simplification of the solution by the inverse dynamics method is achieved through the use of special constructive schemes, for example, walking machines with orthogonal propellers.

The solution of the inverse dynamics method is obtained from the system of differentially-algebraic equations [9, 10]:

$$\begin{cases} M\ddot{x} - D^T p - D_W^T p_W = f(x, \dot{x}, t), \\ D\ddot{x} = h(x, \dot{x}) \\ D_w\ddot{x} = \ddot{w}(t) \end{cases} \tag{1}$$

Here $x = (x_1, x_2, \ldots, x_n)^T$ is the vector of general coordinates of the system, M is the matrix of inertia, $f(x, \dot{x}, t)$ is the vector of external and internal forces, D is the matrix of variable coefficients of kinematics connections equations by a dimension $k \times n$, $h(x, x)$ is the vector of right parts of connections equations, p is the vector of Lagrange multipliers corresponding to kinematic pairs. Control of the system is reduced to moving its points along the trajectories $w(t)$, D_w is the matrix of variable coefficients of the constraint equations for points whose motion is given by functions $w(t)$, p_w is the vector of Lagrange multipliers, corresponding to program paths $w(t)$.

From system (1) values of the generalized coordinates through which it is possible to define the program motions of drives are obtained. The program motions of drives allow organizing the control by deviation

$$u_i(t) = c_i\delta_i(t) + k_i\dot{\delta}_i(t) \tag{2}$$

Here $u_i(t)$ is force in the drive, c_i, k_i are coefficients of the proportional-differential regulator, $\delta_i(t)$ is the difference between the measured and the program values.

For implementing android control by the system (1) and Eq. (2) the equation system (1) should contain the equations determining the motion of the body of the android, the equations defining the motion of the foot points of walking propellers and the equations ensuring the stability of the robot position:

$$D_{w_b}\ddot{x} = \ddot{w}_b$$

$$D_{w_f}\ddot{x} = \ddot{w}_f$$

$$D_{w_s}\ddot{x} = \ddot{w}_s$$

The function w_b specifies the program motion of the robot body points, the function w_f specifies the motion of the foot points of the walking propellers, the function w_s specifies the motion of some auxiliary points that enter the additional equations of links. The function w_b contains six components and determines the spatial motion of the robot body. The parameters of this function can be directly used to control walking through their task by means of operating controls. The function w_f determines the motion of the points of the stepper propeller, taking into account the kinematic parameters of the characteristic points of the robot body, in particular, and the attachment points of the walking propeller to the body. The function w_f implicitly depends on function w_b, which is necessary for planning the step parameters.

The FRUND complex (MBS simulation software), developed at the Faculty of Electronics and Computer systems of VSTU [11] allows solving the Eqs. (1). It allows the analysis of motion parameters of the android when modeling it and also can be used as a part of an android control system working in real time.

3 Stability of the Motion of the Points Foot of the Walking Propeller Along a Given Limit Cycle

The vector $w(t)$ of the system (1) includes components describing the trajectories of the robot's body and the end points of its propellers.

For program motions the function w_f is piecewise continuous. This worsens the quality of control. Moreover it is necessary to use additional methods to ensure the stability of the system (1).

The use of control in the form (2) does not guarantee the stability of the system (1) since control functions depend on essentially nonlinear expressions.

In the program motion of the foot points of the walking propeller, the trajectories consist of near-rectilinear parts. Let us consider a method for the synthesis of stable modes of motion along such trajectories.

For this purpose in $\mathbf{R}^{2n}$ space we will define a layer as follows:

$$\mathbf{D}_1^{2n} \subset \mathbf{D}_2^{2n} \tag{3}$$

where $\mathbf{D}_l^{2n} \subset \mathbf{R}^{2n}$, $l = 1, 2$; the boundaries $\partial \mathbf{D}_1^{2n}$ and $\partial \mathbf{D}_2^{2n}$ of the layer are given by equations:

$$\partial \mathbf{D}_1^{2n} = \left\{ \mathbf{X} \in \mathbf{R}^{2n} \Big| c_1 - \sum_{i=1}^{2n} \frac{x_i^{2m}}{a_i^{2m}} = 0 \right\}, \quad \partial \mathbf{D}_2^{2n} = \left\{ \mathbf{X} \in \mathbf{R}^{2n} \Big| c_2 - \sum_{i=1}^{2n} \frac{x_i^{2m}}{a_i^{2m}} = 0 \right\} \tag{4}$$

For the realization of a condition (3), it is enough that $0 < c_1 < c_2$ was carried out. Thus, the behavior of the controlled system in the following areas is investigated

$$\mathbf{D}_1^{2n} \backslash \{0\} = \left\{ \mathbf{X} \in \mathbf{R}^{2n} : 0 < \sum_{i=1}^{2n} \frac{x_i^{2m}}{a_i^{2m}} < c_1 \right\}, \quad \mathbf{D}_2^{2n} \backslash \mathbf{D}_1^{2n} = \left\{ \mathbf{X} \in \mathbf{R}^{2n} : c_1 < \sum_{i=1}^{2n} \frac{x_i^{2m}}{a_i^{2m}} < c_2 \right\},$$
$$\mathbf{R}^{2n} \backslash \mathbf{D}_2^{2n} = \left\{ \mathbf{X} \in \mathbf{R}^{2n} : c_2 < \sum_{i=1}^{2n} \frac{x_i^{2m}}{a_i^{2m}} \right\} \tag{5}$$

In the neighborhood of the boundaries of such a set, we synthesize a class of smooth polynomial systems for which one of the boundaries is an invariant asymptotically stable set. A typical surface included in $\mathbf{R}^5$ with even integer exponents $2m = 6$ is shown in Fig. 2. Such surfaces have areas close to flat. Under $m = 3$ the system describing the motion along such trajectories is nonlinear, and the phase trajectories of the system consist of near-rectilinear sites.

$$\begin{cases} \dot{x}_{2i-1} = \alpha_{2i} x_{2i}^{2m-1} + \mathbf{U}_{2i-1}(x_{2i-1}, x_{2i}) + \mathbf{V}_{2i-1}(\mathbf{X}), \\ \dot{x}_{2i} = -\alpha_{2i-1} x_{2i-1}^{2m-1} + \mathbf{U}_{2i}(x_{2i-1}, x_{2i}) + \mathbf{V}_{2i}(\mathbf{X}), \end{cases} \tag{6}$$

$$\prod_{k=1}^{2} \left(c_k - \sum_{i=1}^{n} \frac{x_{2i-1}^{2m}(t)}{a_{2i-1}^{2m}} - \sum_{i=1}^{n} \frac{x_{2i}^{2m}(t)}{a_{2i}^{2m}} \right) \xrightarrow{t \to +\infty} 0, \tag{7}$$
$$\mathbf{X} \in \left(\mathbf{D}_1^{2n} \backslash \{0\} \right) \cup \left(\mathbf{D}_2^{2n} \backslash \mathbf{D}_1^{2n} \right) \cup \left(R^{2n} \backslash \mathbf{D}_2^{2n} \right),$$

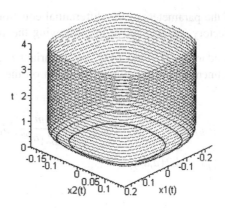

Fig. 2. Integral tube of the limit cycle

The problem of generators synthesis of the program trajectories with asymptotic stability invariant surfaces can be presented in the following form where $i = 1, 2, \ldots, n$; $\mathbf{U}_i(U_{2i-1}(x_{2i-1}, x_{2i}), U_{2i}(x_{2i-1}, x_{2i}), V_{2i-1}(\mathbf{X}), V_{2i}(\mathbf{X}))$ is the desired polynomial smooth control with feedback such that the attraction condition (7) of the problem is satisfied either on the set $\left(\mathbf{D}_1^{2n}\backslash\{0\}\right) \cup \left(\mathbf{D}_2^{2n}\backslash\mathbf{D}_1^{2n}\right)$ or on the set $\left(\mathbf{D}_2^{2n}\backslash\mathbf{D}_1^{2n}\right) \cup \left(R^{2n}\backslash\mathbf{D}_2^{2n}\right)$. Moreover, one of the boundaries of the layer will be an invariant Lyapunov stable surface of the system (6) of our problem on one of the indicated sets. The fulfillment of these conditions is sufficient for the asymptotic stability of one of the invariant boundaries according to the work of Zubov [12] In the conditions of this problem, we will define component of controls as follows

$$U_{2i-1}(x_{2i-1}, x_{2i}) = \beta_{2i,2i}x_{2i}^{4m-1} + \beta_{2i,2i-1}x_{2i-1}^{2m}x_{2i}^{2m-1},$$

$$U_{2i}(x_{2i-1}, x_{2i}) = \alpha'_{2i-1}x_{2i} + \beta_{2i-1,2i-1}x_{2i-1}^{4m-1} + \beta_{2i}x_{2i}^{4m-1} + \gamma_{2i}x_{2i}^{4m+1} + \beta_{2i-1,2i}x_{2i}^{2m}x_{2i-1}^{2m-1} + \beta_{2i-1}x_{2i-1}^{2m}x_{2i} + \gamma_{2i-1}x_{2i-1}^{4m}x_{2i} + \gamma_{2i-1,2i}x_{2i}^{2m+1}x_{2i-1}^{2m},$$

$$V_{2i-1}(\mathbf{X}) = \sum_{\substack{j=1, \\ j\neq 2i-1, j\neq 2i}}^{2n} \beta_{2i,j}x_j^{2m}x_{2i}^{2m-1}, \qquad\qquad (8)$$

$$V_{2i}(\mathbf{X}) = \sum_{\substack{j=1, \\ j\neq 2i-1, j\neq 2i}}^{2n} \left(\beta_{2i-1,j}x_j^{2m}x_{2i-1}^{2m-1} + \beta_j x_j^{2m}x_{2i} + \gamma_j x_j^{4m}x_{2i}\right) + \sum_{\substack{j=1, \\ k\neq j}}^{2n} \sum_{\substack{k=1, \\ j,k\neq 2i-1,2i}}^{2n} \gamma_{j,k}(x_j x_k)^{2m}x_{2i},$$

where i is a number of the nonlinear oscillatory subsystem, $U_{2i-1}(x_{2i-1}, x_{2i})$, $U_{2i}(x_{2i-1}, x_{2i})$ are feedback controls on state vector of a separate subsystem, $V_{2i-1}(\mathbf{X})$, $V_{2i}(\mathbf{X})$ are controls with feedback on the state vector of a multilinked system. The control functions $V_{2i-1}(\mathbf{X})$, $V_{2i}(\mathbf{X})$ provide a non-linear interaction between the subsystems (6).

For justification of the parameters of the differential equations describing a closed almost rectangular trajectory, we will prove the following theorem.

Theorem (1) The boundaries $\partial \mathbf{D}_1^{2n}$ and $\partial \mathbf{D}_2^{2n}$ are invariant manifolds of the system (6) in the case of fulfillment of the following condition on the coefficients of control functions:

$$\alpha'_{2i-1} = \pm c_1 c_2, \quad \beta_{2i,j} = -\frac{4m}{a_{2i}^{2m} a_j^{2m}}, \quad \beta_{2i-1,j} = \frac{4m}{a_{2i-1}^{2m} a_j^{2m}}, \quad \beta_j = \mp \frac{c_1 + c_2}{a_j^{2m}},$$

$$\gamma_j = \pm a_j^{-4m}, \quad \gamma_{j,k} = \pm 2 (a_j a_k)^{-2m} \tag{9}$$

on condition

$$\frac{a_{2i-1}}{a_{2i}} = \sqrt[2m]{\frac{\alpha_{2i}}{\alpha_{2i-1}}}, \tag{10}$$

where $i = 1, 2, \ldots, n; \ j, k = 1, 2, \ldots, 2n, \ j \neq k$ for trajectories with initial conditions are defined on sets $(\mathbf{D}_1^{2n} \backslash \{0\}) \cup (\mathbf{D}_2^{2n} \backslash \mathbf{D}_1^{2n})$ and $(\mathbf{D}_2^{2n} \backslash \mathbf{D}_1^{2n}) \cup (R^{2n} \backslash \mathbf{D}_2^{2n})$, respectively.

(2.1) If in this case, some coefficients of polynomial controls meet the relations:

$$\alpha'_{2i-1} = c_1 c_2, \quad \gamma_j = a_j^{-4m}, \quad \gamma_{j,k} = 2(a_j a_k)^{-2m}, \quad \beta_j = -\frac{c_1 + c_2}{a_j^{2m}} \tag{11}$$

then the boundary $\partial \mathbf{D}_1^{2n}$ is asymptotically stable for trajectories with initial conditions defined inside the manifold $\mathbf{D}_1^{2n} \backslash \{0\}$ and in some layer adjacent to the surface $\partial \mathbf{D}_1^{2n}$ from the outside in $\mathbf{D}_2^{2n} \backslash \mathbf{D}_1^{2n}$.

(2.2) If in this case, some coefficients of polynomial controls meet the relations:

$$\alpha'_{2i-1} = c_1 c_2, \quad \gamma_j = -a_j^{-4m}, \quad \gamma_{j,k} = -2(a_j a_k)^{-2m}, \quad \beta_j = \frac{c_1 + c_2}{a_j^{2m}} \tag{12}$$

then the boundary $\partial \mathbf{D}_2^{2n}$ is asymptotically stable for trajectories with initial conditions defined inside the manifold $\mathbf{D}_2^{2n} \backslash \mathbf{D}_1^{2n}$ and in some layer adjacent to the surface $\partial \mathbf{D}_2^{2n}$ from the outside in $\mathbf{R}^{2n} \backslash \mathbf{D}_2^{2n}$.

Proof of the theorem.

(1) Invariance of the boundary $\partial \mathbf{D}_l^{2n}, \ l = 1, 2$. Consider a sign-definite function
$$\mathbf{F}(\mathbf{X}) = \prod_{k=1}^{2} \left(c_k - \sum_{i=1}^{n} \frac{x_{2i-1}^{2m}(t)}{a_{2i-1}^{2m}} - \sum_{i=1}^{n} \frac{x_{2i}^{2m}(t)}{a_{2i}^{2m}} \right).$$ The total derivative of a function $\mathbf{F}(\mathbf{X})$ on the motion of system (6), taking into account conditions (1) of the theorem on the coefficients, is equal to:

$$\sum_{i=1}^{n} \left(\dot{x}_{2i-1} \frac{\partial F(\mathbf{X})}{\partial x_{2i-1}} + \dot{x}_{2i} \frac{\partial F(\mathbf{X})}{\partial x_{2i}} \right) = \sum_{i=1}^{n} P_{2i} x_{2i}^{2m} \prod_{k=1}^{2} \left(c_k - \sum_{i=1}^{n} \frac{x_{2i-1}^{2m}(t)}{a_{2i-1}^{2m}} - \sum_{i=1}^{n} \frac{x_{2i}^{2m}(t)}{a_{2i}^{2m}} \right) \quad (13)$$

Equality (13) is satisfied if and only if the vector X belongs to the surface $\prod_{k=1}^{2} \left(c_k - \sum_{i=1}^{n} \frac{x_{2i-1}^{2m}(t)}{a_{2i-1}^{2m}} - \sum_{i=1}^{n} \frac{x_{2i}^{2m}(t)}{a_{2i}^{2m}} \right) = 0$. Injected function is of constant signs on sets $\mathbf{D}_1^{2n} \backslash \{0\}$, $\mathbf{D}_2^{2n} \backslash \mathbf{D}_1^{2n}$ `and $R^{2n} \backslash \mathbf{D}_2^{2n}$. The relation is a condition for the invariance of the surface described by equation $\mathbf{F}(\mathbf{X}) = 0$ [8]. That is, the conditions for the invariance of the boundaries $\partial \mathbf{D}_1^{2n}$ and $\partial \mathbf{D}_2^{2n}$ are satisfied for trajectories with initial conditions defined on the sets $\left(\mathbf{D}_1^{2n} \backslash \{0\} \right) \cup \left(\mathbf{D}_2^{2n} \backslash \mathbf{D}_1^{2n} \right)$ and $\left(\mathbf{D}_2^{2n} \backslash \mathbf{D}_1^{2n} \right) \cup \left(R^{2n} \backslash \mathbf{D}_2^{2n} \right)$ respectively. The trajectories of the system starting at the boundary of the manifold $\partial \mathbf{D}_l^{2n}$, $l = 1, 2$, do not leave it at $t \to +\infty$.

(2.1) Asymptotic stability of $\partial \mathbf{D}_1^{2n}$. Let polynomial controls with feedback on the state vector have the above form. The conditions for the parameters of the control functions are fulfilled: $\alpha'_{2i-1} = c_1 c_2$, $\beta_{2i,j} = -\frac{4m}{a_{2i}^{2m} a_j^{2m}}$, $\beta_{2i,j} = -\frac{4m}{a_{2i}^{2m} a_j^{2m}}$, $\gamma_j = a_j^{-4m}$, $\gamma_{j,k} = 2(a_j a_k)^{-2m}$, $\beta_j = -\frac{c_1 + c_2}{a_j^{2m}}$. We calculate the total derivative of the function $\mathbf{F}(\mathbf{X})$ (13) on the set $\left(\mathbf{D}_1^{2n} \backslash \{0\} \right) \cup \left(\mathbf{D}_2^{2n} \backslash \mathbf{D}_1^{2n} \right)$. The total derivative $\frac{d\mathbf{F}(\mathbf{X})}{dt}$ is definitely positive for trajectories with initial conditions defined inside the manifold $\mathbf{D}_1^{2n} \backslash \{0\}$ and in $\mathbf{R}^{2n} \backslash \mathbf{D}_2^{2n}$. Certain positivity means that the trajectories of the system on the set $\mathbf{D}_1^{2n} \backslash \{0\}$ will be directed from within to the boundary $\partial \mathbf{D}_1^{2n}$ and go to infinity at $\mathbf{R}^{2n} \backslash \mathbf{D}_2^{2n}$. In the layer, $\mathbf{D}_2^{2n} \backslash \mathbf{D}_1^{2n}$ the derivative $\frac{d\mathbf{F}(\mathbf{X})}{dt}$ will be definitely negative. And the trajectories defined in this layer will be directed from the outside to the boundary $\partial \mathbf{D}_1^{2n}$. The origin $\mathbf{O} = (0, 0, \ldots, 0)^{\mathrm{T}}$ is a α - limit point and does not belong to the surface $\partial \mathbf{D}_1^{2n}$. According to Zubov's theorem, V.I. [12], the boundary $\partial \mathbf{D}_1^{2n}$ is asymptotically stable for trajectories with initial conditions defined inside the manifold $\mathbf{D}_1^{2n} \backslash \{0\}$ and in some layer adjacent to the surface $\partial \mathbf{D}_1^{2n}$ from the outside in $\mathbf{D}_2^{2n} \backslash \mathbf{D}_1^{2n}$.

(2.2) Asymptotic stability of $\partial \mathbf{D}_2^{2n}$. The conditions for the parameters of the control functions are realized: $a'_{2i-1} = -c_1 c_2$, $\beta_{2i,j} = -\frac{4m}{a_{2i}^{2m} a_j^{2m}}$, $\beta_{2i-1,j} = \frac{4m}{a_{2i-1}^{2m} a_j^{2m}}$, $\gamma_j = -a_j^{-4m}$, $\gamma_{j,k} = -2(a_j a_k)^{-2m}$, $\beta_j = \frac{c_1 + c_2}{a_j^{2m}}$. We calculate the total derivative of the function $\mathbf{F}(\mathbf{X})$ (13) on the set $\left(\mathbf{D}_2^{2n} \backslash \mathbf{D}_1^{2n} \right) \cup \left(R^{2n} \backslash \mathbf{D}_2^{2n} \right)$. The total derivative $\frac{d\mathbf{F}(\mathbf{X})}{dt}$ is definitely positive for trajectories with initial conditions defined inside the manifold $\mathbf{D}_2^{2n} \backslash \mathbf{D}_1^{2n}$. Certain positivity means that the trajectories of the system on the set $\mathbf{D}_2^{2n} \backslash \mathbf{D}_1^{2n}$ will be directed from within to the boundary $\partial \mathbf{D}_2^{2n}$. In set $R^{2n} \backslash \mathbf{D}_2^{2n}$ the derivative $\frac{d\mathbf{F}(\mathbf{X})}{dt}$ will be definitely negative. And the trajectories defined here will be sent from the outside to the boundary $\partial \mathbf{D}_2^{2n}$.

Thus, the boundary $\partial \mathbf{D}_2^{2n}$ is asymptotically stable for trajectories with initial conditions defined inside the manifold $\mathbf{D}_2^{2n} \backslash \mathbf{D}_1^{2n}$ and in some layer adjacent to the surface $\partial \mathbf{D}_2^{2n}$ from the outside in $R^{2n} \backslash \mathbf{D}_2^{2n}$. **The theorem is proved.**

A flat layer geometrically corresponds to the case with two concentrically arranged limit cycles at $i = 1$. The internal limit cycle is a closed curve $\partial \mathbf{D}_1^{2n}$, the outside limit cycle is $\partial \mathbf{D}_2^{2n}$. In Fig. 2 the integral tube obtained in the numerical modeling describes the generator output to the regime of stable self-oscillations with parameters of the inside limit cycle $\partial \mathbf{D}_1^{2n}$ having sites of near-rectilinear motion.

4 Dynamic Stability of the Robot Body Points

Let's consider the additional links which are imposed on the Eqs. (1). They provide stability and the coordinated relative motion of elements. The stability conditions are given by three equations, that is, one equation for each coordinate of the center of mass of the robot. Coordinates x and y of the center of mass are equated to corresponding components of zero moment point, the vertical coordinate can be assigned a special function, for example, envelope surface of variable height. When walking on a flat surface the vertical coordinate is assigned a constant value, selected by calculation from the condition of the minimum angle of the leg fold in the knee joint. Known kinematic schemes of robots contain a foot made in the form of a single element, while during walking the plane of the foot is horizontal. This kinematic scheme allows you to vary the distance from the center of mass of the robot to the foot support area, mainly due to the bending of the leg in the knee. For the same reason, in the posture of readiness and during walking, the legs are bent at the knee that is typical for the known constructions of robots (androids). Motion with the support of the straight legs in the robot construction can be achieved during additional links in the torso or in the foot. For kinematic schemes of robots selected from the condition of a minimum number of hinges and drives, it is possible to step only on the bent legs.

In Fig. 3 calculated positions of the robot at the end of a step are shown with the different height of the center of mass from which it is visible that at a high arrangement of the center of mass the relative turns of links gain have unacceptably great values.

The insolvability of this problem within the framework of the existing kinematic schemes led to kinematic schemes of robots without a knee joint.

In the equations of links for coordinates of the center of mass the precise expressions containing coordinates of all robot elements are used

$$\sum_{i=1}^{n} m_i S_{xi}/M = w_{sx} \tag{14}$$

Here m_i is a mass of the i-th robot body, S_{xi} is coordinate x of the center of mass of the i-th body, M is the complete mass of the robot, w_{sx} is x-coordinate of zero moment point. The Eq. (14) is written for the coordinate x. On other coordinates, equations look like similarly.

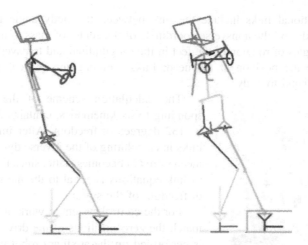

Fig. 3. The calculated positions of the robot at the end of the step with the left foot. The height of the center of mass is 0.57 m (on the left) and 0.61 m (on the right).

Additional link equations are also necessary for specifying a certain mutual motion of individual elements. An additional link is a link between the angle of the longitudinal body and the longitudinal angles of the thighs of both legs

$$U_{yk} + K_y U_{yl} + K_y U_{yr} = 0 \,. \tag{15}$$

Here U_{yk} is the angle of rotation of the robot's body with respect to the transverse axis, U_{yl} is the angle of rotation of the left femur with respect to the transverse axis, U_{yr} is the angle of right femur rotation relative to transverse axis, and K_y is the scale factor. Due to this equation, a change in the average value of the longitudinal body angle is achieved (Fig. 4).

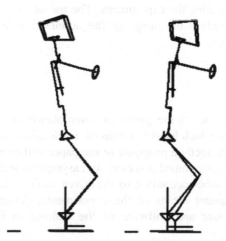

Fig. 4. The change in the longitudinal slope of the hull as a function of the coefficients of Eq. (15). The initial posture phase.

Also, additional links include the link between the body angle relative to the longitudinal axis and the transverse coordinate of the center of mass of the robot; links, zeroing the angles of rotation of the feet in the longitudinal and transverse plane; links that determine the position of the head; links, defining the vertical and transverse distance from hand to body.

Fig. 5. Android AR600E [11]

The calculation scheme of the robot, corresponding to its kinematics, contains 22 bodies, that is, 132 degrees of freedom. After imposing all the links in calculating of the inverse dynamics method, the system (1) becomes static, since the total number of link equations is equal to the number of degrees of freedom of the system.

For the control system to work, it is necessary to match the zero positions of the drive angles, which is performed on the auxiliary robot model.

The robot control system software is implemented as additional modules of the FRUND simulation system [11], which can be connected to the robot via a network or can be installed on the on-board computer of the robot.

By means of the presented control system experiments with the android AR600E motion were made.

Synthesis of the robot's program motion was performed using the inverse dynamics method. The method of synthesis of stable modes of motion for given limit cycles was used to generate trajectories of the foot points of the android AR600E (Fig. 5) and showed its efficiency. Site [11] contains various videos with android walks in different modes, taken during the experiments. The use of the proposed programmatic trajectories helped to reduce the jumps of the acceleration in the robot movement approximately in 2 times.

5   Conclusion

Existing gait generators mainly use piecewise interpolation of program trajectories by trigonometric functions; which leads to jumps of accelerations at the boundaries of the trajectory segments. The method proposed in the paper will ensure a continuity of the functions describing a programmed trajectory and asymptotic stability of motion of foot points of the walking robot according to the given limit cycle. The control system considered is a convenient means of the experimental debugging and operational development of hardware and software of the android to improve the principal specifications.

References

1. Liatsikos, E., Kallidonis, P., Tuerk, I., Anderson, C., Beerlage, H., Stolzenburg, J.-U.: Setup of da Vinci System for Kidney Surgery. Laparoscopic and Robot-Assisted Surgery in Urology. Springer, Heidelberg (2011). ISBN 978-3-642-00890-0.1
2. Vukobratovic, M., Borovac, B.: Biped Locomotion Dynamics, Stability, Control and Application. Springer, Berlin (1990)
3. Carla, M.A., Pinto, J.A., Machado, T.: Fractional central pattern generators for bipedal locomotion. Nonlinear Dyn. **62**, 27–37 (2010)
4. Di Gironimo, G., Pelliccia, L., Siciliano, B., et al.: Biomechanically-based motion control for a digital human. Int. J. Interact. Des. Manuf. **6**, 1 (2012). doi:10.1007/s12008-011-0132-x
5. Santos, C.P., Alves, N., Moreno, J.C.: Biped Locomotion Control through a Biomimetic CPG-based Controller. Nonlinear Dyn. **62**, 27–37 (2010)
6. Gorobtsov, A.S., Ryzhov, E.N., Churzina, A.S.: Detecting of oscillations close to explosive. Biomed. Radioelectronics **8**, 32–34 (2009). (in Russian)
7. Gorobtsov, A., Ryzhov, E., Churzina, A.: Principals of multilinked nonlinear stabilization and lame-manifolds in dynamic systems. Rare Attractors and Rare Phenomena in Nonlinear Dynamics: mater. of the Int. Symposium RA08 Riga Techn. Univ., Inst. of Mechanics RTU [etc.], Riga, pp. 29–32 (2008)
8. Kima, J.-Y., Kimb, J.-H.: Error analysis and effective adjustment of the walking-ready posture for a biped humanoid robot. Adv. Rob. **24**, 2137–2169 (2010)
9. Fumagalli, A., Gaias, G., Masarati, P.: A simple approach to kinematic inversion of redundant mechanisms. In: IDETC/CIE 2007 ASME 2007 International Design Engineering Technical Conferences & Computers and Information in Engineering Conference, Las Vegas, NE, USA (2007)
10. Gorobtsov, A., Ryzhov, E., Polyanina, A.: About formation of the stable modes of the movement of multilink mechanical systems. In: proceedings of 22nd International Conference on Vibroengineering, Vibroengineering Procedia/ Publisher JVE International Ltd. - Kaunas (Lithuania), vol. 8, pp. 522–526 (2016)
11. FRUND - Mathematical modeling in science and engineering [An electronic resource] URL: http://frund.vstu.ru [Date of retrieval 05/05/17]
12. Zubov, V.I.: Stability of movement. The Higher School, Moscow (1973). (in Russian)

Autonomous Locomotion and Navigation of Anthropomorphic Robot

Alexey Titov, Alexey Markov, Andrey Skorikov, Pavel Tarasov,
Andrey E. Andreev$^{(\boxtimes)}$, Sergey Alekseev,
and Alexander S. Gorobtsov

Volgograd State Technical University, Volgograd, Russia
staffofmousecorp@gmail.com, markovalex95@gmail.com,
{scorpion_energy, tarasradio, 2serales96}@mail.ru,
andan2005@yandex.ru, vm@vstu.ru

Abstract. The paper describes a software implementation of the locomotion, autonomous navigation, and voice interface support subsystems for the anthropomorphic robot AR-600E. All these subsystems comprise the integer system which provides the capability for autonomous movement of the biped AR-600E robot. The general architecture of the autonomous movement system, as well as each subsystem features, are presented; much attention is paid to computer vision role in navigation and next step planning. The main specificity of the locomotion support system is the use of FRUND modeling CAE system as a high-level movement controller, conditioning some specific demands to route planning. The performance of the robot onboard computer aimed to support all these subsystems is also assessed. The optimization potential of these subsystems to migrate them to the onboard standalone or augmented with the embedded graphics accelerator computer is revealed. Further directions of the investigations are outlined.

Keywords: Anthropomorphic robot AR-600E · Embedded systems · Locomotion · Computer vision · Path planning · FRUND · OpenCL · GPU · SLAM · Vectorization

1 Introduction

Nowadays, control systems for anthropomorphic robot AR-600E are the subject of development at the Computer Science Faculty of Volgograd State Technical University. To some extent, this robot is similar to the famous robot ASIMO, developed by Honda Corporation [1]. Previously, two techniques, which provide basic autonomous locomotion modes, were developed: an adaptive control system and an interface for operator. The following components are considered as the improvement of the robot: computer vision components, route planning and orientation of a robot, obstacle avoidance, and non-trivial advanced walk modes.

At the moment, the control system is distributed over multiple computers; it leads to difficulties in the maintenance of the system, high costs for data transfer and reduces the overall system performance. Therefore, the aim is to investigate the applicability of robot onboard computer to solve the tasks of locomotion and autonomous navigation of the robot.

© Springer International Publishing AG 2017
A. Kravets et al. (Eds.): CIT&DS 2017, CCIS 754, pp. 242–255, 2017.
DOI: 10.1007/978-3-319-65551-2_18

Thus, the main tasks, to achieve the goal mentioned above, are the following:

- to assess the possibility of simultaneous operation of
  - locomotion;
  - speech support;
  - autonomous navigation based on RGB-D camera Kinect;
- to assess the suitability of the developed subsystems to solve the above problems, including optimizations;
- to select the most required subsystems to be installed in the robot, that is compatible with each other;
- to choose the operating system for the robot, based on the selected subsystems;
- to analyze the performance of the whole system.

2 The Anthropomorphic Robot AR-600E

Robot AR-600E (robot system – RS) is composed of multiple modules responsible for receiving and processing commands from the control program, for the control and management of the drives. It also has an onboard computer, which can be used to run control programs, tracking systems, machine vision, etc [2].

The onboard computer (Avalue) uses modern Intel Core i7 620LM CPU with two cores and clock frequency of 2.0 GHz. The computer has 4 GB of RAM.

The robot is controlled via Gigabit Ethernet interface, the received packets are processed by ARM STM32f4xx series processor and are sent to drives' control boards using the RS485 interface.

The information on power consumption for each channel and the accuracy of reaching the target position of the engines is sent back.

Each drive's control board stores the parameters of the PID regulators and restrictions on location monitors signals from the magnetic encoders and implements the control interface.

The research sample of RS, which was acquired due to the Program of Strategic Development of VSTU in 2014, has about 23 drives in order to investigate and develop autonomous locomotion and navigation control system, described in the following paragraph.

Intermediate results of implementing such system were presented by the authors at the 5th International Skolkovo Robotics Conference, on April 21, 2017.

3 The Structure of the Autonomous Locomotion and Navigation System

3.1 General System Architecture

Figure 1 shows the general structure of the autonomous locomotion and navigation system consisting of three subsystems: computer vision, locomotion control, and speech support.

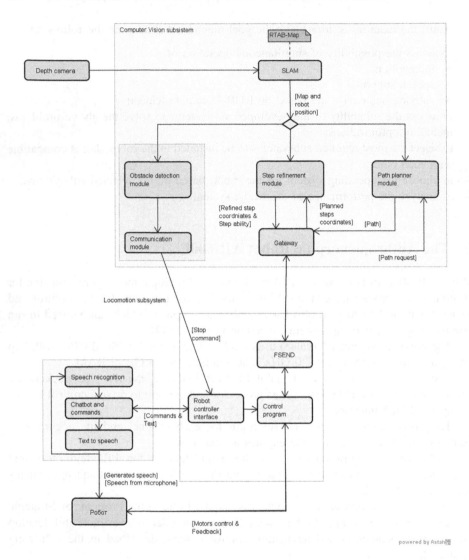

Fig. 1. General control and navigation system architecture

The control system of locomotion allows to generate the laws of motion of the robot in such a way as to provide static balance, to send control commands to the robot and receive data from sensors, such as inertial navigation systems, pressure sensors in the feet, etc.

The computer vision system allows mapping a route for the robot from the initial to the destination point by negotiating obstacles, to adjust each step, taking into account objects on the support surface and stop RS in the case of obstacles ahead.

The speech support system allows to recognize the voice and synthesize it. It gives us possibilities to execute multiple commands for robot control, provides voice informing in a variety of situations (e.g. obstacles) and allows to maintain a conversation using a chatbot. At present, the speech support system does not require a lot of computations. It requires a wide-band Internet connection and substantial disk space for dialog database storage. These requirements have to be reduced in future.

3.2   The Locomotion Control System

The CAE software system FRUND is the basis of locomotion. FRUND stands for forming and solving the equations of nonlinear dynamics. This system is designed to simulate the dynamics of systems of rigid and elastic bodies. The main features of the methods to represent the equations of motion used in the FRUND are: the possibility of the unification of the investigated object design scheme setting with a finite set of types of constituent elements, simple automatic generation of the motion equations and programs for their integration, flexibility in adding new types of specific interactions [3].

FRUND solves the problems of static stability and inverse kinematics.

Locomotion control is performed by a separate external computer with Windows operation system, connected to the robot via Ethernet cable.

3.3   The Computer Vision System

The autonomous navigation of AR600E is quite significant. Therefore, the robot could be adapted to solve specific practical problems, such as area investigation. This solution enables to adapt robot for solving practical problems in the unknown environment.

The general scheme of solving the navigation task for the AR600E robot is shown in Fig. 2.

The computer vision system consists of two main and one additional elements:

1. Navigation and cartography module. It ensures the path planning of the robot in the environment.
2. Module defining parameters of the step. It determines the possibility of performing each step individually, analyzing the proposed location of the step in the presence of small obstacles or other defects that prevent to make a move. It also defines the height of the leg lift and the displacement of the feet relative to the proposed point, to avoid stepping on anything.
3. The assist obstacles identification module.

The data come from Kinnect and are passed to the SLAM (Simultaneous Localization and Mapping) [4] algorithm which provides an area map as a point cloud with the camera location. Then, using the transformations, we get the coordinates of the robot in the cloud. These coordinates and the map are used to build a trajectory of the robot. The trajectory is sent to the control unit (with FRUND software in the particular case). FRUND asks the step parameters detection module for the details of the next step. This module determines the optimal location for the leg of the robot when stepping to the next point of the trajectory. Having received the data, FRUND changes the parameters to make the optimal movement of the robot.

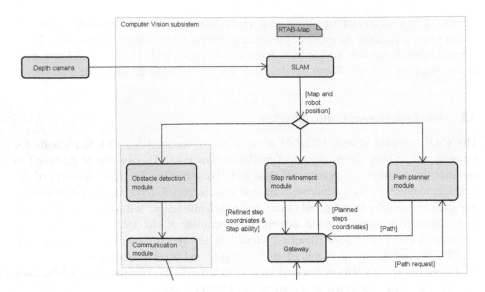

Fig. 2. The subsystem of computer vision structure

Presently, the preliminary scheme of the autonomous navigation system is elaborated, and some of its modules are implemented, namely: the SLAM module, the step parameters detection module. The work is underway to develop a path planning module of the robot and the module of interaction with FRUND via the network.

Robot Operation System (ROS) framework has been chosen as a platform for the implementation of the system. ROS is a flexible framework for the software design for robots [5]. The choice is justified by the fact that ROS provides a large number of open packages and libraries in robotics, as well as the convenient concept of messages, which helps different parts of the system to operate in parallel (in different threads).

ROS is only supported on some Linux distributions (also note that virtual machine is not suitable for some of the libraries used). The fact that FRUND is only supported for Windows OS eliminates the possibility of sharing ROS and FRUND on one PC.

3.3.1   The Problem of Building a Map and Localization

To build a map, we have chosen the implementation of the algorithm from the RTabMap library [6]. It is less resource-intensive than other implementations and can be used in real-time. Furthermore, this algorithm has high-quality results compared to other algorithms (KinFU, KinectFusion) and strong community support. It is also important to note that this library is represented as a package in ROS.

Figure 3 shows a map built with RTAB-Map. The blue line indicates the trajectory of movement of the camera.

3.3.2   Routing Task

To simplify the task of routing we derive the discrete 2D map of obstacles (Fig. 4), where each cell can be in one of 3 states (free, obstacle, unknown), from the original point cloud. This map reduces complex planning in point clouds to a relatively

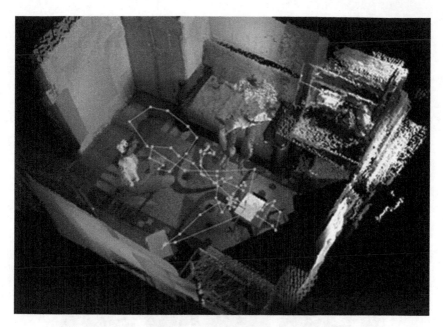

Fig. 3. The results of the implementation of the SLAM algorithm from the RTAB-Maplibrary

computationally simple planning on the plane. The example of this map is shown in Fig. 4, where gray pixels form unknown space, white pixels represent free space and black pixels represent an obstacle.

There are many solutions for route planning. Table 1 presents some of the solutions.

Most of all robot path-planning solutions are applied to wheel robots and use plane trajectory as a simple curve or set of points in 2D-space. This is a simple approach, but it doesn't allow the humanoid robot to step over some obstacles or take the stairs. On the other hand, there is footstep_planner [7]. It is ROS package developed by Humanoid Robots Lab, the University of Freiburg. It provides functionality to plan humanoid robot movement trajectory via a chain of steps. This approach allows the humanoid robot to step over some small obstacles. It uses ARA*, AD* and R* path planning algorithms for efficient path planning [8, 9].

But footstep_planner is not the best solution for our system. It generates a chain of steps and robot should execute this steps, but our locomotion control system generates its own steps using FRUND software to fulfill the condition of static balance. Footstep_planner uses geometrical approach only and doesn't check balance conditions, so we can't use this software as is. We intend to implement our own 2D planner for the obstacles map orientation.

3.3.3 Determining the Optimal Parameters of the Step

The task of computer vision applied to anthropomorphic robot differs from such tasks in general, which address the problem of constructing a trajectory without considering the peculiarities of movement of the robot. The distinction is a discrete mechanism of

Fig. 4. The obstacles map

movement. In addition to the global planning of a trajectory it is necessary to undertake local planning:

- not to step on objects, garbage, etc.
- to plan the height of the step when stepping on a stair or other object.
- to move the leg a bit to choose the optimal stepping point.

This requires checking the possibility of making each step in the given point and to adjust a number of parameters, such as the height of the leg lift and shift of the foot, within certain limits, relative to the originally planned point.

Step planning system receives a coordinate of the planning step from the robot control program. It checks whether it is possible to take a step in this place, and, if necessary, step point can be shifted within certain limits, to choose the optimum surface (Figs. 5 and 6). The possibility to take the step and its parameters (fixed position, the height of leg lift, the angle of the surface) are sent back.

Within the valid step region we have to choose the point:

- which is not too high/low from ground level;

Table 1. SLAM solutions

The name and a brief description	Applicability to our project
The move_base concept, composed of Local and Global planners	This package is more suitable for wheeled robots and is not able to perform effective planning for anthropomorphic robots. The only Global planner is of interest since it can be used to build the trajectory of the robot in the form of a line
footstep_planner	The promising concept for the planning of a trajectory as a set of the feet positions, which you want the robot to follow in the process of passing the trajectory Currently adopted as the basic variant
3d_navigation	Promising project for planning in 3D and developing the idea of move_base. It is not currently used by us since there are no significant benefits in comparison with the planning on a 2D map of obstacles derived from the implementation of the SLAM algorithm from the RTLabMap
MoveIt	The package that enables you to plan robotic motion of any structure in the transition from one position to another considering any obstacles. In our case, FRUND performs the role of this package, so its applicability is reduced to 0

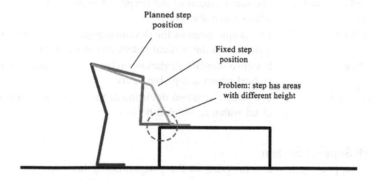

Fig. 5. Illustration of step point correction by height

– which results in not too much slope;
– is on the smooth surface;
– which results in no height difference.

To formalize these requirements, the function of the surface quality, which is a weighted sum of the normalized components corresponding to the above-mentioned requirements (see Table 2) was introduced. The minimum of this function is to be found to select the optimal point.

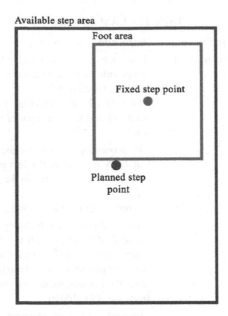

Fig. 6. Illustration of step point correction by shift

Table 2. Surface quality features

Requirement to the surface	Formalization
Not too high/low from the ground level	The sample mean of the heights of points in the point cloud within acceptable limits
Not too much tilt	The sample mean of the deviation angles of the normals to the surface from the vertical within acceptable limits
Smooth surface	Selective standard deviation angles of the normals from the vertical within acceptable limits
There is no height difference	The sample standard deviation of the heights of points in the cloud within acceptable limits

The Speech Support System

The speech support system is a program in the programming language Python 3.*. It can be run both on Windows 7 and above, and on several GNU/Linux distributions.

A large part of the speech support system is not resource-intensive.

The system requires a broadband network since the recognition and synthesis of speech are performed by Google services.

Summary for Subsystems, Computers Used and Performance Assessment

Presently, the system modules are distributed on three computers (see Table 3).

The experiments have shown that the solution of the equations using the onboard computer of RS results in the CPU usage up to 90–100%, which makes it impossible for simultaneous processing of computer vision, SLAM, and speech.

Table 3. Subsystems distributed by computers

Locomotion control	Type	Standalone desktop
	OS	Windows 10
	CPU	Intel Core i7-3770
	RAM	16 Gb
	Storage	128 Gb SSD, 500 Gb HDD
Computer vision	Type	Lenovo notebook
	OS	Ubuntu 14.04
	CPU	Intel Core i5-4200 M
	RAM	4 Gb
	Storage	500 Gb HDD
Speech support	Type	Embedded
	OS	Ubuntu 14.04
	CPU	Intel Core i7-620HQ
	RAM	4 Gb
	Storage	eMMC 16 Gb

In the subsystem of computer vision, the main contribution to the computational load accounts for SLAM RtabMAP library, completely loading one core of CPU. This library does not support multithreading but can use CUDA for specific tasks, which will give about 20% performance gain when using NVidia GPU. Step test and the creation of a trajectory do require high performance. Moreover, they are rarely invoked for each new step and for each re-planning of the route, respectively.

The subsystem of speech support does not overweight the computer. The load is provided only by the chatterbot library, carrying out phrase selection for response and training for new dialogues. The main load is on the disk subsystem when referring to the JSON questions and answers database file. To accelerate its work, the MongoDB database, which is supported by the library, can be used. Significant gains can be obtained when using a solid state drive (SSD).

Thus, the simultaneous launch of all subsystems (locomotion, computer vision, and speech) on an existing onboard computer of RS is impossible because of the lack of computational resources. To migrate the whole system to the onboard computer it is required to find ways to optimize the existing software, either to choose an onboard computer with higher performance or to use embedded boards with GPU accelerators.

4   The Possibility of Using the Onboard Computer

4.1   Optimization of Existing Systems

4.1.1   FRUND

The current stable version of the FRUND solver is written in Fortran language but does not use vectorization. To optimize calculations we intend to use a vectorized version of the solver, written in C++, which is being developed [10]. First and foremost, we could use the AVX/AVX 2 instruction set. This will speed up the implementation of appropriate code fragments in several times. However, the use of AVX is not always possible. In the case when the calculation of model is done on the onboard computer, the AVX instructions are not available due to the architecture of the Intel i7-620 m, which is installed in the robot. This processor supports vector instructions up to SSE 4.2.

When we test the algorithm of the calculation model of the robot and its control program, the onboard computer's CPU is loaded up to 90–95%, while the calculation itself takes about 55% of machine time. Vectorizing with SSE 4.2 can provide speed-up, but even when the calculation is accelerated by 2 times, the total processor use will be reduced to 75%, which is not enough for other tasks such as computer vision and speech support module. To achieve the mobility of robot, it is required to solve the problem of distribution of calculations to other mobile hardware solutions.

4.1.2 SLAM

In the computer vision module, SLAM method is used in the RTLab-Map library. The library is based on more low-level OpenCV, which in turn can be optimized for use with the GPU. However, as the authors of RTLab-Map point out, this method gives a low-speed growth. In addition, you need the accelerator from NVidia, since the vectorized version of the library is implemented on CUDA only.

4.1.3 Computer Vision – Routing

Most of the approaches, offered by the ROS, for path planning and route planning can be optimized only by selecting more appropriate parameters for the algorithms to work in a particular environment. This can lead to increased performance at the expense of precision, which is not always profitable.

The source code of most of the packages is open, allowing you to optimize it. But also the code of the packages is often very complicated and its analysis would take a long time, that will may not justify the resulting speedup of the algorithm in 5–10%.

4.1.4 Computer Vision – Step

Determination of the optimal locations for the step is performed by means of the utility function. The weights of the utility points are compared to each other. According to the measurements, this calculation takes a small amount of computer time. The tests were performed on an Intel i5-4200 M with enabled Hyper-Threading. In the peak of cyclic calculations, the load was 30%. Given the fact that the calculation of the locations for the step can be carried out with low frequency, the load of this module can be considered acceptable for any hardware platform.

4.2 Choice of the Onboard Computer with Higher Performance

As noted, to solve the problem of robot mobility it is required to find efficient hardware platform for the most expensive computational tasks. This requires the platform compact enough to install it in a robot. We can consider a complete embedded system and an individual selection of various components.

4.2.1 NVidia Jetson

JetsonTX2 is planned for release by NVidia Corporation [11]. The stated parameters include low power consumption, compact form factor and high performance of about 1 TFLOPS. The platform consists of a CPU with 4 cores with the ARM A57 dual Denver 2 architecture and GPU with Pascal architecture with 256 CUDA cores. As stated by the manufacturer, the platform is tuned to solve the problem of deep learning and the use of the NVidia library allows to achieve a multiple increasing in performance on these tasks.

The main advantage of this platform is the use of high-performance GPUs. However, the CPU has relatively low performance, so the platform mainly corresponds to solutions, using OpenCL or CUDA. However, there are no such solutions in the current version of our software, but in the future one can face great difficulties with porting code for ARM A57 if you need to use TX2 Jetson.

So, Jetson TX2 is not suited for our tasks like onboard single computer, though it could be considered as an auxiliary onboard computer (if we'll be able to use OpenCL both for FRUND solver and computer vision libraries), still their combining with the main computer in case of considered RS is a kind of challenge.

4.2.2 Self-assembled Platform

The most promising option for increasing performance of robot onboard computer is installing a second computer in the robot. This computer can be assembled on your own with a selection of all the necessary components. It will allow solving all problems related to the insufficient computational power of the main onboard computer.

First, there are requirements for the size of the entire computer subsystem. The most suitable form factor is Mini-ITX. Its dimensions are 120 by 120 mm. This will definitely allow you to place the whole system compactly; moreover, the computer should contain PCIe motherboard that will allow you to increase the computer performance by using the GPU.

There are motherboards with support for Intel desktop processors with the LGA1151 socket. Restrictions on the processor are determined only by the power of the entire computer. In addition, this platform works with fast DDR4 memory maximum up to 32 GB.

The choice of the processor is based on the constraints of the power supply. The approximate power that can be obtained on board is about 100 W. This power should be enough to almost all of the processors on this socket. The best option for this solution is Core i7 7700 as it is the most powerful one. In fact, installing this CPU eliminates any need in the present onboard system. This processor has the performance of 40 GFLOPS in double precision, which is enough for all tasks mentioned, especially in the presence of well-vectorized algorithms.

Installation of the computer with the powerful modern Intel Core i7 CPU on the motherboard with the mini-ITX form factor seems to be the most promising case today.

5 Conclusions

While developing robot's autonomous movement control system the following results have been obtained.

The proposed robot control system consists of three sub-systems: locomotion control, computer vision and speech support.

Locomotion control system allows the robot to execute some walking modes, such as walking forward, backward and side-walking. Now we are investigating sensor feedback to ensure better robot stability and also developing more movement modes.

Computer vision subsystem allows the robot to stop before obstacles. There is a module for tuning of the step position to avoid treat on small obstacles or surface irregularities, but it is not fully integrated with the locomotion subsystem of the robot. The computer vision subsystem also can provide the obstacles map, though whole routing task solving is under development. Known routing approaches are not directly applicable since high-level locomotion system controller is used.

The speech support subsystem allows some basic chat functionality executing some simple commands like "move" and "stop". Further work for this module is focused on the deeper integration of the speech subsystem with other systems, increasing speech recognition quality (for example, in noisy conditions) and adding additional commands.

All of these three subsystems are running on different computers and now the robot depends on external computers for computer vision and locomotion calculations. Our future goal is to transfer all necessary controlling software on one onboard computer to increase robot autonomy. Some assessments for hardware and preferred architectures of such a computer have been made.

Acknowledgement. Work is performed with the financial support of the Russian Foundation for Basic Research - projects ## 16-47-340385, 16-07-00534, 15-01-04577, 15-07-06254 and the financial support of the Administration of Volgograd region.

References

1. Masato, Y., Kenichi, O.: Honda humanoids robot development. Phil. Trans. R. Soc. **365**, 11–19 (2007). doi:10.1098/rsta.2006.1917
2. NPO Androidnaya Technica. http://npo-at.com/products/ar-600e/
3. Mathematical modeling in science and engineering. http://frund.vstu.ru
4. Garimort, J., Hornung, A., Bennewitz, M.: Humanoid Navigation with Dynamic Footstep Plans. In: Proceedings of the IEEE International Conference on Robotics & Automation (ICRA), pp. 3982–3987. IEEE (2011)
5. Robot operation system (ROS) http://robots.ros.org
6. RTLAB-Map. Real-Time Appearance-Based Mapping. http://introlab.github.io/rtabmap/
7. Hornung, A., Dornbush, A., Likhachev, M., Bennewitz, M.: Anytime Search-Based Footstep Planning with Suboptimality Bounds. In: Proceedings of the IEEE-RAS International Conference on Humanoid Robots (HUMANOIDS) (2012). doi:10.1109/HUMANOIDS.2012.6651592

8. Szeliski, R.: Computer Vision: Algorithms and Applications. Springer, London (2011)
9. Jin'ichi, Y., Noboru, K., Atsuo, T., Ichiro, K.: Development of a biped walking robot adapting to the human's living floor. In: Proceedings of the 1996 IEEE International Conference on Robotics & Automation, pp. 232–239 (1996)
10. Andreev, A.E., Getmanskiy, V.V., Nasonov, A.A., Movchan, E.O., Kharkov, E.S.: Vectorization of algorithms for the dynamic stress-strain state analysis using a wide vector registers. In: Proceedings of International Conference PCT 2017 (in Russian) SUSU, Chelyabinsk, 2017, pp. 243–254 (2017)
11. NVidia Jetson Embedded Systems. http://www.nvidia.ru/object/jetson-embedded-systems-ru.html

A Robot Commenting Texts
in an Emotional Way

Liliya Volkova[1,2]([✉]) [iD], Artemy Kotov[3], Edward Klyshinsky[2,4] [iD],
and Nikita Arinkin[1,3]

[1] BMSTU, 2-ya Baumanskaya ul. 5-1, 105005 Moscow, Russia
liliya@bmstu.ru, nikita.arinkin@gmail.com
[2] NRU HSE, MIEM, ul. Myasnitskaya, 20, 101000 Moscow, Russia
eklyshinsky@hse.ru
[3] National Research Center «Kurchatov Institute», pl. Akademika Kurchatova,
1, 123182 Moscow, Russia
kotov_aa@nrcki.ru
[4] Keldysh Institute for Applied Mathematics,
Miusskaya pl. 4, 125047 Moscow, Russia

Abstract. This paper is dedicated to modeling emotional reactions on a computer agent and a robot. The affective agent software is processing a natural language text (currently in Russian) with a syntactic parser and it operates with semantic structures. The latter represent sentences or events meanings and consist of valencies with semantic markers in each. Basing on input semantic structures, the agent changes its emotional state over time, generating expressive remarks along with gestures. The reactions subsystem operates with emotional criteria and matches the input semantic representation to scenarios from its database, consequently, it selects relevant reactions from a set of multimodal templates. A model of the emotional process is discussed, and observations based on a multimodal corpus of human emotional expressive cues are applied to synthesize combined reactions expressed in gestures, mimics (eyes and eyebrows) and text. The reactions synthesized are passed to a robot control subsystem and then rendered on a robot.

Keywords: Emotional computer agents · Emotion modelling · Nonverbal communication

1 The Emotion Modelling Task

The Machine is conducting our future for us not only simply in direct answer to our direct questions but in general answer to the world situation and to human psychology as a whole.

Isaac Asimov

It is quite possible that by the middle of this century the emotional robots era will begin. Fantasts introduced most futuristic ideas to humanity, and engineers keep on implementing their ideas, among them a robot capable of reacting more naturally, closer to a human being: getting compassionate, happy, frustrated and so on. This sort

© Springer International Publishing AG 2017
A. Kravets et al. (Eds.): CIT&DS 2017, CCIS 754, pp. 256–266, 2017.
DOI: 10.1007/978-3-319-65551-2_19

of enriched reactions (ahead of the machine-synthesized voice) makes such AI more common to a human [14]. Creating robotic assistants and companions requires not only commands execution, but also meeting the challenge of modeling more natural reactions supported with research-based cognitive models. Studies in psychology and linguistics allow simulating surface emotional phenomena, and conjugating these with text semantics processing is of most interest (see IBug [17], SEMAINE [43], Greta [13], Max [4, 31]). Such AI task brings up such attractive problems as machine comprehension and synthesizing of humor and irony in the text, as well as implementing emotional monologs with corresponding gestures accompaniment [25]. This article describes an approach towards a model of computer agent connected to a robot reproducing the reactions; the complex as a whole is modeling multimodal emotional response to the interlocutor's remarks.

The system under consideration comprises following subsystems.

(1) A syntactic analyzer for natural language input text, which produces semantic structures. The latter represent sentences or events meanings in frames containing valencies with semantic markers in each.
(2) An affective computer agent which changes its emotional states over time and produces reactions in text and gestures.
(3) A robot control subsystem (RCS) which processes the generated gestures and sends appropriate commands to the robot.
(4) A robot with hands and face (Fig. 1).

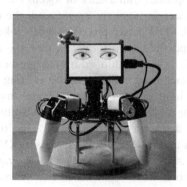

Fig. 1. Emotional robot for the expression of communicative reactions

The four modules of the system are described hereinafter.

A human can see the response to one's phrase in gestures, mimics (eyes, eyebrows and mouth movement on a display which stands for the face) and a remark. The textual part of the reaction is not hard to sound, for the corresponding methods of voice processing exist [30]. At the current stage the Yandex SpeechKit [49, 50] is used for speech recognition and synthesis, but unfortunately, the generated speech intonation is not controlled.

The nonverbal communicative behavior is quite specific for it most often isn't the main channel for the information (though some researchers suggest the value of 60% [12]), but it is of big importance for the personal touch and for transmitting additional information on the attitude toward the addressee or the subject, as well as pragmatics of the message [27]. Creating a so-called emotional agent (so to be referred to) can also be addressed to the problem of captivating human beings [2, 8, 9, 14, 35, 36, 38, 45]. This is important for the production of human assistants and entertaining robots since people lose interest towards a robot quite soon after the acquaintance by reason of limitedness of its reactions specter [18]. One more problem should be taken into consideration: people get scared by androids acting too naturally [33]. Such perception problem could be avoided by means of non-android models acting in a human way, sort of cartoon characters or robots with human reactions simulation, e.g. by hands, eyes, eyebrows. The latter is the reason why the robot described hereinafter is given only hands and face.

2 Machine Comprehension of Text Semantics

Though "it's just lights and clockwork", interlocutors should be convinced that the robot has its mind, for it can produce emotions and change its mood. The first milestone is text semantics interpretation.

The input text is processed by a syntax analyzer (parser) [29] which implements a left-to-right approach and operates with a stack of tokens (word forms) with the help of syntactic rules. On each processing step, the parser reads the next token from the input and applies it to the stack. The parser processes each token with a morphological analyzer to detect all the possible word forms; in case the token is morphologically ambiguous, the number of stacks is multiplied by the number of homonyms. Then the parser tries to reduce the stack head with any of the existing syntactic rules: each rule can reduce a list of tokens in its right-hand side to the left-hand side head: $h \rightarrow$ <a, b, ... n>. Head h can be one of the stack segments, substituting other tokens during reduction, this rule can be defined as $h \rightarrow$ <a, b, h, ... n> or <a, b, h^{head}, ... n>.

Rules are described in an XML-based format – syntXML. In this notation, it is possible for each segment at the stack head to check any grammeme (*check* operator), check the agreement of two or more segments in any grammatic category (*agr* operator), set a grammeme (*set* operator) or copy a grammeme to the rule head h (*copyup* operator). Syntactic rules also assign semantic valencies to the verb and noun phrases: the subject can occupy the "ag" (agents) semantic role, as indicated at the substantive segment head (semval = "ag"). In case several rules can apply to the stack head, the stack is multiplied by the number of applicable rules. It is also possible to control this process through the fork="true/true" statement at the head of each rule. The following rule assigns subject to the head predicate (note the agreement in *number, animation, person,* and *gender* between subject and verb in Russian):

```
<rule name="VFIN-subj-1" fork="true">
  <seg semval="ag">
    <check marker="S"/>
    <check marker="nomn"/>
    <agr type="NMbr"/>
    <agr type="Anim"/>
    <agr type="PErs"/>
    <agr type="GNdr"/>
    <copyup type="Ques"/>
  </seg>
  <seg head ="true">
    <check marker="VFIN"/>
    <check marker="0-Snom-ag"/>
    <agr type="NMbr"/>
    <agr type="Anim"/>
    <agr type="PErs"/>
    <agr type="GNdr"/>
    <set type="Snom-ag" marker="1-Snom-ag"/>
  </seg>
</rule>
```

The parser presently operates with a morphological dictionary of 48,000 lemmas and a grammar with 450 syntactic rules. The result of the syntactic processing is a syntactic dependency tree, where subtrees assign their semantics to specific semantic roles, as indicated by the rules.

The agent is designed as to be influenced with semantic representation: for each lemma, it retrieves semantic markers from a dictionary and assigns the markers to the semantic role. We use a set of 800 marker types, based on [47], which are assigned to lemmas in the dictionary 58,000 times. This procedure allows the agent to construct a shallow semantic representation, i.e. subsets of semantic markers assigned to semantic roles. In this representation "p" is the predicate and is considered as the local head of the semantic representation, and "ag" (agents) and "pat" (patient) are the semantic roles for substantives. Although this representation is quite superficial, it still can be weighted by the possible robot reactions. For the reactions, we use a set of d-scripts (dominant scripts) and r-scripts (rational scripts), represented in [23] and discussed below.

3   The Emotions Model

Emotions are regarded as mediators of conversational content, allowing conversational partners to form the common ground and sometimes to "catch" each other's mood and emotions [10, 48]. Hence, an affective agent would allow initiating such effects with its emotions simulating, which is promising for captivating humans and invoking the sympathy of the audience.

3.1   The Emotions Model Based on Dominating and Rational Scripts

Affect is a general term relating to emotions, moods and other such states with different degrees of activation and valence [22]. Beyond Ekman's basic emotions set, emotions can be represented as points in a continuous two-dimensional space, with valence and activation as axes [41]. Attitudes can be modeled as amalgamations of emotions [22]. Another approach [4] is based on mood changing based on pleasure, arousal and dominance, the weighted combination resulting in an emotion.

For emotions modeling authors of [1] introduced such emotional primitives (referred to as control states) as plans, intentions, wishes, emotions (short-term), preferences, skills, rules and personal characteristics (long-term). The supposition is, agent's actions are defined by concurrence in control states hierarchy, each of the state having its activation degree (changing in time). In this research, the approach of concurrent control states is adapted, in particular, based on the corpus-based observations which allow specifying a set of more low-level control states (emotions or moods) as well.

The agent's structure is two-fold [24–26]. The first level consists of a set of scripts (*if-then* rules as proposed in [32] and implemented in [4, 44]) and is responsible for separate speech reactions. The second level consists of a set of microstates and allows the agent to reply with several phrases (a monolog not bound to the plot) and to distribute the reactions in time, which is the imitation of changing short emotional states. There are *d-scripts* (dominant) for emotions and *r-scripts* for "rational" reactions (considering the situation as a problem to solve or as a source for producing a new rule of acting in such cases), a total of 79 scripts organized to the artificial emotional model. Each script has a variable activation: the input activates all of the scripts with a different degree (also affected by the agent's mood). The script with the maximum activation generates the output reaction in speech and behavior. The agent also simulates mood changes within 10–40 s after the event, i.e. a negative event might initiate getting upset, then blaming itself, and finally thinking rationally about further avoiding such events; the latter is expressed in speech reactions only. Thus, the agent changes several microstates, characterized by a certain emotion. Each microstate is bound to a set of scripts, which are preferred if the agent is in particular microstate. An event may activate several microstates in different degrees, and the activation level fades over time. One of the key goals of this approach is to make reactions most natural; the agent's behavior is not predefined by scenarios but produced in real time depending on events. Tuning the sensitivity of activations and fulfilling the database of emotional reactions is the key to reaching the most adequate model.

Similar to Max [31], the affective agent changes its emotional state in some coordinates, corresponding to emotions. But it is rather a fuzzy logic mechanism, for the d-scripts are dominating each other. This implies a kind of a memory effect: if an emotion was preempted and delayed (wasn't "worked out"), the agent might get back to it later for expressing, in case this emotion didn't fade to zero level. Thus a set of previously activated emotions which didn't lose their activation from a mood, which is similar to more "diffuse" affective states [42] that typically don't have a single antecedent and are of lower intensity than emotions [22].

As to Pepper [36], a remarkable conversational robot, it is considered good at conveying human-like gestures, but it also asks a lot of questions [37]. The agent described in this paper is rather intended to comment texts, for carrying the conversation forward is not limited to questions [10].

The affective agent has a set of communicative strategies comprising gestures and remarks. A strategy might be to shame or to support the interlocutor, to express its discontent or to get embarrassed. The choice of the strategy depends on the initial situation and on the "mood" of the robot. Latest experiments combining the aforesaid strategies resulted in the effect that the robot seems to be torn apart by internal contradictions. This makes the agent one more step closer to human-like behavior.

3.2 The REC Corpus as Research Base

When animating computer agents or robots, the nonverbal communicative behavior modeling is of great importance. Multimodal corpora (containing not only cues but gestures as well) serve as the main research media, allowing to develop such a model (with following verification of it) [39] and for creating an attractive character. Thus, behavior synthesis is a method of verifying the selected markup schema. Focusing on the synthesis of a nonverbal communicative behavior implies the stimuli markup in the corpus, for these will be further used for synthesizing the observed behavior [27].

The Russian Emotional Corpus (REC) [27, 28] is designed for conducting a functional analysis of non-verbal communicative behavior, in particular of emotions-driven reactions. The REC allows studying blended emotions as well as binding the observed communicative reactions not only to emotions but also to communicative intentions of the interlocutor. The mentioned communicative functions are part of the markup in REC, hence the pragmatics of gestures and mimics are under study as well. The REC contains over 200,000 annotations of human emotional behavior in real life [25]. Typical behavior from the corpus is selected for implementation and for further rendering on the robot (see next chapter). For example, a robot can precede speech with simulating thoughtfulness (looking up or aside) as well as expressing its more complex inner states via behavior [26]. If modeling shows that there are some lacunas in communicative strategies, the corpus further accretion will take place in order to enrich robot's pool of communicative behavior.

The gestures selected are stored in the database and processed by the robot control subsystem. The parameterization by means of the mentioned subsystem is one of the key instruments in the research procedure.

4 The Robot Control Subsystem (RCS)

The described theoretical model of communicative behavior is realized for a 3D agent as well as for a corresponding robot. Modeling of agent's behavior serves also as a means of verification of the model developed, e.g., estimation by a human focus group.

The reactions (gestures, mimics, and text) generated in BML (behavior markup language [46]) are sent to the RCS which preprocesses these for further rendering. The RCS broaches the model time [40], decomposes input gestures and forms commands for robot's motors in order to implement current reactions. As BML allows up to 7 phases (including initial phase, swing, peak, finishing), the multi-phase gestures were implemented. Gesture parameterizing is of interest, in particular phases timing and gesture amplitude.

Coordinating both text and gestures is of particular importance when building artificial interlocutors [5]. Human collocutors have been found to align in their facial expressions [11, 21] and gestures [6, 16] to each other, and when communicating with a computer agent they tend to align lexically and to adapt the speech rate to the machine's in order to facilitate the communicative success as well [3, 7].

At this stage of project development, the speech to gesture alignment is performed while preprocessing: the synthesized speech duration is subject to tune to fit the gesture period and keypoints (e.g., gesture peak often corresponds to the phrasal accent, an example being the pointing case). Furthermore, several techniques are under development to conjugate short gesture which can't be prolongated (e.g., a flick of the wrist) with a long speech and vice versa. One more problem to solve is implementing the event memory (perhaps supported with short-term memory for intentions) for interrupted gesture completion (hazardous switching focus might lead to such an interruption). Apart from these research milestones, a quite engineering problem exists: the reverse signal from the robot is not currently taken into account. Its processing will be incorporated into the system on further stages of development in order to avoid motor faults and malfunctions (e.g. when stuck or tangling wires).

Gestures are selected on the base of the REC corpus study. The gestures chosen are first created in Blender to fix motor control points and timing, as well as mimics. Then these are converted into sets of coordinates for a robot; such packs are stored in a database, each attached to a BML label. When a BML frame is received by the RCS, corresponding control points are retrieved from the database (separately for mimics and gestures, if both present in the BML), then parameterized for the adequate synchronization and finally sent to the robot for rendering. Speech is generated by means of Yandex SpeechKit [49, 50] and simply reproduced; still, it is intended to be synchronized with gesture and mimics on further stages of research.

The robot model is based on Dynamixel AX-12 motors and has two hands with 2 degrees of freedom each (for moving upside down and turning hands horizontally in shoulders), a neck with 2 degrees of freedom (nodding and turning left and right) and an LCD display standing for the face. The face is displaying eyes (with pupils moving within), eyebrows and mouth. This model is used to render gestures on it; the database comprises corresponding gestures and mimics, interpreted according to the parameterization of the input gestures by the RCS. The parameterization approach allows adapting gestures not only for the amplitude of the emotion shown but to the start position of the robot as well (e.g., the amplitude of nodding depends on whether the robot starts when looking in front of it or looking up with head up).

Gesture transition smoothing is implemented for gliding on the gestures border without returning to the neutral position.

There is a stand-by mode implemented for the robot. Instead of freezing after having finished acting, the robot can stand for days while simulating breathing, watching the ceiling or its hands, moving slightly, which shows more credible to a human.

5 Conclusion

The affective robot assistant is provided with an ability to simulate emotions and to act sort of natural. First, the agent can comprehend the interlocutor's lines due to the syntax parser extracting semantic data. Second, the robot's mood is modeled: time and semantic representation of input text change the state of the model. Emotions are expressed with text and gestures, which are synthesized and reproduced by means of RCS. While the computer agent produces reactions in a wide specter (and often amuses the developing team while commenting the news), the gestures set for the robot is so far limited, but more gestures are to be implemented. Additionally, the rules-driven reactions will be enriched along with the REC corpus extension (e.g. with reactions in different situations; in particular, a corpus of happy people is under development). This corpus serves media for functional analysis of non-verbal communicative behavior, in particular of emotions-driven reactions, and analysis allows selecting gestures from real-life data.

Bringing in the naturalness of interactions keeps a human interlocutor involved in communication with a robot, beyond the straightforward task of commands completing and efficient processing of factual information [14, 20]. Hence, this research is addressed to social robotics, the agent's communicative ability becomes more and more natural. The non-verbal behavior is a strong mediator of interpersonal alignment [23], the approach presented facilitates the interaction with a machine. Furthermore, the agent's multimodal activity (which is human-like for it is based on a multimodal corpus of human reactions) infers one's engagement in the communication [14, 20]. This makes the aforesaid emotional robot perspective for production due to credible long-term human interest towards it, ascertained by a richer reactions spectrum.

The perspectives of the project include fixing the eyes of the model on the interlocutor or the object of current interest. At the current stage, the eyes movement is implemented for accompanying gesture in a fixed way, but the mechanism of tying the mimics up to the interlocutor position is implied by the designed architecture (i.e. gazing at). The problem of multiparty conversations requires thorough studying and making corresponding project decisions for not only contexts and roles change, but the gesture interpretation and conversation modularity as well. Moreover, gazes and other multimodal signals may indicate the pass of turn or switching the focus of attention [15, 19, 34], modeling of these phenomena is a separate task itself.

References

1. Allen, S.R.: Concern processing in autonomous agents, Ph.D. thesis. University of Birmingham, Birmingham (2001)
2. Andre, E., Dybkjær, L., Minker, W., et al. (eds.): Affective Dialogue Systems. Springer, Berlin (2004)
3. Bell, L., Gustafson, J., Heldner, M.: Prosodic adaptation in human–computer interaction. In: Proceedings of ICPhS-2003. Barcelona, pp. 2453–2456. Cambridge University Press, Cambridge (2003)

4. Becker, C., Kopp, S., Wachsmuth, I.: Simulating the emotion dynamics of a multimodal conversational agent. In: André, E., Dybkjær, L., Minker, W., Heisterkamp, P. (eds.) ADS 2004. LNCS, vol. 3068, pp. 154–165. Springer, Heidelberg (2004). doi:10.1007/978-3-540-24842-2_15

5. Bergmann, K., Branigan, H.P., Kopp, S.: Exploring the alignment space – lexical and gestural alignment with real and virtual humans. Front. ICT. 2(7) (2015). Human-Media Interaction. Frontiers Media S.A., Lausanne

6. Bergmann, K., Kopp, S.: Gestural alignment in natural dialogue. In: Proceedings of the 34th Annual Conference of the Cognitive Science Society, pp. 1326–1331. Cognitive Science Society, Austin (2012)

7. Branigan, H.P., Pickering, M.J., Pearson, J., McLean, J.F., Brown, A.: The role of beliefs in lexical alignment: evidence from dialogs with humans and computers. Cognition 121, 41–57 (2011). Elsevier, Amsterdam

8. Breazeal, C.: Designing Sociable Robots. MIT Press, Cambridge (2002)

9. Cassel, J., Sullivan, J., Prevost, S., et al. (eds.): Embodied Conversational Agents. MIT Press, Cambridge/London (2000)

10. Clark, H.H., Brennan, S.E.: Grounding in communication. In: Lauren, R., Levine, B., John, M., Teasley, S.D. (eds.) Perspectives on Socially Shared Cognition, pp. 127–149. American Psychological Association, Washington (1991)

11. Dimberg, U.: Facial reactions to facial expressions. Psychophysiology 19, 643–647 (1982). Wiley & Sons Ltd., New York

12. Engleberg, I.N., Wynn, D.R.: Communication Principles and Strategies. My Communication Kit Series, p. 133. Allyn & Bacon, Boston (2006)

13. Greta, Embodied Conversational Agent. http://perso.telecomparistech.fr/~pelachau/Greta/. Accessed 10 Apr 2017

14. Han, J.G., Campbell, N., Jokinen, K., Wilcock, G.: Investigating the use of non-verbal cues in human-robot interaction with a Nao robot. In: Proceedings of the 3rd IEEE International Conference on Cognitive Infocommunications (CogInfoCom 2012), Kosice, Slovakia, pp. 679–683. IEEE, Pictasaway (2012)

15. Healey, P.G.T., Battersby, S.A.: The interactional geometry of a three-way conversation. In: Proceedings of the 31st Annual Conference of the Cognitive Science Society, pp. 785–790. Cognitive Science Society Inc., Austin (2009)

16. Holler, J., Wilkin, K.: Co-speech gesture mimicry in the process of collaborative referring during face-to-face dialogue. J. Nonverbal Behav. 35, 133–153 (2011). Springer, Heidelberg

17. i·bug. http://ibug.doc.ic.ac.uk/. Accessed 10 Apr 2017

18. Jokinen, K.: Communicative engagement and autonomous robots: social interaction. In: WikiTalk Software International Symposium Research for Gesturing in Human-Computer Interaction: Robots and Virtual Agents. MSLU, 26 October 2015 (2015)

19. Jokinen, K., Furukawa, H., Nishida, M., Yamamoto, S.: Gaze and turn-taking behavior in casual conversational interactions. ACM Trans. Interact. Intell. Syst. 3(2), 12:1–12:30 (2013)

20. Jokinen, K., Wilcock, G.: Modelling user experience in human-robot interactions. In: Böck, R., Bonin, F., Campbell, N., Poppe, R. (eds.) MA3HMI 2014 Workshop. LNCS, vol. 8757, pp. 45–56. Springer, Heidelberg (2014). doi:10.1007/978-3-319-15557-9_5

21. Likowski, K.U., Mühlberger, A., Gerdes, A.B., Wieser, M.J., Pauli, P., Weyers, P.: Facial mimicry and the mirror neuron system: simultaneous acquisition of facial electromyography and functional magnetic resonance imaging. Front. Hum. Neurosci. 6, 214 (2012). Frontiers Research Foundation, Lausanne

22. Kirby, R., Forlizzi, J., Simmons, R.: Affective social robots. Robot. Auton. Syst. 58, 322–332 (2010). Elsevier, Amsterdam

23. Kopp, S.: Social resonance and embodied coordination in face-to-face conversation with artificial interlocutors. Speech Commun. **52**, 587–597 (2010). Elsevier, Amsterdam
24. Kotov, A.: Simulating dynamic speech behaviour for virtual agents in emotional situations. In: Paiva, A.C.R., Prada, R., Picard, R.W. (eds.) ACII 2007. LNCS, vol. 4738, pp. 714–715. Springer, Heidelberg (2007). doi:10.1007/978-3-540-74889-2_64
25. Kotov, A.: Accounting for irony and emotional oscillation in computer architectures. In: Proceedings of ACII 2009, pp. 506–511. IEEE, Piscataway (2009)
26. Kotov, A.A.: Patterns of emotional communicative reactions: problems of creating a corpus and translating to emotional agents. In: Computational Linguistics and Intellectual Technologies, vol. 8, pp. 211–218. RSUH, Moscow (2009). (in Russian)
27. Kotov, A.A., Zinina, A.A.: Functional analysis of non-verbal communicative behavior. In: Computational Linguistics and Intellectual Technologies, vol. 14, no. 2, pp. 308–320. RSUH, Moscow (2015). (in Russian)
28. Kotov, A.A., Zinina, A.A.: Functional annotation of communicative actions in «REC» corpus (in Russian). In: Proceedings of the International Conference on Corpus Linguistics–2015, pp. 287–295. SPbSU Press, Saint-Petersburg (2015)
29. Kotov, A., Zinina, A., Filatov, A.: Semantic parser for sentiment analysis and the emotional computer agents. In: Proceedings of the AINL-ISMW FRUCT 2015, pp. 167–170. FRUCT Oy, Helsingfors (2015)
30. Lobanov, B.M., Tsirulnik, L.I.: Computer Synthesis and Cloning of Speech. Belorusskaya Nauka, Minsk (2008). (in Russian)
31. Max. http://cycling74.com/products/max/. Accessed 10 Apr 2017
32. Minsky, M.: The Society of Mind. Touchstone Book, New-York/London (1988)
33. Mori, M.: The uncanny valley (MacDorman, K.F., Kageki, N. Trans.). IEEE Robot. Autom. Mag. **19**(2), 98–100. IEEE, Piscataway (1970/2012)
34. Padilha, E.G., Carletta, J.C.: Nonverbal behaviours improving a simulation of small group discussion. In: Proceedings of the 1st International Nordic Symposium of Multi-Modal Communication. Springer, Heidelberg (2003)
35. Paiva, A., Prada, R., Picard, R.W. (eds.): Affective Computing and Intelligent Interaction. LNCS, vol. 4738. Springer, Heidelberg (2007)
36. Pepper. https://www.ald.softbankrobotics.com/en/cool-robots/pepper. Accessed 10 Apr 2017
37. Pepper robot released. http://www.bbc.com/news/technology-33183360. Accessed 10 Apr 2017
38. Picard, R.: Affective Computing. MIT Press, Cambridge/London (2000)
39. Rehm, M., André, E.: From annotated multimodal corpora to simulated human-like behaviors. In: Wachsmuth, I., Knoblich, G. (eds.) Modeling Communication with Robots and Virtual Humans. LNCS, vol. 4930, pp. 1–17. Springer, Heidelberg (2008). doi:10.1007/978-3-540-79037-2_1
40. Rudakov, I.V.: A method for hierarchical investigation of complex discrete structures. Sci. Educ. **6** (2012). (in Russian). BMSTU Press, Moscow. doi:10.7463/0612.0370230
41. Russell, J.: Core affect and the psychological construction of emotion. Psychol. Rev. **110**(1), 145–172 (2003). American Psychological Association, Washington
42. Scherer, K.R.: Psychological models of emotion. In: Borod, J.C. (ed.) The Neuropsychology of Emotion, pp. 137–162. Oxford University Press, Oxford (2000)
43. Semaine Project. http://www.semaine-project.eu/. Accessed 10 Apr 2017
44. Sloman, A., Chrisley, R.: Virtual machines and consciousness. J. Conscious. Stud. **10**(4–5), 133–172 (2003). Imprint Academic, Exeter

45. Tao, J., Tan, T.: Affective computing: a review. In: Tao, J., Tan, T., Picard, Rosalind W. (eds.) ACII 2005. LNCS, vol. 3784, pp. 981–995. Springer, Heidelberg (2005). doi:10.1007/11573548_125
46. Vilhjálmsson, H., et al.: The behavior markup language: recent developments and challenges. In: Pelachaud, C., Martin, J.-C., André, E., Chollet, G., Karpouzis, K., Pelé, D. (eds.) IVA 2007. LNCS, vol. 4722, pp. 99–111. Springer, Heidelberg (2007). doi:10.1007/978-3-540-74997-4_10
47. Wierzbicka, A.: Lingua Mentalis: The Semantics of Natural Language. Academic Press, New York (1980)
48. Wild, B., Erb, M., Bartels, M.: Are emotions contagious? Evoked emotions while viewing emotionally expressive faces: quality, quantity, time course and gender differences. Psychiatry Res. **102**(2), 109–124 (2001). Elsevier, Amsterdam
49. Yandex SpeechKit API. (in Russian). http://api.yandex.ru/speechkit/. Accessed 10 Apr 2017
50. Yandex SpeechKit. Under the hood. (in Russian). https://habrahabr.ru/company/yandex/blog/198556/. Accessed 10 Apr 2017

Pro-active Modeling in Intelligent Decision Making Support

A Medical Decision Support System for the Prediction of the Coronary Artery Disease Using Fuzzy Cognitive Maps

Ioannis D. Apostolopoulos[1]([⊠]), Peter P. Groumpos[2],
and Dimitris I. Apostolopoulos[3]

[1] Department of Electrical and Computer Engineering,
University of Patras, Patras, Greece
apostolopoulos.john.dim@gmail.com
[2] Laboratory for Automation and Robotics/Department of Electrical
and Computer Engineering, University of Patras, Patras, Greece
groumpos@ece.upatras.gr
[3] Division of Clinical Laboratories/Department of Nuclear Medicine,
University of Patras, Patras, Greece
dimap@med.upatras.gr

Abstract. There is a lot discussion nowadays regarding the decision-making problem. The Making decisions and creating computational models using the tools of Fuzzy Cognitive Maps and Neural Systems is presented. The reason is that the contributing factors are several and complicated themselves. The medical problem of coronary artery disease (CAD) is considered and briefly presented. In medicine, factors such as age, symptoms, clinical tests all play their role and have their own importance when it comes to examine a patient, or to decide action. The development of a Medical Decision Support System (MDSS) using fuzzy cognitive maps (FCM) for the first time to study the coronary artery disease (CAD) is formulated. A number of physician experts were used in developing a FCM with thirty concepts. Medical data from a number of real cases were used and simulations were conducted. Interesting results were obtained and discussed. Future directions for this medical application are provided.

Keywords: Coronary artery disease · Medical decision support systems · Fuzzy cognitive maps

1 Introduction

During the last years, there has been a development of an enormous number of medical decision support systems (MDSS). The traditional medical expert systems were equipped with a rule knowledge base which was offered by experts (physicians) [1]. On the basis of rules inserted in the expert system, it is possible to classify new instances of medical observations by matching symptoms to the conditional part of a rule and then to perform forward and backward reasoning to achieve the diagnosis or construct a therapy plan.

© Springer International Publishing AG 2017
A. Kravets et al. (Eds.): CIT&DS 2017, CCIS 754, pp. 269–283, 2017.
DOI: 10.1007/978-3-319-65551-2_20

It is believed that the classic technique of the rule-based knowledge representation in medical DSS has one main disadvantage, which is summarized by its limitation of representing, in reality, some of the more complex associations that may be experienced in medical data. For example, in a rule-based DSS, the representation of the complex phenomenon of causality is, in fact, left to the interpretation and expertise of the doctor [2].

In this work, we illustrate the development for the first time of an MDSS prediction of a very complex medical problem that of Coronary Artery Disease (CAD) using fuzzy cognitive maps (FCM) [3]. FCM is a soft computing technique capable of dealing with situations including uncertain descriptions using a similar procedure such as human reasoning [3, 5, 18]. FCMs are originated from cognitive maps and are used to model knowledge and experience for describing particular domains using nodes-concepts (representing i.e. variables, states, inputs, and outputs) and the relationships between them in order to outline a decision-making process.

What Is Coronary Artery Disease (CAD)?

Coronary artery disease is the most common type of heart disease. It is the leading cause of death all around the world and especially in the United States in both men and women.

For the Physicians, Coronary artery disease, also known as ischemic heart disease (IHD) and by some Acute Coronary Syndrome (ACS), [1, 6, 7] is a group of diseases that include: stable angina, unstable angina, myocardial infarction, and sudden cardiac death. It is within the group of cardiovascular diseases of which it is the most common type [6–9]. This serious condition is a result of plaque buildup in your arteries. The arteries, which start out smooth and elastic, get a plaque on their inner walls, which can make them more rigid and narrowed. This restricts blood flow to your heart, which can then become starved of oxygen. The plaque could rupture, leading to a heart attack or sudden cardiac death. A common symptom is chest pain or discomfort which may travel into the shoulder, arm, back, neck, or jaw. Usually, symptoms occur with exercise or emotional stress, last less than a few minutes, and get better with rest, [12] Shortness of breath may also occur and sometimes no symptoms are present [12]. The first sign is occasionally a heart attack. Other complications include heart failure or an irregular heartbeat. CAD happens when the arteries that supply blood to heart muscle become hardened and narrowed. This is due to the buildup of cholesterol and other material, called plaque, on their inner walls. This buildup is called atherosclerosis. As it grows, less blood can flow through the arteries. As a result, the heart muscle can't get the blood or oxygen it needs. This can lead to chest pain (angina) or a heart attack. Most heart attacks happen when a blood clot suddenly cuts off the hearts' blood supply, causing permanent heart damage.

FCM was chosen because of the nature of the application problem. The medical problem is very complex and depends on many parameters. The prediction of diseases like CAD is a complex process with sufficient interacting parameters and FCMs have been proved suitable for this kind of problems. Similar MDSS have been suggested for the prediction of diseases like pulmonary infection [4].

Before we begin, an introduction to the FCM case is needed and is provided in Sect. 2. Then our medical problem, the Coronary Artery Disease (CAD) is briefly presented in Sect. 3 while Sect. 4 outlines a methodology of a Fuzzy Cognitive Map

(FCM) for Prediction of the Disease (CAD). Simulations for Eleven scenarios and discussion of results are provided in Sect. 5 and Sect. 6 gives conclusions and future research directions.

2 Basics of Fuzzy Cognitive Maps (FCM)

A Fuzzy Cognitive Map (FCM) is a soft computing technique that follows an approach similar to human reasoning and the human decision-making process. Figure 1 shows a simple FCM. An FCM looks like a cognitive map; it consists of nodes (concepts) which interact with each other showing the dynamics of the model. Concepts may represent variables, states, events, trends, inputs, and outputs. The connection edges between concepts are directed and they indicate the direction of causal relationships. A brief overview is very useful. Kosko was the first to introduce the FCMs with the use of fuzzy causal functions, the numbers of which are in $[-1, 1]$ in concept maps [3, 5]. One of the main objectives of building a cognitive map around a problem is the prediction of the outcome, especially in medical applications. This can be done by letting all the issues regarding this problem interact with each other. These predictions can be used in a medical DSS for predicting the possibility of infection in certain diseases. Other research results can be found in [17–20] and many others are easily accessible on the open literature. A brief overview is very useful. The most important element in describing the system is the determination of which concept influences which other and with which degree. Between concepts, there are three possible types of causal relationships that express the type of influence from one concept to another:

(1) Wij > 0, (Ci ↑ → Cj ↑) positive causality
(2) Wij < 0, (Ci ↑ → Cj↓) negative causality
(3) Wij = 0, (Ci, Cj) → no causality

Important remark: We should distinguish Probability and probability density functions versus Fuzzy Logic and Membership functions as well as Correlation versus Causality.

The full procedure of the development of a FCM follows the below steps [18]:

- **Step 1:** Experts select the number and the kind of concepts Ci that constitute the Fuzzy Cognitive Map
- **Step 2:** Each expert defines the relationship between the concepts
- **Step 3:** They define the kind and the value of the relationship between the two nodes
- **Step 4:** Experts describe the existing relationship firstly as "negative" or "positive" and secondly, as a degree of influence using a linguistic variable, such as "low", "medium", "high" etc.

The value of each concept is influenced by the values of the connected concepts with the corresponding causal weights and by its previous value. Mathematically the value of each concept C_i at the iteration step $k + 1$, is calculated applying the following equation:

$$C_i^{(k+1)} = f(C_i^k + \sum_{j=1, j \neq i}^{n} C_j^{(k)} w_{ji}) \tag{1}$$

Where f is the sigmoid function ($\lambda > 0$ steepness of the function):

$$f(x) = \frac{1}{1 + e^{-\lambda x}} \tag{2}$$

In the above equations: the value of concept C (k + 1) is at step k + 1, C(k) is the value of concept C_j at step k, Wji is the weight of the interconnection from concept C_j to concept Ci at step k and f is the threshold function that squashes the result of the multiplication in the interval [0, 1]. This equation indicates that a FCM is free to interact; at every step of interaction, every concept has a new value. FCM approach is based on experts' knowledge for the construction of matrix W_{ij}. This experience is not always reliable though.

That is the reason why the weights need to be trained by a learning algorithm. Several learning principles originally developed for Artificial Neural Networks (ANN) have been applied to FCM. These approaches were based on the concept of Hebbian learning. More specifically Nonlinear Hebbian Learning (NHL) method has been used in many applications. In this learning algorithm, the nodes are triggered simultaneously and interact in the same iteration step with their values to be updated through this process of interaction. The training weight algorithm is computed as follows:

$$w_{ij}^{(k)} = g \cdot w_{ij}^{(k-1)} + h \cdot A_j^{(k-1)} \cdot \left(A_i^{(k-1)} - \mathrm{sgn}(w_{ij}) \cdot w_{ij}^{(k-1)} \cdot A_j^{(k-1)} \right) \tag{3}$$

where the coefficient h is a very small positive scalar factor called learning parameter, and the coefficient g called weight reduction parameter. Two stopping criteria terminate the procedure. The first one concerns the minimization of the sum of the squared differences between each Desired Output Concept i (DOC_i) and a target value T_i. T_i is defined as the mean value of the range of DOC_i = [Timin, Timax]. The second criterion is the minimization of the variation of two subsequent values of Desired Output Concepts. Although we do not use learning on the present paper it is very important to have this in mind when future research on this particular medical problem is to be explored.

3   The Coronary Artery Disease (CAD)

As mentioned above, the CAD includes some risk factors, the presence of which increase the danger of infection. Risk factors include high blood pressure, smoking, diabetes, lack of exercise, obesity, high blood cholesterol, poor diet, and excessive alcohol, among others [12]. Other risks include depression [13]. The underlying mechanism involves atherosclerosis of the arteries of the heart [12]. A number of tests may help with diagnoses including electrocardiogram, cardiac stress testing, coronary computed tomographic angiography, and coronary angiogram, among others [12].

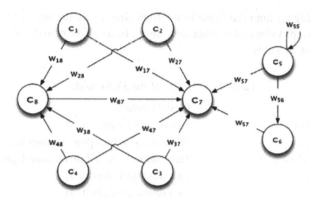

Fig. 1. A generic FCM model

Heart disease is the leading cause of death in developed nations despite known ways to prevent and treat heart problems. One common type of heart disease is called coronary artery disease (CAD). The arteries of the heart (coronary arteries) supply blood flow to the heart muscle. Plaque (buildup of fatty material) damages the coronary arteries, and blood platelets (cells in the blood that help to clot) can stick to these damaged areas, causing blockage of blood flow. This can lead to ischemia (lack of oxygen to the heart muscle cells) or myocardial infarction (heart attack). Risk factors—things that make it more likely for a person to develop coronary heart disease—have been identified through many scientific studies. The most common symptom is chest pain or discomfort, which may travel into the shoulder, arm, back, neck, or jaw. Usually, symptoms occur with exercise or emotional stress, last less than a few minutes, and get better with rest. Other complications include heart failure or an irregular heartbeat [6].

In 2013 CAD was the most common cause of death globally, resulting in 8.14 million deaths (16.8%) up from 5.74 million deaths (12%) in 1990 [7]. In 2015 CAD affected 110 million people and resulted in 8.9 million deaths [14]. It makes up 15.9% of all deaths making it the most common cause of death globally [14]. The risk of death from CAD for a given age has decreased between 1980 and 2010, especially in developed countries [15]. The number of cases of CAD for a given age has also decreased between 1990 and 2010. In the United States in 2010 about 20% of those over 65 had CAD, while it was present in 7% of those 45 to 64, and 1.3% of those 18 to 45 [16]. Rates are higher among men than women of a given age [16].

4   Methodology of a Fuzzy Cognitive Map (FCM) for Prediction of the Disease (CAD)

To begin with, we have to define all the possible input variables of the MDSS. Three physicians-experts were pooled to define the number and type of parameters-factors affecting the possibility of being affected by CAD. These parameters (concepts) are listed in Table 1 and are well documented in the bibliography and represent the main variables that play an important role in the final diagnostic decision of CAD. For this application, concept values take either two, three, four or five possible discrete or fuzzy values, as shown in Table 1.

Table 1. Concepts of the FCM model

Variable	Possible values
A1: Typical angina	Two discrete values [0 1]
A2: Atypical angina	Three fuzzy values [low medium high]
A3: Nonanginal chest pain	Three fuzzy values [low medium high]
A4: Asymptomatic	Two discrete values [0 1]
A5: Gender – male	Two discrete values [0 1]
A6: Gender – female	Two discrete values [0 1]
A7: Age below 40	Two discrete values [0 1]
A8: Age [40 50]	Two discrete values [0 1]
A9: Age [50 60]	Two discrete values [0 1]
A10: Age above 60	Two discrete values [0 1]
A11: Smoking	Three fuzzy values [no light heavy]
A12: Arterial hypertension	Two discrete values [0 1]
A13: Dyslipidemia	Two discrete values [0 1]
A14: Obesity	Two discrete values [0 1]
A15: Family history of coronary artery disease	Two discrete values [0 1]
A16: Diabetes mellitus	Two discrete values [0 1]
A17: Renal insufficiency	Two discrete values [0 1]
A18: Baseline ECG (Electrocardiogram) normal	Two discrete values [0 1]
A19: Baseline ECG (Electrocardiogram) abnormal	Two discrete values [normal abnormal]
A20: Cardiac ultrasound normal	Two discrete values [0 1]
A21: Cardiac ultrasound abnormal	Two discrete values [0 1]
A22: Treadmill exercise test normal	Two discrete values [0 1]
A23: Treadmill exercise test abnormal	Two fuzzy values [ambiguous abnormal]
A24: Dobutamin stress cardiac ultrasound normal	Two discrete values [0 1]
A25: Dobutamin stress cardiac ultrasound abnormal	Two fuzzy values [ambiguous abnormal]
A26: Myocardial perfusion imaging normal	Two discrete values [0 1]
A27: Myocardial perfusion imaging abnormal	Four fuzzy values [ambiguous, mildly abnormal, moderately abnormal, severely abnormal]
A28: Computerized tomography coronary angiography normal	Two discrete values [0 1]
A29: Computerized tomography coronary Angiography abnormal	Three fuzzy values [mildly abnormal, moderately abnormal, severely abnormal]

These variables contain, first of all, information about the patient (i.e. Age, Gender). They also contain information regarding the heaviness of the main symptom, some Comorbidities and predisposing factors for CAD, as well as diagnostic tests that the patient has been submitted to. The main symptom of the disease is angina (chest pain), which is split into four variables (typical, atypical, nonanginal chest pain, asymptomatic). Due to the absence of any other symptoms, angina plays a more important role in the outcome. For example, all experts agree that if the patient has typical angina, then it is almost sure that the patient is affected, regardless of the other parameters.

Age and gender play also an important role, combining with the type of angina of the patient. For example, female patients have less probability of infection, due to biological reasons. In addition, men above sixty years regardless of the type of angina (except for nonasymptomatic), have a high possibility of affection [8]. Moreover, diagnose tests to female patients, especially Cardiac Ultrasound and Myocardial Perfusion Imaging are more susceptible to giving false results [9]. All these factors are been described in guidelines given by experts.

The Decision Concept (A30) represents the possibility of infection and takes four fuzzy values *(a low possibility, medium possibility, high possibility, very high possibility)*.

Some fuzzy sets of the input variables as well as the fuzzy sets of the output decision concept A30 are illustrated in Table 2.

The thirty identified concepts (Table 1) keep relations with each other, in order to characterize the process of assessing infectious diseases and to provide a first front-end decision about the prediction of CAD. After the determination of fuzzy sets, each expert was asked to define the degree of influence among the concepts and describe their interrelationship using if-then rules. To illustrate how the interconnection is translated into numeric values the three experts are asked to describe the relation of the concept A2 (typical angina) with the decision concept A30 in the following example [4]:

Expert 1

"If a small change occurs in the value of concept A2 then a strong change in the value of concept A30 occurs". This means that the influence of A2 to A30 is positive high.

Expert 2

"If a small change occurs in the value of concept A2 then a medium change in the value of concept A30 occurs". This means that the influence of A2 to A30 is positive medium.

Expert 3

"If a small change occurs in the value of concept A2 then a weak change in the value of concept A30 occurs". This means that the influence of A2 to A30 is positive weak.

For the construction of the FCM, three experts are asked to define with the method described above the influence of all the inputs to the final outcome. Afterward, we need to defuzzify the linguistic variables given by experts, in order to fill the final weight of each of the inputs to the output. An algorithm for the comparison of the weights given by experts has been adopted, in order to exclude weights that deviate from the weights given by the other experts. For example if an expert defines the influence from A to B

Table 2. The experts' deffuzified values

	Physician 1	Physician 2	Physician 3	Average
A1	0.875	0.875	0.875	0.875
A2	0.625 0.875	0.375 0.625	0.625 0.875	0.667
A3	0.125 0.375	0.125 0.375	0.125 0.375	0.250
A4	−0.875	−0.625 −0.875	−0.875	−0.813
A5	0.125 0.375	0.125 0.375	0.125 0.375	0.250
A6	−0.125 −0.375	−0.125	−0.375 −0.625	−0.325
A7	−0.375 −0.625	−0.125 −0.375	−0.375 −0.625	−0.417
A8	−0.125 −0.375	−0.125	−0.125	−0.188
A9	0.125 0.375	0.125 0.375	0.125 0.375	0.250
A10	0.375 0.625	0.375 0.625	0.375 0.625	0.458
A11	0.125 0.375	0.375 0.625	0.125 0.375	0.333
A12	0.125	0.125 0.375	0.125	0.188
A13	0.125	0.125 0.375	0.125 0.375	0.225
A14	0.125	0.125 0.375	0.125 0.375	0.225
A15	0.125	0.375 0.625	0.375 0,625	0.425
A16	0.125	0.125 0.375	0.125 0.375	0.225
A17	0.125 0.375	0.375 0.625	0.375 0.625	0.417
A18	−0.375 −0.625	−0.375 −0.625	−0.375 −0.625	−0.500
A19	0.375 0.625	0.625 0.875	0.375 0.625	0.583
A20	−0.375 −0.625	−0.375 −0.625	−0.375 −0.625	−0.500
A21	0.375 0.625	0.625 0.875	0.625 0.875	0.667
A22	−0.375 −0.625	−0.375 −0.625	−0.375 −0.625	−0.500
A23	0.625 0.875	0,625 0.875	0.625 0.875	0.750
A24	−0.375 −0.625	−0.625 −0.875	−0.375 −0.625	−0.583
A25	0.375 0.625	0.375 0.625	0.375 0.625	0.500
A26	−0.375 −0.625	−0.375 −0.625	−0.625 −0.875	−0.583
A27	0.375 0.625	0.625 0.875	0.375 0.625	0.583
A28	−0.375 −0.625	−0.375 −0.625	−0.375 −0.625	−0.500
A29	0.375 0.625	0.625 0.875	0.625 0.875	0.667
A30				

as "positive strong" in opposition to the others who gave a value "negative", then this expert's opinion in not counted to the final outcome and moreover the expert is punished (by reducing his trust from 1 to 0.8 for example). Following the steps of this algorithm, a table including all the weights is created (Table 2). In the last column of the table final weight of its variable is calculated, using centroid defuzzification method. In this technique, we make use of the shape 1 to defuzzify each of the experts proposed weights into their numeric values. Afterward, the final weight is producing by calculating the average of each value.

For example, an expert describes the influence of A2 to the output as "strong". In Fig. 2 we see that the triangle of "strong" is between the values 0.5 and 1. We separate the triangle into two equal triangles and for each one we calculate the median. In this case, the medians are 0.625 and 0.875. We work the same for each expert. To calculate the final weight of each variable we take the average of every expert's deffuzified value. In our example the final weight from A2 to the output is A + B+.../6.

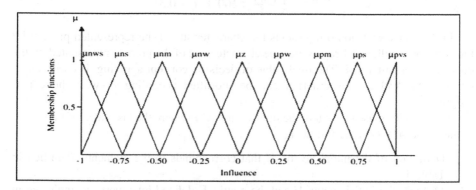

Fig. 2. Defuzzification values

This is the first step in the development of an expert system module that will help in the decision-making process, through the design of the knowledge representation and the design of reasoning with FCM to automate the decision making process. The constructed FCM model is represented in Fig. 3.

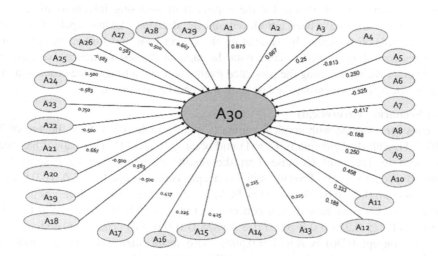

Fig. 3. The constructed FCM for the CAD

In each of the test scenarios, we have an initial vector Ai, representing the presented events at a given time of the process, and a final vector **A30_f**, representing the last state that can be arrived at. For the interpretation of the results, an average only for the output value of the decision concept C30 is computed according to the following criteria [10]:

$$R(x) = \begin{cases} 0, x \leq 0.5 \\ \frac{x-0.5}{0.5} \times 100\%, x > 0.5 \end{cases} \tag{4}$$

In the above equation 0 represents the characteristic of the represented process by the concept is null, and 1 represents, the characteristic of the process represented by the concept is present 100%. The final value of decision concept applying this criterion is denoted by **A30_f**. This criterion can be modified according to with the expert judgment.

The algorithm used to obtain the final vector **A_f** (where the last value of the vector is the value **AD_f**) is the following:

(1) Definition of the initial vector Ai that corresponds to the elements identified in Table 1.
(2) Multiply the initial vector Ai and the matrix **E** defined by experts, as indicated in the previous Sect.
(3) The resultant vector is updating using Eqs. (1)–(2).
(4) This new vector is considered as an initial vector in the next iteration.

5   Simulations and Discussion of Results

After construction of FCM tool for the approach of assessing infectious diseases, a number of scenarios have been introduced and the decision-making capabilities of the technique will be presented by simulating these scenarios and finding the predicted outcomes according to the available data. In each of the test scenarios, we have an initial vector Ai, representing the presented events at a given time of the process, and a final vector **A_f**, representing the last state that can be arrived at.

First Scenario (Theoretical)
We consider a patient with atypical angina (C2 = 1), male (C5 = 5) at the age of 70 (C10 = 1), with dyslipidemia (C13 = 1) and obesity (C14 = 1). This patient has been proceeded to Treadmill Exercise Test the results of which can be described as ambiguous (C23 = 0.25). Thus the initial concept vector is: A (0 1 0 0 1 0 0 0 0 0 1 0 0 1 1 0 0 0 0 0 0 1 0 0 0 0 0 0). After FCM inference, the system converges as in the following state vector named final concept vector: A_f (0 0.667 0 0 0.25 0 0 0 0 0.458 0 0 0.225 0.225 0 0 0 0 0 0 0.1875 0 0 0 0 0 0). The calculated value of decision concept (C30) is A30_f = 0.8985. The result after inserting that value to function (3) suggests that there is a possibility of 79.7% infection, which corresponds after the fuzzification to the linguistic value of "very strong" possibility.

Second Scenario (Theoretical)
We consider a patient with Nonanginal Chest Pain (C3 = 1), Female (C6 = 1) at the age of 65 (C10 = 1), smoker (C11 = 1). That patient were submitted to Treadmill Exercise Test, which was ambiguous (C23 = 0.5) and in Myocardial Perfusion

Imaging, the results of which was characterized as normal (C26 = 1). The initial concept vector is: A (0 0 1 0 0 1 0 0 0 1 1 0 0 0 0 0 0 0 0 0 0 0 1 0 0 1 0 0 0). After FCM inference the final state vector A_f is created, as in the previous scenario. The calculated value of the decision concept (C30) is A30_f = 0.61. Using the function (3) the FCM suggests that there is a 23% possibility of infection, which after the fuzzification would take the linguistic value "low" possibility.

Third Scenario (A Real Scenario)
In this case, an asymptomatic (C4 = 1) patient was analyzed. The patient is male (C5 = 1) at the age of 70 (C10 = 1), smoker (C11 = 1), with Arterial Hypertension (C12 = 1) and Dyslipidemia (C13 = 1). Two tests took place, the results of which were both abnormal (C19 = 1), (C27 = 1). The initial concept vector is: A (0 0 0 1 1 0 0 0 0 1 1 1 1 0 0 0 0 0 1 0 0 0 0 0 0 0 1 0 0). After FCM inference the final state vector A_f is created. The calculated value of the decision concept (C30) is A30_f = 0.8782. Using the function (3) the FCM suggests that there is a 75% possibility of infection, which after the fuzzification would take the linguistic value "high" possibility. After the Invasive Coronary Angiography, the results suggested that the patient was infected by one vessel disease. The extraordinary point of this case is that this patient was infected by the disease even though he had been asymptomatic.

Fourth Scenario (A Real Scenario)
In this scenario, the patient is a man at the age of 79. He has atypical angina, dyslipidemia, arterial hypertension and had been submitted to the test of Myocardial Perfusion Imaging, which is characterized as ambiguous. The initial concept vector is: A (0 1 0 0 1 0 0 0 0 1 0 1 1 0 0 0 0 0 0 0 0 0 0 0 0 0.25 0 0). The calculated value of the decision concept (C30) is A30_f = 0.874. Using the function (3) the FCM suggests that there is a 74.8% possibility of infection, which after the fuzzification would take the linguistic value "high" possibility. In this case, the patient was infected by the disease.

Fifth Scenario (A Real Scenario)
In this very interesting scenario, we have a 59-year-old female patient, smoker, with dyslipidemia and arterial hypertension. The patient had been submitted to Myocardial Perfusion Imaging and Baseline ECG (Electrocardiogram). Both of the tests were characterized as severely abnormal. The initial concept vector is: A (0 0 0 1 0 1 0 0 1 0 1 1 1 0 0 0 0 0 1 0 0 0 0 0 0 0 1 0 0). The calculated value of the decision concept (C30) is A30_f = 0.728. Using the function (3) the FCM suggests that there is a 46% possibility of infection, which after the fuzzification would take the linguistic value "medium" possibility. After the Invasive Coronary Angiography, the results suggested that the patient was infected by one vessel disease. The extraordinary point of this case is that this patient was infected by the disease even though he had been asymptomatic and female. The FCM corresponds satisfactorily in this exceptional scenario, considering that a 46% possibility for a female patient is a relatively high possibility.

Sixth Scenario (A Real Scenario)
Similar to the previous scenario, a female patient at the age of 45 is been examined. The patient has a family history of CAD and had been submitted to Treadmill Exercise Test, which was characterized as abnormal. Thus, the initial vector is A (0 0 0 1 0 1 0 1

0 0 0 0 0 0 1 0 0 0 0 0 0 0 1 0 0 0 0 0 0). The calculated value of the decision concept (C30) is A30_f = 0.2985. Using the function (3) the FCM suggests that there is a 29.85% possibility of infection, which after the fuzzification would take the linguistic value "low" possibility. In this case, the patient was not infected by the disease. Again, in this case, the FCM corresponds satisfyingly, as is predicts a relatively low possibility of risk.

Seventh Scenario (A Real Scenario)

In this case scenario a male patient at the age of 49, with Nonanginal chest pain is been examined. The patient is a smoker and the diagnose tests he underwent were the Treadmill Exercise Test and the Baseline ECG (Electrocardiogram). The first was considered as abnormal and the second as normal. Thus, the initial vector is A (0 0 1 0 1 0 0 1 0 0 0 0 0 0 0 0 1 0 0 0 0 1 0 0 0 0 0 0). The calculated value of the decision concept (C30) is A30_f = 0.71. Using the function (3) the FCM suggests that there is a 66% possibility of infection, which after the fuzzification would take the linguistic value "high" possibility. In this case, the patient was infected by the disease.

Eighth Scenario (A Real Scenario)

A 38-year-old female patient with nonanginal chest pain had been submitted to the Treadmill Exercise Test and the Baseline ECG (Electrocardiogram). As in the previous case, the first was considered as abnormal and the second as normal. Thus, the initial vector is A (0 0 1 0 0 1 1 0 0 0 0 0 0 0 0 0 1 0 0 0 0 1 0 0 0 0 0 0). The calculated value of the decision concept (C30) is A30_f = 0.58. Using the function (3) the FCM suggests that there is a 17.71% possibility of infection, which after the fuzzification would take the linguistic value "very low" possibility. In this case, the patient as it was expected was not infected by the disease.

Ninth Scenario (A Real Scenario)

A diabetic and smoker female patient at the age of 41 with arterial hypertension, obesity and dyslipidemia underwent the Treadmill Exercise Test and the Dobutamine Stress Cardiac Ultrasound test. The first test was considered normal and the second one was considered abnormal. The patient had atypical angina. Thus, the initial vector is A (0 0 1 0 0 1 0 1 0 0 1 1 1 1 0 1 0 0 0 0 0 1 0 0 0 0 0 0). The calculated value of the decision concept (C30) is A30_f = 0.84. Using the function (3) the FCM suggests that there is a 68% possibility of infection, which after the fuzzification would take the linguistic value "high" possibility. In this case, the patient as it was expected was infected by the disease.

Tenth Scenario (A Real Scenario)

A smoker male patient at the age of 67 with arterial hypertension, obesity and dys-lipidemia underwent the Myocardial Perfusion Imaging Test and the Baseline ECG test. The first test was considered abnormal and the second one was considered normal. The patient had nonanginal chest pain and a family history of coronary artery disease. Thus, the initial vector is A (0 0 1 0 1 0 0 0 0 1 1 1 0 0 1 0 0 0 0 0 0 0 0 0 1 0 0). The calculated value of the decision concept (C30) is A30_f = 0.90. Using the function (3) the FCM suggests that there is an 80% possibility of infection, which after the fuzzification would take the linguistic value "high" possibility. In this case, the patient as it was expected was infected by the disease.

Eleventh Scenario (A Real Scenario)
This scenario is similar to the above. Their difference is that the patient is female, at the age of 68 with the other factors to be the same. The first test was considered moderately abnormal and the second one was considered normal. The initial vector is A (0 0 1 0 0 1 0 0 0 1 0 1 0 0 1 0 0 0 0 0 0 0 0 0 0 0 0.55 0 0). The calculated value of the decision concept (C30) is A30_f = 0.69. Using the function (3) the FCM suggests that there is a 30% possibility of infection, which after the fuzzification would take the linguistic value "low" possibility. In this case, there was no infection.

From the above two theoretical scenarios and nine real scenarios, interesting information can be obtained. First of all, it has been proven that the FCM model for the prediction of CAD, which was constructed, is applicable to real scenarios and is responding satisfactorily both into male patients and female patients, despite the fact that there is a complexity as to how each gender affects the risk of infection in real life. Moreover, it has been illustrated that the model is handling well the simultaneous presence of different risk factors and diagnostic tests, notwithstanding the different nature of these concepts. It has been an encouraging attempt to construct a computational model for the prediction of a disease and certainly the future research should deal with the ways of improving the accuracy of the model and its sufficiency in dealing with controversial scenarios.

6 Conclusions and Future Research Directions

The constructed FCM-MDSS model was tested into several real examples, the results of which can't be presented in this paper. The constructed FCM responded satisfactorily to the tests and offered an accurate prediction on the likelihood of infection. One main advantage using the fuzzy cognitive maps is the fact that they can correspond to cases with "missing data" as the scenarios above. The outcome, of course, would be more accurate assuming that all the concept values were inserted into the model. The weight value of each concept that defines the interaction between the concept and the decisive concept A30 are given by the experts. The weights between the concepts play the most decisive role in the procedure. As a matter of fact, the experts must be chosen wisely and moreover, they have to cooperate with each other.

After several simulations, we summarize some weaknesses that could be a field of future research, as to how those weaknesses could be overpassed. One main weakness is that all the factors, from the special characteristics of the patients to the test results are been described as similar type values, though they aren't. The test results, for example, have a completely different nature than the age and the gender of the patient. After the simulation, variable as the age for example and a test result might have the similar numerical influence to the output value. Another disadvantage of the model is that in this level is static. This means that the weights given by experts can't change during the process in order to achieve a more exact result. So for future research directions, this is a very challenging problem and can be investigated using learning algorithms and using the knowledge and expertise of the physician experts [11]. Another future research problem is to take into consideration another parameters and factors of the CAD medical problem such as diet (e.g. Mediterranean), exercise, weight, drinking a lot and other possible diseases such as depression, and some others. Using also intelligent system concepts in connection with FCM modeling approach is a very challenging and promising research topic [19]. Appropriate and more friendly user software tools are needed. One thing is for sure that FCMs will be useful for these future studies.

References

1. Hudson, D.L.: Medical Expert Systems, Encyclopedia of Biomedical Engineering (2006)
2. Pearl, J.: Causality, Models Reasoning and Inference. Cambridge University Press, Cambridge (2000)
3. Kosko, B.: Fuzzy cognitive maps. Int. J. Man Mach. Stud. **24**(1), 65–67 (1986)
4. Papageorgiou, E.I., Papandrianos, N.I., Karagianni, G., Kyriazopoulos, G.C., Sfyras, D.: A fuzzy cognitive map based tool for prediction of infectious diseases. In: FUZZ-IEE 2009, Korea, 20–24 August 2009
5. Kosko, B.: Neural Networks and Fuzzy Systems. Prentice-Hall, Upper Saddle River (1991)
6. Torpy, J.M., Burke, A.E., Glass, R.M.: Coronary heart disease risk factors. JAMA Patient Page **302**, 2388 (2009)
7. Murray, C.J.L.: Global, regional, and national age-sex specific all-cause and cause-specific mortality for 240 causes of death 1990–2013: a systematic analysis for the Global Burden of Disease Study 2013. Lancet (2015). https://www.ncbi.nlm.nih.gov/pmc/articles/PMC4340604/table/T2/
8. Goff Jr., D.C.: ACC/AHA guideline on the assessment of cardiovascular risk: a report of the American College of Cardiology/American Heart Association Task Force on Practice Guidelines, Published online 12 November 2013
9. Sharma, K., Gulati, M.: Coronary artery disease in women: a 2013 update. Global Heart (2013). https://www.ncbi.nlm.nih.gov/pmc/articles/PMC4340604/table/T2/
10. Papageorgiou, E.I., Stylios, C.D., Groumpos, P.: An integrated two-level hierarchical decision making system based on fuzzy cognitive maps (FCMs). IEEE Trans. Biomed. Eng. **50**(12), 1326–1339 (2003)
11. Papageorgiou, E., Stylios, C., Groumpos, P.: Fuzzy cognitive map learning based on nonlinear hebbian rule. In: Gedeon, T.D., Fung, L.C.C. (eds.) AI 2003. LNCS, vol. 2903, pp. 256–268. Springer, Heidelberg (2003). doi:10.1007/978-3-540-24581-0_22
12. Mendis, S., Puska, P., Norrving, B.: Global Atlas on Cardiovascular Disease Prevention and Control. World Health Organization in Collaboration with the World Heart Federation and the World Stroke Organization, pp. 3–18 (2013)
13. Charlson, F.J., Moran, A.E., Freedman, G., Norman, R.E., Stapelberg, N.J., Baxter, A.J., Vos, T., Whiteford, H.A.: The contribution of major depression to the global burden of ischemic heart disease: a comparative risk assessment. BMC Med. **11**, 250 (2013)
14. GBD 2015 Mortality and Causes of Death, Collaborators: Global, regional, and national life expectancy, all-cause mortality, and cause-specific mortality for 249 causes of death, 1980–2015: a systematic analysis for the Global Burden of Disease Study 2015. Lancet **388** (10053), 1459–1544 (2015)
15. Moran, A.E., Forouzanfar, M.H., Roth, G.A., Mensah, G.A., Ezzati, M., Murray, C.J., Naghavi, M.: Temporal trends in ischemic heart disease mortality in 21 world regions, 1980 to 2010: the Global Burden of Disease 2010 study. Circulation **129**(14), 1483–1492 (2014)

16. Centers for Disease Control and Prevention. https://www.cdc.gov/mmwr/prview/mmwrhtml/mm6040a1.htm
17. Glykas, M.: Fuzzy cognitive strategic maps in business process performance measurement. Expert Syst. Appl. **40**(1), 1–14 (2013)
18. Groumpos, P.P.: Fuzzy cognitive maps: basic theories and their application to complex systems. In: Glykas, M. (ed.) Fuzzy cognitive maps. Studies in Fuzziness and Soft Computing, vol. 247, pp. 1–22. Springer, Heidelberg (2010)
19. Groumpos, P.P.: The need for wise decision making support systems (WDMSS) in developing future intelligent Systems, Plenary paper. In: 2016 IEEE ELEKTRO, pp. 3–10 (2016)
20. Groumpos, P.P., Stylios, C.D.: Modelling supervisory control systems using fuzzy cognitive maps. Chaos, Solitons Fractals **11**(1), 329–336 (2000)

Modular Structure of Data Processing in Automated Systems of Risk Management in the Fisheries Industry

Irina Yu. Kvyatkovskaya[1], Irina Kosmacheva[2(✉)], Irina Sibikina[2],
Larisa Galimova[3], Mikhail Rudenko[4], and Elizaveta A. Barabanova[5]

[1] Department of Informational Technology,
Astrakhan State Technical University, Astrakhan, Russia
i.kvyatkovskaya@astu.org
[2] Department of Information Security, Astrakhan State Technical University,
Astrakhan, Russia
ikosmacheva@mail.ru, isibikina@bk.ru
[3] Department of Refrigerating Machines, Astrakhan State Technical University,
Astrakhan, Russia
Galimova_lv@mail.ru
[4] Department of Life Security and Hydromechanics,
Astrakhan State Technical University, Astrakhan, Russia
rudenko@astu.org
[5] Department of Communication, Astrakhan State Technical University,
Astrakhan, Russia
elizavetaAlexB@yandex.ru

Abstract. Decision making in fisheries management takes place in the risk environment having different nature: weather conditions, anthropogenic factors, epidemiological hazards, industrial or information problems. The urgent priority of informatization in the field of fisheries management is the development of mathematical models for decision support systems. The authors proposed a mathematical model for choosing an optimal strategy of the producer behavior of in the field of fisheries management and a fuzzy model of information risk analysis for processing information in information systems. The authors constructed the functions of fuzzy variables "risk degree", "damage degree", "threat level", which are based on the expert data. To evaluate the usefulness of decisions, selection rules are united by various criteria convolutions. The research results have an applied nature and can be used in developments related to the designing information systems, decision support systems for the fishing industry. The presented methods and procedures may be used for the solution of practical tasks.

Keywords: Insurance · Decision making · Criteria · Principle of optimality · Uncertainty · Utility function · Information security management · Risk analysis · Fuzzy simulation

A. Kravets et al. (Eds.): CIT&DS 2017, CCIS 754, pp. 284–301, 2017.
DOI: 10.1007/978-3-319-65551-2_21

1 Introduction

In the field of fisheries, management risks are associated with natural, climatic, environmental problems, disease outbreaks, threats to bioresources from poaching, risks associated with the realization of products, etc. Analysis and management of economic risks are impossible without creating an information system for data collection and processing, which will serve as the basis for making better decisions, including those related to risk insurance.

The degree of information transparency regarding risk factors for the enterprise is important for investors who want to effectively invest their money in the fishing industry, as well as for producers who want to accumulate experience in risk management using analysis of collected information in databases.

The bioresources reproduction processes can be regulated by the managing mechanisms that take into account the demand for certain types of fish products and the profitability of their production. In this situation, government can stimulate the placement and specialization of production using various economic instruments: subsidies, credits, taxes, various risk insurance programs.

Analysis and risk management are carried out using mathematical models. These models can include a large number of factors that take into account both characteristics of producers in the fishing industry and the climatic and environmental conditions of the region, as well as the attitude of the participants of production to risk in the course of business strategy development.

In the light of informatization growth of the fishing industry, information risks are a pressing challenge. This is related to the appearance of geoinformation technologies, automatization of processing, storage, exchange and collection of information concerning the aquaculture facilities, including information obtained from technical sources. The quality of decisions directly depends on the quality of information processed by information systems. It must be characterized by such properties as high integrity, accuracy, accessibility, etc. Management of information risks in the system can be realized by means of the fuzzy inference system in combination with the Delphy techniques.

Currently, the decision support systems are not sufficiently developed to improve the efficiency of fishery industry.

Risk minimization is possible due to risk avoidance, risk insurance and improvement of the quality of management decisions, which can be obtained through the business partners' awareness of information services with the relevant data in the course of their business activities.

Currently, most decision support systems are actualized as smart. Thereby, the actual task is to construct and study mathematical models designed to develop optimal strategies in the field of fish reproduction.

2 Mathematical Model of Selecting the Optimal Strategy

The data collection system concerning risk factors can be enormous. The basis of the information system is formed by the data of risk factors obtained from the current and retrospective information (statistical or expert) [1–4]. Let us make a sample list of factors taken into account for developing solutions, the importance of which can be defined or not defined at the moment of decision making. These factors include: a shortage of specialists in the sector, unrealistic deadlines of the works planned, unrealistic budget, adverse weather and environmental conditions, shortage and poor quality of fish seeds etc.

Risks may be of different nature: the impact of natural phenomena or environmental disasters dangerous for product manufacturing; the penetration and or spread of harmful organisms in aquaculture production; electric or thermal energy supply failure, interruption of water supply resulted from natural disasters etc.

Each of these risks can be compared to the probability P_j of occurrence and possible damage. The probability of events and possible damage can be estimated in terms of statistical data, experience, and knowledge of experts.

As for the solutions concerning the fishing industry, from which the choice is made, there should be appointed:

1. measures to support fishery enterprises;
2. rules for granting subsidies and various privileges to the enterprises;
3. objects of guarantee of priority right to use fish-breeding areas;
4. variants of distributing quotas between fish farms;
5. types of product realization;
6. types of risk insurance.

Agreements about setting fixed prices for future supplies are a traditional practice abroad. These agreements give opportunities to producers to reduce risks and possible losses [2–4]. The developed countries have extensive experience in the application of insurance. For example, multi-risk covers losses; insurance against named risks covers losses of certain aquacultures from certain risks. According to the multi-risk agreement, the manufacturer chooses a certain price of the product which he insures at the beginning of the season. To reduce the cost of insurance, the manufacturer is able to exclude from the coverage certain risk factors that are not typical for his region or for the aquacultures that he reproduces.

The final amount of loss according to the declared insurance contracts is determined after submission of statistical reporting form and other documents (the list of the documents is determined by the insurance contract). When building a model for selecting the optimal strategy of the manufacturer, the insurance program is taken as a strategy (as an example).

Thus, when modeling the processes of insurance in fisheries management, decision-making models in the conditions of uncertainty and risk are applicable [5–8].

There are different types of uncertainty:

- the uncertainty caused by insufficiency of information or its reliability owing to technical, social and other reasons;
- the uncertainty generated by decision-making person owing to a lack of his/her experience and knowledge of factors, influencing on decision-making;
- the uncertainty connected with restrictions in a situation of decision-making (restriction of both time and elements of parameters set which characterizes factors of decision-making);

- the uncertainty caused by the behavior of the environment or an opponent who impact on the decision-making process.

Problem situation of decision-making at risk is formally described by the following model:

- There are alternatives x_k, $k = 1, \ldots, n$, which form a set of solutions $X = \{x_1, \ldots, x_n\}$. In relation to our problem, the following solutions can be x_k: {"To insure according to standard program", "Use index insurance", "Not to insure"}.
- There is a set of states of the environment $S = \{s_1, \ldots, s_q\}$. A decision-making person (DMP) does not know exactly in what state the environment is or will be. In relation to our problem the following environment states may become s_q: {"Insured event took place, confirmation of insurance risk is received", "Insured event took place, confirmation of insurance risk is not received", "Insured event did not take place, confirmation of insurance risk is nt received", "Insured event did not take place, confirmation of insurance risk is received"}.

Characteristic of quality z_i is defined both on the sets of solutions $X = \{x_1, \ldots, x_n\}$ and environment states $S = (s_1, \ldots, s_q)$. This characteristic z_i, is described - by the usefulness function $U_i = \|u_i(x_k, s_j)\|$, $x_k \in X$, $s_j \in S$ (if DMP acts proceeding from the condition of maximization of the function values), or by the function of losses $V_i \|v_i(x_k, s_j)\|$, $x_k \in X$, $s_j \in S$, (if DMP acts proceeding from the condition of minimization).

During evaluating of alternatives quality there is a possibility of one of the following three situations of a DMP's aprioristic knowledge about the environment states:

1. DMP knows the aprioristic distribution of probabilities $p = (p, \ldots, p_q)$ which is defined on the set $A = \left\{ p = (p_1, \ldots p_q), 0 \leq p_j \leq 1, \sum_{j=1}^{q} p_j = 1 \right\}$ on the elements $s_j \in S$ of environment states.

2. The decision-maker knows that the environment actively counteracts his purposes: the environment aspires to choose such states $s_j \in S$ for which (in case the characteristic z_i is described by usefulness function U_i) the environment assumes the state which provides the minimal value of usefulness function among all its maximally possible (on solutions) values. In case the characteristic z_i is described by a function of losses V_k, the environment assumes the state which provides the biggest value of the function of losses among a set of its minimally possible (according to solutions) values.

3. The decision-maker has approximate aprioristic information on conditions of the environment, the information being intermediate between the first and second situations of aprioristic knowledge.

It is required to solve a choice problem – to select the best alternative $x_k \in X$.

The entered function of usefulness U_i is used for assessment of the characteristic of the system z_i. It describes usefulness, benefit, efficiency, the probability of achievement of a purpose etc. In contrast to this, the function of losses V_i is applied to express losses, loss, regrets, damage, risk etc. The type of function is defined by the decision-maker. Sometimes the function of usefulness or losses is to be defined by an expert way.

Formally in the model of decision-making in conditions of uncertainty, it is suitable to present the usefulness function $U_i = \| u_i(x_k, s_j) \|$ or function of losses $V_i = \| v_i(x_k, s_j) \|$, characteristics of quality z_i - in the form of a matrix

Choice of an optimal variant of a solution in conditions of uncertainty - let's present this choice as a generalized algorithm:

1. To form a set of solutions X.
2. To form a set of environment states S.
3. A DMP should define values of characteristics to be evaluated $z_1, \ldots, z_m$, they should be defined as a function of usefulness $U_i = \| u_i(x_k, s_j) \|$, $i = 1, \ldots, m$, or function of losses $V_i = \| v_i(x_k, s_j) \|$, $i = 1, \ldots, m$.
4. A DMP should evaluate and choose appropriate "situation of aprioristic knowledge", which characterize environment behavior.
5. For chosen situation of aprioristic knowledge a DMP should select or construct criteria for evaluation of each characteristic $z_1, \ldots, z_m$ and its function of usefulness $U_i = \| u_i(x_k, s_j) \|$, $i = 1, \ldots, m$, or function of losses $V_i = \| v_i(x_k, s_j) \|$, $i = 1, \ldots, m$.
6. A DMP should select or construct a criterion for joint evaluation of characteristics $z_1, \ldots, z_m$ using principals of optimality.
7. Using received the model, one should decide a problem of choice and to analyze the solution. If necessary, to carry out the correction of made model and solute the problem again.

A large number of types of criteria of the best solution selection makes the problem of selection of the most suitable rule of choice very actual.

Let's consider a problem which aspires to maximize all criteria: $z_i \to \max$, $i = 1, \ldots, m$.

Let's divide all criteria into two groups:

- the first group consists of criteria z_i, $i = 1, \ldots, m'$;
- the second group consists of criteria z_i, $i = m' + 1, \ldots, m$.

On the basis of the first group of criteria a criterion function will be designed, and on the basis of the second group of criteria, the restrictions will be designed. In other words, the principle of the main criterion may be used to these groups. In this case for the first group of criteria, the different convolutions and the corresponding principles of optimality are used. For formation of restrictions the different principles of optimality are applicable:

Principle of ideal point

$$X_1 = \left\{ x_k \ : \ \arg \left(\sum_{i=m'+1}^{m} \gamma_i^p \cdot (z_i^I - z_i(x_k))^p \geq z_{gr} \right) \right\} \tag{1}$$

$p = 1, 2, \ldots$, where z_i^I, $i = m' + 1, \ldots, m$ – coordinates of the ideal point, which are selected for example as large numbers $z_i^I = 10^3$.

Principle of maximin

$$X_2 = \left\{ x_k \; : \; \text{arg (min} \left\{ \begin{array}{l} \gamma_{m'+1} \cdot z_{m'+1}(x_k), \; \ldots, \\ \gamma_m \cdot z_m(x_k) \end{array} \right\} \geq z_{gr}) \right\} \tag{2}$$

Principle of absolute concession

$$X_3 = \left\{ x_k \; : \; \text{arg(} \sum_{i=m'+1}^{m} \gamma_i z_i \geq z_{gr}) \right\} \tag{3}$$

Principle of relative concession

$$X_4 = \left\{ x_k \; : \; \text{arg (} \prod_{i=m'+1}^{m} [z_i(x_k)]^{\gamma_i} \geq z_{gr}) \right\} \tag{4}$$

If $z_i = 0$, then we use $z_i = \varepsilon$, where $\varepsilon > 0$ – small number, for example, $\varepsilon = 10^{-3}$.

Principle of anti-ideal point

$$X_5 = \left\{ x_k \; : \; \text{arg (} \sum_{i=m'+1}^{m} \gamma_i^p \cdot (z_i(x_k) - z_i^{AI})^p \geq z_{gr}) \right\} \tag{5}$$

where z_i^{AI}, $i = m' + 1, \ldots, m$, – coordinates of the anti-ideal point, which are selected for example as $z_i^{AI} = 0$.

Now, using for the first group the following principles of optimality with a combination of different restrictions for the second criteria group, we receive the following combined criteria:

The criterion function and the selection problem definition under different restrictions on the basis of ideal point principle

$$F(x) = \min_{x_k \in X_j} F(x_k) = \min_{x_k \in X_j} \sum_{i=1}^{m'} \gamma_i^p (z_i^I - z_i(x_k))^p \tag{6}$$

$$p = 1, 2, \ldots \quad j = \overline{1, 4},$$

The criterion function and the selection problem definition under different restrictions on the basis of maximin:

$$F(x) = \max_{x_k \in X_j} F(x_k) = \max_{x_k \in X_j} \min_{i \in \{1, \ldots, m'\}} (\gamma_i z_i(x_k))$$

$$j = \overline{1, 4} \tag{7}$$

The criterion function and the selection problem definition under different restrictions on the basis of the principle of relative concession:

$$F(x) = \max_{x_k \in X_j} F(x_k) = \max_{x_k \in X_j} \prod_{i=1}^{m'} [z_i(x_k)]^{\gamma_i}$$

$$j = \overline{1,4}$$

(8)

Except appropriating of a part of criteria to restrictions, it is possible to combine the different principles of optimality, applying them directly to different groups of criteria. We give an optimization problem definition with uses of the principle of an absolute concession (for the first group of criteria) and the principle of ideal point (for the second group of criteria):

$$F(x) = \max_{x_k \in X} F(x) = \max_{x_k \in X} \left(\sum_{i=1}^{m'} (\gamma_k z_i)^p + \lambda \sum_{i=m'+1}^{m} \gamma_i^p (z_i^I - z_i(x_k))^p \right)$$

$$p = 1, 2, \ldots$$

(9)

It is possible to suggest various combinations of principles of optimality.

Criterion of minimum of the usefulness function's mathematical expectation entropy.

The entropy may be a measure of evaluation of uncertainty. Let $s_j \in S$ with probability $p_j, j = 1, \ldots, q$, then the entropy S will be a measure of uncertainty:

$$H_S = -\sum_{j=1}^{m} p_j \ln p_j$$

(10)

Entropy H_S – is a non-negative value. If one from p_j is equal 1 (one), then $H_S = 0$ – situation when there is no uncertainty. When $p_j = 1/q$, entropy value is maximal ($H_s = \ln q$) – situation of full uncertainty.

Assume that $u_i(x_k, s_j) > 0$ for all K and j. The entropy of the mathematical expectation of the utility function for the solution $x_k \in X$ defined as follows:

$$H_i(p, x_k) = -\sum_{j=1}^{q} \frac{p_j u_i(x_k, s_j)}{\sum_{j=1}^{q} p_j u_i(x_k, s_j)} \ln \frac{p_j u_i(x_k, s_j)}{\sum_{j=1}^{q} p_j u_i(x_k, s_j)}$$

(11)

There the probabilities are presented by the weighed normalized values

$$p_j u_i(x_k, s_j) / \sum_{j=1}^{q} p_j u_i(x_k, s_j).$$

It is required to find a solution x^* (or X) from the condition:

$$H_i(p, x) = \min_{x_k \in X} H_i(p, x_k) \tag{12}$$

In case the condition $u_i(x_k, s_j) > 0$ is not fulfilled then for all K and j the transition from values $u_i(x_k, s_j)$ of usefulness function is being done to risks (losses, regret) of the type:

$$\tilde{u}_i(x_k, s_j) = \max_{s_j \in S} u_i(x_k, s_j) - u_i(x_k, s_j)$$
$$x_k \in X \tag{13}$$

In this case, the solution x^* should be found from the condition of the minimum on $x_k \in X$ of entropy of usefulness function's mathematical expectation of the type $H_i(p, x_k)$ when $\tilde{u}_i(x_k, s_j)$:

$$\min_{x_k \in X} H_i(p, x_k)$$

$$= \min_{x_k \in X} \left(-\sum_{j=1}^{q} \frac{p_j \tilde{u}_i(x_k, s_j)}{\sum_{j=1}^{q} p_j \tilde{u}_i(x_k, s_j)} \ln \frac{p_j \tilde{u}_i(x_k, s_j)}{\sum_{j=1}^{q} p_j \tilde{u}_i(x_k, s_j)} \right) \tag{14}$$

Consider for demonstrating the theoretical positions calculated example. For ease of demonstration, we will use the example of low dimension. Let the first group of criteria consists of z1, and the second group consists of z2. Matrix view of a usefulness function $Z_1 = U_1 = \| u_1(x_k, s_j) \|$ are given in Tables 1 and 2.

$$Z_2 = U_2 = \| u_2(x_k, s_j) \|$$

Table 1. Matrix view of a usefulness function

Variants of solutions	Variants of states of environment		
	S_1	S_2	S_3
x_1	10	3	9
x_2	2	0	-7

Table 2. Matrix view of a usefulness function

Variants of solutions	Variants of states of environment		
	S_1	S_2	S_3
x_1	1	11	0
x_2	3	5	8

Use the principle of maximin to design constraints and construction of the target function. Assign characteristics: z1 and z2 the weighting factor, equal to 0.7 and 0.3, respectively.

$$X_2 = \left\{ x_k \ : \ \arg \left(\min \left\{ 0.3 \cdot z_2(x_k) \right\} \geq z_{gr} \right) \right\}.$$

Then $F(x^*) = \max\limits_{x_k \in X_2} F(x_k) = \max\limits_{x_k \in X_2} \min\limits_{i=1}(0.7 \cdot z_1(x_k))$.

Sets the limit value for z_{gr} and find the best option. Other methods can be used analogically. Also important is the study of solutions of different methods on the same input data.

3 Fuzzy Models of Information Risk Analysis

For the creation of an information security system, it is required to solve tasks which are targeted at processing, storage, and protection of the formalized information. In this case, it is possible to form parameters and calculate them rather exactly with the help of methods of the information theory; the parameters reflect the degree of security of an object or system. However, in order to make a complex assessment of security degree, it is often necessary to apply expert methods of estimation for those parameters which can't be calculated by means of theoretic-information approach. A prerequisite for application of fuzzy models is uncertainty due to the absence of information or complexity of the system as well as the presence of qualitative information about the system [9–11].

Formation of an information security system of an object requires solving a number of tasks related to the formalized information - information of interaction in the form of both documents or exchange signals of technical systems. In these cases, methods of the mathematical theory of information are quite applicable, and it is possible to get very exact values of parameters characterizing security of the system. However for a full assessment of security, these parameters should be compared with estimates for information of influence, but this information isn't accessible directly. For example, it is possible to estimate rather accurately the probability of recovery of a separate word in the intercepted speech message, however further it is necessary to establish what probability should be considered admissible. To receive such assessment is possible only in the expert way. To apply methods of the theory of information, in this case, is inefficient as the result completely is defined by the initial assumptions formed actually randomly. For various situations, various contents of phrases, various dictionary structure the expert estimates can yield the results differing much. A prerequisite for application of fuzzy models is the existence of uncertainty due to the absence of information or complexity of the system as well as the existence of qualitative character information about the system [12–15].

The universality of fuzzy systems should be considered their benefit. According to any continuous function can be presented by a fuzzy model with any set accuracy. Special features of systems with fuzzy logic enable to synthesize an object model based on the heuristic information obtained from an expert or as an experiment result. At the same time, fuzzy systems have such shortcomings as both lacks of algorithms of steady models synthesis and low speed of work of the steady models in case of a large number of managing rules.

Creation of fuzzy model is based on a formalization of characteristics of the control system of information security in terms of linguistic variables. The basic concepts of control systems are control algorithm, input and output variables. They are considered as linguistic variables when forming the rule base in systems of fuzzy conclusion.

Now several algorithms of the fuzzy conclusion are offered: algorithm of Mamdani, that of Tsukamoto, Larsen, Sugeno. The simplified algorithm of a fuzzy conclusion formally can be defined as follows:

- Formation of the rule base of fuzzy conclusion
- Fuzzification of input variables.
- Aggregation of subconditions in fuzzy rules of production.
- Activation of sub-conclusions in fuzzy rules of production.
- Accumulation of conclusions in fuzzy rules of production.
- Defuzzification of output variables.

The purpose of creation of a fuzzy model of information security management is: basing on the current status of an object to be protected, to define values of control variables which implementation will provide the necessary protection level.

In the classical theory of control, the basic model is based on the representation of an object and process in the form of some systems. The controlled object is characterized by a finite set of input and output variables. Input variables are created by means of a finite set of sensors. A set of output (controlling) variables is created as an output of control system. Values of controlling variables come to the input of controlled object and make an adequate controlling influence.

If a model of fuzzy control is built, the classical management system is replaced by the system of fuzzy control. A system of the fuzzy conclusion is used to be such system, implementation of all necessary stages being used (Fig. 1). The process of the fuzzy conclusion is being created on the basis of one of the algorithms of fuzzy conclusion.

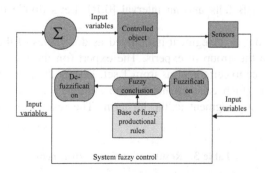

Fig. 1. Scheme of process of fuzzy control

To create a system of fuzzy conclusion there is the Matlab system having rather wide functionality. To assess risks it is necessary to set input variables which are: risk factors such as threat, damage, and vulnerability. Risk degree is an output variable.

However, before starting the creation of fuzzy model it is necessary to construct functions of accessories for each fuzzy variable. Input variables have values in the range from 0 to 1. The closer is an each variable value to 1 – the more strong is the impact of a risk factor on the security system. For the creation of functions of accessory, we suggest to use a method of linguistic scales creation.

Creation of a fuzzy linguistic scale for each of fuzzy variables is carried out in 2 stages:

1. Determination of a set of values of a linguistic variable β_i.
2. Placement of the linguistic variable values on the universal scale [0,1].

At the first stage, we deal with the creation of syntax rule which generates names of values of the linguistic variable. The procedure is performed at the heuristic level. At the same time, experts shall have not really a big number of terms, in order to avoid difficulties when forming preferences while choosing a specific value of the linguistic variable. On the other hand, this number shan't be too small not to roughen sensitivity of expert's estimates [7, 8].

Further, names of terms are selected. The requirement "single-meaning interpretation of these names by most of the experts" is to be fulfilled.

Let's define input linguistic variables: β_1 – "threat level", β_2 – "damage level", β_3 – "vulnerability level".

Let's define the term-set for input variables.

For the variable β_1: term-set $T_1 = \{low, middle, high\}$.

For the variable β_2: term-set $T_2 = \{insignificant, middle, significant\}$

For the variable β_3: term-set $T_3 = \{insignificant, moderate, significant\}$.

At the second stage of creation of fuzzy linguistic scale, a semantic rule is set; the rule matches the name of a linguistic variable with its sense i.e. function of the accessory of the set terms is built.

One of the methods of creation of functions of accessory is the method of statistical experiment. Let's assume that the expert needs to estimate "threat level" in terms of the linguistic variable; the threat variable assumes values ΔB where B is the greatest possible threat and ΔB falls into an interval [0,B]. Let's divide the interval into N segments.

The numbers from each segment interpreted as dot values of the threat degree are randomly shown to the group of experts. The expert (on the basis of personal view) refers the shown value to certain terms from T set. During the experiment, an empirical table is created, in which each element is the summary quantity of reference of a random number from j segment to the ith term. The results of the experiments are presented Table 3.

Table 3. Results of statistic experiment

Linguistic variable value	Interval					
	1	2	...	j	...	N
Low	a_{11}	a_{12}		a_{1j}		a_{1N}
Middle	a_{21}	a_{22}	...	a_{2j}	...	a_{2N}
High	a_{31}	a_{32}	...	a_{3j}	...	a_{3N}

It is obvious that if an equal number of experiments falls to each interval, then the degree of the accessory of some value can be calculated as the relation of the number of experiments in which it was met in a certain interval of a scale, to the number of experiments, maximum for this value, on all intervals. However in practice, this condition is observed not obligatory, for example, an expert finds it difficult to refer the estimated value to any interval.

Let's notice that natural properties of the function of accessory are: the existence of one maximum and smooth fronts, fading to zero. Therefore before processing the obviously wrong data are to be removed from the empirical table. The criterion for remove: the existence of several zero in a line around this element.

Then the value of a function of accessory on the empirical matrix can be calculated according to the following algorithm:

Auxiliary matrix is formed.

$R_{1 \times N} = \{r_1, r_2, \ldots, r_j, \ldots, r_n\}$, where N – the quantity of intervals of splitting (the greatest possible change) $r_j = \sum_{i=1}^{n} a_{ij}$, where n- quantity of terms.

The maximum element $r_{max} = \max_{j=1,\ldots,N} r_j$ is selected from auxiliary matrix.

All elements of the empiric table will be transformed according to the formula

$$c_{ij} = \frac{a_{ij} \cdot r_{max}}{r_j}, i = \overline{1,n}, j = \overline{1,N}$$

For columns, where $r_j = 0$, the linear approximation is applied:

$$c_{ij} = \frac{c_{i(j-1)} + c_{i(j+1)}}{2}, i = \overline{1,n}, j = \overline{1,N}$$

Along lines of empiric table, the maximum elements are selected

$$c_{max} = \max_{j=1,\ldots,N} c_{ij}, i = \overline{1,n}$$

Values of functions of accessory are calculated by formula

$$\gamma_{ij} = \frac{c_{ij}}{c_{imax}}$$

Thus, in result of processing of statistic experiment data we have n discrete fuzzy sets. Discrete functions of accessory can be interpolated by continues functions like $\varphi_j(B)$. Then the semantic rule may be written as follows:

Low = $^\Delta \{ \langle \Delta B_j, \psi_1(\Delta B | \psi_1(\Delta B_j) = \gamma_{1j} \rangle \}$,

Middle = $^\Delta \{ \langle \Delta B_j, \psi_2(\Delta B | \psi_2(\Delta B_j) = \gamma_{2j} \rangle \}$,

High = $^\Delta \{ \langle \Delta B_j, \psi_3(\Delta B | \psi_3(\Delta B_j) = \gamma_{3j} \rangle \}$.

4 Statistic Results of the Experiment on Defining the Functions of Accessory

Changes interval $\beta \in [0,1]$. Experts made decision to divide the interval into 10 segments. Statistic experiment results on defining the functions of accessory for the variable "threat level" are shown in the Table 4.

Table 4. Results of examination

Values for linguistic variable "threat level"	Interval									
	0.1	0.2	0.3	0.4	0.5	0.6	0.7	0.8	0.9	1
Low	10	9	8	1	1	0	0	0	0	0
Middle	0	1	2	9	8	8	0	0	0	0
High	0	0	0	0	1	2	10	10	10	10

Further, according to presented methods the Table 5 is transformed into the Table 5.

Table 5. Transformed matrix

Value	Interval									
	0.1	0.2	0.3	0.4	0.5	0.6	0.7	0.8	0.9	1
Low	10	9	8	2	1	0	0	0	0	0
Middle	0	1	2	8	8	8	6	1	0	0
High	0	0	0	0	1	2	4	9	10	10

A resultant matrix is shown in Table 6.

Table 6. Matrix of functions of accessory for the variable "threat level"

Value	Interval									
	0.1	0.2	0.3	0.4	0.5	0.6	0.7	0.8	0.9	1
Low	1	0.9	0.8	0.3	0,1	0	0	0	0	0
Middle	0	0.125	0.25	0.875	1	1	0.75	0.125	0	0
High	0	0	0	0	0.1	0.2	0.4	0.9	1	1

Functions of accessory for input variables "damage level" and "vulnerability level" are built similarly.

In result of using statistic experiment method for processing of expert data, we get linguistic scales for fuzzy variables, and we can use these scales while creating fuzzy conclusion system in Matlab.

The results of the experiments are presented Table 7.

Table 7. Values of fuzzy variables

Value of term	Value of the variable β_1	Value of term for the variable β_2	Value of the variable β_2	Value of term for the variable β_3	Value of the variable β_3
Low	[0; 0.35]	Insignificant	[0; 0.3]	Insignificant	[0; 0.35]
Middle	[0.35; 0.75]	Middle	[0.3; 0.6]	Moderate	[0.35; 0.7]
High	[0.75; 1]	Significant	[0.6; 1]	Significant	[0.7; 1]

5 Implementation of a Fuzzy Expert System

Elaboration of the fuzzy expert system is implemented as a system of fuzzy conclusion; the system enables to define risk degree on the basis of experts' assessment of threat level, damage level, and vulnerability level.

The graphic interface of the editor of functions of accessory after the setting of input variable "threat level" is shown in Fig. 2. Term-set values of the given input variable are set according to obtained linguistic scales. Variables "damage level" and "vulnerability level" are being set similarly.

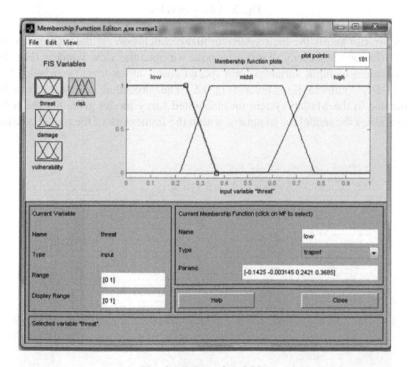

Fig. 2. Editor of variables

Further, the rules for fuzzy conclusions system is set. The graphic interface of the editor of rules after the setting of all rules is shown in Fig. 3.

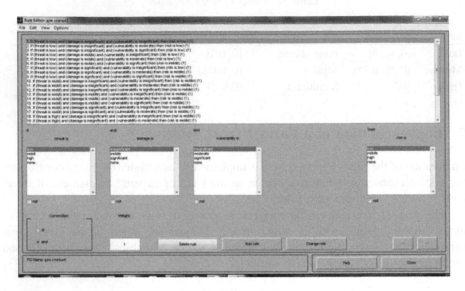

Fig. 3. Editor of rules

Now we can assess the built system of fuzzy conclusion for the task of risk evaluation of information security. For this purpose we open the view window (Fig. 4) and enter the values of input variables for a special case: "threat level" = 0.549; "damage level" = 0.91; "vulnerability level" = 0.512. The procedure of fuzzy conclusion implemented in the Matlab system for elaborated fuzzy model gives the result 0.866, which validates the model for adequacy, within the framework of the model considered.

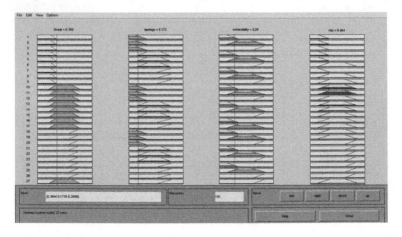

Fig. 4. Editor of view of rules

The process of investigation and analysis of elaborated fuzzy model consists of test fulfillment of fuzzy conclusions for different values of input variables and assessment of obtained results with the aim of making necessary corrections in case of incoordination of some results.

A common analysis of elaborated model enables to obtain a surface of fuzzy conclusion (Figs. 5 and 6).

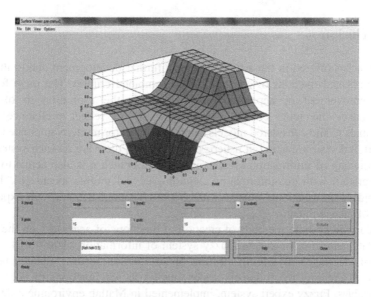

Fig. 5. Surface of fuzzy conclusion (threat-damage-risk)

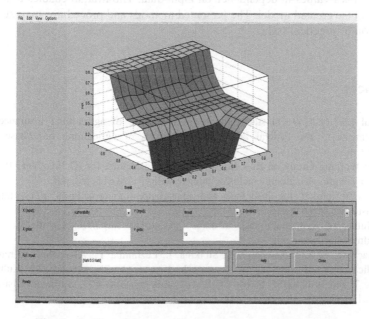

Fig. 6. Surface of fuzzy conclusion (threat-vulnerability-risk)

A prerequisite for application of fuzzy models is existence of uncertainty due to the absence of information or complexity of the system as well as the existence of qualitative character information about the system.

This surface of fuzzy conclusion enables to detect dependence of the "risk degree" output variable values on values of input variables: "threat level", "damage level" and "vulnerability level".

6   Conclusion

The approaches offered in the article may have further development due to the use of more complicated methods of constructing of combined criteria. The main feature of further improvement of approach and methods is the aspiration to offer to a decision-maker the tools enabling most precisely to reflect preferences of the decision-maker. The considered models can be the basis for modern automated systems of support of decision-making in fisheries management, there are no such systems now. While designing of information systems in fisheries branch it is also actual to provide their integration with geo-information technologies and mobile means [6]. This will enrich studied informational objects with spatial characteristics and will expand possibilities of management.

The considered both methods of creation of functions of accessory on the basis of experts data, and modeling of the fuzzy system of information security risks analysis are one of the stages of solving the task of information security management. The procedure of creating the linguistic scales enables to get functions of accessory for fuzzy variables. Fuzzy expert system, implemented in Matlab environment defines the output variables values in dependence on input data. The Matlab enables to assess the adequacy of the created model. The presented methods and procedures may be used for the solution of practical tasks.

References

1. Federal law, N. 260 On state support in the sphere of agricultural insurance and on amendments to the Federal law On development of agriculture. http://base.garant.ru/12188234/
2. Report Working Group on Risk Management in Agriculture for XI Five Year Plan. http://planningcommission.nic.in/whichis/committee/wrkgrp11/wg11_risk.pdf
3. The world market for insurance and reinsurance of agricultural risks. http://www.agroinsurance.com/ru/pratice/?pid=453
4. The future of agricultural risk insurance in Russia. http://raexpert.ru/editions/bulletin/agriculture_ins_future.pdf
5. Kosmacheva, I., Kvyatkovskaya, I., Sibikina, I., Lezhnina, Y.: Algorithms of ranking and classification of software systems elements. In: Kravets, A., Shcherbakov, M., Kultsova, M., Iijima, T. (eds.) JCKBSE 2014. CCIS, vol. 466, pp. 400–409. Springer, Cham (2014). doi:10.1007/978-3-319-11854-3_34

6. Kvyatkovskaya, I., Sibikina, I., Berezhnov, G.: Procedure of the system characteristics competence graph model calculation. World Appl. Sci. J. (Inf. Technol. Mod. Ind. Educ. Soc.) **24**, 111–116 (2013)

7. Barabanov, I., Barabanova, E., Maltseva, N., Kvyatkovskaya, I.: Data processing algorithm for parallel computing. In: Kravets, A., Shcherbakov, M., Kultsova, M., Iijima, T. (eds.) JCKBSE 2014. CCIS, vol. 466, pp. 61–69. Springer, Cham (2014). doi:10.1007/978-3-319-11854-3_6

8. Buldakova, T.I., Mikov, D.A.: Implementation of methods of information security risks assessment in the matlab. In: Voprosykiberbezopasnosti, pp. 53–61(2015)

9. Kosmacheva, I.M.: Algorithm of assessment of risk of information services infringement in an organization. Vestnik of Astrakhan State Technical University. Series: Management, Computing Machinery and Informatics. vol. 2, pp. 58–64 (2015)

10. Sibikina, I.V., Kvyatkovskaya, I.Y.: Creating of linguistic scales for defining of important disciplines forming competences. Vestnik of Astrakhan State Technical University. Series: Management, Computing Machinery and Informatics. vol. 2, pp. 182–186 (2012)

11. Wriggers, P., Kultsova, M., Kapysh, A., Kultsov, A., Zhukova, I.: Intelligent decision support system for river floodplain management. In: Kravets, A., Shcherbakov, M., Kultsova, M., Iijima, T. (eds.) JCKBSE 2014. CCIS, vol. 466, pp. 195–213. Springer, Cham (2014). doi:10.1007/978-3-319-11854-3_18

12. Abdo, H., Flaus, J.-M.: Uncertainty quantification in dynamic system risk assessment: a new approach with randomness and fuzzy theory. Int. J. Prod. Res. **54**(19), 5862–5885 (2016)

13. Yakhyaeva, G., Ershov, A.: Knowledge base system for risk analysis of the multi-step computer attacks. In: Proceedings of the 18th International Conference on Enterprise Information Systems, ICEIS 2016, vol. 2, pp. 143–150 (2016)

14. Inti, S., Tandon, V.: Application of fuzzy preference-analytic hierarchy process logic in evaluating sustainability of transportation infrastructure requiring multicriteria decision making. J. Infrastruct. Syst. **23**(4), Article no. 04017014 (2017)

15. Vytovtov, A.A., Arkhipov, A.D.: Theoretical model of controlled terahertz bandpass filter with isolator properties. Telecommun. Radio Eng. (English translation of Elektrosvyaz and Radiotekhnika) **74**(2), 163–170 (2015)

Creative Tools of Raising the Competitiveness of Business on the Basis of Intellectual Technologies of Decision Support

Victor Kuznetsov[✉], O.V. Trofimov, V.G. Frolov,
Y.A. Sidorenko, and Y.O. Plekhova

N.I. Lobachevsky Nizhny Novgorod State University,
23 Gagarina St., Nizhny Novgorod 603022, Russia
kuznetsov_vic_p@mail.ru

Abstract. The purpose of the article is to determine the perspectives of using the intellectual technologies of decision support in the modern business structures as creative tools for raising their competitiveness. This purpose is achieved with the help of the deductive and inductive methods, synthesis, abstracting, analysis of causal connections, etc. The article offers the creative tools for increasing the competitiveness of business on the basis of intellectual technologies of decision support in the sphere of increasing the quality of business structure's products: automation of the process of innovational & investment decisions and usage of intellectual technologies of decision support in the process of managing the relations with intermediaries. Automation of the decision-making process in the pricing sphere and optimization of the network business with the help of intellectual technologies of decision support are offered. In the sphere of marketing, the formation of the brand of business structures that use the leading technologies is offered; these include the intellectual technologies of decision support and the provision of the possibility of decision making on purchases with the help of the intellectual technologies of decision support. As a result of the research, the authors came to the conclusion that the recent intellectual technologies of support for decision making open new possibilities for development of modern business, as they could be used as creative tools for increasing its competitiveness. Using the intellectual technologies of decision support allows forming the sustainable competitive advantages, strengthening the market positions, and increasing the market share of the business. This is achieved by means of the uniqueness of these technologies and their novelty. The business receives such advantages of using the intellectual technologies of decision support as the expansion of sales markets and receipt of state support for the high innovational activity.

Keywords: Creative tools · An increase of business competitiveness · Intellectual technologies of decision support

1 Introduction

In the modern conditions, most national borders and sectorial barriers are erased, and business structures fill even the remotest and previously closed markets. This inevitably leads to increasing the competition and makes all market players care for supporting

© Springer International Publishing AG 2017
A. Kravets et al. (Eds.): CIT&DS 2017, CCIS 754, pp. 302–316, 2017.
DOI: 10.1007/978-3-319-65551-2_22

their competitiveness. In the 21st century, competition has acquired the unprecedented – global – scale and continues to grow.

It should be noted that even the large business structures, many of which are transnational, make large efforts for the formation and support for their competitive advantages, for there's competition among them, which may be of monopolistic and oligopolistic character; in any case, it predetermines their limited market power and strong dependence on consumer preferences.

Management of competitiveness of modern business is based on high flexibility and innovational activity, as only constant development allows keeping the market positions in the context of dynamic market environment and constant technological leaps. The traditional tools and technologies age quickly and lose their actuality. That's why in the modern innovational economy and information society, creativity comes into the foreground in the management of competitiveness of business.

This article accepts the working hypothesis that the new and active intellectual technologies of decision support open new possibilities for development of modern business, as they could be used as creative tools for increasing its competitiveness. The purpose of the article is to determine the perspectives of using the intellectual technologies of decision support in modern business structures as the creative tools for raising their competitiveness.

2 Background

There are three main directions of increasing the competitiveness of business:

- increasing the product's quality: improvement of its technical characteristics and accompanying service;
- reduction of product's price: minimization of production & distributive and managerial costs;
- strengthening of company's brand and/or its product: increase of consumers' loyalty, the attraction of their interest to the company and its products with the help of innovational elements.

The traditional tools for increasing competitiveness of business are brought down to the following:

- in the sphere of quality: improvement of production, distributive (sales) and organizational & managerial technologies [1–3];
- in the pricing sphere: achieving the "scale effect", saving on raw materials (reduction of price by means of reduction of product's quality) [4–6];
- in the sphere of marketing: PR, advertising [7–9].

These and other tools of management of competitiveness of business are studied in the works of such authors as [10–15] etc. The leading studies in the sphere of intellectual technologies of decision support include the following publications: [16–19] etc.

Analysis of the literature on the topic showed that intellectual technologies of decision support are not used in the process of management of competitiveness of business, which, in our opinion, is a drawback of the modern science and requires further research aimed at formation of the corresponding conceptual basis, as well as methodological and practical recommendations. That is viewed in this article. The purpose is achieved with the help of the deductive and inductive methods, synthesis, abstracting, analysis of causal connections, etc.

3   Creative Tools of Application of Intellectual Technologies of Decision Support in Various Business Spheres

This research offers the following creative tools of increasing the competitiveness business on the basis of intellectual technologies of decision support in the sphere of quality. Firstly, it's automation of the process of making the innovational and investment decisions. Such solutions are characterized by high complexity, so the use of the computer technologies will allow for an increase of their effectiveness.

Due to this, the business structure will sort out the innovational and investment projects and select only the most perspectives ones and those characterized by the optimal ratio of profitability and risk. This will allow increasing the innovational activity of the business, for the risk component of innovational activity will reduce, and increasing the quality of products by means of assigning the additional qualities and improvement of its technical characteristics.

Secondly, the use of intellectual technologies of decision support in the process of managing the relations with intermediaries. Selection of the best intermediaries (suppliers of raw materials, etc.) and business partners for the purpose of creation of integration associations with rivals and R&D organizations is an important task, for it determines the successfulness of this cooperation.

Very often, such decisions must be made quickly, and, as is known, lack of time for thinking leads to mistakes and is a classic manifestation of "human factor" in the economy. Automation of decision making in this sphere will allow bringing such mistakes down to the minimum, due to which a company will be able to select the most profitable intermediaries and business partners.

In the sphere of pricing, we deem it possible to apply the following creative tools for increasing the competitiveness of business on the basis of intellectual technologies of decision support. Firstly, it's automation of the decision-making process in the sphere of pricing. Modern business structures set the prices, not on the basis of cost value and flat-rate benefit on the basis of the targeted profit – they take into account the consumer preferences.

Successful pricing often needs studying the whole demand and offer in the market for determining the readiness of potential buyers to pay and determining the alternatives (substitute products that are cheaper or similar in price and quality), as well as cost value of the associated goods.

Implementation of modern high technologies into the decision-making process will allow minimizing the pricing mistakes, thus increasing the attractiveness of products of a business structure for the consumers. Intellectual technologies of decision support could be also used not only during the establishment of the initial but also of further prices for the products and during the determination of discounts, etc.

Secondly, optimization of the network business with the help of intellectual technologies of decision support. Here we speak of selecting the optimal geographical location of the structural departments of business: production, sales, and the head office, as well as management of transport logistics. It should be noted that such decisions are made by not only transnational business structures but by the national and local ones – during the use of the network model of business.

The complexity of such decisions consists in the fact that it is necessary to find a balance between the contradicting optimization conditions. Thus, for example, provision of the convenience for consumers requires the placement of the sales departments in close proximity, but a large number of such departments and their location in the places with high rental cost leads to high expenses, so the growth of prices may scare the consumers away.

In the sphere of marketing, we offer the following creative tools for increasing the competitiveness of business on the basis of intellectual technologies of decision support. Firstly, the formation of the brand of business structure that uses the leading technologies, which include intellectual technologies of decision support.

Competitive advantages do not have to be based on providing the consumers with any material benefits – sometimes it suffices to provide non-material benefits. Thus, participation in a business that uses leading technologies can be an element of the prestige of consumers and be of some value for them. Using the intellectual technologies of decision support can stimulate strengthening of the brand of the business structure by increasing its products' reliability (as the additional guarantee of quality).

Secondly, providing the consumers with a possibility of making decisions on a purchase with the help of intellectual technologies of decision support. Thus, at the web-site of a business structure, the consumers can see the products in combination with other products, etc.

By the example of clothing, these technologies allow modeling the potential image of the consumer in the clothing, helping him to make a choice between the required products. Intellectual technologies of decision support can advise the consumer, helping to select the optimal goods.

The following intellectual technologies of decision support are offered:

- information search;
- intellectual analysis of data;
- search for knowledge in databases;
- discussions on the basis of precedents;
- imitation modeling;
- evolutional calculations and genetic algorithms;
- neuron networks;
- situation analysis;
- cognitive modeling.

Usage of these technologies provides modern companies with new capabilities: quick and correct innovation and investment decisions, increase of effectiveness of managing relations with intermediaries, elimination of pricing mistakes, increase of effectiveness of network business development, and increase of marketing effectiveness

– which allows solving the existing problems of increase of business competitiveness, namely:

- wrong innovation and investment decisions;
- ineffectiveness of management of relations with intermediaries;
- pricing mistakes;
- ineffectiveness of network business development;
- the complexity of marketing.

4 The Mechanism of Increasing Business Competitiveness on the Basis of Intellectual Technologies of Support for Decision Making

The mechanism of increasing the competitiveness of business on the basis of intellectual technologies of decision support is shown in Fig. 1.

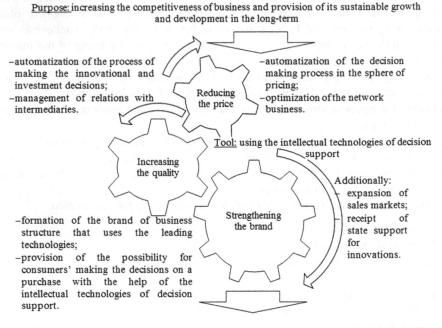

Fig. 1. The mechanism of increasing the competitiveness of business on the basis of intellectual technologies of decision support

As is seen from Fig. 1, the usage of intellectual technologies of decision support allows for the formation of sustainable competitive advantages, strengthening of market positions, and an increase of the market share of the business. This is achieved by means of the uniqueness of these technologies and their novelty. Additionally, the business receives such advantages of using the intellectual technologies of decision support as the expansion of sales markets and receipt of state support for the high innovational activity.

5 Principles and Practical Recommendations

5.1 Principles of Successful Implementation of Creative Tools for Raising Competitiveness of Business on the Basis of Intellectual Technologies of Decision Support

Implementation of intellectual technologies of decision support into the process of company management with the help of developed creative tools is a perspective technical and organizational & managerial innovation with a lot of advantages, which allows raising the competitiveness of business. At the same time, these are new tools, applying which the company may face unexpected difficulties.

As any novelty, implementation of creative tools for raising the competitiveness of business on the basis of intellectual technologies of decision support is subject to risk. Successful management of this risk and provision of a gradual transition of the business from independent company management to the usage of intellectual technologies of decision support requires observation of five principles.

1st principle: selecting a good moment for implementing the intellectual technologies of decision support into the process of company management. Such moment is the period of stability or rise (development) of a company, as it is the time when a business can find additional assets for implementation of innovations, and there's a limit of risk (level of risk is not too high).

Unlike this, in the period of crisis or stagnation the company cannot allow accepting the additional risk, for its level is too high. Also, the company has no free resources for implementing innovations and no possibility for borrowing them. Though, in view of the fact that innovations are an effective tool of crisis management, it would be possible to implement intellectual technologies of decision support in the conditions of recession.

2nd principle: thorough preparation for implementing the intellectual technologies of decision support into the process of company management. This means that before the usage it is expedient to consider all working moment which is to be faced and to provide the competence of the employees who will work with new technologies.

At that, it will not be necessary to just have training courses and receive the corresponding document – it is necessary to possess knowledge and skills, as well as readiness to apply them in practice. That's why not only organizational and educational but also psychological preparation is important. For the purpose of supporting its conduct, it is necessary to start a motivational and stimulation program aimed at stimulating the efforts of the employees working with intellectual technologies of decision support.

3rd principle: stage-by-stage implementation of intellectual technologies of decision support into the process of company management. In order to avoid quick increase of the risk component of business due to quick refusal from old technologies in favor of new technologies, as well as opposition to such quick innovations from personnel, it is better to implement intellectual technologies of decision support gradually.

This means that they should be implemented into separate business processes at first and then distributed to other. At that, it is important to evaluate the effectiveness of their application and compare it to the effectiveness of the traditional technologies of decision support. This is necessary for preserving the sustainability of the business, as it provides time and possibility for the employees to adapt to changes and find solutions to the problems that appear in the process of implementation of any innovations.

4th principle: attentive attitude and thorough control over the use of intellectual technologies of decision support in the process of company management. Monitoring of results should be performed constantly during the whole process of transition from standard technologies of decision support to innovational (intellectual). Evaluation of effectiveness supposes a comparison of the received results (correctness, precision, and actuality of decisions) to the resources spent for usage of intellectual technologies of decision support (time, labor, financial, etc.).

5th principle: temporary termination or full refusal from the usage of intellectual technologies of decision support in the process of company management in case of reduction of its effectiveness. If the effectiveness of intellectual technologies of decision support is lower as compared to traditional technologies, it is expedient to reconsider the approach to implemented innovations or refuse from them – despite the resources spent.

Based on these principles, we offer to use the following algorithm during the implementation of intellectual technologies of decision support into the process of company management (Fig. 2).

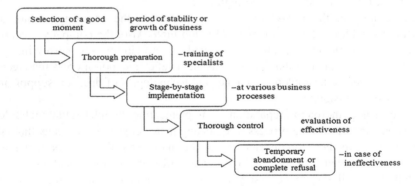

Fig. 2. Algorithm of implementation of intellectual technologies of decision support into the process of company management

5.2   Recommendations for Successful Implementation of Intellectual Technologies of Decision Support in the Sphere of Quality

In the conditions of development of "knowledge economy", innovativeness comes to the foreground among the indicators of products' quality. That's why modern companies often have to make innovational and investment-based decisions. Automation of this process supposes the following sequence of actions.

First off, an innovation is selected for its implementation at the company, depending on the concept of its innovational development, formed on the basis of its needs and requirements dictated by the market. Here it is necessary to specify the spheres in which innovations could be implemented, specify the priority of these spheres for the company, and present the consequences of manifestation of innovational activity in these spheres.

Then, the necessary resources are evaluated (human, material, financial, time, etc.) for the creation of each innovation. At that, it is important to pay attention to all stage of the innovational process: from stimulation of the creative activity of company's employees and promotion of new ideas to direct implementation of innovations into business processes.

Then, the determined necessary resources (needs) are compared to the existing company's resources (its possibilities). At that, it is important to consider that not all company's resources should be used for development of the innovation – only leftovers or a small part of existing resources. In case if the company works with electronic databases and renews them, it is sufficient to enter the information only on the resources that are necessary for the implementation of innovations, whole the information on existing resources will be preserved in the electronic form.

After that, the possible sources for receipt of lacking resources – primarily, investment – are found. Such sources could be borrowed assets of credit organizations, private and corporate investors, and redistribution of profit, as well as a reserve or specialized funds, etc.

If all information is present in the electronic form a specialized program provides the manager with the parameters of the managerial decision:

- innovation or several innovations that are to be implemented at the company in order to support or raise its competitiveness;
- the selected source of innovation: own efforts of the company or purchase of the ready innovations;
- necessity or refusal from the attraction of external investments for the attraction of external investments for the realization of the company's planned innovational project.

Let us view the peculiarities of using the intellectual technologies of decision support in the process of management of relationships with intermediaries. Intermediaries here are seen in a wide sense – as business partners – which can be suppliers of resources, rivals, R&D institutes, and B2B consumers to whom the company sells its products. We distinguished four directions of usage of intellectual technologies of decision support in this case.

1st direction: selection of suppliers of resources from the existing alternatives. For that, it is necessary to specify a large number of parameters of each supplier of resources: their volume, quality, cost, terms of shipment, reliability, and reputation of the supplier, etc. It is possible to pay attention to priorities of these parameters with the help of assigning the weight coefficients.

2nd direction: development of the strategy of behavior in relations with rivals. This could be the strategy of opposition, partial or full cooperation, and integration and reorganization of the business. At that, it is important to take into account not only expected advantages but the drawbacks, problems, and risks of each strategy. Of course, in the case of constant application of intellectual technologies of decision support, the models of such strategies could be created, so it is not necessary to enter the parameters over and over again but renew them.

3rd direction: determining the terms of cooperation with R&D institutes. Here it is necessary to evaluate the readiness of R&D institutes for such cooperation, consider the requirements, and evaluate the potential requirements and profits for this company.

4th direction: optimization of sales of the company's products. Here we speak of the methods of sales (creation of own retail networks or use of intermediaries) and of the sales directions (concentrated sales on a certain territory or diversified sales in all region/country/world).

As a result of using the intellectual technologies of decision support in the process of managing the relationship with intermediaries, the manager receives the following information:

- suppliers of resources, relation with which are most profitable for the company;
- rivals with which the efforts should be joined with the specification of the corresponding spheres;
- R&D institutes with which it's expedient to develop cooperation and the terms on which such cooperation should be conducted;
- B2B consumers for which it's better to sell the company's products.

Logic and structure of the process of decision support in the sphere of quality with the help of intellectual technologies are reflected in Fig. 3.

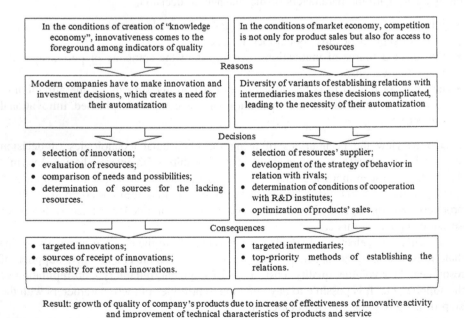

Fig. 3. Causal connections of implementation of intellectual technologies of decision support in the sphere of quality

5.3 Recommendations for Successful Implementation of Intellectual Technologies of Decision Support in the Pricing Sphere

As in the conditions of low market concentration, peculiar for most spheres of modern economic systems, the pricing competition is one of the most important forms of competition, the correctness of decisions in the pricing sphere determine the market success of a company, i.e., its competitiveness. Automation of this process is as follows.

The elasticity of demand for the price is analyzed. For that, based on the existing experience of pricing of the company, the prices, and volumes of products sales are compared. Here it is possible to distinguish various categories of consumers on the basis of the criterion of price elasticity of the demand for the company's products.

The next step is studying the price categories of rivals. Here we speak of the level of prices for the rivals' products as compared to the products of the company and to the supposed future change of rivals' prices. It is also important to take into account the market power and the company's possibilities to influence the price.

Thus, if its market share and, accordingly, market power are small, the possibilities in the pricing sphere will be limited. That's why intellectual technologies of decision support in the pricing sphere are not likely to show high effectiveness.

Then, the prices for substituting and compliment products are analyzed. It is important to see how the current prices, like common pricing tendencies, determined the change of prices in future. It is important to specify the level and strength of connection of compliment products with the products of the company and consider the elasticity of demand, as well as specify the level to which the company's products are subject to replacement by the substituting products.

Then, the possibility for the conclusion of the pricing agreement with intermediaries is assessed. This could be the establishment of special relations with suppliers of resources on the preferential terms of shipment for reducing the products' cost and conclusion of agreements with rivals on the establishment of common prices, as well as ousting the substituting products from the market, etc.

Here it is important to present information on profits and costs of each possible method of the conclusion of a pricing conspiracy with intermediaries, starting with losses, related to the reduction of the freedom of pricing, and finishing with profits from monopolization of the market and the long-term effect.

As a result, the automatized method established the preferential parameters of pricing for the company's products:

- pricing segments of the market that should be created by the company;
- pricing ranges for short-term, mid-term, and long-term periods;
- necessity and parameters of the pricing conspiracy with intermediaries.

Intellectual technologies of decision support also open wide perspectives in the sphere of optimization of network business. For that, the manager has to perform the following main actions. Firstly, it is important to specify the goals of the network business creation. This could be achievement of the "scale effect" by means of increasing the sales volumes, reducing the costs by means of distribution of the company's departments according to the criterion of resources' accessibility, receipt of additional income in the form of royalty from the franchise, reduction of the risk component of business by means of sales diversification, etc.

Secondly, it is necessary to specify the parameters of the variants of network business creation available for the company. These parameters include expenses for networkization of the company for the categories distinguished by the manager and the advantages of networkization (growth of demand, reduction of risk, reduction of costs, etc.).

Thirdly, it is necessary to provide the program with the possible ways of the geographical location of the objects of network business and their characteristics. It is important to take into account a lot of options for expanding the choice range. These could be different spots in one city, different cities, and even different countries. At that, the parameters of each geographical location are given, which allow comparing them.

Fourthly, it is necessary to enter the parameters of various types of the organizational structure of network business. Such types differ according to the level of independence of structural departments of the company and according to constant and variable expenditures. Apart from this, the differences are manifested in the aspects of the distribution of profit between departments and the main office.

As a result, the manager receives the answers to the following questions in the sphere of the creation of network business:

- the preferential method of creation of network business: franchise or creation of own structural departments;
- geographical model of the creation of network business;
- a project of the organizational structure that fits the selected method of network business creation;
- parameters of interaction with the objects of network business (volume of royalty or the withdrawn share of profit, distribution of liabilities in the sphere of marketing and innovations, etc.).

Logic and structure of the process of decision support in the pricing sphere with the help of intellectual technologies are shown in Fig. 4.

5.4   Recommendations for Successful Implementation of Intellectual Technologies of Decision Support in the Sphere of Marketing

For formation of the business structure's brand, which uses the leading technologies, which include intellectual technologies of decision support, we recommend being guided by the following sequence of actions. The first step: preliminary instruction for the public on the following implementation of intellectual technologies into decision support at the company after approving the corresponding plans by the management of the business.

Such instructions could have the form of advertising, the scale of which is selected depending on the company's possibilities (TV, radio, posters, etc.) and the form of information letters (regular mail or e-mail, SMS, etc.). During realization of such marketing communications, it is important to emphasize the uniqueness of such innovation as intellectual technologies of decision support.

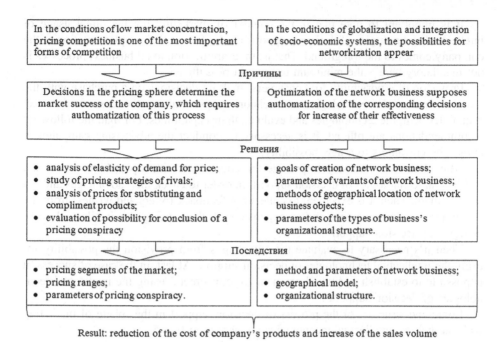

In the conditions of low market concentration, pricing competition is one of the most important forms of competition	In the conditions of globalization and integration of socio-economic systems, the possibilities for networkization appear

Причины

Decisions in the pricing sphere determine the market success of the company, which requires authomatization of this process	Optimization of the network business supposes authomatization of the corresponding decisions for increase of their effectiveness

Решения

• analysis of elasticity of demand for price; • study of pricing strategies of rivals; • analysis of prices for substituting and compliment products; • evaluation of possibility for conclusion of a pricing conspiracy	• goals of creation of network business; • parameters of variants of network business; • methods of geographical location of network business objects; • parameters of the types of business's organizational structure.

Последствия

• pricing segments of the market; • pricing ranges; • parameters of pricing conspiracy.	• method and parameters of network business; • geographical model; • organizational structure.

Result: reduction of the cost of company's products and increase of the sales volume

Fig. 4. Causal connections of implementation of intellectual technologies of decision support in the pricing sphere

The second step: Informing the interested parties on the first results of the implementation of intellectual technologies of decision support at the company. It could be performed in any accessible and preferable way. It is important to inform the targeted audience of the advantages which were reached or are expected to be reached in the near future from the implementation of intellectual technologies of decision support at the company.

The third step: Evaluation of the public reaction to the implementation of intellectual technologies of decision support at the company. It can be performed in the form of sociological survey (in written or electronic form) and financial analysis within which the volume of sales (and loyalty of interested parties) is compared before and after implementation of intellectual technologies of decision support at the company.

The fourth step: a collection of feedback for accepting offers from the public on the expansion of applying the intellectual technologies of decision support at the company. It might be performed in the form of outsourcing. Its main goal consists in the attraction of attention and increase of public's loyalty to the intellectual technologies of decision support.

The fifth step: Informing the interested parties on the long-term results of the implementation of intellectual technologies of decision support in several months (6–12) after the start of the work. It is important for supporting interest to them from the company's targeted audience for getting the maximum profit from such innovative activity.

It is important to note that in the context of marketing not the direct usage of intellectual technologies of decision support but the fact of their implementation at the company comes to the foreground. That is, their application to all business processes is not mandatory here – the minimum use would be sufficient.

Provision of a possibility for consumers' making decisions on a purchase with the help of intellectual technologies of decision support allows the customers to get acquainted with the technologies and evaluate their capabilities. For that, the following recommendations are offered. It is necessary to conduct the advertising campaign to attract the customers to a new possibility.

After that, it is necessary to provide the consumers with a possibility to use the intellectual technologies of decision support, in order to check their advantages and get used to them. Then it is expedient to collect the feedback (offers and wishes) from the consumers on improvement and/or expansion of them using the intellectual technologies of decision support.

Then it's necessary to evaluate the advantages from provision the possibility for using the intellectual technologies of decision support. At last, in the case of success, it is possible to establish additional payment for consumers' using the intellectual technologies of decision support.

Logic and structure of the process of decision support in the sphere of marketing with the help of intellectual technologies are shown in Fig. 5.

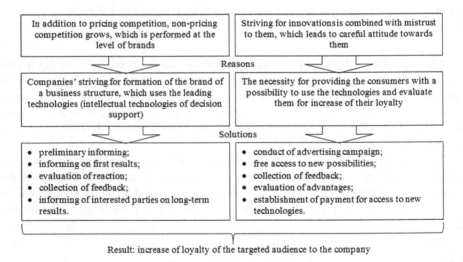

Fig. 5. Causal connections of implementation of intellectual technologies of decision support in the sphere of marketing

6   Conclusion

Thus, intellectual technologies of decision support have wide perspectives for improvement and development of the tools for increasing the competitiveness of business. As was shown in this paper, these technologies can be used by the business structure and provided to the consumer of the product for decision support on the purchase.

The working hypothesis is confirmed in the course of the research and it is proved that intellectual technologies of decision support expand the possibilities of the modern business structures in the sphere of purchase and keeping of competitive advantages, i.e., achievement of sustainable competitiveness in the long-term.

The theoretical significance of the received results consists in the development of the conceptual provisions of the theory of competitiveness of business on the basis of the application of intellectual technologies of decision support. The practical results of the research and its applied value consist in the possibility of using the offered creative tools of increasing the competitiveness on the basis of intellectual technologies of decision support in the economic activity of interested business structures.

Intellectual technologies of decision support are not only one of the leading innovations of modern times but also possess large perspectives in the sphere of development, as the spheres of their application are very wide. This brings them to the rank of such innovations which possess the anti-crisis potential. In other words, intellectual technologies of decision support can become a catalyzer of a new stage of economic growth which is expected in the global economy.

It should be noted that intellectual technologies of decision support do not necessarily have to be costly and accessible only for large business. These technologies are potentially accessible for small and medium business, which allows using them by all market players.

That's why the fact of their use is not sufficient for acquitting and keeping the competitive advantages on the basis of usage of such technologies – it is necessary to use them creatively. Thus, the search for new means of application of intellectual technologies of decision support in the activity of modern business structures is a perspective direction for further scientific and practical research.

References

1. Bakaev, M., Avdeenko, T.: Intelligent information system to support decision-making based on unstructured web data. ICIC Express Lett. **9**(4), 1017–1023 (2015)
2. Belov, A.G., Kravets, A.G.: Business performance management in small and medium businesses and functional automation. World Appl. Sci. J. **24**(24), 7–11 (2013)
3. Ben Yahia, N., Bellamine, N., Ben Ghezala, H.: Towards an intelligent decision making support. In: Abraham, A., Thampi, S. (eds.) Intelligent Informatics. AISC, vol. 182, pp. 81–86. Springer, Heidelberg (2013). doi:10.1007/978-3-642-32063-7_10
4. Cheng, J.L.C., Yiu, D.: China business at a crossroads: institutions, innovation, and international competitiveness. Long Range Plan. **49**(5), 584–588 (2016)
5. Groumpos, P.P.: The need for wise decision making support systems (WDMSS) in developing future intelligent systems plenary paper. In: ELEKTRO 2016 - 11th International Conference: Proceedings, 7512023, pp. 3–10 (2016)
6. Garina, E.P., Kuznetsov, V.P., Egorova, A.O., Garin, A.P., Yashin, S.N.: Formation of the system of business processes at machine building enterprises. Eur. Res. Stud. J. **9**(2), 55–63 (2016)

7. Garina, E., Kuznetsova, S., Semakhin, E., Semenov, S., Sevryukova, A.: Development of national production through integration of machine building enterprises into industrial park structures. Eur. Res. Stud. J. **18**(3), 271–286 (2015)

8. Krioni, N.K., Kolodenkova, A.E., Korobkin, V.V., Gubanov, N.G.: Intelligent decision-making support system using cognitive modeling for project feasibility assessment on creating complex technical systems. Int. J. Appl. Bus. Econ. Res. **14**(10), 7289–7300 (2016)

9. Kamp, B., Parry, G.: Servitization and advanced business services as levers for competitiveness. Ind. Mark. Manag. **60**, 11–16 (2017)

10. Kaur, S.P., Kumar, J., Kumar, R.: The relationship between flexibility of manufacturing system components, competitiveness of SMEs and business performance: a study of manufacturing SMEs in Northern India. Glob. J. Flex. Syst. Manag. **18**(2), 123–137 (2017)

11. Kuznetsov, V.P., Garina, E.P., Semakhin, E.A., Garin, A.P., Klychova, G.S.: Special aspects of modern production systems organization. Int. Bus. Manag. **10**(21), 5125–5129 (2016)

12. Klychova, G.S., Kuznetsov, V.P., Trifonov, Y.V., Yashin, S.N., Koshelev, E.V.: Upgrading corporate equipment as an Asian real option. Int. Bus. Manag. **10**(21), 5130–5137 (2016)

13. Mora, M., Marx-Gómez, J., Wang, F., Gelman, O.: IT service management and engineering: an intelligent decision-making support systems approach. Intell. Decis. Technol. **8**(2), 65–68 (2014)

14. Niaki, M.K., Nonino, F.: Impact of additive manufacturing on business competitiveness: a multiple case study. J. Manuf. Technol. Manag. **28**(1), 56–74 (2017)

15. Nychai, L.: Inovação, sofisticação de negócios e competitividade dos países da América Latina e Caribe | [Innovation, business sophistication and competitiveness of the countries of Latin America and Caribbean]. Espacios **38**(14), 19 (2017)

16. Olevsky, G.M.: Internationalization of business and national competitiveness. World Econ. Int. Relat. **60**(12), 17–26 (2016)

17. Popkova, E.G., Abramov, S.A., Ermolina, L.V., Gandin, E.V.: Strategic effectiveness evaluation as integral part of the modern enterprise management. Asian Soc. Sci. **11**(20), 16–21 (2015)

18. Tweedale, J.W., Phillips-Wren, G., Jain, L.C.: Advances in intelligent decision-making technology support. Smart Innov. Syst. Technol. **42**, 1–15 (2016)

19. Westerlund, M., Isabelle, D.A., Rajala, R., Leminen, S.: Networks, business models, and competitiveness in small Finnish firms. Int. J. Bus. Glob. **18**(1), 9–26 (2017)

Model of Decision-Making Support in Heterarchical System Management of Regional Construction Cluster

Dmitriy Anufriev, Irina Yu. Petrova, and Olga Shikulskaya$^{(\boxtimes)}$

Astrakhan State University of Architecture and Civil Engineering,
18 Tatischeva Str., 414056 Astrakhan, Russian Federation
shikul@mail.ru

Abstract. In this paper, the necessity of creation of a common information space of a regional construction cluster is justified. It is shown that the regional construction cluster is a complex heterarchical system. The heterogeneity of the information environment caused by the fact that the entities as are united in a cluster of the primary production branch, and the accompanying industries, complicates the creation of the common information space supporting activities of a cluster. The functional and information simulation of the system is executed for the purpose of formation of the integrated information and communication environment of the Astrakhan regional construction cluster. The IDEF0 notation is used for business process modeling. Information modeling is executed in the notation of DFD. The model in the IDEF3 notation and the SwimLane diagram are developed for the description of processes logic and vertical and horizontal connections between them. The created models are a basis for the construction cluster portal development.

Keywords: Cluster · Heterarchical system · Holon

1 Introduction

The strategy of social and economic development of the Astrakhan region till 2020 determines improvement of the population life quality as the priority direction, one of its indicators is the creation of comfortable accommodation conditions for the population. One of the main objectives solved in the region remains improvement of housing conditions of the population by means of housing supply increase, achievement of its moderate prices for a population with different income level.

Now the housing stock of the Astrakhan region constitutes 2,2246.6 thousand sq. m, including 15,387.8 thousand sq. m (69.2%) in the city area and 6,585.8 thousand sq. m (30.8%) in the rural zone. The total area of a slum dwelling and emergency housing equal to 10% of the total amount of a housing stock of region [1, 2].

Therefore, the housing problem is one of the most urgent in the social sphere of the Astrakhan region.

© Springer International Publishing AG 2017
A. Kravets et al. (Eds.): CIT&DS 2017, CCIS 754, pp. 317–330, 2017.
DOI: 10.1007/978-3-319-65551-2_23

2 Background of Formation of the Integrated Information and Communication Environment of the Regional Construction Cluster of the Astrakhan Region

Transition to the market relations in the field of housing policy has essentially changed a role of the state in the construction industry and housing and communal services. In the housing market private construction companies, the companies, providing housing and communal services, the solvent purchaser of housing and consumers of housing and communal services interact. In the conditions of market economy, the possibilities of the construction industry management by state and municipal administrative bodies have limited character.

Using concepts of new economy of adaptive systems [3], one may say, that the problem of any transformed economy consists in the ability to adaptation by means of a change of organizational structure to increase the ability to react to unpredictable future changes in the external environment [4, 5].

Development of economy of the region requires the application of such form of the organization and labor co-operation which could provide accumulation and effective use of the territory resources. Clusters belong to such forms.

The founder of cluster approach M. Porter offered the following determination of a cluster. The cluster is a group of geographically adjoining interdependent companies (suppliers, vendors) and the related with them organizations (educational institutions, state bodies, the infrastructure companies) operating in a certain sphere and complementary each other [6].

The significant amount of scientific operations is devoted to a research of regional clusters with hierarchical connections [7–11]. However, the analysis of a construction cluster allowed to reveal both hierarchical (vertical), and market (horizontal) connections between its elements. It allows to say about the existence of the heterarchical connections between elements of a construction cluster.

Thus it is possible to offer the following determination. The regional construction cluster is a set of the territorially localized within the region, interdependent and complementary enterprises of construction and the allied industries integrated by heterarchical connections with local institutions, authorities, the cooperating enterprises for the purpose of the increase in competitiveness of these enterprises and regional economy in general.

It is important to note that a row of works is devoted to questions of determination and functioning of regional construction clusters in Russia. In them, a similar definition of a construction cluster from the point of view of the system approach is given [12–15].

The Astrakhan construction cluster includes more than 811 construction organizations of various forms of ownership the great majority of which is private. Besides, the cluster includes the auxiliary entities and the organizations which are engaged in staff training for a construction industry, the banks and other credit institutions providing the population with available mortgage loans with the guaranteed commissioning time of housing.

For determination of the structure of a regional construction cluster of the Astrakhan region the following types of researches were used:

- research of the movement of material, financial and personnel flows;
- the analysis of information flows in the system of interaction of power, production, scientific and educational and innovative structures in a construction complex of the region;
- the analysis of decision-making processes, their isolation or coherence on the basis of the principles of decisions group;
- the analysis of distribution of the power, division of areas of responsibility, a collectivism in decision-making.

By results of these researches [15] four groups of the main participants of a construction cluster of the Astrakhan region were allocated:

1. Power structures at the level of the region, municipalities.
2. Large enterprises of an industry.
3. The entities interconnected with regional industry vendors.
4. Public structures.

The structure of a construction cluster is heterarchical, and it is still very fragmented, but it intensively develops. The conducted survey of participants of a construction cluster in the Astrakhan region allowed to draw the following conclusions.

The computer park of the entities averages 20–22 computers, and 60% of the computers are of 2011–2015 release, older computers account for 34%, oldest computers account for 66%.

Most of the interviewed entities (93%) have local area networks, i.e. they have a possibility of use of corporate information resources. In all interviewed organizations there is an Internet access, and the allocated communication channels. Speed of data transmission constitutes over 512 KB/sec (37% of respondents), less 512 KB/sec (32% of respondents), less 32 KB/sec (14% of respondents).

Participants of poll define purposes the Internet use as follows:

- work with e-mail accounts for 100%,
- communication with the controlling entity accounts for 86%,
- a search of necessary information accounts for 93%,
- placement of information and advertisement accounts for 71%.

57% of the entities have own websites representing these organizations at networks, however, only 29% of respondents use social networks for placement of information and advertising.

100% of the entities use programs of accounting and inventory accounting. Among them, the line of software products 1C (the Entity, Accounts department, the Warehouse) consists 90%. Besides, programs for calculation of estimates on an asset construction are widely used, for example, "the Grandee the Estimate" is used for 50% of the entities. "Smeta-Bagira" or "RIK" - the programs intended for the automated release of estimate documentation are in certain cases used.

Practically all entities use at the same time several computer-aided engineering systems, and the vast majority of them applies Autocad of various versions (79%) and

Archicad (43%). On the frequency of use 3DMax is on the third place 29%). The programs of new generation allowing to apply information modeling technologies of buildings and industrial facilities, for example, of Revit (Autodesk) are used only in 7% of cases. Similar Russian software products as ACKON are also seldom used. In some cases, SAPR "Lira", "Monomakh", "NormCAD", "SCAD" are used for calculations of building and steel concrete constructions of buildings and constructions.

Legal directory systems are used at most the entities (about 57% of respondents use the Consultant system, 50% - use "Guarantor"). Updating of bases carries based on the signed agreements.

Legal directory systems are used at most of the entities (about 57% of respondents use the Consultant system, 50% of them use "Guarantor"). Updating of bases is executed based on the signed agreements.

All used software is licensed. The programs developed on its own are actively used.

The poll showed that many construction organizations (64%) use electronic document management systems for an internal clerical work, but they practically don't apply project management software (only 14% of the entities use such programs). Many heads would like to use an external information resource for experience exchange with other companies, receipts of information on the implementation of new technologies, new materials, and also for advanced training of employees on the job.

In the nearest future, an essential increase in capacity of information flows in a consequence of active implementation of building information modeling (BIM) is supposed. So since September 1, 2016, provision of Directorate-General for State Environmental Review of Russia has provided services in performing an expert examination of the project documentation and results of engineering researches on the objects financed by means of the federal budget will be performed only in electronic form, and in 2017 similar approach will be applied to regional examinations [16].

The carried-out analysis allows to speak about existence of a large number of the information flows processed by the heterogeneous information systems, in the majority which aren't interacting among themselves that significantly complicates receiving and information processing both from an external environment, and from cluster elements based on which it is possible to work out the controlling decision.

The heterogeneity of the information environment caused by the fact that the entities as are united in a cluster of the primary production branch, and the accompanying industries, complicates the creation of the common information space supporting activities of a cluster [17].

The heterarchical organization of business processes of a construction cluster and heterogeneity of the information environment do a cluster to one of the most difficult objects of informatization.

Solving the situation is the creation of a common information space of the regional construction cluster on the following principles: completeness of information; relevance; predictability; response time; integrity; institutionality; safety.

In this paper, the option of modeling of difficult business processes of a construction cluster taking into account independent static, dynamic and stochastic parameters of this social and economic system with heterarchical communications is provided. It will allow to exercise effective control and management of business processes in a cluster.

3   Modeling of Business Processes of the Construction Cluster

3.1   Business Processes Model of the Construction Cluster in the Notation of IDEF0

The IDEF0 diagrams which are the cornerstone of the methodology of the structural analysis of SADT are the effective instrument of business processes modeling [18, 19].

In view of the developed infrastructure of a construction cluster of the Astrakhan region (see Fig. 1), the modeled system will include both basic processes (directly the construction), and the managing, auxiliary and providing processes. Basic processes (construction) are performing by large enterprises of a construction industry, which are centers of a cluster, and also the small and medium business developing around them.

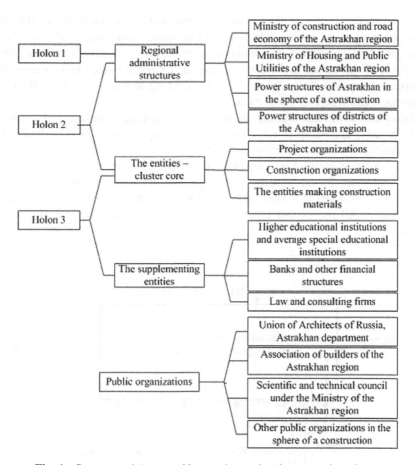

Fig. 1. Structure of the Astrakhan region regional construction cluster

Training and retraining of personnel, consulting services, and financial provision belong to the auxiliary and providing processes. Three large higher education institutions: The Astrakhan state university of architecture and civil engineering, the Astrakhan state university (faculty of Architecture and design), the Astrakhan state technical university (Institute of Town Planning) carry out staff training for the region construction branch. Financial provision is carried out by banks, providing the population with available mortgage loans with the guaranteed terms of new housing supply. Legal structures render consulting services.

Management processes of the construction cluster include 3 control levels. They are carried out by Holon of the administrative management structures and Holon of the business kernels of the cluster [2]. As the system is of heterarchical structure, along with vertical management the decision-making by means of interaction of Holon of the cluster business kernel and the adding enterprises (the financial organizations and legal structures) with the population (customers of production of housing construction) takes place.

Behind borders of the modeled system (the external environment of a cluster), there is a set of factors and objects which are not structural components of a cluster, but which can exert an impact on formation, functioning, and development of certain participants of the cluster and cluster in general. External entities make the revolting impacts on the system. Thus, the model width showing that the system is difficult with heterarchical constructions connections is determined.

The system depth determining the level of its detailing is determined in the simulation process, according to the conditions of an optimum ratio of a detail of the system description and labor input of its development.

The simulation purpose of a regional construction cluster is the description of its business processes for an increase in management efficiency. Context diagram of a business process model of a construction cluster and its decomposition are presented in Figs. 2 and 3. All the system processes are showed on the node tree diagram (see Fig. 4).

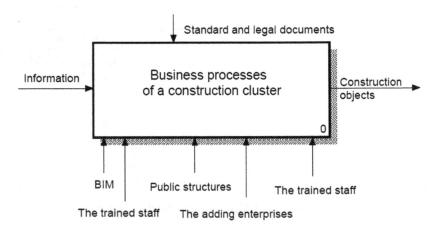

Fig. 2. Context diagram of the construction cluster business process model

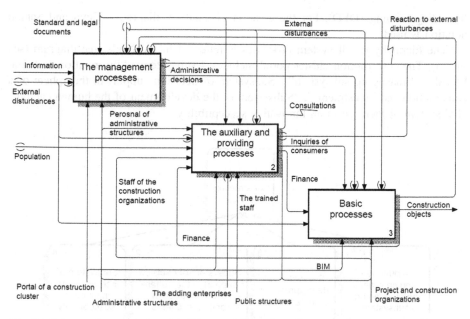

Fig. 3. Context diagram's decomposition of the construction cluster business process model

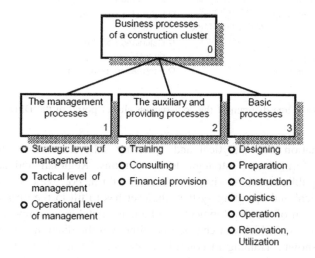

Fig. 4. Node tree diagram of the construction cluster processes

3.2 Information Model of the Construction Cluster Portal in the DFD Notation

Computer support of all business processes of the construction cluster is realized by an information portal for a description of which the appropriate model is necessary. It is expedient to realize simulation of the construction cluster portal in the notation of Data flow diagramming (DFD). For the creation of dataflow diagrams, Geyn and Sarson notation is used.

The hierarchy of all system processes is reflected in the Node tree diagram (see Fig. 5). The construction cluster portal includes 4 subsystems: "Information and analytical and managing subsystem", "Subsystem of decision support in the sphere of a construction and investments", "Subsystem of the development of the human capital", "Subsystem of increase in an innovative susceptibility".

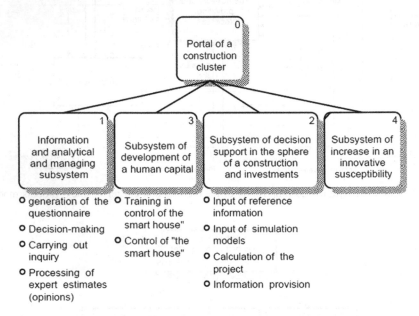

Fig. 5. Node tree diagram of the construction cluster portal in the DFD notation

The information and analytical and operating subsystem serves for computer support of the formation of strategic level solutions. Regional and administrative structures and public structures (Experts) interact with it. For work with the Information and analytical and operating system, the user has to fill in the questionnaire.

The Subsystem of the development of a human capital is decomposed on a set of educational processes which can change over time. On the diagram, as an example, 2 processes are shown: Training in control of "the smart house" and Control of "the smart house". Training of users is made by the supplementing enterprises (educational institutions of different level) [19–25].

The subsystem of decision support in the sphere of a construction and investments includes 4 processes: "Input of reference information", "Input of simulation models", "Calculation of the project" and "Information provision". Regional administrative structures, public structures (experts) and users interact with a subsystem. The first decomposition of the construction cluster portal model is shown in Fig. 6.

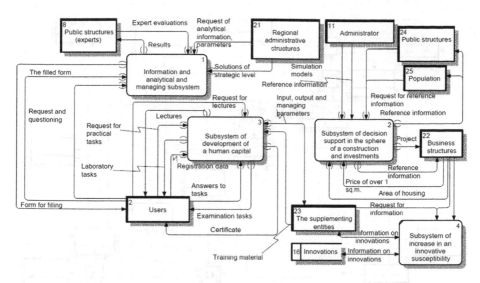

Fig. 6. First decomposition of the construction cluster's portal model

3.3 Business Processes Model of the Construction Cluster in the Notation of IDEF3

Existence in the DFD of elements for the description of sources, receivers and data storages allows to describe document flow process more effectively and visually. However, the notation of IDEF3 – workflow diagramming more is suitable for the description of the logic of information flows interaction.

The construction cluster of the Astrakhan region as early was shown, represents the heterarchical system.

The heterarchy is the method of the organization which isn't either market or hierarchical. While hierarchies assume strict hierarchy on levels and the markets assume the relations of complete independence, a heterarchy assumes the relations of interdependence. It combines both elements of hierarchy and elements of the market relations. In the case of stable functioning of the regulated processes, hierarchical connections more are shown. The hierarchy of processes is well reflected by the developed business process model in the notation of IDEF0. However, in the case of impact on the system of external perturbations, inertial hierarchical control becomes ineffective. The advantage is got by horizontal managing connections which can't be visually provided to models of the IDEF0 notation. For reflection of the logic of processes, and also vertical and horizontal connections the IDEF3 notation was used (see Fig. 7).

For the explicit description of a role and responsibility of performers in specific processes the SwimLane diagram which is a variety of the chart IDEF3 diagram was used. By means of its description, we will display an interaction logic of processes of the heterarchical system of a construction cluster in more detail.

Roles on the SwimLane diagram (see Fig. 8) are defined according to holonic structure of a construction cluster and they correspond both to separate system elements

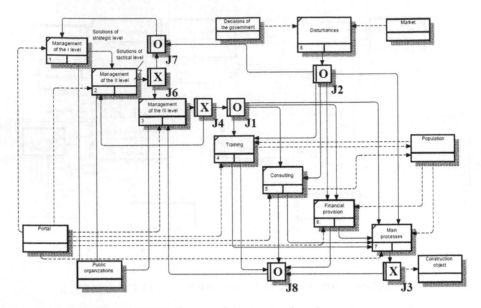

Fig. 7. IDEF3 diagram of the construction cluster processes

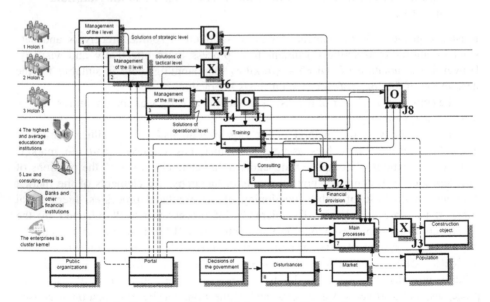

Fig. 8. SwimLane diagram of the construction cluster processes

of the lower level of the hierarchy of management, and to their associations (holon groups) depending on the decision-maker purposes and scale of administrative decisions [26].

Higher education institutions and average special educational institutions, law and consulting firms, banks and other financial institutions, the enterprises — a cluster kernel are presented as separate system elements of the bottom level hierarchy of management. Regional administrative structures are integrated into Holon 1, Holon 2 integrates Holon 1 and the enterprises – a cluster kernel, Holon 3 integrates the enterprises – a cluster kernel and the supplementing entities.

Administrative solutions of tactical level of management arrive on the III management level – the operational level (micro level) displayed on the diagram by process 3. Management of this level is exercised by Holon 3, the business kernel of a cluster and the supplementing entities (the financial organizations and legal structures) formed by the interaction of Holon with the population (customers of production of housing construction). Management of the III level is directed directly to the main and auxiliary processes. For decision-making, the models of the construction cluster portal having the low level of abstraction are used (it is a lot of details, control of flows dynamics, the maximum detailing).

Administrative solutions of all three levels are influenced by the public organizations which are shown by the appropriate referent subject on the diagram.

Auxiliary processes include process 4 of Training, process 5 of Consulting and process 6 of Financial provision.

Owners of Training process are educational institutions. Consulting is realized by law and consulting firms. Objects of these two processes are business structures and the population. Financial provision is realized by banks and other financial institutions. The main processes are realized by the enterprises – the construction cluster kernel. Information support of the main and auxiliary processes is executed by the Portal of a construction cluster.

At impact on the system of the external disturbances generated by the market and the government decisions which are shown by the appropriate referent subject on the diagram, horizontal connections score an advantage. Disturbances through the junction "Asynchronous or" J2 is transferred to the main, auxiliary and operating processes. If owners of these processes by means of internal mechanisms of the level are capable of stabilizing system or to improve its state (to increase its efficiency), their influences are directed to the construction object presented on the diagram by the reference subject.

If resources and powers of this level are not enough for the problems' solution, they through the junction "Asynchronous or" J8 transfer management to Holon 3.

Distributions of flows between a construction object and junction J8 is carried out by means of the junction of "Exclusive or" J3. Depending on possibilities of the operational level of management input control through the junction of "Asynchronous or" is distributed between the main and auxiliary processes, or the control is transferred to tactical level to Holon 2. Distributions of flows are carried out by means of the junction of "Exclusive or" J4. At the tactical level of management in the same way depending on possibilities of this level there is a distributions of flows on the junction of "Exclusive or" J6: or the input control goes to the III (lower) level of management, or the control is transferred to the I (top) level of management. Then hierarchical management begins.

Heterarchical management is more flexible in comparison with hierarchical and it is more organized in comparison with the market relations.

The heterarchical system of a regional construction cluster [3] considered above includes different subjects: investors (developers), builders, contractors, organizations of researchers and designers, and also public authorities and local government. All listed structures (we will define them as elementary (atomic) structures) perform the different functions necessary for a construction object building from "zero" and its delivery in operation form the self-sufficient and balanced system. And, all organizations entering a cluster except for authorities and local government, occupy the economic niches, form and provide own stocks of orders (sometimes even not connected with construction). Now we will assume that in the case of acceptance of certain programs (the federal or regional level) there is a need for the building of construction objects (for example, the program of resettlement from the shabby and hazardous dwelling) [4]. Naturally, under this program, the associations from above-mentioned structures, ready to functionally carry out the created task begin to arise. After execution of the tasks connected to the entered program, temporal associations of structures "break up" and the system reverts to the start state.

4 Conclusions

In the paper, the background of the formation of the integrated information and communication environment of a regional construction cluster of the Astrakhan region is shown. The carried-out analysis of information technologies use by participants of a construction cluster in the Astrakhan region showed existence of a large number of the information flows processed by the heterogeneous information systems, in the majority which aren't interacting among themselves that significantly complicates receiving and information processing, both from an external environment, and from elements of a cluster, necessary for framing of effective managing decisions. The need of creation of a common information space of a regional construction cluster is justified.

The heterarchical organization of business processes of a construction cluster and heterogeneity of the information environment makes the cluster one of the most difficult objects of informatization. So the need of business process modeling for the purpose of formation of the integrated information and communication environment of the regional construction cluster of the Astrakhan region is caused.

In view of the high complexity of system its functional and information modeling in notations of IDEF0 (SADT chart), DFD, IDEF3 is executed, the SwimLane diagram is developed.

The SADT diagram well reflects the hierarchy of processes and hierarchical communications prevailing in case of stable functioning of the regulated processes. However, in the case of impact on the system of external inputs inertial hierarchical control becomes ineffective. The advantage is got by horizontal managing directors of communication which aren't visible in a model of the notation IDEF0. The model in the notation of IDEF3 is developed for reflection of the logic of processes, and vertical and horizontal connections. The SwimLane diagram of business processes of a construction cluster which is a variety of the IDEF3 diagram is developed for the explicit description of a role and responsibility of performers in the specific processes defined according to holonic structure of a construction cluster. For simulation of processes of the Portal of a construction cluster, the notation of DFD is used.

The created models are the basis for the development of the construction cluster portal.

References

1. Anufriev, D.P.: A housing question in social and economic system of the region (on materials of a monitoring sociological research). Soc. Humanitarian Messenger Caspian Reg. 2(5), 17–24 (2016). (In Russian)
2. Anufriev, D.P.: Dwelling as element of social and economic system of the region: experience of applied research. MGSU Bull. 2, 187–195 (2014). (In Russian)
3. Arthur, W.B.: Increasing Returns and Path Dependence in the Economy. University of Michigan Press, Ann Arbor (1994)
4. Grabher, G.: Adaptation at the cost of adaptability? Restructuring the Eastern German regional economy. In: Grabher, G., Stark, D. (eds.) Restructuring Networks: Legacies, Linkages, and Localities in Postsocialism, pp. 107–134. Oxford University Press, London (1997)
5. Grabher, G., Stark, D.: Organizing diversity: evolutionary theory, network analysis, and postsocialist transformations. In: Grabher, G., Stark, D. (eds.) Restructuring Networks: Legacies, Linkages, and Localities in Postsocialism, pp. 1–32. Oxford University Press, London (1997)
6. Porter, M.E.: Competition. Williams Publishing House, Moscow (2005)
7. Akhmetova, M.I.: Analysis of mechanisms of hierarchical interaction of innovation and investment companies. In: Proc. 1st Rus. Sci. Symp. on Regional Economy, vol. 2, pp. 11–14. Institute of Economics of the Ural Division of the RAS Publ., Ekaterinburg (2011). (In Russian)
8. Kovaleva, T.Y., Baleevskih, V.G.: Identification of the educational clusters in the regional economy: theory, methodology and research results (a case study of Perm Krai). J. Econometrics Financ. Manag. 2(4), 153–162 (2014)
9. Persky, Y.K., Dmitriev, D.V.: Interaction and interdetermination of competition processes and information asymmetry on the regional trade market. Econ. Reg. 1, 182–187 (2010)
10. Tupitsyna, M.N.: Improvement of the mechanism of interaction between participants of the credit market as a factor of economic growth. Hierarchical relationships in economic systems: theoretical and applied aspects: collected articles, pp. 120–130. Perm State Univ. Publ., Perm (2005). (In Russian)
11. Zhulanov, E.E.: Theoretical and methodological approach to measuring the results of the hierarchical management of regional socio-economic systems. Econ. Entrepreneurship 2(43), 53–59 (2014). (In Russian)
12. Tokunova, G.F.: Methodology of management of development of a construction complex on a basis of cluster approach. St. Petersburg SUAC, St. Petersburg (2012). (In Russian)
13. Tokunova, G.F.: Basic provisions of methodology of control of development of a construction cluster. Log Leg. Econ. Res. 4, 31–39 (2012)
14. Gumba, H.M., Kuzovlev, I.A., Prokopenkov, V.V.: Economic-mathematical simulation of correlation of factors of development of a building cluster of the region. Messenger IRGTU 5(100), 196–203 (2015). (In Russian)
15. Vakhrusheva, E.A., Gerasimov, V.V.: Conceptual bases of management of innovative development of the housing sphere of the region in Russia on the basis of cluster approach. Creative Econ. 7(31), 68–71 (2009). (In Russian)
16. Anufriev, D.P.: Control of a construction complex as social and economic system: setting of problem. Ind. Civil Eng. 8, 8–10 (2012). (In Russian)
17. Anufriev, D.P.: Regional construction cluster of the Astrakhan region. MGSU Bull. 12(1) (100), 99–106 (2017). (In Russian)

18. Anufriev, D.P.: Business process modeling of a construction cluster of the Astrakhan region as heterarchical system. In: Integration, Partnership and Innovations in Construction Science and Education, pp. 473–478. FGBOOU WAUGH "National Research Moscow State Construction University", Moscow (2017). (In Russian)
19. Anufriev, D.P.: A mathematical model of a regional construction complex. In: Proceedings of the II International Scientific and Practical Conference, pp. 58–73. Astrakhan – The House of The Future, Astrakhan (2010). (In Russian)
20. Anufriev, D.P., Zaripova, V.M., Lezhnina, Y.A., Shikulskaya, O.M., Homenko, T.V., Petrova, I.Y.: Design of elements of the information and measuring and controlling systems for intellectual buildings. ASUACE, Astrakhan (2015). (In Russian)
21. Volkov, A.: General information models of intelligent building control systems: basic concepts, determination and the reasoning. Adv. Mater. Res. **838–841**, 2973–2976 (2014)
22. Volkov, A., Chulkov, V., Korotkov, D.: Intelligent building. Adv. Mater. Res. **1065–1069**, 1606–1609 (2014)
23. Volkov, A.A., Sukneva, L.V.: BIM-technology in tasks of the designing complex systems of alternative energy supply. Procedia Engineering **23**, 377–380 (2014)
24. Volkov, A.A., Batov, E.I.: Simulation of building operations for calculating building intelligence quotient. Procedia Engineering **111**, 845–848 (2015)
25. Volkov, A.A., Batov, E.I.: Dynamic extension of building information model for "smart" buildings. Procedia Engineering **111**, 849–852 (2015)
26. Anufriev, D.P., Holodov, A.Y.: Development of the simulation model of the tactical abstraction layer modeling the business processes arising in case of implementation of shared-equity construction in the regional housing market. Constr. Messenger Caspian Reg. **4**(18), 79–85 (2016). (In Russian)

Intelligent Support of Decision Making in Management of Large-Scale Systems Using Case-Based, Rule-Based and Qualitative Reasoning over Ontologies

Marina Kultsova[✉], Dmitry Litovkin, Irina Zhukova,
and Alexander Dvoryankin

Volgograd State Technical University, Volgograd, Russia
marina.kultsova@mail.ru, {dmitry.litovkin,poas}@vstu.ru

Abstract. The current trend in intelligent support of decision making is an integration of different knowledge representation models and reasoning mechanisms, it allows improving quality and efficiency of obtained decisions. In this paper, we present an ontology-based approach to intelligent support of decision making in the management of large-scale systems using case-based, rule-based and qualitative reasoning. A concept of the reasoning mechanisms integration implies that case-based reasoning (CBR) takes on the role of leading reasoning mechanism, while rule-based (RBR) and qualitative reasoning (QR) support the different phases of CBR-cycle - adaptation and revision phases respectively. The paper describes a modified CBR-cycle and ontological knowledge representation model which supports the proposed concept of reasoning integration. A formal qualitative model of decision making was developed for revision of case solution, it includes the following components: system state model, action model, and assessment model. An ontological representation of the qualitative model was proposed for integration with structural case model in an ontological knowledge base. Implementation of the proposed approach is illustrated by a number of examples of decision making support in various subject domains.

Keywords: Intelligent support of decision making · Knowledge intensive case based reasoning · Ontological case representation · Qualitative model

1 Introduction

All "classical" approaches to control are based on the assumption that it is possible to obtain an exact analytic predetermined form corresponding to the input and output signals of the managed system with a subsequent refinement of the values of the coefficients entering into it. In practice, typically we have to operate with poorly formalized management objects. Their properties are a

© Springer International Publishing AG 2017
A. Kravets et al. (Eds.): CIT&DS 2017, CCIS 754, pp. 331–349, 2017.
DOI: 10.1007/978-3-319-65551-2_24

priori poorly known or change during the object functioning. Due to the lack of knowledge about the object and the environment where it functions, attempts to obtain an accurate model of the behavior of such an object are certain to fail [1].

Recently, a "nonclassical" approach to the theory of management is actively developing. This approach is associated with the use of artificial intelligence methods and algorithms. Use of intelligent decision support system (IDSS) allows to decrease the duration of decision making process and to improve the quality and efficiency of decisions. The current trend in IDSS development is an integration of different knowledge representation models and reasoning mechanisms [2,3] and this paper is devoted to the development of such complex approach to system management.

2   State of the Art

The most complicated systems for analyzing and decision making are those whose features cannot be formally described [4]: (a) description of a decision making problem has a complex and variable structure; (b) components of the problem and solution descriptions can significantly differ in their importance for decision making; (c) there are multiple logical relations between components of problem description; (d) both qualitative and quantitative parameters, which should be interpreted in a context-dependent way (not by absolute value), are taken into account; (e) knowledge about previously solved problems which are similar to the current problem is actively used while decision making.

Based on these features, ontological knowledge representation model, case-based reasoning (CBR), rule-based reasoning and qualitative reasoning can be considered as an appropriate AI technologies for the intelligent decision making. CBR is a problem-solving methodology that aims at reusing previously solved and memorized problem situations, called cases. A case is a concrete problem-solving experience [5].

In many situations, additional knowledge (background knowledge) is required with the case base to cope with the requirements of an application. Knowledge-Intensive CBR (KI-CBR) assumes that cases are enriched and/or coupled with general domain knowledge [6,7]. Ontologies are the useful tool for designing KI-CBR applications because they allow the knowledge engineer to use knowledge already acquired, conceptualized and implemented in a formal language, reducing considerably the knowledge acquisition difficulties. It has powerful abilities in knowledge acquisition, representation, and semantic understanding. Moreover, the reuse of ontologies from a library also benefits from their reliability and consistency. Ontologies provide the creation of complex, multi-relational knowledge structures to support the CBR methods. In CBR, knowledge is distributed among the four knowledge containers: vocabulary, similarity measures, adaptation knowledge and case base. Ontology plays crucial role in representing all of these knowledge containers [5,8].

Employment of ontology coupled with a CBR process is possible in few ways:

1. Ontology as the CBR's domain vocabulary
2. Ontologies as case base and domain vocabulary
3. Domain independent ontological CBR framework
4. XML-based case representation with ontology

In this paper, we focus on the problem-oriented implementation of domain independent ontological CBR framework and suggest a general approach to intelligent support of decision-making on the management of large-scale systems using knowledge-intensive CBR on the base of ontological knowledge representation.

3   Background and Related Work

For more than ten years authors of this paper have been working on the problem of intelligent support of decision-making on the management of large-scale systems in various subject domains. A number of intelligent decision support systems has been designed and implemented using contemporary AI technologies in particular in the field of engineering analysis, waste management, human resource management and water management.

In [9] the automated knowledge-based system for intelligent support of the preprocessing stage of engineering analysis in the contact mechanics domain was presented which employed the CBR mechanism. The case representation model was proposed which was centered on the structured qualitative model of a technical object. The model was formally represented by the OWL DL ontology, it featured the structured representation of engineering analysis cases which was based on the developed integrated qualitative model (QM) of a physical system [12]. QM of a physical system was considered as the main index element of a case description, and properties of an engineering problem formulated for this system, the formal contact problem, and a solution routine were associated with its components.

In [4] we presented the knowledge-based system for intelligent support of decision making in river floodplain management. This system integrated the case based reasoning (CBR), qualitative reasoning (QR) and ontological knowledge base. Proposed knowledge representation model was formally represented by the OWL DL ontology. The case base did not comprise all knowledge required for the correct solution of a new problem, but ontology allowed to formalize general domain knowledge and to reuse it for problem solving. Also, ontology allowed achieving semantic interoperability between case descriptions from different sources. Ontology defined framework for case description which allowed simplifying case retrieving stage of CBR process. And finally, it was recognized that general domain knowledge was necessary at the case adaptation stage. The case revision stage was supported with qualitative reasoning on the base of a qualitative model of case. This model captured qualitative dependencies between components of case solution and case index and allowed assessing proposed solution in terms of the behaviour of case index attributes.

The concept of integration of case-based reasoning and ontology was implemented also for human resource management [10]. According to this concept, ontology described general concepts and rules of the domain, case representation model and contained case base. Ontology as case representation model described the case as a set of individuals and relations. Ontology as domain knowledge base represented domain knowledge in form of DL-rules and provided procedures of knowledge inferring. Ontology as case base stored the cases as a part of domain knowledge.

In [11] a concept of intelligent support of decision making in waste management using knowledge-based approach was presented. To represent domain knowledge in waste management we used an ontological model. The designed ontological model of waste management included the set of DL-rules for the implementation of reasoning over the ontology to generate the waste management strategy. The basic set of these rules can be extended and supplemented for the purpose of operating with the different waste types, management methods, enterprise types.

In this paper, we attempted to generalize the experience in developing intelligent decision support systems in various subject domains and propose a new general approach to the integration of different types of reasoning on the base of ontological knowledge representation model to provide the intelligent support of decision making on the management of the large-scale systems.

4   Decision-Making Process

The task of decision making in the management of the large-scale system is defined as follows.

Input:

- a hierarchy of stakeholders' objectives. There are current qualitative assessments of objectives with their values. Each objective's assessment is qualitative variable with a value. For example, for the problem of floodplain management described in [4], we defined assessment value "Tolerable" for objective "Flood protection", and assessment value "Good" for sub-objective "Strengthening of technical flood protection measures";
- a requirement for each objective: required priority and constraint on assessment value (for example, the objective "Flood protection" has required priority - "High importance", and the constraint on assessment value - "Not less than Good";
- a description of initial system state is represented by the set of numeric and non-numeric attributes and their values (for example, system state attribute "Height of dikes" with value "0.5 m"). Additionally, description determines structural description items and relations between them;

- a set of assessments (and their qualitative values) of initial state associated with the objectives (for example, assessment value "Middle" of initial state attribute "Height of dikes" associated with the objective "Strengthening of technical flood protection measures");
- a set of operations for actions generation. Each operation is described by its own attributes and uses resources. The resource is described by its own attributes (for example, possible operations "Increase height of dikes", "Increase width of dikes", "Rebuild the dike", etc.).

Output: a set of generated actions which are relevant to the requirements for objectives and initial system state. Each action is a sequence of operations with values of their attributes (examples of generated actions are "Increase height of dikes" and "Increase width of dikes").

The general process of actions generation is shown in Fig. 1.

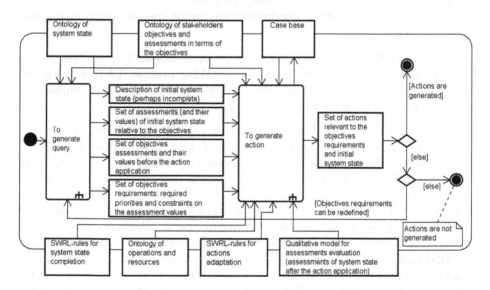

Fig. 1. Decision-making process in management of large-scale system (UML activity diagram)

To implement the proposed decision-making process we need to use the following knowledge:

- domain knowledge about the structure of system state description, the objectives, and their assessments, and also knowledge about operations and resources used for the actions generation;
- the base of cases describing the action application to the various initial states of the system relative to the objectives priorities and constraints on their assessment values;

– a set of completion rules that allow inferring additional attributes values for initial system state. As a result, we get the hypothetical initial state of the system;
– a set of adaptation rules that describe how actions from retrieved similar cases can be adapted to fit the hypothetical initial state of the system, current priorities of the objectives and constraints on their assessment values;
– a qualitative model of decision making for evaluating a set of assessments of system state after applying the action.

To represent, integrate and manage this knowledge, we use OWL DL ontology. In addition to the knowledge mentioned above the ontology should contain following pieces of knowledge:

– a top-level generic, domain-independent concepts. In our case, these are variables, variables domains and inequalities of values;
– case representation that defines case structure;
– a set of rules converting non-qualitative attributes to their qualitative equivalents.

Modified CBR-cycle implementing the decision-making task is presented in Fig. 2. In proposed scheme of the decision-making process, CBR is a leading reasoning mechanism, and QR and RBR carry out knowledge-based support of the main stages of CBR by the following way:

1. A new query is completed using the rules that infer: (a) additional values of attributes of the initial state, (b) instances of the structural description items and relations between them and (c) assessments of the initial system state relative to the objectives. As a result, we get the description of a hypothetical initial state of the system.
2. A completed query is matched with the cases (to be more exact, is matched with case indexes) in the case base and one or more similar cases are retrieved. As a result, we get case solutions and outcomes. Each solution contains: (a) action that has been applied; (b) description of the system result state after action application (set of couples "state attribute - value" and set of qualitative assessments of the result state relative to the objectives). An outcome is a result of action application to the real world situation.
3. If the index of retrieved case is completely similar to the current query (similarity value is equal 1), the solution of this case (the action) is a solution for the current problem.
4. If similarity value of the retrieved case is less than a lower threshold of similarity *LowerThreshold*, the decision-making task has no solution.
5. If similarity value of the retrieved case is between *LowerThreshold* and 1, then the solution of the matching cases is reused and revised. Reusing is implemented by applying adaptation rules that allow inferring how this retrieved solution (the action) can be adapted to the current query. After successful adaptation, the revision stage executes (see details below). Successfully revised actions constitute the decision-making task solution and are used as a solution for the new case.

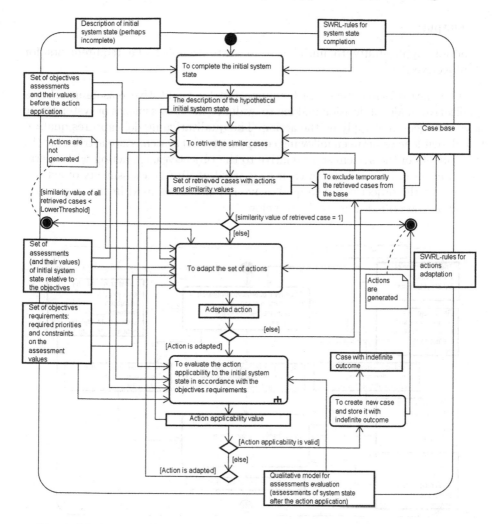

Fig. 2. Modified CBR-cycle for generation of actions (UML activity diagram)

Now let us consider in more detail the case revision stage (or action testing stage) (see Fig. 3). The task of case revision is defined as follows.

Input:

- required priority and constraint on the assessment value for each objective;
- availability of structural description items and relations between them;
- set of the attributes values of the system hypothetical initial state;
- set of the assessments values of the system initial state relative to the objectives;
- action application as a sequence of the applied operations. Each operation is described by its own attributes values and attributes values of used resources.

Output:

– action applicability to initial system state to meet the requirements for objectives.

The case revision stage can be supported by qualitative reasoning using a qualitative model of decision making to evaluate how assessments of system state have changed after applying the action. The qualitative model captures qualitative dependencies between following components: (a) system state attributes; (b) assessments of the system state relative to the objectives; (c) action with operations and used resources (with their own attributes); (d) assessments of actions relative to the objectives. The qualitative dependencies used in the qualitative model are described in more detail below.

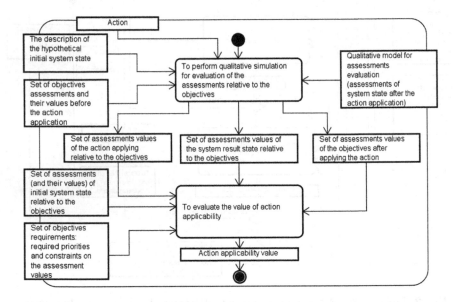

Fig. 3. Evaluation of action applicability to system initial state relative to the objectives (UML activity diagram)

The results of qualitative modeling are:

– set of assessments values of the objectives after applying the action;
– set of assessments values of the system result state relative to the objectives;
– set of assessments values of the applying action relative to the objectives.

Finally based on output assessments values and requirements for objectives a decision on the action applicability is made.

5 Ontological Knowledge Representation Model

To represent, integrate and manage different types of knowledge used in the decision-making process, we developed OWL DL ontology that includes the following components:

1. Domain-independent concepts.
2. General domain concepts:
   2.1. stakeholders objectives;
   2.2. system state description;
   2.3. action description;
   2.4. assessments of the system state and action relative to the stakeholders objectives.
3. Concepts for query description in terms of the task of action generation.
4. Concepts for case structure description.
5. Concepts for the description of the decision-making qualitative model:
   5.1. process fragment of the qualitative model;
   5.2. static fragment of the qualitative model;
   5.3. qualitative description of the system state;
   5.4. qualitative description of the action application;
   5.5. qualitative dependencies between variables and values.

Domain-independent concepts are used by other ontology components as variables, variable domains and inequalities. A variable is a characteristic of some entity the value can be assigned to. Variable domain is the range of values that a variable can take. A numeric domain is defined as the conjunction of intervals of a numerical axis (Fig. 4), an enumerated domain is a finite number of the disjoint values (Fig. 5).

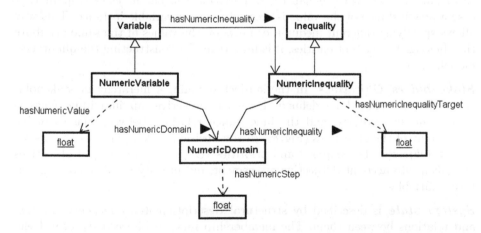

Fig. 4. Numeric variable and its domain (UML class diagram)

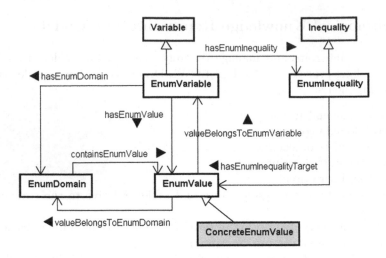

Fig. 5. Enum variable and its domain (UML class diagram)

Unlike an enumerated domain, the values in a qualitative domain form a totally ordered set. Each qualitative value is either a point or an interval [12], and within the domain these two types of qualitative value consecutively alternate (Fig. 6). To set the order of qualitative values, inequalities are used.

Inequalities $(<, \leq, =, \geq, >)$ specify an ordinal relation between two qualitative values or variable and value or two variables (Fig. 7), they also are used for setting the constraints to variables values.

There are different possible ways to specify collections of values (for domains of enum and qualitative values). We used a pattern that defines value collection as disjoint classes which exhaustively partition the parent class [13]. In that case a new instance of the value is created for each variable instance. This way allows specifying different inequalities between the values of the same attribute that belongs to different entities, it is important for constructing the qualitative model.

Stakeholders Objectives. In the subject domain, a hierarchy of stakeholders' objectives should be defined. For each objective, an individual class is created in the ontology, and the inheritance relations between classes define a hierarchy of the objectives (Fig. 8). In the decision making process the assessments (*ObjectiveAssessment*) and priorities (*ObjectivePriority*) of objectives are taken into account. Objective assessment and priority are defined as qualitative variables.

System state is described by structural description items *DescriptionItem* and relations between them. The membership relation between structural elements is obligatory. Using the membership relation we represent the system state in the form of a hierarchy of the description elements, where on the bottom level there are the attributes of the system state (Fig. 9). System

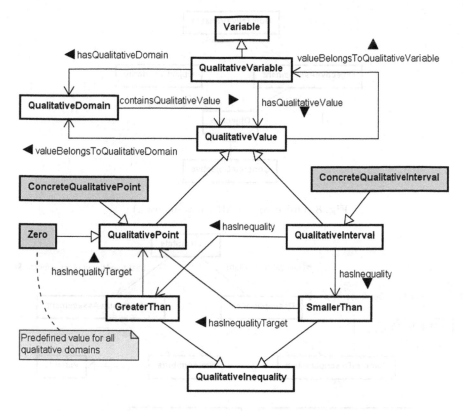

Fig. 6. Qualitative variable and its domain (UML class diagram)

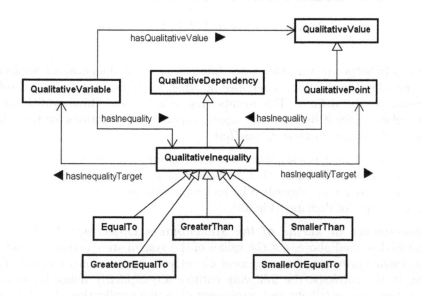

Fig. 7. Qualitative inequalities (UML class diagram)

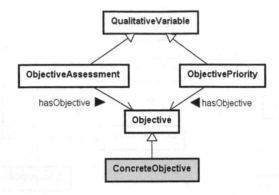

Fig. 8. Objectives (UML class diagram)

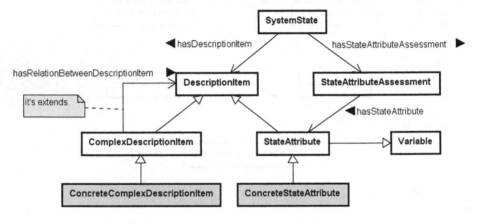

Fig. 9. System state (UML class diagram)

state attributes are variables with different types of domains. In addition to the membership relation, a number of other relations specific to the subject domain can be defined. The membership relation and these additional specific relations are defined as sub-object properties sub-relations for the relation *hasRelationBetweenDescriptionItem*.

Action is specified as a sequence of applied operations. Applying the operations requires the use of resources that are defined as separate entities. Each operation and each resource are described by its own attributes, which are variables with different types of domains (Fig. 10).

Assessments in Terms of the Stakeholders Objectives. In the decision process described above, not the values of the system state attributes, but their assessments in terms of management objectives are taken into account. Therefore, in the ontology, the following entities are explicitly defined: assessment of system state attribute and assessment of action application (Fig. 11). These assessments are qualitative variables.

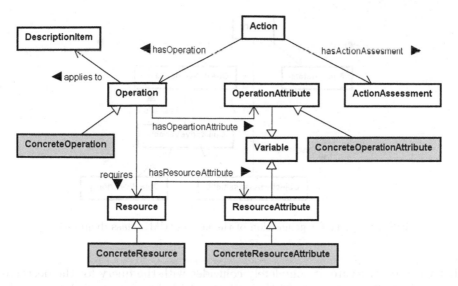

Fig. 10. Action, operations and resources (UML class diagram)

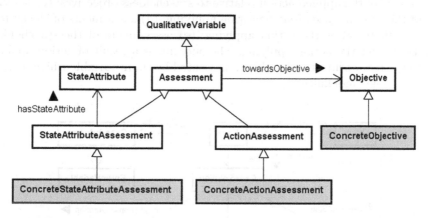

Fig. 11. Assessments of system state and action in terms of the objectives (UML class diagram)

Query for action generation defines the input data for decision-making problem and includes following components: (a) description of the initial system state; (b) subset of the assessments (and their values) of initial system state attributes; (c) assessments (and their values) of the stakeholders objectives before action has been applied; (d) required objectives priorities; (e) expected assessments values of the objectives after the action applying (Fig. 12). Expected assessments values are defined using inequalities described above.

Case consists of (a) index; (b) solution and (c) outcome (Fig. 13). The index defines the criteria for case retrieval and describes the state of the system when the case occurred and, if appropriate, what problem was needed to be solved at

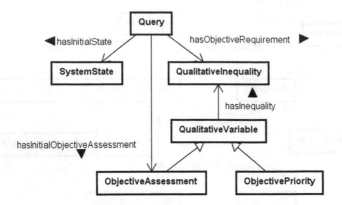

Fig. 12. Query for generation of the action (UML class diagram)

that time. In structure, it completely coincides with the query for the decision-making task. The structure of case solution includes: (a) applied action; (b) assessments of the applied action relative to stakeholders objectives; (c) description of the system state after the action applying; (d) assessments of the system state attributes after the action applying; (e) assessments of the stakeholders objectives after the action applying. The outcome is a result of action application to the real world situation. It is represented by enum variable which domain contains value "indefinite".

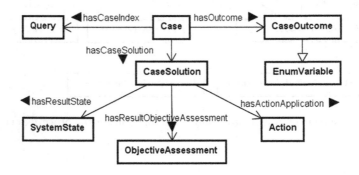

Fig. 13. Case structure (UML class diagram)

Qualitative model is a set of process fragments (Fig. 14). Each *process fragment* describes the change of assessments of the system state attributes, assessments of the action applying and assessments of the stakeholders objectives after the action applying to the initial system state. Process fragments have the form of a rule. This means that model components are incorporated as either conditions or consequences. The conditions include: (a) static fragment and (b) inequalities

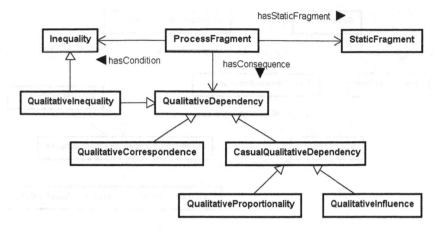

Fig. 14. Process fragment of the qualitative model (UML class diagram)

that set the constraints on the values of static fragment elements. The consequences are the qualitative dependencies between the elements of the static fragment. This means in other words that a dynamic fragment of the model can be applied when the instance of the static fragment exists for which the required constraints are satisfied. If these conditions are met, then the declared qualitative dependencies are applied to the static fragment.

Static fragment includes a structural description of (a) the system state, (b) the action applied, (c) assessments of objectives, and (d) objectives priorities. A structural description specifies only the presence of elements and relations between them. Therefore, static fragment can be represented as a connected graph of variables without values (Figs. 15, 16 and 17). The structure of components (c) and (d) of the static fragment is equivalent to the previously discussed entities. The structure of components (a) and (b) of the static fragment is complemented by qualitative variables that are analogs of the original attributes (Figs. 16 and 17). Analogs are created only for those attributes that participate in the consequences of the process fragment.

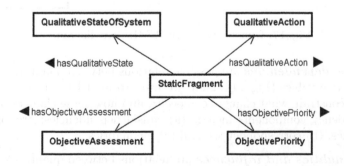

Fig. 15. Static fragment of the qualitative model (UML class diagram)

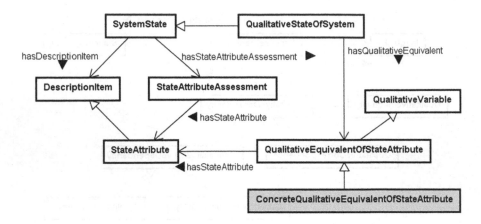

Fig. 16. Qualitative state of the system (UML class diagram)

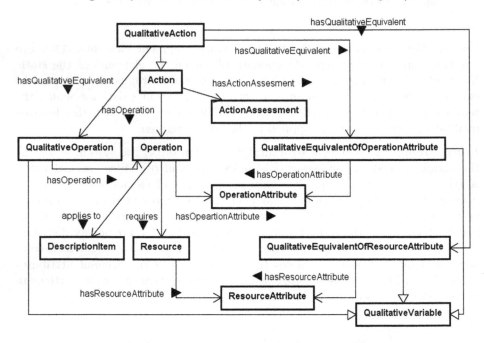

Fig. 17. Qualitative action (UML class diagram)

Qualitative dependencies are possible relations between qualitative variables and qualitative values (Fig. 14). They are used to model the processes causing change, to constrain what changes can occur, and how these changes occur [14]. The dependency components include (a) causal dependencies: proportionality and influence, (b) correspondences, and (c) inequalities.

Proportionalities and influences are relations between qualitative variables which indicate what qualitative variables in a model change (Fig. 18). These relations can be either positive or negative [12]. A positive proportionality indicates that the derivative of the target qualitative variable is positive if the derivative of the origin qualitative variable is positive, and is negative if the derivative of the origin qualitative variable is negative. For a negative proportionality this is just vice versa. A positive influence indicates that the target qualitative variable derivative is positive if the value of the origin qualitative variable is greater than zero, and negative if it less than zero. For the negative influence, this is just the other way around.

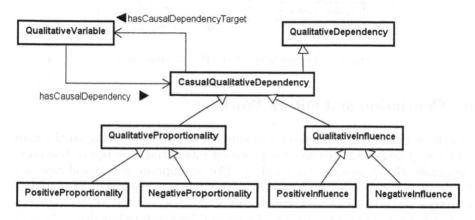

Fig. 18. Casual dependencies (UML class diagram)

Correspondences are relations between qualitative values of different variables (Fig. 19), and can be either directed or undirected [12]. The former means that when value A of variable X corresponds to value B of variable Y, the simulator derives that variable Y has value B when variable X has value A. If the correspondence is undirected, it also derives the value A of variable X when variable Y has value B.

Qualitative inequalities are considered and described above.

The designed ontology provides coupling various knowledge representation models (case model, rules, and qualitative model) used in the modified CBR-based decision-making cycle for system management. The ontology is invariant to the subject domain, it defines the skeleton of domain knowledge base. To use the ontology in the specific subject domain, we should complete it creating the following components: (a) concepts (classes) specific to the subject domain (in the figures they are marked in gray); (b) instances of cases; (c) instances of static and dynamic fragments of the qualitative model; (d) rules for query completion and case adaptation. In addition, it is necessary to design and implement similarity measures for the case retrieval relevant the ontology scheme and the subject domain specifics.

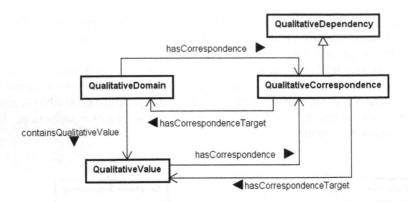

Fig. 19. Correspondences (UML class diagram)

6   Conclusion and Future Work

New knowledge-intensive approach to support of decision-making on the management of large-scale systems was proposed integrating case-based, rule-based and qualitative reasoning over ontology. The appropriate ontological representation for the wide range of used knowledge types was developed. The ontology is extensible, supports knowledge sharing and reuse, as well as the gathering knowledge in the subject domains. The general approach to intelligent decision-making described in the paper provides comprehensive support for all stages of CBR-based decision-making process using rule-based and qualitative reasoning, and general ontological representation of domain knowledge.

Proposed approach was implemented using following software tools: Protege/Stardog [15,16] for ontology development and performing rule-based reasoning over ontology; JColibri Studio [17] for generating CBR-system; Garp3 [18] for building and simulating the qualitative model. To integrate these tools with OWL-ontology, a special converter was designed and implemented. It converts the knowledge stored in OWL-ontology into a format supported by all used environments, and it also allows recording in the OWL-ontology the reasoning results obtained in these environments.

The validity and efficiency of the proposed general approach were proved in a number of test decision-making tasks in the field of ecology and environmental protection. In the nearest future it is planned to apply the developed approach for intelligent support of decision making on Volga-Akhtuba floodplain management.

Acknowledgement. This paper presents the results of research carried out under the RFBR grant 15-07-03541 Intelligent support of decision making in management of large-scale systems on the base of integration of different types of reasoning on ontological knowledge.

References

1. Karpov, L.E., Yudin, V.N.: Adaptivnoe upravlenie po precedentam, osnovannoe na klassifikacii sostoyanii upravlyaemyh ob'ektov. Trudy Instituta sistemnogo programmirovaniya, t.13, Moskva, ISP RAN, pp. 37–57 (2007)
2. Marling, C., Rissland, E., Aamodt, A.: Integrations with case-based reasoning. Knowl. Eng. Rev. **13**, 21–26 (2005)
3. Prentzas, J., Hatzilygeroudis, I.: Categorizing approaches combining rule-based and case-based reasoning. Expert Syst. **24**(2), 97–122 (2007)
4. Wriggers, P., Kultsova, M., Kapysh, A., Kultsov, A., Zhukova, I.: Intelligent decision support system for river floodplain management. In: Kravets, A., Shcherbakov, M., Kultsova, M., Iijima, T. (eds.) JCKBSE 2014. CCIS, vol. 466, pp. 195–213. Springer, Cham (2014). doi:10.1007/978-3-319-11854-3_18
5. El-Sappagh, S.H., Elmogy, M.: Case based reasoning: case representation methodologies. (IJACSA) Int. J. Adv. Comput. Sci. Appl. **6**(11), 192–208 (2015)
6. Díaz-Agudo, B., González-Calero, P.A.: An architecture for knowledge intensive CBR systems. In: Blanzieri, E., Portinale, L. (eds.) EWCBR 2000. LNCS, vol. 1898, pp. 37–48. Springer, Heidelberg (2000). doi:10.1007/3-540-44527-7_5
7. Chen, J., Chen, Y.: Research on operation standard expert system based on ontology and CBR. In: IEEE 18th International Conference on Industrial Engineering and Engineering Management (IE&EM) Part 3, pp. 1932–1936 (2011)
8. Guo, Y., Peng, Y., Hu, J.: Research on high creative application of case-based reasoning system on engineering design. J. Comput. Ind. **64**, 90–103 (2013)
9. Wriggers, P., Siplivaya, M., Joukova, I., Slivin, R.: Intelligent support of the preprocessing stage of engineering analysis using case-based reasoning. Eng. Comput. **24**(4), 383–404 (2008)
10. Zhukova, I., Kultsova, M., Navrotsky, M., Dvoryankin, A.: Intelligent support of decision making in human resource management using case-based reasoning and ontology. In: Kravets, A., Shcherbakov, M., Kultsova, M., Iijima, T. (eds.) JCKBSE 2014. CCIS, vol. 466, pp. 172–184. Springer, Cham (2014). doi:10.1007/978-3-319-11854-3_16
11. Kultsova, M., Rudnev, R., Anikin, A., Zhukova, I.: An ontology-based approach to intelligent support of decision making in waste management. In: 2016 7th International Conference on Information, Intelligence, Systems Applications (IISA), pp. 1–6 (2016)
12. Bredeweg, B., Linnebank, F., Bouwer, A., Liem, J.: Garp3 - workbench for qualitative modelling and simulation. Ecol. Inf. **4**(5–6), 263–281 (2009)
13. Rector, A.: Representing Specified Values in OWL: "value partitions" and "value sets". W3C Working Group Note, World Wide Web Consortium (W3C), May 2005. https://www.w3.org/TR/swbp-specified-values/
14. Liem, J., Bredeweg, B.: Document Type Definition (DTD) for QR Model Fragments Redime (2006). https://staff.fnwi.uva.nl/b.bredeweg/pdf/NNR/D2.3.1.pdf
15. Protege. A free, is open-source ontology editor and framework for building intelligent systems. http://protege.stanford.edu/
16. Stardog. The Enterprise Knowledge Graph. http://www.stardog.com/
17. JColibri Studio. http://gaia.fdi.ucm.es/research/colibri
18. Qualitative Reasoning & Modelling. https://ivi.fnwi.uva.nl/tcs/QRgroup/QRM/index.html

Technical System Modernization During the Operation Stage

Anna V. Matokhina$^{(\boxtimes)}$, Alexey V. Kizim, and Nikita A. Nikitin

Volgograd State Technical University, Volgograd, Russia
matokhina.a.v@gmail.com, {kizim,set.enter}@mail.ru

Abstract. This paper is devoted to such issues as artificial intelligence, ontological engineering, decision support, maintenance and repair, maintenance equipment, life cycle. The paper shows the basic procedure of the modernization and the knowledge representation models that used to organize the process of decision support. In this paper describes the process of developing an ontological knowledge model for general equipment by combining several basic classifiers for industrial equipment. Ontology files generating based on an analysis of the enterprise assets classifier texts showed. The features of each classifier and procedures of their union described. A description of some group's ontology described. The main classes in groups and examples of instances of classes identified. The presented algorithms predicting the state of the technical system. Illustrates the application of the developed methods on the example of the car.

Keywords: Artificial intelligence · Ontological engineering · Decision support · Maintenance and repair · Maintenance equipment · Life cycle

1 Introduction

The task of efficient operation, maintenance, repair and modernization of equipment during its life cycle is important for enterprises and organizations of various industries (general industrial equipment, hoisting, transport, electrical, mechanic, petrochemical, pipelines, boilers, pumping equipment, ventilation systems and other types of engineering).

From modern Russian works of methodological support of the tasks of organizing the operation of technical systems, the most important work is the book of Yashura [10]. But this work has a general methodological orientation and do not provide a complete solution of the problems. In international publications, there is an information of methodologies for improving the efficiency of equipment operation, for example, Failure Modes Effects Analysis (FMEA) and Failure Modes Effects and Criticality Analysis (FMECA) [12], Root Cause Analysis (RCA) [1], System Reliability Analysis, Fault Tree Analysis, Condition Monitoring and Condition Based Maintenance, Preventive Maintenance, Predictive Maintenance, Maintenance Task Analysis, Reliability, Availability, Maintainability and Safety (RAMS), Proactive Maintenance [2]. The most common are Reliability Centered Maintenance (RCM) [3], Total Maintenance Management and Total Productive Maintenance [4, 5]. However, these

A. Kravets et al. (Eds.): CIT&DS 2017, CCIS 754, pp. 350–360, 2017.
DOI: 10.1007/978-3-319-65551-2_25

methodologies also have a common organizational focus and do not include tools for specifying knowledge models about technical and organizational systems, as well as formalizing the positions and algorithms of these methodologies for automatization.

The analysis revealed a number of shortcomings in the methods of maintenance equipment used in enterprises, such as:

- the lack of modern methods for monitoring the condition of the main parameters of operation of the equipment;
- adaptation of permissible deviations of parameters in accordance with the life cycle of equipment;
- lack of methods for forecasting the condition of equipment based on monitoring data;
- not a qualitative system for diagnosing the state of equipment, identifying the failure and problems with identifying ways to eliminate it;
- adaptation of schedules for carrying out planned works to prevent failures, taking into account the results of monitoring and forecasting the condition of the equipment;
- an assessment of the results of the work performed to maintain a working condition, as well as to diagnose and eliminate failures.

As the main problems with solving the modernization task, it should be noted:

- lack of information on examples of solving similar tasks - precedents of modernization;
- difficulties in the forming of the main modernization goal, for the possibility of decomposition of tasks, the election of physical principles of action and structural elements;
- lack of necessary skills and competence for solving the problem of equipment modernization.

To date, there are a large number of devices that allow to monitor the performance of a technical system during operation. Examples include systems for monitoring temperature, pressure, position, engine speed, fluid level, etc. Some technical systems, such as cars, have built-in monitoring and diagnostic systems. But most often, enterprises use systems without built-in sensors.

2 Methods of Modernization of the Technical System at the Operation Stage

Under the modernization of the technical system is meant the replacement of individual units with more advanced ones, in order to increase reliability, durability, maintainability, and efficiency of system operation.

In general, the modernization process takes place with the permanent functional structure of the technical system and includes the following steps:

1. Determination the structure of the whole system.
2. Definition of the main goal of modernization:

(a) monitoring and diagnostics of the state of the technical system;
(b) analysis of parameters for each state of the technical system;
(c) forecasting the state of the technical system;
(d) expert evaluation of the technical system in order to identify the components being upgraded.
3. The formal definition of the of the object's parameters requiring modernization in order to achieve the goal.
4. Determine the components associated with the modifiable and input and output signals of each associated block.
5. Determination of the internal structure of the component to be modified.
6. Identification of the elements of the component that affect the main indicators defined in the modification purpose.
7. Development of modification options:
(a) Replacement of main components;
(b) Entire unit replacement.
8. Determining the possibility of modification.
9. Choosing a variant for modifying the component.
10. Preparation of specification for modernization.

In the process of analysis, the main modernization procedures were identified. Table 1 shows the procedures, decision methods and data and knowledge models planned for use.

Table 1. Procedures for the modernization of the technical system, the methods used in the implementation of procedures and the model for presenting data and knowledge for the implementation of procedures

Procedure	Data models and knowledge models	Solution methods
The definition of functional and parametric and geometric structure of the whole system	Ontology	Automated data entry and knowledge based on the upgraded technical system
Determination of the main modernization goal based on the observation and forecast of the state of the technical system	Ontology, SWRL or production rules	Logical conclusion based on expert knowledge from observations and forecasts
Formal definition of the task of modernization and the parameters of the object requiring modernization in order to achieve the goal	Ontology, CBR models	Search by use case, TIPS
Determination of elements that affect the basic parameters of modernization	Ontology, SPARQL queries	Automated analysis of data and knowledge about the structure, TIPS
Development of modernization options and determination of feasibility	Ontology, CBR models	Search by use case, TIPS
Choosing an option for upgrading the component	Ontology, expert assessments of options	Decision support

According to the results of the survey, ontology is chosen as the main model of knowledge representation about technical systems. The ontological model allows forming a hierarchy of classes of systems, to organize different by nature links among the elements of classes, to assign properties to classes and to use different types of data. In addition, there is an opportunity to enhance the competence of the ontology by appending production rules using SWRL methods, as well as using CBR methods for output on precedents. A taxonomy has been generated for all general industrial equipment described in the classifiers [6–8]. The process of ontology generation and the description of the resulting ontology is presented in [11].

3 Description of the First Step of Modernization and Maintenance Management

For each technical system, it is important to reasonably determine the time for timely maintenance and repair, on the basis of which they develop appropriate procedures and schedules. However, with the course of the life cycle, the performance parameters of the technical system deteriorate, which can lead to failures of technical systems. At the same time, the established planning system becomes inadequate. Thus, support for decision-making in diagnostic tasks becomes an essential stage in the management process in the face of growing amounts of heterogeneous information in modern society and the complexity of management objects.

To increase the effectiveness of diagnostic procedures, approaches combining the achievements of artificial intelligence, fuzzy mathematics, data mining, etc. should be used. One of the main tasks in the development of diagnostic expert systems is the formation and structuring of the knowledge system of the subject domain in question.

Diagnosis of the technical system is related to the analysis of its state. Monitoring the technical system allows obtaining complete information about the status of the technical system. Diagnosis of the state is usually performed by a specialist, which introduces subjectivity into the process and allows the appearance of unnecessary errors, which can lead to additional costs.

The process of diagnosing the technical system begins with monitoring (monitoring and dispatching) of components and complexes of the technical system. At present, self-monitoring and monitoring systems are actively developing and being introduced. Examples include monitoring systems for temperature, pressure, position, engine speed, fluid level, etc. However, their use increases the cost of maintenance and the qualification of personnel. The use of automation systems in the dispatching phase will significantly improve the efficiency, reduce costs of eliminating failures and increase the efficiency of the technical system.

For dispatching, it is suggested to use a multi-agent system, implemented as a software and hardware complex. The main idea of the multi-agent dispatching system is the organization of self-monitoring of the state of the technical system with the help of specialized agents. To implement the system diagnostics state of the technical system, the architecture of the corresponding software support system, shown in Fig. 1.

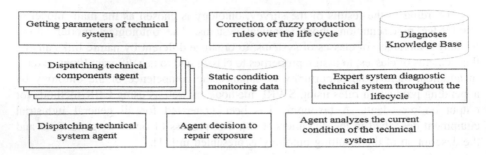

Fig. 1. Architecture of the software support system of diagnostics state of the technical system

4 Example of Multi-agent Systems of Fault Diagnosis and Forecasting of the Condition

Increasing the complexity of technical systems requires increasing the accuracy of determining the presence of malfunctions and their localization, to reduce maintenance costs and downtime of technical systems.

Any developed methods of detection and localization of faults are based on data mining technology.

One of the directions determining the improvement of the quality of information technologies for monitoring and diagnosing a technical condition should be considered intellectualization of the processes of processing diagnostic information using the technology of expert systems that can provide an improvement in the quality of recognition of the technical condition of the object.

Expert systems were the most widely used as decision support systems. Such systems can accumulate knowledge received by a person in various fields of activity. Through expert systems, it is possible to solve many modern problems, including management tasks.

Also, FMEA is used to diagnose faults in technical systems. FMEA (Procedures for Performing a Failure Mode, Effects and Criticality Analysis) is a procedure that analyzes all possible system errors and determines the results or effects on the system in order to classify all errors regarding their criticality for the system.

Forecasting the state of technical systems is presented in. In this paper, we describe the prediction of the state of a technical system using the example of a car brake system. Statistical analysis is used for forecasting.

Also, for the task of forecasting the state of a technical system, time series prediction methods are used.

During the development of the multi-agent systems of fault diagnosis and forecasting of the condition was developed a use case diagram presented in Fig. 2.

The most important component of multi-agent systems of fault diagnosis and forecasting of the condition is data analysis module.

Data analysis module is a class library and implemented in the Java language. This module implements two main functions: diagnostics and forecasting of the state of the technical system.

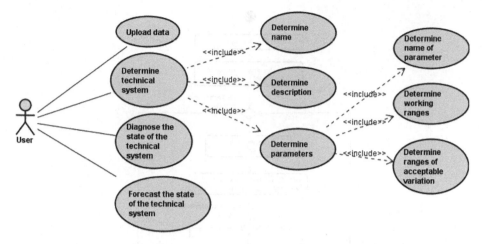

Fig. 2. Use case diagram of the multi-agent systems of fault diagnosis and forecasting of the condition

Algorithm for diagnosing the state of the technical system is shown in Fig. 3 and the algorithms for forecasting the state of the technical system is shown in Fig. 4.

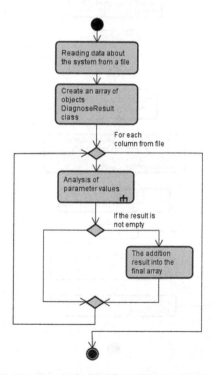

Fig. 3. Algorithms for diagnosing the state of the technical system

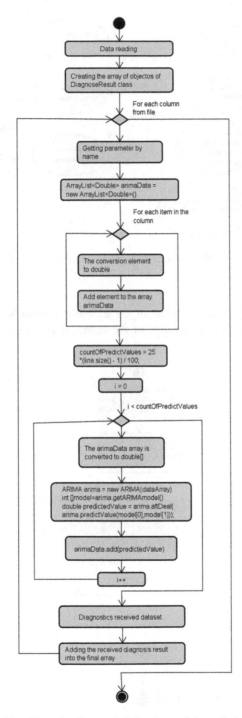

Fig. 4. Algorithms for forecasting the state of the technical system

5 The Experiment

As an experiment, three technical systems were taken, which were simplified for simplicity of analysis.

- Technical system: car. Parameters:
  - Intake Air Temperature. Working range: [21; 25], range of acceptable deviations: [20; 30].
  - Engine Coolant Temperature. Working range: [70; 90], range of acceptable deviations: [50; 110].
- Technical system: personal computer. Parameters:
  - CPU usage. Working range: [0; 50], range of acceptable deviations: [0; 75].
  - ROM usage. Working range: [20; 25], range of acceptable deviations: [0; 70].
- Technical system: printer EPSON L110. Parameters:
  - Print speed. Working range: [20; 25], range of acceptable deviations: [15; 25].
  - The number of black ink. Working range: [25; 100], range of acceptable deviations: [15; 100].

The results of the experiment are shown in Table 2.

Table 2. The results of the experiment

Technical system	Operation	The expected result	Obtained result
Car	Diagnosis of the technical system state	Intake Air Temperature – good condition Engine Coolant Temperature – good condition	Intake Air Temperature – good condition Engine Coolant Temperature – good condition
	Forecasting of the technical system state	Intake Air Temperature – normal condition Engine Coolant Temperature – good condition	Intake Air Temperature – normal condition Engine Coolant Temperature – good
Personal computer	Diagnosis of the technical system state	CPU usage – good ROM usage - normal	CPU usage – good ROM usage - normal
	Forecasting of the technical system state	CPU usage – good ROM usage - bad	CPU usage – good ROM usage - normal
Printer EPSON L110	Diagnosis of the technical system state	Print speed – good The number of black ink - bad	Print speed – good The number of black ink - bad
	Forecasting of the technical system state	Print speed – good The number of black ink - bad	Print speed – good The number of black ink - bad

To analyze the accuracy of forecasting of the technical system was constructed plots of real and predicted values for various parameters of different technical systems.

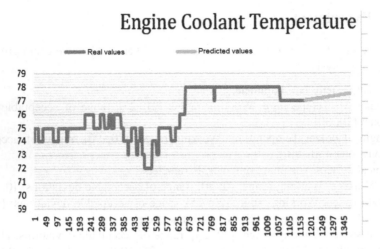

Fig. 5. Plot of the real and the predicted values for the parameter "Engine Coolant Temperature" technical system "Car".

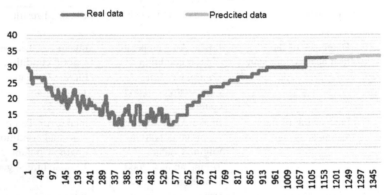

Fig. 6. Plot of the real and the predicted values for the parameter "Intake Air Temperature" technical system "Car".

Figure 5 shows a plot of the real and the predicted values for the parameter "Engine Coolant Temperature" technical system "Car".

Figure 6 shows a plot of the real and the predicted values for "Intake Air Temperature" parameter of the "Car" technical system.

6 Conclusion

In this paper, the software for modernization of the technical system at the operation stage was described. It also described methods of modernization of the technical system, including a description of the most suitable algorithm to different tasks. As the main model of knowledge representation about technical systems was chosen ontology. The ontological model allows forming a hierarchy of classes of systems, to organize different by nature links among the elements of classes, to assign properties to classes and to use different types of data. In addition, there is an opportunity to enhance the competence of the ontology by appending production rules using SWRL methods, as well as using CBR methods for output on precedents.

This work also contains a description of designing and developing multi-agent systems of fault diagnosis and forecasting of the condition. This system was implemented by Java and represents the class library.

During the experiment with this library the following results were obtained:
- diagnostics of the state of the technical system is carried out exactly - the expected and received diagnostic results coincide for all parameters of all technical systems;

The prediction for the "Personal computer" technical system for the "ROM usage" parameter showed a good value, instead of the expected normal, and therefore, forecasting does not always work correctly in all cases. This is a consequence of the fact that methods of predicting time series have some kind of error.

Results obtained with the support of the RFBR (projects numbers 16-07-00635 A, 16-47-340229 r-a).

References

1. Quintela Varajão, J.E., Cruz-Cunha, M.M., Putnik, G.D., Trigo, A. (eds.): CENTERIS 2010. CCIS, vol. 110. Springer, Heidelberg (2010). doi:10.1007/978-3-642-16419-4
2. Fitch, E.C.: Proactive Maintenance for Mechanical Systems. Elsevier Science Publishers, Amsterdam (1992)
3. Ammerman, M.: The Root Cause Analysis Handbook: A Simplified Approach to Identifying, Correcting, and Reporting Workplace Errors. Quality Resources, Clearwater (1998)
4. Cruz-Cunha, M.M.: Social Managerial and Organisational Dimension of Enterprise Information Systems. IGI Global Business Science Reference, Hershey (2009)
5. Ovoeye, D.M., Scherbakov, M.V., Kamaev, V.A.: A photovoltaic output backcast and forecast method based on cloud cover and historical data. In: Power and Energy Systems: Proceedings of the IASTED International Conference, pp. 28–31. Scopus, Phuket (2013)
6. North American Industry Classification System (NAICS). http://www.census.gov/cgi-bin/sssd/naics/naicsrch?chart=2012
7. North American Industry Classification System. http://en.wikipedia.org/wiki/North_American_Industry_Classification_System
8. NAICS Identification Tools | NAICS Association. http://www.naics.com/search/
9. Center for Economic Classifications (2015). http://www.okpd.org/okofvved.htm
10. Yashura, A.I.: System of Maintenance and Repairs of Power Equipment. Handbook, p. 504. NTs ENAS Publishing, Moscow (2006)

11. Kizim, A.V., Matokhina, A.V., Vayngolts, I.I., Shcherbakov, M.V.: Intelligent platform of monitoring, diagnosis and modernization of technical systems at various stages of life cycle. In: Proceedings of the 5th International Conference on System Modeling and Advancement in Research Trends, SMART 2016 (2017)

12. Kizim, A.V.: Justification of the need to automate the repairs and maintenance of equipment. In: VSTU, A Series of "Actual Problems of Management, Computer Science and Informatics Technological Systems", vol. 6, No 6, pp. 118–121, Volgograd (2009)

13. Deerwester, S., Dumais, S.T., Furnas, G.W., Landauer, T.K., Harshman, R.: Indexing by latent semantic analysis. J. Am. Soc. Inf. Sci. **41**, 391–407 (1990)

14. Tyukov, A.P., Brebels, A., Shcherbakov, M.V., Kamaev, V.A.: A concept of web-based energy data quality assurance and control system. In: iiWAS 2012: Proceedings of the 14th International Conference on Information Integration and Web-based Applications & Services (Bali, Indonesia, 3–5 December 2012), pp. 267-271. Association for Computing Machinery, Inc. (ACM), New York (2012)

15. Denisov, M., Kizim, A., Kamaev, V., Davydova, S., Matohina, A.: Solution on decision support in determining of repair actions using fuzzy logic and agent system. In: Kravets, A., Shcherbakov, M., Kultsova, M., Iijima, T. (eds.) JCKBSE 2014. CCIS, vol. 466, pp. 533–541. Springer, Cham (2014). doi:10.1007/978-3-319-11854-3_46

16. Panteleev, V.V., Kamaev, V.A., Kizim, A.V.: Developing a model of equipment maintenance and repair process at service repair company using agent-based approach. Proc. Technol. **16**, 1072–1079 (2014)

17. Panteleev, V., Kizim, A., Kamaev, V., Shabalina, O.: Developing a model of multi-agent system of a process of a tech inspection and equipment repair. In: Kravets, A., Shcherbakov, M., Kultsova, M., Iijima, T. (eds.) JCKBSE 2014. CCIS, vol. 466, pp. 457–465. Springer, Cham (2014). doi:10.1007/978-3-319-11854-3_39

18. Kizim, A.V.: Objectives and methods of maintenance and repairs of equipment throughout its life cycle. In: News VSTU, Series "Actual Problems of Management, Computer Science and Informatics in Technical Systems", vol. 13, No. 4(91), pp. 55–59. Interuniversity Collection of Scientific Articles, Volgograd (2012)

19. Tyukov, A.P., Shcherbakov, M.V., Brebels, A.: Automatic two way synchronization between server and multiple clients for HVAC system. In: The 13th International Conference on Information Integration and Web-based Applications & Services (iiWAS 2011), pp. 467–470. Association for Computing Machinery, Ho Chi Minh (2011)

20. Kizim, A.V., Kamaev, V.A., Denisov, M.V.: Information decision support system (ISPPR) for planning maintenance and repairs of road equipment. Innov. Based Inf. Commun. Technol. **1**, 402–404 (2013)

21. Oliveira, V., Torgo, L.: Ensembles for time series forecasting. In: JMLR: Workshop and Conference Proceedings, ACML, pp. 360–370 (2014)

22. Chatfield, C.: The Analysis of Time Series: An Introduction, 6th edn. CRC Press, Boca Raton (2013)

23. Hyndman, R.J, Khandakar, Y.: Automatic time series forecasting: the forecast package for R. J. Stat. Softw. **27**(3) (2008)

A Model of Control of Expert Estimates Consistency in Distributed Group Expertise

Aleksandr Podvesovskii$^{(\boxtimes)}$ ⓘ, Oksana Mikhaleva ⓘ,
Vladimir Averchenkov, Aleksandr Reutov, and Leonid Potapov

Bryansk State Technical University,
50 let Oktyabrya Ave., 7, 241035 Bryansk, Russia
`apodv@tu-bryansk.ru`

Abstract. The article continues the series of publications of materials of the authors' research in the field of mathematical modeling and computer support of tasks of group expert estimation of objects in conditions of distributed interaction of experts. Main stages of group expertise supporting process in distributed expert networks are considered, and general principles of its modeling are discussed. Methods for assessing the consistency of the set of individual expert judgments, taking into account the degree of competence of experts, as well as procedures for feedback with experts, aimed to achieve a level of consistency sufficient to use individual expert estimates as the basis for determining the final group assessments that satisfy the consistency requirements and solvency are used. Implementation specifics of these methods and procedures are discussed with respect to ordinal and numerical estimate scales. A model is proposed for managing the consistency of expert estimates, which unites methods of assessing consistency and procedures for increasing coherence in a unified management loop based on feedback from experts and taking into account the specific of experts' work in a distributed environment.

Keywords: Decision support · Expert estimates · Group expertise · Consistency of expert estimates · Evaluation of expert competency · Coefficient of concordance · Spectral coefficient of consistency

1 Introduction

With the development of the information society, new information technologies for supporting managerial activities are emerging and are actively developing. One of them is the technology of information and expert-analytical support for the development, analysis, and adoption of management decisions. At the same time, the current level of development of information and communication technologies enables the organization of distributed interaction among experts, as well as with decision-makers (DM) and experts, using modern communication networks and, first of all, the Internet [1]. Thanks to the above circumstances, a new technology of expert evaluation has arisen, called e-expertise, within which expert networks and networked expert communities are actively developing [3, 5].

© Springer International Publishing AG 2017
A. Kravets et al. (Eds.): CIT&DS 2017, CCIS 754, pp. 361–374, 2017.
DOI: 10.1007/978-3-319-65551-2_26

Thus, it is possible to draw a conclusion about the relevance of research aimed at creating and developing mathematical models and information technologies to support e-network activity. Here we can distinguish two groups of tasks:

(1) adaptation of mathematical models and methods for making group decisions to ensure the possibility of their use in a distributed environment;
(2) software support for e-expertise and development and decision-making processes in conditions of distributed interaction between decision-makers and experts.

In [6], authors considered one of the most important and widely used decision-making tasks, the task of group expert estimation of objects, and approaches to its modeling in the distributed work of experts were investigated. For this problem, a generalized algorithm was proposed and an information model of support for group expertise in distributed expert networks was built. On the basis of this, a complex of mathematical models was determined, the development and investigation of which are necessary to provide software support for group expertise in a distributed environment. In this paper, one of these models is proposed, a model for managing the consistency of expert estimates, the purpose of which is to ensure the possibility of using individual expert assessments of objects as a basis for the formation of final group assessments that satisfy the requirements of consistency and substantiality.

2 Statement and Features of Modeling the Task of Group Expert Evaluation in a Distributed Environment

In this section, we give a brief description of the general approach to modeling the processes of supporting distributed group expertise and identify those tasks that will be considered in detail later. The material of the section is based on the results of authors presented in [6].

The task of group expert evaluation allows the following formal representation:

$$< T, D, X, K, F, H, C; X^* > , \qquad (1)$$

Where T is the type of task (selection, ranking or evaluation); $D \in U$ is the subject area of the task; $X = \{x_1, x_2, ..., x_n\}$ is the set of objects of expert evaluation (in the role of which alternatives, outcomes, development scenarios, risks, etc. may appear); K is the criterion on the basis of which the selection, ranking or evaluation of objects is carried out; F is the additional information, depending on the type of task; $H = \{H_1, H_2, ..., H_m\}$ is the set of experts selected to solve the problem; C is the formalized information on the competence of experts in the context of the problem being solved; X^* is the final solution of the problem.

The information C is usually given in the form of a set of degrees of relative competence of experts in the relevant subject area but may have a more complex representation. The additional information F depends on the type of the task and, as a rule, is given in the form of restrictions related to parameters of the evaluation procedure.

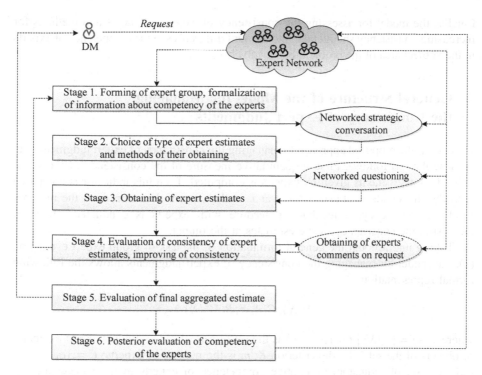

Fig. 1. Diagram of a generalized algorithm for supporting group expertise in a distributed environment (source: [6])

In Fig. 1 a diagram of a generalized algorithm for supporting group expertise in a distributed environment is given. The diagram shows steps corresponding to tasks that arise during this process, as well as e-expert procedures necessary to support their solution.

Analyzing this algorithm, we can note the following. The process of group examination takes passes in three consecutive stages: the preparation for examination (stage 1), the examination itself (stages 2–3) and the processing of examination results (steps 4–6). At the same time, stage 4 plays a key role at the stage of processing the results of the examination, since on it the decision on the possibility of further use of the set of individual expert estimates obtained in the previous stage for calculating a consistent final assessment reflecting the opinion of the expert group as a whole (or detailing some of its significant subsets) is made.

There are many methods for consistency estimate, each of which is focused on working with a specific type of expert estimate [2]. At the same time, along with the choice of the method for estimate the consistency of expert judgments' set, it is also necessary to determine the criterion for assessing its sufficiency (establishing the applicability of this set for further processing). In addition, it is necessary not only to assess the consistency of expert judgments but also to provide measures aimed at enhancing it. Thus, it is required to develop a feedback mechanism that provides the opportunity to promptly adjust expert estimates in the mode of interactive communication with experts.

Finally, the model for assessing the consistency of expert judgments and methods for increasing consistency should take into account differences in the competence of experts in the subject area of the problem being solved.

3   General Structure of the Model for Managing the Consistency of Expert Judgments

In general, the proposed approach to managing the consistency of expert judgments can be described as follows. First, a quantitative measure of the consistency of the set of individual assessments given by experts is computed. Then this indicator is compared with the thresholds established for it and, in the case of deviation from the required level of consistency, a feedback procedure with experts is conducted, aimed at increasing the consistency of the estimates at the output.

Taking into account the general formulation of the task of group expert evaluation (1), the model for managing the consistency of expert judgments allows the following formal representation:

$$< V(X), C, A, Y, B; V^*(X) > ,$$

where $V(X) = \{V_i(X) \mid i = 1, \ldots, m\}$ is the set of formalized individual expert estimates of objects of the set X by the criterion K; m is the number of experts; $C = \{c_1, c_2, \ldots, c_m\}$ is a set of indicators of relative competence of experts in the subject area of expertise, satisfying the conditions of:

$$c_i > 0; \quad \sum_{i=1}^{m} c_i = 1,$$

A is the procedure for estimating the consistency of the set $V(X)$, depending on the type of estimates and taking into account the information C on the competence of experts; Y is the criterion for assessing the sufficiency of consistency, B is the procedure for feedback with experts; $V^*(X)$ is the set of agreed expert estimates.

Depending on the selected evaluation system, the set of evaluations of $V_i(X)$ obtained from the i-th expert may have a different formal representation. In this article, we restrict ourselves to two types of estimates – ordinal and cardinal absolute. Accordingly, for ordinal estimation the set $V_i(X)$ is represented by a set of individual rankings:

$$V_i(X) = R_i = \{r_{ij}\} \; (j = 1, \ldots, n), \tag{2}$$

where r_{ij} is the rank assigned by the i-th expert to the x_j object, and for cardinal absolute estimation by the set of numerical estimates:

$$V_i(X) = W_i = \{w_{ij}\} \; (j = 1, \ldots, n), \tag{3}$$

where w_{ij} is the numerical estimate assigned by the i-th expert to the x_j object.

As it was already noted, the introduction of the feedback mechanism into the model allows, with the insufficient consistency of the set of expert assessments, to carry out their adjustment aimed at increasing the consistency in the mode of interactive interaction with experts. The specified interaction is realized with the help of the e-expert procedure "Obtaining Expert Comments on Demand" (see Fig. 1). In fact, this mechanism implements a control action to reduce the deviation of the degree of consistency of the set of expert judgments from a given threshold value. With this in mind, the model for managing the consistency of expert judgments can be presented in the form of a loop with feedback that implements the principle of deviation management.

The block diagram of this loop is shown in Fig. 2. Here $L_C(V)$ is the quantitative characteristic (coefficient) of the consistency of expert judgments $V(X)$, obtained with the help of procedure A; Z is the estimation of the sufficiency of consistency, calculated on the basis of criterion Y; U is the control action.

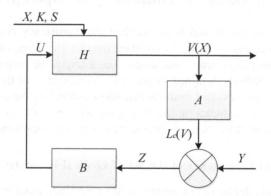

Fig. 2. Representation of a model for managing the consistency of expert judgments in the form of a loop with feedback

Let us consider the general principle of functioning of the proposed loop. The first step after obtaining a set of individual estimates of objects $V(X)$ is to check the consistency of the given set, taking into account the information C on the competence of experts. The result of this check is the calculation of the primary consistency coefficient $L_C(V)$. Further, it is necessary to establish whether the degree of consistency of the set of expert estimates is sufficient to be able to be used to calculate the aggregated estimate. To this end, a criterion for estimating the sufficiency of consistency Y is introduced based on certain threshold values of the consistency coefficient (see below). The value of the consistency coefficient $L_c(V)$ is compared with the threshold values in the comparison block. If the consistency of expert judgments is not sufficient, but it is recognized that it is possible to increase it, then a transition to estimates' correction is made through the feedback procedure B. Within the framework of this procedure, an expert is selected who is invited to change his estimate in a certain direction (the principles for selecting an expert and directions for changing the assessment will be described later) – this is the control effect of U. If the expert agrees to change his estimate, then along with the result of change the coefficient of consistency is recalculated. The expert also has the right not to change his judgment – in this case, the next step will be an attempt to select another expert. The consistency management process continues until a sufficient its level is reached, or until you have exhausted the possibility of appeal to experts. In the latter case, it is concluded that it is not possible to obtain an agreed estimate for the existing expert group.

Thus, in order to formalize the process of managing the consistency of expert judgments, it is necessary to build:

(1) the consistency estimate model based on procedure A using the criterion for assessing the sufficiency of consistency Y;
(2) the model for increasing consistency based on procedure B.

Let us turn to the consideration of each of these models.

4   Model for Assessing the Consistency of Expert Judgments

The main purpose of this model is to calculate the consistency coefficient $L_C(V)$ for a set of individual estimates $V(X)$. As noted earlier, for each type of expert estimates, there are approaches to assessing consistency. Accordingly, the proposed model should be based both on methods designed to assess the consistency of the set of individual rankings (ordinal estimates) and methods that allow evaluating the consistency of a set of numerical values (cardinal absolute estimates). In both cases, an important requirement for these methods is the consideration of the competence of experts.

4.1   Coefficient of Consistency of the Set of Ordinal Estimates

As an estimate of the degree of consistency of the set of individual rankings of the form (2), rank correlation indicators usually appear [4] – the consistency of rankings using these indicators is interpreted as the strength of the relationship between them. In this case, the concordance coefficient is most often used, since it is applicable both to an arbitrary number of evaluated objects and for an arbitrary number of experts. However, a significant limitation of this indicator is the lack of possibility to take into account the competence of experts (it is assumed that all experts have the same competence). A method for overcoming this restriction is proposed in [9], according to which the ranking R_i obtained from the expert H_i is replaced by the set containing k_i of its copies, where k_i is an integer, $c_i = \eta k_i$ ($i = 1, \ldots, m$), η is the greatest common divisor for the competence coefficients of experts $c_i \in C$. As a result of combining the sets obtained in this way for all experts, the task of calculating the concordance coefficient of a set of individual rankings, given by m experts of different competencies, is reduced to the task of determining the concordance coefficient of a set of rankings, given by k experts, each of which has competence η, where

$$k = \sum_{i=1}^{m} k_i.$$

The formula for calculating the corresponding modified concordance coefficient has the form [9]:

$$K_R(V) = \frac{12}{n(n^2-1)} \sum_{j=1}^{n} \left(\frac{n+1}{2} - \sum_{i=1}^{m} c_i r_{ij}\right)^2. \tag{4}$$

Values are taken by this coefficient range from 0 (complete inconsistency of the set of individual rankings) to 1 (complete coincidence of individual rankings).

Thus, the modified concordance coefficient (4) is an adequate model for estimating the consistency of the set of individual rankings of the form (2) if the information on expert competence is represented in the form of a set of coefficients c_j. That is, as the consistency coefficient of the specified set, we take:

$$L_C(V) = K_R(V). \tag{5}$$

4.2 Coefficient of Consistency of the Set of Cardinal (Absolute) Estimates

To assess the consistency of the set of numerical values of the form (3), it is suggested to use the so-called spectral approach [7], whose general idea is to estimate the amount of information contained in the set of individual estimates given by experts to each object $x_j \in X$.

Let there be given a set $W = \{w_i \mid i = 1, \ldots, m\}$ of expert estimates of some object. Elements v_i can be represented as numbers of the scale divisions in which the estimates are measured. Let the total number of divisions be p.

We represent the set W in the form of a weighted spectrum, by which is meant the p-component vector $S = (\sigma_1, \sigma_2, \ldots, \sigma_p)$, where σ_k is the sum of coefficients of relative competence c_i of experts whose estimates are represented by the k-th division of the scale. As an indicator of the consistency of this set, we will use the spectral coherence coefficient [9], calculated using the following formula:

$$K_S(W) = \left(1 - \frac{\sum_{k=1}^{p} \sigma_k \left|k - \sum_{k=1}^{p} k\sigma_k\right| - \sum_{k=1}^{p} \sigma_k \ln(\sigma_k)}{G \sum_{k=1}^{p} |k - (p+1)/2| \ln(p)}\right) z, \tag{6}$$

where $G = m/\ln(m) \, p \, \ln(p)$ is the scale factor;

$$z = \begin{cases} 1 & \text{if } z* = TRUE; \\ 0 & \text{if } z* = FALSE, \end{cases}$$

$$z* = \overline{[k(1) = 1]} \vee \overline{[k(q) = p]} \overset{q-1}{\underset{d=1}{\vee}} \overline{[\sigma_{k(d)} = \sigma_{k(d+1)}]} \overset{q-1}{\underset{d=1}{\vee}} \overline{[k(d) - k(d+1) = const]}. \tag{7}$$

The expression (7) is a Boolean function that defines the necessary and sufficient conditions for the consistency coefficient $K_S(W)$ to be equal to zero. In this case, q is the number of subgroups of experts who gave the same estimates, $k(d)$ is the scale division number corresponding to the evaluation obtained from the experts of the d-th subgroup $(d = 1, \ldots, q)$, $\sigma_{k(d)}$ is the sum of the competence coefficients of experts d-th subgroup.

It can be seen from formulas (6) and (7) that the spectral consistency coefficient takes values within the interval $[0, 1]$, where the value of 1 corresponds to the fully consistent set of expert estimates, and the value 0 is completely inconsistent. More precisely, $K_S(W) = 0$ if each of the following conditions is met:

(a) among the estimates there are scale divisions with minimal and maximal numbers (the first two disjunctive terms of expression (7));
(b) the sum of the competence coefficients of experts who gave each of the estimates is the same (the third disjunctive term of expression (7));
(c) differences between values of two neighboring estimates are the same (estimates are uniformly distributed over the scale – the last disjunctive term of expression (7)).

It should be noted that the spectral consistency coefficient (6) is calculated for a set of expert estimates of an individual object. Hence, in the presence of the set of cardinal estimates presented in the form (3), the consistency of the expert judgments is evaluated separately for each object $x_j(j = 1, \ldots, n)$, and if the consistency is to be increased, the feedback procedure B is also performed separately for each x_j. This is one of the important differences in the case under consideration from the case of ordinal estimates when the consistency assessment and its enhancement are carried out simultaneously for a set of estimates of all objects.

Thus, as the consistency coefficient of the set $V(x_j)$ containing expert estimates of the object x_j, we take the spectral coefficient calculated for the given set, taking into account the competence of experts:

$$L_C\big(V(x_j)\big) = K_S\big(V(x_j)\big). \tag{8}$$

4.3   Evaluation of Sufficiency of Consistency

The sufficiency of the consistency of the set $V(X)$ is estimated using the Y criterion, which is based on the comparison of the calculated $L_C(V)$ consistency coefficient with some specially defined threshold values. As such values, it is suggested to use the detection threshold and the application threshold [7, 9], the first of which establishes the availability of information in the set of expert assessments $V(X)$, and the second - the sufficiency of this information in order to be able to trust the results of the assessment.

More specifically, the detection threshold T_o is the consistency coefficient of the set of expert estimates containing the minimum amount of information (subject to equal expert competence). The threshold of application T_u is the coefficient of consistency of the set of expert estimates, which provides the calculation of the aggregated expert estimate with an allowable accuracy. For each type of assessment (ordinal, cardinal), its own methods of calculating threshold values are used, which will be discussed below.

The result of mapping Z can be used to make a decision about the possibility of further use of the set $V(X)$. There are three possible cases. If

$$L_C(V) < T_o, \tag{9}$$

then the set $V(X)$ does not contain information, and it is necessary to invite all experts to reconsider their estimates of objects or replace the expert group. If

$$T_o \leq L_C(V) < T_u, \tag{10}$$

then the set $V(X)$ contains information, but the degree of its consistency is not sufficient to determine the aggregated estimate with acceptable accuracy, and measures aimed at increasing the consistency are needed. Finally, if

$$L_C(V) \geq T_u, \tag{11}$$

then the consistency of the set $V(X)$ is sufficient to use it to calculate the resulting aggregated estimate.

4.4 Calculation of Threshold Values for a Set of Ordinal Estimates

Following [9], we use the consistency coefficients (5) calculated for the specially constructed ranking sets as threshold values.

We will assume that the set of rankings is completely inconsistent (not containing information) if all objects in it have the same sums of ranks. In this case, according to the formula (4), deviations of the sum of the ranks of all objects from the mean value are equal to zero, and the concordance coefficient takes a zero value.

Obviously, the set of rankings will contain minimal information in the case when the sum of ranks of all objects will differ from the average value by the minimum value. Such set can be obtained from a completely inconsistent set by permuting in one and in only one individual ranking of any two objects having adjacent ranks. Accordingly, as a detection threshold the coefficient of consistency of a given set, calculated under the condition of equal competence of experts is adopted:

$$T_o = \frac{24}{m^2(n^3 - n)}.$$

As the application threshold, the coefficient of consistency of ranking set containing some initial ranking and all rankings obtained from it by a predetermined number of permutations of objects having neighboring ranks is adopted. To formalize this definition, we use the notion of distance between rankings and the set of generated rankings [9].

The distance $l(R_i, R_k)$ between rankings R_i, R_k is the number of permutations of objects having neighboring ranks in the ranking R_j that must be performed in order to convert the ranking R_i into R_k.

The set $Q(R_i, l)$ of rankings generated by the ranking R_i and the distance l is the set of rankings, for each of which the distance to R_i is equal to l. It can be shown that $|Q(R_i, l)| = n - l$.

In view of the concepts introduced, the threshold for application T_u for the set of individual rankings of n objects is defined as the value of the consistency coefficient of ranking set $\{R_i\} \cup Q(R_i, l)$ containing some arbitrary ranking and the set of rankings generated by this ranking and distance l for a number of equally competent experts equal to $(n - l + 1)$. The value of l must satisfy the constraint $l \leq [m/2]$, in practice, it is recommended to use $l = 1$ or $l = 2$ (for the number of experts $m \geq 4$).

It is obvious that the value of the application threshold T_u does not depend on the specific kind of ranking, but is determined by the number n of objects being ranked and the value of l.

4.5   Calculation of Threshold Values for a Set of Cardinal Estimates

Following [7], we use as threshold values spectral consistency coefficients (6) calculated for specially constructed sets of cardinal expert estimates of an object.

As the detection threshold T_o, the coefficient of consistency of the spectrum S_o containing the minimum amount of information (assuming equal competence of experts) is adopted.

By analogy with rankings, we will consider spectrum as completely inconsistent (not containing information) in which each scale division was chosen by exactly one expert as an estimate. From this spectrum, it is possible to obtain the S_o spectrum by shifting one of the estimates along the scale, so that the average value of the obtained spectrum differs from the original one by one scale division. Thus, this spectrum will contain p components, which are specified as follows:

$$s_k = \begin{cases} 0 & 0 \text{ if } k = 1; \\ 2/p & \text{if } k = [0.5p + 1]; \\ 1/p & \text{otherwise.} \end{cases}$$

As a threshold of application T_u, the consistency coefficient of the set of expert estimates is adopted, which ensures the calculation of the aggregated expert judgment with an allowable accuracy. In the role of such set, there may be a set that contains two estimates of equally competent experts, separated by b scale divisions. The choice of the value of b is determined by requirements for the quality of expert judgments (usually $b = 1$ is taken). So, if the scale has p divisions, then for the construction of such spectrum it can be assumed that fissions with numbers $[0.5p]$ and $[0.5p + 1]$ are chosen as estimates.

5 The Model for Increasing the Consistency of the Set of Expert Judgments Based on the Feedback Procedure with Experts

As it was shown above, the result of evaluating the sufficiency of the consistency of a set of expert judgments is the fulfillment of one of the conditions (9)–(11). In this case, the process of increasing the consistency is initiated when condition (10) is satisfied. As it was noted earlier, on the basis of this process is the feedback procedure B, within the framework of which there is a call to the selected expert with a proposal to change his earlier estimate in order to increase the overall consistency of the set $V(X)$.

The process of increasing the consistency of the set of expert assessments is constructed as follows (Fig. 3). Let E be the set of experts to which it is possible to appeal for a change in the estimate. Before starting the process, we believe that this set includes all the experts participating in the assessment, i.e. $E = H$. The expert $H_i \in E$ is chosen (usually from among the least competent ones), and the direction in which this expert needs to change his estimate to increase the $L_C(V)$ consistency coefficient is determined, as a result of which the expert H_i receives a corresponding request. The specific rules for selecting experts and the formation of queries to them depend on the type of assessments (ordinal, cardinal) and will be considered later. If the expert agrees to change the estimate, the set $V(X)$ is corrected accordingly, the new value of the consistency coefficient $L_C(V)$ is calculated, and the fulfillment of conditions (10)–(11) is checked. If condition (11) is satisfied, the process of increasing the consistency is completed, and if condition (10) is still satisfied, then another expert from the set E is selected, and the steps described above are repeated with this expert. If the expert H_i refuses to correct the estimate, then it is excluded from the set E, and another expert is selected with which similar actions are performed.

If at some point, the set E is empty, but the condition (10) is still satisfied, then it means that the possibilities for increasing the consistency of the set of expert estimates have been exhausted, although a sufficient level of consistency has not been achieved. In this case, it is necessary to decide whether to use the existing set of assessments, despite its lack of consistency, or about a complete or partial change in the composition of the expert group and conducting a re-evaluation session.

Let us consider the rules for selecting experts from the set E and generating queries for them for each type of evaluation.

5.1 Rules for Selecting Experts and Generating Queries Using Ordinal Estimates

For ordinal estimates, we use the approach proposed in [10]. From the set E, the expert H_i is chosen with the least coefficient of competence c_i, and for this rank $R_i \in R$ a set Q $(R_i, 1)$ is formed, which contains all possible rankings obtained from R_i by permuting two objects with adjacent ranks – the number of such rankings, as it was noted earlier, is equal to $n - 1$. We denote these rankings as $Q_{ik}(k = 1, \ldots, n - 1)$.

Further, based on the initial set of individual rankings R, the $(n - 1)$ sets $\tilde{R}_{ik}$ are constructed by replacing the R_i ranking by rankings Q_{ik}. For each such set, the

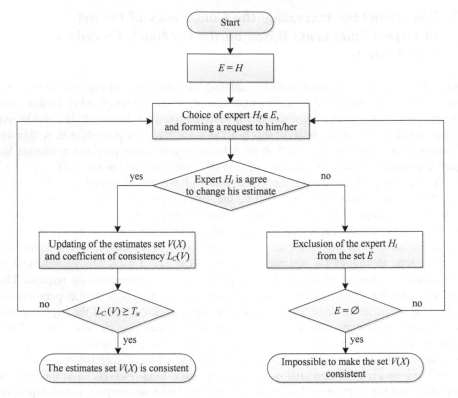

Fig. 3. Scheme of the process of increasing the consistency of the set of expert estimates

consistency coefficient (5) is calculated, and a set $\tilde{R}_{\beta k}$ corresponding to the largest value of this coefficient is selected. The set $\tilde{R}_{\beta k}$ is built on the basis of $Q_{\beta k}$ ranking, which thus sets the permutation of two objects with adjacent rankings, leading to the greatest increase in consistency. Let these be the objects x_k and x_h. Thus, the request to the selected expert H_i should be formed as a proposal to swap the objects x_k and x_h in the ranking.

Accordingly, in the event that the expert H_i refuses to rearrange objects, the next appeal will be addressed to an expert with the lowest coefficient of competence among all experts entering the set E after removing H_i from it.

5.2 Rules for Selecting Experts and Generating Queries Using Cardinal Estimates

In the case of cardinal estimates, we can use the approach proposed in [8]. For the set $W = \{w_1, \ldots, w_m\}$ of estimates of the corresponding object, the average score is calculated taking into account the competence of experts:

$$w_0 = \sum_{i=1}^{m} c_i w_i,$$

and the expert H_i is selected, for which

$$\delta_i = \frac{|w_i - w_0|}{c_i},$$

is the largest value, characterizing the deviation of the given estimate from the average score for the group, taking into account the competence (with a decrease in the competence of the expert, the degree of confidence in his opinion decreases when it differs from the "middle group" one).

Depending on the sign of the difference $(w_i - w_0)$, the direction in which the expert H_i should change the estimate w_i to reduce the value of δ_i is determined. Thus, the request to the expert H_i is formed in the form of a proposal to increase or decrease the estimate of the object given by him. If the expert H_i refuses to change his mind, the next appeal will be addressed to the expert, for which the value of δ_i is the largest among all experts entering the set E after removing H_i from it.

5.3 Experimental Results

We performed a series of simulations with randomly generated sets of expert estimates to test the convergence of the proposed feedback procedure. We consider evaluation tasks with 4 to 8 experts, 4 to 6 objects being ranked (for ordinal estimation), and 7 to 10 scale divisions (for cardinal estimation). The following reduced consistency coefficient was used:

$$R_C(V) = \min\left(\max\left(0, \frac{L_C(V) - T_o}{T_u - T_o}\right), 1\right).$$

It is easy to notice that $R_C(V) \in [0, 1]$. The value of $R_C(V)$ shows the *degree of sufficiency of consistency* for given number of experts and given a number of objects being ranked or scale divisions.

In our simulation, it was found that for $R_C(V)$ values being greater than 0.5, we always managed to make the condition (11) satisfied. The numbers of requests to experts did not exceed 3 (we considered that an expert always agrees to change his estimate). For smaller (but non-zero) $R_C(V)$ values the numbers of requests to experts were 4 and more, and in approximately 30% of the cases we could not make the set of estimates consistent, however, the final values $R_C(V)$ lay between 0.8 and 0.97.

6 Conclusion and Future Work

The article presents a model for managing the consistency of group expert judgments as applied to two types of expert assessments – the ordinal and the cardinal absolute. This model is being implemented within the framework of a software package for decision support in a distributed environment and can be used as a tool to ensure consistency and substantiality of expert assessments in conditions of distributed interaction between decision-makers and experts.

The procedure for feedback from experts that is at the base of the proposed model is human-machine, and therefore its effectiveness inevitably depends on a variety of psychophysiological factors associated with the behavior of experts and that is practically beyond the formal description. With this in mind, the proposed algorithm for increasing consistency is heuristic. Nevertheless, the results of the experimental verification of the given algorithm on a number of test problems available at the current moment make it possible to talk about its convergence and rather high efficiency. In the near future, we are going to publish a more detail study of experimental results, together with the results of trial operation of the above-mentioned software package.

Among the relevant areas of further research, we can distinguish the expansion the set of types of expert assessments supported by the model – in the first place, the support for cardinal relative estimates.

References

1. Cai, J.: A social interaction analysis methodology for improving E-collaboration over the Internet. Electron. Commer. Res. Appl. **4**(2), 85–99 (2005). doi:10.1016/j.elerap.2004.10.007
2. Dong, Y., Xu, J.: Consensus Building in Group Decision Making. Springer, Singapore (2016). doi:10.1007/978-981-287-892-2
3. Gubanov, D., Korgin, N., Novikov, D., Raikov, A.: E-Expertise: Modern Collective Intelligence. Springer International Publisher, Cham (2014). doi:10.1007/978-3-319-06770-4
4. Kendall, M., Gibbons, J.D.: Rank Correlation Methods, 5th edn. Oxford University Press, New York (1990)
5. Liu, X., Wang, G.A., Johri, A., et al.: Harnessing global expertise: a comparative study of expertise profiling methods for online communities. Inf. Syst. Front. **16**, 715–727 (2014). doi:10.1007/s10796-012-9385-6
6. Podvesovskii, A.G., Mikhaleva, O.A.: Features of modeling of group decision-making process in distributed expert networks. Bull. Bryansk State Tech. Univ. **2**(4), 239–250 (2016). doi:10.12737/23242. (in Russian)
7. Totsenko, V.G.: Spectral method for determination of consistency of expert estimate sets. Eng. Simul. **17**, 715–727 (2000)
8. Totsenko, V.G., Tsyganok, V.V., Kachanov, P.T., et al.: Experimental research of methods for obtaining the cardinal expert estimates of alternatives. part 2. methods with expert feedback. J Autom. Inf. Sci. **35**(4), 28–38 (2003). doi:10.1615/JAutomatInfScien.v35.i4.40
9. Totsenko, V.G.: Method of verifying sufficiency of individual ranking consistency in group decision making. J. Autom. Inf. Sci. **38**(8), 1–7 (2006). doi:10.1615/JAutomatInfScien.v38.i8.10
10. Totsenko, V.G.: Group ranking under feedback with experts taking into account their competency. J. Autom. Inf. Sci. **38**(10), 1–8 (2006). doi:10.1615/JAutomatInfScien.v38.i10.10

Systematic Approach to Quality Assessment of Hierarchy Structure in Education for Management Decision Making

Aleksey Godenko[✉], Irina Tarasova, Valeriy Volchkov,
and Vladimir Styazhin

Volgograd State Technical University, Lenin av. 28, 400005 Volgograd, Russia
forstud@vstu.ru, tarasova.irina.aleks@gmail.com,
volchkov38@mail.ru, vstyazhin@yandex.ru

Abstract. A systematic way of assessment of overall quality of the complex hierarchy structure is presented. These qualities form marketability of implementation of foreign students' pre-university training educational programs for ultimate management decision-making. Overall quality of the system is formed through experimentally established individual qualities in accordance with the levels of hierarchy by means of their resultant according to the functional Kolmogorov–Nagumo average. The system analyzed is presented in the form of 4-level structure with 19 parametrical variables, which define 15 system attributes. Quality assessment presented was realized in the form of MathCad files that were organized according to the hierarchy structure of the system. As main criteria to be evaluated several properties were selected with consideration of three criteria: marketability of the brand of the educational institution in the educational services market; the potential of the teaching staff participating in the realization of the educational program and financial stability of the educational program. This approach allows an immediate registration of changes in expert assessment in order to minimize subjective aspect of the decision made.

Keywords: Hierarchy structure · Individual quality · Overall quality · Marketability · Educational programs · Foreign students

1 Introduction

Current Russian system of education can be characterized by fast pace development, which requires timely effective management decisions to be made. The decisions made are often times based on the analyses of underformalized parameters, which characterize the educational system in question. Quite often management decisions are based on the analysis of various diagrams, tables as well as text descriptions of the target. In a number of instances, the latter possess much valued nature, thus creating conditions for subjective management decision to be made. An additional difficulty for objective evaluation of the education system is its hierarchy on the one side and an expert nature of the assessment of the element of the system on all levels on the other side. The main issue is the aggregate of all the assessment into one criterion. Ultimately effective work of any economic branch depends on its competitive ability.

© Springer International Publishing AG 2017
A. Kravets et al. (Eds.): CIT&DS 2017, CCIS 754, pp. 375–385, 2017.
DOI: 10.1007/978-3-319-65551-2_27

The main subject of the analysis of education is the quality of teaching, which is characterised by how the output (students' performance level) meets the requirements of a specific educational system. Many of these questions are described in detail in the works [2, 3, 11]. It is also mentioned in [1], that the definition of quality is quite broad and depends on the situation and aim of the evaluation.

The problem of assessment (in which various statistical methods prevail) of various educational system parameters is described in many works [7, 11].

There are several methods to form overall system quality on the basis of its separate elements analysis. One could point out Saaty pairwise comparison method [10], unified objective function creation on the basis of "desirability" function [4].

In the present article, we chose a partial structure of the educational system, i.e. pre-university training of foreign students.

A lot of works in various fields of economics and technology are dedicated to the analyses of multi-parameter hierarchy systems. The simplest approach is the qualimetry method, which evaluates overall system quality by means of deriving weighed averages on each selected hierarchy level [8, 9] or unified objective function creation on the basis of "desirability" function [4]. Such methods are successfully used in projections of engineering solutions [12]. It is also necessary to mention methods based on Pareto frontier establishment.

As a rule, all these methods were used in static situations. In cases when property values and physical quantities change in time (which defines such characteristics as longevity, repairability etc.) it is necessary to develop methods that would include statistically distributed constituents into the evaluation [12].

In the present article, we chose a partial structure of the educational system, i.e. pre-university training of foreign students.

The Target of Research. In this paper, we present a method of additional educational program implementation - foreign students' pre-university training competitive ability assessment on the basis of the theory of attributes which has been successfully used by the authors for assessment of quality and optimization of various complex subjects in mechanics, chemical engineering, and economics [5].

2   Research Method

Overall system performance is formed by expert-established individual attributes on all levels of hierarchy by means of its convolution according to the functional Kolmogorov–Nagumo average [6].

Pooled overall assessment of competitive ability Q (fourth level) was established by qualitative evaluation of the three integral system properties:

Q_1 – marketability of the brand of the educational institution in the educational services market; Q_2 – potential of the teaching staff participating in the realization of the educational program; Q_3 – financial stability of the educational program.

Integral properties of Q_i are determined by means of system properties convolution (in the case of Q_2, Q_3) or as shown in the case of Q_2, by means of the convolution of qualitative evaluation of the properties, which in turn are the result of the convolution of normalized system properties (two-level convolution):

$$Q_1 = Q_1(q_{11}, q_{12}, q_{13}, q_{14}), \; Q_2 = Q_2(\bar{p}_{11}, \bar{p}_{12}, \bar{p}_{13},), \; Q_3 = P_3(\bar{p}_{14}, \bar{p}_{15})$$

where $q_{11} = q_{11}(\bar{p}_1, \bar{p}_2, \bar{p}_3, \bar{p}_4)$ – qualitative evaluation of university's brand awareness; $q_{12} = q_{12}(\bar{p}_5, \bar{p}_6)$ – qualitative evaluation of the infrastructure, maintaining educational project realization; $q_{13} = q_{13}(\bar{p}_7, \bar{p}_8)$ – qualitative evaluation of the range of educational services in the university/region; $q_{14} = q_{14}(\bar{p}_9, \bar{p}_{10})$ – qualitative evaluation of educational and living expenses in the region; $\bar{p}_i$ – normalized elementary system property, derived from normalization of elementary system property p_i (see Fig. 1).

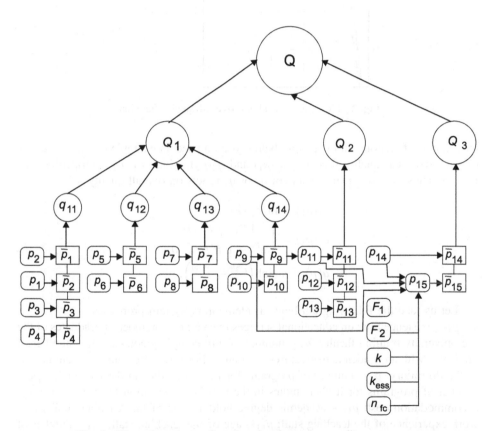

Fig. 1. Hierarchy scheme for educational structure quality assessment

The main idea of this approach is to find local quality functions so even if one of the local qualities has an unacceptable value it will cause overall quality to become undesirable. But if the local quality is good enough (or even better than the others) we should improve (work with) others qualities. This proposal defines the way we choose

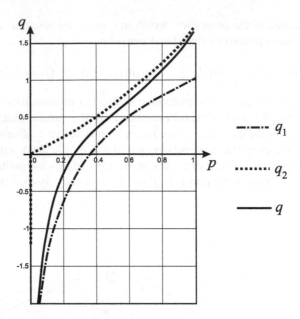

Fig. 2. Example of local and overall quality functions

local quality functions. In the picture below you can see an example of simple quality model: two local quality functions $q_1(p_1)$ and $q_2(p_2)$, where p_1, p_2 – properties (see Fig. 2). Thus, the low quality value of q_1 or q_2 reacts on overall quality q.

$$q_1(p_1) = \ln(p_1 \cdot e),$$
$$q_2(p_2) = \begin{cases} -1.2, \text{ if } p_2 = 0 \\ e^{p_2} - 1, \text{ if } p_2 > 0, \end{cases}$$
$$q(p) = a \, \sinh\left(\frac{e^{p_2(p)} - e^{-q_1(p)}}{2}\right).$$

Let us take the following attributes as elementary system properties:

p_1 – existence time on educational services market; p_2 – number of graduates of the pre-university training faculty; p_3 – number of university's graduates; p_4 – number of graduates with an academic degree; p_5 – dormitory housing per capita; p_6 – remoteness of the dormitory; p_7 – number of programs for further studies in the University; p_8 – number of programs for further studies in the region; p_9 – tuition fees; p_{10} – average accommodation cost; p_{11} – academic degree holders rate of the teaching staff; p_{12} – work experience of the teaching staff; p_{13} – age of the teaching staff: p_{14} – number of foreign students in the pre-university training program; p_{15} – educational program realization profit per 1 group (10 people), which is calculated according to the formula (1), depending on the range of the input parameter, among which there are parameters that are system properties, namely: tuition fees p_9, academic degree holders rate of the teaching staff p_{11}, number p_{14} of foreign students in the program of pre-university training.

Beyond that, educational program realization profit depends on:

- fractions of the assets allotted to the university's centralized funds (k);
- assets, allotted to the educational support staff (ESS) maintenance (k_{ess} – fraction of the salary of the educational support staff of the teaching staff salary);
- established in the university student ratio;
- the annual cost of wages of one labour rate of teaching staff (F_1);
- the annual cost of wages of one labour rate of teaching staff without an academic degree (F_2).

Profit per group of students (10 people) is defined as:

$$p_{15} = \frac{1}{10}\left[(1 - k) \cdot p_9 \cdot p_{14} - (p_{11} \cdot F_1 + (1 - p_{11}) \cdot F_2) \cdot (1 + k_{ess}) \cdot \frac{n_{fc} \cdot p_{14}}{20}\right] \quad (1)$$

Normalized ranges of elementary system properties were expert-defined as p_i^* – border that could be defined as a good value, (i.e. normalized value equals 1), p_i^0 – border, defined as a middling value on the brink of feasible (i.e. normalized value equals 0); the value of property p_i lower than p_i^0 is considered undesirable. In Table 1, there are values of the border p_i^* and p_i^0 is for every elementary system property, as well as normalization of $\bar{p}_i$ elementary properties in formulas. Functions of transition of elementary properties to its normalized properties were expert-selected taking into account the influence of elementary properties on overall system quality. It should be noted that the relation of some elementary properties to the overall quality can be defined as a direct dependence, while for others as the inverse. Properties of p_9, p_{11} are many valued, such as: increasing of the tuition fee (p_9) will lead to a drop in educational program appeal for students, but leads to an increase in cost-effectiveness; similarly an increase in the number of teaching staff with academic degrees (p_{11}) improves the quality of educational service, however teaching staff with academic degrees maintenance costs lead to a drop in cost-effectiveness.

Local quality can be performed by three main types of relations: direct (increasing), reverse (decreasing) and a relation for which the ranges of acceptable values have an interval, and outside the interval the relation can be either direct or reverse or almost constant (see Fig. 3).

Attributes Q_1, Q_2, Q_3 are different through the complexity of its structure. The most complex one is Q_1, which is formed by means of two-level convolution while Q_2, Q_3 are derived from one convolution of elementary standard system properties.

$$q_{11} = -\ln\left(\frac{\alpha_{11}e^{-\bar{p}_1} + \alpha_{12}e^{-\bar{p}_2} + \alpha_{13}e^{-\bar{p}_3} + \alpha_{14}e^{-\bar{p}_4} + }{\alpha_{11} + \alpha_{12} + \alpha_{13} + \alpha_1}\right) \quad (2)$$

$$q_{12} = -\ln\left(\frac{\alpha_{21}e^{-\bar{p}_5} + \alpha_{22}e^{-\bar{p}_6}}{\alpha_{21} + \alpha_{22}}\right) \quad (3)$$

$$q_{13} = \frac{\alpha_{31}\bar{p}_7 + \alpha_{32}\bar{p}_8}{\alpha_{31} + \alpha_{32}} \quad (4)$$

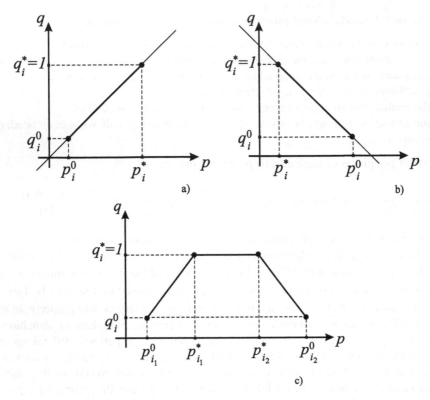

Fig. 3. Basic local quality functions: (a) direct (increasing), (b) reverse (decreasing), (c) piecewise linear function for limited range

Table 1. System attributes.

p_i	Unit of measurement	p_i^0	p_i^*	Description
p_1	Years	3	60	Direct dependence As an example we take Peoples' Friendship University of Russia (RUDN University), its pre-university training program has been on the market for around 60 years. The closer the dimension p_1 is to this property, the closer the value of the corresponding normalized property $\bar{p}_1$ is to 1
p_2	Persons	200	60000	Direct dependence Again, we take as an example Peoples' Friendship University of Russia (RUDN University), its pre-university training program has been on the market for around 60 years. The closer the dimension p_2 to this property, the closer the value of the corresponding normalized property $\bar{p}_2$ is to 1

(*continued*)

Table 1. (*continued*)

p_i	Unit of measurement	p_i^0	p_i^*	Description
p_3	Persons	100	20000	Direct dependence Again, we take as an example Peoples' Friendship University of Russia (RUDN University), its pre-university training program has been on the market for around 60 years. The closer the dimension p_3 to this property, the closer the value of the corresponding normalized property $\bar{p}_3$ is to 1
p_4	Ratio of graduates – Ph.D. to the number of graduates	0	0, 1	Direct dependence According to statistical data, 10% of graduates having an academic degree – excellent property (thus, the closer the value of dimension p_4 to 0, 1, the closer the value of the corresponding normalized property $\bar{p}_4$ is to 1)
p_5	Ratio of number of dormitory places to overall number of students	0, 1	1	Direct dependence The bigger the portion of students provided with dorm accommodations is, the better (thus the closer thus, the value of dimension p_5 to 0, 1, the closer the value of the corresponding normalized property $\bar{p}_5$ to 1)
p_6	Minutes	60	6	Inverse dependence The less time I spent on getting from the dorm to the university, the better. As an ideal situation, we shall take 6 min (the dormitory is in the direct neighbourhood with the University)
p_7	Item	4	40	Direct dependence The more programs of further training of foreign students at the university, the better. (There are approximately *40* of them in Russia)
p_8	Item	8	40	Direct dependence The more programs of further training of foreign students in the region, the better. (There are approximately 40 of them in Russia)
p_9	Rub	130000	80000	In the case when p_9 evaluates brand appeal on the educational services market, the dependence is inverse (the more expensive the service – the less appealing it is to the consumer). The range of tuition fees for pre-university training for foreign students in Russia ranges from 80000 to 130000 rub
				I.e. tuition fees (p_9) is a part of the formula assessing the profit (1), as well as cost-effectiveness (8) thus the dependence is obviously direct: the more expensive the cost of the service provided is the higher the profit from the service realization is

(*continued*)

Table 1. (*continued*)

p_i	Unit of measurement	p_i^0	p_i^*	Description
p_{10}	Rub	20000	7535	Inverse dependence The higher the living wage in the region, the less appealing for the educational service consumer it is, and vice versa. The maximum value of living wage in Russia is approximately 20000 (Moscow), minimum value – 7535 (Voronezh)
p_{11}	The ratio of number of teaching staff with the academic degree to overall teaching staff	0	1	In the case when p_{11} evaluates the potential of teaching staff of the educational program, the dependence is direct (the higher the % of academic degree holders rate – the higher the potential of teaching staff is). Thus the closer the value of dimension p_{11} to 1, the closer the value of the corresponding property $\bar{p}_{11}$ is to 1)
				I.e. academic degree holders rate (p_{11}) is a part of the formula assessing the profit (1), as well as cost-effectiveness (8) thus the dependence is obviously inverse: the higher the rate of academic degree holders, the higher the expenses on teaching staff salary who hold academic degrees, hence the smaller the profit from service realization is
p_{12}	Years (average)	5	$+\infty$	Direct dependence The longer the working experience, the higher the potential of the teaching staff
p_{13}	Years (average)			The dependence has a form of normal distribution with a maximum value 1 that equals 50 years of working experience
p_{14}	Persons	130	200	Direct dependence The bigger the number of students, the bigger the scope of service provided as well as its cost-effectiveness (8) is. For each university, these properties have its own values of the norm. In our case, a middling value is the number of students equalling to 130 persons ($\bar{p}_{14} = 0$), and a good value is – 200 persons ($\bar{p}_{14} = 1$)
				Moreover, the number of students (p_{14}) is a part of the formula assessing the profit (1) as well as financial stability (8), thus the dependence is direct: the bigger the number of students the higher the profit from service realization is, and thus the cost-effectiveness is higher
p_{15}	Thousands of rub	50	500	Direct dependence Profit per group of students (10 persons) is a functional relation with 8 input parameters (1) For each university these dimensions have its own value of norm. In our case, a middling value is a profit of 50 thousand rubles, and a good value is – 500 thousand rubles

$$q_{14} = -\ln\left(\frac{\alpha_{41}e^{-\bar{p}_9} + \alpha_{42}e^{-\bar{p}_{10}}}{\alpha_{41} + \alpha_{42}}\right) \tag{5}$$

Where α_{ij} – is expert-appointed weighting factors that are taking into account the input of each individual attribute into an overall property. This way the qualitative evaluation of the educational institution's brand appeal in the educational services market takes the form:

$$Q_1 = -\ln\left(\frac{\beta_{11}e^{q_{11}} + \beta_{12}e^{-q_{11}} + \beta_{13}e^{-q_{12}} + \beta_{14}e^{-q_{13}} + \beta_{15}e^{-q_{14}}}{\beta_{11} + \beta_{12} + \beta_{31} + \beta_{14} + \beta_{15}}\right), \tag{6}$$

where β_{1j} – are also expert-appointed weighting factors that take into account the input of each individual attribute into an overall property.

Qualitative evaluation of educational program teaching staff potential takes the form of (with weighting factor β_{2i}):

$$Q_2 = -\ln\left(\frac{\beta_{21}e^{-\bar{p}_{11}} + \beta_{22}e^{-\bar{p}_{12}} + \beta_{23}e^{-\bar{p}_{13}}}{\beta_{21} + \beta_{22} + \beta_{23}}\right) \tag{7}$$

Qualitative evaluation of educational program financial stability takes the form (with weighting factor β_{3i})

$$Q_3 = -\ln\left(\frac{\beta_{31}e^{-\bar{p}_{14}} + \beta32e^{-\bar{p}_{15}}}{\beta_{31} + \beta_{32}}\right) \tag{8}$$

Overall system property was derived from the formula:

$$Q = -\ln\left(\frac{\gamma_1 e^{-Q_1} + \gamma_2 e^{-Q_1} + \gamma_3 e^{-Q_3}}{\gamma_1 + \gamma_2 + \gamma_3}\right), \tag{9}$$

where γ_i – weighting factors that take into account property values by attribute groups Q_1, Q_2 and Q_3 in overall system property evaluation. The value of these factors can vary depending on the aims with which the qualitative system evaluation is performed. For example, if system assessment is used for inner aims in order to determine major parameters, which would help optimise it, the value of the attribute Q_3, corresponding with the financial stability of the program shall be considered at a greater value. In contrast, when assessing the system from a superior body (Ministry) point of view this parameter shall be taken with a lesser value and parameters Q_1 and Q_2 shall have an increased value.

The suggested model of competitive ability of additional education program realization (pre-university training of foreign students) assessment was implemented in software package VisSim, in which system hierarchy was presented in a form of correlated MathCad blocks.

In each of selected parameters, the responsiveness of the whole system was evaluated as standard partial derivatives of general objective function for selected parameters. High responsiveness in any of the selected parameters shows that unavoidable ambiguity in expert assessment will highly affect the result of the overall assessment, thus the model can not describe real environment accurately. On the other hand responsiveness on any of the selected parameters, close to zero, indicates that it has little effect on the overall assessment, and thus such example can be excluded from the analysis. The parameters selected in this model provide acceptable responsiveness to the change of the objective function in case of system input parameters change.

3 Results

This model has been used to assess the competitive ability of pre-university training of foreign students using Volgograd State Technical University as an example (VSTU). Given data of the example analysed depicted the following values $Q_1 = 0.676$, $Q_2 = 0.739$, $Q_3 = 0.661$. Concluding property $Q = 0.691432$.

The analysis performed makes it possible to form management decisions for the educational program of foreign students' pre-university training competitive ability improvement.

4 Discussion

This system makes it possible to assess the realization of pre-university training in the random educational institution and to rank university in accordance with the score of their competitive ability assessment. However, in order to compare various universities, it is necessary to include several parameters, which are not accessible to us at the present time. Thus we can consider above described qualitative evaluation of the educational structure as a methodological basis for similar evaluations. In the future, this model can be easily enhanced by means of input of new properties of evaluation. Including a new block that would optimize the objective function will make it possible to find optimal values of parameters of analyzed system management for management decision making.

References

1. Clarke, M.: The sublime objects of education policy: quality, equity and ideology. Discourse: Stud. Cult. Polit. Educ. **35**(4), 584–598 (2014)
2. Creemers, B., Kyriakides, L.: The Dynamics of Educational Effectiveness: A Contribution to Policy, Practice and Theory in Contemporary Schools. Routledge, London (2008)
3. Creemers, B., Kyriakides, L.: Developing, testing, and using theoretical models for promoting quality in education. School Eff. Sch. Improv. **26**(1), 102–119 (2015)
4. Harrington, J.: The desirability function. Ind. Qual. Control **21**, 494–498 (1965)
5. Kidalov, N.A., Volchkov, V.M., Knyazeva, A.S.: Optimization of mixture composition for foundry. In: Kravets, A., Shcherbakov, M., Kultsova, M., Shabalina, O. (eds.) CIT&DS 2015. CCIS, vol. 535, pp. 342–354. Springer International Publishing, Cham (2015). doi:10. 1007/978-3-319-23766-4_27

6. Kolmogorov, A.N.: Matematika i mekhanika. Izbrannye Trudy. Nauka, Moscow (1985)
7. Romiszowski, A.J.: Designing Instructional Systems: Decision Making in Course Planning and Curriculum Design. Routledge, Abingdon (2016)
8. Saaty, T.L.: The Analytic Heararchy Process. McGraw-Hill, New York City (1980)
9. Saaty, T.L.: Prinyatiye reshenii. Metod analiza ierarchiy. Radio I svyaz, Moscow (1989)
10. Saaty, T.L.: Relative measurement and its generalization in decision making why pairwise comparisons are central in mathematics for the measurement of intangible factors the analytic hierarchy/network Process. Revista de la Real Academia de Ciencias Exactas, Fisicas y Naturales. Serie A. Matematicas **102**(2), 251–318 (2008)
11. Skordoulis, M., Chalikias, M., Koniordos, M.: Students' satisfaction from their educational context through DREEM and LOT-R. In: Kravets, A., Shcherbakov, M., Kultsova, M., Iijima, T. (eds.) JCKBSE 2014. CCIS, vol. 466, pp. 113–122. Springer, Cham (2014). doi:10.1007/978-3-319-11854-3_11
12. Tereliansky, P.V.: Extrapolation of Dynamic Systems of Expert's Preferences. The Measurement of Attitude. Chicago Univesity of Chicago Press (1989)

Data Science in Energy Management and Urban Computing

The Passengers' Turnout Simulation for the Urban Transport System Control Decision-Making Process

Ilya V. Stepanchenko$^{(\boxtimes)}$ ⓘ, Elena G. Krushel ⓘ,
and Alexander E. Panfilov ⓘ

Kamyshin Technological Institute, Volgograd State Technical University,
Kamyshin 403874, Russian Federation
stilvi@mail.ru

Abstract. The report deals with the problems of the small city passengers' municipal transport system simulation. The particular purpose of the report concerns to the mathematical model of the passengers' turnout elaboration. The proposed stochastic model of passengers' arrivals at the stops of the transport net as well as the model of the passengers' transition between the stops is applicable to the passengers' turnout simulation for the decision-making on the municipal transport system efficiency raise. The results of the long-term observations of the real transport system operation and the urban transport passengers flow big data cognitive processing have applied for the model parameters identification and adequacy checkup. The model has the form of tabular probability distribution function depending on the passengers' start and destination stops names, the type of the weekday, the number of time interval within the day, and the passengers' social group belonging. The model testing shows the high correlation of the simulated passengers' flow with the real observations results. The confidence level of the accordance between the simulated data probability distribution and the experimental data empiric probability distribution is moderate. In spite of it, the presented model is applicable for the passengers' turnout simulation.

Keywords: Simulation · Passengers' transport system · Passengers flow · Stochastic tabular model · Turnout

1 Introduction

The appropriation of the municipal passengers' transport consists in the passengers' transition within the city bounds. The transport service as well as citizens supplying gas, electricity, and water is the essential social facility, which should be the subject of the municipal checkup and control.

However, the passengers' transition fulfillment sometimes is not profitable for the following reasons. First, the upper level of the trip price may be strictly limited by the citizens' financial possibilities restriction. Second, the fuel and spare parts costs may be over the top acceptable for the profit receiving. Third, the faults of the transport system

© Springer International Publishing AG 2017
A. Kravets et al. (Eds.): CIT&DS 2017, CCIS 754, pp. 389–398, 2017.
DOI: 10.1007/978-3-319-65551-2_28

control may take place, e.g. the high level of the exploitation expenses, the deterioration of the transport facilities, the unsuccessful transport schedule etc.

Nevertheless, the municipal passengers' transport profitability is extremely desirable. The reasonable economic efficiency of the private transport exploitation comparable with the municipal one can offer the indirect proof of the municipal transport profitableness potential attainment.

One of the ways of municipal transport system's efficiency raise consists of the carrying out and further maintenance of the rational transport facilities schedule. Such approach is quite perspective from the control possibilities point of view since the corresponding problems are the part of transport enterprise administration's scope of functions.

The effective schedule of the passengers' transport facilities traffic calls for the passengers' flow simulation instead and in addition to the real experiments since the durable experiments with the operating transport system should disturb the transport service regularity leading to the citizens' dissatisfaction [1–3]. The appropriate model carrying out and further computational experiments execution are based on the general simulation methods of the queue systems study as well as on the random series generation technique. The corresponding model acquisition needs for the real passengers flow reception (e.g. by means of the known passengers' flow observation table method [1]) and further data mining of the observation results.

The passengers' transition model consists of the following submodules. The first submodule presents the model of passengers flow at the stops allocations on municipal transport system net (briefly named further as "model of passengers' arrivals"). The second submodule presents the model of the single transport facility trip. The presented report deals with the first model justified by the real passengers flow observations carried out in the Kamyshin city of Volgograd region, Russia [1].

The problems of the urban transport systems' operation effectiveness raise as well as the urban transport facilities flow control are widely presented in the scientific publications concerning to the motor transport flow simulation and study [4–6]. Particularly, several academic journals deal purely with motor flow's dynamics [7–9] (e.g. "Transportation Research", "Transportation Science"). The analysis is addressed both to the transport nets as a whole and to the separate elements of the net. The discussion touches the following problems:

- Transport nodal points location and transport road crossing control [4–6];
- Effective control of the transport cargo traffic [10];
- Optimization of passengers' routes [11, 12];
- Passengers' behavior strategy estimation and the ways of purposeful on it [13, 14].

Two main approaches have formed historically by now: firstly deterministic and secondly probabilistic (stochastic) ones. The deterministic approach supposes the existence of the dependence between the particular factors (e.g. the correspondence of the rate and distances amongst the motors in the transport flow). The stochastic models treat the transport flow as the probability process.

The small towns possess the set of specific transport problems, which the scientific community almost ignores. The main of them are follows:

- The insufficient approach to the generalized consideration of urban transport control system as a whole, particularly: the lack of the systematic analysis of the motors' utilized capacity, ill-founded motors distribution between the routes, unjustified trip price value, the groundless choice of the motors types etc.
- The low economic efficiency (oftentimes the absence of profitableness) of the municipal transport systems caused by the transport facilities incomplete filling as well as the competition between the social, private, and personal transport facilities.
- The existence of the extremely g-loaded highways' sections between the points of the intensive passengers flows (particularly in the small towns such sections are usually located near the central markets). The exhausts from the motors pipes cause the dangerous pollutant concentrations in the living zones nearby the highways.

2 Problem Statement

The passengers' arrivals model ought to estimate the number of passengers forthcoming to the particular transport's stop during the given time interval and to settle the name of destination stop for each of forthcoming passengers. The number of the forthcoming passengers should depend on the following factors: the start as well the destination stops, the time interval within a day, the weekday name, and the passenger's social group. The factors roster was determined in accordance with the results presented in [1]).

The results of the complete passengers flow observations gave the following model factors details [1]:

- Each start and terminal stop of transport net may treat as the subject of simulation.
- The number of the time interval (its duration is 1 h) lays within the bounds from 5:00 until 20:00 accordingly to the real municipal transport operation mode.
- The weekday name varies from Sunday to Saturday.
- The social groups of passengers are following: pupil, student, worker, unemployed, and pensioner. Each group consists of the two subgroups depending on the availability vs. the absence of the concessionary ticket.

The following efforts are necessary for the model of passengers' arrivals at the stops of the transport system's net elaboration:

- develop the model form and structure for the formal arrival's model reception;
- generalize the data of the passengers' destination stops choose for each stop treated as the start of the passenger's arrivals on the base of the primary observation results [1];
- estimate the statistical characteristics (sufficient for the probability density estimation) of the passengers' arrivals process as well as the destination stop choice depending on the stop allocation, passenger's social group, and daytime;
- analyze the possibility of the parameters' averaged values application instead of the particular parameters values checked up during the real observations;
- justify the model adequacy by means of the simulation results analysis.

The purpose of the parameters' averaged values application consists in the decrease of the parameters number by means of the particular parameters values replacement by the set of the aggregated parameters.

The model justification should be carried out for the several stops with the essential distinction of the passengers' turnout.

The criteria for the model adequacy justification are following:

- The chi-square test and the standard deviation value application as the fitting criteria of the probability laws choice for the simulation of the passengers flow intensity and passengers' social groups belonging.
- The relative error's and the correlation coefficient values application for the validation of mean values of the passengers flows intensity and the number of passengers in the different social groups.

3   The Passengers' Arrivals Model Formalization

3.1   The Formal Model of the Passengers' Arrival

In accordance to [1] the general model form may be presented as follows:

$$x_{i,j,s,k,m} = F(V_i, V_j, T_s, D_k, K_m), \qquad (1)$$

where V is the set of all stops at the urban transport net; i, j are the indices of the start and terminal stops correspondingly, $i, j \in 1 \ldots |V|$; T is the set of the non-overlapping time intervals the join of which cover the whole workday of the municipal passengers transport operation, $s \in 1 \ldots |T|$; D is the weekdays set (from Sunday to Saturday), $k \in 1 \ldots |D|$; K is the set of passengers types classified by the social groups belonging and by the concessionary ticket availability, $m \in 1 \ldots |K|$; $x_{i,j,s,k,m}$ is the number of the mth type passengers arrived at the ith stop during the sth time interval of kth weekday and selected the jth stop as the terminal point.

The abstract function $F(\ldots)$ in (1) belongs to the stochastic functions group. The determination of $F(\ldots)$ in the general mathematical form of the certain random values probability distribution law is possible but the lack of data for its reliable identification should lead to the essential inaccuracy. The acceptable accuracy is obtainable only in the case of the values of four arguments fixation from five ones in (1). Hence, in this case, the number of analyzing functions should raise. Therefore, the choice of the function $F(\ldots)$ should be compromising.

Since the function $F(\ldots)$ describes the certain distribution of the random passengers' arriving at the transport stop, it is reasonable to use the tabular form of $F(\ldots)$ representation.

Although the tabular form of $F(\ldots)$ in (1) ensures the correct approximation of the $x_{i, j, s, k, m}$ probability density function, several disadvantages are attended:

1. The model is able to forecast the passengers' number, the arrivals of which is expected during the sth time interval. However, the exact moment of the individual passenger's arrival within the sth time interval is out of the model's possibilities.

At the same time, just this parameter is necessary for the transport system simulation based on the queue system theory.

2. The tabular form of $F(...)$ requires considerable memory volume to store the corresponding table. Consequently, the speed of simulation process decreases.
3. The adequacy of the model (1) depends on the experimental data representativeness. However, the large-scale observations of the whole set of routes at the whole week and for time intervals within the whole workday is mostly unacceptable because of unreasonable time and resources expenses.

First, of the failings can be eliminated by the appropriate choice of the time scale. Thus, assume the time intervals s in (1) as equal to the simulation time discrete (e.g. one minute). Therefore, the moment of the passengers' $x_{i,\ j,\ s,\ k,\ m}$ arrivals at the sth time discrete becomes fixed and hence the simulation of the passengers' transportation system based on the queue systems theory results would be admissible.

3.2   The Stochastic Parameters Choice

The parameters of the tabular function $F(...)$ in (1) can be determined using the statistical processing of the observations results concerning the data of the passengers' arrivals at the stops and their transition between the stops.

The estimation of the following statistical parameters is in need:

- The expectation of the arrivals number per time unit (a minute in our case) of the passengers from the definite social group at the definite workday for each destination stop:

$$Mx_{i,k,m} = \frac{1}{60 \cdot |T|} \sum_{j=1}^{|V|} \sum_{s=1}^{|T|} x_{i,j,s,k,m};$$ (2)

- The expectation of the arrivals number per time unit (a minute in our case) of the passengers from the definite social group for all days cumulatively (i.e. for observations period as a whole):

$$Mx_{i,m} = \frac{1}{|D|} \sum_{k=1}^{|D|} Mx_{i,k,m};$$ (3)

- The pair correlation coefficient between the expectations' estimates of the arrivals number per time unit (a minute in our case) of the passengers from the definite social group at the differing workdays:

$$rmx_{i,k1,k2} = \frac{E(Mx_{i,k1,m} \cdot Mx_{i,k2,m}) - E(Mx_{i,k1,m}) \cdot E(Mx_{i,k2,m})}{\sqrt{Var(Mx_{i,k1,m}) \cdot Var(Mx_{i,k2,m})}},$$ (4)

where $E(...)$ is the designation of the mathematical expectation function, $Var(...)$ is the designation of the variance, $k1, k2$ are the workdays indices, $k1, k2 \in D$.

- The pair correlation coefficient between expectations' estimates of the arrivals number per time unit (a minute in our case) of the passengers from the definite social group for all days cumulatively:

$$rmx_{i,k} = \frac{E(Mx_{i,k,m} \cdot Mx_{i,m}) - E(Mx_{i,k,m}) \cdot E(Mx_{i,m})}{\sqrt{Var(Mx_{i,k,m}) \cdot Var(Mx_{i,m})}};$$ (5)

- The passengers' arrivals at each hour of the definite workday as the part of the arrivals within the whole of the workday (regardless the passengers' social group):

$$dx_{i,s,k} = \sum_{j=1}^{|V|} \sum_{m=1}^{|K|} x_{i,j,s,k,m} \Bigg/ \sum_{j=1}^{|V|} \sum_{m=1}^{|K|} \sum_{s=1}^{|T|} x_{i,j,s,k,m};$$ (6)

- The passengers' arrivals expectation at each hour as the part of the arrivals within the whole of the workday (regardless the passengers' social group):

$$dx_{i,s} = \frac{1}{|D|} \cdot \sum_{k=1}^{|D|} dx_{i,s,k};$$ (7)

- The pair correlation coefficient between the parts of passengers arrivals for each hour of the differing workdays (regardless the passengers' social group):

$$rdx_{i,k1,k2} = \frac{E(dx_{i,s,k1} \cdot dx_{i,s,k2}) - E(dx_{i,s,k1}) \cdot E(dx_{i,s,k2})}{\sqrt{Var(dx_{i,s,k1}) \cdot Var(dx_{i,s,k2})}};$$ (8)

- The pair correlation coefficient between the parts of passengers' arrivals for each hour of the definite day and the parts of passengers' arrivals for each hour of all days cumulatively (regardless the passengers' social group):

$$rdx_{i,k} = \frac{E(dx_{i,s,k} \cdot dx_{i,s}) - E(dx_{i,s,k}) \cdot E(dx_{i,s})}{\sqrt{Var(dx_{i,s,k}) \cdot Var(dx_{i,s})}};$$ (9)

- The arrivals amount of the passengers transiting to the definite destination stop during the definite day:

$$Kx_{i,j,k} = \sum_{S=1}^{|T|} \sum_{m=1}^{|K|} x_{i,j,s,k,m};$$ (10)

- The expectation's estimate of a number of the passengers transiting to the definite destination stop during all days cumulatively:

$$Kx_{i,j} = \frac{1}{|D|} \cdot \sum_{k=1}^{|D|} Kx_{i,j,k};$$ (11)

- The pair correlation coefficient between the expectations' estimates of the amount of the passengers transiting to the definite destination stop during all days cumulatively and arrivals amount of the passengers transiting to the definite destination stop during the definite day:

$$rkx_{i,k} = \frac{E(Kx_{i,j,k} \cdot Kx_{i,j}) - E(Kx_{i,j,k}) \cdot E(Kx_{i,j})}{\sqrt{Var(Kx_{i,j,k}) \cdot Var(Kx_{i,j})}}. \tag{12}$$

The enumerated above statistical characteristics can be useful also for the detection of the model (1) several arguments independence (e.g. time intervals within the workday, social group of the passenger, weekday, and destination stop). If the justification of the independence should be proofed the decrease of the tabular function $F(...)$ dimension would be decreased.

4 The Passengers' Arrivals Model Simplification

The computation and analysis of the descriptive statistics (2)–(12) based on the actual big data of the urban transport passengers flow to justify the following conclusions:

- Although the number of the passengers depends on the arrivals at the definite starting stop, the arrivals at the differing stops are mutually independent. Therefore, the averaging of the arrivals at starting stops is unacceptable;
- The argument "weekday" almost linearly depends on the other arguments of the model (1) (the correlation coefficient between K and D equals 0.96...0.99, between V and D equals 0.93...0.97, between T and D equals 0.82...0.97). Hence, this argument can be replaced by the constant k_day_k, i.e. the arrivals number at k^{th} day can be estimated as the part of averaged daily arrivals number:

$$x_{i,j,s,k,m} = F(V_i, V_j, T_s, K_m) \cdot k\_day_k; \tag{13}$$

- The social group of the passenger as well as the destination stop name are his individual characteristics. The influence of latter on the passengers' forthcomings is a week and may be neglected:

$$x_{i,s,k} = F_1(V_i, T_s) \cdot k\_day_k; \tag{14}$$

$$v_n = F_2(V_i, T_s, K_m); \tag{15}$$

$$k_n = F_3(V_i, V_j, T_s); \tag{16}$$

where $n = 1...x_{i,s,k}$ is the index of the passenger arriving at the ith stop of kth day's s^{th} minute;

- The destination stop v_n and the passenger's type k_n in (15) and (16) are mutually dependent. As the result, the difficulties of the practical applications may occur because of the uncertainty of the order of these parameters fixing. Substituting (15) in (16) instead V_j, leads to:

$$k_n = F_3(V_i, F_2(V_i, T_s, K_m), T_s) = F_4(V_i, T_s); \qquad (17)$$

i.e. passenger's type k_n is independent of the destination stop V_j. Similarly, the independence of v_n from K_m leads to

$$v_n = F_2(V_i, T_s, F_3(V_i, V_j, T_s)) = F_5(V_i, T_s); \qquad (18)$$

- The correlation coefficients between the definite hour values of passengers' types and their daily averaged values are significant (equal 0.5...0.95). Hence, T_s in $F_4(\ldots)$ can be replaced by the time averaged argument K_sr_t:

$$k_n = F_4(V_i, K\_sr\_t); \qquad (19)$$

- Similarly, the correlation coefficients between the passengers' destination stops per hour and their daily averaged values are significant (equal 0.45...0.95). Hence, T_s in $F_5(\ldots)$ can be replaced by the time averaged argument Vj_sr_t:

$$v_n = F_5(V_i, Vj\_sr\_t). \qquad (20)$$

Thus, the model of the passengers' arrivals at the starting stops and their transit to the destination stops turns into the following form:

$$\begin{cases} x_{i,s,k} = F_1(V_i, T_s) \cdot k\_day_k, \\ k_n = F_4(V_i, K\_sr\_t), \quad n = 1..x_{i,s,k}, \\ v_n = F_5(V_i, V\_sr\_t), \quad n = 1..x_{i,s,k}. \end{cases} \qquad (21)$$

The model (21) contains the reduced arguments number comparable with (1). Hence, the program implementation of (21) and its further application would be easier.

5   The Simulation Results Analysis

In the course of the model adequacy testing, we have passed through ten simulation sessions for each stop of the city's transport net. The results lead to the following conclusions:

1. The model (21) adequacy is better for the stops with significant passengers' turn-over. For example, all adequacy criteria for the stop with 560 average forthcoming passengers for workday are better than for the stop with 130 average forthcomings. In turn, all adequacy criteria of latter are better than for the stop with 50 average forthcomings.

2. The accuracy of the model (21) is best for the case of passengers arrivals distribution via daytime (confidence level value is 0.87). The confidence level values of passengers arrivals distribution at the destination stops and at the passengers' types are comparably less (0.69 and 0.51 correspondingly).

3. The correlation between the real observation data and the simulation data for each of testing distributions is very significant (the corresponding correlation coefficients values are more than 0.83). Hence, the simulation results application is acceptable for the practical applications instead and in addition to the real observations results.

4. The accordance between the empiric probability distribution laws of the real and simulated data (estimated by the chi-square test) is not enough to the confident conclusion on the model (21) adequacy. The best confidence level demonstrates the probability distribution laws of passengers' flow distribution via daytime (0.61...0.83), and the worst one is for the distribution via the passengers' types (0.48...0.51).

5. The model generates random time and corresponding parameters of the passengers' turnover with minor standard deviation. The latter shows the model tolerable accuracy and stability.

Because of the minor statistical accordance, the model (21) is more suited for the passengers' arrivals simulation for the conditions of the abstract workday with the averaged features. The way of model statistical adequacy raise lays in the model (21) complication by means of the refusal from the passengers' forthcoming number averaging accordingly to the types and workday time. However, in this case, the model's dimension should raise significantly while the adequacy would improve for 15-20%.

In spite of slight coinciding of the passengers' arrivals probability distribution laws, the presented model is applicable for the passengers' transition simulation.

6 Conclusion

The report presents the adequate model of the passengers' arrivals at the stops and their transition between the stops of the small city municipal transport net. The model configuration appears as the tabular probability distribution function with the parameters identified by the data acquisition of the passengers' turnout prolonged real observations.

The model shows the high correlation with the real observations results. However, the coinciding of the empiric probability distribution laws of the simulating and real results is not so high. The way of the model adequacy raise lies in the model's complication by means of the refusal from the passengers' forthcomings number averaging accordingly to the passengers' types and workday time.

In spite of slight coinciding of the passengers' arrivals probability distribution laws, the presented model is applicable for the passengers' turnout simulation.

Acknowledgment. The article was based on works supported by grants of Russian Foundation for Basic Research Povolzhie No. 14-07-97011, No. 15-47-02321.

References

1. Krushel, E.G., Stepanchenko, I.V., Panfilov, A.E., Berisheva, E.D.: An experience of optimization approach application to improve the urban passenger transport structure. In: Kravets, A., Shcherbakov, M., Kultsova, M., Iijima, T. (eds.) JCKBSE 2014. CCIS, vol. 466, pp. 27–39. Springer, Cham (2014). doi:10.1007/978-3-319-11854-3_3
2. Parygin, D., Sadovnikova, N., Kravets, A., Gnedkova, E.: Cognitive and ontological modeling for decision support in the tasks of the urban transportation system development management. In: 6th International Conference on Information, Intelligence, Systems and Applications (IISA), Greece, pp. 1–5. IEEE Xplore, Corfu (2015)
3. Sadovnikova, N., Parygin, D., Kalinkina, M., Sanzhapov, B., Ni, T.N.: Models and methods for the urban transit system research. In: Kravets, A., Shcherbakov, M., Kultsova, M., Shabalina, O. (eds.) Creativity in Intelligent, Technologies and Data Science. CCIS, vol. 535, pp. 488–499. Springer, Cham (2015). doi:10.1007/978-3-319-23766-4_39
4. Ding, H., Wang, W., Luo, T., Yang, Z., Li, Y., Li, Z.: Cellular automata based modeling for evaluating different bus stop designs in China. Discrete Dyn. Nat. Soc. **2015**(10) (2015)
5. Di, D., Dongyuan, Y.: Dynamic traffic analysis model of multiple passengers for urban public transport corridor. Adv. Mech. Eng. **7**(11) (2015)
6. Maximey, I.V., Sukach, E.I., Galushko, V.M.: Design modeling of service technology for passenger flow by city transport network. J. Autom. Inf. Sci. **41**(4), 67–77 (2009)
7. Lewe, J.H., Hivin, L.F., Mavris, D.N.: A multi-paradigm approach to system dynamics modeling of intercity transportation. Transp. Res. Part E: Logist. Transp. Rev. **71**, 188–202 (2014)
8. Horn, M.: An extended model and procedural framework for planning multi-modal passenger journeys. Transp. Res. Part B: Methodol. **37**, 641–660 (2003)
9. Herbon, A., Hadas, Y.: Determining optimal frequency and vehicle capacity for public transit routes: a generalized newsvendor model. Transp. Res. Part B: Methodol. **71**, 85–99 (2015)
10. Zheng, Y., Xi, X., Zhuang, Y., Zhang, Y.: Dynamic parameters cellular automaton model for passengers in subway. Tsinghua Sci. Technol. **20**(6), Article no. 7349931, 594–601 (2015)
11. Feng, Y., Li, X., Ma, N.: Research of traffic share in different models of transport based on the Agent theory. In: 2012 Joint Rail Conference, JRC 2012, pp. 813–822. ASME, Philadelphia (2012)
12. Li, D., Yuan, J., Yan, K., Chen, L.: Monte Carlo simulation on effectiveness of forecast system for passengers up and down buses. In: 3rd International Symposium on Intelligent Information Technology Application, IITA 2009, vol. 1, Article no. 5369635, pp. 359–361. IEEE, NanChang (2009)
13. Schelenz, T., Suescun, A., Wikström, L., Karlsson, M.: Application of agent-based simulation for evaluating a bus layout design from passengers' perspective. Transp. Res. Part C: Emerg. Technol. **43**, 222–229 (2014)
14. Bure, V.M., Mazalov, V.V., Plaksina, N.V.: Estimating passenger traffic characteristics in transport systems. Autom. Remote Control **76**(9), 1673–1680 (2015)

Development of Management Principles of Urban Traffic Under Conditions of Information Uncertainty

Yaroslav A. Seliverstov[1(✉)], Svyatoslav A. Seliverstov[1],
Igor G. Malygin[1], Alexander A. Tarantsev[1], Natalja V. Shatalova[1],
Olga Y. Lukomskaya[1], Igor P. Tishchenko[2],
and Alexey M. Elyashevich[3]

[1] Solomenko Institute of Transport Problems of the Russian Academy
of Sciences, St. Petersburg, Russian Federation
silver8yr@gmail.com
[2] Ailamazyan Program Systems Institute of Russian Academy of Sciences,
Pereslavl-Zalesskii, Yaroslavskaya Oblast, Russian Federation
[3] Peter the Great Saint-Petersburg Polytechnic University, St. Petersburg,
Russian Federation

Abstract. New management principles of urban traffic control are presented in this article. A formal model of the urban transportation system is built in the logic-algebraic form related to the graph-analytical model of the urban transportation network. A functional model of the urban transportation system based on the user targets and targets of the urban transportation system is introduced. The user targets are consistent with the Wardrop's first principle and the safe route principle, and the targets of the urban transportation system are consistent with the Wardrop's second principle and the principle of reliable operation. The correctness of the proposed model is demonstrated by practical examples.

Keywords: Intelligent transport systems · Traffic management · Management of urban population mobility · Urban transportation systems · Traffic control system · Principles of traffic control

1 Introduction

Control systems (CS) of urban traffic flows are based on mathematical and software algorithmic models. By now transport models that describe real transport processes with a certain degree of confidence are available Qiao et al. [1]. They are being used to calculate traffic and load on road network elements, to prepare schedules of passenger and freight transportation with the goals of redistributing traffic flows in the most congested areas and enhancing the road safety.

A tendency to successively implement individual components of information traffic management systems into the organization of the urban transportation process in metropolitan areas could not qualitatively increase the safety and manageability of traffic Lord and Mannering [2].

© Springer International Publishing AG 2017
A. Kravets et al. (Eds.): CIT&DS 2017, CCIS 754, pp. 399–418, 2017.
DOI: 10.1007/978-3-319-65551-2_29

The goal of our study was to develop management principles of urban traffic and to build a control model of urban traffic flows that eliminates the above-mentioned disadvantages.

2 Analysis

Among the recent investigations concerning the development of non-equilibrium models, we can point out the following. Zhang [3] described the behavior of vehicles in a traffic flow by using a non-equilibrium gas-dynamic model; Li and Zhang [4] developed a non-equilibrium model of traffic flows based on the Hamilton-Jacobi equation and kinematic wave model in the variational formulation; Hess et al. [5] estimated travel-time savings by using statistical polynomial models with a logistic distribution mixed logit models; Yang and Huang [6] determined the relationship between the system optimum and competitive transport equilibrium for different groups of users; Barth et al. [7] considered the problem of learning the game transport models which are at equilibrium according to Wardrop and proved their convergence with the help of Lyapunov methods, and Costeseque and Lebacque [8] calculated traffic flows at the macro level by using models of the Generic Second Order Modeling family and Lax-Hopf algorithm (Claudel and Bayen [9]);

Xu et al. [10] explored new models of transport equilibrium taking into account ridesharing and their impact on congestion; Daganzo [11] considered linear, gravity and entropy models of distribution of traffic flows; Seliverstov and Seliverstov [12] explained the procedure of constructing matrixes of transport correspondence by the EVA[1] method and evaluated load on the transportation network of St. Petersburg by using simulation; Seliverstov and Seliverstov [13] considered linear, gravity and entropy models of distribution of traffic flows; Daganzo [14–17] and (Newell [18]) considered hydrodynamic models of traffic flows which are still employed.

3 Problem Formulation

Nowadays many research teams are engaged in studies of control models of urban traffic flows in the framework of the behavioral principles of Wardrop [19]. A significant progress has been achieved in the development of theoretical and applied methods and approaches to building intelligent transportation systems (ITS). Many problems of traffic flow control in a metropolis in the model interpretation of ITS (Hasan et al. [20]) have been resolved in a software- algorithmic way, but the efficiency of the control system (CS) for a real urban transportation system (UTS) remains extremely low.

In practice, the redistribution of traffic flows is carried out by informing drivers about the best route. Usually, a driver decides whether to choose a route or maneuver in

---

[1] EVA in German: Erzeugung (Generation), Verteilung (Distribution), Aufteilung (Split).

conditions uncertainty of the external information environment. The uncertainty of the external informational environment is characterized by the lack of information available to drivers, about other participants of the road, condition of their vehicles and the condition of the transportation infrastructure.

Therefore, the behavioral principles of Wardrop do not take into account many factors (the state of the street road network, the behavior of drivers, etc.), and therefore need to be revised. For this reason, the development of management of principles of the behavior of drivers and traffic has an important significance.

4   Formal Model of Urban Transportation System

According to Seliverstov [21], the urban transportation system (TS) is assumed to consist of a multitude of interconnected objects of different classes, which in the general form will be referred to as UTS elements

$$TS : \Xi = \{\xi_i, \ i = 1, \ldots, N\}, \tag{1}$$

where TS is the transportation system, and ξ_i is the UTS element.

The classes in the multitude of the UTS objects will be defined by using the procedure of partitioning f_Ψ^d of the TS set into disjoint of subsets of the following form

$$\overset{d}{\underset{\psi}{}} : \quad TS = \bigcup_\psi TS_\psi, \quad |TS_\psi| = d_\psi, \tag{2}$$

where $\Psi = \{\psi_1, \ldots, \psi_N\}$ is the partition classes, and $d_\psi = 1, \ldots, N$ is the partition class (the number of subclasses of each class).

The classes of the UTS elements are functionally distinct sets of UTS elements, such as objects of transport infrastructure - To, transportation network users[2] - H, street and road transportation networks - Ts, transport vehicles - Tr, goods - Gr, cargo vehicles - Tg, facilities for the transportation process management - Tc, and life support infrastructure - O.

A graphic interpretation of this class partitioning is shown in Fig. 1

For this classification $\Psi = \psi_1, \ldots, \psi_7$, and Eq. (2) acquires the form

$$f_\Psi^d : \quad TS = \bigcup_{\psi_1}^{\psi_7} TS_\psi = H \cup O \cup To \cup Ts \cup Gr \cup Tg \cup Tc \tag{3}$$

The implementation of the transport mobility control in UTS determines the procedure of identification of its elements.

---

[2] User is a user of transport services (passenger, driver and others).

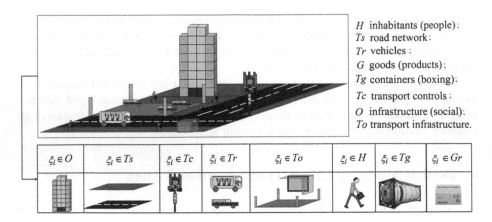

$\xi_i \in O$	$\xi_i \in Ts$	$\xi_i \in Tc$	$\xi_i \in Tr$	$\xi_i \in To$	$\xi_i \in H$	$\xi_i \in Tg$	$\xi_i \in Gr$

Fig. 1. Classes of UTS objects [21]

In the general form, the identifying numbering of the element set *TS* includes f_N which will give a unique number to each object of *TS*:

$$f_N : TS \to I, \tag{4}$$

where $I = \{id_\eta\}$ is the set of unique numbers.

The parameterization of the element set *TS* is given by the operator f_{CH}, which assigns a set of characteristics to each object in the network. The parameterization procedure is as follows

$$f_{CH} : \quad TS \to CH, \tag{5}$$

where $CH = \{ch_\pi^{\xi_i}, \pi = 1, \dots, n; \quad i = 1, \dots, N\}$ is the set of *characteristics* of the UTS elements.

The characteristic $ch_\pi^{\xi_i}$ is given by the sequence $ch_\pi^{\xi_i} = \langle name, \{value\}\rangle$, where *"name"* is the name of the "π" characteristic, and *{value}* is the allowable region. The allowable region is defined by the lists of these values, by the interval, or functionally, by using calculation rules (measurements) and evaluation.

The dynamics of the UTS processes is given by a time operator f_T that assigns a certain time moment or interval to each object of *TS* in the form

$$f_T: \quad TS \to \left[\tau_T^{def} \vee (\tau_T; \tau_{T+1}) \right], \tag{6}$$

where T is the set of time moments or intervals, i.e., $\tau_1 < \tau_2, \dots, \tau_T < \tau_{T+1}; \tau_T^{def} \in T$ is the definite time moment, and $(\tau_T; \tau_{T+1}) \in T$ is the definite time interval.

The elements of the real UTS in the informational presentation of the model of urban traffic flow control will be referred to as $A = \{a_i, i = 1, \dots, N\}$.

Let us take f^{TS-A} which relates each element to an agent.

$$f^{TS-A}: \quad TS = \{\xi_i, \ i = 1, \ldots, N\} \to A = \{a_i, \ i = 1, \ldots, N\}, \tag{7}$$

The condition of element correspondence with take the form

$$\sum_{i=1}^{N} \xi_i = \sum_{i=1}^{N} a_i, \tag{8}$$

Therefore, sets $|TS| = |A|$ are equivalent.

The urban transportation network is given by the graph $\Gamma^{TI}(V; E) \subset B_t(TS)$, where $TI = (To \cup Ts \cup O)$ with a set of nodes $V = \{v\}$ and a set of arcs $E = \{e\}$.

We separate out two subsets in the set of nodes $V = \{v\} \subseteq A \subset B_t(TS)$: generation of traffic flows (sources) $S \subseteq V$ and absorption of traffic flows (sinks) $D \subseteq V$ that satisfy the following condition

$$D, S \subseteq [To \cup Ts \cup O] \subset TS, \tag{9}$$

The subset $S \subseteq V$ contains the UTS elements that generate traffic flows; the subset $D \subseteq V$ contains the UTS elements that absorb traffic flows.

The set of the flow-forming departure-arrival pairs is given by the Cartesian product:

$$W = \{w = (\partial; \alpha) : \partial \in S, \alpha \in D\}, \tag{10}$$

Then the OD matrix will be given by an array $\rho_w : w \in W$ in which each departure-arrival pair $w = (\partial; \alpha) \in W$ will correspond to ρ_w a definite volume of users (passengers, vehicles) which must go from point ∂ (departure) to point α (arrival).

The route (path) connecting nodes ∂ and α is given by the sequence of sections of the street-road network

$$e_1 = (\partial = \Pi_0 \to \Pi_1), \ e_2 = (\Pi_1 \to \Pi_2) \ldots, e_{L-1} = (\Pi_{L-2} \to \Pi_{L-1}),$$
$$e_L = (\Pi_{L-1} \to \Pi_L = \alpha),$$

where $e_\gamma \in E$ at all $\gamma = 1, \ldots, L+1$.

The set of alternative routes by using which for each pair $w = (\partial; \alpha) \in W$ the flow coming from the point of departure ∂ reaches the point of arrival α is defined as

$$P_w = \bigcup_{i=1}^{N} p_i = \bigcup_{i}^{N} \bigcup_{l}^{L} e_{il}, \tag{11}$$

Let us introduce the value x_p of the flow $p \in P$ such that for each pair w the flows x_p satisfy the condition

$$X_w = \left\{ x_p \geq 0 : p \in P_w, \sum_{p \in Pw} x_p = \rho_w \right\}, \qquad (12)$$

Let us introduce a quantitative value y_e of the flow $e \in E$ at the moment of time $t \in T$. Then the flow is calculated as

$$x_p = \sum_{e \in P} \Theta_{ep} y_e, \qquad (13)$$

where $\Theta_{ep} = \begin{cases} 1, & e \cap p \text{ (arc "e" pass through the way "}p\text{")} \\ 0, & e \not\cap p \text{ (arc "e" doesn't pass through the way "}p\text{")} \end{cases}$

Let us define $\Theta = (\Theta_{ep} : e \in E, p \in P)$, i.e., the matrix, and $y = (y_e : e \in E)$, i.e., the vector that describes the load on the network. In the matrix form, the relationship between the flows is described by the equation $y = \Theta x$.

We denote by $G_p = \{g_p\}$ the specific travel cost the path p. Since the travel cost along one route may be affected by loads on other routes, G_p are functions of the load on the total network, i.e., $G_p = G_p(X)$.

5 Functional Model of UTS

The functional model of UTS control contains operators of measurement f_M, regulation f_R, and planning f_Π

$$f_C == \langle f_M; F_R; f_\Pi \rangle, \qquad (14)$$

The operator of the measurement of states $f_M = \left\{ f_M^{\xi_i} \right\} = f_N \cup f_{CH} \cup f_T \cup f^{TS-A}$ correlates each element $\xi_i \in TS$ of UTS at time moment or interval from T under the action $e_{\zeta_i}(t)$ with the registered state $s_{\zeta_i}(t)$ of the form:

$$\forall \ni_i \in TS \quad \exists \quad f_M^{\xi_i} : [t; e_{\zeta_i}(t); \xi_i] \rightarrow [t, e_{\zeta_i}(t), s_{\zeta_i}(t)], \qquad (15)$$

where $s_{\zeta_i}(t) = t \times id_i \times a_i \times ch_\pi^{\zeta_i}$ is the state of control object given by the Cartesian product or tuple at sets TS, I, A, CH, T and determines the real state of control object of UTS in the model interpretation; $e_{\zeta_i}(t) = t \times id_j \times a_j \times ch_\pi^{\zeta_i}, j = 1, \ldots, J$ the effect on control object is given by the Cartesian product or tuple at sets TS, I, A, CH, T and determines the state of the j-th objects and factors of UTS that affect control object:

The operator of regulation of states control object of UTS $f_R = \{f_R^{\zeta_i}\} = f_R^H \cup f_R^{TC}$ correlates each element $\xi_i \in TS$ of UTS at time moment or interval from T to the regulating effect $r_{\zeta_i}(t) \in U(TS)$ of the form:

$$\forall \xi_i \in TS, t \in T \quad \exists \quad f_R^{\zeta_i} : R(TS) \rightarrow r_{\zeta_i}(t_R), \qquad (16)$$

where $f_R^{\xi_i}$ is the operator of regulation of states of control object of UTS; $R(TS)$ is the set of regulating effects of CS UTS; $r_{\xi_i}(t_R)$ is the regulating effect applied to control object $\xi_i \in TS$ at moment $t_R \in T$; f_R^H is the operator of regulation of the states for the UTS users; f_R^{TC} is the operator of regulation of the states for control object of UTS.

The operator of planning of the states of control object of UTS $f_\Pi = \left\{ f_\Pi^{\xi_i} \right\} = f_\Pi^H \cup f_\Pi^{TS/H}$ correlates each object $\xi_i \in TS$ of UTS at time moment or interval from T in the situation $sit_0^{\xi_i}(t) = s_{\xi_i}(t) \cup e_{\xi_i}(t)$ the target state $s_P^{\xi_i}(t_P)$ at time moment $t_P \in T$, i.e.,

$$\forall \xi_i \in TS, t \in T \quad \exists \quad f_\Pi^{\xi_i}: sit_0^{\xi_i}(t) \rightarrow s_P^{\xi_i}(t_P), \tag{17}$$

where $f_\Pi^{\xi_i}$ is the operator of planning of the states of control object of UTS; $sit_0^{\xi_i}(t)$ is the situation in which control object of UTS is found at time moment $t \in T$; $s_P^{\xi_i}(t_P)$ is the target state of control object of UTS at moment $t_P \in T$; f_Π^H is the operator of planning of the states for users of UTS; $f_\Pi^{TS/H}$ is the operator of planning of the states for users of UTS objects.

The correspondence between the UTS state and the required state is estimated through the operator of state control f_{CS} given by

$$f_{CS} = \left\langle f_M \cup f_\psi^d; E_\Xi^{\xi_i}; r_\xi(t_R) \right\rangle, \tag{18}$$

where f_M is the operator of the measurement of the state of control object of UTS; f_ψ^d is the operator of the classification; $r_\xi(t_R)$ is the regulating action or the deviation of the current state from the required one; $E_\Xi^{\xi_i} \in TS$ is the set of UTS elements that affect the element ξ_i.

The control operator f_{CS} contains a system of functions that determine the state of the control object (measurements, acquisition, and refinement of data on the object of management) and assessment of the deviation of the current state from the required one according to the criteria of efficiency.

Therefore, the control operator f_{CS} calculates the deviation $r_{\xi_i}(t_R)$ from the required state $s_P^{\xi_i}(t_P)$ for each ξ_i UTS element which is in the state $sit_0^{\xi_i}(t)$ at moment from T, i.e.,

$$\forall \xi_i \in TS, t \in T \quad \exists \quad f_{CS}^{\xi_i}: \left| sit_0^{\xi_i}(t) - s_P^{\xi_i}(t_P) \right| \rightarrow r_{\xi_i}(t_R), \tag{19}$$

Then, depending on the control operator f_{CS}, the functionally complete operator basis of UTS control is able to realize the functions of control in the regimes of optimal control, control and loss of control, i.e.,

$$
\begin{array}{l}
\xi_i \in TS, \\
\forall f_T, f_{CH}, \quad \exists f_C, U(TS): \\
t = def
\end{array}
\left\{
\begin{array}{l}
f_C^{opt}, U(TS)_{opt} \rightarrow \left\{ \underline{ch_\pi^{AL}} \right\} < \left\{ ch_\pi^{rand} \right\} < \left\{ \overline{ch_\pi^{AL}} \right\} \\
f_C^{AL}, U(TS)_{AL} \rightarrow \left\{ ch_\pi^{rand} \right\} \in CH_\pi^{AL} \\
f_C^F, U(TS)_F \rightarrow \left\{ ch_\pi^{rand} \right\} \notin CH_\pi^{AL}
\end{array}
\right., \tag{20}
$$

where f_C is the control operator of UTS; f_C^{opt} is the operator of optimal control; f_C^{AL} is the operator of admissible control; f_C^F is the operator of loss of control; $\left\{\underline{ch}_\pi^{AL}\right\}$ is the lower boundary of the set of parameters of optimal control; $\left\{\overline{ch}_\pi^{AL}\right\}$ is the upper boundary of the set of parameters of optimal control; $\left\{ch_\pi^{rand}\right\}$ is the values of the set of "π" parameters; CH_π^{AL} is the region of admissible control; $U(TS)$ is the UTS state vector; $U(TS)_{opt}$ is the UTS in the state of optimal control; $U(TS)_{AL}$ is the UTS in the state of admissible control; $U(TS)_F$ is the UTS in the state of loss of control.

6   Target Functions of Control of Mobility Processes in UTS

It is reasonable to build the model of control of dynamic traffic flows on the basis of principles of a distributed control system CS that provide a rational self-organization.

The model of control of urban traffic flows relies on the target function of control of mobility processes in UTS which is realized by the functionally complete operator basis of UTS control.

The target function of control of mobility processes is formed under two components: targets of users $P(H)$ and targets of UTS $P(TS/H)$.

The targets of users rely on the Wardrop's first axiomatic principle and the axiomatic principle of safe route:

(1) Each user of the network non-cooperatively seeks the routes to minimize his cost of transportation (Wardrop's first axiomatic principle), i.e.,

$$\forall h \in H, \; h \to w(\partial; \alpha), w(\partial; \alpha) \to p : \; p \in P_w, \; x_p > 0, \; \Rightarrow$$
$$\Rightarrow G_p(x) = \min_{p_\sum \in P_w} G_p\left(\mathbf{x}_\sum\right) = g_w\left(\mathbf{x}_\sum\right), \tag{21}$$

where $p = e_{1=str}, e_2, \ldots, e_{\ell=fin}$; $g_w\left(\mathbf{x}_\sum\right)$ is the minimum cost of transportation in the routes that connect the pair $w \in W$ in the case the load on the network is determined by the vector $\mathbf{x}_\sum$;

(2) Any trip of each user on the route with a minimum transportation cost takes place in the dynamic region of safe transport mobility.

The dynamic region of safe transport mobility is the region of transportation $D_{h_i}^S$ chosen by the user unilaterally on the basis of available information $I_{TS}^{h_i}$ on the participants of the transport process, traffic rules and the state of transport infrastructure through the information provision function of the type:

$$\forall h_i \in H, w(\partial; \alpha), p = e_{1=H}, \ldots, e_{\ell=k} \quad \exists f_{h_i}^{fs}\left(I_{TS}^{h_i}\right)\big|_{t=def} : h_i \to D_{h_i}^{S}\left(e_{def}\right), \tag{22}$$

The information provision function $f_{h_i}^{fs}\left(I_{TS}^{h_i}\right)$ is formed by CS UTS and provides information on the dynamic region of safe transport mobility to the participants of the transportation process in the following form:

$$D_{h_i}^{S}\Big|_{t=def}^{U} = \left\langle \bigcup_{cl}^{CL} \bigcup_{\psi}^{\psi} \Xi_{\psi cl} \right\rangle_{t=def}^{U} =$$

$$= \left\langle \frac{\left(\{\xi_{11}\} \cup \cdots \cup \{\xi_{\psi 1}\}\right)}{color_{i=1}} \cup \ldots \cup \frac{\left(\{\xi_{1CL}\} \cup \cdots \cup \{\xi_{\psi 1}\}\right)}{color_{i=Z}} \right\rangle_{t=def}^{U}, \tag{23}$$

where $D_{h_i}^{S}$ is the dynamic region of safe transport mobility; $\Xi = \{\xi_i\}$ is the UTS element; $CL = \{cl_i\}$ are hazard classes; $\Psi = \{\psi_i\}$ is the UTS class; $t = def$ is a definite time moment; U is the index that points to CS UTS.

Let us explain Eq. (23) by using Example 1.

Example 1. A participant of the transportation process h_1 drives a vehicle $\xi_{h_i} = tr_1$ along the route e_{def}. By using Fig. 2, it is necessary to determine the dynamic region of safe transport mobility $D_{h_i}^{S}$ at moment $t = t_{def}$.

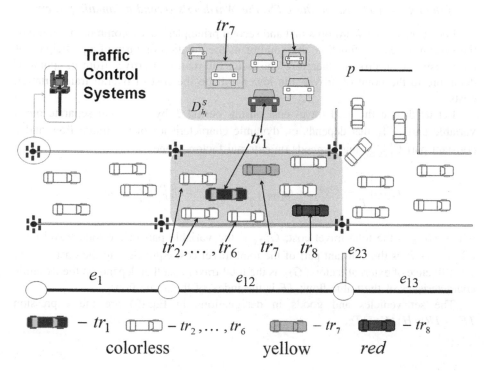

Fig. 2. The dynamic region of safe transport mobility.

For simplicity, we assume that CS UTS separates the UTS elements into 3 hazard classes $CL = \{cl_i,\ i = 1, 2, 3\}$; $|CL| = 3$ such that 1 = colorless; 2 = yellow; 3 = red, and the dynamic region of safe transport mobility (see Fig. 2) contains mobile vehicles of one class ψ ("cars"), the number of which is $tr_2, \ldots, tr_8$.

Solution. A substitution of the initial data into Eq. (23) yields

$$
D^S_{h_1(tr_1)}\Big|^U_{t=def} = \left\langle \bigcup_{cl} \bigcup_{\psi} \ni_{\psi cl} \right\rangle^U_{t=def}
$$

$$
= \left\langle \frac{(\{tr_2; tr_3; tr_4; tr_5; tr_6\})}{color_{i=1}} \cup \frac{(\{tr_7\})}{color_{i=2}} \cup \frac{(\{tr_8\})}{color_{i=3}} \right\rangle^U_{t=def}
$$

Thus, by using CS UTS and having the necessary information on the potential danger from other traffic participants, the participant of the transportation process h_1 unilaterally chooses the route in the traffic flow within the boundaries of the section of the street-road network.

The targets of UTS rely on the Wardrop's second axiomatic principle and the axiomatic principle of UTS safe functioning:

(1) Each user of the network chooses his routes on the basis of the minimization of the total travel costs in the UTS (the Wardrop's second axiomatic principle).

Let us show, that Wardrop's first and second principles have a common optimum of the system which is a function, that minimizes the duration of a trip of a participant of the transportation process; therefore, the faster the road user arrives from the point of departure to the point of arrival, the lower will be the cost of overall transportation costs.

Let us denote the total travel cost during period T by G_{UTS} and separate out a variable part G^{UTS}_{VAR} that depends on dynamic characteristics of the traffic flow and a constant part G^{UTS}_{CONST} that depends on external factors alone

$$
G_{UTS}\Big|_T = \left[G^\Delta_{UTS} + G^\nabla_{UTS}\right]\Big|_T = \left[G_{TF} + G^{UTS}_{EF}\right]\Big|_T \to \min, \tag{24}
$$

where G_{UTS} is the total travel cost; G^Δ_{UTS} is the variable part of the total travel cost; $G^\nabla_{UTS} = G^{UTS}_{EF}$ is the constant part of the total travel cost equivalent to the costs due to the influence of external factors; G_{TF} is the total travel cost that depend on the dynamic characteristics of the traffic flow; TF is the index of the traffic flow.

The set vehicles and goods in designations in Eq. (3) are the expression $TF = TR \cup H \cup Gr \cup Tg$;

We omit the constant part of the total travel cost and obtain:

$$G_{UTS}|_T \sim G_{TF}|_T, \tag{25}$$

Let us consider in more detail the characteristics on which G_{TF} depends. According to [16], they are the value of the flow X, the intensity of the flow M, time of the flow TM, quality of the flow in the network QM; traffic capacity of the network CM. Therefore, G_{TF} acquires the form

$$G_{TF} = G_{TF}(X; M; TM; QM; CM), \tag{26}$$

According to [16], the set of parameters $[X; M; TM; QM; CM]$ correspond to an integral index $TM(X)$, the time of traffic flow, and, hence, the following transition is possible

$$G_{TF}(X; M; TM; QM; CM) \sim G_{TF}(TM(X)), \tag{27}$$

where X is the value of traffic flow; M is the intensity of traffic flow; TM is the time of traffic flow; QM is the quality of traffic flow, and CM is the traffic capacity of UTS.

Then Eq. (27) can be expressed through the function of traffic time limitation (Vrtic et al. [22]):

$$tm_i = \tau_i^0 \left[1 + a \left(\frac{fx_i}{cm_i} \right)^b \right], \tag{28}$$

where τ_i^0 is the time of unconstrained traffic on the "i" route; fx_i is the traffic flow on the "i" route; $cm_i > 0$ is the traffic capacity of the "i" route; $tm_i > 0$ is the travel time of traffic flow on the "i" route; and a, b are calibration coefficients.

If we pass from one route to the UTS, the Wardrop's second principle become accessible at optimization with the limitations the parametric solution of which is given by

$$TM = \min_{fx} \sum_{i=1}^{N} \tau_i^0 \left[1 + a \left(\frac{fx_i}{cm_i} \right)^b \right], \quad X = \sum_i^N fx_i, \, fx_i \geq 0 \tag{29}$$

where $fx = (fx_1, \ldots, fx_i, \ldots, fx_n)$ is the vector of traffic flow distribution X in routes.

Therefore, by comparing Eqs. (21) and (29) we obtain the condition of time optimum

$$g_w \left(x_{\sum} \right) \sim \min \left[tm_w \left(x_{\sum} \right) \right], \tag{30}$$

i.e., the travel time g_w of the traffic flow $x_{\sum}$ in the route connecting the pair $w \in W$ must be minimal.

Under real-time conditions, the traffic participant meets the targets of the user and UTS by choosing the route from the point of departure to the point of arrival that will need the shortest time. The shortest-time route is calculated by car navigation system or a personal planner of the participant of the traffic flow by using the traffic information from traffic control system.

Traffic control system provides the current information on the average speed in the section of the street-road network during the time interval of interest for the user, and car navigation system calculates the shortest-time route by using the Bellman-Ford (Ford Jr., and Fulkerson [23]) or Dijkstra's (Dijkstra [24]) algorithms.

Under real-time conditions Eq. (28) is given by

$$
\mathrm{tm}_l\big|_{\tau=def} = \frac{S_l}{V_l^{\mathrm{avr}}}\Big|_{\tau=def} =
\begin{cases}
n_l \le n_l^{\lim} & V_l^{\mathrm{avr}}\big|_{\tau=def} = V_l^{\mathrm{measured}}\big|_{\tau=def} \le V_l^{\mathrm{permitted}} \\
n_l > n_l^{\lim} & V_i^{\mathrm{avr}}\big|_{\tau=def} = V_l^{\mathrm{measured}}\big|_{\tau=def}
\end{cases}, \quad (31)
$$

and the problem of optimization (29) is

$$
U_{h_i}^{CSUTS}\Big|_{\tau=def} : \quad \left[\{\mathrm{tm}_i(p_i)\}_i^N \to \min_{\{p_i\}} \mathrm{tm}_i(p_i), P_{w=(\partial;\alpha)} = \{p_i\}\right]\Bigg|_{\tau=def}, \quad (32)
$$

where $U_{h_i}^{CSUTS}$ is the functional of car navigation system; $\{\mathrm{tm}_i(p_i)\}$ is the time set for the trip in the route from the point of departure ∂ to the point of arrival α in routes $\{p_i\}$; $\tau = def$ is the access time h_i to the car navigation system.

Let us consider how the first target of UTS is met by using, as an example, the shortest-time route for the user who is planning to go from the point of departure ∂ to the point of arrival α.

Example 2. A traffic participant h_1 at the vehicle is at the crossing of the Ordzhonikidze ave. and Gagarin pr. He is planning to go to the meeting point in the Victory Park (see Fig. 3(A). Technical characteristics of the street-road network and the vehicle and transportation conditions are known (see Fig. 3(B). Find the route which will be recommended by the CS UTS to the traffic participant and its estimated characteristics.

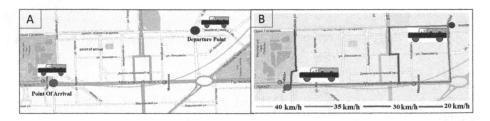

Fig. 3. (A) Route choice (B) Registration of the speed of TC in the SRN (street-road network).

Solution. Having information on the location of the arrival point of the participant of the traffic flow, the speed of the traffic flow at sections of the street-road network in real time, and also technical characteristics of the street-road network, the car navigation system of the participant of the traffic flow will choose the optimal route. The graph of a possible route of the traffic participant is shown in Fig. 4.

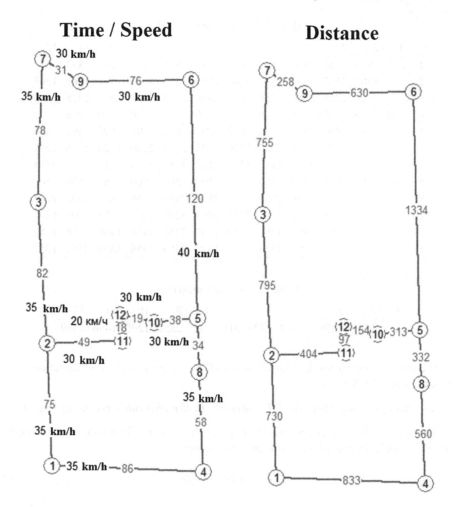

Fig. 4. Graph of the route of the vehicle.

The traffic participant must arrive from node 4 to node 7. Optimization of the route can be performed by CS UTS by using the distance or time parameter. To make the result more reliable, we carry out route optimization by using both parameters. We calculate the shortest route by using the Bellman-Ford and Dijkstra's algorithms. Attention should be paid to the fact that in the case of route optimization by one of the parameters, e.g. distance, the CS UTS can offer the route 4-1-2-3-7 (Tables 1 and 2) with a length of 3133 m (Fig. 5) to the traffic participant.

However, because of the first target of UTS and first target of the user, the system will take into account Eqs. (30)–(32) in the calculations by taking the travel time as a criterion of optimization and will offer the traffic participant the optimal route 4-8-5-6-9-7 (Tables 3 and 4) with a duration of 319 s (Fig. 6).

Table 1. Bellman-Ford algorithm

	1	2	3	4	5	6	7	8	9	10	11	12
1	833	833	833	833	833	833	833	833	833	833	833	833
2	×	1563	1563	1563	1563	1563	1563	1563	1563	1563	1563	1563
3	×	×	2358	2358	2358	2358	2358	2358	2358	2358	2358	2358
4	0	0	0	0	0	0	0	0	0	0	0	0
5	×	892	892	892	892	892	892	892	892	892	892	892
6	×	×	2226	2226	2226	2226	2226	2226	2226	2226	2226	2226
7	×	×	×	3113	3113	3113	3113	3113	3113	3113	3113	3113
8	560	560	560	560	560	560	560	560	560	560	560	560
9	×	×	×	2856	2856	2856	2856	2856	2856	2856	2856	2856
10	×	×	1205	1205	1205	1205	1205	1205	1205	1205	1205	1205
11	×	×	1967	1967	1967	1456	1456	1456	1456	1456	1456	1456
12	×	×	×	2064	1359	1359	1359	1359	1359	1359	1359	1359

Table 2. Dijkstra's algorithm

1	2	3	4	5	6	7	8	9	10	11	12
833	1563	2358	0	892	2226	3113	560	2856	1205	1456	1359

Having considered the first target of CS UTS, we pass to the consideration of the second target of CS UTS.

(2) During the user trip the UTS operates in the allowable reliability region.

The set of values of characteristics CH^{γ_i} of the object γ_i is divided into allowable and irremissible in accordance with the expression:

$$CH^{\gamma_i} = CH^{AL}_{\gamma_i} \cup CH^{IR}_{\gamma_i}, \tag{33}$$

where γ_i denotes the UTS objects (elements) such that $\gamma_i \in (Ts \cup To \cup Tc)$; $CH^{AL}_{\gamma_i}$ is the set of allowable values of characteristics CH^{γ_i} (AL- allowable); and $CH^{IR}_{\gamma_i}$ is the set of irremissible values of characteristics CH^{γ_i} (IR - irremissible);

Thus, the region of allowable and ultimate values of parameters of the UTS objects (elements) the deviation from which leads to deterioration in the functioning and loss of control of UTS is formed.

The condition of operating capability of UTS in the allowable reliability region is written as

$$\forall \gamma_i \in (TS \cup To \cup TC), f_M; f_R; f_\Pi; f_{CS}; f_\psi^d, \forall t, \exists f_C : f_C : u_{\gamma_i} \xrightarrow{r^P_{\gamma_i}(t)(t)} \{ch^{\gamma_i}_\pi, \pi = 1, n\}$$
$$\in CH^{AL}_\pi, \tag{34}$$

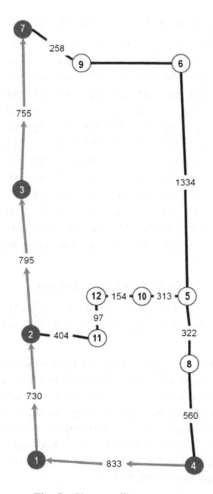

Fig. 5. Shortest-distance route.

where f_{CS} is the operator of control of UTS states; u_{γ_i} is the vector of the object state γ_i; $r_{\gamma_i}^P(t_S)$ is the regulating effect at time moment t_S that keeps the object γ_i in the allowable reliability region by using facilities P.

Equation (34) indicates that for any object γ_i belonging to the set $(Ts \cup To \cup Tc)$ which is in the field of action of UTS operators (operator of measurement of states f_M, operator of regulation of states f_R, operator of planning of changes in states f_Π, operator of control of states f_{CS}, operator of classification of states f_ψ^d) there is an operator of control of the object γ_i which keeps the characteristics of the object γ_i in the allowable reliability region with the help of regulating actions $r_{\gamma_i}^E(t)$. Let us explain how the second target of UTS is met by using as an example the functioning of the control system of the operating condition of the urban street-road network.

Table 3. Bellman – ford algorithm

	1	2	3	4	5	6	7	8	9	10	11	12
1	86	86	86	86	86	86	86	86	86	86	86	86
2	×	161	161	161	161	161	161	161	161	161	161	161
3	×	×	243	243	243	243	243	243	243	243	243	243
4	0	0	0	0	0	0	0	0	0	0	0	0
5	×	92	92	92	92	92	92	92	92	92	92	92
6	×	×	212	212	212	212	212	212	212	212	212	212
7	×	×	×	321	319	319	319	319	319	319	319	319
8	58	58	58	58	58	58	58	58	58	58	58	58
9	×	×	×	288	288	288	288	288	288	288	288	288
10	×	×	130	130	130	130	130	130	130	130	130	130
11	×	×	210	210	210	167	167	167	167	167	167	167
12	×	×	×	228	149	149	149	149	149	149	149	149

Table 4. Dijkstra's algorithm

1	2	3	4	5	6	7	8	9	10	11	12
86	161	243	0	92	212	319	58	288	130	167	149

Example 3. The characteristics registered by CS UTS on section No.1 of the four-lane A class highway with a length of 70 m and a width of 15 m are as follows: there is a damage of the road surface with the total area of $S = 36$ m^2; the level of luminous intensity and illumination from the road lighting systems L1 and L2 in an area of 450 m^2 are $L = 0.2$ cd/m^2 and $E = 1.2$ lm, respectively (see Fig. 7). The maintenance of section No. 1 of the street-road network is carried out by Company. Find the regulating activities suggested by CS UTS in order to restore the operating capability of section No. 1 of the urban street-road network.

Solution. Elements of CS UTS will register the damage of the road surface exceeding the allowable level in 24 times ($36/1.5 = 24$) and a decrease in the required illumination level in 8 times ($1.6/0.2 = 8$).

The regulating action of CS UTS will be to issue the instruction to the road maintenance service to

- carry out urgent repair works on section No.1 to restore a required level of luminous intensity to 1.6 cd/m^2 and illumination up to 20 lm;
- restore the road surface in accordance with the standards - no more than 1.5 m^2 of damages per 1000 m^2;
- issue warning instructions to the participants of the transportation process.

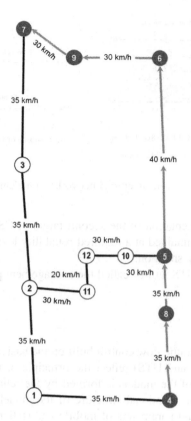

Fig. 6. Shortest-time route.

The formal form of the instructions is

$$
u_{[\text{Section No1}]} = \left\{ \begin{bmatrix} \text{Luminance} \quad L = 0.02\,\text{cd/m}^2 \\ \text{Luminous intensity} \quad E = 1.2\,\text{lm} \\ [\text{Road damage } S = 36\,\text{m}^2] \end{bmatrix} \xrightarrow{r_{[\text{section No1}]}^{[\text{Company}-1]}(t_{\text{repair}})} \begin{bmatrix} L = 1.6\,\text{cd/m}^2 \\ E = 20\,\text{lm} \\ [S = 0.3\,\text{m}^2] \end{bmatrix} \right\}
$$

$$
r_{[\text{section No1}]}^{[\text{Company}-1]}(t_{\text{repair}}) = \begin{bmatrix} \begin{bmatrix} L = 0.02\,\text{cd/m}^2 \xrightarrow{\uparrow} L = 1.6\,\text{cd/m}^2 \\ E = 1.2\,\text{lm} \xrightarrow{\uparrow} L = 20\,\text{lm} \end{bmatrix} \xrightarrow{\text{repair}} L1, L2 \\ \begin{bmatrix} S = 36\,\text{m}^2 \xrightarrow{\downarrow} S = 0.3\,\text{m}^2 \end{bmatrix} \xrightarrow{\text{repair}} \text{SectionNo1} \end{bmatrix}_{T=5days}
$$

$$
r^{[\text{Drivers}]}(\textit{inform}) = \begin{bmatrix} \text{Faulty lighting[Section No1]} \rightarrow \begin{matrix} L = 0.02\,\text{cd/m}^2 \\ E = 1.2\,\text{lm} \end{matrix} \\ \text{Damaged road[Section No1]} \rightarrow S = 36\,\text{m}^2 \end{bmatrix}
$$

where $\uparrow, \downarrow$ denote "to decrease" and "to increase", $\rightarrow$ is the implication sign, and $\wedge$ is the conjunction sign.

Road Class A traffic of more than 3000 vehicles /day

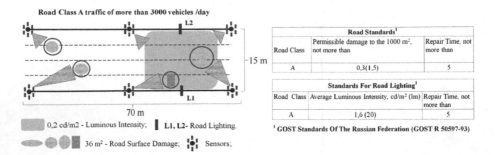

Fig. 7. Section of urban street-road network) with elements of CS UTS.

Therefore, the implementation of the second target of CS UTS allows the state of the UTS objects to be maintained at a required reliability level. It also ensures a quick response to an emergency situation.

Targets of users and UTS will be called the management principles of urban traffic.

7 Conclusions

The models of the urban traffic flow control built on the basis of the target management function (targets of users and UTS) reflect the principle of rational self-organization. The information content of the models is formed by the reliable information from the traffic control system. The functional structure of the models allows one to take into account dynamic states and parameters of mobile and stationary transport facilities.

The implementation of the models we propose is able to increase the capacity of the transportation system of a metropolis by achieving an efficient distribution of traffic flow and to enhance the reliability (Nowakowski [25], Dhillon [26]) and control (Cappelle et al. [27], Zhang and Wang [28]) by informing participants of the transport process (Wahle and Schreckenberg [29], Lequerica et al. [30]).

Acknowledgments. Authors are grateful for financial support to the Russian Foundation for Basic Research. The scientific research was supported by the Russian Foundation for Basic Research within the framework of the project 16-3100306 «Development of the model of intelligent control of urban traffic».

References

1. Qiao, F., Yang, H., Lam, W.H.K.: Intelligent simulation and prediction of traffic flow dispersion. Transp. Res. Part B: Methodol. **35**(9), 843–863 (2001). doi:10.1016/S0191-2615(00)00024-2
2. Lord, D., Mannering, F.: The statistical analysis of crash-frequency data: a review and assessment of methodological alternatives. Transp. Res. Part A: Policy Pract. **44**(5), 291–305 (2010). doi:10.1016/j.tra.2010.02.001

3. Zhang, H.M.: A non-equilibrium traffic model devoid of gas-like behavior. Transp. Res. Part B: Methodol. **36**(3), 275–290 (2002). doi:10.1016/S0191-2615(00)00050-3

4. Li, J., Zhang, H.M.: The variational formulation of a non-equilibrium traffic flow model: theory and implications. Transp. Res. Part B: Methodol. **57**(C), 314–325 (2013). doi:10.1016/j.sbspro.2013.05.019

5. Hess, S., Bierlaire, M., Polak, J.W.: Estimation of value of travel-time savings using mixed logit models. Transp. Res. Part A: Policy Pract. **39**(2–3), 221–236 (2005). doi:10.1016/j.tra.2004.09.007

6. Yang, H., Huang, H.-J.: The multi-class, multi-criteria traffic network equilibrium and systems optimum problem. Transp. Res. Part B: Methodol. **38**(1), 1–15 (2004). doi:10.1016/S0191-2615(02)00074-7

7. Barth, D., Bournez, O., Boussaton, O., Cohen, J.: Distributed learning of wardrop equilibria. In: Calude, C.S., Costa, J.F., Freund, R., Oswald, M., Rozenberg, G. (eds.) UC 2008. LNCS, vol. 5204, pp. 19–32. Springer, Heidelberg (2008). doi:10.1007/978-3-540-85194-3_5

8. Costeseque, G., Lebacque, J.-P.: A variational formulation for higher order macroscopic traffic flow models: numerical investigation. Transp. Res. Part B: Methodol. **70**, 112–133 (2014). doi:10.1016/j.trb.2014.08.012

9. Claudel, C.G., Bayen, A.M.: Lax-Hopf based incorporation of internal boundary conditions into Hamilton-Jacobi equation. Part I: theory. IEEE Trans. Autom. Control **55**(5), 1142–1157 (2010). doi:10.1109/TAC.2010.2041976

10. Xu, H., Pang, J.-S., Ordóñez, F., Dessouky, M.: Complementarity models for traffic equilibrium with ridesharing. Trans. Res. Part B: Methodol. **81**(P1), 161–182 (2015). doi:10.1016/j.trb.2015.08.013

11. Daganzo, C.F.: Urban gridlock: macroscopic modeling and mitigation approaches. Transp. Res. Part B: Methodol. **41**(1), 49–62 (2007). doi:10.1016/j.trb.2006.03.001

12. Seliverstov, Y.A., Seliverstov, S.A.: Methods and models of the construction of transport correspondence matrix. St. Petersburg State Polytech. Univ. J. Comput. Sci. Telecommun. Control Syst. (2–3)(217–222), 49–70 (2015). doi:10.5862/JCSTCS/5. http://ntv.spbstu.ru/humanities/article/T2-3.217-222.2015_05/

13. Seliverstov, Y.A., Seliverstov, S.A.: The distribution modeling and development traffic flows in Megapolises. Izvestiya SPbGETU «LETI» (1)(C) 43–50 (2013). http://www.eltech.ru/assets/files/university/izdatelstvo/izvestiya-spbgetu-leti/LETI_1_13.pdf

14. Daganzo, C.: The cell transmission model: a dynamic representation of highway traffic consistent with the hydrodynamic theory. Transp. Res. **28B**(4), 269–287 (1994). doi:10.1016/0191-2615(94)90002-7

15. Daganzo, C.: The cell transmission model, part II: network traffic. Transp. Res. **29B**(2), 79–93 (1995). doi:10.1016/0191-2615(94)00022-R

16. Daganzo, C.: A variational formulation of kinematic waves: basic theory and complex boundary conditions. Transp. Res. B **39B**(2), 187–196 (2005). doi:10.1016/j.trb.2004.04.003

17. Daganzo, C.: On the variational theory of traffic flow: well-posedness, duality and applications. Netw. Heterogen. Media **1**, 601–619 (2006). http://www.its.berkeley.edu/sites/default/files/publications/UCB/2006/VWP/UCB-ITS-VWP-2006-2.pdf

18. Newell, G.F.: A simplified theory of kinematic waves in highway traffic, part II: queuing at freeway bottlenecks. Transp. Res. B **27B**(4), 289–303 (1993). doi:10.1016/0191-2615(93)90039-D

19. Wardrop, J.: Some theoretical aspects of road traffic research. Proc. Inst. Civil Eng. Part II **1** (36), 352–362 (1952). http://www.icevirtuallibrary.com/doi/abs/10.1680/ipeds.1952.11259

20. Hasan, S.F., Siddique, N., Chakraborty, S.: Intelligent Transport Systems: 802.11-Based Roadside-to-Vehicle Communications, XX, 152 p., Hardcover (2013). doi:10.1007/978-1-4614-3272-2

21. Seliverstov, Y.A.: Formal description of the socio - economic behavior of the urban population using a model classification of agent - based relations for transport systems control of the metropolis. Internet J. Naukovedenie **5**(24), 1–39 (2014). http://naukovedenie.ru/PDF/159TVN514.pdf

22. Vrtic, M., Frohlich, P., Schussler, N., Axhausen, K.W., Lohse, D., Schiller, C., Teichert, H.: Two dimensionally constrained disaggregate trip generation, distribution and mode choice model: theory and application for a Swiss national model. Transp. Res. A **41**, 857–873 (2007). doi:10.1016/j.tra.2006.10.003

23. Ford Jr., L.R., Fulkerson, D.R.: Flows in Networks, p. 216. Princeton University Press, Princeton (1692). https://www.rand.org/content/dam/rand/pubs/reports/2007/R375.pdf

24. Dijkstra, E.W.: A Note on two problems in connexion with graphs. Numer. Math. **1**, 269–271 (1959). http://www-m3.ma.tum.de/foswiki/pub/MN0506/WebHome/dijkstra.pdf

25. Nowakowski, T.: Reliability model of combined transportation system. In: Spitzer, C., Schmocker, U., Dang, V.N. (eds.) Probabilistic Safety Assessment and Management, pp. 2012–2017. Springer, London (2004). doi:10.1007/978-0-85729-410-4_323

26. Dhillon, B.S.: Human Reliability and Error in Transportation Systems. Springer, London (2007). doi:10.1007/978-1-84628-812-8. 182 p.

27. Cappelle, C., Najjar, M., Pomorski, D., et al.: Intelligent geolocalization in urban areas using global positioning systems, three-dimensional geographic information systems, and vision. J. Intell. Transp. Syst. **2010**(14), 3–12 (2012). doi:10.1080/15472450903385999

28. Zhang, Z.X., Wang, Y.H.: Automatic object classification using motion blob based local feature fusion for traffic scene surveillance. Front Comput. Sci. China **2012**(6), 537–546 (2012). doi:10.1007/s11704-012-1296-7. https://link.springer.com/article/10.1007/s11704-012-1296-7

29. Liu, D.: Implementation of intelligent dynamic tracking monitoring system for vehicle transportation-in hazardous goods. In: Jia, Y., Du, J., Zhang, W., Li, H. (eds.) Proceedings of 2016 Chinese Intelligent Systems Conference. LNEE, vol. 404, pp. 119–127. Springer, Singapore (2016). doi:10.1007/978-981-10-2338-5_12

30. Lequerica, I., Ruiz, P.M., Cabrera, V.: Improvement of vehicular communications by using 3G capabilities to disseminate control information. IEEE Netw. **24**(1), 32–38 (2010). doi:10.1109/MNET.2010.5395781

Decision Support System for Urbanization of the Northern Part of the Volga-Akhtuba Floodplain (Russia) on the Basis of Interdisciplinary Computer Modeling

Alexander Voronin, Inessa Isaeva, Alexander Khoperskov$^{(\boxtimes)}$,
and Sergey Grebenjuk

Volgograd State University, Volgograd 400062, Russia
{voronin,khoperskov}@volsu.ru
http://www.volsu.ru/persons/id/?id=000000183,
http://www.infomod.ru/akhoperskov

Abstract. There is a computer decision support system (CDSS) for urbanization of the northern part of the Volga-Akhtuba floodplain. This system includes subsystems of cognitive and game-theoretic analysis, geoinformation and hydrodynamic simulations. The paper presents the cognitive graph, two-level and three-level models of hierarchical games for the cases of uncontrolled and controlled development of the problem situation. We described the quantitative analysis of the effects of different strategies for the spatial distribution of the urbanized territories. For this reason we conducted the territory zoning according to the level of negative consequences of urbanization for various agents. In addition, we found an analytical solution for games with the linear dependence of the average flooded area on the urbanized area. We numerically computed a game equilibrium for dependences derived from the imitational geoinformation and hydrodynamic modeling of flooding. As the result, we showed that the transition to the three-level management system and the implementation of an optimal urbanization strategy minimize its negative consequences.

Keywords: Cognitive analysis · Game theory · Geoinformatics · Numerical modeling · Decision support system

1 Introduction

The Volga-Akhtuba Floodplain (VAF) is a unique natural landscape in the lower reaches of the Volga River and its normal existence is determined by its spring high water. Volzhskaya HPP (VHPP) usually regulates the hydrological regime of the Volga in the interests of hydropower industry, and it has significantly been reducing the spring water volume compared to natural flooding since 11 large dams appeared on the river [1]. In recent years, the Volga-Akhtuba plain has been flooded rarely more than 40% of its total area. Factors of floodplain territory

© Springer International Publishing AG 2017
A. Kravets et al. (Eds.): CIT&DS 2017, CCIS 754, pp. 419–429, 2017.
DOI: 10.1007/978-3-319-65551-2_30

dehydration are the limitation of flood peaks due to the requirements of hydrological safety of expanding agricultural and urbanized territories and natural and anthropogenic degradations of numerous small channels in the interfluve area.

Active and uncontrolled urbanization can significantly accelerate the degradation of the floodplain nature. So, an actual problem is creating the scientifically based decision supporting system for the VAF territory development. This system should ensure the sustainability of the ecosystem, and other interests of population, business entities and authorities. Here we represent the structure of the Decision Support System (DSS) for development of the northern part of the Volga-Akhtuba floodplain and its application for the management of the urbanization process. Subsystems of cognitive and game-theoretic analysis, geoinformation and hydrodynamic simulation modeling are components of our DSS. These subsystems we can use separately or in different combinations to solve various control tasks. Our previous works [2,3] describe the use of this DSS in the management of the flood hydrological regime and hydrotechnical projects in the northern part of the VAF.

2   Structure of the Decision Support System

2.1   The Subsystem of Cognitive Analysis

This subsystem includes a module for PEST + E-analysis, and modules for the construction and analysis of cognitive maps. We identified the following main groups of actors in the system: the collective agent (land buyers in the interfluve), the management centers (municipal and federal level), and the operational and development priorities (hydrological safety, environmental and socio-economic priorities). The general long-term priority is the preservation of the VAF ecosystem, and the short-term priority is the preservation of the flooding area.

We identified the following main factors that influence the urbanization of VAF:

1. The volume of spring flood.
2. The condition of small channels of VAF.
3. The average flooded area ($S_f(S)$).
4. The area of economic lands.
5. The limit of flooded area.
6. The indicator of floodplain ecosystem condition (Φ).
7. The level of economic activity in VAF.
8. The indicator of life's quality in VAF.
9. The level of infrastructure development.
10. The number of inhabitants in VAF.
11. The value of the objective function of the collective agent (f_A).
12. The area of the urbanized territory of VAF (S).
13. The selling price of land (p).
14. The value of the objective function of the municipal authority (f_M).
15. The value of the objective function of the federal center (f_F).

16. The fine rate (R).

17. The maximum area offered for sale.

The cognitive graph of an uncontrolled process contains 15 vertices from the 1st to the 14th and 17th in Fig. 1. In the figure, we graph each link with a solid line and a corresponding symbol "+" or "–", making a decision with a pointed line, and fast interaction with a thin line, slow interaction with a bold line. As we see, the graph contains unstable cycles for the fast interactions $(3 - 17 - 12 - 5 - 3)$ and stable cycles for the slow interactions $(3 - 6 - 8 - 11 - 12 - 10 - 7 - 4 - 2 - 3)$, $(3 - 6 - 16 - 14 - 13 - 11 - 12 - 10 - 7 - 4 - 2 - 3)$, $(3 - 6 - 8 - 11 - 12 - 5 - 3)$.

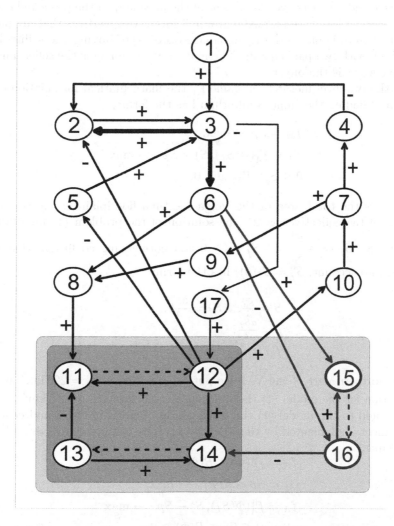

Fig. 1. A fragment of the cognitive graph of the VAF development for the cases of uncontrolled and controlled urbanization of the territory

Our analysis of the graph shows that the slow stabilization of the urbanization process in the case of high effective demand leads to the depletion of the available territory and/or the decline the life quality in the VAF with the degradation of the ecosystem. Vertexes 15, 16 and corresponding edges of the graph (see Fig. 1) describe elements of the mechanisms of environmental and economic management [4–9]. The goal of the management is to change ecological and socio-economic parameters of equilibrium.

2.2   The Subsystem of Game-Theoretic Analysis

The intent of the subsystem of game-theoretic analysis of the situation is a qualitative and quantitative assessment of the adequacy of the projected control mechanisms. In Fig. 1 we marked a group of interacting vertices that are part of the game-theoretic model of the unmanaged process of buying and selling lands of the VAF with two participants. The municipal authority is the seller, and the collective agent is the buyer.

For the two-level hierarchical game Γ_1 the mathematical formulation of the problem of finding the game equilibrium has the form:

$$
\begin{aligned}
& f_M = Sp \to \max_p, \\
& f_A = f_A^0(\Phi(S_f), S) - Sp \longrightarrow \max_S, \\
& 0 \le S \le S_0, \; p \ge 0,
\end{aligned}
\tag{1}
$$

where S_0 is the total area of the Volga-Akhtuba floodplain, f_A^0 is the utility function of the collective agent. The solution of the problem (1) for functions $f_A^0 = aS_f S$, $S_f = -\dfrac{S_f^0}{S_0}S + S_f^0$ ($a \ge 0$ is a normalizing coefficient that takes demand into account, $S_f^0 = S_f(0)$) has the form:

$$
\begin{aligned}
& S = \frac{S_0}{4}, \quad S_f = \frac{3S_f^0}{4}, \\
& p = \frac{aS_f^0}{2}, \\
& f_M = \frac{aS_f^0 S_0}{8}, \quad f_A = \frac{aS_f^0 S_0}{16}.
\end{aligned}
\tag{2}
$$

For the northern part of the VAF we put $S_0 = 867\,\mathrm{km}^2$, $S_f^0 = 220\,\mathrm{km}^2$ and got the solution for the model (1) the solution $S = 217\,\mathrm{km}^2$, $S_f = 165\,\mathrm{km}^2$.

If we add to the model (1) the mechanisms of environmental and economic management implemented by the federal center, we can get a three-level hierarchical game:

$$
\begin{aligned}
& f_F = f_F^0(\Phi) + R(\Phi) \longrightarrow \max_R \\
& f_M = Sp - R(\Phi) \longrightarrow \max_p, \\
& f_A = f_A^0(\Phi(S_f), S) - Sp \longrightarrow \max_S \\
& 0 \le S \le S_0, \quad R(\Phi) \ge 0,
\end{aligned}
\tag{3}
$$

where f_F^0 is a function of the environmental utility of the federal center.

For functions

$$f_A^0 = aS_f S, \quad S_f = -\frac{S_f^0}{S_0} S + S_f^0,$$

$$f_F^0 = bS_f, \quad R = \lambda \left(S_f^0 - S_f \right)$$

(where $b \geq 0$ is a normalizing factor that takes into account the environmental value of the VAF, $\lambda \geq 0$ is an optimized fine rate from the federal government) the solution of problem (3) is equilibrium in the Hermeyer's hierarchical game, and it has the form

$$S = \frac{S_0}{8} (1 - \varepsilon),$$

$$S_f = \frac{S_f^0}{8} (7 + \varepsilon),$$

$$p = \frac{aS_f^0}{4} (3 + \varepsilon),$$

$$\lambda = \frac{aS_0}{2} (1 + \varepsilon),$$

$$f_F = \frac{aS_f^0 S_0}{16} (1 + 14\varepsilon + \varepsilon^2),$$

$$f_M = \frac{aS_f^0 S_0}{32} (1 - \varepsilon)^2,$$

$$f_A = \frac{aS_f^0 S_0}{64} (1 - \varepsilon)^2,$$

$$\varepsilon = \frac{b}{aS_0} \quad (0 \leq \varepsilon \leq 1).$$

(4)

We adopted $a = 5 \cdot 10^5$ RUB/km^4 for numerical estimates.

In the case of $\varepsilon \geq 1$ the solution $S = 0$ is valid. Comparison of (2) and (4) shows that the fines mechanism reduces twice the equilibrium value of the urbanized territory area and also it causes the growth of the average area of flooding even in the case of $\varepsilon = 0$, if the penalty rate is determined by the price of land and $\lambda = \frac{2pS_0}{3S_f^0}$. In addition, the received amounts of fines can be used to finance environmental projects. The municipal center can vary the strategies of offering land properties and determine the actual form of $S_f(S)$ according to the conditions of flooding and the ecological value of these land properties. This function is convex if we use an aggressive urbanization strategy based on the order of the land sale according to their ecological value. In the opposite case, we have a concave function $S_f(S)$.

The exact form of the function $S_f(S)$ is determined by the features of the topography and the flooding regime of the VAF. To simulate the dependences of $S_f(S)$ in the problems (1) and (3), we used here the subsystems of geoinformation and hydrodynamic modeling.

2.3   The Subsystem of Geoinformation Modeling

The basis of our digital elevation model (DEM) for VAF in the form of heights matrix $b(x_i, y_j)$ are SRTM DEM and ASTER GDEM satellite data with a resolution of up to 20 m in the earth's plane and up to 0.5 m vertically. To create the DEM we used the universal geoinformation system "Panorama" and special spatial data software [10]. We perform an annual update of the DEM with new open satellite imagery of the US geological service (Landsat 8 Satellite), and with our own GPS measurements of flooding boundaries.

The current VAF vector map includes a layer of the hydraulic system with 1542 riverbeds, a layer of infrastructure with 118 settlements, and a relief layer with more than 15,000 relief objects. In addition to DEM, this subsystem includes a cadastral digital map and a cadastral database of VAF. Figure 2 shows a digital map of VAF, where the areas of potential urbanization are highlighted with different colors.

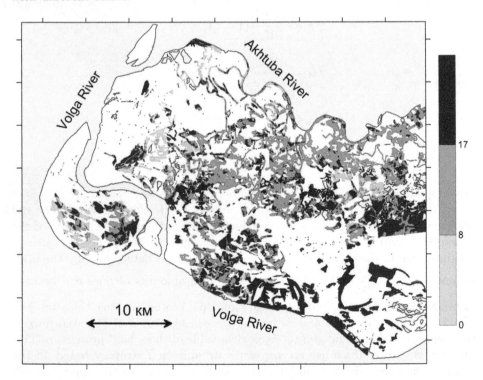

Fig. 2. Map of the territory of the VAF. Different colors show areas of potential urbanization. Numbers show the non-flooding frequency of each map's point for the last 18 years

3   The Subsystem of Hydrodynamic Modeling of Floods

We used a numerical model of the shallow water dynamics and we took into account all the main factors of the territory flooding [11]:

- mode of water supply through the Volga Hydroelectric Power Station (hydrograph);
- surface and underground water sources;
- terrain relief including anthropogenic development of the territory;
- relief of the bottom of reservoirs;
- properties of the underlying surface (bottom friction, infiltration);
- internal viscous friction;
- wind effect;
- rotation of the Earth;
- evaporation.

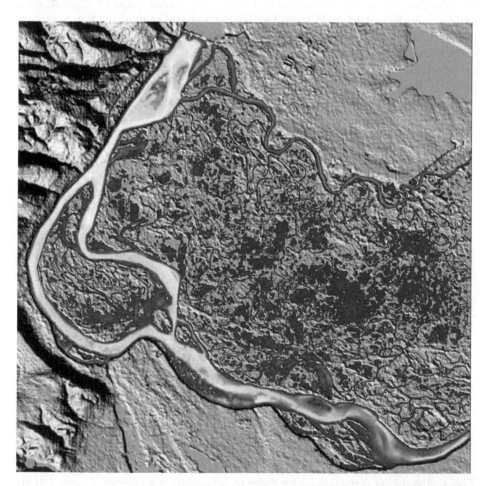

Fig. 3. An example of the spring flood simulation in the northern part of the floodplain

The result of numerical simulations of shallow water is a set of maps of water depth distribution at different times (Fig. 3). To assess the adequacy of the model we compared the results of numerical simulations with the water level observation data at four gauging stations in the northern part of the VAF and we checked the calculated water surface area in 2012–2016 against the Landsat-7 satellite data. We implemented parallel OpenMP, CUDA, OpenMP-CUDA versions of the calculation module for the combined Smoothed Particle Hydrodynamics – Total Variation Diminishing (CSPH-TVD) method, which significantly reduced the required computing resources [12].

4   Simulation Modeling of the Urbanization Process

The subsystem of urbanization imitation modeling makes it possible to analyze the ecological consequences of decisions about the flooding of certain zones. The information basis for analysis is a set of the digital maps of flooding with hydrographs from 1990 to 2016 and a digital cadastral map of the northern part of the VAF. As the result of this module functioning we got the parameters determination for safe and dangerous hydrographs, and the maps of maximum safe flooding of a given part of the VAF. We calculated the frequency of the territory flooding, as well as the predicted value of the average flooding area with guarantee no flooding of this territory.

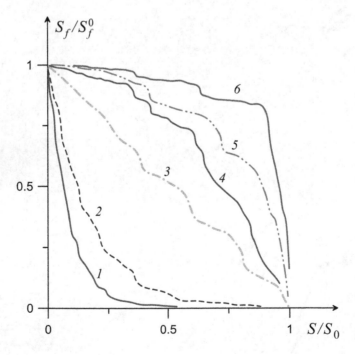

Fig. 4. Simulation dependencies for different urbanization strategies. Curves 1–6 are ordered according to the degree of ecological efficiency

Table 1. The ordering of the three zones in urbanization strategies

Strategy number	1	2	3	4	5	6
Zones order	1 2 3	1 3 2	2 1 3	2 3 1	3 1 2	3 2 1

Let us discuss the results of the consequences analysis for the various urbanization strategies obtained in the interdisciplinary simulation (Fig. 4). The joint analysis of the cadastral and flood maps of the VAF allowed to estimate the frequency of flooding for various sites of potential urbanization. To analyze the impact of urbanization strategies in the VAF on its flooding regime, we built the dependencies $S_f(S)$ for various strategies of lands marketing assignment. The strategies were ordered by the environmental friendliness.

Unsold territory was divided into three zones according to the frequency of flooding: 1 – frequent event, 2 – medium event, 3 – rare event. We numbered the grid nodes of the DEM within each zone randomly in accordance with the information uncertainty. In Table 1 we indicated the ordering of zones in our strategies. For example, in strategy 2, randomly selected areas from zone 1 are subsequently offered for sale. Then we repeat this procedure for zone 3 and then for zone 2.

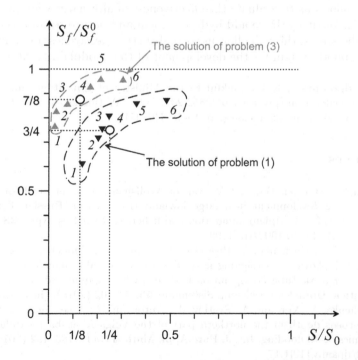

Fig. 5. The solutions of problems (1) and (3) for the simulation dependencies $S_f(S)$ shown in Fig. 4 for $\varepsilon = 0$

We calculated the average value of the flooding area using a set of flood maps for the years 1990–2016, but we excluded the maps where selected urbanized zone is flooded. Figure 4 shows the curves of $S_f(S)$ for the strategies indicated in Table 1. Then, for each of the dependencies $S_f(S)$ (see Fig. 4) we found numerical solutions of problems (1) and (3) for $\varepsilon = 0$. Because of the difficulty in estimating the value of epsilon in numerical experiments we used lower or guaranteed estimates of the functions (4) corresponding to the value of $\varepsilon = 0$. With the growth of ε, the solution of problem (3) locates to the point $(0; 1)$. Figure 5 shows the points that correspond to these solutions. Circles indicate the positions of solutions (2) and (4). Figure 5 demonstrates that the decrease of the equilibrium value S in problem (3) stabilizes the unstable cycle in Fig. 1 for large values of the ecological criterion in comparison with problem (1). In addition, the use of environmental urbanization strategies leads to a significant increase in its effectiveness, both in terms of environmental and socio-economic criterion.

5   Conclusion

The presented simulation results show that the multidisciplinary Computer decision support system on the development of the territory of the Volga-Akhtuba floodplain allows us to evaluate the effectiveness of alternatives for the development of this territory. If we add hydrotechnical and nature restoration projects control subsystems, this will allow us to analyze the effectiveness of an integrated decision support system for the development of the floodplain territory.

Acknowledgments. AK is thankful to the Ministry of Education and Science of the Russian Federation (project No. 2.852.2017/4.6). AV thanks the RFBR grant and Volgograd Region Administration (No. 16-48-340147).

References

1. Gorski, K., van den Bosch, L.V., van de Wolfshaar, K.E., et al.: Post-damming flow regime development in a large lowland river (Volga, Russian Federation): implications for floodplain inundation and fisheries. River Res. Appl. **28**(8), 1121–1134 (2012). doi:10.1002/rra.1499
2. Voronin, A., Vasilchenko, A., Pisareva, M., Pisarev, A., Khoperskov, A., Khrapov, S., Podschipkova, J.: Designing a system for ecological-economical management of the Volga-Akhtuba floodplain on basis of hydrodynamic and geoinformational simulation. Upravlenie Bolshimi Sistemami **55**, 79–102 (2015). (in Russian)
3. Vasilchenko, A., Voronin, A., Svetlov, A., Antonyan, N.: Assessment of the impact of riverbeds depth in the northern part of the Volga-Akhtuba floodplain on the dynamics of its flooding. Int. J. Pure Appl. Math. **110**(1), 183–192 (2016). doi:10.12732/ijpam.v110i1.17
4. Ahmad, S., Simonovic, S.P.: An intelligent decision support system for management of floods. Water Resour. Manag. **20**, 391–410 (2006). doi:10.1007/s11269-006-0326-3

5. Burkov, V.N., Korgin, N.A., Novikov, D.A.: Control mechanisms for organizational-technical systems: problems of integration and decomposition. IFAC-PapersOnLine **49**(32), 1–6 (2016). doi:10.1016/j.ifacol.2016.12.180
6. Novikov, D.: Theory of Control in Organizations. Nova Science Publishers, New York (2013)
7. Haghighi, A.T., Klove, B.: Development of monthly optimal flow regimes for allocated environmental flow considering natural flow regimes and several surface water protection targets. Ecol. Eng. **82**, 390–399 (2015). doi:10.1016/j.ecoleng.2015.05.035
8. Ougolnitsky, G.A.: Game theoretic formalization of the concept of sustainable development in the hierarchical control systems. Ann. Oper. Res. **220**(1), 69–86 (2014). doi:10.1007/s10479-012-1090-9
9. Brunetti, I., Hayel, Y., Altman, E.: State-policy dynamics in evolutionary games. Dyn. Games Appl., 1–24 (2016). doi:10.1007/s13235-016-0208-0
10. Voronin, A.A., Vasilchenko, A.A., Pisarev, A.V., Khrapov, S.S., Radchenko, Y.E.: Designing mechanisms of the hydrological regime management of the Volga-Akhtuba floodplain based on geoinformation and hydrodynamic modeling. Sci. J. Volgogr. State Univ. Math. Phys. **1**(32), 24–37 (2016). doi:10.15688/jvolsu1.2016.1.3. (in Russian)
11. Khrapov, S., Pisarev, A., Kobelev, I., Zhumaliev, A., Agafonnikova, E., Losev, A., Khoperskov, A.: The numerical simulation of shallow water: estimation of the roughness coefficient on the flood stage. Adv. Mech. Eng. **2013**, 11 p. (2013). Article ID 787016. doi:10.1155/2013/787016
12. Dyakonova, T., Khoperskov, A., Khrapov, S.: Numerical model of shallow water: the use of NVIDIA CUDA graphics processors. Commun. Comput. Inf. Sci. **687**, 132–145 (2017). doi:10.1007/978-3-319-55669-7_11

Geoanalytical System for Support of Urban Processes Management Tasks

Svetlana Ustugova[1], Danila Parygin[1(✉)], Natalia Sadovnikova[1],
Vibhash Yadav[2], and Inna Prikhodkova[1]

[1] Volgograd State Technical University, Volgograd, Russia
ustugova.s@gmail.com, dparygin@gmail.com,
npsnl@ya.ru, inna.vt@mail.ru
[2] Krishna Institute of Technology, Kanpur, India
vibhashdsl0@gmail.com

Abstract. Modern approaches to work with big data on urban processes are discussed in the paper, including Data-Driven City and Geoinformation systems (GIS). Analysis of GIS allowed to select their types according to the scope of application and the concept of analytical problems solved by the user. A new approach to support the urban processes management based on geodata analysis is proposed in this study. The concept of the system being developed is based on the idea of combining the functions of GIS and decision support system on the basis of an integrated database. The integration process is based on the ETL process. Typical infrastructure facilities, their characteristics, and geo-referencing become the basis of the geo-analytical system. The method of infographic presentation on an interactive map of data of urban infrastructure typical facilities monitoring at different stages of complex systems research is proposed. The architecture of the created information and analytical platform described. The work of platform prototype considered on an example of information support of processes related to the road repair works in the city.

Keywords: Information integration · Urban data visualization · GIS · Information and analytical platform · Decision support · Geospatial data · Urban processes management · Heterogeneous data · ETL process · Geo database

1 Introduction

The modern urban environment is a complex system. Its effective management requires to use the most current decision support methods.

The directions aimed at using the "Big Data" technologies in the sphere of urban management which have become trends in recent years. The digital revolution and rising internet penetration gave rise to a new phenomenon – the Data-Driven City (DDC). A data-driven city is characterized by the ability of agencies of city management to use technologies for generation of data flows, their processing and analysis aimed for the adoption of solutions for improvement of living standards of residents thanks to the development of social, economic and ecological areas of the urban environment [1].

© Springer International Publishing AG 2017
A. Kravets et al. (Eds.): CIT&DS 2017, CCIS 754, pp. 430–440, 2017.
DOI: 10.1007/978-3-319-65551-2_31

Modern GIS in the field of urban management is a technological platform that provides integration of the spatial, temporal and information component of urban life. They provide the interaction of various information services on a unified basis.

The new concept of decision support in urban management tasks is based on the ability to analyze data related to processes in the city, as well as with new technologies for modeling and forecasting events in space and time. Geoportals are the key resources that combine heterogeneous data from a variety of sources related to geographic location. Thanks to this because solutions to the issues of redistributing the load of transport and engineering networks, forecasting real estate prices, analyzing environmental safety, justifying development plans for the territories, etc. can be found.

Although many research projects about urban data management, knowledge fusion across heterogeneous data and urban data visualization have been done in recent time, there are still quite a few technologies that are missing or not well studied. For example, the problem of integrating heterogeneous data remains one of the most complex. First of all, the data that needs to be integrated is not always structured and has great heterogeneity. In addition, data is often repeated, while having the same semantic meaning but present in different models. The way to access data is an important integration issue. Designing an architecture of integrated data warehouse is another of the top priorities.

A new approach to supporting the urban processes management based on geodata analysis is proposed in this study. Thus, the ability to select data about objects and events on various parameters, analyze regularities, create interactive thematic maps appears.

2 Background

The amount of data related to urban processes is growing every year. The task of combining heterogeneous data becomes relevant for the subsequent joint analysis and use for solving problems of city management, analysis of object states, forecasting situations, development planning, etc. Integration of heterogeneous data into a single information environment provides the possibility of their complex analysis and allows to obtain qualitatively new knowledge about the object of research.

Integration based on geoinformation systems (GIS) is one of the most common ways of organizing data storage about cities. GIS are designed specifically for the management and analysis of spatial relationships and offer many benefits to the city management. The technological basis for such solutions is usually the libraries of programming interfaces such as the Google Maps API, Mapserver Mapscript, Scanex GeoMixer, etc. They provide access to the functions and context of the cartographic elements of web pages such as map visualization tools, thematic data: road network with data on traffic jams, relief, a directory of organizations, goods, and services, etc. [2].

There are a large number of software solutions based on GIS, which allows to solve various city problems. GIS can be divided according to the scope of application and the concept of analytical problems solved by the user:

- Property management and portfolio management. An example of such GIS can be considered Geoinformation System of St. Petersburg [3], geoportal YUGRA [4].
- Management of operation and space. For example, Town-Planning Atlas of the City of Tomsk [5], Zoning Maps of the District of Columbia [6], Current Master Plan Future General Land Use by City of Detroit [7].
- Service management. An example of such a GIS can be the portal Our City [8].
- Management of environmental protection and sustainable development. Examples are the GIS Remote Monitoring Information System of the Federal Forestry Agency [9], GIS Arctic [10], Grand Public Geoportal Luxembourg [11].
- Preparedness for emergency situations. For example, the project Spaceimages-Fires [12].
- Visualization. For example, Geoinformation System of Industrial Parks, Technoparks and Clusters of the Russian Federation [13], Earth [14], Epidemiological Atlas [15].
- Presentation of statistics. Examples of such services exist for individual counties and cities, for example, for Los Angeles, USA [16], Liverpool, England [17] and for whole countries, for example, according to the US census [18] or by key indicators of urban development in the UK [19].

3   Concept and Architecture

The concept of the system being developed is based on the idea of combining the functions of GIS and DSS on the basis of an integrated database. In this connection, it is necessary to create an interactive work environment that will allow to control the process of data collection and integration, their preprocessing and presentation in a single visual space. At the same time, the system should provide decision support functionality for monitoring of urban processes, case management, and development tasks implementation.

The conceptual requirements for the system determined the need for an approach in the presentation of information. In this regard, the method of infographic presentation on an interactive map of data of urban infrastructure typical facilities monitoring at different stages of complex systems research was proposed. The method allows to visually present information about events and processes that occur in different parts of the city and includes the following steps:

1. A single interactive space is organized on a digital cartographic basis.
2. Special point, linear or polygonal markers represent conflict management situations, critical events, processes and infrastructure facilities.
3. Markers are provided with an interactive interface that allows to call up a menu with a situation designation and a list of services whose activities are directly related to the event or process.
4. The timeline is formed using controls in the form of sliders and a calendar that provides the ability to simultaneously view plans and tasks of various services and also the history of events.

5. Viewing standard situations for events that are related to the "season of the year - day of the week - time of day" time conditions is implemented in such a way that it allows you to visualize regular events and forecast critical situations that could affect the implementation of activity plans for various services.
6. Switching between the specialized maps set in the output mode menu on the main screen of additional layers with a display of the infrastructure facilities and the factors of impact (residential buildings, lines of communication, route network, weather radar, information of civil defense and emergency situations, etc.).
7. Control elements of visualization modes are created in the form of sliders, buttons and other tools for filtering output information and allow you to vary color schemes for outputting messages, states, etc.

The architecture of the created Information and Analytical Platform (IAP) will include four complex components (see Fig. 1): a client application, micro services and a web-server for data processing that are linked by XML/JSON HTTP requests to provide for the joint collection, processing and presentation of data, as well as a data warehouse. Microservices includes an unlimited set of mobile and web applications for data collection, their special processing and partial presentation [20]. The client application implements the integrated management of all the information in the system through a single interactive work environment on a digital cartographic basis and access to decision-support tools. The web-server provides management of requests for access to information from the storage with the use of data processing models. The data warehouse implements the integration of information for its subsequent presentation in the format of a Geoinformation system.

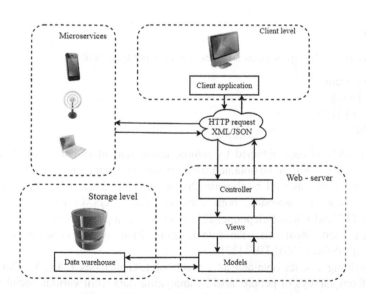

Fig. 1. Architecture of the information and analytical platform

Representational State Transfer (REST) technology is proposed to be used for implementation. Architecture in the style of REST consists of clients and servers. Clients initiate requests to servers. Servers process requests and return appropriate responses. Requests and answers are created based on the transfer of resource representations. REST is originally described in the context of HTTP but is not limited to this protocol. RESTful-type architectures can be based on other application-layer protocols if they already implement an extensive and unified vocabulary for applications that are based on the transmission of meaningful state representations [21]. Thus, in this project, the use of such architecture allows to work with the presentation in various formats, have greater scalability, low embedding costs and a small load of computing resources and also have speed.

4 Integration and Presentation of Data on Geographically Distributed Systems

The tendency of development of modern GIS may be defined as database-driven cartography [2]: "Because GIS has always had the capability of managing data over a wide geographic extent, it includes many tools for map projections and for handling large data volumes. GIS can have different data requirements and behaviors (business rules). The functional elements of GIS include data input, storage, management, retrieval, manipulation, analysis and modeling, output and display". In this regard, the key issue in the design of a geo-analytic system-oriented solution to support the management of urban processes is the development of the database structure.

4.1 Data

Within existing urban processes sources can be distinguished:

- Sensory Data.
- Text Mining.
- Statistical Data.
- GIS Data.

Sensory data is data obtained by remote measurement and the collection of any information [22]. Data can be obtained from sensors that can monitor the level of noise, pollution in the city as well as climatic changes (precipitation, wind, humidity). As a medium for data transmission, both wireless (Radio, GSM/GPRS, ZigBee, WiFi, WiMax, LTE) and wired (telephone, ISDN, xDSL, computer) networks (electrical or optical) are used. Most often the data is transmitted by a text string of the form "NAME_SENSOR = VALUE" [23].

Text mining is data obtained as a result of text analysis [24, 25]. Data can be obtained from surveys of people, also by analyzing data from various social networks [26]. For example, on the website Active citizen [27] weekly survey of residents of Moscow, thanks to which to consider their views on various issues.

Statistical data is a set of objects (observations, events) and attributes (variables) that characterize them [28]. Data can be obtained from a variety of public sources.

For example, on the open data portal of Moscow Government [29] presented different statistical data on the urban infrastructure. Data can be previewed and downloaded in various formats: ".csv", ".xml", ".xlsx", ".json", ".geojson".

GIS data is digital data about spatial objects, including information about their location and properties, spatial and non-spatial attributes [30]. Such data can be obtained from users of various mobile applications and data can be obtained from various specialized sites, such as 2GIS. Another source of data can be social networks in which geotags are used.

4.2 The Concept of Integration

The data integration is the process of combining data from different sources and presenting data to users in a unified form. The integration process is based on the ETL process. The ETL process solves the problems of extracting data from different types of sources, converting them to a form suitable for storage in a certain structure as well as uploading to the appropriate database or data warehouse. In the framework of the problem being solved, the ETL process can be represented in the following form (see Fig. 2).

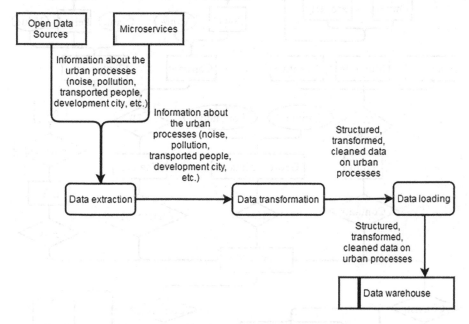

Fig. 2. ETL process

In recent years, there have been many projects focused on the consolidation of data. Among them are iron.io [31], dolater.io [32] and others. All these services help to manipulate data from different sources. However, they provide only remote jobs but do not perform information fusion for researchers. Other services such as Data Lake are oriented to big data analysis and represent a whole system of the data warehouse. Since the information and analytical platform should be an entire data warehouse system and based on the allocated data sources, information processes and tasks that the information and analytical platform should solve, a conceptual data model was constructed, as shown in the Fig. 3.

To describe IAP, it was proposed to use the term "Object". This is the basic value by which the maximum functionality of analytical work with geospatial data is possible. This term implies four basic configurations ("point", "perimeter", "collection" and "line"), whose representation is possible on a cartographic basis.

All objects are tied to the terrain via geographic coordinates and also the converse statement is true, when each coordinate or group of coordinates is some object. Coordinates are always described by the pair "latitude, longitude".

In addition, some objects have constant and temporary characteristics. Time property inherent in all objects and is characterized by a certain feasible time period and measure a value for processes that are important only for its duration.

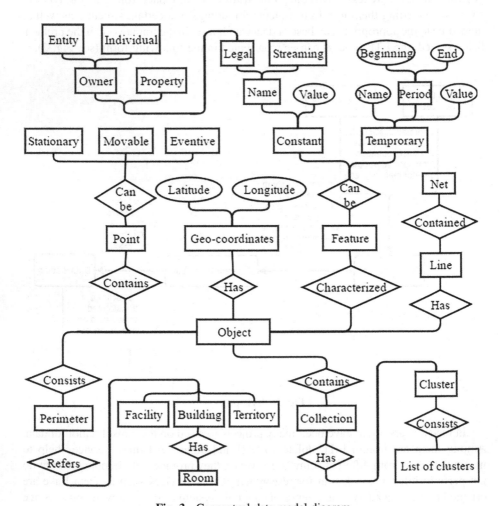

Fig. 3. Conceptual data model diagram

The constant properties are described by the pair "name, value" and have a list of prescribed titles, such as, for example, the legal status of the object, including its subject-object definition. The subjectivity is fixed by the legal status of an individual or organizational affiliation. At the same time for the true ownership of the implementation of the interim specifications, which may denote a constant or rental of property identity.

The basic configuration of the object as a point consists of stationary, mobile and event types and appears to be a single coordinate pair. The stationary type describes locations of equipment and real estate infrastructure, industrial, points, on the ground, etc. Movable type characterizes a temporal location obviously is intended to move objects, machinery, vehicles, people, etc. Vent type includes the location of the actual news, informational or warning messages about accidents, crimes, violations of processes of functioning and providing the required resources etc.

Objects in the form of parameter include territorial structures, buildings, and structures. At the same time, territorial or area structures include, for example, land resources, impact zones, settlements, which may include other objects of different configurations. Buildings are structures that do not have internal premises or have unexploited internal spaces, the main value of which is their integral representation, such as power line supports, monuments etc. Buildings are voluminous structures with a certain number of maintained internal premises which stand out as independent enclosed or making up whole objects.

Objects in the form of a set of points describe structured and chaotic arrays of locations. The formalization of their representation is the clusters included in the lists of clusters.

Linear objects are closed, open, intersecting coordinate sequences that describe structures, one of the main characteristics of which is the value of the flow. Lines can be grouped in a network. Examples of such configurations are roads, routes, power lines, pipelines and utility networks.

5   Example of the Use of the Information and Analytical Platform

The developed platform provides informational and analytical support for effective management solutions based on the objective and multiparameter information. So the IAP allows:

- Receive media information.
- Model visual representation of important facilities.
- Display various city facilities on a map.
- Monitor movement patterns of transport, residents, and other.
- Collect indicators from various sensors and reflect them on a map, etc.

The work of platform prototype can be considered on an example of information support of processes related to the road repair works in the city. In [33] describes a situation related to the repair and temporary block of traffic on the auto-pedestrian bridge in the Central district of the city of Volgograd. Repair work had an impact on the normal operation of various city services and urban processes. Correction of the planned activities of some departments and involving others in solving the related tasks of others was required.

The system identifies this event as critical. The corresponding indication for the problem of territory plot should be displayed on the main screen (see Fig. 4), where all events, like point objects, are displayed with orange icons and linear objects are represented by connected color lines. The marker icon indicates the main source or the basic departmental affiliation of the problem.

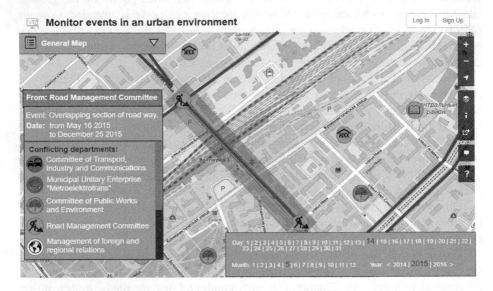

Fig. 4. Output of the request results in the IAP map

The IAP requires information from the data store to display the event in the example on a map basis. The corresponding query to the data store is as follows: http://127.0.0.1:8000/searchrouts/?latitude=48710894&longitude=44517987&start=01.03.2015

In turn, the selection occurs in the data store:

```
object = Object.objects.all()
object.filter(coordinates__ latitude= latitude)
object.filter(coordinates__ longitude= longitude)
object.filter(characteristics__temporary__start= start)
return object
```

6   Conclusion

The implementation of this project will allow to integrate information resources and organize access to all interested parties. Various applications [33, 34] becomes microservices of IAP and supply a wide range of data for the drive of urban development management issues. The proposed concept of data integration is based on the

ETL process and combines data on the city through the links of the simplest elements of space. Typical infrastructure facilities, their characteristics, and geo-referencing have become the basis of the geo-analytical system. The proposed method of representation allows creating a unified working environment. Thus, the informational and analytical platform built on these principles will provide support for solving the most complex tasks of urban management.

Acknowledgements. The reported study was funded by RFBR according to the research projects No. 16-07-00353_a, No. 16-07-00388_a.

References

1. Data-driven cities. From concept to applied solutions. http://www.pwc.ru/en/government-and-public-sector/assets/ddc_eng.pdf
2. Cartographic Design Process: Artistic Interpretation With the Geodatabase. http://www.esri.com/library/whitepapers/pdfs/cartographic-design.pdf
3. Geoinformation system of St. Petersburg. https://gu.spb.ru/188545/mfcservice/
4. The geoportal of UGRA. https://maps.crru.ru/smaps/cmViewer.php
5. The town-planning atlas the city of Tomsk. https://map.admtomsk.ru/main/map_all.html#!system=tomsk_all&bank=1&layers=moLayer_scen,streetLayer_scen&page=home&base=osm
6. Zoning Maps of the District of Columbia. https://maps.dcoz.dc.gov
7. Open Data Portal for the City of Detroit. https://data.detroitmi.gov/Property-Parcels/Current-Master-Plan-Future-General-Land-Use/89q2-aduf
8. Our city. http://gorod.mos.ru/?show=about
9. The information system of remote monitoring of the Federal Forestry Agency. https://nffc.aviales.ru/main_pages/index.shtml
10. The Arctic GIS. http://arctic.rekod.ru/
11. Grand Public Geoportal Luxembourg. http://map.geoportail.lu
12. The project Space images-fires. http://fires.kosmosnimki.ru/
13. Geo-information system of industrial parks, science parks and clusters of the Russian Federation. https://www.gisip.ru/#!ru/
14. Earth. https://earth.nullschool.net/ru/
15. Epidemiological atlas. http://epid-atlas.nniiem.ru/
16. Los Angeles Times. http://maps.latimes.com/neighborhoods/
17. Liverpool City Council. http://liverpool.gov.uk/council/key-statistics-and-data/ward-profiles/ward-map/
18. CensusViewer. http://censusviewer.com/free-maps-and-data-links/
19. The Centre for Cities. http://www.centreforcities.org/data-tool/
20. Golubev, A., Chechetkin, I., Parygin, D., Sokolov, A., Shcherbakov, M.: Geospatial data generation and preprocessing tools for urban computing system development. In: 5th International Young Scientist Conference on Computational Science, pp. 217–226. Elsevier BV, Krakow (2016)
21. REST – architecture. https://html-templates.info/blog/znakomtes-arhitektura-REST
22. Sokolov, A., Tyukov, A., Sadovnikova, N., Zhuk, S., Khrzhanovskaya, O., Brebels, A.: Automatic information retrieval and preprocessing for energy management. In: Kravets, A., Shcherbakov, M., Kultsova, M., Shabalina, O. (eds.) Creativity in Intelligent Technologies and Data Science. CCIS, vol. 535, pp. 462–473. Springer, Cham (2015). doi:10.1007/978-3-319-23766-4_37

23. Finogeev, A.G., Parygin, D.S., Finogeev, A.A.: The convergence computing model for big sensor data mining and knowledge discovery. Hum.-Cent. Comput. Inf. Sci. **7**, Article no. 11 (2017). https://hcis-journal.springeropen.com/articles/10.1186/s13673-017-0092-7
24. Korobkin, D., Fomenkov, S., Kolesnikov, S., Golovanchikov, A.: Technical function discovery in patent databases for generating innovative solutions. In: International Conferences on ICT, Society, and Human Beings 2016, Web Based Communities and Social Media 2016, Big Data Analytics, Data Mining and Computational Intelligence 2016, and Theory and Practice in Modern Computing 2016, pp. 241–245. IADIS International Association for Development of the Information Society, Madeira (2016)
25. Korobkin, D., Fomenkov, S., Kravets, A., Golovanchikov, A.: Patent data analysis system for information extraction tasks. In: 13th International Conference on Applied Computing, pp. 215–219. IADIS International Association for Development of the Information Society, Mannheim (2016)
26. Text mining. https://sites.google.com/site/upravlenieznaniami/tehnologii-upravlenia-znaniami/text-mining-web-mining/text-mining
27. Active citizen. https://ag.mos.ru/
28. The statistical data. http://statlab.kubsu.ru/node/4
29. Open data portal of the Government of Moscow. https://data.mos.ru/opendata
30. GIS data. http://dic.academic.ru/dic.nsf/fin_enc/27995
31. Cloud-based message queuing and async task processing. http://www.iron.io/
32. Simple and hassle free background tasks. http://dolater.io/
33. Parygin, D., Sadovnikova, N., Kalinkina, M., Potapova, T., Finogeev, A.: Visualization of data about events in the urban environment for the decision support of the city services actions coordination. In: 5th International Conference on System Modeling & Advancement in Research Trends, pp. 283–290. CCSIT TMU, Moradabad (2016)
34. Ustugova, S., Parygin, D., Sadovnikova, N., Finogeev, A., Kizim, A.: Monitoring of social reactions to support decision making on issues of urban territory management. In: 5th International Young Scientist Conference on Computational Science, pp. 243–252. Elsevier BV, Krakow (2016)

The Technique of Extracting Knowledge About Buildings' and Constructions' Day Energy Consumption Models

Timur Janovsky[1(✉)], Artyom Kirichuk[1], Anton Tyukov[1],
Maxim Shcherbakov[1], Alexander Sokolov[1], and Adriaan Brebels[2]

[1] Volgograd State Technical University, Volgograd, Russia
janovsky@yandex.ru, mfstarosta@gmail.com,
anton.tyukov@gmail.com, maxim.shcherbakov@gmail.com,
alexander.sokolov.it@gmail.com
[2] Katholieke Universiteit Leuven, Leuven, Belgium
adriaan.brebels@portacapena.com

Abstract. The research paper proposes the methodology of extracting knowledge about the similarity of a certain building's or construction's day energy consumption profiles. The methodology is based on the methods of mathematical statistics. With its help distinguishing of the days in the object's explored past that have the profiles similar to the target day becomes possible. The researcher proposes hypotheses on other features resembling the target day, except for the energy consumption profiles. Having assumed the reasons of the profiles' repetition and distinguished the days consolidated by a certain feature, with the help of the methodology the researcher can verify whether these days are dominating in the set. The acquired knowledge – the set of accepted or rejected hypotheses about the similarity/difference of the past days compared with the target one – allows to identify hidden patterns in the object's energy consumption. They significantly facilitate the important tasks of forecasting, identifying the outliers and managing the energy consumption.

The methodology can be applied to the analysis of buildings and constructions of various functional and typological groups, working by "day/night" mode. The practical aspects of the methodology's application are illustrated with examples, based on the EcoSCADA data.

Keywords: Energy resources consumption · Time series · Consumption profile · Forecasting · Methods of mathematical statistics · Chi-square test · Non-parametric mean rank test

1 Introduction

The aim of energy management of buildings and structures (further called Objects) is the minimization of costs for the business processes' energy supply. Its accomplishment at many industrial and commercial objects is connected to high-quality forecasting [1–4]. For example, the costs of Russia's industrial enterprises for electric power procurement at day-ahead market sector depend on accordance of the actual

© Springer International Publishing AG 2017
A. Kravets et al. (Eds.): CIT&DS 2017, CCIS 754, pp. 441–451, 2017.
DOI: 10.1007/978-3-319-65551-2_32

consumption to the forecast, presented in the applications for the purchase. Focusing on the forecast, energy consumers analyze the effectiveness of its use, monitor the critical differences between the forecast and actual consumption [2], in order to prevent over-expenditure on time, to localize the accident, etc.

What is necessary to make an accurate forecast of the energy consumption?

When answering this question, it should be noted firstly that quality of such a forecast is an objective measure of maturity, the perfection of object's business processes and staff high qualification. Factually, the accurate forecast can't be obtained without discipline and maturity of processes related to loading of energy consuming facilities, monitoring, and awareness of the decision maker on the structure and nature of energy consumption. This awareness includes the analytical work on object's energy consumption schedule on the selected piece of historic data.

This analysis leads to discovering the repeatability of energy consumption profiles [1, 3, 5–7], that is the consequence of repetition of object's business processes. The repeatability may be caused by working schedule of the object, replication of technological equipment's workload and downtime operational plans, other reasons [8, 9]. Reviewing the repeatability allows to achieve a very important knowledge on the actual functioning of the object for effective management and forecasting of its activity and energy consumption.

One more circumstance is to be noted. Energy consumption monitoring and forecasting services are actively developing their client network in many countries [10]. Companies representing this service "run" hundreds of different objects, which functional features either are unknown or can't be taken into consideration under the general analysis and forecasting algorithms. There are some cases when the actual functioning of the object differs from the one forecasted by poorly informed owner or manager. In these conditions automation of energy consumption profiles' repeatability reviewing becomes particularly relevant in solving tasks on acquiring knowledge about the object, monitoring, forecasting and its management. The research paper is devoted to this question.

2   Problem Statement

The target of research is a building or a construction of unrestricted functional-typological affiliation, which business processes, presumably, are inherent in repeatability. To ensure certainty, the object operates in a widespread mode "active daily/non-active at night". Data on its energy consumption is a time series of hourly consumption of a certain energy resource (electrical and heat energy, gas, etc.) for a period of 6 to 12 months.

Energy consumption data of a trade center in Belgium (extracted from EcoSCADA [10], 2016) was used as test data: 7 average energy consumption profiles for each day of the week (Fig. 1) were replicated artificially for 42 weeks, forming a half-year time series.

At the same time, normally distributed interference is superimposed onto hourly parameters of energy consumption specific for each of the 7 profiles. It imitates deviations in energy consumption caused by accidental factors. The standard deviation of this random component is 17–25% from the average number at a stated date and time.

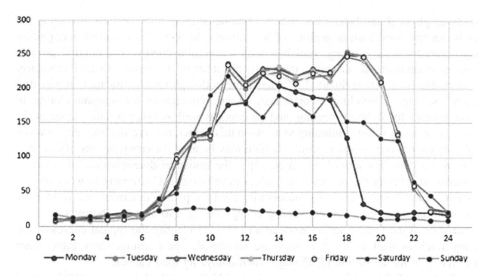

Fig. 1. Average energy consumption profiles of a trade center (kWh)

Reason to use artificial data is simple: objective knowledge about similarity or disparity of profiles of various weekdays is needed to accurately interpret the results of extracting knowledge about the implementation of profiles' similarity methodology on test data.

The aim of research is to offer a researcher an instrument for discovering the repeatability of object's energy consumption profiles and studying its features and causes.

On the reliable basis of statistics, it is necessary to:

1. find a set of days, which energy consumption profile is similar (with an accuracy to accidental interference) to a target day profile in the time period of energy consumption preceding the target day;

2. test the hypothesis of the cause of the profile repeatability characteristic feature in the time before a target day: this reason (feature) accompanies a subset of days the similarity of which to the target ones is systematically greater than that of the others in the found set.

3 Review of the Relevant Approaches and Literature

There is a great amount of scientific publications of the last decade that are devoted to retrieval of information from energy consumption time series and its application to simulating [7, 11], forecasting [5, 7–9, 12], identifying the outliers [5, 7, 11] and objects' dispatch control [5, 13, 14].

There are some publications among them that deserve the particular interest in the context of this paper, as they are the ones where the phenomenon of energy consumption profiles' repeatability is studied. In 2005 Yao and Steemers [8] turn to the study of physical and behavioral factors when developing a method for predicting the daily energy consumption profiles of households. In work [5] a pattern recognition algorithm for distinguishing weekdays with the similar energy consumption profiles and development of dispatch management strategy is represented. Particularly remarkable is the article Stuart [12], where a methodology for identification of potential energy savings in buildings is presented, taking into account the seasonal change in requirements for lighting, heating, and cooling, as well as other weather features. Li et al. [7] in some sense continuing to work on this aspect, analyze the implicit variables of daily energy consumption profiles, which may be used for grouping sets of data into various clusters. The aim of the article [9] is the statistical determination of behavior patterns, supporting the energy user profiles development. Continuing to work on this aspect, in 2012 Abreu et al. [6] successfully used the pattern determination to identify the habitual behavior when consuming energy taking into account the internal characteristics of the family. In the work Jota et al. [15] identify the typical curves of the daily load, as well as the way they are simulated. Their results show rather high efficiency of the clustering technology when analyzing load curves.

Authors of the publication reviewed [1, 11] the methodology of calculation of energy conservation potentials in commercial buildings with the help of the predictive models. Simulation based on the characteristic of repeatability of daily electricity consumption and included the acquiring of statistically based conclusions regarding the division of the time interval under study into a set of time intervals repeating cyclically in a certain order, each of which is characterized by a definite profile of the energy consumption that can be adequately described by the local model [1]. Later, this mathematical-statistical method of identifying repetitive consumption profiles was more thoroughly elaborated and formalized [11].

The peculiarity of the authors' approach [1, 11] to the study of the repeatability of object's energy consumption is that when analyzing the time series of energy consumption: (1) no information on the peculiarities of the object's functioning, except the most general assumptions is used; (2) the phenomenon of repeatability is revealed by mathematical-statistical processing methods of the time series; (3) only after such processing the matching of results with information on the object's functioning is allowed. The approach is applicable when there is a shortage of information about the investigated object, which is relevant for automatic monitoring of a variety of heterogeneous objects. But especially important is the fact that the approach is able to reveal a dangerous discrepancy between the information of the manager or the power engineer about the object of reality ("the object lives its own life").

4 Methodology

According to the objectives the methodology of extracting knowledge about the similarity of daily energy consumption profiles provides the following stages:

1. Determination of the set of days, the energy profile of which coincides with the accuracy of the random deviations with the profile of the target day;

2. Testing hypotheses about the reasons of the repeatability in the past of the target day's profile or about the characteristic features that accompany the repetition of the target day's profile in the past of the object (for example, weekday may be such a feature);

Firstly, the target day is chosen – this is one of the days which energy consumption profile drew the researcher's attention and he wants to test whether there was the repetition of this profile in the past.

First Stage. The target day's profile consisting of the 24 parameters of hourly energy resource consumption, for example, electricity, is compared alternately with each of the profiles in the reviewed past. The statistical measure of the difference between the profiles of the target and the days compared with it, we select [1] the value of the statistic subordinate to the χ^2- distribution:

$$\chi^2 = \sum_{i=1}^{24} \frac{(E_i - \hat{E}_i)^2}{E_i} \tag{1}$$

Here E_i and $\hat{E}_i$ are the amount of measurement units of energy resources, consumed in i-th hour of the target and compared days, respectively. They are interpreted as the expected and observed frequencies of 24 grouping intervals, respectively.

Taking into account the features of the chi-square agreement criterion, correction of the initial values of the consumed energy resource is needed, so that the adjusted values range from 1 to 12–20 according to the recommendations of K. Cochran [16]. A correction factor is used or a transition to another unit of measurement is made, for example, from kWh to mWh.

The hypothesis of statistic agreement of energy consumption profiles of the compared days is performed at the significance level $\alpha = 0.05$, if

$$\hat{\chi}^2 \leq \chi^2_{23,0.05} \tag{2}$$

where $\chi^2_{23,0.05} = 35, 2$ is the parameter of the upper 5% distribution point. Otherwise, the alternative hypothesis about disagreement (disparity) is accepted.

The set of days with energy consumption profiles that have accomplished the similarity test to the target day profile is intended for further analysis. For example, when test data for the target day - Monday 2016/12/19 - are processed, a set of 23 similar days in the past were obtained.

The results (Figs. 2 and 3) confirm the fact known by data construction (Fig. 1) that the Mondays of different weeks have a different energy profile from other weekdays, and even an imposed interference can't hide the strong similarity of Mondays between themselves and their difference from other days of the week. Here the hypothesis of profiles similarity on Mondays does not need verification.

Consider another target day - Saturday 2016/12/24. An increase in the level of the interference overlaid on the 42-week repeated profile (the standard deviation is increased up to 39% of the profile parameters), leads to the result in Fig. 4.

№	Date	Day Of The Week	Chi-Square Stat.	№	Date	Day Of The Week	Chi-Square Stat.
1	2016/11/14	Monday	3,89	13	2016/10/31	Monday	8,93
2	2016/10/24	Monday	4,45	14	2016/8/1	Monday	8,96
3	2016/7/25	Monday	4,74	15	2016/12/12	Monday	9,25
4	2016/11/28	Monday	5,24	16	2016/12/5	Monday	9,80
5	2016/9/19	Monday	5,17	17	2016/7/11	Monday	9,85
6	2016/8/29	Monday	5,59	18	2016/11/7	Monday	11,47
7	2016/10/3	Monday	6,54	19	2016/9/26	Monday	11,57
8	2016/8/15	Monday	6,47	20	2016/10/10	Monday	14,11
9	2016/9/12	Monday	6,71	21	2016/8/8	Monday	14,45
10	2016/10/17	Monday	6,99	22	2016/11/21	Monday	14,39
11	2016/7/18	Monday	7,31	23	2016/9/5	Monday	15,79
12	2016/8/22	Monday	8,55				

Fig. 2. The set of days with energy consumption profile as of the day Monday 2016/12/19

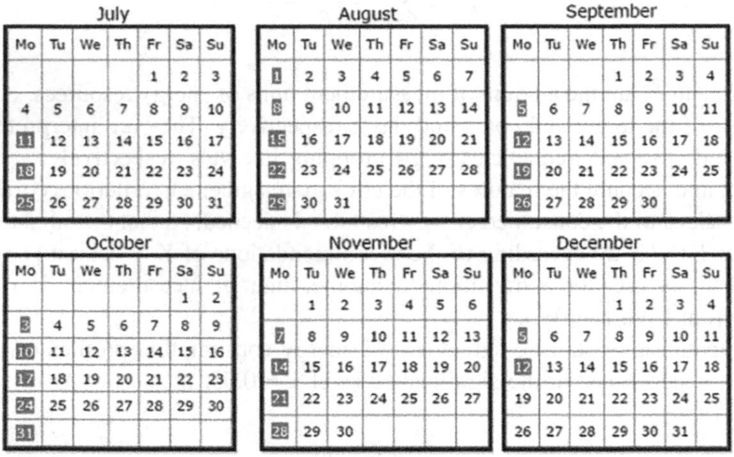

Fig. 3. The set of days with the energy consumption profile similar to Monday 2016/12/19

Here, a set of days similar to the electricity consumption consists not only of Saturdays but also of other days of the week, which similarity to the target day is accidental. This situation is typical: random deviations of energy consumption hide the feature of the profile 2016/12/24 repeatability in the past. This feature is belonging to the same day of the week - Saturday.

Analyzing the set obtained in stage 1, the researcher wants to understand whether there is a pattern in the repetition of the profile so to find the reason for the repeatability or the characteristic feature accompanying the repetition of the profile. Comparing the results of the first stage with additional information about the object or assumptions that are valid for a specific functional-typological group of objects, he can assume a feature or reason - the weekday, the object maintenance by a certain shift of workers, the

№	Date	Day Of The Week	Chi-Square Stat.	№	Date	Day Of The Week	Chi-Square Stat.
1	2016/8/25	Saturday	17,11	16	2016/10/13	Thursday	30,27
2	2016/8/27	Saturday	17,51	17	2016/8/13	Saturday	30,48
3	2016/10/29	Saturday	18,25	18	2016/12/10	Saturday	30,60
4	2016/7/30	Saturday	19,95	19	2016/10/1	Saturday	30,59
5	2016/8/6	Saturday	20,05	20	2016/8/5	Friday	31,00
6	2016/7/16	Saturday	20,49	21	2016/11/18	Friday	31,50
7	2016/10/8	Saturday	20,77	22	2016/11/26	Saturday	31,56
8	2016/9/2	Friday	21,43	23	2016/11/25	Friday	32,04
9	2016/8/12	Friday	23,23	24	2016/8/19	Friday	33,29
10	2016/12/17	Saturday	25,80	25	2016/11/12	Saturday	33,87
11	2016/9/8	Thursday	27,81	26	2016/11/24	Thursday	34,79
12	2016/9/7	Wednesday	27,89	27	2016/8/26	Friday	34,94
13	2016/11/15	Tuesday	28,46	28	2016/9/10	Thursday	34,89
14	2016/12/3	Saturday	29,18	29	2016/10/14	Friday	35,20
15	2016/7/28	Thursday	29,72				

Fig. 4. The set of days with energy consumption profile as in the target day Saturday 2016/12/24

importation of batch for processing on the eve or something else. Then actions can be formalized and supported within the framework of the second stage of the methodology.

Second Stage

A. Assuming a feature or reason for the repeatability in the past of the target day energy profile, it is necessary to distinguish from the set found at the 1st stage a group of days, to which this reason or feature is also immanent. In Fig. 4 Saturdays are already highlighted, as the researcher presumably had drawn attention to the fact that this simplest feature unites many of the selected days with the target one.

The set of similar days is divided into two groups: the first is formed by days united with the target one by the feature under consideration; the second – all other days.

B. The significance of the difference between the two samples is tested. The first is formed by the statistics' $\hat{\chi}^2$ value 2 days from the first group; second sample - the values of $\hat{\chi}^2$ days of the second group.

To test the hypothesis at significance level $\alpha = 0.05$, we apply a nonparametric mean ranks difference criterion [17], that is algebraically equivalent to known criteria – the sums of Wilcoxon ranks and the Mann–Whitney U test:

1. The data of the samples are combined and arranged in ascending order to obtain the ranks of the parameters in the combined set;
2. Average parameters of all ranks for each sample are calculated, R_1 and R_2;
3. The difference $R_2 - R_1$ is determined;
4. The parameter of statistics, which distribution is well approximated by Student's t-distribution, is calculated

$$t_R = \frac{R_2 - R_1}{(n_1 + n_2)\sqrt{\frac{n_1 + n_2 + 1}{12 * n_1 * n_2}}},$$

5. If $t_R \leq t_{\infty, 0.05}(= 1.96)$, the null hypothesis is accepted. Otherwise, the alternative one is.

In the context of the methodology, the acceptance of the null hypothesis means that there is no reason to consider the days distinguished in accordance with a feature or reason "more similar" in terms of energy consumption to a target day than some other days from the set of the similar ones. The acceptance of an alternative hypothesis means that there is a reason to believe so. This certainly increases the practical value of the tested feature or the importance of the anticipated reason, gives basis to regard them as noteworthy.

Let us turn to the samples in Fig. 5. It should be noted that the ranks in the combined set coincide with the row numbers in Fig. 4.

$$R_1 = 10.93 \text{ and } R_2 = 18.8. \ R_2 - R_1 = 7.87. \ \rho = 7.87/3.16 = 2.49.$$

A null hypothesis is declined and an alternative hypothesis is accepted. Hence the similarity of Saturdays to the target day (Saturday) is systematically higher than the similarity of other days.

№	Day Of The Week	Sample 1	№	Day Of The Week	Sample 2
1	Saturday	17,11	1	Friday	21,43
2	Saturday	17,51	2	Friday	23,23
3	Saturday	18,25	3	Thursday	27,81
4	Saturday	19,95	4	Wednesday	27,89
5	Saturday	20,05	5	Tuesday	28,46
6	Saturday	20,49	6	Thursday	29,72
7	Saturday	20,77	7	Thursday	30,27
8	Saturday	25,80	8	Friday	31,00
9	Saturday	29,18	9	Friday	31,50
10	Saturday	30,48	10	Friday	32,04
11	Saturday	30,60	11	Friday	33,29
12	Saturday	30,59	12	Thursday	34,79
13	Saturday	31,56	13	Friday	34,94
14	Saturday	33,87	14	Thursday	34,89
			15	Friday	35,20

Fig. 5. The samples formed on Fig. 4 data

5 Discussion

1. First of all, it should be noted that the presented methodology includes steps of varying degrees of formalization. Easy to formalize: statistical analysis of the profiles of days similarity, testing the hypothesis of a systematically greater similarity to the target set of days combined with a discovered common feature or cause of similarity. But a number of steps are difficult or impossible to formalize. Firstly, it is a search for the reason (feature) of the repetition of the target day's profile in the past. This search involves analyzing the collected set of similar days considering the energy consumption profile and comparing the facts of repeatability with direct or indirect features, possible causes (weekday, end of the month, work of the same shift, repetition of a model work plan). Such work requires the use of additional information about the object, the introduction of various assumptions and can't be formalized. The same can be said about the researcher's extraction of knowledge about the repeatability of energy consumption profiles from the results of a statistical test of the hypothesis in step B of the second stage. It is obvious that testing this hypothesis gives the researcher an objective fact. What does it include? The researcher asks the question: is it true that the feature or cause he found out is accompanied by a discovered set of similar days by a particularly similar group? And he gets an affirmative or negative answer to this question. However, it does not mean that, for example, the true cause or the best feature of repeatability is found. We emphasize that the methodology provides the researcher with certain statistical facts that need to be interpreted and explained before becoming the knowledge. That is something useful for understanding the essence of what is happening or practical application.
2. The nonparametric criterion of the mean ranks difference used in step B of the second stage does not correlate the volumes of the two samples. Although, it could be useful. One matter is when the feature or cause of repeatability assumed by a researcher is inherent in almost the entire set of similar days discovered at the first stage of the methodology. And quite another is when only a tenth of similar days is combined with the feature being analyzed.
3. At the second stage of the methodology, the researcher can consistently introduce and test hypotheses about various causes, features of repeatability. There may be as many repetitions of the second stage as it is necessary.
4. In general, the results obtained from the test data, including those presented in the research paper in the tables and calculations, lead to the belief that the introduced methodology is able to effectively help the researcher even when a significant level of interference caused by random deviations in energy consumption is observed. In a number of tests, the parameters of repeated profiles were superimposed with random interference with standard deviation up to 40% of the profile parameters.

6 Results

The presented methodology of extracting knowledge is able to offer the researcher a kind of outline for research activities, some of which can be fully automated. Using the methodology, the researcher will have a set of objective statistical facts at his disposal:

a set of days with similar energy consumption profiles, measures of the profile similarity, facts of greater similarity of certain groups of days, or lack thereof. Analyzing and comparing them, he can get knowledge about the energy consumption profiles repeatability and use them to improve the energy efficiency of the object.

Acknowledgments. The work has been done in the framework of grant # RFBR 16-37-00387. The reported study was partially supported by RFBR research projects 16-37-60066 mol a dk, and project MD-6964.2016.9.

References

1. Shcherbakov, M., Yanovskiy, T., Brebels, A., Shcherbakova, N.: Methodology for identifying the potential for energy savings based on data mining. Caspian Journal: Management and High Technologies (Прикаспийский журнал: управление и высокие технологии) (2), 51–55 (2011). (in Russian)
2. Shcherbakov, M., Shcherbakova, N., Panchenko, D., Brebels, A., Tyukov, A., Al-Gunayd, M.: Specificity of the application of intelligent data analysis models for improving energy efficiency. In: News of VSTU (Известия ВолгГТУ). Actual problems of management, computer science and informatics in technical systems (Актуальные проблемы управления, вычислительной техники и информатики в технических системах), vol. 9, pp. 72–76. VSTU (2010). (in Russian)
3. Tyukov, A., Brebels, A., Shcherbakov, M., Kamaev, V.: A concept of web-based energy data quality assurance and control system. In: Proceedings of the 14th International Conference on Information Integration and Web based Applications & Services. IIWAS 2012, pp. 267–271, ACM, New York, NY, USA (2012). doi:10.1145/2428736.2428779
4. Shcherbakov, M.V., Kamaev, V.A., Brebels, A., Tyukov, A. P. Shcherbakova, N.L., Janovskiy, T.A.: Implementation of statistical methods and data stream mining approaches in energy management systems for automatic forecasting. In: Proceedings of International Conference Statistics & its Interactions with Other Disciplines, June 2013
5. Seem, J.E.: Pattern recognition algorithm for determining days of the week with similar energy consumption profiles. Energy Build. 37(2), 127–139 (2005). doi:10.1016/j.enbuild. 2004.04.004
6. Abreu, J.M., Pereira, F.C., Ferrão, P.: Using pattern recognition to identify habitual behavior in residential electricity consumption. Energy Build. **49**, 479–487 (2012). doi:10.1016/j. enbuild.2012.02.044
7. Li, X., Bowers, C.P., Schnier, T.: Classification of energy consumption in buildings with outlier detection. IEEE Trans. Industr. Electron. **57**(11), 3639–3644 (2010). doi:10.1109/ TIE.2009.2027926
8. Yao, R., Steemers, K.: A method of formulating energy load profile for domestic buildings in the UK. Int. J. Energy Build. 37(6), 663–671 (2005). doi:10.1016/j.enbuild.2004.09.007
9. Santin, O.G.: Behavioural patterns and user profiles related to energy consumption for heating. Energy Build. **43**(10), 2662–2672 (2011). doi:10.1016/j.enbuild.2011.06.024
10. System for collecting information on resources consumption EcoSCADA. www.ecoscada. com
11. Janovsky, T., Shcherbakov, M., Kamaev, V., Janovsky, A.G.: Automatic identification of repeating energy consumption profiles. World Appl. Sci. J. WASJ Inf. Technol. Mod. Ind Educ. Soc. **24**, 68–73 (2013)

12. Stuart, G., Fleming, P., Ferreira, V., Harris, P.: Rapid analysis of time series data to identify changes in electricity consumption patterns in UK secondary schools. Build. Environ. **42**(4), 1568–1580 (2007). doi:10.1016/j.buildenv.2006.01.004
13. Mathieu, J.L., Price, P.N., Kiliccote, S., Piette, M.A.: Quantifying changes in building electricity use, with application to demand response. IEEE Trans. Smart Grid **2**(3), 507–518 (2011). doi:10.1109/TSG.2011.2145010
14. Al-Gunayd, M., Shcherbakov, M., Kamaev, V., Gerget, O., Tyukov, A.: Decision trees based fuzzy rules. In: Proceedings of III International Scientific Conference Information Technologies in Science, Management, Social Sphere and Medicine' (ITSMSSM 2016), pp. 502–508. Advances in Computer Science Research. Atlantis Press, June 2016. doi: 10. 2991/itsmssm-16.2016.91
15. Jota, P.R., Silva, V.R., Jota, F.G.: Building load management using cluster and statistical analyses. Int. J. Electr. Power Ener. Syst. **33**(8), 1498–1505 (2011). doi:10.1016/j.ijepes. 2011.06.034
16. Lederman, W., Lloyd, E.: Handbook of Applicable Mathematics: Statistics, vol. 6, Parts a & b edn. Wiley, Hoboken (1984)
17. Siegel, A.F.: Practical Business Statistics. Publishing house Williams, 6 edn. (2011)

Design Creativity in CASE/CAI/CAD/PDM

Techniques for Adaptive Graphics Applications Synthesis Based on Variability Modeling Technology and Graph Theory

Alexander Bershadsky[1(✉)], Alexander Bozhday[1], Yulia Evseeva[1],
Alexei Gudkov[1], and Vardan Mkrtchian[2]

[1] Penza State University, Penza, Russia
bam@pnzgu.ru, bozhday@yandex.ru, shymoda@mail.ru,
alexei.gudkov@gmail.com
[2] Triple H Hamalsaran of HHH Technology Inc., HHH University,
Sydney, Australia
hhhuniversity@gmail.com

Abstract. The rapid increase in complexity of software systems in recent decades inevitably leads to a shift in focus of attention from programming techniques and approaches to principles of system engineering. Since complex software systems are quite expensive, they are expected to have a long lifetime. Systems having prolonged lifetime should be able to adapt to changes in the subject area and environment, and contribute to saving human resources as well. The problem of lifetime elongation for interactive software systems using a graphical representation of data (in particular, three-dimensional graphics) such as virtual simulators, training systems, and other similar systems is of current interest. The primary objective is to develop techniques aimed at increasing adaptability of such systems. This will provide further process development of more advanced design technologies for the software having an elongated lifetime. The main challenges of the research under discussion involve: (1) providing an overview of current techniques for adaptive software design; (2) identifying the main issues associated with the development of computer software systems having an elongated lifetime; (3) Suggesting new techniques for synthesis of adaptive software systems using graphical data representation.

Keywords: Feature model · Graph theory · Variability modeling

1 Introduction

Presently the problem of complex systems rapid adaptive development is of particular relevance. Adaptive systems cover a wide class of applications in the world of software. They include computer and intelligent simulators, simulation environments, virtual reality systems, and other similar systems. On the one hand, such applications should provide high detail and realism of graphic data; they are also required to exhibit the properties of architectural and behavioral variability not involving the source code recompiling.

A. Kravets et al. (Eds.): CIT&DS 2017, CCIS 754, pp. 455–466, 2017.
DOI: 10.1007/978-3-319-65551-2_33

Typically, the implementation area of adaptive graphics applications is subject to drastic dynamic changes. Consequently, the variability patterns underlying the adaptive programs should ensure rapid and effective self-adapting application directly at runtime.

The key feature of adaptive software systems is the requirement of automatic identification of land current status (for example, a pilot or a surgeon in virtual simulations) followed by subsequent modifications of the system's state.

Thus, the task to develop techniques and algorithms for synthesis of adaptive programs assumes a special scientific and practical relevance. Its successful advance will provide:

1. reduction of time and resource development costs;
2. elongation of software system lifetime and its continuous runtime;
3. involvement of specialists from different subject areas that do not have special software development skills;
4. improvement of realism and complexity of simulated processes and systems.

The objective of this research is the development of a new method for synthesis of adaptive software systems. The developed method should have the following properties: invariance to the application domain; the possibility of creating CASE-tools on its basis to reduce development time, as well as attracting specialists from other subject scientific areas to the process of program development; using a mathematical apparatus that could allow to implement a wide range of operations and algorithms over the adaptive structure of the application; orientation towards the creation of software systems with pronounced adaptive properties.

These goals can be achieved through the joint application of technology for variability modeling and graph theory. The benefit of using the variability modeling technology is a compact representation capability of all possible states of a software system by means of a unified set. Feature models, in particular, their graphical representation, feature diagrams and make it possible to specify a graphical description of a set of states. Graphical representation of a set of adaptive systems states can be effectively used to automate their design as a basis for corresponding CASE-tools. Turning the compiled set of states into direct hypergraph enables to launch the procedure for automatic generation of adaptive program system states at runtime, the verification procedure of generated states and the procedure of automatic situational choices of the system state at runtime.

2 Background

Currently, there exist several broad method groups used to synthesize adaptive software.

The first group includes approaches based on joint usage of object-oriented design technology and CASE-technologies. Papers [1, 2] discuss the development of such techniques. Both works touch upon delivering the specialized patterns of adaptive software design. The design patterns provided by the authors, such as Sensor Factory, Reflective Monitoring, Adaptation Detector are intended to meet two challenges:

improvement of the efficiency of adaptive software systems development and intensification of their adaptive properties (for example, the capacity for system's self-healing in an emergency).

Another method group is based on multiagent technologies application. The original architectural solution for constructing interactive adaptive system was provided in a paper by Oijen [3]. BDI-agents (belief-desire-intention) appear on the basis of such architecture. The main components of BDI-agent are data structures serving as abstractions of beliefs, desires, and intentions of the intelligent agent, as well as functions that prescind from the process of thinking and justifying the choice of goals and means. The originality of provided approach centers around supplement of classical properties of BDI agent with properties inherent in tools for video games development.

Another "multiagent" techniques for constructing adaptive software systems are featured in the paper by Gemrot et al. [4]. The essence of the approach provided by the authors, like in the previous case, is interoperability between intelligent agents (decision-making system (DMS) agents are used) and gambling tools. However, the task to develop a connecting link between agents and instruments now remains operative. The best decision, in this case, is the one capable of ensuring the interaction between DMS-system and various tools. This will make it possible to use the techniques both for computer games and other types of software.

The third method group for constructing adaptive software systems is based on model-driven development (MDD) approach. The main idea of the approach is to use models as the main application artifacts of software development. Based on the models, the program code is generated and the databases are modified. The model within the framework of MDD concept includes 2 basic elements: notation (a set of graphic primitives listing a model) and metamodel (metadata containing the basic concepts of the model). Using models as the main application artifacts of software system development enables their modification without recompiling of its source code. This can be relevant for constructing systems that are polymorphic at runtime as modifications, in this case, involve mere model, but not the system code. Adaptive methods development based on MDD concept is discussed in [5–7].

The last method group includes techniques that use runtime models. The approach to program development based on the application of runtime models is similar to MDD approach. By contrast, it differs from the latter by the fact that underlying models have a higher level of abstraction and determine both fractional analysis of the system and its behavior over time. However, when developing adaptive systems, the difference between these two approaches is not obvious at all times. Development of techniques for adaptive systems synthesis based on run-time models is discussed in [8–10].

In this paper, new technology for adaptive software systems synthesis is provided based on application of Dynamic Software Product Lines Engineering (DSPLE) technology features. DSPLE technology encapsulates Software Product Lines Engineering (SPLE) extension. While SPLE is designed to effectively manage individual and common components of software product line, DSPLE is focused on solving the problem of dynamic adaptation of software. One of the basic DSPLE models, a feature model, is used in this paper to describe the adaptive behavior of a program.

3 Issues, Controversies, Problems

As the review has shown, none of the current technologies for adaptive software systems synthesis carries in the aggregate the following features:

1. availability of variability modeling;
2. constructed systems capability to respond to changes in the domain;
3. facilities to reuse components;
4. alternative involvement of specialists from other spheres;
5. sustainability of constructed software systems;
6. high degree of development automation and saving resources.

To develop a method characterized by the above-mentioned features, it is necessary to integrate separate principles of technologies and approaches discussed above as well as to use mathematical apparatus that provides algorithmization of the main processes of software system variability. The technique should be based on the universal mathematical model of adaptive software system variability. The available universal and modifiable model at runtime could enable the systems being constructed to respond efficiently to changes in subject area and provide ample opportunities for reusing components. To minimize the resource development costs and simplify the process of adaptive behavior simulation, it is required to deliver specialized visual design aid.

4 Solutions and Recommendations

The core of provided approach is the concept of the general structure of the program system. The concept in question denotes a set of program components (program functions, models, attributes) and interconnections between them. The general structure is initially determined in the framework of specification model, in particular, its visual display, i.e., feature diagram. The feature diagram is an improved AND/OR tree graph, with adaptive program components taken in place of vertices. Tree edges determine the relationship between specifics.

To ensure the automation of further involvement with general structure, the structure is transformed into direct hypergraph. Such a form of feature diagram representation is user-friendly since all possible types of available relations have a unified description in terms of direct hyper-edge. Such an edge connects certain sets of vertices. Each vertex corresponds to some feature of the diagram.

Figure 1 shows feature diagram describing a typical adaptive application, and a direct hypergraph derived from the diagram.

The following mathematical model of software system variability is provided:

$$M = (F, S, X),$$

where F is hypergraph representation of application general structure, initially specified in the form of feature diagram; $S = \{S_1, S_2, S_3, \ldots, S_k\}$ is a set of diagram configurations, each of which is a description of one state of the adaptive system (the subgraph

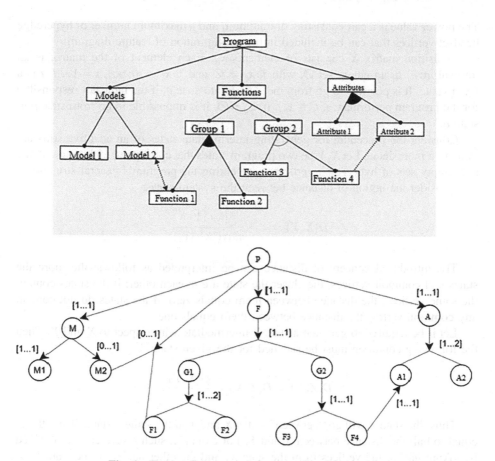

Fig. 1. Feature diagram and corresponding hypergraph

of the original hypergraph); X is a transition matrix from one state of an adaptive software system to another.

The description of application general structure in the form of direct hypergraph (or F-graph) is written as:

$$F = (N, E, \Delta, \Psi),$$

where $N = \{n_1, n_2, n_3, \ldots, n_n\}$ is a bounded set of vertices. $E = \{E_1, E_2, E_3, \ldots, E_m\}$, $E_i \subseteq N \, \forall i = 1, \ldots, m \wedge |H(E_i)| = q_i \wedge |T(E_i)| = 1$ is a set of hypergraph edges. Each edge has its own headset (the set of vertices into which the hyperedge "enters") $H(E_i)$ with power q_i and the tail set (the set of vertices from which the "hyperedge" arises) $T(E_i)$ with power equal to 1; $\Delta \in N$ is a vertex representing the root feature of the diagram; $\Psi : E \to M, M \subset N \times N$ is markup function that assigns a power value $mv(E_i) = (min, max) \in M$ (M is a bounded set of power values of specification model, N is a bounded set of hypergraph vertices) to each direct hyperedge E_i, hence $min, max \in \mathbb{Z} \wedge min \geq 0, _i \, max > 0, min \leq max \wedge max \leq q$ (Z is a set of integer values).

The power value is a pair consisting of minimum and a maximum number of hyperedge headset vertices that can be included in the configuration of feature diagram.

Transition matrix X consists of elements x_{ij}. Each element of the matrix is an interval $[a; b)$ or an empty set $\varnothing$, with $\cap x_{ij} = \varnothing$ and $\cup x_{ij} = [0; \infty)$, $j = 1 \ldots k$, i is a fixed value. It is possible to go from the state p into state q, if the indicator responsible for the program performance, $C \in x_{pq}$. If $x_{pq} = \varnothing$, it is impossible to go from state p to state q.

Consider the procedure for generating intermediate states of an adaptive software system in more detail. Let X, Y be two program states that correspond to the same-name non-empty sets of hypergraph vertices representing the program's general structure.

Consider the notion of distance between the system states:

$$D(X, Y) = 1 - \frac{|X \cap Y|}{max(|X|, |Y|)}.$$

The introduced concept of distance can be interpreted as follows: the more the states and common vertices, the closer the state are to each other; if the states contain the same vertices, the distance between them equals zero; if the states do not contain any common vertex, the distance between them equals one.

Let it be required to generate a state Z intermediate with respect to X and Y. Then the following condition must be satisfied for the given state:

$$D(Z, Y) = D(Z, X) = \frac{D(X, Y)}{2}.$$

Thus, the state Z will go "between" states X and Y at the same distance from them, equal to half the distance between X and Y. For example, such a state can be obtained by taking half of the vertices from the state X, and the other half from the state Y.

If it is required to generate $N \geq 1$ consecutive intermediate states Z_i, $i = 1, 2, \ldots, N$, then the following conditions should be met for these states:

$$D(Z_i, X) = \frac{i}{(N+1)} \cdot D(X, Y),$$

$$D(Z_i, Y) = \frac{(N+1-i)}{(N+1)} \cdot D(X, Y).$$

Thus, intermediate states will be located evenly between the states X и Y.

Since the software systems under consideration are adaptive, steps 3 and 4 of the method in question are performed not only in the process of program design but at runtime as well. Therefore at runtime, specific values are selected from the parameter spaces of the diagram elements specified in step 1 which are based on the information about the user and the environment (in particular, hardware) collected by the system. The verification phase is carried out using specialized algorithmic support, i.e., hypergraph algorithms for searching and fixing errors, the main advantage of which is the correction of the developed structure of software system state at the level of domain concepts.

The algorithm of adaptive program system functioning synthesized by the provided method includes the following steps:

1. Setting the current configuration number $i = 1$.
2. Configuration selection S_i.
3. Computation of computer system performance P

$$
P = \begin{cases} \dfrac{P_R}{P_E}, & \text{if } P_R \le P_E, \\[2mm] 1, & \text{if } P_R > P_E. \end{cases}
$$

where P_R is a performance of a computer on which the program is run; $P_E = k \cdot P_0$ is a performance of a reference computer; k is a coefficient determined by the application author (by default $k = 1$); P_0 is a performance of a computer on which the application was developed.

4. The first stage of parametric synthesis: the corresponding detail level of three-dimensional models is selected, based on obtained system performance factor. In feature diagram, a node corresponding to a three-dimensional object can contain several three-dimensional models of varying granularity of detail. Model data are ordered in ascending detail level. If some object O has n detail levels $(O_1, O_2, \ldots, O_n)$, then when visualizing the object, the pattern O_i will be selected, where $i = \lceil P \cdot n \rceil$, $\lceil x \rceil$ is integer value close to x, $\lceil x \rceil \ge x$.
5. Decompression of subtrees of models, functions, and attributes. Waiting for status to complete.
6. Calculation of the custom performance with the program. When $d > 0$ the calculation formula is as follows:

$$
C = \frac{\left(\dfrac{t_{norm}}{t} + \dfrac{d_{norm}}{d} \right)}{2},
$$

where t is system time in the current state; d is a number of troublesome custom actions that occurred at state runtime; t_{norm} and d_{norm} are normal values for indicators t and d, assumed by the application author for each configuration. If $d = 0$, the formula is replaced by the following one:

$$
C = \begin{cases} \dfrac{\left(\frac{t_{norm}}{t} + 1 \right)}{2}, & \text{if } d_{norm} = 0, \\[2mm] \infty, & \text{if } d_{norm} > 0. \end{cases}
$$

7. The second stage of parametric synthesis: determining the values of attributes used for the functions (the edge "Attributes" of general structure in Fig. 1). These attributes can appertain to one of three data types: integer value, floating-point number, enumerations. In the first two cases, the author should specify a pair of boundary values (x_{init}, x_{end}), within which the attribute can take on its values. In the latter case, the author must list the values $x_1, x_2, \ldots, x_n$. To calculate the attributes it is necessary to compute the normalized index C. In this regard, it is required to map

the interval $[0; \infty]$, which C is found at, to the interval $[0; 1]$. This can be done, for example, using the following transformation:

$$C_{narm} = \begin{cases} \frac{C}{b}, & \text{if } C \leq b, \\ 1, & \text{if } C > b. \end{cases}$$

where $0 < b < \infty$ is the highest value of the indicator C, determined for the current state. Another possible version for transformation is as follows:

$$C_{norm} = 1 - e^{kC},$$

where $k > 0$ is a particular coefficient that enables us to adjust the type of transformation. After the normalized value of custom performance in the state is calculated, the values of attributes used in the next state are computed. If the attribute is an integer value or floating-point number, for which the boundary values are specified (x_{init}, x_{end}), the value of the attribute is found by the formula:

$$x = x_{init} + C_{norm} \cdot (x_{end} - x_{init}).$$

If the attribute is an enumeration, its value is $x = x_i$, where $i = \lceil C_{norm} \cdot n \rceil$, $\lceil x \rceil$ is an integer value, close to x, $\lceil x \rceil \geq x$.

8. If necessary, adjust the transition matrix with regard to the state of the runtime as follows:

$$X = E \cdot X_{ref},$$

where X_{ref} is initial transition matrix specified by the user for E = 1; E is an indicator that determines the status of runtime. This indicator is calculated based on the set of values for the indicator C, characterizing custom performance in several of the latest software system states. If the runtime is too complicated for the user (indicator values C are low according to results of passing the last few states), the value of indicator E decreases and, consequently value ranges located in the cells of matrix get narrowed. If runtime environment becomes more complicated, the value of indicator E increases.

9. If there exists an interval x_{ij}, where $C \in x_{ij}$, then $i = j$ and the transition to point 2 of the algorithm is carried out. Otherwise, the application is terminated.

The features of the proposed method are:

1. The possibility to determine visually the behavioral structure of the program using a feature diagram. This feature allows to significantly reduce the time spent on application development, by reducing the amount of code that must be written manually. The received behavioral structure allows the developer to independently determine the possible states of the adaptive software system, and also set the rules for their automatic generation. The resulting behavioral structure is also invariant to the application domain.

2. Conversion of the obtained behavioral structure into the form of an oriented hypergraph. Hypergraphic representation makes it easy to algorithmize the processes of behavioral structure processing. Such processes include: the process of changing program states during its execution, the process of generating new states, the process of searching and correcting errors in the generated (or determined independently) states.
3. The adaptability of the resulting application. The ability to adapt allows to increase the life cycle of the program because the adaptive application is adapted to changes in the environment (for example, hardware configuration and power consumption conditions).

The proposed mathematical and algorithmic support was implemented as a component of the prototype system for the automated development of adaptive graphics applications. For a full-fledged testing of the system, it is necessary to develop an example that would make full use of the functionality of the system, but which at the same time would be compact enough to the possibility of visual description in the text of the article. For example, the implementation of a special technique for diagnosing the visual intelligence "Kohs blocks" was chosen.

The original version of the Kohs testing consists of 16 cubes, equal in size, with faces of different colors. In each set for testing, cards with patterns are also used, ordered by complexity. The subject is asked to fold the cubes in such a way that the pattern on the upper surface of the cubes corresponds exactly to the pattern on the card.

Unlike original technique, which involves the use of pre-defined tasks (patterns), the developed application assumes the generation of an original pattern at each stage of its own work. The adaptive properties of the developed program are as follows:

1. The ability of graphic objects to change the level of detail, depending on the hardware configuration of the system.
2. The ability of the software system to change the level of complexity of generated patterns depending on the condition of the user.

Figure 2 shows a feature diagram describing the behavioral structure of the program.

The structure includes the following elements:

1. Parameters. The parameters include
   i. k - the dimension of the pattern matrix.
   ii. forbidden_f - an array of faces that are forbidden for use in this step of the application work.
2. Functions. These include:
   i. Function Main_func, which implements the basic logic of the program.
   ii. Function Func_step, prone to variability. Depending on the level of complexity of the application, the function Func_step can be implemented either through the NormMatrix function (generates a medium complexity pattern), HardMatrix (generates a pattern of increased complexity), or SimlpeMatrix (generates a simple pattern).

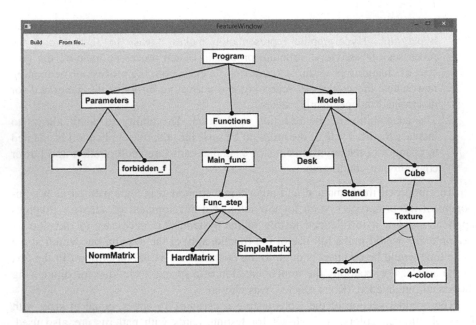

Fig. 2. Feature diagram of Kohs blocks test application

3. Models. Models include
   i. Model of the desk.
   ii. Model of the stand for the cube.
   iii. The cube model, which includes an element that is subject to variability, a texture. The texture can be two-color or four-color.

The main indicator of the quality of the system is its efficiency. Efficiency is the degree of the system's ability to perform all corresponding functions to ensure goal achievement. The most important indicator is the cost-saving efficiency of the system. This indicator characterizes the feasibility of the costs incurred to create and operate the system. To assess the cost-saving efficiency of the implementation of the developed mathematical and algorithmic support, we use a comparison of time is used.

A comparative estimate of the time required to create an application consisting of 9 basic states and 7 states generated during the runtime can be seen in Table 1.

For the most accurate assessment of the increase in the life cycle of the adaptive application, it is necessary to use the developed software system for a long time. For this reason, it was decided to limit experiment to expert evaluations. According to experts, the developed method will have increased the adaptive application life cycle by 20%.

As seen, application of the developed method allows reducing the adaptive software development costs. The life cycle of the software is also increasing.

Table 1. Time costs for the creation of the application

Type of work	Object complexity	Time costs	
		Without system (hours)	With system (hours)
Preparation of the necessary three-dimensional models	73500 polygons	1	1
Development of the visualization module for manipulating objects	476 lines of code	20	0
Development of the module for realizing the adaptive behavior	603 lines of code	26	0
Development of algorithmic basis of functioning	742 lines of code	30	10
Interface development	347 lines of code	16	4
Description of the general feature diagram/ decomposition of the application into components and the definition of the intermodulation	26 nodes, 14 connections	3	1
Description of the individual states of work	17 states (8 intermediate)	3	1
Description of the transitional matrices/determining the relationships between states	9 by 9 lines	3	1
Total		10.5	18.5

5   Future Research Directions

The problem of intellectualization of the procedure for generating intermediate system states is of great interest at this stage of research. Current generation procedure does not fully have regard to the peculiarities of application user's behavior and specifics of the domain. To eliminate these shortcomings, it is proposed to apply artificial intelligence techniques, in particular, machine learning.

Another area of further research is the development of an algorithm for verifying system configuration of the program. The algorithm is mainly designed for search and error correction in program structure at the level of domain concepts.

6   Conclusion

The benefits of the proposed approach involve easy determining the morphological set (in terms of feature diagram) and its simple formalization (transformation into direct hypergraph), the invariance to subject area of software system, the capability to verify the system state, taking into account the domain concepts, the possibility of adaptive program behavior at runtime. Based on provided technology it is possible to implement specialized CASE-tools for adaptive software systems development.

References

1. Ramirez, A.J., Cheng, H.C.: Design Patterns for Developing Dynamically Adaptive Systems. ACM, Cape Town (2010)
2. McKinley, P.K., Sadjadi, S.M., Kasten, E.P., Cheng, H.C.: Composing adaptive software. Computer 37(7), 56–64 (2004)
3. Oijen, J.: Goal-based communication using BDI agents as virtual humans in training: an ontology driven dialogue system. In: Dignum, F. (ed.) Agents for Games and Simulations II, pp. 38–52. Springer, Berlin (2011)
4. Gemrot, J., Brom, C., Plch, T.: A periphery of pogamut: from bots to agents and back again. In: Dignum, F. (ed.) Agents for Games and Simulations II, pp. 19–37. Springer, Berlin (2011)
5. Magableh, B., Barrett, S.: Model-driven productivity evaluation for self-adaptive context-oriented software development. In: International Conference on Next Generation Mobile Applications, Services and Technologies, pp. 87–93, 14–16, September (2011)
6. Becker, M., Luckey, M., Becker, S.: Model-driven performance engineering of self-adaptive systems: a survey'. In: Proceedings of the 8th International ACM SIGSOFT Conference on Quality of Software Architectures, QoSA 2012, pp. 117–122, 25–28, June 2012
7. Vogel, T., Giese, H.: Model-driven engineering of self-adaptive software with EUREMA. ACM Trans. Auton. Adapt. Syst. 8(4), 1–18 (2014)
8. Blair, G., Bencomo, N., France, R.B.: Models@run.time. Computer 42(10), 21–35 (2009)
9. Morin, B., Barais, O., Jezequel, J.M., Fleurey, F., Solberg, A.: Models@ run.time to support dynamic adaptation. Computer 42(10), 44–51 (2009)
10. Vogel, T., Giese, H.: Model-Driven Engineering of Adaptation Engines for Self-Adaptive Software: Executable Runtime Megamodels. Potsdam University Press, Potsdam (2013)

Ontology-Based Decision Support System for the Choice of Problem-Solving Procedure of Commutation Circuit Partitioning

Viktor Kureichik and Irina Safronenkova[✉]

Institute of Computer Technologies and Information Security,
Autonomous Federal State Institution of Higher Education
«Southern Federal University», Taganrog, Russia
kur@tgn.sfedu.ru, safronenkova050788@yandex.ru

Abstract. This paper concerned with an architectural design of ontology-based decision support system intended to optimize the choice of problem-solving procedure of commutation circuit partitioning of the electronic computer during the design phase. Analysis of formal commutation circuit partitioning problems definition against the criteria was performed. A mathematical model of present problem was posed. The fundamental difference of this model is a consideration the criteria of inter-bay wiring and signal delay as local cost functions in the multicriteria optimization problem. In this paper a space of classification attributes of commutation circuit partitioning problems was designed: local cost functions, constraints, and initial data are defined. Data store and databank of ontology-based decision support system are presented as a CCP problems ontology and a problem-solving technique ontology. These domain ontologies were developed and visualized in Protégé 4.2.

Keywords: Ontology · Decision support system · Commutation circuit partitioning problem

1 Introduction

In the market economy conditions, there is a competition for customers between enterprises. This calls for modernizing, upgrading output product and managing customer needs. Agreeably, it's necessary to reduce the time and cost of process engineering, improve development projects. Often an engineer forces to exercise his discretion about the efficiency of possible alternatives and importance of different criteria in the design process. Such way hardly can be applied in the process of correct decision-making [1]. Under the conditions of information gain, a complication of the solving tasks, the relevance of a great number of interrelating factors and changeable demands to the designed object, the actuality of decision support systems (DSS) grows. They are especially effective in situations in which the amount of available information is overall for the intuition of a human decision maker and in which precision and optimality are of importance. Ontologies, by capturing knowledge about a domain and encapsulating constraints about class membership, can offer guidance around a domain and support decision making processes [2]. To automate a creative process completely is impossible. However, the modern methods of artificial intelligence using in its work

© Springer International Publishing AG 2017
A. Kravets et al. (Eds.): CIT&DS 2017, CCIS 754, pp. 467–478, 2017.
DOI: 10.1007/978-3-319-65551-2_34

knowledgebase (KB), lend support to the decision-making process, offering possible alternatives in ill-defined problems [3]. A commutation circuit partitioning problem (CCPP) is the first task at the design stage and it is a source of information for further design stages. The commutation circuit partitioning problem defines quality and efficiency of the whole design process. Here a key factor is an optimum choice of problem-solving procedure of commutation circuit partitioning, which gives a preferable alternative for the decision maker. Each of the existing methods is oriented to solve a certain group of problems, has pros and cons. Nowadays an intellectual technology market includes a great number of Electronics Computer Aided Design systems which are different in functionality, output, cost and used solution methods. Often an engineer runs into difficulties to puzzle out provided products or has to solve other tasks in weakly formalized domains. Decision support system provides the flexibility and adaptability in dealing with ill-defined problems, partial information, and conflicting objectives. Such systems are particularly useful for supporting the solutions of a wide range of semistructured and unstructured problems. Decision support systems intent to improve the processes and outcomes of human decision-making [4]. Although complete elimination of person from the decision-making process is impossible, DSS development for search and recommendation effective or new methods of solution supposes to improve quality and reduce the time of design process. In default of analogs in the modern scientific environment, the authors of this paper suppose that the development of decision support system for the choice of problem-solving procedure of commutation circuit partitioning (further DSSCCP) is an actual task for today. A basic idea of DSSCCP is given bellow. A formal description of some commutation circuit partitioning problem comes on a system input. Then a classification procedure takes place accordingly to an attribute space which is identified early. A result of classification is a subsumption of some CCP problem to a certain ontology class. Then a procedure of subsumption a classified CCP problem to a possible method of the solution takes place. The last step is a recommendation an optimal problem-solving procedure.

Further, the following questions will be observed:

1. An analysis of formal CCP problems representation against the criteria of inter-bay wiring and signal delay. Formulation of CCP problem as a multicriteria optimization problem.
2. A structure synthesis of CCP problem attribute space for further classification.
3. A synthesis of a common DSSCCP architecture.

A present investigation is intended to form a common conception and an operating principle of the decision support system for commutation circuit partitioning. A new mathematical model of the formulation of CCP problem development was performed.

2 Formulation of CCP Problem as a Multicriterion Optimization Problem

A commutation circuit partitioning problem of the electronic computer on stand-alone units is a process of lower level components distribution to a higher level in accordance with a chosen criteria. A major criterion in commutation circuit partitioning problem is a criterion of electromagnetic-hot-wire inter-connectivity of lower level components. Such criterion determines a bearable domain of circuit partition where other criteria are stated. For example a criterion of a number of stand-alone units, a criterion of higher level filling by the lower level components, a criterion of inter-bay wiring, a criterion of test operation simplicity and others. Apparently, that an inter-bay wiring is one of the most important factors. It defines a reliability of electronic computers. Realization of this criterion provides a minimization of reciprocal laying, design simplification ad reliability growth. But in respect of considering expansion in the number of components, size reduction of LSI and VLSI circuits and their speeding, together with the criterion of inter-bay wiring and criterion of stand-alone units, there is need to introduce the criterion of signal delay.

Let pose a CCP problem as an oriented hypergraph partition problem $H = (X, E)$ with weighted edges and nodes into m subschemas. It is required to partition a set X of the hypergraph H into subsets $X_1, X_2, ..., X_m$ such that:

$$X_i \neq \emptyset, i \in I = \{1, 2, \ldots, m\};$$

$$X_k \cap X_l = \emptyset; \bigcup_{k \in I} X_k = X |X_k| = n_k k, l \in I.$$

2.1 A Formulation of CCP Problem Against the Criterion of Inter-bay Wiring

Let S_j - is a j way from one of the initial edge of the hypergraph H to one of the final edge. l_j-a relative length of j way which is defined by a number of subgraphs H where the S_j goes.

$$l_j = \sum_{l=1}^{m} \sum_{k=2}^{t} \alpha_{ki}^{(j)}, \tag{1}$$

where

$$t = |E_j|, E_j = \{e_j | e_j \in S_j\}$$

$$\alpha_{ki}^{(j)} = \left\{ \begin{array}{l} 1, \text{ if } X_{k-1} \subset P_{i,H} o \exists x \in X_k : x \notin P_i \\ 0, \text{ otherwise} \end{array} \right\}.$$

Hence, some constant partition f is characterized by a value

$$\alpha_f = l_{j\max}, \tag{2}$$

which is a maximum number of the subgraphs where through ways from initial edges to final ones go under this partition.

The CCP problem is such partition f, searching from a set of possible F of the hypergraph H that a value α_f is minimized under the given constraints.

$$\Phi = \min \alpha_f \text{ under the restrictions } \left\{ \begin{array}{c} |P_i| \leq B \\ C_i \leq C \end{array} \right\}, \tag{3}$$

where B – is a number of components into the unit;
C – is a number of primary outputs into the unit.

2.2 A Formulation of CCP Problem Against the Criterion of Signal Delay

Let a value of a relevant functional delay (RFD) is assigned for each node and each edge of the oriented hypergraph H. If there is no data about the results of logic-function circuit simulation, then a value of RFD assigns to a certain pitch wave, spreading in the hypergraph, for a node or an edge. The value of RFD in the initial edge is 1. Let us denote RFD of the node r_{xi}, and RFD of the edge r_{ei}, for which a node X_i interprets a component of the schema and is a signal source in the circuit is defined as $r_{ej} = r_{xi} + 1$. RFD of the node X_i is defined as a maximum RFD value incident with lines $E' = \{e_s, e_t, ..., e_f\}$. In this case, a component corresponds a node X_i is not a signal source in the circuits $s, t, ..., f \in I$, so $r_{xi} = \max\limits_{e_j \in E} r_{ej}$.

If the results of logic-function circuit simulation are known, then values assigned to initial edges of the hypergraph H are equal 0. RFD of the edge e_j is defined as

$$r_{ej} = r_{xi} + \Delta r_{xi},$$

where Δr_{xi} - assessed delay value of a component which is assigned a node X_i.

Each subgraph has such characteristic as a range of RFD values of belonging nodes:

$$\Delta R_\gamma = r_{\gamma\max} - r_{\gamma\min}, \tag{4}$$

where

ΔR_γ – a range of RFD values of a subgraph P_γ of the hypergraph H;
$r_{\gamma\max}$ – a maximum value of nodes in subgraph P_γ;
$r_{\gamma\min}$ – a minimum value of nodes in subgraph P_γ.

Any constant partition of the hypergraph H is characterized by a maximum value of the range under this partition:

$$\Delta R_f = \Delta R_{\gamma\max}, \tag{5}$$

In the performance of CCP problem it's necessary to get minimal from all possible values under the given restrictions:

$$\Phi = \min \Delta R_{\gamma max} \text{ under the restrictions } \left\{ \begin{array}{c} |P_i| \leq B \\ C_i \leq C \end{array} \right\}, \tag{6}$$

where

B – a number of components into the unit;
C – a number of primary outputs into the unit.

Allowing for examined criteria a CCP problem is stated as a multicriteria optimization problem and described by cost vector-function which is defined in domain D_x and range of values is $\{F\} = R|F|$:

$$F(X) = (f_1(X), f_2(X)), \tag{7}$$

where $f_1(X)$, $f_2(X)$ – local cost functions;
$\{X\}$ – limited and closed set of accepted values of the parameter vector $D_X = \{X|G(X) \geq 0\} \subset \{X\} = R^{|X|}$.
Let us assume:

$$f_1(X) = \mu_1 K_1, f_2(X) = \mu_2 K_2, \tag{8}$$

where

K_1 – a criterion of inter-bay wiring;
K_2 – a criterion of signal delay;
μ_1, μ_2 – weight number for K_1 and K_2.

Then optimization function is as follows:

$$\begin{aligned} F(X) &= \mu_1 K_1 + \mu_2 K_2 \\ K_1, K_2 &\to \min \end{aligned} \tag{9}$$

Because a decision maker tends to minimize each of cost functions $f_1(X)$, $f_2(X)$ in domain D_x, that

$$\min_{X \in D_X} F(X) = F(X^*) = F^*, \tag{10}$$

where vectors X^*, F^* - a desired solution of optimization problem.

3 A Structure Synthesis of CCP Problem Attribute Space for Further Classification

The goal of this paragraph is a synthesis of an attribute space. According to the main idea of DSSCPP operating, the second step is a procedure of classification formalized CCP problem from the input by any attribute or attribute set. The classification procedure requires that to assign a certain formalized CCP problem to a certain class in the problems ontology. The attribute space should allow classifying any formalizing any CCP problem. So the main task is an adequate choice of the attributes for the formalized CCP problem. Let's consider a classification procedure by the example of CCP problem of the electronic computer. Assume that an initial data is a mathematical model (M) of CCP problem which can be interpreted by graph, multigraph or hypergraph [5]. In the present work, a wiring diagram is presented as a hypergraph. It is known that such presentation is the most representative for the main constructive parameters of the circuit.

Assume that criteria of optimization function are:

– a number of inter-bay wiring;
– a value of signal delay.

These criteria form a cost vector-function (F(X)).

Most often in the performance of the CCP problem, constraints of the maximum number of leading-out wire and a maximum number of a number of components in the unit are used.

– a number of components into the unit (B);
– a number of primary outputs into the unit (C).

Both constraints coupled with a criterion of inter-bay wiring and a criterion of signal delay allow to get an optimum solution for the CCP problem.

Hence, accordingly to (9), there is an attribute space for classification of CCP problem. This attribute space consists of cost vector-function, constraints of variables and initial data:

$$W = (F(X), B, C, M),\tag{11}$$

Such attribute space describes any formalized CCP problem and assigns it to a certain class in the problems ontology.

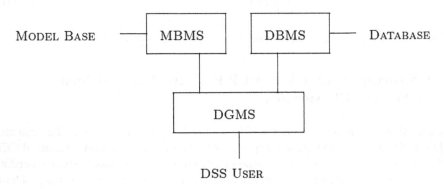

Fig. 1. DSSCCP architecture

4   A Synthesis of a Common DSSCCP Architecture

In accordance with the aim of system work operation, the DSSCCP will have the following architecture (see Fig. 1).

As usual, there are three fundamental components of a decision support system. They are database management system (DBMS), model-based management system (MBMS) and dialog generation and management system (DGMS). A DBMS serves as a data bank for the DSS. It stores large quantities of data that are relevant to the class of problems for which the DSS has been designed and provides logical data structures with which the users interact. It should also be capable of informing the user of the types of data that are available and how to gain access to them. MBMS primary function is providing independence between specific models that are used in a DSS from the applications that use them. The purpose of an MBMS is to transform data from the DBMS into information that is useful in decision making. Since many problems that the user of a DSS will cope with may be unstructured, the MBMS should also be capable of assisting the user in model building. The primary responsibility of a DGMS is to enhance the ability of the system user to utilize and benefit from the DSS. There are two types of automated DSS: universal and special. The universal DSS are automated systems which apply for processing, storage, and analysis of information not only for decision support but also for other purposes. The special DSS - are automated systems which are domain-specific for decision support [6].

The present work introduces to represent a database as a CCP problems ontology (POnt) and a model-base as a problem-solving technique ontology (PSTOnt). Using an ontological approach for data and knowledge storage in DSS is reasoned because there is an opportunity not only to classify and formalize heterogeneous kind of data and knowledge but also to organize an easy access to them. More importantly that developed domain ontologies can be used for others purposes too.

Unstructured and semistructured information explosion, its activity importance and representation of information in the computer resource needs ontological models development. Ontology is a key decision for the unstructured and semistructured information processing. The advantage of ontologies as a method of information processing is a formal structure which simplifies their computer processing. An ontology must be formal and, therefore, machine readable. Formalization of unstructured data is one of the solutions for solving the problem of big data processing. So we may apply the formal ontology - a modern paradigm of computing resources that describe the knowledge of the world and subject areas. This way ontologies can provide a common vocabulary between various applications [6–8]. There are many ontology definitions in academic papers. Some definitions encapsulate a method of ontology development. For example, ontology- is a hierarchically structured set of terms which describe a certain domain. Ontology can be used as an initial structure for a knowledge base. In information technologies, the term ontology denotes explicit specification of a conceptualization, where conceptualization presents a description of a variety of objects and relations between them. In this paper we will use the following formal ontology representation:

$$ONT = \langle C, P, R, F \rangle, \tag{12}$$

where

ONT – is an ontology;
C – is a finite set of terms which denote the domain concepts;
P – is a finite set of attributes of concepts;
R – is a finite set of relations between the concepts;
F – is a finite set of interpretation functions given on the basis of concepts and/or relations of ontology.

Generally, ontologies consist of classes, instances, concepts, attributes, and relations. Instances are the basic components of a low-level ontology. They may represent any physical and abstract objects. Concepts or classes are groups or sets of other objects. Instances of ontology often have attributes. Every attribute has a name, value and store information about the instance. Classes may have subclasses including of combinations of other classes, instances or concepts. Ontology is developed as a net consisted of concepts and relations between them. The relations can be various types such as "is", "consists of", 'is a performer' and so on. As such ontologies contain following types of information: attributes, restrictions to values, exclusive clauses, logical connections between objects. There are some requirements to ontologies:

- clarity (ontology must be translucent, objective and convey the meaning easily);
- sequence (ontology contains statements which don't disagree);
- expansibility (adding new elements without the process of revision of the other elements);
- minimal degree of specialty (absolute subjection is not desirable, it can complicate a late use of ontology) [9, 10].

Nowadays ontology covers a great number of multidisciplinary fundamental scientific theories. Among them, first of all, are new information technologies, artificial intelligence and such its important parts as knowledge bases and stores, knowledge management systems, expert and commendatory as well as classification systems. Development of domain models, information search, and decision-making under uncertain conditions is also important. Currently, all these problems are being solved successfully via ontological models [11–14].

Ontologies can be classified into three classes according to their level of formalization. A formal ontology is a conceptualization whose categories are distinguished by axioms and definitions. Such type of ontologies is stated in logic that can support complex inferences and computations. The second type is prototype-based ontologies whose categories are distinguished by typical instances or prototypes rather than by axioms and definitions in logic. For the instances selection, a similarity metric on instance terms is applied. Terminological ontologies are partially specified by subtype-supertype relations and describe concepts by concept labels or synonyms rather than prototypical instances but lack an axiomatic grounding. Terminological and prototype-based ontologies cannot be used in a straightforward way for inference, but are easier to construct and to maintain [15, 16].

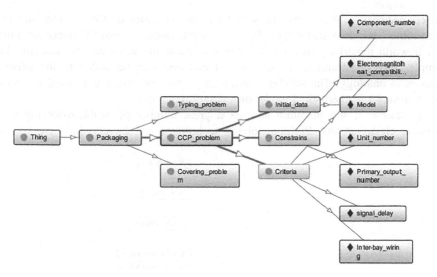

Fig. 2. CCP problems ontology

Ontology visual designer allows visual designing of any domain ontology. In the present work, we used Protégé 4.2. for the ontology models visualization. Ontology is constructed as a network of concepts (vertices of graphs and hypergraphs) and relations (edges and arcs) between them. For the purpose of this paper two domain ontologies were developed: CCP problems ontology (see Fig. 2) and a problem-solving technique ontology (see Fig. 4) [17].

There are three main classes of packaging task are considered in this paper. As can be seen from Fig. 2 a class "Packaging" has three subclasses: "Covering_problem", "Typing_problem" and "CCP_problem". We turn our attention to the subclass "CCP_problem" which has three attributes reviewed above. With the help of relation "has" can be created a relationship between "CCP_problem" and "Criteria", "Constraints" and "Initial_data". The subclass "Criteria" has four instances such that "Inter-bay_wiring", "Signal_delay", "Unit_number" and "Electromagnetic_hot_wire_

Fig. 3. Hierarchy of the problem-solving technique

inter-connectivity". These criteria were detailed considered above. The subclass "Constraints" has two instances: "Primary_output_number" and "Component_number". It worth remarking that a number of constraint instances can be different. For example, such constraint as a total area of elements can be added to the existing instances of ontology. The subclass "Initial_data" has one instance a "Model". In our case, it means a mathematical model of a circuit diagram.

The review of the literature showed a great number of problem-solving CCP technique classifications. Problem-solving techniques can be classified by criteria,

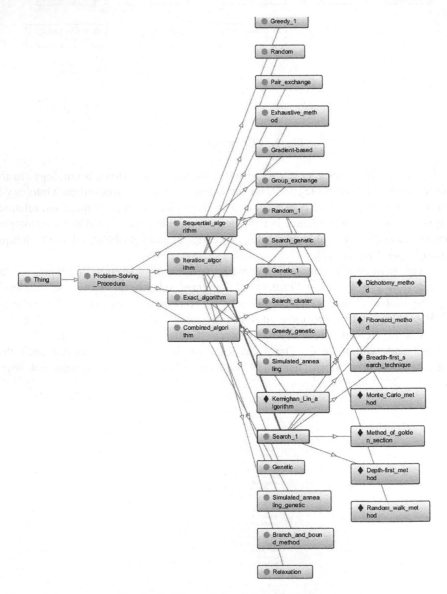

Fig. 4. Problem-solving technique ontology

constraints and computational procedure structure. Authors analyzed known classifications and synthesized a new one. Such classification is the most accurate for the statement of the present work. The full hierarchy of the problem-solving technique is shown in Fig. 3. The classification of the solving-problem CCP technique presents in Fig. 4. As can be seen from Fig. 4 a class "Problem-Solving_Procedure" has four subclasses. They are "Sequential_algorithm", "Iteration_algorithm", "Exact_algorithm" and "Compoused_algorithm". These subclasses describe main existing problem-solving procedure for the CCP problem. Such division is very tentatively and if it is necessary can be classified in another way. Each of these subclasses has a several numbers of subclasses. Let's take a closer look at subclass "Sequential_algorithm". It has five groups of algorithms according to our classification. They are "Random_1", "Search_1", "Greedy_1", "Gradient-based" and "Genetic". This subclass presents the groups of known algorithms for solving an optimization problem. Each of these groups has instances which indicate real algorithms belonging to a certain subclass. For example "Search_1" which means a search algorithm has instances such as "Dichotomy_method", "Fibonacci_method", "Bepth-first_search", "Breadth-first_search", "Monte Carlo_method" and so on [18, 19].

5   Conclusion

The paper describes an architecture of ontology-based decision support system for the choice of problem-solving procedure of commutation circuit partitioning. An analysis of existing formal description CCP problems was carried out and presented a mathematical model of this problems. A new CCP problem model was introduced as a multicriteria optimization problem. Two criteria were taken as a whole: a criterion of inter-bay wiring and a criterion of signal delay. An attribute set was synthesized for further classification procedure. As a data and knowledge storage were used domain ontologies. Hence, two domain ontologies were developed and visualized in Protégé 4.2. To all practical purposes, ontologies realization allows the engineer to avoid ill-defined problems solving. Scientific novelty of the paper is describing an architecture of decision support system which can recommend an optimal choice of problem-solving technique for CCP problems. The obtained recommendation of the DSS expects a new CAD-system development for solving CCP problem efficiently, more reliable and economically-viable. Such DSS is intended to help an engineer to avoid ill-defined problems at the process of decision making, reduce the time and improve the quality of solutions. Of special interest is a situation of work operation multiplicity of classifier (a component of the DSS). For the optimal solution to this problem, authors will pose a modified architecture of DSS. An additional component in the DSS will let to compensate the work operation multiplicity of the classifier and it will be suggested in the future research.

Acknowledgments. We thank collaborators of automated engineering system department for work results discussion. This research is provided by the Russian Foundation for Basic Research through grant #2.5537.2017/VU in Southern Federal University.

References

1. Evgenev, E.B: Intelligence CAD - system. MGTU im. N.Je. Baumana, Moscow (2009) (in Russian)
2. Stevens, R., Lord, P.: Application of ontologies in bioinformatics. In: Staab, S., Studer, R. (eds.) Handbook on Ontologies. IHIS, pp. 735–756. Springer, Heidelberg (2009). doi:10. 1007/978-3-540-92673-3_33
3. Tihonov, A.N., Cvetkov, V.Ja.: Methods and Systems of Decision Making. MAKS Press, Moscow (2001). (in Russian)
4. Chang, C., Lin, J.: Integrated decision support and expert systems in a computer integrated manufacturing environment. Comput. Ind. Eng. **19**(1–4), 140–144 (1990)
5. Kureichik, V.M.: Mathematical Support of Engineering and Production Process With the Help of CAD-Systems. Radio i svjaz', Moscow (1990). (in Russian)
6. Decision Support Systems. http://www.pitt.edu/ ~ druzdzel/psfiles/dss.pdf. Accessed 21 May 2017
7. Zagorulko, G.B.: Development of ontology for intelligent scientific internet resource decision-making support in weakly formalized domains In: Ontology of designing, vol. 6, no. 4(22), pp. 485–500 (2016)
8. Maedchen, A., Staab, S.: Ontology learning. In: Staab, S., Studer, R. (eds.) Handbook on Ontologies Euro-Par 2004. International Handbooks on Information Systems, vol. 2, pp. 173–190. Springer, Heidelberg (2004)
9. Kureychik, V.M., Safronenkova, I.B.: Creation of CAD-systems ontology using Protege 4.2. In: All-Russia Science & Technology Conference "Problems of Advanced Micro- and Nanoelectronic Systems Development", vol.3, pp. 240–245, IPPM RAN (2016)
10. Noy, N., McGuinness, D.: Ontology development 101: a guide to creating your first ontology. stanford knowledge systems laboratory Technical report KSL-01–05 and Stanford Medical Informatics Technical report SMI-2001-0880 (2001)
11. Gruber, T.: Toward principles for the design of ontologies used for knowledge sharing. Int. J. Hum. Comput. Stud. **43**(4–5), 907–928 (1995)
12. Ontology as a knowledge system. http://www.ict.edu.ru/ft/005706/68352e2-st08.pdf. Accessed 10 Jun 2017
13. Ontology Learning from Text. http://www.jlcl.org/2005_Heft2/Chris_Biemann.pdf. Accessed 08 Jun 2017
14. Kureichik, V., Safronenkova, I.: Integrated algorithm of the domain ontology development. In: Silhavy, R., Senkerik, R., Kominkova, O.Z., Prokopova, Z., Silhavy, P. (eds.) Artificial Intelligence Trends in Intelligent Systems. AISC, vol. 573. Springer, Cham (2017). doi:10. 1007/978-3-319-57261-1_15
15. Franconi, E.: Ontologies and databases: myths and challenges. In: PVLDB 2008, 23–28 August 2008, Auckland, New Zealand. VLDB Endowment. ACM (2008)
16. Drumond, L., Girardi, R.: A survey of ontology learning procedures. In: Proceedings of the 3rd Workshop on Ontologies and their Applications. CEUR Workshop Proceedings, vol. 427 (2008)
17. Antoniou, G., van Harmelen, F., Hoekstra, R.: Semantic Web. DMK Press, Moscow (2016)
18. Emeljanov, V.V., Kureichik, V.V., Kureichik, V.M.: Theory and Practice of Evolutionary Modeling. FIZMATLIT, Moscow (2003). (in Russian)
19. Kureichik, V.V., Sorokoletov, P.V.: Composed methods of graph partition. TRTU, Taganrog (2006). (in Russian)

System of Automated Design of Biosensors

Viktoriya M. Zaripova and Irina Yu. Petrova[(⊠)]

Department of CAD and M Systems,
Astrakhan State University of Architecture and Civil Engineering,
Astrakhan, Russia
irapet1949@gmail.com

Abstract. The article considers the creation of two knowledge bases on physicotechnical effects and bioreceptors, which are planned to be used at the stage of conceptual design of biosensors. About 40 physical and technical phenomena are described, a class diagram of the system of automated design of biosensors is included. The classification of physical phenomena in the knowledge base is based on the energy-information model of circuits (EIMS). The automated system for designing of biosensors will expand the amount of specialized knowledge tenfold and reduce the time of creating new solutions by two to three times by reducing the volume of prototyping and full-scale tests due to choosing more efficient options and draft calculation of the significant characteristics of their conceptual models.

Keywords: Biosensor · Conceptual design · Knowledge base · The energy-information method · Physical and technical effect

1 Analysis of Trends in the Development of the Biosensor Market and the Theoretical Foundations of Methods and Technologies for Their Design

Over the last decades, there has been a significant emphasis on developing novel diagnosis systems that enable the analysis of complex samples on site and deliver fast but accurate results. Such demand for innovative and improved analytical methodologies comes mainly from the environmental monitoring, industrial control, and health care fields. Among the sensing strategies, various biosensors, coupling electrochemical or other detectors with biomolecules, have been proposed.

According to the results of marketing research of the American company, Grand View Research Inc. the market of biosensors develops rapidly (Fig. 1) [1]. The main areas of application of biosensors are devices for home health diagnostics, real-time express diagnostics, laboratory research (for example, environmental studies) and the food industry (assessment of product quality and the presence of harmful impurities). According to the forecast of Grand View Research Inc., the volume of the market of biosensors grows annually by 10% and by 2020 it will reach 22,490 million US dollars.

The expected growth of the biosensor market in Russia will be most noticeable in the coming years (about 10%). According to forecasts [2], the market for biosensor devices is expected to reach 26 billion rubles (approximately 470 million US dollars) by 2020.

© Springer International Publishing AG 2017
A. Kravets et al. (Eds.): CIT&DS 2017, CCIS 754, pp. 479–489, 2017.
DOI: 10.1007/978-3-319-65551-2_35

The rapid growth of the market breeds the appearance of a multitude designs of biosensors with improved performance characteristics. Therefore, it is necessary to develop systems for the automated design of biosensors, which make it possible to accelerate the process of creating new structures [3–5].

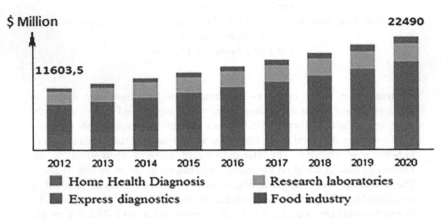

Fig. 1. Dynamics of the global market of biosensors (million US dollars) [1]

2 Automated System for Supporting the Conceptual Design of Biosensors Based on Knowledge Bases on Physicochemical Effects and Bioreceptors

The construction of biosensors belongs to the field of interdisciplinary research, therefore it is necessary to develop a unified system approach that is invariant to the physical nature of the phenomena and processes.

Biosensors are analytical devices that convert a biological response into an electrical signal. Biosensors must be highly specific, independent of physical parameters such as pH and temperature and should be reusable.

A biosensor is a device containing a biological material (enzymes, cells, antibodies, antigens, receptors, DNA fragments) that is in direct contact or embedded in a physicochemical sensor [6]. A generalized scheme for constructing of biosensor devices is shown in Fig. 2.

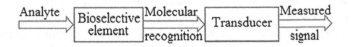

Fig. 2. Generalized biosensor scheme.

1. Bioselective element (bioreceptor). This is a complex of biological molecules in which physicochemical processes occur that transform the properties of the environment into a measured signal (electrical, optical, mechanical, thermal, etc.).

2. Transducer - converts the signal that appears as a result of the interaction of the analyte with the bioselective element, into another signal that is easier to measure. A variety of physicochemical principles of action and the corresponding physicotechnical effects (PTE) are used for the construction of transducers.

The construction of biosensors, in essence, solves two problems related to different fields of science:

1. Creation of a workable biological test object, which has high sensitivity, selectivity, durability, in which a measurable signal should be generated with maximum efficiency. This problem is solved within the biological sciences.
2. Creation of a device for recording and further processing of the signal appearing in the system. This task is solved within the technical sciences.

Analysis of various system approaches to the development of knowledge bases for conceptual design showed that for the systematization of knowledge a specialized method should be used. This method should combine mathematical modeling of processes in a technical device, invariant to the physical nature of these processes, the possibility of processing data about physical effects and phenomena that do not fit into the strict framework of the model, the possibility of the structural description of the physical principle of the device.

This article deals with the design of the knowledge base on physical effects (PTE), in which the systematization of a variety of physical phenomena is based on the energy-information model of chains proposed by the authors in the works [7, 8].

3 The Knowledge Base on Physical and Technical Effects

The majority of usable biosensors today use several types of transducers for converting the action of the bioreceptor into a measurable signal. Transduction can be accomplished via a great variety of methods. Most forms of transduction can be categorized into several classes:

(1) Electrochemical detection methods (amperometric, potentiometric, the change of impedance - conductivity and capacity). The first scientifically proposed as well as successfully commercialized biosensors were those based on electrochemical sensors for multiple analytes. Electrochemical biosensors have been studied for a long time. Principles of the most typical applications of electrochemical biosensors are divided into three types according to the operating principle governing their method of measurement: potentiometric, amperometric and impedimetric transducers [9–13].
(2) Mass detection methods (piezoelectric transducers). Piezoelectric biosensors are of two types: the quartz crystal microbalance and the surface acoustic wave device. They are based on the measurement of changes in resonance frequency of a piezoelectric crystal due to mass changes in the crystal structure [14, 15].
(3) Thermal biosensors measure the thermal energy released or absorbed in biochemical reactions. Thermal activities exist ubiquitously in biological processes,

and thermal biosensing is hence a widely applicable method. Thermal biosensors or calorimetric biosensors are developed by assimilating biosensor materials into a physical transducer [16–18].

(4) A biosensor based on magnetoresistance technology. Magnetic biosensors: miniaturized biosensors detecting magnetic micro- and nanoparticles in microfluidic channels using the magnetoresistance effect have great potential in terms of sensitivity and size [19, 20].

(5) Optical detection methods (photometric). An optical biosensor is a compact analytical device containing a biorecognition sensing element integrated with an optical transducer system. It consists of a light source, as well as numerous optical components to generate a light beam with specific characteristics and to beeline this light to a modulating agent, a modified sensing head along with a photodetector. The basic objective of an optical biosensor is to produce a signal which is proportionate to the concentration of a measured substance (analyte) [21, 22].

(6) Other new methods. Advances in nanotechnology have led to the development of nanoscale biosensors that have big sensitivity and versatility. The ultimate goal of nanobiosensors is to detect any biochemical and biophysical signal associated with a specific disease at the level of a single molecule or cell. Another modern trend is biosensing with paper-based miniaturized printed electrodes. The miniaturized printed electrochemical biosensors are eco-friendly analytical multipurpose tools, disposability and low cost. This allows to develop of point-of-care tests (POCT) i.e., devices that provide non-trained personnel with clinical results within a few minutes, either at home or healthcare services, thereby moving diagnostics from the laboratory to the home [23–25]. The paper electrochemical biosensors trend is an added value to the diagnostic assays since it combines the merits of paper as a solid support, to the high sensitivity and selectivity of bioelectrochemical detection. In fact, the combination of the working electrode with a biological component markedly improves analyte recognition, and the electrochemical transducer provides quantitative readouts, with good detection limits, especially if nanostructured materials such as metal nanoparticles, carbon nanotubes or graphene are used for signal amplification.

However, new types of transducers are constantly being developed for use in biosensors. Each of these classes contains many different subclasses, creating a nearly infinite number of possible transduction methods or a combination of methods. The knowledge base on physical and technical effects (PTE) is designed to synthesize variants of the physical principle of transducers, as well as to store and retrieve information about the decisions. Such information includes a sequential description of all the physic-technical effects included in the chains generated according to the user-defined conditions (the nature and size of the input and output quantity, the number of links in the chain, the permission to repeat the quantity).

The knowledge is presented in a formalized model of the passport of the physical and technical effect. The passport contains a brief and complete description of the physical and technical effect, input, and output quantities, as well as the average typical values of performance characteristics and the formula for calculating the transmission coefficient based on known physical laws, a list of patents in which each effect is present, and values of operational characteristics.

Table 1 lists the following: PTEs included in the base, the PTE formula in terms of the energy-information model, and the formula for the conversion coefficient of the PTE, expressed through known physical parameters of materials, physical constants, and the geometric dimensions of the environment in which this PTE is observed.

Table 1. List of physic-technical effects used in the synthesis of transducers for biosensors.

№	Name of PTE	Formula of PTE	Coefficient of PTE
1.	Tensodiode	$I_e = K_{UmIIe} \cdot U_{ml}$	$K_{UmIIe} = -3J_0 \frac{a}{kT}$ $\left[\frac{A}{N}\right]$
2.	Magnetodiode effect	$U_e = K^n_{QmgUe} \cdot Q_{mg}$	$K^n_{QmgUe} = \frac{\gamma_H \cdot l_e}{S_{mg}}$ $\left[\frac{V}{Wb}\right]$
3.	Pyroelectric effect	$Q_e = K_{UtQe} \cdot U_t$	$K_{UtQe} = \gamma \cdot S$ $\left[\frac{C}{K}\right]$
4.	Mechanocapacitive effect (linear)	$Q_e = K_{QmlCe} \cdot U_e \cdot Q_{ml}$	$K_{QmlCe} = \frac{\varepsilon \varepsilon_0 L}{\tau}$ $\left[\frac{F}{m}\right]$
5.	The effect of amperes	$U_{mg} = K_{IeUmg} \cdot I_e$	$K_{IeUmg} = \omega_e \cdot \omega_{mg}$
6.	The effect of electromagnetic induction	$U_e = K_{ImgUe} \cdot I_{mg}$	$K_{ImgUe} = \omega$
7.	Reverse piezoelectric effect	$Q_{ml} = K_{UeQml} \cdot U_e$	$K_{UeQml} = d$ $\left[\frac{m}{V}\right]$
8.	Magnetostrictive effect	$Q_{ml} = K_{UmgQml} \cdot U_{mg}$	$K_{UmgQml} = \frac{\gamma \mu_0 \mu}{E}$ $\left[\frac{m}{A}\right]$
9.	Piezoelectric effect	$Q_e = K_{UmlQe} \cdot U_{ml}$	$K_{UmlQe} = d$ $\left[\frac{C}{N}\right]$
10	The effect of thermoelectric power (Seebeck effect)	$U_e = K_{UtUe} \cdot U_t$	$K_{UtUe} = \alpha_{12}$ $\left[\frac{V}{K}\right]$
11.	The Peltier effect	$I_t = K_{IeIt} \cdot I_e$	$K_{IeIt} = \alpha_{12}$ $\left[\frac{V}{K}\right]$
12.	Magnetoresistance effect	$U_e = K_{QmgRe} \cdot I_e \cdot Q_{mg}$	$K_{QmgRe} = \frac{K_{MR}(\mu_h)^2 R_0 Q_{mg}}{S_{mg}^2}$ $\left[\frac{1}{s \cdot A}\right]$
13.	The effect of the dependence of the metal resistance on temperature	$U_e = K_{UtRe} \cdot I_e U_t$	$K_{UtRe} = \alpha \cdot R_0$ $\left[\frac{\Omega}{K}\right]$
14.	Varistor effect	$I_e = K_{IeUe} \cdot U_e^\beta$	$K_{IeUe} = A$ $\left[\frac{A}{V^\beta}\right]$
15.	Field effect in a MOSFET	$I_e = K_{QeGe} \cdot U_e \cdot Q_e$	$K_{QeGe} = \frac{\mu_p}{l^2}$ $\left[\frac{1}{\Omega \cdot C}\right]$
16.	Righi-Leduc effect	$U_t = K_{UmgUt} \cdot U_t$	$K_{UmgUt} = S \frac{U_a l_y}{l_x l_z}$ $\left[\frac{K}{A}\right]$
17.	Thermodiode	$U_e = K_{UtUe} \cdot U_t$	$K_{UeUt} = \frac{k}{q} \ln\left(\frac{l_e W_n n_n}{CT^{4-\alpha}}\right)$ $\left[\frac{V}{K}\right]$
18.	The tensoresistive effect in metals	$U_e = K_{QmlRe} \cdot I_e \cdot Q_{ml}$	$K_{QmlRe} = \frac{\rho_0 \cdot \alpha_s}{S}$ $\left[\frac{\Omega}{m}\right]$
19.	Magnetocaloric effect in ferromagnets	$U_t = K_{UmgUt} \cdot U_{mg}$	$K_{UmgUt} = -\frac{T}{Cl_{mg}}\left(\frac{dl_S}{dT}\right)$ $\left[\frac{K}{A}\right]$
20.	Magnetoelectric effect (inverse)	$Q_{mg} = K_{UeQmg} \cdot U_e$	$K_{UeQmg} = \overset{'}{\alpha} \cdot \frac{S}{l}$ $\left[\frac{Wb}{V}\right]$
21.	Magnetoelectric effect	$Q_e = K_{QmgQe} \cdot Q_{mg}$	$K_{QmgQe} = \frac{\overset{'}{\alpha}}{\mu}$ $\left[\frac{C}{Wb}\right]$
22.	Bimetallic effect	$Q_{ml} = K_{UtQml} \cdot U_t$	$K_{UtQml} = k$ $\left[\frac{m}{K}\right]$
23.	Thermoresistive effect in semiconductors (thermistor)	$I_e = K_{UtGe} \cdot U_e \cdot U_t$	$K_{UtGe} = B$ $\left[\frac{1}{\Omega \cdot K}\right]$
24.	The electrocaloric effect	$\Delta Q_t = K_{Ue\Delta Qt} \cdot U_e$	$K_{Ue\Delta Qt} = P \cdot S$ $\left[\frac{J}{V \cdot K}\right]$
25.	The Nernst effect	$U_{ez} = K_{UtxUez} \cdot U_{tx}$	$K_{UtxUez} = \frac{A^{NE} \cdot B \cdot \Delta z}{\Delta x}$ $\left[\frac{V}{K}\right]$
26.	The bimorphic effect (inverse)	$Q_{ml} = K_{UeQml} \cdot U_e$	$K_{UeQml} = \frac{3}{4} \cdot d_{31} \cdot \left(\frac{L}{t}\right)^2$ $\left[\frac{m}{V}\right]$

(*continued*)

Table 1. (*continued*)

№	Name of PTE	Formula of PTE	Coefficient of PTE
27.	Potentiometric PTE	$U_e = U_0 + K_{UdUe} \cdot U_d$	$K_{UdUe} = \frac{1}{n \cdot F} \left[\frac{mol}{C}\right]$
28.	Amperometric PTE	$I_e = K_{Udle} \cdot U_d$	$K_{Idle} = n \cdot F \left[\frac{C}{mol}\right]$
29.	Conductometric PTE	$I_e = K_{UdGe} \cdot U_e \cdot U_d$	$K_{UdGe} = \alpha F v \frac{S}{L} \left[\frac{S \cdot mol}{J}\right]$
30.	Dependence of the capacity of a double electric layer on the concentration of matter	$C_e = K_{UdCe} \cdot U_d^{0,5}$ $I_e = K_{UdCe} \cdot U_d \cdot \dfrac{d(U_e)}{dt}$	$K_{UdCe} = \sqrt{\dfrac{Az^2 e^2 \varepsilon \varepsilon_0 N_A}{kT}} \left[\frac{F}{V^{0,3}}\right]$
31.	PTE of changes in temperature during the biochemical reaction (thermistor)	$\Delta R_e = R_{eo} - \alpha \frac{\Delta H}{C_p} Q_d = R_{e0} + K_{QdRe} Q_d$	$K_{QdRe} = -\alpha \frac{\Delta H}{C_p} \left[\frac{\Omega}{mol}\right]$
32.	The effect of electroosmosis	$I_{ml} = K_{Uelml} \cdot U_e$	$K_{Uelml} = \frac{\varepsilon \varepsilon_0 \zeta}{\eta l} \left[\frac{A}{N}\right]$
33.	Current flow effect	$I_e = K_{Uhle} \cdot U_h$	$K_{Uhle} = \frac{\varepsilon \varepsilon_0 \zeta S}{\eta l} \left[\frac{A \cdot m^2}{N}\right]$
34.	Effect of flow potential	$U_e = K_{UhUe} \cdot U_h$	$K_{UhUe} = \frac{\varepsilon \varepsilon_0 \zeta}{\eta \kappa} \left[\frac{V \cdot m^2}{N}\right]$
35.	Electrophoresis effect	$I_{ml} = K_{Uelml} \cdot U_e$	$K_{Uelml} = \frac{\varepsilon \varepsilon_0 \zeta}{\eta l} \left[\frac{A}{N}\right]$
36.	Sediment current effect	$I_e = K_{Umlle} \cdot U_{ml}$	$K_{Umlle} = \frac{\varepsilon \varepsilon_0 \zeta S}{\eta l} \left[\frac{A \cdot m^2}{N}\right]$
37.	Sedimentation potential effect	$U_e = K_{UmlUe} \cdot U_{ml}$	$K_{UhUe} = \frac{\varepsilon \varepsilon_0 \zeta}{\eta \kappa} \left[\frac{V}{N}\right]$

Notation used:

Input or output quantities: $U_e, U_{mg}, U_{ml}, U_t, U_d, U_h$ - impact quantities; $I_e, I_{mg}, I_{ml}, I, I_d, I_h$ - reaction quantities; $Q_e, Q_{mg}, Q_{ml}, Q_t, Q_d, Q_h$ - charge quantities; $K_{VoutVin}$ - corresponding coefficient of PTE (where V_{in} – input quantity of PTE and V_{out} – output quantity of PTE); J_0 – current density through p-n barrier [A/m^2], – coefficient characterizing the displacement of energy bands [J/Pa], T – temperature [K], k – Boltzmann's constant [J/K]; γH - volt magnetosensitivity, [V/A·T]; B - magnetic induction, [T]; S_{mg} – cross-sectional area of the diode, [m^2]; γ – pyroelectric coefficient [C/m^2 K]; S – area of the face of a pyroelectric [m^2]; ε - the relative permittivity; ε_0 - dielectric constant [F/m]; τ - dielectric thickness [m]; L – capacitor plate width [m]; ω_e – number of windings; ω_{mg} - number of turns of magnetic core; d - piezoelectric module, [m/V]; μ - relative permeability; μ_0 - magnetic constant [H/m]; γ – constant of magnetostriction effect, [A/m]; E – Young's modulus for the magnetostriction material, [N/m^2]; α_{12} - thermo-EMF coefficient [V/K]; K_{MR} - coefficient depending on the properties of the semiconductor; μ_h - charge carrier mobility, [m^2/(V·s)]; ρ_0, ρ_B - the resistivities of a semiconductor material in the absence of a magnetic field and in a field with induction B, [Ω·m]; B - magnetic induction, [T]; Sμ - cross-sectional area of the sample, [m^2]; α - temperature coefficient of resistance [1/K], R_0 – resistance of a thermistor at 0 °C [Ω]; β - varistor non-linearity coefficient; A - constant factor, the value of which depends on the type of varistor and temperature; μ_p - effective mobility of charge carriers in a channel [m^2/(V s)]; 1 - length of the MOSFIT channel [m]; S – constant of the Righi-Leduc effect [m/A]; A^N - constant of the Nernst effect [K·A·m^5/J^2]; n_n – electron concentration [1/m^3]; C – constant, which includes all temperature-independent constants; α - shows

Table 2. The example of the passport of physical and technical effect (PTE).

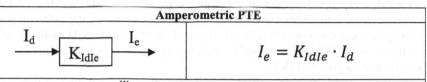

Amperometric PTE	
$I_d \rightarrow \boxed{K_{Idle}} \xrightarrow{I_e}$	$I_e = K_{Idle} \cdot I_d$

Faraday's Law: $I = nF\frac{dN}{dt} = nFSJ$

where dN/dt – oxidation or reduction rate, [mol/s]; F – Faraday constant 96485,33 [C/mol]; n – is the valency number of ions of the substance (electrons transferred per ion); S – area of the electrode [m^2]; J – flux of material per unit surface area [mol/m^2 s].

The equation can be transformed in terms of energy-information model of circuits (EIMS):

$$I_e = K_{Udle} \cdot I_d$$

$I_d = SJ$ - diffusion value of reaction [mol/s];

$I_e = nFI_d$ The electrical value of the reaction (electric current) [A];

$K_{Idle} = nF$ coefficient of physical and technical effects

$$K_{Idle} = n \cdot F \quad [C/mol]$$

F– Faraday constant 96485,33 [C/mol]; n– is the valency number of ions of the substance (electrons transferred per ion); S– area of the electrode [m^2]; J– flux of material per unit surface area [mol/m^2 s].	F=96485,33 [C/mol]; n = 1 -2 S = 1-2 10^{-6} m^2
Sensitivity: 400 - 1800 [A/(моль·м2] Price: 6-10 Reliability: 10-3 – 10-4 [1/час] Error: 5% Nonlineriaty: 10%	Range: 0,05 – 2,50 [мМоль] Speed: 0,05 [с] Losses: 10% Ecology:·10-8 [кг/с] Weight: 0,0005 [кг]

References [27, 28, 29]	
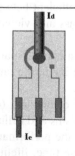	The amperometric method is based on measuring the current density flowing in an electrochemical cell with a constant applied potential. The current density is a function of the electrochemically active particles of the solution, the oxidation or reduction of which occurs on the surface of the working electrode. During electrolysis, the working electrode can be either an anode or a cathode, depending on the nature of the analyte and the applied potential. If a constant electric potential is applied to the electrode, then in the electrochemical electrode/solution system, the charged particles are exchanged. Particularly it is the oxidation and reduction processes. This process obeys the Faraday law.

the dependence of the mobility of electrons and holes on temperature; k – Boltzmann's constant [J/K]; q – electron charge [C]; K – coefficient of tensosensitivity; $\varepsilon_l = \Delta l/L$ – relative linear deformation; R_0 – resistance of the test-object without deformation [Ω]; α'

- coefficient of effect [s/m]; k – bimetal effect coefficient [m/K]; A^{NE} – Nernst coefficient [m^2/s K]; J_k – the diffusion flux of the k-th component, [mol/(m^2·s)]; D_k – diffusion coefficient of the k-th component, [m^2/s]; C_k – concentration of the k-th component, [mol/m^3]; R – gas constant, [J/(mol·K)]; $\Delta_{\mu k}$ – chemical potential, [J/mol]; η – coefficient of viscosity [N·s/m^2]; κ– specific conductivity of a liquid [1/(Ω·m)]; ζ – electrokinetic or zeta potential [V].

The list of physic-technical effects will be supplemented with new effects, which will find application in the design of transducers for biosensor devices.

Optical physic-technical effects can be described based on the energy-information model, Such effects have recently been increasingly used in designing biosensors. The energy-information model for optical polarization phenomena was described in the article [26].

Information about each effect in the database is presented in the form of a passport. An example of a fully completed passport is shown in Table 2.

4 Logical Model of the System of Conceptual Design of Biosensors

The information technology of the conceptual design of biosensors is based on the theoretical positions of energy-information models of circuits that are invariant to the physical nature of processes occurring in technical devices. The process of designing biosensors can be divided into two stages. First is to select a sensitive biological element that recognizes the desired substance in the bioreceptor database and to indicate the output quantity of this bioreceptor. After this, the transducer is synthesized on the basis of the knowledge base data, for which the output quantity of the bioreceptor is the input quantity.

The logical model of the system of the conceptual design of biosensors is presented in the form of a class diagram and demonstrates the classes, their attributes, methods, and interrelations between them (Fig. 3).

1. **PTE passport** - the main attributes of the class are: the name of the physical and technical effect, the input and output quantities, the conversion coefficient between them, the number of inputs (1 or 2). The main methods of the class are: viewing, editing, searching.
2. **Quantity** - attributes of the class are: name, physical nature, qualitative, spatial, temporal and special characteristics of the physical quantity of the input, the range of the magnitude change, the dimension and nature of its change.
3. **Bioreceptor passport** - basic attributes: the type of biochemical component (enzyme, immunosensor, DNA sensors, sensors based on microorganisms and cellular tissues, sensors based on supramolecular cellular structures, etc.), the performance of the bioreceptor (selectivity, sensitivity, linearity, range, response time, lifetime, regeneration time, precision, accuracy, reproducibility), immobilization method (adsorption, microencapsulation, inclusion, crosslinking or covalent binding). Additionally, forbidden combinations of bioreceptors and transducers are indicated. The main methods of the class are: viewing, editing, searching.

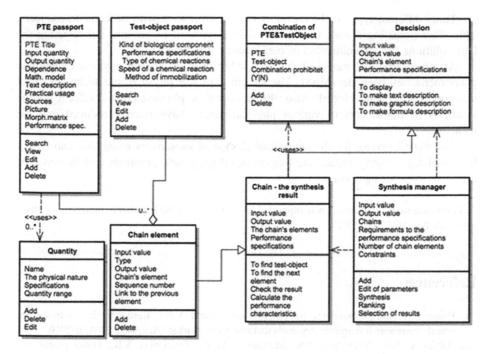

Fig. 3. Class diagram of the system of conceptual design of biosensors.

4. **Chain as synthesis result** – describes an array of elementary links that make up the synthesized structural scheme of the action principle of the designed biosensor. The main methods of the class are: search for a bioreceptor for a given type of test substance (analyte); search for the next element of the chain (PTE from the second base); check for the result of synthesis; checking the limit on the number of elements in the chain; calculation of the main performance characteristics of the synthesized chain. This class uses the auxiliary class **Chain element**, which describes a PTE or a bioreceptor within a synthesized chain. Methods in this class: create and remove a circuit element.

5. **Synthesis Manager** – describes the mechanisms of multicriteria ranking and selection of synthesized circuits based on the aggregate of calculated performance characteristics. Methods: formulation of the synthesis problem, launch of synthesis with calculation of performance characteristics, multicriteria ranking of synthesis results.

6. **Synthesis Decision** - describes the selected and stored user synthesis chain.

5   Conclusion

A study of the world market of biosensors showed a projected annual growth of up to 10%. In Russia, the market of biosensors is also expected to grow up to twenty six billion rubles (approximately 470 million of US dollars) by 2020. Thus, the creation of a system for automated design of biosensors is an urgent task.

Thus, different types of bioreceptors can be combined with different transducers. This allows creating a wide variety of different types of biosensors and selecting the best solutions for a combination of performance characteristics.

An object-oriented model of the knowledge base on known physical effects and phenomena has been developed. The structure of the physical and technical effect passport has been developed. Also, 40 passports of physic-technical effects for the synthesis of transducers of various physical nature have been introduced into the database.

Automated system for the conceptual design of biosensors using this knowledge base will significantly reduce the time of developing new solutions and increase the productivity of design work.

Acknowledgment. This work was supported by a grant from the Russian Foundation for Basic Research No. 16-37-00258\17.

References

1. Biosensors Market Analysis by Application. Grand View Research, Inc. http://www.grandviewresearch.com/industry-analysis/biosensors-market. Accessed 31 Aug 2016
2. Balyakin, A.A., Malyshev, A.S., Mamonov, M.V., Taranenko, S.B.: Development and implementation peculiarities of medical biosensors in Russian Federation. https://www.fundamental-research.ru/ru/article/view?id=35103. Accessed 06 Apr 2017
3. Zaripova, V.M., Petrova, I.Y.: Ontological knowledge base of physical and technical effects for conceptual design of sensors. J. Phys.: Conf. Ser. **588**, 012031 (2015). doi:10.1088/1742-6596/588/1/012031
4. Petrova, I.Y., Zaripova, V.M., Lezhnina, Y.A., Sokolskiy, V.M., Mitchenko, I.A.: Energy and information models of biosensors. Vestn. Astrakhan State Tech. Univ. Ser. Manag. Comput. Sci. Inf. **3**, 35–48 (2015)
5. Petrova, I., Zaripova, V., Lezhnina, Y., Sokolskiy, V.: Modeling of the physical principle of the processes that is occurring in bioselective elements. Int. J. Monit. Surveill. Technol. Res. **3**, 43–61 (2015). doi:10.4018/IJMSTR.2015100103
6. Thevenot, D.R., Toth, K., Durst, R.A., Wilson, G.S.: Electrochemical biosensors: recommended definitions and classification. Biosens. Bioelectron. **16**(1–2), 121–131 (2001)
7. Zaripova, V., Petrova, I.: System of conceptual design based on energy-informational model. In: Selvaraj, H., Zydek, D., Chmaj, G. (eds.) Progress in Systems Engineering. AISC, vol. 366, pp. 365–372. Springer, Cham (2015). doi:10.1007/978-3-319-08422-0_54
8. Zaripova, V., Petrova, I.: Information technology of concept design of biosensors. Indian J. Sci. Technol. (S.l.) (2016). doi:10.17485/ijst/2017/v10i1/109983. http://www.indjst.org/index.php/indjst/article/view/109983. Accessed 03 Mar 2017
9. Monošík, R., Streďanský, M., Šturdík, E.: Biosensors—classification, characterization and new trends. Acta Chim. Slov. **5**(1), 109–120 (2012). doi:10.2478/v10188-012-0017-z
10. Hammond, J.L., Formisano, N., Estrela, P., Carrara, S., Tkac, J.: Electrochemical biosensors and nanobiosensors. Essays Biochem. **60**(1), 69–80 (2016). doi:10.1042/EBC20150008. Estrela, P. (ed.)
11. Pisoschi, A.M.: Potentiometric biosensors: concept and analytical applications-an editorial. Biochem. Anal. Biochem. **5**, e164 (2016). doi:10.4172/2161-1009.1000e164

12. Li, L., Wang, Y., Pan, L., Shi, Y., Cheng, W., Shi, Y., Yu, G.: A nanostructured conductive hydrogels-based biosensor platform for human metabolite detection. Nano Lett. **15**(2), 1146–1151 (2015). doi:10.1021/nl504217p

13. Crescentini, M., Rossi, M., Ashburn, P., Lombardini, M., Sangiorgi, E., Morgan, H., Tartagni, M.: AC and phase sensing of nanowires for biosensing. Biosensors **6**, 15 (2016). doi:10.3390/bios6020015

14. Pohanka, M.: The piezoelectric biosensors principles and applications, a review. Int. J. Electrochem. Sci. **12**, 496–506 (2017). doi:10.20964/2017.01.44

15. Li, X., Wu, X., Shi, P., Ye, Z.-G.: Lead-free piezoelectric diaphragm biosensors based on micro-machining technology and chemical solution deposition. Sensors **16**, 69 (2016). doi:10.3390/s16010069

16. Najib, F.M., Zewar, S., Abdulla, A.M.: A new sensor for thermometric titrations. Talanta **71**, 141–148 (2007)

17. Mehrotra, P.: Biosensors and their applications – a review. J. Oral Biol. Craniofac. Res. **6**(2), 153–159 (2016). doi:10.1016/j.jobcr.2015.12.002

18. Kopparthy, V.L., Tangutooru, S.M., Guilbeau, E.J.: Label free detection of L-glutamate using microfluidic based thermal biosensor. Bioengineering **2**, 2–14 (2015). doi:10.3390/bioengineering2010002

19. Krishna, V.D., Wu, K., Perez, A.M., Wang, J.-P.: Giant magnetoresistance-based biosensor for detection of influenza a virus. Front. Microbiol. **7**, Article ID 400 (2016)

20. Orlov, A.V., Khodakova, J.A., Nikitin, M.P., Shepelyakovskaya, A.O., Brovko, F.A., Laman, A.G., Grishin, E.V., Nikitin, P.I.: Magnetic immunoassay for detection of staphylococcal toxins in complex media. Anal. Chem. **85**(2), 1154–1163 (2013)

21. Eggins, B.R. (ed.): Photometric Applications, in Analytical Techniques in the Sciences: Chemical Sensors and Biosensors. Wiley, Chichester (2002). doi:10.1002/9780470511305.ch6

22. Shen, Q., Han, L., Fan, G., Zhang, J.-R., Jiang, L., Zhu, J.-J.: "Signal-on" photoelectrochemical biosensor for sensitive detection of human T-cell lymphotropic virus type II DNA: dual signal amplification strategy integrating enzymatic amplification with terminal deoxynucleotidyl transferase-mediated extension. Anal. Chem. **87**(9), 4949–4956 (2015). doi:10.1021/acs.analchem.5b00679

23. Vigneshvar, S., Sudhakumari, C.C., Senthilkumaran, B., Prakash, H.: Recent advances in biosensor technology for potential applications – an overview. Front. Bioeng. Biotechnol. **4**, 11 (2016). doi:10.3389/fbioe.2016.00011

24. Sagadevan, S., Periasamy, M.: Recent trends in nanobiosensors and their applications - a review. Rev. Adv. Mater. Sci. **36**, 62–69 (2014)

25. Silveira, C.M., Monteiro, T., Almeida, M.G.: Biosensing with paper-based miniaturized printed electrodes–a modern trend. Biosensors **6**, 51 (2016). doi:10.3390/bios6040051

26. Petrova, I.Y., Kiselev, A.A.: Energy-information model of optical polarization phenomena. Sens. Syst. **6**(C), 26–30 (2005). (in Russian)

27. Freire, R.S., Pessao, C.A., Mello, L.D., Kubota, L.T.: Direct electron transfer: an approach for electro- chemical biosensors with higher selectivity and sensitivity. J. Braz. Chem. Soc. **14**(2), 230–243 (2003). doi:10.1590/S0103-50532003000200008

28. Grieshaber, D., MacKenzie, R., Vöros, J., Reimhult, E.: Electrochemical biosensors—sensor principles and architectures. Sensors **8**(3), 1400–1458 (2008). doi:10.3390/s8031400

29. Pohanka, M., Skládal, P.: Electrochemical biosensors – principles and applications. J. Appl. Biomed. **6**, 57–64 (2008)

The Risk Management Model of Design Department's PDM Information System

Alla Kravets[(⊠)] and Svetlana Kozunova

Volgograd State Technical University, Volgograd, Russian Federation
agk@gde.ru

Abstract. At presented paper, existing methods of risk management are analyzed. It is substantiated that the most rational mechanism for controlling the risks of design department's information system is the risk management model. This mechanism takes into account the specifications of design department's information system and allows reducing the anomalous events that can cause risks. Most modern research is devoted to the problems of managing risks of industrial enterprises and commercial companies. However, the problem of managing the design department's information system and the risks to which such systems may be exposed has not been studied. The authors proposed a new risk management model of design department's information system. The design of such model is based on the process of presenting the risk management of design department's information system as a model of the "black box" and the structural scheme. The architecture of the risk management system of design department's information system is proposed.

Keywords: Design department · Risk · Control loop · Structural scheme · PDM · Diagram · Architecture

1 Introduction

One of the main tasks in managing information flows, protecting information resources and ensuring the fault tolerance of design department's product data management (PDM) information system (DDIS) is risk management. The relevance of the research topic is justified by the need to develop a system of risk management and incidents of DDIS [1–6]. Such system must be able to operate in conditions of uncertainty and risk tolerance. Problems of risk management are considered in the works of authors [1, 5, 6], but it is an open question: the identification of risks in real time, *selection of criteria* for *assessing risks*, accounting *specificity* of the design department, holding of risk optimization. The reason for this is the development of methods for risk management of DDIS is carried out relatively recently. Therefore this area of research is devoted to not a lot of scientific works. As a solution to the problem of the study, we propose a risk management model of DDIS. This model is based on the control loop. The developed risk management model of DDIS is designed to solve problems such as event monitoring of DDIS, management of risks, risk assessment and possible

© Springer International Publishing AG 2017
A. Kravets et al. (Eds.): CIT&DS 2017, CCIS 754, pp. 490–500, 2017.
DOI: 10.1007/978-3-319-65551-2_36

damages, reduce risks. The effectiveness of the use of PDM systems is confirmed by studies [5, 15].

2 Related Work and Existing Solution

In this field of research, we can subdivide the most common practical application and risk management solutions. Standardized methods of risk management are such as ISO, COSO II ERM-Integrated Framework, FERMA, BS and others. Software: GRAMM, RISKWATCH, CORAS, OCTAVE. However, each of these methods does not take into account the features. This greatly complicates the analysts and information technology specialists to carry out a complex risk management and make a decision on the application of measures aimed at reducing the risks. The use of standardized methods described in detail in [7–9, 14]. Algorithms of functioning described in [12, 13].

Let's analyze the most commonly used methods of risk management. The result of analysis displayed in Table 1.

Table 1. Analysis of risk management methods.

Method name	Identification of risks	Risk assessment	Risks analysis	Establishing the risk of criticality	Report on risks
FERMA:2002	+	+	−	−	−
COSO:2004	−	+	−	−	−
ISO 31000:2009	+	+	+	−	−
GRAMM	+	+	−	+	+
BS 7799-3:2006	−	+	+	−	+
OCTAVE	−	+	+	+	−
RiskWatch	−	+	−	+	+
CORAS	+	+	+	−	+

According to the analysis, the maximum number of positive evaluations received GRAMM, CORAS. The greatest number of negative evaluations scored method COSO:2004.

Most scientific research has shown that some scientists have tried to solve the problem of risk management of information security (IS). The authors [5, 11] of a systematic approach has been created, in which the risks of IS are considered in a single system communication. The strategic approach is based on the choice of a particular management strategy [1, 5, 6]. Process approach allows you to manage the processes that can lead to risks of IS [13, 14]. The authors [6] proposed the concept of configuration management. This concept is to carry out of administrative procedures at different levels: corporate, technical and other. In this paper, we propose a new method of risk management of DDIS, which allows managing and optimizing risk tolerance. This method is based on a systematic, strategic and process approach.

3 Structural Scheme of Risk Management Model of Design Department's Information System

Works [1, 2, 10] have shown that for DDIS characterized by the following risks: the economic, the risk of market conditions and the risk of information, technical and catastrophe risks. Thus, it is to manage these risks to develop models.

Structural scheme of risk management model of the DDIS is shown in Fig. 1. The main structural elements of the proposed model are monitoring center, a management agent, logserver, information system, network, mechanism of neutralizing the risks, the risks report generator.

Management agent intercepts the events analyzed and sends them to logserver. Management agent responds to risk events and attempts to block or reduce. So the management agent decides on risk management (selects management strategy). The risks report generator (RRG) shape a report on the risk events and the measures chosen agent for their elimination. Then RRG sends reports to logserver. Next, the management agent carries out risk management procedures of DDIS (Fig. 1). After the management, procedures run neutralization mechanism of risk, which activates the elimination by means of risk. After performing the function of risk management, mechanism of the model is restarted in order to verify the correctness of the IS and the elimination of residual risks.

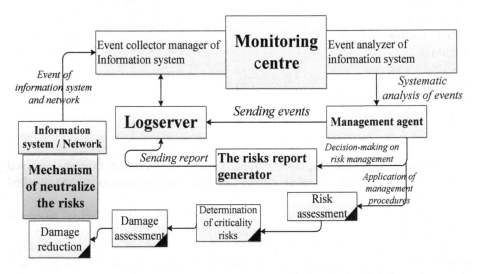

Fig. 1. Structural scheme of risk management model of design department's information system

The risk management process of DDIS can be represented as a "blackbox" (Fig. 2).

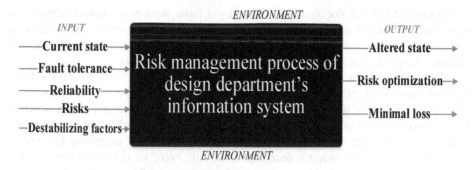

Fig. 2. Risk management process of design department's information system as "blackbox"

Input supplied data to the system such as current state vector, fault tolerance, reliability, risks and destabilizing factors. The output of "blackbox" observed data characterizing the effect of the decision (control functions) such as altered state vector of DDIS, risk optimization, minimal loss. Input signals are input vector data. Environment affects to the DDIS. This influence will call signals to the external environment. The output is the effect of the control actions.

Presentation of the management process as a "blackbox" (Fig. 2) makes it possible to the risk management model take into account the influence of the environment not only in the management process but also on the ability to resist risks of DDIS.

The basis of the construction of model risk - management put the control loop, depicted in Fig. 3. Control loop displays the control signals, which are sent to the management agent. As a management agent acts as the subject of management. The subject of management sends appropriate control actions to control object. In the proposed model. The control object is a risk, information flows of DDIS and its sub-systems, information resources. The subject of management is an information - analytical system of risk management.

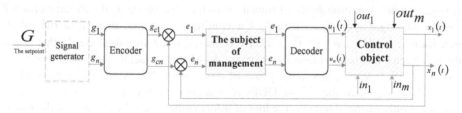

Fig. 3. Control loop of risks of design department's information system

A control loop (Fig. 3) is closed with feedback. Input for the impact of the subject of management it is defining the external impact and internal reference variable. Internal exposure defining an act as control actions. g_1, g_n drive signals; g_{c1}, g_{cn} – coded drive signals; e_1, e_n - error signals; $u_n(t)$ - control signal; $x(t)$ - output; out_m - external disturbance; in_m - internal exposure.

Control object $S = \{s_1, s_2, ..., s_i\}$, where i – a finite number of control subjects. In this way the subject of management is an integral. Control action $U(t) = A_u[e(t)]$, where A_u – operator, which establishes a connection between the master and control actions. $A_u: \{x(t), g(t)\} \rightarrow U(t)$. The error signal is $e(t) = u(t) - x(t)$.

The control object formalized describe how $O = \{o_1, o_2, ..., o_j\}$, where j – finite number control object. The setpoint $G = \{g_1, g_2, ..., g_n\}$, where n – the number of signals, generated by signal generation (SG). The behavior of control object describe through operator B. Operator B determines the behavior of the subject of management. B uses a rule that sets the current value $x(t)$ for the control and disturbing influences. The behavior of control object is described as $B: \{u(t), g(t), x_0, t\} \rightarrow x(t)$, where x_0 – the initial state of the control object, t – time of management. The setpoint G generated by a signal generator (SG). SG forms the setpoint G according to the rule $C: \{t, x(t), u(t)\} \rightarrow gl(t)$. Achieving the management objective - reducing the risk and the blocking of defined quality management K. Output signals control object $x_1 (t), ..., x_n (t) \in X(t)$ when $t \in [t_0, t_n]$, where t_0 – start time, t_n – end time. Quality control criteria $K = \{K_k (x, u, g), k = 1, ..., N\}$.

Control object work can be described by the operator $Y: X(t): \rightarrow u(t)$.

Thus, the method developed risk management of DDIS is based on the method of analysis of the events taking place in IS and qualitative - quantitative risk assessment.

We give a formal description of the risk assessment procedure. Quantitative risk assessment is calculated as $R_r = p_r L_r$, where p_r – probability of risk occurrence, L_r - damage that could cause a risk, r – the serial number of risk. Damage caused by risk L_r can be calculated as $L_r = p_r Cost$, where $Cost$ - the value of the information asset.

The ability to resist risks of DDIS projected based on risk tolerance assessment. Evaluation criteria of risk tolerance of DDIS is defined as formalized $RT = \sum_{r=1}^{N} W_r$, where N - the total number of risk of DDIS, W_r - risk weight. Risk weight calculates as $W_r = \frac{0,5(R-r+1)}{(R+1)R}$. Thus W_r satisfies the following conditions: $W_r \in [0;1]$, $RT = \sum_{r=1}^{N} W_r = 1$.

Risks of DDIS are able to change their state to move from the permissible at a critical risk. Phase (risk condition) through m-transitions describe the way $\alpha(0) \rightarrow \alpha (1) \rightarrow ... \rightarrow \alpha(m)$. The probability of transition to the next phase p_{ij} described as $p_{ij} = P \{\alpha(m + 1) = \alpha_i(\alpha(m)) = \beta_i\}$, where β_i - a condition in which there is a risk of m-transition, $i, j = 1, 2...m$, $m = \overline{0, 3}$. If $m = 0$, then it is a zero-risk phase. In this phase, the risk begins to emerge; therefore, there are destabilizing factors that could lead to the risk of DDIS. If $m = 1$, this initial phase of risk. This risk is acceptable with minimal losses. If $m = 2$, then the risk of DDIS is unacceptable because it can lead to large losses not only financial but also the loss of information assets. When m = 3, the risk of DDIS is critical. This risk can destroy the DDIS recovery without the possibility of functioning.

The developed method allows management to assess the risks of DDIS, categorize events of DDIS on risk levels and to predict damages.

When researching risks, it is important to talk about destabilizing factors (DF). A large number of active DF indicates a strong exposure of DDIS to risks. The authors of the article proposed a diagram showing the relationship of processes to the DDIS with risk-tolerance (Fig. 4). The diagram proposed by the authors reflects typical for DDIS processes and the corresponding DF. The heterogeneity of the processes causes the formation of different information flows. When the DDIS processes a large number of such flows, failures in the functioning of the DDIS system may occur. Thus, one of the measures of risk management is the control of DF.

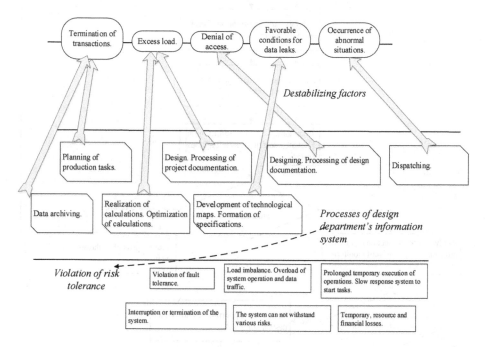

Fig. 4. The diagram of communication processes by the information system with risk-tolerance.

Based on the research [3, 4, 10] and developed model, the authors created a general algorithm for risk management of DDIS. The algorithm is shown in Fig. 5.

Step 1: the beginning, the starting point of the management processes. Steps 2–3: data processing. Step 4: comparison of available data with the capabilities of the management system. Steps 5–12: application of risk management functions. Step 13: display the results of the control system. Step 14: complete the control cycle.

Using the proposed model (Figs. 1, 2, 3, 5), the authors designed the architecture of risk management's DDIS. Designed architecture is shown in Fig. 6.

Architecture is distributed (Fig. 6). The architecture includes several subsystems such as monitoring center, management agent, DDIS, storage system and user input/output interface. The interaction between the components of the risk management system is shown by arrows with double guides.

Management agent includes modules: signal generation module, report generation module, signal encoding and decoding module, build management tasks module.

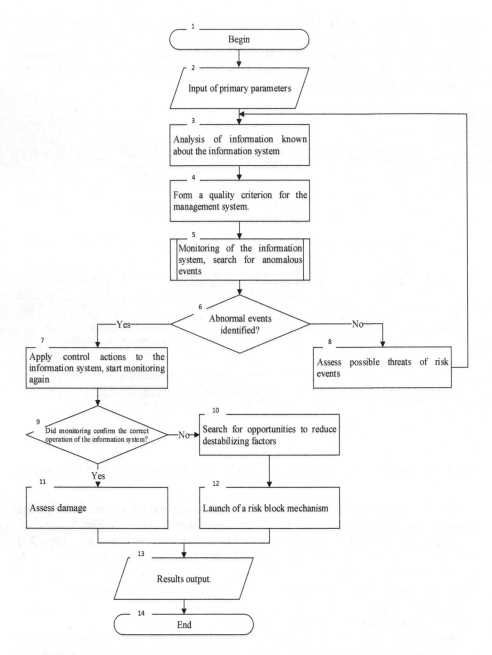

Fig. 5. Algorithm for risk management of design department's information system

Monitoring center includes information collection module, build logic functions module, risk and damages assessment module. Monitoring center provides system event monitoring function of DDIS and network in real time. Information collection

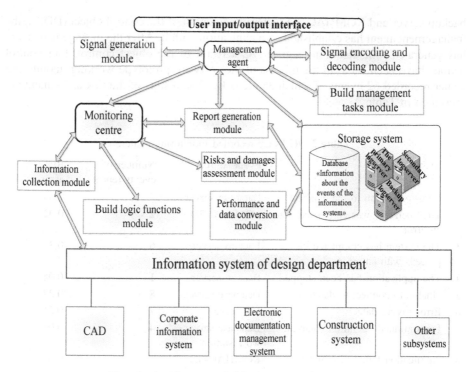

Fig. 6. Architecture of risk management's system

module performs event collection procedures as information on its initial and final states and about the restart of DDIS or about the system operation termination.

Information collection module performs event collection procedure of DDIS: information on its initial and final states, restart the DDIS or the termination of its functioning. Build logic functions module executes the processes handled by the system risk management. Risks and damages assessment module executes the processes handled by the system risk management. This module performs the evaluation and optimization of the IS risks.

Report generation module connects the subsystems and displays the result of each subsystem in the form of reports. Storage system consists of a database "Information about the events of the information system", logserver cluster and performance and data conversion module. Logserver cluster consists of the primary logserver, secondary logserver, backup logserver. Storage system features a third-party memory allocation data and internal data exchange intermediaries.

User input/output interface for the user to not only introduced the input and receive the output but also to call a certain module or component system risk management.

The risk management model of DDIS is implemented in software. Experimental researches of the model were carried out in the network of the company "Reanimator". This company provides services for data recovery. DDIS operates in this subnet. Subnetwork consists of a gateway, switch, router, workstation, hypervisor, file server, database server (MS SQL Server and three databases), access control subsystem, the backup server and КОМПАС-3D. After initialization of the control object (DDIS), the management agent has established communication with it. After the management agent has generated four disturbing signals. As a result of the object control, four control actions have been filed. In the process of the software prototype working, monitoring center recorded 62 events of which 38 are risky. The results of the risk assessment are presented in Table 2.

Table 2. Risks are recorded monitoring center.

#	Risk event	Event source	Number of events repeats	Risk assessment
1	Lost connection to the database	Database server	5	0.05
2	The operation was completed with an error	КОМПАС-3D	2	0.02
3	The system has completed the process with an error	Backup server	6	0.3
4	The application has been stopped	Backup server	1	0.04
5	Unable to connect to database	Database server	8	0.27
6	Error saving data	File server	7	0.21
7	Discontinued operation database	Database server, work station	4	0.08
8	Application failed to initialize	КОМПАС-3D	1	0.012
9	Script execution postponed	Database server services	2	0.008
10	Disconnected to the file server	Workstation	2	0.01

The risk assessment scored the highest assessment events: the system has completed the process with an error, unable to connect to database, error saving data. These events are critical risks. These events can damage the DDIS. The lowest estimate of typed events: disconnected to the file server, the application failed to initialize. These risks are acceptable because of the little effect on the risk tolerance.

Monitoring center produced a collection of events for 16 h of DDIS. The maximum period of time 3 o'clock recorded event categories "unable to connect to database". The experimental results showed that the risk management model is able to manage the risks of DDIS. As a result of software prototypes, it was found that a weak spot in the DDIS is the backup server. The reason for this is that backups are done incorrectly. This leads to the problem of the database server. This work means no backup server failover infrastructure. The results show the effectiveness and quality of the developed method of risk management of DDIS.

4   Conclusion

At the article is shown that it is necessary to manage system risks using a DDIS-oriented method. As such a method, the authors proposed a specialized model.

The result of the study in the direction of "risk management" was developed and formalized a model of risk – management of DDIS. The proposed model solves the problem of minimizing the risks of DDIS. Using such a model can monitor system events and classify events on the critical (risky) and non-critical (non-anomalous for the IS) events. This model allows for complex risk management based on their evaluation of the system and event analysis occurring in the system and network in which the IS works.

The difference model risk - management is the application of a control loop, which describes the change in the signal, and the impact of the subject of management on the control object. The uniqueness of the developed model is that it allows you to take into account the specifics of DDIS.

In Conclusions, based on the developed model, we proposed system architecture of the risk management of DDIS. In the future, we plan to develop a risk management system of design department based on the architecture developed. Designed risk management model of the DDIS model meets all the criteria of the analysis of risk management: risk identification, risk assessment, risk analysis, the establishment of critical risks, and the ability to generate a report on the risks of DDIS. Thus, the analysis of risk management practices, the proposed model scored the maximum score. Risk management model focuses on DDIS. The architecture of risk management's system takes into account of the DDIS. Software testing prototype models have shown that the method of the system.

Acknowledgments. This research was partially supported by the Russian Fund of Basic Research (grant No. 15-07-06254 A).

References

1. Campbell, T.: The information security manager. Practical Information Security Management, pp. 31–42. Apress, Berkeley (2016). doi:10.1007/978-1-4842-1685-9_3
2. Tong, X., Ban, X.: A hierarchical information system risk evaluation method based on asset dependence chain. Int. J. Secur. Appl. **8**(6), 81–88 (2014)
3. Kravets, A.G., Bui, N.D., Al-Ashval, M.: Mobile security solution for enterprise network. In: Kravets, A., Shcherbakov, M., Kultsova, M., Iijima, T. (eds.) JCKBSE 2014. CCIS, vol. 466, pp. 371–382. Springer, Cham (2014). doi:10.1007/978-3-319-11854-3_31
4. Yamamoto, S.: A knowledge integration approach for safety-critical software development and operation based on the method architecture. In: Teufel, S., Min, T.A., You, I., Weippl, E. (eds.) CD-ARES 2014. LNCS, vol. 8708, pp. 17–28. Springer, Cham (2014). doi:10.1007/978-3-319-10975-6_2
5. Saltykov, S., Rusyaeva, E., Kravets, A.: Typology of scientific constructions as an instrument of conceptual creativity. In: Kravets, A., Shcherbakov, M., Kultsova, M., Shabalina, O. (eds.) CIT&DS 2015. CCIS, vol. 535, pp. 41–57. Springer, Cham (2015). doi:10.1007/978-3-319-23766-4_4
6. Kamaev, V.A., Kozunova, S.S.: Incident management system of information security of industrial enterprises. In: Congress IS&IT 2016, Vol. 3, pp. 166–171 (2016)
7. BS 7799-3 – Information security management systems. Guidelines for information security risk management

8. COSO: Enterprise Risk Management—Integrated Framework (2004)
9. ISO 31000: Risk management – Principles and guidelines (2009)
10. Shafiee, M.: Modelling and analysis of availability for critical interdependent infrastructures. Int. J. Risk Assess. Manag. **19**(4), 299–314 (2016)
11. Patacas, J., Dawood, N., Greenwood, D., Kassem, M.: Supporting building owners and facility managers in the validation and visualisation of asset information models (AIM) through open standards and open technologies. J. Inf. Technol. Constr. **21**, 434–435 (2016)
12. Chandrashekhar, A.M., Kurmar, H.S., Huded, Y.: Advances in information security risk practices. Int. j. Adv. Res. Datamin. Cloud Comput. **3**, 47–51a (2015)
13. Behnia, A., Rashid, R.A., Chaudhry, J.A.: A survey of information security risk analysis methods. Smart Comput. Rev. **2**(1), 79–94 (2012)
14. Sokolov, B.V., Yusupov, R.M., Ivanov, D.A.: Conceptual description of integrated risk modelling problems for managerial decisions in complex organisational and technical systems. Int. J. Risk Assess. Manag. **18**(3/4), 288–306 (2015)
15. de Sousa, W.H., Giardino, A., Trezza, M.A.H.: The development of an enterprise resource planning system (ERP) for a research and technology institute: the case of the nuclear and energy research institute – IPEN. JISTEM J. Inf. Syst. Technol. Manag. **8**(1), 5–24 (2011)

View-Dependent Level of Detail for Real-Time Rendering of Large Isosurfaces

Vyacheslav Shakaev, Natalia Sadovnikova, and Danila Parygin[(✉)]

Volgograd State Technical University, Volgograd, Russia
dparygin@gmail.com

Abstract. Isosurface extraction is a widely used method for interactive visualization of volumetric scalar data sets in many scientific, engineering and entertainment applications. When visualizing large isosurfaces, interactive frame rates are enabled by view-dependent level-of-detail rendering techniques. However, these techniques usually require lengthy pre-processing and thus are unsuitable for visualizing procedurally-generated or dynamic data. In this paper, we present an approach for real-time rendering of isosurfaces with the view-dependent level of detail. It is based on a pointerless octree for low-overhead hierarchy management and a modified Dual Contouring algorithm with geomorphing to avoid costly stitching and abrupt level-of-detail transitions at run-time. We demonstrate that our method can render large procedurally-generated surfaces without any precomputation. We show that our algorithm can approximate sharp features, which is an important requirement for many CAD/CAM/CAE applications.

Keywords: Level-of-detail techniques · View-dependent visualization · Isosurface extraction · Real-time rendering

1 Introduction

The need for interactively navigating and inspecting very large volumetric data sets arises in many application domains, such as architectural design and urban planning, driving and flight simulation, geometric modeling and entertainment. Isosurface extraction is one the most popular techniques for visualizing scalar volumetric data. Due to the high amount of storage and computational complexity, visualization of huge isosurfaces at interactive rates requires multi-resolution representations and view-dependent rendering strategies based either on top-down refinement or bottom-up simplification of the original data.

The key to visualizing large and complex isosurfaces in real-time without noticeably losing image quality is employing level-of-detail (LoD) techniques that adjust mesh complexity according to visual importance to the viewer and with respect to the available rendering power. Most of these techniques are based on spatial partitioning and recursively traverse the LoD hierarchy, which often incurs a noticeable CPU overhead when dealing with deep hierarchies. Moreover, those methods usually require time-consuming pre-processing of the original data set and thus are not applicable to visualizing procedurally-generated or dynamically changing data. Furthermore, many

© Springer International Publishing AG 2017
A. Kravets et al. (Eds.): CIT&DS 2017, CCIS 754, pp. 501–516, 2017.
DOI: 10.1007/978-3-319-65551-2_37

approaches rely on expensive and complicated stitching to obtain a continuous mesh in transitional regions (where the level of detail changes), and/or suffer from LoD popping artifacts. Finally, few of them are able to reconstruct sharp corners and edges which are desirable in most CAD/CAM/CAE applications.

In this paper, we propose an approach for real-time rendering of large isosurfaces which does not require any pre-processing. Our non-recursive view-dependent refinement algorithm works on a pointerless octree which allows processing huge LoD hierarchies with very low CPU overhead. Our LoD algorithm is fairly straight-forward to implement and can be used with any LoD metric. We avoid stitching and achieve seamless level-of-detail transitions via geomorphing. As a result, we are able to render very large isosurfaces in real-time without cracks or seams. We also show that our isosurface extraction algorithm can approximate sharp features.

2   Related Work

2.1   Isosurface Extraction

Here we only cover references most relevant to our work and establish terminology; for a comprehensive review, we refer the reader to [1]. Isosurface extraction methods generate a polygonal mesh approximating the surface of the volume. The resulting mesh can then be efficiently rendered by the graphics hardware. We focus on spatial decomposition methods that subdivide the space into disjoint convex (usually, cubic) cells. The cell grid is dual to the voxel grid, i.e., voxel centers are located at cell's corners, and vice versa. Surface components (vertices and triangles) are created only for a boundary, or active cells (i.e. intersecting the isosurface).

Marching Cubes (MC) [2] is the most popular algorithm for isosurface extraction, but it was designed for uniform grids and requires crack-patching [3] or stitching [4] for constructing an adaptive, view-dependent isosurface. Moreover, it is not feature-preserving and tends to produce a lot of skinny triangles.

Dual Contouring (DC) [5] is a unified method to extract crack-free surfaces on both uniform and adaptive grids. DC creates a representative vertex inside each active cell and, for each active edge (i.e. crossing the isosurface), DC connects the vertices of the adjacent cells sharing this edge. When Hermite data (exact intersection points and normals of the isosurface with active edges) is available, DC can reconstruct sharp features by positioning the vertex at the minimizer of the quadratic error function (QEF). Zhang *et al.* [6] described a feature-preserving octree-based extended dual contouring algorithm for interactive visualization of editable isosurfaces, but their approach requires expensive stitching and re-triangulation. [7] developed techniques for LoD generation and isosurface extraction of smooth volumetric terrains using GPU-based dual contouring and stitching for seamlessly joining regions with different levels of detail. [8] described a GPU-based parallel polygonization pipeline using Dual Marching Cubes [9], but didn't address visualization of large-scale models with many levels of detail. More recently, [10, 11] presented a modified MC working on hexa-hedral cells over a coarse-grained conforming tetrahedral subdivision. Their approach is efficient and GPU-friendly, doesn't require stitching/crack patching and produces meshes of better quality than methods operating directly on tetrahedral cells, but, unfortunately, is limited to smooth isosurfaces (i.e. without sharp features).

2.2   View-Dependent Refinement

View-dependent refinement methods extract the relevant portions of the isosurface to invest limited memory and computational resources only where needed. For example, it is usually sufficient to render a highly detailed surface in a small region of interest around the viewer, while the rest can be displayed coarsely. For this purpose, hierarchical space partitioning data structures have been widely used, such as octrees [3, 4, 6, 7] and conformal hierarchies of tetrahedra, often based on longest-edge bisection [10–13]. The latter scheme allows to completely avoid stitching at the cost of increased hierarchy depth and creation of bad-shaped triangles. To improve mesh quality, [10, 11] split each tetrahedron into four hexahedra and extract the surface using a modified MC.

To be able to visualize procedurally-generated content without pre-processing, the LoD hierarchy must be defined in a top-down manner. To our knowledge, [10, 11] is the only published algorithm, which was designed for visualizing large volumetric datasets without any preparation, stitching or crack patching.

3   Non-recursive Level-of-Detail Algorithm

In this section, we describe the data structure for managing the LoD hierarchy and our new algorithm for view-dependent refinement and rendering using this data structure.

3.1   Level-of-Detail Hierarchy

Similar to most previous methods of view-dependent isosurface extraction, we use an octree-based decomposition of the domain space. An octree subdivides the scene into cubic regions of the same resolution and varying size. The root node of the octree encompasses the whole volume. Each node has 8 children, one per each octant of the node's volume. View-dependent Level-of-Detail selection, culling, and rendering is typically performed recursively in a top-down manner, starting from the root node. However, recursive traversals may become expensive when processing deep hierarchies with many levels of detail (e.g. in planetary rendering). Moreover, our seamless isosurface extraction (as well as approaches based on stitching) requires nearest neighbor searching, which is usually a costly operation in traditional pointer-based octrees. We avoid these issues by organizing leaf nodes into a pointerless octree, which allows to update only a single LoD in each frame and enables efficient neighbor finding.

Each octree node can be uniquely identified by its *level* in the LoD hierarchy (zero level corresponds to the smallest nodes or the most detailed LoD) and *coordinates* of the node's minimum corner at this LoD. We use 64-bit node identifiers, where 4 bits are used to represent LoD (allowing up to 16 levels of detail), and the remaining bits store the node's coordinates (allowing for 2^{20} values along each coordinate axis). The Morton code of a node at tree depth D is a bit string created by bit-interleaving the values that comprise the node's *xyz* coordinates:

$$M = z_D y_D x_D \ldots z_1 y_1 x_1 z_0 y_0 x_0.$$

A pointerless, or linear, octree stores only terminal, leaf nodes ordered by their Morton codes, that serve as search keys [14]. In our implementation, the octree consists of an array of *LoD* structures. Each *LoD* represents a single level of detail and stores an array of references to leaf nodes paired with their Morton codes. This array is always kept sorted by Morton codes in increasing order, which has several advantages. First, a binary search can be used to quickly locate leaf nodes by their coordinates at the corresponding level of detail. Second, from the sorted array of child nodes, an array of unique Morton codes corresponding to the parent nodes can be easily built by scanning through the sorted list. (For a node with Morton code M, the parent's code is generated by zeroing out the last three bits of M.) Third, sibling nodes are grouped together, i.e. by finding the index of the first child node we can iterate over the remaining eight children (they form a contiguous block).

Each leaf node contains a pointer to the mesh for rendering and a flag denoting whether the node is currently being refined, which is used to ensure correct execution during view-dependent refinement. Empty leaf nodes (i.e. not intersecting the isosurface and thus having a null mesh pointer) are also stored, and each octree node is always split into exactly 8 smaller nodes during refinement. Figure 1 gives an overview of the data structure.

```
// Represents a leaf node of the LoD octree.
struct Node {
  Mesh* mesh; // memory-resident data
  bool refining; // is a 'Split' operation in progress?
};
// Represents a single Level Of Detail.
struct LoD {
  // leaf nodes sorted by increasing Morton keys
  Array< Pair< UInt64, Node* > > nodes;
};
struct Octree {
  LoD lods[ MAX_LODs ];  // refers to nodes at each LoD
  Pool< Node > nodePool; // memory storage for nodes
};
```

Fig. 1. Basic data structure to represent the LoD hierarchy.

To ensure consistency of the data structure, nodes across different levels of details must not occupy the same space, i.e., if a node exists in LoD $i+1$, then the finer LoD i must not contain the node's children and vice versa. As stated above, node arrays of each LoD are maintained in sorted order. They only temporarily become unsorted at the beginning of a frame when updating the octree during view-dependent refinement.

3.2 View-Dependent Refinement and Coarsening

We begin by creating and initializing the root node of the octree. We decide whether a node should be refined (split into eight children) or coarsened (collapsed to parent) by evaluating a LoD function. The function returns the desired level of detail of the node given the node's current LoD, its coordinates at this LoD, and the camera parameters. If the desired LoD of a node is less than its current LoD, the node should be split. Our prototype implementation uses a simple LoD function based on Chebyshev distance, that causes a square, clip map-like arrangement of octree nodes. For each node, we compute the closest distance d between its bounding box and the viewer under L_∞ metric. To avoid floating-point precision issues, this computation is performed with integers, and d is expressed in units of the finest, most detailed LoD grid. The desired level of detail is then defined as:

$$l_{\text{target}} = \log_2(\max(d, 1)).$$

To ensure a steady frame rate, volume data generation and isosurface extraction run asynchronously in worker threads. The main thread only performs refinement, i.e. determines the appropriate level of detail for each node, issues requests to split and merge nodes, handles completed requests and updates the octree. To amortize the costs of LoD evaluation and octree management, we process only a single LoD of the octree in each frame.

Specifically, we iterate over each leaf node of the LoD L being processed. If the node is marked as *refining* (i.e. it is currently being worked on by a worker thread), it is skipped and excluded from further processing. Otherwise, if $L > 0$ (i.e. L is not the most detailed level), we evaluate the LoD function and request the node to be split if the desired LoD is less than the node's current LoD.

At the same time, we also gather unique Morton codes corresponding to the parent nodes. As already mentioned, building a set of unique parents is simple and fast, as the eight siblings having the same parent are stored contiguously. Again, using the LoD function we test whether any of the parent nodes would satisfy the LoD criterion. If a parent node (which doesn't exist yet) can be rendered at the next LoD (i.e. its desired LoD, as returned by the LoD function, equals $L+1$), then its children (i.e. nodes at the current L) should be collapsed, and then we create a request for merging the eight sibling nodes under this parent.

Split/Merge requests are implemented as asynchronous tasks that are submitted to the task scheduler by the main thread. A "Split" task creates the meshes of the eight children of the node in worker threads and replaces the node with its children on the main thread. A "Merge" task generates the geometry of the node in a worker thread and merges its children in the main thread. These tasks sample the volume, extract the isosurface and produce indexed triangle meshes in the final format ready for rendering. Completed tasks are pushed onto the split and merge queues to be finalized on the main thread. At the beginning of each frame, the main thread handles completed tasks, uploads mesh data to dynamic vertex and index buffers and updates the octree. New octree nodes are added at the end of node arrays, old nodes are marked as deleted, then node arrays are re-sorted.

If the isosurface is very complex or the viewer moves too fast, hundreds of frames can elapse between launching an asynchronous task and receiving the results of the completed task for updating the octree. To prevent the creation of duplicate "Split" tasks, the node to be subdivided is marked as *refining* before issuing the request, and unmarked after the task is finalized on the main thread. Similarly, a set of unique outstanding "Merge" requests is maintained to avoid creating redundant "Merge" tasks. Pseudo-code for our non-recursive LoD algorithm is listed in Fig. 2.

```
function Update_Level_Of_Detail( LoD lod, Observer eye ) {
  NodeID currentParent = ~0;// ID of the current parent
  for each node in lod.nodes {
    if( node.refining )
      continue; // This node is being split right now.
    int iTargetLoD = Get_Desired_LoD( node.id, eye );
    if( iLoD > 0 && iLoD > iTargetLoD ) {
      node.refining = true;
      Request_Split( node.id );
    } else { // if( iLoD <= iTargetLoD )
      const NodeID parentId = Get_Parent_ID( node.id );
      if( parentId != currentParent ) {
        Try_Merge_Node( currentParent );
        currentParent = parentId; // Start a new run.
      }
    }
  }//For each octree node of the LoD being updated.
  if( currentParent.IsValid )
    Try_Merge_Node( currentParent );
}
function Try_Merge_Node( NodeID parentId, Observer eye ) {
  int iTargetLoD = Get_Desired_LoD( parentId, eye );
  if( parentId.LoD <= iTargetLoD ) {
    if( !mergeRequests.Contains( parentId ) ) {
      mergeRequests.Add( parentId );
      Request_Merge_Children( parentId );
    }//If the merge request hasn't been created yet.
  }//If child nodes can be collapsed to this parent.
}
```

Fig. 2. Pseudo-code for octree refinement and coarsening.

Our LoD algorithm can be used with arbitrary refinement criteria, as long as the LoD function guarantees that adjacent nodes do not differ by more than one level of detail. This condition is crucial for our seamless isosurface extraction algorithm, which is detailed in the next section.

4   Isosurface Extraction and Rendering with Multiple Levels of Detail

We use uniform Dual Contouring (DC) to extract the isosurface inside each leaf node of the octree. We modify the original algorithm to eliminate inter-cell dependency between adjacent nodes of the same LoD and to ensure that the generated mesh always stays within the bounds of each node. Seamless continuity between adjacent nodes with differing LoDs is achieved via geomorphing and "central" cracks are filled with additional triangles.

4.1   Algorithm for Contouring Adjacent Nodes of the Same Level of Detail

Being a dual polygonization method, DC introduces the problem of inter-cell dependency: in order to create a single polygon, several adjacent cells must be considered, i.e. to obtain a continuous mesh, each cell can no longer be processed in parallel, without the knowledge of its neighbors. In the context of view-dependent isosurface extraction, this means that dual-contouring each node independently produces cracks and gaps along the boundary between the node and its neighbors (because the node's border cells cannot form polygons with edge-adjacent cells from the node's neighbors). We extend the original DC algorithm using the same approach as CMS [15]: introducing additional vertices on boundary faces and edges of each node for breaking inter-cell dependency along node boundaries.

The input to our algorithm is a set of voxels with associated Hermite data. Each node consists of a dense 3D array of voxels (material indices) and a sparse array of active edges (positions and normals at intersections of the surface with cell edges). Our algorithm relies on the fact that voxels and active edge data are duplicated between adjacent nodes along their borders. This data must be "synchronized" at all times to guarantee a continuous surface.

Each node is expanded with an additional layer of "outer" cells that touch the boundary faces and edges of the node (i.e. if the original node has N^3 cells, after padding it will have $(N+2)^3$ cells). For each active outer cell, a vertex is created which lies precisely on the node's border (i.e. on a face or edge of the node), as illustrated in Fig. 3.

If an outer cell touches a boundary face of the node, the cell's vertex is positioned at the 2D sharp feature on the node's face and clamped to the cell's bounds. As in CMS [15], we sample face-sharp features using the active edges associated with the outer cell, i.e. we gather intersections from active edges of the cell's face (a face can have up

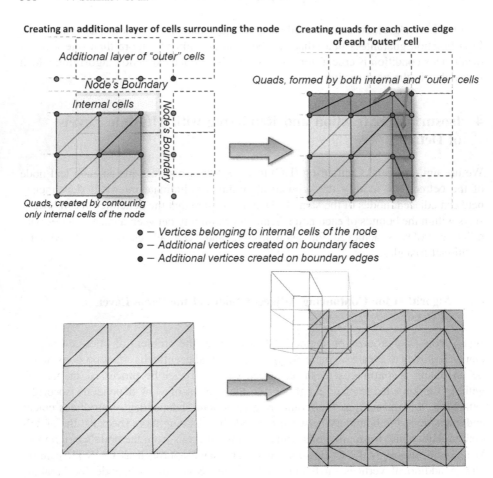

Fig. 3. *Top*: Overview of the modified Dual Contouring algorithm. Each node is padded with a layer of "outer" cells which vertices are placed exactly on boundary faces and edges of the node. Active edges of these cells generate quads that form the node's boundary. *Bottom*: The result of polygonizing a horizontal plane on a grid consisting of 4^3 cells (viewed from above).

to four active edges) and determine the point closest to the tangent planes formed by the intersection points and surface normals at those points, as in standard DC [5].

If an outer cell touches a boundary edge of the node, the cell's vertex is placed at the intersection point of the edge with the surface (i.e. the vertex's position and normal are taken directly from Hermite data).

The outer cells are also included in the process of dual-contouring (i.e. their active edges also generate mesh quads), along with the original, internal cells. Note that we don't need to include additional cells that touch the node's corners because DC creates mesh quads only for cell edges. After executing the above process, the expanded node will neatly contain the generated mesh inside the node's bounding box.

4.2   Geomorphing for Seamless Transitions Between Different Levels of Detail

Rendering nodes of differing resolutions next to each other produce cracks along the mesh boundaries. We use geomorphing [16–19] to achieve seamless transition between adjacent LoD levels. Vertex attributes (positions, normals, texture coordinates, etc.) of each mesh are computed both at the current, *fine* LoD and at the next, *coarse* LoD. During rendering, vertex attributes are interpolated between adjacent LoDs so that to smooth level-of-detail transitions and to maintain connectivity between neighboring nodes. When all vertices of a full-resolution mesh are fully morphed into their low-resolution state, the mesh can be seamlessly replaced by its low-detail version and vice versa. For each vertex, the morph ratio (or geomorph weight) is usually computed based on the distance between the vertex and the viewer and ranges from 0 (corresponding to the fine, full-resolution mesh) to 1 (low-detail, coarse mesh). In order to prevent seams between adjacent nodes, the positions of boundary vertices must match exactly across the nodes' borders.

Geomorphing is typically performed on the graphics hardware in a vertex shader. During rendering, the vertex shader computes the morph ratio and interpolates the primary (fine) and secondary (coarse) vertex position (and other attributes) based on distance from the camera and boundary constraints.

Creating meshes for geomorphing requires being able to establish a correspondence between vertex buffers generated at different levels of detail, where low-detailed meshes are obtained by sub-sampling the original data. While being difficult with primal contouring methods [10, 11], matching mesh vertices across different levels of detail is rather straightforward when using Dual Contouring.

More specifically, when extracting the isosurface for each node, we generate the fine mesh and the coarse vertex buffer. In the fine mesh, the secondary vertex attributes are temporarily used to store the integer coordinates of the corresponding dual cell. After creating the fine mesh, we generate the coarse vertex buffer by running the modified Dual Contouring algorithm on a course, half-resolution grid. Then, for each vertex of the fine mesh, we search for the corresponding vertex of the coarse mesh. Knowing the coordinates of the dual cell in the full-resolution grid (they are stored in the secondary vertex attributes of the fine vertex), we can get the coordinates of the corresponding cell in the half-resolution grid using unsigned division by two with ceiling.

```
UInt3 coarseCellIndex3D = fineCellIndex3D/2u + fineCellIndex3D % 2u.
```

This ensures that boundary vertices of the fine mesh map to the corresponding boundary vertices of the coarse mesh, which is important to prevent cracks during rendering.

If the coarse cell has a vertex, its position and normal are copied into the second position and normal of the fine vertex. If the coarse cell doesn't have a vertex, the secondary position and normal of the fine vertex are set to its primary position and normal. The latter case indicates a topology change between the levels of detail and can happen, for example, when the surface passes through the coarse cell without intersecting any of the cell's edges.

In addition to the primary and secondary positions and normals, each vertex also stores its type that indicates which boundary faces and edges of the node the vertex touches. There are 19 possible vertex types: an internal vertex type and 18 types of boundary vertices which belong to "outer" cells in the modified Dual Contouring. Internal vertices lie in the interior of the node and don't touch the node's boundary, face vertices touch one of the node's 6 faces and edge vertices touch one of the node's 12 edges (or two of its faces). Vertex types are assigned during the execution of our modified Dual Contouring algorithm.

After completing the above process, the fine mesh is now fully self-contained and can be morphed into its coarse version that corresponds to the mesh at the next level of detail.

To avoid boundary cracks during rendering, each node needs to be aware of its neighbors in the octree, and its boundary vertices must be locked to ensure continuity in transitional regions (between nodes with different levels of detail). Therefore, for each node, we calculate an adjacency mask which encodes the difference in LoDs between this node and its neighbors. The bit values of the adjacency mask indicate, for each vertex type, whether the corresponding face- or edge-adjacent node at the next level of detail is being rendered. The adjacency mask is computed using a binary search over the linear octree and placed in the GPU's constant store prior to rendering each node so that the vertex shader can enforce the boundary constraints during geomorphing.

At run-time, during rendering, the vertex shader computes the morph ratio based on the vertex's type and its distance d to the camera. If the vertex lies inside the interior of the node, then the morph ratio is defined as:

$$k_{morph} = \text{lerp}(s, e, d),$$

where s is the start distance for geomorphing, and e is the end distance. In our prototype implementation, s and e are simply the closest and farthest distances between the node's bounding sphere and the camera. This doesn't prevent the "popping" effect of switching between levels of detail. To completely hide level-of-detail transitions, the morph ratio could depend on a time value or on the subdivision status of the node's children [16].

If the vertex lies on the node's boundary, the morph ratio is selected based on its type and the adjacency mask. The boundary vertex type is used to determine whether the corresponding adjacent node exists at the next level of detail. (This is done by ANDing the value, obtained by left-shifting the vertex type, with the adjacency mask.) If so, the morph ratio is set to 1, and the vertex shader will select the secondary, coarse vertex position and normal. Otherwise, the morph ratio is set to 0, and the shader will select the fine vertex position and normal.

After computing the morph ratio, the vertex position and normal are linearly interpolated between their fine and coarse versions, and the normal is renormalized.

In most cases, this algorithm produces a crack-free surface with smooth level-of-detail transitions, as shown in Fig. 4.

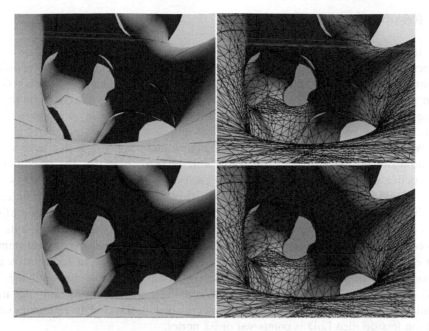

Fig. 4. An isosurface of gyroid rendered with 8 levels of detail. Transitions from lower to a higher level of detail are marked with red color. *Top row*: mesh with cracks and T-junctions. *Bottom row*: all visual artifacts are eliminated with geomorphing. (Color figure online)

However, since the sampling rate differs by two in transitional regions, small cracks or T-junctions occur in the middle of boundary faces between nodes representing different levels of detail. We cover those cracks with new triangles that use existing vertices from both levels of detail and are attached to the low-detail mesh. Each triangle lies on the boundary face of the low-resolution mode and is formed by two of the node's face vertices and an intersection point on the cell's edge between those vertices. While being simple, this method may potentially cause shadowing and lighting artifacts, due to the fact that the new triangle's normal is in stark contrast to the normal vectors of the surrounding triangles. Since the cracks are typically very small, and triangles for covering up the cracks don't significantly affect visual quality (Fig. 5), we leave these triangles as they are in our current implementation.

Fig. 5. From left to right: an isosurface with cracks; a wireframe rendering of the same mesh after crack patching; new triangles are visually unnoticeable. Each node contains 4^3 cells. Level-of-detail transitions are highlighted with red color. (Color figure online)

5 Results

We implemented our view-dependent isosurface extraction algorithm in C++ using Direct3D 11. Our experiments were made on a machine running 64-bit Windows 7, equipped with a 2.8 GHz quad-core processor, 8 GB RAM and an AMD Radeon 6950 with 1 GB memory. In all cases, the geometry for rendering was generated on-the-fly using 3 worker threads. (Recall that our algorithm doesn't require any pre-processing at all.)

We evaluated the scalability of our LoD algorithm by applying it to a large scene. Figure 6 shows a view of the Klein bottle with 12 levels of detail. The resolution of each octree node is 32^3 cells. If the size of each cell were 1 m, the size of the whole scene would be 131 km. The isosurface consists of 2124053 triangles. We achieve an idle frame rate of approximately 98 frames per second. To test the performance of our LoD algorithm, we performed a series of fly-bys at the speed of 2500 world units per second. Since the cost of updating the LoD hierarchy is amortized over several frames, and all heavy tasks are executed in worker threads, we are able to zoom in on any region of interest without any noticeable delays. After the camera stops moving, the LoD hierarchy will eventually stabilize. When the camera remains still, the most detailed LoD consists of 216 octree nodes, intermediate LoDs contain 189 nodes each, and the less detailed LoD is composed of 32 nodes.

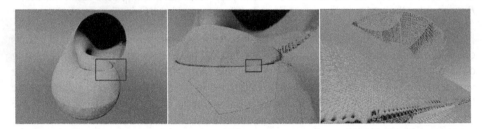

Fig. 6. *Left:* an isosurface of the Klein bottle rendered with our approach. *Middle:* a zoomed-in view on the infinitely thin region around the point of interest. *Right:* the rendered mesh in wireframe when the observer is looking from the point of interest. Notice that the size of triangles in screen space remains approximately constant.

As we support up to 16 levels of detail, we can theoretically render large isosurfaces up to $2^{(16-12)} = 16$ times as big, but, at these scales, we start to observe artifacts due to reduced floating-point precision (dimpled surfaces, incorrectly computed normals, Z-fighting).

Figure 7 shows a synthetic isosurface with sharp features. The scene uses 8 levels of detail and consists of 34871 triangles, each node contains 16^3 cells. The scene is rendered at 134 frames per second. We use flat shading to highlight sharp edges and corners.

Fig. 7. *Left:* an isosurface with sharp features rendered using flat shading. *Middle:* the same mesh shown in wireframe to illustrate view-dependent triangulation. *Right:* a view from the point of interest.

Our method can also visualize conventional, heightmap-based terrains. Figure 8 shows a view of the Grand Canyon dataset rendered with 10 levels of detail and using nodes of 32^3 cells each, which corresponds to 32768 world units. We can render 831609 triangles at over one hundred frames per second. Hermite data for Dual Contouring was obtained by intersecting the heightfield without any pre-processing.

Fig. 8. The Grand Canyon dataset rendered with our approach. *Left:* a bird's-eye view of the terrain. *Middle:* a zoomed-in view on the area around the point of interest. *Right:* the underlying triangular mesh around the region of interest.

6   Discussion

Experiments show that our method can be used to render large isosurfaces without any pre-processing. Unlike previous approaches, we use a non-recursive LoD algorithm working on a pointerless octree, which allows to spread out the LoD computations and octree updates over multiple frames. As a consequence, the overhead of octree management does not grow with the number of all nodes but depends only on the maximum number of leaf nodes in each LoD. As a trade-off, we lose the ability to do hierarchical view-frustum, occlusion and contribution culling.

Compared to existing techniques of large-scale isosurface visualization, our approach provides a unique combination of desirable features:

- **No pre-processing:** Our method doesn't rely on any preparation of the input data and thus is appealing for visualizing procedurally-generated data.

- **Scalability:** Our non-recursive view-dependent refinement algorithm allows to visualize volumetric datasets of virtually unlimited size with low CPU load and memory consumption.
- **Flexibility:** The refinement algorithm can be used with any LoD metric or extended to out-of-core visualization of large datasets.
- **Continuous Level of Detail:** Our rendering algorithm achieves continuous level-of-detail triangulation via geomorphing which doesn't require stitching and smoothes level-of-detail transitions.
- **Sharp feature preservation:** Our isosurface extraction algorithm is based on Dual Contouring and can reconstruct sharp corners and edges, which is important for various CAD/CAM/CAE applications.
- **High-performance rendering:** Our method produces meshes in a form ready for GPU accelerated rendering.
- **Simplicity:** Our LoD algorithm is easier implement than traditional recursive approaches.

Our method has some limitations. First, our LoD metric is not optimal – the refinement criterion only considers viewer distance and it ignores local surface geometry, which leads to an excessive number of triangles in planar regions. Second, our geomorphing technique only ameliorates LoD popping artifacts but does not eliminate the problem. Other obvious downsides brought by geomorphing are increased mesh size and vertex shader complexity. To improve vertex cache utilization during rendering, we could optimize and cache generated meshes. Third, Dual Contouring cannot correctly reconstruct sharp features which are not aligned to the grid (feature chamfering) and often produces non-manifold meshes. Finally, isosurface extraction, the most time-consuming stage of the visualization pipeline, could be ported to GPU to improve performance.

7 Conclusion

In this paper, we presented a solution for real-time rendering of large isosurfaces with view-dependent level-of-detail. Our simple and easy-to-implement, yet effective LoD algorithm uses a pointerless octree for low-overhead non-recursive hierarchy management. During rendering, a coarse isosurface is iteratively refined to build a view-dependent approximation to the original model. Our isosurface extraction algorithm is based on Dual Contouring and thus can reconstruct surfaces with sharp features. Unlike previous methods, our approach does not require stitching and uses geomorphing to achieve seamless level-of-detail transitions. We demonstrated the effectiveness of our method by applying it to view-dependent visualization of large isosurfaces generated on-the-fly.

Our method is suitable for scientific visualization and virtual reality systems where the user is expected to navigate immediately in the virtual environment. Since our method does not require any pre-processing, it can be successfully applied to visualize huge procedurally-generated data sets in real time.

Acknowledgment. The reported study was funded by RFBR according to the research projects No. 16-07-00353_a, No. 16-07-00388_a.

References

1. De Araújo, B.R., Lopes, D.S., Jepp, P., Jorge, J.A., Wyvill, B.: A survey on implicit surface polygonization. ACM Comput. Surv. **47**(4), 1–39 (2015)
2. Lorensen, W., Cline, H.: Marching cubes: a high resolution 3D surface construction algorithm. In: Computer Graphics (SIGGRAPH 87 Proceedings), pp. 163–169 (1987)
3. Westermann, R., Kobbelt, L., Ertl, T.: Real-time exploration of regular volume data by adaptive reconstruction of isosurfaces. Vis. Comput. **15**(2), 100–111 (1999)
4. Lengyel, E.: Voxel-based terrain for real-time virtual simulations. Ph.D. dissertation, University of California at Davis (2010)
5. Ju, T., Losasso, F., Schaefer, S., Warren, J.: Dual contouring of hermite data. ACM Trans. Graph. **21**(3), 339–346 (2002)
6. Zhang, N., Qu, H., Hong, W., Kaufman, A.: SHIC: a view-dependent rendering framework for isosurfaces. In: VV 2004 Proceedings of the 2004 IEEE Symposium on Volume Visualization and Graphics, Washington, DC, USA, pp. 63–70 (2004)
7. Löffler, F., Müller, A., Schumann, H.: Real-time rendering of stack-based terrains. In: Proceedings of 16th International Workshop on Vision, Modeling, and Visualization (VMV), pp. 161–168 (2011)
8. Löffler, F., Schumann, H.: Generating smooth high-quality isosurfaces for interactive modeling and visualization of complex terrains. In: Proceedings of 17th International Workshop on Vision, Modeling, and Visualization (VMV), pp. 79–86 (2012)
9. Nielson, G.: Dual marching cubes. In: Proceedings of the conference on Visualization, pp. 489–496 (2004)
10. Scholz, M., Bender, J., Dachsbacher, C.: Level of detail for real-time volumetric terrain rendering. In: Proceedings of 18th International Workshop on Vision, Modeling, and Visualization (VMV), Vision, Modeling, and Visualization, pp. 211–218 (2013)
11. Scholz, M., Bender, J., Dachsbacher, C.: Real-time isosurface extraction with view-dependent level of detail and applications. Comput. Graph. Forum **34**(1), 103–115 (2014)
12. Gregorsky, B., Duchaineau, M., Lindstrom, P., Pascucci, V., Joy, K.I.: Interactive view-dependent rendering of large iso-surfaces. In: Proceedings of IEEE Visualization, IEEE Computer Society, Washington, DC, USA, pp. 475–484 (2002)
13. Cignoni, P., Ganovelli, F., Gobbetti, E., Marton, F., Ponchio, F., Scopigno, R.: Adaptive tetrapuzzles: efficient out-of-core construction and visualization of gigantic multiresolution polygonal models. ACM Trans. Graph. **23**(3), 796–803 (2004)
14. Samet, H.: Applications of Spatial Data Structures: Computer Graphics, Image Processing, GIS. Addison-Wesley, Reading (1990)
15. Ho, C.-C., Wu, F.-C., Chen, B.-Y., Chuang, Y.-Y., Ouhyoung, M.: Cubical marching squares: adaptive feature preserving surface extraction from volume data. In: EURO-GRAPHICS 2005, vol. 24, no. 3, pp. 537–545 (2005)
16. Hoppe, H.H.: Smooth view-dependent level-of-detail control and its application to terrain rendering. In: IEEE Visualization 1998, pp. 35–42 (1998)
17. Borgeat, L., Godin, G., Blais, F., Massicotte, P., Lahanier, C.: GoLD: interactive display of huge colored and textured models. ACM Trans. Graph. **24**(3), 869–877 (2005)

18. Sander, P.V., Mitchell, J.L.: Progressive buffers: view-dependent geometry and texture for LOD rendering. In: Proceedings of Symposium on Geometry Processing, pp. 129–138. ACM, New York (2005)

19. Strugar, F.: Continuous distance-dependent level of detail for rendering heightmaps. J. Graph. GPU Game Tools **14**(4), 57–74 (2009)

The Method of CAD Software and TRIZ Collaboration

Nikolai Efimov-Soini[✉] and Leonid Chechurin

Lappeenranta University of Technology, Lappeenranta, Finland
nefso@mail.ru, leonid.chechurin@lut.fi

Abstract. This article is devoted to the collaboration of TRIZ function analysis and the engineering CAD software. The presented approach uses the TRIZ function modeling for the system development and improving, meanwhile, it uses the information from the CAD model in the initial source. The case study is illustrated by the industrial example. Its aim is the improving of the electro-magnetic flow meter magnetic system the, created by means of the SolidWorks software. For process automatization the software, created in C# Microsoft Visual Studio by using the SolidWorks API tool. The suggested method proposes the formal mechanism based on the TRIZ methodology for the system devel-oping and improving by means of the CAD model. This one may be used as in the conceptual design, so detail design stages and for patent-around design.

Keywords: TRIZ · CAD · Function analysis · Trimming

1 Introduction and States of the Arts

According to Ullman [1], decisions made during the design process have a great effect on the cost of the product but these decisions cost is very low. Also, about 75% of the manufacturing cost of the typical product is committed by the end of the conceptual phase process. It means that decisions, made after this time, can influence only 25% of the product's manufacturing cost. On the other hand, the Top-down approach [2] permits to create the common Computer-Aided Design (CAD) model on the conceptual design stage. In this case, inventive methods in collaboration with the CAD software may be very effective.

This paper presents the method that combines tool based on the application pro-gramming interface (API) of the SolidWorks software and the Theory of Inventive Solving (TRIZ).

The TRIZ (Russian acronym "Teoriya Reshenia Izobretatelskih Zadach" – the Theory of the Inventive Problem Solving) is an inventive method proposed by the Soviet scientist and the inventor Altshuler (1926–1998) in 1956 [3]. He studied about 40000 patents and drew out the formal processes for some new ideas of the generation and the technical evolution trends. Such methods are 40 inventive principles, contra-dictions, ideality, and patterns of the evolution. In presence, TRIZ is widely used in different areas of industry and science [4–7].

The functional part of the method is based on TRIZ function analysis. There are several types of the function presentation of the system, such as the Functional Flow

© Springer International Publishing AG 2017
A. Kravets et al. (Eds.): CIT&DS 2017, CCIS 754, pp. 517–527, 2017.
DOI: 10.1007/978-3-319-65551-2_38

Block Diagram (FFBD) [8], the Functional Analysis System Technique (FAST) [9], the Integrated Computer Aided Manufacturing DEFinition for Function Modeling (IDEF0) [10], etc. All these methods use the function approach for the system presentation. For example, the FFBD is the function-oriented approach based on the sequential relationship of all system functions. FFBD develops a system from the top to the bottom and it proposes the hierarchal view of the functions across the series of levels. The aim of each one is to identify a single task on a higher level by means of the functional decomposition. Compared with FFBD, the Functional Analysis System Technique (FAST) diagram focuses on functions of the product rather than its specific design. There the system is presented in a tree structure where each function is presented in a verb + noun format.

In contrast to FFBD and FAST, the TRIZ function modeling takes into account the physical interaction between the system elements and the type of this interaction. There are four types of interaction - useful, harmful, insufficient or excessive. In this approach, the system is presented by using the component and function views together. Therefore, it is possible to create a new design pattern and make a new design based on the initial design.

This paper is devoted to two main problems such as the transferring of the CAD model to the TRIZ function model by using the API technology [11] and the Function Model improving by means of the functional analysis. These problems are solved to receive new patterns, to improve the existing design or for patent-around design.

In the area of collaboration between CAD and TRIZ, the proposed approach is not a novelty. In one hand Dr. Ullah proposed the methodology [12] of integrating CAD, TRIZ, and customer needs, but he did not propose any formal integration mechanism. On the other hand, Dr. Bakker and Dr. Chechurin [13, 14] developed the formal mechanism of the collaboration. The proposed approach evolves ideas of the last one by means of the function-oriented approach.

There are different methods for the design improvement and development, such as the topological improvement (e.g. Generative design software Autodesk Within - [15]), using CAI (Computer-Aided Invention, e.g. GoldFire [16]) also the TRIZ approach may be used. The first one proposes the topological optimization without a new design generation. The second one proposes a new design generation but without the collaboration to the CAD model. It is used in additive technologies. The CAI approach uses the function approach, but it doesn't collaborate with the engineering software. This approach is used in the patent-around design. The TRIZ function analysis is the third in the list of the TRIZ tools popular method [17]. There are different approaches in this case. For example, Miao Li's method [18] used in patent around design. It takes into account an each element importance. Gen3 method [19] is used for design improvement and development. This one uses the formal functional approach to rank the importance of each function in the system. Presented method combines these methods and supplements them, also collects the previous works in this domain [20–22].

The remainder of this paper is structured as follow: Sect. 2 is devoted to the method description, in Sect. 3 the method is illustrated by industrial case study – improving the electromagnetic flow meter, Sect. 4 is considered to materials conclusions and finally, Sect. 5 is devoted to the further development.

2   Method Description

The suggested method is based on [13, 14]. There are 3 main steps: the export from the CAD model, the function modeling, and the trimming. In the first step, the information from the CAD model is received. In the second step, the TRIZ function model is created by using information received above. Finally, the trimming of the TRIZ function model is used for system improving and development.

2.1   Export from CAD Model

The API tool is used for the information export from the CAD model. This one is included in the popular CAD software (SolidWorks, Inventor, SolidEdge, Kompas etc.) and permits to receive some information from the model or to work in this software by using commands "outside". In this case, the model structure and the relationship between elements (mates in SolidWorks) are received by using the SolidWorks API. In fact, this step replaces the component analysis in [19]. The translation is completed by using the special software, created in the C# Visual Studio 2017 by using the SolidWorks API tool.

2.2   Function Analysis

The function analysis model is based on [19–21]. There are three formal steps: the component analysis, the interaction analysis, and the function modeling. The first one is devoted to the system decomposition to elements. It is completed above and is similar to [19]. The following algorithm is proposed for the decomposition:

1. The system is decomposed into the main elements, usually to a big assembly. For example, a car consists of a body, an electric system, an engine, etc.
2. User select target element in the system.
3. Decomposed elements are divided into the smaller components. The assembly is divided into the subassembly or parts; the subassembly is divided into parts, etc.
   The main goal of this step is to create a detailed system decomposition model in the area close to the target element of the system.
4. In the final step, the interaction analysis, the trimming is held according to the algorithm presented in Sect. 2.3. If the result is not satisfactory, then the system is additionally decomposed (step 3).

In the second step, the relation between elements is defined. For example, a simple system, which consists of the frame, the shaft, and the gear, is illustrated. The frame interacts with the shaft and doesn't interact with the gear; on the other hand, the gear interacts with the shaft and don't do it with the frame. In this case interaction analysis is based on mates of the CAD model, but may be modified by the user, e.g. he may add or remove elements. For example, the mate "contact" in the CAD model is equal to the function "hold" in the function model, and for bolts and nuts function "hold" is defined as the default. The final step defines the interaction between elements as a function and type of this interaction. There are four types of interaction: useful, harmful, insufficient or excessive. But in this case, one useful function is considered. Also, the function ranking is done.

Finally, the function rank defines an each function importance. It is based on the following formal rules:

1. The rank defines the functional importance. The more useful (or more used) functions obtain the higher rank; the useless (or unused) functions obtain the lower rank.
2. The function rank is defined by the ranking factor (the degree of importance). This one is a rational number and may be positive or negative.
3. The rank is evaluated by integers from 1 to ∞, where the function with the highest rank obtains the value 1. Hence, the higher number has the lower rank.
4. The target function (system main function) obtains the initial rank 0. This function is defined by the user.
5. The system is static in this case; it means that the function rank and the ranking factor are time-independent.
6. If the ranking factor for two functions is equal, the function with a smaller distance between the function carrier and the target element obtains the higher rank. In this instance rank of the function wrote in type: number + letter. For example: 2A, 3B, 7C etc.

The following formula is used for ranking factor calculation:

$$RF = IR - NL + ND + 1 \tag{1}$$

where: RF - Ranking factor, IR-Initial rank, NL - Number of links, ND - Numbers of duplicated functions.

2.3 Trimming

This step is based on formal trimming rules [23]. A function may be trimmed if:

1. An object of the Function does not exist;
2. An object of the Function performs the function itself;
3. Another Engineering System Component performs the useful function of the Function Carrier.

Where an object that performs a function is called the Function Carrier, while the object on which the function is performed is called the Object of the Function. For example in the function "hammer move nail", the hammer is the function carrier, moves – the function, and the nail is an object of the function.

The trimming rules are applied for all function starting with the lowest rank in this case. After an each trimming iteration, the software proposes a user to continue or to finish the trim process. If the trimming is impossible, the process stops.

3   Case Study

The case study is illustrated with the electromagnetic flowmeter magnetic system improvement. The electromagnetic (EM) flow meter is used for the heating, the air conditioning, the water supply and the water treatment, in the drinking water system distribution, the pipelines etc. The main feature of the electric flow meter is its ability to work with any conductive liquid.

In the electromagnetic flowmeter, the magnetic field is generated by coil interaction with water that generates an electric signal. This signal is processed by the flow meter controller, and it displays the measured data on the screen or sends the data to the external server.

This one is presented in the Fig. 1 and consists of two nuts, the stud, the coil and the tube. The stud is welded to the tube and holds the coil in this system. Meanwhile, the coil is fixed in the stud with two nuts. The coil is used to generate the magnetic field into the tube.

3.1   Case Study Export from CAD Model

The special software is developed for information translation. This one is created in the C# Microsoft Visual Studio by using SolidWorks API tool. It permits to create the function model by using following information: the name, the type of component (assembly or part) and mates (interaction between elements). The presented tool replaces component analysis in the functional analysis. The developed software presented in the Fig. 2.

The suggested software works in a semi-automatic manner. It proposes the same ideas to a user, but one can interrupt and each step in this algorithm. On other hand, the user can optimize the software work. - The user may add changes in the process in any step (e.g. add or remove functions, elements, change the type of the relation etc.).

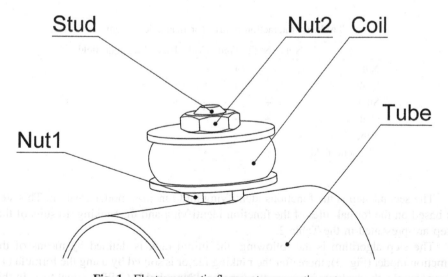

Fig. 1. Electromagnetic flow meter magnetic system.

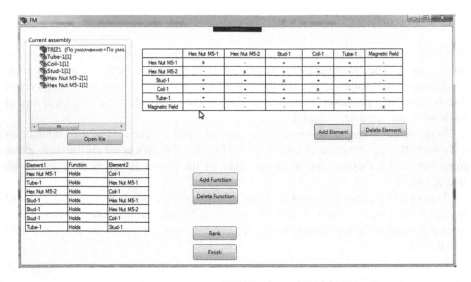

Fig. 2. Software for interaction analysis.

3.2 Case Study Function Analysis

The interaction matrix is created (Table 1) by using information received above; meanwhile, the interaction between elements is based in the mates of the CAD model. Also, the model elements are amplified with the element "magnetic field" (the element of the super system).

For interaction analysis algorithm presented in Sect. 2.2 is used. The mates "contact" and "concentric" are defined is an interaction of the elements in the function model.

Table 1. Interaction matrix for magnetic system

	Nut1	Nut2	Stud	Coil	Tube	Magnetic field
Nut1		−	+	+	+	−
Nut2	−		+	+	−	−
Stud	+	+		+	+	−
Coil	+	+	+		−	+
Tube	+	−	+	−		−
Magnetic field	−	−	−	+	−	

The second step is the functions identifying and function model creation. This step is based on the formal rules of the function identifying and the ranking. Results of this step are presented in the Table 2.

The step algorithm is the following: the initial rank is defined by means of the function model (Fig. 3); thereafter the ranking factor is solved by using the formula (1). For example, the ranking factor for the function "Nut1 holds Coil" is equal to 1. In this case, the function has the initial rank is equal to 1 and the element Nut1 has 3 links (with the tube, the stud and the coil). Additionally, the function is duplicated with two ones. Finally, the ranking factor of the function "Nut1 holds Coil" is equal to the ranking factor of the function "Stud holds Coil", but the distance between elements Stud and Coil is smaller than the second function. The distance between elements is defined as the distance between the centers of the mass in this case.

Meanwhile, the least ranking factor defines the most important function in the system – the Coil generates the Magnetic field. This function receives the higher rank of the system – 1. The remaining function receives the function rank with the increasing of the ranking factor.

In this case, the system is static, this means ranking factor and rank are time-independent. For the dynamic system calculation of the function, ranking factor is similar, but time factor takes into account.

Table 2. The function ranking

Element 1	Function	Element 2	Initial rank	Ranking factor	Final rank
Nut1	Holds	Coil	1	1 − 3 + 3 = 1	4B
Tube	Holds	Nut1	3	3 − 2 + 2 = 3	6
Nut2	Holds	Coil	1	1 − 2 + 3 = 2	5
Stud	Holds	Nut1	2	2 − 4 + 0 = −2	2
Stud	Holds	Nut2	2	2 − 4 + 0 = −2	2
Stud	Holds	Coil	1	2 − 4 + 3 = 1	4A
Tube	Holds	Stud	2	2 − 2 + 0 = 0	3
Coil	Generates	Magnetic field	0	0 − 4 + 0 = −4	1

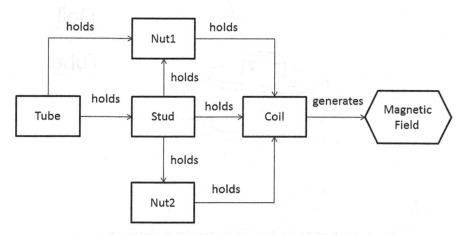

Fig. 3. Magnetic system function model

3.3   Case Study Trimming

The trimming is completed by using Fig. 3 and Table 2. In this case, the algorithm uses three formal trimming rules (Sect. 2.3). It starts with the lowest rank (function – "tube holds nut1") and finishes with the higher rank function (the coil generates a magnetic field). As a result, three functions are highlighted to the trimming. Trimmed functions, these ranks, and trimming rules are presented in the Table 3.

Table 3. Trimmed functions and rules

Function	Rank	Trimming rules
Tube holds Nut1	6	Rule A. Function maybe trim if eliminate object of the function – Nut1
Nut2 holds coils	5	Rule C. Another component of the engineering system performs the useful function of the function carrier – e.g. stud
Nut2 holds coils	4B	Rule C. Another component of the engineering system performs the useful function of the function carrier – e.g. stud

The improved system is presented in the Fig. 4, and the function model is presented in the Fig. 5. The new system consists of the modified stud, the coil, and the tube. The stud holds the coil. The retention diameter of the stud is bigger than the diameter of the hole in the coil. Elements Nut1 and Nut2 are eliminated.

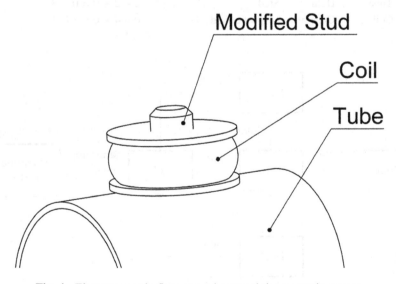

Fig. 4. Electromagnetic flow meter improved the magnetic system.

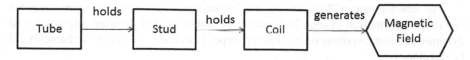

Fig. 5. Function model of improved magnetic system

The presented design of the electromagnetic flow meter is cheaper in mass manufacturing, and very easy to assemble. It means that the cost of an each flow meter in mass-production is lower. Also, this design of this device has small differences with the initial flow meter design. That means the cost of the transition to the new design is tiny.

The improved function model is less complicated and has a smaller number of elements. It means that the presented system is simpler. Ideality of this one is bigger than in initial system.

This example demonstrates that an implementation of the TRIZ-based software can provide the guidelines for the design development and improve, significantly reduce the number of iterations, reduce the design time and the number of errors and unsuccessful design at the in the conceptual design, detail design stages and for the patent around design.

4 Conclusions

In this paper, the method of the system development and improvement is presented with the example of the electromagnetic flow meter. The major steps and the procedures are explained in details.

The presented approach permits to improve and develop the system by means of the CAD model created in SolidWorks. This one permits to receive new design patterns and possibilities of the improvement and the development in the conceptual design, detail design stages and for the patent around design. The suggested method is an effort to transform the informal and uncertain design inventive process into the formal algorithm. The proposed algorithm is easy to use, simple, formal and may be used for all types of the CAD software with API (e.g. Inventor, SolidEdge, Kompas etc.).

The suggested method is an attempt to add the new possibilities in the work of the practical designers and developers. The simplicity of use makes it an ideal candidate for the integration with the different areas of industry and science.

5 Further Development

The further development goes in three areas – the verifying of presented approach, the automating of the trimming step and the design assessment.

For development and the verifying of the function ranking formal mechanism, patent analysis and collaboration with practice engineers will be used. In this instance, different types of system will be used (mechanics, electrics, pneumatics, complex systems etc.).

The development will be focused in the automatic trimming and semi-automatic one in the automatization area. In this case, the automation of the trimming process for dynamic and static systems of the different types (mechanical and not mechanical) will be developed.

For the development of the design assessment algorithm, the method of the collaboration with different techniques, such as Analytic hierarchy process (AHP) [24], Comparison (Pugh's) matrix [2] or other precise and fuzzy techniques [25] will be developed.

Acknowledgments. Authors would like to acknowledge EU Erasmus plus program and its project Open Innovation Platform for University-Enterprise Collaboration: new product, business and human capital development (Acronym: OIPEC, Grant Agreement No.: 2015-3083/001-001) for the support.

References

1. Ullman, D.: The Mechanical Design Process, 4th edn. McGraw-Hill, New York City (2010)
2. Pugh, S.: Creating Innovative Products: Using Total Design: The Living Legacy of Stuart Pugh. Addison-Wesley Publishers, Boston (1996)
3. Altshuller, G., Shapiro, R.: Psychology of inventive creativity. Issues Psychol. **6**, 37–49 (1956)
4. Di Gironimo, G., Carfora, D., Esposito, G., et al.: Improving concept design of divertor support system for FAST tokamak using TRIZ theory and AHP approach. Fusion Eng. Des. **88**, 3014–3020 (2013). doi:10.1016/j.fusengdes.2013.07.005
5. Chechurin, L.: TRIZ in science. Reviewing indexed publications. Proc. CIRP **39**, 156–165 (2016). doi:10.1016/j.procir.2016.01.182
6. Jupp, M.L., Campean, I.F., Travcenko, J.: Application of TRIZ to develop an in-service diagnostic system for a synchronous belt transmission for automotive application. Proc. CIRP **11**, 114–119 (2013). doi:10.1016/j.procir.2013.07.051
7. Yang, C.J., Chen, J.L.: Forecasting the design of eco-products by integrating TRIZ evolution patterns with CBR and simple LCA methods. Expert Syst. Appl. **39**, 2884–2892 (2012). doi:10.1016/j.eswa.2011.08.150
8. Akiyama, K.: Function Analysis: Systematic Improvement of Quality and Performance. Productivity Press Inc., Cambridge (1991)
9. Cooke, J.: TRIZ-based modelling and value analysis of products as processes. In: Trizfuture 2015, pp. 1–11 (2015)
10. Systems Engineering Fundamentals. https://ocw.mit.edu/courses/aeronautics-and-astronautics/16-885j-aircraft-systems-engineering-fall-2005/readings
11. API Support. https://www.solidworks.com/sw/support/api-support.htm
12. Ullah, A.M.M.S., Sato, M., Watanabe, M., Rashid, M.M.: Integrating CAD, TRIZ, and customer needs. Int. J. Autom. Technol. **10**, 132–143 (2016). doi:10.20965/ijat.2016.p0132
13. Chechurin, L.S., Wits, W.W., Bakker, H.M., Vaneker, T.H.J.: Introducing trimming and function ranking to SolidWorks based on functional analysis. In: Proceedings of the TRIZ Future Conference 2011, pp. 215–225 (2011)
14. Bakker, H.M., Chechurin, L.S., Wits, W.W.: Integrating TRIZ function modeling in CAD software. In: Proceedings of the TRIZfest-2011, p. 18 (2011)

15. Generative Design Software. Autodesk Within. http://www.autodesk.com/products/within/overview
16. Goldfire: Advanced Research, Problem Solving & Analytics. https://www.ihs.com/products/design-standards-software-goldfire.html
17. Ilevbare, I.M., Probert, D., Phaal, R.: A review of TRIZ, and its benefits and challenges in practice. Technovation **33**, 30–37 (2013). doi:10.1016/j.technovation.2012.11.003
18. Li, M., Ming, X., He, L., et al.: A TRIZ-based trimming method for patent design around. CAD Comput. Aided Des. **62**, 20–30 (2015). doi:10.1016/j.cad.2014.10.005
19. Ikovenko, S., Litvin, S., Lyubomirskiy, A.: Basic Training Course. GEN3 Partners, Boston (2005)
20. Efimov-Soini, N.K., Chechurin, L.S.: Method of ranking in the function model. Proc. CIRP **39**, 22–26 (2016). doi:10.1016/j.procir.2016.01.160
21. Efimov-Soini, N., Chechurin, L., Renev, I., Elfvengren, K.: Method of time-dependent TRIZ function ranking. In: TRIZ Future Conference 2016: Systematic Innovation and Creativity (2016)
22. Efimov-Soini, N., Uzhegov, N.: The TRIZ-based tool for the electrical machine development. In: Progress in Electromagnetic Research Symposium (2017)
23. Gadd, K.: TRIZ for Engineers: Enabling Inventive Problem Solving, 1st edn. Wiley, Hoboken (2011)
24. Saaty, T.: The Analytic Hierarchy Process: Planning, Priority Setting, Resource Allocation. McGraw-Hill, New York City (1980)
25. Efimov-Soini, N., Kozlova, M., Collan, M., Passi, L.: A multi-criteria decision-making tool with information redundancy treatment for design evaluation. In: Proceedings of NSAIS 2016 Workshop on Adaptive and Intelligent Systems, pp. 73–75 (2016)

A New Method of Search Design of Cooling Systems and Refrigerating Systems Containing a Liquid and Gaseous Working Medium Based on the Engineering Physical Approach

A.A. Yakovlev, V.S. Sorokin[✉], S.N. Mishustina, V.G. Barabanov, and S.V. Shostenko

Volgograd State Technical University,
V I Lenin Ave., 28, Volgograd 400131, Russia
S.o.r.o.k.i.n@mail.ru

Abstract. The article describes a new method of search design of cooling systems and refrigerating systems, the basis of which is represented by a graph model of the physical operating principle based on the thermodynamic description of physical processes. The mathematical model of the physical operating principle has been substantiated, and the basic abstract theorems relatively semantic load applied to nodes and edges of the graph have been represented. The graphic representations of the physical operating principle model of physical phenomena for cooling systems and refrigerating systems have been developed. The necessity and the physical operating principle enough for the given model and intended for the considered device class were demonstrated by the example of an absorption refrigerating plant. The example of obtaining a multitude of engineering solutions of a device for the feeding of lubricating-cooling agent plant has been considered.

Keywords: Searching design · Physical working principle · Cooling system · Working body · Directed graph

1 Introduction

As of today, scientific and technological progress in many branches of industry is characterized by the advanced development of engineering devices compared to the methods of their creation. Traditional design is incapable to provide a radical reduction of the lead time and enhancement of devices. A growing interest in the methodology of design is promoted by the creation and evolvement of design methods and development of computer-aided design (CAD) of more new groups of engineering systems on their basis.

Implementation of similar ideas in the majority of familiar approaches is based on the application of the graph models, which represent physical processes occurring in engineering systems. Therefore, in order to achieve the set goal, it is necessary to solve the following problems: to develop a graph model of the physical operating principle

© Springer International Publishing AG 2017
A. Kravets et al. (Eds.): CIT&DS 2017, CCIS 754, pp. 528–550, 2017.
DOI: 10.1007/978-3-319-65551-2_39

(POP) for the considered class of engineering systems, to verify the adequacy of this model and to form the method of the synthesis of engineering solutions on the basis of the POP model.

2   An Applied Model of the Physical Operating Principle

Among the diversity of methods for generation of the engineering solution, the most perspective is a method based on the POP models. This includes: substance-field analysis (su-field analysis) [27, 28] within the framework of theory of inventive problem solving (Russian abbreviation TRIZ) [1, 3, 4]; combinatorial method for searching of physical operating principle [6, 7]; energy-information method of science-technical creation [8, 9] as well as function-physical method of search design [17, 18]. POP models, which are used in these methods, show the structure of designed device and represent the main physical processes, performed in the technical system. Every POP model is depicted in the form of an oriented graph. However, the semantic load to nodes and edges of the graph is different from each to other. For example, concerning su-field analysis the nodes of the graph are fields and material objects, edges are interactions between material objects by the means of fields [1, 3]. A combinatorial method for searching of physical operating principle is based on the array of physical effects, which is represented in the form of an oriented graph. Nodes present cause and/or result of physical effects (changes of parameter's value of objects). Edges denote the condition for implementation of physical processes. Physical operating principles consist of physical effects, which are described in the form of chains, connected each node to another [6, 7]. In the energy-information method of science-technical creation POP portrayed by way of the parametric structural scheme. This scheme is a complex of elementary converting one physical quantity to another, connected in the certain order [8, 9]. One of the most familiar and theoretically substantiated approaches is a function-physical method of search design [18, 19]. The POP model represented as an oriented graph underlies it. The nodes of such graph are physical objects providing transformation of input and output streams of substance, energy, signals, represented as edges [17].

The analysis of methods for synthesis of engineering solution has revealed that the most important problem of these methods is the difficulty of transition from the structure in the form of POP model's description to the construction of designed device. This is because these methods don't take into consideration displacement routes and the order of interaction of the working medium during the functioning of the environment which is characteristic of the most of the modern cooling and cooling systems and refrigerating systems.

It finds the necessity of model, which allows to adequately representing POP of this class of devices. In this model, the semantic load of nodes and edges must be specified, and an opportunity of representing the displacement routes and the order of interaction of the working medium must be provided.

The most prospective way of solution of this task consists in the use of the conceptual apparatus of phenomenological thermodynamics [21, 22]. This is conditioned by three reasons. First, thermodynamics embraces the totality of natural phenomena, which has made its apparatus maximally distinct and universal and, thus, providing the opportunities of using it for describing possible POP. Secondly, on the basis of engineering thermodynamics, the description of the operation of the majority of (CS and RS) is established. This conditions the conventionality of its terminology when training specialists, designing these devices and facilitates their perception of this model. Third, thermodynamics allows a substitution of a complex real phenomenon for some conditional, elementary ones, which facilitates the process of formalization of POP description.

The theoretical propositions of phenomenological thermodynamics laid the foundation of engineering-physical approach to synthesis for engineering solutions of energy converters. This method involves next main steps: first – making a POP model of designed device as an oriented graph; second - making a matrix of engineering solutions by the way of matching elementary functions with alternative constructive elements. Elementary functions are determined from the POP model; alternative constructive elements may be selected from the patent list and other sources of science and technical literature.

In the proposed model, the nodes designate the spots, so-called characteristic points, where the working medium of CS and RS undergoes the interactions, for which a unified formula of an analytical expression of the generalized work is offered in thermodynamics:

$$dQ = P\,dE, \qquad (1)$$

where P – a generalized force or an intentional which implies such physical values as force, velocity, pressure, absolute temperature, potential difference, chemical potential and etc.; E – a generalized coordinate or an extensor which implies such values as displacement, the number of movements, volume, entropy, electric charge, the mass of a substance and others.

The semantics of edges is determined by the following considerations. Any interactions of the working medium are always connected with the changes of extensor E, that is, they are conditionally compared to the process of transfer over the reference surface of the thermodynamical system of a certain amount of dE. For each interaction, there is typical parameter E which defines explicitly physical properties of the working medium on a qualitative and quantitative side in as much as they are connected to the given interaction [11].

The interactions of the working medium are represented in the graph by edges with the designation of extensors conjugated with them. These edges are incident to those nodes (characteristic points) where corresponding interactions take place [12].

Besides, during an operation process, the substance of the working medium of (CS and RS) can move inside of the plant, which conditions the necessity of introduction of edges of the second type – path ones connecting characteristic points [25].

For the functioning of many (CS and RS), the periodicity of interactions and displacements of the working medium is typical. The examples are gaseous cryogenic machine operating by an inverse Stirling cycle, turbo refrigeration machines and others. In this case, the POP graph is supplemented with a cyclogram for periodic interactions and displacements of the working medium.

When developing the POP model, the characteristic points of (CS and RS), a sequence and types of interactions with them, as well as the order of passing them by the working medium are determined. For all elements of the graph, the following symbols are introduced.

The nodes are marked by letter V with lower and upper indices. The indices indicate the state of the working medium and a serial number of the characteristic point, correspondingly. If the working medium is subsequently passed through several states in one characteristic point, it can have a compound designation consisting of several letters. Edges – interactions are designated by letter E with lower and upper indices which determine the sort of interaction and its serial number. Edges – streams of the working medium are designated by the letter I, which has lower and upper indices as well, determining the components of the working medium and a series number of the edge [26].

So, unlike analogs proposed POP model allows to take into consideration specific and important particular qualities of cooling systems and refrigerating systems. It includes the displacement of working medium from element to element of cooling system during the functioning of the device; the order and duration of the interaction of the working medium during the functioning of the device. These facts essentially increase the relevance of abstract formulation of designed device's structure and its physical processes. The semantics of POP graph is based on the thermodynamic abstractions, such as: thermodynamic system; control surface; the factor of extensiveness; the factor of intensity. It allows making the construction of designed device by the means of elementary functions (look further) connected to the nodes and edges of the POP graph. Aforesaid facts render positive effects to labor efficiency of designers at early stages of designing for CS and RS.

3 Modeling Physical Operating Principles of Cooling Systems and Refrigerating Systems

In spite of large area of application of cooling systems and refrigerating systems, they use the limited quantity of physical phenomena. It includes change of phase (boiling, evaporation, condensation, sublimation, melting), throttling of gases, throttling of liquids, adiabatic expansion, expansion with the performance of external work, vortex effect, absorption of gases, desorption of gases from solutions and ejection [2, 5, 15].

The graphic representations of the POP model of physical phenomena for cooling systems and refrigerating systems have been developed. For example, the boiling of refrigerant is represented in the following way (Fig. 1). The boiling of refrigerant accompanying by the supply of heat from an external heat source is imaged on the Fig. 1a. The same process without a supply of heat is imaged on the Fig. 1b. In the first case, boiling is carried out at a constant temperature. In the second case, the temperature o refrigerant reduces because the evaporation of liquid refrigerant is performed by dint of internal energy. The same way the physical phenomena of evaporation, condensation, sublimation, and melting are represented on the graph model of POP.

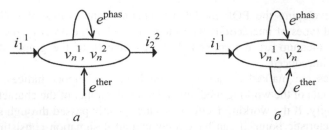

Fig. 1. The graphic representations of boiling process

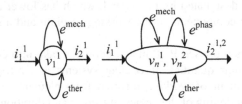

Fig. 2. The graphic representations of the throttling processes of gases and liquids

where v_n^1, v_n^2 – refrigerant in a liquid state and refrigerant in a gaseous state respectively; i_1^1 – the flow of liquid refrigerant; i_2^2 – the flow of gaseous refrigerant; e^{phas} – the factor of extensiveness conjugate to phase form of motion; e^{ther} – the factor of extensiveness conjugate to a thermal form of motion.

The graphic representation of the process of gaseous refrigerant expansion with the performance of external work is imaged on the Fig. 3a. The process of the adiabatic expansion of gaseous refrigerant imaged on the Fig. 3b.

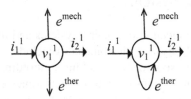

Fig. 3. The graphic representations of the processes of gas expansion

where v_n^1 – gas in the vortex tube; i_1^1 – the flow of high pressure gas in the nozzle input of the vortex tube; i_2^1 – the flow of hot gas; i_3^1 – the flow of cold gas; e^{mech} – the factor of extensiveness conjugate to mechanical form of motion; e^{ther} – the factor of extensiveness conjugate to thermal form of motion; e^{kr} – the factor of extensiveness conjugate to kinetic (rotation) form of motion.

The vortex effect (the Ranka-Hilsch effect), which is realized by vortex tube is imaged on the Fig. 4. As result of this phenomenon, the flow of air is separated into cold and hot flows in the vortex tube (Fig. 2).

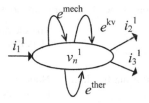

Fig. 4. The graphic representations of the vortex effect (the Ranka-Hilsch effect)

The simplified line diagram of the ejector and graphic representation of the process occurred in ejector are shown on the Fig. 5. Working medium (gas or steam of high pressure) comes out of nozzle 1 (node v_1^1) and enters to mixing chamber 2 (node v_2^1). Sucked medium (gas or steam of low pressure) moves from suction chamber 3 into mixing chamber 2. The mixture of this mediums travels from mixing chamber to diffuser 4 when the kinetic energy of jet is transformed into potential energy. This process is accompanied by an increase of flow pressure.

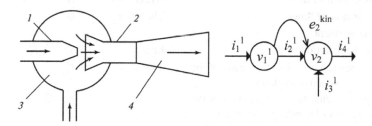

Fig. 5. The graphic representations of processes in ejector

where v_1^1 – working medium in the nozzle of ejector; v_2^1 – working and sucked mediums in the mixing chamber; i_1^1 – input flow of working medium; i_2^1 – flow of working medium from the nozzle; i_3^1 – flow of sucked medium; i_4^1 – output flow of working medium; e^{kin} – the factor of extensiveness conjugate to kinetic form of motion.

Every interaction of working medium with environmental object results in a change of working medium's internal energy. However, its functions in technical systems may be different significantly. In the cooling systems and refrigerating systems, the main environmental objects are «heat givers» and «heat receivers». The thermal interactions of working body with this environmental object result in reduce or increase of working medium's temperature (Table 1).

For implementation, this main processes other interactions are needed as well. The necessity of other interactions is conditioned by two reasons. Firstly: these interactions are needed for alteration of working medium's parameters. Secondly: these interactions are needed for movement of working medium from node to node. All environmental objects are divided into six groups according to the functional purpose:

Table 1. The classification of the elementary functions of constructive elements

Elementary function	The element of POP model	Denomination
Ensuring the process		
1. Enabling the internal degrees of the freedom of working medium	Node, (refrigerant)	f_1
2. Enabling the internal isolation of working medium from unwanted interactions	The same	f_2
3. Enabling the external degrees of the freedom of working medium	Node, (control surface)	f_3
4. Enabling the external isolation of working medium from unwanted interactions	The same	f_4
5. Enabling the internal degrees of freedom for the factor of extensiveness conducted	Edge	f_5
6. Enabling the external isolation for the conductor of the factor of extensiveness from unwanted interactions	The same	f_6
7. The association of flows	Hyper edge	f_7
8. The separation of flows	The same	f_8
Process management		
9. Change the direction of flow	Edge	f_9^1, f_9^2, f_9^3
10. Change the value of flow by means of the resistance of conductive medium	The same	$f_{10}^1, f_{10}^2, f_{10}^3, f_{10}^4, f_{10}^5, f_{10}^6$
11. Change the value of flow by means of the transverse section of conductive medium	–//–	$f_{11}^1, f_{11}^2, f_{11}^3$
12. Change the specific characteristics of flow	–//–	f_{12}

- «heat givers» (HG);
- «heat receivers» (HR);
- realizing the function of altering of working medium's parameters (WMP)
- realizing the function of working medium's transportation (WMT)
- sources of the working medium (SWM);
- the effluent of the working medium (EWM);
- every environmental object may belong to different levels of hierarchy.

In order to substantiate the suggested model of POP for the considered class of devices, the POP models of the main types of modern cooling system and refrigerating systems were built. As an example, Fig. 6 shows the scheme of the absorption refrigerating plant, and Fig. 7 shows its POP model.

The absorption refrigerating plant is intended to cool of water or antifreeze, which is used in the central air conditioning systems. The cooling of water is implemented by means of the refrigeration cycle. The main physical processes of this refrigeration cycle are absorption (e^{abs}) and desorption (e^{des}).

For the organization of refrigeration cycle thermal energy of secondary heat sources, such as hot water, hot steam, the energy generated by the combustion of

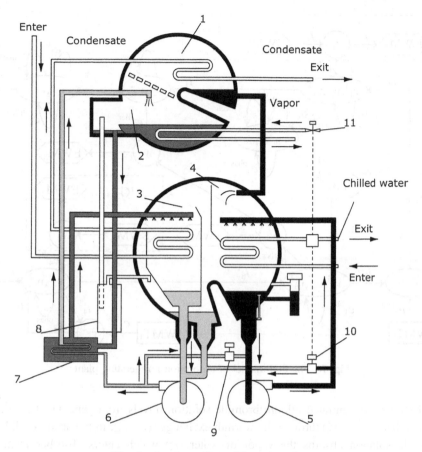

Fig. 6. An absorption refrigerating plant

natural gas etc. is used. The working medium of absorption refrigerating plant is a refrigerant, which transfers the warmth from «heat givers» to «heat receivers». As a rule, in absorption refrigerating plant the water is used by way of working medium and lithium bromide solution is applied as absorbent.

The absorption refrigerating plant contains two chambers. The upper chamber is hot chambers, under high pressure. It comprises the generator and condenser. The lower chamber has the low temperature and pressure. It includes the evaporator and absorber [2].

Due to warmth (e_1^{ther}) the vapor of water (i_1^1) is separated from the lithium bromide solution in the generator (v_1^1, v_1^2, v_1^3) and then enters to the condenser (v_2^1, v_2^2). The vapor of water condenses (e_1^{phas}), gives away the warmth (e_2^{ther}) to the circuit of coolant water (nodes w_1, w_2). Cooled water enter to evaporator (v_4^1, v_4^2) through expansion valve (v_3^1, v_3^2). In the evaporator (v_4^1, v_4^2) water boils in the conditions of low pressure and low temperature and consequently take the warmth (e_4^{ther}) from the cooled object (s_1). The pump of refrigerant (v_5^2) pumps (e_1^{hyd}) the water on the atomizer. It contributes to more intensive warmth exchange.

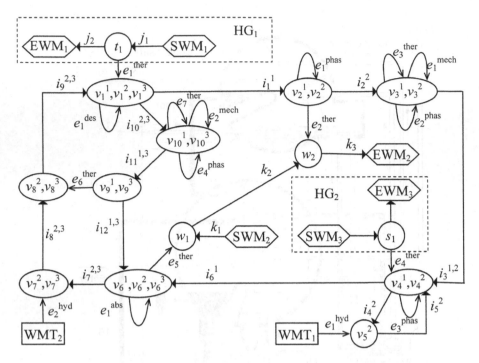

Fig. 7. The POP model of absorption refrigerating plant

Leftover concentrated lithium bromide solution travels from generator (v_1^1, v_1^2, v_1^3) to absorber (v_6^1, v_6^2, v_6^3) through the warmth exchanger (v_9^1, v_9^3). In the absorber, lithium bromide solution absorbs the vapor of water (i_6^1) which enters absorber from the evaporator (v_4^1, v_4^2). In order to intensify this process, the lithium bromide solution is sprayed by the atomizer. The process of absorption is accompanied by the warmth release (e_5^{mep}), so the cooling of absorber by the circuit of coolant water (w_1) is implemented. The solution of lithium bromide and water is pumped ($i_8^{2,3}$, $i_9^{2,3}$) by solution pump (v_7^2, v_7^3) into generator through warmth exchanger (v_8^2, v_8^3). Then cycle repeats.

The similar POP model for the vapour-compressive refrigerating plant, the steam-ejector refrigerating plant, the refrigeration turbine, the engine cooling system has been developed etc. It showed the efficiency of the engineering-physical approach for the considered class of technical systems.

The analysis conducted has completely justified the adequacy of the used model of POP for refrigerating systems. This model allows considering the sequence of displacement and interactions of the working medium in the space and in time and concentrates the designer's attention on the peculiarities of physical processes which determine the CS and RS morphology.

The sequence of the drafting of the POP model is shown in Fig. 8. It's represented in the form of block-diagram, which contains two cycles with post condition. These cycles are performed consistently. The presence of cycles with post condition means that each procedure of cycles must be fulfilled at least once. This structure of method corresponds to the principles of structured programming completely. It enables to realize the method in the form of interactive information searching system for decision-making within the framework of CAD for cooling systems and refrigerating systems.

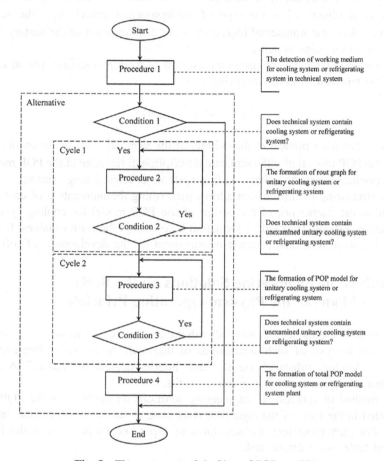

Fig. 8. The sequence of drafting of POP model

The entries of table A1 are made for each characteristic place of the POP model of projected cooling systems or refrigerating systems. The structure of table A1 is represented in the following way:

$$S_{A1} = \{a_1^1,\, a_1^2,\, a_1^3,\, a_1^4,\, a_1^5\}, \tag{2}$$

where a_2^1 – the index number of the column of the table; a_2^2 – the denomination of the characteristic place of the POP model; a_2^3 – the semantic description of the node; a_2^4 – the description of the condition of refrigerant in characteristic place; a_2^5 – the denomination of the unitary cooling systems or refrigerating systems.

The entries of table A2 are made for each source and sink of working medium. The structure of table A2 is represented in the following way:

$$S_{A2} = \{a_2^1, a_2^2, a_2^3, a_2^4, a_2^5\},\qquad(3)$$

where a_2^1 – the index number of the column of the table; a_2^2 – the denomination of the environmental object; a_2^3 – the type of environmental object; a_2^4 – the semantic description of the environmental object; a_2^5 – the denomination of the unitary cooling systems or refrigerating systems.

The entries of table A3 are made for each flow of working medium. The structure of table A3 is represented in the following way:

$$S_{A3} = \{a_3^1, a_3^2, a_3^3, a_3^4\},\qquad(4)$$

where a_3^1 – the index number of the column of the table; a_3^2 – the denomination of the edge of the POP model; a_3^3 – the semantic description of the edge of the POP model; a_3^4 – the denomination of the unitary cooling systems or refrigerating systems.

This structuring of information allows performing the automation of each procedure within the framework of the design of the POP model for cooling systems or refrigerating systems. Herewith, information is formed in the form of tables. It enables using the tools of relational database management for the development of software.

4 Synthesis of Engineering Solutions on the Basis of the Model of the Physical Operating Principle

Each element of the model is connected with the construction functions revealed on the basis of the analysis of such abstractions of thermodynamics as a "thermodynamic system", a "control surface", "external" and "internal degrees of freedom". A detailed description of these functions is given in works.

The method of synthesis of engineering solutions on the basis of the POP model represented in the form of the algorithm consisting of the set of procedures and conditions. For each procedure, the structures of input and output data in the form of relational tables were determined.

The sequence of the implementation of the procedures for the synthesis of engineering solutions is shown in Fig. 9. It contains eight procedures. Procedure activation is determined by two conditions. The condition 1 of the continuation of the cycle is checked after implementation of procedure 1 and procedure 2. Further, cycle body is carried out. Cycle body contains procedure 3–8, which are performed successively. The necessity of recycling is determined by condition 2. This structure of method also corresponds to the principles of structured programming. It includes two consecutions, an alternative, and a cycle. Each of these structures has one point of entry and one exit point.

Table $M1$ is filled out during the determination of elementary functions, related to the nodes and edges of the POP model. The structure of the table M1 is represented in the following way:

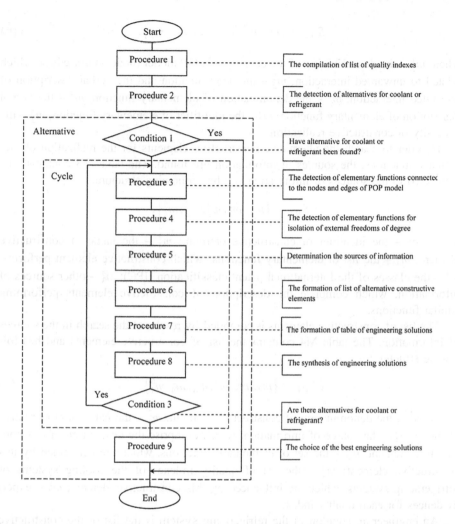

Fig. 9. The sequence of the implementation of procedures for the synthesis of engineering solutions

$$S_{M1} = \left\{ m_1^1, \ m_1^2, \ m_1^3, \ m_1^4, \ m_1^5 \right\}, \tag{5}$$

where m_1^1 – the denomination of the element of the POP model (node and/or edge); m_1^2 – the type of elementary function; m_1^3 – the verbal description of elementary function related to the element of the POP model; m_1^4 – the identifier of elementary function; m_1^5 – the necessity of constructive realization.

Further, unwanted interactions of working medium are determined and elementary functions for protection from them are defined. As result table M2 is filled out. The structure of the table M2 is represented in the following way:

$$S_{M2} = \{m_2^1,\ m_2^2,\ m_2^3,\ m_2^4,\ m_2^5,\ m_2^6\}, \tag{6}$$

where m_2^1 – the denomination of the element of POP model (node and/or edge), which related to unwanted interaction; m_2^2 – the denomination and the verbal description of unwanted interaction; m_2^3 – the denomination of elementary function; m_2^4 – the verbal description of elementary function; m_2^5 – the identifier of elementary function; m_2^6 – the necessity of constructive realization.

In order to search the alternative constructive elements for the realization of elementary functions, the sources of information are found. The table M3 contains date connected to the sources of information and has following structure:

$$S_{M3} = \{m_3^1,\ m_3^2, m_3^3, m_3^4, m_3^5\}, \tag{7}$$

where m_3^1 – the identifier of constructive element; m_3^2 – the name of constructive element; m_3^3 – the list of elementary functions, which constructive element performs; m_3^4 – the classes of the International patent classification (IPC); m_3^5 – other sources of information, which comprise the description of constructive elements performing similar functions.

The list of constructive elements is compiled by results of the search in the sources of information. The table M4 contains the list of constructive elements and has following structure:

$$S_{M4} = \{m_4^1,\ m_4^2, m_4^3, m_4^4, m_4^5, m_4^6\} \tag{8}$$

where m_4^1 – the denomination of constructive element; m_4^2 – the name of constructive element; m_4^3 – the source of information, which comprise the description of this constructive element; m_4^4 – the set of elementary functions, which are performed by this constructive element; m_4^5 – the list of quality indexes of the cooling systems or refrigerating systems, which are influenced by this constructive element; m_4^6 – expert evidences for each quality index.

An engineering solution of the refrigerating system is the list of the constructive element. The elements from this list perform all elementary functions from the tables M1 and M2. For this, the table of engineering solutions is filled in, where the attributes are the names of the elementary functions from Tables 2 and 3. Each line of the table corresponds to one constructive element. The fields of the table contain the values of predicate function P(fi) which possesses a true or false value depending on the performance of corresponding function f_i, specified in the head of the table, by this element. The practice of development and using of these tables has shown that on numerous occasions different constructive elements perform several identical elementary functions. It stipulates incompatibility such constructive elements in one engineering solution. Making out a list of possible engineering solutions consisting of compatible elements is implemented by specific software.

Algorithm for the synthesis of engineering solutions and the method of expert estimate for the level of quality of obtained engineering solutions have been described in the article (Fig. 9).

The quality assessment of projected designs is executed with the aim of:

- the justification of predictable level of design quality;
- the justification of technical requirements for the product;
- the choice of optimal version for production start-up;
- achievement and exceeding the technical level of designed products.

Base quality indexes are defined based on the analysis of known analogs of the developed refrigerating system. Herewith the prospect of technological progress and customer requirements are taken into consideration. Indexes of existing best samples, planned and predictable indexes and the recommendations of international organizations may be base indexes.

During the designing of new cooling systems or refrigerating systems, upon condition, there is no analog of developing a product, all available information up to prospective indexes of a hypothetical sample is used for determination of base indexes. The quality indexes are defined by design project leader involving all necessary specialists. After that, the results are analyzed by an expert commission, which makes a final decision. The values of the accepted quality indexes are defined during the matching of similar basic and prospective indexes.

The coefficients of the significance of quality indexes are determined by means of expert estimate method, which assume formation of the expert group consisted of highly qualified specialists (at least seven experts). The level of competence of each expert is equal to another one.

Table 2. The list of functions connected to the edges of the POP model of absorption refrigerating plant

m_1^1	m_1^2	m_1^3	m_1^4	m_1^5
e_1^{ther}	$f_3(e_1^{ther})$	Enabling the heat feed to the solution in the generator	016	0
e_1^{des}	$f_3(e_1^{des})$	Enabling desorption of the vapor of water from the lithium bromide solution	017	0
e_2^{ther}	$f_3(e_2^{ther})$	Enabling the heat removal from the vapor of water	018	0
e_1^{phas}	$f_3(e_1^{phas})$	Enabling the vapor of water condensation	019	0
e_1^{mech}	$f_3(e_1^{mech})$	Enabling expansion of the vapor of water	020	0
e_2^{phas}	$f_3(e_2^{phas})$	Enabling refrigerating medium evaporation	021	0
e_3^{ther}	$f_3(e_3^{ther})$	Enabling the reduction of the vapor of water temperature	022	0
i_1^1	$f_5(i_1^1)$	Enabling the motion of the vapor of water from the generator to the condenser	031	0
i_2^2	$f_5(i_2^2)$	Enabling the motion of the water from the condenser to the expansion valve	032	1
$i_3^{1,2}$	$f_5(i_3^{1,2})$	Enabling the motion of the vapor and water from the expansion valve to the evaporator	033	0
i_4^2	$f_5(i_4^2)$	Enabling the motion of the water from the evaporator to the working chamber of the refrigerant pump	034	1

Table 3. The list of functions connected to the nodes of the POP model of absorption refrigerating plant

m_1^1	m_1^2	m_1^3	m_1^4	m_1^5
v_1, CO$_1$	$f_3\left(e_1^{ther}\right)$	Enabling the heat feed to the solution in the generator	001	1
v_1	$f_3\left(e_1^{des}\right)$	Enabling desorption of the vapor of water from the lithium bromide solution	002	1
v_2, w_2	$f_3\left(e_2^{ther}\right)$	Enabling the heat removal from the vapor of water	004	1
v_2	$f_3\left(e_1^{phas}\right)$	Enabling the vapor of water condensation	003	1
v_3	$f_3\left(e_1^{mech}\right)$	Enabling expansion of the vapor of water	005	1
v_3	$f_3\left(e_2^{phas}\right)$	Enabling refrigerating medium evaporation	006	1
v_3	$f_3\left(e_3^{ther}\right)$	Enabling the reduction of the vapor of water temperature	007	1
v_4, CO$_2$	$f_3\left(e_4^{ther}\right)$	Enabling the heat feed to the water in the evaporator	008	1
v_4	$f_3\left(e_3^{phas}\right)$	Enabling refrigerating medium evaporation	009	1
v_5, TR$_1$	$f_3\left(e_1^{hyd}\right)$	Enabling the pumping of water	010	1
v_6, w_1	$f_3\left(e_5^{ther}\right)$	Enabling the heat removal of absorption	011	1
v_6	$f_3\left(e_1^{abs}\right)$	Enabling absorption of the vapor of water into lithium bromide solution	012	1
v_7, TR$_2$	$f_3\left(e_2^{hyd}\right)$	Enabling the pumping of the solution of lithium bromide and water	013	1
v_8, v_9	$f_3\left(e_6^{ther}\right)$	Enabling the heat feed to the solution of lithium bromide and water	014	1
v_{10}	$f_3\left(e_2^{mech}\right)$	Enabling expansion of the vapor of water	015	1

Table 2 contains the part of functions connected to the edges of the POP model. Table 3 contains the part of functions connected to the nodes of the POP model of absorption refrigerating plant.

The number of elements in the engineering solution of CS and RS can be different, which differs this approach from a morphological one. In a particular case, when elements perform similar sets of functions, this table is degenerated into a morphological one.

5   Practical Application of New Method of Search Design

Proposed method has been used for the decision of practical industrial problem arisen by initial machining o high-alloyed rough parts (such as bearing collars). At present these rough parts are cooled and lubricated by «sulfofrezol», which presents a mineral oleaginous fluid, containing sulfur. During intensive evaporation of «sulfofrezol» in the point of operation, vapor is generated. This vapor presents douche-colored fog, which is harmful to people's health.

Relative to this problem new technique for delivery of lubricated-cooled agents has been offered. In accordance with the new technique, lubricating and cooling agents are separated. Lubricating agent is ionized air, cooling agent is pulverized water. Lubricating agent is supplied traditionally into the point of operation, whilst cooling agent is supplied to surfaces of the metal-cutting tool and rough part. Development of suchlike cooling systems for multipoint metal-cutting tools (for example, drills and milling cutters) is the most difficult task. For the purpose of development of suchlike devices, POP models and matrix of engineering solutions have been made. Two devices for milling operation and two devices drilling operation have been developed and patented.

Further, POP model, the lists of elementary functions, a matrix of engineering solutions and construction of a device for the feeding of lubricating-cooling agent [24] are shown. Device for the feeding of lubricating-cooling agent contains two unitary cooling systems. The first unitary cooling system is the flow of ionized air; the second unitary cooling system is the flow of pulverized water. According to the new method of search design, the POP model of projected device has been created (Fig. 10).

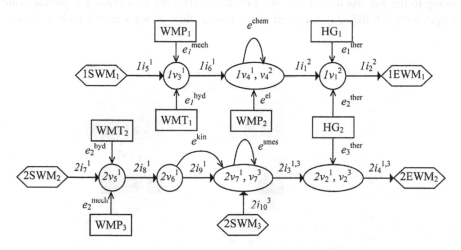

Fig. 10. The POP model of device for feeding of lubricating-cooling agent

Nodes of the POP model are characteristic points of the cooling system and environmental objects. Its present positions of working mediums at elements of the cooling system and objects interacted with working medium. Among these are: position of air at compressor's working chamber ($1v_3^1$, $2v_5^1$), position of air and ionized air at ion-production chamber ($1v_4^1$, v_4^2), position of ionized air at the point of operation ($1v_1^2$), position of air at driving nozzle ($2v_6^1$); positions of pulverized water at ejector's bending chamber ($2v_7^1$, v_7^3), positions of pulverized water at drill's surface ($2v_1^2$, v_2^3); compressor's gears (WMT$_{1-2}$, WMP$_{1-3}$), electricity supply (WMP$_2$), rough part (HG$_1$), drill (HG$_2$), sources of working mediums (1SWM$_1$, 2SWM$_2$, 2SWM$_3$) and effluents of working medium (1EWM$_1$, 2EWM$_2$). Edges of POP model present interactions and displacements of working medium. Among these are: process of generation of corona effect (e^{el}), ionization of air (e^{chem}), movements of air (e_1^{hyd}, e_2^{hyd}), compressions of air (e_1^{mech}, e_2^{mech}), processes of ejection (e^{kin}, e^{smes}), cooling of rough part (e_1^{ther}) and cooling of drill (e_2^{ther}, e_3^{ther}); displacements of air ($1i_5^1$, $1i_6^1$, $2i_7^1$, $2i_8^1$, $2i_9^1$), displacements of ionized air ($1i_1^2$, $1i_2^2$), displacement of water ($2i_{10}^3$) and displacements of pulverized water ($2i_3^{1,3}$, $2i_4^{1,3}$).

Then, on the basis of the POP model matrix (Fig. 11) containing about one hundred and fifty engineering solutions has been made by dint of determination of elementary functions (Tables 4, 5 and 6) and choice of constructive elements. The most perspective engineering solutions have been determined by the method of expert estimates [20] adapted to the new method of search design. In the matrix, the most perspective engineering solutions are denoted by colored cells of the table. One of these has been constructed and patented [24] (Figs. 12, 13, 14 and 15). It corresponds to green cells of a table in the matrix (Fig. 11). In this device lubricated agent is ionized air, which is supplied directly to the point of contact of cutting bit with rough part's juvenile surface. Owing to the constructive organization of device delivery of ionized air into the point of operation is fulfilled in the form of directional flow about a closed path. It doesn't

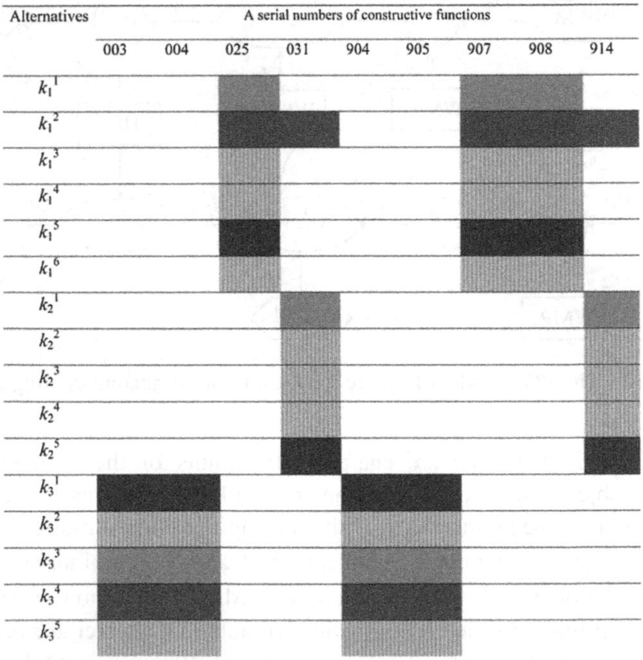

Fig. 11. The table of engineering solutions for device for feeding of lubricating-cooling agent (Color figure online)

allow dispersal of ionized air and improves conditions for its gain access to the point of operation, especially during the drilling of deep holes. Due to these facts, in-contact edge life is increased at the expense of the best efficiency of lubricant group at the point

Table 4. The list of functions connected to the nodes of POP model for device for feeding of lubricating-cooling agent

m_1^1	m_1^2	m_1^3	m_1^4	m_1^5
$1v_3$, WMP$_1$	$f_3\left(e_1^{\text{mech}}\right)$	Enabling the compression of air	001	0
$1v_3$, WMT$_1$	$f_3\left(e_1^{\text{hyd}}\right)$	Enabling the movement of compressed air	002	0
$1v_4$, WMP$_2$	$f_3\left(e^{\text{el}}\right)$	Enabling the generation of corona effect	003	1
$1v_4$	$f_3\left(e^{\text{chem}}\right)$	Enabling the ionization of air	004	1
$1v_1$, HG$_1$	$f_3\left(e_1^{\text{ther}}\right)$	Enabling the heat removal from the rough part	005	0
$1v_1$, HG$_2$	$f_3\left(e_2^{\text{ther}}\right)$	Enabling a heat removal from the drill	006	0
$2v_5$, WMP$_2$	$f_3\left(e_2^{\text{mech}}\right)$	Enabling the compression of air	007	0
$2v_5$, WMT$_2$	$f_3\left(e_2^{\text{hyd}}\right)$	Enabling the movement of compressed air	008	0
$2v_6, v_7$	$f_3(e^{\text{kin}})$	Enabling the transfer of air's kinetic energy to sucked water	009	0
$2v_7$	$f_3(e^{\text{smes}})$	Enabling the mixing of air with water (forming of pulverized water)	010	0
$2v_2$, HG$_2$	$f_3\left(e_3^{\text{ther}}\right)$	Enabling a heat removal from the drill	011	0

Table 5. The list of functions connected to the edges of POP model for device for feeding of lubricating-cooling agent

m_1^1	m_1^2	m_1^3	m_1^4	m_1^5
$1i_1^2$	$f_5\left(1i_1^2\right)$	Enabling the supply of ionized air to the point of operation	023	1
$1i_2^2$	$f_5\left(1i_2^2\right)$	Enabling the moving away of air to the atmosphere	024	0
$2i_3^{1,3}$	$f_5\left(2i_3^{1,3}\right)$	Enabling the supply of pulverized water to drill's surface	025	1
$2i_4^{1,3}$	$f_5\left(2i_4^{1,3}\right)$	Enabling the moving away of pulverized water to the atmosphere	026	0
$1i_5^1$	$f_5\left(1i_5^1\right)$	Enabling the supply of air to compressor's working chamber	027	0
$1i_6^1$	$f_5\left(1i_1^6\right)$	Enabling the supply of air to the ion-production chamber	028	0
$2i_7^1$	$f_5\left(2i_7^1\right)$	Enabling the supply of air to compressor's working chamber	029	0
$2i_8^1$	$f_5\left(2i_8^1\right)$	Enabling the supply of air to the driving nozzle	030	0

Table 6. The list of functions for isolation of the external degrees of freedom for device for feeding of lubricating-cooling agent

m_1^1	m_1^2	m_1^2	m_1^4	m_1^5	m_1^6
$1v_3$	e_{01}^{hyd} – The leakage of air at the compressor	$f_4\left(e_{01}^{hyd}\right)$	The protection of the compressor's working chamber from the leakage of air	901	0
$1v_4$	e_{01}^{el} – The generation of spark-over-initiated discharge at the ion-production chamber	$f_4\left(e_{01}^{el}\right)$	The protection of the ion-production chamber from the generation of spark-over-initiated discharge	902	0
$1v_4$	e_{02}^{el} – The generation of arc-type discharge at the ion-production chamber	$f_4\left(e_{02}^{el}\right)$	The protection of the ion-production chamber from the generation of arc-type discharge	903	0
$1v_4$	e_{03}^{el} – The electrization of machine-tool by the ion-production chamber	$f_4\left(e_{03}^{el}\right)$	The protection of electrization of machine-tool by the ion-production chamber	904	1
$1v_4$	e_{02}^{hyd} – The leakage of ionized air at the ion-production chamber	$f_4\left(e_{02}^{hyd}\right)$	The protection of the ion-production chamber from the leakage of ionized air	905	1
$1i_1^2$	e_{03}^{hyd} –The leakage of ionized air at the conductive channel	$f_6\left(e_{03}^{hyd}\right)$	The protection of the conductive channel from the leakage of ionized air	906	1
$1i_1^2$	e_{01}^{chem} –The important reduction of lubricating-cooling agent's ions concentration at the conductive channel owing to significant distance of place of air's ionization from the point of operation	$f_6\left(e_{01}^{chem}\right)$	The protection of the conductive channel from the important reduction of lubricating-cooling agent's ions concentration owing to significant distance of place of air's ionization from the point of operation	907	1
$1i_6^1$	e_{04}^{hyd} – The leakage of air at the pipeline	$f_6\left(e_{04}^{hyd}\right)$	The protection of the pipeline from the leakage of air	908	0
$2v_5$	e_{05}^{hyd} – The leakage of air at the compressor	$f_4\left(e_{05}^{hyd}\right)$	The protection of the compressor's working chamber from the leakage of air	909	0
$2v_6$	e_{06}^{hyd} – The leakage of air at the driving nozzle	$f_4\left(e_{06}^{hyd}\right)$	The protection of the driving nozzle from the leakage of air	910	0
$2v_7$	e_{07}^{hyd} –The leakage of pulverized water at the bending chamber of ejector	$f_4\left(e_{07}^{hyd}\right)$	The protection of the bending chamber of ejector from the leakage of pulverized water	911	0
$2i_3^{1,3}$	e_{08}^{hyd} – The leakage of pulverized water at the conductive channel	$f_6\left(e_{08}^{hyd}\right)$	The protection of the conductive channel from the leakage of pulverized water	912	1
$2i_8^1$	e_{09}^{hyd} – The leakage of air at pipeline	$f_6\left(e_{09}^{hyd}\right)$	The protection of the pipeline from the leakage of air	913	0
$2i_9^1$	e_{10}^{hyd} – The leakage of air at pipeline	$f_6\left(e_{10}^{hyd}\right)$	The protection of the pipeline from the leakage of air	914	0

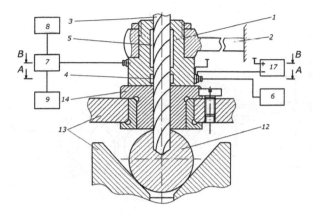

Fig. 12. Device for the feeding of the lubricating-cooling agent. The main view.

A-A

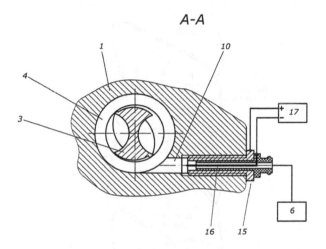

Fig. 13. Device for the feeding of the lubricating-cooling agent. View A-A.

of contact of the instrument with rough part's juvenile surface. The cooled agent is pulverized water, which is supplied to drill shank. In so doing essential gradient of temperature is created and heat is taken away from the whole body of the metal-cutting tool, rough part and from the point of operation. In this way, additional cooling of the metal-cutting tool is established a control base and it increases in-contact edge life.

1 – case; 2 – bracket; 3 – drill; 4, 5 – circular chambers; 6, 8 – sources of feeding of compressed air; 7 – ejector; 9 – sources of feeding of water; 10, 11 – holes; 12 – rough part; 13 – fixture group; 14 – drill bushing; 15 – cylindrical positive electrode; 16 – needle negative electrode; 17 – electricity supply.

B-B

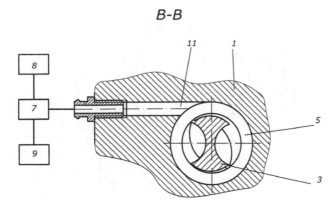

Fig. 14. Device for the feeding of the lubricating-cooling agent. View B-B.

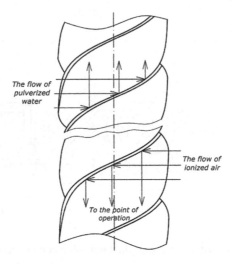

Fig. 15. Device for the feeding of the lubricating-cooling agent. An additional view.

6 Conclusions

The suggested method can be used in case the constructive elements perform different sets of functions and in case the development of morphological tables is hindered or impossible. This is conditioned by the fact that the model of the physical operating principle allows forming a table (Fig. 11), where engineering solutions of the converters are obtained by means of joining functionally compatible elements.

The process of development of the model of the physical operating principle, determination of the multitude of constructive functions and compilation of the table of engineering solutions is implemented according to tough rules and almost does not depend on human intuition. It significantly increases the labor efficiency of designers at early stages of designing that essentially reduces time and cost of engineering developments for CS and RS.

The study of the method does not require mastery of new concepts, and its application – utilizing specialized databases. The descriptions of engineering solutions taken from the patent file and other scientific and technical literature can be used as elements.

The method can be applied as a means of enhancing the labor efficiency of designers at early stages of designing owing to reduction of labor expenditures when choosing the concept of an engineering system for energy transformation, and also as a methodical support for the development of computer-aided design systems.

References

1. Alves, J.F., Navas, H.V.G., Nunes, I.L.: Application of TRIZ methodology for ergonomic problem solving in a continuous improvement environment. In: Arezes, P. (ed.) Advances in Safety Management and Human Factors. AISC, vol. 491, pp. 473–485. Springer, Cham (2016). doi:10.1007/978-3-319-41929-9_43
2. Baranenko, A.V., Bucharin, N.N., Pekarev, V.I., Skakun, V.I., Timofeevskii, L.S.: Cooling Machines, Moscow (1997)
3. Berdonosov, V.D., Kozita, A.N., Zhivotova, A.A.: TRIZ evolution of black oil coker units. Chem. Eng. Res. Des. **103**, 61–73 (2016). doi:10.1016/j.cherd.2015.08.013. Springer, Komsomolsk-na-Amure
4. Chani, J.A., Natasha, A.R., Che Hassan, C.H., Syarif, J.: TRIZ approach for machining process innovation in cryogenic environment. Int. J. Mater. Prod. Technol. **53**, 268–297 (2016). doi:10.1504/IJMPT.2016.079200. Inderscience Enterprises Ltd
5. Dyachek, P.I.: Refrigerating machines and plants, Moscow (2007)
6. Korobkin, D., Fomenkov, S., Kravets, A., Kolesnikov, S., Dykov, M.: Three-steps methodology for patents prior-art retrieval and structured physical knowledge extracting. In: Kravets, A., Shcherbakov, M., Kultsova, M., Shabalina, O. (eds.) Creativity in Intelligent Technologies and Data Science. CCIS, vol. 535, pp. 124–136. Springer, Cham (2015). doi:10.1007/978-3-319-23766-4_10
7. Glazunov, V.N.: The search of physical operating principles of technical systems, p. 143 (1990)
8. Zaripov, M., Zaripova, V., Petrova, I.: System of conceptual design based on energy-informational model. In: Selvaraj, H., Zydek, D., Chmaj, G. (eds.) Progress in Systems Engineering, 23rd International Conference on Systems Engineering, vol. 330, pp. 365–372. Springer, Heidelberg (2002). doi:10.1007/978-3-319-08422-0_1
9. Zaripova, V., Petrova, I.: Knowledge-based support for innovative design on basis of energy-information method of circuit In: 11th Joint Conference on Safety Knowledge-Based Software Engineering, pp. 521–532. Springer, Volgograd (2014) doi:10.1007/978-3-319-11854-3_45
10. Zaripova, V., Petrova, I.: System of conceptual design based on energy-informational model In: Symposium on Education in Measurement and Instrumentation. IMEKO, Wroclaw (2015). doi:10.1007/978-3-319-08422-0_54
11. Kamaev, V.A., Yakovlev, A.A.: Information modelling of the physical operating principle and formation of a multitude of engineering solutions of energy converters In: Information Technologies, vol 1, pp. 2–8 (2006)

12. Zaripova, V.M., Petrova, I.Y., Kravets, A., Evdoshenko, O.: Knowledge bases of physical effects and phenomena for method of energy-informational models by means of ontologies. Commun. Comput. Inf. Sci. **535**, 224–237 (2015)
13. Fomenkov, S.A., Korobkin, D.M., Kolesnikov, S.G., Kamaev, V.A., Kravets, A.G.: The automated methods of search of physical effects Int. J. Soft Comput. **10**(3), 234–238 (2015)
14. Koller, R.: Konstruktionsmethode für den Maschinen – Gerate- und Apparatebau, p. 191. Springer, Berlin (1979)
15. Kurylyov, Y.S., Onosovskii, V.V., Rumyantsev, D.: Refrigerating plants, Moscow (2000)
16. Lezhnina, Y., Khomenko, T., Zaripova, V.: Topological structure for building ontology of energy-information method circuits. In: Kravets, A., Shcherbakov, M., Kultsova, M., Iijima, T. (eds.) Knowledge-Based Software Engineering. CCIS, vol. 466, pp. 185–194. Springer, Cham (2014). doi:10.1007/978-3-319-11854-3_17
17. Polovinkin, A.I.: The automation of search design, Moscow (1981)
18. Polovinkin, A.I.: The method of optimal designing with automatic search of schemes and structures for engineering construction, Moscow (1970)
19. Kravets, A.G., Kravets, A.D., Rogachev, V.A., Medintseva, I.P.: Cross-thematic modeling of the world prior-art state. Rejected Patent Applications Analysis. J. Fundam Appl. Sci. **8** (3S), 2542–2552 (2016)
20. Sadovnikov, V.I.: Quality Management: Educational Aid. Volgograd State Technical University, Volgograd (2002)
21. Veinik, A.I.: Thermodynamics of real processes. Science and Technique, Minsk (1991)
22. Mironenko, A.G., Kravets, A.G.: Automated methods of patent array analysis. In: IISA 2016 - 7th International Conference on Information, Intelligence, Systems and Applications, Article no. 7785341 (2016)
23. Wang, Q.Y., Yang, B.J., Duan, X.L.: Reclassification of standard solution based on su-field model and similarity. Chinese J. Eng. Des. **22**, 520–527 (2015). doi:10.3785/j.issn.1006-754X.2015.06.002. Springer Science + Business Media
24. Yakovlev, A.A., et al.: Ustrojstvo dlja podachi smazochno-ohlazhdajushego technologich-eskogo sredstva. Patent RF, no. 152129 (2015)
25. Yakovlev, A.A., Chursina, S.V., Pozdnyakova, P.E., Sorokin, V.S.: Energy converters with gaseous and liquid working body searching design. World Appl. Sci. J. **24**, 213–219 (2013). doi:10.5829/idosi.wasj.2013.24.itmies.80042. International Digital organization for Scientific Information
26. Yakovlev, A.A., Sorokin, V.S., Mishustina, S.N., Proidakova, N.V., Postupaeva, S.G.: A new method of search design of refrigerating systems containing a liquid and gaseous working medium based on the graph model of the physical operating principle In: International Conference on Information Technologies in Business and Industry. Institute of Physics Publishing, Tomsk (2017). doi:10.1088/1742-6596/803/1/012181
27. Yan, W., Zanny-Merk, C., Rousselot, F., Cavallucci, D.: A heuristic method of using the pointers to physical effects in Su-Field analysis. Proc. Eng. **131**, 539–550 (2015). doi:10.1016/j.proeng.2015.12.448. Elsevier BV
28. Yan, W., Zanny-Merk, C., Rousselot, F., Cavallucci, D., Collet, P.: A new method of using physical effects in su-field analysis based on ontology reasoning. Proc. Comput. Sci. **22**, 30–39 (2013). doi:10.1016/j.procs.2013.09.078. Elsiver BV

Computer Linguistic Approach
for Computational Creativity Tasks

Tatiana V. Khomenko, Irina Yu. Kvyatkovskaya,
Elizaveta A. Barabanova, and Yulia A. Veselova[✉]

Astrakhan State Technical University, Astrakhan, Russia
{t_v_khomenko, veselova-yulia}@mail.ru,
kvyatkovskaya.irina@gmail.com,
elizavetaalexb@yandex.ru

Abstract. At present, information automated systems for finding technical solutions contain a module that allows calculating the values of requirements for synthesized models of the principle of operation to the design object, in an automatic mode. Traditionally, the values of these requirements are presented in the form of quantitative estimates. To extend the capabilities of information automated systems, it is proposed to use requirements whose values are represented as a linguistic variable that is considered given if all elements of the tuple are defined, including the name of the linguistic variable. This problem is complicated by the fact that for different types of representation of input quantities (qualitative - quantitative) as a result of the application of arithmetic and logical operations, the functions of the resulting fuzzy sets can be obtained, which are difficult to identify. The paper proposes a technique that allows the values of the membership function to be associated with their semantic meaning for the representation of the linguistic variable.

To solve this problem, the neural network with adaptive resonance feature is used: to retain plasticity when memorizing new images, and at the same time to prevent the modification of old memory. It is shown that parallel computations of a neural network occur faster and do not increase with the increase in the number of effects models in the chain of the model of the operation principle of the design object.

The developed information automated search system for technical solutions covering the tasks of calculating requirements, both with clear and linguistic values, is applied at the stage of search design of technical objects. The tasks that are considered at this stage relate to the tasks of TSIP (the Theory of solving inventive problems). The use of an automated system for searching technical solutions is aimed at supporting scientists and inventors to quickly find solutions to creative problems in the design of technical objects.

Keywords: Design object · Action principle model · Calculation of requirements values · Qualitative estimates · Linguistic variable · Neural networks · Adaptive resonance

© Springer International Publishing AG 2017
A. Kravets et al. (Eds.): CIT&DS 2017, CCIS 754, pp. 551–561, 2017.
DOI: 10.1007/978-3-319-65551-2_40

1 Introduction

One of the designing technical objects main tasks is the task of outstripping development. To solve this problem at the initial stages of the design in the field of instrument engineering, various methods of TSIP [1], which are the theoretical basis of information automated systems for technical objects designing and constructing [2]. Despite the diversity in the presentation of such systems theoretical aspects of functioning, they all use physical effects database.

The structure composed by the certain rule of the j joint and combined physical effects $F^k := \left(q_j^k \right)$, that provide the transformation of the given input action into output $Y_{\text{MPA}k} = F^k(X_{\text{MPA}k})$, is the model of the $\text{MPA}^k := F^k$ operating principle of the design object and is considered as its technical solution [3].

Currently, the physical effects database contains more than two thousand effects. Such volume of the physical effects database allows automated systems of searching design, with preliminary effect modeling, to synthesize a large enough number of technical solutions different variants of the various types of converters. The models of effects are the models $qkj := <x_j, y_j, K_j>$, showing the transformations K_j, with which the physical effects on the objects X_j lead to the appearance of some actions Y_j (Fig. 1).

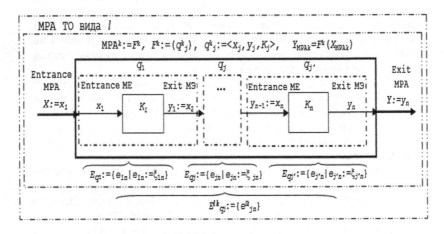

Fig. 1. Model of the design object operating principle

The wrong choice of a technical solution, like the best of the many synthesized solutions and its subsequent constructive implementation, will lead to huge financial losses. To exclude such errors, in modern automated systems of search design, besides forming a set of requirements, according to which the decision is made, the required values are set. If there's no data about operational characteristics of existing technical objects in the reference literature, it is not always possible to specify the values of the requirements for technical solutions in the form of an accurate quantitative assessment.

This situation appears at the initial stages of the technical objects design, where the selection of technical solutions is reduced to the choice of the model and the experts have only one of the possibilities - a verbal description of the requirements for technical solutions.

To extend the potential of automated systems of search design, it is proposed in [4, 5] to use the mathematical apparatus of fuzzy sets and fuzzy logic. The methods of this mathematical apparatus allow performing operations on the values of the requirements specified by experts both in the form of quantitative and in the form of a qualitative assessment, with the representing it as linguistic (fuzzy) variables. In [5, 6], methods for calculating the values of requirements for a technical solution under conditions of different types (clear, fuzzy) of input values are considered. However, as a result of calculating the values of the requirements for the technical solution, the functions of the resulting fuzzy sets can be obtained, for which it is difficult to identify the linguistic variable. The functional structure of informational automated systems of searching design is such that in the procedure of ranking design object's models of the operating principle in automatic mode, fuzzy sets and membership functions are used and represent the linguistic (fuzzy) variable stored in the knowledge base of the automated system. For analysis of technical solutions options and their further processing, the linguistic variable L is used, which is recorded in the passport of the design object's model of the operating principle as the value of the requirement for a technical solution. Therefore, the theoretical basis for identifying the linguistic variable by the output fuzzy set and the corresponding membership function is necessary.

2 Problem Statement

Suppose:

(1) set of variants MPA^k is a design object's models of the operating principle $(k = \overline{1,k'})$, synthesized using an information automated system for searching design for a certain type of design object l ($l = \overline{1,l'}$);

(2) set $E_{q_j}^{lk} := \{e_{ij}^{lk}\}$ is a set of requirements for the design object inherent in technical objects of the form l;

(3) set of values $\zeta := \{\xi_{ij}^{lk}\}$ (quantitative and/or qualitative) of the requirements $e_i^{lk}(i = \overline{1,i'})$ for j model of the q_j ($j = \overline{1,j'}$) effects included in the MPA^k structure over which the calculation operations are performed according to the MPA^k structure;

(4) $\tilde{A}_{ij}^{lk}$ is a set of values and $\mu_{\tilde{A}_{ij}^{lk}}(x)$ are membership functions representing values ξ_{ij}^{lk}, that are presented as linguistic value L_{ij}^{lk};

(5) $\tilde{A}_i^{lk}$ ($k = \overline{1,k'}$) is a fuzzy set obtained as a result of operations on input fuzzy sets $\tilde{A}_{ij}^{lk}$, with corresponding membership function $\mu_{\tilde{A}_i^{lk}}(x)$, representing value ξ_i^{lk} of the requirement i to k model of operating principle MPA^k of the design object l.

Develop: M – rule that allows $\mu_{\tilde{A}_i^{lk}}(x)$ each value to put in correspondence its semantic value $\xi_{ij}^{lk} \in \zeta$, represented by a linguistic variable L_i^{lk}:

$$\mu_{\tilde{A}_i^{lk}}(x) \xrightarrow{M} L_i^{lk} := \left\langle N_i^{lk}, T, G, X_i^{lk}, M \right\rangle.$$

3   Methodology

In [7] methods for presenting verbal evaluation requirements e_i to model j of effect q_j as a linguistic variable L_{ij}^{lk} with defining all the elements of a tuple $\left\langle N_{ij}^{lk}, T, G, X_{ij}^{lk}, M \right\rangle$ are proposed. To determine values ξ_i^{lk} of requirements e_i to model k of operating principle MPA^k of design object l, according to [8] calculating operations are done on values ξ_{ij}^{lk} of requirements e_{ij}^{lk} to models q_j of effects k of a model operating principle MPA^k of design object l.

Suppose: $t_n \in T$ $(n = \overline{1, n'})$ is a base term, such that $X = [X_{\min}; X_{\max}]$:

$$\mu_{\tilde{A}_{t_n}} : t_n \rightarrow x_n, \tag{1}$$

where:

$$\tilde{A}_{t_n} = \{(x_n / \mu(x_n))\} \text{is a fuzzy set}, x_n \in X;$$

$h_{\hbar}^I \in T$ $(\hbar = \overline{1, \hbar'})$ is a modifier of the I kind, for instance, with $m = 1$ – modifier $h_1^I := \text{"not"}$.

Then, considering (1) we have $X = [X_{\min}; X_{\max}]$:

$$\mu_{\tilde{A}_{t_n h_{\hbar}^I}} : t_n h_{\hbar}^I \rightarrow x_m, \tag{2}$$

where:

$$\tilde{A}_{t_n h_{\hbar}^I} = \left\{ \left(x_m / \mu_{\tilde{A}_{t_n h_{\hbar}^I}}(x_m) \right) \right\} \text{ is a fuzzy set}, x_m \in X \ (m = \overline{1, m'}), t_n h_{\hbar}^I \in T \text{ is a}$$ compound term considered as name $N := \text{"}t_n h_{\hbar}^I\text{"}$ of the linguistic variable L_{ij}^{lk}, describing the value ξ_{ij}^{lk} of the requirement e_i to model j of effect q.

Wherein,

$$t_n \xrightarrow{G(t_n; h_{\hbar}^I)} t_n h_{\hbar}^I. \tag{3}$$

Suppose $h_{\varkappa}^{II} \in T$ $(\varkappa = \overline{1, \varkappa'})$ is a modifier of the II kind, for instance, with $\varkappa = 1$ – modifier $h_1^{II} := \text{"increase in"}$.

Then, taking into consideration (1), (2) we have on $X = [X_{\min}; X_{\max}]$:

$$\mu_{\tilde{A}_{t_n h_{\hbar}^I h_{\varkappa}^{II}}} : t_n h_{\hbar}^I h_{\varkappa}^{II} \rightarrow x_c, \tag{4}$$

where:

$$\tilde{A}_{t_n h_{\hbar}^I h_{\kappa}^{II}} = \left\{ \left(x_c / \mu_{\tilde{A}_{t_n h_{\hbar}^I h_{\kappa}^{II}}}(x_c) \right) \right\} \text{ is a fuzzy set, } x_c \in X \ (c = \overline{1, c'}),$$

$t_n h_{\hbar}^I h_{\kappa}^{II} \in T$ – compound term that is considered as a name $N := {}''t_n h_{\hbar}^I h_{\kappa}^{II}{}''$ of linguistic variable L_i^{lk}, describing value ξ_i^{lk} of requirement e_i to model k of operating principle MPA^k of design object l.

Wherein,

$$t_n h_{\hbar}^I \xrightarrow{G(h_{\hbar}^I ; h_{\kappa}^{II})} t_n h_{\kappa}^{II}, \tag{5}$$

then, taking into consideration (3), (5) we have:

$$t_n \xrightarrow{G(t_n ; h_{\hbar}^I ; h_{\kappa}^{II})} t_n h_{\hbar}^I h_{\kappa}^{II}, \text{ where} \tag{6}$$

the following rules are formulated.

T – basic term of the linguistic variable N, where each one's domain is the set X: modifier plays the role of generating a large set of values of a linguistic variable L_i^{lk} from a small set of base terms $t_n \in T$. Therefore: modifier $h_{\hbar}^I \in T$ may be considered as a non-linier operator transforming the fuzzy set $\tilde{A}_{t_n}$ into the fuzzy set $\tilde{A}_{t_n h_{\hbar}^I}$, representing the value ξ_{ij}^{lk}, transforming the value of corresponding terms; modifier $h_{\kappa}^{II} \in T$ may be considered as a non-linier operator transforming the fuzzy set $\tilde{A}_{t_n h_{\hbar}^I}$ into the fuzzy set $\tilde{A}_{t_n h_{\hbar}^I h_{\kappa}^{II}}$, representing the value ξ_i^{lk}, transforming the value of corresponding terms. The construction of membership functions is proposed to be performed based on the membership functions of the basic terms according to certain rules, using a standard set of mathematical descriptions of the base term membership functions. If necessary, the parameters of the membership function are corrected. The coefficients are calculated by the approximation methods of the membership function values [9].

X is a universal set with base variable x: as a result of executing binary operations, according to the rules of fuzzy arithmetic, the interval X of setting the values ξ_i^{lk} of the requirement e_i to the model k of operating principle MPA^k of the design project l changes. To determine which of the base terms $t_n \in T$ in combination with modifiers $h_{\hbar}^I, h_{\kappa}^{II} \in T$ corresponding to the output fuzzy set, it's necessary to consider them at the same intervals. Dividing each element from X by the value of the interval, all values from X will be mapped onto the interval [0, 1], regardless of how many effect models q_j participate in forming of a given MPA^k of the design object l.

G is a syntax rule defined in the form of a context-free grammar that generates the terms of the set T: during the compound term formalizing, the standard precedence rules that apply to the reorganization of Boolean expressions are applied.

Parentheses are used to change the order of precedence. The resulting formalized expressions, unlike Boolean ones, cannot be simplified, since they do not have the Boolean algebra properties: $a \cdot \bar{a} = 0$, $a \vee \bar{a} = 1$, except: $\tilde{a} = 0$ $(\tilde{a} = 1)$, where $\tilde{a} = \mu_{\tilde{A}}(x)$. For the same reason, the resulting compound term formalizations are not represented in the disjunctive (conjunctive) normal form with the help of miniterms (maxiterms), and therefore the idea of representing the action of modifiers on the semantics of the basic terms in the form of operations over the corresponding fuzzy sets is implemented.

The procedure of forming new terms $G(T(\xi_i))$ is performed to assess the requirements for a technical object in the early stages of design, due to the lack of basic terms and high uncertainty of requirements. Thereby the base B is formed. It contains fuzzy sets $\tilde{A}^{lk}$, $\tilde{A}_i^{lk}$, $\tilde{A}_{ij}^{lk}$ and membership functions $\mu_{\tilde{A}^{lk}}(x)$, $\mu_{\tilde{A}_i^{lk}}(x)$, $\mu_{\tilde{A}_{ij}^{lk}}(x)$, representing the values ζ, representing the values, including the reference values, of the requirements E to the models of the operating principle MPA^k of the design objects, where the values ξ_{ij}^{lk}, $\xi_i^{lk} \in \zeta$ are represented as a linguistic variable L_{ij}^{lk} (L_i^{lk}).

To define the name $N_i^{lk} \in \langle N_i^{lk}, T_i^{lk}, G_i^{lk}, X_i^{lk}, M_i^{lk} \rangle$ of the linguistic variable L_i^{lk} we use the feature of neural networks with adaptive resonance: to retain plasticity while memorizing new images, and at the same time to prevent the modification of old memory [10].

A neural network, having an internal detector of novelty, identifies the presented image with a simultaneous refinement modification of the neuron synoptic weights performing the identification. There is an adaptive resonance in the network:

(a) if it's beyond a certain threshold level, the novelty test is considered successful and the image is perceived by the network as new;
(b) if it's within a certain threshold level, the identification test is considered successful and the image is perceived by the network as identified, while the degree of equivalence of the presented image with the image contained in memory is the highest.

The degree of equivalence of the presented image with the image is calculated by the following formula:

$$\mu(\tilde{A}_1, \tilde{A}_2) = v(\tilde{A}_1, \tilde{A}_2) \text{ and } v(\tilde{A}_2, \tilde{A}_1) \tag{7}$$

According to (7), fuzzy sets degree of equivalence is a conjunction of the implication of these fuzzy sets, where each implication represents the degree of nesting of one fuzzy set in another:

$$\mu_{\tilde{A}_1}(x) \rightarrow \mu_{\tilde{A}_2}(x) = 1 \text{ and } \left(1 - \mu_{\tilde{A}_1}(x) + \mu_{\tilde{A}_2}(x)\right) \tag{8}$$

A neural network that implements formula (8) of the second stage may be represented as a network of the following structure (Fig. 2):

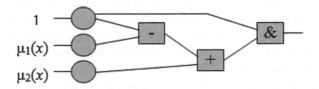

Fig. 2. A neural network that implements implication

The implication as the degree of nesting of fuzzy sets may be considered as a conjunction of implication for all arguments x_n of the indicator vector $\mu_{\tilde{A}^{lk}}(x_n)$, $\mu_{\tilde{A}_i^{lk}}(x_n)$, and interpreted as follows: for every first input, «1» is supplied, for every second - the degree of belonging of the current values fuzzy set $\tilde{A}_i^{lk}$, for every third - the degree of belonging $\mu_{\tilde{A}_i^{lk}}(x_n)$ of the reference value fuzzy set $\tilde{A}^{lk}$. The result is the degree of nesting of the fuzzy set $\tilde{A}_i^{lk}$ in $\tilde{A}^{lk}$. This interpretation may be represented as a network of a certain structure (Fig. 3).

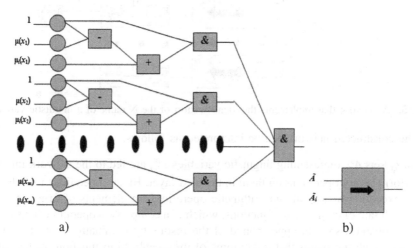

a)   b)

Fig. 3. (a) A network that calculates fuzzy sets degree of nesting; (b) A network that calculates fuzzy sets degree of nesting, presented as a single unit

To calculate the degree of equivalence, fuzzy sets $\tilde{A}^{lk}$ and $\tilde{A}_i^{lk}$ fuzzy sets are distributed and fed into the next layer - layer of implication, after which (in the next layer) the conjunction of the calculated implications $(\tilde{A}^{lk}; \tilde{A}_i^{lk})$ and $(\tilde{A}_i^{lk}; \tilde{A}^{lk})$ are found. A neural network that implements formula (7) may be represented as a network (Fig. 4).

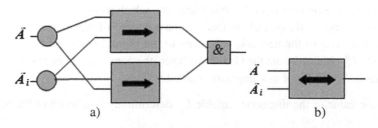

a)   b)

Fig. 4. (a) A network that calculates fuzzy sets degree of equivalence; (b) A network that calculates fuzzy sets degree of equivalence, presented as a single unit

According to the above, the following rule is proposed.

M is a semantic rule that allows each value $\mu_{\tilde{A}_i^{lk}}(x)$ to put in correspondence its semantic value $\xi_{ij}^{lk} \in \zeta$, represented by a linguistic variable L_i^{lk}.

The general network that implements the semantic rule M is shown in Fig. 5.

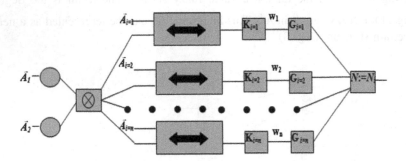

Fig. 5. A network that implements the identification of the N name of a linguistic variable

The constructed network can be interpreted as follows:

1. Fuzzy sets $\tilde{A}_{ij}^{lk}$, representing linguistic variables L_{ij}^{lk}, are fed to the network inputs to perform binary operations on them in the next layer. Binary operations include both the execution of logical and arithmetic operations on elements of fuzzy sets, and convolution of membership functions, which is a comparison operation. This allows us to obtain a smooth upper bound of the results by eliminating from the output fuzzy set all the points that are minima of the membership function of this set.
2. In the «equivalence» block, input №1 is the result of binary operations which is the fuzzy set $\tilde{A}^{lk}$, input №2 of the same block from database B is fuzzy sets of the linguistic variables L_i^{lk} for calculating the degree of their equivalence in the next layer.
3. The results of the calculation (the degree of equivalence) go into the next layer of neurons, similar to the Kohonen neurons: the neuron that receives the maximum value returns the value "1", the rest of the neurons return the value "0".
4. The output data goes into the next layer of neurons similar to Grossberg's neurons, where the weighted sums of the inputs are calculated: only one of the Grossberg layer neurons that receives the value "1" on the input returns the weight connecting it with the neuron of the Kohonen layer; the other neurons, which received the value "0", return "0". This weight is the ordinal number s of the name N_i^{lk} of the linguistic variable L_i^{lk}.
5. In the last layer of the network, according to the ordinal number s of the linguistic variable L_i^{lk} obtained from the Grossberg layer, the name N_s will be taken to identify the name $N_i^{lk} := N_s$ of this linguistic variable.

N is the name of the linguistic variable L_i^{lk} determining as a result of the following steps:

- Performing operations on fuzzy sets $\tilde{A}_{ij}^{lk}$, representing linguistic variables L_i^{lk}, the result of which is a fuzzy set $\tilde{A}_i^{lk}$.

- Performing implication on fuzzy set $\tilde{A}_i^{lk}$ which is the output linguistic variable L_i^{lk} with the name N, that is identified and fuzzy set $\tilde{A}^{lk}$ which is the linguistic variable L^{lk} with the name $N_s \in B$ from database ($s = \overline{1, s'}$).
- Calculating the degree of equivalence v of the fuzzy sets $\tilde{A}_i^{lk}$ which is the linguistic variable L_i^{lk} and $\tilde{A}^{lk}$ which is the linguistic variable $L^{lk} \in B$ from database.
- Assignment: $N_i^{lk} := N_s \leftrightarrow v(\tilde{A}^{lk}, \tilde{A}_i^{lk}) - \max$.

4 Experiments and Results

As an alternative to the use of neural networks, algorithms that lead to the same result may be considered [10, 11]. However, the operations performed in one layer of the neural network are performed in parallel, and the operations implemented by the algorithms are performed sequentially. The speed of execution of binary operations depends on the hardware component of the computer, but since the fastest arithmetic operation is addition, then the elementary unit of calculation time t is the time of the addition operation.

Taking into consideration that the structure of the operating principle model MPA^k of the design object l contains an arbitrary j number of models of q_j effects (the power of MPA^k), then binary operations and identification will be performed as many times as the power of MPA^k. The results of the computational experiment on fuzzy sets of linguistic variables representing the values of the requirements specified in qualitative form are shown in the Table 1.

Table 1. Time comparison from the computational experiment

Operations	Neural network computation time				Algorithm computation time			
	Power of MPA^k							
	1	5	10	20	1	5	10	20
«+»	t				t			
«−»	2t				2t			
«*»	2t				2t			
«>» («&»)	3t				3t			
«→»		9t	9t	9t		33t	63t	123t
«↔»		12t	12t	12t		69t	129t	249t
identification		120t	120t	120t		1177t	2077t	3877t

Obviously, parallel computations of the neural network occur faster and do not increase with the increase of the MPA^k power.

Let's consider the use of the semantic rule M to describe the values of the requirements for the effect model (EM) as a linguistic variable on the example:

EM is the «*Thermomagnetic effect*»,
requirement: e_6 – «*price*».

Suppose:

T is a base term whose alphabet contains a non-empty set of base terms symbols and symbols of modifiers of the I and II kind;

G is a syntax rule defined in the form of a context-free grammar that generates terms of the set T;

$X_6 = [5; 35]$ is a universal set, then on $X_6 = [5; 35]$ we find:

$$\tilde{A}_{t_{1(\textit{низкая})}} = \{(10/1); (15/0{,}98); (17/0{,}05); (20/0{,}01)\};$$

$$\tilde{A}_{t_{2(\textit{средняя})}} = \{(15/0{,}04); (18/0{,}91); (23/0{,}5); (26/0{,}015)\};$$

$$\tilde{A}_{t_{3(\textit{высокая})}} = \{(22/0{,}05); (25/0{,}86); (27/0{,}99); (30/1)\}.$$

Applying the syntax rule we have:

$$G(T(e_{6j}^{lk})) := MORE(\tilde{A}_{t_2}^{lk}) \wedge LESS(\tilde{A}_{t_3}^{lk}).$$

Using the usual precedence rules (valid for the conversion of Boolean expressions) and parentheses (to change the order of precedence), we get:

$$\tilde{A}_j^{lk} = (\tilde{A}_{t_2}^{lk} \mathbin{\tilde{+}} k) \wedge (\tilde{A}_{t_3}^{lk} \mathbin{\tilde{-}} k)$$

Computing the value of the compound term we get:

$$\tilde{A}_{t_n h_\hbar}^{lk} = \{(20/0{,}05); (25/0{,}99); (28/0{,}015)\},$$

the graphical interpretation of which is shown in the Fig. 6.

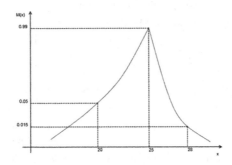

Fig. 6. Graphical interpretation of the fuzzy set membership function.

Applying semantic rule M to the output set $\tilde{A}_{t_n h_\hbar}^{lk}$ with the membership function $\mu_{\tilde{A}_{t_n h_\hbar}^{lk}}(x_c)$, we have:

$$N_{6j}^{lk} = \{\text{more than average, but less than high}\}.$$

5   Conclusion

Thus, having defined all the elements N, T, G, X, M, we can characterize the value of the EM requirement given in the form of a linguistic variable. The received name N_{ij}^{lk} of the linguistic variable L_{ij}^{lk} is registered in the passport of the EM.

The fuzzy set $\tilde{A}_{t_n h_h} = \{(x_m/\mu(x_m))\}$ obtained as a result of the execution of the semantic rule M, describing the value of the EM requirement e_{ij}^{lk} specified in the linguistic form is registered in the database B of the automated system of search design. The use of such system allows to combine different ways of representing requirements values to a design object and apply an automated system to solve creative problems in the early stages of designing technical objects.

References

1. Gin, A.A., Kudryavtsev, A.V., Bubentsov, V.Y., Seredinsky, A.: Theory of Inventive Problem Solving, 129 p. Vita-Press, Moscow (2012)
2. Khomenko, T.V., Petrova, I.Y., Lezhnina, Y.A.: Methodology of Choosing the Optimal Technical Solutions at the Stage of Conceptual Design: Monograph, 176 p. GAOU AS of the HPE, Astrakhan Civil Engineering Institute, Astrakhan (2014)
3. Khomenko, T.V.: Technique of constructing a knowledge space for methods of designing technical systems. Izv. Volgogr. State Tech. Univ. 6(20), 108–113 (2014)
4. Shikulskaya, O.M., Shikulskiy, M.I.: Energy-information modeling of the flat membrane on the fractal approach basis. J. Phys: Conf. Ser. 803(1), 145–157 (2017)
5. Lezhnina, Y., Khomenko, T., Zaripova, V.: Topological structure for building ontology of energy-information method circuits. In: Kravets, A., Shcherbakov, M., Kultsova, M., Iijima, T. (eds.) JCKBSE 2014. CCIS, vol. 466, pp. 185–194. Springer, Cham (2014). doi:10.1007/978-3-319-11854-3_17
6. Petrova, I.Y., Puchkova, A.A., Zaripova, V.M.: Search automation of the generalized method of device operational characteristics improvement. J. Phys: Conf. Ser. 803(1), 115–127 (2017)
7. Murygin, M.A.: Definition and application of the semantic rule in describing the values of operational characteristics of physic technical effects in the form of a linguistic variable. J. Sci. Publ. Post-Grad. Stud. Doc. Stud. (11), 12–16 (2008)
8. Murygin, M.A.: Calculation of operational characteristics of the physical principle of action in the energy-information model of circuits with input values specified by clear/fuzzy values. J. Sci. Publ. Post-Grad. Stud. Doc. Stud. (11), 16–20 (2008)
9. Batyrshin, I.Z., Nedosekin, A.O., Stetsko, A.A., Tarasov, V.B., Yazenin, A.V., Yarushkina, N.G.: Fuzzy Hybrid Systems: Theory and Practice, 208 p. FIZMATLIT, Moscow (2007)
10. Protalinskiy, O.M., Khomenko, T.V., Grigoriev, O.V.: Technical solutions for conceptual design search automation. World Appl. Sci. J. 24(24), 138–144 (2013)
11. Barabanova, E.A., Maltseva, N.S., Barabanov, I.O.: Algorithm for parallel data processing in optical networks. Sci. Bull. Novosib. State Tech. Univ. 56(3), 88–95 (2014)

Optimization and Parallelization of CAE Software Stress-Strain Solver for Heterogeneous Computing Hardware

Victor Getmanskiy, Andrey E. Andreev$^{(\boxtimes)}$, Sergey Alekseev,
Alexander S. Gorobtsov, Vitaly Egunov, and Egor Kharkov

Volgograd State Technical University, Volgograd, Russia
victor.getmanskiy@gmail.com, andan2005@yandex.ru,
{2serales96,vegunov}@mail.ru, vm@vstu.ru,
kharkov.e.s@gmail.com

Abstract. The efficient code development for multibody simulation is considered. The solver is developed for dynamic stress-strain simulation of bodies in complex mechanisms. The mathematical formulation for a stress-strain solver based on discrete elements method is presented. Main aspects of the computational algorithm are considered to reveal possibilities to increase performance. The computational algorithm has limitations of scalability and maximal speedup in a parallel implementation. Further optimization is performed using different sets of vector instructions such as SSE, AVX, AVX2, FMA, IMCI for Intel Xeon Phi coprocessors (KNC) and AVX512 for 2nd generation Intel Xeon Phi processors (KNL). Some advanced techniques are developed and explained for packing matrix and vector data into 512-bit SIMD registers. For parallel implementation, OpenMP is used. For heterogeneous computing hardware, such as GPU and FGA, OpenCL is considered as universal and open standard. The vectorized parallel solver version is tested on Intel Xeon E5, MIC KNC and KNL architectures. OpenCL version is tested on NVIDIA Tesla architecture. Speedup results are achieved and compared with compiler autovectorization feature. Perspectives of future research are summarized and formulated in conclusion.

Keywords: Code optimization · Vectorization · Vector registers · Dynamic stress-strain state · MIC · KNL · SIMD · OpenCL · Heterogeneous computing

1 Introduction

Traditionally quasistatic approaches of the finite-element method (FEM) are used to the calculation of dynamic stresses. The alternative method of the discrete elements (DEM) [1] which doesn't require the solution of a linear equation system and uses an orthogonal grid allows to analyze tension in the speaker and can be effectively vectorized and parallelized when implementing in software.

© Springer International Publishing AG 2017
A. Kravets et al. (Eds.): CIT&DS 2017, CCIS 754, pp. 562–574, 2017.
DOI: 10.1007/978-3-319-65551-2_41

The developed solver module is a part of CAE (computer-aided engineering) software FRUND [2] based on multibody dynamics and multiphysics in which the connected tasks of the analysis of dynamics of construction and physical processes of stress-strain and a heat transfer in its separate details are simulated.

Currently, to perform computing-intensive tasks and simulations with large models there are available various computing architectures, including powerful multicore CPUs, many-core architectures like Intel Many Integrated Cores (MIC) and graphics accelerators (GPU) that are often present in a common heterogeneous environment. There is also a growing interest in computing on FPGA. Researches show the effectiveness of MIC for solving large-scale simulation tasks but in the case of the careful code, optimization using vectorization [3–5]. The same can be said about the second-generation MIC (known as Knights Landing or KNL), which allow in some cases to outperform powerful CPU, but also only with the code optimization [6]. As for graphics co-processors, they also demonstrate high performance in large-scale simulation but require careful attention to reducing the intensity of exchange with the host and minimizing branching in algorithms [7, 8]. For heterogeneous environments, the most preferred technique of using co-processors (at least GPU and FPGA) is probably OpenCL.

The previous researches of authors showed a possibility of accelerating stress-stain solver and similar computations due to vectorization using different vector registers and such instruction sets as SSE, AVX, AVX2 with FMA for Intel CPUs and IMCI (Initial Many-Core Instructions) for 512-bit vector registers of MIC co-processors Xeon Phi (known as Knights Corner or KNC) [9, 10]. In the present research, the results are received for new second generation Intel Xeon Phi processors KNL also with the help of a set of 512-bit registers and AVX-512 instruction set.

2 Discrete Elements Method for Stress-Strain Solver

2.1 Deformable Body Representation and Stress Calculation

Quasi-static approach lacks in the case of dynamic loads. In proposed method deformable body is approximated by rigid discrete elements. The computational domain is regular orthogonal mesh based on CAD geometry of the part. Each mesh node is a discrete element with 6 degrees of freedoms. Each rigid element is connected to adjacent elements by a flexible joint. Regular discrete elements structure greatly simplifies the construction of differential equation system in natural coordinates. The inertia matrix is diagonal and all elements are described by similar ordinary differential equations to within a number of links to adjacent elements. Flexible body has a rigid analog in the multibody model which is called reference body. The system of equations for the flexible body has the following form in the coordinate system of reference body:

$$\mathbf{M}^s\ddot{\mathbf{y}} = \mathbf{q}(\dot{\mathbf{y}}, \mathbf{y}, t) - \mathbf{M}^s\hat{\mathbf{a}}(t) + \mathbf{s}(\dot{\mathbf{y}}, \mathbf{y}), \tag{1}$$

where **y** is a vector of discrete elements coordinates, $\mathbf{M}^s$ is a matrix of inertia for a set of discrete elements, $\hat{\mathbf{a}}$ is a vector constructed of reference body acceleration vector components, $\mathbf{s}(\dot{\mathbf{y}}, \mathbf{y})$ is a stabilizing component. Reference body acceleration is obtained from the multibody model. The function $\mathbf{q}(\dot{\mathbf{y}}, \mathbf{y}, t)$ describes the forces between rigid elements. Stress values are computed from the values of the forces on each iteration. The random perturbing effect makes flexible body model unstable. The additional stabilizing component $\mathbf{s}(\dot{\mathbf{y}}, \mathbf{y})$ is introduced in (1) to constrain the position of discrete elements.

Right-hand sides of the equation are completed with inertia forces taking into account motion of the reference body in the multibody model.

The flexible body is connected to multibody model with joints. To complete the equation it is necessary to add reaction forces in flexible joints to a subset of (1) corresponded to solid elements on contact surfaces. There are two kinds of joints shown in Fig. 1: spring-damper force $f_1 = f$ and stiff joint with reaction force $\mathbf{f}_2 = (\mathbf{r}_x, \mathbf{r}_y, \mathbf{r}_z)$. The equation of motion for boundary discrete element has the following form in case of uniform distribution of reaction force along boundary:

$$\mathbf{M}_i^s \ddot{\mathbf{y}}_i = \mathbf{f}(t)/|F| + \mathbf{q}_i(\dot{\mathbf{y}}, \mathbf{y}, t) - \mathbf{M}_i^s \mathbf{a}_i(t) + \mathbf{s}_i(\dot{\mathbf{y}}, \mathbf{y}), i \in F, \tag{2}$$

where F is a set of node indices of the boundary with applied reaction **f**. So the reference body data obtained from multibody solver is enough to calculate forces of inertia and reactions in joints.

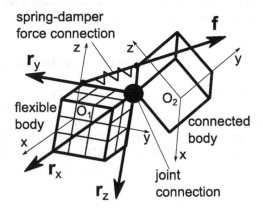

Fig. 1. Flexible body with rigid body connection

Equation (1) is solved using 4-th order Runge-Kutta method (RK4). The data of reference body is transferred to stress solver on sync time steps. Numerical integration time steps of multibody solver (Δt_{main}) and stress solver (Δt_{sub}) are different in general case. For simplification, it is posed that time steps are divisible. If $\Delta t_{sub} < \Delta t_{main,}$ then

$\Delta t_{main} = N \cdot \Delta t_{sub}$, where N is an integer multiplier. There is general time counter with minimal time step $\Delta t = \min(\Delta t_{sub}, \Delta t_{main})$ and coupling time counter with maximal time step $\Delta t_{upd} = \max(\Delta t_{sub}, \Delta t_{main})$. Solver algorithm is presented below.

$t = 0$, $t_{sub} = 0$, $t_{main} = 0$, $\Delta t = \min(\Delta t_{sub}, \Delta t_{main})$, $\Delta t_{upd} = \max(\Delta t_{sub}, \Delta t_{main})$
While $t < T$
    If $t = t_{main}$ Then
        MBS iteration solving for current time t
        $t_{main} = t_{main} + \Delta t_{main}$
    If $t = t_{upd}$ Then
        Right hand-side update for stress-strain solver
        $t_{upd} = t_{upd} + \Delta t_{upd}$
    If $t = t_{sub}$ Then
        Stress-strain solver iteration for time t_{sub}
        $t_{sub} = t_{sub} + \Delta t_{sub}$
    Writing simulation results
    $t = t + \Delta t$

Each iteration of stress solver gives positions of discrete elements. They are used to obtain displacements. Stresses in deformable body in each discrete element can be calculated using formula

$$
\begin{bmatrix} \sigma_{11} \\ \sigma_{22} \\ \sigma_{33} \\ \sigma_{23} \\ \sigma_{13} \\ \sigma_{12} \end{bmatrix} = \begin{bmatrix} \psi & \lambda & \lambda & 0 & 0 & 0 \\ \lambda & \psi & \lambda & 0 & 0 & 0 \\ \lambda & \lambda & \psi & 0 & 0 & 0 \\ 0 & 0 & 0 & \mu & 0 & 0 \\ 0 & 0 & 0 & 0 & \mu & 0 \\ 0 & 0 & 0 & 0 & 0 & \mu \end{bmatrix} \begin{bmatrix} \varepsilon_{11} \\ \varepsilon_{22} \\ \varepsilon_{33} \\ 2\varepsilon_{23} \\ 2\varepsilon_{13} \\ 2\varepsilon_{12} \end{bmatrix}, \tag{3}
$$

where σ_{ij} are stress tensor components, ε_{ij} are strain tensor components, $\psi = \lambda + 2\mu$, $\lambda = E \cdot v/(1 - v^2)$, $\mu = E/(2 \cdot (1 + v))$, E is an elasticity modulus. Equivalent tensile stresses are calculated using von Mises criterion:

$$
\sigma = \sqrt{0.5 \sum_{i=1}^{2} \sum_{j=i+1}^{3} \left((\sigma_{ii} - \sigma_{jj})^2 + 6\sigma_{ij}^2 \right)}, \tag{4}
$$

Formula (4) determines stresses in each element. We can construct color map representation of stress field. An example of a comparative study of stresses in process of plate deformation is shown in Figs. 2 and 3 (It should me mentioned that left and right images have a different resolution, not because of calculation results, but due to different visualizers used).

Fig. 2. DEM (left) and FEM (right) comparison of normal stresses in deformed plate (Color figure online)

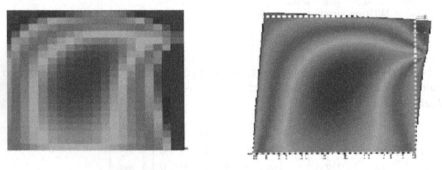

Fig. 3. DEM (left) and FEM (right) comparison of tangent stresses in deformed plate (Color figure online)

2.2 Coordinate Transformation and Matrix-Vector Operations

Right-hand sides of Eq. (1) are the most computationally expensive. They are calculated in several steps. Each calculation is a force of the pair of coupled discrete elements. At first, the rotation matrix of the first element in the pair is calculated to transform all coordinates of the first element to the coordinate system of reference body:

$$\mathbf{A}_{21} = \mathbf{A}_{02}^{\mathrm{T}} \mathbf{A}_{01},$$

where the first digit in the index is a number of the coordinate systems which the transformation is performed to. The second digit is the number of current coordinate system. The main computation is as follows:

$$\mathbf{d}_{s1}^{(1)} = \mathbf{C}_1^{(1)} - \mathbf{A}_{21}^{\mathrm{T}} \mathbf{C}_2^{(2)} - \mathbf{A}_{01}^{\mathrm{T}} (\mathbf{P}_2 - \mathbf{P}_2)^{(0)}, \tag{5}$$

$$\mathbf{d}_{vl}^{(1)} = \mathbf{W}_1^{(1)} \times \mathbf{C}_1^{(1)} - \mathbf{A}_{21}^{\mathrm{T}} \left(\mathbf{W}_2^{(2)} \times \mathbf{C}_2^{(2)} \right) - \mathbf{A}_{01}^{\mathrm{T}} (\mathbf{V}_2 - \mathbf{V}_1)^{(0)}, \tag{6}$$

$$\mathbf{d}_{sa}^{(0)} = \mathbf{R}_1^{(0)} - \mathbf{R}_2^{(0)}, \tag{7}$$

$$\mathbf{d}_{va}^{(0)} = \mathbf{W}_1^{(0)} - \mathbf{W}_2^{(0)}, \tag{8}$$

where $\mathbf{C}_1^{(1)}$ and $\mathbf{C}_2^{(2)}$ – vectors of connecting points in local coordinate systems of first and second bodies (number of body is upper index), $\mathbf{P}_1^{(0)}$ and $\mathbf{P}_2^{(0)}$ – coordinates of center of mass of elements in global coordinate system, $\mathbf{W}_1^{(1)}$ and $\mathbf{W}_2^{(2)}$ – angular velocities, $\mathbf{V}_1^{(0)}$ and $\mathbf{V}_2^{(0)}$ – linear velocities of elements.

Formula (5) computes linear shift of element which is a deformation in this position, formula (6) computes the change of linear velocity, formula (7) computes angular displacement, (8) – computes the change of angular velocity.

So all computational intensive operation is matrix-vector operations with a small number of elements. Such operations are well performed on SIMD architectures in the case of proper memory alignment and use of vector instructions.

3 Vectorization of Dynamic Stress-Strain Solver Using 512-Bits Vector Registers

Prior to vectorization the memory alignment is performed to reduce the time for data loading into cache and registers. Linear memory structure allows to use only 4 element per register. With double precision it is $4 * 64 = 256$ bits which is perfect for AVX registers, but only half-size of KNC and KNL 512-bit registers. The requirement of development of the advanced packing algorithm was revealed. Such procedure was deduced and it multiplies 2 matrices and vectors simultaneously. The registers state is presented at Fig. 4.

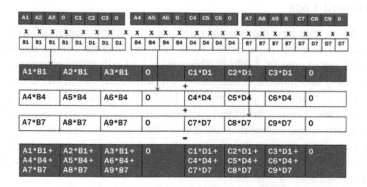

Fig. 4. 512-bits registers matrix multiplication scheme

One of the approaches uses blending intrinsic function is as follows:

```
    zmm08=_mm512_extload_ps(vec+   0,   _MM_UPCONV_PS_NONE,
_MM_BROADCAST_1X16, _MM_HINT_NONE);
    zmm09=_mm512_extload_ps(vec+   4,   _MM_UPCONV_PS_NONE,
_MM_BROADCAST_1X16, _MM_HINT_NONE);
    zmm10=_mm512_extload_ps(vec+   8,   _MM_UPCONV_PS_NONE,
_MM_BROADCAST_1X16, _MM_HINT_NONE);
    zmm11=_mm512_extload_ps(vec+   12,  _MM_UPCONV_PS_NONE,
_MM_BROADCAST_1X16, _MM_HINT_NONE);


    zmm06 = _mm512_mask_blend_ps(mask32_0, zmm08, zmm09);
    zmm07 = _mm512_mask_blend_ps(mask32_1, zmm10, zmm11);
    zmm04 = _mm512_mask_blend_ps(mask32_2, zmm06, zmm07);
```

Other approach uses tricky KNC-KNL instruction swizzle:

```
    zmm04 = _mm512_swizzle_ps(zmm08, _MM_SWIZ_REG_AAAA);
    zmm05 = _mm512_swizzle_ps(zmm08, _MM_SWIZ_REG_BBBB);
    zmm06 = _mm512_swizzle_ps(zmm08, _MM_SWIZ_REG_CCCC);
    zmm07 = _mm512_swizzle_ps(zmm08, _MM_SWIZ_REG_DDDD);
```

The second variant is more optimal because number of instructions is fewer as well as number of registers zmm04–zmm08. So it is less time consuming. This approach was implemented in the stress strain solver.

4   Comparative Study of Optimized and Parallel Algorithms Running on Intel Xeon E5, KNC, KNL, GPU

4.1   Vectorized Code

In modern C++ compilers, the optimizer performs autovectorization of code. It works well in simple cases but in advanced such, as ours, manual tuning can give better results which are shown in Table 1. Three stages of solver are analyzed: rotations, right-hand sides, and numerical integration. For rotations, the SIMD optimization of trigonometric calculations is performed by Intel SVML, an extension which speeds them up 2.5 times. The test problem is a stress-strain state of plate consisted of 4000 discrete elements (plate dimensions are 200×200 discrete elements).

There are comparative results of automatic vectorization (auto) and manual FMA vectorization (XEON FMA) in Table 1. Task was run on a single core of Intel Xeon E5 2650v3. Total speedup is 2 times.

There are the results of the problem run on a single core of Intel Xeon Phi 31s1p coprocessor (KNC) in Table 2. Manual vectorization using KNC 512-bit SIMD gives a total speedup of 1.63 times, but the right-hand sides speed up is much better even than on Xeon E5. The main bottleneck is slow trigonometric calculations in rotations. Column "KNC 512" shows run time with half-registers optimization (it means that we

Table 1. Solver run on single core of Intel Xeon E5 with FMA optimization

1 core	XEON auto, t, s	XEON FMA, t, s	Speedup
Rotations	1.69	1.69	1.00
Right hand sides	33.4	15.33	2.18
Integration	0.65	0.44	1.48
Total	35.74	17.46	2.05

use only half of a whole vector size). Column "KNC 512-2" shows run time with full-registers optimization. A single core of KNC is 28 times slower than a single core of Xeon E5 in our case.

Table 2. Solver run on single core of Intel Xeon PHI 31s1p with KNC optimization

1 core	KNC auto, t, s	KNC 512, t, s	KNC 512-2, t, s	Speedup
Rotations	337.22	339.11	338.25	1.00
Right hand sides	438.1	196.44	139.32	3.14
Integration	10.6	3.42	3.51	3.02
Total	785.92	538.97	481.08	1.63

Table 3. Solver run on single core of Intel Xeon Phi 7210p with KNL optimization

1 core	KNL auto, t, c	KNL FMA, t, c	KNL AVX-512, t, c	Speedup
Rotations	7.4	7.4	7.4	1.00
Right hand sides	131.9	61.7	52.9	2.49
Integration	3.77	0.76	0.61	6.18
Total	143.07	69.86	60.91	2.35

Processor Intel Xeon Phi 7210p with the KNL architecture uses all the previous instruction sets of x86-architecture and besides AVX-512. Table 3 shows the results of the computation time on an Intel KNL. Manual vectorization allows to achieve an overall speedup of 2.35 times. In the column "KNL AVX512" measurements with the optimization are given, using 512-bit registers, in the column "KNL FMA" results for the FMA-optimized code running on KNL are present. One KNL core loses Xeon E5 core in speed for 3.5 times for our task, which is much better than in the case of KNC.

4.2 Parallel Vectorized Code

The architecture of the considered processor unit contains vector registers in each core, so for MIC (many integrated cores) architecture, which includes both KNC and KNL, it makes sense to consider only the execution of parallel code. The code was parallelized using OpenMP standard with the use of loop parallelization.

First, let's consider performing a parallel calculation on the Xeon E5. The results are shown in Table 4. It follows that if we compare the result of executing of autovectorized code on a single core with the code vectorized by hand on 10 cores, the overall effect of this optimization is 11-times speedup of the whole calculation.

Table 4. Solver run on all cores of Intel Xeon E5

All cores/threads	XEON auto 10/1, t, c	XEON FMA 10/10, t, c	XEON, speedup
Rotations	1.69	1.11	1.52
Right hand sides	33.4	2	16.70
Integration	0.65	0.06	10.83
Total	35.74	3.17	11.27

The following result is obtained for KNC and is shown in Table 5.

Table 5. Solver run on all cores of Intel Xeon Phi (KNC)

All cores/threads	KNC auto 60/1, t, c	KNC 512 60/240, speedup	KNC 512 60/60, speedup
Rotations	337.22	21.8	18.01
Right hand sides	438.1	6.52	7.27
Integration	10.6	0.09	0.13
Total	785.92	28.41	25.41

From the presented results it follows that if we compare the result of autovectorized code run on a single core with the code, vectorized by hand on 60 cores, the overall effect of this optimization is 25.41-times speed-up of the whole calculation, but the absolute time result itself is significantly worse than on the Xeon E5. It is because of too slow (20 times slower) operations with the trigonometric functions in the calculation of rotations. Also, testing has shown that using multiple threads per core (hyperthreading) is not justified for this task and does not improve the overall result.

The most interesting result is the calculation on the latest computing architecture from Intel – KNL. Testing was conducted with a maximum load of cores with single and multiple threads. The configuration of fast MCDRAM memory – addressable, the configuration of the grid cores "each with each". Results for KNL are shown in Tables 6 and 7.

Table 6. Solver run on all cores of Intel KNL

Cores/threads	KNL auto, t, s	KNL FMA 64/64, t, s	KNL AVX-512 64/64, t, s	Speedup
Rotations	7.4	3.3	3.3	2.24
Right hand sides	131.9	1.47	1.43	92.24
Integration	3.77	0.06	0.08	47.13
Total	143.07	4.83	4.81	29.74

Table 7. Solver run on all cores of Intel KNL with hyperthreading

Cores/threads	KNL auto, t, s	KNL FMA 64/128, t, s	Speedup
Rotations	7.4	4.84	1.53
Right hand sides	131.9	2.34	56.37
Integration	3.77	0.08	47.13
Total	143.07	7.26	19.71

KNL supports the previous vector instructions and is fully compatible with x86, unlike KNC [6]. Therefore, the comparison was conducted for parallelized vectorized code using FMA and using AVX512, as well as when comparing of vectorized versions. Unlike the first case when parallelizing compiler optimizes the code with FMA the same way as when using AVX512, therefore, complex algorithms for packing multiple rows of the matrices in one vector register not make sense that can be seen from Table 6. Parallel code is executed only 1.5 times slower than on Intel Xeon E5, the acceleration compared to autovectorized code on a single core is 30 times. The use of additional threads per core yields, unlike KNC, to a significant decreasing of performance, so it makes no sense for this task, as seen from Table 7.

The final results of the comparison of the three architectures are shown in Table 8, which shows that KNL architecture is significantly more efficient than KNC, the procedure of calculation of the right-hand sides is even ahead of Intel Xeon E5, but in general both MIC architectures are slower than Xeon E5 architecture for the considered task. KNC is 8 times slower, KNL − 1.5 times.

Table 8. Comparison of best versions run times (shows how much times Intel Xeon Phi is slower than Intel Xeon E5 for the considered task)

	KNC/Xeon E5	KNL/Xeon E5
Rotations	16.23	2.97
Right hand sides	3.64	0.72
Integration	2.17	1.33
Total	8.02	1.52

4.3 OpenCL Implementation for GPU

In order to utilize all the computational power of heterogeneous computing system, both stand-alone and computing cluster node, we need an implementation for host-coprocessor pairs, regardless of the type of the coprocessor (GPU or FPGA, though in this paper we consider GPU only). To obtain such implementation we have chosen OpenCL technology. So, we have developed OpenCL kernels for most computer-intensive parts of the algorithm, still performing branching-intensive calculations on the host (CPU).

An important element when working with OpenCL on the GPU is a limitation of the bus between the host and the device. The PCI Express bus is such "bottleneck" (if we do not consider Systems-On-Crystal (SoC) with integrated CPU and coprocessor cores, which is out of the scope of this paper). On this basis, it is critical to minimize the amount of data transmitted between the GPU and CPU.

Table 9 outlines the major buffers involved in the calculation. Forwarding Stress buffer is necessary to calculate the total stress according to von Mises on the host. DataInternal buffer contains the positions, rotations, the first and second derivatives of these parameters. Sync of DataInternal buffer is necessary for the correct calculation and for detecting errors and overflows, as the tests are performed on the host side. Transfer of Stress occurs whenever the host calculates the intermediate result of stress.

This happens with a certain period during a major iteration. DataInternal must be sent to the device each time since the detection of overflow is done at each iteration, furthermore, the modeling process is saved in a file, where the stresses and the coordinates of each node between major iterations are stored. Buffers BoudaryFixed, BoudaryForces, and LinkedElements are sent every time when the model changes. This creates a reserve for future expansion of functionality, for example, to remove links if you exceed the stress, simulating the destruction of the part.

All secondary buffers and constants are loaded once during initialization and are listed in Table 9.

Table 9. Buffers to transfer memory between host and device (OpenCL implementation)

Memory buffer	Host memory	Content
DataInternal	Read/Write	Linear and angular coordinates and derivatives
Stress	Read/Write	Stresses
BoudaryFixed	Write	Coordinate boundary conditions
BoudaryForces	Write	Boundary conditions for accelerations
LinkedElements	Write	Numbers of linked elements

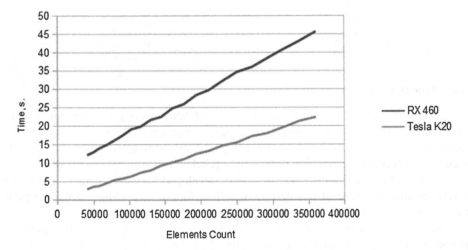

Fig. 5. Computing time chart on AMD RX 460 and Tesla K20 for different task dimensions

Launches were performed on AMD RX460 and NVIDIA TESLA K20 (Fig. 5). GPGPU from NVIDIA exceeds AMD GPU in performance. OpenCL implementation according to our last obtained results works from 1.5 to 2.5 times faster on NVIDIA TESLA K20 than on two Intel Xeon E5 2660 CPUs. So our OpenCL implementation of solver works on GPU quite well and it can be used in heterogeneous computing environment effectively.

5   Conclusions and Future Research Directions

Vectorization of a solver code has shown that the considered problem is solved significantly quicker on the KNL than on KNC. The kernel of KNL concedes in speed to Xeon E5 kernel by only 3.5 times. KNL processor could be used to the full load only when using multithreading on all physical kernels but without hyperthreading.

Manual vectorization has given an acceleration of computation in the solver by 2–3 times in comparison with autovectorization by the modern Intel compiler (Intel Parallel Composer 2017).

In the long term, it is possible to estimate that the parallel version of a code of the considered solver (as a result of further optimization of an algorithm) will work on KNL comparably with 10-core CPU Intel Xeon E5.

Further optimization can be connected with the changes in a multithreading algorithm with the use of multibody model decomposition for lowering the number of synchronizations in a parallel code. It makes a sense also to optimize calculation and application of rotation matrixes. It can yield good result in case of a large number of flows and it is possible to bring computation speed on Phi (on KNL, partly on KNC) closer to computation speed on Intel Xeon E5 CPU and thus to get benefits from using both traditional CPUs and MICs in heterogeneous cluster environment while solving large-scale tasks.

Also, first results obtained from testing OpenCL version of real solver are quite promising – we can speed even pair of fast CPUs at least 1.5 times (up to 2.5 times on large models), and it can be improved in future. What still has to be done besides optimizing each solver (both vectorized one for CPU as well as MIC on one hand and OpenCL for GPU/FPGA on other) is (a) good problem decomposition and load balancing to utilize multiple nodes of a cluster with heterogeneous hardware as well as (b) trying to perform each part of calculations on more appropriate computing subsystem or whole node.

Acknowledgements. Work is performed with the financial support of the Russian Foundation for Basic Research - projects ## 16-47-340385, 16-07-00534, 15-01-04577, 15-07-06254 and the financial support of the Administration of Volgograd region.

All experiments were conducted using a computational cluster of Volgograd State Technical University. The cluster was assembled from the equipment acquired in the course of the implementation of the Strategic University development program, Program of the engineering training for industry and the Development program of the flagship university.

References

1. Getmanskiy, V., Gorobtsov, A., Sergeev, S., Izmailov, D., Shapovalov, O.: Concurrent simulation of multibody systems coupled with stress-strain and heat transfer solvers. J. Comput. Sci. **3**(6), 492–497 (2012)
2. Gorobtsov, A., Getmanskiy, V., Andreev, A., Trung, D.D.: Simulation and visualization software for vehicle dynamics analysis using multibody system approach. Commun. Comput. Inf. Sci. **535**, 378–390 (2015)

3. Kireev, S.E.: Optimization for a cluster with Xeon PHI accelerators the problem of filtration of water-oil mixture through an elastic porous medium. Numer. Methods Program. **16**(2), 177–186 (2015). MSU, Moscow. (In Russian)

4. Heybrock S., Joó, B., Kalamkar D.D., Smelyanskiy M., Vaidyanathan K., Wettig T.: Lattice QCD with domain decomposition on Intel Xeon Phi co-processors (2014). arXiv: 1412.2629v1

5. Murano, K., Shimobaba, T., Sugiyama, A., Takada, N., Kakue, T., Oikawa, M., Ito, T.: Fast computation of computer generated hologram using Xeon Phi coprocessor. Comput. Phys. Commun. **185**(N10), 2742–2757 (2014)

6. Barnes, T.: Evaluating and optimizing the NERSC workload on knights landing. In: Proceedings of the 7th International Workshop on Performance Modeling, Benchmarking and Simulation of High Performance Computing Systems, PMBS 2016, pp. 43–53 (2016). doi:10.1109/PMBS.2016.10

7. Adinetz, A.V.: NUDA: programming graphics processors with extensible languages. Nuclear Electronics & Computing, Varna, Bulgaria (2011)

8. Capuzzo-Dolcetta, R., Spera, M., Punzo, D.: A fully parallel, high precision, N-body code running on hybrid computing platforms. J. Comput. Phys. **236**, 580–593 (2013). doi:10. 1016/j.jcp.2012.11.013

9. Getmanskiy, V.V., Andreev, A.E., Movchan, E.O.: Key features of multibody code vectorization using different instruction sets. In: Proceedings of International Conference Russian Supercomputing Days 2016, MSU, Moscow, pp. 365–372 (2016)

10. Andreev, A., Nasonov, A., Novokshenov, A., Bochkarev, A., Kharkov, E., Zharikov, D., Kharchenko, S., Yuschenko, A.: Vectorization algorithms of block linear algebra operations using SIMD instructions. In: Kravets, A., Shcherbakov, M., Kultsova, M., Shabalina, O. (eds.) CIT&DS 2015. CCIS, vol. 535, pp. 323–341. Springer, Cham (2015). doi:10.1007/ 978-3-319-23766-4_26

Synthesis of the Physical Operation Principles of Technical System

Ilya Vayngolts, Dmitriy Korobkin$^{(\boxtimes)}$ ⓘ, Sergey Fomenkov ⓘ, and Alexander Golovanchikov

Volgograd State Technical University, Volgograd, Russian Federation
dkorobkin80@mail.ru

Abstract. Nowadays using of various computer-aided design systems is the most perspective method of getting new technical solutions. In those systems used special databases, which stored physical knowledge that is represented by Physical Effects (PhE). The physical effect is the connection between two or more physical phenomena, which are characterized by physical quantities. Authors of this paper developed a methodology for calculation of PhE's compatibility, an algorithm for constructing structures of physical operation principle (POP) of new technical systems. Developed software has been implemented and tested for tasks of POP synthesis with enhanced conditions of physical effects compatibility (quantitative compatibility conditions, PhE objects with structural transformation comparing). The developed software is more effective than the POP synthesis softwares such as "Assistant", "Novator", "Intellect", "SAPFIT".

Keywords: Physical effect · Physical phenomena · Design of technical systems · Operation principle of technical system · Physical operation principle

1 Introduction

Nowadays using of various automated systems is the most perspective method of getting new technical solutions. In those systems special databases are used, and they have physical knowledge that are represented by Physical Effects (PhE). A lot of researchers such as Glazunov [1], Petrova [2], Polovinkin [3], Arel [4, 5], Zlotin [6], Rivin [7], Kamaev [8] and others are engaged in problem of formalization the conceptual physical effect models and creating the computer-aided design systems. However, such systems can give to user some solutions that it's impossible to use those solutions in practice. That's why problem of decrease of number of physically impossible technical solutions is actual.

We consider four computer-aided design systems:

- "Novator 4.02" [1]
- "Intellect" [2]
- "SAPFIT" [9]
- "Assistant" [10]

© Springer International Publishing AG 2017
A. Kravets et al. (Eds.): CIT&DS 2017, CCIS 754, pp. 575–588, 2017.
DOI: 10.1007/978-3-319-65551-2_42

We will analyze these systems by two features:

- by the structure of PhE description;
- by the compatibility conditions of the PhE in the physical operation principle (POP) synthesis module.

The criteria for comparing systems by the compatibility conditions of the PhE are:

- presence/absence of quantitative compatibility conditions;
- presence/absence of PhE compare by the object;
- taking into account structural transformation of the object.

Each of the criteria is estimated either 1 (presence) or 0 (absence) (Table 1).

Table 1. The criteria for comparing systems

Criteria	"Novator 4.02"	"Intellect"	"SAPFIT"	"Assistant"
Presence/absence of quantitative characteristics	1	1	1	1
Presence/absence of object	1	0	1	1
Presence/absence of structural transformation of the object	0	0	0	1
Presence/absence of quantitative compatibility conditions	0	0	0	0
Presence/absence of PhE compare by the object	1	0	0	0
Taking into account structural transformation of the object	0	0	0	0

Thus the developed system must meet the following criteria:

- It is necessary to ensure the compatibility of the PhE at the qualitative level (taking into account actions, their characteristics and physical quantities, and characteristics of the object) and the quantitative level (taking into account ranges of changes of physical quantities).
- It is necessary to ensure take into account all input actions of PhE that included in POP structures (it is actual for the initial construction of the linear structure when we have unaffected internal input action of the PhE).
- The system should be implemented as web application with graphical representations of POP structures.

2 Physical Effect

The physical effect is the connection between two or more physical phenomena, which are characterized by physical quantities.

Actions are physical phenomena, they are bound PhE. The input-cause action (A_i) is physical phenomenon that it necessary to transform. The output-effect action (C_i) is physical phenomenon that it necessary to obtain. The object of PhE (B_i) is some physical system (it may be substance or field).

As a result of explorations, which carried out at CAD Department of VSTU, the next structure of PhE has been developed [11]:

$$PhE_i = \left(A_i, B_i^1, B_i^2, C_i\right) \tag{1}$$

where A_i – input cause-action(s) of PhE;
B_i^1 – start state of PhE's object;
B_i^2 – final state of PhE's object;
C_i – output effect-action of PhE.

Example: Physical Effect No 961 "The method of obtaining compact nanocrystalline materials (compacting nanopowders)"

- Input cause-action: Input 1: The force (mechanical) action. Homogeneous. Constant. Pressure (Pa). Increase to 10 GPa. Input 2: The pressure of the discharged inert gas (Pa). Reduction to vacuum.
- Start state of PhE object: A nanocrystalline powder of metal, ceramics at inety gas atmosphere, for example, Al, Fe, Ni, Cu, Pd, Si at He atmosphere, etc.
- Final state of PhE object: The compact nanocrystalline metal, ceramics, for example, Al, Fe, Ni, Cu, Pd, Si, etc.
- Output effect-action: Density of the compact (kg/m^3). Increase.

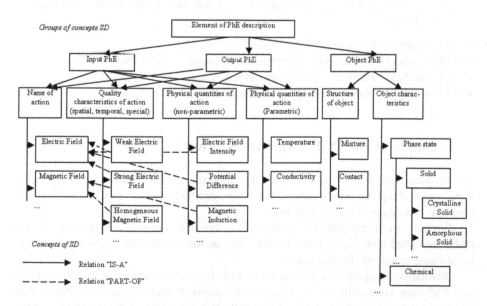

Fig. 1. Taxonomy of SD concepts

3 The Ontology of Subject Domain

Figure 1 represents a taxonomy diagram of "Physical Effect" domain concepts [12, 13]. Describing the subject domain (SD) concepts is used a taxonomy and relations "IS-A" and "PART-OF".

4 Global Database of Physical Effects

The Physical Effects database ("Global Database") [13] contains about 1200 PhE descriptions includes knowledge from different physical domains and also on the base of new discoveries and inventions.

Structure of a Global Database of Physical Effects:

- Educational database (211 PhEs) includes PhEs from General Physics course study in the technological universities.
- Main database (589 PhEs) includes PhEs from additional course of General Physics and special sections of Physics.
- Database of PhEs from patent applications on the basis of physics discoveries - 120 PhEs.
- PhE database which is compiled on the basis of information contained in new scientific publications (1995–2016) in physical journals - 147 PhEs.

Completeness a coverage of various domains of physical knowledge is reached due to invariancy of information filling of PhE database. The PhE Global Database forms a basis for creation of the highly specialized databases focused on the solution of tasks in concrete subject domain.

There are object-oriented PhE databases in addition to the Global Database of Physical Effects:

- PhE database "Properties of rock formation" - 155 PhEs.
- PhE database "Diamond in electronic engineering" - 39 PhEs.
- PhE database "Properties of amorphous materials" - 67 PhEs.
- PhE database "Nanotechnology and nanomaterials" - 42 PhEs.

5 Example of the POP Structure Synthesis

The physical operation principle (POP) is a structure of compatible PhEs that ensure transform of the given input-cause action to the specified output-effect action. The POP structure is a chain of compatible PhEs.

The concept of compatibility of the PhE is that two successively effects PhE_1 and PhE_2 are called compatible if the output-effect action of the PhE_1 C_i is equivalent to input-cause action of the PhE_2 A_{i+1}.

Qualitative compatibility conditions of PhE is that two successively effects PhE_1 and PhE_2 are compatible if the name of the physical quantity and its character of change in the output-effect of the PhE_1 match with the name of the physical quantity and its character of change in the input-cause effect of the PhE_2, and the spatial, temporal and special characteristics of the input-cause effect of the PhE_2 contain all spatial, temporal and special characteristics of the output-effect actions of PhE_1.

The quantitative compatibility conditions of PhE is that the presence of a common interval for the ranges of physical quantities of the output-effect of the PhE_1 and the input-cause of the PhE_2.

Enhanced compatibility conditions of the PhE include qualitative compatibility conditions, quantitative compatibility conditions and compatibility by PhE's objects.

Compatibility by PhE's objects is that two successively effects of PhE_1 and PhE_2 are compatible if for each phase of objects the phase state, chemical composition, magnetic structure, electrical conductivity, mechanical state, optical state and special characteristics of the object PhE_2 contain a phase state, chemical composition, magnetic structure, Electrical conductivity, mechanical state, optical state and special characteristics of PhE_1.

The inverse POP structure is the POP structure that the two successively PhE_1 and PhE_2 effects are compatible if the input-cause action of the PhE_1 is equivalent to the output-effect action of the PhE_2. The PhE, which the construction of the inverse POP structure begins, is compatible with the previous PhE in the direct POP structure if the result of constructing the inverse POP structure. The last PhE of the structure contains all external input-cause actions.

The length of the POP structure is the number of effects from which it consists (without taking into account the effects of inverse POP structures).

The length of the inverse POP structure is the number of effects, of which the inverse POP structure consists.

The rank of the POP structure is a quantity that is proportional to the length of the POP structure. It calculated as follows: the POP structure with a minimum length will be the maximum rank, and for the POP structure with a maximum length will be the minimum rank.

Example of the POP synthesis:

- Input cause-action: Electric field. The electric field strength (V/m);
- Output effect-action: Electricity. The strength of the electric current (A/m); (Fig. 2)

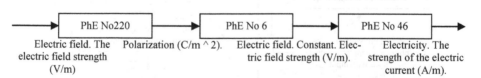

PhE No 220 "Polarization of Electro Electrodes", PhE No 6 "Electric field of electret", PhE No 46 "Corona discharge"

Fig. 2. Example of the POP synthesis

6   Methods of POP Structures Synthesis

Using such structure of PhE we can distinguish two types of checks on compatibility:

- compatibility by actions;
- compatibility by objects.

It's possible the next variations of input and output actions (Fig. 1):

- both actions are parametric;
- both actions are not parametric;

Parametric action is described as follows: type of input/output; the physics section; the name of the physical quantity; the character of the change of physical quantity; the range of change of the physical quantity.

Algorithm of check parametric actions on compatibility has been presented on Fig. 3.

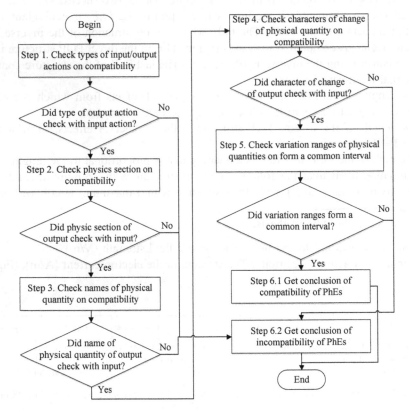

Fig. 3. Algorithm of check compatibility parametric actions

Nonparametric action is described as follows: type of input/output; the name of action; the name of the physical quantity; the character of the change of physical quantity; the range of change of the physical quantity; spatial characteristics; temporary characteristics; special characteristics.

Algorithm of check not-parametric actions on compatibility has been presented on Fig. 4.

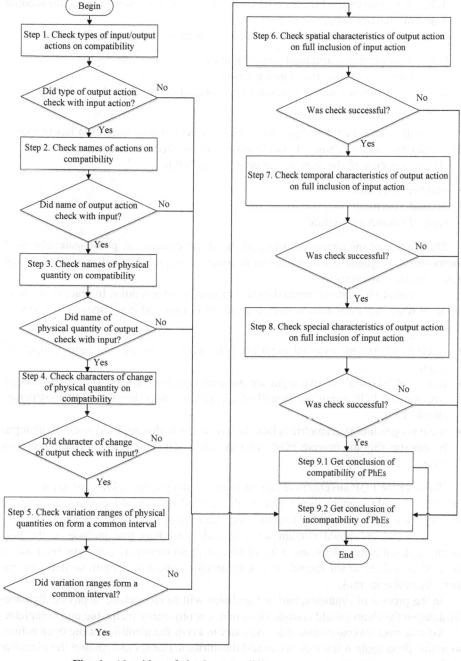

Fig. 4. Algorithm of check compatibility not-parametric actions

It's need check compatibility by objects in two cases:

- output and input actions are not parametric and types of input/output are external;
- output and input actions are parametric.

When we compare the PhE for compatibility by object, we would take into account its structural transformation.

In this regard there are three variants of combinations of combined effects:

- both objects without structural transformation;
- both objects with structural transformation;
- one of the objects without structural transformation and the other with structural transformation.

We will assume that the object that lacks a structural transformation has the same initial and final states. Thus, all combinations are reduced to the second.

The description of the state of the object is as follows:

- number of phases;
- general structure;
- type of contact or mixture.

Description of the general structure of the object consists of: phase state; chemical composition; magnetic structure; electrical conductivity; mechanical condition; optical state; special characteristics.

The most of PhEs from current database have two input actions. In practice we have situation when one from input actions is compatible with nothing ("opened"). To avoid it, we set the next rules:

- in case of "opened" external input not-parametric action we will ignore "opened" input;
- in case of "opened" internal input not-parametric action we need to make up reverse structure of POP using all described algorithms. Max length of such structure should be 3.
- there is open input parametric action: in this case it is also required to close the input by constructing the inverse POP structure, using the same rules as in the previous case.

To store the POP structures results from the synthesis, two tables are required: the first table should contain direct chains, the second one should contain the reverse chains. We call the first table "Chains", the second one call "ReverseChains".

A direct chain should contain a list of PhE identifiers that include it, the task identifier that it corresponds, and a list of reverse chain identifiers that have been added to it. Also, a direct chain should contain information about its length, so that you can then determine its rank.

In the process of synthesis, part of the chains will be recognized as physically unrealizable, so the chain should contain signs that it is physically realizable and complete.

To construct reverse chains, it is necessary to know the identifier of the open action, so in the direct chain it is necessary to add the attribute that should contain the identifier of the open input action.

The reverse chain should contain a list of PhE identifiers that it includes, as well as a sign that it is physically realizable (Fig. 5).

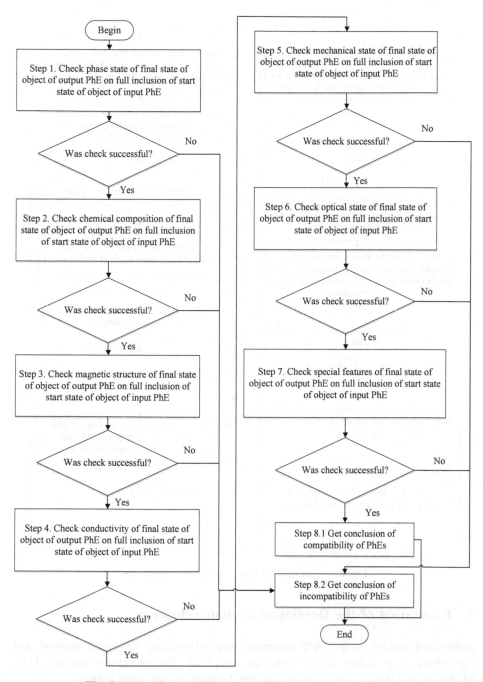

Fig. 5. Algorithm of check compatibility phases of PhE objects

Based on the above-described methodology for comparing PhEs for the compatibility of the POP structure, they should be constructed according to the algorithm presented on Fig. 6.

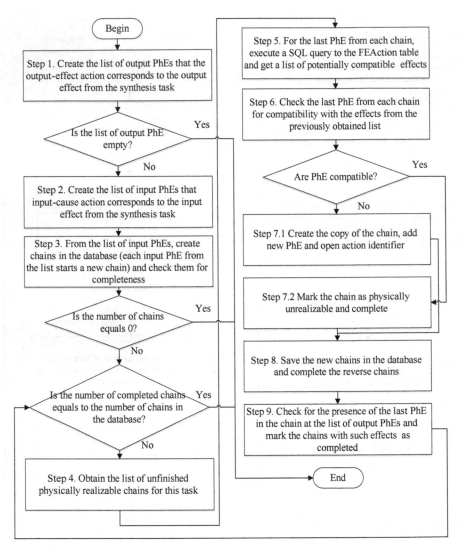

Fig. 6. Algorithm for constructing POP structures

7   Evaluating of the Developed System Efficiency

Automated system of the POP structures synthesis using developed method and algorithms is a "client-server" software with.NET Framework technology [15]. Microsoft SQL Server has been used as the database management system.

The architecture of the system is shown on Fig. 7.

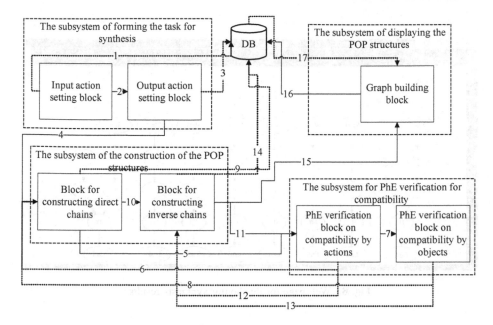

Fig. 7. System architecture

- 1 – saving the input action to the database;
- 2 – calling the output action setting block;
- 3 – saving output action to the database;
- 4 – calling the block for constructing direct chains;
- 5 – calling the PhE verification block on compatibility by actions;
- 6 – transmission to the block for constructing direct chains the result of the compatibility test by actions;
- 7 – calling the PhE verification block on compatibility by objects;
- 8 – transmission to the block for constructing direct chains the result of the compatibility test by objects;
- 9 – saving direct chains to the database;
- 10 – calling the block for constructing return chains;
- 11 – calling the PhE verification block on compatibility by actions;
- 12 – transmission to the block for constructing inverse chains the result of the compatibility test by actions;
- 13 – transmission to the block for constructing inverse chains the result of the compatibility test by objects;
- 14 – saving inverse chains to the database;
- 15 – calling the graph building block;
- 16 – querying the database to retrieve physically realizable chains of the required rank;

- 17 – obtaining from the database records of physically realizable chains of the required rank (Fig. 8).

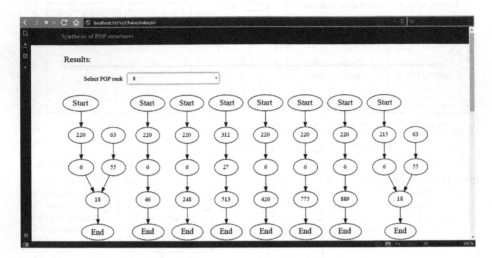

Fig. 8. Web-page for displaying synthesis results

It was realized the comparative analysis of the POP structures obtained as a synthesis result with automated system "Assistant" [10] and developed software (module). Results of tests with the same input and output parameters has been presented on Fig. 9.

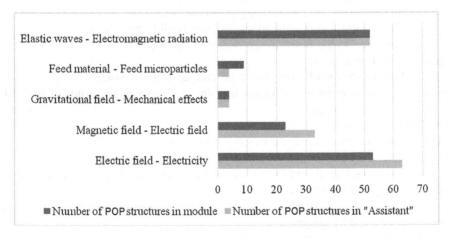

Fig. 9. Results of tests synthesis module

How we can see general number of POP structures, which has been got in "Assistant" is 156, general number of POP structures, which has been got in developed software is 141. The results on Fig. 9 show that methods and algorithms realized in new POP synthesis module could reduce the number of physically unrealizable POP structures more than 1.2 times.

8   Conclusion

As a result of this work, the following tasks were accomplished:

- has been analyzed of existing CAD systems for the compatibility conditions of the PhE;
- has been developed a methodology for compare PhE compatibility;
- the algorithm for constructing POP structures has been developed;
- has been implemented and tested the system of synthesis of the physical operation principle of technical systems with enhanced conditions of physical effects compatibility

The developed module is more effective than the POP synthesis module in the "Assistant" at 1.2 times, the average operating time of the module is 3–6 min.

Acknowledgements. The research has been performed with the financial support from the RFBR (Projects No. 15-07-09142-A and No. 15-47-02383-r_povolzhye_a).

References

1. Glazunov, V.N.: Technology of ideas: expert systems "Innovator" and "Edison" (2015). http://www.trizland.ru/trizba/pdf-articles/system_novator.pdf
2. Zaripova, V., Petrova, I.: Knowledge-based support for innovative design on basis of energy-information method of circuits. J. Commun. Comput. Inf. Sci. (2014)
3. Dvoryankin, A.M., Polovinkin, A.I., Sobolev, A.N.: Automating the search for operation principles of technical systems on the basis of a bank of physical phenomena. J. Cybern. **14**, 79–86 (1978)
4. Arel, E., Verbitsky, M., Devoino, I., Ikovenko, S.: TechOptimizer Fundamentals. Invention Machine Corporation, Boston (2002)
5. Arel, E.: Goldfire Innovator. Patents and Innovation Trend Analysis User Guide, vol. 2, Invention Machine Corporation, Boston, MA (2004)
6. Zlotin, B., Zusman, A.: Directed Evolution: Philosophy, Theory and Practice. Ideation International (2001)
7. Fey, V., Rivin, E.: Innovation on Demand: New Product Development Using TRIZ. Cambridge University Press, Cambridge (2005)
8. Fomenkov, S.A., Korobkin, D.M., Kolesnikov, S.G., Kamaev, V.A., Kravets, A.G.: The automated methods of search of physical effects. Int. J. Soft Comput. **10**, 234–238 (2015). doi:10.3923/ijscomp.2015.234.238

9. Korobkin, D.M., Kolesnikov, S.G., Fomenkov, S.A., Golovanchikov, A.B.: Evaluating an operation principle practicability of new technical system. In: 6th International Conference on Information, Intelligence, Systems and Applications (IISA). IEEE (2015). doi:10.1109/IISA.2015.7388068

10. Korobkin, D.M., Fomenkov, S.A., Kolesnikov, S.G., Lobeyko, V.I.: Synthesis of new technical solutions with physical effects database. In: 7th International Conference on Information, Intelligence, Systems & Applications (IISA). IEEE (2016). doi:10.1109/IISA.2016.7785397

11. Korobkin, D., Fomenkov, S., Kolesnikov, S., Lobeyko, V., Golovanchikov, A.: Modification of physical effect model for the synthesis of the physical operation principles of technical system. In: Kravets, A., Shcherbakov, M., Kultsova, M., Shabalina, O. (eds.) First International Conference on Creativity in Intelligent Technologies & Data Science (CIT&DS), vol. 535, pp. 368–378. Springer, Cham (2015)

12. Hirsch, E.: Physical-object ontology, verbal disputes and common sense. Quantifier Variance and Realism: Essays in Metaontology. Oxford University Press, Oxford (2011)

13. Parygin, D., Sadovnikova, N., Kravets, A., Gnedkova, E.: Cognitive and ontological modeling for decision support in the tasks of the urban transportation system development management. In: Sixth International IEEE Conference on Information, Intelligence, Systems and Applications (IISA), pp. 1–5. IEEE (2015). doi:10.1109/IISA.2015.7388073

14. Fomenkov, S.A., Kolesnikov, S.G., Korobkin, D.M., Kamaev, V.A., Orlova, Y.A.: The information filling of the database by physical effects. J. Eng. Applied Sci. 9, 422–426 (2014)

15. Sadovnikova, N., Parygin, D., Kalinkina, M., Sanzhapov, B., NiNi, T.: Models and methods for the urban transit system research. In: Kravets, A., Shcherbakov, M., Kultsova, M., Shabalina, O. (eds.) Creativity in Intelligent Technologies and Data Science. Communications in Computer and Information Science, vol. 535, pp. 488–499. Springer, Cham (2015)

Intelligent Internet of Services
and Internet of Things

Heuristic Anticipation Scheduling for Efficient and Fair Resources Allocation in Grid VOs

Victor Toporkov and Dmitry Yemelyanov$^{(\boxtimes)}$

National Research University "MPEI",
ul. Krasnokazarmennaya, 14, Moscow 111250, Russia
{ToporkovVV,YemelyanovDM}@mpei.ru

Abstract. In this work, a job-flow scheduling approach for Grid virtual organizations (VOs) is proposed and studied. Users' and resource providers' preferences, VOs internal policies, resources geographical distribution along with local private utilization impose specific requirements for efficient scheduling according to different, usually contradictive, criteria. With increasing resources utilization level the available resources set and corresponding decision space are reduced. In order to improve overall scheduling efficiency, we propose an anticipation scheduling heuristic. It includes a predetermined (anticipated) pattern solution definition and a special replication procedure for efficient and feasible resources allocation. A proposed anticipation algorithm is compared against conservative backfilling variations using such criteria as average jobs' response time (start and finish times) as well as users' and VO economic criteria (execution time and cost).

Keywords: Scheduling · Grid · Utilization · Heuristic · Job batch · Virtual organization · Cycle scheduling scheme · Anticipation · Replication · Backfilling

1 Introduction and Related Works

In distributed environments with non-dedicated resources such as utility Grids the computational nodes are usually partly utilized by local high-priority jobs coming from resource owners. Thus, the resources available for use are represented with a set of slots - time intervals during which the individual computational nodes are capable to execute parts of independent users' parallel jobs. These slots generally have different start and finish times and a performance difference. The presence of a set of slots impedes the problem of coordinated selection of the resources necessary to execute the job-flow from computational environment users. Resource fragmentation also results in a decrease of the total computing environment utilization level [1,2].

Two established trends may be outlined among diverse approaches to distributed computing. The first one is based on the available resources utilization and application level scheduling [3]. As a rule, this approach does not imply

© Springer International Publishing AG 2017
A. Kravets et al. (Eds.): CIT&DS 2017, CCIS 754, pp. 591–603, 2017.
DOI: 10.1007/978-3-319-65551-2_43

any global resource sharing or allocation policy. Another trend is related to the formation of user's virtual organizations (VO) and job-flow scheduling [4,5]. In this case a metascheduler is an intermediate chain between the users and local resource management and job batch processing systems.

Uniform rules of resource sharing and consumption, in particular based on economic models, make it possible to improve the job-flow level scheduling and resource distribution efficiency. VO policy may offer optimized scheduling to satisfy both users' and VO common preferences. The VO scheduling problems may be formulated as follows: to optimize users' criteria or utility function for selected jobs [6,7], to keep resource overall load balance [8,9], to have job run in strict order or maintain job priorities [10], to optimize overall scheduling performance by some custom criteria [11,12], etc.

VO formation and performance largely depends on mutually beneficial collaboration between all the related stakeholders. However, users' preferences and VO common preferences (owners' and administrators' combined) may conflict with each other. Users are likely to be interested in the fastest possible running time for their jobs with least possible costs whereas VO preferences are usually directed to available resources load balancing or node owners' profit boosting. Thus, VO policies in general should respect all members and the most important aspect of rules suggested by VO is their fairness.

A number of works understand fairness as it is defined in the theories of cooperative games and mechanism design, such as fair job-flow distribution [8], fair quotas [13,14] or fair user jobs prioritization [10]. The cyclic scheduling scheme (CSS) [15] implements a fair scheduling optimization mechanism which ensures stakeholders interests to some predefined extent.

The downside of a majority centralized metascheduling approaches is that they loose their efficiency and optimization features in distributed environments with a significant workload. In such conditions of a *limited resources supply* overall job-flow execution makespan and individual jobs' finish time minimization become essential scheduling criteria. For example in [2], a traditional backfilling algorithm provided better scheduling outcome when compared to different optimization approaches in resource domain with a minimal performance configuration.

A main contribution of this paper is a CSS-based heuristic anticipation approach which retains scheduling efficiency and at the same time minimizes job-flow processing time. Initially this heuristic generates a near optimal but infeasible (anticipated) schedule. A special replication procedure is proposed and studied to ensure and provide a feasible scheduling solution.

The rest of the paper is organized as follows. Section 2 describes a general CSS fair scheduling concept. The proposed anticipation scheduling technique is presented in Sect. 3. Section 4 contains simulation experiment setup and results of comparison with conservative backfilling variations. Finally, Sect. 5 summarizes the paper.

2   Cyclic Alternative-Based Fair Scheduling Model and Limited Resources

Scheduling of a job-flow using CSS is performed in time cycles known as scheduling intervals, by job batches [15]. The actual scheduling procedure during each cycle consists of two main steps. The first step involves a search for alternative execution scenarios for each job or simply alternatives [16]. During the second step the dynamic programming methods [15] are used to choose an optimal alternatives' combination (one alternative is selected for each job) with respect to the given VO and user criteria. This combination represents the final schedule based on current data on resources load and possible alternative executions.

An example for a user scheduling criterion may be a minimization of overall job running time, a minimization of overall running cost, etc. This criterion describes user's preferences for that specific job execution.

Alongside with time (T) and cost (C) properties each job execution alternative has a user utility (U) value: user evaluation against the scheduling criterion. We consider the following relative approach to represent a user utility U. A job alternative with the minimum (best) user-defined criterion value Z_{min} corresponds to the left interval boundary $(U = 0\%)$ of all possible job scheduling outcomes. An alternative with the worst possible criterion value Z_{max} corresponds to the right interval boundary $(U = 100\%)$. In the general case for each alternative with value Z of user criterion, U is set depending on its position in $[Z_{min}; Z_{max}]$ interval using the following formula:

$$U = \frac{Z - Z_{min}}{Z_{max} - Z_{min}} * 100\%. \tag{1}$$

Thus, each alternative gets its utility in relation to the "best" and the "worst" optimization criterion values user could expect according to the job's priority. And the more some alternative corresponds to user's preferences the smaller is the value of U.

For a fair scheduling model the second step VO optimization problem could be in form of: $C \rightarrow \max$, $\lim U$ (maximize total job-flow execution cost, while respecting user's preferences to some extent); $U \rightarrow \min$, $\lim T$ (meet user's best interests, while ensuring some acceptable job-flow execution time) and so on.

First step of CSS requires allocation of a multiple *nonintersecting* in terms of slots alternatives for each job. Otherwise irresolvable collisions for resources may occur if different jobs will share the same time-slots. Sequential alternatives search and resources reservation procedures help to prevent such scenario. However in an extreme case when resources are limited or overutilized only at most one alternative execution could be reserved for each job. In this case alternatives-based scheduling result will be no different from FIFO resources allocation procedure without any optimizations [2].

3   Heuristic Anticipation Scheduling

3.1   General Scheme

In order to improve scheduling efficiency for job batch the following heuristic is proposed. It consists of three main steps.

1. First, a set of all possible execution alternatives is found for each job not considering time slots intersections and without any resources reservation. The resulting intersecting alternatives found for each job reflect a full range of different job execution possibilities user may expect on the current scheduling interval. It may be noticed that this set is guaranteed to include the best and the worst alternatives according to any scheduling criterion including user and VO criteria.
2. Second, CSS scheduling procedure is performed to select alternatives combination (one alternative for each job of the batch) optimal according to VO fairshare policy. The resulting alternatives combination most likely corresponds to an infeasible scheduling solution as possible time slots intersection will cause collisions on resources allocation stage.

   The main idea of this step is that obtained infeasible solution will provide some heuristic insights on how each job should be handled during the scheduling. For example, if time-biased or cost-biased execution is preferred, how it should correspond to user criterion and VO administration policy and so on.
3. Third, a feasible resources allocation is performed by replicating alternatives selected in step **2**. The base for this replication step is an Algorithm searching for Extreme Performance (AEP) described in details in [16]. In the current step AEP helps to find and reserve required resources most similar to those selected in the near-optimal infeasible solution.

After these three steps are performed the resulting solution is both feasible and efficient as it reflects scheduling pattern obtained from a near-optimal reference solution from step **2**.

The following subsections will discuss these scheduling steps in more details.

3.2   Finding a Near Optimal Infeasible Scheduling Solution

CSS scheduling results are strongly depend on diversity of alternatives sets obtained for batch jobs. The task of finding all possible execution alternatives for each job of the batch may become impractical as number of all different resource allocations may reach combination of p things m at a time, where p is a total number of different available resource types and m is a number of resources requested by user. Moreover as we consider non-dedicated resources this task is additionally complicated by a local resources utilization. In this case not every resources combination may be available during the scheduling cycle.

However, as we need to find alternatives for an apriori infeasible reference solution a reasonable diverse set of possible execution alternatives will do. One important feature of this set is that it should contain extreme execution alternatives according to different criteria, i.e. the most expensive, the least time-consuming alternative and so on. Further this set of possible alternatives may be used to evaluate actual user job execution against the job execution possibilities according to Eq. (1).

We used AEP modification to allocate a diverse set of execution alternatives for each job. Originally AEP scans through a whole list of available time slots and retrieves one alternative execution optimal according to the user custom criterion. During this scan, AEP estimates every possible and sufficient slots combination against user criterion and selects the one with the best criterion value. In order to retrieve all possible execution alternatives we save all distinct intermediate AEP search results to a dedicated list of possible alternatives.

After sets of possible execution alternatives are independently allocated for each job a CSS scheduling optimization procedure selects an optimal alternatives combination according to VO and users criteria [15]. More details on alternatives combination selection procedure were provided in Sect. 2.

3.3 Replication Scheduling and Resources Allocation

The resulting near-optimal scheduling solution in most cases is infeasible as selected alternatives may share the same time slots and thus cause resource collisions. However we propose to use it as a reference solution and replicate into a feasible resources allocation.

For the replication purpose a new *Execution Similarity* criterion is introduced. It helps AEP to find a window with minimum *distance* to a reference pattern alternative. Generally we define a *distance* between two different alternatives (windows) as a relative difference or *error* between their significant criteria values. For example if reference alternative has C_{ref} total cost, and some candidate alternative cost is C_{can}, then the relative cost error E_C is calculated as $E_C = \frac{|C_{\text{ref}} - C_{\text{can}}|}{C_{\text{ref}}}$. If one need to consider several criteria the *distance* D between two alternatives may be calculated as a linear sum of criteria errors:

$$D_m = E_C + E_T + \ldots + E_U, \tag{2}$$

Or as a geometric distance in a parameters space:

$$D_g = \sqrt{E_C^2 + E_T^2 + \ldots + E_U^2}. \tag{3}$$

AEP with *Execution Similarity* scans through a whole list of available time slots, for every possible slots combination calculates it's distance from a reference alternative and selects the one with the minimum distance to a reference.

For a feasible job batch resources allocation AEP consequentially allocates for each job a single execution window with a minimum *distance* to a reference alternative (2)–(3). Time slots allocated for the i-th job are reserved and excluded from the slot list when AEP search algorithm is performed for the following jobs $i + 1, i + 2, \ldots$. Thus, this procedure prevents any conflicts for resources and provides scheduling solution which in some sense reflects near-optimal reference solution.

3.4 Replication Reference Setup

Anticipated near-optimal scheduling solution provides a heuristic insight on how each job should be executed with a reference to other users criteria, VO optimization policy and a current computing domain composition and utilization level. Basically this solution suggests what kind of resources should be allocated for each job in terms of performance and cost. Thus, available resources can be consistently distributed between the user jobs according to their performance or cost optimization targets.

At the same time the anticipated solution can't provide any meaningful reference on jobs' start and finish times. As anticipation procedure independently allocates a set of possible execution alternatives for each job, it does not consider resources reservation and utilization by other jobs. Thus, resulting anticipated jobs' start and finish times are randomly distributed on a whole scheduling interval with a bias towards the interval's start. In this way anticipation scheduling scheme can't provide neither adequate estimation on jobs' starting times, nor the common jobs' execution order.

In order to improve the anticipated reference solution we use backfilling algorithm to provide practical values for jobs start and finish times. Backfilling is able to minimize the whole job-flow execution makespan as well as to generally follow the initial jobs relative queue order. These features make backfilling scheduling solution a good reference target for the anticipation scheduling scheme. Thus, for the replication step we set infeasible CSS solution as a reference for jobs execution runtime and cost, and backfilling solution - for jobs start and finish times.

Additionally we use a finish time approximation coefficient K_t to relate the anticipated finish times to backfilling reference solution. For example when $K_t = 1$ we use exact jobs finish times provided by backfilling as a reference for a replication step. $K_t = 0.5$ means that we strive to execute the job-flow twice as faster compared to backfilling. $K_t = 1.5$ allows anticipation scheme to use 50% longer scheduling interval compared to backfilling makespan. So just by changing K_t we are able stretch resulting anticipation solution on a desired time interval.

4 Simulation Study

4.1 Simulation Environment Setup

An experiment was prepared as follows using a custom distributed environment simulator [2,15–17]. For our purpose, it implements a heterogeneous resource domain model: nodes have different usage costs and performance levels. A space-shared resources allocation policy simulates a local queuing system (like in GridSim or CloudSim [18]) and, thus, each node can process only one task at any given simulation time. The execution cost of each task depends on its running time which is proportional to the dedicated node' performance level. The execution of a single job requires parallel execution of all its tasks.

During each experiment new instances for the computing environment and the job flow are automatically generated. VO and computing environment generation properties used for the simulation are the following:

We considered different resource domains with 25, 30 and 40 heterogeneous computational nodes to simulate a relatively limited resources supply.

A base cost of a node is an exponential function of its performance value, so any two nodes of the same resource type and performance have the same base cost. Effective node cost during the scheduling interval is then calculated by adding a variable distributed normally as ± 0.6 of a base cost, simulating discounts or extra charges up to 60%. The scheduling interval length is 3000 time quanta. The initial 5% to 10% resource load with owner jobs is distributed hyper-geometrically over the whole scheduling interval.

The job batch properties are specified as follows. Jobs number in a batch is 75. Nodes quantity needed for a job is an integer number distributed evenly on $[2; 5]$. Node reservation time is an integer number distributed evenly on $[100; 600]$. Job budget varies in the way that some of jobs can pay as much as 160% of base cost whereas some may require a discount. Every request contains a specification of a custom criterion which is one of the following: *job execution runtime* or *overall execution cost*.

During each experiment a VO resource domain and a job batch were generated and the following scheduling algorithms were simulated and studied.

1. First we ran a conservative backfilling algorithm BF_s to obtain an exemplary job-flow scheduling solution. Conservative backfilling consequently starts each job as soon as possible on condition it does not delay execution of higher priority jobs.
2. Next, we ran a conservative backfilling modification BF_f, which instead of minimizing jobs' start times, performs each job finish time minimization with the same restriction to delay high priority jobs. For this purpose we used AEP algorithm with a finish time minimization criterion to find and allocate suitable resources for each job.
3. Original CSS scheduling was performed with a $C \rightarrow \max$, $\lim U_a = 10\%$ policy. U_a stands for average user utility for one job, i.e. $\lim U_a = 10\%$ means that at average resulting deviation from the best possible outcome for each user did not exceed 10%. Thus, VO policy provides individual jobs execution optimization depending on user criteria: job runtime minimization or job cost minimization.
4. Anticipation scheduling procedure ANT with a $C \rightarrow \max$, $\lim U_a = 10\%$ policy was performed using BF_f scheduling results as a jobs *start* time reference.
5. Finally we performed anticipation scheduling procedure $ANT_{\min}$ with a $C \rightarrow \max$, $\lim U_a = 10\%$ policy and a general time minimization setup. For this purpose we used BF_f scheduling results as a jobs *finish* time reference and decreased jobs runtime references with a 0.8 factor. Additionally we considered different approximation coefficient values $K_t \in \{0, 0.1, 0.5, 1, 1.1, 1.5\}$ (see Sect. 3.4). Different K_t values for $ANT_{\min}$ are supposed to specify an

importance of backfilling scheduling results over anticipated near-optimal scheduling solution. For example, when $K_t = 0$ only backfilling scheduling results are replicated and no individual jobs optimization is performed.

4.2   Simulation Results

More then 1500 scheduling cycles were simulated to obtain average job-flow scheduling results for BF_s, BF_f and ANT.

Figure 1 shows average jobs' start time for CSS, BF_f and ANT in resource domains with 25, 30 and 40 computational nodes. Here we used BF_f scheduling results as a reference for ANT jobs *start* time. As expected average jobs start time decreases gradually with increasing number of available computational nodes for all considered scheduling approaches.

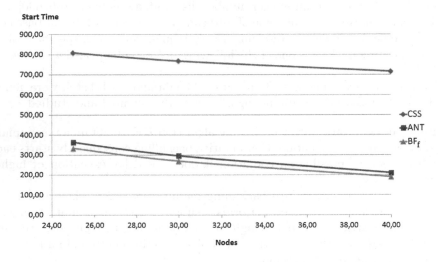

Fig. 1. Simulation results: average job execution start time

The main result presented on Fig. 1 is that ANT has start times almost half of that provided by original CSS algorithm. Indeed, CSS used the whole scheduling interval for the most efficient resources allocation according to $C \rightarrow$ max, lim $U_a = 10\%$ policy without any conditions on start or finish times. ANT on the contrary had additional reference factor for jobs start time and, thus, provided *only* 10% longer average jobs start time compared to BF_f.

At the same time ANT was able to allocate available resources according to VO users criteria. For example Fig. 2 shows average job execution cost for BF_f, ANT and separately for jobs with cost (ANT_C) and time (ANT_T) minimization criteria from ANT scheduling solution. As it can be seen ANT_C jobs have 6–8% less execution cost compared to ANT_T and 4–6% less compared to backfilling.

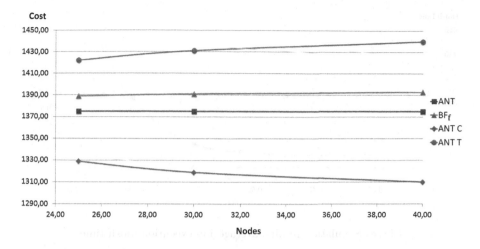

Fig. 2. Simulation results: average job execution cost

The following experiment series were simulated in resource domain with 25 heterogeneous computational nodes using ANT_{min} anticipation procedure setup to reduce a job flow average start time even more.

Figures 3 and 4 show average job-flow average starting and finishing times as a function of K_t parameter. BF_s and BF_f scheduling results are independent from K_t and hence are represented by a horizontal lines.

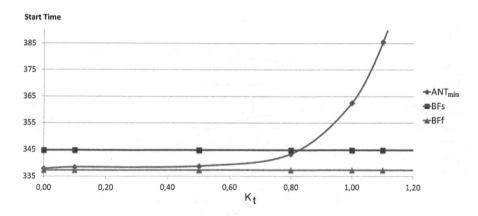

Fig. 3. Simulation results: average job execution start time

First it should be noted that BF_f algorithm at average provided 2% earlier jobs start times and 7% earlier finish times compared to a simple BF_s implementation. Thus, considered backfilling modification BF_f provides an even higher scheduling standard then a traditional conservative backfilling. At the same time ANT_{min} provided earlier jobs finishing times compared to BF_s for all

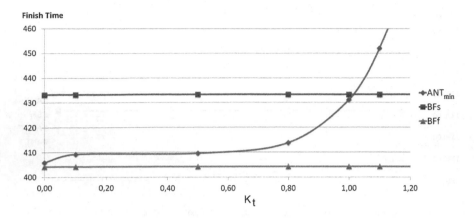

Fig. 4. Simulation results: average job execution finish time

$0 < K_t \leq 1$. In case when $K_t > 1$, by K_t definition, $ANT_{\min}$ jobs finish times are expected to be longer then in a reference backfilling solution.

It can be observed on Figs. 3 and 4 that by decreasing K_t $ANT_{\min}$ job-flow average start and finish times are decreasing and tends almost to BF_f result. In an extreme case when $K_t = 0$ and no job-flow optimization is performed, BF_f advantage is less then 1%. On the other hand with $0 < K_t \leq 1$ values $ANT_{\min}$ with a 2–7% longer job-flow finishing time is still able to perform job-flow scheduling optimization (Figs. 5 and 6).

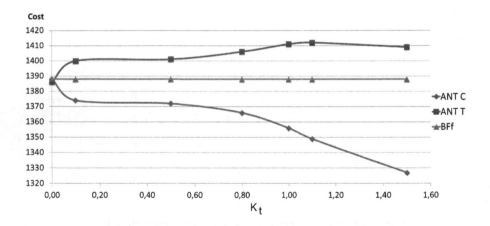

Fig. 5. Simulation results: average job execution cost

Figure 5 shows average jobs execution cost for jobs with a cost minimization (ANT_C) and runtime minimization (ANT_T) criteria obtained by $ANT_{\min}$ and by backfilling modification BF_f. As expected with $K_t = 0$ ANT_C, ANT_T and BF_f have the same jobs execution cost as no job-flow optimization is performed by anticipation scheme. However when $0 < K_t \leq 1$ anticipation algorithm allocates resources according to scheduling policies and hence ANT_C jobs has 1–2% less execution cost compared to backfilling and 2–4% less compared to ANT_T.

A similar picture is presented on Fig. 6 for an average jobs' execution runtime. With a relatively small values $K_t < 0.8$ ANT_T provides up to 6% shorter jobs runtime compared to backfilling and 20% shorter compared to ANT_C jobs. With increasing K_t ANT_T advantage over backfilling increases and reaches 22% when $K_t = 1.5$.

At the same time ANT_C jobs runtime noticeably decreases when $K_t > 1$. It can be explained by a $C \to$ max, lim $U_a = 10\%$ scheduling policy, decreased $ANT_{\min}$ runtime reference and a larger number of computational resources available for a job-flow scheduling optimization.

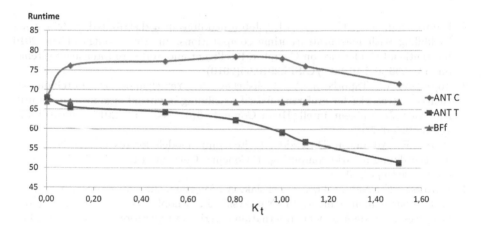

Fig. 6. Simulation results: average job execution runtime

Summarizing the results, anticipation scheduling algorithm is able to perform an efficient and fair resources allocation and at the same time provide competitive job-flow execution completion time. This achieved by a replication procedure which uses backfilling and CSS scheduling results combination as a reference target solution.

5   Conclusions and Future Work

In this paper we study the problem of a fair job batch scheduling with a relatively limited resources supply. We introduce a heuristic scheduling scheme which uses combination of a fair share scheduling policy with a common backfilling algorithm as a reference to allocate a feasible accessible solution.

Computer simulation was performed to study anticipation scheduling scheme and to evaluate it's efficiency. We considered different anticipation scheduling setups to express and predetermine suitable job-flow execution scenario. The obtained results show that the new heuristic approach provides flexible solutions for different fair scheduling scenarios while job-flow execution time is only 1–10% longer compared to backfilling solution.

Future work will be focused on replication algorithm study and it's possible application to fulfill complex user preferences expressed in a resource request.

Acknowledgments. This work was partially supported by the Council on Grants of the President of the Russian Federation for State Support of Young Scientists and Leading Scientific Schools (grants YPhD-2297.2017.9 and SS-6577.2016.9), RFBR (grants 15-07-02259 and 15-07-03401) and by the Ministry on Education and Science of the Russian Federation (project no. 2.9606.2017/8.9).

References

1. Dimitriadou, S.K., Karatza, H.D.: Job scheduling in a distributed system using backfilling with inaccurate runtime computations. In: Proceedings of the 2010 International Conference on Complex, Intelligent and Software Intensive Systems, pp. 329–336. doi:10.1109/CISIS.2010.65(2010)

2. Toporkov, V., Toporkova, A., Tselishchev, A., Yemelyanov, D., Potekhin, P.: Heuristic strategies for preference-based scheduling in virtual organizations of utility Grids. J. Ambient Intell. Hum. Comput. **6**(6), 733–740 (2015). doi:10.1007/s12652-015-0274-y

3. Buyya, R., Abramson, D., Giddy, J.: Economic models for resource management and scheduling in Grid computing. J. Concurr. Comput. **14**(5), 1507–1542 (2002). doi:10.1002/cpe.690

4. Kurowski, K., Nabrzyski, J., Oleksiak, A., Węglarz, J.: Multicriteria aspects of grid resource management. In: Nabrzyski, J., Schopf, J.M., Węglarz, J. (eds.) Grid Resource Management. International Series in Operations Research & Management Science, vol. 64, pp. 271–293. Springer, Boston (2004). doi:10.1007/978-1-4615-0509-918

5. Rodero, I., Villegas, D., Bobro, N., Liu, Y., Fong, L., Sadjadi, S.M.: Enabling interoperability among Grid meta-schedulers. J. Grid Comput. **11**(2), 311–336 (2013). doi:10.1007/s10723-013-9252-9

6. Ernemann, C., Hamscher, V., Yahyapour, R.: Economic scheduling in grid computing. In: Feitelson, D.G., Rudolph, L., Schwiegelshohn, U. (eds.) JSSPP 2002. LNCS, vol. 2537, pp. 128–152. Springer, Heidelberg (2002). doi:10.1007/3-540-36180-4_8

7. Rzadca, K., Trystram, D., Wierzbicki, A.: Fair game-theoretic resource management in dedicated Grids. In: IEEE International Symposium on Cluster Computing and the Grid (CCGRID 2007), pp. 343–350 (2007). doi:10.1109/ccgrid.2007.52

8. Penmatsa, S., Chronopoulos, A.T.: Cost minimization in utility computing systems. Concurr. Comput.: Practice Experience, Wiley **16**(1), 287–307 (2014). doi:10.1002/cpe.2984

9. Vasile, M., Pop, F., Tutueanu, R., Cristea, V., Kolodziej, J.: Resource-aware hybrid scheduling algorithm in heterogeneous distributed computing. J. Future Gener. Comput. Syst. **51**, 61–71 (2015). doi:10.1016/j.future.2014.11.019

10. Mutz, A., Wolski, R., Brevik, J.: Eliciting honest value information in a batch-queue environment. In: 8th IEEE/ACM International Conference on Grid Computing, pp. 291–297. IEEE Computer Society (2007). doi:10.1109/grid.2007.4354145

11. Blanco, H., Guirado, F., Lrida, J.L., Albornoz, V.M.: MIP model scheduling for multi-clusters. In: Proceedings of the Euro-Par 2012, pp. 196–206 (2012). doi:10.1007/978-3-642-36949-022

12. Takefusa, A., Nakada, H., Kudoh, T., Tanaka, Y.: An advance reservation-based co-allocation algorithm for distributed computers and network bandwidth on QoS-guaranteed grids. In: Frachtenberg, E., Schwiegelshohn, U. (eds.) JSSPP 2010. LNCS, vol. 6253, pp. 16–34. Springer, Heidelberg (2010). doi:10.1007/978-3-642-16505-4_2

13. Carroll, T., Grosu, D.: Divisible load scheduling: an approach using coalitional games. In: Proceedings of the Sixth International Symposium on Parallel and Distributed Computing (ISPDC 2007), pp. 36–36 (2007). doi:10.1109/ispdc.2007.16

14. Kim, K., Buyya, R.: Fair resource sharing in hierarchical virtual organizations for global Grids. In: Proceedings of the 8th IEEE/ACM International Conference on Grid Computing, pp. 50–57 (2007). doi:10.1109/grid.2007.4354115

15. Toporkov, V., Yemelyanov, D., Bobchenkov, A., Tselishchev, A.: Scheduling in grid based on VO stakeholders preferences and criteria. In: Zamojski, W., Mazurkiewicz, J., Sugier, J., Walkowiak, T., Kacprzyk, J. (eds.) Dependability Engineering and Complex Systems. AISC, vol. 470, pp. 505–515. Springer, Cham (2016). doi:10.1007/978-3-319-39639-2_44

16. Toporkov, V., Toporkova, A., Tselishchev, A., Yemelyanov, D.: Slot selection algorithms in distributed computing. J. Supercomput. 69(1), 53–60 (2014). doi:10.1007/s11227-014-1210-1

17. Toporkov, V., Tselishchev, A., Yemelyanov, D., Bobchenkov, A.: Composite scheduling strategies in distributed computing with non-dedicated resources. Procedia Comput. Sci. 9, 176–185 (2012). doi:10.1016/j.procs.2012.04.019

18. Calheiros, R.N., Ranjan, R., Beloglazov, A., De Rose, C.A.F., Buyya, R.: CloudSim: a toolkit for modeling and simulation of cloud computing environments and evaluation of resource provisioning algorithms. J. Softw.: Pract. Exp. 41(1), 23–50 (2011). doi:10.1002/spe.995

A Mobile Botnet Model Based on P2P Grid

Marek Šimon$^{(\boxtimes)}$, Ladislav Huraj, and Marián Hosťovecký

Department of Applied Informatics and Mathematics,
University of SS. Cyril and Methodius, Trnava, Slovak Republic
{marek.simon,ladislav.huraj,marian.hostovecky}@ucm.sk

Abstract. Along with the rise of mobile devices the threat of adopting the mobile devices for cyber-attacks has increased. The sheer number of smartphones would be more than a billion in the world. Such amount of devices has strong communication potential. Moreover, running of open operating systems such as Google Android on mobile devices results in including the mobile platform into botnet network and mobile devices begin to be more interesting for attackers. The question how the mobile devices can be dangerous for a particular network, especially DDoS (Distributed Denial of Service) attacks carried from mobile devices, is a great challenge to security for computer networks.

This paper illustrates a testbed model based on a P2P grid in order to straightforward include mobile devices to testbed environment and to understand DDoS attack carried on mobile devices such as smartphones, tablets or other mobile personal computers. Testbed model based on P2P grid built on OurGrid environment creates a framework behaving as a hybrid botnet and is able to execute commands from a botmaster and consequently to test a real network system on mobile devices threats.

The article presents a possibility how to use of mobile devices and their computational resources the P2P grid nodes for computational tasks, and it shows abilities of mobile devices for the real DDoS attack. For this purpose, we benchmarked the framework, performed a real DDoS attack on existing web server assisted by several mobile devices. Moreover, analysis of the results is provided.

Keywords: Mobile devices · DDoS attack · OurGrid · Testbed · Botnet

1 Introduction

Mobile devices are increasingly adopted because of their development and diffusion and they have become an important and crucial element of people lives. Through mobile devices, users can easily connect to the Internet using access points distributed along the territory and via different technologies of network types (Wi-Fi, LTE, 3G). Mobile devices are able to execute most tasks and operations typically operated by a common personal computer (e.g. web browsing, playing audio and video files or other multimedia contents, sending/receiving e-mails, file sharing, etc.). But the potential of mobile devices is exploited by cybercrime as well; developing special malicious applications such as spyware or worm, as well as exploiting of compromised network nodes for attacks and including the nodes in botnets is used by cybercrime [1].

© Springer International Publishing AG 2017
A. Kravets et al. (Eds.): CIT&DS 2017, CCIS 754, pp. 604–615, 2017.
DOI: 10.1007/978-3-319-65551-2_44

Botnets as a collection of infected computers running autonomously and automatically are a new phenomenon of last decade. The growth of the power of mobile devices increases also interest in their collection into botnet where hackers control and group together such infected computers or other devices and perform various attacks like spamming, infection spreading, identity theft and distributed denial of service (DDoS). One of the threats most frequently culpable of unavailability of internet services is especially the DDoS attack.

Based on the interest to investigate the attack potential offered by mobile devices from the point of view of the real network as well as to use the offensive potential from the perspective of the hackers, a tool to test the state of real networks is needed.

To develop a DDoS testbed environment, three major approaches are used [2]. The first approach is the use of a network simulator, for example, OPNET, ns-2 or ns-3; then a simulation of the environment is specified and instantiated on a particularly powerful machine. The second approach is to produce an emulation of the environment through a connection between real computers to a required topology. The third approach is to use the real network and to execute real experiment despite the fact that the network could not match all requests of the experiment or the network could be infected or damaged.

Nowadays, experimentation laboratory platforms for example DETER, Emulab or PlanetLab are used to develop an emulation environment [3]. But a secure and isolated platform is needed to reproduce a comprehensive attack, compared with our case where real live pseudo-attack is leaded and monitored from administrator side.

Additionally, more realistic consequences are met when testbed for the DDoS attack is based on live experimentation rather than either emulation or simulation [4]. Moreover, environmental parameters of the experiment are under the greater control of researchers and therefore a careful consideration with larger modification of environmental parameters can be carried out.

The rest of the paper is structured as follows: Sect. 2 describes how computational P2P grid and botnet works. Section 3 introduces the structure of the proposed model. In Sect. 4, the experimental outcomes are described. Finally, Sect. 5 reports about the conclusions and possible future work.

2 Background

In this section, we briefly describe the background of two main mechanisms: computational P2P grid and DDoS attack. The whole framework, for the mobile computational grid as well as for mobile DDoS testbed is based on OurGrid middleware [5]. OurGrid is an open source environment generating a peer-to-peer architecture.

2.1 Computational P2P Grid

Distributed computing models such as peer-to-peer networks and grids collect computers into networks that offer or consume available distributed resources. A grid as a geographically distributed computation framework offers a set of heterogeneous machines accessible through a single interface. On the other hand, a peer-to-peer network does not require fixed clients and servers and uses a decentralized collaboration of nodes where each node can act both as a server and a client. The combination of P2P and grids into a computational P2P grid accelerates progress in both platforms; it enables a new approach to solving a problem in which each node provides resources into distributed systems while using resources provided by other nodes in the network of involving nodes [6].

The OurGrid environment allows the formation of a computational P2P grid to accelerate computing of Bag-of-tasks applications. In Bag-of-tasks model, several parallel independent jobs can be executed separately not communicating with each other during their performance, tolerating network delays and faults. Despite their simplicity, the Bag-of task applications are used in a variety of scientific domains, such as simulations, parameter sweeps, fractal calculations, computer imaging or computational biology and they are able to exploit the computing power provided by the framework [7].

A special part of OurGrid called Broker is responsible for interaction of each user with the particular OurGrid community. Moreover, the heterogeneity of P2P grid structure is hidden through this part. Furthermore, compared to traditional grids, the computational P2P grids are more accessible from different social and geographical settings, which offers opportunities to new areas such as emergency communication, management of disasters or battlefields, the entertainment industry, e-healthcare, e-learning, etc. [8–10].

Computational tasks and specific nodes called Peers are scheduled by the Broker through discovery services; the Peers are responsible for allocation of each task to end-use nodes called Workers which process particular jobs. The Peers connects other Peers in the individual group in order to detect idle resources to jobs. The Broker utilizes gained information about existing idle resources provided by the Peers for the scheduling [11, 12].

Mobile devices can serve as nodes of the computational P2P grid as well. Although mobile devices are usually limited by reduced CPU, memory, secondary storage, and bandwidth capabilities and individual devices are resource-limited, collected resources from a number of mobile devices can establish significant capacity for involving them for calculation in a computational P2P grid or as a part of the framework for computer attacks.

2.2   Botnet

Bot nodes or bot machines are compromised computers controlled by the attacker in the network called botnet. There could be thousands of bot-nodes in a botnet. Powerful distributed computing ability and abundant information resources reserve is obtained by the attacker by controlling these bot-nodes. The control of botnet gives to attacker called botmaster an opportunity to perform numerous kinds of attacks such as theft of privacy, phishing, spam, spyware bulk distribution, Trojans and, last but not least, distributed denial of service attack (DDoS). Botnet research constitutes an important network security hotspot as major security threats on the Internet.

In the recent years, just DDoS attacks are one of the most significant threats run from botnets. The DDoS attack is run indirectly through many distributed infected computers as coordinated attacks on the availability of services. The major objective of the cyber-attack is a performance reduction of the victim, i.e. the network bandwidth decrease, and computational resources reduction and so to reduce the quality of provided services to legitimate clients. A set of servers, hosts, networks or other systems whose services the attacker wishes to block is possible to conceive as the victim [13].

Because of easy instantiation of DDoS attacks, the attacks are usually extremely efficient and problematic to mitigate, even if the attacker knows the only little technical background of them [14]. Instead, simulating of DDoS attacks through artificial traffic generators is not the ideal way to research them, regardless of whether software or hardware generator is used [15]. Furthermore, direct physical representation of DDoS testing requires a need of massive amount of infected computers to operate the attack [16].

Special kind of botnet is a P2P botnet. The model is based on peer-to-peer systems where nodes that can act both as a server and as a client in communication with each other, create the P2P system. The main benefit of such model inherited from the P2P network structure is a very high level of anonymity and reliability of nodes, which is harder to detect. P2P botnets are more difficult to trace. On the other hand, the main shortcoming of such botnet is that firewalls and network address translation systems can obstacle botnet communications, e.g. a peer behind a network address translation without a public IP address could not act as a server and receive inbound connections coming from other peers [1].

Mobile platforms enable to develop a version of a mobile botnet. Mobile botnets make it possible to botmaster similarly to perform numerous kinds of attacks like usual botnet which increases the interest of attackers in mobile devices and also increases the number of attacks to property security and privacy of smartphones [17, 27]. Moreover, the mobile devices are more vulnerable to be compromised and to be involved into botnet than common computers.

3   Mobile P2P Grid Design

Formation of mobile workers through OurGrid environment enables to join mobile devices into P2P grid environment. Although the OurGrid environment provides relatively simple and clear connection of new workers into the P2P grid, the environment is primarily oriented to static nodes. An implementation of mobile workers to OurGrid requires dealing mainly with the question of implementation under operating systems because OurGrid is running only under OS Linux or MS Windows, while common mobile devices are running under OS Android.

Our solution was based on the following applications and the OurGrid environment was running with their support:

- application *GNURoot Debian* providing a method to install and use OS Debian and its associated applications/packages alongside OS Android without rooting of the mobile device; but inside GNURoot Debian it is possible to create a root file system, launch into it, or delete it; and the application *GNURoot WheezyX (xterms)* allowing to create and launch a Debian Wheezy roots again without rooting the device when used along with GNURoot,

- three supporting applications on a mobile device are required: (i) application *tightvncserver* under OS Debian, package provides a server to which X clients can connect and the server generates a display that can be viewed with a vncviewer, (ii) OS Debian should have *Java virtual machine* installed that is necessary for correct running of OurGrid environment, (iii) application *VNC Viewer* under OS Android for remote access to Linux computer from localhost to view the computer's graphical desktop and control its mouse and keyboard.

From this moment, it is possible to utilize mobile devices as computational workers and to distribute to them the particular jobs through Broker node.

3.1 Mobile P2P Grid Design for DDoS Attack

The botnet structure was an inspiration for DDoS testbed design based on OurGrid environment. To receive and response commands from a botmaster to infected machines, the botnet uses several architectures to hide its detection starting with central architecture and ending with a combination of P2P with Hyper Text Transfer Protocol (HttP2P botnet). Implementation of the traditional central architecture of botnet which uses one or two hosts as central controllers is straightforward but easy detectable by intrusion detection mechanism or firewall. On the other hand, an implementation of a hybrid combination of HttP2P botnet can better bypass detection mechanisms but it is difficult to manage [18].

OurGrid environment as the P2P grid has characteristics closely resembling those of the hybrid P2P botnet. In hybrid P2P botnet, some bots are used as botnet controllers (servent bots), which resembles the super node in the current P2P network and they behave as both clients and servers. Client bots are remaining bots and they perform the DDoS attack to target. Client and servent bots use their peer lists in order to actively contact the servent bots to receive commands. A botmaster injects commands through social websites where servent bots periodically connect to the website in bot groups, retrieve commands from the social websites issued by their botmaster and forward the commands to all client bots to subsequently execute it, Fig. 1 [19–21].

The P2P grid based on the OurGrid environment has a similar design to receive and response commands. The Broker node is analogue to botmaster in botnet where the jobs are scheduled using discovery service; the Peers nodes correspond to servent bots where jobs are distributed to Worker nodes; and Worker nodes correspond to client bots where the jobs are executed and the target is attacked, Fig. 1. Therefore, it is comparatively desirable to exploit proposed testbed for botnet attacks and to monitor impacts of such attacks on the real network.

Moreover, incorporation of mobile devices into the model gives the possibility to explore aspects of the impact of mobile botnet from the point of view of the network as well as from the point of view of mobile devices and their workload and it is possible to propose countermeasures. As mentioned in Sect. 2.1, some special applications should be installed for this purposes on mobile devices. On the other hand, it is not required to root or otherwise modify rights of the mobile devices to simulate mobile botnet as is the practice in the case of real botnets.

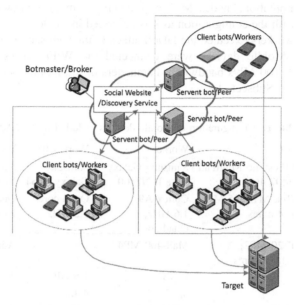

Fig. 1. Analogy of structure of hybrid P2P botnet and OurGrid scheme

Corresponding to a real mobile botnet and its client bots, each mobile device as a Worker in P2P grid shall have installed OurGrid software what is the same manner as for each infected machine in a botnet. After that receiving and responding to commands taken by a Worker node can be quite simple as well as the setting up and maintaining of the whole OurGrid environment. The testbed experiments do not require to hide the existence of the simulated botnet, therefore, the messages between the Broker node and Worker nodes do not have to be masked. Likewise, it is not possible to solve social engineering means to infect the machines.

As mentioned above, the main shortcoming of the OurGrid environment is the limitation to perform only bag-of-tasks model and the Worker nodes are not able to communicate with each other during executing the calculation. On the other hand, hybrid P2P botnet also does not use direct communication between bots, involving mobile devices, and therefore the bag-of-tasks and OurGrid environment are applicable for botnet experiments.

4 Performance Tests

We conducted a preliminary evaluation to value the feasibility of our approach in situations where each input data for the distributed tasks is small (the size is less than 1 kB). The performance tests are from the point of view of: (i) suitability to use mobile devices for computing tasks as a part of the P2P grid, (ii) efficiency of the DDoS attack led from mobile devices.

For both scenarios, four mobile devices were used. We operated different kinds of equipment to demonstrate the ability of the OurGrid environment to hide heterogeneity of particular computational nodes. More specifically, we monitored two tablets and two mobile phones with the configuration as it is described in Table 1. The mobile devices as the OurGrid workers executed the DDoS attack to the web server and their capacity was measured. Mobile devices were connected via WiFi access point 2.4 GHz 802.11b/g/n with 100 Mb/s bandwidth. Parameters of the mobile botnet attack are in detail described in Subsect. 4.2.

Table 1. Configuration of mobile devices included into P2P grid

	Worker 01	Worker 02	Worker 03	Worker 04
Mobile device	Tablet Prestigio MultiPad Wize 3407 4G	Samsung Galaxy Note II N7100	Samsung Galaxy Tab4	Samsung Galaxy Note III N9005
CPU	MediaTek MT8735 M, 1 GHz, 4 cores	Cortex-A9, 1.6 GHz, Quad-core	Quad core 1.2 GHz	Quad-core 2.3 GHz Krait 400
GPU	Mali-T720 MP2, 416 MHz, 2 cores	Mali-400 MP4		Adreno 330
RAM	1 GB	2 GB	1.5 GB	3 GB
Android	5.1	4.4.2	4.4.2	5
Debian	aarch64, 3 cores	ARMv7, 3 cores	ARMv7, 4 cores	ARMv7, 4 cores

4.1 Mobile Devices as a Computational P2P Workers

The first experiment was oriented to measure if the mobile devices are suitable to perform the computational task during common operation of the devices in the P2P grid. We applied the LinpackJava benchmark [22] for calculating the total capacity of the mobile devices. The Linpack Benchmark is an open source Java application that includes a numerically intensive test to measure the floating point performance of computers. Linpack benchmarks measure how fast the system can solve linear equations with Gaussian elimination; it is measured in Millions of Floatingpoint Operations per Second (MFLOPS). Analogous measuring for P2P grid through LinpackJava can be found for example in [23, 24].

In Fig. 2 we determine the amount of MFLOPS by LinpackJava that was performed on each mobile device during performing the DDoS attack. As can be seen from the graph, there is still enough computational capacity to compute another task and the mobile device owners could not notice that the attack was led by their devices, except battery consumption of the mobile device. There is also shown by the dashed line the maximal capacity in MFLOPS of each mobile device determined by LinpackJava benchmark in the Fig. 2.

As an outcome of this experiment, the concrete potentials of using mobile devices influencing the performance perceived by users can be known as well as the amount of MFLOPS as a metric established that identifies the capacity of each mobile device to support the computation of parallel bag-of-tasks based on a P2P grid.

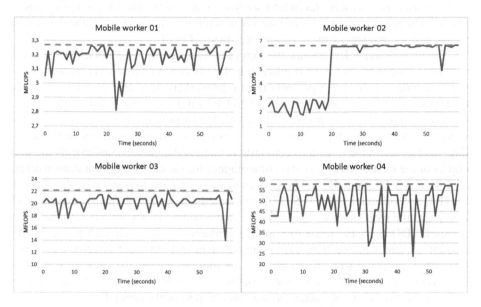

Fig. 2. LinpackJava benchmark for mobile devices

4.2 Mobile Botnet Attack

In this experiment, a DDoS attack led only by mobile devices was investigated. The prototype of our P2P grid testbed enables to include the mobile devices and to carry out an attack from them as from bots in a botnet. For our case study, we executed HTTP Get flood attack led to our web server. Basic GET requests are used to barrage the web-server in the HTTP Get flood attack. The main aim is to overwhelm the computing resources of the web server, i.e. the CPU of the web server. Such kind of attack is led in the application layer and does not exercise reflection techniques, nonstandard packets or spoofing. We employed a single-threaded computer benchmark ApacheBench for performance measuring of HTTP web servers [25]. The benchmark tool was configured to set up one hundred number of connections to the web server during 60 s. The ApacheBench tool sends a request to URL on every connection and waits until the web server processes it. Subsequently, it sends next request to URL.

In order to compare the efficiency of mobile devices for the DDoS attack, two different attacks have been prototyped, first from mobile Worker nodes and the same one led from static Worker nodes with the same amount of four attacking nodes. The length of the attacks was 60 s. OS Debian7 with OurGrid worker framework was running on all attacking static workers. OS CentOS6, CPU 3.3 GHz Pentium, 1 GB RAM was running on the victim server. In our previous research [12, 26] we showed that it is possible to overload such tested web server even just with 40 static workers with HTTP Get flood attack to HTTP URLs.

Two main metrics were taken into account in the study outcomes in both cases of attacks. The load1 of the victim web-server was the first metric, Fig. 3, and the second metric was the amount of received and sent bytes, Fig. 4.

The Figs. 3 and 4 demonstrate the impact of both attacks led from mobile workers and from static workers on the bandwidth and CPU consumption of the victim server. Since the attack was carried out only from four workers in mobile devices attack, the HTTP Get flood attack carried out to HTTPS URLs did not result in full overloading of the whole target server. Conversely, the attack led from static workers overloaded the web server to an extent that the web server was ceasing to execute additional requests, Fig. 4b. The measured outcomes demonstrate some valuable assumptions: (i) the load impact of the victim server was eight times higher for the attack led from static workers than the attack led from the mobile devices workers; (ii) just four static worker through HTTP Get flood attack to HTTPS URLs consumed the computational resources in such a way that the web server was ceasing to execute additional requests corresponding to successful DDoS attack; while four mobile workers did not reach such point, (iii) the amount of sent and received data is approximately by a third smaller for mobile workers as for static workers. In general, the mobile devices have shown the ability significantly to jeopardize the running of the web server. Let us note that a botnet includes hundreds or thousands of bots and experiments depend on a number of available mobile devices appropriated for the testing.

OurGrid today represents beneficial environment for testing of mobile distributed denial of service attacks.

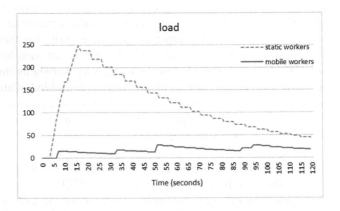

Fig. 3. System load average during the attack

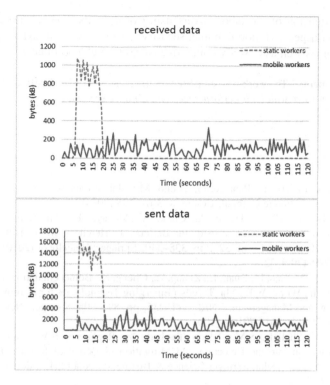

Fig. 4. Amount of bytes (a) received (b) transmitted to the network by the web server

5 Conclusions and Future Work

The fast growth of mobile devices and also of mobile internet cause some security problems. Our paper showed the design and development of testbed environment for mobile botnet based on a P2P grid. The mobile botnet is constructed to perform and test DDoS attack usually followed by reduction of network bandwidth and victim's resources.

The paper demonstrated in practice the suitability to use a P2P grid with the assistance of mobile devices as a testbed for mobile botnet and to execute real experimental DDoS flood attack as well as the feasibility of common mobile devices act as computational P2P workers. This fact puts mobile devices from the point of the P2P grid at the same level with other common computers.

Results prove that although mobile device workers in P2P grid produces lower attack force than common static P2P workers, their attack executions have a significant impact. Involving of mobile nodes into P2P grid gives to the botnet possibility to extend DDoS attack effects. Moreover, once the mobile testbed scheme under OurGrid environment is constructed it can be used for testing of various cyber-attacks led from mobile devices. The OurGrid hides the heterogeneity also of mobile devices and a mobile device can act as regular Worker node in the P2P grid.

Future extension of the labor covers using of the experimental mobile botnet to examine other aspects of mobile botnet security, e.g. a network aimed at spam or malware diffusion as well as to study countermeasures to such coordinated vulnerabilities.

Acknowledgements. The work was supported by the grant KEGA 011UMB-4/2017 *Increasing competencies in work with high performance computing ecosystem.*

References

1. Farina, P., Cambiaso, E., Papaleo, G., Aiello, M.: Mobile botnets development: issues and solutions. Int. J. Future Comput. Commun. **3**(6), 385 (2014)
2. Schmidt, D., Suriadi, S., Tickle, A., Clark, A., Mohay, G., Ahmed, E., Mackie, J.: A distributed denial of service testbed. In: Berleur, J., Hercheui, M.D., Hilty, L.M. (eds.) CIP/HCC -2010. IAICT, vol. 328, pp. 338–349. Springer, Heidelberg (2010). doi:10.1007/978-3-642-15479-9_32
3. Lin, B., Hao, Q., Xiao, L., Ruan, L., Zhang, Z., Cheng, X.: Botnet emulation: challenges and techniques. In: Wong, W.E., Ma, T. (eds.) Emerging Technologies for Information Systems, Computing, and Management. LNEE, vol. 236, pp. 897–908. Springer, New York (2013). doi:10.1007/978-1-4614-7010-6_100
4. Schmidt, D., Shalinie, S.M.: DDoS Testbed. In: Raghavan, S.V., Dawson, E. (eds.) An Investigation into the Detection and Mitigation of Denial of Service (DoS) Attacks, pp. 115–129. New Delhi, Springer Science & Business Media (2011). doi:10.1007/978-81-322-0277-6_4
5. Ourgrid Project. http://www.ourgrid.org
6. Domenico, T., Trunfio, P.: Toward a synergy between P2P and grids. IEEE Internet Comput. **7**(4), 96–95 (2003)
7. Da Silva, M., Nesmachnow, S.: Heterogeneous resource allocation in the ourgrid middleware: a greedy approach. In: HPCLatAm, pp. 49–60 (2013)
8. Hrmo, R., Kristofiakova, L., and Kučerka, D.: Developing the information competencies via e-learning and assessing the qualities of e-learning text. In: 15th International Conference on Interactive Collaborative Learning, Villach, Austria (2012)
9. Ölvecký, M., Gabriška, D.: Motion capture as an extension of web-based simulation. Appl. Mech. Mater. **513**, 827–833 (2014)
10. Horváthová, D., Siládi, V., Lacková, E.: Phobia treatment with the help of virtual reality, In: 13th International Scientific Conference on Informatics. IEEE (2015)
11. Zhao, H., Liu, X., Li, X.: A taxonomy of peer-to-peer desktop grid paradigms. Clust. Comput.: J. Netw. Softw. Tools Appl. **14**(2), 129–144 (2011). Springer
12. Simon, M., Huraj, L., Siládi, V.: Analysis of performance bottleneck of P2P grid applications. J. Appl. Math. Stat. Inform. **9**(2), 5–11 (2013)
13. Singh, S., Gyanchandani, M.: Analysis of botnet behavior using queuing theory. Int. J. Comput. Sci. Commun. **1**(2), 239–241 (2010)
14. Hosnieh, R., Meinel, C.: Privacy and security in IPv6 networks: challenges and possible solutions. In: Proceedings of the 6th International Conference on Security of Information and Networks. ACM (2013)
15. Bhatia, S., Schmidt, D., Mohay, G., Tickle, A.: A framework for generating realistic traffic for Distributed Denial-of-Service attacks and Flash Events. Comput. Secur. **40**, 95–107 (2014)

16. Gupta, B., Joshi, R., Misra, M.: Prediction of number of zombies in a DDoS attack using polynomial regression model. J. Adv. Inf. Technol. **2**(1), 57–62 (2011)
17. Sun, F., Zhai, L., Du, Y., Wang, P., Li, J.: Design of mobile botnet based on open service. Int. J. Digit. Crime Forensics (IJDCF) **8**(3), 1–10 (2016)
18. Ullah, I., Khan, N., Aboalsamh, H.A.: Survey on botnet: its architecture, detection, prevention and mitigation. In: 10th IEEE International Conference on Networking, Sensing and Control (ICNSC), pp. 660–665 (2013)
19. Lu, T., Liao, H., Chen, M.: An advanced hybrid P2P botnet 2.0. World Acad. Sci. Eng. Technol. **81**, 595–597 (2011)
20. Wang, P., Sparks, S., Zou, C.C.: An advanced hybrid peer-to-peer botnet. IEEE Trans. Dependable Secur. Comput. **7**(2), 113–127 (2010)
21. Zeidanloo, H.R., Manaf, A.A.: Botnet command and control mechanisms. In: Second International Conference on Computer and Electrical Engineering, ICCEE 2009, vol. 1. IEEE (2009)
22. Linpack Benchmark – Java Version. http://www.netlib.org/benchmark/linpackjava/
23. Veiga, L., Rodrigues, R., and Ferreira, P.: GiGi: an ocean of gridlets on a "Grid-for-the-Masses". In: Proceedings of the Seventh IEEE International Symposium on Cluster Computing and the Grid. pp. 783–788 (2007)
24. Gómez, C.E., Díaz, C.O., Forero, C.A., Rosales, E., Castro, H.: Determining the Real Capacity of a Desktop Cloud. In: Osthoff, C., Navaux, P.O.A., Barrios Hernandez, C.J., Silva Dias, P.L. (eds.) CARLA 2015. CCIS, vol. 565, pp. 62–72. Springer, Cham (2015). doi:10.1007/978-3-319-26928-3_5
25. ab - Apache HTTP server benchmarking tool. http://httpd.apache.org/docs/2.0/programs/ab.html
26. Šimon, M., Huraj, L., Hosťovecký, M.: IPv6 Network DDoS Attack with P2P Grid. In: Kravets, A., Shcherbakov, M., Kultsova, M., Shabalina, O. (eds.) Creativity in Intelligent, Technologies and Data Science, pp. 407–415. Springer International Publishing, Cham (2015). doi:10.1007/978-3-319-23766-4_32
27. Juhasova, B., Halenar, I., Juhas, M.: Design and implementation of autonomous mobile device with adaptive control. In: 17th International Conference International Conference on Mechatronics - Mechatronika (ME). IEEE, Prague (2016)

The Impact of Generation Y's Customer Experience on Emotions: Online Banking Sector

Sandra Maria Correia Loureiro[1] and Eduardo Moraes Sarmento[2,3(✉)]

[1] Instituto Universitário de Lisboa (ISCTE-IUL) Business Research Unit
(BRU/UNIDE), Lisbon, Portugal
sandramloureiro@netcabo.pt
[2] CEsA/ISEG (Lisbon School of Economics and Management,
Lisbon University), ULHT, Lisbon, Portugal
emoraessarmento@gmail.com
[3] ESHTE, Estoril, Portugal

Abstract. Recently, banking sector focused on attracting Generation Y (individuals born between 1980 and 2000) because they have emerged as a huge force with growing spending power which will unavoidably rival with Baby Boomers' market dominance. They try to attract them through a unique customer experience, especially the ability of differentiation.

Using the Mehrabian & Russell's model of stimulus (S) - organism (O) - response (R), this study developed the Generation Y customer experience framework that intends to explain their consumer emotional responses toward customer experience attributes in a bank through three aspects: pleasure, dominance, and arousal toward online banks.

Empirical evidence, based on data from a survey suggests that the overall customer experience attributes in the bank had a positive relation with emotional responses in different ways. "Value for money", "Getting things right the first time" and "Put the consumer first" emerged as the most important attributes for Generation Y in experiencing a bank.

Keywords: Customer experience · Generation Y · Stimulus-organism-response model · Pleasure · Dominance · Arousal · Banking sector

1 Introduction

In a global and competitive world, searching for competitive advantage through product differentiation in the banking sector is increasingly difficult because products and services are very quickly copied forcing banks to find new ways and opportunities of identifying and developing relationships with customer and enhancing positive feelings about them. Today, banking is a consumer-oriented service industry, and their business increasingly depends on the quality of the consumer service provided and overall satisfaction of the customer.

Therefore, experiences have become a critical aspect to corporate banking success. Today, customers expect a high level of experience from banks, which, if fulfilled,

© Springer International Publishing AG 2017
A. Kravets et al. (Eds.): CIT&DS 2017, CCIS 754, pp. 616–639, 2017.
DOI: 10.1007/978-3-319-65551-2_45

could result in significantly improved customer satisfaction, and potentially retention levels [1]. Furthermore, the Brand experience has been as the outcome of an attribute drove information processing in which consumers are engaged rationally and emotionally. Therefore, when creating a brand experience, the key is to engage all senses and to evoke emotional as well as an intellectual reaction towards a brand [2].

Generation Y (Gen Y) is considerably less likely to have positive experiences, compared to all other age groups due to the high expectations they have toward banks' digital capabilities. Gen Y is far more interested in using mobile banking compared to other age groups, placing additional importance on the development of this channel [3]. Customer experience acts as an emerging opportunity in this fast-paced highly competitive world especially in the new horizon of experience economy since customers with positive experiences are three to five times more likely to refer others and purchase additional products [4].

Prior studies with bank institutions revealed a gap because they didn't properly analyze which stimuli of online bank experience could influence positively the emotions. Therefore, the research question is: which stimuli of bank experience can influence the emotions of Generation Y (or Gen Y)?

We will try to understand the impact of Generation Y customer experience in the banking sector through the stimulus (S) - organism (O) - response (R) model developed by Mehrabian and Russell (1974). This model is a key component in focusing the various dimensions that may stimulate consumers, as well as postulating the various emotional responses of consumers. All those aspects are affected by stimulus variables. The emotional responses represent the outcomes of the bank marketing effort which include three variables: pleasure, dominance, and arousal.

This article is organized into three parts. The first one gives the theoretical background and it starts with the Stimulus–Organism–Response model that will be relied on this study as well as the analysis of the topic of Sensory Marketing and Co-creator, Experience and Brand experience, and Stimulus as Customer experience. We also present the description to the topic of Generation Y as a focus segment in this study. The second part is related to the research design and methodology and the last part analyses the results and conclusions.

2   Theoretical Framework

2.1   Stimulus–Organism–Response Model

The stimulus–organism–response model (S-O-R) was introduced into marketing by Donovan and Rossiter in 1982. When applied to a retail setting the stimulus is operationalized as the atmospheric cues, organism as emotional and cognitive states of consumers, and response as approach or avoidance behaviors such as re-patronage, store search, and various in-store behaviors [6].

The stimuli in the S-O-R framework are represented by a set of attributes that affect the perceptions of the consumer [7]. These attributes are the starting point of the consumer behavioral process and are cues that enter a consumer's cognition and arouse or incite him (as a recipient) consciously or subconsciously into action. The attributes entered into a consumer's mind in a traditional retail environment include social factor such as the people in the store, customers, and employees, design factors such as visual cues of layout, clutter, cleanliness, and color, and ambient factor such as non-visual cues including smells and sounds [8]. The organism, the second component in the S–O–R framework, refers to the intervening internal process between the stimuli and reaction of the consumer. It is a process in which, the consumer converts the stimuli into meaningful information and utilizes them to comprehend the environment before making any judgment or conclusion. The third component, the response, is the final outcome or reaction of the consumers, including psychological reactions such as attitudes and/or behavioral reactions [9].

In other words, a stimulus is something outside consumers' control, which can include marketing mix variables or other inputs from the environment. Those stimuli will affect consumers' internal states [10]. The organism is described as the internal processes and structures intervening between stimuli, external to the person, and the final actions, reactions, or responses emitted [11]. Finally, the response is defined as the output in the form of the reaction of consumers toward the stimuli [11].

In examining Generation Y experience in the banking sector, "stimuli" or environmental cues will be conceptualized as Customer Experience attributes. More specifically accessibility, ease of doing business, execution excellence, personalized offering, staff engagement, value for money, and reputation. "Organism" will be described as the internal state, using the Pleasure-Arousal-Dominance scale to measure the affective and emotional state of consumers, as well as a satisfactions scale, which ultimately reflects upon the attitudinal state of the consumers while engaging with particular experience attributes given by the bank.

2.2 Customer Experience in Banking Sector

By monitoring competitive scenario that happens in different business sectors, customer experience has turned out to be a hotspot in the growth cycle of any organizations. The concept of customer experience first appeared in marketing studies in 1982 by Holbrook and Hirschman and became generalized in marketing literature by Pine II and Gilmore in 1998. Nowadays, creating and delivering superior customer experience has become one of the prime objectives of organizations. Since traditional Marketing views the customer as rational decision making, who care about benefit and functional feature of products/service [12].

The term started gaining increasing interest among academicians and practitioners, especially because of turn from service- based economy to experience- based economy. In other words, as goods and services become commoditized, the customer experiences that companies create will matter most. An experience occurs when a company intentionally uses services as the stage, and goods as props, to engage individual customers in a way that creates a memorable event [13].

Customer experience is defined as the internal and subjective response customers must any direct or indirect contact with a company. Direct contact generally occurs during purchase, use, and service and is usually initiated by the customer. Indirect contact most often involves unplanned encounters with representatives of a company's products, service or brands and takes the form of word-of-mouth recommendations or criticisms, advertising, news reports, reviews and so forth [14]. In other words, Customer experience is the user's interpretation of his or her total interaction with the brand [15].

In considering customer experience, it is appropriate to consider two perspectives of consumer behavior: the traditional "information processing and decision oriented" perspective and the "experiential" perspective. The first perspective sometimes referred to as the cognition affect and behavior approach; this cognitive view suggests that the customer is engaged primarily in goal-directed activities such as searching for information, evaluating available options and deciding whether to buy a particular product or service or not [16]. In another hand, the experiential view of consumption has broadened this perspective considerably. Consumption includes the flow of fantasies, feelings, and fun where such behavior may not necessarily be goal [17]. Customer experience needs to be seen from both an information-processing approach that focuses on memory-based activities and on processes that are more sub-conscious and private in nature [18].

The nature of service encounter and kind of service provider do an essential function because the customers not just purchase the service delivered by the business, however, purchases "experience" from that business, too. The main reason to work on the experiences of the banks' customers is that the prosperity of any bank depends upon its number of existing customers [19]. For services, it has been demonstrated that the creation and delivery of an emotion-rich experience provide brand differentiation and influences sales, consumer loyalty, and promotion of the brand [20].

In studying of customer experience factors in banking, a customer requires convenience at its every contact point with the organization as regarding the location of the bank, available parking facilities, speed, hygienic environment and alike [21]. According to (AHP) approach, the factor "convenience" possesses maximum weight it shows that though customer takes cognitive decisions regarding "monetary aspect" but still requires "convenience" in every aspect while dealing with the organization. In addition, employees, online functional elements, and servicescape possess distinctively higher weights than the other factors such as service process, marketing mix, Customer interaction and online hedonic elements [19].

The research results about banking by Chahal and Dutta study revealed that core service experience comprising cognitive, affective and behavioral factors is most significant dimension followed by relational experience and sensory experience dimensions. The cognition items affecting banking customer experience include knowledge of bank products, competitive interest on loans and information sharing. Bank managers when respect customer's time and give special attention to knowledge, speed and service process, can generate positive behavioral experience. Similarly, effective items in the core service factor include problem handling, responding quality, aesthetic, and empathy, which have a significant impact on creating customer experience in banking sector. Behavioral characteristics affecting customer experience include concern and caring attitude, prompt customer service and error free bank services [22].

2.3   Organism - Internal Emotional States

In this section, we will focus on three variables that will represent the organism component in SOR model; pleasure, arousal, and dominance.

Russell and Mehrabian presented pleasure-arousal-dominance scale as it relates to Consumer's affective state while engaged with the stimuli. Pleasure relates to how good a consumer feels about the retail environment. While arousal is the extent, to which a consumer feels excited or stimulated. Then finally, dominance is an effective state that relates to control in regards to the retail environment [5].

Donovan and Rossiter used the P-A-D model to examine the relationship between affective states provoked by store environment and the consumer behavioral intention in those environments. The study found that pleasure created a willingness to purchase while arousal created a positive desire to interact with the store environment, as well likelihood to return to the same environment. Furthermore, it has been examined that dominance variable is strongly related to usability attribute of websites, which ultimately affect pleasure and arousal states of consumers while engaging with a retailer [23].

Pleasure measures people's general positive or negative reaction to the environment. Pleasure is defined as the degree to which a person feels good, joyful, happy, or satisfied in a situation [8]. According to Menon and Kahn (1995), if consumers do not have any specific goals for evaluation, they may use their affective feelings as a guide while evaluating any target. In doing so, they may mistakenly attribute a pre-existing pleasure state as a reaction towards the target stimuli. This suggests that pre-existing emotions may increase favorable evaluations of novel stimuli more than familiar stimuli, thus increasing the approach behavior [24]. In addition, Sherman et al. (1997) demonstrated that pleasure has a positive influence on how much a consumer likes a store and the money spent in the store, but has no significant impact on the number of items purchased or time spent in the store [10].

Arousal refers to the extent to which a person feels stimulated, active, or excited [8]. The current study introduces a two-dimensional concept of arousal; there are at least two different types of arousal; energetic arousal and tense arousal. Energetic Arousal refers to the extent to which a person feels active, energetic, alert or vigorous ranging from subjectively defined feelings of energy and vigor to the opposite feelings of sleepiness and tiredness and varies in a circadian rhythm. Meanwhile, tense arousal refers to the extent that an individual feels anxious, jittery, tense, or nervous ranging from subjective tension to placidity and quietness [25]. In this study; Energetic Arousal just will be used.

Dominance defined by Russell and Mehrabian (1976) as the extent that a person feels powerful vis-à-vis the environment that surrounds him/her. According to them, a person feels dominant when he/she is able to influence or control the situation he/she is in. He/she feels submissive when the environment influences him/her [5]. In a service environment, dominance refers to the degree of power and influence on the service specification, realization, and outcome. Service providers can influence consumers' perceived dominance in the environment. The proximity of the store, the control of the shopper's movement through the store layout, available and personalized stock and service can increase the consumers' perceived dominance [26].

2.4   Generation Y

The Generation Y segment comprises individuals who were born between 1980 and 2000. They are also referred to as Millennials, net generation and Echo Boomers [27]. Individuals in this segment were typically raised in a secure and goal-driven environment. The competitive environment at home is mild. They are also called "trophy kids" as they have several accomplishments. Generation Y likes to work in a team and in a culture that is organized, integrated and growth-oriented. They believe that this would help them to accomplish their goals more easily than when working individually. However, they are eager to achieve their objectives within a short time period and are receptive to continuous feedback [28].

Generation Y is influenced by western culture and is eager to spend money. They experiment with and adapt to new products and brands. They usually spend on personal services and consumer goods. While they have high brand awareness, they are generally not brand loyal. They are hence called "brand switchers." However, it is important to note that the purchasing power of this young segment will only increase over time [29]. Gen Y's use of social media is already changing the marketplace, the workplace, and society; it will ultimately lead to new business models, processes and products [30].

Younger customers are more likely to change their banks easily, so if retail banks want to retain younger customers, they need to offer more meaningful incentives to younger customers than they offer to older customers. In terms of practice, the findings of this research highlight the need for managers to design different switching barrier packages for each customer age group [31].

The study by Robert Rugimbana has shown that cultural values and perceptual variables may have significant implications for marketing practice particularly where Generation Y is concerned. Given that e-banking services are designed essentially to suit individuals who prefer convenience, quicker service, more frequent and less face-to-face retail banking services, one would expect that Generation Y individuals, more likely to use these e-banking services, would be those who are socialized in more individualistic and consumption orientations. These individuals would be expected to use the e-services more regularly given that individualistic societies tend to be more consumption-oriented and therefore more encouraging towards spending [32].

Bilgihan (2016) report that generation Y group likes to travel and prefers to spend money on experiences rather than materialistic items. Their responses to online marketing are expected to be different as they process website information five times faster than older generations and are the most emotional and least loyal customers compared to all other generations. In addition, Bigham demonstrated that trust is the most important antecedent of e-loyalty in online shopping for Gen Y customers. Brand equity is also a key precursor of e-loyalty. Finally, a positive online experience (flow) is also a significant precursor of e-loyalty for this cohort [33].

2.5   Banking Sector

For several years now, the banking sector has been facing several challenges. One of the biggest challenges is keeping pace with ongoing development technology. In this part, we will deliver brief information about Internet Banking & Mobile-Banking, Banking for generation Y and show worldwide examples about banking experience for Generation Y.

2.5.1   Internet Banking and Mobile-Banking

The Internet has transformed the ways in which individuals, groups, organizations communicate, obtain information, access entertainment, and conduct their economic and social activities. Looking forward, by 2018 almost 3.6 billion people, i.e. half of the world's population will be connected to the internet or the mobile internet [34].

In response to market competition and with relatively low setup costs, traditional banks have adopted a policy of enhancing the possibilities of their online services. Interactive banking services have currently become a common practice, ubiquitously performed all over the world and are now an integral part of the modern commercial environment [35].

It is widely recognized that the nature of banking services is changing rapidly, due to the diverse advances offered by the revolutionary information technologies of the Internet. This significant change extends across all levels of service in the banking industry – from global business to individual concerns. Advances in technology, globalization, and customization have created a dynamic banking environment, in an attempt to improve service quality and satisfy customers' need for faster, easier, independent and real-time service [36].

Internet banking as a medium of delivery of banking services and as a strategic tool for business development has gained wide acceptance internationally and is fast catching up with more and more banks entering the fray [37]. Internet banking services can be defined as the provision of information or services by a bank to its customers via the computer, cellular phone or other Internet-oriented devices [42]. The online banking penetration in the European Union (EU 28) showed that in 2007 it was 25% and in 2015 it was 46%. In 2015, 46% of all individuals used the internet for online banking, but usage was higher among those who had used the internet within the last three months, at 57%.

Sahoo and Swain [37] reported main benefits from Internet banking for both Banks and customers being the most important its availability 24 h a day and 7 days a week. Customer's perception and lifestyle play an important role in the growth of Internet banking system: (i) banks are succeeded to reduce this queue through uses of latest technology. Also, banks are going to utilize internet facility for customer's transactions this method will reduce paperwork and will give a quick response to the customer while they remain in their office or at home; (ii) E- Banking, i.e., the liberation of bank's services to a customer at his workplace or domicile using Electronic Technology, makes it easier for customers to compare banks' services and products. Also, it can augment competition among banks, and authorizes banks to penetrate new markets and thus inflate their geographical reach; (iii) customers in e-banking era can access services more easily from banks abroad and through wireless communication systems, which are developing more rapidly than traditional "wired" communication network and that provides enormous benefits to consumers regarding the ease and cost of transactions.

Thus, mobile has become an intrinsic and vital part of bank customers' everyday life, and they expect banks to respond rapidly to their demands and provide the level of service they want [38]. According to the second annual Trends in Consumer Mobility report of Bank of America, of those consumers who use a mobile banking app, nearly two-thirds (62%) access it at least a few times a week or more, while one in five (20%) check once a day or more [39].

Mobile Banking covers some areas, from apps to mobile financial services and even mobile payments in the future, and from smartphones to smart TVs (and eventually all devices will become 'smart' and connected). These are all part of the rapidly evolving mobile ecosystem [38]. Most consumers check their balance or statement (74%), view transactions (63%) via their mobile banking app and 72% of Millennials ages 25–34 generation report using mobile bank check deposit. Additionally, nearly four in 10 (38%) pay bills, almost one-third (32%) use it to locate a branch or ATM, and 15% manage investments [39].

Other issues also need to be considered, such as the opportunities and challenges posed by the social media; the development of mobile wallets; and the role of payments. Mobile payments are often seen as being a separate discipline from mobile banking. However, there are a few signs that there could soon be a level of convergence between the two areas, which will lead to a larger mobile ecosystem [38].

Despite the huge worldwide migration towards the use of mobiles in recent years, mobile banking is still really in its infancy. There is a lot to be discovered, and many challenges to overcome – and meanwhile, the whole mobile ecosystem is continuing to grow and evolve [38].

2.5.2 Banking for Generation Y

As banks target technology-friendly Gen Y customers, they must focus on developing products and services in unique and innovative ways. Gen Y customers are more likely to be attracted by innovation, quality of service, and accessibility to various products and services such as payment systems and banking accounts. To that end, effectively utilizing mobile and social media tools are powerful ways to engage Gen Y [3]. Generations often hold common values shaped by shared experiences during their key developmental years. Social media allows experiences and attitudes to be wide - nearly instantly - shared. The reasons that younger generations patronize banks is that they offer more sophisticated - online and mobile- banking services and is more convenient access to ATMs. Online or mobile banking is an influential factor for about 25% of younger generations, but only 18% of Older Boomers or Matures. Gen Y is more likely to pay attention to what their friends are saying, texting or perhaps entering on their Facebook page about the bank than what the bank is saying about itself. Gen Y prefers to receive communications via the bank's online banking site (after login), e-mail to their computers or the bank's website more than by "snail mail." Gen Y also is more receptive than others to communications via the bank's ATM machines or their mobile phones [1].

According to Capgemini report (2014) called "What Makes Gen Y-Stick with a Bank?", Gen Y Requirements & Demands are the following: (i) they choose banks that charge lower fees and are more interested in products and services that offer low fees and charges; (ii) tend to shop around for the best price, and are willing to switch banks to obtain higher rates on savings accounts; (iii) they prefer banks whose processes are more streamlined and offer a high level of convenience; (iv) they are aware of a bank's quality of service and will select a bank that delivers the greatest value and benefit to them; (v) they seek added convenience in terms of services, not only through bank branches but also online and through mobile channels [40].

However, according to World Retail Banking Report (2014), one finds some important facts when comparing Gen Y and other age groups: (i) Gen Y customers who do have positive experiences are somewhat less likely to engage in profitable behaviors; (ii) Gen Y are slightly less likely to refer a friend, and a similar trend exists regarding the likelihood of Gen Y to purchase another product [3].

For that and to encourage an ongoing mutually valuable relationship with Gen Y customers, banks need to focus on four key areas that could increase Gen Y Customer Stickiness [40]: (i) Banks should introduce Gen Y-specific checking and savings accounts that offer competitive interest rates and a high level of online and mobile banking convenience. Banks should provide attractive long-term savings, pension, and securities and insurance products and services to meet this need. This may encourage Gen Y customers to stay with a bank over the long term; (ii) Gen Y customers have unique preferences in the way they prefer to make payments, so banks should bundle payment instruments because bundled payments offer a high level of convenience. For example, the emerging digital wallet payment system enables customers to access payment systems remotely anytime and anywhere, increasing convenience; (iii) Gen Y customers seek access to banking services anytime, so they are among the most likely segments to use the Internet for online and mobile banking. This technology (mobiles and internet) allows them to check account balances, make purchases, and conduct payment transactions on their mobile devices or the Internet. Gen Y customers are always connected to the world via their smartphones, and they are increasingly adopting smartphones and Internet banking, so banks should focus on enhancing their online and mobile channels; (iv) To improve brand awareness and increase customer retention, banks need to embrace social media platforms to engage Gen Y customers who are more likely to trust experiences posted on social media by other customers and use social networks and platforms to voice their opinions. Before making a purchase, these customers are more apt to conduct extensive research on social media and the Internet, collecting expert opinions and feedback from friends and relatives.

To ensure how important the relationship between the banking sector and young generation is, the Child and Youth Finance International (CYFI) issued 'The Child and Youth Friendly Banking Product Certificate.' The Certificate is awarded to Banking Products that meet specific standards, including Availability and accessibility for children and youth, Maximum control to children and youth, the Positive financial incentive for children and youth, A Financial education component, and Monitoring of child and youth satisfaction. Core Principles of CYFI movement are focused firmly on increasing the financial protection and empowerment of all children and youth across the world. Also, CYFI is leading a global movement which seeks to facilitate access to child and youth friendly bank accounts and holistic financial education for 100 million children and youth in 100 countries by 2015 [41].

3   Research Model and Hypotheses

In order to explore the impact of Customer Experience attributes on generation Y's behavior in the banking sector, we defined the following conceptual model and research hypotheses based on several studies previously developed. From those studies, important information was retrieved and selectively used to adequately match the aims of the present study.

The research model (see Fig. 1), was developed on stimulus-organism-response (S-O-R) theory. The stimulus aspects are represented by Customer Experience attributes. The Customer Experience attributes encompass: Accessibility, Ease of doing business, Executional excellence, Personalized offering, Staff engagement, Value for money, and Reputation affect the organism. The organism is defined by the affective state that includes pleasure, dominance, and arousal.

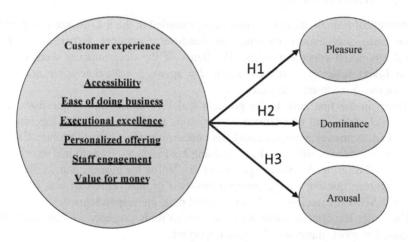

Fig. 1. Research model (Source: authors' elaboration)

The overall hypotheses proposed for this study are the following:

H1: **Customer Experience**, that is, Accessibility (H1a), Ease of doing business (H1b), Executional excellence (H1c), Personalized offering (H1d), Staff engagement (H1e), Value for money (H1f), and Reputation (H1g) **positively affects pleasure of Generation Y in experiencing the bank**.

H2: **Customer Experience**, that is, Accessibility (H2a), Ease of doing business (H2b), Executional excellence (H2c), Personalized offering (H2d), Staff engagement (H2e), Value for money (H2f), and Reputation (H2g) **positively affects Dominance of Generation Y in experiencing the bank**.

H3: **Customer Experience**, that is, Accessibility (H3a), Ease of doing business (H3b), Executional excellence (H3c), Personalized offering (H3d), Staff engagement (H3e), Value for money (H3f), and Reputation (H3g) **positively affects Arousal of Generation Y in experiencing the bank**.

3.1   Data Collection

We collected secondary data through a revision of previous researches related to the topic. With the support of the theoretical background and in order to collect primary data an on-line survey was created and launched via the umfrageonline website, being available during February and March 2016. Therefore, it was chosen and online survey because (i) it allows a quick response and it possible to reach a higher number of Generation Y's customers in a small period of time in different places; (ii) the study is aimed at Generation Y that is also known as the Internet generation, increasing the importance of using an on-line survey. The survey was spread to customers via Facebook. We posted the survey's link on several Facebook pages like universities and youth organizations.

3.2   Questionnaire Design

The theoretical framework of this study was grounded in the S-O-R framework [5]. The questionnaire was mainly designed to measure: Customer Experience attributes, internal emotional consumer states. The items of the questionnaire were rated on a 5-point Likert scale: (1 = strongly agree, 2 = agree, 3 = Neither agree nor disagree, 4 = disagree, 5 = strongly disagree).

Hence, in the first part, the respondent had four demographic questions: gender, age, marital status and educational background. In the second part, the respondents were asked to answer eighteen questions concerning the seven Customer Experience attributes (1 - Accessibility, 2 - Ease of doing business, 3 - Executional excellence, 4 - Personalized offering, 5 - Staff engagement, 6 - Value for money, and 7 - Reputation). Those eighteen questions were grouped into two groups. This part was based on the study of KMPG International [42]. In the third part, the respondents were asked to rank that Customer Experience attributes according to its importance to them according to the scale 1 = most important, 7 = less important.

In the fourth part, the respondents were asked to answer questions about emotional states. The emotional state (pleasure, arousal, and dominance) were based on a scale developed by Koo and Lee [6].

3.3   Sample Profile

The sample of this study consisted of Generation Y customers of banks from different countries around the world. In order to achieve the target sample, an online survey was spread through Facebook with URL embedded that lead the respondents to the survey.

Almost 550 questionnaires were spread over a two-month period in 2016. Thereby, we gathered a sample of 211 respondents. The data consists of 205 usable survey participants (120 male - 58%; 85 female - 42%). Most of the answers are from individuals aged between 21–25 (46.8%) and between 26–30 (35.1%) followed by 31–35 (13%) and 18–20 (5%). Regarding the marital status, most the respondents were single (180), and the others 25 were married.

Finally, regarding the education level, most of the sample is doing or already has University degree (100–49%), 41% were doing or already had a Master degree, 3% has a Ph.D. degree, and 7% had a senior high school degree.

4 Discussion: Research and Results

In this section, we divided the results into three parts: the descriptive statistics, reliability, multiple regressions and custom table.

4.1 Descriptive Statistics and Reliability

We go through all the Customer Experience items (1 - Accessibility, 2 - Ease of doing business, 3 - Executional excellence, 4 - Personalized offering, 5 - Staff engagement, 6 - Value for money, 7 - Reputation) analyzing means and standard deviations for all of them.

Cronbach's alpha was calculated to confirm the construct reliability of the scales for the following customer experience Items (Executional excellence, Staff engagement, and Reputation). For the others customer experience items (Accessibility, Ease of doing business, Personalized offering and Value for money) we do not apply the reliability test using the Cronbach's Alpha because those items had only two statements.

Stimuli-Online Bank Experience

1. Accessibility

As we can see in Table 1, the item 1CE1 is the one that shows the highest agreement, with an average response of 2.09 (where 2 = agree, in 5-point Likert scale). Moreover, regarding variability **1CE2** shows the highest value, with a standard deviation of 0.95.

Table 1. Accessibility (Source: authors' elaboration)

Items	Mean	Std. deviation
1CE1: in my Bank, the physical proximity/ease of access is good	2.09	0.85
1CE2: in my Bank, the availability of services (around the clock) is good	2.27	0.95

2. Ease of doing business

As shown in Table 2, the item 2CE2 is the one that shows the highest agreement, with an average response of 2.44 and 2CE1 shows the highest variability with a standard deviation of 0.92.

Table 2. Ease of doing business (Source: authors' elaboration)

Items	Mean	Std. deviation
2CE1: my Bank has services and products that are easy to understand	2.47	0.92
2CE2: it is ease of getting issues/queries/complaints resolved	2.44	0.89

3. Executional excellence

Concerning the Execution excellence. We can see in Table 3 below that the item **3CE1** shows the highest agreement rate, with an average response of 2.04 (where 2 = agree). Moreover, in terms of variability, 3CE2 shows the highest value, with a standard deviation of 0.93.

Moreover, we can conclude that the internal dimensions of the items do have consistency and can be used for statistical analysis since the value 0,762 observed for the Cronbach's Alpha is considered a respectable value.

Table 3. Executional excellence (Source: authors' elaboration)

Items	Mean	Std. deviation	Cronbach's Alpha
3CE1: it is fast to make an inquiry/transaction	2.04	0.86	**0.762**
3CE2: my Bank is fast in resolving a complaint/resolving a query	2.46	0.93	
3CE3: I get things right from the first time	2.47	0.85	
3CE4: the services are Consistent – continuity in communications or interactions	2.34	0.82	

4. Personalized offering

As we can see in Table 4, the item **4CE1** is the one that shows the highest agreement, with an average response of 1.95 (where 2 = agree), and **4CE2** shows the highest variability, with a standard deviation of 0.93.

Table 4. Personalized offering (Source: authors' elaboration)

Items	Mean	Std. deviation
4CE1: my Bank offers products and services that can be tailored to my specific needs	1.95	0.92
4CE2: my Bank rewards my choice to do business with it	2.98	0.93

5. Staff engagement

Concerning the Staff engagement. We show in Table 5 that the item 5CE1 shows the highest agreement rate, with an average response of 2.21. Also, regarding variability, 5CE2 shows the highest value, with a standard deviation of 0.89.

Table 5. Staff engagement (Source: authors' elaboration)

Items	Mean	Std. deviation	Cronbach's Alpha
5CE1: in my Bank, the staff has a positive attitude	2.21	0.80	0.711
5CE2: the staff are honest and tell the truth	2.32	0.89	
5CE3: my Bank offers high quality of advice and service	2.41	0.85	

Moreover, we can conclude that the internal dimensions of the items do have consistency and can be used for statistical analysis since the value 0,711 observed for the Cronbach's Alpha is considered a respectable value.

6. Value for money

In term of value for money, we can see in Table 6 that the item **6CE1** shows the highest agreement rate, with an average response of 2.77. Also, in terms of variability, **6CE1** shows the highest value, with a standard deviation of 1.08.

Table 6. Value for money (Source: authors' elaboration)

Items	Mean	Std. deviation
6CE1: The fees/charges are fair and appropriate (Value for money)	2.77	1.08
6CE2: The rewards and promotions are available	2.85	0.89

7. Reputation

In term of value for money, we can see in Table 7 that the item 7CE1 shows the highest agreement rate, with an average response of 2.27. Also, regarding variability, 7CE1 also shows the highest value, with a standard deviation of 1.03.

Concerning the Cronbach's Alpha, the value of 0.65 – that appear in Table 9 below is considered the minimally acceptable value hence, we can infer that the internal dimensions of the items do have consistency and can be used for statistical analysis.

Table 7. Reputation (Source: authors' elaboration)

Items	Mean	Std. deviation	Cronbach's Alpha
7CE1: my Bank is well regarded in the media	2.27	1.03	0.65
7CE2: I trust that my Bank does the right thing	2.62	0.91	
7CE3: my Bank puts the consumer first	2.79	0.96	

Organism - Internal Emotional States

Regarding descriptive analysis of organism variables, we went through all the items (1 - Pleasure, 2 - Dominance, 3 - Arousal). Cronbach's alpha was calculated to confirm the construct reliability of the Credibility items. For the others organism variables, we didn't apply the reliability test (Cronbach's Alpha) because those items had only two statements for each.

1. Pleasure

As shown in Table 8, the item **PL2** is the one that shows the highest agreement, with an average response of 2.54 (closer to 2 = Agree on a 5-point Likert scale) and shows the highest variability, with a standard deviation of 0.89.

Table 8. Pleasure (Source: authors' elaboration)

Items	Mean	Std. deviation
PL1: when I am dealing with my Bank, I feel (Pleased)	2.58	0.89
PL2: when I am dealing with my Bank, I feel (Contented)	2.54	0.84

2. Dominance

From the Table 9, we can infer that the item DO1 is the one that shows the highest agreement, with an average response of 2.65 and DO2 shows the highest variability, with a standard deviation of 0.85.

Table 9. Dominance (Source: authors' elaboration)

Items	Mean	Std. deviation
DO1: when I am dealing with my Bank, I feel (Acted) in control of the environment	2.65	0.80
DO2: When I am interacting with my Bank, I feel (Influential) in control of the environment	2.77	0.85

3. Arousal

From the Table 10, we can infer that the item **AR2** is the one that shows agreement, with an average response of 2.80. In addition, in terms of variability, **AR2** shows the highest value, with a standard deviation of 0.88.

Table 10. Arousal (Source: authors' elaboration)

Items	Mean	Std. deviation
AR1: when I am interacting with my Bank, I feel (Energetic)	3.04	0.85
AR2: when I am interacting with my Bank, I feel (Active)	2.80	0.88

4.2 Multiple Regressions

In order to test the hypothesized relationships of H1 through H3, multiple regression analysis was used since we wanted to determine relationships between two or more independent variables and one dependent variable.

Multiple regression analysis compares data and then prioritizes the effects. In this case, multiple regression determined the relative importance as well as the significance of the relationship between customer experience, the organism state, and responses.

To achieve this a transformation was employed for each of the latent variables presented: **Stimulus variables** (Customer Experience; Accessibility, Ease of doing business, Executional excellence, Personalized offering, Staff engagement, Value for money, Reputation) and **Organism variables** (Pleasure, Dominance, and Arousal). In order to detect multicollinearity among independent variables, the Variance Inflation Factor (VIF) was examined. All VIF values among independent variables in multiple regression models in this study were within acceptable range (VIF values were below 10).

Tolerance and Durbin-Watson values were tested for all the following regressions. For all of them, Tolerance values are superior to 0.1. Given the sample's dimension, it can be considered that the Durbin-Watson test is at the inclusion zone (close to 2).

H1: Customer Experience Positively Affects the Pleasure of Generation Y in Experiencing the Bank

In order to test the Hypothesis 1, multiple regression analysis was used. The seven attributes of Customer Experience; Accessibility, Ease of doing business, Executional excellence, Personalized offering, Staff engagement, Value for money and Reputation were used as independent or predictor variables while pleasure was the dependent or outcome variable.

In Table 11, results show that there is a significant positive relationship between the Customer Experience and pleasure ($p < .05$). The seven customer experience attributes help to explain 38.7% of the variability of Pleasure.

Table 11. H1: customer experience positively affects pleasure of Generation Y in experiencing the bank (Source: authors' elaboration)

F(sig.) = 19.384 (p = .000)	Adjusted R^2 = .387			Durbin-Watson = 1.852		
	Unstandardized coefficients B	Standardized coefficients beta	t	p(Sig.)	Collinearity statistics	
					Tolerance	VIF
(Constant)	.206		.612	.542		
Accessibility	−.044−	−.041	−.634−	.527	.728	1.374
Ease of doing business	.017	.017	.242	.809	.626	1.598
Executional excellence	.151	.277	3.699	.000	.537	1.862
Personalized offering	.138	.130	2.030	.044	.738	1.356
Staff engagement	.145	.188	2.750	.007	.644	1.552
Value for money	.118	.123	1.990	.048	.785	1.274
Reputation	.129	.187	2.862	.005	.701	1.427

However, only the Executional excellence ($\beta = .277$, p $\leq$ .05), Personalized offering ($\beta = .130$, p $\leq$ .05), Staff engagement ($\beta = .188$, p $\leq$ .05), Value for money ($\beta = .123$, p $\leq$ .05) and the Reputation ($\beta = .187$, p $\leq$ .05) are important to explain the Pleasure. The Accessibility and Ease of doing business do not significantly contribute to explain the Pleasure.

H2: Customer Experience Positively Affects Dominance of Generation Y in Experiencing the Bank

Hypothesis 2 was tested with the seven attributes of **Customer Experience**; Accessibility, Ease of doing business, Executional excellence, Personalized offering, Staff engagement, Value for money and Reputation as independent or predictor variables, while **Dominance** was the dependent or outcome variable.

In Table 12, results show that there is a significant positive relationship between the Customer Experience and Dominance (p < .05) and the seven customer service attributes used in the study help to explain 31.9% of the variability of Dominance.

Table 12. H2: customer experience positively affects dominance of Generation Y in experiencing the bank (Source: authors' elaboration)

F(sig.) = 14.633 (p = .000)	Adjusted R^2 = .319				Durbin-Watson = 1.957	
	Unstandardized coefficients B	Standardized coefficients beta	t	p(Sig.)	Collinearity statistics	
					Tolerance	VIF
(Constant)	1.026		3.192	.002		
Accessibility	.086	.087	1.289	.199	.728	1.374
Ease of doing business	.235	.248	3.397	.001	.626	1.598
Executional excellence	.005	.010	.122	.903	.537	1.862
Personalized offering	.111	.115	1.708	.089	.738	1.356
Staff engagement	.098	.140	1.944	.053	.644	1.552
Value for money	.015	.017	.256	.798	.785	1.274
Reputation	.136	.217	3.145	.002	.701	1.427

However, only the Ease of doing business (**$\beta = .248$, p $\leq$ .05**) and the Reputation (**$\beta = .217$, p $\leq$ .05**) are important to explain the Dominance. The Accessibility, Executional excellence, Personalized offering, Staff engagement, and Value for money do not significantly contribute to explaining the Dominance.

H3: Customer Experience Positively Affects Arousal of Generation Y in Experiencing the Bank

In order to test the Hypothesis 3, multiple regression analysis was used. The seven attributes of Customer Experience; Accessibility, Ease of doing business, Executional excellence, Personalized offering, Staff engagement, Value for money and Reputation were used as independent or predictor variables while Arousal was the dependent or outcome variable.

Table 13 shows that there is a significant positive relationship between the Customer Experience and Arousal (p < .05). Arousal is explained by the seven predictors by 32.4%.

Table 13. H3: customer experience positively affects arousal of Generation Y in experiencing the bank (Source: authors' elaboration)

F(sig.) = 14.999 (p = .000)	Adjusted R^2 = .324				Durbin-Watson = 1.903	
	Unstandardized coefficients B	Standardized coefficients beta	t	p(Sig.)	Collinearity statistics	
					Tolerance	VIF
(Constant)	1.157		3.363	.001		
Accessibility	.060	.057	.850	.396	.728	1.374
Ease of doing business	.244	.240	3.299	.001	.626	1.598
Executional excellence	.034	.065	.822	.412	.537	1.862
Personalized offering	.222	.213	3.186	.002	.738	1.356
Staff engagement	.063	.084	1.173	.242	.644	1.552
Value for money	.007	.008	.118	.906	.785	1.274
Reputation	.113	.168	2.446	.015	.701	1.427

However, only the Ease of doing business (β = .240, p $\leq$ .05), Personalized offering (β = .213, p $\leq$ .05), and Reputation (β = .168, p $\leq$ .05) are important to explain the Arousal variable. The Accessibility, Executional excellence, Staff engagement, and Value for money do not significantly contribute to explaining the Arousal.

4.3   Custom Table - Rank the Customer Experience Attributes

In order to find out how important the Bank customer experience attributes for Gen Y customer, we asked them to rank the seven attributes that represent the seven categories of customer experience. The customer experience attributes are: Value for money (i.e. fair and appropriate fees and charges), Getting things right the first time, Put the consumer first, Staff who are honest and tell the truth, Ease of getting issues/queries/complaints resolved), Availability of services (around the clock), and Offers products and services that can be tailored to my specific needs [42].

To test the data, a custom Table 14 was created. From this Table 15 below that shows the number and percentage of respondents for each rank, the results determined that the majority of respondents mentioned Value for money (i.e. fair and appropriate fees and charges) as the most important attribute (rank 1) (68 respondents - 33.2%). The least important for most of the respondents (rank 7) was Offers products and services that can be tailored to my specific needs (90 respondents - 43.9%).

Table 14. Custom table (Source: authors' elaboration)

Customer experience attributes	Rank 1		Rank 2		Rank 3		Rank 4		Rank 5		Rank 6		Rank 7		Column Total	
Availability of services (around the clock)	21	10.2%	31	15.1%	18	8.8%	25	12.2%	22	10.7%	57	27.8%	31	15.1%	205	100%
Offers products and services that can be tailored to my specific needs	13	6.3%	13	6.3%	18	8.8%	27	13.2%	21	10.2%	23	11.2%	90	43.9%	205	100%
Value for money (i.e. fair and appropriate fees and charges)	68	33.2%	29	14.1%	31	15.1%	22	10.7%	22	10.7%	19	9.3%	14	6.8%	205	100%
Getting things right the first time	39	19.0%	39	19.0%	30	14.6%	31	15.1%	25	12.2%	25	12.2%	16	7.8%	205	100%
Put the consumer first	37	18.0%	41	20.0%	51	24.9%	26	12.7%	23	11.2%	20	9.8%	7	3.4%	205	100%
Staff who are honest and tell the truth	19	9.3%	37	18.0%	29	14.1%	42	20.5%	29	14.1%	29	14.1%	20	9.8%	205	100%
Ease of getting issues/queries/complaints resolved	8	3.9%	15	7.3%	28	13.7%	32	15.6%	63	30.7%	32	15.6%	27	13.2%	205	100%

As well we can notice from the Table 15, in rank (2) there are two attributes (Getting things right the first time and Put the consumer first) that have a close number of respondents 39–41 respectively.

Table 15. Rank the customer experience attributes (Source: authors' elaboration)

Customer experience attributes	Rank	Nr. of respondents who gave this rank	% of respondents who gave this rank
Value for money (i.e. fair and appropriate fees and charges)	1	68	33.2%
Getting things right the first time	2	39	19.0%
Put the consumer first	3	51	24.9%
Staff who are honest and tell the truth	4	42	20.5%
Ease of getting issues/queries/complaints resolved)	5	63	30.7%
Availability of services (around the clock)	6	57	27.8%
Offers products and services that can be tailored to my specific needs	7	90	43.9%

5   Conclusions and Managerial Implications

In order to go further in understanding how customer experience of Gen Y could affect the outcomes of the banking sector's efforts from a marketing perspective (the relationship between the Gen Y customer experience attributes with the Internal States of customers -pleasure-arousal-dominance and Gen Y satisfaction from a customer perspective) we used a Russell and Mehrabian (1974)'s S-O-R theoretical framework.

In this article, we used the 30 attributes of customer experience categorized in seven main categories by KPMG International that focus on financial organizations. Those categories are (i) Accessibility; (ii) Ease of doing business; (iii) Executional excellence; (iv) Personalized offering; (v) Staff engagement; (vi) Value for money; (vii) Reputation. In general, by considering the descriptive statistics, we noticed that all attributes had positive agreement rates. The highest agreement rates were for "Accessibility" and "Staff engagement" with an average response of 2.18 and 2.31 respectively, meaning that the Accessibility and Staff engagement bank's experience of the sample was positive. On the other hand, the lowest agreement rates were for "Value for money" (2.81) and "Reputation" (2.65).

In the same context, to know the most and less important customer experience attributes, we consider the results in the table (Rank the Customer Experience attributes). We saw that "Value for money" (i.e. fair and appropriate fees and charges) was the most important attribute (with 33.2% of respondents). Moreover, the least important attribute was "Offers products and services that can be tailored to my specific needs" with the 43.9% of respondents gave this rank. Those results are consistent with the ones found by KPMG International for banks [42]. The only difference is that Gen Y in this sample gave "Getting things right the first time" and "Put the consumer first" attributes were more important than "Staff who are honest and tell the truth".

In the descriptive statistics and looking in the internal state: Pleasure - Dominance - Arousal scale results, we see overall positive agreement rates. However, this rate is low and closer to "neither agree nor disagree = 3" than to "agree = 2." The highest agreement rate is for "Pleasure," with an average response of (2.56) on a 5-point Likert scale. Further, the lowest agreement rate is for "Arousal" with an average response of (2.92), notably the lowest item rate "When I am interacting with my Bank, I feel (Energetic)" with an average response of (3.04). That means the banking experience of the sample members does not matter for the Gen Y internal state that much.

Moreover, for the Gen Y bank experience outcomes - Satisfaction, Credibility, Loyalty, Word-of-mouth and Brand equity - we can infer that there is an overall positive agreement rate, which means that banks provided a positive experience for the Gen Y customer. Moreover, both "Credibility2" and "Satisfaction" showed the highest agreement rate among the sample's members (2.30, 2.31 respectively) while Word-of-mouth and Loyalty got the lowest agreement rate among all the outcomes, with 2.68 and 2.56 respectively. Those results are consistent with the studies that said Gen Y is less loyalty [3, 43].

To test the relationship in all the study hypotheses, we resorted to multiple linear regressions. All the hypotheses showed significant results, meaning that there is a significant positive relationship between the dependent variables and at least one of the independent or outcome variables. In other words, all customer experience attributes (Accessibility, Ease of doing business, Executional excellence, Personalized offering, Staff engagement, Value for money, and Reputation) had a positive impact on internal state (Pleasure - Dominance – Arousal), Satisfaction and Credibility. Furthermore, those variables, internal state, satisfaction, and credibility had a positive effect on Loyalty, Word-of-mouth, and Brand equity.

The first research hypothesis has been confirmed. This hypothesis estimates Customer Experience attributes; Accessibility (H1a), Ease of doing business (H1b), Executional excellence (H1c), Personalized offering (H1d), Staff engagement (H1e), Value for money (H1f), and Reputation (H1g) have a positive impact on pleasure. Those results are consistent with the ones found by Murugiah and Akgam (2015) that said subjective emotions and experience are getting more and more important in bank sector [44]. However, only the Executional excellence, Personalized offering, Staff engagement, Value for money and the Reputation significantly contribute to explaining the pleasure by 38.7%. Although The Accessibility and Ease of doing business do not significantly contribute to explaining the pleasure.

We also confirmed the second research hypothesis related to Customer Experience attributes; Accessibility (H2a), Ease of doing business (H2b), Executional excellence (H2c), Personalized offering (H2d), Staff engagement (H2e), Value for money (H2f), and Reputation (H2g) had a positive impact on dominance of Gen Y in experiencing a bank. However, not all the items significantly contribute to explaining the dependent variable, only the Ease of doing business and the Reputation do.

The third research hypothesis has been confirmed. This hypothesis stated that Customer Experience attributes; Accessibility (H3a), Ease of doing business (H3b), Executional excellence (H3c), Personalized offering (H3d), Staff engagement (H3e), Value for money (H3f), and Reputation (H3g) had a positive impact on Arousal. However, we found that only the Ease of doing business, Personalized offering, and Reputation significantly contribute to explaining the Arousal by 32.4%. While, The Accessibility, Executional excellence, Staff engagement, and Value for money do not significantly contribute to explaining the Arousal.

In sum, by examining relationships from stimulus to organism and then to behavioral response, significant relationships were identified in this study. From that, it is determined that the seven underlying stimulus dimensions (customer experience attributes) predict the studied behavioral responses; Loyalty, Word-of-mouth, and Brand equity.

We can conclude from the figure below that "Ease of doing business", "Executional excellence", "Personalized offering", and "Reputation" are primary predictor variables for all dimensions of behavioral response (Loyalty, Word-of-mouth, and Brand equity) through different organism variables.

"Reputation" plays a key role in predicting all the organism variables; Pleasure, Dominance, and Arousal. On the other hand, "Dominance" is a dimension not identified as a predictor variable for any of the measured behavioral responses in this article. It can be concluded that "Dominance" in itself can be seen as the resulting stage to an experience.

This study contributes to understanding the importance of customer experience concept in the banking sector for Gen Y and also to develop a new model for banks that focus on the emotional side of the interaction between Gen Y and banking sector.

Therefore, Banks need to be aware of the importance of the value for money for Gen Y as a first reason to stay or leave the Bank. Another important issue is the need to put the consumer first and Getting things right the first time play a crucial role in building a positive Gen Y customer experience. Furthermore, attention should also be paid to the Reputation because it plays the leading role to achieve marketing efforts outcomes and it is the foundation to any relationship between Gen Y and banks.

A genuine personalized offering along with excellence performance is a critical issue for Gen Y in the banking sector. It was also noticed that the Gen Y does not feel active or energetic when experiencing the bank environment as he/she does in other industries. So, bank's managers should consider turning the process of the interaction between Gen Y and the bank more entertainment for example.

In sum, banks need to work in making Gen Y customer experience unique. This must be done with customized services and products tailored answering to the special needs of this segment along with ongoing innovations that benefit from continuing IT development.

References

1. Putnam, M.: Attracting and retaining Gen Y and Gen X. Fis strategic insights, vol 6, March 2012. Slideshare.net. (2012). http://www.slideshare.net/pmcadam/fis-strategic-insights-vol-6-march-2012. Acceseed 8 May 2016
2. Brakus, J., Schmitt, B., Zarantonello, L.: Brand experience: what is it? How is it measured? Does it affect loyalty? J. Market. **73**(3), 52–68 (2009)
3. Capgemini and Efma: World Retail Banking Report 2014. Capgemini and Efma (2014). https://www.capgemini.com/resources/world-retail-banking-report-2014-from-capgemini-and-efma
4. Capgemini and Efma: World Retail Banking Report 2015 (2015). https://www.capgemini.com/thought-leadership/world-retail-banking-report-2015
5. Russell, J., Mehrabian, A.: Evidence for a three-factor theory of emotions. J. Res. Pers. **11**(3), 273–294 (1977)
6. Koo, D., Lee, J.: Inter-relationships among dominance, energetic and tense arousal, and pleasure, and differences in their impacts under online vs. offline environment. Comput. Hum. Behav. **27**(5), 1740–1750 (2011)
7. Mazursky, D., Jacoby, J.: Exploring the development of store image. J. Retail. **62**(2), 145–165 (1986)
8. Eroglu, S., Machleit, K., Davis, L.: Empirical testing of a model of online store atmospherics and shopper responses. Psychol. Market. **20**(2), 139–150 (2003)
9. Koo, D., Ju, S.: The interactional effects of atmospherics and perceptual curiosity on emotions and online shopping intention. Comput. Hum. Behav. **26**(3), 377–388 (2010)
10. Sherman, E., Mathur, A., Smith, R.: Store environment and consumer purchase behavior: Mediating role of consumer emotions. Psychol. Market. **14**(4), 361–378 (1997)
11. Bagozzi, R.: Principles of Marketing Management. Science Research Associates Inc., Chicago (1986)
12. Schmitt, B.: Experiential Marketing. J. Market. Manag. **15**(1–3), 53–67 (1999)
13. Pine II, B., Gilmore, J.H.: Welcome to the experience economy. Harv. Bus. Rev. (1998)
14. Meyer, C., Schwager, A.: Understanding customer experience. Harv. Bus. Rev., 117–126 (2007)
15. Ghose, K.: Thought Leaders International Conference on Brand Management. Birmingham Business School, England (2007)
16. Frow, P., Payne, A.: Towards the 'perfect' customer experience. J. Brand Manag. **15**(2), 89–101 (2007)
17. Payne, A., Storbacka, K., Frow, P.: Managing the co-creation of value. Acad. Market. Sci. **36**(36), 83–96 (2007)
18. Holbrook, M., Hirschman, E.: The experiential aspects of consumption: consumer fantasies, feelings, and fun. J. Consum. Res. **9**(2), 132 (1982)

19. Garg, R., Rahman, Z., Qureshi, M., Kumar, I.: Identifying and ranking critical success factors of customer experience in banks. J. Model. Manag. **7**(2), 201–220 (2012)
20. Morrison, S., Crane, F.: Building the service brand by creating and managing an emotional brand experience. J. Brand Manag. **14**(5), 410–421 (2007)
21. Jain, R., Bagdare, S.: Determinants of customer experience in new format retail stores. J. Market. Commun. **5**(2), 34–44 (2009)
22. Chahal, H., Dutta, K.: Measurement and impact of customer experience in banking sector. Decision **42**(1), 57–70 (2014)
23. Mathwick, C., Rigdon, E.: Play, flow, and the online search experience. J. Consum. Res. **31**(2), 324–332 (2004)
24. Menon, S., Kahn, B.: The impact of context on variety seeking in product choices. J. Consum. Res. **22**(3), 285 (1995)
25. Matthews, G., Davies, D., Holley, P.: Extraversion, arousal and visual sustained attention: the role of resource availability. Personal. Individ. Differ. **11**(11), 1159–1173 (1990)
26. Lunardo, R., Mbengue, A.: Perceived control and shopping behavior: the moderating role of the level of utilitarian motivational orientation. J. Retail. Consum. Serv. **16**(6), 434–441 (2009)
27. Valentine, D., Powers, T.: Generation Y values and lifestyle segments. J. Consum. Market. **30**(7), 597–606 (2013)
28. Viswanathan, V., Jain, V.: A dual-system approach to understanding "Generation Y" decision making. J. Consum. Market. **30**(6), 484–492 (2013)
29. Jurisic, B., Azevedo, A.: Building customer–brand relationships in the mobile communications market: the role of brand tribalism and brand reputation. J. Brand Manag. **18**(4–5), 349–366 (2010)
30. Bolton, R., Parasuraman, A., Hoefnagels, A., Migchels, N., Kabadayi, S., Gruber, T., et al.: Understanding Generation Y and their use of social media: a review and research agenda. J. Serv. Manag. **24**(3), 245–267 (2013)
31. Tesfom, G., Birch, N.: Do switching barriers in the retail banking industry influence bank customers in different age groups differently? J. Serv. Market. **25**(5), 371–380 (2011)
32. Rugimbana, R.: Generation Y: how cultural values can be used to predict their choice of electronic financial services. J. Financ. Serv. Market. **11**(4), 301–313 (2007)
33. Bilgihan, A.: Gen Y customer loyalty in online shopping: an integrated model of trust, user experience and branding. Comput. Hum. Behav. **61**, 103–113 (2016)
34. Nagurney, A.: Cyber security and financial services. In: INFORMS Conference on Business Analytics and Operations Research. Isenberg School of Management, University of Massachusetts Amherst, Boston, Massachusetts 01003 (2014). https://supernet.isenberg. umass.edu/visuals/Boston_Analytics_INFORMS_Cybersecurity_Nagurney.pdf
35. Levy, S.: Does usage level of online services matter to customers' bank loyalty? J. Serv. Market. **28**(4), 292–299 (2014)
36. González, M., Mueller-Dentiste, R., Mack, R.: An alternative approach in service quality: e-banking case. Qual. Manag. J. **15**(1), 41–58 (2008)
37. Sahoo, R., Swain, S.: Study of perceived value and performance of e-banking in India with a special reference to Punjab National Bank. Indus J. Manag. Soc. Sci. **5**(1), 64–75 (2012)
38. EFMA: Mobile banking: the dawn of a new era for retail banks, pp. 6–8. EFMA (2014). https://www.efma.com/ressources/studies/2014/1-YQ1TH_E_study.pdf
39. Bank of America: Trends in Consumer Mobility Report, pp. 3–7. Bank of America (2015). http:// newsroom.bankofamerica.com/files/doc_library/additional/2015_BAC_Trends_in_Consumer_ Mobility_Report.pdf

40. Capgemini: What Makes Gen Y Stick with a Bank? Explore how banks can increase acquisition and foster retention of Gen Y customers, pp. 9–12. Capgemini (2014). https://www.capgemini.com/resource-file-access/resource/pdf/gen_y_whitepaper.pdf
41. The Child and Youth Finance International: Child and Youth Friendly Banking Product Certificate. The Child and Youth Finance International, Amsterdam (2012). http://childfinanceinternational.org/library/cyfi-publications/Child-and-Youth-Friendly-Banking-Product-Certificate-CYFI.pdf
42. KPMG International: Customer Experience Barometer. KPMG Network, Switzerland (2014). https://www.kpmg.com/dutchcaribbean/en/Documents/Publications/customer-experience-barometer-v1-fs.pdf
43. Syrett, M., Lamminman, J.: Advertising and millennials. Young Consum. 5(4), 62–73 (2004)
44. Murugiah, L., Akgam, H.: Study of customer satisfaction in the banking sector in Libya. J. Econ. Bus. Manag. 3(7), 674–677 (2015)

Towards More Context-Awareness in Reactive Digital Ecosystems

Alexandru Averian[(⊠)]

Politehnica University of Bucharest, Bucharest, Romania
aaverian@gmail.com

Abstract. Ecosystems are open adaptive systems with self-organizing properties; they are based on a local interaction of the composing elements and generating a general end-result. Digital ecosystems incorporate these features in context-aware applications that work together for the efficient solving of complex dynamic problems. This article considers the digital ecosystems as being open-system of applications with a certain degree of context-awareness. It also presents Econtxt a programming model for the context used by context-aware applications running in digital ecosystems. An implementation of the proposed context model is presented and analysed in the final part of the article.

Keywords: Context · Digital ecosystems · Context-awareness

1 Introduction

The term "ecosystem" is a concept that evolved ever since its first utilization in the field of biology and ecology. Today this term represents a largely used expression which defines a wide range of systems, including social systems, technological systems, and economic systems - defined by data, relations and rules, and the systems they are made of. The term digital comes as a transposition of the systems and of their resources in the digital environment in order to obtain a representation in the form of a digital open platform. Ecosystems are considered to be adaptive complex systems consisting of the various elements which interact at the local level, adapt to the environment (they operate in) and evolve on the basis of selection processes [1]. The most interesting features of an ecosystem are self-organization, the ability to adapt to the environment and the tendency to achieve a dynamic balance. These properties can exploit in digital ecosystems to solve complex dynamic problems. Self-organization and adaptation to an always-changing environment require the existence of context-aware applications that interact together in order to achieve the predefined global goal.

   A context-aware application has the ability to autonomously adapting to the present context, which is a continuous change with the aim to provide a response and an optimal experience for the user. In this article, a digital ecosystem is considered as an open collaboration platform, scalable, of reactive and context-aware applications and a model of the context used in the programming of this type of applications is presented.

© Springer International Publishing AG 2017
A. Kravets et al. (Eds.): CIT&DS 2017, CCIS 754, pp. 640–654, 2017.
DOI: 10.1007/978-3-319-65551-2_46

2   Related Work

A digital ecosystem is a new techno-social platform and collaborative environment derived from properties observed in natural ecosystems. Such properties as openness, loosely-coupling, auto-control, auto-organization and niche orientation could be used to design new types of applications.

In the design of the digital ecosystems, a series of architectures have been taken into account. In [2, 3] Briscoe presents the first applications in the area of the neural computing that bring together, in a new approach, elements of theory with service-oriented architectures, multi-agent systems, and distributed computing. The proposed digital ecosystems provide support for the business environment.

In [4, 5] Chang and Wood continue research in digital ecosystems domain, enlarging the scope of their implementation in areas such as education and health, in [6] an implementation of a digital ecosystem in health realm, based on multi-agent architecture is presented. All examples suppose the presence of a communication medium and the presence of intelligent agents or context-aware applications which react to the changes occurring in the environment.

A wide range of approaches of the context has been presented in the specialized literature, in particular in the field of Ubiquitous Computing. There are key-value models, with objectional representation, based on logic, based on ontologies, using graphic representation or markup. A classification of the context models can be found in [7]. The construction of a context-aware application, as part of an open ecosystem, involves several factors; in particular, we must answer the following questions:

- In what domain will the application run and what is the relevant context information?
- How will it be obtained and how will the required information in relation to the selected domain be interpreted?
- How will the application adapt to the changes of context?

We shall try to answer these questions by introducing a programming model of the context for the digital ecosystems.

3   The Econtxt Model

Digital ecosystems can be considered as clusters of context-aware reactive applications having different levels of context awareness. Econtxt is a programming model that provides an abstraction of context data for context-aware applications running in digital ecosystems. The main objective pursued in the design of Econtxt model was to facilitate the development of an open, scalable system of applications, domain oriented and with the possibility of involving many actors, in the form of a digital ecosystem.

The main element in the proposed context model is represented by the consource – an object that abstracts a source of context data. More specifically, a consource represents one single source of data, actually a type of context data for the application. Any context information may be represented as a consource object type. Consource objects together with the filtering, composition and aggregation operations defined with the data streams constitute the starting basis in constructing the context-aware applications present in a digital ecosystem.

3.1 Architecture of Econtxt

Context information is the data describing the situation in which application runs and which are relevant to the interaction between the user and the application, while the context can include both the user and the application [8–10]. To be able to access all types of relevant context information we use an instance (an object) consource which represents a generic way to access the sources of context data. From the application's perspective, the way the context information is obtained is not relevant, this being encapsulated in consource objects.

The application interacts with the consource objects using an interface that allows the extraction of the necessary data without effectively knowing the method of obtaining them; this way we have a separation between the applications which use the context and the mechanisms used in acquiring the context data. This separation allows the modification of the objects that capture the context and also accomplish the aggregation of the data without modifying, and even without recompiling the applications which use the context. Under this aspect, consource objects are similar with context widget introduced by Dey in [9] and also with ambient components introduced in [11]. The proposed model differs from the fact that the consource object is not associated with a data source but with a context data type. Any new issuer of that type will be "sensed" by the consource object. By using the consource object the application will be able to extract different types of data such as local data from the sensors, text messages, information from various local or remote data sources. The context data can be primary data coming directly from sources of data or obtained by processing/combining the primary data extracted from other consources. The processing context data algorithms called in the composition process of the sources are also context-aware.

In general, both the data processing and the queries in the digital ecosystem carried out by the user will be contextualized and they will take into account the evolution of the context. As presented in [8] there are several context categories:

- **physical context:** location and time, environment data, weather conditions, altitude, brightness, other specific information, the trend of the stock exchange shares, the exchange rate evolution;
- **user context:** personal information related to the health conditions and the state of mind, the activity carried out by the user, social context, group membership, social relationships;
- **digital context or calculated:** contains information concerning the environment in which a particular service runs, system status, network speed, a capacity of the calculation resources, memory, application's condition/status, performed operations, executed queries.

An ideal programming model of the context of a digital ecosystem applications should offer the possibility to define the context in a simple and explicit way, using a design that unifies in one single representation several context types. Using the Econtxt model, the context-aware applications can process multiple types of context data, some of them are taken from external sources of data and events; other types of context can be computed based on the former types. By definition, in the Econtxt model, each instance of a context source and each consource object has associated a name, a type and a series of metadata (such as QoS). A consource object may use other consource objects in a complex processing network of data streams, this way new context information being generated. The data resulting from the consouce streams get in the application by setting the value of a variable. If the application needs a certain piece of information coming from the context it's enough to access that specific variable and it will obtain the last available value; there is no need to execute complex interrogations.

There are situations in which, on the basis of such variables that retain the contextual information, new values are defined and generally they are obtained via calculations. For example, if we have a value from the context that remembers the temperature of the environment and another value from the context that remembers the humidity, we could combine the two values in order to obtain a temperature index. Typically, this index should be recalculated each time when the values on which this is based on change. We have two options:

- In the first case, we recalculate the index each time regardless if two data values changed or not; consequently, it will end up with many useless calculations;
- In the second case, we use a callback mechanism, which updates our index only in case the context data change. In this case, the major disadvantage is given by the utilization of the callback function itself which leads to a code too difficult to follow, debug and maintain.

The solution adopted in Econtxt is given by the use of the reactive variables as defined in [12], the first implementation for C++ is available at [13] address.

3.2 Consource Objects

As one can see in Fig. 1, consource objects abstract a context data stream which originates from one or more sources of context such as sensors, various data or events sources. Also, these objects may be combined to build complex processing networks for context data.

Every consource object has a name, an associated a type (topic) and or quality of service (QoS). These parameters defining the consource objects are established in the design stage and remain unchanged. Consource objects are associated with a specific topic and are part of specific and well-defined domains. In other words, a classification of the context data for several domains is done; within each domain, the context data sources will be divided into several partitions.

If the field is identified by a fixed ID, the partitions can be changed by the program, which makes it possible for the context source to migrate from one partition to another within the specific domain. Below, the main features and the operating mode of the consource objects are presented. If a supplier (publisher) of context data, let's say a sensor, enters the partition on which is defined a consource object of the same type

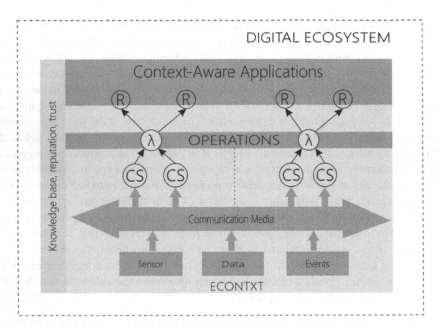

Fig. 1. Econtxt model

(i.e. the same topic) then when it is automatically recognized. Therefore, consource objects automatically discover the sources which transmit/issue context data.

Consource objects are universal relative to the data source. If in other modelling systems the context of a context object abstract a single context data with which is connected during the initialization, in Econtxt model consource objects abstract a specific context type and does not select a specific provider of the contextual information. This makes possible a separation between the source of the actual data and consource "widget" which receives the data and supply them to the application. We also need to add that context data can come from the local system, from the systems connected to the local network, or from the applications located in other networks (habitats).

In some cases we face situations where the objects which supply the context data need to be migrated from one computer to another; in our case, thanks to the separation between consource object and its actual source, we can move the data sources without affecting the functionality. In addition, due to this separation can we remove some of the sources of data and add new ones without the need of reconfiguration of the consource objects, which "follows" the context data type.

Consource objects are replicable. Multiple consource instances running in different working environments, possibly in different physical locations can "listen" for the same type of context data. If the application is located at a given moment in the same domain/partition, i.e. in the same environment, then they will receive the same context information.

Consource objects may also be composed in such a way so we can obtain a new context information from the composing data. The new source of data can be directly delivered to the application or can be exposed back in the environment under the form of a new consource instance. This composing operation represents a method for building a series of sophisticated schemes for processing contextual information.

3.3   Operations

A digital ecosystem is an open system consisting of a group of users and a set of "similar" applications which use data and services from the environment, and produce data and provide various services to the other participants. The common environment in which applications run allows context data exchange by all applications in the group.

From the communication environment's perspective, a consource object is a "listener" of the context data; from the Econtxt's perspective, it is seen as a data stream. From this latter perspective, we will define a series of operations that operates with data streams.

The operations defined with consource objects allow the transformation of the data, but also the generation of new context data; a part of the new latter data can return to the environment and can be used by other applications.

In various systems of context data, modelling registration mechanisms are utilized in central context source register so that they can be found. A series of select type operations are used to identify the context data sources based on a chosen criteria are proposed; the current values are extracted through special retrieval operations [14].

In Econtxt model's case, the data sources are not registered in a central register and the selection operation does not exist. Practically, the data source and the consource object define a common type of data, a topic that will use to transport the context data. To be able to communicate in addition to the topic and domain, the partition and the communication mode are also set. The operations that can be performed with the consource objects are the operation of filtering data (filter), transformation (mapping), deduction applied to several consource objects (inference), concatenation, combining (merge), aggregation and convolution (.zip).

1. The filtering operation allows the selection of context data which comply with a specific criterion. This way a series of data which are not relevant for the application shall be deleted. Each time a context information is available, a verification is performed to validate if this complies with the specified condition in the criterion from filter's definition; if the information is compliant, it is transferred to the application. The filtering operation will be involved in queries that are more complex in order to eliminate a part of irrelevant data; consequently, the complexity of later calculations is reduced.
2. The mapping operation allows the changing of the type of context data and their delivery in a new format. This operation allows the adaptation of the data type so that it will be supported by certain applications; also, the context data can be converted in such a way that they would be compatible, i.e. it turns into a common type in order to be able to apply other operations such as concatenation or merging.
3. The deduction operation applied to consource objects allows the application of algorithms for various data source types with the intention to produce new results

deducted after the calculations. The deduction algorithm is executed every time new data are available regardless of the originating selected sources for the calculations.

4. Aggregation applies an algorithm to a set of data coming from the same source. The modeling of the context data in the form of a stream gives us the ability to carry out a number of calculations on data sets, which come from the same stream. We can say that the data stream provides us a history of data. The aggregation may produce a series of new data such as the average of the last values, minimum or maximum value, etc. The aggregation algorithm is executed whenever a new set of data is available from the connected context data stream. The size of the data set can be specified as a maximum number of items (elements) or as a time period for executing the algorithm. Usually, the aggregation is applied to data that have been selected by means of filtering operations so that the result of the aggregation makes sense.

5. The merging and concatenation of context data are possible in the case of *compatible* data sources. The concatenation of the context data sequences is possible in the case of extraction of finite length sequences from several sources. Combining or mixing multiple data in a new context data stream can be applied to the data sources after a prior transformation (mapping) operation is performed on them in such a way so they are compatible (of the same type). In fact, if an object follows a type of context data and there are several data sources providing this type then the type of data will be automatically merged.

6. Combining the data from several sources and generating a new type of context is achieved by convolution (.zip); in other words, from a tuple of sequences, we will obtain a sequence of tuples representing the context data.

The operations described above may be repeatedly applied to the consource objects. Each operation can be carried out in a separate thread, if appropriate, so such applications can access the context data if required without be being blocked until obtaining them. Effectively we can use a mechanism based on callback functions, also we can use a promise-future scheme type, option present in C++11. The actual implementation presented below uses the reactive variables. For the environment (and communication) we can use a P2P network or a DDS (Date Distribution Service) [15], such systems are used more often as a development base for applications in industrial IOT domain.

3.4   Reactive Variables

The reactive variables, noted with the symbol R in Fig. 1, are objects, which permit the propagation of data changes in a push model. In other words, if a variable R depends on some other variables a_1, a_2, ..., a_n then any change of one of the variables a_1, a_2, ..., a_n will imply the recalculation of R. In a pull model, this happens every time when we need the value of R, which involves a set of useless calculations. Using a push model we can avoid repeated calculations if by changing one of the variables a_1, a_2, ..., a_n the value of R is recalculated (and of all variables which depend on R) as one can see in Fig. 2. So, whenever we need the value of R this is available without needs to be recalculated. We can say that a reactive variable allows the concurrent execution of multi-level coordinated callback functions. Practically reactive variables simplify programming using the callback functions offering a model for declarative programming. This guarantees that they will perform a minimum number of calculations per update, in a thread safe manner. For more details can be consulted [13].

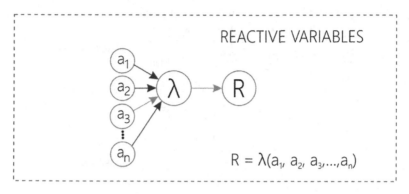

Fig. 2. Reactive variables in Econtxt model

4 Econtxt Implementation

In the Econtxt model, the context data may originate from a number of sensors, the external sources of data or events. The flow of context data comes from the environment, the operations applied to context data is happening in the context area where the values of reactive variables are updated. The application can access the reactive variables at any time. If its data has not arrived yet the variable will have a default value set at initialization. Context data will be represented by a structure, which may contain more fields of different types. If a certain structure of data will be delivered by several sources then it is recommended to use a special field that will have the role to identify the origin of the context data. In this way, the structure resembles a recording from a database, and the field for the identification of the source plays the role of the primary key.

We can consider that we deal with a context that works with key type data– value similar to the model introduced in [16]. If, for instance, in a swarm of drones (UAV - unmanned aerial vehicles) each drone issues in the environment the geographical coordinates of its own position and the other participants can know its position at any given moment. The registration itself is a value that changes over time and therefore it can be considered a separate stream of data. The context data defined this way and generated from multiple suppliers constitute a mix of data streams that can be received by a consoure object. This is where its name comes. If the operator wants to follow the trajectory of drones he can introduce a filter in order to select only the data stream coming from the object of interest. In addition, the data can be filtered by applying a criterion to the fields that make up the structure of the context data (Fig. 3).

For example, suppose we have a set of UAVs which perform a surveillance operation and image taking of a piece of land. There is a number of studies which address the coordination of the flight of a group of UAV systems. In [17] it is tackled the problem of

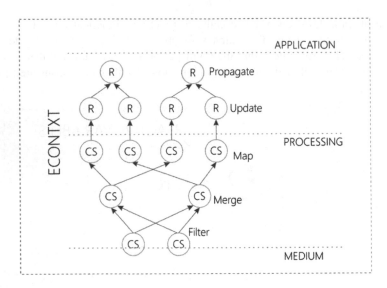

Fig. 3. Context data processing in Econtxt model

replanning of a flight in case of the appearance of a hostile object. The system presented is formed by a coordinator (the algorithm used is the same), a trajectory planning component, an optimization component (smoothing the computed trajectory) which makes possible that the determined trajectory can be used for the flight, and, finally, the autopilot. All vehicles communicate with each other at the supervisor level, changing the information related to the position, altitude, and speed; in case an obstacle appears, the information is immediately communicated to the other participants. The trajectory planner generates a set of possible (candidate) routes that are adjusted by the coordinator in order to avoid overlaps with the trails of flight participants; the routes go through a smoothing operation and are sent to the autopilot (Fig. 4).

All transferred data represents context information transferred and processed in real-time. Every flight object calculates its route individually, taking into account of the received context date. If it receives the replanning command, this is communicated to all participants. The trip planner may use an evolutionary algorithm for calculating the routes, in the source mentioned an algorithm of type ACO (Ant Colony Optimization) with enhanced strategy. For more details, please refer to [18]. Modeling of data types used for the transmission of the context, we will adopt an approach of the components based programming. As can be seen in Listing 1, for the transfer of the context data we have defined a structure Position by means of the IDL language. The IDL compiler converts the description of the structure in a source code, obtaining a projection of the Position structure (in C++ language) under the form of a type that will be used for reading or writing context data.

After compiling the source files obtained, a dynamic library is generated and it will be used both by the context-aware application and the context data suppliers. The module will contain the work functions with the Position through which the application can read and write the data structure in the communication environment. Figure 5

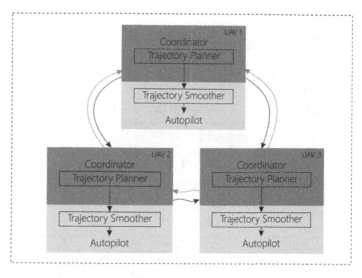

Fig. 4. The components of a flight coordination system [17]

shows the other classes involved in the construction of the context and the relations between the context, application, and ecosystem.

```
module CtxSource
{
  struct Position
  {
    long pid;
    long pLat;
    long pLong;
    long pAlt;
    long pSpeed;
  };
  #pragma keylist Position pid
};
```

Listing 1. IDL specification of Position structure

As one can see in the next listing, for extracting and processing of the context data we use streams from the RxCpp library. Next, we shall present the implementation of Connect function of the ConSource class. The utilization of NetworkContext procedure which contains a loop for the interception of the environment and which is rolled in a separate thread of execution. The next function creates an observer connected to the environment (Network), it activates and connects it a client (subscriber) which will be notified when the context data gets into the environment. The Start function is similar (see Listing 3) it returns the observing object without connecting a client to it. This way it is possible to apply stream data operations by connecting filtering mapping and

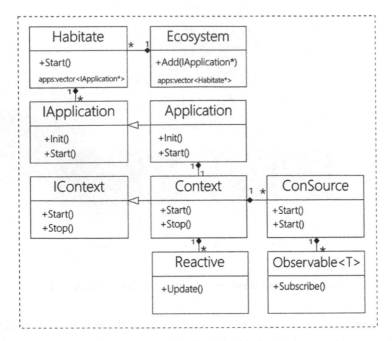

Fig. 5. Main classes of Econtxt model

another type of operations; then, using the subscribe method, connects to a client which it will be notified when the data arrives. This updates the reactive variables and this leads to an automatic recalculation of all the data, which are dependent on the context.

```
template<typename FUNC>
auto Connect( FUNC && func ){
   auto keys = rx::observable<>::create<T>(NetworkContext)
     .subscribe_on( rx::synchronize_new_thread())
    .publish();
 // run the loop in create in new thread
 auto k1 = keys.connect_forever();
}
```

Listing 2. Connect function of the ConSource class

In the code listed below is (partially) defined the class Context in which we see the two ConSource<T> type objects which bring context data in the application. posx0 and posy0 reactive variables represent the position of the current vehicle; posx and posy represent the position of the another flight vehicle.

Type **SignalT<int>** dist variable represents the distance (we use a simplified form) between the two objects. We can notice the declarative expression mode of the calculations that update the value of dest, yet the executing callback functions cannot be observed. The code is simpler, more easy to understand and to maintain.

```
using Type = CtxSource::Position;
class Context final: public IContext
{
 //Our position
 VarSignalT<int>  posx0 = MakeVar<R>( 1 );
 VarSignalT<int>  posy0 = MakeVar<R>( 1 );
 //peer position
 VarSignalT<int>  posx = MakeVar<R>( 1 );
 VarSignalT<int>  posy = MakeVar<R>( 1 );

 SignalT<int> dist = (posx-posx0) * (posx-posx0)
      + (posy-posy0) * (posy-posy0);
 ConSource<Type> cs0; //our position
 ConSource<Type> cs1; //peer position
 public:
 virtual int Connect(){
  auto stream0 = cs0.Start(); //start listening
  auto Filter0 = []( Type t ) {
   return t.pid() == 0;
  };
  auto Activate0 = [&]( Type t ) {
   DoTransaction<R>( [&]
   {
    posx0 <<= t.pLat();
    posy0 <<= t.pLong();
   } );
  };
  stream0 >> rxo::filter( Filter0 ) >>
rxo::subscribe<Type>( Activate0 );

  auto stream1 = cs1.Start(); //start listening
  auto Filter1 = []( Type t ){
   return t.pid() != 0;
  };
  auto Activate1 = [&]( Type t ){
   DoTransaction<R>( [&] {
    posx <<= t.pLat();
    posy <<= t.pLong();
   } );
  };
  stream1 >> rxo::filter( Filter1 ) >>
rxo::subscribe<Type>( Activate1 );
  return 0;
 }
};
```

Listing 3. Source code of Context class

The context-aware application can read any information managed by Context class presented in the 3rd listing. The main program can execute any algorithm and if necessary, it can utilize the data from the class Context. In order to illustrate this, we set an observer, which will signal any modification of the reactive variable dist; this latter variable is automatically updated each time when one of the variables on which it depends changes its value.

```
void Application::run()
{
Context ctx;
ctx.Connect();
//this observer will observe any change
Observe( ctx.dist, [ this ]( int v ){
  cout << app_id << " Distance: " << v << endl;
});
while( CanRun() ) {
  //use ctx
  UpdateTrajectory(ctx);
  //Sleep( 100 );
}
}
```

Listing 4. The main function of the application

The introduced implementation of the Econtxt model is carried out using programming language C++, consource objects and the operations done with these were implemented using Reactive Library Extensions (RxCpp). The communication environment is given by a real-time data distribution service [19], the implementation used in the experiment is OpenSplice from PrismTech.

5 Conclusion

This work follows the study conducted in [20] and continues the research that was presented in the respective paper. The model introduced is based on the use of consource objects that receives and processes the context data coming from various sources (sensors) or events. There is no fixed association between the sources of data and the receiving consource objects; they recognize each other and automatically communicate if define the same data type and the same communication parameters. Therefore, we can extend the ecosystem by adding new data context sources in a specific domain and the running application will automatically recognize them. Consource objects can be combined in various ways using the defined operations of filtering, deduction, aggregation, concatenation, merge and join. The proposed model has been implemented using as a communication medium a real-time data distribution system, namely a DDS standardized by OMG [15]. OpenSplice is the implementation that has been used. The internal data streams have been carried out using Reactive

Extensions library for C++ (RxCpp). The first experiments show that the system can be applied to real-time applications. The future research will analyze the stability and scalability of the proposed solution.

Acknowledgements. The work has been funded by the Sectoral Operational Programme Human Resources Development 2007-2013 of the Ministry of European Funds through the Financial Agreement POSDRU/159/1.5/S/132395.

References

1. Levin, S.A.: Ecosystems and the biosphere as complex adaptive systems. Ecosystems **1**(5), 431–436 (1998)
2. Briscoe, G.: Digital ecosystems: evolving service-orientated architectures, no. 507953 (2006)
3. Briscoe, G., Sadedin, S.: Natural science paradigms. Digit. Bus. Ecosyst., 48–55 (2007)
4. Chang, E., West, M.: Digital ecosystems a next generation of the collaborative environment. Eight Int. Conf. **214**, 3–23 (2006)
5. Chang, E., West, M.: Digital ecosystems and comparison to existing collaboration environment. WSEAS Trans. Environ. Dev. **2**(11), 1396–1404 (2006)
6. Serbanati, L.D., Ricci, F.L., Mercurio, G., Vasilateanu, A.: Steps towards a digital health ecosystem. J. Biomed. Inform. **44**, 621–636 (2011)
7. Strang, T., Linnhoff-Popien, C.: A context modeling survey graph models. In: Workshop, no. 4, pp. 1–8 (2004)
8. Dey, A.K.: Understanding and Using Context. Pers. Ubiquit. Comput. J. **1**(5), 4–7 (2001)
9. Dey, A.K.: Providing architectural support for building context-aware applications, November 2000
10. Dey, A.K., Abowd, G.D., Salber, D.: A context-based infrastructure for smart environments. In: Nixon, P., Lacey, G., Dobson, S. (eds.) Managing Interactions in Smart Environments, pp. 114–128. Springer, London (1999). doi:10.1007/978-1-4471-0743-9_11
11. Jacquet, C., Bourda, Y., Bellik, Y.: A component-based platform for accessing context in ubiquitous computing applications. J. Ubiquit. Comput. Intell. **1**(2), 163–173 (2007)
12. Salvaneschi, G., Hintz, G., Mezini, M.: REScala: bridging between object-oriented and functional style in reactive applications. In: Proceedings of the 13th International Conference Modularity - Modularity 2014, pp. 25–36 (2014)
13. Jeckel, S.: Documentation of C++React. http://schlangster.github.io/cpp.react/. Accessed 01 Jan 2017
14. Sehic, S., Li, F., Nastic, S., Dustdar, S.: A programming model for context-aware applications in large-scale pervasive systems. In: International Conference on Wireless and Mobile Computing, Networking and Communications, pp. 142–149 (2012)
15. Data Distribution Service for Real-time Systems, OMG (2015). http://www.omg.org/spec/DDS/1.4/
16. Schilit, B., Adams, N., Want, R.: Context-aware computing applications. In: Mobile Computing Systems and Applications, pp. 85–90 (1994)
17. Duan, H.B., Zhang, X.Y., Wu, J., Ma, G.J.: Max-min adaptive ant colony optimization approach to multi-UAVs coordinated trajectory replanning in dynamic and uncertain environments. J. Bionic Eng. **6**(2), 161–173 (2009)

18. Duan, H., Li, P.: Bio-inspired Computation in Unmanned Aerial Vehicles. Springer, Heidelberg (2014). doi:10.1007/978-3-642-41196-0
19. Corsaro, A., Schmidt, D.C.: The data distribution service. In: Tech, pp. 1–19 (2012)
20. Averian, A.: Digital ecosystems software modeling from a niche perspective. Mathematics-Informatics Series. Annals of Spiru Haret University, vol. 10, pp. 37–47 (2014). (CNCSIS B+)

Monitoring of Road Transport Infrastructure for the Intelligent Environment «Smart Road»

Alexey Finogeev[1(✉)], Anton Finogeev[1], and Sergey Shevchenko[2]

[1] Penza State University, Penza, Russia
alexeyfinogeev@gmail.com, fanton3@ya.ru
[2] National Technical University "Kharkiv Polytechnic Institute",
Kharkiv, Ukraine
sv_shevchenko@mail.ru

Abstract. In the article, the issues of monitoring the road transport infrastructure based on a distributed network of photoradar complexes for fixing traffic accidents have been considered. This paper discusses tools for collection of road accident's photo and video data fixation, data mining and forecasting of transport incidents, depending on various factors (meteorological, social, operational, etc.). The connection between the complexes and the data processing center is established to ensure secure data transmission using a heterogeneous transport network. In the process of monitoring, tasks of spatial and intellectual analysis, evaluation, and forecasting of traffic accidents and transport situations for preventive response, notification and warning road users are solved. The monitoring system is an integral part of Smart Road intellectual environment within the framework of the Smart & Safe City concept. A multi-agent model of convergent data processing is implemented for big sensor data, which integrates cloud, fog, and mobile computing technologies.

Keywords: Monitoring · Data mining · Decision support · Streaming data processing · Deep machine learning · Wireless sensor networks · Big sensor data · Multiagent approach · Smart Road · Smart and safe city · Intelligent Transportation System · Convergent data processing

1 Introduction

The modern trend of increase of efficiency and safety of the vital processes in the urban environment is the introduction of new information systems and technologies in the form of smart environments [1]. Currently, there is a Smart & Safe City concept [2] in terms of the project's implementation such as Smart Manufacturing, Smart Houses, Smart Light, Smart Energy, Intelligent Transportation System, Smart Road etc. This concept involves the development of an intelligent information and computing environment for solving the problems of distributed monitoring and support of municipal

The reported study was funded by RFBR according to the research project № 15-07-01720, 16-07-00031.

A. Kravets et al. (Eds.): CIT&DS 2017, CCIS 754, pp. 655–668, 2017.
DOI: 10.1007/978-3-319-65551-2_47

management processes with the necessary level of life activity [3]. The smart environment will combine various factors for the development of urban area elements into a single system to ensure universal access to information, computing and telecommunication resources. The main direction is the development and implementation of smart big data processing technologies, which are collected from distributed sensors, measuring devices and automation devices in the Internet of Things (IoT) [4]. The result of the synthesis of Smart & Safe City intelligent environment should be to ensure maximum comfort and safety of human life in the urban infrastructure and highly efficient production in the industrial sector.

The paradigm of an intelligent multimodal environment includes three basic concepts: (a) Ubiquitous (Pervasive) Computing and Networking [5]; (b) Intellectual Assistant (Ambient Intelligence) [6]; (c) Smart Environments [7]. Synthesis of the intellectual multimodal environment includes wide introduction and application of technologies:

- remote control of objects and processes in automatic mode in real time,
- wireless sensor data exchange,
- secure collection of information through sensor networks,
- intellectualization of sensors, automation devices, home appliances, etc.,
- multi-agent big data processing,
- predictive modeling of situations for decision-making,
- convergence of information, computing and telecommunication technologies,
- standardization of inter-machine interactions between components of the intellectual environment, etc.

The key components of the intellectual environment are:

1. Intelligent sensors (sensors, measuring devices, photo, and video fixation devices) capable of by the built microcontroller to data processing, change modes and actuate with monitoring object.
2. Telecommunication networks of broadband data transmission (fiber-optic and wireless) and mobile communication systems.
3. Satellite navigation systems.

2 Intelligent Transportation Systems and Smart Road

In the Smart & Safe City concept, the important task is to solve the problem related to the development of intelligent transport systems (ITS) and intellectual environment Smart Road [8, 9]. The terms mean the presence of built-in intellectual functionality in vehicles and on objects of the road and transport infrastructure, as well as an intelligent monitoring system for the purpose of automated traffic management and security. In fact, ITS is a system, which uses innovations in the transport system modeling [10] and traffic management, providing end customers informative and safety. The level of interaction between participants (ITS) in the movement growing compared to conventional transport systems.

ITS differ in their technology - from simple car navigation systems, regulation of traffic lights, systems for regulating cargo transportation, information placard systems, car number recognition systems and vehicle speed registration to video surveillance systems, parking management, weather services, etc.

The main classes of ITS are:

(1) In-vehicle ITS. Includes sensors, microprocessor cards, and displays, which provide drivers geospatial information on traffic situations.
(2) Infrastructure-based ITS. They present various information, including meteorological information, by the roadside information panels, as well as control the traffic flow.
(3) Cooperative ITS. Inter-machine interaction is carried out between road infrastructure objects and vehicles (vehicle to infrastructure, V2I), between vehicles (vehicle to vehicle, V2V).

The Smart Road intellectual environment are handled large amounts of data in real time, the bulk of which are photos and video streams from surveillance cameras and photoradar systems. The aim of Smart Road component is to influence the behavior of cars and drivers to optimize the use of transport routes and vehicles, to prevent abnormal and emergency situations and to improve road safety.

Three types of factors affect the risks of road accidents:

(1) Anthropogenic factors, which can be caused by changes in the behavior of drivers and pedestrians, speed of movement, health status at a particular moment, etc.
(2) Technogenic factors, which are determined by possible problems with vehicles in the process of movement.
(3) Infrastructural factors, which are dependent on changes in the state of road transport infrastructure.

Smart Road components need to reduce risks promptly perform such monitoring tasks:

− monitoring of the road surface state,
− meteorological monitoring,
− monitoring of traffic flows and speeds of transport units,
− monitoring violations of traffic rules,
− rapid detection of traffic accidents.

Monitoring results should be transmitted to road users through traffic channels, cellular, trunk and satellite radio communication channels, information boards and dynamic road signs.

The main components of the Smart Road environment are:

− Intelligent monitoring system (IMS) for traffic management,
− a system of road users warning,
− feedback system to take into account social reactions of road users and other people,
− intelligent traffic lights and other signaling systems,
− intelligent video surveillance cameras and photo and video-fixing complexes of road accidents,

- satellite systems of transport monitoring,
- intelligent parking and loading areas,
- road sensor systems for unmanned vehicles,
- cars with built-in intelligent transport system,
- electronic payment systems for road services, etc.

In Russia, the development of ITS is now at the stage of active implementation of primary elements, such as vehicle monitoring system based on GLONASS [11], emergency care system drivers ERA-GLONASS, dynamic maps of public transport, etc. Currently, there are no ready commercial solutions in the field of communication systems between machines (V2V) and communication systems between machines and intellectual infrastructure (V2I).

3 Convergent Model for Processing Big Sensor Data in Smart Road Environment

For the interaction of the components of Smart Road, a transportable wireless environment is required in the form of a segment of the Internet of Things [12], which is designed to provide information exchange of complexes, data center servers, ITS, aerial surveillance systems, mobile users.

For interaction, Smart Road component a transport wireless environment is required in the form of an Internet of things network segment, which is designed to provide information exchange complexes, servers, data centers, ITS, air surveillance systems, mobile communications. Such a medium is heterogeneous, as it is realized through various technologies: wireless sensor networks, cellular networks, WiFi networks, satellite navigation systems. In this environment, a secure data exchange mechanism is implemented. The heterogeneous transport environment for the collection and processing of photo and video data is realized within the framework of the convergent model of computing and data storage [13].

Convergence is defined as the interlinking of computing and storage technologies such as media, content and communication networks that have arisen as a result of evolution and popularization of the internet as well as activities, products, and services in the digital media space. Convergence also refers to the phenomena of a group of technologies which are developed for one use but is being utilized in many different contexts.

Convergence of technology happens due to the digitization of content. The content can be text, graphics, video, animation, and audio. Digital technology allows the use of multiple communication modes in a single network. The reason of convergence is the rapid advancement in the field of the internet along with the emergence of various products and services, the availability of carrier technology with high bandwidth.

Term convergence of networks means telecommunications technology convergence process with the appearance of similar characteristics in network equipment, communication channels, network standards and protocols, data transfer processes [14]. The result of convergence in this aspect is the synthesis and development of a heterogeneous transport environment with the integration of a variety of information and computing services for the big sensor data processing. An example of a convergent platform for collecting and transmitting sensory data is the Internet of things built into the Internet.

The convergence of distributed computing and storage technologies can be used to implement processing big sensor data from photoradar complexes and video cameras.

Four models of distributed computing can be distinguished: GRID computing; cloud computing; fog computing, mobile computing. GRID calculations are based on the architecture of computer networks of the individual compute nodes (Fig. 1).

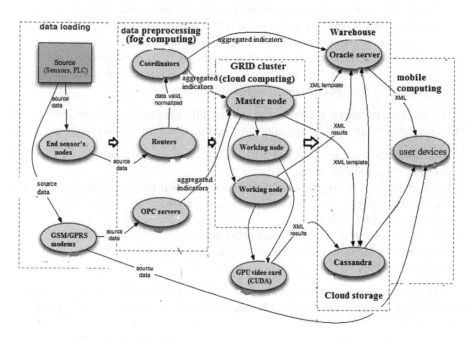

Fig. 1. The data flow diagram of convergence computing model

Computing process provides for a distribution separate parts for the task to currently free network computing resources. This approach is used for tasks too complex for a single node. Cloud computing - is not only the allocation of tasks on the network nodes of computing resources. This model is used for the ubiquitous network access to a common pool of configurable resources (software, server, information, platform, etc.) at any time. The user uses the technology of "thin" client as a means of access to applications, platforms, and data, and the entire infrastructure of the information system is located at the provider of cloud services. Fog computing - is the virtual platform of distributed computing and data storage services on end-terminal devices and network services for data transmission, storage, and processing [15]. Computation is performed terminal devices with limited computing and energy resources - including controllers, industrial equipment, household appliances with microprocessors equipment, sensor network nodes. Mobile computing is human–computer interaction by which a computer is expected to be transported during normal usage, which allows for the transmission of data, voice, and video. Mobile computing involves mobile communication, mobile hardware, and mobile software. Communication issues include ad hoc networks and infrastructure networks as well as communication properties, protocols, data formats and mobile technologies.

The reasons for the development of a converged model of distributed computing are existing problems in the plan of information processes:

(1) The information's opacity, which is associated with the closed data formats of information systems from various developers.
(2) Mismatch of sensor data and protocols that are associated with the use of the manufacturers proprietary systems for collecting and data processing.
(3) Duplication and synchronization information. Similar sensor data necessary for solving various tasks are duplicated in databases in its own storage formats.
(4) Mismatch of sensor data streams, associated with the use of different network technologies and telecommunications solutions.

To solve the problems, the cloud, fog, and mobile computing technologies are used. The convergence networks architecture may include five hardware and software levels:

1. The sensor nodes are associated with industrial controllers and sensors, directly implementing fog computing.
2. Clusters network segments with coordinators, cellular modems, router, which collects and transfers sensor data into the data warehouse.
3. Cloud computing clusters.
4. Warehouse of sensor data and monitoring results.
5. The user mobile devices for the organization of access to computing and information resources.

The convergence results are defined more specifically as the coming together of telecommunications, computing, and broadcasting into a single digital bit-stream.

4 Tools for Monitoring Road Transport Infrastructure

Intelligent monitoring road infrastructure and transport is based on collection and analysis of sensor multimedia data that are collected from various ground platforms, air and space surveillance equipment. As a ground-based platform for collecting information, road video cameras and photo and video fixing tools for traffic violations are used, for example, photoradar complexes with photo-fixing "Cordon" and complexes with video recording "Cordon-Temp". Complexes can allocate and recognize objects in photos and in a video stream (Fig. 2).

The main functions of the complex is a measure vehicle speeds in the control zone, automatically capture and save violators' photos, recognize license plates and events, collect and transmit such information to a data center, as: recognized number, fixed speed of the vehicle, type of violation, direction of movement, date and time of the violation, value of the permissible speed, name of the controlled area, geographical coordinates, etc. A large number of the data makes it necessary to develop a monitoring system with multi-agent distributed data processing and intelligent analysis tools for

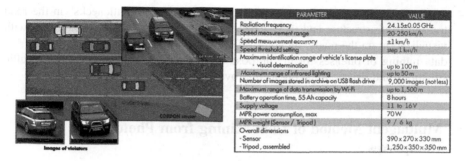

PARAMETER	VALUE
Radiation frequency	24.15±0.05 GHz
Speed measurement range	20-250 km/h
Speed measurement accuracy	±1 km/h
Speed threshold setting	step 1 km/h
Maximum identification range of vehicle's license plate · visual determination	up to 100 m
Maximum range of infrared lighting	up to 50 m
Number of images stored in archive on USB flash drive	9,000 images (not less)
Maximum range of data transmission by Wi-Fi	up to 1,500 m
Battery operation time, 55 Ah capacity	8 hours
Supply voltage	11 to 16 V
MPR power consumption, max	70 W
MPR weight (Sensor / Tripod)	9 / 6 kg
Overall dimensions - Sensor	390 x 270 x 330 mm
- Tripod, assembled	1,250 x 350 x 350 mm

Fig. 2. Operation of photoradar systems

forecasting of traffic situations using multi-agent approach [16], the model converged computing, streaming technologies for sensor data processing and machine learning algorithms (Fig. 3).

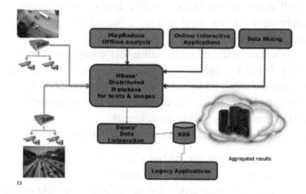

Fig. 3. Distributed processing and data mining system

Monitoring system with multi-agent distributed data processing and intelligent analysis tools performs the following functions:

- detection and identification of moving vehicles on the controlled road section with speed measurement;
- automatic photo-video recording of violations of traffic rules;
- data about traffic flow collection in all controlled areas and transfer to the data processing center via communication channels;
- vehicles detection and tracking them with visualization of routes of their movements on a cartographic basis;
- photographs and video materials processing about road accidents and violations;
- statistical data accumulation and processing about violations for the time periods to identify and analyze changes in dependency violations of traffic accidents from the influence of various factors (weather conditions, traffic volume, repair work, city events, time of day, seasonal factors, etc.);

- spatial analysis of offenses to identify critical areas and "bottlenecks" in the road transport infrastructure and their dependence on changes in traffic conditions with visualization on the map with color differentiation zones;
- data mining of offenses for the purpose of forecasting the development of traffic situations and decision-making to improve traffic safety.

5 Multiagent Method of Data Mining from Photoradar Complexes

The multiagent method involves the use of software agents to solve problems of alerting road users about the current and projected traffic situation in the location areas through mobile communication applications and vehicle navigation equipment [17].

A lot of agents work with the expert server component to provide users with alternative routes and recommendations for choosing the best route with customization to the wishes of users. Set of agents includes driver alert agents, warning traffic agents on the routes (collisions, speed modes, traffic lanes, traffic signs, markings, etc.), parking zone information agents, road service information agents, information agents about loading areas for trucks, etc.

Processing sensor data obtained with photoradar complexes can be implemented in the fog computing layer by agents that are loaded into integrated sensor nodes. Wireless sensor nodes ZigBee [18] are connected to complexes for solving simple problems of analyzing photos and video data, search and detection of vehicles in video streams, localization and tracking their movements.

The method of multi-agent processing of sensory data includes:

- a model of convergent processing of big sensor data,
- a way to load software agents into sensor nodes,
- a technique for analyzing time series for forecasting possible situations,
- a technique of detection, localization, and tracking of vehicles,
- a technique of remote diagnosis of photoradar complexes and the forecast of performance parameters.

The hypervisor management is consolidated computing resources in a multiprocessor system for distributed processing of big sensor data. Software agents are operated in the sensor nodes and interacted with the data acquisition modules, other agents, and brokers. In this model, computing agent is software template for parallel processing.

The intelligent agent responds to requests, decides on the selection of data processing functions, clone and migrate to other nodes in the network. The agents exchange messages with each other and brokers, which send protected data to the central network coordinator, and receive from them control commands.

The model of intellectual brokers is offered to agent interaction with server applications at the data center. The broker is an agent that runs on routers and realizing the storage, data protection, and transmission functions. The message Query Telemetry Transport protocol is used for the implementation of information exchange with limited energy resources [18]. Collect cloud computing results entering from sensor segments ZigBee network [19] is performed by using the broker MQTT, loaded into computing network gateway cluster, that provides interaction ZigBee protocol stack and MQTT-client. The gateway is implemented on a central coordinator ZigBee network or modem pool cellular network. The broker's functions are sensor data and aggregates processing, entering in the coordinator; conversion frames with this information to be integrated into the data warehouse; data encryption; support «sliding» window algorithm to ensure reliable transmission, etc.

The results of data processing by agents in the process of monitoring traffic accidents are transferred to the data center, where more complex spatial and intellectual analysis tasks are solved in the second layer of cloud computing and storage.

6 Results of Monitoring

Consider the results of monitoring and analysis of traffic accidents, fixed by an intelligent monitoring system with photoradar complexes, which are installed on the main highways of the Penza region. To accumulate statistics, their spatial and intellectual analysis, synthesis of graphs and reports to support decision making, the system employs a special agent for remote polling of photo-video fixing complexes and automatic upload of data on administrative violations (Fig. 4). This software agent is provided by developers of photo-video complexes "Cordon-Temp".

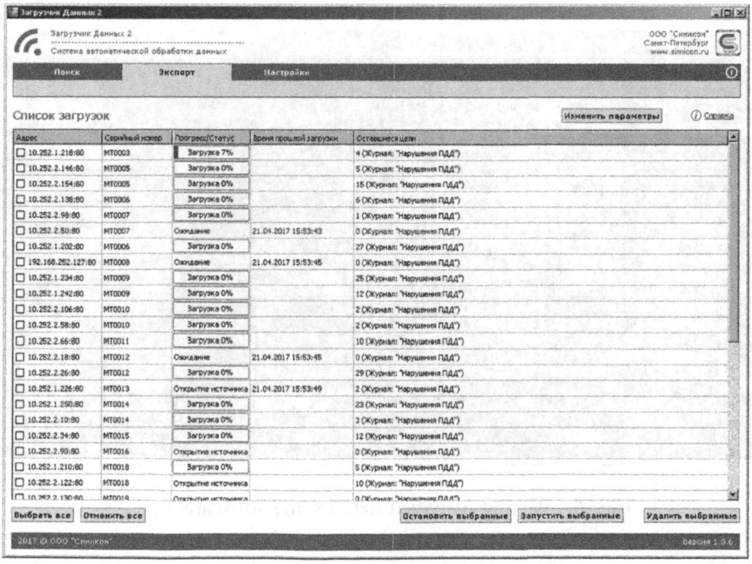

Fig. 4. Operation of the software upload agent

The agent collects and downloads multimedia data such as photos and frames with violators from the video stream, as well as various telemetric data on traffic parameters, for example, time series with changes in the average speed of vehicles in the controlled area. These time series are represented by the visualization agent in the form of graphs (Fig. 5).

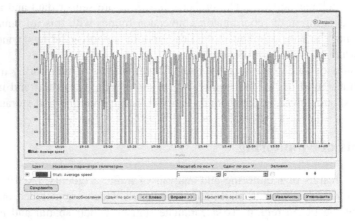

Fig. 5. Time series of average speed of vehicles

The results of automatic collection and unloading of photo-video data are recorded in the database during the parsing process (Fig. 6).

```
C:\Ruby23-x64\bin\ruby.exe
No new records at CSV violations/m1.csv file
No new records at CSV violations/m10.csv file
No new records at CSV violations/m11.csv file
1 records at CSV violations/m12.csv file adding to database
No new records at CSV violations/m13.csv file
No new records at CSV violations/m14.csv file
No new records at CSV violations/m15.csv file
No new records at CSV violations/m16.csv file
No new records at CSV violations/m17.csv file
No new records at CSV violations/m18.csv file
No new records at CSV violations/m19.csv file
No new records at CSV violations/m2.csv file
1 records at CSV violations/m3.csv file adding to database
No new records at CSV violations/m4.csv file
1 records at CSV violations/m5.csv file adding to database
No new records at CSV violations/m6.csv file
No new records at CSV violations/m7.csv file
1 records at CSV violations/m8.csv file adding to database
No new records at CSV violations/m9.csv file
4 records at CSV violations/p1.csv file adding to database
7.432425
```

Fig. 6. Parsing of paged data by the software agent

The database is hierarchical and is located on the data center servers according to the cloud storage model (Fig. 7).

The data mining results and reporting data are also stored in the hierarchical cloud storage database in the server cluster of the data center. To provide operators and other

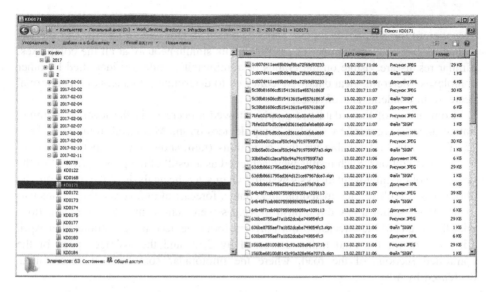

Fig. 7. Fragment of the physical layer structure of the hierarchical database

decision-makers with data, the unloading data and monitoring results are extracted from the storage and presented as a data mart.

As an example, consider the results of the intellectual analysis of unloading data collected from 10 complexes in a month's time in comparison with meteorological data in order to reveal the patterns of variation in the number and severity of road incidents. Figure 8 shows the graphs of the dynamics of the detected incidents by 6 complexes in a month.

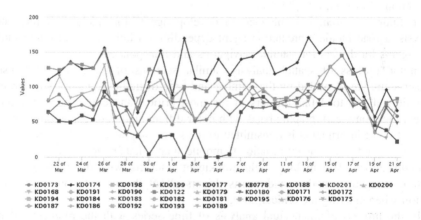

Fig. 8. Graphs of the dynamics of road incidents by 6 complexes from 22 March to 22 April 2017

Analysis of the data presented on the graphs showed some anomaly. It is seen that for a month on 5 complexes (KD0173, KD0174, KD0183, KD0122, KD0180), the number of road incidents is fixed, which on the average is about 60–70 units with the exception of the KD0201 complex, which is installed. However, after April 17 there is a sharp decrease in the number of road incidents simultaneously at all the complexes. Similar results are visible on the graphs of administrative offenses identified by other complexes. Meteorological data were collected to determine the causes of an abnormal decrease in incidents and offenses.

Comparison of these data and graphs showed a decrease in the level of administrative offenses recorded by Cordon-Temp devices on the M-5 (Ural) route after April 15. These days, unfavorable weather conditions (rain, snow, low temperatures) have led to icy conditions. Such results were achieved as a result of the pilot operation of the prototype of the intelligent analysis system, when after the analysis of the data from the photoradar complexes and meteorological data a forecast of unfavorable situations was made. Next, within a few days, push messages were sent to mobile communications with the results of the forecast to warn drivers about the need to be cautious after April 15. As a result, the road traffic decreased by 20% and the average speed of the controlled sections of the road, where the photoradar complexes were installed, decreased by 40%.

7 Conclusions and Future Work

Currently, there is a prototype of a monitoring and intellectual analysis system with a limited set of functions. The system functionality is implemented by several agents that perform data cleaning, clustering of incidents, comparing time series of road accidents with meteorological data, downloading data from the complexes, retrieving data from the storage for visualization in a data mart in the form of a dynamic hypertable, preparing charts and reports, generating push notifications to mobile client for the prevention of drivers, etc. [20, 21].

In future research, it is planned to develop agents for spatial and intellectual analysis, a road incident prediction agent depending on human mobility and mobile alert agents for drivers for satellite navigators and transponders.

In the process of spatial analysis, similar sections of the road and transport infrastructure are identified by the number and type of traffic accidents. Clustering of such sites allows to define clusters of the most critical and emergency sites and to present them on a cartographic basis with color differentiation of dangerous zones for motorists. The information is transmitted to the server application, which in turn shall forward a coordinate zone information to mobile agents that are downloaded to the user communications. The mobile application-agent interacts with the GPS/GLONASS satellite navigation module and warns drivers about the need to observe extreme caution when entering the critical zone.

In the process of intellectual analysis of time series with the moments of road incidents, time intervals are determined, in which an abnormal deviation of the number of incidents from average indicators occurs. Next, various data are collected on environmental changes at these time intervals. Such data include the results of meteorological observations, information on past events, information on repair work in controlled areas, a calendar of working hours, information about seasonal factors, etc.

As a result of the comparison of time series and various factors, factors that are highly likely to become determinants for an abnormal change in the traffic situation in various controlled areas are identified. The goal is to identify critical time zones and factors that cause the occurrence and implementation of road accident risks. The results of the analysis are transferred to decision-makers and mobile users' applications to warn about the increase in the risks of incidents at specific times and the factors of these risks.

To infer traffic accident, a direct way is to predict whether it will happen or not. However, by performing some analysis on traffic accident data, we have found that it is difficult to forecast the occurrence deterministically under given conditions since traffic accidents are caused by complex factors. Some of these factors such as driver's maneuver and distraction cannot be observed in advance. Therefore, we have decided to diagnose the risk of traffic accidents. The risk of a traffic accident can be reflected by frequency and severity. We define risk level as the cumulative severity of set traffic accident record. For example, the risk level is 6 if six injury accidents have happened or one fatal accident has happened in the control zone of the photoradar complex in the corresponding time interval. Regions with highest risk level can be regarded as critical zones for the time interval. Traffic accidents are possible to happen with human mobility, like walking, biking or driving, which can be reflected by the density of GPS records. Therefore, another goal of the intellectual analysis is to identify how human mobility will affect traffic accident risk, to develop a model for forecasting traffic accident risk with real-time data.

Funding. The reported study was funded by RFBR according to the research projects № 15-07-01720 and № 16-07-00031.

References

1. European Commission Green Paper: Towards a new culture for urban mobility. Publication European Commission, Brussels (2007). 551 final
2. Batty, M., Axhausen, K.W., Giannotti, F., et al.: Smart cities of the future (2013). http://www.complexcity.info/files/2013/08/BATTY-EPJST-2012.pdf
3. Zheng, Y., Capra, L., Wolfson, O., Yang, H.: Urban computing: concepts, methodologies and applications. ACM Trans. Intell. Syst. Technol. (TIST) 5(3), 38 (2014)
4. Voevodin, Y.V., Kirichek, R.V.: Overview of unique software and hardware parameters of various internet technologies things. Inf. Technol. Telecommun. (IT&T) 4(12), 40–47 (2015). http://www.sut.ru/doci/nauka/review/4-15.pdf
5. Ouzounis, G., Portugali, Y.: Smart cities of the future. Eur. Phys. J. Spec. Top. **214**(1), 481–518 (2012)
6. Cook, D., Das, S.: Smart Environments. Technologies, Protocols And Applications. Wiley-Interscience, Hoboken (2005)
7. Nakashima, H., Aghajan, H., Augusto, J.C.: Handbook of Ambient Intelligence and Smart Environments. Springer, New York (2010)
8. About ITS. http://www.its.dot.gov/its_program/about_its.htm

9. Nowacki, G.: Development and standardization of intelligent transport systems. Int. J. Mar. Navig. Saf. Sea Transp. **6**(3), 403–411 (2012)
10. Castro, P.S., Zhang, D., Li, S.: Urban traffic modelling and prediction using large scale taxi GPS traces. In: Kay, J., Lukowicz, P., Tokuda, H., Olivier, P., Krüger, A. (eds.) Pervasive 2012. LNCS, vol. 7319, pp. 57–72. Springer, Heidelberg (2012). doi:10.1007/978-3-642-31205-2_4
11. Finogeev, A.G., Botvinkin, P.V., Kamaev, V.A., Nefedova, I.S.: On information of security risk management for GPS/GLONASS-based ground transportation monitoring and supervisory control automated navigation systems. Soc. Sci. **10**(2), 201–205 (2015)
12. Hersent, O., Boswarthick, D., Elloumi, O.: The Internet of Things: Key Applications and Protocols. Willey, Hoboken (2012)
13. Finogeev, A.G., Parygin, D.S., Finogeev, A.A., et al.: A convergent model for distributed processing of Big Sensor Data in urban engineering networks. J. Phys: Conf. Ser. **803**, 1–6 (2017). In: Proceedings of the International Conference on Information Technologies in Business and Industry
14. Finogeev, A.G., Parygin, D.S., Finogeev, A.A.: The convergence computing model for big sensor data mining and knowledge discovery. Hum.-Centric Comput. Inf. Sci. **7**, 11 (2017). doi:10.1186/s13673-017-0092-7
15. Stojmenovic, I., Wen, S.: The fog computing paradigm: scenarios and security issues. In: Proceedings of the Federated Conference on Computer Science and Information Systems (ACSIS), vol. 2, pp. 1–8 (2014)
16. Finogeev, A.G., Skorobogatchenko, D.T., Trung, D.A., Kamaev, V.A.: Application of indistinct neural networks for solving forecasting problems in the road complex. ARPN J. Eng. Appl. Sci. **11**(16), 9646–9653 (2016)
17. Finogeev, A.G., Parygin, D.S., Finogeev, A.A., et al.: Multi-agent approach to distributed processing of big sensor data based on fog computing model for the monitoring of the urban infrastructure systems. In: Proceedings of the 5th International Conference on System Modeling & Advancement in Research Trends, vol. 1, pp. 305–310 (2016)
18. OASIS. MQTT version 3.1.1. OASIS Standard (2014). http://docs.oasis-open.org/mqtt/mqtt/v3.1.1/os/mqtt-v3.1.1-os.pdf
19. ZigBee Specification Overview. http://www.zigbee.org/Specifications/ZigBee/Overview.aspx
20. Sadovnikova, N.P., Finogeev, A.G., Parygin, D.S, Finogeev, A.A., et al.: Visualization of data about events in the urban environment for the decision support of the city services actions coordination. In: Proceedings of the 5th International Conference on System Modeling & Advancement in Research Trends, vol. 1, pp. 283–290 (2016)
21. Sadovnikova, N.P., Finogeev, A.G. Parygin, D.S., et al.: Monitoring of social reactions to support decision making on issues of urban territory management. In: Proceedings of the 5th International Young Scientist Conference on Computational Science, vol. 101, pp. 243–252

Data Science in Social Networks Analysis

Engineering an Elite in Social Networks Through Semiolinguistics' Data Mapping: A Fantasy or Reality?

Andrew Olyanitch[1]([⊠]), Zaineta Khachmafova[2],
Tatiana Ostrovskaya[2], and Susanna Makerova[2]

[1] Volgograd State Agrarian University, Volgograd, Russian Federation
aolyanitch@mail.ru
[2] Adyge State University, Maycop, Republic of Adyge, Russian Federation
zaineta@nextmail.ru

Abstract. The article highlights major possible means of engineering an elite by way of social networks data mapping with the use of semiolinguistics' methods. Given is the definition of an elite; described are its parameters and means of its construing. We enumerate the possible locations and institutions involved into elite's construing as well as resources applied and personalities participating in the elite engineering process. The article also describes the model elite person and presents the mapping algorithm according to which the process of elite engineering is possible within social networks. Cognitive portrait of an elite person is also taken into consideration both in aspects of ancestry and being brought-up (construed). The semiotic locations within which an elite person may obtain habitation and social activity are considered. Major features of an elite person to be construed, such as proficiency of the discursive activity, mental health, tendency to religious or groups' confession, ritualism, specific externality, special habits and stereotypes, preferences in food, sport as well as bacchius preferences. While construing a model elite person through mind mapping also considered are the gender aspect, ability to leadership, tendency to tolerance, possibility of being a sociopath. Norm/deviation from a norm as a concept is also taken into consideration. The role of social networks' impact in construing (engineering) an elite is also observed.

Keywords: Cognitive approach · Construing · Discourse · Elite · Engineering · Mind mapping · Model elite person · Social network · Semiolinguistics · Semiotics · Sign

1 Introduction

What is an elite? The dictionary defines it as: "a. a group or class of persons or a member of such a group or class, enjoying superior intellectual, social, or economic status. b. The best or most skilled members of a group" [11]. The discourse-forming concept of the elite is realized in the forms accepted by social groups: intellectual elite, creative elite, business elite, military elite, religious elite, etc. The change in the semantics of the word is traced by Tom Bottomore in the book "Elites and Society": in

A. Kravets et al. (Eds.): CIT&DS 2017, CCIS 754, pp. 671–682, 2017.
DOI: 10.1007/978-3-319-65551-2_48

the 17th century, the word "elite" was used only for goods of the highest quality, and only from the XIX century - to identify individuals and groups at the top of the social hierarchy [1].

In Russian, the word "элита/elite" appeared only in the 1920s. In the "Explanatory dictionary of the Russian language" ed. D.N. Ushakov - this word is fixed in three meanings: Elite1. Selected Society (rare books); 2. Collective. The best, selective specimens of some plants or animals, characterized by such qualities that provide a rich reproduction (agricultural production). Elite selection; 3. The very selection of such plants or animals (agricultural). Elite Method [4].

At present, the term "elite" belongs to several areas of humanities - linguistics, sociolinguistics, psychology, philosophy, political science, anthropology. Consequently, a look at the concept of "elite" requires taking into account the focus of the researcher's interests; in a fairly full extent, the concept is realized in numerous lexicographical sources. In linguistics, the concept of the elite is traditionally associated only with an elitist linguistic personality, so the article is directly describing the phenomenon of the elite which is missing in linguistic dictionaries and encyclopedias.

Modern dictionaries avoid the classical definitions of the term "elite", which existed until the beginning of the twentieth century: the true elite is the bearer of values that are grounded in higher, sacred origin and serving high ideals. On these grounds, the elite stands out from the masses.

Another question is, how does elite come to life? How does it appear? The point is if it is of an inborn status, or it is brought-up or cultivated? There are arguments for both visions.

1.1 An Inborn Status of an Elite Vision

Yes, one can be born an elitist person: an elite by birth exists, because each newly born member of an elitist group inherits high social status, gets involved into elite's activities, performs a certain role in institutional processes etc. If you are born as a prince or princess, you "maintain the ruling line", i.e. you continue to perform the same functions as your predecessor does or did. The succession dwells until the elite family continues to emit new members. The same happens in military elites when the kids go on to perform the military functions as their fathers did; elites of art and literature remain to flourish in case their offspring become famous while they continue to create art masterpieces or write outstanding literary chef-d'oeuvres. An elite remains an elite until the succession line brakes: when it happens, an elite dies.

1.2 A Cultivated Elite: A Vision of Elite's Engineering/Construing

In case the elite is not born, there might be ways to create it artificially, by means of engineering. Here comes a vast field of research for computer science which can prove that cultivation of an elite may find its way in computer engineering, or, computer-based construing. Actually, the process of engineering seems to be fulfilled socially, by ways of upbringing. The computer technologies cannot perform the human functions of instructor, tutor, educator or mentor. What they really can offer are models, algorithms, and schemes according to which the elitist person can be created (engineered, construed). Computer can, on the basis of input information, such as necessary parameters of an elitist person, required environment for the elite construed, required field of an elitist person's feature applications etc., comprise a cognitive portrait of such person and forward it to people who will follow its recommendations and create an elite person by person. Is this a fantasy or might happen in reality? Hereby we are going to discuss the method of mind mapping, or, a cognitive computer-based method of semantic (semiotic) maps that might be used in construing a cognitive portrait of an elitist person.

2   Methodology

In the cognitive zone of a particular linguistic person lacunae of knowledge always need to be present, which need to be gradually filled in as the person, led by certain every day, demanding, professional, aesthetic and other intentions/motives, faces the need to build communicative, behavioral and linguistic algorithms for realizing these intentions and motives. Faced with the unknown, a person intuitively and consciously formulates an action plan for mastering a new reality, with which he has to deal. He needs to get full information about the object of his interest, to master it, to try on the current state of affairs and phenomena, among which there is this object-phenomenon, to scan its parameters in a peculiar way and turn these parameters into instruments of its influence on society, nature, environment etc. In other words, the formation/ formulation of a strategic action plan is taking place, which is nothing more than a cognitive map of human existence.

Review of the theory of mental maps in cognitive psychology can be found in an article by Redtenbaher [10]. The same problem sets itself in the article by Hartl [7]. One of the newest collections of research of mental maps in cognitive psychology that integrates articles of geographers and psychologists is published by Portugal [6]. A useful introduction to the theory of mental models, which should rank as well as mental maps, is found in the work of Dutke [2].

A mental or semantic map is a didactic (explanatory) tool to reach the end of the path or to achieve a result - the most optimal route of cognition, which simplifies and facilitates the very movement towards cognition [8]. The basis of mental cartography is the principle of the catechism - the answer to why-questions, step by step allowing you to master someone else's reality and someone else's mentality. Today, this principle is relevant to the point that it is used as didactics in the compilation of textbooks (for example, grammatical algorithms in the American textbook "Side by Side"), lexicographers in the compilation of activator-type dictionaries (for example, Longman English Activator), and the media. Thus, became extremely popular a Russian weekly "Vsyo jasno" ("Everything is clear"), in which diagrams and algorithmized illustrations responding to the questions "What is this?", "How is it done?", "How does it work?", "What will happen next?", etc., make a complete picture of the reality presented to the study and information is given.

As an example of semantic mapping as a way of algorithmizing intercultural knowledge, we present a semantic map of the English-language sub-concept "Jury" as part of the "Court" concept. Basic information about this sub-concept is contained in the following text from the Encarta encyclopedia:

"**Jury**, in law, a body of people who are chosen to decide the truth of factual evidence in an action or legal proceeding and, on the instruction of the **court**, to apply the law to the facts. Traditionally, a **trial** jury consists of 12 people.

Jurors are selected according to statutory and constitutional provisions. Each state has its own qualifications for those who may serve on a jury. In general, all jurors must be United States citizens, local residents, of majority age, of approved integrity, and of reasonable intelligence. Both the defense and the prosecution have the right to eliminate undesirable members from the jury, based on perceived circumstances that would affect a juror's decisions, such as bias or self-interest.

In general, during the progress of a trial, all questions of law are determined by the court; questions of fact are determined by the jury. Whether evidence is properly **admissible** or not is a question for the court, but the weight and **credibility** of the evidence admitted are determined by the jury.

After all the **evidence** has been presented, the **two counsels**, first for the **defendant** and then for the **plaintiff** or **prosecution**, address the jury, reviewing the evidence in the **case**. The judge then makes a charge to the jury. The charge is a statement of the rules of law applicable to the evidence in that particular case. The jury then retires from the courtroom to begin **deliberations**. These deliberations continue until an agreement as to the **verdict** is **reached**, or until the **judge** deems that the jury cannot reach an agreement. The latter case is known as **a hung jury**. In the event that no agreement is reached, a new trial may be called. All members of a jury must agree on a verdict, which in a civil trial may be "for the plaintiff" or "for the defendant," and in a criminal trial **"guilty"** or **"not guilty."** In some states, however, the verdict in a **civil trial** need not be **unanimous**. In a civil trial, the jury is then empowered to set the amount of any damages" [3].

The mental map of mastering this reality consists of the following algorithm (Fig. 1):

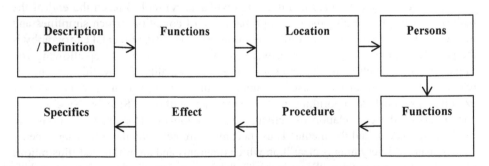

Fig. 1. An algorithm of mental mapping

Description/Definition: **Jury**, in law, a body of people who are chosen to decide the truth of factual evidence in an action or legal proceeding and, on instruction of the **court**

Functions: to apply the law to the facts

Location: Court

Persons: after all the **evidence** has been presented, the **two counsels**, first for the **defendant** and then for the **plaintiff** or **prosecution**, address **the jurors** (12 people), reviewing the evidence in the **case**. **The judge** then makes a charge to the jury.

Procedure: The jury then retires from the courtroom to begin **deliberations**.

Effect: These deliberations continue until **an agreement** as to the **verdict** is **reached**, or until the judge deems that the jury cannot reach an agreement.

Specifics: The latter case is known as **a hung jury**. In the event that no agreement is reached, a new **trial** may be called. All members of a jury must agree on a verdict, which in a civil trial may be "for the plaintiff" or "for the defendant," and in a criminal trial **"guilty"** or **"not guilty."** In some states, however, the verdict in a **civil** trial need not be **unanimous**. In a civil trial, the jury is then empowered to set the amount of any damages.

Structuring the text according to this algorithm allows you to fix in the mind the basic components of another's reality, which are then gradually revealed and explained.

As it can be assumed, the computer-based algorithm may follow these steps when solving the problem of construing an elitist person portrait: first, it should gather information on necessary parameters that should characterize an elitist person; second, get aware of the necessary environment for an elitist person; third, draw a whole map of an engineering process with defining of an elitist person, indication of personalities involved, location where the process takes place, description of the whole procedure, stating of its effect(s) and notification of specific features of the process.

All necessary parameters were gathered through posting questions in such social networks as Facebook, Vkontakte and Telegram, as well as by questioning different groups in WhatsUp. Finally, all answers after an analysis comprised the following set of necessary parameters to determine a scope of what elitist person is.

3 Discussion: Research and Results

By questioning our respondents in social networks we have determined the scope of necessary parameters of an elitist person. We made it a point to create an elitist person whose elite abilities lie in the sphere of education, i.e. we decided to construe an elite teacher, or instructor who might be evaluated as top-ranked in the higher education system of foreign language teaching - one who is able to create "a cosmopolitan" personality able to speak a foreign language with the highest level - "proficiency". Our respondents enumerated the following parameters to be present while considering such person as an "elitist teacher of a foreign language":

- ability to speak certain language proficiently;
- ability to easy communication;
- ability to perform an ethical communication;

– never curse;
– the vast horizon of knowledge, including the knowledge of the countries where this language is spoken (geography, sociology, culture, traditions, food preferences, art, literature, Bacchus preferences, travel traditions, economics, history, legislative base, media, etc.);
– tolerance;
– computer usage habits;
– ability to conduct leadership;
– mental health;
– physical health;
– openness;
– preferably masculine gender;
– ability to discursive impact (ability to persuade);
– creativity both in action, image and language;
– attractive exterior;
– sportive;
– ability to listen and to react adequately;
– having a very close circle of friends;
– ability to keep polite distance with the students;
– be the God for students!

Most and foremost feature of proficient communication that an elitist foreign language instructor must obtain is ethical communication. Here we inevitably draw to the analysis of the achievement of communicative pragmatics, postulating the principles of effective, logically built and full-fledged ethical communication. These principles were formulated by linguists Paul Grice and Jeffrey Leach in the form of a series of maxims.

At the core of Paul Grice's maxim [5] - the rules expected of the speaker - lies the principle of cooperation: make your contribution as is required, when it is required, your communicative contribution to This step of the dialogue should be the same as that required by the jointly adopted goal - direction - of this dialogue). On the basis of this principle, P. Grice singles out:

(1) the maximum of quality: to contribute only what you know to be true. Do not say false things; Do not say things for which you lack evidence (do not say what you think is false, do not say what you do not have good reasons for);
(2) the maximum of the quantity: make your contribution as informative as is required; Do not say more than is required (your statement should contain as much information as required, your statement should contain no more information than required);
(3) maximum relevance: make your contribution relevant (do not deviate from the topic);
(4) maximum manners: (a) avoid obscurity (avoid confusing expressions); (b) avoid ambiguity (avoid ambiguity); (c) be brief (be brief); (d) be orderly (be organized).

In the modern pragmatics of communication to the principle of cooperation, the principles of relevance (relevance principle) and quantitative sufficiency (quantity principle, as much information as you can, without violating the maxim of quality and the principle of relevance) are added.

Leach [9], formulating the principle of courtesy as the principle of the interposition of the speakers speaking in the structure of the speech act, provided the following maxims:

(a) maximum tact (assumes the boundaries of the personal sphere of the interlocutor - minimize the expression of beliefs which imply a cost to other; maximize the expression of beliefs which imply benefit to other);

(b) the maxim of generosity maxim (non-repayment of the interlocutor, in fact, it protects the interlocutors from dominance in the course of the speech act - minimize the expression of beliefs that express or imply benefit to self; maximize the Expression of beliefs that express or imply a cost to self);

(c) the maximum approval [approbation maxim] (the positivity in assessing others; the discrepancy with the interlocutor in the direction of assessing the world has a very strong effect on the possibility of implementing one's own communication strategy - minimize the expression of beliefs which express dispraise of other; Of other);

(d) the maximum modesty [modesty maxim] (rejection of self-praise; realistic self-esteem is one of the conditions for the success of the deployment of a speech act - minimize the expression of praise of self;

(e) maximum agreement [agreement maxim] (instead of deepening the contradiction that has arisen in the course of communication, this maxim recommends the search for consent in order for the communication act to be productive completion - minimize the expression of disagreement between self and other; Maximize the expression of agreement between self and other);

(f) maximum sympathy maxim (recommends benevolence, it is a condition for the action of other maxims, it also protects speech acts from conflict - minimize antipathy between self and other; maximize sympathy between self and other).

Compliance with the principle of courtesy creates an environment of positive interaction, provides a favorable background for the implementation of communicative strategies. As we see, the basic criterion of the ethical nature of communication, according to J. Leach, is a measure of minimizing the negative (N) and maximizing the positive (P) during the interaction, which in terms of logic is semioticized by the mutual exclusion log: $\{N_{min} \rightarrow 0\} \leftrightarrow \{P_{max} \rightarrow \infty\}$. Evidently also an ethically conditioned centripetal motion to Conventions in the course of the interaction, where the intentions (Int) of communicants X and Y, observing and mutually sharing norms and rules for effective interaction, vectorically tend to each other, forming a convention of consent (Conv) - the log $\{Int_{(x)} \rightarrow Conv_{(x+y)} \leftarrow Int_{(y)}\}$. Communication turns out to be an ethical failure if the convention is not formed because of a critical misalignment of intentions, and this situation is displayed by the rejection log: $\{Int_{(x)} \leftarrow Conv_{(x \leftrightarrow y)} \rightarrow Int_{(y)}\}$.

This type of communication must prevail, whereas the other features seem to be most desirable.

Next mapping step is the determination of an environment (location). Where can these elitist teacher's qualities get most vivid explicitness? Which location is most productive? Respondents were unanimous: NOT IN CLASS! They set as the most friendly environment the locations of outdoor "hiding" places, such as plein air, a park, street, even a café! Some chose a quiet place in a library or a museum! Some demanded a space in the University's winter garden - away from the classroom! Anyway, this choice discloses the immortal intention to communicate in 'natural' sites, or, for some, this natural site is a computer site or computer-based environment like a messenger! Some student victimized face-to-face interaction for the sake of distant socializing!

Another question here is the construing the environment in which the elitist foreign language teacher might be brought-up. Here we cannon against the dilemma - whether the above-mentioned qualities are in-born, or they are obtained within the didactic process. We tend to accept the education and up-bringing an elitist teacher, so here cognitive computer-based mapping might be applied.

A computer-generated map must be organized according to the following algorithm (Fig. 2):

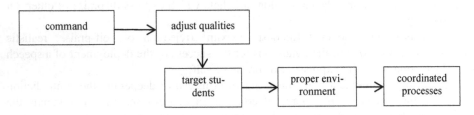

Fig. 2. A computer-generated map

Mapping according to this algorithm would create the chain of possible adjustments of necessary qualities with personalities of students who might accept or agree with such elitist teacher's qualities together with the appropriate environment in which these qualities should be developed, and the appropriate process in which these qualities might be developed.

Thus, step by step, the computer-based technology seems to be able to coordinate the developed quality with resources available or needed; for example, a command "find the environment in which a tolerant teacher can be brought-up" the machine starts to seek for variants of such environment, say, "multicultural space", "non-Caucasian race-friendly space" etc. Same with more complicated qualities of an elitist language teacher, such as the foreign language proficiency knowledge: to develop this parameter the computer must be commanded to seek for necessary resources that facilitate the task, like, specific books or courses, specifically chosen instructors or schools, specific environment semiosis filled with special signs that make the process easier etc. Anyway, the mapping would somehow help to create a program which would summarize necessary elitist foreign language teacher's parameters, find an appropriate environment in which they will be brought-up, determine the necessary resources for the process of such up-bringing and, finally, create a cognitive portrait of such model teacher.

4 Conclusion

These days when mankind is expecting a breakthrough in the field of artificial intellect and seeks for ideal improving human abilities, much is talked about the necessity to engineer elite societies which play the part of an avant-garde in forwarding ideas to a further humanity progress. In a post-industrial society, economic relations are pushed to the background and experts play a decisive role. The process of "production of knowledge" comes first. Hence, hegemony must belong to the elite of knowledge - the most capable, most useful people in society.

Another important characteristic of the new era is the modification of the role of time and space: electronic means allow you to use communication technologies that change the essence of physical mobility - you can manage global corporations online. Spatial ligaments begin to weaken. First of all, they are released, i.e. globalized, elites, they are transformed into a globally mobile class, into "new nomads", "tourists" who move freely with their money, which is also completely mobile, all over the world. Thus, "mobility" turns out to be a concept allowing to reflect the essence of the transformation of social space (social practices of the elite) in the era of late modernity.

Today we witness the emergence of an extremely eclectic class of a new, trans-boundary elite - masters of free arts, graduates of prestigious and not so prestigious universities, intellectuals, intelligentsia. People who control the meanings, the goal-setting of society, the images of its future, codes of conduct, information-financial flows, geo-economic compositions (rather than, say, commodity or industry elements of practice). People associated with non-material production, which in their own way, differently than the previous "third estate" elite, read the notions of freedom, transnationality, universalism, and culture.

The scientific value lies in the description of a discursive national elitist personality in terms of a cognitive stereotype concept of «national elite» in the global discursive space. It is hypothesized that the discourse of the national elite in the globalization era represents a superinstitutional construct displaying a tendency towards the fusion of culture-bound concepts, elitist thinking, semantics, and semiotics of the national elites.

The purpose of the project is to solve the following research problems: to identify the content and boundaries of the discourse of the national elite; to expose the constitutive and systemic features of the discourse of the national elite; to detect the content of the basic concepts of the discourse of the national elite; to define the notion of the discursive national elitist personality; to determine the properties of verbal, nonverbal and transverbal means of the discourse of the national elite; to analyze the evolution and modification of the discourse practices of the modern national elite in the globalization era; to identify the role of intertextuality and interdiscoursiveness in connection with the widening of the discursive space of the national elite.

The expected results of the project are:

1. The development a scientific conception of the discourse of the national elite in the globalization era, evidence from the elitist personality in the situation of bilingualism and polylinguism.

2. The identification of cognitive, communicative and semiotic features of the discourse of the national elite, communicative strategies of the national elitist language personality and the cognitive stereotype of the notion of «national elite».
3. The exposure of the specifics of the national elitist mind and the categorization of the national elite. The description of discourse practices of the national elitist personality in the global socio-cultural discourse.
4. The analysis of the modification of the discourse practices of the national elite alongside with the modification of social practices.
5. The definition of the place of the national elites in the global elite. The definition of the notion of the behavioural discourse of the national elitist personality.

The justification for research of the project is determined by the following factors:

1. The concept of discourse is currently a matter of scientists' interest, besides, the system-making features of the discourse of the national elite; its discursive-cognitive space and a systematic linguistic description of the discourse of the national elite have never been studied before.
2. The research of the discourse of the national elite as a semiotic space is of much relevance as it includes verbal and nonverbal signs in a particular communicative sphere alongside with transverbal signs of the discourse in which, within the scope of symbolic interactionism, speech and behavioral reactions of the elitist personality are manifested.
3. The considered problem of the discourse of the national elite does not solely lie in the field of linguistics, but, thanks to its polyparadigmatic nature, attracts the attention of many researchers. General discourse studies and social discourse, in particular, remaining in the focus of attention of Russian and foreign scientists as linguistics is closely associated with other branches of knowledge, such as sociology, philosophy, psychology, and study of culture.

Firstly, it is to expose cultural and verbal codes as well as the role and place of the national elitist personality in the modern multicultural society. In the research, the above-mentioned issues are studied in the combination of nonverbal and transverbal means of the specific discursive strategy, which appears to be a very important task of modern linguistics.

Secondly, it is to describe the national discursive elitist personality through the analysis of its verbal, nonverbal, transverbal components representing its communicative models and nonverbal behavioral patterns which constitute the discourse of the national elitist personality.

Thirdly, to analyze the evolution and modification of the discourse practices of the national elite alongside with the modification of social practices; to identify extralinguistic factors affecting the formation and variation of the discourse practices of the national elite.

Fourthly, it is to determine substantive and pragmatic characteristics of the discourse of the national elite; to expose conceptual dominants of the discourse of the national elite and give the parameters of its discursive-cognitive space.

Scientific novelty of this project is that for the first time this research work suggests the systematic linguistic description of the national elite discourse.

Connection with significant changes of social practices in the globalization era of modern society.

The following general scientific methods are suggested for solving the urgent problems within the project:

conceptual and introspective analyses, a method of observation, content analysis, intent analysis, critical discourse analysis, alongside with linguistic methods such as contextual and interpretative analyses,

etymological analysis, componential analysis, conceptual analysis and semiotic analysis.

Combined application of several approaches in the investigation of the national elite discourse practices suggests the usage of descriptive approach with its comparative analysis of the informative part of the text, intentional socially oriented discourse-analysis that reveals the usage of language as a means of domination in the society.

Multidimensionality and integrity are important for the methodology of the project survey which allows to use the complex discourse analysis, the theory of speech acts and other research methods within the synergetic paradigm.

These days much is discussed about social engineering; it exists, and this is not a fantasy. Researchers denote both its negative and positive potentials. Same with construing an elite: on the one hand, an ideal elitist person recommended by a computer may rise a wave of resistance; on the other - computers only offer a possible model and recommend ways to achieve it. Time will tell: anyway, mapping a process of creating an elitist person may be of great use. We believe that offered algorithm is far from fantastic notions.

References

1. Bottomore, T.B.: Elites and Society. Penguin Books, Harmondsworth (1976)
2. Dutke, S.: Mentale Modelle: Konstrukte des Wissens und des Verstehens. Kognitionspsychologische Grundlagen fur die Software-Ergonomie. Göttingen (1994)
3. Encarta® 98 Desk Encyclopedia © & 1996–97 Microsoft Corporation. All rights reserved
4. Explanatory dictionary Ushakov online [Electronic resource]. http://ushakovdictionary.ru
5. Grice, H.P.: Logic and conversation. In: Cole, P., Morgan, J.: Syntax and Semantics: Speech Acts, pp. 41–57. Academic Press, New York (1975)
6. Portugali, J. (ed.): The Construction of Cognitive Maps. Springer, Dordrecht (1996). doi:10.1007/978-0-585-33485-1
7. Hartl, A.: Kognitive Karten und kognitives Kartieren. In: Freksa, C., Habel, C. (eds.) Repräsentation und Verarbeitung räumlichen Wissens. Informatik-Fachberichte (Subreihe Künstliche Intelligenz), vol. 245. Springer, Heidelberg (1990). doi:10.1007/978-3-642-84235-1_4
8. Saltykov, S., Rusyaeva, E., Kravets, A.G.: Typology of scientific constructions as an instrument of conceptual creativity. In: Kravets, A., Shcherbakov, M., Kultsova, M., Shabalina, O. (eds.) Creativity in Intelligent Technologies and Data Science. Communications in Computer and Information Science, vol. 535, pp. 41–57. Springer, Cham (2015). doi:10.1007/978-3-319-23766-4_4

9. Leech, G.: Principles of Pragmatics. Longman Group Ltd., London (1983)
10. Redtenbacher, C.: Kognitive Karten im Spielfilm. In: Vitouch, P., Tinchon, H.-J. (Hg.). Cognitive Maps und Medien. Formen mentaler Repräsentation bei der Medienwahrnehmung. Frankfurt/ M., pp. S.15–S.72, especially S.27–S.47 (1996)
11. The American Heritage® Dictionary of the English Language, Third Edition ©. Houghton Mifflin Company (1996)

Structures and Cluster Technologies of Data Analysis and Information Management in Social Networks

Anver K. Enaleev and Vladimir V. Tsyganov[✉]

V.A. Trapeznikov Institute of Control Sciences, Russian Academy Sciences,
65, Profsoyuznaya Street, 117997 Moscow, Russia
anver.en@gmail.com, bbc@ipu.ru

Abstract. One of the important types of intellectual management in social engineering is information management. Information management structures and cluster technologies in social networks are characterized. The problems of analysis and optimal synthesis of information management structures in social networks have been set. Methods for solving these problems are proposed, in particular, the coordination of interests and the determination of the number of centers and boundaries of information management structures. A model for coordinating the boundaries of different types of information management clusters in social networks is considered. Algorithms for analyzing data on the social network and determining the boundaries of information management clusters are developed.

Keywords: Information · Conflicts · Alignment of interests · Hierarchy · Network structure · Division of the graph · Consistency of partitions

1 Introduction

As the global contradictions deepen in the world, accelerating changes and reaching the limits of growth, information confrontation in social networks becomes acuter [1, 2]. To solve the emerging problems is widely used information management, which is one of the most important types of intellectual management [2–4]. For example, information management is used to solve the problems of socio-economic stagnation under the constraints of global growth [5] and improve the safety of large-scale social systems [6].

Information management is activity, which based on information technology impact on the object- personality, group, organization, society. In this case, the control actions (resources, plans, incentives) are connected with the information impact. The subject of information management is information struggle, operations, and wars, and the goal is the mastery of capital and power [4]. The instrument of its achievement is the information impact on partners, competitors and other persons.

In the individual, group and organizational information management, agitation is especially important, and in the social information management- propaganda.

A. Kravets et al. (Eds.): CIT&DS 2017, CCIS 754, pp. 683–696, 2017.
DOI: 10.1007/978-3-319-65551-2_49

Information management uses both formal and informal structures. Social information management is often carried out with the help of parties [4].

Depending on the field of activity, information management in a social network can be economic or political. Economic one is aimed at capturing the capital of social network elements. An important type of it is advertising management, which allows to manage the behavior of consumers through advertising campaigns in social networks. For this, corporate information management used, including Public Relations.

Technologies and structures of information management of social networks have their own peculiarities, caused by a large number of related and geographically distributed processes. In this regard, there is a need for a multi-level organizational information management system (such as national and regional security systems [6]). The need to optimize the information management system generates the problem of splitting social networks into subnets (clusters) - areas of responsibility of regional information management bodies. This problem relates to the mathematical problem of partitioning a graph.

Generally speaking, a considerable number of publications are devoted to the partition of a graph into subgraphs, in which various applications of these problems are considered. For example, in [7, 8] a problem of the graph of the partition describing a calculation process in order to create an efficient system of parallelization is considered. Authors of [9] propose the decomposition of PCB into layers having the minimum number of links. We note that the problem of partitioning a graph into connected subgraphs is NP-complete [10].

In this article, we study the problems of partitioning social networks in organizational information management systems, taking into account the increase in their structural and functional complexity [11]. The criterion for such partitioning is to ensure equal complexity of information management for each subnet (or equal costs of such management). When partitioning social networks in information management systems, there are two types of problem. The first type of problem is connected with the construction of methods and algorithms for analyzing data about a social network and an equal (equal-cost) subnet partition. The second type of problem is the harmonization of different types of partitions of the same network, in order to reduce costs for the interaction and deletion of conflict between subnets of different types of partitions. To explain the essence of the problematic of this type of problem, we give the following interpretation.

Many social networks are managed not only on the basis of the established regional decentralization but also on the basis of the required functional division. In practice, different groups manage the transfer of information and maintenance of the network infrastructure. Thus, there are at least two types of regional partition net, by types of support services. For the given above example, this partition, generally speaking, into different systems of social network clusters (for servicing the network infrastructure and for organizing the transmission of information on the network). Given the interdependence of different information management functions, must align structures of different types of network partitions belonging to these functions, in order to maximize the efficiency of the social network.

Another type of problem arising in the decomposition of the social network into clusters of information management and the formation of the corresponding hierarchical organizational structure, due to the appearance of elements in the structure of their own purposes (because the network is present people with their own interests). As a result, when the elements of the system interact in the context of conflicting goals, problems arise with deliberate distortion of the information circulating in the system.

When considering mathematical models and productions of the problem, the methodology of synthesis of optimal hierarchical structures [12–15] and organizational management [16–18] is used.

2 Model Description

The paper considers a hierarchical system of information management of a social network, including a Center and its subordinate functional information management centers (FIMC). Each FIMC manages, within the framework of its functional responsibility (regional subnet). In turn, each of the regional subnets has its own regional information management body (RIMB). Next, for simplicity, we shall consider the case when there are only two FIMCs. Regional subnets, to which the social network is divided, will be called clusters of the social network of information management. Note that the network can be broken up in different ways for each of the FIMC. Partitions related to the first FIMC will be called a partition of the first type, and to the second FIMC, respectively, of the second type.

Consider the network S consisting of n vertices. For each of the FIMC, which carries out its own kind of activity, it is necessary to break up the network into a subsystem of clusters of the social information management network. As already noted, for each FIMC, network breakdowns into social network clusters may vary. Let us denote $g^1 = \{g_i^1\}$ the partition of the network S into the first FIMC on N^1 clusters of the social network of the first type, where $i = 1,..., N^1$, and denote $g^2 = \{g_i^2\}$ the partition of the network S by the second FIMC on N^2 clusters of the social network of the second type, where $i = 1,..., N^2$.

Let us suppose that the partitioning into social network clusters satisfies the conditions $\bigcup_{i=1}^{N^m} g_i^m = S$ and $g_i^m \cap g_j^m = \emptyset$, where is the number of the partition type (in the case under consideration $m = 1$ or $m = 2$). The boundaries of each of the partitions pass through the vertices of the network. We supplement the network at each vertex with an edge that is a loop. For each type of partition, the loop at the vertex through which the boundary passes can only refer to one cluster of the corresponding type.

Within each cluster, in one of its vertices is the RIMB of this cluster. This means that we have N^1 RIMB of the first type and N^2 RIMB of the second type.

We denote by G^1 and G^2 the sets of admissible partitions of the first and second types, respectively. Let for each partition of the m-th type a generalized indicator characterizing the complexity of information management (CIM) by the social network for the considered FIMC (CIM by the whole network, including m-th FIMC) for a given partition is given:

$$K(g^m) = \overline{K}(K_0^{g^m}, K_1^{g^m}, \ldots, K_i^{g^m}, \ldots, K_{N^m}^{g^m}), \tag{1}$$

where $K_0^{g^m} = K_0^{g^m}(N^m)$ is the indicator characterizing the CIM by the social network for the m-th FIMS, $K_i^{g^m} = K_i^{g^m}(\bar{l}_i^m)$ an indicator characterizing the CIM for the i-th RIMB in the partition g^m, $i = 1, \ldots, N^m$. Here $\bar{l}_i^m$ is the set of parameters of the CIM for the elements of the i-th cluster in the partition g^m (the meaning of these parameters will be clarified below). We assume that the function $\overline{K}(\ldots)$ is nondecreasing. This means that the magnitude of the generalized CIM index $K(g^m) = \overline{K}(K_0^{g^m}, K_1^{g^m}, \ldots, K_i^{g^m}, \ldots, K_{N^m}^{g^m})$ does not decrease in magnitudes, $i = 0, \ldots, N^m$. We also assume that the functions $K_0^{g^m} = K_0^{g^m}(N^m)$, $K_i^{g^m} = K_i^{g^m}(\bar{l}_i^m)$ do not decrease in their arguments. A particular case of such a generalized indicator is additive: $K(g^m) = K_0^{g^m}(N^m) + \sum_{i=1}^{N^m} K_i^{g^m}(\bar{l}_i^m)$.

Content (1) means that the overall complexity of the information management during the partitioning is composed of the CIM by the clusters of the social network for RIMB, as well as the CIM for the m-th FIMC.

Suppose that there are restrictions on the maximum values of the CIM indicators:

$$0 \le K_0^{g^m}(N^m) \le K_0^{max}, \; 0 \le K_i^{g^m} \le K_i^{max}, \; i = 1, \ldots, N^m. \tag{2}$$

In addition, restrictions on the CIM $K(g^m) = \overline{K}(K_0^{g^m}, K_1^{g^m}, \ldots, K_i^{g^m}, \ldots, K_{N^m}^{g^m})$ on the whole set of admissible partitions G^m can be given. With an additive CIM index (1), these constraints are:

$$K(g^m) = K_0^{g^m}(N^m) + \sum_{i=1}^{N^m} K_i^{g^m}(\bar{l}_i^m) \le \overline{K}^{max}, \tag{3}$$

where $\overline{K}^{max} < K_0^{max} + \sum_{i=1}^{N^m} K_i^{max}$.

Suppose that the cost functions $Z_0^m(K_0^{g^m})$, $Z_i^m(K_i^{g^m})$, where $i = 1, \ldots, N^m$ are defined on the set of admissible values of the CIM index. Suppose that the cost functions are increasing and convex. The task of choosing the optimal partition g^m minimizing total costs is:

$$Z_0^m(K_0^{g^m}) + \sum_{i=1}^{N^m} Z_i^m(K_i^{g^m}) \underset{g^m \in G^m}{\to} \min \tag{4}$$

under the constraints (2)–(3).

Note that (2)–(4) is the problem of optimal resource allocation if the CIM is considered as the latter. Due to the condition $g^m \in G^m$, the CIM indicators are discrete values, making difficult to obtain estimates of the optimal distribution of the CIM between FIMC and RIMB. Nevertheless, in some cases, considering the CIM indicators as continuous values and solving the classical problem of resource allocation (2) – (4), it is possible to obtain acceptable approximate estimates of the optimal distribution of the CIM between the FIMC and RIMB.

In the case where the cost functions are linear. This means that $Z_0^m(K_0^{g^m}) = K_0^{G^m}$, and $Z_i^m(K_i^{g^m}) = \gamma_i^m K_i^{g^m}$ where the inverse $1/\gamma_i^m$ of the coefficient γ_i^m has the meaning of "power" of the i-th RIMB. Further, for simplicity, without loss of generality, these coefficients will be assumed equal to 1.

For this linear case, the solution of the problem of minimizing management costs corresponds to a uniform distribution of the complexities between the elements of the system under consideration and is a justification of the principle of the equal complexity of information management: the difference in CIM organizational structures should be minimal.

The principle of equal complexity of information management reflects the condition for minimizing the maximum CIM: it is necessary for a given type of partition m to define a partition into N^m of social network clusters $\bar{g}^m$ from an admissible set that satisfies the relation

$$\min_{g^m \in G^m} \max_{1 \leq i \leq N^m} K_i^{g^m}(\bar{l}_i^m) = R^{\bar{g}^m}, \tag{5}$$

The value $\max\limits_{1 \leq i \leq N^m} K_i^{g^m}(\bar{l}_i^m)$ determines the maximum cluster CIM in the given partition. We say that a partition satisfying (5) is balanced if, with such a partitioning, all information management clusters have a CIM as close to a value as possible. In other words, the difference between the CIM of social network clusters in an equilibrated partition (briefly by the E-partition) is negligible for the conditions of the problems under consideration.

3 Problem Statement

Next, we will assume that the network contains E-partitions.

Problem 1. Formation of a system of clusters of the equal complexity of a social information management network for each type of partitioning separately.

Suppose that for each m there are restrictions on the number of clusters of the social network $N_{min}^m \leq N^m \leq N_{max}^m$. The problem of determining the optimal E-partition has the form:

$$\min_{N_{min}^m \leq N^m \leq N_{max}^m} [K_0(\bar{g}^m) + N^m R^{\bar{g}^m}] \tag{6}$$

In essence, it is necessary to define a partition ensuring the minimum value of the CIM for the E -partitions. At the same time, the minimization is carried out according to the number of RIMB.

Thus, the problem of determining the optimal solution (1), (2) consists in calculating the optimal number of RIMB and optimizing the boundaries (distribution to balanced subnets). The structure of the problem (5), (6) allows us to decompose it into 2 subproblems in order to find a solution approximating to the optimum:

- determination of the number of RIMB, or clusters of a social network,
- defining the boundaries of balanced clusters of social networks.

Their consistent solution allows us to approach the optimum (the method of such decomposition will be considered below).

The following statements of the problem are also possible. The search is not for an exact optimal solution, but for an approximate one, with a weakening of the requirements for the equilibrium of the partition. The concept of an absolute equilibrium indicator for a given partition is introduced: $\Delta^{g^m} = \max\limits_{1 \leq i \leq N^m} K_i^{g^m}(\bar{I}_i^m) - \min\limits_{1 \leq i \leq N^m} K_i^{g^m}(\bar{I}_i^m)$,

as well as the relative equilibrium index: $\delta^{g^m} = \Delta^{g^m} / \max\limits_{1 \leq i \leq N^m} K_i^{g^m}(\bar{I}_i^m)$. The smaller the

values of these indicators, the more balanced is the partition. Setting an acceptable indicator of poise Δ^* or δ^*, it is possible to limit the number of options to be sorted.

Extension of the Model 1. Suppose that for each vertex and edge of the network S there are given the indexes of complexity corresponding to each RIMB. This means that the indexes of complexity are corresponding to the type of network partition. We denote l_{ij}^m the complexity indices of the edge (i, j) in the given network for the m-th type of partitions. Note that $l_{ij}^m = l_{ji}^m$. In the case where the i-th vertex is not connected to the j-th vertex by an edge in the network under consideration, we supplement the network with an edge (i, j) of zero complexity. It means that $l_{ij}^m = 0$. The complexity of the i-th vertex $(i = 1,..., n)$ is defined as $w_i^m = l_{ii}^m$ where m = 1 or 2, i.e. The complexity of the vertex is given by the complexity of the edge (loop) (i, i).

We denote $Q_{k^1}^1$ the set of edges (i, j) and vertices (i, i) of the cluster with the number k^1 for the first type of partition and, respectively, the cluster $Q_{k^2}^2$ with the number k^2 for the second type of partition. The numbers k^1 and k^2 correspond to the RIMB numbers of the clusters of the social network of partitions. We define the complexity of informational management of clusters of a social network $L^{k^1}(Q_{k^1}^1) = \sum\limits_{(i,j) \in Q_{k^1}^1} l_{ij}^1$, and

$L^{k^2}(Q_{k^2}^2) = \sum\limits_{(i,j) \in Q_{k^2}^2} l_{ij}^2$, as well as the complexity of coordinating work with a first type

cluster k^1 with a second type of cluster k^2

$Z_{k^1}^1(Q_{k^1}^1, Q_{k^2}^2) = (\sum\limits_{(i,j) \in Q_{k^1}^1 \cap Q_{k^2}^2} z_{ij}^{k^1 k^2})(\sum\limits_{(i,j) \in Q_{k^2}^2 \setminus Q_{k^1}^1} l_{ij}^2)$, where $z_{ij}^{k^1 k^2}$ the additional com-

plexity of coordinating actions on the edge (i, j) by the cluster's governing body of the first type with the cluster's governing body of the second type. Thus, the CIM $K_{k^1}^{g^1}$ by

the cluster k^1 is equal to $W^{k^1}(Q_{k^1}^1, Q_{k^2}^2) = L(Q_{k^1}^1) + Z^{k^1}(Q_{k^1}^1, Q_{k^2}^2)$.

Further, to simplify the problem, we assume that the number of clusters of the social network for each type of partition is given and $N = N^1 = N^2$.

Problem 2. Formation of systems of clusters of equal complexity on the social information management network with matching costs: finding the g^{1*} and g^{2*} partitions that are the solution of the problem $W^{*k^1}(g^1, g^2) = \min\limits_{g^1, g^2 \in G} \max\limits_{1 \le k^1 \le N, 1 \le k^2 \le N}$ $W^{k^1}(Q^1_{k^1}, Q^2_{k^2})$. Here $W^{*k^1}(g^1, g^2)$ determines the equal complexity of the clusters in the first type partitioning, taking into account the costs of reconciling with the clusters of the partitioning of the second type. Here G denotes a given set of admissible partitions of the first and second types, which determines the variety of sets $Q^1_{k^1}, Q^2_{k^2}$.

Similarly, the other task is to determine the clusters of the equal complexity of the second type.

Problem 3. Harmonization of the boundaries of clusters of a social network of different types. Determine the conditions under which the boundaries of the clusters of the equal complexity of the first and second types coincide. This means that $Q^1_k = Q^2_k$ for k = 1,..., N.

The Maximum Coordination Condition of the Boundaries of Social Network Clusters

Statement. Let there be given two types of network partitioning into N social network clusters. If for any pair of partitions of different types $g^1 = \{g^1_i\}$, $g^2 = \{g^2_i\}$ the condition for all i, j = 1,..., n is fulfilled, then the partitioning into clusters of different types is the same. This means that $Q^1_k = Q^2_k$ for k = 1,..., N. The coincidence of the partitions corresponds to their maximum consistency.

This statement corresponds to the condition of "strong fines" for deviating the state from the plan, which is considered in the works on the theory of active systems [16]. In [19] this problem was investigated in the case when it is not necessary to fulfill the condition, but the 1st RIMB should agree on its choice and take into account the interests of the 2nd RIMB.

Extension of the Model 2. In the model described above, it was assumed that the definition of the complexity of the edges and vertices given by the matrix $L^m = \left\| l^m_{ij} \right\|_n$ is unique. In practice, one can face the fact that for different RIMB the representations of the matrix of complexities $L^m_{k^m} = \left\| l^m_{ijk^m} \right\|_n$ are different. This means that for each RIMB its own matrix is defined, where m = 1,..., N.

Suppose that the network is divided into clusters of a social network by the Center on the basis of its information about the CIM of the vertices and edges of the network. Let us consider a simpler case where the costs of coordinating the interaction of clusters of a social network of different types of partitions are absent or so large (see the assertion stated above) that divisions of different types obviously coincide. This means that Problem 1 of partitioning into clusters of equal complexity for each of the types of partitioning is solved independently. In this case, for both FIMC, the partition problem is identical. Therefore, we can consider the task of splitting into clusters of a social network for each FIMC independently.

The main difference between the model is that the Center does not know exactly the magnitude of the CIM of vertices and edges for each type of partition. Suppose that each RIMB knows its CIM values. This means that, in fact, the elements of the matrix $L_{k^m}^m = \left\| l_{ijk^m}^m \right\|_n$. Therefore, Center requests from each RIMB the relevant information. Denote $V_{k^m}^m = \left\| v_{ijk^m}^m \right\|_n$ the information reported by the k^m-th RIMB in the values.

There are two possible cases. In the first case, all RIMB, as well as Center, are interested in a partition of clusters of equal complexity and, therefore, are interested in reporting reliable information about their matrix $L_{k^m}^m = \left\| l_{ijk^m}^m \right\|_n$.

Problem 4. Construct clusters of equal complexity for the case of different RIMB views of the CIM, expressed by matrices $L_{k^m}^m = \left\| l_{ijk^m}^m \right\|_n$.

In the second case, we will assume that each RIMB has its own interests in including certain edges and vertices of the network in its cluster. We will describe these interests for each k^m-th RIMB using the matrix of benefits $F_{k^m}^m = \left\| f_{ijk^m}^m \right\|_n$. Suppose that the benefit matrix is known to Center. Suppose also that Center has a compensation fund of B, which he can use to encourage those RIMB for which "unprofitable" clusters of the social network are formed. The benefit of a cluster is determined by the sum of the benefits of the edges and vertices that are included in the cluster, determined by the matrix $F_{k^m}^m = \left\| f_{ijk^m}^m \right\|_n$.

Let's designate $P^{k^m}(Q_{k^m}^m) = \sum_{(i,j) \in Q_{k^m}^m} f_{ijk^m}^m + B^{k^m}$ the benefit of the k^m RIMB, where B^{k^m} is the amount of compensation for the k^m RIMB.

Problem 5. To determine the minimum compensation fund B and its distribution among all the RIMB, in which all RIMB are profitable to report reliable information,

$$V_{k^m}^m = \left\| v_{ijk^m}^m \right\|_n = L_{k^m}^m = \left\| l_{ijk^m}^m \right\|_n.$$

This task is closely connected with the problems of synthesis of optimal control mechanisms in organizational systems [16, 17]. In it, the procedure for forming the boundaries of clusters of a social network and the distribution of a compensation fund can be linked to the construction of coordinated planning and incentive mechanisms. Let's consider some approaches to solving the presented problems.

4 The Optimal Number of Social Network Clusters Estimation

As mentioned above, Problem 1 can be decomposed into two subproblems. One of them is the estimation of the number of clusters of a social network. First, assume that the CIM of the entire network is equal to the sum of the CIM of its subnets (3). Suppose also that the partition is balanced, and the CIM of the different organizational structures are approximately equal $\min\limits_{g^m \in G^m} \max\limits_{1 \leq i \leq N^m} K_i^{g^m}(\bar{l}_i^m) = R^{\bar{g}^m}$. Then we assume that the CIM of all RIMB is the same and equal to the total CIM of the entire social network $\tilde{L} = NR^{\bar{g}^m}$.

The FIMC spends time and money on monitoring the work of each RIMB. Therefore, one of the components of the CIM FIMC - $a_1 N$ is proportional to the number of subordinate organizational structures - clusters of the social network. In addition, the FIMC coordinates the interaction of the RIMB pairs. Therefore, another component of its FIMC can be estimated by a quadratic function $a_2 N^2$. Coefficients a_1 and a_2 characterize, for example, the time spent managing each RIMB and coordinating their interactions. Thus, the CIM FIMC is estimated by the sum $K_0(\bar{g}^N) = a_1 N + a_2 N^2$. Then problem (6) can be represented as a minimization with respect to N of the expression $K_0(\bar{g}^N) + NR^{\bar{g}} = a_1 N + a_2 N^2 + \tilde{L}$.

Consider the problem of minimizing costs (4). Suppose that the costs of the equisyllabic clusters of a social network are described using an incremental cost function $\tilde{Z}(\tilde{L}/N)$. Then the problem of determining the conditionally optimal number of clusters of the social network for the m-th FIMC can be represented as minimization of the N expression $K_0(\bar{g}^N) + NR^{\bar{g}} = a_1 N + a_2 N^2 + N\tilde{Z}(\tilde{L}/N)$.

Let us approximate the cost function in the form of a quadratic function [16], namely $\tilde{Z}(\tilde{L}/N) = b_1 \tilde{L}/N + b_2 \tilde{L}^2/N^2$. Then from the condition, it is possible to determine the estimate of the optimal number of organizational structures N^*. From the necessary conditions of the extremum, we obtain the equation for estimating N^*: $a_1 + 2a_2 N = b_2 L^2/N^2$ under the condition $N_{min} \leq N \leq N_{max}$.

5 Network Compression

By compression (reduction) of a network, we call the transformation of the initial network to a simpler one, with a smaller number of edges and vertices, due to

- the union of some edges and vertices;
- a prior binding of individual edges and vertices to certain centers;
- restrictions on the ability to bind individual edges and vertices to certain centers. In this case, the centers (and, respectively, the clusters of the social network) are defined, only to which one or another vertex or edge can be assigned in the process of forming the boundaries.

Let's single out two modes of network compression.

The first mode determines the initial compression (reduction) of the network in order to reduce the size of the task and to take into account non-formalized factors that impose restrictions on the formation of clusters of the social network.

The network compression in the first reduction mode is based on the analysis of a specific network, taking into account its specificity, technological features of information transfer, points of "origin and repayment" of information impacts (origination and receipt of messages), types of security (data format), Taking into account the technological interdependence of individual sections of the network.

The second compression mode used in the typical step, which is used in the algorithms of analyzing data on the social network offered below and the successive formation of clusters of the social network. Compression and the typical step of these algorithms described by the following procedure.

After carrying out the first compression mode, renumber the vertices of the received network so that the first N numbers receive the selected vertices (RIMB), $i = 1,\ldots,N,\ldots,n$.

For ease of writing, this section omits an index characterizing the type of partition. It means network transformations considered for the case when there is a single FIMC. In the case of two FIMC, an index corresponding to the number of the FIMC is added.

Suppose that for the complexity l_{ij} of the edge (i, j) is true $l_{ij} = l_{ji}$. The complexity of the i-th vertex $(i = 1,\ldots, n)$ is defined as $w_i = l_{ii}$. We denote $L^0 = \left\| l_{ij}^0 \right\|_n$ the initial matrix of arcs and vertices of the network under consideration. Here, the superscript denotes the step number in consecutive network compression. Note that this matrix is symmetric, has dimension n, and its elements take non-negative values. In the case where the i-th vertex is not connected to the j-th vertex by an edge in the network under consideration, we supplement the network with an edge (i, j) of zero complexity. It means $l_{ij} = l_{ji} = 0$. Suppose that the selected vertices are not joined by edges of nonzero length.

Formation of social network clusters is represented as a consecutive assignment of edges and vertices to one or another selected vertex, which is the RIMB of the cluster, and the formation of a new network with a smaller number of vertices per unit (network compression). This transforms the matrix $L^0 = \left\| l_{ij}^0 \right\|_n$ into a n-1 matrix $L^1 = \left\| l_{ij}^1 \right\|_{n-1}$ at the first step, and at the second step $L^2 = \left\| l_{ij}^2 \right\|_{n-2}$ in dimension n-2 and so on, until we obtain a matrix $L^{n-N} = \left\| l_{ij}^{n-N} \right\|_N$ of dimension N at the (n-N) -th step. At the compression step, it is allowed to attach only one vertex and, possibly, several edges incident to the attached vertex.

Consider the first step of compression. Let the unselected vertex with the number j $(j > N)$ connected to the edge (i, j) be attached to the selected vertex with the number i $(i \le N)$, and $l_{ij} > 0$. Then the transformation of the complexities of vertices and edges of the network will be determined by the following relations $w_i^1 = w_i + w_j + l_{ij} + l_{jk}$, $l_{jk}^1 = 0$ where k ¬ is the number of the unseparated vertex such that $l_{ik} > 0$. Similar to the first step, the following compression steps are performed. The complexity recalculation formulas at the τ-th step have the form $w_i^{\tau+1} = w_i^\tau + w_j^\tau + l_{ij}^\tau + l_{jk}^\tau$ where $\tau = 1,\ldots,$ n-N.

Note that the compression formulas reflect the linear transformation of the matrix $L^\tau = \left\| l_{ij}^\tau \right\|_{n-\tau}$ into a matrix $L^{\tau+1} = \left\| l_{ij}^{\tau+1} \right\|_{n-\tau-1}$. Thus, the τ-th compression step can be represented as a transformation $L^{\tau+1} = B^\tau L^\tau B^{\tau T}$, where B^τ is the transformation matrix at the τ-th step of dimension n-τ on n-τ-1, $B^{\tau T}$ is its transposed matrix. The transformation under consideration translates a symmetric matrix $L^\tau = \left\| l_{ij}^\tau \right\|_{n-\tau}$ into a symmetric matrix $L^{\tau+1} = \left\| l_{ij}^{\tau+1} \right\|_{n-\tau-1}$ in which there is no j-th row and column in the original numbering of rows and columns.

Thus, as a result of the entire sequence of steps described, we can write the final reduction of the original matrix L^0 to L^{n-N} in the form $L^{n-N} = BL^0B^T$, where $B = B^{n-N}B^{n-N-1}...B^1$ and $B^T = (B^{n-N})^T(B^{n-N-1})^T(B^1)^T$. As a result, by construction, we obtain a diagonal matrix L^{n-N}, and the quantities on the diagonal set the values of the information management complexity indicators of the constructed social network clusters $K_i^{g^N} = w_i^* = w_i^{n-N}$, where $i = 1,..., N$. The described reduction procedure can be used in the basic step in algorithms for analyzing data on a social network and locally optimal partitioning based on the directional construction of clusters of a social network.

The described procedure for sequential network reduction, applied to Problem 1, corresponds to obtaining the smallest difference in the values of the diagonal elements $K_i^{g^N} = w_i^* = w_i^{n-N}$ of the matrix L^{n-N} when choosing the partition.

6 Analyzing Data Algorithms on the Social Network and Determining the Boundaries of Information Management Clusters

Construction of heuristic algorithms for analyzing social network data based on local optimization. Some initial partitioning is determined, and then procedures for its sequential improvement are based on a directed search of options and sequential expansion of subnets until a complete network partition is obtained. The process of such an expansion is directed to improve at each step the indicator of the equilibrium of social network clusters.

Analyzing Data Algorithm "Nearest Center of the Social Network". Consider the method of forming social network clusters for the case of different matrices $L_{k^m}^m = \left\| l_{ijk^m}^m \right\|_n$. Let the net already reduced at some τ-th step be given. We compute the CIM of the reduced distinguished vertices $w_\theta = w_{k^\theta}^\tau$, where $\theta = 1,..., N$ (we shall omit the reduction order in the notation since it is not important in the description of this algorithm). In the calculation of the CIM, a representation of the matrix of complexities $L_{k^\theta}^\theta = \left\| l_{ijk^\theta}^\theta \right\|_n$ related to the θ RIMB is used.

Steps of the Algorithm. We define the shortest distances between all RIMB (distinguished vertices) between the s-th and t-th RIMB of the reduced network in two variants, using matrices $L_s = \left\| l_{ijs}^s \right\|_n$ and $L_t = \left\| l_{ijt}^t \right\|_n$, respectively, s, t = 1,..., N. If the shortest distance between centers is 0, this means that at the appropriate point the clusters of the social network that they manage are neighboring. This fact is fixed, but the edge of zero length is excluded from further consideration in the algorithm. We also denote the shortest distances $\widetilde{\lambda}_{st} > 0$ and $\widetilde{\lambda}_{ts} > 0$ between the s-th and t-th, as well as the t-th s-th and the centers of the reduced network. Note that, generally speaking, $\widetilde{\lambda}_{st} \neq \widetilde{\lambda}_{ts}$ by force $L_s \neq L_t$. Let us determine the minimum distance between all pairs of centers $\widetilde{\lambda}_{j^*i^*} = \min_{j \neq i} \widetilde{\lambda}_{ji}$. Let it be a couple with numbers j^*, i^*. We will compare CIM by clusters of a social network corresponding to these reduced centers – w_{j^*} and w_{i^*}. Let $w_{j^*} > w_{i^*}$. Then in the reduction of the vertex i^* we add an edge incident to the vertex i^* along the considered shortest path, and also a vertex connected by this edge to the center i^*. After this, we recalculate the CIM of the corresponding clusters of the social network. Then we again compare the CIM w_{j^*} and w_{i^*} then add the edge and the vertex to the reduction of the center where the CIM was smaller. In the case of equality of CIM, we arbitrarily choose one of the centers. As a result of the described reduction along the shortest path, we obtain the distance between the centers j^*, i^* equal to zero. This zero edge is excluded from consideration.

The data analysis algorithm is completed when, after the next reduction, there are no shortest distances of non-zero length. The final reduction determines the partitioning into social network clusters.

Analyzing Data Algorithm "Nearest Social Network Boundary"

Steps of the Algorithm. We define t such that $w_t = \min_{1 \le j \le N} w_j$. Let us consider the reduction of the allocated RIMB. This reduction is a subnet that is reduced ("compressed") to the reduced center t. Using the representation $L_t = \left\| l_{ijt}^t \right\|_n$ of the t-th RIMB for the network subnet, we define the minimum "radius", which is defined as the shortest path from RIMB to the "periphery". The boundary of the network is determined by the vertices with which the edges that are not part of the reduction in question are an incident. To the vertex of the boundary corresponding to the minimal radius, we add an edge incident to this vertex. This edge and the associated vertex are added to the reduction of the t-th RIMB. This addition is carried out only from the number of edges not included in the reduction of other vertices. If there are several such edges, then the selection rule from these edges establishes a modification of the considered algorithm. This completes the algorithm step. We pass again to the beginning of the described step. If we do not succeed in adding an edge (since the neighboring edge is in the reduction of another RIMB), we believe that a point of contact between neighboring clusters of the social network has been found. This point is excluded from the boundary points to which the radius is calculated. The data analysis algorithm ends when all edges that are not included in any reductions are exhausted.

Analyzing Data Algorithm "Reducing Social Networks Order". At each step of this algorithm, reduction (compression) of the subnet with minimal $w = w_j$ is considered. In this reduction, we add an edge and the corresponding vertex, which does not change the order of reduction of the distinguished RIMB considered, after which we recalculate $w = w_j$. If in the reduction under consideration it is not possible to find an edge that does not change the order of reduction, then we go on to consider the reduction of another RIMB with the next largest increase w. If such RIMB was not found, then we increase the reduction order of the RIMB with a minimum w. And so on, until the entire network is broken down into organizational structures.

7   Conclusions

Systems, structures, and technologies of information management of social networks have their own peculiarities, caused by a large number of related and geographically distributed processes. In this regard, there is a need for a multi-level organizational system of information management. The necessity of its optimization generates the problem of splitting social networks into subnets (clusters) - areas of responsibility of regional information management bodies. The paper describes the model and presents the problems of optimizing the number of centers and boundaries of organizational structures (clusters) of information management on the network. The notion of the complexity of information management is introduced. The problem of optimal network partitioning into information management clusters is set as the problem of minimizing the complexity of information management, due to its equalization. The ways of the approximate solution of the problem are determined on the basis of its decomposition into determining the number of clusters and forming their boundaries on the basis of the proposed principle of equal complexity. Algorithms for analyzing data from a locally optimal partition are developed, based on a directional search of options, including algorithms for analyzing data for the formation of cluster boundaries, given the number and location of organizational information management structures on the network. The latter include heuristic data analysis algorithms: the nearest-center data analysis algorithm; analyzing the data algorithm of the nearest boundary; the algorithm for data analysis of the order of reduction.

References

1. Kile, F., Dimirovski, G.: Choices for global social stability. In: Reports of the 17th IFAC World Congress, Seoul, pp. 6669–6674 (2008)
2. Gubanov, D.A., Novikov, D.A., Chkhartishvili, A.G.: Social Networks: Models of Information Influence, Management and Confrontation. Fizmatgiz, Moscow (2010)
3. Kulba, V.V., Kononov, D.A., Malyugin, Y.D., Tsyganov, V.V.: Theoretical basis of information management. Inf. Wars. Moscow. **2**, 16–25 (2008)
4. Tsyganov, V.V., Bukharin, S.N.: Information Management. Dictionary & Directory. Academic Project, Moscow (2009)
5. Tsyganov, V.V.: Limits of global growth, stagnation, creativity and international stability. Artif. Intell. Soc. J. Knowl. Cult. Commun. **29**, 259–266 (2013). Springer-Verlag, London
6. Shultz, V.L., Tsyganov, V.V.: Modernization of the National Security System. Nauka, Moscow (2010)
7. Kalyaev, I.A., Levin, I.I.: Reconfigurable multicopy computing systems for solving streaming problems of information processing and control. In: Reports of the 5th Conference "Parallel Computing and Control Problems", pp. 23–37. IPU RAS, Moscow (2010)
8. Kalyaev, I.A., Levin, I.I., Semernikov, E.A., Shmoilov, V.I.: Reconfigurable Multicopy Computing Structures. UNSC RAS, Rostov (2009)
9. Kureichik, V.M., Glushan, V.M., Shcherbakov, L.I.: Combinatorial Hardware Models and Algorithms in CAD. Radio and Communication, Moscow (1990)
10. Papadimitriou, C.H., Steiglitz, K.: Combinatorial Optimization: Algorithms and Complexity. Mir, Moscow (1985)

11. Heylighen, F.: The Growth of structural and functional complexity during evolution. In: Heylighen, F., Aerts, D. (eds.) The Evolution of Complexity, pp. 17–44. Kluwer, Dordrecht (1999)
12. Novikov, D.A.: Theory of Management of Organizational Systems. Fizmatlit, Moscow (2007)
13. Voronin, A.A., Gubko, M.V., Mishin, S.P., Novikov, D.A.: Mathematical Models of Organizations. Lenand, Moscow (2008)
14. Mishin, S.P.: Optimal Hierarchies of Management in Economic Systems. PMsoft, Moscow (2004)
15. Gubko, M.V.: Mathematical Models of Optimization of Hierarchical Structures. Lenand, Moscow (2006)
16. Burkov, V.N.: Fundamentals of the Mathematical Theory of Active Systems. Nauka, Moscow (1977)
17. Mechanism Design and Management: Mathematical Methods for Smart Organizations/Business Issues, Competition and Enterpreneurship. NOVA Publishers, New York (2013)
18. Enaleev, A.K.: Optimal Incentive Compatible Mechanism in a System with Several Active Elements. Autom. Remote Control 78, 146–158 (2017). Moscow
19. Enaleev, A.K.: Coordinated splits in network organizational structures. Manag. Prob. 6, 18–25 (2016). Moscow

Community Cut-off Attack on Malicious Networks

Iveta Dirgová Luptáková[✉] and Jiří Pospíchal

Faculty of Natural Sciences, University of SS. Cyril and Methodius in Trnava,
917 01 Trnava, Slovak Republic
iveta.dirgova@ucm.sk, jiri.pospichal@gmail.com

Abstract. This paper aims to provide an efficient algorithm for quick disabling of known malicious network by sequential removal or incapacitation of their nodes. The nodes are selected for deletion in such a sequence, that the network is swiftly separated into small disjoined parts. We propose using a community detection based on random walks. For all the divisions of the found communities into two separate sets we create bigraphs defined by the edge set with each edge's node in different community and use Koenig's theorem to find the best vertex cut (set of vertices to be deleted). This community detection and their separation is used recursively on a currently maximal component of the network. The effectiveness of our algorithm is tested on both real-world and model networks by quantifying network robustness measure R based on the size of maximum component. Its results compare favorably against standard centrality based attack strategies.

Keywords: Complex networks · Attack strategy · Community detection · Minimum vertex cut · Bigraph · Koenig's theorem · Betweenness

1 Introduction

Social, biological or technological networks and networking is ordinarily regarded desirable or at worst neutral, as an effective way to communicate and distribute knowledge or resources [2, 25]. Typically, attacks on networks have been studied from the defender's point of view, where the goal was to design a topology of network in such a way that would ensure its robustness against either random failures or intentional attacks [1, 18].

However, there are many cases, where the goal of a network is malevolent or its result unintentionally harmful. As examples can serve terrorist networks, malevolent fake-news spreading networks, the spread of disease, cascading failures in power networks, malnets used in DDoS attack [22, 32, 33] or spreading worms and viruses, dark nets distributing child pornography or involved in other criminal activities, etc. [7, 8, 10–12, 26, 38].

To study such networks in general, their structure is narrowed to graphs composed of nodes and edges. The only difference from an ordinary graph is then in their topological properties. Unlike ordinary graphs, the real world networks tend to have a

© Springer International Publishing AG 2017
A. Kravets et al. (Eds.): CIT&DS 2017, CCIS 754, pp. 697–708, 2017.
DOI: 10.1007/978-3-319-65551-2_50

few nodes with a very high degree (the degree distribution has a "heavy tail"), a high clustering coefficient expressing the fact that neighbors of a node are likely connected themselves, and a community structure [2, 25].

In order to shut down or incapacitate such networks, one can formally delete edges or nodes, sequentially or at once. In graph theory, removing a smallest possible set of nodes at once to split the graph roughly into halves is called balanced minimum vertex cut problem (also known as the vertex separator problem), it belongs to graph partitioning problems and it is NP-hard [14]. Another approach related to graph partitioning is community detection, but while in graph partitioning the number of partitions is set in advance, in most community detection algorithms the number and the size of the communities is determined from network's topology [2].

In our case, we shall consider sequential deletion of nodes. There exist various strategies for selecting nodes for deletion, mainly based on local centrality measures like vertex degree or its betweenness. Sequences of vertices with decreasing values of degrees or betweenness [15] can be calculated at once for the complete network (initial degree/betweenness distribution), or recalculated iteratively when the vertex with maximum value is deleted. The iterative strategies (sequence targeted attack or recalculated centrality) for degree/betweenness (RD/RB) require more computational resources, but provide better results [19], therefore they will be used as reference attack strategies.

Measures, how to calculate the incapacitation of the network, are mainly based on average length of paths between vertices, degrees of remaining nodes or size of connected components of the network [13, 36]. In our paper, we use network robustness measure R based on the size of a maximum component after each node deletion for quantifying the attack effectiveness of the whole sequence [17, 31, 34, 35], defined as:

$$R = \frac{1}{N+1} \sum_{Q=0}^{N} S(Q) \tag{1}$$

where N is the initial number of nodes in the network, $S(Q)$ is the fraction of nodes in the largest connected component after deletion of $Q = Nq$ nodes and q is a current fraction of deleted nodes vs. N.

At the core of our attack strategy is Module-Based Attack, its idea originating from [16], later developed by [9] and further by [30]. We have adapted their strategy by merging the found communities into such two supersets, which have the best ratio of size of the removed superset against the number of removed bridges, which we recalculate iteratively.

There are many methods for community detection, based on various principles. Edge betweenness uses the number of shortest paths through it in [23]. Fast greedy uses local optimization in [6]. Node labels are updated by majority voting in the neighborhood of the node in [28]. The leading non-negative eigenvector of the modularity matrix is calculated by [24]. The modularity measure and a hierarchical approach are used in Louvain method [4]. The modularity maximization is transformed into an integer programming problem in [5]. Spin-glass model and simulated annealing is used by [29], and random walks are utilized in "walktrap" [27]. We have tried all the methods with the equally good best results provided by edge betweenness [23], optimal [5], spinglass [29] and walktrap [27]. In further calculations, we shall use a community detection method walktrap with reasonable robustness and runtime complexity [39].

2 Community Cut-off Attack Strategy

The module- or community-based attack strategy, which was studied by da Cunha [30], was defined as partially simultaneous attack, which first finds nodes in intercommunity connections and then removes them. The selection of the nodes to be removed is determined only on the bases of their betweenness and on sequential removal of the intercommunity node, whose counterparts on the other side were already removed. The strategy, according to [30], is as follows:

1. Extract communities using a heuristic detection algorithm.
2. Make a list of the nodes that participate in intercommunity connections.
3. Sort the list in descending betweenness centrality order.
4. Delete nodes one by one, starting from the first in the list.
5. When a node from a link between two communities is deleted, its counterpart is removed from the list, unless it also participates in other intercommunity connections.
6. The attack is always restricted to the largest connected component of the network. In other words, if at some point the next node in the list does not belong to the remaining largest connected component that node is skipped.

While this strategy is effective, sometimes it is not optimal. To illustrate the problem, due to a scarcity of benchmark malicious networks, we shall show it on a network of the "contiguous USA graph". Its nodes represent the contiguous 48 states of the United States plus the District of Columbia (DC) and its edges connect pairs of states (plus DC) that are connected by at least one drivable road [20, 37], see Fig. 1. The nodes representing states are labeled by their postal abbreviations and clustered into 7 communities by the walktrap algorithm [27], the clusters are shown by the colored regions. The community attack specified above would start to attack the nodes MO, PA, KY, TN, NY, NE, ... In the lower part of the figure are betweenness values of the nodes. The deletion would start with nodes of values 403, 328, 321, 256, 253, 180,.. so after 6 deletions only nodes VT, NH, ME, MA, CT, RI would be cut off. The size of the largest component would be 4 times repeatedly diminished by 1, only the deletion of the fifth node NY would cut-of 6 nodes. In minimization of R value, we are trying to maximize the following ratio:

$$\frac{number\_of\_cut - off\_nodes + number\_of\_deleted\_nodes}{number\_of\_deleted\_nodes} \tag{2}$$

In this case, the ratio is $(6 + 6)/6 = 2$, which means, that in average for one deleted node we cut of one other node from the largest component. After deletion of 6 nodes, the size of the largest connected component is $49-12 = 37$. If we look at the network, just by deleting NY node marked by red framed square we can cut off 6 other nodes, VT, NH, ME, MA, CT, and RI, which gives the ratio 7. By further deletion of nodes

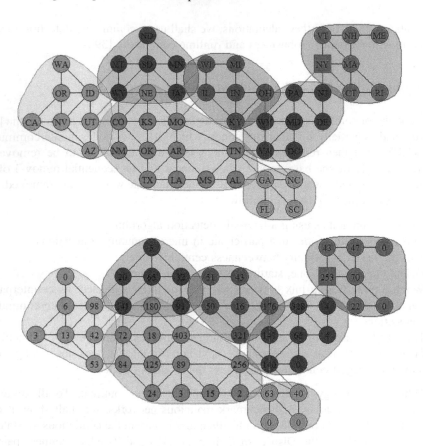

Fig. 1. Contiguous USA neighboring states, clustered by walktrap algorithm. The lower figure shows betweenness values of nodes.

MN, IA, MO, TN and AL we can cut of further 16 nodes, with a ratio (16 + 5)/5 = 4.2. After deletion of just 6 nodes, the size of the largest connected component is only 49−(6 + 16 + 6) = 21. The algorithm of [30] could therefore certainly be improved. The Fig. 2 shows the partial results after deletion of only 6 nodes, on the left for the algorithm [30] resulting in the largest component with 37 nodes, on the right improvement with the largest component of 19 nodes (improved even comparing to original community cut off by iterative recalculating of communities after deletion of each node).

However, this brings us to the question, how to decide, which communities should be cut-off from the rest and which of the nodes incident with intercommunity edges should be deleted?

When the number of communities is reasonably small, the answer is simply combinatorial enumeration. In our case, if we label the initially found 7 communities shown in Fig. 1 by A-G, we can partition the set of the communities into all possible

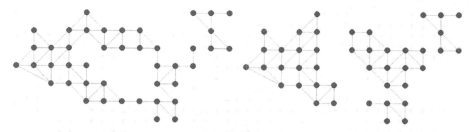

Fig. 2. Contiguous USA neighboring states, after deletion of 6 nodes. The left figure shows the result of the antecedent algorithm [30], the second result of the new one.

couples of proper subsets {{A},{B,C,D,E,F,G}}, {{B},{A,C,D,E,F,G}}, ..., {{G}{A, B,C,D,E,F}}, {{A,B},{C,D,E,F,G}}, {{A,C},{B,D,E,F,G}},..., {{F,G}{A,B,C,D, E}}, {{A,B,C},{D,E,F,G}}, ..., {{E,F,G},{A,B,C,D}}, which makes 63 partitions. However, from these we can omit those partitions, which do not induce connected networks. If, say, communities A and B are not connected by an edge, then there is not much point in analyzing which nodes are best to be cut off from {{A,B},{C,D,E,F,G}}, since it would be in most cases already covered by {{A},{B,C,D,E,F,G}}, {{B},{A,C, D,E,F,G}}. In our case, it will reduce the number of partitions to analyze just to 21, see Fig. 3. Occasionally, there may exist a few cases, when e.g. a node from a subset {C,D, E,F,G} could be connected both to A and B. For instance, cutting of {A} from {B,C,D, E,F,G} would require deletion of 2 nodes, cutting of {B} from {A,C,D,E,F,G} would require deletion of 2 nodes, but cutting of {A,B} from {C,D,E,F,G} would require only 3 nodes, since one in C is connected to both A and B, even though A is not connected with B. Analyzing these cases in optimization would require too much computational overload, so we choose to ignore them. Their inclusion would only slightly shift the order, in which the communities are cut off.

In order to separate two parts of a partition, we take edges with one end in each part of partition. These edges induce a bipartite graph.

Hopcroft–Karp algorithm takes as input a bipartite graph and produces as output a maximum cardinality matching – a maximum set of edges when no two edges share a node. It runs in $O(|E|\sqrt{N})$ time in the worst case, typical time is linear. Finding nodes to delete to disconnect the bipartite graph means to find a minimum vertex cover from the matching. By application of König's theorem [3, 21] it can be done in logarithmic time. When more possible minimum vertex cover sets exist, we take the one, which has more nodes in the larger community, so that the size of resulting largest connected component is further diminished.

Compared with the algorithm [30], communities are extracted anew after each removal of a node. This does not have to be the case, when we order the gains for partitions in decreasing order and delete all the nodes of their minimum vertex covers in that order. This would substantially accelerate the computation, but only slightly increase the resulting R value. Similarly, if the number of found communities would be too large in order to analyze all the partitions, it can be artificially decreased by merging smallest most connected communities. Nevertheless, in our calculations we did not find it necessary.

Fig. 3. Contiguous USA neighboring states, all possible partitions of communities into two subsets (when each subset induces a connected graph) colored red and blue, nodes to be deleted to separate the partitions are marked by squares. (Color figure online)

On the other hand, if we would like to get even better results of R value, in the following pseudocode we can skip the removing partitions with an unconnected graph induced by its subset of nodes, slightly improving results at a great computational cost. Further, finding communities anew after deleting each node is advantageous most of the time, but not always. The algorithm might be improved by remembering old minimum vertex covers with their gains and compare the new gains with the old ones.

The pseudocode of the adapted modular based attack strategy is as follows:

```
Program AdaptedModuleAttack:
BEGIN
INPUT network
WHILE number of edges in network>0
    Find largest connected component CC
    IF CC is tree THEN
        Delete its node with maximum betweenness
    ELSE
        Extract communities in CC using a heuristic detection algorithm.
        IF only one community is found THEN
            delete its node with maximum betweenness,
        ELSE
        Generate all possible partitions of the communities in two
        nonempty subsets.
        FOR each partition:
            IF either set the nodes from communities in the two subsets
            does not induce a connected component, THEN
                Remove the partition
            ELSE
                Define both subsets of communities as new communities, find
                edges that are incident with nodes from both communities
                Create a bipartite graph induced by these edges
                Using Hopcroft-Karp algorithm and König's theorem, find
                the minimum vertex cover for the bipartite graph, which
                has more nodes in the larger community
                Calculate gain of the partition from eq. (2), when number
                of deleted nodes equals the cardinality of the minimum
                vertex cover and the number of cut-off nodes is the number
                of nodes in the currently smaller of the two partition
                communities after eventual deletion of the minimum vertex
                cover
            ENDIF
        ENDFOR
        Find partition with maximum gain; delete the node with maximum
        degree from its minimum vertex cover.
        ENDIF
    ENDIF
    Calculate S(Q) from eq. (1)
ENDWHILE
Print network robustness measure R and plot S(Q) sequence
END
```

3   Experimental Results

The effectiveness of the adapted algorithm (AMBA - Adapted Module Based Attack) was compared against iterative strategies recalculating degree (RD) and betweenness (RB) on selected networks. Since we do not have access to the code of [30], it would not be fair to compare our adapted algorithm against our version of their code and the published results of the original module-based attack [30] are unfortunately only in graphical form. However, there is no reason why our adapted algorithm should be worse.

Apart of the contiguous USA graph described previously, we tested attack strategies to attack Barabási–Albert (BA) preferential attachment model, generated by starting with a triangle and adding each time a node together with 3 edges. Another test

Table 1. R-values for various combinations of attacks and networks

Network	ContiguousUSA	Barabási–Albert	Geometric random
Attack strategy	R	R	R
RD	0.2873	0.2525	0.3866
RB	0.1820	0.2294	0.2792
AMBA	0.1751	0.2431	0.2564

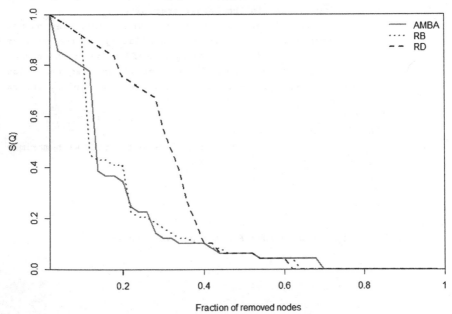

Fig. 4. S(Q) values for RD, RB and our AMBA attacks on contiguous USA neighboring states network. (Color figure online)

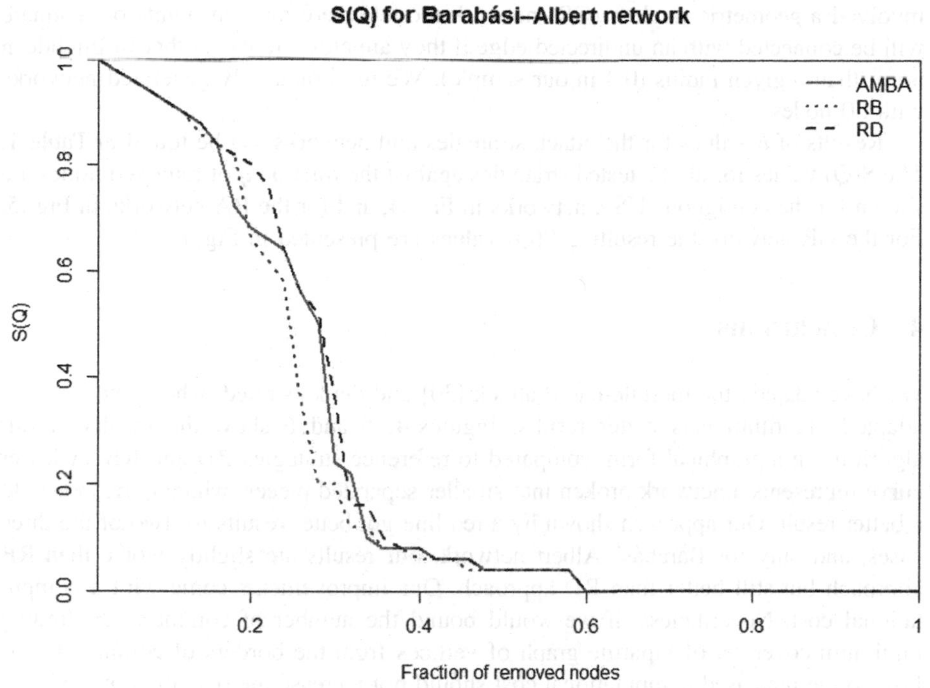

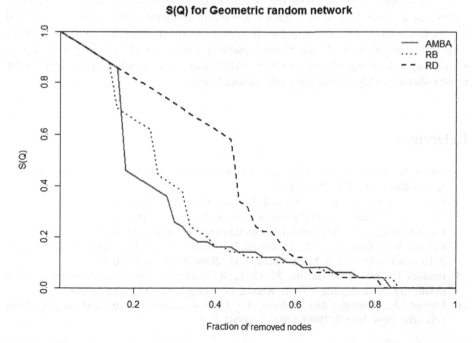

Fig. 5. S(Q) values for RD, RB and our AMBA attacks on Barabási–Albert network. (Color figure online)

Fig. 6. S(Q) values for RD, RB and our AMBA attacks on Geometric random network. (Color figure online)

involved a geometric random (GR) network model where random points on a square will be connected with an undirected edge if they are closer to each other in Euclidean norm than a given radius (0.3 in our sample). We used randomly generated networks with 50 nodes.

Results of R values for the attack strategies and networks can be found in Table 1. The S(Q) values for all the tested strategies against the fraction q of removed nodes are shown for the contiguous USA networks in Fig. 4, and for the BA networks in Fig. 5. For the GR network the resulting S(Q) values are presented in Fig. 6.

4   Conclusions

We have adapted the module-based attack [30] and demonstrated, where and why the adapted algorithm gets better results. Figures 4, 5 and 6 show the results of our algorithm in a graphical form, compared to reference strategies RD and RB. A lower curve represents a network broken into smaller separated pieces, which corresponds to a better result. Our approach shown by a red line got better results for two of the three cases, and only for Barabási–Albert network, our results are slightly worse than RB approach but still better than RD approach. Our improvements come with a computational cost. Nevertheless, if we would bound the number of communities, finding minimum cover set of bipartite graph of vertices from the borders of communities is fast, so the increased computational cost should not increase the overall complexity of the module-based attack approach.

The choice, if to use our adapted algorithm, depends on how soon the results are needed and what type and how big is the attacked network. In case of cascading failures of a power grid or wi-fi malnet, the original algorithm providing less optimal results faster might be more suitable. In case of terrorist networks, immunization of disease, or any network based at least partially on real world Euclidean distances, which support emergence of modular architecture, our approach providing better results should justify the higher computational cost.

References

1. Albert, R., Jeong, H., Barabási, A.L.: Error and attack tolerance of complex networks. Nature **406**(6794), 378–382 (2000)
2. Barabási, A.-L., Pósfai M.: Network Science. Cambridge University Press, Cambridge (2016). http://barabasi.com/networksciencebook. Accessed 7 Apr 2017
3. Bipartite minimum vertex cover. http://tryalgo.org/en/matching/2016/08/05/konig/
4. Blondel, V.D., Guillaume, J.L., Lambiotte, R., Lefebvre, E.: Fast unfolding of communities in large networks. J. Stat. Mech: Theory Exp. **2008**(10), P10008 (2008)
5. Brandes, U., Delling, D., Gaertler, M., Gorke, R., Hoefer, M., Nikoloski, Z., Wagner, D.: On modularity clustering. IEEE Trans. Knowl. Data Eng. **20**(2), 172–188 (2008)
6. Clauset, A., Newman, M.E., Moore, C.: Finding community structure in very large networks. Phys. Rev. E **70**(6), 066111 (2004)

7. Cohen, R., Erez, K., Ben-Avraham, D., Havlin, S.: Breakdown of the Internet under intentional attack. Phys. Rev. Lett. **86**(16), 3682 (2001)
8. Cohen, R., Havlin, S., Ben-Avraham, D.: Efficient immunization strategies for computer networks and populations. Phys. Rev. Lett. **91**(24), 247901 (2003)
9. De Meo, P., Ferrara, E., Fiumara, G., Provetti, A.: On Facebook, most ties are weak. Commun. ACM **57**(11), 78–84 (2014)
10. D'Orsogna, M.R., Perc, M.: Statistical physics of crime: A review. Phys. life Rev. **12**, 1–21 (2015)
11. Duijn, P.A., Kashirin, V., Sloot, P.M.: The relative ineffectiveness of criminal network disruption. Sci. Rep. **4**, 4238 (2014)
12. Duijn, P.A.C., Klerks, P.P.H.M.: Social network analysis applied to criminal networks: recent developments in Dutch law enforcement. In: Masys, A. (ed.) Networks and Network Analysis for Defence and Security. LNCS. Springer, Cham (2014). doi:10.1007/978-3-319-04147-6_6
13. Ellens, W., Kooij, R.E.: Graph measures and network robustness. arXiv preprint arXiv:1311.5064 (2013)
14. Feige, U., Hajiaghayi, M., Lee, J.R.: Improved approximation algorithms for minimum weight vertex separators. SIAM J. Comput. **38**(2), 629–657 (2008)
15. Freeman, L.: A set of measures of centrality based on betweenness. Sociometry **40**, 35–41 (1977)
16. Granovetter, M.S.: The strength of weak ties. Am. J. Sociol. **78**(6), 1360–1380 (1973)
17. Hong, C., He, N., Lordan, O., Liang, B., Yin, N.: Efficient calculation of the robustness measure for complex networks. Phys. A: Stat. Mech. its Appl. **478**, 63–68 (2017)
18. Huang, X., Gao, J., Buldyrev, S.V., Havlin, S., Stanley, H.E.: Robustness of interdependent networks under targeted attack. Phys. Rev. E **83**(6), 065101 (2011)
19. Iyer, S., Killingback, T., Sundaram, B., Wang, Z.: Attack robustness and centrality of complex networks. PLoS ONE **8**(4), e59613 (2013)
20. Knuth, D.E.: The Art of Computer Programming, Volume 4, Fascicle 0: Introduction to Combinatorial Functions and Boolean Functions. Addison-Wesley, Upper Saddle River (2008). p. 15
21. Kőnig, D.: Gráfok és mátrixok. Matematikai és Fizikai Lapok **38**, 116–119 (1931)
22. Korytar, M., Gabriska, D.: Integrated security levels and analysis of their implications to the maintenance. J. Appl. Math. Stat. Inf. **10**(2), 33–42 (2014)
23. Newman, M., Girvan, M.: Finding and evaluating community structure in networks. Phys. Rev. E **69**, 026113 (2004)
24. Newman, M.: Finding community structure using the eigenvectors of matrices. Phys. Rev. E **74**, 036104 (2006)
25. Newman, M.: Networks An Introduction. Oxford University Press, Cambridge (2010)
26. Pastor-Satorras, R., Vespignani, A.: Immunization of complex networks. Phys. Rev. E **65**(3), 036104 (2002)
27. Pons, P., Latapy, M.: Computing communities in large networks using random walks. In: Yolum, P., Güngör, T., Gürgen, F., Özturan, C. (eds.) International Symposium on Computer and Information Sciences, LNCS, vol. 3733, pp. 284–293. Springer, Berlin Heidelberg (2005)
28. Raghavan, U.N., Albert, R., Kumara, S.: Near linear time algorithm to detect community structures in large-scale networks. Phys. Rev. E **76**, 036106 (2007)
29. Reichardt, J., Bornholdt, S.: Statistical mechanics of community detection. Phys. Rev. E **74**, 016110 (2006)

30. da Cunha, B.R., González-Avella, J.C., Gonçalves, S.: Fast fragmentation of networks using module-based attacks. PLoS ONE **10**(11), e0142824 (2015). doi:10.1371/journal.pone. 0142824

31. Schneider, C.M., Moreira, A.A., Andrade, J.S., Havlin, S., Herrmann, H.J.: Mitigation of malicious attacks on networks. Proc. Natl. Acad. Sci. **108**(10), 3838–3841 (2011)

32. Šimon, M., Huraj, L., Čerňanský, M.: Performance evaluations of IPTables firewall solutions under DDoS attacks. J. Appl. Math. Stat. Inf. **11**(2), 35–45 (2015)

33. Šimon, M., Huraj, L., Hosťovecký, M.: IPv6 network DDoS attack with P2P grid. In: Kravets, A., Shcherbakov, M., Kultsova, M., Shabalina, O. (eds.) Creativity in Intelligent Technologies and Data Science. Communications in Computer and Information Science, vol. 535. Springer, Cham (2015). doi:10.1007/978-3-319-23766-4_32. (pp. 407–415)

34. Tambouratzis, T., Souliou, D., Chalikias, M., Gregoriades, A.: Maximising accuracy and efficiency of traffic accident prediction combining information mining with computational intelligence approaches and decision trees. J. Artif. Intell. Soft Comput. Res. **4**(1), 31–42 (2014)

35. Tambouratzis, T., Souliou, D., Chalikias, M., Gregoriades, A.: Combining probabilistic neural networks and decision trees for maximally accurate and efficient accident prediction. In: The 2010 International Joint Conference on Neural Networks (IJCNN), pp. 1–8. IEEE (2010)

36. Van Mieghem, P., Doerr, C., Wang, H., Hernandez, J.M., Hutchison, D., Karaliopoulos, M., Kooij, R.E.: A framework for computing topological network robustness. Delft University of Technology, report20101218 (2010)

37. Weisstein, E.W.: Contiguous USA Graph. From MathWorld–A Wolfram Web Resource. http://mathworld.wolfram.com/ContiguousUSAGraph.html

38. Xu, J., Chen, H.: The topology of dark networks. Commun. ACM **51**(10), 58–65 (2008)

39. Yang, Z., Algesheimer, R., Tessone, C.J.: A comparative analysis of community detection algorithms on artificial networks. Sci. Rep. **6**, 30750 (2016). doi:10.1038/srep30750

Creativity and Game-Based Learning

Structures, Frameworks and Assessments for Student Exercises for Creative Thinking in Design

David C. Moffat[1] and Olga A. Shabalina[2(✉)]

[1] Glasgow Caledonian University, Glasgow, UK
D.C.Moffat@gcu.ac.uk
[2] Volgograd State Technical University, Volgograd, Russia
O.A.Shabalina@gmail.com

Abstract. Students of engineering and design would benefit from an improved understanding of their own and each others' creativity. We can exercise students by setting challenges, and asking them to evaluate their work, for novelty and quality. This is to help them to develop and become familiar with their own creative processes; but also to appreciate the different styles of creative thinking that others can have, the properties that society generally values in creative design, and how their own work may be appreciated. In order to achieve this in higher education, it is useful to develop frameworks in which student work can be assessed for creativity in particular, and to offer ways in which work can be assigned to students so that they may produce design concepts and then peer-assess them for their mutual benefit.

In this paper we summarise how creativity is evaluated or measured by psychologists and educationalists, as well as more recent proposals by researchers in the new field of computational creativity. We consider how these notions may be applied in the classroom context, to evaluate the creativity of student work. The suggestions are illustrated with our recent assignments to students to produce and assess creative design concepts for serious games. A general framework is proposed, which has been used in two universities for game design students.

Keywords: Creativity · Education · Innovation · Design engineering · Torrance tests for creative thinking · Peer assessment · Creative concepts · Serious games

1 Design Thinking in Industry

In many European countries there is an increasing demand for graduates that are able to think more creatively. In the UK, for example, there was a large survey conducted by the Confederation of British Industry, which was to inquire about the key factors for innovation. The results confirmed a demand for more science and engineering graduates, that should be educated to better understand

© Springer International Publishing AG 2017
A. Kravets et al. (Eds.): CIT&DS 2017, CCIS 754, pp. 711–722, 2017.
DOI: 10.1007/978-3-319-65551-2_51

the nature of the sector, and its need for innovation. They should also be able to identify, develop and adopt new ideas.

We believe that engineering is a creative endeavour, but are aware that it is not usually seen that way by society at large, and is not considered to be one of the "creative industries." However, engineering is more than mere calculation. Engineering becomes seen as more creative when it turns to design; and in that guise at least it demands that education institutions should attempt to foster the creative awareness of its students.

One leading international design house is IDEO [1], which believes that it is possible to develop the creativity of its clients, and works with them to design solutions for them. Their directors highlight the centrality of *divergent thinking* in producing new design ideas. This is a kind of thinking in which ideas are produced that do not lie in the typical lines for the domain problem. It is also related to "lateral thinking" [9]; or in a common idiom: "thinking out of the box." Not only is divergent thinking characteristic of creativity in the popular imagination, but it also forms the basis of the most common tests for human creativity, as we shall see later.

In advice to clients and other designers more generally, Tom Kelley of the IDEO consultancy suggests ways in which people can improve their divergent thinking [14,15]. He recommends keeping a journal by the side of the bed for any ideas that may occur when half asleep, for example. There is also advice more related to emotion management, such as adopting a freer attitude of mind in which there is a playful attitude to the problem, rather than too much focus on outcomes, or the pressing need for a solution. "Gain some mental distance" is one recommendation; and "switch off self-criticism" so that your new ideas have a chance. Such advice is quite typical, and may well be helpful for others wanting to become more confidently creative, to adopt such attitudes if they can; as it surely has been for Kelley himself. It may also be helpful for HE (Higher Education) students in design and other creative disciplines; but we would like to explore the possibility of more structured interventions that could take place in a formal lesson plan, or a coursework assignment in HE.

2   Creative Thinking in a Social Context

In his research into creativity, the psychologist Csikszentmihalyi conducted extensive interviews over several years with creative people of many kinds, from musicians and artists to scientists [8]. He was searching for the essential characteristics of human creativity, and found that it has a core experience, which he named *flow* [7].

This work has become very influential, and is now one of the most important ways to understand the components and conditions of creativity. Components of the flow experience include task characteristics that encourage a creative state of mind; and aspects of the experience relating to attention, such as focus of attention on the task itself, and lack of attention to the surrounding context or the passage of time.

While *flow* is a very important theory in the psychology of creativity, and it does have relevance to education [6] it is also more descriptive of everyday experience. Rather like the helpful adivce of designers like Kelley, then, the *flow* concept in itself has limited direct application to formal teaching contexts. It has been argued that the industrial context can work against the mental states that have been associated with creativity. The educational context could also prevent the state of "flow" [11, 19].

However there is another way in which Csikszentmihalyi's research is helpful to our project. He developed a model in which creativity is viewed as a cultural and social construct, as well as a cognitive process [5]. He argued that there is a field of "gatekeepers" (*teachers*, *peers*, *editors* and *critics*) who decide what is and what is not creative in the context of the domain. In the framework we propose below, the teachers and peers (other students in the class) are the gatekeepers that criticise and judge the creative value of the concepts that the students make. This emulates the outside world in the way that creative products are judged in society.

Cultural systems are described as comprising related domains and social criticism is viewed as necessary to validate creative value. Innovative design benefits from the generation of a high number of creative ideas [3, 10], and the idea generation process can be particularly fruitful within collaborative environments [2, 16].

Csikszentmihalyi draws relationships between the creative, talented person, the work domain with its related professionals, who collaborate to develop the ideas or validate them, and the wider society that may or may not use the end products.

On this basis we argue that a collaborative, knowledge-sharing teaching and learning approach is needed, and the framework we present below will achieve this.

3   Psychological Measures of Creativity

In Higher Education (HE) it is important to assess the advance of students, and in the sphere of creativity this should include some kind of measurement of creativity.

The most influential research in measuring creativity has focused on *divergent thinking*, and led to psychometric tests by Guilford and Torrance [22, 26], now generally called the *Torrance Tests for Creative Thinking* (TTCT).

The tests take the form of short questionnaires, which ask the person to think of as many relevant answers as they can in the short time allowed. There are several types of question. The "unusual uses" question would ask for ways in which an everyday object could be put to use, that are not the normal one. For example, "How many ways can you think of to use a brick?" Answers should be logical in some sense, but are scored by counting up how many alternatives are given. A brick could be used to hold a door open, for example; or to stop a stationary car from rolling down a hill; or to keep the corners of a picnic rug in place on a windy day; and so on. The only legitimate use that would not be counted would be to use the brick to build a wall, because that is the usual purpose.

Another type of question is the "consequences task," in which an impossible situation is described and the person is asked to list as many consequences as possible. For example, if animals could talk, there might be more pet shops, and vegetarians; fewer abattoires; earthquake and avalanche victims could be found much quicker by dogs and mice; and so on.

The answers are scored by enumerating the valid alternatives, which lessens the need for subjective judgement, and makes the TTCTs more reliable measures of divergent thinking. The scores may be for different forms of creative thinking, including *fluency*, *flexibility* and *originality*. These are respectively to capture a person's mental capcities to think of many relevant possibilities, to think of possibilities of different categories; and to be original compared to the rest of the population.

These are good ways to assess a person's capacity for creative thinking. They could be used in an educational setting, for example to help teachers to guide students to appropriate careers for them. As a regular part of the curriculum, however, they leave something to be desired. For one thing, they bring out a view of creativity as a personal characteristic that is relatively permanent, like intelligence. Again like intelligence scores, administered with an IQ test, there are sensitive issues associated with a simplistic categorisation of students into more or less creative or intelligent types. The purpose of education is not merely to categorise people, but to help them to become the best they can be, given the range of talents they have.

Rather than focus on the student as a more or less talented person, therefore, we focus on the products they make with the aptitude, skills and knowledge they have so far learned. Instead of testing the individual for creative capacity, we should assess the work produced for its creative content.

4   Assessing Creativity of Ideas and Artefacts

People make products in some context, generally, and by following some procedure. Creative thinking comes to fruition in the artefact that is made, and so there is creativity in the product, as well as the person and process [13,24]. An artefact does not itself think creatively, but it does embody ideas that were thought up by people. If we can assess the creative value of artefacts (and ideas) then the students and other people who produced them may benefit from the feedback, and learn to think more creatively.

In order to assess creativity in products and ideas, a definition is first needed. Two criteria are most commonly given, which we refer to as *novelty* and *value* [4,25]. It is obvious that novelty is essential to creative ideas; and is the basis of the TTCT measures for a person's capacity for divergent thinking (see above). In those, the particular measures of *fluency*, *flexibility* and *originality* can be seen as variants of *novelty*. The last of these refers to the ideas of other people and society, and thus involves some small degree of expertise to judge it.

What is *valuable* in an idea depends on the domain, and depends significantly on expert judgement in that domain. For example, what is valuable in music is that it should be enjoyable and pleasant to listen to. What is valued in the architecture of a house is that it is a good place to live in, healthy and convenient for people, sturdy and durable, safe and not expensive to build. In science we value theories and knowledge that can explain the world effectively without making too many assumptions. Generally we find that artistic products are pleasing; while engineering products are more useful.

While originality and value are common criteria of creativity, some researchers propose additional criteria. Boden also includes a third criterion, for example, which is *surprise* [4], meaning that the idea should not be obvious to us. We might also suggest other possibilities, such as *elegance*, referring to how well the ideas in an artefact are put together. This is an aesthetic quality that would apply to engineering or design. In addition to the usefulness of the artefact, it may be aesthetically pleasing in itself; but more interestingly it can be elegant in its conception, which would be a more cognitive/affective aspect of appreciation.

Education could thus benefit from the assessment of students' creations; but there is a similar focus on the artefact in the new field within AI (Artificial Intelligence) of "computational creativity," to which we turn next.

5   Evaluation in Computational Creativity

Within AI (Artificial Intelligence) there has recently arisen a strong interest in the use of software to generate outputs that would normally be considered creative, if people produced them. The field includes the computer generation of the visual arts, and the other arts, including music [27]. It includes the automatic generation of virtual worlds for 3D games, known in video game technology as "procedural content generation." Software is also used to create stories, and even poetry [17]. Much of this work can be seen at the international conference series on computational creativity (ICCC, see http://computationalcreativity.net/).

We intend that our framework, for exercising and assessing student creativity in HE (Higher Education), should align with suitable frameworks for evaluating creativity in CC (computational creativity), as far as is appropriate. This is because in both cases there is an emphasis on assessing the creativity of products; and because we expect that computers will be used to augment human creativity and not only to replace it. In that eventuality we shall need a single unified framework that can assess the creativity of artefacts made by machines, by people, or by both working together. Another reason we suggest this unifying approach is because creative assessments have a similar role in both cases. In HE we wish to assess the creativity of student work to help them to improve (with so-called "formative feedback"), as well as to certify how skillful they are (by "summative feedback"). In CC there are the same purposes, but to improve software (by incrementally re-programming it) instead of people; and even the same terms have been imported from education into CC [12].

Boden has been influential in this field of CC (computational creativity) [4], especially in setting up the conceptual frameworks, including the important criteria that define creativity, as above. More recently, Ritchie has extended analysis of those concepts to help set out some elements of methodology that he proposes for the field of CC. We follow principally Boden's and Ritchie's (forthcoming) analyses here [4, 23].

One distinction is between "loose" and "strict" notions of creativity. The way that society generally refers to the "creative industries" is a loose notion, because the artefacts there produced are said to be creative merely because of who made them (e.g. music, film, and the dramatic arts). They may also be creative in a strict sense, meaning that they are genuinely novel and valuable artefacts; but strict creativity flourishes in other industries as well, including science and engineering, where it might not be so quickly recognised by society at large. In our domain of education in general, we are interested in the *strict* notion of creativity.

Another distinction is between "creativity" and "Creativity", or little-c and big-C notions of creativity. This refers to the significance of the idea or artefact. Many new ideas can be quite useful in an everyday context; such as trying a new recipe, for example; or finding a new route to commute to work everyday. Those ideas are little-c creative; but we reserve big-C "Creativity" to refer to the best or greatest ideas and artefacts (and people). The *Mona Lisa* is a Creative work, for example; and Leonardo was a big-C Creative person.

In our case of education, we wish to encourage students to try to produce works that are creative with a bigger C. The ambitions that researchers in CC have for their software are obviously similar: to make systems that are capable of better, more creative products.

Another distinction Ritchie makes is between "internal" and "external" evaluation. An obvious need that CC has is to make software that can evaluate its own products, while they are being produced; Only when they are good enough, should it announce them to the world as outputs. Then "external" evaluation is how we may assess the creative value of the outputs. This is important because in the end it is always experts, and then society at large, who judge the creative value of an artefact. A focus of the field of CC is just how this kind of external evaluation may be done. It is crucially important for CC because ordinary people will usually be skeptical about claims that a piece of software is actually creative in any real sense.

How should this external evaluation proceed? As before, Ritchie follows Boden in proposing the key criteria of *novelty*, *value*, and *surprise*. At least the first two of these are universal in all research on creativity. The aspect of *novelty* can be qualified. An idea might be novel to the person who thought of it, and for whom it is therefore "P-novel" (P for personally). A more creative idea could be new to a larger group of people, or even to all people in history, and is then "H-novel" (H for historically). In general an idea can only be creative if it is at least P-novel. Novelty is fairly clear to understand and evaluate.

The question of *value* or quality is less clear. It is now recognised within CC that this criterion is essential to creative evaluation; but is also in need of closer examination in order to clarify it. We cannot easily state what value is, because for one reason it is often quite subjective; and for another reason it is dependent on the domain or culture that it is part of. Because of this criterion of *value*, in particular, we have to accept that there is a social character to the assessment of creativity. In the sphere of education, and HE especially, this means that we should teach our students not only to become more creative themselves; but also to assess their own and each others' creativity; and to understand how society in the end will judge their own work.

In the following framework, we aim to support students in their development of "strict" Creativity (with a "big-C"). They should generate ideas that are novel to them personally, "P-novel"; and possibly to the other students in their class. It would generally be unreasonable to expect their ideas to be H-novel though, if they are also to be somewhat valuable. Finally the students will also be encouraged to evaluate each other's work, as peers in the same small creative community.

6   A Framework for Creative Thinking Exercises in HE

As an example of a creative domain, we take the case of a class of students of serious game design. They are learning how to make better "serious games" which are video games or board games that are not only entertaining, but also have a serious purpose, such as education or health awareness.

The framework, or conceptual apparatus we propose, takes creative thinking to be productive of new, valuable ideas and artefacts. In creative exercises students can be asked to think creatively with particular attention. To focus time and energy on the creative thinking itself, in the chosen domain, we suggest that it is most efficient to produce design concepts, and not to go forward to make them as well. Although it does involve creativity to make a video game, much of the effort is directed towards technicalities and not at the creative pursuit itself. Therefore we propose to set a larger number of smaller challenges: to create game concepts only, and not to make a single, full game. Each challenge is specified by a "client brief" which is a description of what sort of artefact is wanted, by the real or pretend client; and what problem they have that it should solve for them. A "creative concept" is a short document of text and possibly pictures, to describe what the intended serious game (or other artefact) would be like, and why it would be a good solution to the client's need.

Each creative concept can be done fairly quickly, because it only needs the ideas to be generated and worked into an appropriate solution. To do that, and then write it out in a couple of pages, can be achieved in a half hour quite comfortably. The task can be set individually, or groups of students can work together on the concepts. Students will then get more insight into their own creative processes; or into their classmates', and the way in which groups can work together to produce new design ideas.

The task can be done on paper, or quite easily on computers. It can be done in class-time; or at home in the student's own time. These variations allow the exercises to fit into the curriculum quite flexibly.

Table 1. Framework stages and effects on student learning

Teacher does	Students do	Students learn
Assign client brief (what concept is to do)	Creative Concepts (CCs) (half-hour, two pages each)	How they respond to challenge to "be creative" in a short time and without any resources
Assess the CCs (for novelty, value, surprise)	[If returned to them] Read their feedback	[If returned] How creative their concepts were thought to be, in those criteria
Anonymise the CCs and group into sets. Assign each set to a group of students	Evaluate the CCs in their set	The standards and range of work by their fellow students. Also how their own compares.
Anonymise the peer evaluations. Assess them for accuracy and consistency	[If returned to them] Read their feedback from other students. Also from teacher on accuracy.	[If returned] How creative they were, compared to others in the class. Also how well they understand what creativity means in field.

Assessment of the concepts then takes place, in which the key criteria of *novelty, value* and possibly *surprise* are applied. This would initially be done by the teacher of the class; but it can profitably be done by the students themselves. Students can assess each other's concepts, if they are anonymised first by the teacher. This helps the students to understand and appreciate the range of creative ideas that were possible, in response to the client's brief. Students may come to value group work more when they see that others are as capable of generating exciting ideas; but they may also acquire more self-confidence when they see how their own work measures up to that of their peers.

The framework is summarised by steps in Table 1. In a final step, students can have their own concepts returned to them, with the assessments from the teacher and/or peers. From this they can see how their own work was appreciated by others, and reflect on how they achieved that. With a wider discussion about what went well or not, and further iterations of the exercises, it may be that students could learn to improve their strategies for creative and design thinking. That remains a question for future research, however.

The two criteria of *novelty* and *value* have been mentioned as standard in the literature for creativity. In order to evaluate novelty, a suitable scale for the small society that is relevant would be the class itself. An idea could be counted new if nobody else in the class had it. This scale is intermediate between "P-novelty" and "H-novelty" — but is quite appropriate for the education context.

In order to evaluate the *value* of the concepts, there will inevitably be more discussion. While students may disagree about the value of a concept, and that can make their peer assessments seem unfair or wrong, it is still a worthwhile discussion to have. It exposes the subjective element that is essential to creativity anyway, so that students may become accustomed to it, and be able to tolerate the judgements of others even when they seem to be unfair or uncomprehending. More usefully, discussion of the value of an artefact must go directly to the deepest aims of the chosen domain. In a sense, that is what the education curriculum is all about. In the domain of serious game design, for example, students will reflect on what makes a serious game a good one. They will need to discuss whether a particular game concept adequately describes the intended artefact, whether that would be an enjoyable game, and whether a player would get the intended serious benefit from it. Being able to answer these questions goes to the heart of the subject of serious game design; and so the discussion both tests and further develops this crucial expertise in the students.

In other domains, the same framework should apply in the same way. Only the content of the client briefs and the concepts would be different. The structure of the exercises would not need to change, for other design and engineering domains. The domain-specific details typically stay encapsulated in the general criteria of novelty and value. The framework is thus perfectly general.

7   Initial Trials of the Framework

The above framework was used as a basis for student exercises in classes for serious game design, at two universities, in the UK and Russia. The students were able to produce several creative concepts in a fairly short time, and to evaluate each other's work afterwards. This allowed them to experience the pressure of needing to produce new ideas that would be seen and judged by their peers. They would then evaluate the concepts of other students, without knowing whose they were.

Those initial trials were reported in previous publications [20,21], which give more details. To summarise, the framework was found to help students to produce a fairly significant number of creative concepts in only a single module of work (representing in itself about one sixth of the work for an entire academic year). In addition they managed to evaluate the creativity of other students' concepts reasonably well, although with some inconsistencies that were difficult to explain, and are the subject of further study. Their experience appeared to be a positive one, according to their final reflections on the exercises at the end of the module. Some of them valued the opportunities to work with and observe their fellow students in their thought processes as they attempted to produce new valuable work. It seemed that had a beneficial effect on their own self-knowledge as well as appreciation for the unique skills of their friends and colleagues that could serve them well in professional life later on.

8   Conclusion

The need for creative thinking in industry these days demands that we should aim to develop it in our students if we can. While it is often said that you cannot teach creativity, most would agree that you can *exercise* it, at least in a given domain; and that it will become strengthened as a result.

We have surveyed the notion of creativity, and ways in which it is measured by psychologists. Those were not quite appropriate for our education needs, and so we turned to evaluate the creativity in artefacts made or designed by students. The framework we drew up to enable this was drawn from the general literature on creativity; but more particularly from the new field of CC (computational creativity), as it shares many of the same goals already, and we predict this overlap to strengthen in future.

The proposed framework allows students to quickly and efficiently produce many creative concepts in a class, and to focus on the creativity of their thought processes. It allows them to see and assess the work of other students and to receive feedback from them in return. The innovation here is that the framework is to explicitly support the development and training of student creative skills, from production and collaboration to evaluation of ideas. This can be applied to engineering education, but also potentially to creative skills in other fields, as the framework was designed to be generic.

With a focus on the two chief criteria of *novelty* and *value*, the students can evaluate concepts for different aspects of creativity. The criteria will help to guide them, but still allow freedom within them to fit their judgements to the relevant domain. Students without guidance will not know how to answer a question like "is this concept creative?" On the other hand, a framework that is fitted too closely to some particular domain will be both detailed and unwieldy, and not applicable to other domains. The framework proposed here is structured enough to give students some guidance in their peer assessments; but also general enough to be relevant to any design or engineering domains.

In future work it would be interesting to see how well students manage with the limited guidance given them in the framework, as well as how they experience the exercises, the peer assessment and the feedback from other students. Most important would be the question of the method's success: do students indeed improve their capacity for and/or confidence in their own creative thinking?

In related work we have also found that students can perform at a higher creative level in some ways, after playing some kinds of video game for a short time [18]. That work also asks for further research, as it yielded some interesting and encouraging results, but not uniformly. Creativity was found to improve, reliably; but only in some limited measures. It remains to be seen whether the psychological effects are robust or broad enough to support truly creative work.

Taken together, these studies imply that there is good scope to develop creative skills in students, in production and assessment of novel and valuable ideas in their chosen field. There may also be scope to temporarily increase their creative capacity in the classroom, and so enable them to produce better quality work. These implications are tentative at this stage however, and they ask for further research to be done to establish and refine them.

Acknowledgements. The work was partially supported by RFBR, research project No. 16-07-00611

References

1. IDEO. http://www.ideo.com/. Accesed 21 Apr 2017
2. Alves, J., Marques, M.J., Saur, I., Marques, P.: Creativity and innovation through multidisciplinary and multisectoral cooperation. Creativity Innov. Manag. **16**(1), 27–34 (2007)
3. Amabile, T.: The Social Psychology of Creativity. Springer, Heidelberg (2012). doi:10.1007/978-1-4612-5533-8
4. Boden, M.A.: Creativity. Artificial Intelligence, pp. 267–291. Elsevier (1996). http://dx.doi.org/10.1016/b978-012161964-0/50011-x
5. Csikszentmihalyi, M.: A systems perspective on creativity. Creative Manag. **11** (2001)
6. Csikszentmihalyi, M., Wolfe, R.: New conceptions and research approaches to creativity: implications of a systems perspective for creativity in education. The Systems Model of Creativity, pp. 161–184. Springer, Dordrecht (2014). doi:10.1007/978-94-017-9085-7_10
7. Csikszentmihalyi, M.: Flow: The Psychology of Optimal Experience. HarperCollins, New York City (1990)
8. Csikszentmihalyi, M.: Creativity: Flow and The Psychology of Discovery and Invention. HarperCollins, New York City (1996)
9. De Bono, E.: Serious Creativity: Using the Power of Lateral Thinking to Create New Ideas. HarperColins, New York (1992)
10. Dym, C.L.: Engineering Design: A Synthesis of Views. Cambridge University Press, Cambridge (1994)
11. Gray, E., Moffat, D.C.: Fostering creativity for the changing demands of innovative industry. In: Kravets, A., Shcherbakov, M., Kultsova, M., Shabalina, O. (eds.) Creativity in Intelligent Technologies and Data Science. Communications in Computer and Information Science, vol. 535. Springer, Cham (2015). doi:10.1007/978-3-319-23766-4_1
12. Jordanous, A.: A standardised procedure for evaluating creative systems: computational creativity evaluation based on what it is to be creative. Cogn. Comput. **4**(3), 246–279 (2012). http://dx.doi.org/10.1007/s12559-012-9156-1
13. Jordanous, A.: Four perspectives on computational creativity in theory and in practice. Connection Sci. **28**(2), 194–216 (2016). http://dx.doi.org/10.1080/09540091.2016.1151860
14. Kelley, T.: Tom Kelley on Creativity. http://www.youtube.com/watch?v=xQmQnSpH47g. Accessed 21 Apr 2017
15. Kelley, T.: The Art of Innovation: Lessons in Creativity from IDEO, America's Leading Design Firm. Doubleday, New York (2001)
16. Kratzer, J., Lettl, C.: A social network perspective of lead users and creativity: an empirical study among children. Creativity Innov. Manag. **17**(1), 26–36 (2008)
17. Méndez, G., Gervás, P., León, C.: On the use of character affinities for story plot generation. In: Kunifuji, S., Papadopoulos, G.A., Skulimowski, A.M.J., Kacprzyk, J. (eds.) Knowledge, Information and Creativity Support Systems. AISC, vol. 416, pp. 211–225. Springer, Cham (2016). doi:10.1007/978-3-319-27478-2_15
18. Moffat, D.C., Crombie, W., Shabalina, O.: Some video games can increase the player's creativity. Int. J. Game-Based Learn. **7**(2), 35–46 (2017). http://dx.doi.org/10.4018/ijgbl.2017040103

19. Moffat, D.C., Gray, E.: The need for creative skills in design engineering, and how education can develop them. In: 2015 6th International Conference on Information, Intelligence, Systems and Applications (IISA), pp. 1–5, July 2015. http:// ieeexplore.ieee.org/xpl/articleDetails.jsp?reload=true&arnumber=7387985

20. Moffat, D.C., Shabalina, O.: Assessing creativity of game design students. In: 7th International Conference on Information, Intelligence, Systems & Applications (IISA) (2016). http://dx.doi.org/10.1109/iisa.2016.7785337

21. Moffat, D.C., Shabalina, O.: Student creativity exercises in designing serious games. In: European Conference on Games Based Learning, pp. 470–478. Academic Conferences International Limited (2016)

22. Phillips, V.K., Torrance, E.P.: Levels of originality at earlier and later stages of creativity test tasks. J. Creative Behav. **11**(2), 147 (1977). http://dx.doi.org/10.1002/j.2162-6057.1977.tb00602.x

23. Ritchie, G.: The evaluation of creative systems. In: Veale, T., Cardoso, F.A. (eds.) Computational Creativity: The Philosophy and Engineering of Autonomously Creative Systems. Computational Synthesis and Creative Systems. Springer International Publishing, Heidelberg (2017)

24. Simonton, D.K.: Scientific creativity as constrained stochastic behavior: the integration of product, person, and process perspectives. Psychol. Bull. **129**(4), 475–494 (2003). http://dx.doi.org/10.1037/0033-2909.129.4.475

25. Simonton, D.K.: Taking the US patent office criteria seriously: a quantitative three-criterion creativity definition and its implications. Creativity Res. J. **24**(2–3), 97–106 (2012). http://dx.doi.org/10.1080/10400419.2012.676974

26. Torrance, E.P.: Scientific views of creativity and factors affecting its growth. Daedalus, pp. 663–681 (1965)

27. Wiggins, G.A., Pearce, M.T., Müllensiefen, D.: Computational modeling of music cognition and musical creativity, Oxford Handbooks Online. Oxford University Press (2011). http://dx.doi.org/10.1093/oxfordhb/9780199792030.013.0019

Focused Visualization in Interactive Applications for Surgery Training

Anton Ivaschenko[1(✉)], Nickolay Gorbachenko[1],
and Alexandr Kolsanov[2]

[1] Samara National Research University,
Moskovskoye Shosse 34, Samara, Russia
anton.ivashenko@gmail.com
[2] Samara State Medical University, Chapayevskaya, 89, Samara, Russia

Abstract. The paper introduces basic principles of focused visualization for adaptive data presentation in interactive software solutions according to the user's activity in real time. It is proposed to study the challenge of targeting the 4P goals (performance, persistence, perception, and personalization) in interactive applications. This problem traditionally requires much creativity of software developers that need to balance visualization quality and computational complexity. In order to meet these goals, the system should capture and analyze the user's actions, compare it with typical scenarios captured in a knowledge base and generate user's attention attractors in order to provide the focused visualization. There is presented a formal ontological model and technology of visual scene complexity management based on levels of detail (LOD) coordination. Implementation is illustrated by anatomy training and surgery simulation applications: "Inbody Anatomy" anatomic atlas and laparoscopy training suite that require simulating complex 3D scenes and sustainable simulating scenarios.

Keywords: Simulation · Virtual reality · Ontology · Surgery training

1 Introduction

Interactive visualization is strongly required in various software solutions that provide decision-making support. The areas of its useful application include medical diagnostics and simulation, industrial enterprises and transportation logistics management, situational scheduling of resources, geo-monitoring, project planning, and others. One of the most challenging areas of its application is surgery training that needs to provide maximum educational efficiency using 3D simulators. Considering the volumes and complexity of anatomy simulation, which is Big Data according to key features, there should be developed a special solution that provides pre-processing, adaptation and demonstrative visualization.

Interactive applications should be user-friendly. This means not only an attractive and convenient UI but also an ability to correspond to the changing user's needs caused by external events and provide game based learning. In this regard, modern interactive applications should be able to adapt their logic for each user individually targeting his or her attention to the content being the most important at the moment. Interactive IT

© Springer International Publishing AG 2017
A. Kravets et al. (Eds.): CIT&DS 2017, CCIS 754, pp. 723–734, 2017.
DOI: 10.1007/978-3-319-65551-2_52

devices, including VR and AR goggles, tablets and panels allow tracking the user's activity, which can be used to understand the user's behaviour aspects and patterns and adapt the interactive application logic of data presentation. In this paper there proposed such a solution based on focused visualization of data for decision-making support.

2   State of the Art

Major modern trends of data visualization are explored in [1, 2]. These papers deal with medical data presentation, still, the conclusions can be extrapolated over the other problem domains that require clear visualization of complex systems. Particularly one of the main goals of data presentation is to combine several data sets to analyze multiple layers of a complex system at once. The system should interlink all related data sets (e.g., images, text, measured values, scans) and offer visual analytics to support experts. This approach supports the idea of maximum effective visualization of complex data for professionals instead of automatic decision-making.

This concept gains a foothold and is taken further in [3]. In this paper, there is presented the "human-in-the-loop" approach, according to which the humans (decision makers) are not only involved in pre-processing, by selecting data or features but actually during the learning phase, directly interacting with the algorithm. The main reason is that in case the set of parameters needed for decision-making is big in size and vary in type, it becomes problematic to present them in a single picture. Therefore it is proposed to involve the decision maker into the process of data processing and visualization by means of continuous interacting with the system, which helps to optimize the learning behavior of both humans and algorithms.

The idea of deep involvement of actors or subjects in business processes organization and management are studied in S-BPM concept [4], which conceives a process as a collaboration of multiple subjects organized via structured communication. Some approaches to implementation of interactive user interfaces are given in [5]. Special aspects of the implementation of information technologies in adaptive education and game dynamics are addressed in [6, 7].

Consequently, medical data should be considered as Big Data [8]. Addressing the multiple-V problem of Big Data analysis and visualization there can be formulated a 4P goals problem of interactive visualization:

- Performance: 3D picture should be processed and visualized in real time using preferably personal or mobile hardware;
- Persistence: separate parts of one picture should correspond to each other with minimum conflicts, caused by data variance, but not data format difference;
- Perception: the picture should be understandable and explicitly interpretable by the user;
- Personalization: the picture should adapt to personal particular aspects of behavior in terms of cognition, knowledge, and skills.

Multi-agent technologies [9] that implement interaction of software and human actors with autonomous behavior using ontology as a knowledge base [10] provide developing the intelligent solutions that meet the specified requirements. The virtual world of the 3D scene can be modeled and built as a complex network of continuously running and co-evolving intelligent agents.

Our experience of interactive applications development with major attention given to adaptive visualization is given in [11–13]. There should be also mentioned a 3D web-based anatomical visualization tool using virtual reality (VR) technology [14].

Focused visualization deals with adaptation. Within this context, the term "adaptation" describes the possibility of scenarios to consider random factor and users' progress and evaluate accordingly. This allows introducing computational complexity optimization. At the early beginning of simulation not all the models with maximum detail are loaded, but only those that are contextually required. Later with user's intervention progress, the detailed models are uploaded instead of simple substitutes, which allow simulating more complicated surgery.

This logic is described by "Level of detail (LOD)" term, which comes from computer graphics [15, 16] and game development and describes the process of decreasing the complexity of 3D models representation as it moves away from the viewer or according to other metrics such as object importance, viewpoint-relative speed or position.

3 The Model of Surgery Simulation Scenes

The proposed solution is based on users' behavior analysis in the context of an expected scenario that defines a sequence of possible user's behavior. For example, surgery intervention scenario includes a sequence of actions that should be performed by a surgeon over the simulated human body parts. This sequence is standard in general but can differ in details depending on the surgery case, patient state, and doctor's qualification. Simulation software should consider these factors in order to increase the educational effect.

Let us propose a formal model for these cases. The scene, in general, contains a number of real and virtual objects combined into a semantic network, which forms a knowledge base (ontology). This can be implemented using the Augmented Reality goggles or interactive display that depicts a certain situation. The data that is presented to the user is reviewed and analyzed according to the expected scenario and result in some decision. The system needs to identify possible gaps in viewer's perception when no required attention is given to certain scene objects at necessary times.

To be able to evaluate the quality of decision-making, the software must have the information about the expected actions order and parameters. To reach this goal the scenario must be described using the machine-readable language, so the specialized knowledge base must be created. The knowledge base must contain the information about the simulated objects themselves (behavior aspects of surgery instruments, aircraft, valves etc.) and the possible interaction aspects between the user and the modeled objects.

Let us call the particular set of objects and conditions used in the scenario the case. Every case is created on the base of a scene denoted by z_k where k is the identifier of the scene. The scene contains objects that we will denote as

$$b_{k,m}, \text{ with } m = 1..N_b(z_k). \tag{1}$$

Every scene object has its visual representation and a set of attributes which we will denote by

$$a_{k,m,n}, \text{ with } n = 1..N_a(b_{k,m}). \tag{2}$$

Attributes transformation in time is formalized as:

$$\psi_{k,m}(\Delta t) = \psi(\{\{a_{k,m,n}\}, \Delta t\} \rightarrow \{a'_{k,m,n}\}). \tag{3}$$

Now we can define the scene as a set of objects and their attributes:

$$z_k = \{\{b_{k,m}\}, \{a_{k,m,n}\}, \{\psi_{k,m}\}\}. \tag{4}$$

Depending on the boundary values of objects attributes, the scene may be in one of the states. We consider the elementary states denoted by $h^0_{k,m,w}, w = 1..N_{h^0}(b_{k,m})$ which describe the single object's behavior aspect and the composite states denoted by $h_{k,m,w}, w = 1..N_h(b_{k,m})$, which describe many aspects of object's behavior and are composed of the elementary ones. The superposition of all objects states on the scene is called the scene state $s_{k,j}$.

The scene can change its current state during the simulation process. The transitions between the scene states will be denoted by:

$$v_{k,j_1,j_2} = v\left(\begin{array}{c} s_{k,j_1} \rightarrow s_{k,j_2}, \\ \{a_{k,m,n}\} \rightarrow \{a'_{k,m,n}\} \end{array} \right), \tag{5}$$

where $\{a'_{k,m,n}\}$ are the new values of scene objects' attributes.

The transition between the scene states occurs as a reaction to user actions or as a reaction to some internal event (e.g. blood loss during the surgery simulation reached its critical value). The same scene state transitions may be triggered by different user actions.

Let us denote the educational case scenario by p_x. Each scenario contains the set of events. The occurrence of the event may change the current state of the scene. Let us define the event as follows:

$$e_{x,i} = e(z_k, v_{k,j_1,j_2}, g_{x,i}, \tau_{x,i}, t_{x,i}) = \{0, 1\}, \tag{6}$$

where $g_{x,i}$ is an event type, $\tau_{x,i} = \left[t^{start}_{x,i}, t^{fin}_{x,i} \right)$ is the time interval during which the event occurrence is expected, $t_{x,i}$ is the exact event occurrence time defined during the simulation process. There are events of two types: external ($g_{x,i} = 1$) and system ($g_{x,i} = 0$) events.

External events are generated when the user performs some actions. System events are generated by the simulator software to represent the reaction on performed actions or to make the user perform the particular actions.

The simulation is finished when the scene comes to a terminal state. To distinguish the terminal states from the ordinary ones we introduce the terminality attribute:

$$\gamma_{k,j} = \begin{cases} 1, & s_{k,j} \text{ is terminal}; \\ 0, & else. \end{cases}$$

This attribute allows us to determine if the simulation must be finished or the scene is in the infeasible state from which there are no transitions defined.

Now we can define the scenario as follows:

$$p_x = \{z_k, \{s_{k,j}\}, \{\gamma_{k,j}\}, \{v_{k,j_1,j_2}\}, \{e_{x,i}\}\}, \tag{7}$$

where $s_{k,j}$ is the state of the scene that contains the objects z_k with transitions between the scene states v_{k,j_1,j_2} caused by the events $e_{x,i}$, $\gamma_{k,j}$ is the terminality attribute of the state.

It should be considered that the single scene may have multiple scenarios defined involving its objects. Let us now define the operations on scenes and scenarios using the terms described above. We can define the union of the scenes as follows:

$$z_{k_1} + z_{k_2} = z_{k_3} \left(\begin{array}{c} \{b_{k_1,m_1}\} \cup \{b_{k_2,m_2}\}, \\ \{a_{k_1,m_1,n_1}\} \cup \{a_{k_2,m_2,n_2}\} \\ \{\psi_{k_1,m_1}\} \cup \{\psi_{k_2,m_2}\} \end{array} \right) \tag{8}$$

The resulting scene z_{k_3} consists of all objects of scenes z_{k_1} and z_{k_2}, so it also contains all attributes of these objects and all their own behaviors.

Let us define the union operation for the scenarios. There can be different scenarios defined and these scenarios may share some objects. But these objects can have different logical states in different contexts. So after the union of two scenarios the logical states of objects presented in both of them are combined into a Cartesian product of all their presented logical states.

Considering the concept of elementary and the composite states we may define the states union operation as follows:

$$(h_{k,m,j_1}, h_{k,m,j_2}) \rightarrow h'_{k,m,j_3}, \tag{9}$$

$$h'_{k,m,j_3} = \left\{h^0_{k,m,j_1}\right\} \cup \left\{h^0_{k,m,j_2}\right\},$$

where h_{k,m,j_1} and h_{k,m,j_2}- the states of an object in first and second scenarios, $\{h^0_{k,m,j_1}\}$ and $\{h^0_{k,m,j_2}\}$ – corresponding elementary states sets, h'_{k,m,j_3} – the object state in the resulting scenario.

The scene states after the union of scenarios are defined as:

$$s'_{k,i} = \{h'_{k,m,j}\}. \tag{10}$$

The transitions between resulting scene states are defined as follows:

$$v_{k,j_1,j_2} \rightarrow \{v'_{k,l,m}\}, \tag{11}$$

$$v'_{k,l,m} = v\left(\begin{array}{c} s'_{k,l} \rightarrow s'_{k,m} \\ \{a_{k,m,n}\} \rightarrow \{a'_{k,m,n}\} \end{array} \right).$$

where $s'_{k,l}$, $s'_{k,m}$ – scene states in the resulting scene, v_{k,j_1,j_2} – transition in the initial scenario, $v'_{k,l,m}$ – transition in the resulting scenario.

The terminality feature of resulting states is determined according to the rule:

$$\gamma'_{k,j_3} = \gamma_{k,j_1} \vee \gamma_{k,j_2}, \tag{12}$$

where γ_{k,j_1} and γ_{k,j_2} – terminality features of states s_{k,j_1} and s_{k,j_2} in the initial scenarios. If any of the initial states was terminal, the resulting state will also be terminal.

Events' set is transformed in the following way:

$$\{e_{x_1,i}\}, \{e_{x_2,j}\} \rightarrow \{e_{x_3,j}\}, \tag{13}$$

$e_{x_3,i} = e\left(z_k, v'_{k,j_1,j_2}, g_{x_3,i}, \tau_{x_3,i}, t_{x_3,i} \right);$

$\tau_{x_3,i} = \tau_{x_1,i}$, if $e_{x_3,i}$ is produced from $e_{x_1,i}$,

$\tau_{x_3,i} = \tau_{x_2,i}$, else wise;

$g_{x_3,i} = g_{x_1,i}$, if $e_{x_3,i}$ is produced from $e_{x_1,i}$;

$g_{x_3,i} = g_{x_2,i}$, else wise.

Now we can denote the scenarios union operation as

$$p_{x_1} + p_{x_2} = p_{x_3} \tag{14}$$

The proposed model is used to describe the basic scenarios and to produce a more complex description of user's behavior. The mentioned scenarios and events were implemented in corresponding classed and the logic of their processing provides the required functionality of game-based simulation learning.

More details of software architecture are provided below.

4 Solution Vision

Practical implementation of interactive applications for surgery simulation is concerned with a number of problems caused by performance, visibility and layout, informational value and conciseness issues. The information is presented for the decision maker should be useful and clear at a certain moment of time, which makes the process of guide data processing a complex technical problem.

The proposed solution is based on users' behavior analysis according to the introduced scenario-based model. Embedded software with intelligent decision-making support captures the user's behavior in the form of event chains and compares them with typical scenarios of maintenance and repair. The analysis is produced at a time frame of the standardized procedure using cross-correlation functions. Such analysis allows identification possible gaps in viewer's perception when no required attention is given to certain scene objects at necessary times. This knowledge is captured in the form of rules in knowledge base linked to specified types of scene objects and steps of maintenance scenarios. As a result, the scenarios are supplied by virtual entities (textual items, marks or highlights) that attract user's attention to the required scene objects when needed.

The proposed approach is illustrated by Fig. 1. There are presented two modules that process knowledge base on user's actions and maintenance scenarios in the form of Ontology, and a couple of modules for decision-making support that produces user's actions analysis and focus attraction. User behavior can also be identified by capturing the head and eyes move in case the headset or goggles spectacles are used as AR devices.

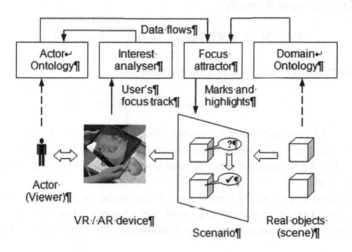

Fig. 1. Focused visualization solution vision.

The results of the proposed approach testing and practical use prove the necessity to study and manage the ways of limited but yet effective data representation using AR. The main benefit of accented visualization is the personification of AR, which allows minimization of the additional information added to the scene view.

In general, to model, the user's behavior extended by virtual entities realistically the function $\Psi_{k,m}(\Delta t)$ includes the complex transformations requiring much computation power. To improve the computational efficiency several different 3d-models may be used instead of a single universal one (considering all real behavior aspects). These models differ in terms of the level of detail (LOD) and can be adaptively selected based on the current scene state and events set. We propose an extension that allows us to implement such behavior.

The scene object will be denoted as $b_{k,m}, m = 1..N_b(z_k)$. Each object can have one or several levels of detail denoted as ξ. The attributes set will now be associated with the particular LOD instead of the body in common. The attributes set associated with the particular LOD will be denoted as:

$$a_{k,m,\xi,n_\xi}, \xi = 1..N_\xi(b_{k,m}), n_\xi = 1..N_a(b_{k,m}, \xi). \tag{15}$$

Current LOD ξ can be changed to the new LOD ξ' in the result of emitting events on the scene. This results in attributes set changes. The attributes that belong to the both levels of detail are left unchanged. The attributes associated only with the new level of detail are calculated based on the values of the old level of detail attributes set. In common, the transformations set is defined for every object:

$$\varphi_{k,m}(\xi, \xi') = \varphi(\{a_{k,m,\xi,n_\xi} \rightarrow a_{k,m,\xi',n_{\xi'}}\}). \tag{16}$$

These transformations map the attributes values of ξ to the attributes values of ξ' after changing the current LOD.

Considering ξ we will specify:

$$\Psi_{k,m}(\Delta t, \xi) = \Psi(\{\{a_{k,m,\xi,n_\xi}\}, \Delta t\} \rightarrow \{a'_{k,m,\xi,n_\xi}\}) \tag{17}$$

The expression for the scene will be rewritten as:

$$z_k = \{\{b_{k,m}\}, \{a_{k,m,\xi,n_\xi}\}, \{\Psi_{k,m}\}, \{\varphi_{k,m}\}\}. \tag{18}$$

The proposed extension allows describing the object's behavior with several levels of detail in a generic way. It also allows describing the "seamless" transitions between the different LOD's because it defines the transformations between the attributes values on different levels.

We also need to extend the logical part of our model since the interactions of the objects are described using scenarios. Considering changes introduced to the scene we extend the transition between scene states introducing the transition between the level of details:

$$v_{k,j_1 j_2} = v \begin{pmatrix} s_{k,j_1} \rightarrow s_{k,j_2} \\ \{a_{k,m,\xi,n_\xi}\} \rightarrow \{a'_{k,m,\xi,n_\xi}\} \\ \{\xi_{k,m}\} \rightarrow \{\xi'_{k,m}\} \end{pmatrix}. \tag{19}$$

For every LOD of the scene object, we have the separate states set described. The states in one of these sets are independent of the states in all other sets, i.e. the state "organ is bleeding" on LOD 1 and the similar state "organ is bleeding" on LOD 2 are considered as completely different states.

The proposed model extension allows producing more computational efficient educational cases comparing to the original model. As an example, let us consider the simple abstract surgery operational case. In the initial state, all organs are in the rest state and are not moving. We do not need to physically simulate such behavior so on the first LOD, we can model the objects as a static 3d-model. When we touch the organ with an instrument it is deformed and its parts start to move. We have to use the soft body dynamics to simulate this movement.

The static vertices positions of the original static model are translated to the positions of dynamic vertices of the physical tetrahedral grid using $\{\phi_{k,m}\}$ and the first LOD is switched to the second LOD. On this level of details, the transformation $\Psi_{k,m}(\Delta t, \xi)$ considers the spring forces between the vertices and models the deformation. But we still do not need to know the internal structure of the organ so it can be modeled only statistically. When we make a cut on the organ we can see it's internals, so we need to use the third LOD, where all internal details are modeled precisely. The positions of soft body vertices are used to initialize the initial values of internal forces in the organ using $\{\phi_{k,m}\}$.

It must be considered that the transitions between LOD's are not always bidirectional. In the example above the transition between the first and the second LOD's is bidirectional, i.e. when the instrument leaves the operational area, the organ will come in the rest state. After that, we do not need to simulate the soft body behavior and we can use the first LOD again. Obviously, we need to translate the attribute values of the second LOD to the attribute values of the first LOD. But when we cut the organ and go to the third LOD we can't return to the second LOD because it results in unrealistic and unexpected behavior. Figure 2 illustrates this thesis.

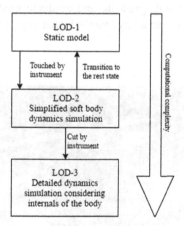

Fig. 2. A load of details complexity management.

5   Implementation in Surgery Training

Medical data is a major source of human health observation and at the same time a challenging object for simulation and visualization. Virtualization of the human body is one of the effective examples of implementation of focus-based visualization in interactive applications.

The idea of human body digital prototyping and visualization is inspired by forthcoming IT technologies like graphical interfaces, display panels, visual dashboards, virtual and augmented reality devices and other innovations. 3D models of the human body can be used to display the results of medical diagnostics in an informative way and simulate medical treatment like e.g. surgery intervention for better decision-making support.

Still, implementation of this idea in practice is concerned with a challenge to provide both high realities of anatomic 3D scenes together with a high performance that allows functioning in real time.

The proposed virtual scene processing and the display are based on the common principle of focused visualization. In addition to the basic software, there is introduced an intelligent module that monitors and captures the user's behavior and operates the visualization procedure. The displayed scene options are presented in the knowledge base in the form of a semantic network that describes 3D models of human body parts with different granularity. These 3D models have a different level of detail (LOD) and are interchangeably loaded to visualization scenes, which leads to high adaptation of them for each user individually. This allows decreasing the computational complexity of 3D models processing in real time.

The proposed approach balancing the 4P target goals of medical data visualization: Performance, Persistence, Perception, and Personalization.

The example of its successful implementation in practice is "Inbody Anatomy" anatomic atlas (see Fig. 3) and laparoscopy surgery training suite (see Fig. 4).

These solutions use an interactive software implementing a clear-structured natural science study program for undergraduate and graduate medical specialists, including such study fields as applied anatomy, morbid anatomy, forensic medicine, surgical studies, etc.

Fig. 3. "Inbody Anatomy" interactive application.

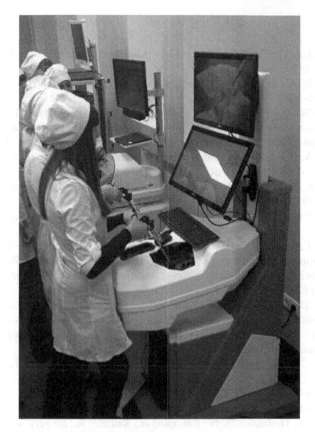

Fig. 4. Laparoscopy surgery training suite.

The software was developed in C ++ using NET C# as a platform for user interface and infrastructure support. It provides a realistic simulation of surgical intervention with the usage of different laparoscopic instruments and video camera – endoscope in 3D scenes.

6 Conclusion

The proposed approach of focused visualization can be used in different interactive applications that provide decision-making support. Based on LOD control it provides the managed complexity of the displayed VR and AR scenes that allows effective balancing of the 4P target goals of data visualization: performance, persistence, perception, and personalization.

The provided example illustrates the benefits of the proposed solution in medicine. High perspectives of the proposed approach motivate further developments in this area.

References

1. Holzinger, A.: Extravaganza tutorial on hot ideas for interactive knowledge discovery and data mining in biomedical informatics. In: Ślęzak, D., Tan, A.-H., Peters, J.F., Schwabe, L. (eds.) BIH 2014. LNCS, vol. 8609, pp. 502–515. Springer, Cham (2014). doi:10.1007/978-3-319-09891-3_46
2. Sturm, W., Schreck, T., Holzinger, A., Ullrich, T.: Discovering medical knowledge using visual analytics – a survey on methods for systems biology and *omics data. In: Eurographics Workshop on Visual Computing for Biology and Medicine (VCBM), pp. 71–81 (2015)
3. Holzinger, A.: Interactive machine learning for health informatics: when do we need the human-in-the-loop? Brain Inf. **3**(2), 119–131 (2016)
4. Fleischmann, A., Schmidt, W., Stary, C. (eds.): S-BPM in the Wild. Springer, Cham (2015). doi:10.1007/978-3-319-17542-3
5. Rusev, I., Ruisev, R., Vassilev, T.: An approach for implementing an intelligent user interface. Int. J. Inf. Technol. Secur. **6**(4), 43–50 (2014)
6. Uyulur, A., Karahoca, D., Karahoca, A., Güngör, A.: Measuring cognitive load of e-learning students for improving efficiency of learning. Int. J. Inf. Technol. Secur. **7**(4), 35–44 (2015)
7. Gaftandzhieva, S.: Automated evaluation of students' satisfaction. Int. J. Inf. Technol. Secur. **8**(1), 31–40 (2016)
8. Bessis, N., Dobre, C. (eds.): Big Data and Internet of Things: A Roadmap for Smart Environments. SCI, vol. 546. Springer, Cham (2014). doi:10.1007/978-3-319-05029-4
9. Gorodetskii, V.I.: Self-organization and multiagent systems: I models of multiagent self-organization. J. Comput. Syst. Sci. Int. **51**(2), 256–281 (2012)
10. Kostadinov, S.: Ontology guided assistance for three dimensional scenes. Int. J. Inf. Technol. Secur. **6**(3), 13–20 (2014)
11. Kolsanov, A.V., Ivaschenko, A.V., Kuzmin, A.V., Cherepanov, A.S.: Virtual surgeon system for simulation in surgical training. Biomed. Eng. **47**(6), 285–287 (2014)
12. Ivaschenko, A., Gorbachenko, N., Kolsanov, A., Kuzmin, A.: Surgery scene representation in 3D simulation training SDK. In: Proceedings of the 18th FRUCT & ISPIT Conference, 18–22 April 2016, St. Petersburg, Russia, pp. 75–84 (2016)
13. Ivaschenko, A., Kolsanov, A., Nazaryan, A., Kuzmin, A.: 3D surgery simulation software development kit. In: Proceedings of the European Simulation and Modeling Conference 2015, EUROSIS-ETI, Leicester, UK, pp. 333–240. (2015)
14. Said, C.S., Shamsudin, K., Mailok, R., Johan, R., Hanaif, H.F.: The development and evaluation of a 3D visualization tool in anatomy education. EDUCATUM – J. Sci. Math. Technol. **2**(2), 48–56 (2015)
15. Glander, T., Döllner, J.: Abstract representations for interactive visualization of virtual 3D city models. Comput. Environ. Urban Syst. **33**, 375–387 (2009)
16. Biljecki, F., Ledoux, H., Stoter, J., Zhao, J.: Formalisation of the level of detail in 3D city modelling. Comput. Environ. Urban Syst. **48**, 1–15 (2014)

Immersive Natural EEG Neurofeedback to Stimulate Creativity

Alin Moldoveanu[1], Ana-Karina Nazare[1],
and Maria-Iuliana Dascălu[2(✉)]

[1] Faculty of Automatic Control and Computers,
University POLITEHNICA of Bucharest, Bucharest, Romania
alin.moldoveanu@cs.pub.ro,
nazare.ana.karina@gmail.com
[2] Department of Engineering in Foreign Languages,
University POLITEHNICA of Bucharest, Bucharest, Romania
maria.dascalu@upb.ro

Abstract. We propose a natural, 3D immersive and real-time representation of the mental state acquired through EEG. Unlike most other neurofeedback methods currently in use, which are mostly simplistic, synthetic representations, our approach will make use of rich natural visual metaphors, presented immersivity and user-centric. This powerful approach will stimulate deep neurofeedback-based learning and opens a wide range of applications, from the personal training of various mental capabilities (relaxation, focus, etc.) to psychological or psychiatric treatment. In this paper, we present the general concept of the system (acquiring the EEG data, it's processing, mapping, and rendering) and discuss one of its most promising applications - in stimulating users' creativity. There is detailed a training protocol to enhance neurological processes related to the creative activity, based on researched studies.

Keywords: EEG · Brain waves · Brain-computer interface · Neurofeedback · Virtual reality · Procedural animation and generation

1 Introduction

Creativity is a rare psychological trait, due to its complexity: it includes intelligence, perseverance, unconventionality, the ability to adapt, to express etc. [1]. While none of these traits are rare, the combination of them is not so common [2]. A creative idea is both adapted to context and original and very often consists of novel combinations of preexisting elements.

Kris proposed that creative individuals have better abilities to alternate between primary process (free-associative, analogical, appearing in normal states – dreaming and reverie – and abnormal states – psychosis and hypnosis) and secondary process modes of thought than uncreative people (abstract, logical, reality-oriented thought of waking consciousness) [3]. Creative inspiration involves a regression to a primary process of the state of consciousness, facilitating the discovery of new combinations of mental elements. On the other hand, creative elaboration involves a return to a

© Springer International Publishing AG 2017
A. Kravets et al. (Eds.): CIT&DS 2017, CCIS 754, pp. 735–749, 2017.
DOI: 10.1007/978-3-319-65551-2_53

secondary process state. There can be drawn a parallel between cortical activation as measured in electroencephalography (EEG) and the state of consciousness: as one moves from alert wakefulness through fantasy, and reverie to sleep, cortical activation measured directly by EEG frequency and inversely by EEG amplitude decreases. This suggests a parallel with the secondary process-primary process continuum [4]. Thus, in creative subjects there is more variance on the primary-secondary process continuum, then it should be present on the arousal continuum as well.

This article presents possibilities of data retrieval regarding the mental and emotional states of the participant and their representation as parametrized graphical structures. It proposes a 3D virtual reality model which maps in real-time the brain waves activity (EEG signals) in an immersive e-environment.

The following section describes the electromagnetic brain activity data reading and processing. It also broadly explains the technologies to support EEG. The third section proposes graphical constructions on which to perform transformations that reflect the electromagnetic activity of the brain. These will be categorized in user-centered scenes (where the environmental surroundings are changed according to the data reading) and object-oriented scenes (which contain objects which are animated).

As a neurofeedback immersive and artistic application, the presented model creates a perfect medium for training creative patterns of brain waves. The users may influence the environment by reducing it to a state of peace or may try to train different emotional responses to directly visualize their effects. They can switch between different states of cortical activation by trying to simulate the creative process.

2 Brain Computer Interface and Emotion Detection

A brain-computer interface (BCI) is a novel human-computer interface, which establishes an interactive channel between the human brain and external electronic devices. BCIs are able to identify the user's intentions directly through electrophysiological signals of the brain and to translate them into corresponding commands to the electronic devices [5].

Such an interface firstly requires a recording device which collects the biological data and then interprets them for further processing based on the purpose of the system. BCI hardware records brain signals either non-invasively (e.g. electroencephalography (EEG), magnetoencephalography (MEG), functional near-infrared spectroscopy (fNIRS) or invasively (e.g. electrocorticography (ECoG), local field potentials (LEP), single-unit activity) using a bio-signal amplifier and analog-digital converter. It may be used for communication, for accessing or controlling the computer or the control of prosthetic devices such as robotic arms or wheelchairs. Another use regards the psychological or psychiatric treatment [6].

In studying creativity, both fMRI and EEG approaches in this field are challenged to decompose its complex construct into measurable cognitive processes that can be adequately investigated. In the same time, they need to capture "real-life creativity" to the best possible extent. Concerning the latter issue, the EEG environment might provide slightly better conditions for creativity than studies using fMRI, in which participants are required to lie supine in the noisy scanner [7].

2.1 Electroencephalography

The electroencephalogram (EEG) is the graphical recording of spontaneous fluctuations of the electrical potential of the membranes of the neurons from the cerebral cortex. The graphical structure of an EEG is a record of electrical potential fluctuations on EEG tracks located between two electrodes placed on the scalp. The reading is macroscopic and follows a large number of neurons (approximately one million) on the path that responds synchronously. Based on the particularity of EEG tracks, an electroarhitectonic map of the cortex can be developed, by delimiting homogeneous regions.

By using the microelectrodes introduced in the interior cortex (or other gray matter formations), the electrical activity of different layers and even separate neurons, registering fast potential having durations of approximately 1 ms. The absence of these fast oscillations in the tracks registered on the scalp is due to the derivative action of the superior cortex layers, of the meningeal envelope and the cerebrospinal fluid, as well to the small number of the fast potential generating neurons in the superficial cortical layers, rich in thin dendric branches. The genesis of EEG slow oscillations is explained by different theories: the synaptic theory –explaining their generation by the summation of the postsynaptic potentials, or the dendritic theory -considering the emergence of slow potentials in apical dendrites, glial or chemical theories, etc. [8].

Brain Waves. EEG signals are encoded in frequency, amplitude, and shape, characterizing normal biological states. Visible deviations in these features are due to external stress factors or pathological states. In the absence of special stimuli, rhythmic oscillations of the cerebral potentials are seen as a manifestation characteristic of current body functions, such as the activity of cardio-vascular apparatus, respiration, digestion and so on. It represents the fundamental rhythm or the basic electrical activity of the brain. The frequency of oscillations of the main EEG potentials varies widely (0.5–50 oscillations per second). Amplitude, expressed in microvolts (μV) oscillates between 5 μV and 300 μV.

Table 1. Characteristics of the main EEG potentials

Rythm	Frequency (Hz)		Amplitude (μV)		Duration (ms)
	Mean	Limits	Mean	Limits	
Delta	2	0.1–4	100	50–300	250–1000
Theta	5	4–8	70	30–100	130–250
Gamma	70	40–100	13	10–15	20–40
Beta	20	12–40	20	10–30	40–75
Alpha	10	8–12	50	30–100	75–125

In a healthy waking person, the Alpha rhythm will prevail, which is a characteristic of the bioelectric activity of the brain in rest – see Table 1. Alpha waves correspond to a state of physical and mental relaxation, but an alert in which long-term memory is activated and learning is quick and easy. In the normal adult, in a state of vigilance, without being subjected to special stimulation, these rhythms represent approx. 90% of all recorded rhythms. Beta waves are emitted in conscious states, alert, or in states of agitation, tension or fear. Short-term memory is used, and body and mind are active Theta waves betray a deep relaxation state in which creativity and intuition are increased, and the subconscious becomes accessible. They play an important role in childhood, and increased activity in maturity indicates pathological problems. Delta and Sigma rhythms are associated with deep sleep, unconsciousness or catalepsy [9].

Quantitative Electroencephalogram. The brain is a system whose functioning is controlled by feedback. Thus, the brain has to organize its entire activity at time-relevant scales of behavior. Behavioral demands call for a brain organization that provides a response as quickly as possible and in a non-wider band of instability limit (in controlled systems, it translates to hazard). In the case of the brain, it is reasonable to consider which functional deficiencies are associated with various types of irregularities in the field of this (lack of response, delayed response) or in the frequency domain (irregularities of the activity of the cortical zones are overactivation, inactivation or inactivation).

Quantitative EEG (QEEG) is the quantitative recording of cortical electrical activity highlighted by cerebral waves. This representation is obtained by interpreting the EEG records. The main measurement instrument is a computing platform on which a program for calculating the quantitative characteristic (power) of the EEG signal of a given frequency is implemented and its association with a position in the brain, depending on the recording path [10].

The mathematical tool for calculating QEEG is Fourier transform; this transforms the measured signals E (t) (signal amplitude per time) into processing signals Q (ω), representing the wave power as a function of frequency. Conversion of the characteristics of the brain waves: the amplitude, frequency, spatial coordinates and their subsequent representation as topographical statistical maps of the brain can be done via appropriate software.

Event-Related Potential. An event-related potential (ERP) analysis involves analyzing the neuronal response to a stimulus such as a sound or an image. This is done by analyzing the same type of information collected for a QEEG (quantitative electroencephalogram), with the difference that the data is collected during a subject engagement in an activity. The response is then decomposed into independent components, and their characteristics are compared to a normative database.

ERPs are of two types: exogenous and endogenous. The exogenous (or sensory) ones are obtained in the first 100 ms from the onset of the stimulus and its characteristics depend on the physical nature of the stimulus. In contrast, the exogenous (or cognitive) ones are obtained later and depend on the information received and how it is processed. The largest value is represented by the ERP component called P3 or P300. This is associated with stimulus evaluation [11].

P300 appears as a positive deviation of the voltage of 2–5 μV with a latency of 250–400 ms since receiving the stimulus. Because the ERP potential is relatively small, it is usually obscured by noise and not visible in a typical electroencephalogram. Therefore, in order to obtain a visible ERP, a certain number of EEG segments (containing singular ERPs called epochs) are mediated by repeating the same experiment.

During the analysis, the averaged EEG wavelength of the target period (in which the stimulus to which the participant has to respond occurs) is compared to that of the non-target periods (occurrence of the stimuli to be ignored). If the experiment was successful, then the potential-response ERP is distinguished.

Neurofeedback. Neurofeedback is a technique consisting in measuring neural physiological activity by using a technical interface to extract a certain parameter of interest, which is then represented real-time to the participant. It is intended that they will consciously modify this parameter thus training their cognitive abilities [12].

Studies have shown that creative people perform relatively worse at neurofeedback tasks [2]. Therefore, the low levels of arousal that creative people show during creative inspiration are evidently not due to self-control. We propose a training program which may rise the ability of consciously controlling the creative process.

2.2   Emotion Detection

While affective computing is an ever-rising topic within the human-computer interaction, the field of recognizing emotions by BCIs is its youth. Nonetheless, in human communication, nonverbal information such as intention and emotion plays a key role. Even more, the exact emotional state isn't always readable from the face. Therefore, even though emotion recognition rates are 50–60% in emotional speech recognitions [13–15], and 80–90% in facial expressions [16–18], there is a need to expand the recognition techniques using physiological indexes. Physiological changes according to exciting emotions affect the body surface and/or the autonomic nervous system and can be observed by reading data regarding skin conductivity, electrocardiogram, electromyogram, blood pressure or even pupil movement.

Furthermore, the use of brain waves reading proves to be effective, since the emotions are excited in the limbic system and are deeply related to cognition process. By gathering data from multiple subjects and using learning based recognition methods, it is possible to achieve person independent emotion recognition, at a rate of 60% [19].

Emotions as Discrete Categories. The discrete emotion theory claims that there is a small number of core emotions. In 1962 Silvan Tolkins [20] concluded the existence of eight basic emotions: surprise, interest, joy, rage, fear, disgust, shame, and aguish.

His idea was influenced by Darwin's concept, i.e. the vast variety of human emotions evolve from a limited number of pancultural basic emotions or "affect programs".

The fact that the integrity of this theory depends on cultural differences represents a disadvantage, therefore there is a need of differentiating emotions without naming them [21].

The Spatial Model of Emotions. Psychological studies show that there is a direct link between the amount of electromagnetic activity in the left frontal lobe and the right frontal lobe and the resulting emotion [22, 23]. This method gives only a one-dimensional solution, a more active frontal lobe indicating a positive reaction, while an active right anterior lobe indicates negative affect. The explanation consists of the response to the stimuli; if the response is one of rejection, the right hemisphere would be excited.

Another name for this process is identifying the frontal asymmetry index. In short, this "approach-avoidance" effect reflects someone's motivation [24]. Relatively increased left-frontal activity is an index of approach motivation or related emotion (e.g. joy), while a right-frontal increased activity denotes a withdrawal motivation or related emotion (e.g. disgust, fear).

The frontal asymmetry index can be computed relatively simply from raw EEG data. After pre-processing the data to attenuate artifacts, the data is split into epochs. Scientific studies recommend overlapping the periods with each limited to a duration of 1–2 s. Then each epoch is converted in the frequency-time domain by computing the Fast Fourier Transform, to determinate which frequencies underlie the actual data, allowing extraction of the power in a specific frequency band. The equation to be solved to obtain the frontal asymmetry index is:

$$Frontal\ Asymmetry\ Index = log\left(\frac{alpha\ power_{right} - alpha\ power_{left}}{alpha\ power_{right} + alpha\ power_{left}}\right) \quad (1)$$

The calculation implies that higher scores are indicative of approach behavior, while lower scores are indicative of avoidance motivation [25] (Fig. 1).

Fig. 1. The circumflex model of emotion (source: Nazare [26])

The circumflex model developed by James Russel [27] distributes emotions in a two-dimensional circular space containing arousal and valence. Ulterior research has added dimensions to the model. Robert Plutchik [28] offers a tridimensional model that arranges emotions in concentric circles whose complexity grows eccentrically. In 2011,

Lövheim [29] proposed a three-dimensional model represented by a cube, where the signal substances form the aces of a coordinate system, and the eight basic emotions of Silvan Tomkins are placed in its corners. In practice, the two-dimensional models are preferred to the three-dimensional ones, as the third dimension may be calculated using the cross product between the vectors of the first two. As previously given, the Beta waves associate to an alert or excited state, while the Alpha waves predominate in relaxed mental states. The activity of the Alpha waves has also been associated with cerebral inactivation. Therefore, the Beta/Alpha ratio is an acceptable indicator of the arousal state of a person. Assuming a direct link between affective valence and motivational direction, this is an effective method of determining emotional valence.

3   Graphical Representations of Mental State

We propose a graphical representation of the QEEG by passing values of interest to the construction of the scene or animation parameters and the emotional state by changing the color palette or the shape of certain graphical elements.

Emotion view and perception have been inspected in multiple concepts in the past decades. In 2005, Liu [30] uses an affective bar that codes emotions into colors, while Stahl [31] proposes a representation based on symbols and colors. In another paper, the affective state of the use is represented trough real-time animated scenes through objects movement or through the fractal generation of objects, by using parameters which are modified from generation to generation depending on the received data [32].

We propose an immersive feedback environment, which engages the user and instantaneously responds to the input (corresponding to the enhancing program corresponding to the neurofeedback protocol).

3.1   Scene-Oriented Models

The user is placed in the center of the scene, with which he interacts through his brain waves, influencing the scene morphology. The objects of interest can be animated by periodic or cyclic functions.

Ocean Waves. The first proposed model contains a seemingly never-ending body of water on whose surface are projected waves. Their shape and frequency depend of the neural activity of the subject. To represent Beta waves there are used sharp, abrupt and rife waves, characterizing a thawing, stormy water corresponding to an agitated state, while Alpha waves will be mapped into rhythmic, calm waves. For this purpose is used the Gerstner [33] model. Parameters such as amplitude, speed or shape of the waves are dependant on the EEG recorded data (Fig. 2).

The aim of this scene is to calm the water through mental and affective relaxation.

Fractal Generation of a Psychedelic Pattern. Another representation proposes a hemisphere (the upper hemisphere of the virtual world), on which is projected an animated texture.

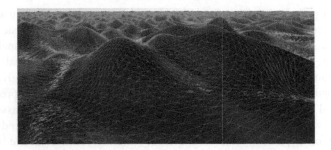

Fig. 2. Wave simulation using the Gestner model (Source: Pevans [33])

The center of the dome is situated above the camera and it defines a partition in regions of generation of individual fractals (for example, hexagons in polar coordinates), each having a generation seed (starting from which the fractal is generated) in its geometrical center. The pattern creation itself is asymmetrical and it propagates (using an energy parameter whose value decreases with each propagation) from cell to cell, starting from a region corresponding to an active EEG zone (Fig. 3).

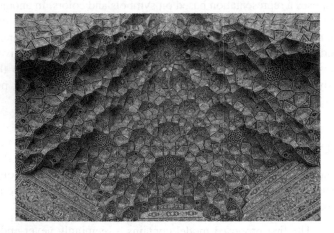

Fig. 3. The model would resemble a traditional mosque ceiling. In the picture, there is the ceiling of the mosque in Shiraz, Iran (Source: BoredPanda, Schneider [34])

The generation speed of the new generation depends on the intensity of EEG, while the shape and color of the elements from each generation depend on the perceived affective state. From generation to generation, the size of the graphical elements is smaller and smaller, the fractal always being enclosed in the cell. The users' goal is to correlate the activity of specific regions of the dome (for protocols targeting activation areas and coherence) or to control the area as a whole.

Plant Growth Simulation. There are multiple methods of simulating plant growth, such as the space colonization algorithm that uses attractors toward which the plants tend to reach, object-oriented, fractalic, or recursive, through simple functions or using L-systems (Lindenmayer rewrite systems [35], conceived especially for describing plant growth).

For therapeutical purposes, the model is being developed so the plants may continue to grow only in relaxed states of the user. Conversely, the territorial distribution may evolve differently – the colonization may be favored by an increase in the electromagnetic brain activity (Fig. 4).

Fig. 4. Space spreading of colonial plants depending on the light intensity (in the picture the lightness of the gray indicates the luminance of the corresponding zones) (Source: Mech and Prusinkiewicz [35])

3.2 Object-Oriented Scenes

In this category of models, a focus point is an object with animatable characteristics on which the user acts through consciously changing his mental state.

Development of a Plant. This model can faithfully track the effects of mental states on physical development. In the biological reality, stress affects the development of all living creatures. The body isn't capable of growth in states which require that its resources are allocated to protection, fight or flight.

The model will track the photosynthetic products synthesis and transmission along the plant body, as well as the raw sap distribution. In an alert state, the plant will grow only short segments of branches and roots, it will process and transport sap; however, the notable growth, the production of leaves and flowers takes place only in moments of relaxation (Fig. 5).

Fig. 5. Trees simulated using L-systems (Source: Wikipedia [36])

Sphere with Bumps. Asimple solution consists in a sphere with bumps which heights fluctuate depending on the read data. The EEG activity may be directly translated in the height modification of sharp tips such as spikes. The purpose is to smooth the surface. The simple implementation of this model is by bump-mapping, or the processing of texture coordinates, i.e. normals and tangents to surfaces (Fig. 6).

Fig. 6. The discussed sphere during an agitated state of the user (Source: ToxicLab [37])

Storm Cloud. Intuitively, the dark couloir and lightning effects of the cloud will indicate a negative and agitated state. In order to bring the cloud to a state of equilibrium, the user pursues his calming.

One way to construct the cloud is to create a volume on which are applied both a fluid animation (for example using the Navier-Stokes equations), and a function of modifying the normal to its surface, causing a texture noise with a vaporous effect.

Another one uses particle emission in 3D containers.

Generating an Auroreal Storm. In this model, the user may create and keep an auroreal curtain only in states of concentration. When he loses focus, the aurora is scattered.

For simplicity, we consider a single aurora curtain. It can be decomposed into a 2D function that describes its shape in plan and one height-dependent one that characterizes the luminous intensity of the particles in the atmosphere according to altitude (Fig. 7).

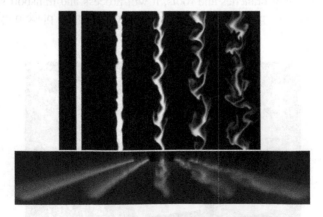

Fig. 7. Auroreal curtain 2D footprint and 3D model on different stages of applied fluid dynamics (Source: Lawlor and Genetti [38])

The curtain's shape is given by its projection on the planet's surface and is represented by a spline curve on which are applied fluid dynamics simulation equations (Navier-Stokes in 2D). The curtain dissipates with the breaking the of spline curve at reaching the threshold values of the deviation given by the generated swirls.

4 A Model to Stimulate Creativity Through Graphical Representation-Based Neurofeedback

As Martindale stated, "Creativity is a matter of having the right brain waves." Hardt's and Gale's study [39] suggests that there are at least two distinct categories of beneficial results from feedback training to increase EEG alpha: increased creativity and reduced anxiety. Training by recessing consciously to hypnagogia (the half-dream state, measured by an Alpha/Theta rate) [40] has been proved to stimulate creativity.

A highly relevant line of research has related mindfulness meditation practice to reduced default mode network activity and functional connectivity [41–43]. Mindfulness meditation is a technique of remaining aware and noticing the salient features of present experience while refraining from judgmental processes, elaboration of concepts or mind wandering [44].

The proposed models and modes of interaction are perfect for developing a training program designed to augment creativity. While having an object to focus on, and synchronously getting feedback from the EEG readings, the subject experiences a new type of neurofeedback that allows multiple exercises and types of interaction.

The brief instructions are written in each subsection of Sect. 3 **Graphical Representations of Mental State** describe possible neurofeedback tasks that train the cognitive abilities of the user.

The neurofeedback protocol firstly gathers information in the current state of the subject; the purpose of the system being learning of self-control and augmenting certain mechanisms, while simultaneously remembering and responding to the evolution of the user's performance in time. The first concept which must be defined is the target neurological state or mechanisms.

Knowing brain patterns characteristic to creative processes by extracting ERPs during receiving and completing tasks there may be isolated the specific brain waves generations to be entrained. Problem-solving tasks, in which there are multiple solutions to a certain problem, are used in creativity research that tries to measure fluency, flexibility originality, and elaboration. Studies on the higher cognitive process have shown that during the solving of tasks with the effort the prefrontal cortex is activated [45]. There have been several proposals that intelligence and executive functions are implemented in a common neural circuitry and depend on the prefrontal cortex [46]. Such functions involve processes such as reasoning, decision-making, and performing operations on mental representations in absence of external referents. Given the possible importance of executive functions in creativity, the studies indicate that the prefrontal cortex plays a significant role in creative tasks [47, 48].

The analysis techniques that have been used in creativity research are spectral analysis and coherence analysis.

4.1 Spectral Analysis

Spectral analysis is typically performed with EEG segments by computing the Discrete Fourier Transform.

An important function for EEG analysis is the autocorrelation function, containing information about the expected frequency content of the random process, used for deducing the power spectral density (PSD) function.

Spectral analysis of EEG has shown that insight preparation (in performing tasks that included insight) was associated with less Alpha power (i.e. greater brain activity) in the range of 9–10 Hz especially in the mid-frontal cortex and left-anterior temporal cortex [49]. Other studies have shown an increase in Alpha power associated with creative tasks. Recordings have also revealed a sudden burst of high-frequency (Gamma band) neural activity prior to insight solutions in the right hemisphere anterior superior temporal gyrus [50]. The change in the Alpha power may depend on the nature of the creative task and the employment to different types of creative tasks [51]. Other studies have shown that the higher the EEG complexity is during divergent than convergent thinking could be the result of concurrent activation of a greater number of independently oscillating processing units [52].

The coherence spectrum is obtained by computing the Fourier transform of the cross-correlation function, for specific frequency bands between two electrodes. Higher coherence values indicated higher cooperative processing different regions [53].

4.2 Coherence Analysis

There have been computed three indices based on general synchronization, based on generalized synchronization, mean phase coherence and phase synchrony based on entropy in order to study phase synchronization in artists and non-artists. An effect of hemispherical asymmetry was also obtained with more synchronization in the right hemisphere for visual artists and higher phase synchrony (Gamma band) for musicians [54, 55]. There has also been noted a synchronization in the frontal areas in divergent thinking tasks [56].

5 Conclusions

It has been briefly presented a state-of-the-art technique of reading EEG and detecting affect, as well as several artistic possibilities of representing the psychological state of the subject in real-time. The numerous applications of such a medium of interaction include training and healing trough neurofeedback, communication, meditation aid and video games immersion factor [57].

Lastly, but not least, the complex neural – psychological trait of creativity may be trained by using the proposed model, i.e. using a training program based on controlling the Alpha and Theta waves consciously or through mindfulness meditation, consciously synchronizing activity in certain areas of the brain or generating Gamma waves.

Acknowledgements. This work has received funding from the TRAVEE grant of the Romanian Executive Agency for Higher Education, Research, Development and Innovation Funding - UEFISCDI, Joint Applied Research Projects program, project number PN-IIPT-PCCA-2013-4-1580.

References

1. Piirto, J.: Understanding Those Who Create, 2nd edn. Gifted Psychology Press, Scottsdale (1998)
2. Martindale, C.: Biological Bases of Creativity. Cambridge University Press, Cambridge (1998)
3. Kris, E.: Psychoanalytic Explorations in Art. International Universities, New York (1952)
4. Armstrong, J., Martindale, C.: The relationship of creativity to cortical activation and its operant control. J. Genet. Psychol. **124**(2), 311–320 (1973)
5. Hassanien, A.E., Azar, A.T.: Brain-Computer Interfaces. Current Trends and Applications. Springer, Berlin (2015)
6. Brunner, P., Bianchi, L., Guger, C., Cincotti, F., Schalk, G.: Current trends in hardware and software for brain-computer interfaces (BCIs). J. Neural Eng. **8**, 025001 (2011)
7. Fink, A., Benedek, M.: EEG alpha power and creative ideation. Neursci. Biobehav. Rev. **44**(100), 111–123 (2014)
8. Nanu, M.: Structura Activității Bioelectrice Al Creierului. 3.Frontierele Muzicii Curcubeului, October 2009. https://mariananu.wordpress.com/psihologie/1-structura-activitatii-bioelectrice-al-creierului/. Accessed 01 May 2017
9. Sanei, S., Chambers, J.: EEG signal processing. In: International Conference on Digital Signal Processing, Cardiff, Wales (2008)
10. Budzynski, T.H., Budzynski, H.K., Evans, J., Abarbanel, A.: Introduction to Quantitative EEG and Neurofeedback, Soquel. Academic Press, California (2008)
11. Sinha, V., Sur, S.: Event-related potenital: an overview. Ind. Psychiatry J. **18**, 70–73 (2009)
12. Sherlin, L., Arns, M., Lubar, J., Heinrich, H., Kerson, C., Strehl, U., Sterman, M.: Neurofeedback and basic learning theory: implications for research and practice. J. Neurother. **15**, 292–304 (2011)
13. Chen, L., Huang, T.: Emotional expressions in audovisual human computer interaction. In: Proceedings of 2000 IEEE International Conference on Multimedia and Expo (2000)
14. Dellaert, F., Polzin, T., Waibel, A.: Recognizing emotion in speech. In: Proceedings of Fourth IEEE International Conference on Spoken Language Processing (1996)
15. Nicolson, J., Takahashi, K., Nakatsu, R.: Emotion recognizing in speech using neural networks. Neural Comput. Appl. **9**(4), 290–296 (2000)
16. Sarode, N., Bharia, S.: Facial expression recognition. Int. J. Comput. Sci. Eng. **2**(05), 1552–1557 (2010)
17. Busso, C., Deng, Z., Yildirim, S., Bulut, M., Lee, C., Kazemzadeh, A., Lee, S., Neumann, U., Narayanan, S.: Analysis of emotion recognition using facial expressions, speech and multimodal information. In: Proceedings of the 6th International Conference on Multimodal Interfaces, New York (2004)
18. Edwards, J., Jackson, H., Pattison, P.: Emotion recognition via facial expression and affective prosody in schizophrenia: a methodological review. IEEE Trans. Pattern Anal. Mach. Intell. **22**(8), 1267–1285 (2002)
19. Takahashi, K.: Remarks on emotion recognition from bio-potential signals. In: Second International Conference on Autonomous Robots and Agents, Palmerston North (2004)

20. Tomkins, S.S.: Affect Imagery Consciousness: Volume I: The Positive Affects, vol. I. Springer, Heidelberg (1962)
21. Eid, M., Diener, E.: Norms for experiencing emotions in differnet culture: inter- and intranational differences. J. Pers. Soc. Psychol. **81**(5), 869–885 (2001)
22. Niemic, C.: Studies of emotion. a theoretical and empirical review of psychophysiolocial studies of emotion. J. Undergrad. Res. **1**(1), 12–18 (2002)
23. Watson, D., Tellegen, A.: Toward a consensual structure of mood. Psychol. Bull. **98**, 219–235 (1985)
24. Harmon-Jones, E., Gable, P.A., Peterson, C.K.: The role of asymmetric frontal cortical activity in emotion-related phenomena: a review and update. Biol. Psychol. **84**, 451–462 (2010)
25. iMotions: Frontal Asymmetry 101 - How to Get Insights on Motivation and Emotions from EEG, 18 August 2015. https://imotions.com/blog/frontal-asymmetry-101-get-insights-motivation-emotions-eeg/. Accessed 01 May 2017
26. Nazare, A.: Researh Report on Immersive Natural EEG Neurofeedback, University Politehnica of Bucharest (2017)
27. Russel, J.: A circumplex model of affect. J. Pers. Soc. Psychol. **39**, 1161–1178 (1980)
28. Plutchik, R.: The Nature of Emotions. American Scientist, July 2001
29. Lövheim, H.: A new three-dimensional model for emotions and monoamine neurotransmitters. Med. Hypotheses **78**(2), 341–348 (2012)
30. Liu, H., Selker, T., Lieberman, H.: Visualising the affective structure of a text document. In: Extended Abstracts on Human Factors in Computing Systems, pp. 740–741. ACM Press, New York (2005)
31. Stahl, A., Sunstorm, P., Hook, K.: A foundation for emotional expressivity. In: Conference for Designing for User Experience, New York (2005)
32. Fraga, T., Pichiliani, M., Louro, D.: Experimental art with brain controlled interface. In: Stephanidis, C., Antona, M. (eds.) UAHCI 2013. LNCS, vol. 8009, pp. 642–651. Springer, Heidelberg (2013). doi:10.1007/978-3-642-39188-0_69
33. Pevans, B., Gerstner Wave Implementation, 24 August 2016. https://opengllair.wordpress.com/2016/08/24/gerstner-wave-implementation/. Accessed 01 May 2017
34. Schneider, A.: 20+ Mesmerizing Mosque Ceilings That Highlight The Wonders of Islamic Architecture (2015). http://www.boredpanda.com/mosque-ceilings/. Accessed 15 June 2017
35. Mech, R., Prusinkiewicz, P.: Visual models of plants interacting with their environment. In: Computer Graphics Proceedings, New Orleans (1996)
36. User: Solkoll: L-system, 17 February 2005. https://commons.wikimedia.org/wiki/File:Dragon_trees.jpg. Accessed 01 May 2017
37. Neckmasher, U.: 3DS MAX Micro Cells Tutorial, 23 January 2006. http://www.tutorialized.com/tutorial/Micro-Cells/10774. Accessed 01 May 2017
38. Lawlor, O., Genetti, J.: Interactive volume rendering aurora on the GPU. J. WSCG **19**(1), 25–32 (2011)
39. Hardt, J.V., Gale, R.: Creativity Increases in Scientist through Alpha EEG Feedback Training (1993)
40. Leach, J.: EEG Neurofeedback as a Tool to Modulate Creativity in Music Performance. Goldsmiths, London (2014)
41. Berkovich-Ohana, A., Harel, M., Hahamy, A., Arieli, A., Marach, R.: Alternations in task-induced activity and resting-state dluctuations in visual and DMN areas revealed in long-term medidators. NeuroImage **135**, 125–134 (2016)
42. Brewer, J., Worhunsky, P., Gray, J., Tang, Y., Weber, J., Kober, H.: Meditation experience is associated with differences in default mode activity and connectivity. Proc. Natl. Acad. Sci. U.S.A. **108**(50), 20254–20259 (2011)

43. Hasenkamp, W., Barsalou, L.: Effects of meditation experience on functional connectivity of distributed brain networks. Front. Hum. Neurosci. **6**, 1–14 (2012)
44. Kabat-Zinn, J.: Mindfulness-based interventions in context: past, present and future. Clin. Psychol. Sci. Pract. **10**(2), 144–156 (2003)
45. Ashby, G., Valentin, V., Turken, A.: Emotional Cognition: From Brain to Behaviour. John Benjamins, Amsterdam (2002)
46. Conway, A., Kane, M., Engle, R.: Working memory capacity and its relation to general intelligence. Trends Cogn. Sci. **12**(7), 547–552 (2003)
47. Dietrich, A.: The cognitive neuroscience of creativity. Psychon. Bull. Rev. **11**, 1011–1026 (2004)
48. Srinivasan, N.: Cognitive neuroscience of creativity: EEG based approaches. Methods **1**(42), 109–116 (2007)
49. Kounios, J., Frymiare, J., Bowden, E., Fleck, J., Subramaniam, K., Parrish, T., Jung-Beeman, M.: The prepared mind: neural activity prior to problem presentation predicts subsequent solution by sudden insight. Psychol. Sci. **17**(10), 882–890 (2006)
50. Jung-Beeman, M., Bowden, E., Haberman, J., Frymiare, J., Arambel-Liu, S., Greenblatt, R., Reber, P., Kounios, J.: Neural activity when people solve verbal problems with insight. Psychol. Sci. **17**(10), 882–891 (2004)
51. Cooper, N., Croft, R., Dominey, S., Burgess, A., Gruzelier, J.: Paradox lost? Exploring the role of alpha oscillations during externally vs. internally directed attention and the implications for idling and inhibition hypotheses. Int. J. Psychophysiol. **1**(47), 65–74 (2003)
52. Molle, M., Marshall, L., Wolf, B., Fehm, H., Born, J.: EEG complexity and performance measures of creative thinking. Int. J. Psychophysiol. **36**(1), 95–104 (1999)
53. Bazanova, O., Mernaya, E.: 3rd International Congress on Brain and Behaviour. Annals of General Psychiatry, Thessaloniki (2008)
54. Bhattacharya, J., Petsche, H.: Phase synchrony analysis of EEG during music perception reveals changes in functional connectivity due to musical expertise. Sig. Process. **85**, 2161–2177 (2005)
55. Fink, A., Benedek, M.: EEG alpha power and creative ideation. Neurosci. Behav. Rev. **44**(100), 111–123 (2014)
56. Fink, A., Grabner, R., Benedek, M., Reishofer, G., Hauuswirth, V., Fally, M., Neuper, C., Ebner, F., Neubauer, A.: The creative brain: investigation of brain activity during creative problem solving by means of EEG and fMRI. Hum. Brain Mapp. **3**(30), 734–748 (2009)
57. Moldoveanu, A., Gradinaru, A., Ferche, O.M., Stefan, L.: The 3D UPB mixed reality campus: challenges of mixing the real and the virtual. In: Proceedings of 18th International Conference on System Theory, Control and Computing (ICSTCC), pp. 538–543 (2014)

Expert System Based Diagnostic Application for Medical Training

Yumchmaa Ayush[1,2(✉)], Uranchimeg Tudevdagva[2,3],
and Michael Grif[1]

[1] Novosibirisk State Technical University, Novosibirsk, Russia
yumchmaa@must.edu.mn, grifmg@mail.ru
[2] Mongolian University of Science and Technology, Ulaanbaatar, Mongolia
uranchimeg.tudevdagva@informatik.tu-chemnitz.de
[3] Chemnitz University of Technology, Chemnitz, Germany

Abstract. This paper discusses the main concept of the medical expert system (MES) and its algorithm and application. The algorithm based on an expert system which consists of two main diagnose parts: the traditional medicine, part "E" (Tibetan or eastern medicine) and the European medicine, part "W". This paper will focus only on "E" part of the system. Part "E" designed as MES. Part "E" includes a basic questionnaire. By this questionnaire system, it will collect data from the user. The questionnaire is set of questions 26 by 3, and this is new approach test to estimate diagnose by innate nature of human. Collected data processes by MES knowledge rules. Then outcome of "E" part will be compared with the outcome of "W" part. Comparison part will compute the probability of diagnose. One of the new ideas of this MES is, we are using "E" part results into "W" part result to do decision about diagnose that's "Is this really serious illness? If it had some probability could be a serious illness, then the system looks for a reason. May be a general balance of the human body is damaged, and patient not yet ill. If it is real illness, then what is system calculating the probability of correctness of diagnoses by the methodology of "E" part".

We are developing an application for this MES with a mission to use it in the training of medical students. It will help students to learn basics of eastern medicine methodology to estimate diagnose of the patient. Application designed to be easy to understand and use for users without special computer skills.

Keywords: Expert system · Eastern medicine · Western medicine · Training application · Knowledge database

1 Introduction

Technology is developing rapidly and researchers trying to gain more benefits from the result of science in human daily life. One of the key points of this way is to use advantages of technology into learning and teaching. E-learning or distance learning is now not new for any level of education. The Early stage of digital learning technology researchers focused more on engineering science and natural sciences. In our days, this is spreading out to all fields. We can see the significant influence from virtual reality usage into medical science and training. Technology benefits opened a lot of

© Springer International Publishing AG 2017
A. Kravets et al. (Eds.): CIT&DS 2017, CCIS 754, pp. 750–761, 2017.
DOI: 10.1007/978-3-319-65551-2_54

opportunities to medical teaching and learning a lot of opportunities and now many researchers working in this field. In some example, we refer to [1, 10, 14].

The expert system developed early 1970's. Mid 1970's, Stanford University, USA developed successfully MYCIN: a rule-based system for medical diagnosis [3]. More details about expert system history we refer to [12, 16]. Nowadays mobile devices like, tablets and smart phones become one of the main channels to support learners for motivation to their study. Especially medicine is the longest and hardest way for studying. We hope that final version of our application can be a tool for training of medical students.

Generally, we started with an idea to develop special medical equipment, which can offer, diagnose to the user, based on the traditional eastern methodology: palpation. Palpation is one of the main diagnostic techniques used in eastern medicine and involves pulse diagnosis. In addition, pulse diagnosis applies in Western medicine, too. Especially, changes of pulse wave used to assist eastern doctors to predict the pathological changes of particular organs. Subjective pulse diagnosis is very difficult to learn and requires from doctors many years of experiences and special feeling techniques. In the book, it says that experienced doctor is capable of distinguishing more than 360 different pulse waves. In starting years of our study, we focused on a method based on palpation. Meantime our main goal was to define a method, which can distinguish different pulse rhythm of the patient by special medical device [8, 9, 20, 21].

In the practice of Western medicine, more considers to individual symptoms of diseases. The difference of the eastern medicine from the Western medicine is consideration of any diagnose based on the whole body as a complex unified system (innate nature of human). Proper identification of any diagnosis should consider basics of the human's lifestyle and healthy conditions. Regarding eastern medicine methodology such as information will give a sign to doctor to estimate human diseases and to offer more correct treatment for a human. The goal of our research is to develop MES based on eastern medicine to support decision-making process for diagnose of patients. We are expecting to use the developed application in various cases such as: training of students as future medical doctors, self-diagnose of interested people, to support decision-making process from distance in urgent cases and so on. Moreover, we hope that new application will help people to learn and hear own body early as possible to avoid a late hard diagnosis of different diseases.

2 The State of the Art

Western and Eastern medicine uses completely different methodologies to make a diagnosis for a human. The main method of western medicine is to collect many possible symptoms from human by questions and measures all possible quantitative value which producing the human body. From here we can do summary that diagnosis of western medicine is the result of observation on collected quantitative data from the human body. A diagnosis by western medicine is to diagnose for physical body only and here playing the main role collected data by medical apparatus. Therefore, treatment with western medicine is a different kind of counted medicines depending on the age and weight of the human. Nevertheless, nowadays we know that any medicine has some kind of side effects to human body. One medicine can be good for one disease but we have no guarantee for that same medicine leads to another disease. Such as development requested from researchers think about a new way to make most correct cure in acceptable time also to provide human organ-friendly medicines.

One of the possible solutions to the above-defined problem is to use traditional medicine methodology, which more used in Asian countries. Some Asian countries still using this method presently, we can refer here to Tibetan medicine.

Next possible solution for giving problem can be to develop medical expert systems to provide not only medical doctors to support early self-diagnosis of any disease by interested citizens. In introduction section, we shortly mentioned about the development of the medical expert system in general. The medical expert system is still developing but in limited interested people and research groups. The new direction of expert system development is to apply advantages of artificial intelligence algorithms in the expert system. Researchers working on an advanced medical expert system where used eastern methodology to estimate diagnosis of human and treatment portions. For example, Suryani Lukman, Yulan He and Siu-Cheung Hui worked on calculation method to combine advantages of western and eastern medicine into the diagnose system [17]. They developed calculation methods to use eastern medicine methodology into the medical software to support decision-making about the diagnosis.

From the middle of 1960, scientists and programmers developed various different expert systems for medical diagnosis. Since the 80 s the development of expert systems, both in theory and practice have gained tremendous success and development and demonstrated its great vitality and value [25]. Usage of the expert system depends on the implementation field and can be different in application. Various types of expert systems are used for decision-making support to define medical diagnosis [15, 18, 19, 22–24] and treatments.

Development of computational technologies gives the chance to reach a new level at present visually the course of a disease according to mathematical models. Technology development opens us big opportunities to develop a new type of expert system where we can visualize self-diagnosis by the expert system to users. One of the main differences of eastern medicine from Western, diagnosis method is more focused on the innate nature of human in depth relation to the observation of patient behavior and lifestyle. For example, we refer to [2, 11]. In this work, the author gives recommendations on proper nutrition and a healthy lifestyle from the example of Tibetan medicine.

Zhambaldagbaev and Zandanova developed a two-mode expert system based on Tibetan medicine, so-called "Emchi" [11]. Eastern medicine methodology used survey which created by the knowledge base of "Chzhud-shi". "Chzhud-shi" is the expert system which developed by Boronoyev Expert system "Chzhud-shi" is in the composition of the automated system of pulse diagnostics, based on the knowledge laid down in the canonical treatise "Chzhud-shi" and representing two of the methods of diagnosis used in Tibetan medicine: questioning and inspection [2].

3   The Architecture of Training Application

Training application (TA) architecture consists of the main parts (Fig. 1).

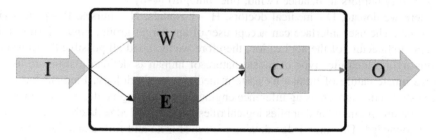

Fig. 1. Architecture of TA

Here we donate, I - input of application, W - Western medicine diagnosis, E - Eastern medicine diagnosis, C - comparison unit and O - the output of the application. In this section, we will focus on the "E" part, only.

Figure 2 shows the architecture of "E" part. The "E" part consists of two main parts: User interface and Request processing part.

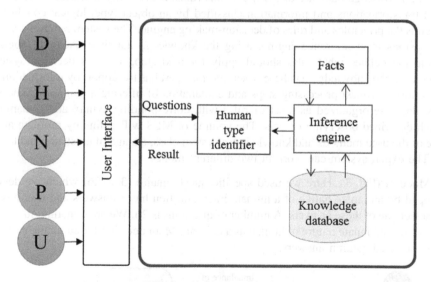

Fig. 2. Architecture of MES

- User interface divided into different target groups: medical doctors, hospitals, nurses, patient, and user.
- Request processing element includes sub-functions: facts, identification of innate nature of human, explanation engine, database, rules and knowledge database.

The MES has both: database and knowledge database. Knowledge database stores rules based on eastern medicine methodology. Rules related to innate nature of human for making the decision for diagnose. Innate nature of human idea discussed in work of Dr. Choijinnimaeva. The fundamental concepts of the Tibetan medicine are to keep the three bodily humors in balance (wind, bile, phlegm) [4–6].

Here we donate, D - medical doctors, H – hospitals, N – nurses, P – patient and U – users. The user interface can accept user of any target group. Figure 2 shows the general architecture of the application, therefore we included all possible target groups in this figure. Identifier type of innate nature of human is defined a structure to recognize innate nature of human by eastern medicine methodology. Element facts produce estimated diagnose using inference engine. Inference engine defines conclusion of innate nature of human and applies logical rules to the knowledge database and reduced new knowledge. The knowledge database is set of facts and formulated knowledge of experts and organized by a collection of data about special characteristics of innate nature of human and diseases.

Main architecture bases in one fundamental structure of request processing part and switches off some obligatory parts. In the literature on an expert system, three key components described. All these components are in each expert system: knowledge database (KDB), inference engine (IE) and user interface (UI). Any expert systems are based on the set of knowledge structured for simplification of the process of decision-making [7].

The knowledge database of MES contains rules, data of this area describing expedient transformations and information classified by an object type, logical conclusion contains the principles and rules of decision-making engine. The system receives logical conclusions from inference engine, using the knowledge database. Actually, logical conclusion defines what rules should apply for next step, and this decision system accesses to the knowledge database. User interface part has to support by information to users during request processing steps and explanation of offering a diagnosis. Knowledge database organized as a set of rules with corresponding syntax and semantics, which described observing objects. The volume of MES will define by problem area, type of the used methods and knowledge, a system class, a stage of existence and tools.

The expert system can work in two different modes.

- Mode A (Fig. 3). Here we used specific questionnaire (3 × 26) which we developed by an innate native of a human. Each question has 3 answers and user has to select one of these answers. A number of questions is 26. We are donating questions as row and innate nature of human as a column. Main decision based on the number of selected column answers.

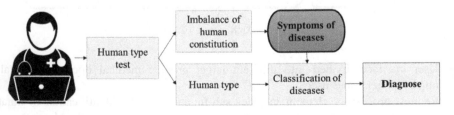

Fig. 3. System in mode A

- Mode B (Fig. 4). Here user (target groups) would be used as the questions, and the answer would be a diagnosis of the user's disease.

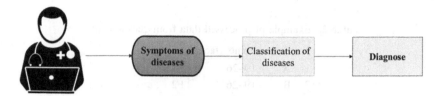

Fig. 4. System in Mode B

We are focusing in mode A. For example, if a human has a dominant type so-called "wind" then more likely suffer disease and it can be related to the neurological and cardiovascular system. It partly explained by own properties of wind element, that more support human mental activity. Accordingly, the system is able to give an admissible result for users that it chosen from the selected group of classification of diseases, which have more exposure to highly probability match for diagnosis.

To define a 3 × 26 set of questions we worked on the innate native of a human with the cooperation of medical doctor (Dr. Enkhtuvshin, N. - Mongolian national center for maternal and child health) who has many years of experiences in both types of medicine: Western and traditional. New aspect of this MES is we are not only defining innate native of human, moreover we are comparing estimated diagnosis from part "E" with part "W". By other words, this is our first time that we are trying to compare two diagnoses of patient by both type of medicine: by western and eastern medicine. Part "C" of our system will calculate correct probability by offered diagnosis.

4 Calculation Rule for Inference Engine

In the eastern medicine, all people are divided into three types by innate nature of human: wind, bile, and phlegm. Moreover, depending on type each person has specific properties. Table 1 shows these specific properties by main three types.

Table 1. Human type and their specific properties

Human type	Specific properties by innate native of human
Wind	Stooped, skinny, dark blue complexion, over talkative, unable to endure cold and the wind, shuffling of joints when walk, small in stature, poor strength of the body, little sleeper, love to sing, to dance, grapple and to bet. Like sweet, sour and bitter foods
Bile	Tend to be more rounded often hungry and thirsty, yellow complexion, yellow hair, intelligent, arrogant, and sweaty with the putrid smell, middle in stature and strength. Like sweet, bitter, eager, fresh drink
Phlegm	A Little heat in the body, heavy, pale complexion, with the thrown back arrogant, burly, able-bodied, able to endure protracted hunger and thirsty, sleeper, quiet. Like sour, musty, heavy foods

Data from Table 1 used for inference engine of MES. Based on this data we defined 3×26 matrix questionnaire for MES. Depending on the feedback of user, MES making the decision for diagnose (Table 2).

Table 2. Example of processed data from questionnaire

№	Signs	Points (facts)	Indicators
1	A	19–26	F1
2	B	19–26	F2
3	C	19–26	F3
4	A	9–18	F4
5	B	9–18	F5
6	C	9–18	F6
7	A	0–8	F7
8	B	0–8	F8
9	C	0–8	F9

Outcome of MES is divided into three types (Table 3).

Table 3. Human own natural behavior types

Types	MES definition	Hints from MES by definition
T1	Predominant human behaviors	The highest numbers show leading disorder and human own behavior, and second points secondary
T2	Mixed human behaviors	Two disorders approximately in equal (points)
T3	Composite human behavior	All three disorders in equal (points)

Most people have one disorder predominant, a few have two disorders approximately equal and fewer will have all three disorders in equal proportion. For instance, if MES defined as the wind than bile and phlegm, it would show that human has a wind disorder is predominant.

Suppose that in our example, the information received will give the following directions (Fig. 5). For example:

- User selected simultaneously facts F1 AND F8 OR F9 then MES should show type T1.

$$F1 \cdot [F8 + F9] \rightarrow T1$$

- User selected simultaneously F2 AND F7 OR F9 without F1 AND F3 then MES should show T2.

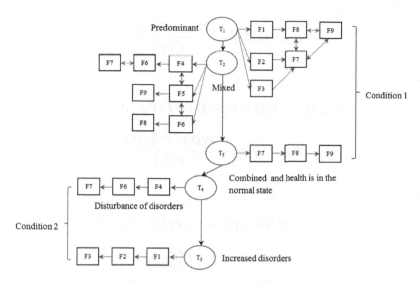

Fig. 5. Calculation rule with decision-making tree diagram

$$F2 \cdot [F7 + F9] \cdot \overline{F_1} \cdot \overline{F_3} \to T2$$

- If all 3 facts in equal, that's mean type T3.

$$[F7 \cdot F8 \cdot F9] \to T3$$

Assume that we have set D of diagnosis with symptoms S. Based on these input expert to have to estimate diagnose for the patient. Each diagnose can have some hypothesis, where $\{S_j\}, j = \overline{1, m}$ – set of symptoms. For every S_j we will consider that, giving some symptom or no symptoms - $\overline{S_j}$.

Input data are:

- $P(D_i), i = \overline{1, n}$ - a priori probability of diagnosis, with $P(\overline{D_i}) = 1 - P(D_i)$.

We donate:

- $P(S_j/D_i)$ – the conditional probability of a symptom, if observed some symptoms from the patient.
- $P_{apost}(S_j/D_i)$ – a posteriori probability of diagnosis.

The probability of MES diagnose is calculating by next formula:

$$\{P(S_j/D_i)\}; \{P(\overline{S_j}/D_i)\}; \{P(S_j/\overline{D_i})\}; \{P(\overline{S_j}/\overline{D_i})\}$$

Evaluating a posteriori probability with positive and negative answers by symptom: $P_{apost}(D_i)$ and $P_{apost}(\overline{D_i})$.

$$P_{apost}(D_i/S_j) = \frac{P(D_i) \cdot P(S_j/D_i)}{P(S_j)} \tag{1}$$

where,

$$P_{apost}(S_j) = P(D_i) \cdot P(S_j/D_i) + P(\overline{D_i}) \cdot P(S_j/\overline{D_i}) \tag{2}$$

$$P_{apost}(S_j/D_i) = \frac{P(D_i) \cdot P(\overline{S_j}/D_i)}{P(\overline{S_j})} \tag{3}$$

where,

$$P(\overline{S_j}) = P(D_i) \cdot P(\overline{S_j}/D_i) + P(\overline{D_i}) \cdot P(\overline{S_j}/\overline{D_i}) \tag{4}$$

$$P(\overline{D_i}/S_j) = 1 - P(D_i/S_j) \tag{5}$$

$$P_{apost}(\overline{D_i}/\overline{S_j}) = 1 - P_{apost}(D_i/\overline{S_j}) \tag{6}$$

5   Application Design and Test

The user interface of the application designed to be easy for everyone. Figure 6 shows how to register a new user in first access to the application. Registration and opening account (Login) is similar to every user oriented application.

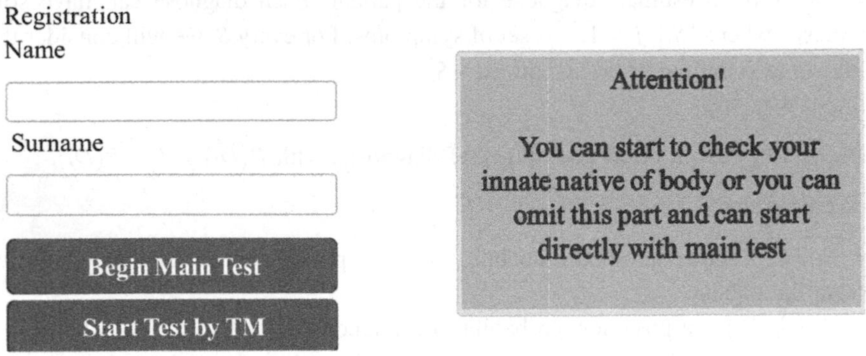

Registration
Name

Surname

Begin Main Test

Start Test by TM

Attention!

You can start to check your innate native of body or you can omit this part and can start directly with main test

Fig. 6. Login page of user

The user should answer all 26 questions then MES will process collected data and open the result of processing in new windows (Fig. 7).

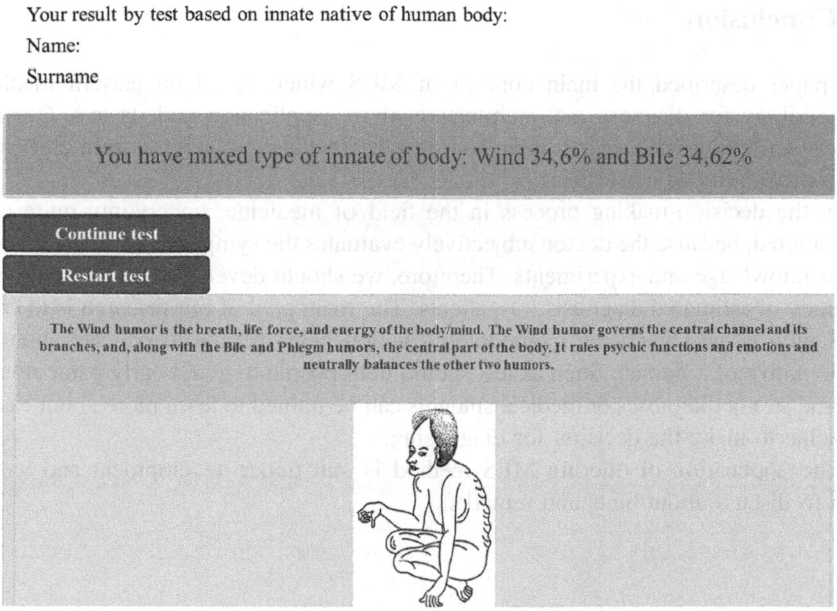

Your result by test based on innate native of human body:

Name:

Surname

You have mixed type of innate of body: Wind 34,6% and Bile 34,62%

Continue test

Restart test

The Wind humor is the breath, life force, and energy of the body/mind. The Wind humor governs the central channel and its branches, and, along with the Bile and Phlegm humors, the central part of the body. It rules psychic functions and emotions and neutrally balances the other two humors.

Fig. 7. Result of MES

If the user wants to repeat, the test can do it and all process will start from the beginning. Moreover, the application has down list menu for user:

- Save of result
- Continue test
- Restart test
- See hints about question
- Select criteria

After the test, MES calculates the probability of diagnosis (Table 4). From this result, the user can get information about own innate native human properties and estimated diagnoses with calculated probabilities.

Table 4. Calculated probabilities for estimated diagnoses

#	Code	Diagnose	Probability
1	18	Pneumoconiosis	0.500250125062531
2	3	Sinusitis	0.476190476190476
3	25	Gastric ulcer	0.476190476190476
4	46	Coronary heart disease	0.444691495275153
5	45	Epilepsy	0.444691495275153

6 Conclusion

The paper described the main concept of MES which based on eastern medicine methodology for diagnose and architecture of the application and its test. Our new aspect of offering MES is a comparison of western diagnose with eastern and calculating probability of correctness.

In the decision-making process in the field of medicine, uncertainty quite often encountered, because the doctor subjectively evaluates the symptoms of illnesses based on his knowledge and experiments. Therefore, we should develop MES to increase the accuracy of estimated diagnosis for patients. The main goal of our research is to create MES with eastern medicine methodology, which helps people to educate about the innate native of a human. Such as test should help people to avoid early panic relating to some strong diagnoses or medical students can be trained to learn more about eastern medicine to make the decision for diagnosing.

The application of offering MES method is still under development and we are open to discuss about hints and remarks.

References

1. Asefeh, B.H., et al.: Information and communication technology in medical education: an experience from a developing country. J. Pak. Med. Assoc. **62**(3), 71–75 (2012)
2. Boronoyev, V.V.: Practical implementation of the method of diagnosis by the pulse of tools. Int. J. Appl. Fundam. Res. **12**(1), 188–192 (2015). https://www.applied-research.ru/ru/article/view?id=7844. Accessed 25 Apr 2017
3. Bruce, G.B., Edward, H.S.: Rule-Based Expert Systems: The MYCIN Experiments of the Stanford Heuristic Programming Project. Addison Wesley, Boston (1984)
4. Choijinnimaeva, S.G.: Diseases of Nervous People, or Where Blows Wind. Press Astral, Russia (2010)
5. Choijinnimaeva, S.G.: Diseases of Big People, or What is the Phlegm. Press Piter, Russia (2016)
6. Choijinnimaeva, S.G.: Diseases of Strong People, or How Bridle Bile. Press Astral, Russia (2010)
7. Echeverría, F.R., Echeverría, C.R.: Application of expert systems in medicine. In: Proceedings of Conference on Artificial Intelligence Research and Development, pp. 3–4. IOS Press, Amsterdam (2006)
8. Grif, M.G., Yumchmaa, A.: Application of expert system by pulse diagnostics. In: Articles of Novosibirsk State Technical University, vol. 3, no. 81, pp. 114–133. Press NGTU, Russia (2015)
9. Grif, M.G., Yumchmaa, A.: Data analysis of expert system by pulse diagnosis. In: Proceedings of 11th International Forum of Strategic Technology (IFOST), Russia, vol. 1, pp. 329–332 (2016)
10. Izet, M., et al.: Information technologies (ITs) in medical education. J. Adv. Med. Educ. Professionalism **19**(3), 161–167 (2011)
11. Zhambaldagbaev, N.C., Zandanova, G.I.: Two-mode expert system based on Tibetan medicine: "EMCHI-1". In: Proceedings of Russian Scientific and Technical Conference on Diffraction and Wave Propagation, Russia, pp. 234–236 (1996)

12. Keith, D.: A brief historical review of explanation in expert system applications. In: Proceedings of the 25th IASTED International Multi-Conference: Artificial Intelligence and Applications, pp. 604–609. Press Anaheim, USA (2007)
13. Mcleish, M., Cecile, M.: Enhancing medical expert systems with knowledge obtained from statistical data. Ann. Math. Artif. Intell. **2**, 261–276 (1990). Springer, Heidelberg
14. Naeem, M., et al.: Blended learning' as an effective teaching and learning strategy in clinical medicine: a comparative cross-sectional university-based study. J. Taibah Univ. Med. Sci. **8**(1), 12–17 (2013)
15. Patra, P.S.K., Sahu, D.P., Mandal, I.: An expert system for diagnosis of human diseases. Int. J. Comput. Appl. **1**(13), 71–73 (2010)
16. Puppe, F.: Systematic Introduction to Expert Systems. Springer, Heidelberg (1993)
17. Suryani, L., Yulan, H., Siu-Cheung, H.: Computational methods for traditional chinese medicine: a survey. Comput. Methods Programs Biomed. **88**, 283–294 (2007)
18. Uranchimeg, T., Javzandulam, D.: An opportunity to use expert system in medicine. In: Proceeding of Scientific Seminars of PES, MUST, pp. 25–27. Press of MUST, Mongolia (2006)
19. Uranchimeg, T., Munh-Ochir, N.: Usage of the object oriented method in the decision making process for expert system. In: Proceeding of Scientific Seminars of PES, MUST, pp. 15–17. Press of MUST, Mongolia (2009)
20. Yumchmaa, A., et al.: The automatic diagnostic by pulse based on the expert system. In: Proceedings of IBS International Summer School, pp. 17–20. TUD Press, Germany (2015)
21. Yumchmaa, A.: Aspects of medical experts system by pulse. In: Proceedings of the 2016 Summer School on Information and Communication Technology, China, vol. 1, pp. 22–25 (2016)
22. Yumchmaa, A., Uranchimeg, T.: Decision support expert system for medical engineers, problems and solutions. In: Proceeding of Health and Young Researchers Scientific Conference, pp. 19–24. Press of MUST, Mongolia (2009)
23. Zahra, S., Fagnza, T., Rahmatalan, A.: The role of educational technology in medical education. J. Adv. Med. Educ. Professionalism **2**(4), 179–183 (2014)
24. Zahrani, N.M.A., Soomro, S., Memon, A.G.: Breast cancer diagnosis and treatment of prophetic medicine using expert system. J. Inf. Commun. Technol. **4**(2), 20–26 (2010)
25. The evolution of expert systems. https://ru.scribd.com/document/297691212/F030-The-Evolution-of-Expert-System-by-Noran. Accessed 14 June 2017

Game-Based Learning Platform
for Integrating International IT-Students
into the Russian Educational Environment

Anna V. Matokhina, Olga A. Shabalina$^{(\boxtimes)}$, Natalia V. Kharlamova,
and Eugenie A. Kulikov

Volgograd State Technical University, Volgograd, Russia
matokhina.a.v@gmail.com, o.a.shabalina@gmail.com,
{gorkovskaya, fl_kulikov}@mail.ru

Abstract. Success in training foreign students in Russian universities strongly depends on the level of Russian language the students have mastered before they start their study. Teaching Russian language as foreign (RaF) has some special requirements that should be taken into consideration while teaching young people who are going to study at Russian universities. One of the promising approaches for studying foreign languages is the use of educational computer games. The authors of this paper have developed a game-based learning platform for studying RaF based on the idea of immersing a user into a virtual language environment in different life situations. The platform includes a set of games, each game is devoted to one topic that is necessary to know while studying at the university in a foreign country. The games consist of different game levels, each game level includes several lexical and grammatical tasks. For creating certain tasks corresponding templates with empty text boxes are created. To protect viewing right answers before playing the game, an encryption algorithm based on a pyramid permutation cipher and double inversion of the text lines is developed. An example of the game implementation is described and the results of testing developed platform showing significant improvement in speaking, reading, writing, audition, and even communication skills are presented.

Keywords: Educational game · Russian as a foreign · RaF · Assignment template · Level map · Web application

1 Introduction

Success in training foreign students in Russian universities strongly depends on the level of Russian language the students have mastered before they start their study. To help students adapt to a new language environment some Russian universities organize special departments where potential students are teached Russian language and prepared to study in Russia.

Teaching Russian language as foreign (RaF) young people who are going to study at Russian universities has some special requirements that should be taken into consideration:

© Springer International Publishing AG 2017
A. Kravets et al. (Eds.): CIT&DS 2017, CCIS 754, pp. 762–773, 2017.
DOI: 10.1007/978-3-319-65551-2_55

- in most cases the language training should start «from scratch», without using the student's native language;
- the very first lessons should provide the **lexical and grammatical knowledge** that would be enough for the quick adaptation of the students for living in Russia;
- the topics for the lessons should help students to faster adapt to a new cultural and linguistic environment and to be ready to study at the university.

2 Related Work

One of the promising approaches for studying foreign languages is the use of educational computer games. By now, digital game-based technologies for studying RaF have been implemented in a number of desktop and mobile applications. Game-based technologies are used for instance in the "1C: Tutor. Russian as a foreign language" [1], and such mobile apps as "Russian Lessons", "Learning Russian language", etc.

However, the most part of such applications are intended for teaching Russian language as a discipline, and they are not focused on adapting international students who are supposed to come to a new language environment (Fig. 1).

Fig. 1. Examples of RaF game

3   Methodology

3.1   Platform Structure

The authors of this paper have developed a game-based learning platform for studying RaF based on the idea of immersing a user into a virtual language environment in different life situations. The platform includes a set of games, each game is devoted to one topic that is necessary to know while studying at the university in a foreign country. The structure of the platform content is shown in Fig. 2.

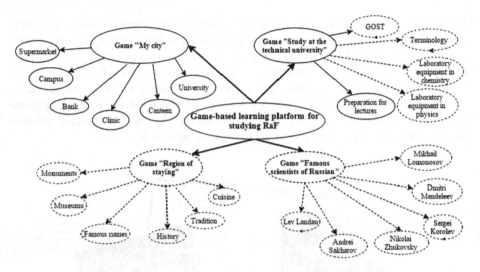

Fig. 2. The structure of the platform content.

Each game consists of different game levels, each level is matched to a corresponding section of the basic part of the educational standard for studying RaF. Each game level includes several lexical and grammatical tasks. The lexical tasks are the following:

- sorting Russian words by type;
- placing the words or their combinations to the right place in the text;
- selecting the right type of the word.

- Grammatical tasks:

- inserting words to the text in right time or case;
- agreeing words in the sentence;
- constructing correct sentences from words and their combinations.

The development process started from the development of two games - "My City" and "Study at the Technical University", devoted to the topics, the authors consider to be the most important ones for the newcomers.

3.2   Functionality

All the games allow to choose a game character for each game, and also select a part and view the results of the missions the player in stages, and in the whole parts of the game. Knowing the insight of students and their quick adaptation to new information technologies, that's why tasks in the game are encrypted, answers the repeated passage of the levels are shuffled randomly (Fig. 3).

The game's content was created by the staff of the faculty of foreign specialist preparation in the Department of Russian of VSTU.

The application is written in PHP 7.0 (HTML/CSS/JS) without third-party frameworks and uses the user's browser for input\output data. Not required for operation of the DBMS, but need a web server with support for mod_php (Apache/NGINX).

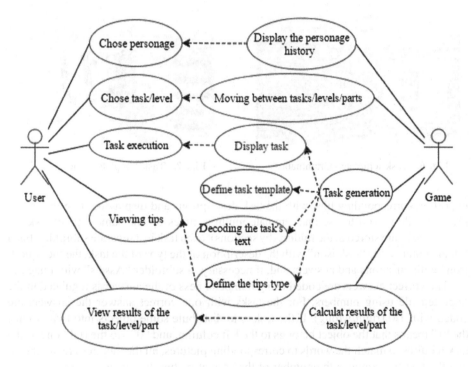

Fig. 3. Use case game diagram

3.3   Data Templates and Structures

As noted above, each game contains different types of game tasks for each game level. For creating certain tasks corresponding templates with empty text boxes have been created. Such approach allows to use the same template several times for the same type of assignment or to load different files for filling out the assignment text fields, depending on the number of player attempts. The database of tasks, level scripts and graphical content for each section has been created. Some examples of the templates are shown in Figs. 4, 5, 6 and 7. A special program function has been developed for

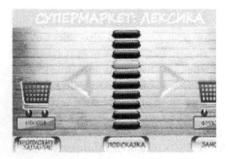

Fig. 4. Task template "Lexical"

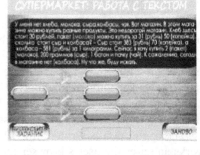

Fig. 5. Task template "Working this text"

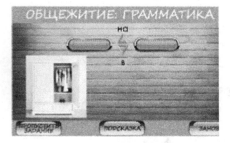

Fig. 6. Task template "Grammatics"

Fig. 7. Task template "Vocabulary"

importing corresponding files with the task descriptions and displaying it on the screen [2]. This allows you to use one template multiple times for the same type of task.

The tasks are stored in the folders (by sections), each task in a separate subfolder. Each folder contain a file "task.json" with the description of the type of the task, the file "quest. json" with questions and answers and, if necessary, a subfolder "Assets" with images.

The correct answers are coded using numbers. ness of the answer is regulated in the imported file using numbers. For the tasks with one correct answer the answers are coded with 1/0 (right/wrong). If the task is to distribute some objects into two groups, the "1" means that the object belongs to the left column, and "0" - to the right one. If the task requires to match the words to corresponding pictures, all the pictures are numbered and the text file contains the number of the correct picture that matches to the word.

In each section there is a file "level.json" with the name and description of the level, as well as with the background image. The root of the structure is the file "map.json", in which the level map is stored with the order of tasks and the transition between them (Fig. 8).

When the button is clicked, the function of determining the correctness of the answer and switching to the next screen is called.

The following types of tasks are used in the game:

– to sort the names of food by types (for example, fruits: apples, oranges, etc., vegetables: cucumbers, tomatoes, etc.)

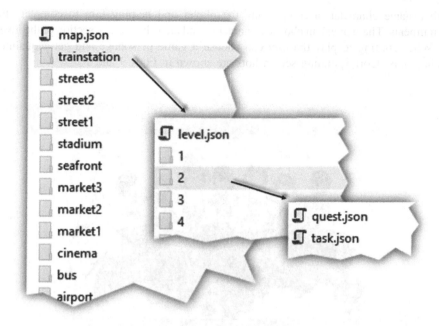

Fig. 8. Level-data structure

- to put an object in relation to another object in accordance with the meaning of the given preposition (for example, in the table, on the table, etc.)
- to choose correct ending of the word (for example, depending on the case of the word, personal endings of verbs, etc.)
- to fill in the blanks in the text with words in the right rect case and with the right prepositions, etc.)
- to match a noun to the object or profession.

A set of hints presented in a form of a table is attached to each block. The tables include prepositional-case system for selecting the right cases, the tables of right verbs to the concrete case, etc.

There is also a button "Start over" which has been always active. If the user wants to restart the task, he returns back to the beginning of the block, but in this case he gets an updated task (the sequence of answers for the task is changed).

4   An Example of Implementation. The Game "My City"

The game "My city" consists of seven levels. Each level consists of several sections devoted to a specific real life situation with a set of tasks of increasing complexity for writing or translating some words, phrases or sentences. For each type of assignment used a template with empty text fields, for importing files with corresponding data and their on-screen display implemented special functions, described above. Each level is matched with a game character, accompanying the player and helping him to complete the assignments. The player can choose a character, and also choose any section of the level.

When starting to play the user can choose a game personage and get acquainted his/her story. Corresponding screenshots are shown in Figs. 9 and 10.

Fig. 9. Start page of the game.

Fig. 10. Splash screen part "My city" and a fragment of the personage history.

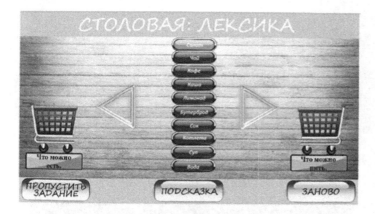

Fig. 11. The tasks in the level "Canteen: Vocabulary"   **Fig. 12.** The tasks in retry

In the game "My City", each section includes four sets of tasks: vocabulary on a given topic, lexical, grammar working on the case and the text or exercises in which there are verbs that are used with this case.

For instance, in the vocabulary task of the level "Canteen", the player is asked to sort products by those that can be consumed and those that can be drunk (Fig. 11). If for some reasons the player clicks the "Start over" button, he gets the same list of products, but in a different order (Fig. 12).

After each block of tasks, the system displays the result. Depending on the accumulated points, the player may proceed to a block of grammar, or pass the task on vocabulary again (Fig. 13).

Fig. 13. Result example

The player can anytime ask for a tip. Depending on the task it can be, for instance, the list of the names of the products in English language, the words in right cases. The examples of the tips are given in Figs. 14 and 15.

Fig. 14. Tip in level "Supermarket: Vocabulary"

Fig. 15. Tip in level "Bank: Grammatics"

5 Experiment

To evaluate the effectiveness of the suggested approach an experiment was conducted at the preparatory department of Volgograd State Technical University (VSTU). Two groups of students from Iraq, Jordan, Congo, Guinea-Bissau (14 people in each group), who studied the basics of Russian language, took part in the experiment. The first group of students used the developed games while studying Russian language, the students from the second group studied the language in a traditional way. At the end of studying the level of spoken Russian and communicative skills of the students in both groups was evaluated.

To estimate the results of studying a system of standardized tests designed by the staff of the preparatory department was used. The subject of evaluation was the correctness of the use of lexical and grammatical rules of modern Russian language.

The experiment showed that the students that used the games in comparison to their classmates who did not used them distinguished lexical units much easier, correctly, practically without errors used prepositional-case forms of the names and verbal forms; faster and better build simple and complex proposals.

The results of the test in the "Lexicon. Grammar" are shown in Fig. 16

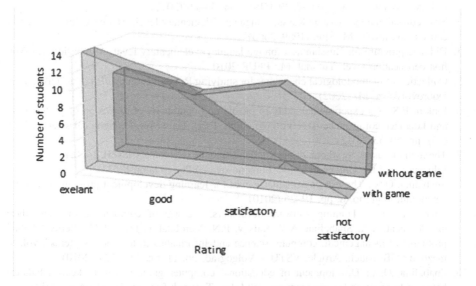

Fig. 16. Graph the assessment of students knowledge on results of study of basic level of Russian language proficiency with and without the use of the game (the data for the 2016–2017 academic year)

The results of testing developed games showed not only the significant improvement in mastering the Russian language, but also the students interest and enthusiasm while playing the game. Almost all students confirmed that the game really helped them to train their speaking, reading, writing, audition, and even communication skills.

6 Conclusions

The platform interface was designed using iterative testing on the target group of international students of VSTU. Currently, the platform is used in VSTU for training the Russian language skills, preparing for Russian language tests and exams, to improve the conversational vocabulary of international students. The aggregated results of the game application will be used to evaluate the effectiveness of the proposed technology of teaching RaF and to develop the next levels of the game.

Results obtained in the support of the RFBR project number 16-07-00611\16-a.

References

1. 1C: Tutor. Russian as a foreign language. CD-ROM, 2005 (N Rumyantsev. M., Tsareva N. Y.)
2. The use of gaming technologies for teaching Russian as a foreign language in high school. A.V. Matokhin, N. In: Kharlamov, O.A., Shabalina, E.V., Tyumentseva, E.K. Proverok. Izvestia Volggtu. Ser. Actual problems of management, computer science and Informatics in technical systems. – Volgograd, № 1(196), pp. 83–89 (2017)
3. State educational standard on Russian language. Elementary level. At a basic level. 1, 2, 3, 4 certification levels. M: SPb. (1999–2000)
4. Didactic program for Russian as a foreign language: elementary level. At a basic level. The first certification level. Tutorial. M.: PFUR 2010
5. Collection of methodological challenges for studying Russian language/E.I. Vasilenko, V.V. Dobrovolskaya. M. (2002)
6. Ionkin, E.S.: An experimental study of factors and conditions of formation of professional and language competence. Izv. Volgogr. GOS. PED. Univ. Ser. Pedagogical science, № 1 (65), pp. 50–53 (2012)
7. The road to Russia. Textbook of the Russian language (elementary level). 2-e Izd., Rev. – M.: Education and the University. M.V. Lomonosov. – SPb.: "Zlatoust", 344 p. (2003)
8. Shabalina, O.A.: The use of computer games for learning development programme ensure. Open education, no. 6, pp. 19–26 (2010)
9. Shabalina, O.A.: Training software developers: the use of computer games and their development. S.A. Shabalina, A.V. Kataev, P.N. Vorobkalov, Izv. VSTU. Series "Actual problems of management, computer science and Informatics in technical systems", vol. 9: mezhvuz. SB. nauch. Article. VSTU. - Volgograd, no. 11, pp. 117–124 (2010)
10. Shabalina, O.A.: Development of educational computer games: how to keep a balance between learning and game components? Educ. Technol. Soc. **16**(3), 586–602 (2013)
11. Parygin, D.S.: Model out intercommunication system meet the needs of residents. In: Proceedings of the Volgograd State Technical University: series actual problems of control, computer science and Informatics in technical systems, vol. 17: mezhvuz. SB. nauch. article/VSTU. – Volgograd: VSTU IUNL, № 14(117), pp. 90–95 (2013)
12. 3I-approach to the development of computer games for learning technical subjects us Shabalina O.A., Vorobkalov, P.N., Kataev, A.V. J. Comput. Inf. Technol. **4**, 45–51 (2011)
13. Kryuchkova, L.S.: Practical methods of teaching Russian as a foreign language: textbook. L.S. Kryuchkov, N. In: Mosinska. – M.: Flinta: Nauka (2011)
14. Novikova, O.A., Shurygin, A.I., Chaikina, T.A.: Methodological support independe-Yateley foreign students pre-University training. International cooperation in education: Materials of IV International scientific-practical conference. Part 2. SPb: Izd-vo SPbSPU, 300 p. (2004)
15. Kharlamova, N.: In: Filimonova, N. Yu., Gorky, V.D.: The Importance of role-playing games in teaching Russian as a foreign language. Current issues of vocational education, T. 10. no. 13(116), pp. 152–154 (2013)

16. Serova, L.K.: Computer technology at the initial stage of teaching Russian as a foreign language. Traditions and innovations in the professional activity of teacher of Russian as a foreign language: an Educational monograph. Under the General editorship of Jabroni, S.A. Noah, T.M. Balykhina. - M.: Russian University of peoples friendship (2002)
17. Kryuchkova, L.S.: Practical methods of teaching Russian as a foreign language: textbook. In: Handbook – 2nd edn. – M.: Flinta: Nauka (2011)
18. Glenaroua, R.: Application of games on the Russian language lessons/Russian language as foreign and methodology of its teaching: the XXI century. – Moscow state pedagogical University, h. 1 (2007)

Designing of an Internet Portal for Scaffolding and Development of Network Educational Communities

Svetlana Gerkushenko[1(⊠)], Georgy Gerkushenko[2], Olga Khudobina[3], and Igor Fedulov[1]

[1] Volgograd State Socio-Pedagogical University, Volgograd, Russian Federation
svetlana@gerkushenko.ru, infedoulov@mail.ru
[2] Volgograd State Technical University, Volgograd, Russian Federation
georgiy@gerkushenko.ru
[3] Volgograd State Medical University, Volgograd, Russian Federation
Olga_hdb@mail.ru

Abstract. The article is devoted to the problem of finding effective means and methods of arranging the process of education in the network professional learning communities. The communities are an important phenomenon of modern education system. Their appearance is obliged to a global development of web technologies. The authors describe one of the possible ways of solving the problem, associated with working out a program of the scaffolding of pedagogical activities in the network of modern learning communities. There are considered theoretical and practical aspects of arranging interactive creative forms of the instruction based on game learning. Developed by the authors and launched into operation an Internet portal for methodological scaffolding of teachers of preschool educational institutions is an effective illustration of the importance of such educational tools, as media project.

Keywords: Internet portal · Professional learning community · Instructional scaffolding · Joint training · Network educational community · Professional education · Professional cooperation · Game-based learning

1 Introduction

The main peculiarity of professional activity in the sphere of preschool training is its polyfunctionality, including both organization of preschool education and scaffolding, and advising parents. It also stipulates conducting research activities, a comprehensive evaluation, and self-concept of educational outcomes. Under the circumstances, it becomes evident the necessary to arrange permanent « training» of the staff for the purpose of achieving educational goals and tasks. The most effective way of arranging the «joint training» is the close and productive cooperation of colleagues. The phenomenon of the involvement of a specialist in a certain professional community appears great potential for self-development of the teacher and results in improved quality of education. To understand better the specific character of the functioning of the community they should provide insight into the described phenomenon.

© Springer International Publishing AG 2017
A. Kravets et al. (Eds.): CIT&DS 2017, CCIS 754, pp. 774–791, 2017.
DOI: 10.1007/978-3-319-65551-2_56

In the research work, there is considered the following understanding of the concept «professional learning community».

Firstly, professional learning community (PLC) is a group of specialists working together in the same sphere of schooling and collaborating with each other to get better educational results and that of upbringing within modern educational standards [4]. Secondly, PLC is a team or a number of teams working together, interacting on the basis of mutual responsibility and doing their best to attain a common objective [3]. Thirdly, PLC is a group of specialist aimed at continuing education, a group of people focused on a proper result and being guided by the principle of collective nature [3].

Thus, the essential characteristic of the community is the productive interaction of professionals consolidated by a common idea in the sphere of their professional activities.

Nowadays professional pedagogical activity teems with uncertainties and novelties of educational tools, methods, and technologies. The situation requires expansion of the sphere of professional interaction from communication between colleagues within the same institutions to regional, national and even international levels. At the same time, the development of telecommunication technologies has led to the emergence of networks among teachers of different educational establishments, parents, children, spontaneously formed social enterprises of a new type of network community [6].

There is also introduced a new certain term network methodological community, which characterizes the community of specialists of the education system, united by telecommunication. Its purpose is to support professional activities through a joint network of practical activities in the framework of the set requirements to the quality of education, institutional constraints and existing resource provision of the local area [5]. The network methodological communities are arranged to offer an opportunity for - self-realization and self-empowerment of teachers through joint network activities; - development and realization of creative abilities of the community members; -creation of innovative educational environment and support new educational initiatives. Online communication in these communities takes place through a variety of Web 2.0 services such as social networks, wiki-systems, chats, blogs, video services etc. [1, 8, 12].

1.1   Functions of the Network Communities

Communicative Function
This is a key function of the network communities. There are two main components in the structure of the function according to Volokhonskiy's opinion. They are communication itself and expansion of the sphere of communication [11]. The function allows participants of the communities to keep up their conversation and share joint interests easily due to technological facilities of the network communities. During the conversation, the factor of virtuality in communication manifests itself more vividly. The lack of eye contact activates the ability to communicate in a virtual design image of each other [5]. Users give each other properties and characteristics, which are called the parameters of mediated communication. This communication is the subject – subject character.

Network communities can provide a very valuable personal and professional communication between members of the community, in which there is an active interaction on issues of a professional nature and perception as part of remote communication that allows the participants of the Internet community to know each other by learning profile, as well as direct communication with chat and video channel.

Gnostic Function

The inclusion in a network community according to the thematic interests allows people to communicate with others involved in this community and to gain all necessary, verified, relevant information qualitatively supervised by the members of the community and transformed into the knowledge. Thus, there is considered the gnostic function of the network communities thanks to which the person has the opportunity to acquire professional knowledge and experience of other members of the community, as well as, share their own professional experience and information.

Function of Self-presentation

Network communities became a so-called personal environment where everybody can find all necessary technical and social basis for the creation of their own virtual self. Each user gets an opportunity to communicate, create, and share the products of his creative work with the community audience or any other network resource. The publicity of the web page demands from the author to continue the process of communication, to deal with people competently and help them to understand better current events. Thus, the user of the community has a great opportunity to develop his professional self-concept. Professional self-concept reveals one's professional attitude and competence.

1.2 Review of Existing Network Educational Communities

The idea of creating the data portals for research, methodological support, and scaffolding of educational establishments is very popular all over the world. For example, in the USA there has been created a data portal of methodological support for professional development of teachers called «Solution Tree» (www.solutiontree.com). The portal is designed for teachers of all levels of education (preschool, primary, secondary school etc.) and provides information, coordination, counseling and other support educational institutions, professional learning communities and individual teachers in developing strategies for successful learning.

Nowadays in Russia, there are no projects with similar functionality, but some ideas are partially implemented on the following websites: Методисты.Ru (there is no scientific information and counseling support, the site does not divide educational organizations into clusters, there is no information for preschool learning); Педагогический мир www.pedmir.ru (there is no focus on creating a community of teachers, the site does not provide the users with scientific, informational and counseling support); educational system "Школа 2100" www.school2100.ru (one of the largest educational portals with a lot of functionality, however, directed at the scientific and information support of only one educational program, there is no functionality for students, besides the portal is not responsible for coordinating communities of teachers).

The situation determines the relevance of the work on the creation of a portal for scaffolding of teachers and students in the education cluster Higher Educational Establishment and Preschool educational establishment.

In the article, there is described a solution to the problem of finding effective ways and methods of arranging and scaffolding of educational activities of students and teachers within the network educational communities. There are considered some aspects of organizing such interactive form of learning, as a media project.

2 Methodology

2.1 Network Educational Communities

Let us consider the main definitions of the concept «network community» found in modern research works.

The concept «network community» is defined as a collection of people in interaction with a common objective, values, and activities. Common purposes, interests, needs, resources, discourse, and thesaurus are important factors composing the concept. Cyberspace is a communicative environment of the community [10].

Network community is a group of people interacting on the basis of Internet communication and capable of joint activity and self-reflection [10].

Network community is a basic unit of social organization of users of telecommunication networks with a stratification system, accepted social standards, roles, and statuses of participants. The organization includes in its membership at least three authors exercising through the use of appropriate hardware and software artifacts on a regular basis for social interactions, as well as having access to the shared content and other resources [2].

In modern Russian research works, there are revealed reflections and correlations between education and Internet technologies. The central element of the correlation is a network community, which operates on the basis of Internet technologies [5]. The community is aimed at solving pedagogical tasks and operates in the network of pedagogical technologies. Thus, the network community is a connecting link between instruction and Internet and it allows us to talk about network learning communities.

Network communities are built on the basis of social network services. Social network service is a virtual area connecting people in the online communities with the help of software, computers integrated into the network of Internet and network of documents. Social network services are the very means that help people to interact with modern online network communities. They are classified as follows:

1. **Blogs**. Visitors can publish their opinion using typical blogs. It makes blogging an efficient environment for network communication. Blogs can cover the requirements of the community, whose participants inside the blogosphere can carry out the following actions:

- write own messages;
- read messages published by other authors;
- comment upon the messages written by other members of the blog;
- reply to comments written in the messages;
- connect messages and comments together using hypertext links.

Volokhonskiy, analyzing psychological mechanisms and motivation of using blogs and highlights two different contents of the process — reading blogs and authorship [11]. People, who use the communicative possibilities of blogs outside the context of running their own blog, noted the possibility of communicating with people with whom they are not able to communicate directly.

2. «WikiWiki» is a website with variation structure and content which users can change with the help of special instruments provided by the site itself. Technologies of the wiki are very convenient both for teachers and learners. Users can place teaching material in open access, arrange discussions on various issues, encourage students to work independently on further development of online resources. Wiki-sites create good opportunities for conducting joint development projects, involving the creation of electronic materials, their location, and discussion on the Internet.

Wiki is characterized by:

- the ability to correct texts repeatedly by means of the environment of the site itself without the usage of special tools on behalf of the editor;
- a special markup language — the so-called wiki-markup permitting to mark structural elements and hyperlinks easily and quickly, to format and arrange definite elements;
- taking into account changes of pages: the ability to compare versions and restore the previous ones;
- the emergence of changes just after making them;
- separation of content on named pages;
- contextual hyperlinks;
- a lot of authors. Some wikis can be edited by all the site visitors.

2.2   Designing of the Network Educational Community

According to Bondarenko, to describe the technology of the network learning community we should firstly create software and then invite its potential users. Over time a new social structure appears due to the process of interaction of regular users of the resource. Designers of the resource should orient to groups of future users even at the stage of choosing the software and technical solutions [2].

Let us consider essential characteristics of each stage of creating a network educational community.

1. *Creating software for a network community.*

It is built up as a website and is based on fundamental principles of generating online communities described by Smith [9]:

- Identification – the ability to give personal information.
- Presence on the site – the ability to see the users who are currently on the website and to speak to them.
- Relationships — the ability to describe relations between two users – friends, family members etc.

- Communication — the ability to communicate with other members of the network. For example, send them personal messages, comment on the content.
- Groups — the ability to generate inside the social network communities of interest.
- Reputation — the ability to know the status of other users and observe their behavior within the social network.
- Information exchange — the ability to exchange the materials, photos, references, presentation etc.

There are several options for creating a shell:

- *Professional level.* The option is suitable for experienced specialists who are good at dealing with information technologies because the work implies a high qualification in working out all the components of the shell.
- *Standard level.* Suitable for experienced users and consists of a choice of ready-made solutions for managing the content, for example, JomSocial for CMS Joomla, BuddyPress for CMS Wordpress etc.

2. The involvement of participants in the community.

After the software created in the community raises the question of how to attract the first members of the community. Most often, the expansion of the participants is identified with the development of the community network that is implemented on the basis of "promotion" of an existing social and information resource on the Internet. The participants are involved in the work not to develop Internet resources but to create a special educational environment for a definite community of teachers and students and to arrange special conditions for their successful studying and personal growth.

3. Design and organization of interaction between community members.

The principal measure of generating such interaction is a project activity, in particular, the usage of media projects. According to the definition of Polat [7], media project may be considered as an activity organized on the basis of web media having common problems, objectives, and methods aimed at achieving a joint result of the activity. Today, web media can be called web2.0 technology: network communities, blogs, forums, wikis etc.

Let us consider the typological features of analyzed media-projects having built on the basis of main principals described by Polat [7], Bondarenko [2] (see Table 1).

The structure of the media project includes four stages:

1. Pre-project stage. At the stage, it is necessary to carry out a study (diagnostics) to reveal the main problem of the project, its aims, duration and to prepare all necessary resources (including the development of a technological platform, connect Internet resources), etc.
2. Stage of design (project implementation). The leading task of this stage is to put the activity directly, which means discussing the ideas of the project, dividing the trainees into groups, determining the general rules and terms for developing their own materials, the criteria for their evaluation etc.

Table 1. Typology of media projects

Signs of media projects	Types of media projects
The dominant activity in the project	Research media project Game-based media project Creative media project Educational and cognitive media project
Subject matter area	Mono-project Inter-subject media project
Nature of project coordination	Media project with open coordination Media project with hidden coordination
Nature of contacts	Group media project School media project University media project City media project Regional media project International media project
Number of project participants	Microsocial media project Macrosocial media project
Duration of the project	Short term media project Long term media project
Technological platform of the project	Not network media project Network media project
Nature of attracting new participants (only for network media projects)	With private participation With open participation

3. Reflective stage. Reflection on the design of the project, its progress and results (the conformity of the result with the initial plan, the quality of the product obtained, the quality of the joint activity and relations, the prospects for using the product and the development of the project).
4. Post-project stage. Approbation, dissemination of the results and products of the project activity; finding new ways and ideas for creating new projects within the same community.

What happens with a network community after finishing media-project? We suppose that the educational media project results in a *new stage* of the network community. Hence it becomes possible to talk about the *scaffolding of the network educational community as the new stage of its creating.*

3   Discussion: Research and Results

3.1   Designing of the Informational and Analytical Internet Portal

In accordance with the purpose and objectives of the study, the team of authors conducted the following work and obtained the following results: software was developed, installed and tuned to ensure the functioning of a scientific information and analytical Internet portal.

The Internet portal consists of several websites and has the following features and capabilities:

1. *Web-site "International Centre for the Childhood and Education"* (www. preschool-center.ru) *(Fig. 1).*

Fig. 1. Interface of the web-site "International Centre for the Childhood and Education"

The site includes the following information services and sections:

1.1. «Social network».
1.2. «Virtual museum of children's creativity».
1.3. «Competitions». There is generated a special informational system to assist the process of holding the competitions (www.konkurs.preschool-center.ru).
1.4. «Library».
1.5. «Media collection of pedagogical experience».
1.6. "Virtual employment office".
1.7. "Webinars".

2. *The web-site of electronic journal "Child and Society"* (www.childandsociety.ru) for teachers and students involved in Early childhood instruction (Fig. 2).

There is used a system of automatic reception of author's issues and there is worked out a system that provides additional services for dealing with reviewers (receiving documents, notification of a new reviewer). The journal was registered with ISSN and indexed in the Google Scholar database. There are generated groups in social networks such as Twitter, Facebook, LinkedIn, ВКонтакте.

3. *Web-site «Counselling and methodological center for preschool instruction»* (www.kidworlds.ru) (Fig. 3).

Fig. 2. Interface of the web-site "Electronic journal Child and Society"

Fig. 3. Interface of the web-site «Counselling and methodological center for preschool instruction»

The menu panel provides access to other sites of the Portal. It contains the following information services and sections:

3.1. «Web library».
3.2. «Catalog of sites of pre-school educational institutions and other organizations of a pre-school profile in Volgograd and Volgograd region with photos and geolocation.
3.3. «Forum».
3.4. «On –line consultant», which provides users with scientific and methodological support in the field of preschool instruction.
3.5. «Information materials».

Let us describe the authors' technology of creation and scaffolding the network educational community within the designed portal.

The First Stage. Creation the Software for Network Community. Authors have constructed a technological web platform that covers all communicational capabilities for social network services. It was created on the basis of the research laboratory "International Centre for Childhood and Education Problems" at the Volgograd State Social and Pedagogical University (VSSPU) at the chair of Preschool Education.

To generate the portal the authors have chosen open source software. During the process of registration, the user can identify himself in the network, set up a personal page, place a picture, photo albums, create groups, participate in groups, maintain a personal electronic blog - Diary, download the information and exchange it with the colleagues through personal messages and correspondence.

The Second Stage. Involvement of Participants in the Technological Platform. To attract community members, regional and international scientific and practical training seminars were held with the employees of the pre-school education system, teachers and students of the pre-school department of VSSPU to familiarize themselves with the portal and learn how to interact in the network community.

The Third Stage. Organization of Interaction within the Network Community. The stage of registering the users in the network community and analyzing their activity in the latter. To achieve the aim of the stage there were created and held different media projects based on game learning for the students of VSSPU. The first game-based media project was «Photo cross in the country Detsadia (kindergarten land)». The project «Photo cross in the country Detsadia» was conducted in the form of a business game. The task of the students was to create their own country Detsadia and to present in their creative work photos of the most interesting kindergartens, according to the nominations presented in the cross-list: the most beautiful kindergarten in the country of Detsadia; the best teacher of kindergarten of the country of Detsadia; the best health-saving technology for working with preschoolers; creativity and innovation of the country of Detsadia etc. There were generated groups of students and further, they, together with the teacher as the project manager, discussed text messages, worked on the blog and also commented on the ideas of the other members of the group. This practice contributed to the intensification of cooperation between the group members.

Figure 4 shows the albums of student teams. The album's name corresponds to the name of each group of students.

If we open the album we can consider all the creative activities of the students of one group as a whole and read comments on it (Fig. 5) of the contestants, as well as ask them questions or leave their feedback.

Internet voting was also conducted for the work they liked. The winners of the competition were determined on the basis of the conclusion of the competitive commission. At the post-project stage, the results of the media project were summed up. The students were interested and motivated to work in a game form. The work done by the students was highly appreciated by the practitioners in the community.

Later on the initiative of students, a **game-based media project «I am the head of the preschool educational establishment»** was developed. At the pre-project stage,

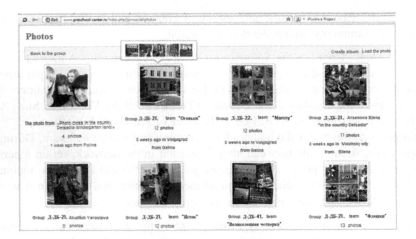

Fig. 4. Albums of students within network community

Fig. 5. Students' comments within created community

students, during an active discussion in the network community, formed the ideas of a new project design. Together with the teacher, the position of the project was formed and project activities were defined. The team captains of the previous project became the unofficial leaders of the community, they were assigned the function of moderating the community at the time of the project (Fig. 6).

Fig. 6. The page of students' media-project

During this game implementation the students solved the following design tasks:

1. Identify the mission of the organization.

The task of this game was to formulate the mission of the pre-school organization. All assignments and training materials for project activities were displayed in the project coordinator group.

2. External attributes.

In this part of the game, students developed and placed on the page of their group versions of the logo, image symbols of the educational organization. The students identified in their group some roles: an artist, an idea generator, and a project protection specialist. This division of roles has led to the creation of a quality unique and interesting product.

3. The image of the personnel (qualifications, personal qualities, appearance, competence).

On this project decision, the students analyzed the qualification and other requirements for the pre-school teacher, personal correspondence, and discussed with the colleagues their new knowledge and developed their point of view. Then they created blog entries in the form of a small essay in which each group defined the staff of their pre-school organization.

4. Style of organization and quality of services.

The content of the work in this part of the project included the following actions:

(A) Selecting the target audience.
   Each group had to analyze and determine the target audience, who would "advertise" their services (parents, social partners, media).

(B) Work on the visual identity of the pre-school organization, traditions, educational program (where necessary). This work required the inclusion of students in other professional network communities, which students chose for themselves (for example, Metodisty.ru), registering on the network and already having experience in such a community, students analyzed the materials and work experience.

As a result, students have mastered the principle of working in network educational communities. Many of the students (56%) went beyond the proposed network community and had their own accounts in other professionally-oriented network communities.

All media-projects used different sections of the Internet Portal. For example, all groups of described games were placed at the **"Social Network"** section of the Portal. The section **"Media collection of pedagogical experience"** was filled by the students and teachers after the conducted educational seminars and was dedicated to the experience of implementing media projects in preschool educational organizations of Volgograd and the Volgograd region. Teachers had the opportunity to comment on the materials of their colleagues and to help them with downloading the materials. Some teachers created their own groups of their professional interests to exchange all necessary experience and information.

The unique section **"Virtual Employment Bureau"** was created as a service for communication of the students and employers. This section allows placing on the site a unified electronic student resume that contains the basic part, as well as the possibility of attaching portfolio files. In addition, the service allows posting information from the employer containing the name of the organization, contact information, type of job, category and job description.

The functionality of the service "Virtual Employment Bureau" provides for the following functions in the context of the roles of the employer, the applicant, and the system administrator:

- control panel for the employer
- packages for the employer
- the resume search interface. Resume search by application name, name, nationality, sex, availability, category, type of assignment, salary range, education, experience

Employer:

- control panel for the employer;
- packages for the employer;
- the resume search interface; resume search by application name, nationality, sex, availability, category, type of assignment, salary range, education, experience;
- saving resume search;
- create a company profile;
- download company logotype;
- departments;
- vacancies;
- description of meta and meta keywords for work;
- integration with Google Map and YouTube videos;
- list of candidates;

- send a message to the employer;
- professional job search screen and resume;
- download the resume files;
- export to PDF;
- my statistics;
- notification of company approval/rejection.

Applicant:

- control panel for applicants;
- job listing by category;
- company job listing;
- job listing filter by type of location, category, and job;
- saving filters for users;
- job search by name of the company, salary range, job status, experience, publication date etc.;
- save job search;
- manager's resume;
- cover letter to a manager;
- allow multiple cover letters;
- my vacancies;
- my statistics;

Administrator:

- admin control panel;
- management of job types;
- management of work status;
- management of companies;
- management of offices;
- job management.

The Fourth Stage. The Scaffolding of the Network Community. Organization of educational counseling, which is conducted in several areas: (1) diagnostics, assistance in the implementation of pedagogical projects and giving required recommendations; (2) assistance in finding necessary solutions; (3) assistance in the implementation of self-organization and self-development; organization of joint activities to solve a problem. Work with teachers in the network of web journal plays an important part in the research. Its creation allows teachers to improve the quality of professional interactions within the created cluster of higher educational establishment – preschool educational institutions and to increase the publication activity of the teachers.

For scaffolding the community there was generated and installed software to conduct **webinars and video conferences** based on the Big Blue Button platform. The software contains a control panel to maintain the list of users and assign roles (a participant/a guide); send invitations to webinar participants (indicating the date, time, roles, themes, login and a password; enabling/disabling webinar recording; creating and modifying webinar schedules; maintaining a list of previous webinars and their viewing (Fig. 7).

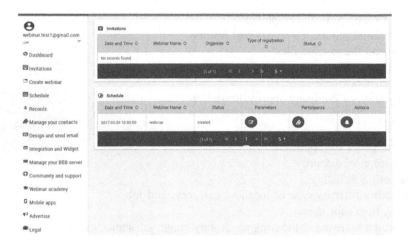

Fig. 7. The control panel for webinars

The approbation of the service took place during the International video conference and regional webinars with kindergarten teachers and university students.

3.2   Diagnostic of Early Childhood Education Teachers' and Students' Readiness for Interaction in Network Educational Communities

An important condition for the effective communication of teachers and students is their readiness for cooperation in the network of the Internet communities [5]. The authors have developed a questionnaire to study the readiness of the teachers and students engaged in preschool instruction to interact in the network community. The questionnaire allows analyzing the following components of the readiness: motivational, informational and cognitive. The authors defined purposes and frequency of using the network educational communities and social professional sites by teachers and students; Internet services used for professional communication with colleagues and experts in their professional field; the need for a specialized portal to provide the scaffolding of professional activities.

Having analyzed the questionnaires of the participants, the authors found out the following levels of readiness for professional cooperation in the network of the Internet communities:

Low level - low activity in the use of computer technologies for educational/professional purposes; Disinterest in the use of professionally-oriented portals and services on the Internet; Weak awareness of existing professional communities in the network.

Medium level - high user activity in computer technologies for educational/professional purposes; interest in methodological support of educational/professional activities through specialized Internet portals and communities; poor information about educational services and services on the Internet; low level of skills of using Internet services for professional communication.

High level - high user activity in computer technologies for educational/ professional purposes; interest in methodological support of educational/professional activities through specialized Internet portals and communities; high awareness of educational services and services in the Internet; use of specialized portals for communication with colleagues, participation in professionally significant projects, competitions, for professional self-presentation; great variability in the use of Internet services for professional communication: chats, webinars, social networks, specialized portals, e-mail, etc.

Having analyzed the answers of the respondents there were received the following results of their readiness for cooperation in the network of the Internet communities (See Table 2).

Table 2. The results of the respondents' readiness for cooperation in the network educational communities

Levels	Beginning of the experiment		Final stage of the experiment	
	Students	Teachers	Students	Teachers
Low	35%	22%	5%	0%
Medium	45%	55%	28%	44%
High	20%	23%	67%	56%

Finally, there was revealed positive dynamics of the levels of readiness of the respondents for working in the network. Respondents' activity highly increased and their principal position as the members of the network professional learning communities has changed from exploitative treatment to creative one.

4 Conclusion

Thus, in modern conditions of globalization and transition to a post-industrial economy, the society needs new teaching approaches using outstanding achievements of science and technologies. There are observed the changes in the structure of the society and that of the pedagogical environment. Under the circumstances, it becomes evident the necessity to arrange permanent «joint training» of the staff for the purpose of achieving educational goals and tasks. The most effective way of organizing the «joint training» is the close and productive cooperation of colleagues on the basis of the network methodological community, which characterizes the community of specialists of the education system, united by telecommunication. Online communication in these communities takes place through a variety of web services such as social networks, wiki-systems, chats, blogs, video services etc.

The principal measure of generating such interaction was a project activity, in particular, the use of media projects. For the purpose there was developed a software, it was installed and tuned to ensure the functioning of a scientific information and analytical Internet portal. The Internet portal was created on the basis of the research laboratory "International Centre for Childhood and Education Problems" at the Volgograd State Social and Pedagogical University (VSSPU) at the chair of Preschool Education. The authors have implemented the following sites within the portal: *1. Website "International Centre for Childhood and Education Problems"* (www.preschool-center.ru*); 2. The web-site of electronic scientific and practical journal "Child and Society"* (www.childandsociety.ru) for teachers and students involved in Early childhood instruction; *3. Web-site «Counselling and methodological center for preschool instruction»* (www.kidworlds.ru). There were created and held different media projects based on game learning for the students of VSSPU - «Photo cross in the country Detsadia», «I am the head of the preschool educational establishment» etc.

There were revealed the conditions for effective adoption by teachers and students engaged in the sphere of preschool instruction the ideas of professional methodological communities as an effective means of continuing professional education. An important condition for the effective communication of teachers and students is their readiness for cooperation in the network of the Internet communities. The authors have developed a questionnaire to study the readiness of the teachers and students engaged in preschool instruction to interact in the network community.

Having analyzed the answers of the respondents there were received the following results: at the beginning of the study showed that 18% of the participants not only do not participate in professionally-oriented Internet communities but also do not know about their existence. They are not users, but 22% of respondents are aware of the existence of such communities. 41% of respondents use information published in communities, but they are not registered in them, that is, they occupy a passive position, being only consumers of someone's professional experience. 19% of students and teachers were active users of communities that have their own account and participated in the life of a professionally oriented Internet group, most of whom are educators who are interested in exchanging information and ideas for professional use.

So the majority of students (75%) indicated the search for information as the main goal of visiting such Internet resources, while among the practitioners, only the informational purpose of visiting communities was 32%. Teachers of preschool institutions use professional Internet portals and services mainly to participate in competitions and projects (25%), as well as to communicate with colleagues and exchange ideas on professional issues (16%). Finally, there was revealed positive dynamics of the levels of readiness of the respondents for working in the network methodological communities.

Thus, the authors are convinced of the high efficiency of cooperating within network educational communities in comparison with the traditional forms of organizing a pedagogical activity.

References

1. Attwell, G.: Web 2.0 and the changing ways we are using computers for learning: what are the implications for pedagogy and curriculum (2014). https://www.researchgate.net/publication/264857678_Web_20_and_the_changing_ways_we_are_using_computers_for_learning_what_are_the_implications_for_pedagogy_and_curriculum

2. Bondarenko, S.V.: Social structure of virtual network communities. Publishing house of the Russian State University. Rostov-on-Don, pp. 68–69 (2004). (in Russian)
3. Downes, S.: Learning networks in practice. J. Emerging Technol. Learn. **2**, 19–27 (2007)
4. Dufour, R., et al.: Learning by Doing: A Handbook for Professional Learning Communities at Work, 2nd edn. Solution Tree Press, Bloomington (2010)
5. Gerkushenko, G., Gerkushenko, S., et al.: Comparative analysis on personal learning environment of Russian and Slovakian students. In: The Proceedings of the European Conference on Social Media ECSM 2014, University of Brighton, Brighton, UK, 10–11 July 2014 (2014)
6. Klamma, R., Chatti, M.A., Duval, E., Hummel, H., Hvannberg, E.H., Kravcik, M.: Social software for life-long learning. J. Educ. Technol. Soc. **10**(3), 72–83 (2007)
7. Polat, E.S.: Typology of telecommunication projects. J. Sci. Sch. **4**, 12–17 (1997). (in Russian)
8. Richardson, W.: Blogs, Wikis, Podcasts, and other Powerful Web Tools for Classrooms. Sage, Thousand Oaks (2010)
9. Smith, G.: «Atomiq: Folksonomy: social classification», 3 August 2004. http://atomiq.org/archives/2004/08/folksonomy_social_classification.html
10. Taratukhina, Y.V., Maltseva, S.V.: Networking communities: communication aspects. J. Autom. Modern Technol. **2**, 21–25 (2011). (in Russian)
11. Volokhonsky, V.L.: Psychological mechanisms and foundations of the classification of blogs. In: Volokhonsky, V.L. (ed.) Personality and Interpersonal Interaction in the Network Internet, Blogs: A New Reality. Publishing House of St. Petersburg State University. St. Petersburg (2006). (in Russian)
12. Vossen, G., Hagemann, S.: Unleashing Web 2.0: From Concepts to Creativity. Elsevier, Amsterdam (2010)

Intelligent Assistive Technologies:
Software Design and Application

Elderly Consumers' Perceptions on Self-medication Using Over the Counter Medicines

Dimitra Chatziathanasiou, Miltiadis Chalikias,
and Michalis Skordoulis$^{(\boxtimes)}$

Department of Business Administration, School of Business and Economics,
Piraeus University of Applied Sciences, 250 Thivon & Petrou Ralli Av.,
12244 Egaleo, Greece
mskordoulis@gmail.com

Abstract. Elderly people are the largest consumers of over the counter medicines (OTC) worldwide. They are using OTC medicines, on a daily basis, to treat minor health issues; however little is known regarding the attitudes and beliefs of the elderly consumers in Greece regarding the purchase and use of OTC drugs and how decisions to self-medicate are made. The OTC medicine market constitutes a key source of business expansion and leads to a significant competitive advantage. The aim of this paper is to examine the attitudes of third age Greek consumers in over the counter medicines market. We have used the Theory of Planned Behavior to explore the influence of beliefs about Medicines – particularly the OTC medicines (Beliefs about Medicines Questionnaire), the influence of subjective norms and perceived behavioral control, as predictors of intent to self-medicate. Beliefs about medicines –OTC medicines emerged as the most significant predictor of intent to self-medicate, while subjective norms and perceived behavioral control were found to be secondary factors in the decision to self-medicate. Furthermore, intent to self-medicate significantly predicted (Self - Medicating Scale - SMS) the attitude of purchase and use of OTC medicines for self-medicating minor health issues. The results of the statistical analysis have shown that third age consumers in Greece do not use often OTC medicines, unlike consumers in the same age group of other countries. A significant positive correlation between the frequency of the use of OTC medicines and chronic diseases is recorded while a negative one is recorded effect among variables of the frequency of OTC medicines use and the health status of participants. The results of the survey indicate that self-medication with OTC is more likely when necessity regarding their use outweigh the concerns arising from their use.

Keywords: Over the counter medicines · Elderly · Self-medication · Health behavior · Theory of Planned Behavior · Self-Medicating Scale

1 Introduction

Over the counter medicines (OTC) are the pharmaceutical products, which consumers can obtain without a prescription. Many people use OTC medicines worldwide to face mild health issues. However, few things are known about how decisions are made to

© Springer International Publishing AG 2017
A. Kravets et al. (Eds.): CIT&DS 2017, CCIS 754, pp. 795–804, 2017.
DOI: 10.1007/978-3-319-65551-2_57

make consumers self-medicate with OTC. Despite the economic crisis, the sales of OTC medicines keep growing, mainly due to the growing trend toward self-medication, the increased access through the expansion of distribution channels, and the conversion of many prescription medicines to OTC medicines (Tisman 2010).

Many people worldwide use OTC medicines to face mild health issues. However, few things are known about how decisions are made to make consumers self-medicate with OTC. The use of OTC is connected directly to the consumer shift towards self-medication. Today self-medication with OTC is also known as OTC-ness (Soller 1998) and is significantly developed worldwide. Since the 1990s, the growing need for people to manage and treat a large proportion of diseases was recognized, without contributing always a health professional (WSMI 2010). The reasons that self-care was increased are many and multidimensional. Briefly, the socio-economic factors can be mentioned: the changing lifestyle, the easier access to medicines, the increased potential for the management of certain diseases through self-medication, the improvement of public health and environmental factors, the greater availability of medicines and the demographic and epidemiological factors (WHO 1988).

The tendency to self-medicate with OTC is continuously increasing in recent years for the same reasons that self-care has grown, and also for the increasing conversion of many prescription medicines to OTC. Elderly people are the largest consumers of OTC medicines.

Many of them tend to self-medicate with OTC in order to deal with health conditions such as cold, pain, diarrhea and constipation (DeBrew et al. 1998). The most common self-medication practices meet the following health conditions: fever, snuffles, sore throat, cough, nausea, diarrhea, constipation, indigestion, headache, muscle pain and arthralgia (Amoako et al. 2004).

The OTC medicine market constitutes a key source of business expansion and leads to a significant competitive advantage. In Europe, there are observed dynamics that lead to new development opportunities in some mature markets, but also in the emerging markets of Central and Eastern Europe. The prospects are good, but the challenges are many and the identification of better opportunities is not easy.

The OTC medicine market is foreseen to continue expanding in the future, for many reasons, such as (DeLorme et al. 2010):

1. The increase of OTC medicines and self-medication provide an easy and economical way to face mild health problems.
2. The regulatory change of prescription medicines to OTC medicines will continue, making more medicines available without a prescription.
3. The use of OTC medicines is encouraged by health systems, as they offer treatment without wasting public money.
4. The knowledge of patients on issues related to their health will increase as the use of the Internet, as an information tool, is expanding.

Globally, Western Europe and the US remain the largest OTC medicine markets, having the 43% of sales in the industry, but now the driving forces are the continuously growing markets of Southeast Asia, Latin America and Central and Eastern Europe. These emerging markets now represent the 77% of global OTC growth, while in 2010 they had only the 36.6% of the OTC share sales.

Among the key trends that assist the global OTC medicine market is the major changes in the distribution of these products, which is characterized by the adoption of the innovative multi-channel distribution model of the United Kingdom. In the USA, OTC medicines are available in various retail stores. On the contrary, in Europe, the traditional model of the independent pharmacy dominates as a distribution channel for OTC medicines and many countries are trying to gradually evolve towards a wider distribution and access to OTC medicines, following new models beyond the rigorous character of traditional pharmacies.

The five categories of OTC medicines dominating worldwide are cold and cough medicines, vitamins, analgesics, medicines for the digestive system (e.g. antacids), and dermatological. OTC medicines in Greece hold a considerable share of total sales to pharmacies, with an increasing trend in the period 2009–2011. Indeed, according to the available data, the size of the OTC medicines market was formed in 2011 to €569 million, close to previous years (Fig. 1).

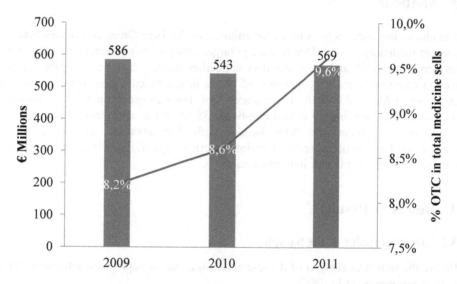

Fig. 1. OTC medicines share in Greece (for total sales except for hospitals).

OTC medicines share in Greece (for total sales except for hospitals) is among the lowest in comparison with other members of the European Union. It should be noted that this share depends on the range of medicines that are in each country OTC, and the rate of parallel exports as well, which are included in total sales.

Analgesics were the most important category of OTC medicines in Greece in 2011, while formulations for cold treatment also had significant shares.

OTC medicine market in Greece currently consists of 1,284 formulations, 115 of different pharmaco-technical forms and salts, and their combinations as well. Granted only by pharmacies and carry an identification-authenticity tape, similar to that of medicines (of a different color), in order to facilitate their traceability. Finally, their price is determined by the state, in contrast to 24 out of the 28 members of the European Union, which are sold freely, with a price determined by the manufacturer.

Adopting the Theory of Planned Behavior, this research will try to explore the factors that lead to the intention and ultimately to self-medication of mild health problems with OTC, among third age people (65 years old and over). The theory suggests that the intention is determined by the individual's attitudes toward the behavior, the subjective standards that indicate the adoption and the perceived behavioral control, which refers to the perception of the person on the ability to adopt a particular behavior. A Central factor in the theory of planned behavior is the individual's intention to perform a certain behavior (Ajzen and Fishbein 1980; Ajzen 1991). The present study examined whether beliefs about OTC medicines correlate with the intention of the person to self-medicate or not.

2 Methods

The aim of this paper is to examine the attitudes of third age Greek consumers over the counter medicines market. Due to the age target group of this research, which focuses on people aged 65 and over, the data collection method that was adopted are the face-to-face interviews to people over 65 living in the Attica region from January 14, 2016, up to March 23, 2016. The research tool that was used is a strictly structured questionnaire consisting 40 closed questions, 38 of which were "closed-ended questions" and 2 of them were "closed-ended with short answers". The questionnaire consists of four sections, self-medication practices, questions relating to consumer behavior, health profile and individual data.

3 Research Results

3.1 Demographics of the Sample

Before the statistical analysis of the research results, demographic characteristics of the sample are presented in details.

From the 138 questionnaires collected, there is a complete balance of women and men in the sample.

Specifically, the 50% were women and the other 50% were men. Regarding the age of the respondents, approximately the 54% were less than 70 years old, about 15% were between 70 and 74 years old, the 11% belonged to the age group from 75 to 79 years old, the 13% to the group from 80 to 84 years old, while the remaining 7% belonged to the group of 85 years old and above.

Concerning the health profile, respondents' perceptions are shown in Table 1.

Table 1. Respondents' health profile.

Health condition	Categories	% Percent
Current health condition	Bad	7.2%
	Regular	25.4%
	Good	31.9%
	Very good	31.9%
	Excellent	3.6%
Health condition, compared to others of the same age	Much worse	0.7%
	Wore	9.4%
	The same	22.5%
	Better	57.2%
	Much better	10.1%
Health condition obstructs participation in activities	Very much	5.1%
	Much	9.6%
	Moderatery	16.2%
	A little	30.9%
	Not at all	38.2%
Chronic disease	Yes	52.9%
	No	47.1%

3.2 Perceptions on Self-medication Practices Using OTC

The first section of the questionnaire includes questions about self-medication practices. The first question concerns the purchasing frequency of OTC medicines
(Table 2).

Table 2. Purchasing frequency of OTC medicines.

	% Percent
Not so often	31.6%
Quite often	31.6%
Often	22.7%
Very often	14.1%

The second question to be analyzed concerns the type of OTC medicines that are
bought by the consumers (Fig. 2).

The next session to be analyzed concerns consumers' perceptions on OTC
medicines and self-medication. Figure 3 shows respondents perceptions on OTC
medicines and self-medication.

According to Fig. 3, most of the respondents think that their health does not depend
on OTC medicines, their life could be normal without them and they will not depend on
them in the future. Furthermore, the majority of the respondents seem to have worries
about OTC medicines negative effects. The most common usage of OTC medicines is
for self-medication of mild health problems.

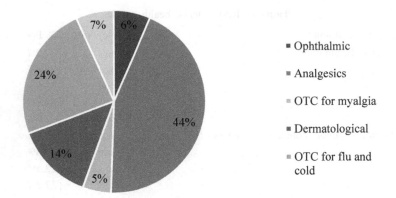

Fig. 2. Types of OTC medicines bought.

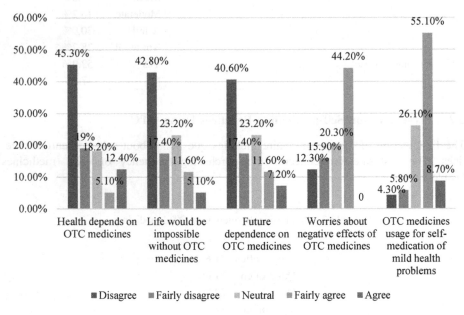

Fig. 3. Perceptions on OTC medicines and self-medication.

To examine the necessity of OTC medicines to the lives of third age consumers, the factors representing the attitudes - beliefs about OTC medicines consumer, namely the BMQ (Beliefs about Medicines Questionnaire) Specific, "Concern" and "necessity", were adjusted. The study of the international literature helped for the confirmation or refutation of the case (Pineles and Parente 2013). The aim was to get a total sum for each variable or factor.

The total rates in each specific BMQ factor range between 5 and 25. High rates on the factor "concern" indicate high concern about the side effects of medicines. High rates on the factor "necessity" show strong convictions in the necessity and effectiveness of

OTC. Since the rates of the factor of necessity and the factor of concern, are significantly associated as found, the rating is calculated as the difference of rates of these two groups (necessity - concern differential - NCD). The NCD rating was calculated by subtracting the rate of the factor "concern" by the rate of the factor "necessity" with a possible range from −20 up to +20. The overall rating of NCD is similar to a cost-benefit analysis for each participant, for whom the costs (concerns) outweighs the expected benefits (necessity) (Neame and Hammond 2005). A positive NCD rating indicates the positive person's attitude on taking OTC medicines (necessity), while a negative rating indicates the negative person's attitude (concerns) on taking OTC medicines (Table 3).

Table 3. BMQ score "necessity", BMQ score "Concern", Necessity Concern Differential score.

	BMQ necessity	BMQ concern	NCD score
Other types of OTC	1328	1494	−166

From all this process, it was found that the results of the factor "concern" are larger than the factor "necessity", which shows that Third age consumers have negative attitudes towards OTC.

To examine whether the attitudes - perceptions, the subjective norms and the perceived behavioral control affect third age consumer intention, for the purchase and use of OTC, in order to self-medicate mild health problems, a multiple regression analysis was performed.

Attitudes -beliefs about OTC- BMQ, the Subjective Norms and the Perceived Behavioral Control were considered as independent factors. The factors of the intention for SMS Scale (Self Medicating Scale) were considered as dependent factors.

Initially concerning as dependent variable the factor "unwillingness to self-medicate", multiple regression analysis was performed, using all the independent variables. The aim was to determine the percentage of the dependent factor, which interprets the independent variable. The results of multiple regression showed that the dependent factor correlates significantly only with the group of BMQ Specific scale "Concern" where $b = 0.277$ (p-value = 0.002), showing a significant positive impact direction.

Subsequently concerning as dependent variable the factor "self-medication without a second thought", multiple regression analysis was performed, using all the independent variables. The results here showed that the dependent factor was significantly associated only with the group of BMQ Specific scale "necessity" where $b = 0.312$ (p-value = 0.001), showing a significant positive impact direction.

Finally, concerning as dependent variable the factor "continues its progress along", multiple regression analysis was performed, using all the independent variables. The results showed that the dependent factor was significantly associated with the group of BMQ Specific scale "necessity" where $b = -0.222$ (p-value = 0.018), showing a significant negative direction of effect, but with the factor "subjective criteria" where $b = 0.213$ (p-value = 0.022), showing this time a significantly positive direction of effect.

To check if the intention to self-medicate predicts the final third age consumer behavior, for the purchase and use of OTC medicines, in order to self-medicate mild health problems, multiple regression was performed. The variables listed on the intention to self-medicate- SMS Scale (Self Medication Scale) were considered as the independents, while those indicated in the final consumer behavior were considered as the dependent ones.

Initially, concerning as dependent the variable "I purchase of OTC medicines in order to self-medicate, when I have to deal with mild health problems", a multiple regression analysis was performed, using all the aforementioned independent variables. The results of multiple regression showed that the first r-squared coefficient explains the 28.4% of the variance, as perceived by the participants of the sample. More specifically, it was observed that the dependent variable was significantly associated only with the SMS Scale (Self Medicating Scale), "self-medication without a second thought", where b = 0.409 (p-value = 0.000), showing a significantly positive direction of effect.

Finally, concerning as dependent the "how much money do you spend every month on the purchase of OTC medicine?" multiple regression analysis was performed, using all the independent variables. The results showed that the dependent one is also correlated significantly only with the factor of the SMS Scale (Self Medication Scale), "self-medication without a second thought" where b = 0.347 (p-value = 0.001), showing a significantly positive direction of effect.

4 Conclusions

Third age consumers in Greece do not use often OTC medicines, unlike consumers in the same age group of other countries, according to studies conducted in the past (Amoako et al. 2004). Most of the USA elderly use often OTC medicines and only a few recognized the precautions associated with them (Conn 1992).

Third age consumer's beliefs towards OTC medicines play an important role in this difference, which in this case is positive because the necessity scale is not significantly associated with the intention to purchase and use OTC medicines in order to self-medicate mild health issues. It also seems that their concerns toward OTC medicines are greater than their necessity for use, and for this reason, the frequency of use is lower compared with other studies carried out abroad. For this attitude, it should be taken into consideration that OTC medicines were legislatively delineated as a separate category just in 2006 and that their distribution frame (only through pharmacies) and promotion is more stringent compared to that of other countries of Europe and America. Many formulations marketed in other countries, under the arrangements of OTC medicines, have not yet been converted from Prescription medicines to OTC medicines in Greece.

This study, like many others in the past, has shown that the most popular OTC medicines category among the third age consumers is that of analgesics (Soller et al. 1994). The 44.5% of the participants reported that they are using or have used more analgesics in the past. This finding is confirmed by the theoretical part of this research which shows that, according to literature, the category of analgesics is the most popular OTC medicine category in the world and not only for third age consumers.

The assumption that attitudes - beliefs about OTC medicines predict the intention to self-medicate mild health problems with OTC medicines is partially supported by the results because only the factors of the BMQ Specific scale: "concern" is significantly associated with the intention to self-medication. More specifically, the score of the variable: "concern", outperforms the score of the variable: "necessity", which expresses and supports negative beliefs about OTC medicines. This is confirmed by the correlation of "concern" with the factor of Self - Medicating Scale, "unwillingness for self-medication". Therefore, third age Greek consumers maintain negative beliefs about OTC and these, in turn, affect negatively their intention to self-medicate with OTC. This finding agrees with the Theory of Planned Behavior, which states that a person's attitude toward a behavior affects the intention to perform this behavior. The analysis of the BMQ Specific scale can be described as a cost-benefit analysis, in the first person, regarding medication intake.

There was no significant correlation with the factors of Self-Medicating Scale and the perceived behavioral control. Therefore, the perceived behavioral control is not regarded as a significant effect on the intention to self-medicate with OTC medicines.

In the case of subjective standards, a significant positive correlation only with the factor of Self-Medicating Scale was found. This data shows that the greater the influence of subjective standards, the stronger the decision of third age consumers not to self-medicate with OTC and allow the body to fight alone with any health problem.

Additionally, a statistically significant negative effect among variables of the frequency of OTC medicines use and the health status of participants is recorded. As expected from previous studies, those who believed that was in good health condition were using OTC medicines less often.

Of course, other factors described in the Theory of Planned Behavior should be taken into consideration to identify in more detail the factors that affect the intention and ultimately the decision to self-medicate with OTC medicines, such as the earlier behavior, and also other socio-economic and psychological factors. Considering that from the three variables of the factor of Self-Medicating Scale, the one expressing the intention to self-medication is: "self-medication without second thought" and considering the declaration of the final behavioral statement, namely "I purchase of OTC medicines in order to self-medicate, when I have to deal with mild health problems", it is observed that there is a significant positive correlation. This result is also confirmed by the Theory of Planned Behavior which states that the intention to perform a behavior, predicts the final behavior.

According to the findings of the research is shown that beliefs about medicines are expressed through the BMQ Specific scale, represent a significant proportion of the variance of intention to self-medicate. The predictive value of the positive NCD score indicates that a person intends to self-medicate when the rating of the sub-scale of necessity is larger than that of the sub-scale of concern. This data gives a lot of information for the decision making process.

The research results could be used for the assessment of self-medication practices with OTC medicines in order to determine the use or misuse of pharmaceutical products by consumers and take the appropriate prevention and/or remedy measures.

Namely, campaigns of public and scientific information transmission via primary health care operators can affect the consumer attitudes and behavior towards the medicines use. Specific targeted campaigns to identify and prevent possible misuse of medicines could save millions of dollars in healthcare costs in order to deal with situations arising from the undesirable medicine side effects (Budnitz et al. 2011).

Given that science and medicine are fields that constantly evolve, more and more treatment options with OTC medicines are available to consumers. Information relevant to consumers' decision to self-medicate mild health problems with OTC medicines, have important applications in the approval from the competent authorities and therefore the movement of OTC medicines as well as the marketing mix that will be selected for their promotion to consumers. Recording patients' views on health care services combined with results from clinical studies can provide solid conclusions (Chalikias et al. 2016).

References

Ajzen, I., Fishbein, M.: Understanding Attitudes and Predicting Social Behavior. Prentice-Hall, Englewood Cliffs (1980)

Ajzen, I.: The theory of planned behaviour. Organ. Behav. Hum. Decis. Process. **50**(2), 179–211 (1991)

Amoako, E., Richardson-Campbell, L., Kennedy-Malone, L.: Self-medication with over the counter drugs among elderly adults. J. Gerontol. Nurs. **29**(8), 10–15 (2004)

Budnitz, D.S., Lovegrove, M.C., Crosby, A.E.: Emergency department visits for overdoses of acetaminophen-containing products. Am. J. Prev. Med. **40**(6), 585–592 (2011)

Chalikias, M., Drosos, D., Skordoulis, M., Tsotsolas, N.: Determinants of customer satisfaction in healthcare industry: the case of the Hellenic Red Cross. Int. J. Electron. Mark. Retail. **7**(4), 311–321 (2016)

Conn, V.S.: Self - management of over the counter medications by older adults. Public Health Nurs. **9**(1), 129–136 (1992)

DeBrew, J., Barba, B.E., Tesh, A.S.: Assessing medication knowledge and practices of older adults. Home Healthcare Nurse **16**(10), 686–692 (1998)

DeLorme, D., Huh, J., Reid, L.N., Soontae, A.: The state of public research an over the counter drug advertising. Int. J. Pharm. Healthcare Mark. **4**(3), 208–231 (2010)

Neame, R., Hammond, A.: Beliefs about medications: a questionnaire survey of people with rheumatoid arthritis. Rheumatol. (Oxford) **44**, 762–767 (2005)

Pineles, L.L., Parente, R.: Using the theory of planned behaviour to predict self-medication with over-the-counter analgesics. J. Health Psychol. **18**(12), 1540–1549 (2013)

Soller, R.W.: Evolution of self-care with over the counter medications. Clin. Ther. **20**(3), 134–140 (1998)

Soller, P.E., Forster, E.L., Portugal, A.S.: Older people's recommendations for treating symptoms: repertoires of lay knowledge about disease. Med. Care **32**(8), 852–860 (1994)

Tisman, A.: The Rising Tide of OTC in Europe: Trends, Challenges and New Potential in a Rapidly Evolving Market. IMS Health, Norwalk (2010)

WHO: The Role of the Pharmacist in Self-care and Self-medication. WHO, The Hague (1988)

WSMI: The Story of Self-care and Self-medication. 40 Years of Progress 1970–2010. WSMI Publications, Ferney-Voltaire (2010)

A Two-Phase Method of User Interface Adaptation for People with Special Needs

Marina Kultsova[✉], Anastasiya Potseluico, Irina Zhukova,
Alexander Skorikov, and Roman Romanenko

Volgograd State Technical University, Volgograd, Russia
`marina.kultsova@mail.ru, poas@vstu.ru`

Abstract. The paper is devoted to a problem of increasing accessibility of mobile applications for people with disabilities, that requires the creation of specialized adaptive user interfaces. A knowledge-intensive approach to the design of adaptive user interface was proposed on the basis of integration of ontological user modeling and design pattern approach. An ontological model of the adaptive user interface and interface pattern model were developed as well as an ontological knowledge base and pattern database. A two-phase method of user interface adaptation for people with special needs based on the ontological user model, rule-based reasoning over ontology and interface design patterns was developed. The method was implemented in a software tool for user interface developers. The application of the proposed approach is illustrated by a number of examples of user interface design and adaptation for people with special needs.

Keywords: Assistive technologies · Adaptive user interface · Mobile applications · Ontological user modeling · Interface patterns

1 Introduction

A problem of socialization for people with disabilities becomes more important from year to year. According to recent researches [1] over a billion people have some form of disability, this number is equal to 15% of the world's population. Moreover, the report brought the facts that amount of people with disabilities will be raised due to chronic health conditions increasing and population ageing.

Despite on a large number of social adaptation programs, people with disabilities still experience a lot of difficulties in everyday life because of social barriers [2]. Besides political and economic barriers, shortage of social services, this group of people experiences the lack of communication, what makes the social barrier around them. Therefore the significant challenge for society is increasing accessibility level of infrastructure objects and services in priority spheres of life for people with disabilities and low mobility groups. This is also considered as eliminating the social gap between people with disabilities and other citizens.

The wide spread of mobile technologies can provide numerous services for solving a great part of the everyday life problems for people with disabilities.

© Springer International Publishing AG 2017
A. Kravets et al. (Eds.): CIT&DS 2017, CCIS 754, pp. 805–821, 2017.
DOI: 10.1007/978-3-319-65551-2_58

The main negative aspect of these services is their low usability for people with disabilities. Most applications can not be useful for people with health problems because of disease's peculiarities in physical, emotional and cognitive aspects. A person with a certain disease can face several difficulties in interaction with the graphical interface of mobile applications. As a result, the people with disabilities have limited access to the useful mobile applications, which can reduce the impact of communication and information barriers on their life. The important step for resolving this issue is converting electronic resources and mobile applications into accessible for people with special needs. In order to do this, the electronic resources and mobile applications must have software user interfaces that take into account the special characteristics of people with disabilities.

The design of such user interfaces is a complicated task for user interface developer. A developer has to know the standards and the requirements for developing user interfaces of mobile applications for people with disabilities and to follow them. Furthermore, the great variety of physical, sensory and cognitive disabilities, that people with special needs may encounter, requires personalized customization of mobile application user interfaces for different types of users. In existing user interface editors, the process of creating interfaces for people with disabilities takes a long time and has a high complexity, and does not take into account the necessary specialized knowledge required for the development of such interfaces.

The usability problem appears when developers and interface designers do not consider the requirements to interfaces for people with disabilities. Firstly, it takes a lot of resources to create an interface, which would satisfy the most of the common requirements for a wide set of diseases of different nature. Secondly, the developers do not exactly know all requirements to graphical interfaces for people with special needs. Finally, the developers often can not meet fully the individual requirements of all application users. Thus, the actual task is to develop the specialized software tool for creating interfaces of mobile applications for people with disabilities, which will allow to reduce time and complexity of design process and improve the quality of the developed user interfaces.

Our research is focused on the problem of interface adaptation and development of the personalized adaptive user interfaces for people with disabilities. This paper describes a two-phase method of the interface adaptation on the basis of the ontological user model, rule-based reasoning over ontology and interface design patterns as well as its implementation in the software tool for user interface developers.

2   State of the Art

A lot of new approaches are recently appeared to improve the life of people with disabilities in the sphere of computer technologies. Numerous researchers are devoted to the development of user models including ontological user model to provide the adaptivity and personalization of user interface.

In the framework of AEGIS project [13] the Open Accessibility Framework (OAF) was developed including the set of ontologies, which are providing accessibility knowledge about the user with special needs. A number of domain ontologies are joined into meta-ontology [14]. The first one is Accessible ontology, which has been developed as a result of EU project Accessible and contains characteristics of users with disabilities according to the "International Classification of Functioning, Disability, and Health (ICF)" of the WHO5, descriptions of assistive devices and software applications, web accessibility standards and guidelines (WAI-ARIA and WCAG 2.0), also mapping user requirements and constraints. The second great set of ontologies is LOCO (The Learning Object Context Ontologies). This is a group of ontologies developed for an e-learning framework to ease the exchange of data among multiple educational services. The last related ontology is ADOOLES (Ability and Disability Ontology for Online Learning and Services) that has been developed to annotate learning resources. ADOOLES represents knowledge in the domain of e-learning and includes a set of users disability concepts.

An ontology as a user model is used in EGOKI Adaptive System [7]. This application allows creating the adaptive user interface in XML format. Ontology model also contains some extra information about the software and hardware components of user's device, localization and personal preferences in interface usage such as preferred color, font, etc.

One more ontology-based approach to the development of adaptive user interface is described in [6]. This research is directed to the personalization of context-aware applications within mobile. Ontological user model contains the important information for context such as user activities and capabilities, an area of interests and preferences, health conditions, user location, etc.

Another view on the graphical interface adaptation is presented in MyUI Adaptation Framework [5]. This framework creates adaptive graphical interfaces for the interactive TV set. The main idea of the approach is to use the best practice patterns in the adaptation process. All patterns are divided into four groups: generic patterns for defining the global settings of TV interface such as font size or color; interaction patterns for providing the suitable interactive elements for each person; common patterns for defining the stable features as screen orientation or basic layout; and transition patterns for defining the mechanism of switching between common or interaction patterns. During the process of user interaction with TV, the framework collects information about the user, when the conditions of certain pattern become true the pattern is applied to the interface. It continues until the user turns off the TV.

We have considered some more approaches to interface adaptation [4, 8, 10] and concluded that ontology-based approach is not usable for real-time adaptation and adaptation on the base of user behavior analysis whereas interface design patterns approach seems to be a good solution to implement this process. The ontology-based approach can be extended with interface patterns for the purpose of supporting these types of interface adaptation. In this paper, we propose a two-phase method of interface adaptation which uses both the ontological user model and the interface patterns.

3   Ontological Model of Adaptive User Interface for Special Needs

The ontological model of the adaptive user interface is described in detail in [11] and is used for representing knowledge about the users' restrictions, the problems, which are occurred during the process of user interaction with the interface, and the possible interface solutions. The inference over ontology on the base of semantic rules allows obtaining the appropriate interface profile for the user with special needs. The meta-ontology of the adaptive user interface for people with disabilities (Fig. 1) was developed to integrate and manage the domain ontologies. The meta-ontology integrates all the ontologies described below and defines the relations between them:

$$M = <O_M, C, Inst, R, I>, \tag{1}$$

where M - meta-ontology; $O_M = \{O_{User}, O_{Dis}, O_{Int}, O_{Dev}\}$ – a set of domain ontologies, O_{User} - user ontology, O_{Dis} - user disease ontology, O_{Int} – interface ontology, O_{Dev} – device ontology; C – a finite set of meta-ontology concepts, $C = \varnothing$; $Inst$ – a finite set of meta-ontology instances, $Inst = \varnothing$; $R = \{has, impacts\ on\}$ – a finite set of relations between meta-ontology components; I - a finite set of interpretation rules, $I = \varnothing$.

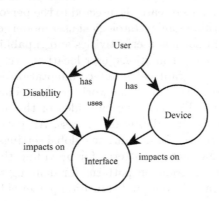

Fig. 1. Meta-ontology of adaptive user interface (IDEF5 diagram)

The ontology of user disease (Fig. 2) represents a variety of physical and cognitive problems which are caused by diseases. This ontology was developed with the assistance of the medical staff of Regional rehabilitation center "Nadezhda" for children with disabilities (Volzhsky, Russia).

The disease ontology is defined as follows:

$$O_{Dis} = <C_{Dis}, Inst_{Dis}, R_{Dis}, I_{Dis}>, \tag{2}$$

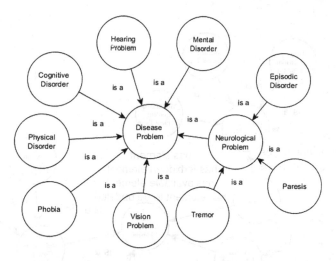

Fig. 2. Fragment of disease ontology (IDEF5 diagram)

where C_{Dis} – finite set of concepts of the disease ontology; $Inst_{Dis}$ – finite set of the disease ontology instances, $Inst = \varnothing$; R_{Dis} – finite set of relations between the disease ontology components; I_{Dis} - finite set of interpretation rules.

The ontology of interface (Fig. 3) represents the relations between interface use cases and design solutions for user interface adaptation.

The interface ontology is defined as follows:

$$O_{Int} = <C_{Int}, InstInt, R_{Int}, I_{Int}>, \tag{3}$$

where C_{Int} – finite set of concepts of the interface ontology; $Inst_{Int}$ – a finite set of interface ontology instances, $Inst = \varnothing$; R_{Int} – a finite set of relations between the interface ontology components; I_{Int} – a finite set of interpretation rules.

During the research, the ontology of users device was developed. The full description of it can be found in [3]. But that ontology does not have concrete instances of special devices and there was no access to experts in the area of hardware and software for people with disabilities. To resolve this problem it was decided to use ontology model of the device from AEGIS project [13]. The ontology model of the device (Fig. 4) is represented as an aggregate of software applications for devices and hardware extra appliances for users device.

Each class of devices has concrete instances, for example, speech device class has two instances with the brief description: J-Say and IBM Embedded ViaVoice. Every instance has a relation with the disease.

To use this ontology model in our project we need to connect software and hardware components with users problems caused by disabilities. Also, we need to notice the impact of using appropriate software or hardware on interface elements. It can be achieved by adding extra rules to the meta-ontology.

The user ontology was created to store the information about users with disabilities, it is a simple taxonomy of the instances.

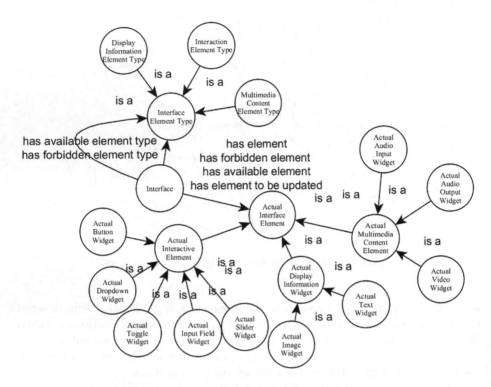

Fig. 3. Fragment of interface ontology (IDEF5 diagram)

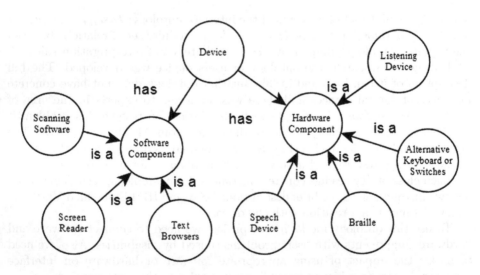

Fig. 4. Device ontology of AEGIS project (IDEF5 diagram)

Developed ontological model provides extensibility and modularity, supports the accumulation, reusing and sharing the knowledge in the development of the interface for the user with special needs and allows implementing the rule-based reasoning over ontology, it is implemented using Jena Rules library. Rules are written in the special form - Turttle language. An example of the rule is introduced below (4).

$$[deafnessForbiddenTypes : (?usermain : hasDiseaseProblem$$
$$dis : Deafness), (?usermain : hasInterface?interface),$$
$$(?interfaceinterface : hasElement?element),$$
$$(?elementrdf : type$$
$$interface : ActualMultimediaContentElement) \rightarrow$$
$$\rightarrow (?interfaceinterface : hasForbiddenActualElement?element)] \quad (4)$$

where $?user, ?interface, ?element$ – Jena variables; $main : hasDiseaseProblem$, $main : hasInterface$, $dis : Deafness$; $interface : hasElement$, $rdf : type$– ontology relations with ontology prefixes; $ActualMultimediaContentElement$ – ontology instance of $Interface$ domain.

This rule means that if the user has deafness and has the interface for usage and this interface contains some elements from the multimedia content area then these elements are not allowed for this user.

Now two groups of Jena rules are developed which are included in disease ontology, some examples of the rules are described in more detail in [11]. The total number of rules is 75 in the first group and 176 in the second group. The first group provides knowledge about interface elements types which are allowed or not allowed. The second group provides knowledge about current interface elements and decides which are allowed, not allowed or need to be updated.

4 Interface Design Patterns

The interface design patterns contain the best practices of interface constructions for people with special needs (most of them are described in [9]) and the knowledge of experts about requirements to interfaces for people with disabilities. They specify global interface settings (such as font sizes and interactive fields sizes, a preferred mode of information presentation, etc.) according to the given user type (the list of physical, sensory and cognitive disabilities that the target end user group has). After all of the settings is applied we get customized interface best fitting to the needs of users with given disabilities.

The difficulty in pattern-based approach lies in the phase of extracting knowledge for the development of interface patterns database. However, given such database, the application of patterns to create user interface is performed automatically. The modularity is another advantage of this approach - new patterns can be added without changing the structure of the application and interface adaptation algorithm. This approach allows to start with a small subset of proven solutions (interface patterns) and then it is possible to supplement and increase pattern database in the process of gaining new knowledge.

To implement this design pattern approach we proposed the interface pattern model and developed the interface pattern database, as well as the interface adaptation algorithm using these model and database.

The following interface pattern model was suggested:

$$Pattern = <PatternName, Problem, PatternGroup, Context, Solution>$$

where PatternName - unique pattern name;

Problem - description of the problem, that this pattern solves;

PatternGroup - name of the group, that this pattern belongs to;

Context $= \{(userProblem_1 : value_1), \ldots (userProblem_n : value_n)\}$ - description of the rules, under the fulfillment of which this pattern is applied, where UserProblem is the set of user disabilities, value is their severity;

Solution $= \{setting_1 : value1), \ldots (setting_n : value_n)\}$ - solution of the problem, which is a set of interface profile variables with the values to be assigned to them.

The example of pattern description in accordance with the proposed model is represented in the Table 1.

Table 1. The example of pattern description

Pattern	Font size - large
Problem	People with vision impairment need enlarged font size
Pattern group	Font size
Context (condition)	$2 \leq visualimpairment < 3$
Solution	bodyTextFontSize $= 51$
	complementaryTextFontSize $= 32$

Patterns are grouped depending on interface settings they define (for example, all patterns defining font size are in the same group). Pattern group model can be described as follows:

$$PatternGroup =$$
$$<GroupName, Problem, Context, SetVariables, Patterns, DefaultPattern>$$

where GroupName - unique name of the pattern group;

Problem - a description of the problem, that this pattern solves;

Context - a description of the selection conditions of pattern in text form;

SetVariables - $\{variable_1, \ldots variable_n\}$ - set of interface profile variables, that are determined by the patterns of this group;

Patterns - $\{pattern_1, \ldots pattern_n\}$ - set of the patterns, contained in this group;

DefaultPattern - element from Patterns used as a default.
An example of pattern group description is given in the Table 2.

Table 2. Pattern group "font size"

Name	Font size
Problem	Different users need different font size for comfortable perception
Patterns	Font size - small
	Font size - medium
	Font size - large
Set variables	bodyTextFontSize
	complementaryTextFontSize
Default pattern	Font size - small
Context	If the visual impairment is absent use small size
	If the visual impairment is minor use medium size
	If the visual impairment is severe use large size

The developed pattern model allows to use a modular approach to interface design, and also determine the unified form of rules for solution descriptions of different problems with interface design for people with disabilities. According to described models, the test interface pattern database had been developed, including 4 pattern groups: font size, interactive area size, availability of text input fields and preferred mode of presentation (text or pictures).

5 Two-Phase Method of User Interface Adaptation

The proposed approach to user interface adaptation combines both the use of ontology as a user model and interface design patterns.

The adaptation method consists of two phases: the phase 1 – an initial adaptation based on the ontological user model; the phase 2 – interface adaptation based on the analysis of data about user behavior and applying the appropriate patterns.

The first phase of the method begins when a caregiver defines the user profile of a person with disabilities. The reasoning mechanism allows obtaining the interface solutions for the current user in accordance with his/her peculiarities and parameters of his/her mobile device. At that, the conflicting situations are taken into account, when the user has multiple diseases which require applying the mutually exclusive interface solutions. Pseudocode of the phase 1 is presented in Phase 1.

As a result of the phase 1 execution, the common interface is generated, which is suitable for the user disease or set of diseases.

Algorithm 1. Phase 1 - Initial graphical interface adaptation

```
for all disease ∈ User'sDiseases do
    Get all physical Problems of disease.
    for all problem ∈ Problems do
        Check problem on compatibility with current graphical interface.
        if problem appears during interface interaction then
            Add problem to Interface Problems
        end if
    end for
end for
for all interfaceproblem ∈ InterfaceProblems do
    Get Interface Solutions for problem.
    for all solution ∈Interface Solutions do
        Check solution on consistency with other solutions.
        if solution is not contrary to other solutions then
            Add solution to Current Interface Solutions.
        else
            Resolve conflict situation according to resolving rules.
        end if
    end for
end for
for all solution ∈Current Interface Solutions do
    Apply solution to current graphical interface.
end for
```

The phase 2 of the adaptation method runs within the process of interaction between user and application during trial operation. Pseudocode of the phase 2 is presented in Phase 2.

Some parameters, like a number of clicking on object or region near this object, a time between clicking on two buttons, time of text input are caught by the application. After that, the flow of events is analyzed and some valuable interaction parameters are saved into the event database. The process of collecting and analyzing data on user behavior will continue during the whole period of trial operation. Then it should be checked if the saved events have changed the pattern conditions in the pattern database. If it happened, the appropriate patterns must be applied to the user interface. From each pattern group, the most appropriate pattern is selected - it is defined by the checking context rules in each pattern of the group. If the context does not match to any pattern then the default pattern must be selected as an active. As a result of this step, we obtain the set of best fitting patterns by one from each group. After that, each pattern from the set of active patterns should be applied to the current interface, it means that the interfaces profile variables are setting up in accordance with the values from pattern solution. All of the interface elements update their parameters according to the new interface profile values.

As a result of the phase 2, the personal adaptive interface is generated, which takes into account all users' peculiarities.

Algorithm 2. Phase 2 - Fine-tuning interface adaptation

while Application is running **do**
    Catch *event* of user's interaction.
    Save *event information* to *Event Database.*
    if *event information* triggered *pattern* in *Pattern Database* **then**
        Apply *pattern* to current graphical interface.
    end if
end while

The procedure of interface adaptation can be introduced by the following example. People after ischemic stroke have some physical problems and can not serve themselves in everyday life. For example, a user with lacunar syndrome subcortical stroke (LACS) has several post-effects such as pure sensory stroke, ataxic hemiparesis and unilateral weakness of face and arm. In addition to this, the user has middle vision impairment.

Suppose that user with these post-effects needs to perform the following interface task - to enter his name and press accept button. The inference over the developed ontology [11] shows that user with LACS disease can not easily perceive visual information and work with a touch screen to input text or push the buttons. Therefore the interface developers should design the interface using audio as a way for data output to avoid the use of visual data and should use audio or some special devices (for example trackballs) for data input to avoid the use of touch screen as a way of data input. Design patterns for building this interface are shown below in Tables 3, 4 and 5.

Table 3. Example of a design pattern: "Interface Element Audio Output"

Pattern name	Interface element audio output
Problem	User can't recognize *Interface Element* to read text on it
Context	*Vision Impairment Range* > Medium **and** *User's Device* has speakers
Solution	Replace *Interface Element* with *Audio Output Interface Element*

At the first phase of adaptation method, the suitable patterns according to the user's problems should be retrieved. The current user has problems in the perception of visual information, so he can not read text on the interface or input it in appropriate fields. Moreover, the user has problems with motoric, so he can not click on buttons or choose interface elements for text input without problems. Suppose that user's mobile device has microphone and audio dynamics. The conditions of two described patterns became true, that means that adapted interface should include audio input element and audio output element (Tables 3

Table 4. Example of a design pattern: "Interface Element Audio Input"

Pattern name	Interface element audio input
Problem	User can't use *Interface Element* to input data into it
Context	(*Vision Impairment Range* > Medium **or** *Motorics Impairment Range* > Low) **and** *User's Device* has microphone
Solution	Replace *Interface Element* with *Audio Input Interface Element*

and 4). At the second phase, the interface which was generated at the first phase should be improved to make it more personalized for the current user. Suppose that the user did not hear audio output information. In that case, if the application would not get any feedback from user during the next 30 s, then the condition of the third pattern became true, and according to this pattern, the solution is to repeat the last audio information louder (Table 5).

Table 5. Example of an improvement pattern: "Repeat Audio Output Command"

Pattern name	Audio output volume increasing
Problem	User can't hear *Feedback* from application
Context	*Time of Waiting* >30 s **and** *User's Device* has speakers
Solution	Repeat *Last Command* with *Current Volume* + 20%

The Interface editor on the base of the algorithm described above was created as a plug-in for Unity using following technologies and tools: Unity 5.1.3 for plug-in development and interface creation (.NET 3); Visual Studio 15 for developing C# application; NetBeans IDE 8.2 for creating JAVA application for working with ontology; Protege 5.0.0 for creating ontology; Jena 3.1.1 for reasoning over ontology via JAVA application; Video player plug-in for Unity to create Video widget; JUnit library for developing tests for JAVA application. The architecture of developed software tool is shown in Fig. 5.

The editor can generate recommendations to current interface using Java standalone application for connecting to the ontology via Jena Framework. The screenshot of the main working window of the editor is presented in Fig. 6, green buttons show that interface elements are available to use and red buttons show that developer can not use these elements for current user with a certain set of problems. After choosing ranges of disabilities (mental and motor) the available and forbidden interface elements are shown.

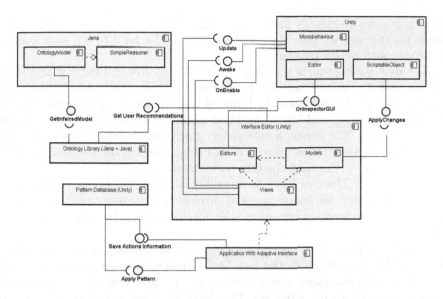

Fig. 5. Architecture of interface editor (UML notation).

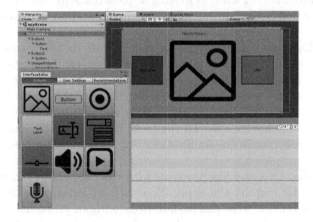

Fig. 6. Main working window of interface editor (Color figure online)

The developed Interface editor allows to create a mok-up of the adaptive user interface and gives some recommendations for interface developer, so it is not forbidden to use other interface elements or change element properties.

6   Testing Results

To test the correctness of the proposed approach the simple application was created which provides a set of pictures illustrating different kinds of activities and two buttons to identify preferences of the user. The use of this application is simple for the user without disabilities, but it can be hard to use such interface for people with health problems.

End user testing was held in MPI Oosterlo [15], five end users with a different range of disabilities were involved in testing the application created using Interface editor. All test users had mental disabilities, three of them had mild cognitive disabilities, and two of them had moderate and severe cognitive disabilities accordingly. The person with severe cognitive disabilities had also problems with motor function. Below there is a brief description of the users' peculiarities and problems in performing the task with the interface.

User 1 - Bart. This user has mild mental disabilities, but he can read and use a tablet without help. He understood the purpose and the result of the application usage, also he understood how to use the application and he performed the task well.

User 2 - Francis. This user has problems with mobility and mild cognitive disorders. He tried to finish the task as fast as possible. He was clicking both buttons and did not think about pictures and his preferences. He can read but can not concentrate his attention. The delay time between two clicks was set according the recommendations of the proposed system. He was not able to click buttons one after another without looking at pictures. After interface adaptation, he did the task well but he always need the help of assistant to explain the picture meaning.

User 3 - Dimitry. This user has problems with mobility, motor functions, also he has severe mental disorders. He can not read and understand how to use application. It was difficult for him to push buttons. The suitable adaptation, in that case, was to set the delay time between two clicks on buttons, because he did not do a click, he just pressed the button and was waiting for next picture. After setting the delay time he did the task. Also, it was recommended by our system not to use text in the application. So, all text on buttons was replaced with pictures.

User 4 - Jelle. This user has problems with reading, vision and has mild mental disabilities. He can use the application without assistance. But he does not have motor disabilities, so he can push buttons without problems. The developed system recommended increasing font size of text elements. He did the task well after increasing the font size on buttons and in the description to the pictures.

User 5 - Tallal. This user has problems with reading and has moderate mental disabilities. He can not use the application without assistance. He does not have motor disabilities. The developed system recommended using pictures instead of text elements. He did the task well, he understood the meaning of pictures on buttons but he needed a help of an assistant to explain each picture.

Testing process showed the availability of the developed approach. Firstly system gives recommendations to developers, then interface can be personally set to the unique user. For example, interface for a user without disabilities is shown below (Fig. 7). It contains two buttons with text elements and the

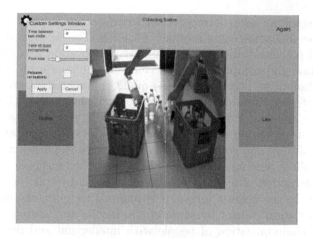

Fig. 7. Interface before adaptation

picture of activity. If developer chooses the moderate mental disabilities and motor disabilities for user, interface will change according to set of Jena rules (Fig. 8).

Fig. 8. Interface after adaptation

Also, the result of adaptation can be seen in the settings window. Appropriate problem changes the value int settings field. So after adaptation user with motor problems will get the specified button work which can lately be set again personally.

7   Conclusion and Future Work

The two-phase method of user interface adaptation was developed, it includes the process of initial interface adaptation on the basis of the ontological user model and reasoning over ontology, and interface adaptation on the base of analysis of user behavior using interface patterns. The developed software tool using created pattern database and suggested adaptation algorithm allows to reduce the time and complexity of interface customization of applications for people with disabilities and improves the quality of created interfaces. Therefore the number of such applications will grow, what means that the accessibility level of mobile application for people with disability will increase.

Next, we are planning to extend the interface pattern database, and add the methods of resolving conflicts during the pattern application. Also, we will improve the editor functionality and add the statistical methods for adaptation during the interaction of a user with the application by collecting statistics on user behavior. In the nearest future, it is planned to apply the developed approach for adaptation of user interface of the mobile application for support of mobility and communication of people with intellectual and development disabilities 'Travel and Communication Assistant' [12]. The main provisions of the proposed approach to interface adaptation are planned to be used for the development of software tool for designers and developers of mobile interfaces for people with special needs.

Acknowledgment. The authors would like to thank the staff of Regional Rehabilitation Center "Nadezhda" (Russia) for children with disabilities, most notably psychologist S. Karpova, for their help in designing and testing the ontological model and creating the base of interface patterns.

Also, we would like to thank the staff and clients of MPI Oosterlo (Belgium) for their help in testing the developed interface editor, and prof. J. Dekelver for his support in the organization of the software testing.

This paper presents the results of research carried out under the RFBR grant 15-07-03541 Intelligent support of decision making in the management of large scale systems on the base of integration of different types of reasoning on ontological knowledge.

References

1. WHO official website: World Health Statistics 2015. http://www.who.int/gho/publications/world_health_statistics/EN_WHS2015_Part1.pdf
2. WHO official website: World Disability Report 2011. http://www.who.int/gho/disabilities/world_report/2011/
3. Kultsova, M., Romanenko, R., Anikin, A., Poceluico, A.: An ontology-based adaptation of user interface for people with special needs. In: Proceedings of the AINL FRUCT 2016 Conference, November 2016
4. Abascal, J., Aizpurua, A., Cearreta, I., Gamecho, B., Garay, N., Minon, R.: A modular approach to user interface adaptation for people with disabilities in ubiquitous environments. Internal Technical report, no. EHU-KAT-IK-01-11, January 2011
5. Peissner, M., Schuller, A., Spath, D.: A design patterns approach to adaptive user interfaces for users with special needs. In: Jacko, J.A. (ed.) HCI 2011. LNCS, vol. 6761, pp. 268–277. Springer, Heidelberg (2011). doi:10.1007/978-3-642-21602-2_30

6. Skillen, K.-L., Chen, L., Nugent, C.D., Donnelly, M.P., Burns, W., Solheim, I.: Ontological user profile modeling for context-aware application personalization. In: Bravo, J., López-de-Ipiña, D., Moya, F. (eds.) UCAmI 2012. LNCS, vol. 7656, pp. 261–268. Springer, Heidelberg (2012). doi:10.1007/978-3-642-35377-2_36
7. Gamecho, B., Minon, R., Aizpurua, A., Cearreta, I., Arrue, M., Garay-Vitoria, N., Abaskal, J.: Automatic generation of tailored accessible user interfaces for ubiquitous services. IEEE Trans. Hum.-Mach. Syst. **45**(5), 612–623 (2015)
8. Llinás, P., Montoro, G., García-Herranz, M., Haya, P., Alamán, X.: Adaptive interfaces for people with special needs. In: Omatu, S., Rocha, M.P., Bravo, J., Fernández, F., Corchado, E., Bustillo, A., Corchado, J.M. (eds.) IWANN 2009. LNCS, vol. 5518, pp. 772–779. Springer, Heidelberg (2009). doi:10.1007/978-3-642-02481-8_117
9. Office of the Government Chief Information Officer: Mobile Application Accessibility Handbook. The Government of the Hong Kong Special Administrative Region (2011)
10. Castillejo, E., Almeida, A., Lopez-de-Ipina, D.: Ontology-based model for supporting dynamic and adaptive user interfaces. Int. J. Hum.-Comput. Interact. **30**, 771–786 (2014)
11. Kultsova, M., Romanenko, R., Anikin, A., Poceluico, A.: An ontology-based approach to automated generation of adaptive user interface based on user modeling. In: Proceedings of the IISA2016 Conference, July 2016
12. Kultsova, M., Romanenko, R., Zhukova, I., Usov, A., Penskoy, N., Potapova, T.: Assistive mobile application for support of mobility and communication of people with IDD. In: Proceedings of the MobileHCI 2016 Conference, September 2016
13. AEGIS Ontology. http://www.aegis-project.eu
14. Elias, M., Lohmann, S., Auer, S.: Towards an ontology-based representation of accessibility profiles for learners. In: Proceedings of the Second International Workshop on Educational Knowledge Management, vol. 1780, November 2016
15. MPI Oosterlo official website. http://www.mpi-oosterlo.be

LIT: Labour Interest Test for People with Intellectual Disabilities

Annemie Bos[1], Jan Dekelver[1], Wendy Niesen[1],
Olga A. Shabalina[2(✉)], Dmitriy Skvaznikov[2], and Raf Hensbergen[3]

[1] Thomas More University College, Geel, Belgium
{annemie.bos,jan.dekelver,wendy.niesen}@thomasmore.be
[2] Volgograd State Technical University, Volgograd, Russia
o.a.shabalina@gmail.com, orkich@gmail.com
[3] MPI Oosterlo, Geel, Belgium
Raf.Hensbergen@mpi-oosterlo.be

Abstract. The LIT (Labour Interest Test) for people with intellectual disabilities is an online test that probes interest for different labour opportunities. This test is based upon an earlier test, made by Lamings and Hezemans, a test which is frequently used for career counseling and guidance of people with intellectual disabilities, but which lacks theoretical basis and empirical validation. Therefore, in-dept interviews with the job coaches, observations during the test and statistical analysis led to suggestions for improvement and updating the test which were tested in several iterations. This paper focuses on the process through which these changes were made and the stakeholders who were involved in this process.

Keywords: People with intellectual disabilities · Inclusion · User-centered design · Labour interest test · Web application

1 Introduction: Intellectual Disabilities

The American Association on Intellectual and Developmental Disabilities (AAIDD) defines Intellectual Disability (ID) as "a disability characterized by significant limitations both in intellectual functioning and in adaptive behavior, which covers a range of everyday social and practical skills. This disability originates before the age of 18" [1].

Intellectual functioning refers to general mental capacity, such as learning, reasoning, problem solving, and so on. Adaptive behaviour is the collection of conceptional, social, and practical skills that are learned and performed by people in their everyday lives. For example: language and literacy, money, time and number concepts (conceptual), interpersonal skills, social responsibility, self-esteem, social problem solving, the ability to follow rules/obey laws and to avoid being victimized (social), personal care, occupational skills, healthcare, travel/transportation, schedules/routines, safety, use of money, use of the telephone (practical).

The definition by the American Psychiatric Association is comparable: "Intellectual Disability (Intellectual Developmental Disorder) is a disorder with onset during the developmental period that includes both intellectual and adaptive functioning deficits in

A. Kravets et al. (Eds.): CIT&DS 2017, CCIS 754, pp. 822–832, 2017.
DOI: 10.1007/978-3-319-65551-2_59

conceptual, social, and practical domains" [2]. The diagnostic term Intellectual Disability is the equivalent term for the ICD-11 diagnosis of Intellectual Developmental Disorders (IDD). The International Classification of Diseases (ICD) is the standard diagnostic tool for epidemiology, health management and clinical purposes as defined by the World Health Organization. ICD is used by physicians, nurses, other providers, researchers, health information managers and coders, health information technology workers, policy-makers, insurers and patient organizations to classify diseases and other health problems recorded on many types of health and vital records, including death certificates and health records [3].

The concept of intellectual disability has evolved over the last years into an ecological and social context-based notion.

The current paradigm is an adaptive one that applies when an individual has difficulties performing specific tasks in its environment, and from it, a notion of support actions to mitigate or annul these barriers comes into place. Those support actions are envisioned as tools or formal/informal support that allow achieving a certain task. They can be continuous or applied in an initial formation phase depending on the individual characteristics of the person in need of the support actions.

Estimates of worldwide and country-wide numbers of individuals with intellectual or developmental disabilities are problematic. Notwithstanding the varying approaches taken to defining disability, demographers agree that the world population of individuals with IDD is very large. According to the World Health Organization, almost 200 million people of the world's population have intellectual disabilities [4], being the biggest group within the disability population. Epidemiological studies suggest that the overall prevalence of severe intellectual disabilities (approximating to IQ < 50) is between 0.3 and 0.4% people of all ages, implying that in the 27 countries of the European Union (total population 504 million) between 1.5 and 2 million people have severe intellectual disabilities [5]. A meta-analysis of population-based studies showed that the prevalence of intellectual disability across all 52 studies included in the meta-analysis was 10.37/1000 population [6].

Labour is a very important means to inclusion and a lot of people with intellectual disabilities do not have access to it. This is problematic and in contradiction with Convention on the Rights of Persons with Disabilities that recognizes the right of persons with disabilities to work, on an equal basis with others; this includes the right to the opportunity to gain a living by work freely chosen or accepted in a labour market and work environment that is open, inclusive and accessible to persons with disabilities [7]. The labour market, in general, is not very receptive to people with intellectual disabilities who themselves experience problems to imagine what a job will require from them. On the other hand, it is essential to involve people with disabilities in the decisions that affect their lives [8].

It remains difficult for them to match personal goals, ambitions, strengths, and weaknesses to a new labour environment. Guidance and support are needed to support a pathway to employment. A test to map personal preferences to existing jobs is one of the many tools that can help to find a good match.

2 Methods to Screen for Labour Interests

2.1 Summary of Existing Methods for Labour Interests

General Introduction. Many of the contemporary methods to identify the labour interests of a person are based on the RIASOC model of Holland [9]. According to this model, there are six general occupational themes that categorise people according to their personality: realistic, intellectual, artistic, social, entrepreneurial and conventional type. Holland states that people perform at their best in an environment that fits their personality.

Other, but seldom used models are the hierarchical interest structure of Gati [10] and an alternative hierarchical model by Rounds and Tracey [11].

Questionnaires that identify ones interests are seldom used in the context of selection as they contain too many irrelevant domains (Lievens 2006). Moreover, no straightforward association with job performance is found.

These questionnaires are more often used in the context of career guidance and counseling. The most frequently used questionnaires are the Self-Directed Search (SDS), Jackson Vocational Interest Survey (JVIS), Kuder Occupational Interest Inventory (KOIS) and the Strong Interest Inventory (SII) [12].

Interest Tests for People with Intellectual Disabilities. People with intellectual disabilities perceive it as even more difficult to formulate their job and career preferences, given the broad array of options [13]. As such, career questions need to be specified and administered in a methodological way. Only then will an instrument prove to be a useful tool in guiding the career choices of people with intellectual disabilities. Methods that fulfill this requirement and offer visual and/or auditive help include the SWIT, KIT-V, RFVII, WBT and ABI test. Each of these tests focuses on a specific target group (intellectual disability, autism spectrum disorder...).

2.2 The AIT Test

The AIT Test as Developed by Cor Lamings and George Hesemans. In the book "Aan het werk, arbeid voor mensen met een verstandelijke beperking" (At work, labour for people with intellectual disabilities), Lamings and Hesemans [13] start with the statement that job satisfaction is not an obvious goal for PID. Skills, needs, and availability, are key factors in finding a good match. There is an important task for coaches to make sure that PID find a job that matches. The book presents a model to find a good fit between the interests and capabilities of PID and options for work. Lamings and Hesemans suggest the AIT as an intake instrument that and initial source of information that offers opportunities to map labour interest.

The test itself consists of 12 areas with five tasks per area. In total 60 tasks are part of the test. Tasks are presented in series of 3 tasks, selected out of different areas of interest. For each task, a representative picture is used.

The 12 areas are: semi-industrial work, domestic work, housekeeping, preparing food, administrative work, services, textile crafts, animal care, gardening, creative work, healthcare, arts and crafts, customer services.

Five tasks are linked to each area. As an example, we name tasks linked to housekeeping: clean windows, fold laundry, mop, clear the tables, vacuum. A picture is added to each task.

A test candidate looks at a total of 100 series of 3 tasks. At first, the test candidate is asked to select the preferred task out of the 3 presented tasks. After going through the test a first time, the test candidate is asked to select one of the two remaining tasks. The result presents a good basis to get information on the different interest areas of the test candidate (Fig. 1).

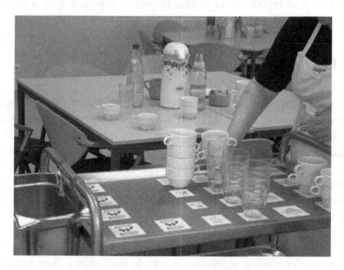

Fig. 1. Picture to illustrate the task: clear tables.

Test Results Based on AIT Test. The concepts for the AIT, as developed by Lamings and Hesemans, were transformed into a computer application by a volunteer and used by different organisations, working with PID in Flanders. The AIT was available only in Dutch. The results from one of the organisations where the test was taken from different test persons (n = 55) over a period of several years. All test persons were people who, due to their disability, are not able to work in an ordinary job. The results do not consider 7 test users because they did not finish the test. From the remaining 28 test persons, 15 were male, 33 female.

A recent psychometric analysis of the different scales [10], each representing a specific work area reveals that not all scales show sufficient internal consistency, as demonstrated by a Chronbach's alfa below .70. More specifically, the scales administrative work (α = .31), gardening (α = .58), creative work (α = .58), arts and crafts (α = .53) and customer services (α = .60) lack internal consistency. This implies that not all items- in this case: pictures – of these subscales that propose to measure the same construct produce similar scores. For the other scales, internal consistency was sufficient to high.

Results show that some work areas are preferred more than other work areas: preparing food (M = 64, 67), semi-industrial work (M = 62, 92) are lost likely to be selected by a random test user, while animal care (M = 36, 38) and gardening (M = 36, 38) are least likely to be selected. As the test does not include norm groups, it is impossible to compare the score of an individual with scores of a reference group.

The importance of comparing individual scores to a reference group is demonstrated by comparing the scores for each work area between male and female respondents. For the areas of domestic work, preparing food, textile crafts, animal care, gardening and arts and crafts large gender differences were found.

Finally, correlations between scales varied, implying that some scales are more related and hinting at higher-factor scales. However, research with a larger sample is needed to test this.

3 The LIT Approach

Remarks Concerning the AIT Test Method. The results of the empirical study suggest that an adaptation of the AIT test is needed in which inter-scale correlations, internal consistency, and reference groups are taken into consideration. Besides these psychometric considerations, other remarks concerning the current test method can be made. First, in-depth interviews with job coaches reveal that the duration of the test poses a problem for people with intellectual disabilities: those for who the test is designed, find it difficult to remain focused on the test and often need a break to be able to complete the test. Second, the 3-choice option unnecessarily complicates the choice for the test persons as he/she has to make two choices simultaneously: (1) whether he/she likes each of the three activities presented and (2) which activity he/she likes most. This creates confusing situations in which the subject likes none or all three activities but is forced to choose one. This forced-choice option is unlikely to aid in offering an accurate picture of the labour interests of the respondent. A better alternative is to give respondents with intellectual disabilities the possibility to give a Like-Dislike rating of each item. This allows the respondent to focus on one item and express both an explicit liking or disliking of the activity.

4 Programming of LIT

4.1 User Requirements

After testing the initial implementation of AIT, it was decided to migrate the app to Web, to improve the testing process, to update the interface and to extend the functionality of the app. The following improvements of the testing process were made: decreasing the number of pictures for each question from three to one, adding the ability to interrupt the current test and resume it later using the previously saved state.

The Web app needed to keep all features from the initial version, such as testing and evaluating the test results. In addition to the basic functionality, it was decided to implement the following Web-site features:

- managing the database of tests;
- storing the state of suspended tests and the results of completed tests: the date and time when the test was taken, the time spent in answering each question and the number of changed answers to each question;
- manual editing of test results by the tutor;
- visualizing the result of each test using tables and charts;
- recording the result of each test to an Excel file;
- adding sound support to enable the use of the app by visually impaired people;
- protecting the app from spam-bots.

Moreover, it was deemed necessary to distinguish the following types of users: super-administrator, local administrator, tutor, and student. Local administrator and user can create and manage the profiles for students. Super administrator, in addition, can create profiles for the administrators and teachers. Each category of managers can suspend/restore student accounts if necessary.

In addition, a dummy test for training end users and manuals for super-administrators, local administrators and tutors were supposed to be developed.

4.2 Database Structure

The Web app is intended to be used by the following categories of people: students, teachers, administrators. In addition, the app should have access to tests and test results. To store this information, including corresponding objects and attributes, a database has been developed. The structure of the database is shown in Fig. 2.

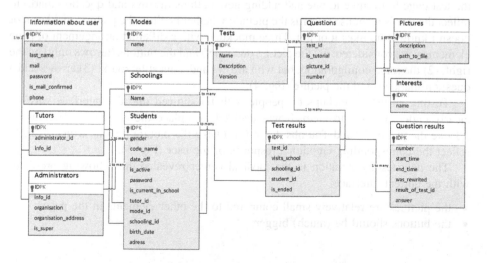

Fig. 2. Database structure.

The "Tutor" and "Administrator" tables have identical fields that are placed into a separate table "Info" which stores the following attributes: email, password hash, phone and some system information. The table "Student" stores FKs referring to the test's settings and students' personal data. Test results are stored in two tables: the main table and a table with the information about a certain question. The main table included the FK to a student being tested and the information whether the test has been completed. The second table keeps the question ID, testing time, answer selected by the student (Yes/No/n/a), the number of re-answers.

The tests themselves are stored in a similar way, in the main table and related table with corresponding question description. Each question keeps the key to the corresponding image. Each image can be linked to many questions and many professional interests.

4.3 User Interface

For developing the user interface Iterative design was used. Testing iterations were organized in MPI Oosterlo, a service centre for people with intellectual disabilities in Flanders, Belgium. The centre offers its clients professional service tailored to the individual client and co-determined by them. MPI Oosterlo works together with partners in the region to offer a service that meets the real needs for support and guidance. Secondly, the centre wants to support social changes, allowing people with intellectual disabilities to realize their right to full-fledged citizenship. The testing was conducted by Mr. Raf Hensbergen, a job-coach who helps mentally disabled people to find and keep a suitable (voluntary) job.

In the initial implementation of the user interface of AIT the test page had three pictures (shown in Fig. 3), matching their corresponding tasks, the progress bar and the following GUI controls Previous arrow, Settings, and Exit icons.

The design of a new Web interface began by decreasing the number of pictures on the test page from three to one and adding new buttons (arrows and question mark) to reflect the user's response towards the picture: whether he likes the picture, dislikes it or doesn't know if he likes it or not. Three mockups with a different arrangement of page elements were considered: (1) the picture on the left and the buttons (arrows only) on the right, (2) the same configuration, but with arrows and a question mark, (3) arrows and a question mark around the picture (Fig. 4).

Testing all three mockups on people with ID showed that the interface was not clearly understandable to them. It was decided to replace the arrows by Thumbs up ("I like the picture"), and Thumbs down ("I dislike the picture") icons which visually reflect the corresponding emotional response of the user (Fig. 5).

The next testing iteration in the medical center revealed the following problems with the current interface:

- the pictures are relatively small compared to the other elements in the page;
- the buttons should be (much) bigger;

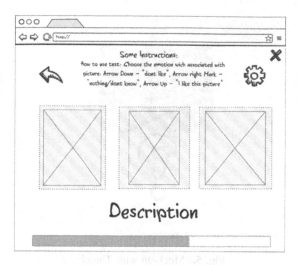

Fig. 3. The first version of the AiT app interface.

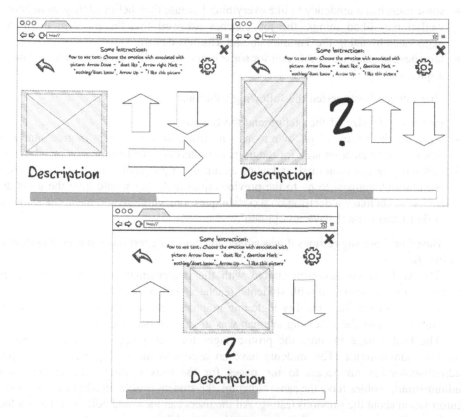

Fig. 4. Mock-ups with one picture

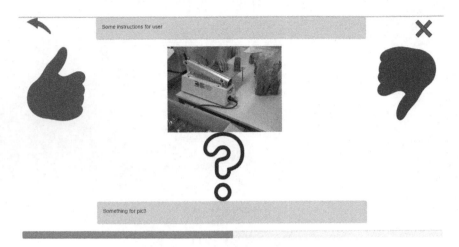

Fig. 5. Mock-up with Thumbs.

- some users had a tendency to like everything because they believed they were doing well if they liked things (the job coaches assumed that the problem might be aggravated by using the Thumbs up and Thumbs down);
- the question mark was confusing for some users, they might understand it as 'I have a question'.

The job coach suggested the following solutions:

- increasing the size of the picture and the buttons;
- replacing the Thumbs Up/Down icons with (more neutral) circles in green and red that should be clear enough for the users to understand the meaning of each button;
- removing the question mark and using an arrow for proceeding to the next question (similar to the arrow to go to the previous question), that would give the users an option to not make a decision on a certain question, which would mean the same as 'I don't know' or 'I have no opinion'.

Based on those suggestions it was agreed to change the test page interface to shown in Fig. 6.

The Web-site development started with the implementation of a minimal user functionality and testing it with students, teachers, and administrators. In the second iteration, the overall functionality including graphics, user search, TTS-text to speech was improved and the following sitemap was developed (see Fig. 7).

The Profile page includes the profile pages for each category of users: student, teacher, administrator. The students have an access to the testing page. The super administrator has an access to the pages for the tests settings. The teacher and administrator profiles have the same structure; the student profile, in addition, stores the information about the previous testing. All the users can view and edit their data on the corresponding pages. A special page was developed for viewing and editing the test results. The information is displayed in the form of tables, charts, and graphs.

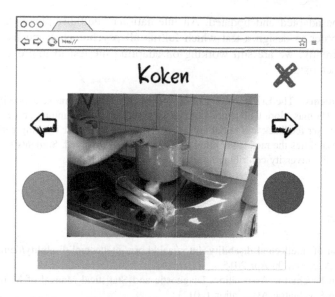

Fig. 6. Mock-up with arrows and coloured circles. (Color figure online)

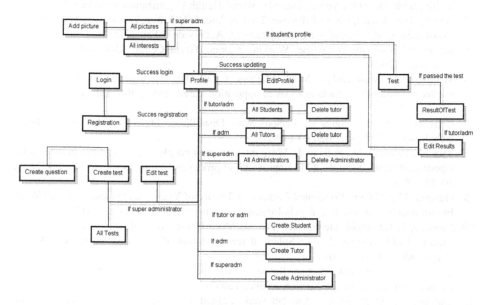

Fig. 7. Sitemap.

5   Conclusion

Performing activities that fit your interests is important for everyone's well-being, this being equally the case for persons with intellectual disabilities. In order to adequately measure their interests, the frequently used AIT designed by Laming en Hezemans needed to be adapted and updated. An international multidisciplinary team led this process in order to design a test which fulfills all psychometric and user-experience criteria. Currently, we are still working on adapting the test to improve the psychometric characteristics.

Acknowledgments. The LIT research and development is a collaborative action between many stakeholders. Thomas More University College provided the initial funding and accommodation and organized user feedback and initial testing. As community partner working with people with intellectual disabilities the medical centre MPI Oosterlo was involved. Students from Volgograd State Technical University contributed during an Erasmus Exchange.

References

1. Definition of intellectual disability. http://aaidd.org/intellectual-disability/definition#.VSIvy UZ9fTt. Accessed 06 Apr 2015
2. American Psychiatric Association. Diagnostic and Statistical Manual of Mental Disorders. American Psychiatric Association (2013)
3. World Health Organization. International statistical classification of diseases and related health problems. 10th revision, 2nd edn. World Health Organization, Geneva (2004)
4. WHO | The global burden of disease: 2004 update. WHO. http://www.who.int/healthinfo/ global_burden_disease/2004_report_update/en/. Accessed 05 Feb 2015
5. Intellectual disability in Europe: Working papers. Tizard Centre, University of Kent at Canterbury (2003)
6. Maulik, P.K., Mascarenhas, M.N., Mathers, C.D., Dua, T., Saxena, S.: Prevalence of intellectual disability: a meta-analysis of population-based studies. Res. Dev. Disabil. **32**(2), 419–436 (2011)
7. Convention on the Rights of Persons with Disabilities. http://www.un.org/disabilities/ default.asp?id=150. Accessed 05 Feb 2015
8. Vilà, M., Pallisera, M., Fullana, J.: Work integration of people with disabilities in the regular labour market: what can we do to improve these processes? J. Intellect. Dev. Disabil. **32**(1), 10–18 (2007)
9. Holland, J.L.: Making Vocational Choices: A Theory of Vocational Personalities and Work Environments, 3rd edn. Fla: Psychological Assessment Resources, Odessa (1997)
10. Diouane, I.: De arbeidsinteressetest. Thomas More University College, Antwerp (2015)
11. Tracey, T.J.G., Rounds, J.: The Spherical representation of vocational interests. J. Vocat. Behav. **48**(1), 3–41 (1996)
12. Lievens, F.: Handboek Human Resource Management: Back to Basics. Den Haag: LannooCampus; Academic Service, Leuven (2007)
13. Laming, C., Hezemans, G.: Aan het werk. Arbeid voor mensen met een verstandelijke beperking. Lib Edits, Tilburg (1996)

Data-Driven Approach for Modeling of Control Action Impact on Anemia Dynamics Based on Energy-Informational Health State Criteria

Olga Gerget[1](✉), Dmitry Devyatykh[1], and Maxim Shcherbakov[2]

[1] Tomsk Polytechnic University, 30, Lenina Ave., Tomsk 634050, Russia
gerget@tpu.ru
[2] Volgograd State Technical University, 28, Lenina Ave.,
Volgograd 400066, Russia

Abstract. In this work, spatial and time parameters were used to estimate the state of a biosystem on the strength of all attributes from integral criteria based on the Kullback information metric that is considered as a metric of a preferential behavior of a bio-object. Proximity of observed and preferential (reference) states is analyzed in the attribute space, where the proximity is normalized in the Mahalanobis model by an intraset distance of the reference state. Proposed approach can be considered as decision support instrument for medical experts evaluating possible outcomes of several treatment procedures. By modeling dynamics of individual integral criteria, the authors demonstrated the possibility of predicting the impact of sorbifer durules and mecsidol on the health state of pregnant women diagnosed with anemia. Experimental data included 8 blood properties from 92 pregnant women at different gestation periods measured at 3 timesteps: before; while; after applying treatment defined by medical experts. Treatment was considered as control action on biosystem and implicitly embedded into basic machine learning models such as linear regression and multilayer perceptrone. "Brute" approach to cross-validation identified several unique cases that could not be learned by models, due to lack of representativeness in original dataset and not model's relative simplicity. Revealed anomalies were proven to be correct by medical experts from Tomsk neonatal health center.

Keywords: Integral criteria · Anemia · Kullback metrics · Identification · Prediction · Decision support system

1 Introduction

Nowadays, problems of identification and prediction of biosystems states are actively discussed [1, 2]. Biosystems systems function normally if factors (functional variables) deviate a little from their equilibrium state. Such deviations define a homeostatic region. The fact when functional variables have excessive values indicates the violation of the conditions of self-regulation in a homeostatic region, in other words, degradation of the whole system. Thus, the state of a dynamic biosystem can be estimated on the

© Springer International Publishing AG 2017
A. Kravets et al. (Eds.): CIT&DS 2017, CCIS 754, pp. 833–846, 2017.
DOI: 10.1007/978-3-319-65551-2_60

basis of its integral energy-information parameters. These parameters can be used not only to identify functioning of an organism under various conditions but also to predict its adaptive capacity during preassessment and modeling.

Significant physiological changes in pregnant woman body ensure the correct development of fetuses and keep the woman organism in order. However, during the perinatal period, a pregnant woman is under additional stress, which leads to complications or/and exacerbation of chronic diseases. Based on statistics, 968 out of 1000 pregnant women suffer from different diseases. This fact highlights the necessity of monitoring and evaluation health status of pregnant women.

Among many other diseases that precede and complicate labor, anemia is ranked at the first place. In this regard, the crucial issue is the development of methods for detecting abnormalities in the health status of women who have anemia in their anamnesis. Methods should help to generate timely adopted preventive, organizational and control actions.

The completeness and quality of collected data are very crucial for accurate identification and prediction of the health status of pregnant women. In the paper, commonly used approaches to estimating the information capacity of the energy and information indicators has been selected.

In the energy approach, information capacity is estimated by the magnitude of the indicator. However, this approach fails in the case when the parameter having the greatest value among other attributes is relatively the same in all considered classes. In this case, there is no clarity regarding the significance of such parameter for diagnostic purposes. In this regard, information approach to estimating the information capacity of medical data has been proved more reliable as it considers information about each parameter as a significant difference between classes of objects in the space of characteristics. Within the framework of the information approach, there are several methods to determine informative parameters:

- the method of accumulated frequencies;
- Shannon method;
- Kullback method.

The method of accumulated frequencies and the Kullback method are used to determine the information capacity of the parameters that participate in the recognition of two classes, while the Shannon method makes it possible to determine the information capacity of the parameters that recognize an arbitrary number of classes.

The contribution of the paper lies in the development of decision support making system for pregnancy diagnostics; modeling of treatment impact based on dynamics of energy-informational health state criterion.

2 Background

Depending on associated tasks, there are several types of medical decision support systems that can be defined [3]: consulting; educational; researching. The complex approach, based on merging these approaches is a possible and perspective way of building advanced systems.

Common medical decision support systems are aimed to algorithmize physician's activity based on sickness patterns. Mathematical apparatus of such systems includes: multidimensional classification [4, 5], fuzzy-logic [6–8], case-based reasoning [9, 10].

Integral criteria based approaches process rate of decay of the oscillating transient characteristics and the deviation of the managed parameters from the norm [11]. Such approach solves the problem of finding a single quantitative indicator that would sufficiently reflect the various aspects of such a complex phenomenon as health. In a number of researches [12, 13] performed by Kochegurov, Konstantinova, Gerget, a generalized assessment of the health state of the biosystem, was determined using the mean geometric index.

Interest in the development of integral criteria is more closely related to the modern development of human physiology and the need to quantify the response of the whole organism to changes occurring under the influence of the internal and external environment.

3 Data-Driven Health State Modeling

3.1 Main Objective

This project is aimed at developing a clinical decision support system that can be used to identify functional states of biosystems in the context of energy-information processes. Overall objectives are following:

1. To characterize behaviors of biological systems in clearly defined functional states (diagnostics);
2. To define control actions that can minimize the risk of system transition into adverse conditions.

A solution of the objectives is supposed to be achieved by following the algorithm:

1. Collect the data, preprocess it by detecting spiking cases with anomaly set of features or dynamics;
2. Construct individual integral criteria I_{adapt} for each sample in dataset, if data had temporal structure then I_{adapt} is a vector, including independent values for each time-step;
3. Build intervals of criteria values that correspond to particular health state;
4. Evaluate effectiveness of control action by researching dynamics of health state proportions;
5. Build regression model, which takes I_{adapt} value at t-timestep and possible control action outputs future criteria value as result of treatment impact;
6. Perform decision support by evaluation each control action impact on health state.

3.2 Features, Control Actions, and Health State

While building a mathematical model of organism adaptation and treatment reaction the dichotomy properties of an organism have to be considered. On the one hand functioning organism being affected by environment and treatment requires set of specific features to be stable, on the other hand, the organism is not supposed to be constant but to demonstrate adaptation.

According to Kochgurov and Gerget [14] – metabolic, life-sustaining processes follow fundamental law of conservation of energy [2], life itself may be considered from the point of second law of thermodynamics. Thus, to describe organism functioning terms from control theory can be used, denoting: state vector as $X(x_1, \ldots, x_n)$, environmental and treatment impact as $V(v_1, \ldots, v_m)$, output vector as $Y(y_1, \ldots, y_z)$. The latter includes informative values, which characterize tension of additional mechanism, which keeps homeostasis. Information theory provides several approaches for estimating organism functioning deviation from some ideal condition.

Integral Criteria. In this paper, organism deviation is estimated using [2] approach which is based on Kullback-Leibler divergence. The preferable state is described as Eq. (1):

$$I = \sum_{j=1}^{n} P_0(x_j) \ln \frac{P_0(x_j)}{P_1(x_j)}, \tag{1}$$

where n denotes the number of informative features.

$P_0(x_j)$ is the "preferable" probability of object state, i.e. case when j-th feature deviation from physiological norm equals 0. As for such term as "norm", there is no uniform definition, it may be formed by experts or can be based on average statistical values of homogeneous samples.

$P_1(x_j)$ stands for the probability that x_j matches the "norm" and is calculated according to Eq. (2):

$$P_1(x_j) = P(|x_j - a| < \delta) = 2\Phi\left(\frac{\delta}{\sigma}\right) - 1, \tag{2}$$

where: a – expected value of x_j; δ – deviation from a; σ – standard deviation; $\Phi(\cdot)$ – $\frac{1}{2}erf\left(\frac{\cdot}{\sqrt{2}}\right)$.

In (1) $P_0(x_j) = 1$ because "preferable" state requires δ = 0, thus "preferable" probability may be described with Eq. (3):

$$P_0(x_j) = 1 - \left[2\Phi\left(\frac{0}{\sigma}\right) - 1\right] = 1 \tag{3}$$

Thus individual adaptation capabilities can be described with Eq. (4):

$$I_{adapt} = \frac{1}{n}\sum_{j=1}^{n} \ln \frac{1}{P_1(x_j)}. \tag{4}$$

This criterion can be used to estimate deviation of the object's current state from its preferential state. The following principles serve the basis for the estimation: if varying parameters change randomly and no regularity is observed, then the system remains in the same state, and its information parameters remain within a set range. When the information parameters exceed its predefined level, the system's state undergoes significant changes.

Deviation from the Norm. Integral criterion depends on average statistics of the group and its homogeneity. In case data provided by experts is supplemented with an interval of normal values for each property, actual mean values of x_j may be changed to closest borderline or interval's mean (denoted as ς), thus altering (4). Expert's thresholds leave several questions open about δ function: is it symmetrical; linear; does it depend on mean threshold value or interval?

In our case both approaches were used, the pair of deviations was calculated according to Eqs. (5 and 6):

$$\delta^{mean}(x_j) = |x_j - \varsigma|, \tag{5}$$

$$\delta^{closest}(x_j) = \begin{cases} |x_j - \varsigma^{bot}|, & x_j < \varsigma^{bot}, \\ |x_j - \varsigma^{top}|, & x_j > \varsigma^{top}, \\ 0, & \varsigma^{bot} \le x_j \le \varsigma^{top}. \end{cases} \tag{6}$$

Graphical representation of several hypothetic δ-functions (see Fig. 1) demonstrates that being inferior or exceeding the threshold may have a different impact on health state in general or integral criteria in particular. At the current stage of research, we suppose that deviation function for each feature is symmetrical and linear, though both authors and medical experts agreed that further research on the approximation of deviation function is required.

Prediction of Control Action Impact. One of the author's main hypothesis is that health state dynamics in accordance with treatment proposed by medical experts may be modeled and thus predicted. Moreover, by predicting future health state, the effectiveness of treatment can be assumed. Finding such control action that would bring

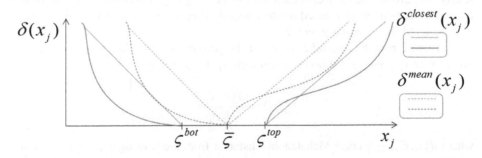

Fig. 1. Family of deviation functions

organism closer to an equilibrium state in future, is a key feature of decision support system being developed. Control action impact on integral criterion can be written as Eq. (7):

$$F(X(t), V(t), w) = I^*_{adapt}(t+k), \quad k \in \mathbb{N}. \tag{7}$$

F-values may be obtained using various of models: from linear regression to LSTM-network. It should be mentioned that (7) does not find ideal treatment, but predict possible impact of each control action included into V.

Embedding Control Action. Dynamic machine learning proposes 2 general [16] approaches for time embedding into a model: explicit suggests concatenating input vector X and the exact time value; implicit uses short-term memory in the form of additional weights, thus distributing time impact all over parameters of the model. The same principle may be applied for modeling impact of treatment or control actions.

While explicit approach, vectors of features and control actions are concatenated. Their dot product with the vector of model parameters can be used as an F argument. In this case, there is a single model that consequently takes several input vectors, gained in a result of the concatenation of feature vector and each control impact coded. The output of such single model is a vector of integral criteria predictions, which indexes correspond to control action.

Using implicit approach means that each prediction is generated by the separate model, trained to simulate precise control action. Thus, each model with a unique set of weights takes only one feature vector as an input.

Mahalanobis Distance Based Estimation of the Functional State as an Integral Parameter. Homogeneous groups can be formed on the basis of individual trajectories to estimate functional states of biosystems if sufficient information is available. Quantitative assessment of a functional state can be based on the analysis of proximity between the observed biosystem and the states described within the research [17].

Qualitative data on a functional state can be used not only to estimate relative deviation of its variables from their permissible values but also to consider objects' relative positions, the location of objects' maximum concentrations and their spacing relative the investigated object in each homogeneous group at each time interval. In this approach the estimation in based on the integral criterion, where Mahalanobis distance is considered as a proximity metric.

Let us express the integral criterion of the proximity of the functional state of the object x_j to the state of the homogeneous group C_0 as follows:

$$I_{C_0}(x_j) = \frac{d(x_j, C_0)}{D_{C_0}},$$

where $d(x_j, C_0)$ – average Mahalanobis distance from the investigated object x_j to the equilibrium state C_0:

$$d(x_j, C_0) = \frac{1}{M_{C_0}} \sum_{i=1}^{M_{C_0}} d_M(x_j, x_i),$$

where x_i, $(i = 1, \ldots, M_{C_0})$ – object entering the set of the equilibrium state C_0,
$d_M(x_j, x_i) = \sqrt{(x_j - \mu)^T S^{-1} (x_j - \mu)}$, $x_j = (x_1, x_2, \ldots, x_n)^T$ – the vector of the bio
object's state j; $\mu = (\mu_1, \mu_2, \ldots, \mu_M)^T$ – set of average values (vector of average values)
in the homogeneous group C_0; S – covariance matrix.

For independent attributes with a normal distribution, covariance matrix $S = I$ (I – identity matrix), the Mahalanobis distance coincides with the Euclidean distance. In this case, the metric of proximity for an object x_j to the equilibrium state C_0 is numerically equal to the square Euclidean distance from the object to the center of the area occupied by the set:

$$(x_j, C_0) = \frac{1}{M_{C_0}} \sum_{i=1}^{n} (x_{j,l}, \bar{x}_l)^2,$$

where $\bar{x}_l$ — average value of the 1st attribute of the state C_0 :

$$\bar{x}_l = \frac{1}{M_{C_0}} \sum_{i=1}^{M_{C_0}} x_{i,l},$$

D_{C_0} – metric of the area occupied by bio-objects from the homogeneous group C_0.
    The compactness metric takes the following form:

$$D_{C_0} = \frac{1}{M_{C_0}(M_{C_0} - 1)} \sum_{k=1}^{M_{C_0}} \sum_{i=1}^{M_{C_0}} d(x_k, x_i)$$

where M_{C_0} – number of bio-objects that describe the state C_0;
    The metric of the area occupied with bio-objects from a homogeneous group is an average distance among all objects that compose the group of the equilibrium state C_0. Therefore, D_{C_0} is a compactness metric that specifies spacing of objects among attributes of a homogeneous group.
    Approach [6], where information metric is used as a metric of bio object's preferential behavior, was used on the basis of the method to form integral estimates in decision-making support system.

4   Experimental Data and Results

Dataset consists of 92 records; each record represents the data about a particular woman under observation. Features for each record belong to one of 8 blood properties blocks: hemoglobin (HGB); erythrocytes (RBC); reticulocytes (RT); leucocytes (WBC); serum iron (FES); total iron binding capacity (TIBC); transferrins (TF);

transferrin receptors (TFRC). Each feature was measured 3 times: before treatment is the first time stamp; when treatment method being applied is the second time stamp; after the treatment is the third time stamp.

Dataset was split into three subsets based on treatment approach and the health state. There is a control group with 30 cases; sorbifer durules treatment group with 31 cases; and sorbifer durules and mecsidol combination group with 31 cases. Each of these none overlapping subsets was used for training and testing corresponding model.

Blood properties measured at the first timestamp were used as inputs. The integral criteria calculated using blood features measured at the third time stamp were used as desired outputs. For explicit control action embedding, inputs were concatenated with vectors that included binary encoded control actions.

Low representatives of the dataset caused by including only 92 patients make machine learning process sensitive to train-test split ratio. Low amount of initial information justified the decision to create all possible pairs of train/test samples with the minimal ratio for the test sample. Each element of the subset was presented in all folds excluding one training samples. Each test sample included only one record.

To mitigate the impact of random initialization, each model was given an array of initial weights. The model performance was evaluated as mean accuracy all over the train/test samples and initial weights.

4.1 Linear Regression Model

Linear regression model (LRM) is a well-known and commonly used model in medicine domain. The Linear regression model is trained to minimize mean-squared error. In the research, mean absolute percentage error (MAPE) was used for performance evaluation. It allows interpreting the model results and adequacy in a better way.

Input for each model was based on blood properties measured at the first time stamp, a pair of desired outputs was calculated using (4) for integral criteria and (5) for δ, σ. Pair of deviations were calculated using mean of normal interval and closest borderline value as $\bar{x}$.

The First Group (Sorbifer Durules) Analysis Using LRM. Figure 2 shows the histogram of error measures for the first group subset (left side) and percentage errors for particular cases in the test sample (right side). Mean average statistics of modeling integral criteria are:

- deviation from normal interval – mean error: 11.36%; std: 14.53%;
- deviation from the center of normal interval – mean error: 18.47%; std: 21.63%.

The Second Group (Sorbifer Durules + Mecsidol) Analysis Using LRM. Figure 3 represents the histogram of error measures for the second group subset (left side) and percentage errors for particular cases in the test sample (right side). Mean average statistics for modeling integral criteria based on:

- deviation from normal interval – mean error: 15.28%; std: 17.32%;
- deviation from the center of normal interval – mean error: 19.26%; std: 21.14%.

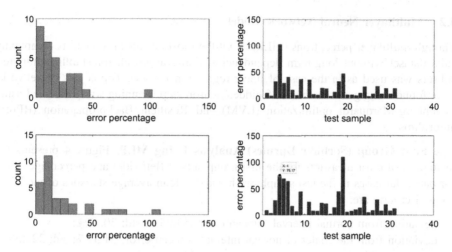

Fig. 2. First group integral criteria linear regression accuracy results: (top) based on deviation from borderline of the normal interval; (bot) based on deviation from the center of the normal interval.

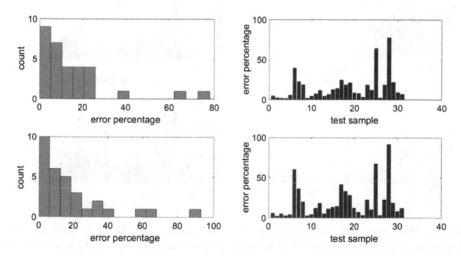

Fig. 3. Second group integral criteria linear regression accuracy results: (top) based on deviation from borderline of the normal interval; (bot) based on deviation from the center of the normal interval.

LRM Performance Evaluation. Predictions of integral criteria based on deviation from the center of the interval is less accurate in comparison to criterion, that was based on deviation from borderlines.

The high amount of experiments and combinatory approach to splitting dataset in train/test samples allowed to make the conclusion that errors of modeling are inherent in specific test cases because of high data variability and lack of additional information.

4.2   Multilayer Neural Network Model

Though multilayer perceptrons (MLP) is not the most advanced model, its complexity suits dataset without long-term dependencies. Same approach for shuffling train/test subsets was used as in the case of linear regression models. Topologies of networks were found using grid-search with 5 hidden neuron step. Training was performed using Levenberg-Marquardt optimization (LVM) and Resilient Backpropagation (RProp) algorithms.

The First Group (Sorbifer Durules) Analysis Using MLP. Figure 4 presents the histogram of error measures for the first group subset (left side) and percentage errors for particular cases in the test sample (right side). Mean average statistics of modeling integral criteria are:

- deviation from normal interval – mean error: 43.25%; std: 30.47%;
- deviation from the center of normal interval – mean error: 51.57%; std: 32.45%.

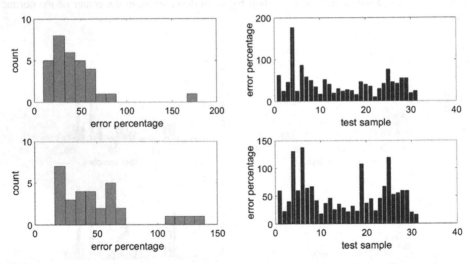

Fig. 4. First group integral criteria mlp accuracy results: (top) based on deviation from borderline of the normal interval; (bot) based on deviation from the center of the normal interval.

The Second Group (Sorbifer Durules + Mecsidol) Analysis Using MLP. Figure 5 represents the histogram of error measures for the second group subset (left side) and percentage errors for particular cases in the test sample (right side). Mean average statistics for modeling integral criteria based on:

- deviation from normal interval – mean error: 25.83%; std: 14.8%;
- deviation from the center of normal interval – mean error: 33.55%; std: 20.99%.

Multilayer Perceptron Performance. Despite adding nonlinear features, regression based on the neural network was considerably less accurate in the case of modeling impact of first treatment. It is worth mentioning that both neural network and linear regression models provided the least performance using same train/test samples. This fact demonstrates that specific cases (such as 28-th from 2-nd subset) are worth being attended by medical experts.

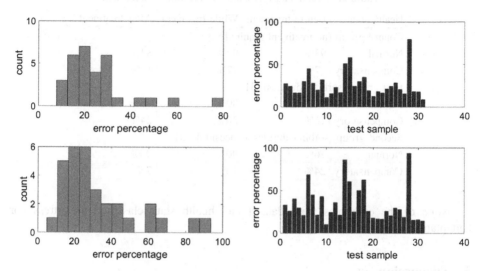

Fig. 5. Second group integral criteria mlp accuracy results: (top) based on deviation from borderline of the normal interval; (bot) based on deviation from the center of the normal interval.

4.3 Integral Criteria Critical Values

Machine learning based prediction of integral criteria is not enough for assessing the effectiveness of treatment. Unlike blood properties, integral criteria have no expertly predefined interval of values related to a health state. Interpretation of integral criteria relation with adaptive capabilities of an organism is as important as modeling its dynamics according to treatment.

Table 1 contains the dataset integral criteria critical values calculated according to [5]. Being lower or exceeding interval, defined by "normal" and "compensatory" matches significant health state decline.

Table 1. Integral criteria critical values in accordance with health state

I		Health state
0.9514		Normal
0.7817	1,18302	Compensatory
0.6434	1,48021	Stress
0.3465	1,67257	Adaptation failure, critical stress

To estimate the effectiveness of each kind of treatment on all three groups, health state dynamics was calculated. Each cell in Table 2 includes the percentage of patients whose adaptive capabilities were classified according to Table 1.

Table 2. Health states dynamics in reaction to treatment

Health state	Before treatment	While treatment	After treatment
Control group (no treatment required): 30			
Normal	93%	93%	84%
Compensatory	7%	7%	16%
First group (sorbifer durules): 31			
Normal	84%	80%	76%
Compensatory	16%	20%	24%
Second group (sorbifer durules + mecsidol): 31			
Normal	76%	90%	93%
Compensatory	24%	10%	7%

None of the examples from dataset had health state classified as "stress" or "adaptation failure".

5 Discussion

Experimental results demonstrated that health state of pregnant women diagnosed with anemia is measurable with the individual integral criterion. Its dynamics allows estimating treatment procedures effectiveness.

Integral criteria dynamics based on blood properties of the control group indicates the physiological changes happening in the body of healthy pregnant women. Positive dynamics of the health states were observed in the 2nd group, which indicates that adding mecsidol to treatment complex was a reasonable decision. Excluding the drug from treatment nullified effectiveness of sorbifer durules, this fact is verified by dynamics of 1-st group integral criteria values.

Predicting dynamics of individual integral criteria provides additional information for medical experts, thus treatment procedure assignation becomes more substantiate decision. Mathematical core of regression was based on linear and neural network models.

The performance of both models depends on splitting the dataset into train/test subsets. Cross-validation help to detect anomaly cases, which could not be properly analyzed by any model. While most cases reaction to treatment could be predicted by linear regression with error 10-20% according to mean absolute percentage error measurement.

However, neither linear regression nor MLP model could predict an integral value for a 28-th patient in the second group (see Figs. 3 and 5, bottom-right diagrams). A lot of experiments with various model's parameters brought us to the conclusion that this particular patient possesses unique blood properties and their dynamics. Anomaly reaction to treatment could not be modeled due to unique values of TF and TFRC features. Even with correct treatment iron balance was not fixed because of iron receptors lacking. Such rare case of anemia did not have enough time to cause severe harm to mother or fetus. Harm was prevented due to diagnostics based on a combination of blood features expert's analysis and cross-validation approach to machine learning train/test.

Such problematic cases are hard to detect manually, but several models cross-check, cross-validation approach to test/train sampling allows identify such cases by standing out MAPE value. To improve the performance of machine learning such cases can be investigated from the statistical point of view, excluded from the dataset or form a new subclass of reactions to particular treatment. Unique cases can become the foundation for future preproduction function working as a gate in the following way – if the patient possesses blood properties that are similar to specific cases from the dataset, then none of the already trained model can answer how effective the treatment would be and such case is worth attention of a medical expert.

6 Conclusion

In the case of various health issues, integral criteria can be considered as health state indicators. Such criteria dynamics characterize organism recovering flow according to a particular treatment. By predicting future values of criteria with mathematical models, the most efficient way from a list of possible treatments was determined.

Control action was implicitly represented in linear regression and MLP models. Linear regression model adequacy was significantly higher, especially for first group integral criteria prediction.

Currently, we are facing dataset representativeness issues, that were partially avoided by minimal test ratio and "brute" approach to building train-test pairs. Cross-validation approach for train/test data splitting detected several anomaly cases with unique blood features combination. These cases could not be learned by any of model used in the current stage of researching. All models despite initial weights demonstrated low accuracy for several specific cases, but low accuracy had triggered a manual investigation of anomaly cases. Medical experts explained resistance to common treatment as a combination of specific blood features, preventing the organism from fixing its iron balance.

Thus, the even extremely low accuracy of prediction specific case's integral criteria can perform clusterization of datasets revealing anomalies. The satisfactory mean accuracy of predicting control action impact will become a solid base for future researches with more advanced machine learning models.

Acknowledgments. The reported study was partially supported by RFBR, research project No. 16-37-60066 and research project MD-6964.2016.9.

This work was in part supported by the Russian Federation Governmental Program "Nauka" No. 17.8205.2017/BCh.

References

1. Jia, P., Zhang, L., Chen, J., Zhao, P., Zhang, M.: The effects of clinical decision support systems on medication safety: an overview. PLoS ONE **11**(12), e0167683 (2016)
2. Evans, J., Wilhelmsen, K., Berg, J., Schmitt, C., Krishnamurthy, A., Fecho, K., Ahalt, S.: A new framework and prototype solution for clinical decision support and research in genomics and other data-intensive fields of medicine. eGEMs (Gener. Evid. Methods Improv. Patient Outcomes), **4**(1) (2016)
3. Atkov, O., Kudrjashov, J., Prohorov, A., Kasimov, O.: Support system of clinical decisions. Inf. Technol. Phys. **6**, 8 (2013)
4. Kobrinskij, B.: System of decision support in health care. Doct. inf. Technol. **2**, 39–45 (2010)
5. Zaripova, G., Bogdanova, J., Kataev, V.: Actual models of support systems for medical decision-making in surgical practice. Int. Res. J. **53**(11), 137–142 (2016)
6. Spichyarin, A.A.: The issue of the use of cloud technologies in the decision-making systems. In: Spichyarin, A.A., Elizarov, D.E., Burkovskij, V.L. (eds.) Applied Mathematics, Mechanics and Control Processes, vol. 150. PNIPU, Perm (2014)
7. Simankov, V.S., Cherkasov, A.N.: Analysis and synthesis of the decision support system based on intellectual systems of the situational center. Sci. Bus.: Ways Dev. **12**(42), 93–98 (2014)
8. Ivanov, A.V., Mishustin, V.N., Lazurina, L.P., Serebrovskij, V.I.: Fuzzy mathematical model of the system of decision support for the decision of task of prognostication of acute pancreatitis. Doct. Inf. Technol. **6**, 60–66 (2013)
9. Korenevskij, N.A.: Prediction, early diagnosis and assessment of severity of acute cholecystitis based on fuzzy logic decisionmaking. Bull. Voronezh State Tech. Univ. **5**, 150–155 (2009)
10. Yudin, V.N., Karpov, L.E., Vatazin, A.V., Zulkarnaev, A.B.: Two approaches to software for physician's decision support. Almanac Clin. Med. **30**, 88–90 (2014)
11. Grigoriev, Y.G., Vasin, A.L., Grigoriev, O.A., Nikitina, V.N., Pokhodzey, L.V., Rubtcova, N.B.: Harmonization options for EMF standards: proposals of Russian national committee on non-ionizing radiation protection (RNCNIRP). In: 3rd International EMF Seminar in China: Electromagnetic Fields and Biological Effects, Guilin, China, p. 55, 13–17 October 2003
12. Gerget, O., Kochegurov, V.: Mathematical modeling of complex homeostatic systems. Sci. Bull. Novosib. State Tech. Univ. **4**, 89–94 (2014)
13. Konstantinova, L.I., Konstantinova, L.I., Kochegurov, V.A., Shumilov, B.M.: Nonlinear differential equations: parametric identification by exact polynomial spline schemes. Autom. Remote Control **58**(5), 756–764 (1997)
14. Kochgurov, V., Gerget, O.: Modeli i Informatsionnie Tekhnologii v Zadachakh Lechebno-Vosstanovitel'noii Meditsiny: Monografiia. Tomsk: Tomskii gos. politekhnicheskii universitet, Tomsk, Russia (2012).
15. Andreev, S., Batalov, R., Popov, S.: Modeling algorithms of excitation waves transmission in myocardium on the basis of cellular automation. In: ESC Congress, Munich (2004)
16. Devyatykh, D., Gerget, O.: Extraction of the fetal electrocardiogram using dynamic neural networks. Biomed. Eng. **50**(6), 371–375 (2017)
17. Alifirova, V., Brazovskii, K., Zhukova, I., Pekker, Y., Tolmachev, I., Fokin, V.: A method for quantitative evaluation of the results of postural tests. Bull. Exp. Biol. Med. **161**(3), 439–441 (2016)

Dynamics of Health Care Quality Indicators at Inpatient Hospitals of the Volgograd Region Estimated by an Automated Information System

Tamara Dyachenko[1], Victoria Ivanenko[1], Boris Lempert[1(✉)],
and Natalia Salnikova[2]

[1] Volgograd State Medical University, Volgograd, Russian Federation
ozz-volggmu@yandex.ru, bal4224@mail.ru
[2] Volgograd Institute of Management - Branch of the Russian Presidential
Academy of National Economy and Public Administration,
Volgograd, Russian Federation
ns3112@mail.ru

Abstract. The aim of this work is the scientific substantiation, development, and implementation of an automated information system for assessing the results of the expertise of quality of medical care in hospitals in the Volgograd region. A unified formalized expert card for assessing the quality of medical care; the groups of procedural indicators and an integrated indicator had been developed. On this platform, an automated information system for evaluating the care quality in a hospital was implemented demonstrating the effectiveness of its use in hospitals. A database was formed, containing the results of expertise which was carried out in the context of individual institutions and the Volgograd region as a whole. The quality of provided care was improved for all indicators in the dynamics for 2008–2015 as a result of monitoring, analysis of information received, development and adoption of management decisions.

Keywords: Quality of health care · Expert assessment · Expert card · Automated computer systems · Health management · Database

1 Introduction

The search for effective management methods which are able to optimize the activities of medical and preventive institutions became, in modern conditions, one of the strategic directions of healthcare in Russian Federation. Improvement of the quality and accessibility of medical care is one of the main objectives in the field of public health, according to the Concept of the Development of the Health Care System in the Russian Federation for the period until 2020. When improving the quality of medical care (QMC), one of the key issues is the way to get information about the QMC. Among the existing approaches to the assessment of the QMC (on the process, the result, the structure, according to patient satisfaction), the most complete information about the quality of the professional activities of doctors, medical offices and agencies provides a process approach, a necessary component of the modern concept of total quality management (Total Quality Management - TQM).

© Springer International Publishing AG 2017
A. Kravets et al. (Eds.): CIT&DS 2017, CCIS 754, pp. 847–857, 2017.
DOI: 10.1007/978-3-319-65551-2_61

All existing methods for research of medical care quality which are actually used originate from the analysis of individual cases to assist physicians without the use of a special technology. A qualified physician, skilled in clinical experience and professional knowledge, can assess the quality of another doctor's activity and present the results in the form of findings, conclusions, and the characteristics of the QMC [1, 2].

The main goal of QMC examination is to discover problems which exist while medical care provided. Next step is revealing of system reasons which cause this problem. Finally, the managerial decisions should be generated to eliminate discovered problems in future [3].

The assessment of quality must rest on a conceptual and operationalized definition of what the "quality of medical care" means. Many problems are present at this fundamental level, for the quality of care is a remarkably difficult notion to define. Perhaps the best-known definition is that offered 80 years ago by Lee and Jones [4] in the form of eight "articles of faith," some stated as attributes or properties of the process of care and others as goals or objectives of that process. These "articles" convey vividly the impression that the criteria of quality are nothing more than value judgments that are applied to several aspects, properties, ingredients or dimensions of a process called medical care. As such, the definition of quality may be almost anything anyone wishes it to be, although it is, ordinarily, a reflection of values and goals current in the medical care system and in the larger society of which it is a part.

Which of a multitude of possible dimensions and criteria are selected to define quality will, of course, have a profound influence on the approaches and methods one employs in the assessment of medical care [5].

Many ways to estimate the quality of medical care were suggested and used at different periods of time [6, 7]. The most popular among them are:

(a) Expert analysis of the quality of care providing process without the use of a method;
(b) Assessment of the care quality based on list of criteria for particular disease;
(c) Assessment of the care quality based on quality indicators;
(d) Association of quality of diagnostic and treatment process with negative outcomes;
(e) Methods based on research algorithms;
(f) Formal methods using describing of expert judgments;
(g) Methods of direct quantitative assessment of the medical care quality.

The qualimetric method, which essentially consists of the immediate quantifiable quality estimation by experts, lies at the heart of the last approach. Quality assessment methods included in this group involve compulsory structuring of medical process for information acquisition blocks such as diagnosis, treatment, and in some cases - to ensure continuity. Each of included blocks may be further divided into sub-blocks. For example, the obtaining of information is divided into sub-blocks of questioning, physical examination, laboratory, instrumental diagnostics, expert advice. Evaluation mechanism lies in the scoring of subjective expert opinion on the quality of performance of each sub-unit of medical action in accordance with the scale of assessments, the calculation of mean value for each block and integrated index for a whole case. The

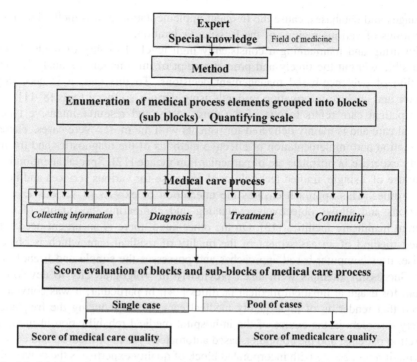

Fig. 1. Model of medical care process quality assessment based on direct quantitative expert evaluations

model of medical care process quality assessment based on direct quantitative expert evaluations is shown in Fig. 1.

Methods developed within the framework of this approach are the following: an integrated quality assessment method, an assessment of the quality of treatment, an assessment of the quality of diagnosis and treatment, and other modifications which differ on the estimated number of medical process blocks (sub-blocks), quantifying rules; principles of calculation of integrated indicators and QMC ranking. Some methods involve the need for expert comments in the form of descriptions of errors which cause a scoring reduction in expert cards. This kind of comments may serve as a basis for generalization of data on medical errors committed.

Thus, this approach requires the participation of highly skilled experts in the certain clinical specialty. Intermediate actual data are a quantitative evaluation of elements of the medical process that are fixed in the expert cards or computer programs. A number of techniques provide a description of the error which causes a score reduction.

Examples of the use of methods of this group are widely represented in the activities of medical facilities. The advantage of this approach is considered the possibility of a comparative analysis of quantitative indicators in different groups of doctors in different diseases. Easy handling of the material by the method of integrated quality assessment, easiness of integration into existing systems of processing and accounting for medical and economical information, based on common programming languages and databases, cause the frequent implementation of this method in medical institutions of various regions of the Russian Federation.

Ensuring and maintaining a consistently high level of quality of medical care is impossible without the timely and prompt receipt of information, its analysis and the adoption of evidence-based management decisions. To this end, it is necessary to monitor and analyze information in depth using various software tools [8–11].

In-patient care refers to one of the most costly and resource-intensive types of medical care and is mainly delivered for patients with the most severe cases. Therefore the creation and implementation of effective methods of the diagnostics and treatment quality expertise in hospitals are of particular importance [12]. Special attention is paid to the use of a single, unified technology of expertise for various services and hospital care profiles. This approach ensures the interaction of experts of various levels and directions and allows objectively evaluating and comparing the quality of care in different healthcare facilities [13]. On the other hand, there is an urgent need for the unified method of an assessment of the quality of medical care which is objective, precise, uses computer-based approaches and possesses the simple and friendly interface. Successful attempts were taken previously in Volgograd city to develop such system for usage at inpatient medical facilities [14]. In particular, it was convincingly proved that rendering of high-quality medical care allows reducing the frequency of anxiety disorders in the course of the in-hospital medical rehabilitation in myocardial infarction patients, and the computer-based automated system of medical and economic information processing with incorporated block of quality expertise is the powerful tool for timely detection of medical care quality defects and violation of the treatment standard [15].

2 Automated Computer System for Assessment of Health Care Quality

The aim of this work is the scientific substantiation, development, and implementation of an automated information system for assessing the results of the expertise of quality and technology of medical care in hospitals in the Volgograd region. Assessment of the care quality based on quality indicators has become the core of algorithm of automated system because this approach is considered to be the most effective when it's necessary to found the reason of care defects and to make decisions to prevent them [16].

To achieve this goal, a unified formalized expert card for assessing the quality and technology of medical care; the groups of procedural indicators and an integrated indicator; and a mathematical model of its weight characteristics, had been developed. On this platform, an automated information system for evaluating the care quality and technology in a hospital was designed and implemented. The following indicators were used in the process of evaluation of health care quality:

(a) the quality of documentation;
(b) diagnostic procedures;
(c) the accuracy of diagnosis;
(d) correspondence of treatment and diagnostic procedures to standards;

(e) providing of consultations;
(f) continuity of care;
(g) the analysis in the case of lethal outcome.

A database was formed, containing the results of expertise which was carried out in the context of individual institutions and the Volgograd region as a whole. An outline flowchart of this system is shown in Fig. 2.

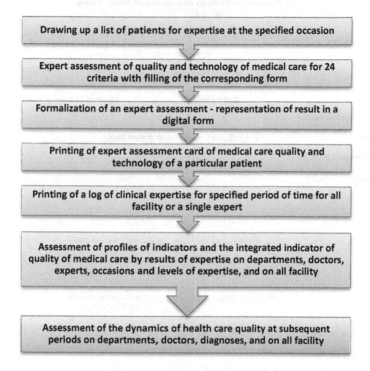

Fig. 2. An outline flowchart of AIS KMP "Hospital" software

The proposed questionnaire is an expert tool for assessing the quality of care. After filling in the personal data of the patient (Fig. 3) an expert is encouraged to answer 30 formalized questions choosing the variant which mostly match the situation. Based on the results of the examination, problem areas are identified in the procedural, organizational and technological aspects of medical care, defects in the activities of the services are established and systematized, and the causes of these violations are eliminated. The continuity of the various stages of the treatment and diagnostic process is also evaluated along with its adequacy, completeness, timeliness, and validity of diagnostic and therapeutic measures. The summarized result of the assessment of QMC is generated in conclusion.

All questions of the expert card are divided into 7 sections according to the logic of physician's job: A - the quality of documentation; B – diagnostic procedures; C – accuracy of diagnosis; D - treatment and prophylactic procedures; K - consultations; P – continuity of care; R - expert opinion in case of lethal outcome. The quantification

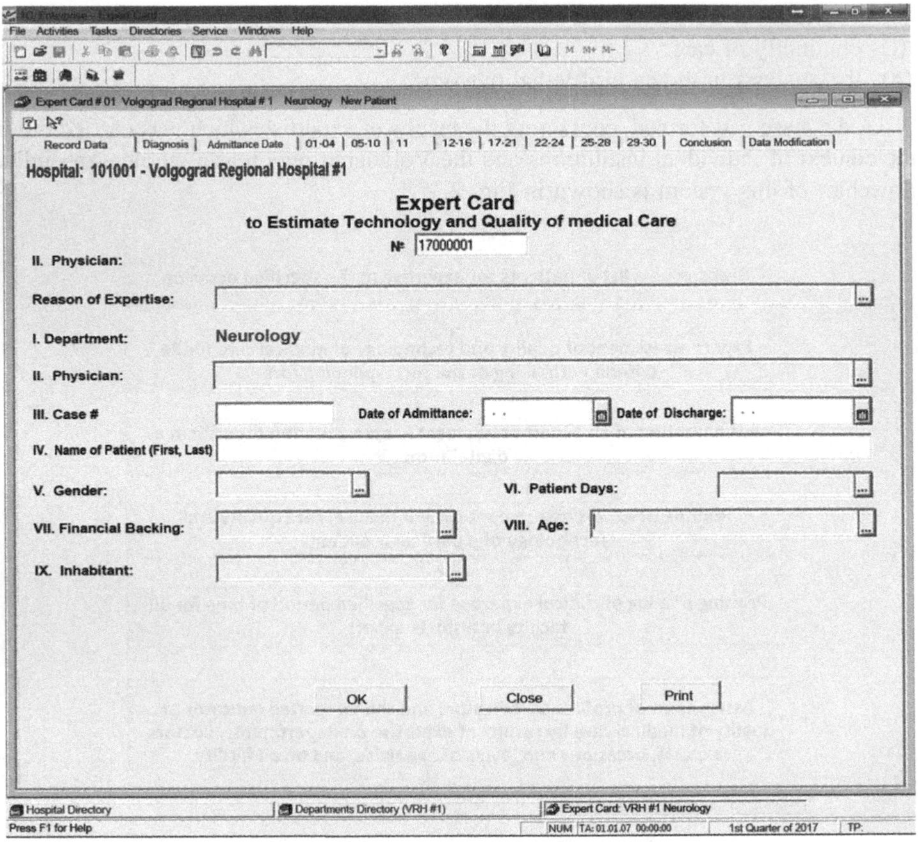

Fig. 3. An example of patient's personal data page (fields are blank for confidentiality)

method, i.e. evaluation of the quality level in a quantitative equivalent, was used to analyze the information obtained, and quantify the qualitative characteristics. Each of the variants of answers to the questions posed to the expert is assigned a ranked score from 0 to 1. The resulting evaluation is calculated for each of these sections of the examination, allowing separately evaluating the different stages and aspects of medical care, analyzing the work of medical services at all levels in detail, and identify defects at specific stages of the process. The resulting assessment of the quality of care for each section is the average of all subsections. It is converted to more familiar five-point assessment by mathematical processing.

The integrated index (E) of health care quality and technology is calculated at each case of expertise, according to the analysis of all the sections. The indicator is defined as the sum of the resulting estimates of the sections divided by the estimated number of sections of the questionnaire. An example of a report generated for one of the multi-field hospitals in Volgograd city is shown in Fig. 4.

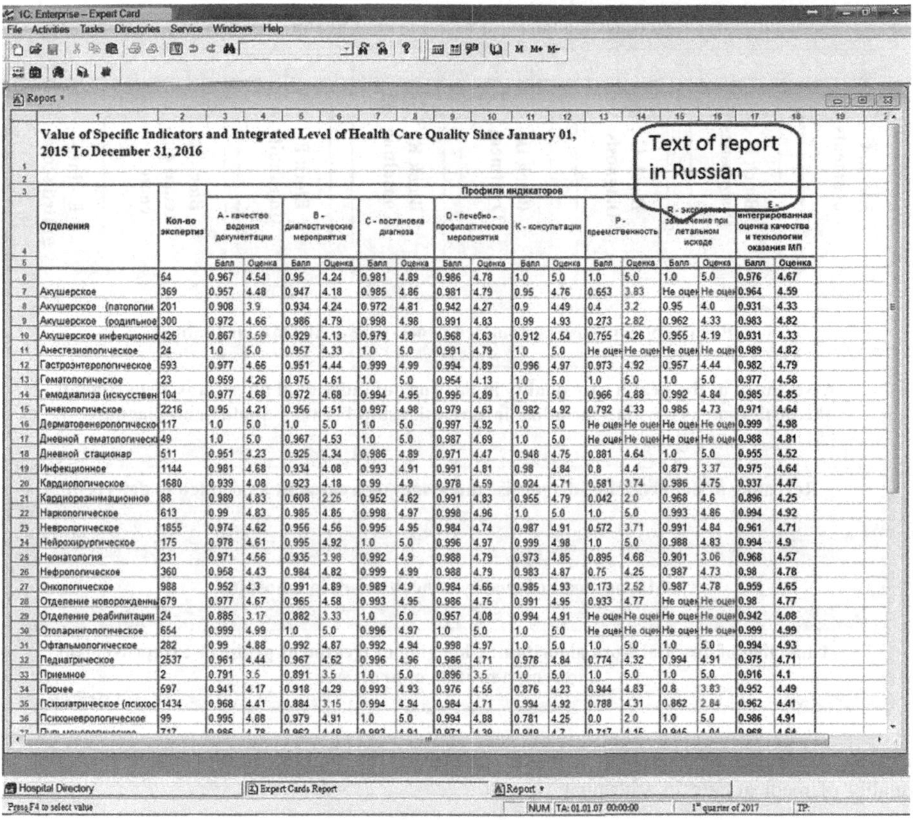

Fig. 4. A report on results of care quality expertise generated by software

The proposed method allows assessing the same expert case at different levels of expertise for a more objective and effective identification, analysis, and elimination of defects. After the examination of the quality of care and creating a database, an integrated score is calculated in different directions, allowing identifying and fixing defects due to the work of a certain physician, department, and facility in general. The analysis of errors and implementation of measures to correct them can be done afterward. Thus, a real possibility appears to manage the quality of care when the automated system is used. The algorithm of examination results processing is shown in Fig. 5.

The processing of information received, statistical analysis and the formation of a final expert opinion, containing conclusions, proposals and recommendations are important for making managerial decisions. In modern conditions, the processing of information based on the results of the QMC expertise implies the use of automated information systems. An automated system based on «built-in quality» statistical evidence (AIS KMP "Hospital") was developed for analyzing the quality of medical care. It's able to process a large amount of data contained in the expert questionnaire, allowing to assess objectively the level of care quality and make adequate management decisions improving the work of health and preventive facilities [9, 17].

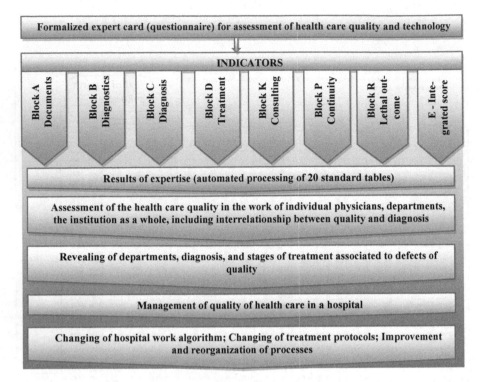

Fig. 5. Algorithm of examination results processing to suggest administrative decisions on quality of medical care in a hospital

Being introduced, this automated system made possible:

- calculation of individual indicators and an integrated indicator for quality and technology of medical care;
- assessment of the quality of medical care at homogeneous groups of patients on specific parameters (diagnosis, gender, age, social status, the severity of the state, etc.);
- monitoring and comparative analysis of the health care quality in the work of individual physicians, departments, the institution as a whole;
- creation of a database with the results of the examinations.

Unified way to access the information resources provided by the system is realized through a single desktop and ensures input, editing, and search for information. Unified access, automatically created a custom entry and search forms, specialized ways of presenting information, greatly simplify the work of users and administrators of the health care quality monitoring system in the hospital. Integrated technology of expertise ensures the interaction of experts of different levels and directions.

3 Results of Monitoring of Health Care Quality and Their Analysis

The software was launched in 2007. At this time, 108 inpatient hospitals (99%) were equipped with an automated information system for assessing the quality and technology of medical care of the AIS QMC "Hospital" in the Volgograd Region. The continuous monitoring of the QMC and analysis of the results obtained began in 2008. The dynamics of the number of cases carried out to assess the QMC using the AIS of the In-Patient Hospital since 2008 to 2015 is shown in Fig. 6. In the first two years (2008–2009), work was carried out to teach the top management of medical institutions to work with analytical data obtained as a result of monitoring the quality of medical care, to find the root causes of defects, and to develop evidence-based management solutions for their elimination and prevention. In the future, the number of examinations was increased especially at the first level of expertise, i.e. held by the heads of departments of hospitals. In 2014–2015 it was decided to reduce the number of examinations in order to improve the quality of the examination. The number of expertise of the first level has been reduced by more than 2 times and the main attention has been paid to the expertise held by the deputy heads of in-patient hospitals, responsible for quality (second level of expertise).

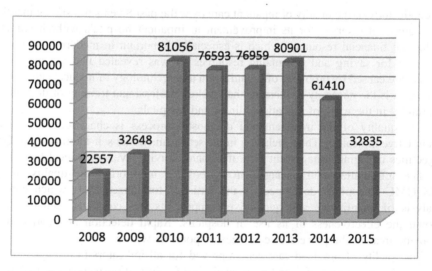

Fig. 6. The dynamics of the number of examinations carried out to assess the quality and technology of medical care using the AIS of the In-Patient Hospital for the period of 2008–2015

All the results obtained during the monitoring of the quality of care were analyzed taking into account the dynamics of the indicator profiles and the distribution structure of the estimates obtained.

When analyzing the results of assessing the quality of care, it was noted that the main criticism of experts throughout the study period was related to the quality of medical records. Defects were detected when checking the scope of the description of the patient's condition, the documentation, the completeness of the epicrisis, etc.

The organization and scope of diagnostic activities, the quality and timeliness of their conduct, and the interpretation of the results obtained also required improvement and correction. Based on the results of the analysis of the QMC in different medical facilities, a joint work was conducted with the participation of clinical pharmacologists, aimed at increasing the rationality of combinations of drugs used in treatment. Managerial decisions were taken to optimize the timing of treatment and bring it in accordance with standards. Among them was a correction of staff lists, optimization of salary increments, improvement of working timetable at emergency rooms, labs, X-ray departments etc.

The compliance of diagnosis to the classification of the ICD-X, accountable in the "Placing of Diagnosis" block, didn't, as a rule, cause significant criticism by experts. No significant defects were either found while evaluating the consultative work in hospitals, in particular with the participation of Regional Health Care Committee chief consultants in different fields of medicine. Positive dynamics was noted in the continuity of the work of inpatient hospitals, which was the result of a corresponding adjustment of this section during the first three years of monitoring.

4 Conclusion

In-depth study of the quality of inpatient care over the past 8 years has shown that there are significant reserves for its improvement in inpatient hospitals without attracting additional financial resources, which is especially important in modern conditions of the need for saving and optimizing resources. It was revealed that the majority of defects are caused by problems of organization and technology of medical care. No less important is the necessity to increase the level of professional training of doctors, and continuity in the work of outpatient clinics and hospitals.

The quality of the treatment and diagnostic process is characterized by many quantitative indicators. Their inclusion in the set of functional self-monitoring of QMC objectifies collegial management of professional activity level of medical facilities.

The information and management system for monitoring the quality of care AIS QMC "Hospital" developed on the basis of formalized tools which combine analysis of quantitative and qualitative components and computer technology has shown the effectiveness of its use in hospitals. Rapid detection and correction of problem areas in the process of care became possible with it.

The quality of provided care was improved for all indicators in the dynamics for 2008–2015 as a result of monitoring, analysis of information received, development and adoption of management decisions, and implementation of measures to eliminate and minimize the identified defects in hospitals of the Volgograd region.

A provision can be made to differentiate the remuneration of physicians, depending on the quality of their work, based on the analytical information obtained with the use of the AIS QMC "Hospital".

References

1. Dratcheva, T.I., Egorova, I.A.: The program indicator-based assessment in the system of governance and management of QMC in the Altai Territory. Development of a system to ensure the quality of care in the present conditions and problems of optimizing the structure of health care. In: Vth Semashko Institute Conference, pp. 105–108. Moscow (2000)
2. Donabedian, A.: The Criteria and Standards of Quality. Health Administration Press, Ann-Arbor (1982)
3. Klimenko, V.F., Lobachev, S.L., Petrovskiy, V.S.: Improving the analytical work as a mechanism for increasing the efficiency of external control of quality of medical care. Vestn. OMS **3**, 17–24 (2002)
4. Lee, R.I., Jones, L.W.: The Fundamentals of Good Medical Care. University of Chicago Press, Chicago (1933)
5. Donabedian, A.: Evaluating the quality of medical care. Milbank Q. **83**(4), 691–729 (2005)
6. Methods of Assessing the Quality of Care. http://www.medlinks.ru/sections.php?op=viewarticle&artid=3355
7. Trifonova, N.Y., Gabrielyan, A.R., Kasapov, K.I.: Evaluation of quality of medical care in medical facilities at contemporary stage. Soc. Aspects Health Popul. Electron. J. **33** (2013). http://www.vestnik.mednet.ru/content/view/508/30/lang,ru/
8. Vyalkov, A.I., Groisman, V.A.: Information technologies in management of health care and prophylaxis facilities under obligate medical insurance. Vestn. OMS **1**, 4–8 (2001)
9. Nazarenko, G.I., Polubentseva, E.I.: Quality of Medical Care, Management, Measuring Security Information. Medicine XXI, Moscow, (2004)
10. Sabanov, V.I., Golubev, A.N., Ivanenko, V.V.: Development and implementation of information system for inpatient control of health care quality. Volgograd J. Med. Sci. **3**, 8–11 (2008)
11. Sabanov, V.I., Ivanenko, V.V., Kokorina, L.V., Demidenko, Y.A.: Automated Information System for Assessment of Results of Expertise of Inpatient Health Care Quality and Technology. User Handbook. Volgograd State Medical University, Volgograd (2007)
12. Stolbov, A.P., Tronin, Y.N.: Informatization of System of Obligate Medical Insurance. A Textbook. Elit, Moscow (2008)
13. Sabanov, V.I., Ivanenko, V.V.: Monitoring of health care quality at inpatient hospital using formalized expert cards. Quest. Expert. Health Care Qual. **12**, 16–19 (2006)
14. Salnikova, N.A., Lempert, B.A., Lempert, M.B.: Integration of methods to quantify the quality of medical care in the automated processing systems of medical and economic information. In: Kravets, A., Shcherbakov, M., Kultsova, M., Shabalina, O. (eds.) Creativity in Intelligent Technologies and Data Science. CCIS, vol. 535, pp. 307–319. Springer, Cham (2015). doi:10.1007/978-3-319-23766-4_25
15. Lempert, B.A, Statsenko, M.E., Shilina, N.N., Lempert, L.B., Shabalina, O.A.: Anxiety disorders in the early post-myocardial infarction: adaptol treatment and the relationship with the quality of medical care evaluated by computer-based system. In: 7th International Conference on Information, Intelligence, Systems & Applications (IISA), pp. 1–6. IEEE Conference Publications (2016). doi:10.1109/IISA.2016.7785415
16. Yuriev, A.S., Avksentiyeva, M.V., Vorobyev, P.A., Gorbunov, S.N.: Methodological approaches to formation of actual indicators of quality of medical care. Probl. Stand. Health Care **8**, 1–15 (2005)
17. Dyachenko, T.S., Ivanenko, V.V., Gonik, M.I., Kulichkin, A.S.: Assessment of health care quality in gastrointestinal departments of inpatient hospitals in volgograd region for 2013–2014 years. Volgograd J. Med. Sci. **52**, 3–6 (2016). (in Russian)

Creating a Virtual Machine in Matlab as Part of Business Game for Educating People with Special Needs

Alena Khaperskaya[1](✉) , Olga Berestneva[1] ,
Olga Marukhina[1,3] , Elena Mokina[1] , Artur Mitsel[2] ,
Natalia Kozlova[3] , and Lyudmila Petrova[4]

[1] Tomsk Polytechnic University, 634050 Lenin Avenue, 30, Tomsk, Russia
khape@mail.ru
[2] Tomsk State University of Control Systems and Radio electronics,
634050 Lenin Avenue, 40, Tomsk, Russia
[3] Tomsk State University, 634050 Lenin Avenue, 36, Tomsk, Russia
[4] State University of Humanities and Technology,
Green Street 22, Orekhovo-Zuyevo, Russia

Abstract. The paper addresses the problem of adapting people with special needs to their future working environment. We support the idea that organizing courses and business cases on a virtual machine will be a solution to this problem. The analysis of people with special needs behavior in the actual learning process and their e-learning experience shows their ability to adjust their actions and develop adaptation skills relevant to any environment. Then, we analyze their behavior and the ways to involve them in the virtual setting activities, thus enabling them to feel that they are productive employees and members of the society. As the key evidence, we give an algorithm for creating a virtual business game that can engage people of any professions and social niches. We present the detailed algorithm of competences design and instruments of LSA- method, which helps to create a virtual machine for the decision-making process. Participants, including those with special needs, can also correct their decisions, which help them develop their abilities to adapt to their future working environment in a company. The work is interdisciplinary at the confluence of the disabled people behavior analysis and application of the key e-learning technologies. The main advantage of arranging such courses on the virtual machine is that people with special needs acquire the adaptation, communication, and decision-making skills as a part of distance learning.

Keywords: Data mining · Artificial intelligence · LSA-algorithm · Business case · Disable people · Virtual machine

1 Introduction

The present-day system of professional education does not only aim to improve the quality of professional training and competitive strength of university graduates but also to form new ways of thinking and intellect adapted to fast-changing technological,

© Springer International Publishing AG 2017
A. Kravets et al. (Eds.): CIT&DS 2017, CCIS 754, pp. 858–871, 2017.
DOI: 10.1007/978-3-319-65551-2_62

social, economic and information environment. When someone enters a working environment for the first time, they often have to face conflicts in the organization, solve complex problems, work in a team, be a leader and make important decisions that will affect the future of the organization as well as consider other social aspects. Not everyone, however, knows how to act in these situations. This problem can be solved by arranging business games in a virtual machine. This type of activity is also gaining popularity as an effective supplementary form of social support for people with special needs. Virtual business games make it possible for all people including those who are mobility challenged to actualize their economic, political and creative subjectness.

A potentially useful intelligent tool for researchers is the opportunity to establish the connection between the facts which aren't connected with each other, and, as a result, the new ideas, approaches, and hypotheses appear. This process is known as the analysis of the text (or intellectual data analysis if it is aimed at not bibliographic data set).

Data mining (text mining) includes the analysis of the big collection of the digital elements, which are often not connected with each other on a systematic basis and there is the process of the unknowns' detection before the facts, which could serve further as templates. If being guided by traditional manual search it would be extremely difficult to find complex couplings between the objects.

Now the ability of text recognition and data mining is the accelerator of the research process and the effective operation which was done in the past. Nevertheless, a row of features or conditions arises before starting such type of activity [2]. These include:

- access to a huge set of information on scientific research in the sequential and compatible form;
- free access without prohibitive monitoring of authentication;
- the digitized text, data, and other media sources;
- data which aren't protected by copyright, etc.

The diversity, value, and speed of data increase every year [3]. To track and process the changing data these hardware opportunities also should undergo essential changes.

As data mining is not a single operation, but a set of steps, theories, and algorithms, the hardware can be partitioned into a row of components. Changes in components aren't always synchronous with the increase in demand in data mining, machine training and big analytical problems solving. A hardware system of data mining must be balanced in relation to components to give users the best solution to their analytical problem.

Data mining of any scale can't be made without specialized software or virtual machine.

2 Benefits and Impact of Business Games Realized in Virtual Machine on the Development of Adaptation Skills of People with Special Needs

Business game on a virtual machine is essentially a method that makes use of an especially organized activity of implementing theoretical knowledge, so it is not a mechanical accumulation of information but an active discovery of a domain of a human reality.

Business games can be classified into three groups in terms of their functions [4]:

1. educational or training games meant for developing abilities and skills of transferring book knowledge into practice;
2. production games creating a forecast for the future and testing the current (innovative) mechanisms of the enterprise;
3. research games meant for checking new standards or principles of work; also used when implementing new technologies.

The business game embraces all the three functions. Since it is conducted on a virtual machine, we can add such functions as:

1. Electronic logbook as an effective control method;
2. Timely analysis of disabled people's actions in the course of the business game and an opportunity to correct them.
3. Knowledge of tools of information technologies.

One of the benefits of virtual business games is that a game can engage those who could not be present at a certain place at a certain time. The authorized leader gets an opportunity to see the viewpoints of all the participants in the chat window, analyze them and make a decision without any outside interference. The probability of making the right decision increases since there is an established communication system and information from the source reaches the target in the form of a chat message virtually without any data losses. Without a direct contact with their teacher, students feel free to express themselves. Many plug-ins enable us to adapt blogs to specific disabled people needs without much of an effort.

Another undoubted benefit is the automation of all the educational process planning and control as well as the communication among participants of the educational process, which reduces the time it takes for the teacher to control disabled people activities and correct their possible mistakes [5].

Social, psychological and professional adaptation is of key importance for successful work in an organization. This involves a wide range of topical problems under investigation [6]. These types of adaptation have a complex hierarchy and their own special dynamics of intercorrelation at different stages of learning. In the end, however, they integrate into a single adaptation process, in which the adaptation medium and the adapting element (disable people) interact to engender the adaptive situation encouraging the adaptive need in students.

The theoretical analysis and practical investigation into the adaptation factors of people with special needs helped us identify the organizational and pedagogical conditions of the efficiency of each adaptation type [7]:

1. Forming cognitive motivation and professional activity of disabled people with due consideration of the virtual environment of the teaching process;
2. Forming a disabled people group with a favorable social and psychological climate; psychological comfortable, moral satisfaction of students with themselves and with their teamwork;
3. Forming a steady focus on acquiring a professional qualification.

To implement the first condition, we need to center around the systematic forming of students' mental efforts and the approach to differentiating the levels of learning and cognitive activities of disable people. With this in mind, the first stage of the adaptive process incorporates the formation of cognitive activity at the reproductive level; the second stage is devoted to the heuristic level and the third one focuses on the creative level.

Since it is important to consider the nature of the computer information environment of the learning process, when forming the cognitive activity of disable people, the first pedagogical condition is provided by purpose-designed virtual business games. There are detailed methodology guidelines uploaded to the university's corporate portal for both teachers and students. Thus, students have free access to the whole set of cutting-edge learning tools including those for distance learning and virtual training.

The implementation of the second pedagogical condition of social and psychological adaptation for disabled people is associated with the following:

1. Arranging teamwork for students with a favorable social and psychological climate through involving them in active creative cooperation;
2. Providing psychological comfort as well as the moral satisfaction of students with themselves and being a part of the team [8].

The leading role in this type of adaptation falls on supervisors and dean's office representatives responsible for discipline as well as subject teachers.

The third pedagogical condition—providing a stable focus on the acquisition of professional qualification (professional adaptation)—is especially important for further development of professional competences. A stable focus on professional qualification comes from a positive attitude to the profession as well as features of character that are professionally in demand. The implementation of the above pedagogical conditions will result in the development of skills listed in Fig. 1. It also outlines the outcomes of developing this or that skill.

In this paper, we address the problem of disabled people adaptation to their future working environment in a company and offer ways to solve it in the form of virtual games and various business cases in the online setting. This field is also supplemented by the analysis and integration of people with special needs to the virtual environment. Thereby, it gives them the opportunity to feel the real organization as a full unit of society. As the key evidence, we have given an example of a virtual business game, whose participants can be representatives of any professions and niches in the society. We have also identified the pedagogical conditions of social and psychological adaptation of disabled people and people with special needs. The research has shown that the provision of these conditions will result in the development of skills specified in Fig. 1.

Thus, despite the active research into the impact of the global network on various sides of the society, the investigation into the influence of business games in an electronic setting on social adaptation of students and physically challenged people is still largely overlooked by most scientists [9–12].

Individual skills	
Being able to single out specific objective crucial for achieving the main goals.	Forming independent judgment
Developing personal interest	Acquiring self-organization skills
Deepening the knowledge in a certain sphere	
Seeing the prospects of developing practical skills	Creating something individual
Performing activities that are of practical use	Creating something unique
Developing the ability to adapt to critical situations	Collecting and analyzing new information
Explore problem solving strategies (algorithms) and integrate them into practice	Analyzing and evaluating other people's work
Learning to motivate yourself at work	Developing personal proactivity
Interdisciplinary skills	
Applying one's knowledge beyond a specific field	Integrating the knowledge acquired from different sources
Learning to perceive different situations, approach them from different standpoints and be able to adapt to them	Being able to perceive criticism and being ready for contradictory statements and arguments.
Teamwork skills	
Learning to work in a team	Being able to be a team leader and having organization skills
Developing diplomacy and tact	Supervising and guiding other people's activity
Taking part in the decision-making process	Acquiring cooperation skills
Work with self-awareness	
Doing one's own SWOT analysis (strengths, weaknesses, opportunities, and threats)	Acquiring satisfaction with the job done
Objectively estimating one's abilities in terms of solving the set objective	Striving for the feeling of autonomy and freedom in one's professional field
Communication skills	
Improving the perception of information the electronic format and formulation of questions while digesting this information	Writing a comprehensive and clear progress report
Offering one's work to other people's criticism (both written and oral)	Improving leadership and persuasion skills following a logical line of reasoning

Fig. 1. Skills acquired by disabled people when playing a business game on the virtual machine

3   Algorithm of the Intellectual Search of Tasks for the Competence Development

On the basis of the intelligent data processing methods, we can create a semantic core that contains all the keywords associated with a particular competence. Figure 2 shows the interface result, which contains the relevant words database, where the user can enter his query. Then, the task will be identified or recognized on the basis of the entered competence. After studying and passing the mentioned tasks the user will be able to develop this competence.

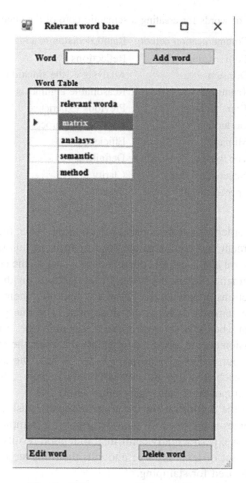

Fig. 2. Relevant words base for users

This program, which shows a Relevant word base for users, was developed in Matlab.

As an example, we can consider this kind of competence to be a communication activity, as well as rapid decision-making. Table 1 shows the examples of two competencies, as well as a few words related to the development of these competencies, which can be found in a business game, business case, problem situation, etc. All the keywords related to this concept are presented in Table 1.

According to the competence, such as communication activity, entered in the search, several business cases containing binders with this word concept were issued. On a rather small fragment of the business case, it can be seen that the program found a binding word, for example - "negotiating skills" and issued the task, after studying which the user can develop communication activity.

That is, general adapted software has been created to search for competency development tasks. The program produces a semantic analysis of the documents that

Table 1. Set of words for creating a semantic core of a certain competence.

Communication activity	Rapid decision-making
Conversation	Reflections
Decision	Analysis of the situation
Teamwork	Reasonable arguments
Teambuilding	Previous experience
Gestures	Improve the process
Mimicry	Efficiency
The words	Definition
Negotiating skills	Clarity
Speeches	Speed

are on the server, in order to find this or that information. Also, the program parses the text inside the document and compares the request to it. In this way, we can create a semantic core. When we add a specific document or a task to the core, it is indexed; the program builds a semantic image by some criteria based on the information in the header and some sections, identifies the keywords and uses them to form a tree cloud which highlights the semantic core of the document. The query can be formed in a natural form and then when it is converted into a semantic tree, it is compared with the database. If the inclusion occurs, certain documents that meet the request will be issued.

The first step in our proposed algorithm is to exclude the stop symbols, that is, words that occur in each text, but do not carry any meaning, for example, all conjunctions, particles, prepositions and many other words.

The next step in the algorithm for creating automated task search for the development of competencies is the need for the operation of a stamping operation. It is not mandatory, it has been experimentally confirmed that good results are obtained without it. In addition, if the set of texts is large enough, then this step can be skipped. The Porter algorithm was used for stamping.

The final step of the algorithm for an automated search of tasks for the development of competencies will be the exclusion of words that occur in a single case. This step is also optional; it does not have any significant effect on the final result, but greatly simplifies mathematical calculations. As a result, after all the steps are done, the indexed (relevant) words remain. In the figure, they are shown in bold type (See Fig. 3).

Figure 3 presents the result of the search that was created using the proposed algorithm, as well as the LSA algorithm applied to detect hidden patterns or non-obvious dependencies.

3.1   LSA Algorithm Used to Implement the Program

Among a huge number of algorithms that are used to search and analyze information, a special place is occupied by those of them whose purpose is to detect hidden patterns or non-obvious dependencies [13,14].

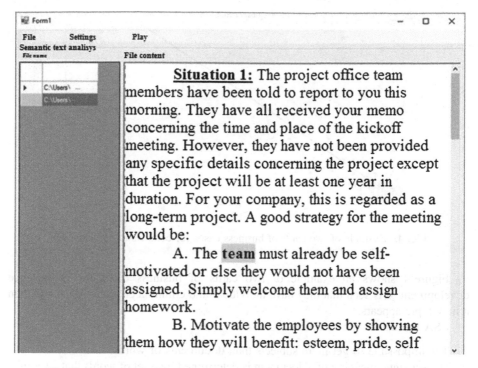

Fig. 3. An example of searching for a text fragment using the LSA algorithm

Using them, we can say, for example, that two texts are similar, even if this similarity is expressed indirectly. Or, for example, the words "skis" and "car" belong to different categories, but being used together they can be interpreted in such categories as "sports" and "rest".

One of such kinds of methods used for recommendation systems (collaborative filtering), information semantic search, the separation of texts on subjects without training and many others will be described later. This method is called latent-semantic analysis (LSA).

But in real life there are a lot of documents and words and there arise the following problems:

- dimensionality (computation of proximity between vectors becomes a slow procedure);
- noisiness (for example, small foreign text insertions should not affect the subject m);
- low level (most cells in the table will be zero ones).

In this case, the following idea is quite logical: instead of using the word-document table, the term-subject and the subject-document should be applied. The solution of this problem is offered by the LSA. But, unfortunately, the interpretation of the results can be difficult.

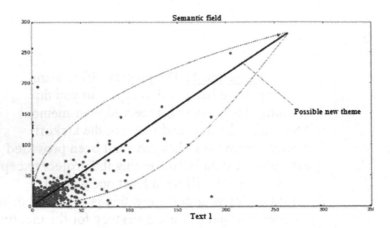

Fig. 4. Example of two cards of business cases for competence development

Figure 4 shows an example of two cards of business cases for competence development. It is seen that they have individual and common characteristics, and then a new topic appears.

LSA limitations are as follows:

1. It is impossible to get more subjects than documents or words.
2. The semantic meaning of a document is determined by a set of words that, as a rule, go together.
3. Documents are viewed as simple sets of words. The order of words in documents is ignored. It is only important how many times a word occurs in the document.
4. Every word has a single meaning.
5. A disadvantage of the LSA is the assumption that the word map in the documents does not have the form of a normal distribution. Other modifications of the method cope with this problem [3].

The LSA includes the following steps:

1. The process of stop words removing, stamping or lemmatization of words in documents;
2. The exclusion of words that occur in a single copy;
3. Matrix word-document building (binary existence or absence of a word, the number of occurrences or tf-idf);
4. The expansion of the matrix by SVD (A = U * V * WT). According to the competence, entered in the search, such as communication activity, several business cases containing binders with this word concept were issued. On a rather small fragment of the business case, it can be seen that the program found a binding word, for example, "negotiating skills" and issued a task, after studying which the user can develop communication activity. We receive the result of singular decomposition (Fig. 4).

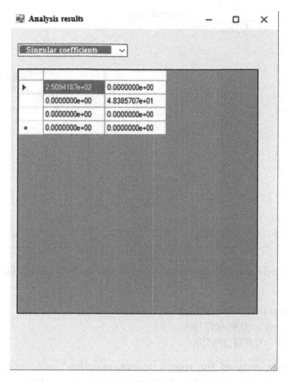

Fig. 5. Singular decomposition of competence "negotiating skills"

In this case, the main advantage of singular decomposition is that it highlights the key components of the matrix, allowing a user to ignore the noise. According to the simple rules for the product of matrices, it can be seen that the columns and rows corresponding to the smaller singular values give the smallest contribution to the final product. For example, you can drop the last columns of the matrix U and the last rows of the matrix WT, leaving only the first ones. It is important that the optimality of the product obtained is guaranteed. An expansion of this kind is called a two-dimensional singular decomposition (Fig. 5).

There is one more example: let's assume that there are three documents, each on a different subject (the first is about the competence, the second is about sports and the third is about computers). Using LSA, we will depict a two-dimensional representation of the semantic field, and how words (in red), requests (green) and documents (blue) will be represented in it. As we remember all the words in the documents and queries have passed the procedure of lemmatization or stamping (Fig. 6).

It is evident that the theme "adaptation" has been separated from the other two themes. But "negotiations" and "team building" are quite close to each other. For each topic revealed there are special keywords. In the picture, the green color shows a request for "communication activity". Its relevance to documents is as follows:

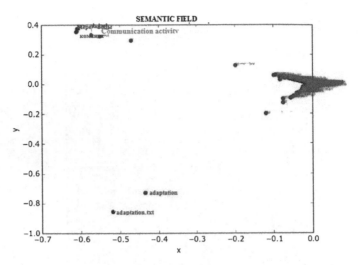

Fig. 6. Two-dimensional representation of semantic field (Color figure online)

1. 'communication.txt' - 0.99990845
2. 'teambuilding.txt' - 0.99987185
3. 'adaptation.txt' - 0.031289458

Due to the proximity of the topics "communication" and "team building," it is rather difficult to determine exactly which topic it belongs to. But certainly, it does not belong to "adaptation." If the system, trained on these documents, tries to determine the relevance to the emerging themes of the word "market", then we get 0 in response, because this word in the documents did not occur once.

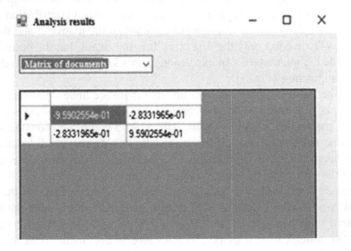

Fig. 7. Matrix of documents

Thus, the results are as follows:

1. LSA allows a user to reduce the dimensionality of data. You do not need to store the entire matrix of the word document, just a relatively small set of numerical values for describing each word and document is enough;
2. We get a semantic representation of words and documents, which allows to find unobvious connections between words and documents. Figure 7 shows the matrix of documents.

The disadvantage of this algorithm is a very large computational complexity of the method.

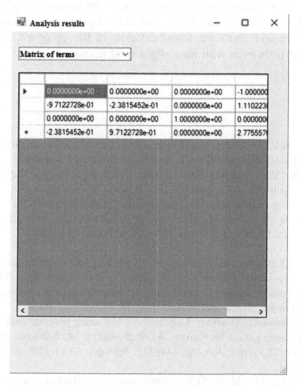

Fig. 8. Analysis results of term matrix

So, according to the developed algorithm, a task search system was developed for the development of competencies, where the analysis results look like a matrix of terms (Fig. 8).

4   Conclusion

The task of competencies development has been solved in this work with the help of machine learning. It is relevant for the system of general and professional education. The relevance of the study is determined by the need for further training and skills development, as well as the introduction of information technologies in the education process. The solution of this problem allows improving the methods and ways of developing competences with the help of an automated search system.

The analysis of the subject area was carried out, and the main problems of creating automated systems for searching competency development tasks were considered.

The methods that are used for reference systems (collaborative filtering), information semantic search, and separation of texts on topics without training are presented. Application of the method of LSA is described. The developed algorithm can be used in other areas that require text analysis, for example, in search of plagiarism testing systems. The application of the developed algorithm in the system of antiplagiarism will be more effective than the widespread method of "shingles", a significant disadvantage of which is the lack of the possibility of processing synonyms. Using text filtering, stamping and character transformation in the proposed algorithm allows finding borrowed texts even with their slight modification.

References

1. Khaperskaya, A.V.: Creating a virtual enterprise as part of a business game for adaptation of students and people with special needs. In: 8th International Conference, EDULEARN 2016, pp. 5779–5783. Education and New Learning Technologies, Spain, Barselona (2016)
2. Dekelver, J., Kultsova, M., Shabalina, O., Borblik, J., Pidoprigora, A., Romanenko, R.: Design of mobile applications for people with intellectual disabilities. In: Kravets, A., Shcherbakov, M., Kultsova, M., Shabalina, O. (eds.) Creativity in Intelligent Technologies and Data Science. CCIS, vol. 535, pp. 823–837. Springer, Cham (2015). doi:10.1007/978-3-319-23766-4_65
3. Saltykov, S., Rusyaeva, E., Kravets, A.: Typology of scientific constructions as an instrument of conceptual creativity. In: Kravets, A., Shcherbakov, M., Kultsova, M., Shabalina, O. (eds.) Creativity in Intelligent Technologies and Data Science. CCIS, vol. 535, pp. 41–57. Springer, Cham (2015). doi:10.1007/978-3-319-23766-4_4
4. Ogar, O., Shabalina, O., Davtyan, A., Kizim, A.: Mastering programming skills with the use of adaptive learning games. In: Kravets, A., Shcherbakov, M., Kultsova, M., Iijima, T. (eds.) JCKBSE 2014. CCIS, vol. 466, pp. 144–155. Springer, Cham (2014). doi:10.1007/978-3-319-11854-3_14
5. Berestneva, O.G., Marukhina, O.V., Fisochenko, O.N., Romanchukov, S.V.: Information technology assessment of competence of technical university students. In: International Siberian Conference on Control and Communications (SIBCON), pp. 1–4. IEEE Russia Siberia Section, Novosibirsk (2015)
6. Berestneva, O.G., Marukhina, O.V., Benson, G.F., Zharkova, O.S.: Students' competence assessment methods. Proc. – Soc. Behav. Sci. **166**, 296–302 (2015)
7. Berestneva, O.G., Marukhina, O.V., Kozlova, N.V., Lombardo, C.: Modeling coping strategies of technical university students. In: Kravets, A., Shcherbakov, M., Kultsova, M., Shabalina, O. (eds.) Creativity in Intelligent Technologies and Data Science. CCIS, vol. 535, pp. 81–90. Springer, Cham (2015). doi:10.1007/978-3-319-23766-4_6
8. Bermus, A.G.: Problems and prospects for implementing a competence approach in education. www.eidos.ru/journal/2005/0910-12.htm. Accessed 21 Nov 2016

9. Eisner, J.M.: Three new probabilistic models for dependency parsing: an exploration. In: Proceedings of the 16th Conference on Computational Linguistics, pp. 340–345. Association for Computational Linguistics (1996)
10. Iomdin, L., Petrochenkov, V., Sizov, V., Tsinman, L.: Papers from the Annual International Conference «Dialogue», pp. 830–853. ETAP parser: state of the art (2012)
11. Gaifman, H.: Dependency systems and phrase-structure systems. Inf. Control **8**, 304–337 (1965)
12. Gallant, S.I.: Connectionist expert system. Commun. ACM **31**, 152–169 (1988)

The Development of Medical Diagnostics Module for Psychotherapeutic Practice

Alla Kravets[1], Olga Poplavskaya[2], Lev Lempert[2],
Natalia Salnikova[3(✉)], and Irina Medintseva[3]

[1] Volgograd State Technical University,
28 Lenin av., Volgograd 400005, Russia
agk@gde.ru
[2] Volgograd State Medical University,
1 Pavshikh Bortsov Sq., Volgograd 400131, Russia
poplavok9@rambler.ru, faust807@mail.ru
[3] Volgograd Institute of Management – Branch of the Russian Presidential
Academy of National Economy and Public Administration,
8 Gagarin St., Volgograd 400131, Russia
ns3112@mail.ru, medinira@yandex.ru

Abstract. The article deals with the problems of establishing the diagnosis by psychiatrist and psychotherapist using standard questionnaires for mental status assessing and history taking, along with computer versions of diagnostics instruments. A full-scale automation of establishing the diagnosis is offered, based on techniques of artificial intellect. The class of clinical decision supporting systems was selected for modeling of psychiatrist's reasoning in course of interpretation of the test results. The apparatus of fuzzy logic has been selected to increase acceptance of decision making by experts in medical diagnostics, due to plenty of fuzzy and approximate reasoning in the process of establishing the diagnosis. Comparative analysis of well-known and most used algorithms for fuzzy inference, such as Mamdani and Sugeno, was held on to select the algorithm for medical diagnostics task. The Mamdani algorithm was selected due to the simplicity of implementation. An example of the fuzzy logic module using for establishing the diagnosis by a psychiatrist was considered.

Keywords: Medical diagnostics unit · Psychiatry · Establishing diagnosis · Expert systems · Decision support systems · Base of knowledge · Fuzzy logic theory · Fuzzy logic algorithms

1 Introduction

In psychiatric practice, a comprehensive study of the patient is crucial for correct diagnosis. This study consists of a past history of the patient, the subjective and objective medical history, its course, the study of the patient's mental condition, neurological status, and physical, laboratory, instrumental data.

Such a comprehensive study of the patient require that physicians have to take a great care and sensitivity to the patient's statements, deliberation while making conclusions, in-depth study of the patient's individuality, and true interpretation of his

© Springer International Publishing AG 2017
A. Kravets et al. (Eds.): CIT&DS 2017, CCIS 754, pp. 872–883, 2017.
DOI: 10.1007/978-3-319-65551-2_63

behavior. The necessity of early detection and prevention of diseases in the population entails the need to use modern information technologies in health care, in particular, the creating of the systems for differential diagnosis [1, 2]. A special place is given to systems which help to improve the quality of medical care [3, 4]. The software approach to modeling of medical knowledge representation in expert systems of differential diagnosis seems to be the most relevant.

Diagnosis is an important aspect of understanding the patient, allowing to use methods and tools of psychological help and to plan a strategy to work with the patient, more adequately. Attempts to use information technologies in the diagnosis of mental illness were made repeatedly [5, 6], but it's clear now that full-scale automation of this process is only possible when based on the methods of artificial intellect. This fact makes the actuality of this work.

2 The Specificity of Mental Diseases Diagnosis

The diagnosis is essential in the activity of practitioner in any clinical discipline, including psychiatry. The process of taking anamnesis, being always the main method of evaluation in psychiatry, will be replaced by standard questionnaires within the framework of evidence-based research. The standardized and structured partially and fully instruments conforming the criteria and algorithms to ICD-10 and DSM-IV has been developed abroad thereby. Doctors gather information by asking the standard questions during the planned interviews, regardless of the specific symptoms of patients. Among structured instruments the most valid is "Composite International Diagnostic Interview" (CIDI) and "Scheme of Diagnostic Interview" (DIC) and among semi-structured – "Scale for Affective Disorders and Schizophrenia" (SADS), "Schemes of Clinical Examination in Neuropsychiatry" (SCAN) and "Structured Clinical Interview for the classification of DSM" (SCID). The standardized survey scheme "Present State Examination" (PSE); "Schedule of Affective Disorder and Schizophrenia" (SADS); "Diagnostic Interview Schedule" (DIS) and others are provided also. All of them contain a set of symptoms that need to be identified, as well as their definitions and assessment of the disease severity.

The result and the final stage of the diagnostic process are the diagnoses of the patients, established on the basis of the analysis and synthesis of individualized facts revealed during questioning and observation. Thus, the purpose of diagnosis (diagnostic process) is the "medical conclusion about the nature of the disease and the patient status, expressed in terms of modern medical science", realized in the form of establishing of the individual diagnosis, which determines the choice of treatment and rehabilitation activities and prognosis of the disease.

3 Review of Computer Diagnostics Tools

Computer versions of diagnostics instruments are spread widely, although most of these systems, allowing to automate the processing of data, only simulate generating of psychological conclusion, substituting the process by compiling values of aggregate diagnostic signs (reproducing by this way the logic of C student) [7, 8]. A full-scale automation of the procedure is possible only relying on artificial intellect techniques as it involves modeling of psychologist reasoning in the interpretation of test results, and the transfer of knowledge and experience of the diagnostician to some structures, perceived by a computer [9–11].

Attempts to create an expert system (ES) in psychiatric diagnosis were held in 2007–2008 years. A model of psycho-diagnostic examination has been implemented in software [12] and has become the basis of expert system prototype "Psycho" introduced in 2009 in the Moscow Psychological and Pedagogical University.

In the USA, expert systems were developed for the detection and evaluation of some disorders obstructing successful schooling (e.g. ES DYSLEXPERT [13] and others). An example of this type of ES is FEARDEX (Fear Diagnostic Expert System), diagnosing phobias. The system interface is designed for contact with the testing subjects while demonstrating them picturesque and animated material. According to the authors, when conclusions formulated by FEARDEX and compiled by psychologists have been compared, the differences were revealed for subtle cases (system overestimates the figures); the differences disappeared in the case of more severe phobias [14].

4   Formulation of the Problem

The present level of development of artificial intellect allows to design the software not only processing the application tasks of the same type but also being also able to support decision-making in complicated situations. For example, for the needs of medicine, such programs work as physician assistants to help to analyze the patient's data collected for reasonable interpretation.

A task was placed before the authors to develop a medical diagnostics expert module, including a database for patient's surveys and a knowledge base of clinical symptoms. Module requests patient's data and then responds by providing a set of relevant diagnoses. The diagnostic module should provide support for decision-making by psychiatrists placing the diagnosis according to questionnaires, ensuring a reduction in the complexity and timing of routine job and increasing the efficiency of psychotherapists and psychiatrists. The final user of the software is a psychiatrist. Regulating of access to electronic medical records is prerequisite due to the problem of medical confidentiality [15].

The actuality of developed software is proved by its ability to save the experience of mental illnesses diagnosing by a psychiatrist, assisted by a module developed. Decisions on placing diagnosis are made by a doctor on his own, taking into account or ignoring the conclusion of diagnostic module.

4.1   Requirements for the Functional Characteristics

The scope of the study is the medical diagnosis of mental diseases. Automation of diagnosis of mental disorders is based on case studies. The following objectives are necessary to achieve greater coherence of decision-making experts in course of placing diagnosis: to provide authentication of users (admin and physicians) in the module, and user registration in the software; to organize the output of questionnaires and survey fields, the storage of diagnostic questionnaires and survey results, and records of patients; to develop an interface for carrying out the survey; to be able to work with fuzzy knowledge of questionnaire fields and fuzzy inference rules; to create a graphical user interface for input/editing of fuzzy rules; to ensure the generation of patient diagnoses based on fuzzy logic and the ability to analyze the survey results.

4.2 The Problems can be Solved with the Help of Medical Diagnostics Module for Psychiatric Practice

The task was placed in the course of this work to develop a module of medical diagnosis of mental illnesses to psychiatrists based on fuzzy logic.

Clinical decision support system is oriented to knowledge management so that a correct diagnosis and recommendation for treatment should be based on a collected patient's data a reasonable interpretation of the results of medical examination should be offered.

The following problems were solved in the course of medical diagnostics module developing:

- a comprehensive method for determination of psychiatric diagnoses and appropriate treatment recommendations was established;
- a reasonable choice of fuzzy inference algorithm was held on for medical diagnostics and interpretation of the investigation results;
- the concept and architecture of decision support system for medical diagnosis on the basis of fuzzy inference was developed.

The diagnostic module should provide support for decision-making by psychiatrists during diagnosis placing, according to patient profiles, ensuring a reduction in the complexity and timing of the diagnostics, and improvement of efficiency of psychiatrists.

The end user of the program is a psychiatrist. The necessity to regulate access to electronic medical records is prerequisite due to the problem of medical confidentiality.

5 Clinical Decision Support Systems

The developers of fuzzy logic medical diagnostics module should improve the decision-making experts' consistency in course of medical diagnostics. This system belongs to the class of clinical decision support systems (CDSS) based on the information technologies. The definition of such systems has been proposed by Robert Hayward of the Centre for Health Evidence: "Clinical decision support systems combine patient's monitoring data and special knowledge of the physicians to select the best mode of treatment to improve health". CDSS constitute the main topic in the field of artificial intellect in medicine [16].

In 2005, studies have shown increasing an interest among physicians to medical CDSS by 64%. Using CDSS led to improved patient outcomes by 13% [17, 18]. The 2005 annual review notes: "Systems supporting decision making had significantly improved clinical practice in 68% of tests". Features of CDSS, which have an impact on the success of the use of systems are:

- CDSS is integrated into the clinical trial;
- CDSS uses electronic templates instead of paper ones;
- CDSS provides support for decision-making in the real time mode, not after the patient has gone;
- CDSS provides (active) voice guidance on care, not just diagnosis.

However, other system reviews are less optimistic about the use of the CDSS. In particularly it was mentioned in 2011: "There is a large gap between stated and real benefits of CDSS and other e-health systems, their cost-effectiveness has not yet been demonstrated" [16].

Clinical decision support systems are defined as "active knowledge system that uses two or more data elements for the diagnosis of patients in each particular case" [18]. This means that the CDSS is a system of decision support focused on knowledge management in a way that would establish the correct diagnosis and treatment based on patient's data.

The main goal of modern CDSS is to help physicians in the diagnosis. This means that doctors can interact with CDSS, for a complete analysis and diagnosis operating on patient's data.

The earliest CDSS were conceived as a decision support system for the doctor. The implication was that the doctor will enter the information and wait for diagnosis placed by CDSS. Modern technology of CDSS bases on co-operation with a physician, in order to use both pools of knowledge, for a deeper analysis of patient's data.

There are two main types of CDSS [19]:

- based on knowledge;
- Systems that do not use the knowledge.

An example of how CDSS can be used by a physician is a specific type of clinical decision support systems, named diagnostic decision support system (DDSS). DDSS requests some data of patients and in response provides a set of relevant diagnoses. The doctor then analyses the data received from DDSS to determine which diagnoses are relevant and which are not, and what further research is needed to narrow down the diagnosis row.

Most CDSS consists of three parts: a knowledge base, an inference engine and dialogue mechanism (Fig. 1).

The knowledge base contains the rules and associations, made up of data, which usually take the form of IF–THEN rules. If it's, for example, a system for determining drug interactions, the rule may be of the form:

IF X and Y drugs are used THEN notify the user.

While using the interface, the advanced user can edit the knowledge base to keep it up to date with new drugs. Output mechanism combines the rules of the knowledge base with the patient's data. Dialogue mechanism allows the system to show the results to the user, as well as to provide data input and access to the system [18, 19].

CDSS, which do not use the knowledge base use a form of artificial intellect, which is called machine learning [20]. This form allows computers to use past experience to

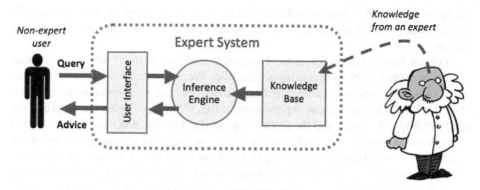

Fig. 1. The main components of CDSS

find patterns in clinical data. This eliminates the need for writing rules. However, as systems based on machine learning can't explain the reasons for its conclusions (they are the so-called "black boxes"), most doctors do not use them for diagnosis [21, 22]. However, they may be useful as after diagnostic systems.

Three types of learning mechanisms are used in these systems: vector machines, artificial neural networks and genetic algorithms [23].

Artificial neural networks use artificial neurons and weighted links between them, for the analysis of samples obtained among patient's data to determine the relationship between symptoms and diagnosis.

Genetic Algorithms (GA) are based on simplified evolutionary processes using directional selection for optimum results. Selection algorithms assess the components of random sets of solutions to the problem. Solutions that are chosen as the best recombine and mutate, and then the process starts all over again. It happens again and again, as long as the correct solution will not be detected. GA is functionally similar to neural networks, being also a "black box" that work with data of patients.

Such DDSS are often centered on a narrow list of symptoms, such as symptoms of one disease, in contrast to the approach based on the knowledge which covers the diagnosis of various diseases [18, 19].

6 Comparative Characteristics of the Fuzzy Inference Algorithms

Fuzzy sets theory has been chosen for this task solution. The concepts of fuzziness were first proposed by Lotfi Zadeh in 1965. Zadeh wrote in his work on the application of fuzzy set theory in medicine: "The most likely area of application of this theory is medical diagnostics and to a lesser extent the description of biological systems" [24]. The main reason for the emergence of this theory was the abundance of fuzzy and approximate reasoning in the description of the processes, systems, facilities. Fuzzy logic is a computing paradigm that provides mathematical methods for handling uncertainty and inaccuracy which are typical to human reasoning process. The main feature of fuzzy logic is the ability to express knowledge in a linguistic form, namely in the form of a set of simple-to-understand rules. Fuzzy logic can improve the classification models, based on the rules of fuzzy sets using to determine the overlapping classes.

Typical fuzzy classifier consists of rules set, such as "if, then" with fuzzy prerequisites, and class marked according to the rule. Prerequisites of the rules divide the space of sign values to a number of fuzzy areas. The rules' aftermaths describe the classifier output in these areas. Application of fuzzy "if, then" rules can improve the interpretability of results, and the ability to penetrate into the structure of the classifier in the decision-making process. Fuzzy classifiers use a gradual change in the degrees of belonging to several classes. Due to the fact that the fuzzy sets allow us to introduce the concept of continuity in deductive reasoning, the behavior of the fuzzy system becomes closer to the normal reality of traditional medical diagnostics. At the same time, fuzzy sets have all the advantages of symbolic models.

Among the fuzzy inference algorithms, Mamdani and Sugeno algorithms are probably the best known and most used. A simple comparison of these algorithms should be done applied to the problem of continuous functions of one variable approximation, to choose one for medical diagnostics An example of results of comparing is shown in Table 1.

Table 1. Results of the approximation function $F(x) = x^3$

i	1	2	3	4	5	6	7	8	9
x_i	−1	−0.75	−0.5	−0.25	0	0.25	0.5	0.75	1
$F(x_i)$	−1.000	−0.422	−0.125	−0.016	0	0.016	0.125	0.422	1.000
Based on the algorithm Mamdani	−0.962	−0.441	−0.136	−0.021	0	0.021	0.136	0.441	0.962
Based on the algorithm Sugeno	−0.976	−0.433	−0.133	−0.019	0	0.019	0.133	0.433	0.976

These results allow us to conclude:

- the A and B error of approximation using Sugeno algorithm is somewhat less than with Mamdani algorithm at all things being equal and parameters are optimal;
- Mamdani algorithm is preferable in terms of a software implementation.

Given the only slight advantage of Sugeno algorithm error, Mamdani algorithm has been selected, guided by its easiness of implementation.

7   Development Tools and Software Design

A professional tool Visual Paradigm for UML was selected as a simulation tool, supporting full software lifecycle – object-oriented analysis, object-oriented design, coding, testing and deployment of software.

UML modeling helps to improve the quality of software builds, to increase the speed of development. It allows making a quality product at a lower cost. This tool can draw all types of class diagrams and reverse code, generate code from diagrams, and create documentation.

The Visual Paradigm for UML works in addition to key industry standards, such as Systems Modeling Language (SysML), graphical notation of business process modeling (BPMN), XML standards, etc. Visual Paradigm for UML supports the entire operating cycle of development including object-oriented analysis, requirements fixing, planning, modeling, testing, and much more. With the tools of this application, you can draw all kinds of diagrams, browse code in reverse, and generate documentation and code from diagrams. Product Visual Paradigm for UML is designed for a wide range of users, including system and business analysts, systems engineers and architects, and other professionals involved in the software creating. Visual Paradigm is free; having great functionality at the same time.

MS SQL Server was selected to work with a relational database, being powerful and at the same time, allowing users to perform all necessary operations in plain language. Currently, SQL is implemented in almost all commercial relational databases.

7.1   Module Design

At the designing phase of the module, charts using Visual Paradigm for UML were created. Basic requirements for the module are shown in Fig. 2.

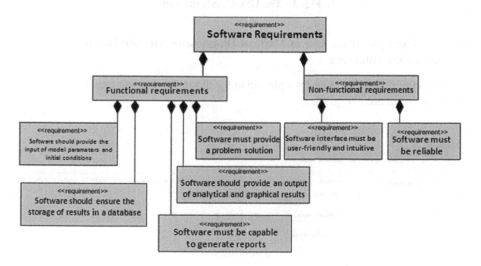

Fig. 2.   Chart of requirements

The module must be easy to use, have an intuitive interface, to be a reliable and practical in addition to the implementation of different scenarios of usage. A USE-CASE diagram is shown in Fig. 3.

As seen in Fig. 3, the basic features of the software are:

- Data input (medical card of the patient, the base of inference rules);
- Placing of diagnosis;
- Data storage in the database;
- Creating and viewing the results of a survey of patients.

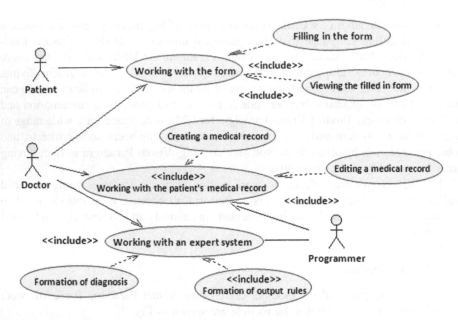

Fig. 3. The USE-CASE diagram

7.2 An Example of the Use of Medical Diagnostics Module Based on Fuzzy Inference

The option of using a module by a physician for diagnosis placing based on the patient survey is considered (Fig. 4).

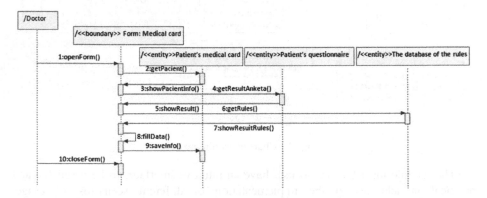

Fig. 4. The sequence diagram of a diagnosis placing process based on the patient survey

Diagram of basic software process activity is shown in Fig. 5. Diagram of classes for the system main functions is shown in Fig. 6.

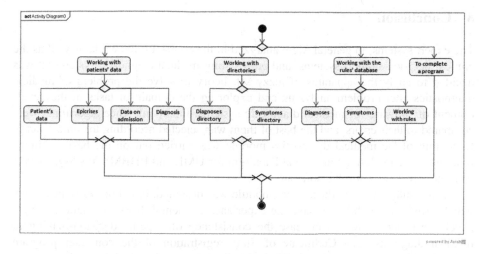

Fig. 5. Activity diagram

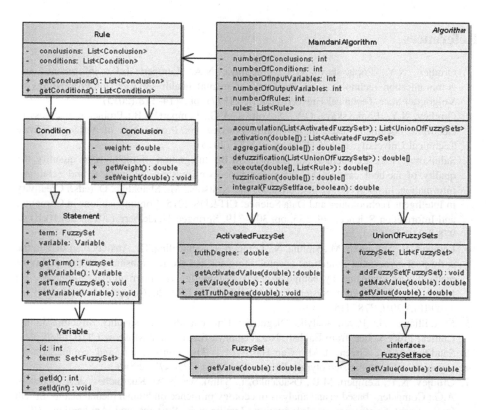

Fig. 6. Diagram of classes for the operation with fuzzy rules functions

8 Conclusion

The expert systems, in general, were analyzed in the course of this work, as well as the clinical decision support systems, and pre-existing medical diagnostic systems. It was decided to apply the apparatus of fuzzy set theory to solve the problem of medical diagnostics after problem analyzing and exploring the domain of tasks in the development of software for medical diagnostic systems. Fuzzy inference algorithms were compared to their errors, and the best of them was selected according to some criteria. Designing of the medical diagnostics module was carried out on the basis of fuzzy inference. The modeling tool Visual Paradigm for UML and RDBMS MS SQL Server were chosen to develop the software.

As a result, a medical diagnostics module was designed, based on fuzzy inference, which provides the ability to save the experience of mental illnesses diagnosing by a psychiatrist, and allows to increase the consistency of experts' decision-making in medical diagnosis. The Certificate of State registration of the computer program #2016619951 from September 1, 2016 "Medical diagnostics module on fuzzy inference based on" has been obtained [25].

References

1. Orudjev, N.Y., Poplavskaya, O.V., Chernaya, N.A., Lempert, L.B.: Information and communication technologies in the work of mental health services. In: Proceedings of Volgograd State Technical University, no. 13 (177), pp. 114–118 (2015)
2. Orudjev, N.Y., Poplavskaya, O.V., Sokolova, A.G., Lempert, L.B.: Problems of access to electronic documents used in psychiatric practice. In: Proceedings of Volgograd State Technical University, no. 14 (178), pp. 74–77 (2015)
3. Salnikova, N.A., Lempert, B.A., Lempert, M.B.: Integration of methods to quantify the quality of medical care in the automated processing systems of medical and economic information. In: Kravets, A., Shcherbakov, M., Kultsova, M., Shabalina, O. (eds.) Creativity in Intelligent Technologies and Data Science, CIT&DS 2015. Communications in Computer and Information Science, vol. 535, pp. 307–319. Springer, Heidelberg (2015). doi:10.1007/978-3-319-23766-4_25
4. Lempert, B., Statsenko, M., Shilina, N., Lempert, L., Shabalina, O.: Anxiety disorders in the early post-myocardial infarction: adaptol treatment and the relationship with the quality of medical care evaluated by computer-based system. In: 7th International Conference on Information, Intelligence, Systems and Applications, (IISA 2016), pp. 1–6 (2016). doi:10.1109/IISA.2016.7785415
5. McWilliams, N.: Psychoanalytic Diagnosis: Understanding Personality Structure in the Clinical Process. Per. from English, Nezavisimaya firma Klass, Moscow (2001). 480 p.
6. Sandifer, M.G., Green, L.M., Carr-Harris, E.: The construction and comparison of psychiatric diagnostic stereotypes. Behav. Sci. 11(6), 471–477 (2006)
7. Orudjev, N.Y., Lempert, M.B., Osaulenko, I., Salnikova, N.A., Kuzmichev, A.A., Kravets, A.G.: Computer - based visual analysis of ecology influence on human mental health. In: 7th International Conference on Information, Intelligence, Systems and Applications (IISA 2016), pp. 1–6 (2016). doi 10.1109/IISA.2016.7785416

8. Orudjev, N.Y., Poplavskaya, O.V., Lempert, L.B., Salnikova, N.A., Kultsova, M.B.: Problems of introducing information technologies in practice of psychiatric service. In: 7th International Conference on Information, Intelligence, Systems and Applications (IISA 2016), pp. 1–6 (2016). doi 10.1109/IISA.2016.7785417

9. Zaripova, V.M., Petrova, I.Y., Kravets, A.G., Evdoshenko, O.: Knowledge bases of physical effects and phenomena for method of energy-informational models by means of ontologies. Commun. Comput. Inf. Sci. **535**, 224–237 (2015)

10. Sadovnikova, N., Parygin, D., Gnedkova, E., Kravets, A., Kizim, A., Ukustov, S.: Scenario forecasting of sustainable urban development based on cognitive model. In: Proceedings of the IADIS International Conference ICT. Society and Human Beings 2013. Proceedings of the IADIS International Conference e-Commerce 2013, pp. 115–119 (2013)

11. Kravets, A.G., Titova, O.V., Shabalina, O.A.: E-learning practice-oriented training in physics: the competence formation. In: Proceedings of the International Conference e-Learning, pp. 351–355 (2013)

12. Kan, L.V., Kuznetsova, Y.M., Chudova, N.V.: Expert systems in the field of psycho-diagnostics. In: Artificial Intelligence and Decision Making, Moscow, pp. 26–35 (2010)

13. Blonk, A.M., Bercken, J.H.L., Den, V., De Bruyn, E.E.J.: Evaluation of DYSLEXPERT: a comparison of a knowledge-based system with experienced clinicians in the diagnosis of dyslexia. Comput. Hum. Behav. **12**(4), 567–586 (2006)

14. Amosig, J.M., Escara, E.J., Martinez, R., Paculanang, E.: Feardex: Fear Diagnostic Expert System (2008). http://www.shvoong.com

15. Orudjevv, N.Y., Poplavskaya, O.V., Lempert, L.B., Salnikova, N.A.: Problems of medical confidentiality while using electronic documents in psychiatric practice. In: Proceedings of the 2016 Conference on Information Technologies in Science, Management, Social Sphere and Medicine, ITSMSSM 2016, vol. 51, pp. 120—125. Atlantis Press (2016)

16. Rutkowski, L.: Methods and Techniques of Artificial Intelligence. Per. with the floor. I. D. Rudinsky, Hot line, Telecom, Moscow (2010). 520 p.

17. Kostrov, B.V., Campfires, B.V., Ruchkin, V.N., Fulin, V.A.: Artificial Intelligence and Robotics: Dialog-MIFI, 224 p., Moscow (2008)

18. Chulyukov, V.A., et al.: Artificial intelligence systems. In: Astakhova, J.F., (ed.) Practical Course: Training Benefit, 292 p., Binom, Knowledge Lab, Moscow (2008)

19. Smolin, D.V.: Introduction to Artificial Intelligence: Lecture Notes, 2nd edn. FIZMATLIT, Moscow (2007). 260 p.

20. Sahabetdinova, L.A., Babushkina, T.A.: The theory, technology, models and application of methods of artificial intelligence. In: Lebedev, V.G. (ed.) Institute of Exercise Problems Them, V.A. Trapeznikov, RAS, Scientific and Engineering, Bk; comp., Moscow, vol. 4 (2008). 189 p.

21. Kravets, A.G., Belov, A.G., Sadovnikova, N.P.: Models and methods of professional competence level research. Recent Pat. Comput. Sci. **9**(2), 150–159 (2016)

22. Saltykov, S., Rusyaeva, E., Kravets, A.G.: Typology of scientific constructions as an instrument of conceptual creativity. In: Kravets, A., Shcherbakov, M., Kultsova, M., Shabalina, O. (eds.) Creativity in Intelligent Technologies and Data Science. Communications in Computer and Information Science, vol. 535, pp. 41–57. Springer, Heidelberg (2015). doi:10.1007/978-3-319-23766-4_4

23. Jackson, P.: Introduction to Expert Systems, 3rd edn. Williams, Moscow (2001). 624 p.

24. Strickland, E.: IBM's Watson Goes to Med School E. Strickland. IEEE Spectr. **12**, 243 (2012)

25. Lempert, L.B., Kravets, A.G., Poplavskaya, O.V., Salnikova, N.A.: RF, Module for Medical Diagnostics on the Basis of Fuzzy Inference. Certificate of State Registration of the Computer no. 2016619951, 1 September 2016

Author Index

Printed in the United States
By Bookmasters

Printed in the United States
By Bookmasters